standard catalog of

WORLD PAPER MONEY

Third Edition
Volume Three – Modern Issues
1961-1997

Colin R. Bruce II
Senior Editor

George S. Čuhaj
Managing Editor

Special Consultants
Weldon D. Burson, Arnoldo Efron, Lee Shin Song
William McNatt, Tony Pisciotta, Jan Vandersande, Robert Wilhite,
Christof Zellweger

The seeds of knowledge may be planted in solitude,
but must be cultivated in public. – *Johnson.*

krause publications

Published in the United States by Krause Publications, Inc.
700 E. State Street, Iola, WI 54990
Telephone: 715-445-2214 • FAX: 715-445-4087
Internet: www@krause.com

Library of Congress Catalog Card Number: 95-76858
International Standard Book Number: 0-87341-496-9

Printed in the United States of America

TABLE OF CONTENTS

ACKNOWLEDGMENTS

The contributions to this catalog have been many and varied, and to recognize them all would be a volume in itself. Accordingly, we wish to acknowledge these invaluable collectors, scholars and dealers in the world paper money field, both past and present, for their specific contributions to this work through the submission of notes for illustration, improved descriptive information and market valuations.

E. K. Aboagye
Julio Acosta Pedraza
Esko Ahlroth
Jan Alexandersson
Paulo Almeida
Milan Alusic
Carl A. Anderson
Dr. Jorge E. Arbelaez
Donald Arnone
Norman Athy
Bene Attila
David B. August
Keith Austin
Cem Barlok
Yuri Barshay
Richard Bates
Adriaan C. F. Beck
Milt Blackburn
Gilles Blançon
Ed Bohannon
Joseph E. Boling
Arthur John Boyko
Wilfried A. Bracke
Jean Bricaud
Dr. Alejandro Brill
Robert J. Brooks
Christopher J. Budesa
Weldon D. Burson
Valikonagi Caddesi
Ramiro O. Casanas
Lance K. Campbell
David Carlson
Arthur D. Cohen
George Conrad
Scott E. Cordry
Guido Crapanzano
Jehangir B. Dalal
Howard A. Daniel III
Paul N. Davis
A. A. C. de Albergaria Pinheiro
Ricardo de Leon-Tallavas
Daniel Denis
C. M. Desai
J. B. Desai
Bob Diedrich
Duane D. Douglas
Vladimir Duic
Dundar Numismatik
Arnoldo Efron
Wilhelm Eglseer
Jos F. M. Eijisermans

Esko Ekman
Jean Michel Engels
Paul Simon Essof
Edward Feltcorn
Jack G. Fischer
Guvendik Fisekcioglu
George A. Fisher, Jr.
Mark Fox
Ian Fraser
W. A. Frick
Hubert Fritzinger
Gary Ganguillet
Richard L. Gatto
Brian Giese
Yves Gilles
Bernardo Gonzales-White
Lee Gordon
Carlos Alberto Graziadio
Rune Gustafsson
Mario Gutierres Minera
John S. Haas
Ray Hackett
Edmond Hakimiam
Agus Halim
Murray Hanewich
Brian Hannon
Flemming Lyngbeck Hansen
Len Harsel
Sergio Heise Fuenzalida
William G. Henderson
Melvin P. Hennisch
Dick Herman
Anton Holt
Armen Hovsepian
Nicolae Hridan
Mikhail Istomin
Tomasz Jazwinski
Edouard Jean-Pierre
Walter Jellum
Erik Johanson
William M. Judd
Alex Kaglyan
Olaf Kiener
Josef Klaus
Ladislav Klaus
Michael E. Knabe
Tristan Kolm
Lazare N. Kouame
Michael Kvasnica
Michael Lang
David Laties

Morris Lawing
Akos Ledai
Lee Shin Song
Allan L. Lewis
George Lill III
Claire Lobel
L.K. Loimaranta
Alan Luedeking
Ma Tak Wo
Ranko Mandic
Rolf Marklin
Ian A. Marshall
John T. Martin
Arthur C. Matz
Leo May
Scott McNatt
William McNatt
Juozas Minikevicius
Lazar Mishev
Howard Mitchell
Ernest J. Montgomery
Richard Murdoch
Tanju Mutlu
Colin Narbeth
Son Xuan Nguyen
Andrew Oberbillig
Geoffrey P. Oldham
Julian Papenfus
Frank Passic
Juan Jose Paris
Antonio E. Pedraza
Juan Pena
Tony Pisciotta
Steve Pomex
Miguel Angel Pratt Mayans
Yahya J. Qureshi
Nazir Rahemtulla
Mircea Raicopol
Jerome H. Remick
Rudolph Richter
Leo Reich
Nicholas Rhodes
Duane C. Riel
Thomas P. Rockwell
William M. Rosenblum
D.E. Royer
Jose Louis Rubio
Arnaldo Russo
Alan Sadd
Karl Saethre
David M. Salem

E. Schnepf
Dr. Wolfgang Schuster
Hartmut Schoenawa
Christian Selvais
Alan Sealey
Narendra Sengar
Joel Shafer
Neil Shafer
Ladislav Sin
Saran Singh
George Slusarczuk
Gary F. Snover
Dimas S. Souza
Jimmie C. Steelman
Jeremy Steinberg
Mel Steinberg
Tim Steiner
Georg H. Stocker A.
Zeljko Stojanovic
Roger B. Stolberg
Mark Strumpf
Imre Szatmari
Steven Tan
David Tang
Mike Tiitus
Andrew Timofee
Guillermo Triana Aguiar
Eduardo R. Trujillo B.
Anthony Tumonis
G. van Caelnbergh
W. J. van der Drift
Jan Vandersande
Grobljar Vanjo
Dr. Karel Vanka
Igor Victorov-Orlov
James Warmus
A. Wang
Chien-Yu Wang
Stewart Westdal
Dr. Heinz Wirz
S. C. Wong
Michael J. Whelihan
Yu Chien Hua
Joseph Zaffern
Christof Zellweger
Igor Zhuravliov

INSTITUTIONS AND PUBLICATIONS

American Numismatic Association
American Numismatic Society
International Bank Note Society
Smithsonian Institution
Note Printing Australia

Ceska Narodni Banka
Banco Central de la Republica Dominicana
Central Bank, Iceland
Reserve Bank of New Zealand

Banco Central de Reserva del Peru
Narodowry Bank Polski
National Bank of Romania
Banco Central del Uruguay
Bank of Slovenija

Nardona Banka Slovenska
National Bank of Macedonia
Central Bank of Samoa
L.A.N.S.A.

The Stateman's Year-Book, 1996-97
  133rd Edition
  by Brian Hunter, editor, The Stateman's Year-Book Office, The Macmillan Press Ltd., 4-6 Crinan Street, London N1 9SQ, England.
  (Statistical and Historical Annual of the States of the World).

Le Change des Monnaies Etrangers
  by R. L. Martin. 12, rue Poincaré, F 55800 Revigny, France.
  (Illustrated guide of current world bank notes.)

MRI Bankers' Guide to Foreign Currency
  by Arnoldo Efron, Monetary Research Institute, P.O. Box 3174, Houston, Texas, U.S.A., 77253-3174.
  (Quarterly illustrated guide of current world bank notes and travelers checks.)

INTRODUCTION

Welcome to this third edition of the *Standard Catalog of World Paper Money, Modern Issues - 1961 to 1997.*

A change users familiar with the Standard Catalog series will notice is the format of the listings. The maps, introductions and listings of rulers, monetary system and the like are all here, but in slightly larger typesizes, hopefully making it easier to read. In addition to the larger typesize for the listings, they are structured with the catalog number and denomination listings on a separate line from that of the date, descriptive, and price information giving more space for all fields of information. Finally, extensive variety revision has been added when it has been noted within the collecting community to affect prices. These varieties could be as basic as the addition of listings for the availability of specimens or proofs; or extensive runs of signature combinations or dates where there have been increased interest and value changes for short print runs.

For the ease of identification, notes are listed under their historic country name (British Honduras is no longer hidden within Belize). Notes of a particular bank are listed in release date order, and then grouped in ascending denomination order. In the cases of countries where more than one issuing authority is in effect at a single time, follow the bank headings in the listings and it will become apparent if that country's listing is by date or alphabetical by issuing authority. In the cases where a country has changed from a kingdom to a republic all the banknotes of the kingdom's era would be listed before that of the republic's.

Catalog numbers have become the hobby's shorthand for listing a banknote in an inventory booklet or dealer advertisement. Catalog numbers in this book have been extensively changed within many countries in order to retain a consecutive system that most people have become comfortable with. It will cause many to look at their collections again and compare listings to update catalog numbers and varieties; but at the same time, those collectors should be pleasantly surprised at the current market valuation listings.

An Invitation

Users of this catalog may find a helpful adjunct is the *Bank Note Reporter,* the only monthly newspaper devoted exclusively to North American and world paper money. Each issue presents up-to-date news, feature articles and information - including appearances of the *World Paper Money Update* on the latest world paper money releases and discoveries. Listings in these presentations are all keyed to the Standard Catalog numbering system utilized in this catalog. All purchasers of this catalog are invited to subscribe to the *Bank Note Reporter.* Requests for a sample copy should be addressed to *Bank Note Reporter*, 700 East State Street, Iola, WI, 54990-0001.

A review of paper money collecting

Paper money collecting is undoubtedly nearly as old as paper money itself, this segment of the numismatic hobby did not begin to reach a popularity approaching that of coin collecting until the latter half of the 1970's. While coins and paper money are alike in that both served as legal obligations to facilitate commerce, long-time paper money enthusiasts know the similarity ends there.

Coins were historically guaranteed by the intrinsic value of their metallic content - at least until recent years when virtually all circulating coins have become little more than legal tender tokens, containing little or no precious metal - while paper money possesses a value only when it is accepted for debts or converted into bullion or precious metals. With many note issues, this conversion privilege was limited and ultimately negated by the imposition of redemption cutoff dates.

Such conditions made collecting of bank notes a risky business, particularly with notes possessing a high face value. This is why in most instances, except where issued were withdrawn shortly after release or became virtually worthless due to hyperinflation, early high denomination notes are extremely difficult to locate, especially in choice to uncirculated grades of preservation.

The development of widespread collector interest in paper money of most nations were long inhibited by a near total absence of adequate documentary literature. No more than three and a half decades ago collectors could refer to only a few catalogs and dealer price lists of limited scope, most of which were incomplete and difficult to acquire, or they could build their own knowledge through personal collecting pursuits and contact with fellow collectors.

This situation was somewhat corrected over the past 30 years with a number of special catalogs covering the more popular collected countries. Still, many areas remained uncataloged, and no single volume existed which provided comprehensive, detailed, illustrated listings of issues from all countries of the world.

The early catalogs authored by Albert Pick chronicled issues of Europe and the Americas and were assembled as stepping stones to the ultimate objective which became reality with publication of the first *Standard Catalog of World Paper Money* in 1975. That work provided collectors with near complete listings and up-to-date valuations of all recorded government note issues of the 20th century, incorporating Pick's previously unpublished manuscripts on Africa, Asia and Oceiana, plus many earlier issues.

This completely revised and updated 3rd Edition of Volume III, Modern Issues, along with the companion Eighth Edition Volume II General Issues presents a substantial extension of the cataloging effort initiated in 1975 and revised in succeeding editions. As the most comprehensive world paper money reference ever assembled, it fully documents the many and varied legal tender paper currency issued circulated by nearly 300 past and current governments of the world from 1375 to present.

Dates and Date Listing Policy

In previous editions of this work it was the goal to provide a sampling of the many date varieties that were believed to exist. In recent times, as particular dates (and usually signature combinations) were known to be scarcer, that particular series was expanded to include listings of individual dates. At times this idea has been fully incorporated, but with some series it is not practicable, especially when just about every day in a given month could have been an issue date for the notes.

Accordingly, where it seems justifiable that date spans can be realistically filled with individual dates, this has been done. In order to accommodate the many new dates, the idea of providing small letters to break them up into narrower spans of years has been used. Within these small letter date spans, the aim has been to include no more than five of six dates. If it appears that there are too many dates for a series, with no major differences in value, then a general inclusive date span is used (beginning and ending) and individual dates within this span are not shown.

For those notes showing only a general date span, the only important dates become those that expand the range of years, months or days; earlier or later. But even they would have no major value change.

Because a specific date is not listed does not necessarily mean it is rare. It may be just that it has not been reported. Those date varieties which are known to be scarcer are cataloged separately. Newly reported dates in a wide variety of listings are constantly being reported. This indicates that research into the whole area is very active, and a steady flow of new dates are fully expected upon publication of this edition.

Abbreviations

Certain abbreviations have been adopted for words occurring frequently in note descriptions. Following is a list of these:

#	—	number (catalog or serial)
bldg.	—	building
ctr.	—	center
dk.	—	dark
FV	—	face value
Gen.	—	General
govt.	—	government
Kg.	—	king
l.	—	left
lg.	—	large
lt.	—	light
m/c	—	multicolored
ND	—	no date
ovpt.	—	overprint
portr.	—	portrait
Qn.	—	queen
r.	—	right
sign.	—	signature or signatures
sm.	—	small
unpt.	—	underprint (background printing)
wmk.	—	watermark
w/	—	with
w/o	—	without

Valuations

Valuations are given for most notes in three grades. Earlier issues are usually priced in the grade headings of Good, Fine and Extremely Fine; later issues take the grade headings of Very Good, Very Fine and Uncirculated. While it is ... early notes cannot be priced in Extremely Fine ... notes have no premium value in Very Good, it is ... coverage provides the best uniformity of value da... ... lecting community. There are exceptional cases where headings are adjusted for either single notes of a series which really needs special treatment. We have endeavored to print the Grade Headings often for ease of reference.

Valuations are determined generally from a consensus of individuals submitting prices for evaluation. Some notes have NO pricing, but this does not necessarily mean they are expensive or even rare; but it shows that no pricing information was forthcoming. A number of notes have a 'Rare' designation, and no values. Such notes are generally not available on the market, and when they do appear the price is a matter between buyer and seller. No book can provide guidance in these instances except to indicate they are rare.

Valuations used in this book are based on the IBNS grading standards and are stated in U.S. Dollars. They serve only as aids in evaluating paper money since actual market conditions throughout the world wide collector community is constantly changing. In addition, particularly choice examples of many issues listed may bring higher premiums to values listed.

Unless otherwise presented, values are given for types only, without regard for date or signature. In a number of instances there could be dates or signature varieties worth a substantial premium over the listed value.

FV (for Face Value) is used as a price designation on older but still redeemable legal tender notes in lower conditions. FV may appear in one or both condition columns before Uncirculated, depending on the relative age and availability of the note in question.

Collection care

The proper preservation of a collection should be of paramount importance to all in the hobby - dealers, collectors and scholars. Only a person who was housed notes in a manner giving pleasure to himself and others will keep alive the pleasure of collecting for future generations. The same applies to the way of housing as to the choice of the collecting specialty: it is chiefly a questions of what most pleases the individual collector.

Arrangement and sorting of a collection is most certainly a basic requirement. Storing the notes in safe paper envelopes such as those used in the philatelic trade for stamps and boxes should, perhaps, be considered only when building a new section of a collection; for accommodating varieties or for reasons of saving space when the collection has grown quickly.

The grouping of notes on large sheets and fixing them into position with photo corners had been a method practiced for many years. The collector could arrange the notes to his own taste, identify and otherwise embellish them. Difficulties arise in the accommodation of supplements and the exchanging of notes for examples in better condition, since even slight differences in the format will necessitate detaching and most likely remaking a whole page.

Most paper money collections are probably housed in some form of plastic-pocketed album which are today manufactured in many different sizes and styles to accommodate many types of world paper money.

Because of the number of bank note collectors has grown continually over the past twenty-five years, some specialty manufacturers of albums have developed a paper money selection. The notes, housed in clear plastic pockets, individually or in

...ups, can be viewed and exchanged without difficulty. These albums are not cheap, but the notes displayed in this manner do make a lasting impression on the viewer. A large collection will hardly be accommodated in its entirety in this manner, thus many collectors limit themselves to partial areas or especially valuable notes which are displayed thus. A word of concern: certain types of plastic and all vinyl used for housing notes may cause notes to become brittle over time, or cause a irreversible and harmful transfer of oils from the vinyl onto the bank notes.

The high demands which stamp collectors make on their products cannot be transferred to the paper money collecting fraternity. A postage stamp is intended for only a single use, then it is relegated to a collection. With paper money, it is nearly impossible to acquire uncirculated specimens from a number of countries due to export laws or just because of internal bank procedures. Bends from excessive counting, or even staple holes are commonplace. Once acquiring a circulated note, the collector must endeavor to maintain its state of preservation.

The face that there is a classification and value difference between notes with greater use or even damage is a matter of course. It is part of the opinion and personal taste of the individual collector to decide what he will consider worthy of collecting and what will pay for such items.

For the purposed of strengthening and mending torn paper money, under no circumstances should one use plain cellophane tape or a similar material. These tapes warp easily, with sealing marks forming at the edges, and the tape frequently discolors. Only with the greatest of difficulty (and often not at all) can these tapes be removed, and damage to the note or the printing is almost unavoidable. The best material for mending tears is an archival tape recommended for the treatment and repair of documents.

There are collectors who, with great skill, remove unsightly spots, repair badly damaged notes, replace missing pieces and otherwise restore or clean a note. Before venturing to tackle such work, one should first experiment with cheap duplicates and not endanger a collection piece. Really difficult work of this nature should be left to the experienced restorer. There is also the question of morality of tampering with a note to improve its condition, either by repairing, starching, ironing, pressing or other methods to possibly deceive a potential future buyer. Such a question must, in the final analysis, be left to the individual collector.

COMPANION CATALOGS

Volume I - Specialized Issues
Volume II - General Issues 1650-1950

The Companion Catalogs in the Standard Catalog of World Paper Money series include a volume on Specialized Issues of the world - listed are those banknotes which were issued on a limited circulation basis rather than the nationally-franchised note issues detailed in this work. The Specialized volume is currently in its 7th edition, and it is updated periodically. The General Issues, 1650-1960 volume lists national notes dated and issued before 1961. It is a bi-annual publication currently in its 8th edition. Inquiries on the availability of both these volumes are invited to contact Book Department, Krause Publications, 700 East State Street, Iola, WI 54990-0001 or you may call 1-800-258-0929 or www.krause.com.

IBNS
GRADING STANDARDS
FOR
WORLD PAPER MONEY

The following introduction and Grading Guide is the result of work prepared under the guidance of the Grading Committee of the International Bank Note Society (IBNS.) It has been adopted as the official grading standards of that society.

Introduction

Grading is the most controversial component of paper money collecting today. Small differences in grade can mean significant differences in value. The process of grading is so subjective and dependent on external influences such as lighting, that even a very experienced individual may well grade the same note differently on separate occasions.

To facilitate communication between sellers and buyers, it is essential that grading terms and their meanings be as standardized and as widely used as possible. This standardization should reflect common usage as much as practicable. One difficulty with grading is that even the actual grades themselves are not used everywhere by everyone. For example, in Europe the grade 'About Uncirculated' (AU) is not in general use, yet in North America it is widespread. The European term 'Good VF' may roughly correspond to what individuals in North America call 'Extremely Fine' (EF).

The grades and definitions as set forth below cannot reconcile all the various systems and grading terminology variants. Rather, the attempt is made here to try and diminish the controversy with some common-sense grades and definitions that aim to give more precise meaning to the grading language of paper money.

How to look at a banknote

In order to ascertain the grade of a note, it is essential to examine it out of a holder and under a good light. Move the note around so that light bounces off at different angles. Try holding it up obliquely so that the not is almost even with your eye as you look up at the light. Hard-to-see folds or slight creases will show up under such examination. Some individuals also lightly feel along the surface of the note to detect creasing.

Cleaning, Washing, Pressing of Banknotes

a) Cleaning, washing or pressing paper money is generally harmful and reduced both the grade and the value of a note. At the very least, a washed or pressed note may loose its original sheen and its surface may become lifeless and dull. The defects a note had, such as folds and creases, may not necessarily be completely eliminated and their telltale marks can be detected under a good light. Carelessly washed notes may also have white streaks where the folds or creases were (or still are).

b) Processing of a note which started out as Extremely Fine will automatically reduce it at least one full grade.

Unnatural Defects

Glue, tape or pencil marks may sometimes be successfully removed. While such removal will leave a cleaned surface, it will improve the overall appearance of the note without concealing any of its defects. Under such circumstances, the grade of that note may also be improved.

The words "pinholes", "staple holes", "trimmed", "writing on face", "tape marks" etc. should always be added to the description of a note. It is realized that certain countries routinely staple their notes together in groups before issue. In such cases, the description can include a comment such as "usual staple holes" or something similar. After all, not everyone knows that certain notes cannot be found otherwise.

The major point of this section is that one cannot lower the overall grade of a note with defects simply because of the defects. The price will reflect the lowered worth of a defective note, but the description must always include the specific defects.

The Term *Uncirculated*

The word *Uncirculated* is used in this grading guide only as a qualitive measurement of the appearance of a note. It has nothing at all to do with whether or not an issuer has actually released the note to circulation. Thus, the term About Uncirculated is justified and acceptable because so many notes that have never seen hand to hand use have been mishandled so that they are available at best in AU condition. Either a note is uncirculated in condition or it is not; there can be no degrees of uncirculated. Highlights or defects in color, centering and the like may be included in a description but the fact that a note is or is not in uncirculated condition should not be a disputable point.

GRADING GUIDE —
Definitions of Terms

UNCIRCULATED: A perfectly preserved note, never mishandled by the issuing authority, a bank teller, the public or a collector.

Paper is clean and firm, without discoloration. Corners are sharp and square, witout any evidence of roudning. (Rounded corners are often a tell-tale sign of a cleaned or "doctored" note.)

An uncirculated note will have its original, natural sheen.

NOTE: Some note issuers are most often avaialble with slight eveidence of very light counting folds which do not "break" the paper. Also, French-printed notes usually have a slight ripple in the paper. Many collectors and dealers refer to such notes as AU-UNC.

ABOUT UNCIRCULATED: A virtually perfect note, with some minor handling. May show very slight evidence of bank counting folds at a corner or one light fold through the center, but not both. An AU note cannot be creased, a crease being a hard fold which has usually "broken" the surface of the note.

Paper is clean and bright with original sheen. Corners are not rounded.

NOTE: Europeans will refer to an About Uncirculated or AU note as "EF-Unc" or as just "EF". The Extremely Fine note described below will often be referred to as "GVF" or "Good Very Fine".

EXTREMELY FINE: A very attractive note, with light handling. May have a maximum of three light folds or one strong crease.

Paper is clean and bright with original sheen. Corners may show only the slightest evidence of rounding. There may also be the slightest sign of wear where a fold meets the edge.

VERY FINE: An attractive note, but with more evidence of handling and wear. May have several folds both vertically and horizontally.

Paper may have minimal dirt, or possible color smudging. Paper itself is still relatively crisp and not floppy.

There are no tears into the border area, although the edges do show slight wear. Corners also show wear but not full rounding.

FINE: A note which shows considerable circulation, with many folds, creases and wrinkling.

Paper is not excessively dirty but may have some softness.

Edges may show much handling, with minor tears in the border area. Tears may not extend into the design. There will be no center hole because of excessive folding.

Colors are clear but not very bright. A staple hole or two would not be considered unusual wear in a Fine note. Overall appearance is still on the desirable side.

VERY GOOD: A well used note, abused but still intact.

Corners may have much wear and rounding, tiny nicks, tears may extend into the design, some discoloration may be present, staining may have occurred, and a small hole may sometimes be seen at center from excessive folding.

Staple and pinholes are usually present, and the note itself is quite limp but NO pieces of the note can be missing. A note in VG condition may still have an overall not unattractive appearance.

GOOD: A well worn and heavily used note. Normal damage from prolonged circulation will include strong multiple folds and creases, stains, pinholes and/or staple holes, dirt, discoloration, edge tears, center hole, rounded corners and an overall unattractive appearance. No large pieces of the note may be missing. Graffiti is commonly seen on notes in G condition.

FAIR: A totally limp, dirty and very well used note. Larger pieces may be half torn off or missing besides the defects mentioned under the Good category. Tears will be larger, obscured portions of the note will be bigger.

POOR: A "rag" with severe damage because of wear, staining, pieces missing, graffiti, larger holes. May have tape holding pieces of the note together. Trimming may have taken place to remove rough edges. A Poor note is desirable only as a "filler" or when such a note is the only one known of that particular issue.

STANDARD INTERNATIONAL GRADING TERMINOLOGY AND ABBREVIATIONS

U.S. and ENGLISH SPEAKING LANDS	UNCIRCULATED	EXTREMELY FINE	VERY FINE	FINE	VERY GOOD	GOOD	POOR
Abbreviation	UNC	EF or XF	VF	FF	VG	G	PR
BRAZIL	(1) DW	(3) S	(5) MBC	(7) BC	(8)	(9) R	UTGeG
DENMARK	0	01	1+	1	1÷	2	3
FINLAND	0	01	1+	1	1?	2	3
FRANCE	NEUF	SUP	TTB or TB	TB or TB	B	TBC	BC
GERMANY	KFR	II / VZGL	III / SS	IV / S	V / S.g.E.	VI / G.e.	G.e.s.
ITALY	FdS	SPL	BB	MB	B	M	
JAPAN	未使用	極美品	美品	並品	—	—	—
NETHERLANDS	FDC	Pr.	Z.F.	Fr.	Z.g.	G	
NORWAY	0	01	1+	1	1÷	2	3
PORTUGAL	Novo	Soberbo	Muito bo	—	—	—	—
SPAIN	Lujo	SC, IC or EBC	MBC	BC	—	RC	MC
SWEDEN	0	01	1+	1	1?	2	—

BRAZIL

FE	— Flor de Estampa
S	— Soberba
MBC	— Muito Bem Conservada
BC	— Bem Conservada
R	— Regular
UTGeG	— Um Tanto Gasto e Gasto

DENMARK

0	— Uncirkuleret
01	— Meget Paent Eksemplar
1+	— Paent Eksemplar
1	— Acceptabelt Eksemplar
1	— Noget Slidt Eksemplar
2	— Darlight Eksemplar
3	— Meget Darlight Eskemplar

FINLAND

00	— Kiitolyonti
0	— Lyontiveres
01	— Erittain Hyva
1+	— Hyva
1?	— Keikko
3	— Huono

FRANCE

NEUF	— New
SUP	— Superbe
TTB	— Tres Tres Beau
TB	— Tres Beau
B	— Beau
TBC	— Tres Bien Conserve
BC	— Bien Conserve

GERMANY

VZGL	— Vorzüglich
SS	— Sehr schön
S	— Schön
S.g.E.	— Sehr gut erhalten
G.e.	— Gut erhalten
G.e.S.	— Gering erhalten Schlect

ITALY

Fds	— Fior di Stampa
SPL	— Splendid
BB	— Bellissimo
MB	— Molto Bello
B	— Bello
M	— Mediocre

JAPAN

未使用	— Mishiyo
極美品	— Goku Bihin
美品	— Bihin
並品	— Futuhin

NETHERLANDS

Pr.	— Prachtig
Z.F.	— Zeer Fraai
Fr.	— Fraai
Z.g.	— Zeer Goed
G	— Good

NORWAY

0	— Usirkuleret eks
01	— Meget pent eks
1+	— Pent eks
1	— Fullgodt eks
1-	— Ikke Fullgodt eks
2	— Darlig eks

ROMANIA

NC	— Necirculata (UNC)
FF	— Foarte Frumoasa (VF)
F	— Frumoasa (F)
FBC	— Foarte Bine Conservata (VG)
BC	— Bine Conservata (G)
M	— Mediocru Conservata (POOR)

SPAIN

EBC	— Extraordinariamente Bien Conservada
SC	— Sin Circular
IC	— Incirculante
MBC	— Muy Bien Conservada
BC	— Bien Conservada
RC	— Regular Conservada
MC	— Mala Conservada

SWEDEN

0	— Ocirkulerat
01	— Mycket Vackert
1+	— Vackert
1	— Fullgott
1?	— Ej Fullgott
2	— Dalight

BANKNOTE PRINTERS

Printers' names, abbreviations or monograms will usually appear as part of the frame design or below it on face and/or back. In some instances the engravers name may also appear in a similar location on a note. The following abbreviations identify printers for many of the notes listed in this volume:

ABNC .... American Bank Note Company (USA)
BABN(C) .... British American Bank Note Co., Ltd. (Canada)
B&S .... Bouligny & Schmidt (Mexico)
BEPP .... Bureau of Engraving & Printing, Peking (China)
BF .... Banque de France (France)
BFL .... Barclay & Fry Ltd. (England)
BWC .... Bradbury, Wilkinson & Co. (England)
CABB .... Compania Americana de Billetes de Banco (ABNC)
CBC .... Columbian Banknote Co. (USA)
CBNC .... Canadian Bank Note Company (Canada)
CCBB .... Compania Columbiana de Billetes de Banco (CBC)
CdM- .... Casa da Moeda (Brazil)
CdM- .... Casa de Moneda (Argentina, Chile, etc.)
CHB .... Chung Hua Book Co. (China)
CMN .... Casa de Moneda de la Nacion (Argentina)
CMPA .... Commercial Press (China)
CNBB .... Compania Nacional de Billetes de Banco (NBNC)
CONB .... Continental Bank Note Company (USA)
CPF .... Central Printing Factory (China)
CSABB .... Compania Sud/Americana de Billetes de Banco
.... (Argentina)
CS&E .... Charles Skipper & East (England)
DLR .... De La Rue (England)
DTB .... Dah Tung Book Co., and Ta Tung Printing (China)
E&C .... Evans & Cogwell (CSA)
EAW .... E. A. Wright (USA)
FLBN .... Franklin-Lee Bank Note Company (USA)
FNMT .... Fabrica Nacional de Moneda y Timbre (Spain)
G&D .... Giesecke & Devrient (Germany)
HBNC .... Hamilton Bank Note Company (USA)
HKB .... Hong Kong Banknote (Hong Kong)
HKP .... Hong Kong Printing Press (Hong Kong)
H&L .... Hoyer & Ludwig, Richmond, Virginia (CSA)
HLBNC .... Homer Lee Bank Note Co. (USA)
H&S .... Harrison & Sons Ltd. (England)
IBB .... Imprenta de Billetes-Bogota (Columbia)
IBSFB .... Imprenta de Billetes-Santa Fe de Bogota (Columbia)
IBNC .... International Bank Note Company (USA)
JBNC .... Jeffries Bank Note Company (USA)
JEZ .... Johan Enschede en Zonen (Netherlands)
K&B .... Keatinge & Ball (CSA)
KBNC .... Kendall Bank Note Company, New York (USA)
LN .... Litografia Nacional (Columbia)
NAL .... Nissen & Arnold (England)
NBNC .... National Bank Note Company (USA)
OCV .... Officina Carte-Valori (Italy)
ODBI .... Officina Della Banca D'Italia (Italy)
OFZ .... Orell Fussli, Zurich (Switzerland)
P&B .... Perkins & Bacon (England)
PBC .... Perkins, Bacon & Co. (England)
PB&P .... Perkins, Bacon & Petch (England)
SBNC .... Security Banknote Company (USA)
TDLR .... Thomas De La Rue (England)
UPC .... Union Printing Co. (China)
UPP .... Union Publishers & Printers Fed. Inc. (China)
USBNC .... United States Banknote Corp. (USA)
WDBN .... Western District Banknote Fed. Inc.
W&S .... Waterlow & Sons Ltd. (England)
WPCo .... Watson Printing Co. (China)
WWS .... W. W. Sprague & Co. Ltd. (England)

International Bank Note Society

The International Bank Note Society (IBNS) was formed in 1961 to promote the collecting of world paper money. A membership in excess of 2,000 in over 100 nations around the globe draw on the services of the Society in advancing their knowledge and collections.

The benefits of Society membership include the quarterly IBNS Journal, a magazine featuring learned writings on the notes of the world, their history, artistry and technical background. Additionally each member receives a directory which lists the membership by name as well as geographic location. Collector specialties are also given. A newsletter is published, to announce events in a timely fashion, as well a semi-annual auctions of bank notes. Finally, an attribution service is offered by the society for persons with paper money they could not identify.

One of the greatest benefits of IBNS membership is the facility for correspondence with other members around the world, for purposes of exchanging notes, information and assistance with research projects.

DATING

Determining the date of issue of a note is a basic consideration of attribution. As the reading of dates is subject not only to the vagaries of numeric styling, but to variations in dating roots caused by the observation of differing religious eras or regal periods from country to country, making this determination can sometimes be quite difficult. Most countries outside the North Africa and Oriental spheres rely on Western date numerals and the Christian (AD) reckoning, although in a few instances note dating has been tied to the year of a reign or government.

Countries of the Arabic sphere generally date their issues to the Muslim calendar which commenced on July 16, 622 AD when the prophet Mohammed fled from Mecca to Medina. As this calendar is reckoned by the lunar year of 354 days, it is a year 3.03% shorter than the Christian year. A conversion formula requires you to subtract the percent from the AH date, and then add 621 to gain the AD date.

The Muslim calendar is not always based on the lunar year (AH), however, causing some confusion. Afghanistan and Iran (Persia) used a calendar based on a solar year (SH) introduced around 1920. These dates can be converted to AD by simply adding 621. In 1976 Iran implemented a solar calendar based on the founding of the Iranian monarchy in 559 BC. The first year observed on this new system was 2535(MS) which commenced on March 20, 1976.

Several different eras of reckoning, including the Christian (AD) and Muslim (AH) have been used to date paper money of the Indian subcontinent. The two basic systems are the Vikrama Samvat (VS) era which dates from October 18, 58 BC, and the Saka (SE) era the origin of which is reckoned from March 3, 78 AD. Dating according to both eras appear on notes of several native states and countries of the area.

Thailand (Siam) has observed three different eras for dating. The most predominant is the Buddhist (BE) era which originates in 543 BC. Next is the Bangkok or Ratanakosind-sok (RS) era dating from 1781 AD (and consist of only 3 numerals), followed by the Chula-Sakarat (CS) era which date from 638 AD, with the latter also observed in Burma.

Other calendars include that of the Ethiopian (EE) era which commenced 7 years, 8 months after AD dating, and that of the Hebrew nation which commenced on October 7, 3761 BC. Korea claims a dating from 2333 BC which is acknowledged on some issues.

The following table indicates the years dating from the various eras which correspond to 1997 by the Christian (AD) calendar reckoning. It must be remembered that there are overlaps between the eras in some instances:

Christian Era (AD)	— 1997
Mohammedan era (AH)	— AH1418
Solar year (SH)	— SH1376
Monarchic Solar era (MS)	— MS2556
Vikrama Samvat era (VS)	— SE2054
Saka era (SE)	— Saka 1919
Buddhist era (BE)	— BE2540
Bangkok era (RS)	— RS216
Chula-Sakarat era (CS)	— CS1359
Ethiopian era (EE)	— EE1989
Jewish era	— 5757
Korean era	— 4330

Paper money of Oriental origin - principally Japan, Korea, China, Turkestan and Tibet generally date to the year of the government, dynastic, regnal or cyclical eras, with the dates indicated in Oriental characters which usually read from right to left. In recent years, however, some dating has been according to the Christina calendar and in western numerals reading from left to right.

More detailed guides to the application of the less prevalent dating systems than those described, and others of strictly local nature, along with the numeral designations employed are presented in conjunction with the appropriate listings.

Some notes carry dating according to both the locally observed and Christian eras. This is particularly true in the Arabic sphere, where the Muslim date may be indicated in Arabic numerals and the Christian date in western numerals.

In general the date actually carried on a given paper money issue is indicated. Notes issued by special Law or Decree will have a L or D preceding the date. Dates listed within parentheses are dates of issue which may differ from the date appearing on the note, but which is documented by other means. Undated notes are listed with ND, followed by a year when the year of actual issue is known.

Timing differentials between the 354 day Muslim and the 365 day Christian year cause situations whereby notes bearing dates of both eras have two date combinations that may overlap from one or the other calendar system.

China – Republic 9th year, 1st month, 15th day (15.1.1920), read r. to l.

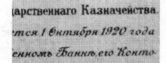

Russia – 1 October 1920

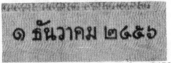

Thailand (Siam) – 1 December 2456

Korea – 4288 (1955)

Poland – 28 February 1919

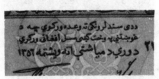

Afghanistan – Solar year 1356

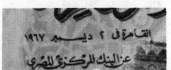

Israel – 1973, 5733

Indonesia – January 1950

Egypt – 1967 December 2

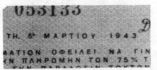

Greece – 5 March 1943

HEJIRA DATE CONVERSION CHART
HEJIRA DATE CHART

HEJIRA (Hijra, Hegira), the name of the Mohammedan era (A.H. = Anno Hegirae) dates back to the Christian year 622 when Mohammed "fled" from Mecca, escaping to Medina to avoid persecution from the Koreish tribesmen. Based on a lunar year the Mohammedan year is 11 days shorter.

*= Leap Year (Christian Calendar)

AH Hejira	AD Christian Date
1010	1601, July 2
1011	1602, June 21
1012	1603, June 11
1013	1604, May 30*
1014	1605, May 19
1015	1606, May 9
1016	1607, April 28
1017	1608, April 16*
1018	1609, April 6
1019	1610, March 26
1020	1611, March 16
1021	1612, March 4*
1022	1613, February 21
1023	1614, February 11
1024	1615, January 31
1025	1616, January 20*
1026	1617, January 9
1027	1617, December 29
1028	1618, December 19
1029	1619, December 8
1030	1620, November 26*
1031	1621, November 16
1032	1622, November 5
1033	1623, October 25
1034	1624, October 14*
1035	1625, October 3
1036	1626, September 22
1037	1627, September 12
1038	1628, August 31*
1039	1629, August 21
1040	1630, August 10
1041	1631, July 30
1042	1632, July 19*
1043	1633, July 8
1044	1634, June 27
1045	1635, June 17
1046	1636, June 5*
1047	1637, May 26
1048	1638, May 15
1049	1639, May 4
1050	1640, April 23*
1051	1641, April 12
1052	1642, April 1
1053	1643, March 22
1054	1644, March 10*
1055	1645, February 27
1056	1646, February 17
1057	1647, February 6
1058	1648, January 27*
1059	1649, January 15
1060	1650, January 4
1061	1650, December 25
1062	1651, December 14
1063	1652, December 2*
1064	1653, November 22
1065	1654, November 11
1066	1655, October 31
1067	1656, October 20*
1068	1657, October 9
1069	1658, September 29
1070	1659, September 18
1071	1660, September 6*
1072	1661, August 27
1073	1662, August 16
1074	1663, August 5
1075	1664, July 25*
1076	1665, July 14
1077	1666, July 4
1078	1667, June 23
1079	1668, June 11*
1080	1669, June 1
1081	1670, May 21
1082	1671, May 10
1083	1672, April 29*
1084	1673, April 18
1085	1674, April 7
1086	1675, March 28
1087	1676, March 16*
1088	1677, March 6
1089	1678, February 23
1090	1679, February 12
1091	1680, February 2*
1092	1681, January 21
1093	1682, January 10
1094	1682, December 31
1095	1683, December 20
1096	1684, December 8*
1097	1685, November 28
1098	1686, November 17
1099	1687, November 7
1100	1688, October 26*
1101	1689, October 15
1102	1690, October 5

AH Hejira	AD Christian Date
1103	1691, September 24
1104	1692, September 12*
1105	1693, September 2
1106	1694, August 22
1107	1695, August 12
1108	1696, July 31*
1109	1697, July 20
1110	1698, July 10
1111	1699, June 29
1112	1700, June 18
1113	1701, June 8
1114	1702, May 28
1115	1703, May 17
1116	1704, May 6*
1117	1705, April 25
1118	1706, April 15
1119	1707, April 4
1120	1708, March 23*
1121	1709, March 13
1122	1710, March 2
1123	1711, February 19
1124	1712, February 9*
1125	1713, January 28
1126	1714, January 17
1127	1715, January 7
1128	1715, December 27
1129	1716, December 16*
1130	1717, December 5
1131	1718, November 24
1132	1719, November 14
1133	1720, November 2*
1134	1721, October 22
1135	1722, October 12
1136	1723, October 1
1137	1724, September 20*
1138	1725, September 9
1139	1726, August 29
1140	1727, August 19
1141	1728, August 7*
1142	1729, July 27
1143	1730, July 17
1144	1731, July 6
1145	1732, June 24*
1146	1733, June 14
1147	1734, June 3
1148	1735, May 24
1149	1736, May 12*
1150	1737, May 1
1151	1738, April 21
1152	1739, April 10
1153	1740, March 29*
1154	1741, March 19
1155	1742, March 8
1156	1743, February 25
1157	1744, February 15*
1158	1745, February 3
1159	1746, January 24
1160	1747, January 13
1161	1748, January 2
1162	1748, December 22*
1163	1749, December 11
1164	1750, November 30
1165	1751, November 20
1166	1752, November 8*
1167	1753, October 29
1168	1754, October 18
1169	1755, October 7
1170	1756, September 26*
1171	1757, September 15
1172	1758, September 4
1173	1759, August 25
1174	1760, August 13*
1175	1761, August 2
1176	1762, July 23
1177	1763, July 12
1178	1764, July 1*
1179	1765, June 20
1180	1766, June 9
1181	1767, May 30
1182	1768, May 18*
1183	1769, May 7
1184	1770, April 27
1185	1771, April 16
1186	1772, April 4*
1187	1773, March 25
1188	1774, March 14
1189	1775, March 4
1190	1776, February 21*
1191	1777, February 9
1192	1778, January 30
1193	1779, January 19
1194	1780, January 8*
1195	1780, December 28*
1196	1781, December 17
1197	1782, December 7
1198	1783, November 26
1199	1784, November 14*
1200	1785, November 4
1201	1786, October 24
1202	1787, October 13
1203	1788, October 2*
1204	1789, September 21
1205	1790, September 10
1206	1791, August 31
1207	1792, August 19*
1208	1793, August 9

AH Hejira	AD Christian Date
1209	1794, July 29
1210	1795, July 18
1211	1796, July 7*
1212	1797, June 26
1213	1798, June 15
1214	1799, June 5
1215	1800, May 25
1216	1801, May 14
1217	1802, May 4
1218	1803, April 23
1219	1804, April 12*
1220	1805, April 1
1221	1806, March 21
1222	1807, March 11
1223	1808, February 28*
1224	1809, February 16
1225	1810, February 6
1226	1811, January 26
1227	1812, January 16*
1228	1813, January 4
1229	1813, December 24
1230	1814, December 14
1231	1815, December 3
1232	1816, November 21*
1233	1817, November 11
1234	1818, October 31
1235	1819, October 20
1236	1820, October 9*
1237	1821, September 28
1238	1822, September 18
1239	1823, September 7
1240	1824, August 26*
1241	1825, August 16
1242	1826, August 5
1243	1827, July 25
1244	1828, July 14*
1245	1829, July 3
1246	1830, June 22
1247	1831, June 12
1248	1832, May 31*
1249	1833, May 21
1250	1834, May 10
1251	1835, April 29
1252	1836, April 18*
1253	1837, April 7
1254	1838, March 27
1255	1839, March 17
1256	1840, March 5*
1257	1841, February 23
1258	1842, February 12
1259	1843, February 1
1260	1844, January 22*
1261	1845, January 10
1262	1845, December 30
1263	1846, December 20
1264	1847, December 9
1265	1848, November 27*
1266	1849, November 17
1267	1850, November 6
1268	1851, October 27
1269	1852, October 15*
1270	1853, October 4
1271	1854, September 24
1272	1855, September 13
1273	1856, September 1*
1274	1857, August 22
1275	1858, August 11
1276	1859, July 31
1277	1860, July 20*
1278	1861, July 9
1279	1862, June 29
1280	1863, June 18
1281	1864, June 6*
1282	1865, May 27
1283	1866, May 16
1284	1867, May 5
1285	1868, April 24*
1286	1869, April 13
1287	1870, April 3
1288	1871, March 23
1289	1872, March 11*
1290	1873, March 1
1291	1874, February 18
1292	1875, February 7
1293	1876, January 28*
1294	1877, January 16
1295	1878, January 5
1296	1878, December 26
1297	1879, December 15
1298	1880, December 4*
1299	1881, November 23
1300	1882, November 12
1301	1883, November 2
1302	1884, October 21*
1303	1885, October 10
1304	1886, September 30
1305	1887, September 19
1306	1888, September 7*
1307	1889, August 28
1308	1890, August 17
1309	1891, August 7
1310	1892, July 26*
1311	1893, July 15
1312	1894, July 5
1313	1895, June 24
1314	1896, June 12*

AH Hejira	AD Christian Date
1315	1897, June 2
1316	1898, May 22
1317	1899, May 12
1318	1900, May 1
1319	1901, April 20
1320	1902, April 10
1321	1903, March 30
1322	1904, March 18*
1323	1905, March 8
1324	1906, February 25
1325	1907, February 14
1326	1908, February 4*
1327	1909, January 23
1328	1910, January 13
1329	1911, January 2
1330	1911, December 22
1331	1912, December 11*
1332	1913, November 30
1333	1914, November 19
1334	1915, November 9
1335	1916, October 28*
1336	1917, October 17
1337	1918, October 7
1338	1919, September 26
1339	1920, September 15*
1340	1921, September 4
1341	1922, August 24
1342	1923, August 14
1343	1924, August 2*
1344	1925, July 22
1345	1926, July 12
1346	1927, July 1
1347	1928, June 20*
1348	1929, June 9
1349	1930, May 29
1350	1931, May 19
1351	1932, May 7*
1352	1933, April 26
1353	1934, April 16
1354	1935, April 5
1355	1936, March 24*
1356	1937, March 14
1357	1938, March 3
1358	1939, February 21
1359	1940, February 10*
1360	1941, January 29
1361	1942, January 19
1362	1943, January 8
1363	1943, December 28
1364	1944, December 17*
1365	1945, December 6
1366	1946, November 25
1367	1947, November 15
1368	1948, November 3*
1369	1949, October 24
1370	1950, October 13
1371	1951, October 2
1372	1952, September 21*
1373	1953, September 10
1374	1954, August 30
1375	1955, August 20
1376	1956, August 8*
1377	1957, July 29
1378	1958, July 18
1379	1959, July 7
1380	1960, June 25*
1381	1961, June 14
1382	1962, June 4
1383	1963, May 25
1384	1964, May 13*
1385	1965, May 2
1386	1966, April 22
1387	1967, April 11
1388	1968, March 31*
1389	1969, March 20
1390	1970, March 9
1391	1971, February 27
1392	1972, February 16*
1393	1973, February 4
1394	1974, January 25
1395	1975, January 14
1396	1976, January 3*
1397	1976, December 23*
1398	1977, December 12
1399	1978, December 2
1400	1979, November 21
1401	1980, November 9*
1402	1981, October 30
1403	1982, October 19
1404	1983, October 8
1405	1984, September 27*
1406	1985, September 16
1407	1986, September 6
1408	1987, August 26
1409	1988, August 14*
1410	1989, August 3
1411	1990, July 24
1412	1991, July 13
1413	1992, July 2*
1414	1993, June 21
1415	1994, June 10
1416	1995, May 31
1417	1996, May 19*
1418	1997, May 9
1419	1998, April 28
1420	1999, April 17
1421	2000, April 6*

Language	January	February	March	April	May	June	July	August	September	October	November	December
English	January	February	March	April	May	June	July	August	September	October	November	December
Albanian	Kallnuer	Fruer	Mars	Prill	Maj	Qershuer	Korrik	Gusht	Shtatuer	Tetuer	Nanduer	Dhetuer
Czech	Leden	Unor	Brezen	Duben	Kveten	Cerven	Cervenec	Srpen	Zari	Rijen	listopad	Prosinec
Danish	Januar	Februar	Maart	April	Maj	Juni	Juli	August	September	Oktober	November	December
Dutch	Januari	Februari	Maart	April	Mei	Juni	Juli	Augustus	September	Oktober	November	December
Estonian	Jaanuar	Veebruar	Marts	Aprill	Mai	Juuni	Juuli	August	September	Oktoober	November	Detsember
French	Janvier	Fevrier	Mars	Avril	Mai	Juin	Jillet	Aout	Septembre	Octobre	Novembre	Decembre
Finnish	Tammikuu	Helmikuu	Maaliskuu	Huhtikuu	Toukokuu	Kesakuu	Heinakuu	Elokuu	Syyskuu	Lokakuu	Marraskuu	Joulukuu
German	Januar	Februar	Marz	April	Mai	juni	Juli	August	September	Oktober	November	Dezember
Hungarian	Januar	Februar	Marcius	Aprilis	Majus	Junius	Julius	Augusztus	Szeptember	Oktober	November	December
Indonesian	Djanuari	Februari	Maret	April	Mai	Djuni	Djui	Augustus	September	Oktober	Nopember	Desember
Italian	Gennaio	Fabbraio	Marzo	Aprile	Maggio	Giugno	Luglio	Agosto	Settembre	Ottobre	Novembre	Dicembre
Lithuanian	Sausis	Vasaris	Kovas	Balandis	Geguzis	Birzelis	Liepos	Rugpiutis	Rugsejis	Spalis	Lapkritis	Gruodis
Norwegian	Januar	Februar	Mars	April	Mai	Juni	Juli	August	September	Oktober	November	Desember
Polish	Styczen	Luty	Marzec	Kwiecien	Maj	Cerwiec	Lipiec	Sierpien	Wrzesien	Pazdziernik	Listopad	Grudzien
Portuguese	Janerio	Fevereiro	Marco	Abril	Maio	Junho	Julho	Agosto	Setembro	Outubro	Novembro	Dezembro
Romanian	Ianuarie	Februarie	Martie	Aprilie	Mai	Iunie	Iulie	August	Septembrie	Octombrie	Noiembrie	Decembrie
Croatian	Sijecanj	Veljaca	Ozujak	Travanj	Svibanj	Lipanj	Srpanj	Kolovoz	Rujan	Listopad	Studeni	Prosinac
Spanish	Enero	Febrero	Marzo	Abril	Mayo	Junio	Julio	Agosto	Septiembre	Octubre	Noviembre	Diciembre
Swedish	Januari	Februari	Mars	April	Maj	Juni	Juli	Augusti	September	Oktober	November	December
Turkish	Ocak	Subat	Mart	Nisan	Mayis	Haziran	Temmuz	Agusto	Eylul	Ekim	Kasim	Aralik
Arabic-New (condensed)	يناير	فبراير	مارس	ابريل	مايو	يونيو	يوليو	اغسطس	سبتمبر	اكتوبر	نوفمبر	ديسمبر
Persian (Solar)	فروردین	اردیبهشت	خرداد	تیر	مرداد	شهریور	مهر	آبان	آذر	دی	بهمن	اسفند
(Lunar)	محرم	صفر	ربيع الأول	ربيع الآخر	جمادى الأولى	جمادى الآخرة	رجب	شعبان	رمضان	شوال	ذو القعدة	ذو الحجة
Chinese	一月	二月	三月	四月	五月	六月	七月	八月	九月	十月	十一月	十二月
Japanese	一月	二月	三月	四月	五月	六月	七月	八月	九月	十月	十一月	十二月
Greek	Ιανουάριος	Φεβρουάριος	Μάρτιος	Απρίλιος	Μάιος	Ιούνιος	Ιούλιος	Αύγουστος	Σεπτέμβριος	Οκτώβριος	Νοέμβριος	Δεκέμβριος
Russian	ЯНВАРЬ	ФЕВРАЛЬ	МАРТ	АПРЕЛЬ	МАИ	ИЮНЬ	ИЮЛЬ	АВГУСТ	СЕНТЯБРЬ	ОКТЯБРЬ	НОЯБРЬ	ДЕКАБРЬ
Serbian	Јануар	Фебруар	Март	Април	Мај	Јун	Јул	Август	Септембар	Октобар	Новембар	Децембар
Ukranian	Січень	Лютий	Березень	Квітень	Травень	Червень	Липень	Серпень	Вересень	Жовтень	Листопад	Грудень
Yiddish	יאַנואַר	פֿעברואַר	מאַרץ	אַפּריל	מיי	יוני	יולי	אויגוסט	סעפּטעמבער	אקטאבער	נאוועמבער	דעצעמבער
Hebrew (Israeli)	ינואר	פברואר	מרץ	אפריל	מאי	יוני	יולי	אוגוסט	ספטמבר	אוקטובר	נובמבר	דצמבר

Note: Word spellings and configurations as represented on actual notes may vary significantly from those shown on this chart.

STANDARD INTERNATIONAL NUMERAL SYSTEMS © 1997 BY KRAUSE PUBLICATIONS
PREPARED ESPECIALLY FOR THE STANDARD CATALOG OF WORLD PAPER MONEY

WESTERN	0	½	1	2	3	4	5	6	7	8	9	10	50	100	500	1000
ROMAN			I	II	III	IV	V	VI	VII	VIII	IX	X	L	C	D	M
ARABIC-TURKISH	٠	١/٢	١	٢	٣	٤	٥	٦	٧	٨	٩	١٠	٥٠	١٠٠	٥٠٠	١٠٠٠
MALAY—PERSIAN	٠	١/٢	١	٢	٣	۴	۵	۶ or ٧	٧	٨	٩	١٠	۵٠	١٠٠	۵٠٠	١٠٠٠
EASTERN ARABIC	o	½	1	૨	૩	૭	୯	Ƴ	٦	٩	9	1o	୯o	1oo	୯oo	1ooo
HYDERABAD ARABIC	o	¼	١	٢	٣	୵	۵	५	<	٨	٩	1o	۵o	1oo	۵oo	1ooo
INDIAN (Sanskrit)	0	૪/૨	૧	૨	૩	૪	૫	૬	૭	૮	૯	૧૦	૪૦	૧૦૦	૪૦૦	૧૦૦૦
ASSAMESE	0	৸/2	৵	২	৩	৪	৫	৩	৭	৮	২	৵০	50	৵০০	৩০০	৵০০০
BENGALI	0	৩/২	১	২	৩	৪	৫	৬	৭	৮	৯	১০	৫০	১০০	৫০০	১০০০
GUJARATI	0	૧/૨	૧	૨	૩	૪	૫	૬	૭	૮	૯	૧૦	૪૦	૧૦૦	૪૦૦	૧૦૦૦
KUTCH	0	૧/૨	1	૨	૩	૪	૪	૬	૭	੭	૨	10	૪0	100	૪00	1000
DEVAVNAGRI	0	૧/૨	૧	૨	૩	૪	૫ or ૬	७	৩	८ or ८	૯	૧૦	૪૦	૧૦૦	૪૦૦	૧૦૦૦
NEPALESE	0	½	૧ or ૧	૨	૩	૪	૪ or ૫	૬	૭	८ or ८	५ or ६	૧૦	૪૦	૧૦૦	૪૦૦	૧૦૦૦
TIBETAN	o	⁷/₂	໑	২	३	৮	୳	৬	੭	৴	৮	໑০	৮০	໑০০	৮০০	໑০০০
MONGOLIAN	0	%2	໑	੨	੩	੦	੫	੬	੭	੭	੭	໑০	੫০	໑০০	੫০০	໑০০০
BURMESE	o	⅔	০	၂	၃	၄	၅	၆	၇	၈	၉	၁၀	၅၀	၁၀၀	၅၀၀	၁၀၀၀
THAI-LAO	0	%2	๑	๒	๓	๔	๕	๖	๗	๘	๙	๑๐	๕๐	๑๐๐	๕๐๐	๑๐๐๐
JAVANESE	o		꧑	꧒	꧓	꧔	꧕	꧖	꧗	꧘	꧙	꧑꧐	꧕꧐	꧑꧐꧐	꧕꧐꧐	꧑꧐꧐꧐
ORDINARY CHINESE JAPANESE-KOREAN	零	半	一	二	三	四	五	六	七	八	九	十	十五	百	百五	千
OFFICIAL CHINESE			壹	貳	參	肆	伍	陸	柒	捌	玖	拾	拾伍	佰	佰伍	仟
COMMERCIAL CHINESE			〡	〢	〣	〤	〥	〦	〧	〨	〩	十	〥十	〡百	〥百	〡千
KOREAN		반	일	이	삼	사	오	육	찰	팔	구	십	오십	백	오백	천

GEORGIAN

			1	2	3	4	5	6	7	8	9	10	20	30	40	50
			ა	ბ	გ	დ	ე	ვ	ზ	ჱ	თ	ი	კ	ლ	მ	ნ

11	20	30	40	50	60	70	80	90	100	200	300	400	600	700	800
ჲ	ო	პ	ჟ	რ	ს	ტ	უ	ფ	ქ	ღ	ყ	შ	ჩ	ც	ძ

ETHIOPIAN

1	2	3	4	5	6	7	8	9	10	20	30	40	50	60	70	80	90
፩	፪	፫	፬	፭	፮	፯	፰	፱	፲	፳	፴	፵	፶	፷	፸	፹	፺
									100	200	300	400	600	700	800		
									፻	፪፻	፫፻	፬፻	፮፻	፯፻	፰፻		

HEBREW

1	2	3	4	5	6	7	8	9	10	100	500	1000
א	ב	ג	ד	ה	ו	ז	ח	ט	י	ק	תק	תתק

20	30	40	60	70	80	90	200	300	400	600	700	800
כ	ל	מ	ס	ע	פ	צ	ר	ש	ת	תר	תש	תת

GREEK

A	B	Γ	Δ	E	Σ	T	Z	H	Θ	I	N	P	O	Ϟ

20	30	40	60	70	80	200	300	400	600	700	800
K	Λ	M	Ξ	O	Π	Σ	T	Y	X	Ψ	Ω

SPECIMEN NOTES

To familiarize private banks, central banks, law enforcement agencies and treasuries around the world with newly issued currency, many issuing authorities provide special 'Specimen' examples of their notes. Specimens are actual bank notes, complete with consecutive or all zero serial numbers, proper signatures and bearing an overprint or pin-hole perforation of the word SPECIMEN, sometimes in English, or in the language of the nation of issue or choice of the printing firm.

Some countries have made specimen notes available to collectors. These include Cuba, Czechoslovakia, Poland and Slovakia. Aside from these collector issues, specimen notes usually command higher prices than regular issue notes of the same type, even though there are far fewer collectors of specimens. In some cases notably older issues in high denominations, specimens may be the only form of such notes available to collectors today. Specimen notes are not legal tender or redeemable, thus have no real 'face value' which also is indicated on some examples.

The most unusual form of specimens were produced by the firm of Waterlow and Sons Ltd. They printed the notes with a company seal, and very often printed them in several different color combinations in addition to the regularly approved colors. These were intended to be mounted in salesman's sample books. Generally these are not included in the scope of this catalog.

Some examples of how the word SPECIMEN is represented in other languages or on notes of other countries follow:

AMOSTRA: Brazil
COMPIONE: Italy
CONTOH: Malaysia
EKSEMPLAAR: South Africa
ESPÉCIME: Portugal and Colonies
ESPECIMEN: Various Spanish-speaking nations
GIAY MAU: Vietnam
MINTA: Hungary
MODELO: Brazil
MODEL: Albania
MUSTER: Austria, Germany
MUESTRA: Various Spanish-speaking nations
NUMUNEDIR GECMEZ: Turkey
ORNEKTIR GECMEZ: Turkey
ОБРАЗЕЦ or **ОБРАЗЕЦЪ:** Bulgaria, Russia
PARAUGS: Latvia
PROFTRYK: Sweden
SPEZIMEN: Switzerland
UZORAK: Croatia
VZOREC: Slovenia
WZOR: Poland
ЗАГВАР: Mongolia

نموذج or نموذج : Arabic

نمونه : Persian

نمونہ : Pakistan

דוגמא : Israel

ແບບປ່າງ : Laos

Specimen of face of a Taiwan Bank year 53 (1964) dated note with perforated ancient Chinese seal script characters.

Specimen of a Bermuda Monetary Authority 1978 dated note with punched normal serial numbers having been created at a later date for sale to collectors.

樣本 : China (printed or perforated)

見本 : Japan

 : Cambodia

 : Korea (old)

 : Korea (old)

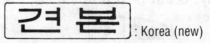
견본 : Korea (new)

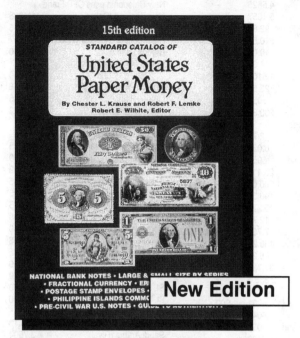

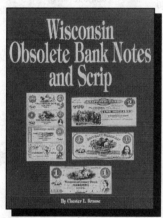

Foreign Exchange Table

The latest foreign exchange fixed rates below apply to trade with banks in the country of origin. The left column shows the number of units per U.S. dollar at the official rate. The right column shows the number of units per dollar at the free market rate.

Country	Official #/$	Market #/$
Afghanistan (Afghan)	4,750	5,300
Albania (Lek)	102.50	–
Algeria (Dinar)	55.489	66.00
Andorra uses French Franc and Spanish Peseta		
Angola (Readjust Kwanza)	201,994	
Anguilla uses E.C. Dollar	2.70	–
Antigua uses E.C. Dollar	2.70	–
Argentina (New Peso)	.9998	–
Armenia (Dram)	420.00	–
Aruba (Florin)	1.79	–
Australia (Dollar)	1.2726	–
Austria (Schilling)	10.635	–
Azerbaijan (Manat)	4,230	–
Bahamas (Dollar)	1.00	–
Bahrain Is. (Dinar)	.377	–
Bangladesh (Taka)	42.61	43.00
Barbados (Dollar)	2.01	–
Belarus (Ruble)	11,500	–
Belgium (Franc)	31.13	–
Belize (Dollar)	2.00	2.00
Benin uses CFA Franc West	510.57	–
Bermuda (Dollar)	1.00	–
Bhutan (Ngultrum)	35.74	39.00
Bolivia (Boliviano)	5.18	–
Bosnia-Herzegovina (New Dinar)	141.00	–
Botswana (Pula)	3.629	–
British Virgin Islands uses U.S. Dollar	1.00	–
Brazil (Real)	1.034	–
Brunei/Ringgit	1.39	–
Bulgaria (Lev)	248.71	–
Burkina Faso uses CFA Fr. West	510.57	–
Burma (Kyat)	5.81	110.00
Burundi (Franc)	216.31	–
Cambodia (Riel)	2,300	–
Cameron uses CFA Fr. Central	510.57	–
Canada (Dollar)	1.3301	–
Cape Verde (Escudo)	82.97	91.00
Cayman Is. (Dollar)	0.8282	–
Central African Rep.	510.57	
CFA Franc Central	510.57	
CFA Franc West	510.57	
CFP Franc	92.83	
Chad uses CFA Franc Central	510.57	
Chile (Peso)	417.95	
China, P.R. (Renminbi Yuan)	8.297	
Colombia (Peso)	1,000.75	
Comoros (Franc)	382.93	–
Congo uses CFA Franc Central	510.57	–
Cook Islands (Dollar)	1.47	–
Costa Rica (Colon)	216.5	–
Croatia (Kuna)	5.371	–
Cuba (Peso)	20.00	35.00
Cyprus (Pound)	.4611	–
Czech Republic (Koruna)	26.909	–
Denmark (Krona)	5.81	–
Djibouti (Franc)	165.00	–
Dominica uses E.C. Dollar	2.70	–
Dom. Rep. (Peso)	13.78	–
East Caribbean (Dollar)	2.70	–
Ecuador (Sucre)	3,365.00	–
Egypt (Pound)	3.3928	–
El Salvador (Colon)	8.75	–
England (Sterling Pound)	.6050	–
Equatorial Guinea uses CFA Franc Central	510.57	
Eritrea, see Ethiopia		
Estonia (Kroon)	12.06	–
Ethiopia (Birr)	6.231	7.25
European Currency Unit	.7869	–
Falkland Is. (Pound)	.6050	–

Country	#/$	#/$
Faroe Islands (Krona)	5.811	–
Fiji Islands (Dollar)	1.39	–
Finland (Markka)	4.5625	–
France (Franc)	5.1057	–
French Polynesia uses CFP Franc	92.83	–
Gabon (CFA Franc)	510.57	–
Gambia (Dalasi)	10.04	–
Georgia/Lari	1.30	–
Germany (Mark)	1.5103	–
Ghana (Cedi)	1,723.50	–
Gibraltar (Pound)	.6050	–
Greece (Drachma)	238.39	–
Greenland uses Danish Krona		
Grenada uses E.C. Dollar	2.70	–
Guatemala (Quetzal)	6.039	–
Guernsey uses Sterling Pound	.6050	–
Guinea-Bissau (Peso)	23,418	–
Guinea Conakry (Franc)	1,000.00	–
Guyana (Dollar)	140.30	–
Haiti (Gourde)	15.271	–
Honduras (Lempira)	12.70	–
Hong Kong (Dollar)	7.732	–
Hungary (Forint)	159.21	–
Iceland (Krona)	66.22	–
India (Rupee)	35.739	–
Indonesia (Rupiah)	2,333.5	–
Iran (Rial)	3,000	5,000
Iraq (Dinar)	.31	1,200
Ireland (Eire) (Punt)	.6046	–
Isle of Man uses Sterling Pound	.6050	–
Israel (New Sheqalim)	3.2438	–
Italy (Lira)	1,521.25	–
Ivory Coast uses CFA Fr. West	510.57	–
Jamaica (Dollar)	34.00	38.00
Japan (Yen)	111.96	–
Jersey (Sterling Pound)	.6050	–
Jordan (Dinar)	.709	–
Kazakhstan (Tenge)	65.00	–
Kenya (Shilling)	55.75	–
Kiribati uses Australian Dollar		
Korea-PDR (Won)	2.15	–
Korea-Rep. (Won)	829.0	–
Kuwait (Dinar)	.299	–
Kyrgyzstan (Som)	11.05	–
Laos (Kip)	920.00	–
Latvia (Lat)	.55	–
Lebanon (Pound)	1,551.00	–
Lesotho (Maloti)	4.685	–
Liberia/Dollar "JJ"	1.00	30.00
"Liberty"	–	49.00
Libya (Dinar)	.3555	1.00
Liechtenstein uses Swiss Franc		
Lithuania (Litas)	4.00	–
Luxembourg (Franc)	31.13	–
Macao (Pataca)	7.988	–
Macedonia (New Denar)	40.298	–
Madagascar (Franc)	3,950	–
Malawi (Kwacha)	15.325	16.50
Malaysia (Ringgit)	2.521	–
Maldives (Rufiya)	11.77	–
Mali uses CFA Franc West	510.57	–
Malta (Lira)	.3565	–
Marshall Islands uses U.S. Dollar		
Mauritania (Ouguiya)	138.92	140.00
Mauritius (Rupee)	20.205	–
Mexico (Peso)	7.925	–
Moldova (Leu)	4.55	–
Monaco uses French Franc		
Mongolia (Tugrik)	466.67	–
Montenegro uses Yugo New Dinar		
Montserrat uses E.C. Dollar	2.70	–
Morocco (Dirham)	8.675	–
Mozambique (Metical)	11,140.5	–
Myanmar (Burma) (Kyat)	5.81	110.00
Namibia (Rand)	4.685	–
Nauru uses Australiian Dollar		
Nepal (Rupee)	56.775	–

Country	#/$	#/$
Netherlands (Gulden)	1.6937	–
Netherlands Antilles (Gulden)	1.79	–
New Caledonia uses CFP Franc		
New Zealand (Dollar)	1.4085	–
Nicaragua (Cordoba Oro)	8.775	–
Niger uses CFA Franc West	510.57	–
Nigeria (Naira)	79.00	–
Northern Ireland uses Sterling Pound	.6050	–
Norway (Krone)	6.346	–
Oman (Rial)	.385	–
Pakistan (Rupee)	40.22	–
Palau uses U.S. Dollar		
Panama (Balboa) uses U.S. Dollar		
Papua-New Guinea (Kina)	1.3395	–
Paraguay (Guarani)	2,100	–
Peru (Nuevos Soles)	2.589	–
Philippines (Peso)	26.255	–
Poland (Zloty)	2.8105	–
Portugal (Escudo)	155.875	–
Qatar (Riyal)	3.639	–
Romania (Leu)	3,450	–
Russia (Ruble)	5,458	–
Rwanda (Franc)	323.85	–
St. Helena (Pound)	.6050	–
St. Kitts uses E.C. Dollar	2.70	–
St. Lucia uses E.C. Dollar	2.70	–
St. Vincent uses E.C. Dollar	2.70	–
San Marino uses Italian Lira		
Sao Tome e Principe (Dobra)	2,385.13	–
Saudi Arabia (Riyal)	3.7504	–
Scotland uses Sterling Pound	.6050	–
Senegal uses CFA Franc West	510.57	–
Seychelles (Rupee)	5.0008	–
Sierra Leone (Leone)	750	–
Singapore (Dollar)	1.3985	–
Slovakia (Sk. Koruna)	30.937	–
Slovenia (Tolar)	137.88	–
Solomon Is. (Dollar)	3.6063	–
Somalia (Shillin)	2,620	12,000
Somaliland (Somali Shillin)	N/A	100
South Africa (Rand)	4.685	–
Spain (Peseta)	127.14	–
Sri Lanka (Rupee)	57.05	–
Sudan (Dinar)	146	980.00
Surinam (Guilder)	410.00	–
Swaziland (Lilangeni)	4.685	–
Sweden (Krona)	6.6255	–
Switzerland (Franc)	1.2733	–
Syria (Pound)	41.95	–
Taiwan (NT Dollar)	27.24	–
Tajikistan uses Russian Ruble		
Tanzania (Shilling)	602.50	–
Thailand (Baht)	25.475	–
Togo uses CFA Franc West	510.57	–
Tonga (Pa'anga)	1.2141	–
Transdniestra (New Ruble)	N/A	30,000
Trinidad & Tobago (Dollar)	6.045	–
Tunisia (Dinar)	.9725	–
Turkey (Lira)	97,479.00	–
Turkmenistan (Manat)	195	–
Turks & Caicos uses U.S. Dollar		
Tuvalu uses Australian Dollar		
Uganda (Shilling)	1,096	–
Ukraine (Hryvnia)	1.844	–
United Arab Emirates (Dirham)	3.672	–
Uruguay (Peso Uruguayo)	8.51	–
Uzbekistan (Som)	24.00	40.00
Vanuatu (Vatu)	111.31	–
Vatican City uses Italian Lira		
Venezuela (Bolivar)	471.51	–
Vietnam (Dong)	11,030	–
Western Samoa (Tala)	2.4295	–
Yemen Rial	130.00	145.00
Yugoslavia (Novikh Dinar)	5.034	–
Zaire (Nouveaux Zaire)	29,226.5	–
Zambia (Kwacha)	1,275.00	–
Zimbabwe (Dollar)	10.665	–

AFGHANISTAN

The Islamic Republic of Afghanistan, which occupies a mountainous region of Southwest Asia, has an area of 250,000 sq. mi. (647,497 sq. km.) and a population of 16.6 million. Presently about a fourth of the total population reside mostly in Pakistan in exile as refugees. Capital: Kabul. It is bordered by Iran, Pakistan, Russia, and Peoples Republic of China's Sinkiang Province. Agriculture and herding are the principal industries; textile mills and cement factories are recent additions to the industrial sector. Cotton, wool, fruits, nuts, sheepskin coats and hand-woven carpets are exported but foreign trade has been interrupted since 1979.

Because of its strategic position astride the ancient land route to India, Afghanistan - formerly known as Aryana and Khorasan - was conquered by Darius I, Alexander the Great, various Scythian tribes, the Arabs, the Turks, Genghis Khan, Tamerlane, the Mughals, the Persians, and in more recent times by Great Britain.

It was a powerful empire under the Kushans, Hephthalites, Ghaznavids and Ghorids. The name Afghanistan, "Land of the Afghans," came into use in the eighteenth and ninteenth to describe the realm of the Afghan kings. Previously this mountainous region was the eastern most frontier of the Iranian world, with strong cultural influences from the Turks and Mongols to the north and India to the south.

The first Afghan king, Ahmad Shah Abdali, founder of the Durrani dynasty, established his rule at Qandahar in 1747. He conquered large territories in India and eastern Iran, which were lost by his grandson Zaman Shah. A new family, the Barakzays, drove the Durrani king out of Kabul, the capital, in 1819, but the Durranis were not eliminated completely until 1858. Further conflicts among the Barakzays prevented full unity until the reign of 'Abd al-Rahman in 1880. In 1929 the last Barakzay was Saqao, "Son of the Water-Carrier," who ruled as Habib Allah for less than a year before he was defeated by Muhammad Nadir Shah, a relative of the Barakzays. The last king, Muhammad Zahir, became a constitutional, though still autocratic, monarch in 1964. In 1973 a coup d'etat displaced him and created the Republic of Afghanistan. A subsequent military coup established the pro-Soviet Democratic Republic of Afghanistan in 1978. Mounting resistance in the countryside and violence within the government led to the Soviet invasion of late 1979 and the installation of Babrak Kamal as prime minister. A brutal civil war ensued, which continues to the present, even after soviet forces withdrew in 1989 and Kamal's government was defeated in 1992. Various militant Islamic movements have had control on and off since. Troops of President Rabbani regained possession of Kabul in March, 1995.

RULERS:
Muhammad Zahir Shah, SH1312-1352/1933-1973AD

MONETARY SYSTEM:
1 Amani = 20 Afghani 1925-
1 Afghani = 100 Pul

KINGDOM

BANK OF AFGHANISTAN

1961-63 ISSUES
#37-42 Kg. Muhammad Zahir at l. and as wmk. Printer: TDLR. 156 x 66mm.

37	10 AFGHANIS	VG	VF	UNC
	SH1340 (1961). Brown on m/c unpt.	.50	1.00	5.00

38	20 AFGHANIS	VG	VF	UNC
	SH1340 (1961). Blue on m/c unpt.	.50	1.00	6.00

39	50 AFGHANIS	VG	VF	UNC
	SH1340 (1961). Green on m/c unpt.	1.00	3.00	11.00
40	100 AFGHANIS			
	SH1340 (1961). Red on m/c unpt.	5.00	10.00	22.50
40A (41A)	500 AFGHANIS			
	SH1340 (1961). Orange on m/c unpt.	30.00	75.00	150.00

41	500 AFGHANIS	VG	VF	UNC
	SH1342 (1963). Olive-brown on m/c unpt.	15.00	45.00	85.00

42	1000 AFGHANIS	VG	VF	UNC
	SH1340 (1961); SH1342 (1963). Blue-gray on m/c unpt.			
	a. 8 Digit serial #. SH1340.	40.00	100.00	250.00
	b. Prefix serial #. SH1342.	35.00	90.00	225.00

1967 ISSUE
#43-46 Kg. Muhammad Zahir at l. and as wmk. W/o imprint.

43	50 AFGHANIS	VG	VF	UNC
	SH1346 (1967). Green on m/c unpt.	1.25	2.50	7.50

44	100 AFGHANIS	VG	VF	UNC
	SH1346 (1967). Lilac on m/c unpt.	2.00	4.00	12.00
45	500 AFGHANIS			
	SH1346 (1967). Blue on m/c unpt.	10.00	30.00	90.00
46	1000 AFGHANIS			
	SH1346 (1967). Brown on m/c unpt.	30.00	100.00	300.00

REPUBLIC
SH1352-1358/1973-1979 AD

BANK OF AFGHANISTAN

1973-78 ISSUE
NOTE: #47-53 Pres. Muhammad Daud at I. and as wmk.

NOTE: It is possible that all notes #47-53 dated SH1354 are replacements. Small quantities of the above filtered into the market via Pakistan recently.

			VG	VF	UNC
47	**10 AFGHANIS**				
	SH1352 (1973); SH1354 (1975); SH1356 (1977). Green on m/c unpt.		.25	.75	2.25

			VG	VF	UNC
48	**20 AFGHANIS**				
	SH1352 (1973); SH1354 (1975); SH1356 (1977). Violet on m/c unpt.		.30	1.00	3.00

			VG	VF	UNC
49	**50 AFGHANIS**				
	SH1352 (1973); SH1354 (1975); SH1356 (1977). Green on m/c unpt.		.50	1.50	4.50

			VG	VF	UNC
50	**100 AFGHANIS**				
	SH1352 (1973); SH1354 (1975); SH1356 (1977). Brown-lilac on m/c unpt.		.65	2.00	6.00

			VG	VF	UNC
51	**500 AFGHANIS**				
	SH1352 (1973); SH1354 (1975). Blue on m/c unpt.		1.00	4.00	12.50
52	**500 AFGHANIS**				
	SH1356 (1977). Brown on m/c unpt. Like #51.		2.00	8.00	25.00

			VG	VF	UNC
53	**1000 AFGHANIS**				
	SH1352 (1973); SH1354 (1975); SH1356 (1977). Brown on m/c unpt.		1.25	5.00	15.00

DEMOCRATIC REPUBLIC
SH1357-1370/1978-1992 AD

DA AFGHANISTAN BANK

1978 ISSUE

			VG	VF	UNC
54	**50 AFGHANIS**				
	SH1357 (1978). Blue-green on m/c unpt. Arms w/star at top, and Arabic legend. Bldg. on back.		.30	1.50	8.50

1979 ISSUE
NOTE: #55-61 arms w/horseman at top on face.

			VG	VF	UNC
55	**10 AFGHANIS**				
	SH1358 (1979). Green and blue on m/c unpt. Mountain road scene on back.		.15	.25	.75

			VG	VF	UNC
56	**20 AFGHANIS**				
	SH1358 (1979). Purple on m/c unpt. Bldg. and mountains on back. Sign. varieties.		.20	.40	1.25

			VG	VF	UNC
57	**50 AFGHANIS**				
	SH1358- (1979-). Greenish black with black text on m/c unpt. Similar to #54.				
	a. SH1358 (1979). 2 sign. varieties.		.10	.30	1.00
	b. SH1370 (1991).		.15	.20	2.00

58 100 AFGHANIS
SH1358- (1979-). Deep red-violet on m/c unpt. Farm worker in wheat field at r. Dam in mountains at ctr. on back.

		VG	VF	UNC
a.	SH1358 (1979). 2 sign. varieties.	.15	.40	1.25
b.	SH1369 (1990).	.35	1.00	3.50
c.	SH1370 (1991).	.35	1.00	3.50

59 500 AFGHANIS
SH1358- (1979). Violet and dk. blue on m/c unpt. Horsemen competing in Buzkashi at r. Fortress at Kabul on back.

	VG	VF	UNC
	1.00	3.50	9.00

60 500 AFGHANIS
SH1358- (1979-). Like #59 but reddish brown, deep green and deep brown on m/c unpt. Back deep green on m/c unpt.

		VG	VF	UNC
a.	SH1358 (1979).	.30	1.25	3.00
b.	SH1369 (1990).	.65	1.75	5.00
c.	SH1370 (1991).	.25	1.00	3.00

61 1000 AFGHANIS
SH1358- (1979-). Dk. brown and deep red-violet on m/c unpt. Mosque at r. Shrine w/archways at l. ctr. on back.

		VG	VF	UNC
a.	SH1358 (1979).	1.25	4.00	10.00
b.	SH1369 (1990).	.25	1.00	3.00
c.	SH1370 (1991)	.35	1.50	4.50

1993 ISSUE

62 5000 AFGHANIS
SH1372 (1993). Violet, dk. brown and black on m/c unpt. Mosque w/minaret at r. Mosque at ctr. on back. Wmk: Arms.

VG	VF	UNC
FV	FV	6.50

63 10,000 AFGHANIS
SH1372 (1993). Dk. blue, deep olive-green and black on m/c unpt. Gateway between minarets at r. Arched gateway at ctr. on back. Wmk: Arms.

VG	VF	UNC
FV	FV	12.50

The Republic of Albania, a Balkan republic bounded by the rump Yugoslav state of Montenegro and Serbia, Macedonia, Greece and the Adriatic Sea, has an area of 11,100 sq. mi. (28,748 sq. km.) and a population of 3.3 million. Capital: Tirana. The country is predominantly agricultural, although recent progress has been made in the manufacturing and mining sectors. Petroleum, chrome, iron, copper, cotton textiles, tobacco and wood products are exported.

Since it had been part of the Greek and Roman Empires, little is known of the early history of Albania. After the disintegration of the Roman Empire, Albania was overrun by Goths, Byzantines, Venetians and Turks. Skanderberg, the national hero, resisted the Turks and established an independent Albania in 1443, but in 1468 the country again fell to the Turks and remained part of the Ottoman Empire for more than 400 years.

Independence was re-established by revolt in 1912, and the present borders established in 1913 by a conference of European powers which, in 1914, placed Prince William of Wied on the throne; popular discontent forced his abdication within months. In 1920, following World War I occupancy by several nations, a republic was set up. Ahmet Zogu seized the presidency in 1925, and in 1928 proclaimed himself king with the title of Zog I. King Zog fled when Italy occupied Albania in 1939 and enthroned King Victor Emanuel of Italy. Upon the surrender of Italy to the Allies in 1943, German troops occupied the country. They withdrew in 1944, and communist partisans seized power, naming Gen. Enver Hoxha provisionaly president. In 1946, following a victory by the communist front in the 1945 elections, a new constitution modeled on that of the USSR was adopted. In accordance with the constitution of Dec. 28, 1976, the official name of Albania was changed from the People's Republic of Albania to the People's Socialist Republic of Albania. A general strike by trade unions in 1991 forced the communist government to resign. A new government was elected in Mar. 1992.

MONETARY SYSTEM:
- 1 Lek = 100 Qindarka 1948-1965
- 1 "heavy" Lek = 10 old Leke, 1965-1992
- 1 Lek Valute = 50 Leke, 1992-1993

PEOPLES REPUBLIC

BANKA E SHTETIT SHQIPTAR

1964 ISSUE
#33-39 arms at upper r. on back. Wmk: Curved *BSHSH* repeated.

33 1 LEK

		VG	VF	UNC
1964. Green and deep blue on m/c unpt. Peasant couple at ctr. Hillside fortress at l. ctr. on back.				
a.	Issued note.	.15	.50	1.50
s.	Specimen ovpt: *MODEL*.	—		3.00

34 3 LEKE

		VG	VF	UNC
1964. Brown and lilac on m/c unpt. Woman w/basket of grapes at l.				
a.	Issued note.	.20	.65	2.25
s.	Specimen ovpt: *MODEL*.	—		4.00

35 5 LEKE

		VG	VF	UNC
1964. Lilac and blue on m/c unpt. Truck and steam train. Ship at l. on back.				
a.	Issued note.	.25	.90	3.00
s.	Specimen ovpt: *MODEL*.	—		5.00

36 10 LEKE

		VG	VF	UNC
1964. Dk. green on m/c unpt. Woman working w/cotton spinning frame. People at l. ctr., male portr. at upper r. on back.				
a.	Issued note.	.35	1.20	4.00
s.	Specimen ovpt: *MODEL*.	—	—	6.00

37 25 LEKE

		VG	VF	UNC
1964. Blue-black on m/c unpt. Peasant woman w/sheaf at l., combine and truck at ctr. Farm tractor at l. ctr. on back.				
a.	Issued note.	.60	2.00	7.00
s.	Specimen ovpt: *MODEL*.	—	—	7.50

38 50 LEKE

		VG	VF	UNC
1964. Red-brown on m/c unpt. Soldiers on parade at l. ctr., bust of Skanderbeg at upper r. Rifle and pick axe at l., modern bldg. under construction at l. ctr.				
a.	Issued note.	1.00	3.50	12.00
s.	Specimen ovpt: *MODEL*.	—	—	8.50

39   100 LEKE
1964. Brown-lilac. Worker and boy at the coffer dam at l. ctr. Steel
worker and well rigger at ctr. on back.

	VG	VF	UNC
a. Issued note.	2.25	7.50	25.00
s. Specimen ovpt: *MODEL*.	—	—	10.00

PEOPLES SOCIALIST REPUBLIC

BANKA E SHTETIT SHQIPTAR

1976 ISSUE
#40-46 wmk: Bank name around radiant star, repeated.

40   1 LEK
1976. Green and deep blue on m/c unpt. Like #33.

	VG	VF	UNC
a. Issued note.	.10	.25	.75
s1. Red ovpt: *SPECIMEN* w/all zeros serial #.	—	—	3.50
s2. Red ovpt: *SPECIMEN* w/normal serial #.	—	—	.50
s3. Lg. blue ovpt: *SPECIMEN* on face. Black ovpt: *E PRANUESHME* on back.	—	—	—
s4. Lg. blue ovpt: *SPECIMEN* on face. Black bank 25th anniversary rectangular ovpt. on back. Possibly a private ovpt.	—	—	—

41   3 LEKE
1976. Brown and lilac on m/c unpt. Like #34.

	VG	VF	UNC
a. Issued note.	.10	.30	1.00
s1. Red ovpt: *SPECIMEN* w/all zeros serial #.	—	—	4.00
s2. Red ovpt: *SPECIMEN* w/normal serial #.	—	—	.75

42   5 LEKE
1976. Lilac and blue on m/c unpt. Like #35.

	VG	VF	UNC
a. Issued note.	.10	.35	1.50
s1. Red ovpt: *SPECIMEN* w/all zeros serial #.	—	—	4.50
s2. Red ovpt: *SPECIMEN* w/normal serial #.	—	—	1.00
s3. Lg. blue ovpt: *SPECIMEN* on face. Black ovpt: *E PRANUESHME* on back.	—	—	—
s4. Lg. blue ovpt: *SPECIMEN* on face. Black bank 25th anniversary rectangular ovpt. on back. Possibly a private ovpt.	—	—	—

43   10 LEKE
1976. Dk. green on m/c unpt Like #36.

	VG	VF	UNC
a. Issued note.	.10	.40	2.00
s1. Red ovpt: *SPECIMEN* w/all zeros serial #.	—	—	5.50
s2. Red ovpt: *SPECIMEN* w/normal serial #.	—	—	1.25

44   25 LEKE
1976. Blue-black on m/c unpt. Like #37.

	VG	VF	UNC
a. Issued note.	.15	.50	3.50
s1. Red ovpt: *SPECIMEN* w/all zeros serial #.	—	—	6.50
s2. Red ovpt: *SPECIMEN* w/normal serial #.	—	—	1.75

45   50 LEKE
1976. Red-brown on m/c unpt. Like #38.

	VG	VF	UNC
a. Issued note.	.25	.75	8.50
s1. Red ovpt: *SPECIMEN* w/all zeros serial #.	—	—	7.50
s2. Red ovpt: *SPECIMEN* w/normal serial #.	—	—	2.50
s3. Lg. blue ovpt: *SPECIMEN* on face. Black ovpt: *E PRANUESNHME* on back.	—	—	—
s4. Lg. blue ovpt: *SPECIMEN* on face. Black bank 25th anniversary rectangular ovpt. on back. Possibly a private ovpt.	—	—	—

46   100 LEKE
1976. Brown-lilac on m/c unpt. Like #39.

	VG	VF	UNC
a. Issued note.	.30	1.50	15.00
s1. Red ovpt: *SPECIMEN* w/all zeros serial #.	—	—	8.50
s2. Red ovpt: *SPECIMEN* w/normal serial #.	—	—	3.00

1991 Issue

#47-48 wmk: Bank name around radiant star, repeated.

47 100 Leke
1991. Deep brown and deep purple on pale orange and m/c unpt.
Steel workers at l., steel mill at r. Refinery at l. ctr., arms at upper r. on
back.

		VG	VF	UNC
a.	Issued note.	.50	2.00	5.00
s.	Specimen.	—	—	5.00

48 500 Leke
1991. Purple, red and blue-green on lt. blue and lt. orange unpt.
Peasant woman by sunflowers at l. ctr. Evergreen trees, mountains at
l. ctr., arms at upper r. on back.

VG	VF	UNC
1.25	5.00	10.00

1992 Issue

#49-50 Steelworker at ctr., electrical transmission towers at l., arms at upper ctr., hydro-electric generator
at r. on back. Wmk: *B.SH.SH.* below star, repeated.

NOTE: Many examples of #49 have mismatched serial #s. No additional premmium should be given for
such.

49 10 Lek Valute (= 500 Leke)
ND (1992). Deep green and purple on m/c unpt.

VG	VF	UNC
2.00	5.00	12.00

50 50 Lek Valute (= 2500 Leke)
ND (1992). Deep brown-violet and gray-green on m/c unpt.

		VG	VF	UNC
a.	W/serial #.	5.00	20.00	55.00
b.	W/o serial #.	2.00	5.00	12.00
s.	Specimen.	—	—	25.00

REPUBLIC

BANKA E SHQIPERISE

1992 Issue

#52-54 wmk: Repeated ring of letters *B.SH.SH.*

#51 Held in reserve.

52 200 Leke
1992. Deep reddish-brown and m/c unpt. I. Qemali at l. Citizens
portrayed in double-headed eagle outline on back.

VG	VF	UNC
FV	FV	4.50

53 500 Leke
1992. Deep blue on blue and m/c unpt. N. Frasheri at l. Rural
mountains at l., candle at ctr. on back.

VG	VF	UNC
FV	FV	12.00

54 **1000 LEKE**

	VG	VF	UNC
1992. Deep green and green on m/c unpt. Skanderbeg at l. Hillside fortress tower at l., crowned arms at ctr. on back.	FV	FV	22.00

1993-94 ISSUE

55 **100 LEKE**

	VG	VF	UNC
1993-94. Purple on m/c unpt. L. Kombetar at l. Mountain peaks at l. ctr., falcon at ctr. on back.			
a. 1993.	FV	FV	3.25
b. 1994.	FV	FV	2.75
s. Specimen.	—	—	2.50

56 **200 LEKE**

	VG	VF	UNC
1994. Like #52.			
a. Issued note.			3.50
s. Specimen.	—	—	4.00

57 **500 LEKE**

	VG	VF	UNC
1994. Like #53.			
a. Issued note.	FV	FV	8.00
s. Specimen.	—	—	6.50

58 **1000 LEKE**

	VG	VF	UNC
1994. Like #54.			
a. Issued note.	FV	FV	16.00
s. Specimen.	—	—	13.00

FOREIGN EXCHANGE CERTIFICATES

BANKA E SHTETIT SHQIPTAR

1965 ISSUE

#FX21-FX27 arms at r. Bank arms at ctr. on back.

FX21 **.05 LEK**

	VG	VF	UNC
1965. Deep blue-green on pink and pale yellow-orange unpt.	—	—	50.00

FX22 **.10 LEK**

	VG	VF	UNC
1965. Deep olive-brown on pink and pale blue unpt.	—	—	50.00

FX23 **1/2 LEK**

	VG	VF	UNC
1965. Deep purple on pink and lilac unpt.	—	—	50.00

FX24 1 LEK   VG   VF   UNC
  1965. Blackish green on pale yellow and pale yellow-orange unpt. —   —   50.00

FX25 5 LEK   VG   VF   UNC
  1965. Blue-black on pale yellow-green. unpt.   —   —   140.00

FX26 10 LEK   VG   VF   UNC
  1965. Blue-green on pale yellow and pale grayish green unpt. —   —   140.00

FX27 50 LEK   VG   VF   UNC
  1965. Deep red-brown on pink and pale yellow unpt.   —   —   140.00

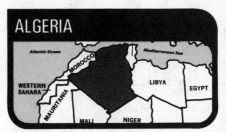

ALGERIA

The Democratic and Popular Republic of Algeria, a North African country fronting on the Mediterranean Sea between Tunisia and Morocco, has an area of 919,595 sq. mi. (2,381,741 sq. km.) and a population of 25.3 million. Capital: Algiers (Alger). Most of the country's working population is engaged in agriculture although a recent industrial diversification, financed by oil revenues, is making steady progress. Wines, fruits, iron and zinc ores, phosphates, tobacco products, liquified natural gas, and petroleum are exported.

Algiers, the capital and chief seaport of Algeria, was the site of Phoenician and Roman settlements before the present Moslem city was founded about 950. Nominally part of the sultanate of Tlemcen, Algiers had a large measure of independence under the amirs of its own. In 1492 the Jews and Moors who had been expelled from Spain settled in Algiers and enjoyed an increasing influence until the imposition of Turkish control in 1518. For the following three centuries Algiers was the headquarters of the notorious Barbary pirates. The French took Algiers in 1830, and after a long and wearisome war completed the conquest of Algeria and annexed it to France, 1848. Following the armistice signed by France and Nazi Germany on June 22, 1940, Algeria fell under Vichy Government control until liberated by the Allied invasion forces under the command of Gen. Dwight D. Eisenhower on Nov. 8, 1942. The inability to obtain equal rights with Frenchmen led to an organized revolt which began on Nov. 1, 1954 and lasted until a ceasefire was signed on July 1, 1962. Independence was proclaimed on July 5, 1962, following a self-determination referendum.

* * *NOTE: This section has been renumbered.* * *

RULERS:
  French to 1962

MONETARY SYSTEM:
  1 Franc = 100 Centimes to 1960
  1 Nouveaux Franc = 100 Old Francs, 1960-64
  1 Dinar = 100 Centimes, 1964-

FRENCH INFLUENCE

BANQUE DE L'ALGÉRIE

1959 PROVISIONAL ISSUE

118	**5 NOUVEAUX FRANCS**	VG	VF	UNC
(47)	1959. Green and m/c. Ram at bottom ctr., Bacchus at r.	10.00	60.00	150.00
	a. 31.7.1959; 18.12.1959.	10.00	70.00	200.00
	s. Specimen. 31.7.1959.	—	—	160.00

119	**10 NOUVEAUX FRANCS**	VG	VF	UNC
(48)	1959-61. Brown and yellow. Isis at l.			
	a. 31.7.1959-2.6.1961.	15.00	85.00	210.00
	s. Specimen. 31.7.1959.	—	—	165.00

120	**50 NOUVEAUX FRANCS**		VG	VF	UNC
(49)	1959. M/c. Pythian Apollo at r.				
	a. 31.7.1959; 18.12.1959.		35.00	125.00	325.00
	s. Specimen. 31.7.1959.		—	—	250.00

121	**100 NOUVEAUX FRANCS**				
(50)	1959-61. Blue and m/c. Seagulls w/city of Algiers in background.				
	a. 31.7.1959; 18.12.1959.		65.00	175.00	350.00
	b. 3.6.1960; 25.11.1960; 10.2.1961; 29.9.1961.		22.50	75.00	225.00
	s. Specimen. 31.7.1959.		—	—	175.00

REPUBLIC

BANQUE CENTRALE D'ALGÉRIE

1964 ISSUE
#122-125 wmk: Emir Abd el-Kader.

122	**5 DINARS**		VG	VF	UNC
(51)	1.1.1964. Violet and lilac. Vultures perched on rocks at l. ctr. Native objects on back. 2 styles of numerals in date and serial #.		1.25	5.00	15.00

123	**10 DINARS**		VG	VF	UNC
(52)	1.1.1964. Lilac and m/c. Pair of storks and minaret. Native craft on back. 2 styles of numerals in date and serial #.		1.50	6.50	20.00

124	**50 DINARS**				
(53)	1.1.1964. Lt. brown and m/c. 2 mountain sheep. Camel caravan on back.		3.50	16.50	50.00

125	**100 DINARS**		VG	VF	UNC
(54)	1.1.1964. M/c. Harbor scene. Modern bldg. complex at l. ctr. on back. 2 styles of numerals in date and serial #.		7.50	15.00	40.00

1970 ISSUE
#126 and 127 wmk: Emir Abd el-Kader.

126	**5 DINARS**		VG	VF	UNC
(55)	1.11.1970. Blue and m/c. Warrior w/shield and sword at ctr. r. Fox head at l. ctr., village in background at ctr. r. on back. Sign. varieties.		.75	2.00	7.50

127	**10 DINARS**		VG	VF	UNC
(56)	1.11.1970. Red-brown. Sheep at l., peacock at r. Seated elderly man at l., ornate bldg. at r. on back. Minor plate varieties in legend.		1.35	4.00	12.50

131 **100 DINARS**
(60) 1.11.1981. Dk. blue and blue on lt. blue unpt. Village w/minarets at l.
Man working w/plants at ctr. on back.

	VG	VF	UNC
	1.00	3.00	12.50

128 **100 DINARS**
(57) 1.11.1970. 2 men at l., wheat ears at r. Scenery w/antelope at r. on
back.

	VG	VF	UNC
a. Deep brown, brown-orange, blue-gray and pale yellow-orange.	3.50	10.00	25.00
b. Lt. brown, brown-orange, blue-gray and pale yellow-orange.	3.50	10.00	25.00

1982-83 ISSUE
#132-135 wmk: Eir Abd el-Kader.

132 **10 DINARS**
(61) 2.12.1983. Black on brown and blue-green unpt. Diesel passenger
train at ctr. Back blue, blue-green and brown; mountain village at ctr.

	VG	VF	UNC
	FV	.20	2.00

129 **500 DINARS**
(58) 1.11.1970. Purple. View of city. Ships on back.

	VG	VF	UNC
	7.50	30.00	75.00

1977; 1981 ISSUE
#130 and 131 wmk: Emir Abd el-Kader.

133 **20 DINARS**
(62) 2.1.1983. Red-brown on ochre unpt. Vase at l. ctr., handcrafts at r.
Tower at ctr. on back.

	VG	VF	UNC
	FV	.25	2.50

130 **50 DINARS**
(59) 1.11.1977. Dk. green on m/c unpt. Shepherd w/flock at lower l. ctr.
Tractor on back. Sign. varieties.

	VG	VF	UNC
	.75	2.50	10.00

134 **100 DINARS**
(64) 8.6.1982. Pale blue and gray. Similar to #131 but w/o bird at upper r.

	VG	VF	UNC
	FV	20.00	50.00

135	**200 DINARS**	VG	VF	UNC
(65)	23.3.1983. Brown, dk. green on m/c unpt. Monument at l. Canyon at ctr., amphora at r. on back.	FV	6.00	17.50

BANQUE D'ALGÉRIE

1995-96 ISSUE

136	**50 DINARS**	VG	VF	UNC
				Expected New Issue
137	**100 DINARS**			
	21.5.1992 (1996).	FV	FV	6.00
138	**200 DINARS**			
	21.5.1992 (1996).	FV	FV	10.00
139	**500 DINARS**			
(66)	21.5.1992 (1996). Deep purple, violet and red-violet on m/c unpt. Hannibal's troops and elephants engaging the Romans at ctr. r. Waterfalls at l., ruins of tomb of the Numid Kg. Massinissa at l. ctr., elephant mounted troops at ctr. r. on back. Wmk: Elephants.	FV	FV	22.50

140	**1000 DINARS**	VG	VF	UNC
(67)	21.5.1992 (1995). Red-brown and orange on m/c unpt. Tassili cave paintings of animals at lower ctr., bull's head at r. Hoggar cave painting of antelope at l., ruins at ctr. on back.	FV	FV	35.00

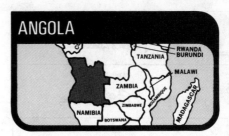

ANGOLA

The Peoples Republic of Angola, a country on the west coast of southern Africa bounded by Zaïre, Zambia and Namibia (South-West Africa), has an area of 481,354 sq. mi. (1,246,700 sq. km.) and a population of 10.4 million, predominantly Bantu in origin. Capital: Luanda. Most of the people are engaged in subsistence agriculture. However, important oil and mineral deposits make Angola potentially one of the richest countries in Africa. Iron and diamonds are exported.

Angola was discovered by Portuguese navigator Diogo Cao in 1482. Portuguese settlers arrived in 1491, and established Angola as a major slaving center which sent about 3 million slaves to the New World.

A revolt against Portuguese rule, characterized by guerrilla warfare, began in 1961 and continued until 1974, when a new regime in Portugal offered independence. The independence movement was actively supported by three groups, the National Front, based in Zaïre, the Soviet-backed Popular Movement, and the moderate National Union. Independence was proclaimed on Nov. 11, 1975.

RULERS:
Portuguese to 1975

MONETARY SYSTEM:
1 Escudo = 100 Centavos, 1954-77
1 Kwanza = 100 Lwei, 1977-95
1 Kwanza Reajustado = 1,000 "old" Kwanzas, 1995-

	SIGNATURE VARIETIES	
	Governor	**Administrator**
1		
	Governor	**Administrator**
2		
	Governor	**Administrator**
3		
	Governor	**Vice-Governor**
4		
	Governor	**Vice-Governor**
5		
	Governor	**Vice-Governor**
6		
	Governor	**Administrator**
7		
	Governor	**Administrator**
8		
	Governor	**Administrator**
9		
	Governor	**Administrator**
10		
	Governor	**Vice-Governor**
11		

	Governor	Administrator
12		

	Governor	Administrator
13		

	Governor	Vice-Governor
14		

	Vice-Governor	Vice-Governor
15		

	Governor	Vice-Governorr
16		

	Governor	Vice-Governor
17		

	Governor	Vice-Governorr
18		

	Governor	Vice-Governorr
19		

	Governor	Administrator
20		

PORTUGUESE INFLUENCE

BANCO DE ANGOLA

1962 ISSUE
#92-96 portr. A. Tomas. at l. or r. Printer: TDLR.

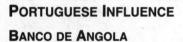

92	20 ESCUDOS	VG	VF	UNC
	10.6.1962. Black on m/c unpt. Portr. Porto at r., dock at l. Gazelle running on back. Sign. 1.	1.00	3.50	10.00

93	50 ESCUDOS	VG	VF	UNC
	10.6.1962. Lt. blue on m/c unpt. Portr. H. de Carvalho at r., airport at l. Various animals at water hole on back. Sign. 2.	1.50	4.50	15.00

94	100 ESCUDOS	VG	VF	UNC
	10.6.1962. Lilac on m/c unpt. Salazar bridge at l. Elephants at watering hole on back. Sign. 3.	2.00	10.00	45.00
95	500 ESCUDOS			
	10.6.1962. Red on m/c unpt. Port of Luanda at ctr. 2 rhinoceros on back. Sign. 4.	6.00	25.00	150.00
96	1000 ESCUDOS			
	10.6.1962. Blue on m/c unpt. Dam at ctr. Herd on back. Sign. 4.	8.00	35.00	225.00

1970 ISSUE
#97-98 printer: TDLR.

97	500 ESCUDOS	VG	VF	UNC
	10.6.1970. Red on m/c unpt. Like #95. Sign. 5.	5.00	15.00	65.00
98	1000 ESCUDOS			
	10.6.1970. Blue on m/c unpt. Like #96. Sign. 5.	7.50	30.00	110.00

1972 ISSUE
#99-103 M. Carmona at ctr. r. Printer: TDLR.

99	20 ESCUDOS	VG	VF	UNC
	24.11.1972. Red, brown and m/c unpt. Flowers on back. Sign. 7.	.50	1.00	5.00

100 **50 ESCUDOS**
24.11.1972. Green, brown and m/c. Plants on back. Sign. 8.

	VG	VF	UNC
	.35	.65	5.00

101 **100 ESCUDOS**
24.11.1972. Lt. and dk. brown and m/c. Tree and plants on back. Sign. 7.

	VG	VF	UNC
	.50	1.00	5.50

102 **500 ESCUDOS**
24.11.1972. Blue and m/c. Rock hill w/huts on back. Sign. 8.

	1.50	4.50	12.50

103 **1000 ESCUDOS**
24.11.1972. Purple and m/c. Waterfalls on back. Sign. 6.

	2.00	7.00	25.00

1973 ISSUE
#104-108 Luiz de Camoes at r.

104 **20 ESCUDOS**
10.6.1973. Blue, purple and green. Cotton plant on back. Sign. 10.

	VG	VF	UNC
	.50	2.00	7.50

105 **50 ESCUDOS**
10.6.1973. Blue and brown. Plant on back. Sign. 9.

	VG	VF	UNC
	.35	.75	3.50

106 **100 ESCUDOS**
10.6.1973. Brown and maroon. Back green and maroon; tree at l. Sign. 10.

	VG	VF	UNC
	.75	1.50	4.00

107 **500 ESCUDOS**
10.6.1973. Brown and purple. Rock hill on back. Sign. 11.

	VG	VF	UNC
	1.50	3.50	9.50

108 **1000 ESCUDOS**
10.6.1973. Olive, blue and m/c. Waterfalls on back. Sign. 11.

	VG	VF	UNC
	2.00	7.50	17.50

PEOPLES REPUBLIC

BANCO NACIONAL DE ANGOLA

1976 ISSUE
#109-113 Agostinho Neto at r. Arms at lower l. on back.

109 **20 KWANZAS**
11.11.1976. Brown, green and orange. Field soldiers on back. Sign. 12.

	VG	VF	UNC
	1.00	2.50	5.00

110 **50 KWANZAS**
11.11.1976. Purple, brown and black. Field workers on back. Sign. 12.

	VG	VF	UNC
	.75	1.50	4.00

111 **100 KWANZAS**
11.11.1976. Green. Cloth factory workers on back. Sign. 12.

	VG	VF	UNC
	1.00	2.00	4.50

112	**500 KWANZAS**	**VG**	**VF**	**UNC**
	11.11.1976. Blue. Cargo ships dockside on back. Sign. 12.	2.00	7.00	15.00

113	**1000 KWANZAS**	**VG**	**VF**	**UNC**
	11.11.1976. Red. School class on back. Sign. 12.	2.00	7.00	17.50

1979 ISSUE

#114-117 w/Z serial #. Sign. titles, date of independence added under bank name on face. Arms at lower l. on back.

114	**50 KWANZAS**	**VG**	**VF**	**UNC**
	14.8.1979. Purple, brown and black. Like #110. Sign. 13.	.80	1.75	5.00

115	**100 KWANZAS**	**VG**	**VF**	**UNC**
	14.8.1979. Green. Like #111. Sign. 13.	.80	1.75	5.00

116	**500 KWANZAS**	**VG**	**VF**	**UNC**
	14.8.1979. Blue. Like #112. Sign. 13.	2.50	15.00	50.00

117	**1000 KWANZAS**	**VG**	**VF**	**UNC**
	14.8.1979. Red. Like #113. Sign. 13.	3.00	12.00	30.00

1984-87 ISSUE

Replacement notes: #118-125: ZA, ZB, ZC, etc., prefix letters.

#118-125 conjoined busts of Jose Eduardo Dos Santos and Antonio Agostinho Neto at r. Arms at lower l. on back. Wmk. (weak): bird.

#118 dated 11.11.1987 may exist (see #122).

#119 dated 1987 was only issued w/ovpt. (see #125).

#120 and 121 wmk: Sculpture.

118	**50 KWANZAS**	**VG**	**VF**	**UNC**
	7.1.1984. Deep brown and green on lt. green and tan unpt. Classroom and teacher on back. Sign. 14.	.40	1.00	3.00

119	**100 KWANZAS**	**VG**	**VF**	**UNC**
	7.1.1984; 11.11.1987. Deep blue, violet and brown on lt. blue and m/c unpt. Picking cotton on back. Sign. 14.	1.50	5.00	10.00

120	**500 KWANZAS**	**VG**	**VF**	**UNC**
	1984; 1987. Black, red-brown and red on lilac and m/c unpt. Offshore oil platform at l., worker at r. on back.			
	a. Sign. 14. 7.1.1984.	3.00	10.00	25.00
	b. Sign. 15. 11.11.1987.	3.00	10.00	25.00

121 1000 KWANZAS

	VG	VF	UNC
1984; 1987. Purple, blue-black and blue on lt. blue and m/c unpt. Soldiers embarking dockside and soldier on back.			
a. Sign. 14. 7.1.1984.	3.00	8.50	30.00
b. Sign. 15. 11.11.1987.	3.00	8.50	30.00

1991 PROVISIONAL ISSUE

122 50 NOVO KWANZA ON 50 KWANZAS

	VG	VF	UNC
ND (-old date 11.11.1987). Ovpt. *NOVO KWANZA* on unissued date of #118. Sign. 15.		Reported Not Confirmed	

123 500 NOVO KWANZA ON 500 KWANZAS

	VG	VF	UNC
ND (-old date 11.11.1987). Ovpt. *NOVO KWANZA* in lt. green on #120. Sign. 15.	10.00	30.00	—

124 1000 NOVO KWANZA ON 1000 KWANZ

	VG	VF	UNC
ND (-old date 11.11.1987). Ovpt. *NOVO KWANZA* in red on #121. Sign. 15.	5.00	17.50	50.00

125 5000 NOVO KWANZA ON 100 KWANZA

	VG	VF	UNC
ND (-old date 11.11.1987). Ovpt. *NOVO KWANZA 5000* in brown on unissued date of #119. Sign. 15.	35.00	100.00	—

1991 ISSUE

Replacement notes: #126-131: AZ, BZ, CZ, DZ, EZ prefix letters.

#126-134 portr. conjoined busts of J. E. Dos Santos and A. A. Neto at r. and as wmk. Arms at lower l. on back.

126 100 KWANZAS

	VG	VF	UNC
4.2.1991. Purple, green and brown. Rock formation at Pungo Andongo at l. ctr. Tribal mask at r. on back. Sign. 16.	.25	1.00	2.50

127 500 KWANZAS

	VG	VF	UNC
4.2.1991. Blue and violet. Back blue, violet, green and brown. Like #126. Specimen.	—	—	—

128 500 KWANZAS

	VG	VF	UNC
4.2.1991. Purple and deep blue-green on m/c unpt. Serra de Leba at l. ctr.; native pot at r. on back.			
a. Sign. 16.	.75	3.00	7.50
b. Sign. 17.	.50	2.00	5.00
c. Sign. 18.	.75	3.00	7.50

129 1000 KWANZAS

	VG	VF	UNC
4.2.1991. Brown, orange, purple and red-violet on m/c unpt. Banco Nacional at l. ctr, native doll at r. on back.			
a. Sign. 16.	1.00	4.00	10.00
b. Sign. 17.	.75	3.00	7.50
c. Sign. 18.	1.00	4.00	10.00

130 5000 KWANZAS

	VG	VF	UNC
4.2.1991. Dk. green, blue-green and dk. brown on m/c unpt. Waterfalls and stylized statue of "The Thinker" on back.			
a. Sign. 16.	1.50	6.00	15.00
b. Sign. 17.	1.00	4.00	10.00
c. Sign. 18.	1.50	6.00	15.00

131 10,000 KWANZAS

		VG	VF	UNC
4.2.1991. Red, olive-green and purple on m/c unpt. Palanca Negra, antelope herd and shell on back.				
a.	Sign. 17.	.50	2.00	5.00
b.	Sign. 18.	.50	2.00	5.00

132 50,000 KWANZAS

	VG	VF	UNC
4.2.1991. Bright green, yellow-green and dk. brown on m/c unpt. Like #130. Sign. 18.	1.00	2.50	6.00

133 100,000 KWANZAS

		VG	VF	UNC
4.2.1991 (1993). Orange and aqua on emerald green and m/c unpt. Like #129 except for value. Sign. 18.				
a.	Microprint around wmk area reads: *100000 BNA*, latent print: *100000 CEM MIL*. Wmk: *100000*.	1.50	6.00	15.00
x.	Microprint around wmk. area reads: *10000 BNA*, latent print: *10000 DEZ MIL*. Wmk: *10,000*. (error).	2.00	8.00	20.00

134 500,000 KWANZAS

	VG	VF	UNC
4.2.1991 (1994). Red, brown and violet on m/c unpt. Rhineceros at l. on back. Sign. 19.	.50	2.00	5.00

1995 ISSUE

#135-137 portr. conjoined busts of J. E. Dos Santos and A. A. Neto at r. Arms at lower l., mask at upper r. on back. Wmk: Sculpture.

135 1000 KWANZAS REAJUSTADO

	VG	VF	UNC
1.5.1995. Black and blue on m/c unpt. Palauca Negra Real, antelope at l. on back. Sign. 20.	FV	FV	4.00

136 5000 KWANZAS REAJUSTADO

	VG	VF	UNC
1.5.1995. Green and brown on m/c unpt. Banco Nacional at l. on back. Sign. 20.	FV	FV	12.50

137 10,000 KWANZAS REAJUSTADO

	VG	VF	UNC
1.5.1995. Red and purple on m/c unpt. Off shore oil platform at l. on back. Sign. 20.	FV	FV	8.50

ARGENTINA

The Argentine Republic, located in southern South America, as an area of 1,068,301 sq. mi. (2,766,889 sq. km.) and a population of 32.6 million. Capital: Buenos Aires. Its varied topography ranges from the subtropical lowlands of the north to the towering Andean Mountains in the west and the windswept Patagonian steppe in the south. The rolling, fertile pampas of central Argentina are ideal for agriculture and grazing, and support most of the republic's population. Meat packing, flour milling, textiles, sugar refining and dairy products are the principal industries. Oil is found in Patagonia, but most of the mineral requirements must be imported.

Argentina was discovered in 1516 by the Spanish navigator Juan de Solis. A permanent Spanish colony was established at Buenos Aires in 1580, but the colony developed slowly. When Napoleon conquered Spain, the Argentines set up their own government in the nane of the Spanish king on May 25, 1810. Independence was formally declaired on July 9, 1816.

MONETARY SYSTEM:
1 Peso (m/n) = 100 Centavos to 1970
1 New Peso (Ley 18.188) = 100 Old Pesos (m/n), 1970-83
1 Peso Argentino = 10,000 Pesos, (Ley 18.188) 1983-85
1 Austral = 100 Centavos = 1000 Pesos Argentinos, 1985-92
1 Peso = 10,000 Australes, 1992-

REPUBLIC

BANCO CENTRAL

Signature Titles:

A - *GERENTE GENERAL*

B - *SUBGERENTE GENERAL*

C - *GERENTE GENERAL* and *PRESIDENTE*

D - *SUBGERENTE GENERAL* and *VICE-PRESIDENTE*

E - *SUBGERENTE GENERAL* and *PRESIDENTE*

F - *VICE PRESIDENTE* and *PRESIDENTE*

G - *PRESIDENTE B.C.R.A.* and *PRESIDENTE H.C. SENADORES*

H - *PRESIDENTE B.C.R.A.* and *PRESIDENTE H.C. DIPUTADOS*

1960-67 ND ISSUE

W/o Ley

#275-277, 279-280 Portr. Gen. José de San Martin in uniform at r. Sign. varieties.

Replacement notes: *R* prefix.

275	**5 PESOS**	VG	VF	UNC
	ND (1960). Brown on yellow unpt. People gathering before bldg. on back. Printer: CMN.			
	a. Sign. titles: D.	.30	1.35	5.00
	b. Sign. titles: C.	.75	3.25	10.00
	c. Sign. titles: E.	.40	1.65	5.00

276	**50 PESOS**	VG	VF	UNC
	ND (1969). Green on m/c unpt.	.40	1.65	5.00

277	**100 PESOS**	VG	VF	UNC
	ND (1967). Brown on m/c unpt. 2 sign. varieties.	.40	1.65	5.00

278	**500 PESOS**	VG	VF	UNC
	ND (1964). Blue on m/c unpt. Portr. elderly Gen J. de San Martin in uniform at r. Grand Bourg House in France on back. 4 sign. varieties.			
	a. Sign. titles: E.	1.00	4.00	12.00
	b. Sign. titles: C.	.75	3.25	10.00

279	**1000 PESOS**	VG	VF	UNC
	ND (1966). Violet on m/c unpt. Portr. young Gen. J. de San Martin in uniform at r. Saling ship on back. 3 sign. varieties.			
	a. Sign. titles: E.	1.00	3.50	12.00
	b. Sign. titles: C.	1.00	3.00	10.00

280	**5000 PESOS**	VG	VF	UNC
	ND (1962). Brown on yellow-green unpt. Portr. young Gen. J. de San Martin in uniform. Capitol on back. 6 sign. varieties.			
	a. Sign. titles: E.	4.50	13.50	40.00
	b. Sign. titles: C.	4.00	12.00	36.00

281 10,000 PESOS
ND (1961). Red-brown on m/c unpt. Portr. elderly Gen J. de San
Martin not in uniform at r. Armies in the field on back. 5 sign.
varieties.

	VG	VF	UNC
a. Sign. titles: E.	4.50	13.50	40.00
b. Sign. titles: C.	2.50	10.00	30.00

1969 ND PROVISIONAL ISSUE
Ley 18.188

282 1 PESO ON 100 PESOS
ND (1969). Ovpt: New denomination on #277.

VG	VF	UNC
.20	.50	1.75

283 5 PESOS ON 500 PESOS
ND (1969). Ovpt: New denomination on #278. 2 sign. varieties.

VG	VF	UNC
1.00	4.00	12.00

284 10 PESOS ON 1000 PESOS
ND (1969). Ovpt: New denomination on #279.

1.00	4.00	12.00

285 50 PESOS ON 5000 PESOS
ND (1969). Ovpt: New denomination on #280.

VG	VF	UNC
1.50	6.50	20.00

286 100 PESOS ON 10,000 PESOS
ND (1969). Ovpt: New denomination on #281. 2 sign. varieties.

VG	VF	UNC
6.00	15.00	45.00

LEY 18.188; 1970 ISSUE
#287-289 Gen. Manuel Belgrano at r. Printer: CMN. Many sign. varieties. W/o colored threads in paper.
#290-292 Gen. José de San Martin at r. Colored threads in paper.
Replacement notes: R prefix.

287 1 PESO
ND (1970-73). Orange on m/c unpt. Scene of Bariloche-Llao Llao on
back. 5 sign. varieties.

VG	VF	UNC
.15	.40	2.00

288 5 PESOS
ND (1971-73). Blue on m/c unpt. Monument to the Flag at Rosario on
back. 2 sign. varieties.

VG	VF	UNC
.25	1.00	4.00

289 10 PESOS
ND (1970-73). Violet on m/c unpt. Waterfalls at Iguazu on back. 6
sign. varieties.

VG	VF	UNC
.20	.75	3.00

290 50 PESOS
ND (1972-73). Black and brown on m/c unpt. Hot springs at Jujuy on
back. 3 sign. varieties.

1.00	3.00	10.00

291 100 PESOS
ND (1971-73). Red on m/c unpt. Coastline at Ushuaia on back. 4 sign.
varieties.

1.50	5.00	15.00

292 500 PESOS
ND (1972-73). Green on m/c unpt. Army monument at Mendoza on
back. 2 sign. varieties.

2.00	6.50	20.00

LEY 18.188/69; 1973-74 ISSUE
#293-295 Gen. Manuel Belgrano at r. Backs like #287-292. Sign. varieties. W/o colored threads in paper
  (varieties). Wmk. varieties.
#296-299 Gen. José de San Martin at r. Sign. varieties. Colored threads in paper.
Replacement notes: R prefix.

293 1 PESO
ND (1974). Orange on m/c unpt.

VG	VF	UNC
.15	.65	2.00

294 5 Pesos
ND (1974-76). Blue on m/c unpt. 2 sign. varieties.

	VG	VF	UNC
	.15	.65	2.00

295 10 Pesos
ND (1973-76). Violet on m/c unpt. 4 sign. varieties.

	VG	VF	UNC
	.15	.65	2.00

296 50 Pesos
ND (1974-76). Black and brown on m/c unpt. 3 sign. varieties.

	VG	VF	UNC
	.15	.65	2.00

297 100 Pesos
ND (1974-76). Red on m/c unpt. 3 sign. varieties.

	VG	VF	UNC
	.25	1.00	3.00

298 500 Pesos
ND (1974-75). Green on m/c unpt. 2 sign. varieties.

	VG	VF	UNC
	1.00	3.00	7.00

299 1000 Pesos
ND (1973-76). Brown on m/c unpt. Plaza de Mayo in Buenos Aires on back. 3 sign. varieties.

	VG	VF	UNC
	1.25	5.00	15.00

1976 ND Issue

W/o Decreto or Ley
#301-310 Gen. José de San Martin at r. Sign. and wmk. varieties.
#305-310 w/colored threads.
Replacement notes: *R* prefix.

300 10 Pesos
ND (1976). Violet on m/c unpt. Gen. M. Belgrano at r.

	VG	VF	UNC
	.05	.20	1.00

301 50 Pesos
ND (1976-78). Black and brown on m/c unpt. 2 sign. varieties.

	VG	VF	UNC
a. No colored threads in paper.	1.25	5.00	15.00
b. Colored threads in paper.	.15	.65	2.00

302	**100 Pesos**	VG	VF	UNC
	ND (1976-78). Red on m/c unpt.			
	a. No colored threads in paper. 2 sign. varieties.	.15	.65	2.00
	b. Colored threads in paper. 2 sign. varieties.	.10	.20	.75

303	**500 Pesos**	VG	VF	UNC
	ND (1977-82). Green on m/c unpt. 4 sign. varieties.			
	a. Wmk: Arms. No colored threads in paper.	.10	.20	1.00
	b. Wmk: Arms. Colored threads in paper.	.15	.65	2.00
	c. Wmk: Multiple sunbursts. Colored threads. Back lithographed.	.05	.20	1.00

304	**1000 Pesos**	VG	VF	UNC
	ND (1976-82). Brown on m/c unpt. 5 sign. varieties.			
	a. Wmk: Arms. No colored threads in paper.	.10	.30	1.50
	b. Wmk: Arms. Colored threads in paper. 2 sign. varieties.	.05	.20	1.00
	c. Wmk: Multiple sunbursts. Back engraved.	.05	.20	1.00
	d. Wmk: Multiple sunbursts. Back lithographed.	.05	.20	1.00

305	**5000 Pesos**	VG	VF	UNC
	ND (1977-83). Blue and green on m/c unpt. Coastline of Mar del Plata on back.			
	a. Wmk: Arms. 2 sign. varieties.	.20	.50	3.50
	b. Wmk: Multiple sunbursts. 2 sign. varieties.	.10	.20	.75

306	**10,000 Pesos**	VG	VF	UNC
	ND (1976-83). Orange on m/c unpt. National park on back. 4 sign. varieties.			
	a. Wmk: Arms. 3 sign. varieties.	.25	.75	3.00
	b. Wmk: Multiple sunbursts.	.20	.50	1.25

307	**50,000 Pesos**	VG	VF	UNC
	ND (1979-83). Brown on m/c unpt. Banco Central bldg. at l. ctr. on back. Wmk: Arms. 2 sign. varieties.	.30	1.00	3.00

308	**100,000 Pesos**	VG	VF	UNC
	ND (1979-83). Gray on m/c unpt. Mint bldg. at l. ctr. on back.			
	a. Wmk: Arms.	.50	1.50	6.00
	b. Wmk: Multiple sunbursts.	.30	1.00	3.00

309	**500,000 Pesos**	VG	VF	UNC
	ND (1980-83). Green and brown on m/c unpt. Founding of Buenos Aires on back. Wmk: Multiple sunburst. 2 sign. varieties.	.30	1.00	4.50

310	**1,000,000 Pesos**	VG	VF	UNC
	ND (1981). Pink and blue on m/c unpt. Independence Declaration w/25 de Mayo on back. Wmk: Multiple sunbursts. 2 sign. varieties.	1.00	3.00	22.50

1983-85 ISSUE

#311-316 wmk: Multiple sunbursts. Printer: CdM.

#311-317 have face design w/San Martin at r. #311-315 have back designs like #287-291. #311-319 w/colored threads.

Replacement notes: *R* prefix.

		VG	VF	UNC
317	**1000 PESOS ARGENTINOS** ND. Blue-green and brown on m/c unpt. *El Paso de los Andes* battle scene on back.			
	a. Wmk: San Martin (1983). 2 sign. varieties.	.40	1.25	5.00
	b. Wmk: Multiple sunbursts (1984).	.25	.75	1.75
318	**5000 PESOS ARGENTINOS** ND (1984-85). Red-brown on m/c unpt. J. B. Alberdi at r. Constitutional meeting of 1853 on back. Wmk: Young San Martin.	.35	1.50	6.00
319	**10,000 PESOS ARGENTINOS** ND (1985). Blue-violet on m/c unpt. M. Belgrano at r. Creation of Argentine flag on back. Wmk: Young San Martin.	1.25	3.50	12.50

		VG	VF	UNC
311	**1 PESO ARGENTINO** ND (1983-84). Red-orange and purple on m/c unpt. 2 sign. varieties.	.05	.15	.75

1985 PROVISIONAL ISSUE

#320-322 ovpt. on Peso Argentino notes.

		VG	VF	UNC
312	**5 PESOS ARGENTINOS** ND (1983-84). Brown-violet and black on m/c unpt. 2 sign. varieties.	.05	.20	1.00

		VG	VF	UNC
313	**10 PESOS ARGENTINOS** ND (1983-84). Black and red-brown on green and m/c unpt. 2 sign. varieties.	.05	.20	1.00
314	**50 PESOS ARGENTINOS** ND (1983-85). Brown on m/c unpt. 2 sign. varieties.	.10	.20	1.00
315	**100 PESOS ARGENTINOS** ND (1983-85). Blue on m/c unpt. 2 sign. varieties.	.15	.35	1.25

		VG	VF	UNC
320	**1 AUSTRAL** ND (1985). New denomination ovpt. in numeral and wording in box, green on face and blue on back. Ovpt. on #317b. Series D.	.15	.60	2.50

		VG	VF	UNC
316	**500 PESOS ARGENTINOS** ND (1984). Violet on m/c unpt. Town meeting of May 22, 1810 on back.	.15	.45	1.75

		VG	VF	UNC
321	**5 AUSTRALES** ND (1985). New denomination ovpt. as #320, purple on face and brown on back. Ovpt. on #318, Series B.	.35	1.50	6.00

322   10 AUSTRALES
ND (1985). New denomination ovpt. as #320. Ovpt. on #319.

		VG	VF	UNC
a.	Blue ovpt. on face and back. Wmk: San Martin. Series A.	1.00	4.00	8.00
b.	Like a. but wmk: Multiple sunburses. Series B.	.45	1.75	4.00
c.	Blue ovpt on face, lt. olive-green ovpt on back. Series B; C.	.75	3.00	10.00

1985-89 ISSUE
#323-330 latent image "BCRA" on face. Liberty (Progreso) w/torch and shield seated at l. ctr. on back. Printer: CdM. Sign. varieties.

Replacement notes: *R* prefix.

323   1 AUSTRAL
ND (1985). Blue-green and purple on m/c unpt. B. Rivadavia at ctr. Wmk: Multiple sunbursts.

		VG	VF	UNC
a.	Sign. titles: E. Series A.	.10	.50	2.00
b.	Sign. titles: C. Series B; C.	.05	.20	.50

324   5 AUSTRALES
ND (1986). Brown and deep olive-green on m/c unpt. J. J. de Urquiza at ctr. Wmk: Multiple sunbursts.

		VG	VF	UNC
a.	Sign. titles: E. Series A.	.10	.25	.75
b.	Sign. titles: C. Series A.	.05	.20	.50

325   10 AUSTRALES
ND (1986). Dk. blue and purple on m/c unpt. S. Derqui at ctr. Wmk: Multiple sunbursts.

		VG	VF	UNC
a.	Coarse portrait in heavy horizontal wavy lines. Sign. titles: E. Series A.	.25	1.00	3.00
b.	Modified portrait in finer horizontal wavy lines. Sign. titles: C. Series A; B; C.	.05	.25	.75

326   50 AUSTRALES
ND (1986). Violet and deep brown on m/c unpt. B. Mitre at ctr. Wmk: Multiple sunbursts.

		VG	VF	UNC
a.	Sign. titles: E. Series A.	.75	3.00	10.00
b.	Sign. titles: C. Series A.	.10	.25	.75

327   100 AUSTRALES
ND (1985). Dk. red and purple on m/c unpt. D. F. Sarmiento at ctr. Wmk: Multiple sunbursts.

		VG	VF	UNC
a.	Sign. titles: E. Series A.	.50	2.00	6.00
b.	Sign. titles: C. Engraved back. Series A; B.	.10	.50	2.00
c.	Sign. titles C. Back pink and lithographed; w/o purple and blue. Series C; D.	.05	.20	.50

328   500 AUSTRALES
ND (1988). Pale olive-green on m/c unpt. N. Avellaneda at ctr. Sign. titles: C.

		VG	VF	UNC
a.	Metallic green guilloche by *500*. Back olive-green, black and m/c. Wmk: Liberty. Series A. (1988).	.10	.50	2.00
b.	Dk. olive-green guilloche by *500*. Back pale olive-green and m/c; lithographed (w/o black). Wmk: Multiple sunbursts. Series A. (1990).	.05	.20	.75

329   1000 AUSTRALES

	VG	VF	UNC
ND (1989). Violet-brown and purple on m/c unpt. J. A. Roca at ctr. Sign. titles: *GERENTE GENERAL* and *PRESIDENTE*.			
a. Vertical green guilloche near *1000*. Wmk: Liberty. Series A.	.15	.75	2.50
b. Vertical brown-violet guilloche near *1000*. Wmk: Multiple sunbursts. Series B.	.10	.45	1.50
c. Like b. but sign. titles: F. Series C.	.10	.45	1.50

330   5000 AUSTRALES

	VG	VF	UNC
ND (1989). Dk. brown and red-brown on m/c unpt. M. Juarez at ctr.			
a. Green shield design at upper ctr. r. Sign titles: E. Wmk: Liberty. Series A.	.75	3.00	10.00
b. Green shield design at upper ctr. r. Sign titles: C. Wmk: Liberty. Series A.	1.25	5.00	15.00
c. Dk. brown shield design at upper ctr. r. Sign. titles: E. Wmk: Liberty. Series B.	.60	2.50	8.00
d. Dk. brown shield design. Sign. titles: E. Wmk: Liberty. Series B.	.50	2.00	6.00
e. Dk. brown shield design. Sign. titles: F. Lithographed back. Wmk: Multiple sunbursts. Series C.	.20	1.00	3.00

1989-91 PROVISIONAL ISSUE

#331-333 use modified face plates from earlier issue. Wmk: Multiple sunbursts. Series M. Printer: CdM.
Replacement notes: R prefix.

331   10,000 AUSTRALES

	VG	VF	UNC
ND (1989). Black-blue, deep blue-green and brown on m/c unpt. Face similar to #306. Ovpt. value in olive-green in box at l. Word "PESOS" at ctr. blocked out. Denomination repeated in lines of text and ovpt. value at r. on back. Sign. titles: C.	2.00	7.50	20.00

332   50,000 AUSTRALES

	VG	VF	UNC
ND (1989). Deep olive-green and blue on m/c unpt. Face similar to #307. Ovpt. value in violet in box at l. Word "PESOS" at ctr. blocked out. Back similar to #331. Value in lt. brown at r. Sign. titles: E.	2.00	8.00	25.00

333   500,000 AUSTRALES

	VG	VF	UNC
ND (1991). Black, purple and red on m/c unpt. Face similar to #309. Ovpt. value in box at l. Word "PESOS" at bottom r. blocked out. Back similar to #331. Value at r. Sign. titles: F.	10.00	30.00	75.00

1989-91 ISSUE

#334-338 Progreso on back. Wmk: Liberty head. Printer: CdM.
Replacement notes: *R* prefix.

334   10,000 AUSTRALES

	VG	VF	UNC
ND (1989). Black on deep blue, brown and m/c unpt. w/brown diamond design at upper ctr. R. C. Pellegrini at ctr.			
a. Sign. titles: C. Series A; B.	.40	1.25	3.50
b. Sign. titles: F. Series C.	.50	1.50	4.50

335   50,000 AUSTRALES

	VG	VF	UNC
ND (1989). Black on ochre, olive-green and m/c unpt. w/black flower design at upper ctr. r. L. Saenz Peña at ctr. Sign. titles: C. Series A; B.	1.50	6.00	15.00

339 1 PESO

		VG	VF	UNC
ND (1992-). Black and violet-brown on m/c unpt. C. Pelligrini at r. Back gray on m/c unpt; National Congress bldg. at l. ctr.				
a. Sign. titles: F. (1992).		FV	FV	3.00
b. Sign. titles: G. (1993).		FV	FV	2.75

336 100,000 AUSTRALES

		VG	VF	UNC
ND (1990-91). Dk. brown and reddish-brown on pale brown and m/c unpt. Coarsely engraved portr. of J. Evaristo Uriburu at ctr. Black sign. titles: F. Series A; B.		2.50	10.00	30.00

340 2 PESOS

		VG	VF	UNC
ND (1992-). Deep blue and red-violet on m/c unpt. B. Mitre at r. Back lt. blue on m/c unpt; Mitre Museum at l. ctr.				
a. Sign. titles: F. (1992).		FV	FV	4.00
b. Sign. titles: H. (1993).		FV	FV	4.00

337 100,000 AUSTRALES

		VG	VF	UNC
ND (1991). Dk. brown and reddish-brown on brown and m/c unpt. Finely engraved portr. of J. Evaristo Uriburu at ctr. Brown sign. titles. Series B.		2.00	8.00	25.00

341 5 PESOS

		VG	VF	UNC
ND (1992-). Deep olive-green and red-orange on m/c unpt. Gen. J. de San Martin at r. Back lt. olive-gray on m/c unpt; monument to the Glory of Mendoza at l. ctr.				
a. Sign. titles: F. (1992).		FV	FV	10.00
b. Sign. titles: G. (1993).		FV	FV	9.00

338 500,000 AUSTRALES

		VG	VF	UNC
ND (1990). Black-violet, red and blue on m/c unpt. M. Quintana at ctr. Series A.		5.00	25.00	75.00

1992 ISSUE

#339-341 wmk: Multiple sunbursts. Printer: CdM.
#342-343 wmk: Liberty head. Printer: CdM-Argentina.
#344-345 portr. as wmk.
Replacement notes: R prefix.

342 10 PESOS

		VG	VF	UNC
ND (1992-). Deep brown and dk. green on m/c unpt. M. Belgrano at r. Monument to the Flag - Rosario w/city in background at l. ctr. on back.				
a. Sign. titles: F. (1992).		FV	FV	18.50
b. Sign. titles: H. (1993).		FV	FV	17.50

343 20 PESOS
 ND (1992-). Carmine and deep blue on m/c unpt. J. Manuel de Rosas
 at r. *Vuelta de Obligado* battle scene on back.

	VG	VF	UNC
a. Sign. titles: F. (1992).	FV	FV	32.50
b. Sign. titles: G. (1993).	FV	FV	32.50

344 50 PESOS
 ND (1992-). Black and red on m/c unpt. D. Faustino Sarmiento at r.
 Government office w/monuments, palm trees in foreground at l. ctr.
 on back.

	VG	VF	UNC
a. Sign. titles: F. (1992).	FV	FV	75.00
b. Sign. titles: H. (1993).	FV	FV	75.00

345 100 PESOS
 ND (1992-). Violet, lilac, green and m/c. J. A. Roca at r. and as wmk.
 Back violet and m/c; *La Conquista del Desierto* scene.

	VG	VF	UNC
a. Sign. titles: F. (1992).	FV	FV	140.00
b. Sign. titles: G. (1993).	FV	FV	140.00

The Republic of Armenia (formerly Armenian S.S.R.) is bounded in the north by Georgia, to the east by Azerbaijan and to the south and west by Turkey and Iran. It has an area of 11,490 sq. mi. (29,800 sq. km) and a population of 3.3 million. Capital: Yerevan. Agriculture including cotton, vineyards and orchards, hydro-electricity, chemicals - primarily synthetic rubber and fertilizers, and vast mineral deposits of copper, zinc and aluminum and production of steel and paper are major industries.

The earliest history of Armenia records continuous struggles with expanding Babylonia and later Assyria. In the sixth century B.C. it was called Armina. Later under the Persian empire it enjoyed the position of a vassal state. Conquered by Macedonia, it later defeated the Seleucids and Greater Armenia was founded under the Artaxis dynasty. Christianity was established in 303 A.D. which led to religious wars with the Persians and Romans who divided it into two zones of influence. The Arabs succeeded the Persian Empire of the Sassanids which later allowed the Armenian princes to conclude a treaty in 653 A.D. In 862 A.D. Ashot V was recognized as the "prince of princes" and established a throne recognized by Baghdad and Constantinople in 886 A.D. The Seljuks overran the whole country and united with Kurdistan which eventually ran the new government. In 1240 A.D. onward the Mongols occupied almost all of western Asia until their downfall in 1375 A.D. when various Kurdish, Armenian and Turkoman independent principalities arose. After the defeat of the Persians in 1516 A.D. the Ottoman Turks gradually took control over a period of some 40 years, with Kurdish tribes settling within Armenian lands. In 1605 A.D. the Persians moved thousands of Armenians as far as India developing prosperous colonies. Persia and the Ottoman Turks were again at war, with the Ottomans once again prevailing. The Ottomans later gave absolute civil authority to a Christian bishop allowing them free enjoyment of their religion and traditions.

Russia occupied Armenia in 1801 until the Russo-Turkish war of 1878. British intervention excluded either side from remaining although the Armenians remained more loyal to the Ottoman Turks, but in 1894 the Ottoman Turks sent in an expeditionary force of Kurds fearing a revolutionary movement. Large massacres were followed by retaliations, then amnesty was proclaimed which led right into WW I and once again occupation by Russian forces in 1916. After the Russian revolution the Georgians, Armenians and Azerbaijanis formed the short lived Transcaucasian Federal Republic on Sept. 20, 1917 which broke up into three independent republics on May 26, 1918. Communism developed and in Sept. 1920 the Turks attacked the Armenian Republic; the Russians soon followed suit from Azerbaijan routing the Turks. On Nov. 29, 1920 Armenia was proclaimed a Soviet Socialist Republic. On March 12, 1922, Armenia, Georgia and Azerbaijan were combined to form the Transcaucasian Soviet Federated Socialist republic, which on Dec. 30, 1922, became a part of U.S.S.R. On Dec. 5, 1936, the Transcaucasian federation was dissolved and Armenia became a constituent republic of the U.S.S.R. A new constitution was adopted in April 1978. Elections took place on May 20, 1990. The Supreme Soviet adopted a declaration of sovereignty in Aug. 1991, voting to unite Armenia with Nagorno-Karabakh. This newly constituted "Republic of Armenia" became fully independent by popular vote in Sept. 1991. It became a member of the CIS in Dec.1991.

Fighting between Christians in Armenia and Muslim forces of Azerbaijan escalated in 1992 and continued through early 1994. Each country claimed the Nagorno-Karabakh, an Armenian ethnic enclave, in Azerbaijan. A temporary cease-fire was announced in May, 1994.

REPUBLIC

ARMENIAN REPUBLIC BANK

1993-95 ISSUE
#33-38 wmk: Decorative design.

33 10 DRAM
 1993. Dk. brown, lt. blue and pale orange on m/c unpt. Statue of David
 from Sasoun, and main railway station in Yerevan. Mt. Ararat on back.

	VG	VF	UNC
	FV	FV	.60

34 25 DRAM
 1993. Brown, yellow and blue. Frieze w/lion from Erebuni Castle and
 cuneiform tablet. Ornament on back.

	VG	VF	UNC
	FV	FV	1.25

35   **50 DRAM**   **VG**   **VF**   **UNC**
1993. Blue, red and violet. State Museum of History and National   FV   FV   2.00
Gallery at upper l. ctr. Parliament bldg. at upper ctr. r. on back.

36   **100 DRAM**   **VG**   **VF**   **UNC**
1993. Violet, red and blue. Mt. Ararat at upper ctr. Zvarnots Temple at   FV   FV   2.25
l. ctr. Opera and ballet theater in Yerevan on back.

37   **200 DRAM**   **VG**   **VF**   **UNC**
1993. Brown, green and red. St. Hegine Temple in Echmiadzin at   FV   FV   3.50
upper ctr. Circular design on back.

38   **500 DRAM**   **VG**   **VF**   **UNC**
1993. Dk. green and red-brown on m/c unpt. Tetradachm of Kg.   FV   FV   6.50
Tigran II the Great at l. ctr. and Mt. Ararat at upper ctr. Open book and
quill pen at upper ctr. r. on back.

39   **1000 DRAM**   **VG**   **VF**   **UNC**
1994. Dk. brown and brown on m/c unpt. Ancient statue at l. Ancient   FV   FV   11.00
ruins on back. Wmk: Arms.

40   **5000 DRAM**
1995. Brown-violet on m/c unpt. Temple of Garni at ctr. Goddess   FV   FV   30.00
Anahid on back.

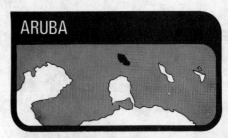

ARUBA

Aruba, formerly a part of the Netherlands Antilles, achieved on Jan. 1, 1986 a special status "status aparte" as the third state under the Dutch crown, together with the Netherlands and the remaining five islands of the Netherlands Antilles. On Dec. 15, 1954 the Netherlands Antilles were given complete domestic autonomy and granted equality within the Kingdom of the Netherlands.

Aruba was the second-largest island of the Netherlands Antilles and is situated near the Venezuelan coast. The island has an area of 74 1/2 sq. mi. (193 sq. km.) and a population of 68,000. Capital: Oranjestad, named after the Dutch royal family. Chief industry is tourism. For earlier issues see Curaáao and the Netherlands Antilles. During Jan. 1986 the banknotes of the Netherlands Antilles were redeemed at a ratio of 1 to 1.

MONETARY SYSTEM:
1 Florin = 100 Cents

DUTCH INFLUENCE

BANCO CENTRAL DI ARUBA

1986 ISSUE
#1-5 flag at l., coastal hotels at ctr. Arms of Aruba at ctr. on back. Printer: JEZ.

1   **5 FLORIN**   **VG**   **VF**   **UNC**
1.1.1986. Green.   FV   FV   6.50

2   **10 FLORIN**   **VG**   **VF**   **UNC**
1.1.1986. Green.   FV   FV   12.50

3   **25 FLORIN**   **VG**   **VF**   **UNC**
1.1.1986. Green.   FV   FV   28.50

4	**50 FLORIN**	**VG**	**VF**	**UNC**
	1.1.1986. Green.	FV	FV	55.00

5	**100 FLORIN**	**VG**	**VF**	**UNC**
	1.1.1986. Green.	FV	FV	110.00

CENTRALE BANK VAN ARUBA

1990 ISSUE

#6-10 geometric forms with pre-Columbian Aruban art on back. Wmk: Stylized tree. Printer: JEZ.

6	**5 FLORIN**	**VG**	**VF**	**UNC**
	1.1.1990. Purple and m/c. Tortuga Blanco (sea turtle) at ctr. r.	FV	FV	6.00

7	**10 FLORIN**	**VG**	**VF**	**UNC**
	1.1.1990. Blue and m/c. Calco Indjian snail at ctr r.	FV	FV	11.00

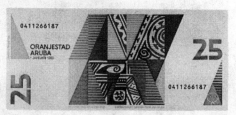

8	**25 FLORIN**	**VG**	**VF**	**UNC**
	1.1.1990. Brown and m/c. Cascabel snake at r.	FV	FV	22.50

9	**50 FLORIN**	**VG**	**VF**	**UNC**
	1.1.1990. Red-brown and m/c. Shoco owl at ctr. r.	FV	FV	42.50

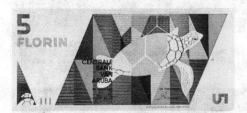

10	**100 FLORIN**	**VG**	**VF**	**UNC**
	1.1.1990. Olive-green and m/c. Frog on back.	FV	FV	80.00

1993 (1996) ISSUE

#11-15 like #7-10 but w/text: *Wettig Betaaimiddel* (legal tender).

11	**10 FLORIN**	**VG**	**VF**	**UNC**
	16.7.1993 (1996). Like #7.	FV	FV	10.00
12	**25 FLORIN**			
	16.7.1993 (1996). Like #8.	FV	FV	21.50
13	**50 FLORIN**			
	16.7.1993 (1996). Like #9.	FV	FV	40.00
14	**100 FLORIN**			
	16.7.1993 (1996). Like #10.	FV	FV	75.00
15	**500 FLORIN**			
(11)	16.7.1993. Blue and m/c. Mero fish at ctr r.	FV	FV	335.00

COLLECTOR SERIES

CENTRALE BANK VAN ARUBA

1995 ISSUE

CS1	**1990 (1995) 5-100 FLORIN**	**ISSUE PRICE**	**MKT.**	**VALUE**
	#6-10 w/matched serial # in special presentation set.	—		200.00

AUSTRALIA

The Commonwealth of Australia, the smallest continent and largest island in the world, is located south of Indonesia between the Indian and Pacific oceans. It has an area of 2,967,909 sq. mi. (7,686,849 sq. km.) and a population of 16.8 million. Capital: Canberra. Due to its early and sustained isolation, Australia is the habitat of such curious and unique fauna as the kangaroo, koala bear, platypus, wombat and barking lizard. The continent possesses extensive mineral deposits, the most important of which are gold, coal, silver, nickel, uranium, lead and zinc. Livestock raising, mining and manufacturing are the principal industries. Chief exports are wool, meat, wheat, iron ore, coal and nonferrous metals.

The first whites to see Australia probably were Portuguese and Spanish navigators of the late 16th century. In 1770, Captain James Cook explored the east coast and annexed it for Great Britain. The Colony of New South Wales was founded by Captain Arthur Phillip on Jan. 26, 1788, a date now celebrated as Australia Day. Dates of creation of six colonies that now comprise the states of the Australian Commonwealth are: New South Wales, 1823; Tasmania, 1825; Western Australia, 1838; South Australia, 1842; Victoria, 1851; Queensland, 1859. A constitution providing for federation of the colonies was approved by the British Parliament in 1900; the Commonwealth of Australia came into being in 1901. Australia passed the Statute of Westminster Adoption Act on Oct. 9, 1942, which officially established Australia's complete autonomy in external and internal affairs, thereby formalizing a situation that had existed for years.

During WWII Australia was the primary supply and staging area for Allied forces in the South Pacific Theatre. Japan had included Australia in its failed plan of the Co-prosperity Sphere of occupied areas.

Australia is a member of the Commonwealth of Nations. The Queen of England is Chief of State.

Australia's currency system was changed from pounds - shillings - pence to a decimal system of dollars and cents on Feb.14, 1966.

RULERS:
British

MONETARY SYSTEM:
1 Shilling = 12 Pence
1 Pound = 20 Shillings to 1966
1 Dollar = 100 Cents, 1966-

COMMONWEALTH OF AUSTRALIA

RESERVE BANK

1960-61 ISSUE

#33-36 w/title: *GOVERNOR/RESERVE BANK OF AUSTRALIA* below lower l. sign.

			VG	VF	UNC
33	**10 SHILLINGS**				
	ND (1961-65). Brown. M. Flinders at r. Parliament in Canberra on back. Sign. H. C. Coombs and R. Wilson.		1.25	3.50	27.50

			VG	VF	UNC
34	**1 POUND**				
	ND (1961-65). Green. Qn. Elizabeth II at r. Portr. C. Sturt and H. Hume on back. Sign. H. C. Coombs and R. Wilson.		2.00	5.00	30.00

			VG	VF	UNC
35	**5 POUNDS**				
	ND (1960-65). Blue. Sir J. Franklin at r. Cattle, sheep and agricultural products on back. Sign. H. C. Coombs and R. Wilson.		10.00	22.50	75.00

			VG	VF	UNC
36	**10 POUNDS**				
	ND (1960-65). Red. Gov. Philip at l. Symbols of science and industry on back. Sign. H. C. Coombs and R. Wilson.		20.00	35.00	190.00

1966-67 ISSUE

#37-41 w/text: *COMMONWEALTH OF* in heading. Wmk: Capt. James Cook.

			VG	VF	UNC
37	**1 DOLLAR**				
	ND (1966-72). Orange and brown. Arms at ctr., Qn. Elizabeth II at r. Stylized Aboriginal figures and animals on back.				
	a. Sign. H. C. Coombs and R. Wilson. (1966).		1.50	4.00	30.00
	b. Sign. H. C. Coombs and R. J. Randall. (1968).		4.00	17.50	180.00
	c. Sign. J. G. Phillips and R. J. Randall. (1969).		FV	3.00	20.00
	d. Sign. J. G. Phillips and F. H. Wheeler. (1972).		FV	2.00	12.50

38 2 DOLLARS

		VG	VF	UNC
ND (1966-72). Green and yellow. J. MacArthur at r., sheep at ctr. Farrer at l., wheat at ctr. on back.
	a. Sign. H. C. Coombs and R. Wilson. (1966).	FV	2.50	15.00
	b. Sign. H. C. Coombs and R. J. Randall. (1967).	3.00	8.50	50.00
	c. Sign. J. G. Phillips and R. J. Randall. (1968)	FV	2.50	12.50
	d. Sign. J. G. Phillips and F. H. Wheeler. (1972).	FV	2.50	15.00

39 5 DOLLARS

ND (1967-72). Deep purple and m/c. Sir J. Banks at r., plants at ctr. C. Chisholm, ship, bldgs., and women on back.
	a. Sign. H. C. Coombs and R. J. Randall. (1967).	FV	6.00	37.50
	b. Sign. J. G. Phillips and R. J. Randall. (1969).	FV	5.00	37.50
	c. Sign. J. G. Phillips and F. H. Wheeler. (1972).	FV	4.00	27.50

40 10 DOLLARS

		VG	VF	UNC
ND (1966-72). Blue and orange. F. Greenway at r., village scene at ctr. H. Lawson and bldgs. on back.
	a. Sign. H. C. Coombs and R. Wilson. (1966).	FV	9.00	25.00
	b. Sign. H. G. Coombs and R. J. Randall. (1967).	FV	20.00	120.00
	c. Sign. J. G. Phillips and R. J. Randall. (1968).	FV	9.00	25.00
	d. Sign. J. G. Phillips and F. H. Wheeler. (1972).	FV	10.00	30.00

41 20 DOLLARS

		VG	VF	UNC
ND (1966-72). Red and yellow. K. Smith at r. Hargrave at l., aeronautical devices on back.
	a. Sign. H. C. Coombs and R. Wilson. (1966).	FV	17.50	35.00
	b. Sign. H. G. Coombs and R. J. Randall. (1968).	35.00	100.00	600.00
	c. Sign. J. G. Phillips and R. J. Randall. (1968).	FV	16.00	32.50
	d. Sign. J. G. Phillips and F. H. Wheeler. (1972).	FV	16.00	32.50

AUSTRALIA, RESERVE BANK

1973; 1984 ISSUE

#42-48 w/o text: *COMMONWEALTH OF* in heading.
#42-46 like #37-41, wmk: Capt. James Cook.

42 1 DOLLAR

		VG	VF	UNC
ND (1974-83). Orange and brown.
	a. Sign. J. G. Phillips and F. H. Wheeler. (1974).	1.00	2.50	12.00
	b. Sign. H. M. Knight and F. H. Wheeler. (1976).	1.00	1.75	8.00
	c. Sign. H. M. Knight and J. Stone. (1979).	1.00	1.50	3.50
	d. Sign. R. A. Johnston and J. Stone. (1983).	1.00	1.50	2.50

43 2 DOLLARS

		VG	VF	UNC
ND (1974-85). Green and yellow.
	a. Sign. J. G. Phillips and F. H. Wheeler. (1974).	FV	3.00	17.50
	b. Sign. H. M. Knight and F. H. Wheeler. (1976). 2 serial # varieties.	FV	2.00	8.50
	c. Sign. H. M. Knight and J. Stone. (1979).	FV	2.00	5.00
	d. Sign. R. A. Johnston and J. Stone. (1983).	FV	2.00	4.00
	e. Sign. R. A. Johnston and B. W. Fraser. (1985).	FV	2.00	4.00

44 5 DOLLARS

		VG	VF	UNC
ND (1974-91). Deep purple and m/c.
	a. Sign. J. G. Phillips and F. H. Wheeler. (1974).	FV	8.00	45.00
	b. Sign. H. M. Knight and F. H. Wheeler. (1976).	FV	4.50	15.00
	c. Sign. H. M. Knight and J. Stone. (1979). 2 serial # varieties.	FV	FV	9.00
	d. Sign. R. A. Johnston and J. Stone. (1983).	FV	FV	9.00
	e. Sign. R. A. Johnston and B. W. Fraser. (1985). 2 serial # varieties.	FV	FV	7.00
	f. Sign. B. W. Fraser and C. I. Higgins. (1990).	FV	FV	7.00
	g. Sign. B. W. Fraser and A. S. Cole. (1991).	FV	FV	7.00

45   10 DOLLARS
ND (1974-91). Blue and orange.

	VG	VF	UNC
a. Sign. J. G. Phillips and F. H. Wheeler. (1974).	FV	14.00	100.00
b. Sign. H. M. Knight and F. H. Wheeler. (1976).	FV	9.00	20.00
c. Sign. H. M. Knight and J. Stone. (1979). 2 serial # varieties.	FV	FV	25.00
d. Sign. R. A. Johnston and J. Stone. (1983).	FV	FV	22.50
e. Sign. R. A. Johnston and B. W. Fraser. (1985).	FV	FV	13.50
f. Sign. B. W. Fraser and C. I. Higgins. (1990).	FV	FV	13.50
g. Sign. B. W. Fraser and A. S. Cole. (1991).	FV	FV	13.50

46   20 DOLLARS
ND (1974-). Red and yellow on m/c unpt.

	VG	VF	UNC
a. Sign. J. G. Phillips and F. H. Wheeler. (1974).	FV	FV	75.00
b. Sign. H. M. Knight and F. H. Wheeler. (1975).	FV	FV	40.00
c. Sign. H. M. Knight and J. Stone. (1979). 2 serial # varieties.	FV	FV	35.00
d. Sign. R. A. Johnston and J. Stone. (1983).	FV	FV	35.00
e. Sign. R. A. Johnston and B. W. Fraser. (1985) 2 serial # varieties.	FV	FV	25.00
f. Sign. M. J. Phillips and B. W. Fraser. (1989).	FV	FV	25.00
g. Sign. B. W. Fraser and C. I. Higgins. (1989).	FV	FV	25.00
h. Sign. B. W. Fraser and A. S. Cole. (1991).	FV	FV	25.00
i. Sign. B. W. Fraser and E. A. Evans. (1994).	FV	FV	23.50

47   50 DOLLARS
ND. (1973-). Yellow-brown and green on m/c unpt. Teaching implements at ctr., Sir W. Florey at r., I. Clunies-Ross at l., space research at ctr. on back.

	VG	VF	UNC
a. Sign. J. G. Phillips and F. H. Wheeler. (1973).	FV	45.00	90.00
b. Sign. H. M. Knight and F. H. Wheeler. (1975).	FV	45.00	100.00
c. Sign. H. M. Knight and J. Stone. (1979).	FV	FV	70.00
d. Sign. R. A. Johnston and J. Stone. (1983).	FV	FV	70.00
e. Sign. R. A. Johnston and B. W. Fraser. (1985). 2 serial # varieties.	FV	FV	75.00
f. Sign. M. J. Phillips and B. W. Fraser. (1989).	FV	FV	65.00
g. Sign. B. W. Fraser and C. I. Higgins. (1989).	FV	FV	60.00
h. Sign. B. W. Fraser and A. S. Cole. (1991).	FV	FV	60.00
i. Sign. B. W. Fraser and E. A. Evans. (1994).	FV	FV	57.00

48   100 DOLLARS
ND (1984-). Blue and gray on m/c unpt. Sir Douglas Mawson at ctr. J. Tebbutt at l. ctr. on back.

	VG	VF	UNC
a. Sign. R. A. Johnston and J. Stone. (1984).	FV	FV	135.00
b. Sign. R. A. Johnston and B. W. Fraser. (1985).	FV	FV	120.00
c. Sign. B. W. Fraser and C. I. Higgins. (1990).	FV	FV	110.00
d. Sign. B. W. Fraser and A. S. Cole. (1992).	FV	FV	105.00
e. Sign. as d. Red serial #. (900 issued).	FV	FV	200.00

1988 COMMEMORATIVE ISSUE
#49 Bicentennial of British Settlement, 1988.

49   10 DOLLARS
1988; ND. Brown and green on m/c unpt. Capt. Cook OVD at upper l., colonists across backgr ound; Cook's ship supply at lower r. shoreline. Aboriginal youth, rock painting and ceremonial " Morning Star" pole at ctr. on back. Sign. R. A. Johnston and B. W. Fraser. Plastic.

	VG	VF	UNC
a. 26.1.1988. Serial # prefix AA.	FV	FV	20.00
b. ND. Serial # prefix AB.	FV	FV	14.00

1992-96 ISSUES
#50-55 polymer plastic.

50   5 DOLLARS

1992; ND. Black, red and lilac on m/c unpt. Branch at l., Qn. Elizabeth II at ctr. r. Back black on lilac and m/c unpt., the old and the new Parliament House in Canberra at ctr. Sign. B. W. Fraser and A. S. Cole.

		VG	VF	UNC
a.	7.7.1992.	FV	FV	10.00
b.	ND.	FV	FV	6.00

51   5 DOLLARS
(55)

ND (1995). Like #50 but diagonal white lines in orientation bands in upper and lower margins. Red and ornage circular unpt. on back. Sign. B. W. Fraser and E. A. Evans.

		VG	VF	UNC
a.	W/4 diagonal white lines.	FV	FV	6.50
b.	W/11 diagonal white lines.	FV	FV	6.00

52   10 DOLLARS
(51)

1993; ND. Purple on dk. blue m/c unpt. Man on horseback at l., 'Banjo' Paterson at ctr., windmill OVD in transparent window at lower r. Dame M. Gilmore at ctr. r. on back. Sign. B. W. Fraser and E. A. Evans.

		VG	VF	UNC
a.	Red serial # 1993.	FV	FV	15.00
b.	Black serial # ND.	FV	FV	9.00

53   20 DOLLARS
(52)

1994; ND. Black and red on orange and pale green unpt. Biplane at l., Rev. J. Flynn at ctr. r., camel back at r. Sailing ship at l., M. Reiby at ctr. on back. Compass OVD in transparent window at lower r. Sign. B. W. Fraser and E. A. Evans.

		VG	VF	UNC
a.	Red serial #. 1994.	FV	FV	30.00
b.	Black serial #. ND.	FV	FV	23.50

54   50 DOLLARS
(53)

1995; ND. Yellow-brown and green on m/c unpt. D. Unaipon at l. ctr., Mission Church at Point McLeay at lower l., patent drawings at upper ctr. r., Southern Cross constellation OVD in transparent window at lower r. Portr. E. Cowan, foster mother w/children at ctr., W. Australia's Parliament House at upper l., Cowan at lectern at r. Sign. B. W. Fraser and E. A. Evans.

		VG	VF	UNC
a.	1995.	FV	FV	52.50
b.	ND.	FV	FV	50.00

55   100 DOLLARS
(54)

1996; ND. Black and green on orange and m/c unpt. Opera stage at l. Dame N. Melba at ctr., stylized peacock OVD in transparent window at lower r. Sir J. Monash and WWI battle scenes and insignia on back. Sign. B.W. Fraser and E.A. Evans.

		VG	VF	UNC
a.	Red serial #. (900 issued). 1996.	FV	FV	200.00
b.	Normal serial #. Green date. (3000 issued). 1996.	FV	FV	120.00
c.	Normal serial #. ND.	FV	FV	100.00

COLLECTOR SERIES

AUSTRALIA, RESERVE BANK

Special printings:

#44f was issued in uncut vertical pairs and blocks of 4, 1000 half sheets (20 subjects) and 500 full sheets (40 subjects).

#44g was released in horizontal and vertical pairs of U.S. $24 and in blocks of four subjects at U.S. $45 at three different coin fairs in 1992 as the last paper $5 note w/special serial prefix *#XXV-000001* thru *XXV-020000*. Only the note at l. was ovpt.: *5th ANNIVERSARY/1967 - 1992.*

#45g was issued in uncut form, vertical pairs, plain blocks of four, and blocks of four w/ovpt: NAAIC & BF held in Sydney in 1991.

#46f was issued as uncut strips of ten subjects (five double rows), to a total of 36 strips.

#47f was issued in uncut blocks of four, to a total of 72 blocks.

#47h was issued in 100 vertical pairs and 100 blocks of four w/gold serial #, also vertical pairs and blocks of four w/red serial #.

#47i was issued in uncut pairs and blocks of four to a total of 500 pairs and 250 blocks.

#48d includes 150 blocks of four and 300 pairs w/red serial # and 500 blocks of four and 700 pairs w/black serial #.

#49a was issued in a souvenir folder for U.S. $11, and also in sheets of 4, 12 and 24 subjects.

#50a was issued in a souvenir folder containing a plastic and a paper note (#44g) for U.S. $14. This issue marked the 25th anniversary of the $5 banknote.

#52 includes 900 matched serial # sets of two $10 notes, paper and plastic in "prestigiously packaged" por-folio; a set of $10 notes in an "embossed collector folder," issue 9,000 sets; a set of $10 notes in a "presentation/collector" folder, larger quantities available.

#55 includes sets of two $100 notes w/matched serial # in premium packaging, issue 900 sets. Another set includes notes w/normal serial #, new note w/date in green.

#55 was issued in uncut blocks of 4 in special folders at U.S. $50.00. A total of 2200 blocks were available. Uncut pairs were also sold.

1993 ISSUE

#CS1 and CS2 - 3000 notes were prepared for the International Coin and Banknote Fair held in Brisbane. A printing of 5000 is reported for the 80th anniversary of the first banknotes of the Commonwealth of Australia w/red serial # and beginning w/M000001.

		ISSUE PRICE	MKT. VALUE
CS1	**20 DOLLARS**		
	Ovpt: *NAAIC & BF* on #46h. Red serial #M000001-M000500.	—	55.00
CS2	**20 DOLLARS**		
	As #CS1, but higher serial #.	—	35.00

AUSTRIA

The Republic of Austria (Oesterreich), a parliamentary democracy located in mountainous central Europe, has an area of 32,374 sq. mi. (83,849 sq. km.) and a population of 8 million. Capital: Vienna. Austria is primarily an industrial country. Machinery, iron and steel, textiles, yarns and timber are exported.

The territories later to be known as Austria were overrun in pre-Roman times by various tribes, including the Celts. Upon the fall of the Roman Empire, the country became a margravate of Charlemagne's Empire. Ottokar, King of Bohemia, gained possession in 1252, only to lose the territory to Rudolf of Habsburg in 1276. Thereafter, until World War I, the story of Austria was that of the ruling Habsburgs, German emperors from 1438-1806. From 1815-1867 it was a member of the "Deutsche Bund" (German Union).

During World War I, the Austro-Hungarian Empire was one of the Central Powers with Germany, Bulgaria and Turkey. At the end of the war, the Empire was dissolved and Austria established as an independent republic. In March 1938, Austria was incorporated into Hitler's short-lived German Third Reich. Allied forces of both East and West liberated Austria in April 1945, and subsequently divided it into four zones of military occupation. On May 15, 1955, the four powers formally recognized Austria as a "sovereign," independent democratic state.

MONETARY SYSTEM:
1 Schilling (= 10,000 Kronen) = 100 Groschen, 1924-38; 1945-

REPUBLIC

OESTERREICHISCHE NATIONALBANK

AUSTRIAN NATIONAL BANK

1956-65 ISSUES

		VG	VF	UNC
136	**20 SCHILLING** 2.7.1956. Brown on red-brown and olive unpt. A. von Welsbach at r., arms at l. Village Maria Rain, Church and Karawanken mountains on back.	1.50	7.00	12.00

		VG	VF	UNC
137	**50 SCHILLING** 2.7.1962. Purple on m/c unpt. R. Wettstein at r., arms at bottom ctr. Mauterndorf castle in Salzburg, on back.	1.50	6.50	15.00

		VG	VF	UNC
138	**100 SCHILLING** 1.7.1960. Dk. green on violet and m/c unpt. Violin and music at lower l., J. Strauss at r., arms at l. Schönbrunn Castle on back.	5.00	14.00	30.00

		VG	VF	UNC
139	**500 SCHILLING** 1.7.1965. Red-brown on m/c unpt. J. Ressel at r. Steam powered screw propeller ship *Civetta* at l., arms at lower r. on back.	FV	FV	85.00

		VG	VF	UNC
140	**1000 SCHILLING** 2.1.1961. Dk. blue on m/c unpt. V. Kaplan at r. Dam and Persenburg Castle, arms at r. on back. 148 x 75mm.	350.00	800.00	1200.
141	**1000 SCHILLING** 2.1.1961. Dk. blue on m/c unpt. Like #140 but w/blue lined unpt. up to margin. 158 x 85mm.	35.00	100.00	200.00

1967-70 ISSUE

		VG	VF	UNC
142	**20 SCHILLING** 2.7.1967. Brown on olive and lilac unpt. C. Ritter von Ghega at r., arms at lower ctr. Semmering Railway bridge over the Semmering Pass (986 meters) on back.	FV	FV	4.00

146   100 SCHILLING
2.1.1969. Like #145 but w/ovpt: *2 AUFLAGE* (2nd issue) at upper l.

	VG	VF	UNC
	FV	FV	16.00

143   50 SCHILLING
2.1.1970. Purple on m/c unpt. F. Raimund at r., arms at l. Burg Theater in Vienna at l. ctr. on back.

	VG	VF	UNC
	FV	6.00	10.00

147   1000 SCHILLING
1.7.1966. Blue-violet on m/c unpt. B. von Suttner at r. ctr. Leopoldskron Castle and Hohensalzburg Fortress on back.

	VG	VF	UNC
	FV	110.00	185.00

1984-85 ISSUE
#148-153 Federal arms at upper l. Wmk: Federal arms and parallel vertical lines.

144   50 SCHILLING
2.1.1970. Like #143 but w/ovpt. *2. AUFLAGE* (2nd issue) at lower l. ctr.

	VG	VF	UNC
	FV	6.00	10.00

148   20 SCHILLING
1.10.1986. Dk. brown and brown on m/c unpt. M. Daffinger at r. Vienna's Albertina Museum on back.

	VG	VF	UNC
	FV	FV	4.00

145   100 SCHILLING
2.1.1969. Dk. green on m/c unpt. A. Kauffmann at r. Large house on back.

	VG	VF	UNC
	FV	FV	20.00

149   50 SCHILLING
2.1.1986. Purple and violet on m/c unpt. S. Freud at r. Vienna's Medical School *Josephinum* on back.

	VG	VF	UNC
	FV	FV	8.00

150 100 SCHILLING
2.1.1984 (1985). Dk. green, gray and dk. brown on m/c unpt. E. Böhm
v. Bawerk at r. Academy *Wissenschaften* at l. ctr. on back.

	VG	VF	UNC
	FV	FV	15.00

151 500 SCHILLING
1.7.1985 (1986). Dk. brown, deep violet and orange-brown on m/c
unpt. Architect O. Wagner at r. Vienna's Post Office Savings Bank on
back.

	VG	VF	UNC
	FV	FV	70.00

152 1000 SCHILLING
3.1.1983. Dk. blue and purple on m/c unpt. E. Schrödinger at r. Vienna
University at l. on back.

	VG	VF	UNC
	FV	FV	125.00

153 5000 SCHILLING
4.1.1988. Lt. brown and purple on m/c unpt. W. A. Mozart at r.
Vienna's Opera House at ctr. on back.

	VG	VF	UNC
	FV	FV	565.00

AZERBAIJAN

The Republic of Azerbaijan (formerly Azerbaijan S.S.R.)
includes the Nakhichevan Autonomous Republic and Nagorno-
Karabakh Autonomous Region
(which was abolished in 1991).
Situated in the eastern area of
Transcaucasia, it is bordered in
the west by Armenia, in the north
by Georgia and Dagestan, to the
east by the Caspian Sea and to
the south by Iran. It has an area
of 33,430 sq. mi. (86,600 sq. km.)
and a population of 7.1 million.
Capital: Baku. The area is rich in mineral deposits of aluminum, copper, iron, lead, salt and zinc,
with oil as its leading industry. Agriculture and livestock follow in importance.

In ancient times home of Scythian tribes and known under the Romans as Albania and to the
Arabs as Arran, the country of Azerbaijan formed at the time of its invasion by Seljuk Turks a prosperous state under Persian suzerainty. From the 16th century the country was a theatre of fighting
and political rivalry between Turkey, Persia and later Russia. Baku was first annexed to Russia by
Czar Peter I in 1723 and remained under Russian rule for 12 years. After the Russian retreat the
whole of Azerbaijan north of the Aras River became a khanate under Persian control until Czar
Alexander I, after an eight-year war with Persia, annexed it in 1813 to the Russian empire.

Until the Russian Revolution of 1905 there was no political life in Azerbaijan. A Mussavat
(Equality) party was formed in 1911 by Mohammed Emin Rasulzade, a former Social Democrat.
After the Russian Revolution of March 1917, the party started a campaign for independence, but
Baku, the capital, with its mixed population, constituted an alien enclave in the country. While a
national Azerbaijani government was established at Gandzha (Elizavetpol), a Communist-con-
trolled council assumed power at Baku with Stepan Shaumian, an Armenian, at its head. The
Gandzha government joined first, on Sept. 20, 1917, a Transcaucasian federal republic, but on
May 28, 1918, proclaimed the independence of Azerbaijan. On June 4, 1918, at Batum, a peace
treaty was signed with Turkey and a Turko-Azerbaijani force started an offensive against Baku,
but it was occupied on Aug. 17, 0918 by 1,400 British troops coming by sea from Anzali, Persia.
On Sept. 14 the British evacuated Baku, returning to Anzali, and three days later the Azerbaijan
government, headed by Fath Ali Khan Khoysky, established itself at Baku.

After the collapse of the Ottoman empire the British returned to Baku, at first ignoring the
Azerbaijan government. A general election with universal suffrage for the Azerbaijan constituent
assembly took place on Dec. 7, 1918 and out of 120 members there were 84 Mussavat supporters; Ali Marden Topchibashev was elected speaker, and Nasib Usubekov formed a new government. On Jan. 15, 1920, the Allied powers recognized Azerbaijan de facto, but on April 27 of the
same year the Red army invaded the country, and a Soviet republic of Azerbaijan was proclaimed
the next day. Later it became a member of the Transcaucasian Federation joining the U.S.S.R. on
Dec. 30, 1922; it became a self-constituent republic in 1936.

The Azerbaijan Communist party held its first congress at Baku in Feb. 1920. From 1921 to
1925 its first secretary was a Russian, S.M. Kirov, who directed a mass deportation to Siberia of
about 120,000 Azerbaijani "nationalist deviationists," among them the country's first two premiers.

In 1990 it adopted a declaration of republican sovereignty, and in Aug. 1991 declared itself
formally independent; this action was approved by a vote of referendum in Jan. 1992. It
announced its intention of joining the CIS in Dec. 1991, but a parliamentary resolution of Oct.
1992 declined to confirm its involvement. Communist President Mutaibov was relieved of his
office in May, 1992. A National Council replaced Mutaibov and on June 7 elected Abulfez Elchibey
in the first democratic election in the country's history. Surat Huseynov led a military coup against
Elchibey and seized power on June 30, 1993. Huseynov became prime minister with former communist Geidar Aliyev, president.

Fighting commenced between Muslim forces of Azerbaijan and Christian forces of Armenia in
1992 and continued through early 1994. Each faction claimed the Nagorno-Karabakh, an Armenian ethnic enclave, in Azerbaijan. A cease-fire was declared in May, 1994.

REPUBLIC

AZERBAYCAN MILLI BANKI

1992 ND ISSUE
#11-13 Maiden Tower at ctr. Wmk: 3 flames.

11 1 MANAT
ND (1992). Deep olive-green on m/c unpt.

	VG	VF	UNC
	.10	.50	1.50

12 10 MANAT
ND (1992). Deep brown-violet on m/c unpt.

	VG	VF	UNC
	.20	1.00	3.00

13 250 MANAT
ND (1992). Deep blue-gray on m/c unpt.

	VG	VF	UNC
	1.50	7.50	55.00

ND; 1994-95 ISSUE
#14-18 different view Maiden Tower ruins at ctr.
#14-20 Ornate "value" backs. Wmk: 3 flames.

14 1 MANAT
ND (1993). Deep blue and tan on dull orange and green unpt.

	VG	VF	UNC
	FV	FV	1.00

15 5 MANAT
ND (1993). Deep brown and pale purple on lilac and m/c unpt.

	VG	VF	UNC
	FV	FV	2.00

16 10 MANAT
ND (1993). Deep grayish blue-green on pale blue and m/c unpt.

	VG	VF	UNC
	FV	FV	2.50

17 50 MANAT
ND (1993). Brownish red and tan on ochre and m/c unpt.

	VG	VF	UNC
	FV	FV	3.00

18 100 MANAT
ND (1993). Red-violet and pale blue on m/c unpt.

	VG	VF	UNC
	FV	FV	4.00

19 500 MANAT
ND (1993). Deep brown on pale blue, pink and m/c unpt. Portr. N. Gencevi at r.

	VG	VF	UNC
	FV	FV	8.50

20 1000 MANAT
ND (1993). Dk. brown and blue on pink and m/c unpt. M. E. Resulzado at r.

	VG	VF	UNC
	FV	FV	7.50

21 10,000 MANAT
1994. Dull dk. brown and pale violet on m/c unpt. Mosque at ctr. r.
Wmk: AMB repeated.

	VG	VF	UNC
a. Security thread.	FV	FV	30.00
b. Segmented foil over security thread.	FV	FV	10.00

22 50,000 MANAT
1995. Blue-green on m/c unpt. Tomb ruins. Carpet design at l. on back. Segmented foil over security thread.

	VG	VF	UNC
	FV	FV	25.00

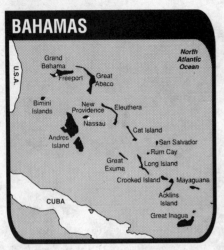

BAHAMAS

The Commonwealth of The Bahamas is an archipelago of about 3,000 islands, cays and rocks located in the Atlantic Ocean east of Florida and north of Cuba. The total land area of the 800-mile (1.287 km.) long chain of islands is 5,380 sq. mi. (13,935 sq. km.). They have a population of 255,000. Capital: Nassau. The Bahamas imports most of their food and manufactured products and exports cement, refined oil, pulpwood and lobsters. Tourism is the principal industry.

The Bahamas were discovered by Columbus in October, 1492, but Spain made no attempt to settle them. British influence began in 1626 when Charles I granted them to the lord proprietors of Carolina. They continued under British proprietors until 1717, when the civil and military governments were surrendered to the King and the islands designated a British Crown Colony. The Bahamas obtained complete internal self-government under the constitution of Jan. 7, 1964. Full independence was achieved on July 10, 1973. The Bahamas is a member of the Commonwealth of Nations. The Queen of England is Chief of State.

RULERS:
British

MONETARY SYSTEM:
1 Shilling = 12 Pence
1 Pound = 20 Shillings to 1966
1 Dollar = 100 Cents 1966-

COMMONWEALTH

GOVERNMENT OF THE BAHAMAS
Replacement notes: Z prefix.

1965 CURRENCY NOTE ACT
#17-25 Qn. Elizabeth II at I. Sign. varieties. Wmk: shellfish. Printer: TDLR.
NOTE: #23-25 w/3 sign. exist in specimen form.

			VG	VF	UNC
17	**1/2 DOLLAR**		.75	1.35	5.00
	L.1965. Purple on m/c unpt. Straw market on back.				

			VG	VF	UNC
18	**1 DOLLAR**				
	L.1965. Green on m/c unpt. Sea garden on back.				
	a. 2 sign.		1.35	2.50	20.00
	b. 3 sign.		1.50	5.00	32.50

			VG	VF	UNC
19	**3 DOLLARS**				
	L.1965. Red on m/c unpt. Paradise Beach on back.				
	a. Sign. Sands and Higgs.		4.00	7.50	20.00
	b. Sign. Francis and Higgs. Specimen.		—	—	200.00

			VG	VF	UNC
20	**5 DOLLARS**		8.00	15.00	55.00
	L.1965. Green on m/c unpt. Government House on back.				
21	**5 DOLLARS**				
	L.1965. Orange on m/c unpt. Like #20.				
	a. 2 sign.		10.00	25.00	225.00
	b. 3 sign.		15.00	55.00	400.00

			VG	VF	UNC
22	**10 DOLLARS**				
	L.1965. Dk. blue on m/c unpt. Flamingos on back.				
	a. 2 sign.		15.00	35.00	385.00
	b. 3 sign.		25.00	100.00	750.00
23	**20 DOLLARS**		35.00	120.00	625.00
	L.1965. Dk. brown on m/c unpt. Surrey on back.				
24	**50 DOLLARS**		75.00	225.00	950.00
	L.1965. Brown on m/c unpt. Produce market on back.				
25	**100 DOLLARS**		150.00	400.00	1500.
	L.1965. Blue on m/c unpt. Deep sea fishing on back.				

BAHAMAS MONETARY AUTHORITY

1968 MONETARY AUTHORITY ACT
#26-33 Qn. Elizabeth II at I. Wmk: Shellfish. Printer: TDLR.

			VG	VF	UNC
26	**1/2 DOLLAR**		.65	1.25	3.50
	L.1968. Purple on m/c unpt. Back similar to #17.				

27 1 DOLLAR
L.1968. Green on m/c unpt. Back similar to #18.

VG	VF	UNC
1.25	2.25	12.50

28 3 DOLLARS
L.1968. Red on m/c unpt. Back similar to #19.

VG	VF	UNC
3.50	5.50	15.00

29 5 DOLLARS
L.1968. Orange on m/c unpt. Back similar to #20.

VG	VF	UNC
7.00	20.00	135.00

30 10 DOLLARS
L.1968. Dk. blue on m/c unpt. Back similar to #22.

22.50	70.00	500.00

31 20 DOLLARS
L.1968. Dk. brown on m/c unpt. Back similar to #23.

VG	VF	UNC
37.50	175.00	850.00

33 100 DOLLARS
L.1968. Blue on m/c unpt. Back similar to #25.

185.00	400.00	2250.

CENTRAL BANK OF THE BAHAMAS

1974 CENTRAL BANK ACT
#35-41 Qn. Elizabeth II. Wmk: Shellfish. Printer: TDLR.

35 1 DOLLAR
L.1974. Dk. blue-green on m/c unpt. Back similar to #18.
  a. Sign. T. B. Donaldson.
  b. Sign. W. C. Allen.

VG	VF	UNC
1.25	2.00	8.50
1.50	7.50	22.50

37 5 DOLLARS
L.1974. Orange on m/c unpt. Back similar to #20.
  a. Sign. T. B. Donaldson.
  b. Sign. W. C. Allen.

VG	VF	UNC
5.50	8.50	35.00
8.50	25.00	200.00

38 10 DOLLARS
L.1974. Dk. blue on m/c unpt. Back similar to #22.
  a. Sign. T. B. Donaldson.
  b. Sign. W. C. Allen.

VG	VF	UNC
11.00	22.50	125.00
20.00	80.00	350.00

39 20 DOLLARS
L.1974. Dk. brown on m/c unpt. Back similar to #23.
  a. Sign. T. B. Donaldson.
  b. Sign. W. C. Allen.

VG	VF	UNC
22.50	30.00	225.00
37.50	125.00	575.00

40 50 DOLLARS
L.1974. Brown on m/c unpt. Back similar to #24.
  a. Sign. T. B. Donaldson.
  b. Sign. W. C. Allen.

55.00	125.00	525.00
65.00	200.00	1000.

41 100 DOLLARS
L.1974. Blue on m/c unpt. Back similar to #25.
  a. Sign. T. B. Donaldson.
  b. Sign. W. C. Allen.

110.00	185.00	900.00
135.00	300.00	1500.

1974 CENTRAL BANK ACT; 1984 ISSUE
#42-49 map at l., mature portr. Qn. Elizabeth II at r., ctr. Arms at r. on back. Wmk: Sailing ship. Printer: TDLR.

42 1/2 DOLLAR
L.1974 (1984). Green on m/c unpt. Baskets at l. Woman and market on back. Sign. W. C. Allen.

VG	VF	UNC
FV	FV	1.50

43   1 DOLLAR

	VG	VF	UNC
L.1974 (1984). Deep green on m/c unpt. Fish at l. Police band at ctr. on back.			
a. Sign. W. C. Allen.	FV	FV	3.50
b. Sign. F. H. Smith.	FV	FV	3.00

44   3 DOLLARS

	VG	VF	UNC
L.1974 (1984). Red-violet on m/c unpt. Beach at l. Sailboats on back. Sign. W. C. Allen.	FV	FV	5.00

45   5 DOLLARS

	VG	VF	UNC
L.1974 (1984). Orange on m/c unpt. Statue at l. Native dancers *Junkanoo* at ctr.			
a. Sign. W. C. Allen.	FV	6.00	20.00
b. Sign. F. H. Smith. 2 horizontal serial #.	FV	FV	12.50

46   10 DOLLARS

	VG	VF	UNC
L.1974 (1984). Pale blue on m/c unpt. 2 flamingos at l. Lighthouse and shoreline on back.			
a. Sign. W. C. Allen.	FV	12.00	30.00
b. Sign. F. H. Smith. 2 horizontal serial #.	FV	15.00	40.00

47   20 DOLLARS

	VG	VF	UNC
L.1974 (1984). Red and black on m/c unpt. Horse and carriage at l. Nassau harbor on back.			
a. Sign. W. C. Allen.	FV	25.00	85.00
b. Sign. F. H. Smith. 2 horizontal serial #.	FV	22.50	55.00

48   50 DOLLARS

	VG	VF	UNC
L.1974 (1984). Purple, orange and green on m/c unpt. Lighthouse at l. Bank on back.			
a. Sign. W. C. Allen.	FV	65.00	185.00
b. Sign. F. H. Smith. 2 horizontal serial #.	FV	75.00	300.00

49   100 DOLLARS

	VG	VF	UNC
L.1974 (1984). Deep blue on m/c unpt. Sailboat at l. Blue marlin on back. Sign. W. C. Allen.	FV	125.00	300.00

1992 COMMEMORATIVE ISSUE

#50, Quincentennial of First Landfall by Christopher Columbus.

50   1 DOLLAR

	VG	VF	UNC
ND (1992). Dk. blue and deep violet on m/c unpt. Commercial seal at l., bust of C. Columbus r. w/compass face behind. Birds, lizard, islands outlined, ships across back w/arms at lower r. Printer: CBNC.	FV	FV	2.75

1974 CENTRAL BANK ACT; 1992-95 ISSUE

#51-56 wmk: Caravel sailing ship. Sign. F.H. Smith.

#52, 54-56 printer: TDLR.

51   1 DOLLAR

	VG	VF	UNC
L.1974 (1992). Deep green on m/c unpt. Like #43b but w/serial # vertical and horizontal. Printer: BABN.	FV	FV	2.50

52   5 DOLLARS

	VG	VF	UNC
L.1974 (1995). Dk. brown, brown and orange on m/c unpt. Sir C. Wallace-Whitfield at r., statue at l. Back similar to #45.	FV	FV	12.50

53   10 DOLLARS

	VG	VF	UNC
L.1974 (1992). Pale blue on m/c unpt. Like #46b but w/serial # vertical and horizontal. Printer: CBNC.	FV	FV	17.50

54   20 DOLLARS

	VG	VF	UNC
L.1974 (1993). Black and red on m/c unpt. Sir M. B. Butler at r., horse drawn surrey at l. Aerial view of ships in Nassau's harbor at ctr., arms at r. on back.	FV	FV	40.00

55	**50 DOLLARS**		**VG**	**VF**	**UNC**
	L.1974 (1992). Brown, blue-green and on m/c unpt. Like #48b but w/serial # vertical and horizontal.		FV	FV	80.00

56	**100 DOLLARS**		**VG**	**VF**	**UNC**
	L.1974 (1992). Purple, deep blue and red-violet on m/c unpt. Like #49 but w/serial # vertical and horizontal.		FV	FV	185.00

1974 CENTRAL BANK ACT; 1996 ISSUE
at lower l.

#57 and 62 mature bust of Qn. Elizabeth II. Ascending serial

57	**1 DOLLAR**		**VG**	**VF**	**UNC**
	1996. Similar to #51. Printer: BABN.		FV	FV	2.50
58	**5 DOLLARS**				Expected New Issue
59	**10 DOLLARS**				Expected New Issue
60	**20 DOLLARS**				Expected New Issue
61	**50 DOLLARS**				Expected New Issue
62	**100 DOLLARS**				
	1996. Similar to #56. Printer: BABN.		FV	FV	150.00

COLLECTOR SERIES

BAHAMAS GOVERNMENT

1965 ISSUE

CS1	**1/2-100 DOLLARS**	**ISSUE PRICE**	**MKT. VALUE**
	ND (1965). #17-25 ovpt: *SPECIMEN*. (100 sets).	—	1000.

BAHAMAS MONETARY AUTHORITY

1968 ISSUE

CS2	**1/2-100 DOLLARS**	**ISSUE PRICE**	**MKT. VALUE**
	ND (1968). #26-33 ovpt: *SPECIMEN*.	—	100.00

BAHRAIN

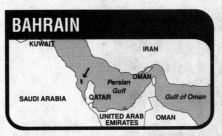

The State of Bahrain, a group of islands in the Persian Gulf off Saudi Arabia, has an area of 258 sq. mi. (622 sq. km.) and a population of 538,000. Capital: Manama. Prior to the depression of the 1930s, the economy was based on pearl fishing. Petroleum and aluminum industries and transit trade are the vital factors in the economy today.

The Portuguese occupied the islands in 1507 but were driven out in 1602 by Arab subjects of Persia. They in turn were ejected by Arabs of the Ataiba tribe from the Arabian mainland who have maintained possession up to the present time. The ruling sheikh of Bahrain entered into relations with Great Britain in 1805 and concluded a binding treaty of protection in 1861. In 1968 Great Britain decided to terminate treaty relations with the Persian Gulf sheikhdoms. Unable to agree on terms of union with the other sheikhdoms, Bahrain decided to seek independence as a separate entity and became fully independent on August 15, 1971.

RULERS:
Isa Bin Sulman al-Khalifa, 1961-

MONETARY SYSTEM:
1 Dinar = 1000 Fils

STATE

BAHRAIN CURRENCY BOARD

AUTHORIZATION 6/1964
#1-6 sailboat at l., arms at r. Wmk: Falcon's head.

1	**100 FILS**		**VG**	**VF**	**UNC**
	L.1964. Ochre on m/c unpt. Palm trees on back.		.25	1.00	7.50

2	**1/4 DINAR**		**VG**	**VF**	**UNC**
	L.1964. Brown on m/c unpt. Oil derricks on back.		.50	1.50	9.00

3	**1/2 DINAR**		**VG**	**VF**	**UNC**
	L.1964. Purple on m/c unpt. Ships on back.		1.00	2.00	10.00

4 **1 DINAR**
L.1964. Reddish brown on m/c unpt. Minarets on back.

	VG	VF	UNC
	FV	4.00	15.00

5 **5 DINARS**
L.1964. Blue on m/c unpt. Sailboats on back.

	VG	VF	UNC
	FV	40.00	150.00

6 **10 DINARS**
L.1964. Green on m/c unpt. Aerial city view on back.

	VG	VF	UNC
	FV	35.00	100.00

BAHRAIN MONETARY AGENCY

AUTHORIZATION 23/1973

#7-11 map at l., sailboat at ctr., arms at r. Wmk: Falcon's head.

7 **1/2 DINAR**
L.1973. Brown on m/c unpt. Cow mask at lower l. Factory at l. on back.

	VG	VF	UNC
	FV	FV	4.00

8 **1 DINAR**
L.1973. Red on m/c unpt. Tower at l. Bahrain Monetary Agency bldg. on back.

	VG	VF	UNC
	FV	FV	7.00

8A **5 DINARS**
L.1973. Blue on m/c unpt. Mosque at l. Pearl fishing scene on back.

	VG	VF	UNC
	FV	FV	30.00

9 **10 DINARS**
L.1973. Green on m/c unpt. Wind tower at l., dry dock on back.

		VG	VF	UNC
a.	2 horizontal serial #.	FV	30.00	50.00
b.	Serial # vertical and horizontal.	FV	35.00	60.00

10 **20 DINARS**
L.1973. Reddish brown on m/c unpt. Tower at l. Bldg. on back.

	VG	VF	UNC
	FV	85.00	185.00

11 20 DINARS
   L.1973. Face like #10, but w/symbol changed at r. of map. Silvering
   added at lower l. denomination. Back has open frame and symbol
   around wmk. area. Also various color differences.

	VG	VF	UNC
a. 2 horizontal serial #.	FV	FV	90.00
b. Serial # vertical and horizontal.	FV	40.00	100.00

AUTHORIZATION 23/1973; 1993 ISSUE
#12-16 arms at ctr., outline map at l. Wmk: Antelope's head.

12 1/2 DINAR
   L.1973 (1993). Deep brown, violet and brown-orange on m/c unpt.
   Man weaving at r. "Aluminum Bahrain" facility at l. ctr. on back.

VG	VF	UNC
FV	FV	3.50

13 1 DINAR
   L.1973 (1993). Violet and red-orange on m/c unpt. Ancient seal at r.
   Bahrain Monetary Agency bldg. at l. ctr. on back.

VG	VF	UNC
FV	FV	6.00

14 5 DINARS
   L.1973 (1993). Blue-black and deep blue-green on m/c unpt. Fortress
   at r. Bahrain International Airport at l. ctr. on back.

VG	VF	UNC
FV	FV	25.00

15 10 DINARS
   L.1973 (1993). Deep olive-green and green on m/c unpt. Dhow at r.
   Aerial view of Kg. Fahad Causeway at l. ctr. on back.

VG	VF	UNC
FV	FV	45.00

16 20 DINARS
   L.1973 (1993). Purple and violet m/c unpt. Govt. bldg. at r. Mosque at
   l. ctr. on back.

VG	VF	UNC
FV	FV	85.00

COLLECTOR SERIES

CS1 100 FILS - 20 DINARS
   ND (1978). #1-6 and 10 w/ovpt: *SPECIMEN* and Maltese cross prefix
   serial #.

ISSUE PRICE	MKT. VALUE
14.00	50.00

BANGLADESH

The Peoples Republic of Bangladesh (formerly East Pakistan), a parliamentary democracy located on the Bay of Bengal bordered by India and Burma, has an area of 55,598 sq. mi. (143,998 sq. km.) and a population of 118.7 million. Capital: Dacca. The economy is predominantly agricultural. Jute products and tea are exported.

British rule over the vast Indian sub-continent ended in 1947 when British India attained independence and was partitioned into the two successor states of India and Pakistan. Pakistan consisted of East and West Pakistan, two areas united by the Moslem religion but separated by culture and 1,000 miles of Indian territory. Restive under the de facto rule of the militant but fewer West Pakistanis, the East Pakistanis unsuccessfully demanded greater economic benefits and political reforms. The inability of the leaders of East and West Pakistan to resolve a political breakdown occasioned by the East Pakistan success in the general elections of 1970 precipitated massive civil disobedience in East Pakistan which West Pakistan sought to suppress militarily. East Pakistan seceded from Pakistan, March 26, 1971, and with the support of India declared an independent Peoples Republic of Bangladesh. Bangladesh is a member of the Commonwealth of Nations. The president is the Head of State and of Government.

MONETARY SYSTEM:
1 Rupee = 100 Paise to 1972
1 Taka = 100 Poisha 1972-

REPUBLIC

PEOPLES REPUBLIC OF BANGLADESH

1971 ND PROVISIONAL ISSUE

#1-3 w/*BANGLADESH* ovpt. in English or Bengali on Pakistan notes. The Bangladesh Bank never officially issued any Pakistan notes w/ovpt. These are considered locally issued by some authorities.

		VG	VF	UNC
1	**1 RUPEE** ND (1971). Blue. Purple *BANGLADESH* ovpt. on Pakistan #9.	10.00	30.00	90.00

		VG	VF	UNC
1A	**1 RUPEE** ND (1971). Blue. Purple Bengali ovpt. on Pakistan #9.	10.00	30.00	90.00

		VG	VF	UNC
2	**5 RUPEES** ND (1971). Brown-violet. Purple Bengali ovpt. on Pakistan #15.	10.00	30.00	90.00

		VG	VF	UNC
3	**10 RUPEES** ND (1971). Brown. Purple Bengali ovpt. on Pakistan #13.	10.00	30.00	90.00

1972-89 ND ISSUES

		VG	VF	UNC
4	**1 TAKA** ND (1972). Brown. Map of Bangladesh at l.	.25	.75	3.00

		VG	VF	UNC
5	**1 TAKA** ND (1973). Violet and ochre. Hand holding rice plants at l. Arms at r. on back.			
	a. W/wmk.	.20	.50	2.00
	b. W/o wmk. (different sign.).	.20	.50	2.00

		VG	VF	UNC
6	**1 TAKA** ND (1974). Violet. Woman preparing grain at l. Hand holding rice plants at ctr., arms at r. on back.	.15	.45	1.50

		VG	VF	UNC
6A	**1 TAKA** ND (1980). Violet and m/c. Arms at r. Deer at l. ctr. on back.	.10	.20	.75
6B	**1 TAKA** ND (1984). Violet and m/c. Similar to #6A but no printing on wmk. area at l. Also, different tiger wmk.	FV	FV	.50

		VG	VF	UNC
6C	**2 TAKA** ND (1989). Black on green and orange unpt. Monument at r. Bird on branch at l. on back.	FV	FV	.75

BANGLADESH BANK

1972 ND ISSUE

#7-9 map of Bangladesh at l., portr. Mujibur Rahman at r.

7	**5 TAKA**	VG	VF	UNC
	ND (1972). Purple on m/c unpt.	.50	1.50	7.50

8	**10 TAKA**	VG	VF	UNC
	ND (1972). Blue on m/c unpt.	.75	2.00	8.00

9	**100 TAKA**	VG	VF	UNC
	ND (1972). Green on m/c unpt.	2.00	7.50	22.50

1973 ND ISSUE

#10-12 Mujibur Rahman at l. Wmk: Tiger's head.

10	**5 TAKA**	VG	VF	UNC
	ND (1973). Red. Lotus plants at ctr r. on back.	.25	1.00	4.00

11	**10 TAKA**	VG	VF	UNC
	ND (1973). Green. River scene on back.			
	a. Serial # in Western numerals.	.50	2.50	10.00
	b. Serial # in Bengali numerals.	.50	1.75	7.00

12	**100 TAKA**	VG	VF	UNC
	ND (1973). Brown. River scene on back.	.75	3.00	10.00

1974 ND ISSUE

#13-14 Mujibur Rahman at r. Wmk: Tiger's head.

13	**5 TAKA**	VG	VF	UNC
	ND (1974). Red. Aerial view of factory on back.	.25	.75	4.00

14	**10 TAKA**	VG	VF	UNC
	ND (1974). Green. Rice harvesting on back.	.50	1.50	7.50

1976-77 ND ISSUE

#15-19 ornate bldg. at r. Wmk: Tiger's head.

NOTE: For similar 500 Taka but w/o printing on wmk. area, see #30.

15	**5 TAKA**	VG	VF	UNC
	ND (1977). Lt. brown. Back like #13.	.15	.35	3.00

16	**10 TAKA**		**VG**	**VF**	**UNC**
	ND (1977). Purple. Back like #14.		.25	.75	5.00

17	**50 TAKA**		**VG**	**VF**	**UNC**
	ND (1976). Orange. Harvesting scene on back.		1.00	4.00	12.50

21	**10 TAKA**		**VG**	**VF**	**UNC**
	ND (1978). Purple. Mosque at r. Back like #14.		.20	.50	2.00

18	**100 TAKA**		**VG**	**VF**	**UNC**
	ND (1976). Blue-violet on m/c unpt. Bldg. at l. Back like #12.		3.00	8.00	17.50

22	**20 TAKA**		**VG**	**VF**	**UNC**
	ND (1980). Blue-green. Bldg. at r. Harvesting scene on back.		.50	1.50	3.50

19	**500 TAKA**		**VG**	**VF**	**UNC**
	ND (1977). Blue and lilac. Government bldg. on back.		15.00	50.00	110.00

23	**50 TAKA**		**VG**	**VF**	**UNC**
	ND (1980). Orange on m/c unpt. Bldg. at r. Women harvesting on back.		.75	1.75	6.50

1978-82 ND ISSUE
#20-24 wmk: Tiger's head.

20	**5 TAKA**		**VG**	**VF**	**UNC**
	ND (1978). Lt brown on m/c unpt. Doorway at r. Back like #13.		.15	.25	1.00

24	**100 TAKA**		**VG**	**VF**	**UNC**
	ND (1982). Blue-violet, deep brown and m/c. Bldg. at r. Unpt. throughout wmk. area at l. Ruins of mosque at l. on back.		1.00	5.00	12.50

1982-88 ND Issue
#25-32 wmk: Different tiger's head. Sign. varieties.

			VG	VF	UNC
25	**5 Taka**	ND (1983). Similar to #20 but no printing on wmk. area at l. on face.			
	a.	Black sign. Lg. serial #.	.15	.25	1.25
	b.	Black sign. Sm. serial #.	FV	.15	1.00
	c.	Brown sign. Sm. serial #.	FV	FV	.50

			VG	VF	UNC
29	**100 Taka**	ND (1984). Similar to #24 but no printing on wmk. area at l. on face.	FV	FV	8.50

			VG	VF	UNC
26	**10 Taka**	ND (1982). Violet on green and m/c unpt. Bldg. at r. Hydroelectric dam at ctr. on back. 3 sign. varieties.	.30	.50	2.00

			VG	VF	UNC
30	**500 Taka**	ND (1984). Gray, blue, violet and m/c. Similar to #19 but no printing on wmk. area at l. on face.			
	a.	W/o segmented foil.	FV	FV	42.50
	b.	W/segmented foil security thread.	FV	FV	25.00

1989-93 ND Issue

			VG	VF	UNC
31	**2 Taka**	ND (1989). Black on green and orange unpt. Monument at r. Back: Bird.	FV	FV	.75

1992-93 ND Issue
#33 *Deleted.* See #30b.

			VG	VF	UNC
27	**20 Taka**	ND (1988). Design like #22 but no printing on wmk. area.			
	a.	Black sign. Lg. serial #.	FV	FV	2.75
	b.	Green sign. Sm. serial #.	FV	FV	2.25

			VG	VF	UNC
32	**100 Taka**	ND (1992). Like #29 but w/circular toothed border added around wmk. area on face and back.			
	a.	W/o segmented foil.	FV	FV	6.50
	b.	W/segmented foil over security thread.	FV	FV	6.00

			VG	VF	UNC
28	**50 Taka**	ND (1986). Black, red and deep green on m/c unpt. Monument at ctr. Modern bldg. at ctr. on back.	FV	FV	4.00

Barbados, an independent state within the British Commonwealth, is located in the Windward Islands of the West Indies east of St. Vincent. The coral island has an area of 166 sq. mi. (431 sq. km) and a population of 258,600. Capital: Bridgetown. The economy is based on sugar and tourism. Sugar, petroleum products, molasses and rum are exported.

Barbados was named by the Portuguese who achieved the first landing on the island in 1563. British sailors landed at the site of present-day Holetown in 1624. Barbados was under uninterrupted British control from the time of the first British settlement in 1627 until it obtained independence on Nov. 30, 1966. It is a member of the Commonwealth of Nations. The Queen of England is Chief of State.

Barbados was included in the issues of the British Caribbean Territories - Eastern Group and later the East Caribbean Currency Authority until 1973.

RULERS:
British to 1966

MONETARY SYSTEM:
1 Dollar = 100 Cents, 1950-

AUTONOMOUS

CENTRAL BANK OF BARBADOS

1973 ND ISSUE
#29-33 arms at l. ctr. Trafalgar Square in Bridgetown on back. Wmk: Map of Barbados. Printer: DLR.
Replacement notes: *Z1* prefix.

29	1 DOLLAR	VG	VF	UNC
	ND (1973). Red on m/c unpt. Portr. S. J. Prescod at r.	FV	.75	2.75

30	5 DOLLARS	VG	VF	UNC
	ND (1973). Green on m/c unpt. Portr. S. J. Prescod at r.	FV	4.00	13.50

31	10 DOLLARS	VG	VF	UNC
	ND (1973). Dk. brown on m/c unpt. Portr. C. D. O'Neal at r.			
	a. Sign. C. Blackman.	FV	7.00	15.00
	b. Sign K. King.	FV	6.00	11.50
32	20 DOLLARS			
	ND (1973). Purple on m/c unpt. Portr. S. J. Prescod at r.	FV	12.00	27.50
33	100 DOLLARS			
	ND (1973). Gray, blue on m/c unpt. Portr. Sir G. H. Adams at r. Treetops are grayish blue on back. Serial # to E 3,200,000.	FV	70.00	125.00

1975-80 ND ISSUE
#34 *Deleted.* See #36.
#35-40 arms at l. ctr. Trafalgar Square in Bridgetown on back. Wmk: Map of Barbados. Printer: DLR.
Replacement notes: *Z1* prefix.

35	2 DOLLARS	VG	VF	UNC
	ND (1980). Blue on m/c unpt. Portr. J. R. Bovell at r.			
	a. Sign. C. Blackman.	FV	1.50	3.50
	b. Sign. K. King.	FV	FV	2.75

36	5 DOLLARS	VG	VF	UNC
	ND (1975). Dk. green on m/c unpt. Portr. Sir F. Worrell at r.			
	a. Sign C. Blackman.	FV	3.50	7.50
	b. Sign. K. King.	FV	FV	6.50

1988-94 ND ISSUE

37	10 DOLLARS	VG	VF	UNC
	ND (1994). Dk. brown and green on m/c unpt. Like #31 but seahorse in rectangle at l. on face, at r. on back.	FV	FV	12.50

38   20 DOLLARS
ND (1988). Purple on m/c unpt. Like #32, but bird emblem in
rectangle at l. on face, at r. on back. Sign. K. King.

FV   FV   22.50

	VG	VF	UNC
39 50 DOLLARS ND (1989). Orange, blue and gray on m/c unpt. Portr. Prime Minister E. W. Barrow at r.	FV	FV	50.00

40   100 DOLLARS
ND (1986). Brown, purple and gray-blue on m/c unpt. Like #33, but
seahorse emblem in rectangle at l. on face, at r. on back. Treetops on
back are green. Serial # above E 3,200,000.

	VG	VF	UNC
a. Sign. C. Blackman.	FV	60.00	100.00
b. Sign. K. King.	FV	FV	85.00

1995-96 ND ISSUE

#41-44 like #35-38 but w/enhanced security features. Ascending serial # at upper l. Sign. C. H. Springer.

		VG	VF	UNC
41	**2 DOLLARS** ND (1995). Blue on m/c unpt. Like #35.	FV	FV	2.50
42	**5 DOLLARS** ND (1995). Dk. green on m/c unpt. Like #36.	FV	FV	5.50
43	**10 DOLLARS** ND (1995). Dk. brown and green on m/c unpt. Like #37.	FV	FV	10.00
44	**20 DOLLARS** ND (1996). Red-violet and purple on m/c unpt. Like #38.	FV	FV	18.50
45	**50 DOLLARS** ND (1996). Orange, blue and gray on m/c unpt. Like #39.		Expected New Issue	
46	**100 DOLLARS** ND (1996). Brown, purple and blue-gray on m/c unpt. Like #40.	FV	FV	80.00

Belarus (Byelorussia, Belorussia, or White Russia - formerly the Belorussian S.S.R.) is situated along the Western Dvina and Dnieper, bounded in the west by Poland, to the north by Latvia and Lithuania, to the east by Russia and the south by the Ukraine. It has an area of 80,134 sq. mi. (207,600 sq. km.) and a population of 4.8 million. Capital: Minsk. Peat, salt, agriculture including flax, fodder and grasses for cattle breeding and dairy products, along with general manufacturing industries comprise the economy.

There never existed an independent state of Byelorussia. When Kiev was the center of Rus, there were a few feudal principalities in the Byelorussian lands, those of Polotsk, Smolensk and Turov being the most important. The principalities, protected by the Pripet marshes, escaped invasion when, in the first half of the 13th century, the Tatars destroyed the Kievan Rus, but soon they were all incorporated into the Grand Duchy of Lithuania. The Lithuanian conquerors were pagan and illiterate but politically wise. They respected the Christianity of the conquered and gradually Byelorussian became the official language of the grand duchy. When this greater Lithuania was absorbed by Poland in the 16th century, Polish replaced Byelorussian as the official language of the country. Until the partitions of Poland at the end of 18th century, the history of Byelorussia is identical with that of greater Lithuania.

When Russia incorporated the whole of Byelorussia into its territories in 1795, it claimed to be recovering old Russian lands and denied that the Byelorussians were a separate nation. The country was named Northwestern territory and in 1839 Byelorussian Roman Catholics of the Uni-

ate rite were forced to accept Orthodoxy. A minority remained faithful to the Latin rite. The German occupation of western Byelorussia in 1915 created an opportunity for Byelorussian leaders to formulate in Dec. 1917 their desire for an independent Byelorussia. On Feb. 25, 1918, Minsk was occupied by the Germans, and in the Brest-Litovsk peace treaty of March 3 between the Central Powers and Soviet Russia the existence of Byelorussia was ignored. Nevertheless, on March 25, the National council headed by Lutskievich, Vatslav Lastovski and others proclaimed an independent republic. After the collapse of Germany the Soviet government repudiated the Brest treaties and on Jan. 1, 1919, proclaimed a Byelorussian S.S.R. The Red army occupied the lands evacuated by the Germans, and by February all Byelorussia was in Communist hands. The Polish army started an eastward offensive, however, and on Aug. 8 entered Minsk. In Dec. 1919 the Byelorussian National council gathered there but a split occurred in its ranks: Lastovski formed a pro-Soviet government, while Lutskievich formed an anti-Communist council. The Lastovski "government" soon took refuge in Lithuania, and later in Czechoslovakia. The peace treaty between Poland and the U.S.S.R. in March 1921 partitioned Byelorussia. In its eastern and larger part a Soviet republic was formed, which in 1922 became a founder member of the U.S.S.R. The eastern frontier was identical with the corresponding section of the Polish-Russian frontier before 1772. The first premier of the Byelorussian S.S.R., Dmitro Zhylunovich, persuaded Lastovski to return. Both perished in the purges of the 1930s. On Sept. 17, 1939, in accordance with the secret treaty partitioning Poland signed on Aug. 23 between Germany and the U.S.S.R., the Soviet army occupied eastern Poland, where a western Byelorussian people's assembly was elected on Oct. 22. The assembly "unanimously" demanded the incorporation of western Byelorussia into the U.S.S.R. On Nov. 2 the supreme soviet of the union proclaimed the unification of all Byelorussia. However, when the Moscow treaty of Aug. 16, 1945, fixed the Polish-Soviet frontier, it left Bialystok to Poland. From Jan. 1, 1955, the republic was divided into 7 oblasti or provinces; Minsk, Brest, Grodno, Molodechno, Mohylev (Mogilev), Homel (Gomel) and Vitebsk. On Aug. 25, 1991, following an unsuccessful coup, the Supreme Soviet adopted a declaration of independence, and the "Republic of Belarus" was proclaimed in Sept. Later in Dec. it became a founder member of the CIS.

MONETARY SYSTEM:
1 Rubel = 100 Kapeek

REPUBLIC

КУПОН РЭСПУБЛІКА БЕЛАРУСБ

BELARUS REPUBLIC

1991 FIRST RUBEL CONTROL COUPON ISSUE

#A1 and A2 full sheet of 28 coupons of various denominations w/guilloche in unpt. in registry at ctr. Uniface.

1991 SECOND RUBEL CONTROL COUPON ISSUE

#A3-A8 w/o unpt. in registry at ctr. Uniface.

#A4-A7 full sheet of 28 coupons of various denominations.

		VG	VF	UNC
A3	**20 RUBLEI**			
	ND (1991). Black text on olive-green unpt. Sheet of 12 coupons of various denominations.			
	a. Issued full sheet.	—	2.00	4.00
	b. Coupon.	—	—	.10
	r. Remainder full sheet.	—	.75	1.50

		VG	VF	UNC
A1	**75 RUBLEI**			
	ND (1991). Black text on blue and yellow unpt.			
	a. Issued full sheet.	—	2.00	4.00
	b. Coupon.	—	—	.05
	r. Remainder full sheet.	—	.75	1.50
A2	**100 RUBLEI**			
	ND (1991). Black text on pale red-orange and yellow unpt.			
	a. Issued full sheet.	—	2.00	4.00
	b. Coupon.	—	—	.05
	r. Remainder full sheet.	—	.75	1.50

		VG	VF	UNC
A4	**50 RUBLEI**			
	ND (1991). Black text on lt. blue unpt.			
	a. Issued full sheet.	—	2.00	4.00
	b. Coupon.	—	—	.05
	r. Remainder full sheet.	—	.75	1.50

A5	75 RUBLEI		VG	VF	UNC
	ND (1991). Dk. brown text on pale purple unpt.				
	a.	Issued full sheet.	—	2.00	4.00
	b.	Coupon.	—	—	.05
	r.	Remainder full sheet.	—	.75	1.50
A5A	100 RUBLEI				
	ND (1991).				
	a.	Issued full sheet.	—	2.00	4.00
	b.	Coupon.	—	—	.05
	r.	Remainder full sheet.	—	.75	1.50
A6	200 RUBLEI				
	ND (1991). Black text on pink unpt.				
	a.	Issued full sheet.	—	2.00	4.00
	b.	Coupon.	—	—	.05
	r.	Remainder full sheet.	—	.75	1.50

A7	300 RUBLEI		VG	VF	UNC
	ND (1991). Black text on pale red-orange unpt.				
	a.	Issued full sheet.	—	2.00	4.00
	b.	Coupon.	—	—	.05
	r.	Remainder full sheet.	—	.75	1.50

A8	500 RUBLEI		VG	VF	UNC
	ND (1991). Black text on pink, purple and yellow unpt.				
	a.	Issued full sheet.	—	2.00	4.00
	b.	Coupon.	—	—	.05
	r.	Remainder full sheet.	—	.75	1.50

НАЦЫЯНАЛЬНАIА БАНКА БЕЛАРУСI

BELARUS NATIONAL BANK

1992-95 РАЗЛIКОВЫ БIЛЕТ - EXCHANGE NOTE ISSUE

#1-10 "Pagonya," a defending warrior wielding sword on horseback at ctr. Wmk. paper.

1	50 KAPEEK	VG	VF	UNC
	1992. Red and brown-orange on pink unpt. Squirrel at ctr. r. on back.	FV	FV	.10

2	1 RUBEL	VG	VF	UNC
	1992. Yellow on green, purple and blue unpt. Rabbit at ctr. r. on back.	FV	FV	.40

3	3 RUBLEI	VG	VF	UNC
	1992. Green, red-orange and pale olive-green on m/c unpt. 2 beavers at ctr. r. on back.	FV	FV	.20

4	5 RUBLEI	VG	VF	UNC
	1992. Deep blue on lt. blue, lilac, violet and m/c unpt. 2 wolves at ctr. r. on back.	FV	FV	.30

5	10 RUBLEI	VG	VF	UNC
	1992. Deep green on lt. green, orange and m/c unpt. Lynx w/kitten at ctr. r. on back.	FV	FV	.20

6	25 RUBLEI	VG	VF	UNC
	1992. Violet on red, green and m/c unpt. Moose at ctr. r. on back.	FV	FV	.30

7	**50 RUBLEI**	**VG**	**VF**	**UNC**
	1992. Deep purple on red and green unpt. Bear at ctr. r. on back.	FV	FV	.30

8	**100 RUBLEI**	**VG**	**VF**	**UNC**
	1992. Brown, gray and tan on m/c unpt. Wisent (European Bison) at ctr. on back.	FV	FV	.30

9	**200 RUBLEI**	**VG**	**VF**	**UNC**
	1992. Deep brown-violet, orange, green and ochre on m/c unpt. City view at ctr. r. on back.	FV	FV	.60

10	**500 RUBLEI**	**VG**	**VF**	**UNC**
	1992. Violet, tan, lt. blue and orange on m/c unpt. Victory Plaza in Minsk at ctr. r. on back.	FV	FV	1.75

11	**1000 RUBLEI**	**VG**	**VF**	**UNC**
	1992 (1993). Blue, olive-green and pink. Back black, dk. blue and dk. green on m/c unpt.; Academy of Sciences bldg. at ctr. r. on back.	FV	FV	.50

12	**5000 RUBLEI**	**VG**	**VF**	**UNC**
	1992 (1993). Purple and red-violet on m/c unpt. Back brown-violet and olive-green on m/c unpt. Bldgs. in Minsk lower city at ctr. r.	FV	FV	2.00

13	**20,000 RUBLEI**	**VG**	**VF**	**UNC**
	1994. Dk. brown on m/c unpt. National Bank bldg. at l. ctr. on back. Wmk: old tower and tree.	FV	FV	4.00

14	**50,000 RUBLEI**	**VG**	**VF**	**UNC**
		FV	FV	10.00

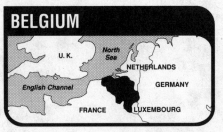

BELGIUM

1995. Dk. brown on m/c unpt. War memorial at ctr. r. City gate at l., tapestry at ctr. r. on back. The Kingdom of Belgium, a constitutional monarchy in northwest Europe, has an area of 11,779 sq. mi. (30,513 sq. km.) and a population of 10.1 million, chiefly Dutch-speaking Flemish and French-speaking Walloons. Capital: Brussels. Agriculture, dairy farming, and the processing of raw materials for re-export are the principal industries. "Beurs voor Diamant" in Antwerp is the world's largest diamond trading center. Iron and steel, machinery, motor vehicles, chemicals, textile yarns and fabrics comprise the principal exports.

The Celtic tribe called "Belgae," from which Belgium derived its name, was described by Caesar as the most courageous of all the tribes of Gaul. The Belgae eventually capitulated to Rome and the area remained for centuries as a part of the Roman Empire known as Belgica.

As Rome began its decline, Frankish tribes migrated westward and established the Merovingian, and subsequently, the Carolingian empires. At the death of Charlemagne, Europe was divided among his three sons Karl, Lothar and Ludwig. The eastern part of today's Belgium lay in the Duchy of Lower Lorraine while much of the western parts eventually became the County of Flanders. After further divisions, the area was absorbed into the Duchy of Burgundy from whence it passed into Hapsburg control when Marie of Burgundy married Maximilian of Austria. Phillip I (the Fair), son of Maximilian and Marie, then added Spain to the Hapsburg empire by marrying Johanna, daughter of Ferdinand and Isabella. Charles and Ferdinand, sons of Phillip and Johanna, began the separate Spanish and Austrian lines of the Hapsburg family. The Burgundian lands, along with the northern provinces which make up present day Netherlands, became the Spanish Netherlands. The northern provinces successfully rebelled and broke away from Hapsburg rule in the late 16th century and early 17th century. The southern provinces along with the Duchy of Luxembourg remained under the influence of Spain until the year 1700 when Charles II, last of the Spanish Hapsburg line, died without leaving an heir and the Spanish crown went to the Bourbon family of France. The Spanish Netherlands then reverted to the control of the Austrian line of Hapsburgs and became the Austrian Netherlands. The Austrian Netherlands along with the Bishopric of Liege fell to the French Republic in 1794.

At the Congress of Vienna in 1815 the area was united with the Netherlands but in 1830 independence was gained and the constitutional monarchy of Belgium was established. A large part of the Duchy of Luxembourg was incorporated into Belgium and the first king was Leopold I of Saxe-Coburg-Gotha. It was invaded by the German army in Aug. 1914 and the German forces carried on a devastating occupation of most of the territory until the Armistice. Belgium joined the League of Nations. On May 10, 1940 it was invaded again by Nazi German armies. The Belgian and Allied forces were quickly overwhelmed and were evacuated through Dunkirk. Allied troops reached Belgium again in Sept. 1944. Prince Charles, Count of Flanders assumed King Leopold's responsibilities until his liberation by the U.S. army in Austria on May 8, 1945. From 1920-1940 and since 1944 Eupen-Malmedy went from Germany to Belgium.

* * *NOTE: This section has been renumbered. * * *

RULERS:
Baudouin I, 1951-93
Albert II, 1993-

MONETARY SYSTEM:
1 Franc = 100 Centimes

KINGDOM

BANQUE NATIONALE DE BELGIQUE

1961-71 ISSUE
#61, 64 and 65 replacement notes w/Z1 prefix.

134 (58)	**100 FRANCS**	**VG**	**VF**	**UNC**
	1.2.1962-30.4.1975. Violet on m/c unpt. Lombard at l. Allegorical figure on back. 4 sign. varieties. Wmk: Baudoiun I.	FV	3.50	6.00

135 **500 FRANCS**
(61)   2.5.1961-28.4.1975. Blue-gray and m/c. B. Van Orley at ctr. Margaret of Austria on back. 4 sign. varieties.

VG	VF	UNC
FV	20.00	30.00

136 **1000 FRANCS**
(64)   2.1.1961-11.12.1975. Brown and blue. Kremer (called Mercator) at l. Atlas holding globe on back. 4 sign. varieties.

VG	VF	UNC
FV	37.50	55.00

137 **5000 FRANCS**
(65)   6.1.1971-15.9.1977. Green. A. Vesalius at ctr. r. Statue and temple on back. 4 sign. varie ties.

VG	VF	UNC
FV	185.00	250.00

ROYAUME DE BELGIQUE - KONINKRIJK BELGIE

TRÉSORERIE - THESAURIE TREASURY NOTES BRANCH

1964-66 ISSUE
#138 and 139 replacement notes w/*Z1* prefix.

138 **20 FRANCS**
(67)   15.6.1964. Black on blue, orange and m/c unpt. Kg. Baudouin at l. and as wmk., arms at lower r. Atomic design at r. on back. Wmk: Baudoiun I. 3 sign. varieties.

VG	VF	UNC
.25	.50	2.00

139 **50 FRANCS**
(69)   16.5.1966. Brown-violet and orange-brown on m/c unpt. Arms at lower l. ctr., Kg. Baudouin and Qn. Fabiola at r. Parliament bldg. on back. Wmk: Baudouin I 4 sign. varieties.

VG	VF	UNC
.25	.75	2.50

1978; 1980 ISSUE
#140-145 sign. varieites. Wmk: Kg. Baudouin.

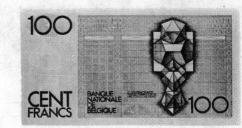

140 **100 FRANCS**
(70)   ND (1978-81). Maroon, blue and olive-green on m/c unpt. H. Beyaert at ctr. r. Architectural view and plan at l. Geomoetric design on back. Sign. on back. 2 sign. varities.

VG	VF	UNC
FV	4.00	6.00

141 **500 FRANCS**
(72)   ND (1980-81). Deep blue-violet and deep green on blue and m/c unpt. C. Meunier at l. ctr. Unpt. of 2 coal miners and mine conveyor tower at r. Five circular designs on back. Sign. on back.

VG	VF	UNC
FV	FV	25.00

1981-82 ISSUE

142 **100 FRANCS**
(71)   ND (1982-94). Like #70 but w/sign. on face and back. 7 sign. varieties.

VG	VF	UNC
FV	4.00	5.00

143 **500 FRANCS**
(73)   ND (1982-). Like #72 but w/sign. on face and back. 7 sign. varities.

VG	VF	UNC
FV	FV	20.00

144 **1000 FRANCS**
(74)   ND (1981-). Brown and m/c. A. Gretry at l., viol in background. Tuning forks and sound wave designs on back. 7 sign. varieties.

VG	VF	UNC

		VG	VF	UNC
a.	Name: *Andre Ernest Modeste Gretry. 1741-1813.*	FV	FV	40.00
x1.	Error name: *André... Gretry, 1741-1813.*	FV	100.00	200.00
x2.	Error name: *Andre . . . Gretry, 1741-1813.*	FV	40.00	80.00

151 **10,000 FRANCS**
(77) ND (1992-). Grayish-purple on m/c unpt. Kg. Baudouin and Qn. Fabiola at l. aerial map as unpt. Flora and greenhouses at royal residence at Lacken at ctr.

VG	VF	UNC
FV	FV	350.00

145 **5000 FRANCS**
(76) ND (1982-). Green. G. Gezelle at l. ctr. Tree and stained glass window behind. Back green, red and brown; dragonfly and leaf. 5 sign. varieties.

	VG	VF	UNC
	FV	FV	200.00

1992-95 ND ISSUE

146 **100 FRANCS**
(78) ND (1995-). Red-violet and black on m/c unpt. J. Ensor at l. and as wmk., masks at lower ctr. and at r. Beach scene at l. on back.

VG	VF	UNC
FV	FV	4.50

147 **200 FRANCS**
(79) ND (1995). Black and brown on yellow and orange unpt. A. Sax at l., saxophone at r. Saxophone players outlined at l.; bldg. outlined at lower r. on back.

VG	VF	UNC
—	—	8.00

148 **500 FRANCS**
ND.

Expected New Issue

149 **1000 FRANCS**
ND.

Expected New Issue

150 **2000 FRANCS**
(75) ND (1994-). Purple and blue-green on m/c unpt. Baron V. Horta at l. and as wmk. Flora and *Art Nouveau* design at l. on back.

VG	VF	UNC
FV	FV	75.00

The British Colony of Belize, formerly known as British Honduras, a self-governing dependency of the United Kingsom is situated in Central America south of Mexico and east and north of Guatemala. It has an area of 8,867 sq. mi. (22,965 sq. km.) and a population of 193,000. Capital: Belmopan. Sugar, citrus fruits, chicle and hard woods are exported.

The area, site of the ancient Mayan civilization, was sighted by Columbus in 1502, and settled by shipwrecked English seamen in 1638. British buccaneers settled the former capital of Belize in the 17th Century. Britian claimed administrative right over the area after the emancipation of Central America from Spain, and declared it a colony subordinate to Jamaica in 1862. It was established as the separate Crown Colony of British Honduras in 1884. The anti-British People's United Party, which attained power in 1954, won a constitution, effective in 1964 which established self-government under a British appointed Governor. British Honduras became Belize on June 1, 1973, following the passage of a suprize bill by the People's United Party, but the consititional relationship with Britain remained unchanged.

In Dec. 1975, the U.N. General Assembly adopted a resolution supporting the right of the people of Belize to self-determination, and asked Britian and Guatemala to renew their negotiations on the future of Belize. They obtained independence on Sept. 21, 1981.

* * *NOTE: This section has been renumbered. * * *

BELIZE

GOVERNMENT OF BELIZE

1974-75 ISSUE
#33-37 arms at., portr. Qn. Elizabeth II at r.

33	1 DOLLAR	VG	VF	UNC
(16)	1974-76. Green.			
	a. 1.1.1974.	.75	2.50	17.00
	b. 1.6.1975.	.75	2.25	15.00
	c. 1.1.1976.	.75	2.00	13.00
34	2 DOLLARS			
(17)	1974-76. Violet and lilac.			
	a. 1.1.1974.	2.00	6.00	35.00
	b. 1.6.1975.	2.00	5.50	25.00
	c. 1.1.1976.	2.00	5.00	20.00

35	5 DOLLARS	VG	VF	UNC
(18)	1.6.1975; 1.1.1976. Red.	3.00	8.50	50.00

36	10 DOLLARS	VG	VF	UNC
(19)	1974-76. Black on m/c unpt.			
	a. 1.1.1974.	6.00	20.00	200.00
	b. 1.6.1975.	6.00	20.00	175.00
	c. 1.1.1976.	6.00	20.00	150.00

37	20 DOLLARS	VG	VF	UNC
(20)	1974-76. Brown.			
	a. 1.1.1974.	12.00	37.50	475.00
	b. 1.6.1975.	12.00	37.50	350.00
	c. 1.1.1976.	12.00	37.50	300.00

MONETARY AUTHORITY OF BELIZE

ORDINANCE NO. 9 OF 1976; 1980 ISSUE
#38-42 linear border on arms in upper l. corner, Qn. Elizabeth II at ctr. r. 3/4 looking l., underwater scene w/reef and fish in ctr. background. House of Representatives in Belize on back. Wmk: Carved head of the "sleeping giant."

38	1 DOLLAR	VG	VF	UNC
(21)	1.6.1980. Green and m/c.	FV	1.25	5.00

39	5 DOLLARS	VG	VF	UNC
(22)	1.6.1980. Red and m/c.	FV	4.50	15.00

40	10 DOLLARS	VG	VF	UNC
(23)	1.6.1980. Violet and m/c.	FV	8.50	40.00

41	20 DOLLARS	VG	VF	UNC
(24)	1.6.1980. Brown and m/c.	FV	17.50	95.00

42	100 DOLLARS	VG	VF	UNC
(25)	1.6.1980. Blue and m/c.	FV	100.00	400.00

CENTRAL BANK OF BELIZE

1983 ISSUE
#43-45 Similar to #38-42. Wreath broder on arms at upper l.

		VG	VF	UNC
43 (26)	**1 DOLLAR** 1.7.1983. Green and m/c.	FV	1.50	7.50

		VG	VF	UNC
44 (28)	**10 DOLLARS** 1.7.1983. Gray and m/c.	FV	7.00	35.00

		VG	VF	UNC
45 (29)	**20 DOLLARS** 1.7.1983. Brown on m/c unpt.	FV	15.00	100.00

1983-87 ISSUE
#46-50 like #38-42. Lg. tree behind arms at upper l. Sign. varieties.

		VG	VF	UNC
46 (30)	**1 DOLLAR** 1.11.1983; 1.1.1986; 1.1.1987. Green and m/c.	FV	FV	3.00

		VG	VF	UNC
47 (31)	**5 DOLLARS** 1987; 1989.			
	a. 1.1.1987.	3.50	15.00	75.00
	b. 1.1.1989.	FV	3.00	12.00

		VG	VF	UNC
48 (32)	**10 DOLLARS** 1987; 1989.			
	a. 1.1.1987.	FV	6.00	22.00
	b. 1.1.1989.	6.00	15.00	85.00

		VG	VF	UNC
49 (33)	**20 DOLLARS** 1.1.1986; 1.1.1987.	FV	12.50	32.50

		VG	VF	UNC
50 (34)	**100 DOLLARS** 1983; 1989.			
	a. 1.11.1983.	FV	85.00	250.00
	b. 1.1.1989.	FV	85.00	250.00

1990 ISSUE
#51-57 older facing portr. of Qn. Elizabeth II at r. Wmk: Carved head of the "sleeping giant." Printer: TDLR.

		VG	VF	UNC
51 (35)	**1 DOLLAR** 1.5.1990. Green on lt. brown, blue and m/c unpt. Crustacean at l. Back green and red; marine life of Belize across ctr.	FV	FV	2.00

		VG	VF	UNC
52 (36)	**2 DOLLARS** 1.5.1990; 1.6.1991. Purple on lt. green, blue and m/c unpt. Carved stone pillar at l. Mayan ruins of Belize on back.	FV	FV	3.00

		VG	VF	UNC
53 (37)	**5 DOLLARS** 1.5.1990; 1.6.1991. Red-orange, orange and violet on m/c unpt. Columbus medallion at l. St. George's Caye, coffin, outline map and bldg. on back.	FV	FV	5.50

54   **10 DOLLARS**   **VG**   **VF**   **UNC**
(38)   1.5.1990; 1.6.1991. Black, olive-brown and deep blue-green on m/c   FV   FV   9.00
      unpt. Court House clock tower at I. Government House, Court House
      and St. John's Cathedral on back.

55   **20 DOLLARS**   **VG**   **VF**   **UNC**
(39)   1.5.1990. Dk. brown on m/c unpt. Jaguar at I. Fauna of Belize on back.   FV   FV   17.00

56   **50 DOLLARS**   **VG**   **VF**   **UNC**
(40)   1.5.1990; 1.6.1991. Purple, brown and red on m/c unpt. Boats at I.   FV   FV   40.00
      Bridges of Belize on back

57   **100 DOLLARS**   **VG**   **VF**   **UNC**
(41)   1.5.1990; 1.6.1991; 1.5.1994. Blue-violet, orange and red on m/c   FV   FV   95.00
      unpt. Toucan at I. Birds of Belize on back.

1996-97 ISSUE

#58-62 like #53-57 but w/segmented foil over security strip and ascending serial # at upper r. Printer: TDLR.

			VG	VF	UNC
58	**5 DOLLARS**				
	1.3.1996. Red-orange, orange and violet on m/c unpt. Like #53.		FV	FV	4.50
59	**10 DOLLARS**				
	1.3.1996. Black, olive brown and deep blue-green on m/c unpt. Like #54.		FV	FV	8.50
60	**20 DOLLARS**				
	(1997). Like #55.				Expected New Issue
61	**50 DOLLARS**				
	(1997). Like #56.				Expected New Issue
62	**100 DOLLARS**				
	(1997). Like #57.				Expected New Issue

COLLECTOR SERIES

CENTRAL BANK OF BELIZE

1984 ISSUE

NOTE: The Central Bank of Belize will exchange these notes for regular currency only in Belize (It is illegal to export the currency afterwards). Value is thus speculative.

CS1   **ND (1984) COLLECTION**   **ISSUE PRICE**   **MKT. VALUE**
       Stamped from paper bonded within gold foil. Denominations: $1 (1   —   350.00
       pc.), $2 (2 pcs.) $5 (3 pcs.), $10 (4 pcs.), $20 (2 pcs.), $25 (6 pcs.),
       $50 (7 pcs.), $75 (5 pcs.), $100 (6 pcs.). Total 36 pcs. All have QE II
       and bldg. on face, different animals, ships, fish, birds etc. on backs.

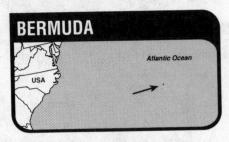

BERMUDA

Atlantic Ocean

USA

The Parliamentary British Colony of Bermuda, situated in the western Atlantic Ocean 660 miles (1,062 km.) east of North Carolina, has an area of 20.6 sq. mi. (53 sq. km.) and a population of 60,470. Capital: Hamilton. Concentrated essences, beauty preparations, and cut flowers are exported. Most Bermudians derive their livelihood from tourism.

Bermuda was discovered by Juan de Bermudez, a Spanish navigator, in 1503. British influence dates from 1609 when a group of Virginia-bound British colonists under the command of Sir George Somers was shipwrecked on the islands for 10 months. The islands were settled in 1612 by 60 British colonists from the Virginia Colony and became a crown colony in 1684. Internal autonomy was obtained by the constitution of June 8, 1968.

In February, 1970, Bermuda converted from its former currency, the English pound, to a decimal currency, termed a dollar, which is equal to one U.S. dollar. On July 31, 1972, Bermuda severed its monetary link with the British pound sterling and pegged its dollar to be the same gold value as the U.S. dollar.

RULERS:
British

MONETARY SYSTEM:
1 Shilling = 12 Pence
1 Pound = 20 Shillings, to 1970
1 Dollar = 100 Cents, 1970-

BRITISH INFLUENCE

BERMUDA GOVERNMENT

1952-66 ISSUE
#18-22 Printer: BWC.

18 (13)	5 SHILLINGS	VG	VF	UNC
	1952; 1957. Brown on m/c unpt. Portr. Qn. Elizabeth at upper ctr. Hamilton Harbor in frame at bottom ctr.			
	a. 20.10.1952.	3.00	10.00	70.00
	b. 1.5.1957.	2.00	7.50	50.00

19 (14)	10 SHILLINGS	VG	VF	UNC
	1952-66. Red on m/c unpt. Portr. Qn. Elizabeth at upper ctr. Gate's Fort in St. George in frame at bottom ctr.			
	a. 20.10.1952.	5.00	35.00	225.00
	b. 1.5.1957.	3.00	15.00	100.00
	c. 1.10.1966.	4.00	20.00	225.00

20 (15)	1 POUND	VG	VF	UNC
	1952-66. Blue on m/c unpt. Portr. Qn. Elizabeth at r. Bridge at l.			
	a. 20.10.1952.	7.50	30.00	225.00
	b. 1.5.1957. W/o security strip.	5.00	20.00	225.00
	c. 1.5.1957. W/security strip.	3.50	15.00	185.00
	d. 1.10.1966.	3.00	13.00	140.00

21 (16)	5 POUNDS	VG	VF	UNC
	1952-66. Orange on m/c unpt. Portr. Qn. Elizabeth at r. Ship entering Hamilton Harbor at l.			
	a. 20.10.1952.	25.00	120.00	600.00
	b. 1.5.1957. W/o security strip.	17.50	75.00	450.00
	c. 1.5.1957. W/security strip.	15.00	70.00	425.00
	d. 1.10.1966.	15.00	55.00	375.00

22 (17)	10 POUNDS	VG	VF	UNC
	28.7.1964. Purple on m/c unpt. Portr. Qn. Elizabeth at r. Bermuda arms at ctr. on back. BWC.	100.00	400.00	1500.

1970 ISSUE
#23-27 Qn. Elizabeth II at r. 3/4 looking l., arms at l. ctr. Wmk: Tuna fish.

23 (18)	1 DOLLAR	VG	VF	UNC
	6.2.1970. Dk. blue on tan and aqua unpt. Sailboats on back.	FV	1.50	9.00

24 (19)	5 DOLLARS	VG	VF	UNC
	6.2.1970. Red-violet on aqua and m/c unpt. Lighthouse at l., bldgs. at ctr. r. on back.	FV	6.00	17.50

25 **10 DOLLARS**
(20)   6.2.1970. Purple on brown and m/c unpt. Bird, seashell and beach on back.

		VG	VF	UNC
25 (20)	10 DOLLARS 6.2.1970. Purple on brown and m/c unpt. Bird, seashell and beach on back.	FV	12.50	40.00
26 (21)	20 DOLLARS 6.2.1970. Green on m/c unpt. Sailboat and bridge on back.	FV	25.00	85.00
27 (22)	50 DOLLARS 6.2.1970. Brown on m/c unpt. Lighthouse and map on back.	FV	70.00	200.00

BERMUDA MONETARY AUTHORITY

1974-82 ISSUE

#23-28 Qn. Elizabeth II at r., 3/4 looking l. Wmk: Tuna fish. Like #23-27. Replacement notes: *Z/1* prefix.

		VG	VF	UNC
28 (23)	**1 DOLLAR** 1975-88.			
	a. Sign. titles: *CHAIRMAN* and *MANAGING DIRECTOR*. 1.7.1975; 1.12.1976.	FV	2.50	15.00
	b. 1.4.1978; 1.9.1979; 2.1.1982; 1.5.1984.	FV	1.50	7.50
	c. Sign. titles: *CHAIRMAN* and *GENERAL MANAGER*. 1.1.1986.	FV	1.50	7.00
	d. Sign. titles: *CHAIRMAN* and *DIRECTOR*. 1.1.1988.	FV	1.50	6.50

		VG	VF	UNC
29 (24)	**5 DOLLARS** 1978-88.			
	a. Sign. titles: *CHAIRMAN* and *MANAGING DIRECTOR*. 1.4.1978.	FV	6.50	17.50
	b. 2.1.1981.	FV	6.00	15.00
	c. Sign. titles: *CHAIRMAN* and *GENERAL MANAGER*. 1.1.1986.	FV	6.00	15.00
	d. Sign. titles: *CHAIRMAN* and *DIRECTOR*. 1.1.1988.	FV	6.00	12.50
30 (25)	**10 DOLLARS** 1978; 1982.			
	a. 1.4.1978.	FV	17.50	75.00
	b. 2.1.1982.	FV	15.00	65.00

		VG	VF	UNC
31 (26)	**20 DOLLARS** 1974-86.			
	a. 1.4.1974.	25.00	45.00	185.00
	b. 1.3.1976.	FV	25.00	95.00
	c. 2.1.1981; 1.5.1984.	FV	FV	37.50
	d. Sign. title: *GENERAL MANAGER* at r. 1.1.1986.	FV	FV	37.50
32 (27)	**50 DOLLARS** 1974-82.			
	a. 1.5.1974.	60.00	150.00	600.00
	b. 1.4.1978; 2.1.1982.	FV	85.00	225.00

		VG	VF	UNC
33 (28)	**100 DOLLARS** 1982-86. Orange and m/c. House of Assembly on back.			
	a. 2.1.1982.	FV	FV	185.00
	b. Sign. title: *GENERAL MANAGER* ovpt. at r. 14.11.1984.	FV	FV	175.00
	c. Sign. title: *GENERAL MANAGER* at r. 1.1.1986.	FV	FV	165.00

1988-89 ISSUE

#34-39 older facing portr. of Qn. Elizabeth II at r. Back similar to #23-28 but w/stylistic changes; arms added at upper l. Sign. titles: *CHAIRMAN* and *DIRECTOR*. Wmk.: Tuna fish. Replacement notes: *Z/1* prefix.

		VG	VF	UNC
34 (29)	**2 DOLLARS** 1.10.1988; 1.8.1989. Blue-green on green and m/c unpt. Dockyards clock tower bldg at l., map at ctr., arms at ctr. r. on back.	FV	FV	4.00

35 (30) 5 DOLLARS
20.2.1989. Red-violet and purple on m/c unpt.

		VG	VF	UNC
a.	Sign. title: *DIRECTOR* on silver background at bottom ctr.	FV	7.00	20.00
b.	Sign. title: *DIRECTOR* w/o silver background.	FV	FV	10.00

36 (31) 10 DOLLARS
20.2.1989. Purple, blue and ochre.

VG	VF	UNC
FV	FV	20.00

37 (32) 20 DOLLARS
20.2.1989. Green and red.

VG	VF	UNC
FV	FV	32.50

38 (33) 50 DOLLARS
20.2.1989. Brown and olive on m/c unpt.

VG	VF	UNC
FV	FV	85.00

39 (34) 100 DOLLARS
20.2.1989. Orange and brown on m/c unpt.

VG	VF	UNC
FV	FV	145.00

1992 COMMEMORATIVE ISSUE
#40, Quincentenary of Christopher Columbus.

40 50 DOLLARS
12.10.1992. As #44 but w/commemorative details. Maltese cross as serial # prefix at upper l., c/c fractional prefix at r., and ovpt: *Christopher Columbus/Quincentenary/ 1492-1992* at l.

VG	VF	UNC
FV	FV	100.00

1992-93 ISSUE
#41-45 issued under Bermuda Monetary Authority Act 1969. Like #34-39 but w/Authorization text in 3 lines at ctr. Wmk: Tuna fish.

41 (35) 5 DOLLARS
12.11.1992; 25.3.1995. Like #35 but new 3-line text under value at ctr.

VG	VF	UNC
FV	FV	8.50

42 (36) 10 DOLLARS
4.1.1993. Like #36 but w/new text as #40.

VG	VF	UNC
FV	FV	15.00

43 (37) 20 DOLLARS
199x.

Expected New Issue

44 (38) 50 DOLLARS
12.10.1992; 25.3.1995. Dk. blue, brown and red on m/c unpt. Face similar to #38 but w/new text similar to #35. Scuba divers, shipwreck at l., island outline at upper r. above arms.

VG	VF	UNC
FV	FV	75.00

45 (39) 100 DOLLARS
199x.

Expected New Issue

1994 COMMEMORATIVE ISSUE
#46, 25th Anniversary Bermuda Monetary Authority.

46 (41) 100 DOLLARS
20.2.1994. Orange and brown on m/c unpt. Similar to #39 but new 3-line text under value. Ovpt: *25th Anniversary*....

VG	VF	UNC
FV	FV	140.00

COLLECTOR SERIES

BERMUDA MONETARY AUTHORITY

1978-84 DATED ISSUES (1985)

CS1 1978-84 1-100 DOLLARS
#22-33 w/normal serial #, punched hole cancelled, ovpt: *SPECIMEN* (1985).

ISSUE PRICE	MKT. VALUE
—	30.00

CS2 1981-82 1-100 DOLLARS
#28-33 w/all zero serial #, punched hole cancelled in all 4 corners, ovpt: *SPECIMEN* (1985).

—	30.00

BHUTAN

The Kingdom of Bhutan, a landlocked Himalayan country bordered by Tibet, India, and Sikkim, has an area of 18,147 sq. mi. (47,000 sq. km.) and a population of 600,000. Capital: Thimphu; Paro is the administrative capital. Virtually the entire population is engaged in agricultural and pastoral activities. Rice, wheat, barley, and yak butter are produced in sufficient quantity to make the country self-sufficient in food. The economy of Bhutan is primitive and many transactions are conducted on a barter basis.

Bhutan's early history is obscure, but is thought to have resembled that of rural medieval Europe. The country was conquered by Tibet, which still claims sovereignty over Bhutan, in the 9th century, and subjected to a dual temporal and spiritual rule until the mid-19th century, when the southern part of the country was occupied by the British and annexed to British India. Bhutan was established as a hereditary monarchy in 1907, and in 1910 agreed to British control of its external affairs. In 1949, India and Bhutan concluded a treaty whereby India assumed Britain's role in subsidizing Bhutan and conducting its foreign affairs.

RULERS:

Jigme Singye Wangchuk, 1972-

MONETARY SYSTEM:

1 Ngultrum (= 1 Rupee) = 100 Chetrums, 1974-

KINGDOM

ROYAL GOVERNMENT OF BHUTAN

1974-78 ND ISSUE

		VG	VF	UNC
1	**1 NGULTRUM**			
	ND (1974). Blue on m/c unpt.	.20	.75	3.50

		VG	VF	UNC
2	**5 NGULTRUMS**			
	ND (1974). Brown on m/c unpt. J. Singye Wangchuk at ctr. Simtokha Dzong palace on back.	1.50	8.00	25.00

		VG	VF	UNC
3	**10 NGULTRUMS**			
	ND (1974). Blue-violet on m/c unpt. J. Dorji Wangchuk at ctr. Paro Dzong palace on back.	5.00	20.00	110.00

		VG	VF	UNC
4	**100 NGULTRUMS**			
	ND (1978). Green and brown on m/c unpt. Portr. J. Singye Wangchuk at ctr., circle w/8 good luck symbols at r. Tashichho Dzong palace on back.	300.00	—	—

1981 ND ISSUE

#5-11 have serial # at upper l. and r.

		VG	VF	UNC
5	**1 NGULTRUM**			
	ND (1981). Blue on m/c unpt. Royal emblem at ctr. Simtokha Dzong palace on back.	.10	.20	1.25

		VG	VF	UNC
6	**2 NGULTRUMS**			
	ND (1981). Brown and green on m/c unpt. Royal emblem at ctr. Simtokha Dzong palace on back.	.15	.50	2.50

7 5 NGULTRUMS
ND (1981). Brown on m/c unpt. Birds l. and r., royal emblem at ctr.
Paro Dzong palace on back.

	VG	VF	UNC
	.35	1.00	5.00

8 10 NGULTRUMS
ND (1981). Blue-violet on m/c unpt. Portr. J. Singye Wangchuk at r.,
roya l emblem at l. Paro Dzong palace on back.

	VG	VF	UNC
	.65	2.00	10.00

9 20 NGULTRUMS
ND (1981). Olive on m/c unpt. Jigme Dorji Wangchuk at r. Punakha
Dzong palace on back.

	VG	VF	UNC
	1.20	3.50	17.50

10 50 NGULTRUMS
ND (1981). Purple, violet and brown on m/c unpt. J. Dorji Wangchuk
at r. Tongsa Dzong palace on back.

	VG	VF	UNC
	3.25	10.00	50.00

11 100 NGULTRUMS
ND (1981). Dk. green, olive-green and brown-violet on m/c unpt. J.
Singye Wangchuk at r., royal emblem at l., bird at ctr. Tashichho
Dzong palace on back.

	VG	VF	UNC
	7.50	22.50	110.00

ROYAL MONETARY AUTHORITY OF BHUTAN

1985-92 ND ISSUE

#12-18 similar to #5-11 but reduced size w/serial # at lower l. and upper r.

12 1 NGULTRUM
ND (1986). Blue on m/c unpt.

	VG	VF	UNC
	FV	FV	.75

13 2 NGULTRUMS
ND (1986). Brown and green on m/c unpt.

	VG	VF	UNC
	FV	FV	1.50

14 5 NGULTRUMS
ND (1985). Brown on m/c unpt.

	VG	VF	UNC
	FV	FV	3.00

15   10 NGULTRUMS
ND (1986; 1992). Blue-violet on m/c unpt.

		VG	VF	UNC
a.	Serial # w/fractional style prefix. (1986).	FV	FV	4.50
b.	Serial # w/2 lg. letters as prefix (printed in China). (1992).	FV	FV	3.00

16   20 NGULTRUMS
ND (1986; 1992). Olive on m/c unpt.

		VG	VF	UNC
a.	Serial # w/fractional style prefix. (1986).	FV	FV	6.00
b.	Serial # w/2 lg. letters as prefix (printed in China). (1992).	FV	FV	4.00

17   50 NGULTRUMS
ND (1986; 1992). Purple, violet and brown on m/c unpt.

		VG	VF	UNC
a.	ND. Serial # w/fractional style prefix.	FV	3.00	15.00
b.	ND. Serial # w/2 large letters as prefix (printed in China). (1992).	FV	2.00	10.00

18   100 NGULTRUMS
ND (1986; 1992). Green and brown on m/c unpt.

		VG	VF	UNC
a.	Serial # w/fractional style prefix. (1986).	FV	5.00	25.00
b.	Serial # w/2 lg. letters as prefix (printed in China). (1992).	FV	4.00	17.50

1994 ND ISSUE
#19 and 20 similar to #17 and 18 but with modified unpt. including floral diamond shaped registry design at upper ctr. Wmk: Wavy repeated text: *ROYAL MONETARY AUTHORITY*.

19   50 NGULTRUMS
ND (1994). Purple, violet and brown on m/c unpt.

VG	VF	UNC
FV	FV	5.00

20   100 NGULTRUMS
ND (1994). Green and brown on m/c unpt.

VG	VF	UNC
FV	FV	9.00

1994 COMMEMORATIVE ISSUE
#21, National Day.

21   500 NGULTRUMS
ND (1994). Orange on m/c unpt.

VG	VF	UNC
FV	FV	35.00

On May 27, 1967, Gen. Yakubu Gowon, head of the Federal Military Government of Nigeria, created three states from the Eastern Region of the country. Separation of the region, undertaken to achieve better regional and ethnic balance, caused Lt. Col. E. O. Ojukwu, Military Governor of the Eastern Region, to proclaim on May 30, 1967, the independence of the Eastern Region as the "Republic of Biafra." Fighting broke out between the Federal Military Government and the forces of Lt. Col. Ojukwu and continued until Biafra surrendered on Jan. 15, 1970. Biafra was then reintegrated into the republic as three states: East- Central, Rivers, and South-Eastern.

For additional history, see Nigeria.

MONETARY SYSTEM:
1 Shilling = 12 Pence
1 Pound = 20 Shillings

REPUBLIC

BANK OF BIAFRA

1967 ND ISSUE
#1-2 palm tree, lg. rising sun.

1	5 SHILLINGS	VG	VF	UNC
	ND (1967). Blue on lilac unpt. Color varies from orange to yellow for rising sun. 4 girls at r. on back.			
	a. Serial #.	.75	3.00	10.00
	b. W/o serial #.	Reported Not Confirmed		

2	1 POUND	VG	VF	UNC
	ND (1967). Blue and orange. Back brown; arms at r.	1.75	15.00	90.00

1968 ND ISSUE
#3-7 palm tree and small rising sun at l. to ctr.

3	5 SHILLINGS	VG	VF	UNC
	ND (1968-69). Blue on green and orange unpt. Back similar to #1.			
	a. Serial #.	1.00	3.00	12.50
	b. W/o serial #.	2.00	6.00	20.00

4	10 SHILLINGS	VG	VF	UNC
	ND (1968-69). Green on blue and orange unpt. Bldgs. at r. on back.			
	a. Serial #.	1.00	3.00	10.00
	b. W/o serial #.	Reported Not Confirmed		

5	1 POUND	VG	VF	UNC
	ND (1968-69). Dk. brown on green and brown unpt. Back similar to #2.			
	a. Serial #.	.10	.20	.50
	b. W/o serial #.	.50	2.00	9.50

6	5 POUNDS	VG	VF	UNC
	ND (1968-69). Violet on m/c unpt. Arms at l., weaving at l. ctr. on back.			
	a. Serial #.	4.00	12.00	45.00
	b. W/o serial #.	2.00	6.00	25.00

7	10 POUNDS	VG	VF	UNC
	ND (1968-69). Blue and brown on m/c unpt. Arms at l., carver at l. ctr. on back.			
	a. Serial #.	4.00	12.00	45.00
	b. W/o serial #.	2.50	7.50	30.00

BOLIVIA

The Republic of Bolivia, a landlocked country in west central South America, has an area of 424,165 sq. mi. (1,098,581 sq. km.) and a population of 7.6 million. Capitals: La Paz (administrative); Sucre (constitutional). Mining is the principal industry and tin the most important metal. Minerals, petroleum, natural gas, cotton and coffee are exported.

The Incas, who ruled one of the world's greatest dynasties, incorporated the area that is now Bolivia into their empire about 1200AD. Their control was maintained until the Spaniards arrived in 1535 and reduced the predominantly Indian population to slavery. When Napoleon occupied Madrid in 1808 and placed his brother Joseph on the Spanish throne, a fervor of revolutionary activity quickened in Bolivia, culminating with the 1809 proclamation of independence. Sixteen years of struggle ensued before the republic, named for the famed liberator Simon Bolivar, was established on August 6, 1825. Since then, Bolivia has had more than 60 revolutions, 70 presidents and 11 constitutions.

RULERS:
Spanish to 1825

MONETARY SYSTEM:
1 Peso Boliviano = 100 Centavos, 1962-1987
1 Boliviano = 100 Centavos, 1987-

REPUBLIC

BANCO CENTRAL DE BOLIVIA

LEY DE 13 DE JULIO DE 1962 - FIRST ISSUE
#152-157 old and new denomination on back at bottom. Arms at l. Sign. varieties. Printer: TDLR.

		VG	VF	UNC
152	**1 PESO BOLIVIANO**			
	L.1962. Black on m/c unpt. portr. Campesino at r. Agricultural scene at ctr. r. on back. Series A-E.			
	a. Issued note.	1.00	2.00	7.50
	s. Specimen. Ovpt: *SPECIMEN*.	—	—	—

		VG	VF	UNC
153	**5 PESOS BOLIVIANOS**			
	L.1962. Blue on m/c unpt. Portr. G. Villarroel at r. Petroleum refinery on back. Sereis A-C1.			
	a. Issued note.	.75	2.50	10.00
	b. Uncut sheet of 4 signed notes.	—	—	60.00
	s. Specimen. Ovpt: *SPECIMEN*.	—	—	—

		VG	VF	UNC
154	**10 PESOS BOLIVIANOS**			
	L.1962. Olive-green on m/c unpt. Portr. Busch at r. Mountain of Potosí on back.			
	a. Issued note.	.10	.40	.85
	b. Uncut sheet of 4 signed notes. Series U2.	—	—	25.00
	c. Uncut sheet of 4 specimen notes. Series U2.	—	—	20.00
	s. Specimen. Ovpt: *SPECIMEN*.	—	—	—

		VG	VF	UNC
155	**20 PESOS BOLIVIANOS**			
	L.1962. Purple on m/c unpt. Portr. Murillo at r. La Paz mountain on back. Series A.			
	a. Issued note.	.75	4.00	25.00
	s. Specimen. Ovpt: *SPECIMEN*.	—	—	—

		VG	VF	UNC
156	**50 PESOS BOLIVIANOS**			
	L.1962. Orange on m/c unpt. Portr. A. J. de Sucre at r. Puerta del Sol on back. Series A.			
	a. Issued note.	15.00	45.00	100.00
	s. Specimen. Ovpt: *SPECIMEN*.	—	—	—

		VG	VF	UNC
157	**100 PESOS BOLIVIANOS**			
	L.1962. Red on m/c unpt. Unpt. w/green at l., blue at r. Portr. Bolívar at r. Red serial #, and security thread at l. ctr. Back: Darker red, engraved; scene of the declaration of the Bolivan Republic. Series A.			
	a. Issued note.	12.00	40.00	80.00
	s. Specimen. Ovpt: *SPECIMEN*.	—	—	—

LEY DE 13 DE JULIO DE 1962 - SECOND ISSUE
#158-163 only new denomination on back. Sign. varieties. Printer: TDLR.
#159, 160 held in reserve.

		VG	VF	UNC
158	**1 PESO BOLIVIANO**	.30	1.00	5.00
	L.1962. Like #152. Series F-F1.			
161	**20 PESOS BOLIVIANOS**			
	L.1962. Like #155. Series B-H.			
	a. Issued note.	.30	1.00	7.50
	s. Specimen. Ovpt: *SPECIMEN*.	—	—	—

		VG	VF	UNC
162	**50 PESOS BOLIVIANOS**			
	L.1962. Like #156.			
	a. Issued note.	.10	.25	1.00
	b. Uncut sheet of 4 signed notes. Series L2, V2.	—	—	40.00
	c. Uncut sheet of 4 notes w/sign. at top of notes. Series L2. (error).	—	—	40.00
	d. Uncut sheet of 4 unsigned notes. Series AZ.	—	—	12.50
	s. Specimen. Ovpt: *SPECIMEN*.	—	—	—

		VG	VF	UNC
163	**100 PESOS BOLIVIANOS**			
	L.1962. Like #157 unpt. w/green at l. and r. on face. Brighter red back, engraved. Lower # prefixes (from B to 10D; ZX; ZY).			
	a. Issued note.	.10	.25	.85
	b. Uncut sheet of 4 signed notes. Series X4; D5; U5.	—	—	40.00
	c. Uncut sheet of 4 unsigned notes. Series AZ.	—	—	12.50
	s. Specimen. Ovpt: *SPECIMEN*.	—	—	—

		VG	VF	UNC
164	**100 PESOS BOLIVIANOS**			
	L.1962 (1983). Design like #163.			
	a. Back dull red, lithographed w/poor detail. Black serial # and no security thread. Prefixes #10E-13D; ZZ.	.25	.50	2.00
	b. Like #163 including engraved back, security thread and red serial #. Higher # prefixes (13E-19T) than for #164a.	.10	.25	1.00
	r. Unsigned remainder, prefix #12H.	—	—	15.00

1981-84 VARIOUS DECREES

		VG	VF	UNC
165	**500 PESOS BOLIVIANOS**			
	D. 1.6.1981. Deep blue, blue-green and black on m/c unpt. Arms at ctr., portr. Avaroa at r. and as wmk. at l. Back blue on m/c unpt. View of Puerto de Antofagasta, ca. 1879 at ctr. Series A; Z. Printer: ABNC.			
	a. Issued note.	.10	.25	1.00
	x. Error w/o series, decreto or sign. overprinting.	25.00	45.00	75.00
	s. Specimen. Ovpt: *MUESTRA SIN VALOR*.	—	—	—
166	**500 PESOS BOLIVIANOS**			
	D. 1.6.1981. Like #165 but Series B; C; Z. Printer: TDLR.	.10	.25	1.25

		VG	VF	UNC
167	**1000 PESOS BOLIVIANOS**			
	D. 25.6.1982. Black on m/c unpt. Arms at ctr., portr. Juana Z. de Padilla at r. and as wmk. at l. House of Liberty on back. Sign. varieties. Printer: TDLR. Series A-Z9; ZY; ZZ; (6 digits) A-L; (8 digits) each only to 49,999,999); Z (8 digits).			
	a. Issued note.	.10	.25	1.25
	s. Specimen. Ovpt: *SPECIMEN*.	—	—	—

168 5000 PESOS BOLIVIANOS
D. 10.2.1984. Deep brown and m/c. Arms at ctr., Marshall J. Ballivian
y Segurola at r. and as wmk. at l. Stylized condor and leopard on back.
Printer: BDDK. Series A; Z.

	VG	VF	UNC
a. Issued note.	.20	.40	1.50
s. Specimen. Ovpt: *MUESTRAS SIN VALOR* or pin-holed cancelled: *SPECIMEN*.	—	—	—

169 10,000 PESOS BOLIVIANOS
D. 10.2.1984. Blackish purple and purple w/dk. green arms on m/c
unpt. Arms at ctr. Portr. Marshall A. de Santa Cruz at r. and as wmk. at
l. Back brown, bluish purple and green; Legislative palace at ctr.
Printer: BDDK. Series A; Z.

	VG	VF	UNC
a. Issued note.	.10	.30	1.00
s. Specimen. Ovpt: *MUESTRAS SIN VALOR*.	—	—	—

170 50,000 PESOS BOLIVIANOS
D. 5.6.1984. Deep green on m/c unpt. Arms at l., portr. Villaroel at r.
Petroleum refinery on back. Printer: TDLR. Series A; B; Z.

	VG	VF	UNC
a. Issued note.	.10	.25	.75
s. Specimen. Ovpt: *MUESTRAS SIN VALOR*.	—	—	—

171 100,000 PESOS BOLIVIANOS
D. 5.6.1984. Brown-violet on m/c unpt. Arms at l., Portr. Campesino
at r. Agricultural scene at ctr. r. on back. Printer: TDLR. Sereis A; B; Z.

	VG	VF	UNC
a. Issued note.	.15	.30	1.00
s. Specimen. Ovpt: *MUESTRAS SIN VALOR*.	—	—	—

1982-86 MONETARY EMERGENCY
BANCO CENTRAL DE BOLIVIA
W/O BRANCH
DECRETO 28.7.1982 - CHEQUES DE GERENCIA

172 5000 PESOS BOLIVIANOS
D.1982.

	VG	VF	UNC
a. Stub w/text attached at r.	—		15.00
b. W/o stub at r.	—		10.00

173 10,000 PESOS BOLIVIANOS
D.1982.

	VG	VF	UNC
a. Stub w/text attached at r.	—		10.00
b. W/o stub at r.	—		7.00

SANTA CRUZ BRANCH
1984 ISSUE
#176; 178 black, Mercury in green circular unpt. at ctr.

176 50,000 PESOS BOLIVIANOS
4.6.1984; 7.6.1984.

	VG	VF	UNC
a. Issued note.	—	—	—
b. Ovpt: *ANULADO* (cancelled) across face.	20.00	40.00	100.00

178 1,000,000 PESOS BOLIVIANOS
4.6.1984; 7.6.1984.

	VG	VF	UNC
a. Issued note.	—	—	—
b. Ovpt: *ANULADO* across face.	30.00	60.00	120.00

LA PAZ BRANCH
1984 ISSUE
#180-182 like #176-178.

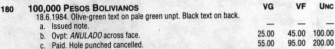

180	**100,000 PESOS BOLIVIANOS**	**VG**	**VF**	**UNC**
	18.6.1984. Olive-green text on pale green unpt. Black text on back.			
	a. Issued note.	—	—	—
	b. Ovpt: *ANULADO* across face.	25.00	45.00	100.00
	c. Paid. Hole punched cancelled.	55.00	95.00	200.00

181	**500,000 PESOS BOLIVIANOS**	**VG**	**VF**	**UNC**
	4.6.1984; 18.6.1984.			
	a. Issued note.	—	—	—
	b. Ovpt: *ANULADO* across face.	30.00	60.00	120.00
	c. Paid. Hole punched cancelled.	40.00	90.00	210.00

182	**1,000,000 PESOS BOLIVIANOS**	**VG**	**VF**	**UNC**
	18.6.1984.			
	a. Issued note.	—	—	—
	b. Ovpt: *ANULADO* across face.	35.00	70.00	140.00
	c. Paid. Hole punched cancelled.	75.00	140.00	175.00

DECRETO SUPREMO NO. 20272, 5 JUNE 1984, FIRST ISSUE

#183-185 brown on pink unpt. Mercury at upper l. Series A. Printer: JBNC. Usable for 90 days after date of issue (Spanish text at lower r. on back).

NOTE: Unpt. of "B.C.B." and denom. boxes easily fade to lt. tan to pale yellow.

183	**10,000 PESOS BOLIVIANOS**	**VG**	**VF**	**UNC**
	D.1984.	2.00	5.00	12.50

184	**20,000 PESOS BOLIVIANOS**	**VG**	**VF**	**UNC**
	D.1984.	5.00	25.00	60.00

185	**50,000 PESOS BOLIVIANOS**	**VG**	**VF**	**UNC**
	D.1984.	1.25	4.00	8.50

DECRETO SUPREMO NO. 20272, 5 JUNE 1984, SECOND ISSUE

#186-187 like #183-185 but w/o 90 day use restriction text on back.

186	**10,000 PESOS BOLIVIANOS**	**VG**	**VF**	**UNC**
	D.1984. Lt. blue on pink unpt. Series A.	1.00	2.50	7.50

187	**20,000 PESOS BOLIVIANOS**	**VG**	**VF**	**UNC**
	D.1984. Green on pink unpt. Series A.	1.00	2.50	7.50

188	**100,000 PESOS BOLIVIANOS**	**VG**	**VF**	**UNC**
	21.12.1984. Reddish brown on lt. blue and lt. reddish brown unpt.			
	Series A. Imprint and wmk: CdMB.			
	a. Issued note.	.10	.50	1.75
	x. Error. Face only, back blank.	1.00	2.50	10.00

W/O BRANCH

DECRETO SUPREMO NO. 20272, DE 5 DE JUNIO DE 1984

189 **500,000 PESOS BOLIVIANOS**
D.1984. Deep green on green and peach unpt. No 90-day clause on back. Wmk: CdMB. (W/o imprint.)

		VG	VF	UNC
a.	Issued note.	.15	.60	3.00
b.	Error. Face only, back blank.	1.00	2.50	10.00

DECRETO SUPREMO NO. 20732, 8 MARCH 1985; FIRST ISSUE

190 **1 MILLION PESOS BOLIVIANOS**
D.1985. Blue on yellow and pale blue unpt. Similar to previous issue. No 90-day restriction clause at lower r. on back. Series A. Wmk: CdMB. W/o imprint.

VG	VF	UNC
.25	1.00	4.50

191 **5 MILLION PESOS BOLIVIANOS**
D.1985. Brown-orange and red-brown on m/c unpt. Similar to previous issues but higher quality printing and appearance. M/c back; bank initials in ornate guilloche at ctr. No 90-day restriction clause.

		VG	VF	UNC
a.	Issued note.	2.00	6.50	12.50
s.	Specimen. Ovpt: SPECIMEN.	—	—	—

191A **5 MILLION PESOS BOLIVIANOS**
D.1985. Similar to #191.

	VG	VF	UNC
	.85	2.50	5.50

192 **10 MILLION PESOS BOLIVIANOS**
D.1985. Rose and blue on tan unpt. Similar to #191.

		VG	VF	UNC
a.	Issued note.	3.00	8.00	18.00
s.	Specimen. Ovpt: SPECIMEN.	—	—	—

192A **10 MILLION PESOS BOLIVIANOS**
D.1985. Rose, violet and purple on m/c unpt. Similar to #192.

VG	VF	UNC
.75	3.25	8.50

DECRETO SUPREMO NO. 20732, 8 MARCH 1985; SECOND ISSUE

A193 **1 MILLION PESOS BOLIVIANOS**
D.1985. Blue and m/c. Lg. guilloche at l., Mercury head in unpt. at r. Series L.

		VG	VF	UNC
a.	Issued note.	.20	.75	3.00
s.	Specimen. Ovpt: MUESTRAS SIN VALOR.			

193 **5 MILLION PESOS BOLIVIANOS**
D.1985. Brown w/reddish brown text on m/c unpt. Similar to #A193. Series N.

		VG	VF	UNC
a.	Issued note.	.75	3.25	6.50
s.	Specimen. Ovpt: MUESTRAS SIN VALOR.			

194 **10 MILLION PESOS BOLIVIANOS**
D.1985. Violet w/lilac text on m/c unpt. Similar to #A193. Series M.

		VG	VF	UNC
a.	Issued note.	3.00	6.00	15.00
s.	Specimen. Ovpt: MUESTRAS SIN VALOR.	—	—	—

REPUBLIC, POST 1986

BANCO CENTRAL DE BOLIVIA

1987 PROVISIONAL ISSUE

			VG	VF	UNC
195	**1 CENTAVO ON 10,000 PESOS BOLIVIAS**		.15	.35	1.25
	ND (1987). Ovpt. at r. on back of #169.				

			VG	VF	UNC
196	**5 CENTAVOS ON 50,000 PESOS BOLIVIAS**		.15	.35	1.25
	ND (1987). Ovpt. at r. on back of #170.				
196A	**10 CENTAVOS ON 100,000 PESOS BOLIVIAS**		.50	1.50	5.00
	ND (1987). Ovpt. on #171.				

			VG	VF	UNC
197	**10 CENTAVOS ON 100,000 PESOS BOLIVIAS**		.15	.40	1.50
	ND (1987). Ovpt. at r. on back of #188.				

			VG	VF	UNC
198	**50 CENTAVOS ON 500,000 PESOS BOLIVIAS**		.15	.35	1.00
	ND (1987). Ovpt. at r. on back of #189.				

			VG	VF	UNC
199	**1 BOLIVIANO ON 1,000,000 PESOS BOLIVIAS**		.25	.60	2.25
	ND (1987). Ovpt. at r. on back of #A193.				

			VG	VF	UNC
200	**5 BOLIVIANOS ON 5,000,000 PESOS BOLIVIAS**				
	ND (1987). Ovpt. at l. or r. on back of #191A.				
	a. Issued note.		.50	2.50	5.00
	x. Error. Inverted overprint on left end.		1.00	5.50	15.00

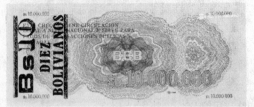

			VG	VF	UNC
201	**10 BOLIVIANOS ON 10,000,000 PESOS BOLIVIAS**		1.00	4.00	12.00
	ND (1987). Ovpt. at l. on back of #192A.				

LEY 901 DE 28.11.1986; 1987-90 ISSUES

#202-208 arms at lower l. or ctr. Printer F-CO.
#202-206 wmk: S. Bolívar.
Series A sign. titles: *PRESIDENTE BCB* and *MINISTRO DE FINANZAS*. Serial # suffix *A*.
Series B sign. titles: *PRESIDENTE DEL B.C.B.* and *GERENTE GENERAL B.C.B.* Serial # suffix *B*.

202 2 BOLIVIANOS

	VG	VF	UNC
L.1986. Black on m/c unpt. A. Vaca Diez at r. Trees and bldgs. at ctr. on back.			
a. Series A (1987).	FV	FV	3.00
b. Series B. (1990).	FV	FV	4.00
s. Specimen. Ovpt: *ESPECIMENS.*	—	—	—

203 5 BOLIVIANOS

	VG	VF	UNC
L.1986. Olive-green on m/c unpt. Adela Zamudio at r. Religious shrine at l. ctr. on back.			
a. Series A (1987).	FV	FV	5.00
b. Series B (1990).	FV	FV	6.50
s. Specimen. As a w/ovpt: *ESPECIMENS.*	—	—	—

204 10 BOLIVIANOS

	VG	VF	UNC
L.1986. Blue-black on m/c unpt. C. Guzman R. at r. Figures overlooking city view on back.			
a. Series A (1987).	FV	FV	9.50
b. Series B (1990).	FV	FV	12.50
s. Specimen. As a. w/ovpt: *ESPECIMENS.*	—	—	—

205 20 BOLIVIANOS

	VG	VF	UNC
L.1986. Orange and brown-orange on m/c unpt. P. Dalence at r. Bldg. at ctr. on back.			
a. Series A (1987).	FV	FV	20.00
b. Series B (1990).	FV	FV	25.00
s. Specimen. As a w/ovpt: *ESPECIMENS.*	—	—	—

206 50 BOLIVIANOS

	VG	VF	UNC
L.1986 (1987). Purple on m/c unpt. M. Perez de Holguin at r. Tall bldg. at ctr. on back. Series A.			
a. Issued note.	FV	FV	50.00
s. Specimen. Ovpt: *ESPECIMENS.*	—	—	—

207 100 BOLIVIANOS

	VG	VF	UNC
L.1986 (1987). Red and orange on m/c unpt. G. Rene Moreno at r. and as wmk. University bldg. at ctr. on back. Series A.			
a. Issued note.	FV	FV	100.00
s. Specimen. Ovpt: *ESPECIMENS.*	—	—	—

208 200 BOLIVIANOS

	VG	VF	UNC
L.1986 (1987). Brown and dk. brown on m/c unpt. F. Tamayo at r. and as wmk. Ancient statuary on back. Series A.			
a. Issued note.	FV	FV	200.00
s. Specimen. Ovpt: *ESPECIMENS*	—	—	—

LEY 901 DE 28.11.1986; 1993 ISSUE

#209-214 similar to #203-208 but many stylistic differences. Sign. titles: *PRESIDENTE BCB* and *GERENTE GENERAL BCB*. Serial # suffix C.

#209-212 wmk: S. Bolívar.

209	5 BOLIVIANOS		VG	VF	UNC
	L.1986 (1993). Series C.		FV	FV	4.00

210	10 BOLIVIANOS		VG	VF	UNC
	L.1986 (1993). Series C.		FV	FV	6.50

211	20 BOLIVIANOS		VG	VF	UNC
	L.1986 (1993). Series C.		FV	FV	11.00

212	50 BOLIVIANOS		VG	VF	UNC
	L.1986 (1993). Series C.		FV	FV	22.50

213	100 BOLIVIANOS		VG	VF	UNC
	L.1986 (1993). Series C.		FV	FV	45.00

214	200 BOLIVIANOS		VG	VF	UNC
	L.1986 (1993). Series C.		FV	FV	90.00

LEY 901 DE 28.11.1986; 1995 FIRST ISSUE

#215, 216 like #209 and 210. Wmk: S. Bolívar. Printer: TDLR.

215	5 BOLIVIANOS		VG	VF	UNC
	L. 1986 (1995). Series C.		FV	FV	3.00
	a. Issued note.		FV	FV	5.00
	s. Specimen. Ovpt: *MUESTRAS SIN VALOR.*		—	—	—

216	**10 Bolivianos**	**VG**	**VF**	**Unc**
	L. 1986 (1995). Series C.	FV	FV	5.50
	a. Issued note.	FV	FV	10.00
	s. Specimen. Ovpt: *MUESTRAS SIN VALOR*.	—	—	—

Ley 901 de 28.11.1986; 1995-96 Issue
#217-222 like #209-214 but w/o 4 control #s. Printer: TDLR.

217	**5 Bolivianos**	**VG**	**VF**	**Unc**
	L. 1986 (1995). Series D.	FV	FV	3.00

218	**10 Bolivianos**	**VG**	**VF**	**Unc**
	L. 1986 (1995). Series D.	FV	FV	5.00

219	**20 Bolivianos**	**VG**	**VF**	**Unc**
	L. 1986(1995). Series D.	FV	FV	8.00

220	**50 Bolivianos**	**VG**	**VF**	**Unc**
	L. 1986(1995). Series D.	FV	FV	17.50
221	**100 Bolivianos**			
	L. 1986 (1996). Series D.	FV	FV	32.50
222	**200 Bolivianos**			
	L. 1986 (1996). Series D.	FV	FV	60.00

The Republic of Bosnia-Herzegovina borders Croatia to the north and west, Serbia to the east and Montenegro in the southeast with only 12.4 miles of coastline. The total land area is 19,735 sq. mi. (51,129 sq. km.). They have a population of 4,366,000. Capital: Sarajevo. Electricity, mining and agriculture are leading industries. Bosnia's first ruler of importance was the Ban Kulin, 1180-1204. Stephen Kotromanió was invested with Bosnia, held loyalty to Hungary and extended his rule to the principality of Hum or Zahumlje, the future Hercegovina. His daughter Elisabeth married Louis the Great and he died in the same year. His nephew Tvrtko succeeded and during the weakening of Serbian power he assumed the title "Stephen Tvrtko, in Christ God King of the Serbs and Bosnia and the Coastland." Later he assumed the title of "King of Dalmatia and Croatia," but died before he could consolidate power. Successors also asserted their right to the Serbian throne.

In 1459 the Turks invaded Serbia. Bosnia was invaded in 1463 and Hercegovina in 1483. During Turkish rule Islam was accepted rather than Catholicism. During the 16th and 17th centuries Bosnia was an important Turkish outpost in continuing warfare with the Hapsburgs and Venice. When Hungary was freed of the Turkish yoke, the Imperialists penetrated into Bosnia, and in 1697 Prince Eugene captured Sarajevo. Later, by the Treaty of Karlowitz in 1699, the northern boundary of Bosnia became the northernmost limit of the Turkish empire while the eastern area was ceded to Austria, but later restored to Turkey in 1739 lasting until 1878 following revolts of 1821, 1828, 1831 and 1862. On June 30, 1871 Serbia and Montenegro declared war on Turkey and were quickly defeated. The Turkish war with Russia led to the occupation by Austria-Hungary. Insurgents attempted armed resistance and Austria-Hungary invaded in mass, quelling the uprising in 1878. The Austrian occupation provided a period of prosperity while at the same time prevented relations with Serbia and Croatia. Strengthening political and religious movements from within forced the annexation by Austria on Oct. 7, 1908. Hungary's establishment of a dictatorship in Croatia following the victories of Serbian forces in the Balkan War roused the whole Yugoslav population of Austria-Hungary to feverish excitement. The Bosnian group, mainly students, devoted their efforts to revolutionary ideas. After Austria's Balkan front collapsed in Oct. 1918 the union with Yugoslavia developed and on Dec. 1, 1918 the former Kingdom of the Serbs, Croats and Slovenes was proclaimed (later to become the Kingdom of Yugoslavia on Oct. 3, 1929).

After the defeat of Germany in WW II during which Bosnia was under the control of Pavelic of Croatia, a new Socialist Republic was formed under Marshal Tito having six constituent republics all subservient, quite similar to the constitution of the U.S.S.R. Military and civil loyalty was with Tito. In Jan. 1990 the Yugoslav government announced a rewriting of the constitution, abolishing the Communist Party's monopoly of power. Opposition parties were legalized in July 1990. On Oct. 15, 1991 the National Assembly adopted a Memorandum on Sovereignty that envisaged Bosnian autonomy within a Yugoslav Federation. In March 1992 an agreement was reached under EC auspices by Moslems, Serbs and Croats to set up 3 autonomous ethnic communities under a central Bosnian authority. Independence was declared on April 5, 1992. The 2 Serbian members of government resigned and fighting broke out between all 3 ethnic communities. The Dayton (Ohio, USA) Peace Accord was signed in 1995 which recognized the Federation of Bosnia-Herzegovina and the Srpska (Serbian) Republic. Both governments maintain seperate military forces, schools, etc. providing humanitarian aid while a recent peace treaty allowed NATO "Peace Keeping" forces be deployed in Dec. 1995 replacing the United Nations troops previously acting in a similar role.

MONETARY SYSTEM:
1 Dinar = 100 Para 1918-1941, 1945-
1 Kuna = 100 Banica 1941-1944

REPUBLIKA BOSNA I HERCEGOVINA

НАРОДНА БАНКА БОЧНЕ И ХЕРЦЕГПВИНЕ

NARODNA BANKA BOSNE I HERCEGOVINE

1992 FIRST PROVISIONAL ISSUE

#1-2 violet handstamp: *NARODNA BANKA BOSNE I HERCEGOVINE*, also in Cyrillic, around Yugoslav arms, on Yugoslav regular issues. Handstamp varieties exist.

#3, 4 held in reserve.

1	500 DINARA	GOOD	FINE	XF
	ND (1992). 31mm handstamp on Yugoslavia #107.			
	a. Handstamp w/o numeral.	12.50	35.00	90.00
	b. Handstamp w/numeral: *1*.	12.50	35.00	90.00
	c. Handstamp w/numeral: *2*.	12.50	35.00	90.00

2	1000 DINARA	GOOD	FINE	XF
	ND (1992). 48mm handstamp on Yugoslavia #108.			
	a. Handstamp w/o numeral.	12.50	35.00	90.00
	b. Handstamp w/numeral 1.	12.50	35.00	90.00
	c. Handstamp w/numeral 2.	12.50	35.00	90.00

1992 SECOND PROVISIONAL ISSUE

#5-9 issued in various Moslem cities. Peace Dove at upper l. ctr. Example w/o indication of city of issue are remainders.

6	100 DINARA	GOOD	FINE	XF
	1992. Deep pink on gray and yellow unpt.			
	a. Handstamped: *BREZA* on back.	3.00	9.00	25.00
	b. Circular red handstamp: *FOJNICA* on back.	2.50	7.50	22.50
	c. Rectangular purple handstamp on face, circular purple handstamp: *KRESEVO* on back.	6.50	20.00	60.00
	d. Handstamped: *TESANJ* on back.	6.50	20.00	60.00
	e. Handstamped: *VARES* on back.	2.50	7.50	22.50
	f. Handstamped: *VISOKO* on back (2 varieties).	2.00	6.00	18.00
	g. Circular red ovpt: *ZENICA*, 11.5.1992. on back r. W/printed sign. at either side.	1.00	3.00	9.00
	r. Remainder, w/o handstamp or ovpt.	.30	1.00	3.00

7	500 DINARA	GOOD	FINE	XF
	1992. Pale greenish-gray on gray and yellow unpt.			
	a. Handstamped: *BREZA* on back.	2.50	8.00	24.00
	b. Circular red handstamp: *FOJNICA* on back.	2.50	7.50	22.50
	c. Handstamped: *KRESEVO* on back.	6.50	20.00	60.00
	d. Handstamped: *TESANJ* on back.	2.50	7.50	22.50
	e. Handstamped: *VARES* on back.	6.50	20.00	60.00
	f. Circular red handstamp: *VISOKO* on back.	4.50	14.00	42.00
	g. Circular red handstamp on back, details as #6g: *ZENICA* (small or large), 11.5.1992.	1.00	3.00	9.00

8	**1000 DINARA**	GOOD	FINE	XF
	1992. Blue on gray unpt.			
	a. Handstamped: *BREZA* on back.	5.00	16.00	48.00
	b. Handstamped: *FOJNICA* on back.	5.00	16.00	48.00
	c. Handstamped: *KRESEVO* on back.	8.00	25.00	75.00
	d. Handstamped: *TESANJ* on back.	6.50	20.00	60.00
	e. Handstamped: *VARES* on back.	6.50	20.00	60.00
	f. Handstamped: *VISOKO* on back (small or large).	2.00	6.00	18.00
	g. Handstamped: *ZENICA* on face, no date on stamping.	8.00	25.00	75.00
	h. Circular red ovpt. on back, details as 6g: *ZENICA*, 11.5.1992.	1.25	4.00	12.00

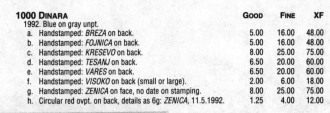

12	**50 DINARA**	VG	VF	UNC
	1.7.1992. Blue-black on red-violet unpt. Mostar stone arch bridge at r. on back.			
	a. Issued note.	.20	.60	1.50
	s. Specimen.	—	—	30.00

9	**5000 DINARA**	GOOD	FINE	XF
	1992. Dull brown on gray and yellow unpt.			
	a. Handstamped: *BREZA* on back.	4.00	12.00	36.00
	b. Circular red handstamp: *FOJNICA* on back.	3.25	10.00	30.00
	c. Handstamped: *KRESEVO* on back.	6.50	20.00	60.00
	d. Handstamped: *TESANJ* on back.	10.00	30.00	—
	e. Handstamped: *VARES* on back.	3.25	10.00	30.00
	f. Handstamped: *VISOKO* on back (3 varieties).	2.00	6.00	18.00
	g. Handstamped: *ZENICA* on face, w/o date in stamping.	6.50	20.00	60.00
	h. Circular violet ovpt. on back, details as 6g: *ZENICA*, 11.5.1992.	1.00	3.00	9.00
	r. Remainder, w/o handstamp or ovpt.	5.00	16.00	48.00

1992-93 ISSUES

#10-15 guilloche at l. ctr. 145x73mm. Wmk: Repeated diamonds. Printer: Cetis (Celje, Slovenia).
#10-18 serial # varieties.

13	**100 DINARA**	VG	VF	UNC
	1.7.1992. Dull black on olive-green unpt. Crowned arms at ctr. r. on back.			
	a. Issued note.	.25	.75	1.75
	s. Specimen.	—	—	30.00

10	**10 DINARA**	VG	VF	UNC
	1.7.1992. Purple on pink unpt. Mostar stone arch bridge at r. on back.			
	a. Issued note.	.10	.40	1.00
	s. Specimen.	—	—	30.00

14	**500 DINARA**	VG	VF	UNC
	1.7.1992. Dull violet-brown on pink and ochre unpt. Crowned arms at ctr. r. on back.			
	a. Issued note.	.50	1.50	3.50
	s. Specimen.	—	—	30.00

11	**25 DINARA**	VG	VF	UNC
	1.7.1992. Blue-black on lt. blue unpt. Crowned arms at ctr. r. on back.			
	a. Issued note.	.50	.50	1.25
	s. Specimen.	—	—	30.00

15   1000 DINARA

	VG	VF	UNC
1.7.1992. Deep purple on lt. green and lilac unpt. Mostar stone arch bridge at r. on back.			
a. Issued note.	.55	1.75	4.50
s. Specimen.	—	—	30.00

16   5000 DINARA

	VG	VF	UNC
25.1.1993. Pale olive-green on yellow-orange unpt.			
a. Issued note.	1.00	3.00	7.50
b. W/ovpt: SDK.	1.75	5.00	15.00

17   10,000 DINARA

	VG	VF	UNC
25.1.1993. Brown on pink unpt.			
a. Issued note.	1.25	3.50	8.50
b. W/ovpt: SDK.	1.75	5.00	15.00

1992-93 BON ISSUE

#21-27 shield at l. on back. Issued for the Sarajevo area. Grayish-green or yellow unpt on back.

21   10 DINARA

	VG	VF	UNC
1.8.1992. Violet.			
a. Issued note.	3.25	10.00	25.00
s. Specimen.	—	—	30.00

22   20 DINARA

	VG	VF	UNC
1.8.1992. Blue-violet.			
a. Issued note.	2.00	6.00	15.00
s. Specimen.	—	—	30.00

23   50 DINARA

	VG	VF	UNC
1.8.1992. Pink.			
a. Issued note.	2.00	6.00	15.00
s. Specimen.	—	—	30.00

24   100 DINARA

	VG	VF	UNC
1.8.1992. Green.			
a. Issued note.	3.25	10.00	25.00
s. Specimen.	—	—	30.00

25   500 DINARA

	VG	VF	UNC
1.8.1992. Orange. Back red-orange on pale purple and grayish green unpt.			
a. Issued note.	3.25	10.00	25.00
s. Specimen.	—	—	30.00

26   1000 DINARA

	VG	VF	UNC
1.8.1992. Brown.			
a. Issued note.	2.00	6.00	15.00
s. Specimen.	—	—	30.00

27   5000 DINARA

	VG	VF	UNC
1.8.1992. Violet.			
a. Issued note.	2.25	7.00	18.00
s. Specimen.	—	—	30.00

		VG	VF	UNC
28	**10,000 DINARA** 6.4.1993. Lt. Blue.	2.25	7.00	18.00
29	**50,000 DINARA** 1.5.1993. Pink.	5.00	15.00	25.00
30	**100,000 DINARA** 1.8.1993. Green on m/c unpt. Back green on gray unpt.	1.65	5.00	12.00
31	**100,000 DINARA** 1.8.1993. Green. Back green on yellow unpt.	2.50	7.50	18.50

1993 EMERGENCY BON ISSUE

			VG	VF	UNC
32	**100,000 DINARA** 1993 (-old date 1.7.1992). Rectangular crenalated framed ovpt: *NOVCANI BON 100,000*...on face and back of #10.				
	a. Purple ovpt. 1.9.1993.		.50	7.00	18.00
	b. Blue ovpt. and lt. blue sign. ovpt. 10.11.1993.		.50	3.50	9.00
33	**1 MILLION DINARA** 10.11.1993 (old date-1.7.1992). Blue-violet ovpt. on #11. (Not issued?)	—	12.50	27.50	

		VG	VF	UNC
34	**10 MILLION DINARA** 10.11.1993 (old date-1.7.1992). Blue-violet ovpt. on #12. (Not issued?)	—	8.00	24.00
35	**100 MILLION DINARA** 10.11.1993 (old date-1.7.1992). Blue-violet ovpt. on #12. (Not issued?)	—	8.00	24.00

1994 FIRST ISSUE
#36 Deleted.

		VG	VF	UNC
37	**500,000 DINARA** 1.1.1994. Brown. Back: Brown on pale yellow-green unpt.	2.50	7.50	18.50
38	**1 MILLION DINARA** 1.1.1994. Red.	2.00	5.00	15.00

1994 SECOND ISSUE
1 New Dinar = 10,000 Old Dinara
#39-46 alternate with shield or Mostar stone bridge at ctr. r. on back.

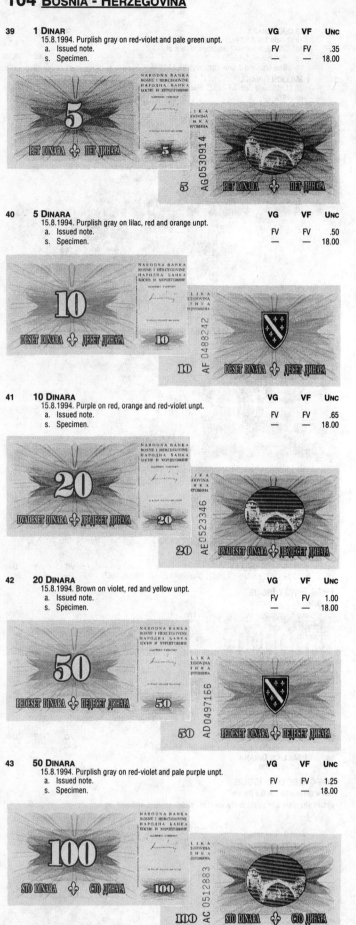

39   1 Dinar
15.8.1994. Purplish gray on red-violet and pale green unpt.

	VG	VF	Unc
a. Issued note.	FV	FV	.35
s. Specimen.	—	—	18.00

40   5 Dinara
15.8.1994. Purplish gray on lilac, red and orange unpt.

	VG	VF	Unc
a. Issued note.	FV	FV	.50
s. Specimen.	—	—	18.00

41   10 Dinara
15.8.1994. Purple on red, orange and red-violet unpt.

	VG	VF	Unc
a. Issued note.	FV	FV	.65
s. Specimen.	—	—	18.00

42   20 Dinara
15.8.1994. Brown on violet, red and yellow unpt.

	VG	VF	Unc
a. Issued note.	FV	FV	1.00
s. Specimen.	—	—	18.00

43   50 Dinara
15.8.1994. Purplish gray on red-violet and pale purple unpt.

	VG	VF	Unc
a. Issued note.	FV	FV	1.25
s. Specimen.	—	—	18.00

44   100 Dinara
15.8.1994. Dull black on aqua, yellow and olive-green unpt.

	VG	VF	Unc
a. Issued note.	FV	FV	1.75

---

s. Specimen.	—	—	18.00

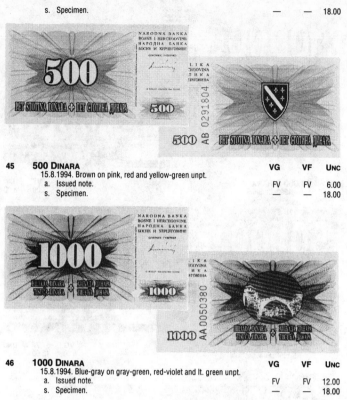

45   500 Dinara
15.8.1994. Brown on pink, red and yellow-green unpt.

	VG	VF	Unc
a. Issued note.	FV	FV	6.00
s. Specimen.	—	—	18.00

46   1000 Dinara
15.8.1994. Blue-gray on gray-green, red-violet and lt. green unpt.

	VG	VF	Unc
a. Issued note.	FV	FV	12.00
s. Specimen.	—	—	18.00

Srpska (Serbian) Republic

НАРОДНА БАНКА ЧРПЧЕ РЕПУБЛИКЕ БОЧНЕ И ХЕРЦЕГОВИНЕ

Narodna Banka Srpske Republike

Bosne I Hercegovine

National Bank of the Serbian

Republic of Bosnia-Herzegovina

1992-93 Banja Luka Issue

#133-139 arms at l., numerals in heart-shaped design below guilloche at ctr. r. Curved artistic design at l. ctr., arms at r. on back.

#133-135 wmk: Portr. of a young girl.

#136-140 wmk: Portr. of a young boy.

NOTE: For similar notes to #136-140 but differing only in text at top, sign., and Knin as place of issue, see Croatia-Regional.

#142-144 wmk: Portr. of a young girl.

133   10 Dinara
1992. Deep brown or orange and silver unpt. Back with ochre unpt.

	VG	VF	Unc
a. Issued note.	.10	.35	1.00
s. Specimen.	—	—	12.50

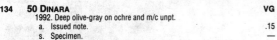

134 50 DINARA
1992. Deep olive-gray on ochre and m/c unpt.

	VG	VF	UNC
a. Issued note.	.15	.40	1.25
s. Specimen.	—	—	12.50

135 100 DINARA
1992. Dk. blue on lilac and silver unpt.

	VG	VF	UNC
a. Issued note.	.35	1.00	3.00
s. Specimen.	—	—	12.50

136 500 DINARA
1992. Dk. blue on pink and m/c unpt.

	VG	VF	UNC
a. Issued note.	.65	2.00	6.00
s. Specimen.	—	—	12.50

137 1000 DINARA
1992. Slate gray on pink and tan unpt. Back with orange unpt.

	VG	VF	UNC
a. Issued note.	.40	1.20	3.50
s. Specimen.	—	—	12.50

138 5000 DINARA
1992. Violet on lilac and lt. blue unpt.

	VG	VF	UNC
a. Issued note.	.40	1.20	3.50
s. Specimen.	—	—	12.50

139 10,000 DINARA
1992. Gray on tan and lt. blue unpt.

	VG	VF	UNC
a. Issued note.	.40	1.20	3.50
s. Specimen.	—	—	12.50

140 50,000 DINARA
1993. Brown on olive-green and m/c unpt.

	VG	VF	UNC
a. Issued note.	1.00	5.00	15.00
s. Specimen.	—	—	12.50

141 100,000 DINARA
1993. Purple on brown and m/c unpt. Wmk: Portr. of young woman w/headcovering.

	VG	VF	UNC
a. Issued note.	.40	1.35	4.00
s. Specimen.	—	—	15.00

142 1 MILLION DINARA
1993. Dp. purple on pink, yellow and m/c unpt.

	VG	VF	UNC
a. Issued note.	.40	1.35	4.00
s. Specimen.	—	—	15.00

143 5 MILLION DINARA
1993. Dk. brown on lt. blue and yellow-orange unpt.

	VG	VF	UNC
a. Issued note.	.40	1.50	4.50
s. Specimen.	—	—	15.00

144 10 MILLION DINARA
1993. Dk. blue-violet on olive-green and yellow-orange unpt.

	VG	VF	UNC
a. Issued note.	.50	1.50	4.50
s. Specimen.	—	—	15.00

НАРОДНА БАНКА РЕИТБЛИКЕ ЧРПЧКЕ

NARDONA BANKA REPUBLIKE SRPSKE

NATIONAL BANK OF THE SERBIAN REPUBLIC

1993 BANJA LUKA FIRST ISSUE

145 50 MILLION DINARA
1993. Dk. brown on pink and gray unpt.

	VG	VF	UNC
a. Issued note.	.85	2.50	7.50
s. Specimen.	—	—	15.00

146	100 MILLION DINARA	VG	VF	UNC
	1993. Pale blue-gray on lt. blue and gray unpt.			
	a. Issued note.	.50	1.65	5.00
	s. Specimen.	—	—	15.00

147	1 MILLIARD DINARA	VG	VF	UNC
	1993. Orange on pale blue and lt. orange unpt.			
	a. Issued note.	.65	2.00	6.00
	s. Specimen.	—	—	15.00

148	10 MILLIARD DINARA			
	1993. Black on pink and pale orange unpt.			
	a. Issued note.	1.00	3.00	9.00
	s. Specimen.	—	—	15.00

1993 BANJA LUKA SECOND ISSUE

149	5000 DINARA	VG	VF	UNC
	1993. Red-violet and purple on pale blue-gray unpt.			
	a. Issued note.	.35	1.00	3.00
	s. Specimen.	—	—	15.00

150	50,000 DINARA	VG	VF	UNC
	1993. Brown and dull red on ochre unpt.			
	a. Issued note.	.50	1.25	4.00
	s. Specimen.	—	—	15.00

151	100,000 DINARA	VG	VF	UNC
	1993. Violet and blue-gray on pink unpt.			
	a. Issued note.	.40	1.35	4.00
	s. Specimen.	—	—	15.00

152	1 MILLION DINARA	VG	VF	UNC
	1993. Black and blue-gray on pale purple unpt.			
	a. Issued note.	.65	2.00	6.00
	s. Specimen.	—	—	15.00

153	5 MILLION DINARA	VG	VF	UNC
	1993. Orange and gray-blue on pale orange unpt.			
	a. Issued note.	.90	2.75	8.50
	s. Specimen.	—	—	15.00

154	100 MILLION DINARA			
	1993. Dull grayish green and pale olive-brown on lt. blue unpt.			
	a. Issued note.	1.20	3.50	10.00
	s. Specimen.	—	—	15.00

155	500 MILLION DINARA	VG	VF	UNC
	1993. Brown-violet and grayish green on pale olive-brown unpt.			
	a. Issued note.	1.20	3.50	10.00
	s. Specimen.	—	—	15.00

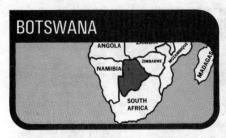

The Republic of Botswana (formerly Bechuanaland), located in south central Africa between Southwest Africa, (Namibia) and Zimbabwe has an area of 231,805 sq. km.) and a population of 1.35 million. Capital: Gaborone. Botswana is a member of a Customs Union with South Africa, Lesotho, and Swaziland. The economy is primarily pastoral with a rapidly developing mining industry, of which diamonds, copper and nickel are the chief elements. Meat products and diamonds comprise 85 percent of the exports.

Little is known of the origin of the peoples of Botswana. The early inhabitants, the Bushmen, did not develop a recorded history and are now dying out. The ancestors of the present Botswana probably arrived about 1600 AD in Bantu migrations from the north and east. Bechuanaland was first united early in the 19th century under Chief Khama III to more effectively resist incursions by the Boer trekkers from Transvaal and by the neighboring Matabeles. As the Boer threat intensified, appeals for protection were made to the British Government, which proclaimed the whole of Bechuanaland a British protectorate in 1885. In 1895, the southern part of the protectorate was annexed to Cape Province. The northern part, known as the Bechuanaland Protectorate, remained under British administration until it became the independent Republic of Botswana on Sept. 30, 1966. Botswana is a member of the Commonwealth of Nations. The president is Chief of State and Head of Government. British administration until it became the independent Republic of Botswana on Sept. 30, 1966. Botswana is a member of the Commonwealth of Nations. The president is Chief of State and Head of Government.

MONETARY SYSTEM:
1 Pula (Rand) = 100 Thebe (Cents)

	SIGNATURE VARIETIES				
1	*O. Masire* *signature*		**4**	*P. S. Mmusi* *signature*	
2	*O. Masire* *signature*		**5**	*P. S. Mmusi* *signature*	
3	*P. S. Mmusi* *signature*		**6**	*signature* *signature*	

REPUBLIC

BANK OF BOTSWANA

1976-79 ND ISSUE
#1-5 Pres. Sir Serese Khama at l., arms at upper r. Wmk: Rearing zebra. Printer: TDLR. Replacements notes: *Z/1* prefix.

			VG	VF	UNC
1	**1 PULA**				
	ND (1976). Brown and m/c. Milking cow on back.		.50	1.50	3.75

			VG	VF	UNC
2	**2 PULA**				
	ND (1976). Blue and m/c. Various workers on back. Printer: TDLR.		1.00	3.00	7.00

			VG	VF	UNC
3	**5 PULA**				
	ND (1976). Purple and m/c. Gemsbok antelope on back.		2.50	7.00	22.50

			VG	VF	UNC
4	**10 PULA**				
	ND (1976). Green and m/c. Lg. bldg. on back.				
	a. Sign. 1.		5.00	17.50	55.00
	b. Sign. 2.		10.00	60.00	165.00
5	**20 PULA**				
	ND (1979). Red and m/c. Mining conveyors on back.				
	a. Sign. 1.		15.00	75.00	200.00
	b. Sign. 2.		20.00	100.00	285.00

1982-83 ND ISSUE
#7-10 Pres. O. Masire at l., arms at upper r. Wmk: Rearing zebra. Replacement notes: *Z/1* prefix.

			VG	VF	UNC
6	**1 PULA**				
	ND (1983). Dk. brown. Pres. O. Masire at l. Animals, plants and arms at ctr. on back.		.15	1.00	3.00

			VG	VF	UNC
7	**2 PULA**				
	ND (1982). Blue and m/c. Bird at ctr.				
	a. Sign. 3.		FV	1.75	6.00
	b. Sign. 4.		FV	1.75	5.00
	c. Sign. 5.		FV	1.50	4.00
	d. Sign. 6.		FV	1.50	3.00

			VG	VF	UNC
8	**5 PULA**				
	ND (1982). Deep violet and m/c. Bird at ctr.				
	a. Sign. 3.		FV	4.25	10.00
	b. Sign. 4.		FV	4.25	9.00
	c. Sign. 5.		FV	4.00	8.50

9 **10 PULA**
ND (1982). Green and m/c. Bird at ctr.

		VG	VF	UNC
a.	Sign. 3.	FV	7.00	20.00
b.	Sign. 4.	FV	7.00	17.50
c.	Sign. 5.	FV	7.00	15.00
d.	Sign.6.	FV	7.00	13.00
s.	Specimen, punched hole cancelled.	—	—	5.00

10 **20 PULA**
ND (1982). Red and m/c. Ostrich at ctr.

		VG	VF	UNC
a.	Sign. 3.	FV	15.00	32.50
b.	Sign. 4.	FV	15.00	30.00
c.	Sign. 5.	FV	15.00	28.50
d.	Sign. 6.	FV	15.00	27.50
s.	Specimen, punched holed cancelled.	—	—	5.00

1992-93 ISSUE
#11-15 Pres. O. Masire at l., arms at upper r. Wmk: Rearing zebra. Metallic thread to r. of portr.

#11-13 printer: Harrison.

		VG	VF	UNC
11	**5 PULA**	FV	FV	6.00
	ND (1992). Similar to #8; sm. stylistic differences. Sign. 6.			
12	**10 PULA**	FV	FV	10.00
	ND(1992). Similar to #9; sm. stylistic differences. Sign. 6.			
13	**20 PULA**	FV	FV	18.00
	ND (1993). Similar to #10.			

		VG	VF	UNC
14	**50 PULA**	FV	FV	35.00
	ND(1992). Dk. brown and dk. green on m/c unpt. Bird at ctr., arms at upper r. Man in canoe and bird w/fish on back. W/o imprint.			
15	**100 PULA**	FV	FV	60.00
	ND (1993). Blue-violet on tan and m/c unpt. Diamond and eagle at ctr. Worker sorting rough diamonds on back. Printer: TDLR.			

COLLECTOR SERIES

BANK OF BOTSWANA

1979, 1982 ISSUE

		ISSUE PRICE	MKT. VALUE
CS1	ND (1979) 1-20 PULA	14.00	25.00
	#1-5 ovpt: *SPECIMEN* and Maltese cross prefix serial # .		
CS2	ND (1982) 1-20 PULA	—	28.50
	#1-5 ovpt: *SPECIMEN* w/4 punched hole cancellation.		
CS3	ND (1982) 1-20 PULA	—	18.50
	#6-10 ovpt: *SPECIMEN* w/ 4 punched hole cancellation.		

BRAZIL

The Federative Republic of Brazil, which comprises half the continent of South America, is the only Latin American country deriving its culture and language from Portugal. It has an area of 3,286,470 sq. mi. (8,511,965 sq. km.) and a population of 146 million. Capital: Brasília. The economy of Brazil is as varied and complex as any in the developing world. Agriculture is a mainstay of the economy, although but 4 percent of the area is under cultivation. Known mineral resources are almost unlimited in variety and size of reserves. A large, relatively sophisticated industry ranges from basic steel and chemical production to finished consumer goods. Coffee, cotton, iron ore and cocoa are the chief exports.

Brazil was discovered and claimed for Portugal by Admiral Pedro Alvares Cabral in 1500. Portugal established a settlement in 1532 and proclaimed the area a royal colony in 1549. During the Napoleonic Wars, Dom Joao VI established the seat of Portuguese government in Rio de Janeiro. When he returned to Portugal, his son Dom Pedro I declared Brazil's independence on Sept. 7, 1822, and became emperor of Brazil. The Empire of Brazil was maintained until 1889 when a republic was established. The Federative Republic was established in 1946 by terms of a constitution drawn up by a constituent assembly. Following a coup in 1964 the armed forces retained overall control under a dictatorship until a civilian government was restored on March 15, 1985. The current constitution was adopted in 1988.

MONETARY SYSTEM:
1 Cruzeiro = 100 Centavos, 1942-1966
1 Cruzeiro Novo = 1000 Old Cruzeiros, 1966-1985
1 Cruzado = 1000 Cruzeiros Novos, 1986-1989
1 Cruzado Novo = 1000 Cruzados, 1989-1990
1 Cruzeiro = 1 Cruzado Novo, 1990-1993
1 Cruzeiro Real (pl. Reais) = 1000 Cruzeiros, 1993-

SIGNATURE VARIETIES

1	CLAUDIONNR S. LEMOS HORÁCIO LAFER	**6**	CLAUDIONNR S. LEMOS LUCAS LOPES
2	CLAUDIONNR S. LEMOS OSWALDO ARANHA	**7**	AFFONSO ALMINO LUCAS LOPES
3	CLAUDIONNR S. LEMOS EUGENIO GUDIN	**8**	SEBASTIÃO P. ALMEIDA CARLOS A. CARRÍLHO
4	CLAUDIONNR S. LEMOS JOSÉ M. WHITAKER	**9**	CLEMENTE MARIANI CARLOS A. CARRÍLHO
5	CLAUDIONNR S. LEMOS JOSÉ MARIA ALKIMIN	**10**	WALTER M. SALLES REGINALDO F. NUNES

REPUBLIC

TESOURO NACIONAL, VALOR RECEBIDO

ESTAMPA 3

		VG	VF	UNC
166	**5 CRUZEIROS**			
	ND (1961-62). Dk. brown and brown. Raft w/sail at l., male Indian at r. Flower on back. Printer: CdM-B.			
	a. Sign. 8. Series #1-75.	.10	.30	1.00
	b. Sign. 10. Series #76-111.	.10	.30	1.00

TESOURO NACIONAL, VALOR LEGAL

ESTAMPA 1A
#167-173 dk. blue on m/c guilloches, 2 printed sign. Printer: ABNC.

		VG	VF	UNC
167	**10 CRUZEIROS**			
	ND (1961-63). Portr. G. Vargas at ctr. Back green; allegory of "Industry" at ctr.	—	Unc	.00
	a. Sign. 9. Series #331-630.	.15	.50	1.50
	b. Sign. 11. Series #631-930.	.15	.50	1.50
168	**20 CRUZEIROS**			
	ND (1961-63). Portr. D. da Fonseca at ctr. Back red; allegory of "the Republic" at ctr.			
	a. Sign. 9. Series #461-960.	.15	.50	2.00
	b. Sign. 11. Series #961-1260.	.15	.50	2.00

		VG	VF	UNC
169	**50 CRUZEIROS**			
	ND (1961). Portr. Princess Isabel at ctr. Back purple; allegory of "Law" at ctr. Sign. 9. Series #721-1220.	.15	.65	3.50

		VG	VF	UNC
170	**100 CRUZEIROS**			
	ND (1961-64). Portr. D. Pedro at ctr. Back red-brown; allegory of "National Culture" at ctr.			
	a. Sign. 9. Series #761-1160.	.30	1.25	5.50
	b. Sign. 12. Series #1161-1360.	.30	1.00	5.00
	c. Sign. 13. Series #1361-1560.	.30	1.50	6.00
171	**200 CRUZEIROS**			
	ND (1961-64). Portr. D. Pedro at ctr. Back olive-green; battle scene at ctr.			
	a. Sign. 9. Series #671-1070.	.50	1.50	7.50
	b. Sign. 12. Series #1071-1370.	.50	1.50	6.50
	c. Sign. 13. Series #1371-1570.	.50	1.50	7.50

		VG	VF	UNC
172	**500 CRUZEIROS**			
	ND (1961-62). Portr. D. Joao VI at ctr. Back blue-black; allegory of "Maritime Industry" at ctr.			
	a. Sign. 9. Series #261-660.	1.00	3.00	12.50
	b. Sign. 10. Series #661-1460.	.75	2.50	12.00
173	**1000 CRUZEIROS**			
	ND (1961-63). Portr. P. Alvares Cabral at ctr. Back orange; scene of the "First Mass" at ctr.			
	a. Sign. 9. Series #1331-1730.	.75	3.00	27.50
	b. Sign. 10. Series #1731-3030.	.75	3.00	18.50
	c. Sign. 11. Series #3031-3830.	1.00	4.00	15.00

		VG	VF	UNC
174	**5000 CRUZEIROS**			
	ND (1963-64). Blue-grayish. Portr. Tiradentes at r. Back red; Tiradentes in historical scene at ctr. Printer: ABNC.			
	a. Sign. 11. Series #1-400.	1.00	4.50	18.50
	b. Sign. 12. Series #401-1400.	1.00	4.00	16.00
	c. Sign. 13. Series #1401-1650.	1.75	7.00	27.50

ESTAMPA 2A; 1962-63
#176-182 2 printed sign. Printer: TDLR. #175 Deleted, see #182A.

		VG	VF	UNC
176	**5 CRUZEIROS**			
	ND (1962-64). Brown on m/c unpt.			
	a. Sign. 10. Series #2301-3500.	.10	.25	.65
	b. Sign. 11. Series #3501-3700.	.10	.25	1.75
	c. Sign. 12. Series #3701-3748; 4149-4180; 4201-4232.	.10	.25	3.00
	d. Sign. 13. Series #3749-4148; 4181-4200; 4233-4700.	.10	.25	.65
177	**10 CRUZEIROS**			
	ND (1962). Green on m/c unpt. Like #167. Sign. 10. Series #2365-3055.	.10	.25	.75

		VG	VF	UNC
178	**20 CRUZEIROS**			
	ND (1962). Red-brown. Like #168. Sign. 10. Series #1576-2275.	.15	.30	1.00
179	**50 CRUZEIROS**			
	ND (1963.) Purple on m/c unpt. Like #169. Sign. 11. Series #586-785.	.25	1.00	4.00
180	**100 CRUZEIROS**			
	ND (1963). Red. Like #170. Sign. 11. Series #216-415.	.35	1.50	6.00

181 1000 CRUZEIROS
ND (1963). Orange on m/c Unpt. Like #173. Sign. 11. Series #791-1590.

	VG	VF	UNC
	.50	1.50	8.00

182 5000 CRUZEIROS
ND (1963-64). Red. Like #174. Sign. at l. w/*Director Caixa de Amortizacao.*

	VG	VF	UNC
a. Sign. 11. Series #1-400.	1.00	3.50	15.50
b. Sign. 12. Series #401-1400.	.85	3.00	15.00
c. Sign. 13. Series #1401-1700.	1.50	5.00	25.00

BANCO CENTRAL DO BRASIL

1965-66 ISSUE

A182 5000 CRUZEIROS
ND (1965). Red on m/c unpt. like #174. Sign. D. Nogueira w/title: *Presidente do Banco Central* and O. Gouvea de Bulhoes. Series #1701-2200.

	VG	VF	UNC
	1.00	3.50	16.50

182A 10,000 CRUZEIROS
ND (1966). Gray on m/c unpt. Portr. S. Dumont at r. Back blue; early airplane at r. Sign. 14. Printer: ABNC.

	VG	VF	UNC
a. Series #1-493.	4.00	16.00	40.00
b. Series #561-590.	20.00	80.00	200.00

1966-67 PROVISIONAL ISSUE

#183-190 black circular ovpt: *BANCO CENTRAL* and new currency unit in black circle on Tesouro Nacional notes.

183 1 CENTAVO ON 10 CRUZEIROS
ND (1966-67). Green on m/c unpt. Ovpt. on #177. Sign. 14.

	VG	VF	UNC
a. Error: *Minstro* below r. sign. (2 types of 1 in ovpt.) (1966). Series #3056-3151.	.10	.20	.60
b. *Ministro* below r. sign. (1967). Series # 3152-4055.	.10	.20	.50
s. As b. Specimen. Ovpt: *MODELLO.*	—	—	—

184 5 CENTAVOS ON 50 CRUZEIROS
ND (1966-67). Purple on m/c unpt. Ovpt. on #179. Sign. 14.

	VG	VF	UNC
a. Type of #183a. Series #786-1313.	.10	.20	.60
b. Type of #183b. Series #1314-1885.	.10	.20	.50

185 10 CENTAVOS ON 100 CRUZEIROS
ND (1966-67). Red on m/c unpt. Ovpt. on #180. Sign. 14.

	VG	VF	UNC
a. Type of #183a. Series #416-911.	.10	.30	.85
b. Type of #183b. Series #912-1515.	.10	.30	.85

186 50 CENTAVOS ON 500 CRUZEIROS
ND (1967). Blue on m/c unpt. Ovpt. on #172. Sign. 14. Series: 1461-2360.

	VG	VF	UNC
	.20	.50	2.00

187 1 CRUZEIRO NOVO ON 1000 CRUZEIROS
ND (1966-67). Blue on m/c unpt. Ovpt. on #173.

	VG	VF	UNC
a. Sign. 13. Series #3831-3930.	.25	.65	3.00
b. Sign. 14. Series #3931-4830.	.25	.60	2.50

188 5 CRUZEIROS NOVOS ON 5000 CRUZEIROS
ND (1966-67). Blue-green on m/c unpt. Ovpt. on #174.

	VG	VF	UNC
a. Sign. 13. Series #1651-1700.	1.00	4.50	15.00
b. Sign. 14. Series #1701-2900.	.75	3.00	10.00

189 10 CRUZEIROS NOVOS ON 10,000 CRUZEIROS
ND (1966-67). Gray on m/c unpt. Bold or semi-bold ovpt. on 182A. Printer: ABNC.

	VG	VF	UNC
a. Sign. 14. Series #494-560 and 591-700.	1.00	4.00	15.00
b. Sign. 15. Series #701-1700.	.75	3.00	10.00
c. Sign. 16. Series #1701-2700.	.75	3.00	10.00

190 10 CRUZEIROS NOVOS ON 10,000 CRUZEIROS
ND (1967). Brown, pink and m/c. Like #182A. Printer: TDLR.

	VG	VF	UNC
a. Sign. 15. Series #1-1000.	.75	3.00	10.00
b. Sign. 16. Series #1001-2100.	.75	3.00	10.00

1970 ISSUES

#191-195 portr. as wmk. Sign. varieties. 5 digit series # above serial #.

#191-194, 195A printer: CdM-B.

191 1 CRUZEIRO
ND (1970-72). Dk. green and Blue. Banco Central bldg. at l. on back.

		VG	VF	UNC
a.	Medallic Liberty head at r. in brown. Serial # prefix A (1970-72). Series #1-3000.	.20	.50	3.00
b.	Medallic Liberty head in green. Serial # prefix B (1972-81). Series #1-18094.	.10	.25	.50

191A 1 CRUZEIRO
ND (1972-81). Dk. green w/medallic Liberty head in green. Serial # prefix B (1972-81). Series #1-18094.

a.	Issued note.	.10	.25	.50
s.	Specimen. Ovpt. and perforated: *MODELLO*.	—	—	—

192 5 CRUZEIROS
ND (1970). Blue on orange and green unpt. Portr. D. Pedro I at r. Back maroon; parade square at l.

		VG	VF	UNC
a.	Back darkly printed. Serial # prefix A (1970-71.) Series #1-107.	.10	.60	8.00
b.	Back lightly printed. Serial # prefix B (1973-79). 3 sign. varieties. Series #1-6841.	.10	.25	1.00
s.	As a. Specimen. Ovpt: *SEM VALOR* perforated: *MODELLO*.	—	—	—

193 10 CRUZEIROS
ND (1970-80). Grayish purple and dk. brown on orange-brown blue-green and m/c unpt. Portr. D. Pedro II at r. Back green, violet and brown; statue of the Prophet Daniel.

		VG	VF	UNC
a.	Back darkly printed. Serial # prefix A (1970-78). 2 sign. varieties. Series #1-7745.	.10	.50	2.50
b.	Back lightly printed. Serial # prefix B (1979-80). 2 sign. varieties. Series #1-5131.	.10	.25	1.00

194 50 CRUZEIROS
ND (1970-81). Black, purple, blue-black and violet on lilac and m/c unpt. Portr. Mal. Deodora da Fonseca at r. Back brown, lilac and blue; coffee loading at l. 3 sign. varieties. Series #1-5233.

VG	VF	UNC
.10	.50	2.00

195 100 CRUZEIROS
ND (1970-81). Purple and violet on pink and m/c unpt. Portr. Marshal F. Peixoto at r. Back blue, brown and violet; National Congress at l. Printer: TDLR. Series #1-00500.

VG	VF	UNC
1.00	3.00	25.00

195A 100 CRUZEIROS
ND. Like #195. Printer: CdM-B. 2 sign. varieties. Series #00501-12681.

VG	VF	UNC
.25	.75	3.50

1972 COMMEMORATIVE ISSUE
#196, 150th Anniversary of Brazilian Independence

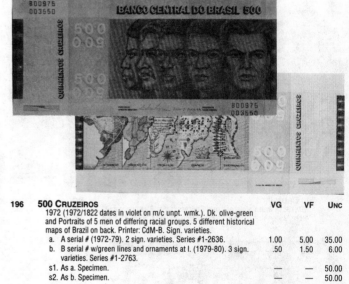

196 500 CRUZEIROS
1972 (1972/1822 dates in violet on m/c unpt. wmk.). Dk. olive-green and Portraits of 5 men of differing racial groups. 5 different historical maps of Brazil on back. Printer: CdM-B. Sign. varieties.

		VG	VF	UNC
a.	A serial # (1972-79). 2 sign. varieties. Series #1-2636.	1.00	5.00	35.00
b.	B serial # w/green lines and ornaments at l. (1979-80). 3 sign. varieties. Series #1-2763.	.50	1.50	6.00
s1.	As a. Specimen.	—	—	50.00
s2.	As b. Specimen.	—	—	50.00

1978 ISSUE

197 1000 CRUZEIROS
ND (1978-80). Green and brown. B. do Rio Branco and as wmk. *BANCO CENTRAL DO BRASIL* in 2 lines. Double view of machinery on back. Also, small plate modification on back. 3 sign. varieties. Series #1-3297.

	VG	VF	UNC
	1.00	5.00	25.00

1981-85 ISSUE
#198-205 portr. as wmk. Sign. varieties. Printer: CdM-B. Series # is first 4 digits of serial #.
#198-202 double portr. and vignettes.

198 100 CRUZEIROS
ND (1981). Red, purple and m/c. D. de Caxias. Back gray-blue and red; battle scene and sword. 2 sign. varieties. Series #1-8176.

	VG	VF	UNC
	.10	.15	.25

199 200 CRUZEIROS
ND (1981). Green, violet and m/c. Princess Isabel. Back brown and green; 2 women cooking outdoors. 2 sign. varieties. Series #1-4960.

	VG	VF	UNC
	.10	.15	.30

200 500 CRUZEIROS
ND (1981). Blue, brown and m/c. D. da Fonseca. Back pink, brown and purple; group legislators. 2 sign. varieties. Series #1-4238.

	VG	VF	UNC
	.05	.20	.50

201 1000 CRUZEIROS
ND (1981). Brown, dk. olive and m/c. Similar to #197, but bank name in 1 line. Back tan and blue. 3 sign. varieties. Series A-B: 1-9999; B-B: 1-0788.

	VG	VF	UNC
	.10	.20	.50

202 5000 CRUZEIROS
ND (1981). Purple, brown and m/c. C. Branco. Back brown, purple and blue; antennas. 3 sign. varieties. Series A-A: 1-9999; B-A: 1-2342.

	VG	VF	UNC
	.10	.30	1.00

203 10,000 CRUZEIROS
ND (1984). Brown on m/c unpt. Desk top at ctr., Rui Barbosa at r. Conference scene on back. 2 sign. varieties. Series #1-3696.

	VG	VF	UNC
	.20	.60	3.00

204 50,000 CRUZEIROS
ND (1984). Violet on m/c unpt. Microscope at ctr., O. Cruz at r. Cruz Institute at at ctr. on back. 3 sign. varieties.

	VG	VF	UNC
a. Issued note. Series #1-1673; 2171-3290.	.50	2.50	8.00
x. Error, titles and sign. in revreversed position so that *President, Banco Central* is at l. Series #1674-2170.	1.00	5.00	15.00

205 100,000 CRUZEIROS
ND (1985). Black on blue, gold and m/c unpt. Electric power station at ctr., Pres. J. Kubitschek at r. Old and modern bldgs. at ctr. on back. Series #1-4347.

VG	VF	UNC
.50	2.50	7.50

1986 PROVISIONAL ISSUE
#206-208 black circular ovpt: *Banco Central Do Brazil* and new currency unit on #203-205.

206 10 CRUZADOS ON 10,000 CRUZEIROS
ND (1986). Ovpt. on #203. Series #3697-5124.

VG	VF	UNC
.10	.20	.60

207 50 CRUZADOS ON 50,000 CRUZEIROS
ND (1986). Ovpt. on #204. Series #3291-4592.

VG	VF	UNC
.20	.75	2.50

208 100 CRUZADOS ON 100,000 CRUZEIROS
ND (1986). Ovpt. on #205. Series #4348-6209.

VG	VF	UNC
.20	.75	3.00

1986 ISSUE
#209-211 printer: CdM-B.

209 10 CRUZADOS
ND (1986). Similar to #203 except for denomination. 2 sign. varieties. Series #1-1505.

VG	VF	UNC
.10	.20	.50

210 50 CRUZADOS
ND (1986). Similar to #204 except for denomination. 2 sign. varieties. Series #1-2051.

VG	VF	UNC
.10	.25	.75

211 100 CRUZADOS
ND (1986). Similar to #205 except for denomination. 4 sign. varieties. Series #1-3059.

VG	VF	UNC
.10	.25	.75

1986 COMMEMORATIVE ISSUE
#212, Birth Centennial of H. Villa-Lobos

212   500 CRUZADOS
ND (1986). Blue-green on m/c unpt. H. Villa-Lobos at r. and as wmk.
Villa-Lobos at l. ctr. on back. Printer: CdM-B. 4 sign. varieties. Series
#1-8309.

	VG	VF	UNC
	.10	.20	.50

1988 ISSUE

#213-215 portr. as wmk. Printer: CdM-B. Series # are first 4 digits of serial #.

213   1000 CRUZADOS
ND (1988). Purple and brown-violet on m/c unpt. J. Machado at r.
Street scene from old Rio de Janeiro on back. 2 sign. varieties. Series
#1-9919.

	VG	VF	UNC
	.15	.75	2.50

214   5000 CRUZADOS
ND (1988). Blue and m/c. Portion of mural at ctr., C. Portinari at r.
Examples of his artwork on back. Series #1-1757.

	VG	VF	UNC
	.35	1.75	5.00

215   10,000 CRUZADOS
ND (1989). Red and brown on m/c unpt. C. Chagas at r. Chagas w/Lab
instruments on back. Series #1-1841.

	VG	VF	UNC
	.75	3.50	10.00

1989 PROVISIONAL ISSUE

#216-218 black triangular ovpt. of new currency unit on #213-215.

216   1 CRUZADO NOVO ON 1000 CRUZADOS
ND (1989). Ovpt. on #213. Purple and brown-violet on unpt. Series A-
A: 9920-9999; B-A: 1-1792.

	VG	VF	UNC
	.10	.20	.30

217   5 CRUZADOS NOVOS ON 5000 CRUZADOS
ND (1989). Ovpt. on #214. Series #1758-4502.

	VG	VF	UNC
	.15	.50	1.75

218   10 CRUZADOS NOVOS ON 10,000 CRUZADOS
ND (1989). Ovpt. on #215. Red and brown on m/c unpt. Series #1842-
4502.

	VG	VF	UNC
	.15	.60	4.00

1989 ISSUE

#219-220, 222 printer: CdM-B. Wmk: Liberty head.

219   50 CRUZADOS NOVOS
ND (1989). Brown and black on m/c unpt. C. Drummond de Andrade
at r. Back black, red-brown and blue; de Andrade writing poetry. 2
sign. varieties. Series #1-3358.

	VG	VF	UNC
	.10	.50	2.50

220   100 Cruzados Novos

		VG	VF	UNC
	ND (1989). Orange, purple and green on m/c unpt. C. Meireles at r. Back brown, black and m/c; child reading and people dancing. Series #1-8794.	.15	.65	3.00

1989 COMMEMORATIVE ISSUE
#221, Centenary of the Republic

221   200 Cruzados Novos

		VG	VF	UNC
	ND (1989). Blue and black on m/c unpt. Political leaders at ctr., sculpture of the Republic at ctr. r., arms at r. Oil painting "Patria" by P. Bruno w/flag being embroidered by a family on back. Wmk: Liberty head. Printer: CdM-B. Series #1-1964.	.20	1.00	3.50

1990 ISSUE

222   500 Cruzados Novos

		VG	VF	UNC
	ND (1990). Green and purple on m/c unpt. Orchids at ctr., A. Ruschi at r. Back lt. orange, purple and blue; hummingbird, orchids and A. Ruschi at ctr. Series #1-3700.	.75	3.00	7.50

1991-92 PROVISIONAL ISSUE
#223-226 black rectangular ovpt. of new currency unit on #219-222.

223   50 Cruzeiros on 50 Cruzados Novos

		VG	VF	UNC
	ND (1991). Ovpt. on #219. Series #3359-5338.	.10	.20	.60

224   100 Cruzeiros on 100 Cruzados Novos

		VG	VF	UNC
	ND (1991). Ovpt. on #220. Series #8795-9447.	.10	.30	1.00

225   200 Cruzeiros on 200 Cruzados Novos

		VG	VF	UNC
	ND (1991). Ovpt. on #221. Series #1965-2668.	FV	FV	1.00

226   500 Cruzeiros on 500 Cruzados Novos

		VG	VF	UNC
	ND (1991). Ovpt on #222.			
a.	Series #3111.	1.25	5.00	25.00
b.	Series #3701-7700.	.10	.40	1.50

1991-93 ISSUE
#228-231 similar to #220-223 but w/new currency unit and new sign. titles.
#228-236 printer: CdM-B.
#235-236 wmk: Sculptured head of *"Brasillia."*

227   5000 Cruzeiros

		VG	VF	UNC
	ND (1992). Deep olive-green and deep brown on m/c unpt. Liberty head at r. and as wmk. Arms at l. on back. Printer: CdM-B. Provisional type. Series #1-1520.	.20	.75	3.00

228   100 Cruzeiros

		VG	VF	UNC
	ND (1992). Like #220. Series #1-1045.	.10	.20	.80

229   200 CRUZEIROS

	VG	VF	UNC
ND (1992). Like #221. Series #1-1646.	.10	.25	1.00

230   500 CRUZEIROS

	VG	VF	UNC
ND (1992). Like #222. Series #1-0210.	.30	.75	3.00

231   1000 CRUZEIROS

ND (1992). Dk. brown, brown, violet and black on m/c unpt. C. Rondon at r., native hut at ctr., map of Brazil in background. 2 Indian children and local food from Amazonia on back. Wmk: Liberty head.

	VG	VF	UNC
a. Upper sign. title: *MINISTRA DA ECONOMIA*,... Series #1-4268.	.10	.50	2.00
b. Upper sign. title: *MINISTRO DA ECONOMIA*,... Series #4269-.	.05	.15	.75

232   5000 CRUZEIROS

ND (1992). Blue-black, black and deep brown on lt. blue and m/c unpt. C. Gomes at ctr. r., Brazilian youths at ctr. Statue of Gomes seated, grand piano at ctr. on back. 3 sign. varieties.

	VG	VF	UNC
a. Upper sign. title: *MINISTRA DA ECONOMIA*,... Series #1-5501.	.10	.50	2.00
b. Upper sign. title: *MINISTRO DA FAZENDA*,... Series #5502-6041.	.05	.25	1.00

233   10,000 CRUZEIROS

	VG	VF	UNC
ND (1992). Black and brown-violet on m/c unpt. V. Brazil at r. and as wmk. Extracting poisonous venom at ctr. One snake swallowing another at ctr. on back. 3 sign. varieties. Series #1-7365.	.05	.25	1.00

234   50,000 CRUZEIROS

ND (1991). Dk. brown and red-orange on m/c unpt. C. Cascudo at ctr. r. and as wmk. 2 men on raft at l. ctr. background. Folklore dancers at l. ctr. on back. Series #1-6289.

	VG	VF	UNC
a. Upper sign. title: *MINISTRO DA ECONOMIA*,...	.10	.35	1.50
b. Upper sign. title: *MINISTRO DA FAZENDA*,...	.10	.35	1.50

235   100,000 CRUZEIROS

	VG	VF	UNC
ND (1992). Hummingbird feeding nestlings at ctr., butterfly at r. Butterfly at l. Ignacu cataract at ctr. on back. 3 sign. varieties.			
a. Upper sign. title: *MINISTRO DA ECONOMIA,...* Series #1-6052.	.30	1.50	5.00
b. Upper sign. title: *MINISTRO DA FAZENDA,...* Series #6053-6733.	.10	.35	1.50

236   500,000 CRUZEIROS

	VG	VF	UNC
ND (1993). Red-violet, brown and deep purple on m/c unpt. M. de Andrade at r., native indian art in unpt. Bldg., de Andrade teaching children at ctr. on back. 3 sign. varieties. Series #1-8291.	.25	1.00	4.50

1993 PROVISIONAL ISSUE
#237-239 black circular ovpt. of new value on #234b-236b.

237   50 CRUZEIROS REAIS ON 50,000 CRUZEIROS

	VG	VF	UNC
ND (1993). Ovpt. on #234b. Series #6290-6591.	.05	.25	1.50

238   100 CRUZEIROS REAIS ON 100,000 CRUZEIROS

	VG	VF	UNC
ND (1993). Ovpt. on #235b. Series #6734-7144.	.10	.40	1.75

239   500 CRUZEIROS REAIS ON 500,000 CRUZEIROS

	VG	VF	UNC
ND (1993). Ovpt. on #236b. Series A:#8292-9999; B:#1-0607.	.10	.50	3.00

1993-94 ISSUE
#240-242 wmk: Sculptured head of *"Brasillia."* Printer: CdM-B.

240   1000 CRUZEIROS REAIS

	VG	VF	UNC
ND (1993). Black, dk. blue and brown on m/c unpt. A. Teixeira at ctr. r. "Parque" school at l. ctr. Children and workers on back. Series #1-2515.	.10	.50	2.50

241   5000 CRUZEIROS REAIS

	VG	VF	UNC
ND (1993). Black, red-brown and dk. olive-green on m/c unpt. Gaucho at ctr. r., ruins of São Miguel das Missões at l. ctr. Back vertical; gaucho, horseback, roping steer at ctr. Series #1-9999.	.50	2.50	10.00

242   50,000 CRUZEIROS REAIS

	VG	VF	UNC
ND (1994). Deep purple and brown-violet on m/c unpt. Native dancer and Baiana at l. and ctr. r. Back vertical; Baiana Acarajé preparing food at ctr. Series #1-1200.	FV	25.00	50.00

1994 ISSUE
#243-247 Sculpture of the Republic at ctr. r. and as wmk. Printer: CdM-B or w/additional imprint of secondary printer. Series # is first 4 digits of serial #.

243   1 REAL

	VG	VF	UNC
ND (1994). Black and green on m/c unpt. Hummingbirds on back. 4 sign. varieties.			
a. W/o text. Series #1-3833.	FV	FV	3.00
b. W/text: *DEUS SEJA LOUVADO.* Series #3834-.	FV	FV	2.25

244 5 REAIS
ND (1994). Purple and blue on m/c unpt. Crane on back. 5 sign. varieties.

		VG	VF	UNC
a.	W/o text or G&D imprint. Series A-A: #0001-1411.	FV	FV	11.00
b.	W/o text. Printer: G&D. Series A-B:#1-1411.	FV	FV	10.00
c.	W/text: *DEUS SEJA LOUVADO*. Series A-A: #1412-.	FV	FV	8.50

245 10 REAIS
ND (1994). Dk. brown and red-orange on m/c unpt. Arara bird on back. 5 sign. varieties.

		VG	VF	UNC
a.	W/o text or TLDR imprint. Series A-A: #1-1817.	FV	FV	20.00
b.	W/o text. Printer: TDLR. Series #A-B: #1-0713.	FV	FV	18.50
c.	W/text: *DEUS SEJA LOUVADO*. Series #1818-.	FV	FV	15.00

246 50 REAIS
ND (1994). Dk. brown and red-brown on m/c unpt. Onca pintada leopard on back. 5 sign. varieties.

		VG	VF	UNC
a.	W/o text or F-CO imprint. Series A-A: #1-1338.	FV	FV	80.00
b.	W/o text. Printer: F-CO. Series A-B: #1-1249.	FV	FV	75.00
c.	W/text: *DEUS SEJA LOUVADO*. Series #1339-.	FV	FV	70.00

247 100 REAIS
ND (1994). Blue-green and purple on m/c unpt. Garoupa fish on back. 4 sign. varieties.

		VG	VF	UNC
a.	W/o text. Series #1-1201.	FV	FV	140.00
b.	W/text: *DEUS SEJA LOUVADO*. Series #1201-.	FV	FV	125.00

The British Caribbean Territories (Eastern Group), a currency board formed in 1950, comprised the British West Indies territories of Trinidad and Tobago; Barbados; the Leeward Islands of Anguilla, Saba, St. Christopher, Nevis and Antigua; the Windward Islands of St. Lucia, Dominica, St. Vincent and Grenada; British Guiana and the British Virgin Islands. As time progressed, the members of this Eastern Group varied.
For later issues see the East Caribben States.

RULERS:
British

MONETARY SYSTEM:
1 Dollar = 100 Cents

BRITISH INFLUENCE

BRITISH CARIBBEAN TERRITORIES, EASTERN GROUP

1953 ISSUE
#7-12 map at lower l., portr. Qn. Elizabeth II at r. Printer: BWC.

7	**1 DOLLAR**	VG	VF	UNC
	1953-64. Red on m/c unpt.			
a.	Wmk: Sailing ship. 5.1.1953.	6.00	35.00	150.00
b.	Wmk: Qn. Elizabeth II. 1.3.1954-2.1.1957.	3.00	15.00	75.00
c.	2.1.1958-2.1.1964.	1.50	12.00	60.00
8	**2 DOLLARS**			
	1953-64. Blue on m/c unpt.			
a.	Wmk: Sailing ship. 5.1.1953.	20.00	175.00	450.00
b.	Wmk: Queen Elizabeth II. 1.3.1954-1.7.1960.	7.50	55.00	325.00
c.	2.1.1961-2.1.1964.	3.00	35.00	250.00

9	**5 DOLLARS**	VG	VF	UNC
	1953-64. Green on m/c unpt.			
a.	Wmk: Sailing ship. 5.1.1953.	22.50	185.00	450.00
b.	Wmk: Queen Elizabeth II. 3.1.1955-2.1.1959.	10.00	65.00	375.00
c.	2.1.1961-2.1.1964.	7.50	50.00	350.00

10   10 DOLLARS
1953-64. Brown on m/c unpt.

	VG	VF	UNC
a. Wmk: Sailing ship. 5.1.1953.	37.50	300.00	1500.
b. Wmk: Queen Elizabeth II. 3.1.1955-2.1.1959.	20.00	150.00	950.00
c. 2.1.1961; 2.1.1962; 2.1.1964.	15.00	110.00	525.00

11   20 DOLLARS
1953-64. Purple on m/c unpt.

	VG	VF	UNC
a. Wmk: Sailing ship. 5.1.1953.	50.00	400.00	2000.
b. Wmk: Queen Elizabeth II. 2.1.1957-2.1.1964.	25.00	200.00	1000.

12   100 DOLLARS
1953-63. Black on m/c unpt.

	VG	VF	UNC
a. Wmk: Sailing ship. 5.1.1953.	375.00	1250.	—
b. Wmk: Queen Elizabeth II. 1.3.1954; 2.1.1957; 2.1.1963.	225.00	750.00	—

The British colony of Belize, formerly British Honduras, a self-governing dependency of the United Kingdom situated in Central America south of Mexico and east and north of Guatemala, has an area of 8,867 sq. mi. (22,965 sq. km.) and a population of 209,000. Capital: Belmopan. Sugar, citrus fruits, chicle and hard woods are exported.

The area, site of the ancient Mayan civilization, was sighted by Columbus in 1502, and settled by shipwrecked English seamen in 1638. British buccaneers settled the former capital of Belize in the 17th century. Britain claimed administrative right over the area after the emancipation of Central America from Spain, and declared it a colony subordinate to Jamaica in 1862. It established as the separate Crown Colony of British Honduras in 1884. The anti-British People's United Party, which attained power in 1954, won a constitution, effective in 1964 which established self-government under a British appointed governor. British Honduras became Belize on June 1, 1973, following the passage of a surprise bill by the Peoples United Party, but the constitutional relationship with Britain remained unchanged.

In Dec. 1975, the U.N. General Assembly adopted a resolution supporting the right of the people of Belize to self-determination, and asking Britain and Guatemala to renew their negotiations on the future of Belize. They obtained independence on Sept. 21, 1981.

Bank notes of the United States circulated freely in British Honduras until 1924.

*** This section has been renumbered. ***

RULERS:
British

MONETARY SYSTEM:
1 Dollar = 100 Cents

BRITISH HONDURAS

GOVERNMENT OF BRITISH HONDURAS

1952-53 ISSUE
#28-32 arms at l., portr. Qn. Elizabeth II at r.

28   **1 DOLLAR**
(11)   1952-73. Green on m/c unpt.

	VG	VF	UNC
a. 15.4.1953-1.10.1958.	4.00	25.00	125.00
b. 1.1.1961-1.5.1969.	2.00	10.00	50.00
c. 1.1.1970-1.1.1973.	1.50	7.00	35.00

29   **2 DOLLARS**
(12)   1953-73. Purple on m/c unpt.

	VG	VF	UNC
a. 15.4.1953-1.10.1958.	7.50	40.00	350.00
b. 1.10.1960-1.5.1965.	3.00	20.00	125.00
c. 1.1.1971-1.1.1973.	2.00	15.00	55.00

	30	**5 DOLLARS**	**VG**	**VF**	**UNC**
(13)		1953-73. Red on m/c unpt.			
		a. 15.4.1953-1.1.1958.	10.00	50.00	350.00
		b. 1.3.1960-1.5.1969.	5.00	30.00	225.00
		c. 1.1.1970-1.1.1973.	4.50	20.00	150.00

31	**10 DOLLARS**	**VG**	**VF**	**UNC**
(14)	1953-73. Black on m/c unpt.			
	a. 15.4.1953-1.10.1958.	15.00	100.00	700.00
	b. 1.5.1965-1.5.1969.	10.00	50.00	500.00
	c. 1.1.1971-1.1.1973.	7.50	35.00	375.00

32	**20 DOLLARS**			
(15)	1952-73. Brown on m/c unpt.			
	a. 1.12.1952-1.10.1958.	30.00	150.00	1000.
	b. 1.3.1960-1.5.1969.	20.00	120.00	750.00
	c. 1.1.1971-1.1.1973.	15.00	100.00	675.00

Negara Brunei Darussalam (The State of Brunei), a British protected state on the northwest coast of the island of Borneo, has an area of 2,226 sq. mi. (5,765 sq. km.) and a population of 256,500. Capital: Bandar Seri Begawan. Crude oil and rubber are exported.

Magellan was the first European to visit Brunei in 1521. It was a powerful state, ruling over Northern Borneo and adjacent islands from the 16th to the 19th century. Brunei became a British protectorate in 1888 and a British dependency in 1905. The Constitution of 1959 restored control over internal affairs to the sultan, while delegating responsibility for defense and foreign affairs to Britain.

The island of Labuan (formerly Sultana), located 6 miles off the northwest coast of Borneo, has an area of 35 sq. mi. (90.6 sq. km.) and a population of 10,000. It is now part of Sabah (British North Borneo), and consequently of Malaysia. The East India Co. sought to make Labuan a trading station in 1775, but the island reverted to a pirate refuge. In 1846 it was ceded by the sultan of Brunei to Britain. Labuan was a crown colony from 1848 to 1890, when its administration was handed over to British North Borneo, which ruled it until 1905, when it became part of the Straits Settlements. Labuan became a part of Sabah in 1946.

RULERS:
Sultan Sir Omar Ali Saifuddin III, 1950-1967
Sultan Hassanal Bolkiah I, 1967-

MONETARY SYSTEM:
1 Dollar = 100 Sen to 1967
1 Ringgit (Dollar) = 100 Sen, 1967-

STATE

KERAJAAN BRUNEI

GOVERNMENT OF BRUNEI

1967 ISSUE
#1-5 Sultan Omar Ali Saifuddin III w/military cap at r. and as wmk. Mosque on back.

1	**1 RINGGIT**	**VG**	**VF**	**UNC**
	1967. Dk. blue on m/c unpt. Back gray, lavender and pink.	1.25	7.00	28.50

2	**5 RINGGIT**	**VG**	**VF**	**UNC**
	1967. Dk. green on m/c unpt. Back green and pink.	5.00	12.50	50.00
3	**10 RINGGIT**			
	1967. Red on m/c unpt. Back red.	9.00	15.00	60.00
4	**50 RINGGIT**			
	1967. Dk. brown on m/c unpt. Back olive.	42.50	70.00	175.00

5	100 RINGGIT	VG	VF	UNC
	1967. Blue on m/c unpt. Back purple.	15.00	140.00	350.00

1972-79 ISSUE

#6-10 Sultan Hassanal Bolkiah I in military uniform at r. and as wmk.

6	1 RINGGIT	VG	VF	UNC
	1972-88. Blue on m/c unpt.			
	a. 1972; 1976; 1978.	FV	1.50	6.00
	b. 1980; 1982.	FV	1.00	4.00
	c. 1983-1988.	FV	.85	3.00

7	5 RINGGIT	VG	VF	UNC
	1979-86. Green on m/c unpt.			
	a. 1979; 1981.	FV	5.00	16.50
	b. 1983; 1984; 1986.	FV	4.00	12.50

8	10 RINGGIT	VG	VF	UNC
	1976-86. Red on m/c unpt.			
	a. 1976; 1981.	FV	9.00	21.50
	b. 1983; 1986.	FV	7.50	18.50

9	50 RINGGIT	VG	VF	UNC
	1973-86. Dk. brown on m/c unpt.			
	a. 1973.	FV	45.00	100.00
	b. 1977; 1982.	FV	37.50	80.00
	c. 1986.	FV	FV	60.00

10	100 RINGGIT	VG	VF	UNC
	1972-88. Blue on m/c unpt.			
	a. 1972; 1976.	FV	90.00	200.00
	b. 1978; 1980.	FV	80.00	140.00
	c. 1982; 1983; 1988.	FV	75.00	135.00

1979; 1987 ISSUE

#11-12 Sultan Hassannal Bolkiah I in royal uniform at r. and as wmk. Mosque on back.

11	500 RINGGIT	VG	VF	UNC
	1979; 1987. Orange on m/c unpt. Mosque at ctr. on back.			
	a. 1979.	FV	425.00	700.00
	b. 1987.	FV	400.00	650.00

12	1000 RINGGIT	VG	VF	UNC
	1979; 1987. Gray, brown and greenish-blue. Brunei Museum on back.			
	a. 1979.	FV	850.00	1350.
	b. 1987.	FV	800.00	1250.

NEGARA BRUNEI DARUSSALAM

1989 ISSUE

#13-20 Sultan Bolkiah at r. and as wmk.

13	1 RINGGIT	VG	VF	UNC
	1989-94. Purple on m/c unpt. Aerial view on back.	FV	FV	2.50

14	**5 RINGGIT**	**VG**	**VF**	**UNC**
	1989-91; 1993. Blue-gray and deep green on m/c unpt. Houses and boats on back.	FV	FV	6.50

15	**10 RINGGIT**	**VG**	**VF**	**UNC**
	1989-92. Purple and red-orange on m/c unpt. Houses and mosque on back.	FV	FV	12.50

16	**50 RINGGIT**	**VG**	**VF**	**UNC**
	1989-91. Brown, olive-green, and orange on m/c unpt. People in power launch on back.	FV	FV	52.50

17	**100 RINGGIT**	**VG**	**VF**	**UNC**
	1989-92; 94. Blue and violet on m/c unpt. River scene on back.	FV	FV	90.00

18	**500 RINGGIT**	**VG**	**VF**	**UNC**
	1989-92. Red-orange, purple, olive and black on m/c unpt. Woman in boat on back.	FV	FV	425.00
19	**1000 RINGGIT**			
	1989-91. Red-violet, purple, olive and blue-green on m/c unpt. Waterfront village on back.	FV	FV	775.00
20	**10,000 RINGGIT**			
	1989. Green and yellow on m/c unpt. Aerial view of harbor on back.	FV	FV	7650.

1992 COMMEMORATIVE ISSUE
#21, 25th Anniversary of Accession

21	**25 RINGGIT**	**VG**	**VF**	**UNC**
	1992. Brown, lilac, green and m/c. Royal procession at ctr., Sultan at r. and as wmk. at l. Crown at l., coronation at ctr. on back. Dates *1967* and *1992* wi1th text at top.	FV	FV	35.00

1996 ISSUE
#22-24 Sultan Bolkiah I at r., arms at upper l. Polumar plastic. Printer: NPA (w/o imprint).

22	**1 RINGGITT**	**VG**	**VF**	**UNC**
	1996. Blue-black and deep green on m/c unpt. Riverside simpur plant at l. ctr. Back blue and m/c; rainforest waterfall at l. ctr.	FV	FV	FV
23	**5 RINGGIT**			
	1996. Black and green on m/c unpt. Pitcher plant at l. ctr. Rainforest floor on back.	FV	FV	6.00
24	**10 RINGGIT**			
	1996. Bk. brown on m/c unpt. Purple leafed forest yam at l. ctr. rainforest canopy on back.	FV	FV	11.50

BULGARIA

The Republic of Bulgaria (formerly the Peoples Republic of Bulgaria), a Balkan country on the Black Sea in southeastern Europe, has an area of 44,365 sq. mi. (110,912 sq. km.) and a population of 8.47 million. Capital: Sofia. Agriculture remains a key component of the economy but industrialization, particularly heavy industry, has been emphasized since the late 1940's. Machinery, tobacco and cigarettes, wines and spirits, clothing and metals are the chief exports.

The area now occupied by Bulgaria was conquered by the Bulgars, an Asiatic tribe, in the 7th century. Bulgarian kingdoms continued to exist on the peninsula until it came under Turkish rule in 1395. In 1878, after nearly 500 years of Turkish rule, Bulgaria was made a principality under Turkish suzerainty. Union seven years later with Eastern Rumelia created a Balkan state with borders approximating those os present-day Bulgaria. A Bulgarian kingdom fully independent of Turkey was Sept. 22, 1908.

During WWI Bulgaria had been aligned with Germany. After the Armistice certain land concessions were granted to Greece and Romania. In 1934 King Boris III suspended all political parties and established a dictatorial monarchy. In 1938 the military began rearming through the aide of the Anglo-French loan. As WWII developed Bulgaria again supported the Germans but Boris protected their Jewish community. Boris died mysteriously in 1943 and Simeon II became king at the age of six. The country was then ruled by a pro-Nazi regency until it was invaded by Soviet forces in 1944. The monarchy was abolished and Simeon was ousted by plebiscite in 1946 and Bulgaria became a People's Republic in the Soviet pattern. Following demonstrations and a general strike the communist government resigned in Nov. 1990. A new government was elected in Oct. 1991.

TITLES:
Bulgarian People's Republic: НАРОДНА РЕПУБЛИКА БЪЛГАРИЯ
Bulgarian National Bank: БЪЛГАРСКАТА НАРОДНА БАНКА
State banknote: ЦАРСТО ЪБЛГАРИЯ
Cashier's bond: ЦКАЧОБЪ БОВЪ

MONETARY SYSTEM:
1 Lev ЛЕВ = 100 Stotinki СТОТИНКИ

PEOPLES REPUBLIC

БЪЛГАРСКАТА НАРОДНА БАНКА

BULGARIAN NATIONAL BANK

1962 ISSUE
#88-92 arms at l.

88	1 LEV 1962. Brown-lilac. Tower on back.	VG	VF	UNC
	a. Issued note.	.10	.25	2.00
	s. Specimen.	—	—	17.50

89	2 LEVA 1962. Green. Woman picking grapes in vineyard on back.	VG	VF	UNC
	a. Issued note.	.20	.40	3.00
	s. Specimen.	—	—	18.50
90	5 LEVA 1962. Red-brown. Coastline village.			
	a. Issued note.	.25	.50	5.00
	s. Specimen.	—	—	20.00
91	10 LEVA 1962. Blue. Factory. Dimitrov on back.			
	a. Issued note.	.35	.70	10.00
	s. Specimen.	—	—	22.50
92	20 LEVA 1962. Brown-lilac. Factory. Dimitrov on back.			
	a. Issued note.	.50	1.00	20.00
	s. Specimen.	—	—	25.00

1974 ISSUE
#93-97 modified arms w/dates *681-1944* at l.
#93-95 wmk: Decorative design.
#96 and 97 wmk: Hands holding hammer and sickle.

93	1 LEV 1974. Brown. Like #88.	VG	VF	UNC
	a. Issued note.	.10	.20	1.00
	s. Specimen.	—	—	17.50

94	2 LEVA 1974. Green. Like #89.	VG	VF	UNC
	a. Issued note.	.10	.25	2.50
	s. Specimen.	—	—	18.50

95	5 LEVA 1974. Red-brown. Like #90.	VG	VF	UNC
	a. Issued note.	.15	.30	3.00
	s. Specimen.	—	—	20.00

96	10 LEVA 1974. Blue. Like #91.	VG	VF	UNC
	a. Issued note.	.25	.75	7.50
	s. Specimen.	—	—	22.50

97	20 LEVA	VG	VF	UNC
	1974. Brown-lilac. Like #92.			
	a. Issued note.	.50	1.00	10.00
	s. Specimen.	—	—	25.00

1989-90 ISSUES

Note: #98 was withdrawn from circulation shortly after its release.

NOTE: #99 carries the name of the Bulgarian Peoples Republic, probably the reason it was not released. An estimated 500-600 pieces were "liberated" from the recycling process.

98	50 LEVA	VG	VF	UNC
	1990. Brown and dk. blue on m/c unpt. Arms at l. ctr. Back brown and dk. green; castle ruins at ctr. r. on back. Wmk: Hands holding hammer and sickle.			
	a. Issued note.	1.00	10.00	75.00
	s. Specimen.	—	—	100.00

99	100 LEVA	VG	VF	UNC
	1989. Purple on lilac unpt. Arms at l. ctr. Horseman w/2 dogs at ctr. r. on back. Wmk: Rampant lion. (Not issued).	—	—	300.00

REPUBLIC

БЪЛГАРСКАТА НАРОДНА БАНКА

BULGARIAN NATIONAL BANK

1991-96 ISSUE

100	20 LEVA	VG	VF	UNC
	ND(1992). Blue-black and blue-green on m/c unpt. Dutchess Sevastokrat oritza Desislava on l. ctr. Boyana Church at r. on back.	FV	FV	1.00

101	50 LEVA	VG	VF	UNC
	1992. Purple and violet on m/c unpt. Khristo G. Danov at l. Platen printing press at r. on back.	FV	FV	2.25

102	100 LEVA	VG	VF	UNC
	1991. Dk. brown and maroon on m/c unpt. Zhary Zograf (artist) at l. ctr. Wheel of life at r. on back. Cream paper.	FV	FV	4.00

103	200 LEVA	VG	VF	UNC
	1992. Deep violet and brown-orange on m/c unpt. Ivan Vazov at l. village in unpt. Lyre w/laurel wreath at r. on back.	FV	FV	7.50

104	500 LEVA	VG	VF	UNC
	1993. Dk. green and black on m/c unpt. D. Hristor at l. and as wmk. Opera house in Varna at ctr. r., sea gulls at lower r. on back.	FV	FV	18.00

105   1000 LEVA
1994. Dk. green and olive-brown on m/c unpt. V. Levski at l. and as wmk., Liberty w/flag, sword and lion at upper ctr. r. Monument and writings of Levski at ctr. r. on back.

	VG	VF	UNC
	FV	FV	35.00

106   2000 LEVA
1994. Black and dk. blue on m/c unpt. N. Ficev at l. and as wmk., bldg. outlines at ctr., wide hologram foil strip at l. Steeple, bldg. plans at ctr. r. on back.

	VG	VF	UNC
	FV	FV	65.00

107   5000 LEVA
3.7.1996. Red-violet on m/c unpt. Z. Stoyanov at l. and as wmk.; quill pen at ctr. r. Monument and *Proclamation to the Bulgarian People* (of 1885) on back.

	VG	VF	UNC
	FV	FV	140.00

108   10,000 LEVA
(1996).   Expected New Issue

BURMA

Burma, now called the Socialist Republic of the Union of Myanmar, a country of Southeast Asia fronting on the Bay of Bengal and the Andaman Sea, has an area of 261,789 sq. mi. (676,552 sq. km.) and a population of 41.5 million. Capital: Rangoon. Myanmar is an agricultural country heavily dependent on its leading product (rice) which embodies two-thirds of the cultivated area and accounts for 40 per cent of the value of exports. Petroleum, lead, tin, silver, zinc, nickel, cobalt and precious stones are exported.

The first European to reach Burma, about 1435, was Nicolo Di Conti, a merchant of Venice. During the beginning of the reign of Bodawpaya (1782-1819AD) the kingdom comprised most of the same area as it does today including Arakan which was taken over in 1784-85. The British East India Company, while unsuccessful in its 1612 effort to establish posts along the Bay of Bengal, was enabled by the Anglo-Burmese Wars of 1824-86 to expand to the whole of Burma and to secure its annexation to British India. In 1937, Burma was separated from India, becoming a separate British colony with limited self-government. The Japanese occupied Burma in 1942, and on Aug. 1, 1943 Burma became an "independent and sovereign state" under Dr. Ba Maw who was appointed the Adipadi (head of state) which collpased with the surrender of Japanese forces. Burma became an independent nation outside the British Commonwealth on Jan. 4, 1948, the constitution of 1948 providing for a parliamentary democracy and the nationalization of certain industries. However, political and economic problems persisted, and on March 2, 1962, Gen. Ne Win took over the government, suspended the constitution, installed himself as chief of state, and pursued a socialistic program with nationalization of nearly all industry and trade. On Jan. 4, 1974, a new constitution adopted by referendum established Burma as a "socialist republic" under one-party rule. The country name was changed to Union of Myanmar in 1989.

MONETARY SYSTEM:
1 Kyat = 100 Pya, 1943-1945, 1952-

REPUBLIC

PEOPLES BANK OF BURMA

1965 ND ISSUE
#52-55 portr. Gen. Aung San at ctr. Wmk. pattern throughout paper. Printed in East Berlin. Replacement notes are special Burmese characters.

52   1 KYAT
ND (1965). Violet and blue. Back violet; fisherman at ctr. Serial # varieties.

	VG	VF	UNC
	.15	.30	1.00

53   5 KYATS
ND (1965). Green and lt. blue. Back green; man w/ox at ctr.

	VG	VF	UNC
	.15	.40	1.50

54 **10 KYATS**
ND (1965). Red-brown and violet. Back red-brown, woman picking
cotton at r.

VG	VF	UNC
.20	.50	2.00

55 **20 KYATS**
ND (1965). Brown and tan. Back brown; farmer on tractor at ctr. r.

VG	VF	UNC
.40	1.00	3.00

UNION OF BURMA BANK

1972-79 ND ISSUE
#56-61 various military portrs. of Gen. Aung San at l. and as wmk.

56 **1 KYAT**
ND (1972). Green and blue on m/c unpt. Ornate native wheel
assembly on back.

VG	VF	UNC
.10	.15	.60

57 **5 KYATS**
ND (1973). Blue and purple on m/c unpt. Palm tree on back.

VG	VF	UNC
.15	.35	.75

58 **10 KYATS**
ND (1973). Red, violet and m/c. Native ornaments on back.

VG	VF	UNC
.15	.40	1.00

59 **25 KYATS**
ND (1972). Brown and tan on m/c unpt. Mythical winged creature at
ctr. on back.

VG	VF	UNC
.25	.60	1.50

60 **50 KYATS**
ND (1979). Brown and violet on m/c unpt. Mythical dancer on back.

VG	VF	UNC
2.00	5.00	17.50

61 **100 KYATS**
ND (1976). Blue and green on m/c unpt. Native wheel and musical
string instrument at l. ctr. on back.

VG	VF	UNC
1.50	4.00	15.00

1985-87 ND Issue
#62-66 smaller notes. Various portr. Gen. Aung San as wmk.

62   15 KYATS
ND (1986). Blue-gray and green on m/c unpt. Gen. Aung San at l. ctr.
Mythical dancer at l. on back.

VG	VF	UNC
FV	.65	1.25

63   35 KYATS
ND (1986). Brown-violet and purple on m/c unpt. Gen. Aung San in
military hat at l. ctr. Mythical dancer at l. on back.

VG	VF	UNC
FV	1.00	2.50

64   45 KYATS
ND (1987). Blue-gray and blue on m/c unpt. Po Hla Gyi at r. 2 workers
w/rope and bucket, oil field on back.

VG	VF	UNC
FV	FV	3.00

65   75 KYATS
ND (1985). Brown and m/c. Gen. Aung San at l. ctr. Dancer at l. on
back.

VG	VF	UNC
FV	1.00	2.50

66   90 KYATS
ND (1987). Brown and green on m/c unpt. Seya San at r. Farmer
plowing w/oxen and rice planting on back.

VG	VF	UNC
FV	FV	4.00

The Republic of Burundi, a land-locked country in central Africa, was a kingdom with a feudalistic society, caste system and Mwami (king) for more than 400 years before independence. It has an area of 10,759 sq. mi. (27,834 sq. km.) and a population of 5.3 million. Capital: Bujumbura. Plagued by poor soil, irregular rainfall and a single-crop economy - coffee - Burundi is barely able to feed itself. Coffee, tea and cotton are exported.

Although the area was visited by European explorers and missionaries in the latter half of the 19th century, it wasn't until the 1890s that it, together with Rwanda, fell under European domination as part of German East Africa. Following World War I, the territory was mandated to Belgium by the League of Nations and administered with the Belgian Congo. After World War II it became a U.N. Trust Territory. Limited self-government was established by U.N.-supervised elections in 1961. Burundi gained independence as a kingdom under Mwami Mwambutsa IV on July 1, 1962. The republic was established by military coup in 1966.

RULERS:
Mwambutsa IV, 1962-1966
Ntare V, 1966

MONETARY SYSTEM:
1 Franc = 100 Centimes

KINGDOM

BANQUE D'EMISSION DU RWANDA ET DU BURUNDI

1964 ND PROVISIONAL ISSUE
#1-7 lg. *BURUNDI* ovpt. on face.

		VG	VF	UNC
1	**5 FRANCS** ND (1964 - old dates 15.5.1961; 15.4.1963). Lt. brown. Black ovpt. on Rwanda-Burundi #1.	25.00	70.00	210.00

		VG	VF	UNC
2	**10 FRANCS** ND (1964 - old date 5.10.1960). Gray. Red ovpt. on Rwanda-Burundi #2.	27.50	75.00	225.00

		VG	VF	UNC
3	**20 FRANCS** ND (1964 - old date 5.10.1960). Green. Black ovpt. on Rwanda-Burundi #3.	30.00	80.00	235.00

		VG	VF	UNC
4	**50 FRANCS** ND (1964 - old date 1.10.1960). Red. Black ovpt. on Rwanda-Burundi #4.	35.00	95.00	325.00

		VG	VF	UNC
5	**100 FRANCS** ND (1964 - old dates 1.10.1960; 31.7.1962). Blue. Red ovpt. on Rwanda-Burundi #5	27.50	75.00	225.00
6	**500 FRANCS** ND (1964 - old date 15.5.1961). Lilac brown. Black ovpt. on Rwanda-Burundi #6.	175.00	650.00	—

		VG	VF	UNC
7	**1000 FRANCS** ND (1964 - old date 31.7.1962). Green. Black ovpt. on Rwanda-Burundi #7.	125.00	550.00	1250.

BANQUE DU ROYAUME DU BURUNDI

1964 ISSUE

#8-14 arms at ctr. on back.

NOTE: #11b was prepared but apparently not released w/o ovpt. See #16b.

		VG	VF	UNC
8	**5 FRANCS** 1.10.1964; 1.12.1964; 1.5.1965. Lt. brown on gray-green unpt. 2 young men picking coffee beans at l.	2.00	6.00	30.00

		VG	VF	UNC
9	**10 FRANCS** 20.11.1964; 25.2.1965; 20.3.1965; 31.12.1965. Dk. brown on lilac-brown unpt. Cattle at ctr.	3.50	9.00	35.00

		VG	VF	UNC
10	**20 FRANCS** 20.11.1964; 25.2.1965; 20.3.1965. Blue-green. Dancer at ctr.	10.00	30.00	100.00

11   50 FRANCS

	VG	VF	UNC
1964-66. Red-orange. View of Bujumbura.			
a. Sign. titles: *LE VICE PRESIDENT* and *LE PRESIDENT*. 1.10.1964-31.12.1965.	18.00	75.00	165.00
b. Sign. titles: *L'ADMINISTRATEUR* and *LE PRESIDENT*. 1.7.1966.	—	—	—

12   100 FRANCS

	VG	VF	UNC
1964-66. Bluish purple. Prince Rwagasore at ctr.			
a. Sign. titles: *LE VICE PRESIDENT* and *LE PRESIDENT*. 1.10.1964; 1.12.1964; 1.5.1965.	6.00	35.00	165.00
b. Sign. titles: *L'ADMINISTRATEUR* and *LE PRESIDENT*. 1.7.1966.	—	—	—

13   500 FRANCS

	VG	VF	UNC
5.12.1964; 1.8.1966. Brown on yellow unpt. Bank at r.	45.00	175.00	—

14   1000 FRANCS

	VG	VF	UNC
1.2.1965. Green on m/c unpt. Kg. Mwami Mwambutsa IV at r.	150.00	450.00	—

REPUBLIC

BANQUE DE LA RÉPUBLIQUE DU BURUNDI

1966 PROVISIONAL ISSUE

#15-19 black ovpt: *DE LA REPUBLIQUE* and *YA REPUBLIKA* on face only of Banque du Royaume notes.
NOTE: Ovpt. on #17 has letters either 3, 2 or 2.6mm high.

15   20 FRANCS

	VG	VF	UNC
ND (1966 - old date 20.3.1965). Ovpt. on #10.	15.00	45.00	150.00

16   50 FRANCS

	VG	VF	UNC
ND (1966 - old dates 1.5.1965; 31.12.1965; 1.7.1966).			
a. Ovpt. on #11a.	17.50	60.00	225.00
b. Ovpt. on #11b.	35.00	85.00	260.00

17   100 FRANCS

	VG	VF	UNC
ND (1966).			
a. Ovpt. on #12a. (- old date 1.5.1965).	15.00	45.00	150.00
b. Ovpt. on #12b. (- old date 1.7.1966).	15.00	45.00	150.00

18   500 FRANCS

	VG	VF	UNC
ND (1966 - old dates 5.12.1964; 1.8.1966). Ovpt. on #13.	90.00	250.00	—

19   1000 FRANCS

	VG	VF	UNC
ND (1966 - old date 1.2.1965). Ovpt. on #14.	200.00	550.00	—

1968-75 ISSUES

Sign. varieties.

20   10 FRANCS

	VG	VF	UNC
1968; 1970. Red on green and blue unpt. "Place De La Revolution" monument at r. Sign. titles: *L'ADMINISTRATEUR* and *LE PRESIDENT*.			
a. 1.11.1968.	1.25	3.00	10.00
b. 1.4.1970.	.15	.50	2.50

21   20 FRANCS

1968-73. Blue on green and violet unpt. Dancer at ctr. Text on back.

	VG	VF	UNC
a. Sign. titles: *LE PRESIDENT* and *LE VICE-PRESIDENT*. 1.11.1968.	3.00	10.00	32.50
b. Sign. titles: *LE PRESIDENT* and *L'ADMINISTRATEUR*. 1.4.1970; 1.11.1971; 1.7.1973.	1.75	5.00	25.00

22   50 FRANCS

1968-73. Pale red on m/c unpt. Drummer at l. ctr.

	VG	VF	UNC
a. Sign. titles: *L'ADMINISTRATEUR* and *LE PRESIDENT*. 15.5.1968; 1.10.1968.	3.50	15.00	65.00
b. Sign. titles: *ADMINISTRATEUR* and *PRESIDENT*. 1.2.1970; 1.8.1971; 1.7.1973.	2.50	10.00	35.00

22A   50 FRANCS

	VG	VF	UNC
1.6.1975. Brown. Like #22b.	5.00	20.00	70.00

23   100 FRANCS

1968-75. Brown on pale orange, lilac and blue unpt. Prince Rwagasore at r.

	VG	VF	UNC
a. Sign. titles: *LE VICE-PRESIDENT* and *LE PRESIDENT*. 15.5.1968; 1.10.1968.	5.00	25.00	85.00
b. Sign. titles: *ADMINISTRATEUR* and *LE PRESIDENT*. 1.2.1970; 1.8.1971; 1.7.1973; 1.6. 1975.	4.00	15.00	65.00

24   500 FRANCS

1968-75. Brown. Bank at r.

	VG	VF	UNC
a. Sign. titles: *LE PRESIDENT* and *LE VICE-PRESIDENT*.1.8.1968.	50.00	150.00	450.00
b. Sign. titles: *LE PRESIDENT* and *L'ADMINISTRATEUR*. 1.4.1970; 1.8.1971.	50.00	150.00	450.00
c. Sign. titles: *LE PRESIDENT* and *LE VICE-PRESIDENT*. 1.7.1973; 1.6.1975.	50.00	150.00	500.00

25   1000 FRANCS

1968-75. Blue and m/c. Bird and flowers. Back blue and lt. brown; cattle at ctr.

	VG	VF	UNC
a. Sign. titles: *L'ADMINISTRATEUR* and *LE PRESIDENT*. 1.4.1968; 1.5.1971; 1.2.1973.	45.00	150.00	425.00
b. Sign. titles: *LE VICE-PRESIDENT* 1.6.1975; 1.9.1976.	45.00	150.00	425.00

26   5000 FRANCS

1968; 1971; 1973. Blue. Pres. Micombero in military uniform at r. Loading at dockside on back.

	VG	VF	UNC
a. Sign. titles: *LE VICE-PRESI ESIDENT* and *LE PRESIDEN T*.1.4.1968; 1.7.1973.	100.00	300.00	800.00
b. Sign. title: *L'ADMINISTRATEUR*. 1.5.1971.	110.00	325.00	875.00

1975-78 ISSUE

#27-31 face like #20-26. Arms at ctr. on back.

27   20 FRANCS

1977-91. Red on m/c unpt. Face design like #21. Sign. titles: *LE GOUVERNEUR* and *L'ADMINISTRATEUR*.

	VG	VF	UNC
a. 1.7.1977; 1.6.1979; 1.12.1981.	FV	.50	2.00
b. 1.12.1983; 1.12.1986; 1.5.1988; 1.10.1989; 1.10.1991.	FV	FV	1.00

28   50 FRANCS

1.7.1977-1.5.1993. Brown on m/c unpt. Face like #22.

	VG	VF	UNC
a. 1.7.1977; 1.8.1979.	.15	.75	2.50
b. 1.12.1981; 1.12.1983.	FV	.50	2.00
c. 1.5.1988; 1.10.1989; 1.10.1991; 1.5.1993.	FV	.35	1.00

29   100 FRANCS

1977-93. Purple. Face design like #23. Sign. titles: *L'ADMINISTRATEUR* and *LE GOUVERNEUR*.

	VG	VF	UNC
a. 1.7.1977; 1.5.1979.	FV	1.00	3.50
b. 1.1.1981; 1.11.1982; 1.11.1984; 1.11.1986.	FV	.85	2.75
c. 1.5.1988; 1.7.1990; 1.5.1993.	FV	.65	1.75

30   500 FRANCS
1977-88. Dk. blue on m/c unpt. Face design like #24. Numeral and
date style varieties. Sign. titles: *LE GOUVERNEUR* and *LE VICE-
GOUVERNEUR.*

		VG	VF	UNC
a.	1.7.1977; 1.9.1981.	FV	6.00	22.50
b.	1.7.1985; 1.9.1986; 1.5.1988.	FV	5.00	15.00

31   1000 FRANCS
1977-91. Dk. green on m/c unpt. Like #25.

		VG	VF	UNC
a.	Sign. titles: *LE VICE-GOUVERNEUR* and *LE GOUV-ERNEUR.*1.7.1977; 1.1.1978; 1.5.1979; 1.1.1980.	FV	12.50	30.00
b.	1.1.1981; 1.5.1982; 1.1.1984; 1.12.1986.	FV	10.00	27.50
c.	Sign. titles: *L'ADMINISTRATEUR* and *LE VICE-GOUVERNEUR.* 1.6.1987.	FV	7.50	35.00
d.	Sign. titles: *LE VICE-GOUVERNEUR* and *LE GOUVERNEUR.* 1.5.1988; 1.10.1989; 1.10.1991.	FV	FV	20.00

32   5000 FRANCS
1978-95. Dk. brown and grayish purple on m/c unpt. Arms at upper
ctr.; bldg. at lower r. Ship dockside on back.

		VG	VF	UNC
a.	1.7.1978; 1.10.1981.	30.00	60.00	175.00
b.	1.1.1984; 1.9.1986.	FV	28.00	85.00
c.	1.10.1989; 1.10.1991.	FV	FV	70.00
d.	Sign titles: *LE 1ER VICE-GOUVERNEUR* and *LE GOUVERNEUR.* 10.5.1994; 25.5.1995.	FV	FV	62.50

1979-81 ISSUES

33   10 FRANCS
1981-95. Blue-green on tan unpt. Map of Burundi w/arms
superimposed at ctr. Text on back. Sign. titles: *LE GOUVERNEUR* and
ADMINISTRATEUR.

		VG	VF	UNC
a.	1.6.1981; 1.12.1983.	FV	FV	.75
b.	1.12.1986; 1.5.1988; 1.10.1989; 1.10.1991.	FV	FV	.50
c.	25.5.1995.	FV	FV	.35

34   500 FRANCS
1.6.1979; 1.1.1980. Tan, blue, violet and green. Back purple, brown
and orange. Similar to #30. Sign titles: *LE GOUVERNEUR* and *LE
VICE-GOUVERNEUR.*

VG	VF	UNC
5.00	12.50	40.00

1993-94 ISSUE
#37 *Deleted*, see #32d.

35   100 FRANCS
1.151993. Dull purple on m/c unpt. Similar to #29. Arms at lower l.,
brick home construction at ctr. on back. Sign. titles: *LE 1ER VICE-
GOUVERNEUR* and *LE GOUVERNEUR.*

VG	VF	UNC
FV	FV	3.00

36   1000 FRANCS
19.5.1994. Greenish black and brown-violet on m/c unpt. Steers at l.,
arms at lower ctr. Monument at ctr. on back. Sign. titles: *LE
GOUVERNEUR* and *LE 1ER VICE-GOUVERNEUR.* Wmk: Pres.
Micombero.

VG	VF	UNC
FV	FV	15.00

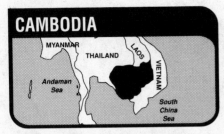

CAMBODIA

Cambodia, formerly known as Democratic Kampuchea and the Khmer Republic, a land of paddy fields and forest-clad hills located on the Indo-Chinese peninsula fronting on the Gulf of Thailand, has an area of 69,898 sq. mi. (181,035 sq. km.) and a population of 12 million. Capital: Phnom Penh. Agriculture is the basis of the economy, with rice the chief crop. Native industries include cattle breeding, weaving and rice milling. Rubber, cattle, corn, and timber are exported.

The region was the nucleus of the Khmer empire which flourished from the 5th to the 12th century and attained an excellence in art and architecture still evident in the magnificent ruins at Angkor. The Khmer empire once ruled over much of Southeast Asia, but began to decline in the 13th century as the Thai and Vietnamese invaded the region and attached its territories. At the request of the Cambodian king, a French protectorate attached to Cochin-China was established over the country in 1863, saving it from dissolution, and in 1885, Cambodia was included in the French Union of Indo-China. France established a constitutional monarchy for Cambodia within the French Union in 1949. The 1954 Geneva Convention resulted in full independence for the Kingdom of Cambodia. King Sihanouk abdicated to his father and won the office of Prime Minister.

Prince Sihanouk was toppled by a bloodless coup led by Lon Nol in March of 1970. Sihanouk moved to Peking to head a government-in-exile. On Oct. 9, 1970, Cambodia became the Khmer Republic, and Lon Nol its President. The government of Lon Nol was in turn toppled, April 17, 1975, by the Khmer Rouge insurgents who took control of the government and renamed the country Democratic Kampuchea.

The Khmer Rouge completely eliminated the economy and created a state without money, exchange or barter. Everyone worked for the state and was taken care of by the state. The Vietnamese supported People's Republic of Kampuchea was installed in accordance with the constitution of January 5, 1976. The name of the country was changed from Democratic Cambodia to Democratic Kampuchea, afterwards reverting to Cambodia.

In the early 1990's the UN attempted to supervise a ceasefire and in 1992 Norodom Sihanouk returned as Chief of State.

*** This section has been partially renumbered. ***

RULERS:
Norodom Sihanouk, (as Chief of State), 1960-1970
Lon Nol, 1970-1975
Pol Pot, 1975-1979
Heng Samrin, 1979-92
Norodom Sihanouk (as Chief of State), 1992-

MONETARY SYSTEM:
1 Riel = 100 Sen to 1975
1 New Riel = 10 Kak = 100 Su, 1975-

SIGNATURE VARIETIES			
GOVERNOR [លេខាធិការ]	**CHIEF INSPECTOR** [អគ្គនិរ្តេស]	**ADVISOR** [ទីប្រឹក្សាមួយនាក់]	**DATE**
1				28.10.1955
2				1956
3				1956
4				Late 1961
5				Mid 1962
6				1963
7				1965
8				1968
9				1968
10				1969
11				1970
12				1972

13				1972
14				1974
15				March, 1975 (Printed 1974)

CAMBODIA - KINGDOM

BANQUE NATIONALE DU CAMBODGE

1956 ND ISSUE
#6 Deleted. See #3a in Volume II, General Issues.

4	**1 RIEL**	VG	VF	UNC
	ND (1956-72). Grayish green on m/c unpt. Boats dockside in port of Phnom-Penh. Royal palace throne room on back. Printer: BW (w/o imprint).			
	a. Sign. 1.	1.00	3.00	15.00
	b. Sign. 2; 6; 7; 8; 10; 11.	.15	.25	1.25
	c. Sign. 12.	.10	.15	.25

5	**20 RIELS**	VG	VF	UNC
	ND (1956-72). Brown. Combine harvester at r. Phnom Penh pagoda on back. Wmk: Buddha. Printer: BWC (w/o imprint).			
	a. Sign. 3; 6; 8; 10.	.25	1.00	5.00
	b. Sign. 12.	.15	.25	1.25

7	**50 RIELS**	VG	VF	UNC
	ND (1956-72). Blue and orange. Fishermen fishing from boats w/lg. nets in Lake Tonle Sap at l. and r. Back blue and brown; Angkor Wat. Wmk: Buddha. Printer: TDLR (w/o imprint).			
	a. Western numeral in plate block designator. Sign. 3.	1.00	3.00	7.00
	b. Cambodian numeral in plate block designator. 5-digit serial #. Sign. 7; 10.	.25	.75	3.00
	c. As b. Sign. 12.	1.00	3.00	7.00
	d. Cambodian serial # 6-digits/ Sign. 12.	.10	.20	.35
	e. Cambodian & Western numeral in plate block designator. 6 digit serial #. Sign. 12.	.25	.75	2.00

8   100 RIELS
ND (1956-72). Brown and green on m/c unpt. Statue of Lokecvara at l. Long boat on back. Wmk: Buddha.

		VG	VF	UNC
a.	Imprint: *Giesecke & Devrient Munchen, AG.* Sign. 3; 7; 8; 11.	.50	1.50	8.00
b.	Imprint: *Giesecke & Devrient Munchen.* Sign. 12.	.10	.20	.65
c.	As b. Sign. 13.	.10	.20	.75

9   500 RIELS
ND (1956-70). Green and brown on m/c unpt. Sculpture of 2 royal women dancers "Devatas" at l. 2 dancers in ceremonial costumes on back. Wmk: Buddha. Printer: G&D.

		VG	VF	UNC
a.	Sign. 3; 6.	5.00	20.00	75.00
b.	Sign. 9.	.25	.75	5.00

1956-62 ND FIRST ISSUE

10   100 RIELS
(13)   ND (1956-72). Blue on m/c unpt. 2 oxen at r. 3 ceremonial women on back.

		VG	VF	UNC
a.	Printer: ABNC w/ imprint on lower margins, face and back. Sign. 3.	3.00	20.00	90.00
b.	W/o imprint on either side. Sign. 12.	.05	.25	1.00

11   500 RIELS
(14)   ND (1956-72). M/c. Farmer plowing w/2 water buffalo. Pagoda at r., doorway of Preah Vihear at l. on back. Wmk: Buddha. Printer BdF (w/o imprint).

		VG	VF	UNC
a.	Sign. 3.	.50	3.00	10.00
b.	Sign. 5; 7.	.50	2.00	8.00
c.	Sign. 9.	.50	1.50	6.00
d.	Sign. 12.	.15	.50	1.00
x.	Lithograph counterfeit; wmk. barely visible. Sign. 3; 5.	20.00	65.00	110.00
y.	As x. Sign 7; 9.	15.00	55.00	90.00

1956-62 ND SECOND ISSUE

12   5 RIELS
(10)   ND (1956-72). Red on m/c unpt. Bayon stone 4 faces of Avalokitesvara at l. Pagoda on back.

		VG	VF	UNC
a.	Sign. 4.	1.00	4.00	40.00
b.	Sign. 6; 7; 8; 11.	.20	.50	2.00
c.	Sign. 12.	.10	.25	.65

13   10 RIELS
(11)   ND (1962). Brown on m/c unpt. Temple of Bantael Srei. Bldg. at l. on back.

		VG	VF	UNC
a.	Sign. 5.	.25	.85	5.00
b.	Sign. 6; 7; 8; 11; 12.	.20	.40	1.00

14   100 RIELS
(12)   ND (1962). Blue-black, dk. green and dk. brown on m/c unpt. Sun rising behind Temple of Preah Vihear at l. Back blue, green and brown, w/distant view of road to a city on mountaintop. Wmk: Statue head. Printer: G&D.

		VG	VF	UNC
a.	Sign. 6.	1.00	3.00	20.00
b.	Sign. 13. (Not issued).	.10	.20	.60

KHMER REPUBLIC

BANQUE NATIONALE DU CAMBODGE

1973 ISSUE

15	100 RIELS	VG	VF	UNC
	ND. Purple on m/c unpt. Carpet weaving. Angkor Wat on back. (Not issued).			
	a. Sign. 13.	.10	.20	.75
	b. Sign. 14.	1.00	2.50	9.00

16	500 RIELS	VG	VF	UNC
	ND (1973). Green on m/c unpt. Girl w/vessel on head at l. Rice paddy scene on back.			
	a. Sign. 13; 14.	.15	.25	1.00
	b. Sign. 15.	.10	.20	.75

17	1000 RIELS	VG	VF	UNC
	ND. Green on m/c unpt. School children. Large sculptured head on back. Sign. 13. Printer: BWC. (Not issued).	.10	.20	.75

KAMPUCHEA

BANK OF KAMPUCHEA

1975 ISSUE

#18-24 prepared by the Khmer Rouge but not issued. New regime under Pol Pot instituted an "agrarian moneyless society." All notes dated 1975.

#20-24 wmk: Angkor Wat.

18	0.1 RIEL (1 KAK)	VG	VF	UNC
	1975. Purple, green, and orange on m/c unpt. Mortar crew l. Threshing rice on back.	.20	.50	2.00

19	0.5 RIEL (5 KAK)	VG	VF	UNC
	1975. Red on lt. green and m/c unpt. Troops marching at l. ctr. Ancient sculpture at l., machine and worker at r. on back.	.20	.50	2.00

20	1 RIEL	VG	VF	UNC
	1975. Red-violet and red on m/c unpt. Farm workers. at l. ctr. Woman operating machine on back.	.20	.50	2.00

21	5 RIELS	VG	VF	UNC
	1975. Deep green on m/c unpt. Ancient temples of Angkor Wat at ctr. r. Landscaping crew on back.	.20	.40	1.50

22	10 RIELS	VG	VF	UNC
	1975. Brown and red on m/c unpt. Machine gun crew at ctr. r. Harvesting rice on back.	.20	.50	2.00

23 50 RIELS
1975. Purple on m/c unpt. Planting rice at l., ancient sculpture at r. Woman's militia at ctr. r. on back.

	VG	VF	UNC
	.50	2.00	10.00

24 100 RIELS
1975. Deep green on m/c unpt. Factory workers at l. ctr. Back black; harvesting rice.

	VG	VF	UNC
	.50	2.25	12.00

STATE BANK OF DEMOCRATIC KAMPUCHEA

1979 ISSUE
#25-32 issued 20.3.1980 by the Vietnamese-backed regime of Heng Samrin which overthrew Pol Pot in 1979.

25 0.1 RIEL (1 KAK)
1979. Green on blue unpt. Arms at ctr. Water buffalos on back.

	VG	VF	UNC
	.10	.15	.25

26 0.2 RIEL (2 KAK)
1979. Dk. green on tan unpt. Arms at ctr. Rice workers on back.

	VG	VF	UNC
	.10	.20	.50

27 0.5 RIEL (5 KAK)
1979. Red-orange on yellow unpt. Arms at l., train at r. Men fishing from boats w/nets on back.

	VG	VF	UNC
	.10	.20	.50

28 1 RIEL
1979. Brown on yellow and m/c unpt. Arms at ctr. Women harvesting rice on back.

	VG	VF	UNC
a. Issued note.	.10	.20	.50
s. Specimen.	—	—	35.00

29 5 RIELS
1979. Dk. brown on lt. green and m/c unpt. 4 people at l., arms at r. Independence monument on back.

	VG	VF	UNC
a. Issued note.	.10	.30	1.00
x. Counterfeit.	.25	1.00	4.00

30 10 RIELS
1979. Gray and blue on m/c unpt. Arms at l., harvesting fruit trees at r. School on back.

	VG	VF	UNC
	.20	.50	2.00

31 20 RIELS
1979. Violet on pink and m/c unpt. Arms at l. Water buffalos hauling logs on back. Wmk: Arms.

	VG	VF	UNC
a. Issued note.	.10	.35	1.50
x. Lithograph counterfeit.	—	—	2.00

32 50 RIELS
1979. Red on green and m/c unpt. Arms at l., Bayon stone head at ctr. Angkor Wat on back. Wmk: Arms.

	VG	VF	UNC
	.10	.25	.75

1987 ISSUE

33 5 RIELS
1987. Like #29 but red and brown on lt. yellow and lt. green unpt. Back red on pale yellow unpt.

	VG	VF	UNC
	.10	.35	1.25

34 10 RIELS
1987. Like #30 but green on lt. blue and m/c unpt. Back deep green and lilac on lt. blue unpt.

	VG	VF	UNC
	.10	.35	1.50

CAMBODIA

NATIONAL BANK OF CAMBODIA -STATE BANK

1990-92 ISSUE

35 50 RIELS
1992. Dull brown on m/c. Arms at ctr., male portrait at r. Ships dockside on back. Wmk: Floral design. Printer: NBC.

	VG	VF	UNC
	FV	FV	.50

36 100 RIELS
1990. Dk. green and brown on lt. blue and lilac unpt. Independence monument at l. ctr., Achar Mean at r. Rubber trees on back. Wmk: Crowned monogram C-C. Issuer: State Bank.

	VG	VF	UNC
	FV	FV	1.00

37 200 RIELS
1992. Deep olive-green and brown on m/c unpt. Floodgates at r. Sculpture in Angkor Wat at ctr. on back. Wmk: Floral design. Printer: NBC.

	VG	VF	UNC
	FV	FV	1.50

38 500 RIELS
1991. Red, purple and brown-violet on m/c unpt. Arms above Angkor Wat at ctr. Animal statue at l., cultivating with tractors at ctr. on back. Wmk: Sculptured heads.

	VG	VF	UNC
	FV	FV	3.00

39 1000 RIELS
1992. Dk. green, brown and black on m/c unpt. Temple ruins in Angkor Wat. Fisherman fishing in boats w/lg. nets in Lake Tonle Sap on back. Wmk: Chinze. (Not released).

	VG	VF	UNC
	—	—	1.25

40 2000 RIELS
1992. Black on dp. blue and violet-brown and m/c unpt. Prince N. Sihanouk at l., and as wmk., Temple portal at r. (Not released).

	VG	VF	UNC
	—	—	3.25

1995 ISSUE

#41-47 printer F-CO.

#41 and 42 wmk: Cube design.

#43-45 N. Sihanouk at r. and as wmk.

41 100 RIELS
1995. Green on rose unpt. Lion statue, ancient tower at r. Tapping rubber trees on back.

	VG	VF	UNC
	FV	FV	.25

42 200 RIELS
1995. Dk. olive-green and brown on m/c unpt. Similar to #37.

	VG	VF	UNC
	FV	FV	.50

43 500 RIELS
1996. Red and purple on m/c unpt. Angkor Wot at r. Mythical animal at l., rice fields at ctr. on back.

	VG	VF	UNC
	FV	FV	1.10

44 1000 RIELS
(41)

	VG	VF	UNC
ND (1995). Blue-green on m/c unpt. Bayon stone 4 faces of Avalokitesvara at l. Back green on m/c unpt.; Prasat Chan Chaya at r.	FV	FV	2.00

45 2000 RIELS
(42)

	VG	VF	UNC
ND (1995). Reddish brown on m/c unpt. Fishermen fishing from boats w/nets in Lake Tonie Sap at l. and r. Temple ruins at Angkor Wat on back.	FV	FV	3.50

46 5000 RIELS
(43)

	VG	VF	UNC
ND (1995). Deep purple and blue-black w/black text on m/c unpt. Temple of Banteai Srei at lower l. ctr. New market in Phnom-Penh on back.	FV	FV	6.50

47 10,000 RIELS
(44)

	VG	VF	UNC
ND (1995). Blue-black and dk. green on m/c unpt. Statue of Lokecvara at lower l. ctr. People rowing long boat during the water festival at lower ctr. on back.	FV	FV	12.00

48 20,000 RIELS
(45)

	VG	VF	UNC
ND (1995). Violet and red on m/c unpt. Boats dockside in Port of Phnom-Penh at ctr. Throne Room in National Palace on back.	FV	FV	20.00

49 50,000 RIELS
(46)

	VG	VF	UNC
ND (1995). Dk. brown, brown and deep olive-green on m/c unpt. Preah Vihear Temple at ctr. Road to Preah Vihear Temple on back.	FV	FV	50.00

50 100,000 RIELS
(47)

	VG	VF	UNC
ND (1995). Green, blue-green and black on m/c unpt. Kg. and Qn. receiving homage of people on back.	FV	FV	95.00

REGIONAL

KHMER ROUGE INFLUENCE

1970 ND ISSUE
#R1-R4 w/sign. of Pres. Khieu Samphan.

R1 5 RIELS

	GOOD	FINE	XF
ca. 1970. M/c. Children harvesting vegetables at ctr., temple carvings at l. and r. Caravan of ox carts at ctr., temple carvings at l. on back.	125.00	300.00	500.00

R2 10 RIELS

	GOOD	FINE	XF
ca. 1970. M/c. Village at r. River village, boats at ctr., temple carvings at r. on back.	135.00	325.00	550.00

R3 20 RIELS

ca. 1970. M/c.	150.00	365.00	600.00

R4 50 RIELS
(R3)

ca. 1970. M/c.	165.00	400.00	650.00

			GOOD	FINE	XF
R5 (R4)	**100 RIELS** ca. 1970. M/c. Field workers at ctr., temple carvings at l. Temples of Angkor Wat at ctr., temple carvings at l. and r. on back.		175.00	425.00	700.00

FOREIGN EXCHANGE CERTIFICATES

MINISTERE DU TOURISME DU CAMBODGE

1961 BON TOURISTIQUE ISSUE

			VG	VF	UNC
FX1	**1 RIEL** ca. 1960's.		1.00	4.00	12.00

			VG	VF	UNC
FX2	**5 RIELS** 1961. Lt. green and violet w/black text. Black text on back.				
FX3 (FX2)	**5 RIELS** ca. 1960's.		1.00	4.00	12.00
FX4 (FX3)	**10 RIELS** ca. 1960's.		1.00	4.00	12.00

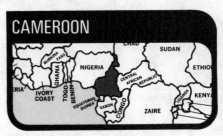

The United Republic of Cameroon, located in west-central Africa on the Gulf of Guinea, has an area of 185,568 sq. mi. (475,442 sq. km.) and a population of 12.2 million. Capital: Yaounde. About 90 per cent of the labor force is employed on the land; cash crops account for 80 per cent of the country's export revenue. Cocoa, coffee, aluminum, cotton, rubber and timber are exported.

European contact with what is now the United Republic of Cameroon began in the 16th century with the voyage of Portuguese navigator Fernando Po. The following three centuries saw continuous activity by Spanish, Dutch and British traders and missionaries. The land was spared colonial rule until 1884, when treaties with tribal chiefs brought German domination. After Germany's defeat in WWI, the League of Nations in 1919, divided the Cameroons between Great Britain and France, with larger eastern area going to France. The French and British mandates were converted into United Nations trusteeships in 1946. French Cameroon became the independent Cameroon Republic on Jan. 1, 1960. The federation of East (French) and West (British) Cameroon was established in 1961 when the southern part of British Cameroon voted for reunification with the Cameroon Republic, and the northern part for union with Nigeria.

See also Central African States, French Equatorial Africa and Equatorial African States.

* * *NOTE: This section has been renumbered.* * *

MONETARY SYSTEM:
1 Franc = 100 Centimes

SIGNATURE VARIETIES:
Refer to introduction to Central African States.

RÉPUBLIQUE DU CAMEROUN

BANQUE CENTRALE

1961 ND ISSUE
#7-9 denominations in French only, or French and English.

			GOOD	FINE	XF
7 (1)	**1000 FRANCS** ND (1961). M/c. Man w/basket harvesting cocoa. Sign. 1A.		150.00	500.00	1200.
8 (2)	**5000 FRANCS** ND (1961). M/c. Pres. A. Ahidjo at r. Sign. 1A.		75.00	250.00	900.00

			GOOD	FINE	XF
9 (2A)	**5000 FRANCS** ND. Like #2 but denomination also in English words at lower l. ctr. Sign. 1A.		150.00	500.00	1200.

RÉPUBLIQUE FÉDÉRALE DU CAMEROUN

BANQUE CENTRALE

1962 ND ISSUE
#10-13 denominations in French and English.
#11 and 12 exist as Engraved or lithographed. No price difference.

10	100 FRANCS	VG	VF	UNC
(3)	ND (1962). M/c. Pres. of the Republic at l. Ships on back. Sign. 1A.	5.00	25.00	75.00

11	500 FRANCS	VG	VF	UNC
(4)	ND (1962). M/c. Man w/2 oxen. Man w/bananas, road w/truck, 2 ships on back. Sign. 1A.	12.00	40.00	150.00

12	1000 FRANCS	VG	VF	UNC
(5)	ND (1962). M/c. Like #7 but w/title: *RÉPUBLIQUE FÉDÉRALE . . .* on back. Sign. 1A.	15.00	60.00	200.00
13	5000 FRANCS			
(6)	ND (1962). M/c. Like #9 but w/title: *RÉPUBLIQUE FÉDÉRALE . . .* on back. Sign. 1A.	50.00	150.00	450.00

1972 ND Issue

14	10,000 FRANCS	VG	VF	UNC
(7)	ND (1972). M/c. Pres. A. Ahidjo at l., fruit at ctr., wood carving at r. Statue at l. and r., tractor plowing at ctr. on back. Sign. 2.	35.00	75.00	200.00

RÉPUBLIQUE UNIE DU CAMEROUN

BANQUE DES ÉTATS DE L'AFRIQUE CENTRALE

1974 ND Issue

15	500 FRANCS	VG	VF	UNC
(8)	ND (1974; 1984); 1978-83. Red-brown and m/c. Woman wearing hat at l., aerial view of modern bldgs. at ctr. Mask at l., students and chemical testing at ctr., statue at r. on back.			
	a. Sign. titles: *LE DIRECTEUR GÉNÉRAL* and *UN CENSEUR.* Engraved. Wmk: Antelope in half profile. Sign. 3. ND (1974).	15.00	60.00	150.00
	b. As a. Sign. 5.	FV	6.00	15.00
	c. Sign. titles: *LE GOUVERNEUR* and *UN CENSEUR.* Wmk: Antelope in profile. Sign. 10. 1.4.1978.	FV	4.00	10.00
	d. Sign. 12. 1.6.1981; 2; 1.1.1983.	FV	3.00	7.50
	e. Sign. 12. 1.1.1982.	5.00	25.00	75.00

16	1000 FRANCS	VG	VF	UNC
(9)	ND (1974); 1978-82. Blue and m/c. Hut at ctr., girl w/plaits at r. Mask at l., trains, planes and bridge at ctr., statue at r. on back.			
	a. Sign. titles: *LE DIRECTEUR GÉNÉRAL* and *UN CENSEUR.* Engraved. Wmk: Antelope in half profile. Sign. 5. ND (1974).	FV	8.00	25.00
	b. Sign. titles like a. Lithographed. Wmk. like c. Sign. 8. ND (1978).	20.00	55.00	135.00
	c. Sign. titles: *LE GOUVERNEUR* and *UN CENSEUR.* Lithographed. Wmk: Antelope in profile. Sign. 10. 1.4.1978, 1.7.1980.	FV	5.00	18.00
	d. Sign. 12. 1.6.1981; 1.1.1982; 2; 1.1.1983.	FV	4.50	15.00

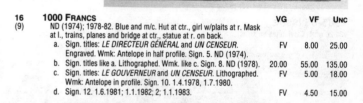

17	5000 FRANCS	VG	VF	UNC
(10)	ND (1974). Brown and m/c. Pres. A. Ahidjo at l., railway loading equipment at r. Mask at l., industrial college at ctr., statue at r. on back.			
	a. Sign. titles: *LE DIRECTEUR GÉNÉRAL* and *UN CENSEUR.* Engraved. Sign. 3. ND (1974).	50.00	175.00	375.00
	b. Like a. Sign. 5.	30.00	60.00	200.00
	c. Sign. titles: *LE GOUVERNEUR* and *UN CENSEUR.* Sign. 11; 12.	FV	35.00	60.00
18	10,000 FRANCS			
(11)	ND (1974; 1978; 1981). M/c. Pres. A. Ahidjo at l. Similar to #7 except for new bank name on back.			
	a. Sign. titles: *LE DIRECTEUR GÉNÉRAL* and *UN CENSEUR.* Sign. 5. ND (1974).	FV	50.00	130.00
	b. Sign. titles: *LE GOUVERNEUR* and *UN CENSEUR.* Sign. 11; 12. ND (1978; 1981).	FV	45.00	100.00

1981 ND ISSUE

19   **5000 FRANCS**   VG   VF   Unc
(12)   ND (1981). Brown and m/c. Mask at l., woman carrying bundle of   FV   15.00   50.00
     fronds at r. Plowing and mine ore conveyor on back. Sign. 12.

20   **10,000 FRANCS**   VG   VF   Unc
(13)   ND (1981). Brown, green and m/c. Stylized antelope heads at l.,   FV   30.00   80.00
     woman at r. Loading of fruit onto truck at l. on back. Sign. 12.

RÉPUBLIQUE DU CAMEROON

BANQUE DES ÉTATS DE L'AFRIQUE CENTRALE

1984 ND ISSUE

21   **1000 FRANCS**   VG   VF   Unc
(14)   1.6.1984. Blue and m/c. Like #9 except for new country name. Sign.   2.50   7.00   20.00
     12.

22   **5000 FRANCS**
(15)   ND (1984; 1990; 1992). Brown and m/c. Like #19 except for new   FV   12.50   35.00
     country name. Sign. 12; 13; 15.

23   **10,000 FRANCS**
(16)   ND (1984; 1990). Brown, green and m/c. Like #20 except for new   FV   25.00   60.00
     country name. Sign. 12; 13.

1985-86 ISSUE

#24-26 wmk: Carving (as on notes).

24   **500 FRANCS**   VG   VF   Unc
(17)   1985-. Brown on m/c unpt. Carving and jug at ctr. Man carving mask
     at l. ctr. on back.
     a.   Sign. 12. 1.1.1985-1.1.1988.   FV   2.50   5.00
     b.   Sign. 13. 1.1.1990.   FV   FV   4.00

25   **1000 FRANCS**   VG   VF   Unc
(18)   1.1.1985. Dk. blue on m/c unpt. Carving at l., small figurines at ctr.,   FV   5.00   18.50
     man at r. Incomplete map of Chad at top. Elephant at l., carving at r.
     on back.

26   **1000 FRANCS**   VG   VF   Unc
(19)   1986-. Like #18 but w/completed outline map of Chad at top ctr.
     a.   Sign. 12. 1.1.1986-1.1.1989.   FV   4.00   10.00
     b.   Sign. 13. 1.1.1990.   FV   4.50   11.00
     c.   Sign. 15.1.1.1992.   FV   3.75   8.00

CANADA

Canada is located to the north of the United States, and spans the full breath of the northern portion of North America from Atlantic to Pacific oceans, except for the State of Alaska. It has a total of 3,850,000 sq. mi. (9,971,550 sq. km.) and a population of 28.4 million. Capital: Ottawa.

Jacques Cartier, a French explorer, took possession of Canada for France in 1534, and for more than a century the history of Canada was that of a French colony. Samuel de Champlain helped to establish the first permanent colony in North America, in 1604 at Port Port Royal, Acadia - now Annapolis Royal, Nova Scotia. Four years later he founded the settlement in Quebec.

The British settled along the coast to the south while the French, motivated by a grand design, pushed into the interior. France's plan for a great American empire was to occupy the Mississippi heartland of the country, and from there to press in upon the narrow strip of English coastal settlements from the rear. Inevitably, armed conflict erupted between the French and the British; consequently, Britain acquired Hudson Bay, Newfoundland and Nova Scotia from the French in 1713. British control of the rest of New France was secured in 1763, largely because of James Wolfe's great victory over Montcalm near Quebec in 1759.

During the American Revolution, Canada became a refuge for great numbers of American Royalists, most of whom settled in Ontario, thereby creating an English majority west of the Ottawa River. The ethnic imbalance contravened the effectiveness of the prevailing French type of government, and in 1791 the Constitutional act was passed by the British parliament, dividing Canada at the Ottawa River into two parts, each with its own government: Upper Canada, chiefly English and consisting of the southern section of what is now Ontario; and Lower Canada, chiefly French and consisting principally of the southern section of Quebec. Subsequent revolt by dissidents in both sections caused the British government to pass the Union act, July 23, 1840, which united Lower and Upper Canada (as Canada East and Canada West) to form the Province of Canada, with one council and one assembly in which the two sections had equal numbers.

The union of the two provinces did not encourage political stability; the equal strength of the French and British made the task of government all but impossible. A further change was made with the passage of the British North American act, which took effect on July 1, 1867, and established Canada as the first federal union in the British Empire. Four provinces entered the union at first: Upper Canada as Ontario, Lower Canada as Quebec, Nova Scotia and New Brunswick. The Hudson's Bay Company's territories were acquired in 1869 out of which were formed the provinces of Manitoba, Saskatchewan and Alberta. British Columbia joined in 1871 and Prince Edward Island in 1873. Canada took over the Arctic Archipelago in 1895. In 1949 Newfoundland came into the confederation. Canada is a member of the Commonwealth of Nations. The Queen of England is Chief of State.

MONETARY SYSTEM:
1 Dollar = 100 Cents

DOMINION OF CANADA

BANQUE DU CANADA / BANK OF CANADA

"Devil's face"

Retouched

1954 'MODIFIED HAIRDO' ISSUE

		VG	VF	UNC
74	**1 DOLLAR**			
	1954 (1955-72). Black on green unpt. Qn.'s hair in modified style. Back green. Western praire scene. Printer: CBNC.			
	a. Sign. Beattie-Coyne. (1955-61).	1.25	3.00	12.50
	b. Sign. Beattie-Rasminsky. (1961-72).	1.00	1.50	7.50
75	**1 DOLLAR**			
	1954. (1955-73). Like #74. Printer: BABNC.			
	a. Sign. Beattie-Coyne. (1955-61).	1.00	2.00	12.50
	b. Sign. Beattie-Rasminsky. (1961-72).	1.00	1.50	5.00
	c. Sign. Bouey-Rasminsky. (1972-73).	1.00	1.50	5.00
	d. Sign. Lawson-Bouey. (1973).	1.00	1.50	5.50

		VG	VF	UNC
76	**2 DOLLARS**			
	1954. (1955-73). Black on red-brown unpt. Qn's hair in modified style. Back red-brown. Quebec scenery. Printer: BABNC.			
	a. Sign. Beattie-Coyne. (1955-61).	2.00	5.50	25.00
	b. Sign. Beattie-Rasminsky. (1961-72).	2.00	3.50	10.00
	c. Sign. Bouey-Rasminsky. (1972-73).	2.00	3.50	11.00
	d. Sign. Lawson-Bouey. (1973).	2.00	3.00	9.50

		VG	VF	UNC
77	**5 DOLLARS**			
	1954 (1955-72). Black on blue unpt. Qn.'s hair in modified style. Back blue; river in the north country. Printer: CBNC.			
	a. Sign. Beattie-Coyne. (1955-61).	7.50	15.00	45.00
	b. Sign. Beattie-Rasminsky. (1961-72).	5.00	7.50	27.50
	c. Sign. Bouey-Rasminsky. (1972).	5.00	7.50	27.50
78	**5 DOLLARS**			
	1954 (1955-61). Like #77. Sign. Beattie-Coyne. Printer: BABNC.	7.50	15.00	45.00

		VG	VF	UNC
79	**10 DOLLARS**			
	1954 (1955-72). Black on purple unpt. Qn.'s hair in modified style. Back purple; Rocky Mountian scene. Printer: BABNC.			
	a. Sign. Beattie-Coyne. (1955-61).	10.00	12.50	65.00
	b. Sign. Beattie-Rasminsky. (1961-72).	10.00	12.50	40.00

80　20 DOLLARS

		VG	VF	UNC
1954 (1955-69) Black on olive green unpt. Qn's hair in modified style. Back olive green. Laurentian hills in winter. Printer: CBNC.				
a. Sign. Beattie-Coyne. (1955-61).		22.50	27.50	100.00
b. Sign. Beattie-Rasminsky. (1961-69).		20.00	25.00	75.00

81　50 DOLLARS

		VG	VF	UNC
1954 (1955-71). Black on orange unpt. Qn's hair in modified style. Back orange; Atlantic coastline. Printer: CBNC.				
a. Sign. Beattie-Coyne. (1955-61).		50.00	65.00	165.00
b. Sign. Beattie-Rasminsky. (1961-72).		50.00	65.00	150.00
c. Sign. Lawson-Bouey. (1973-75).		50.00	85.00	275.00

82　100 DOLLARS

		VG	VF	UNC
1954 (1955-75). Black on brown unpt. Qn.'s hair in modified style. Back brown; mountain lake. Printer: CBNC.				
a. Sign. Beattie-Coyne. (1955-61).		100.00	135.00	250.00
b. Sign. Beattie-Rasminsky. (1961-72).		100.00	125.00	235.00
c. Sign. Lawson-Bouey. (1973-75).		100.00	135.00	250.00

83　1000 DOLLARS

		VG	VF	UNC
1954 (1955-87). Black on rose unpt. Qn's hair in modified style. Back rose; Central Canadian landscape.				
a. Sign. Beattie-Coyne. (1955-61).		1000.	1200.	1750.
b. Sign. Beattie-Rasminsky. (1961-72).		950.00	1100.	1750.
c. Sign. Bouey-Rasminsky. (1972-72).		950.00	1100.	1500.
d. Sign. Lawson-Bouey. (1973-84).		900.00	1050.	1350.
e. Sign. Thiessen-Crow. (1987).		950.00	1100.	1500.

1967 COMMEMORATIVE ISSUE
#84, Centennial of Canadian Confederation.

84　1 DOLLAR

		VG	VF	UNC
1967. Black on green unpt. Qn. Elizabeth II at r. Back green; First Parliament Building. Sign. Beattie-Rasminsky.				
a. *1867-1967* replacing serial #.		1.00	1.50	3.50

		VG	VF	UNC
b. Regular serial #'s.		1.00	1.50	4.50

1969-75 ISSUE
#85-91 arms at l.

85　1 DOLLAR

		VG	VF	UNC
1973. Black, lt. green on m/c unpt. Qn. Elizabeth II at r. Parliament Building as seen from across the Ottawa river on back.				
a. Sign. Lawson-Bouey.		FV	1.00	3.50
b. Sign. Crow-Bouey.		FV	1.00	2.50

86　2 DOLLARS

		VG	VF	UNC
1974. Red-brown on m/c unpt. Qn. Elizabeth II at r. Inuits preparing for hunt on back.				
a. Sign. Lawson-Bouey.		FV	2.00	6.50
b. Sign. Crow-Bouey.		FV	2.00	6.00

87 5 DOLLARS
1972. Blue on m/c unpt. Sir Wilfred Laurier at r. Serial # on face.
Salmon fishing boat at Vancouver Island on back.

	VG	VF	UNC
a. Sign. Bouey-Rasminsky.	FV	6.00	25.00
b. Sign. Lawson-Bouey.	FV	6.00	22.50

88 10 DOLLARS
1971. Purple on m/c unpt. Sir John A. MacDonald at r. Oil refinery at
Sarnia, Ontario, on back.

	VG	VF	UNC
a. Sign. Beattie-Rasminsky.	FV	12.00	40.00
b. Sign. Bouey-Rasminsky.	FV	12.00	45.00
c. Sign. Lawson-Bouey.	FV	FV	25.00
d. Sign. Crow-Bouey.	FV	FV	22.50
e. Sign. Thiessen-Crow.	FV	FV	20.00

89 20 DOLLARS
1969. Green on m/c unpt. Arms at l. Qn. Elizabeth II at r. Serial # on
face. Alberta's Lake Moraine and Rocky Mountains on back.

	VG	VF	UNC
a. Sign. Beattie-Rasminsky.	FV	22.50	70.00
b. Sign. Lawson-Bouey.	FV	22.50	65.00

90 50 DOLLARS
1975. Red on m/c unpt. W. L. MacKenzie King at r. Mounted Police in
Dome formation (from their Musical Ride program) on back.

	VG	VF	UNC
a. Sign. Lawson-Bouey.	FV	55.00	100.00
b. Sign. Crow-Bouey.	FV	50.00	95.00

91 100 DOLLARS
1975. Brown on m/c unpt. Sir Robert Borden at r. Lunenburg, Nova
Scotia harbor scene on back.

	VG	VF	UNC
a. Sign. Lawson-Bouey.	FV	105.00	160.00
b. Sign. Crow-Bouey.	FV	100.00	150.00

1979 ISSUE
#92 and 93 arms at l.

92 5 DOLLARS
1979. Blue on m/c unpt. Similar to #87, but different guilloches on
face. Serial # on back.

	VG	VF	UNC
a. Sign. Lawson-Bouey.	FV	FV	15.00
b. Sign. Crow-Bouey.	FV	FV	22.50

93 20 DOLLARS
1979. Deep olive-green on m/c unpt. Similar to #89, but different
guilloches on face. Serial # on back.

	VG	VF	UNC
a. Sign. Lawson-Bouey.	FV	FV	60.00
b. Sign. Crow-Bouey.	FV	FV	45.00
c. Sign. Thiessen-Crow.	FV	FV	25.00

1986-91 ISSUE
#94-100 arms at upper l. ctr.

94	**2 DOLLARS**	VG	VF	UNC
	1986. Brown on m/c unpt. Qn. Elizabeth II, Parliament Bldg. at r. Pair of robbins on back.			
	a. Sign. Crow-Bouey.	FV	FV	4.00
	b. Sign. Thiessen-Crow.	FV	FV	3.00
	c. Sign. Bonin-Thiessen.	FV	FV	2.50

95	**5 DOLLARS**	VG	VF	UNC
	1986. Blue-gray on m/c unpt. Sir Wilfred Laurier, Parliament bldgs. at r. Kingfisher on back.			
	a. Sign. Crow-Bouey.	FV	FV	9.00
	b. Sign. Thiessen-Crow.	FV	FV	7.00
	c. Sign. Bonin-Thiessen.	FV	FV	5.50

96	**10 DOLLARS**	VG	VF	UNC
	1989. Purple on m/c unpt. Sir John A. Macdonald. Parliament bldgs. at r. Osprey in flight on back.			
	a. Sign. Thiessen-Crow.	FV	FV	13.00
	b. Sign. Bonin-Thiessen.	FV	FV	11.00

97	**20 DOLLARS**			
	1991. Deep olive-green and olive-green on m/c unpt. Green foil optical device w/denom. at upper l. Qn. Elizabeth II, Parliament library at r. Loon on back.			
	a. Sign. Thiessen-Crow.	FV	FV	21.00
	b. Sign. Bonin-Thiessen.	FV	FV	20.00

98	**50 DOLLARS**	VG	VF	UNC
	1988. Red on m/c unpt. W. L. MacKenzie King, Parliament bldg. at r., gold optical device w/denomination at upper l. Snowy owl on back.			
	a. Sign. Thiessen-Crow.	FV	FV	50.00
	b. Sign. Bonin-Thiessen.	FV	FV	47.50

99	**100 DOLLARS**	VG	VF	UNC
	1988. Dk. brown on m/c unpt. Sir R. Bordon, Parliament bldg. at r., green optical device w/denomination at upper l. Canadian goose on back.			
	a. Sign. Thiessen-Crow.	FV	FV	95.00
	b. Sign. Bonin-Thiessen.	FV	FV	90.00

100	**1000 DOLLARS**	VG	VF	UNC
	1988. Pink on m/c unpt. Qn. Elizabeth II, Parliament library at r. Optical device w/denomination at upper l. Pine grosbeak pair on branch at r. on back.			
	a. Sign. Thiessen-Crow.	FV	FV	900.00
	b. Sign. Bonin-Thiessen.	FV	FV	875.00

CAPE VERDE

The Republic of Cape Verde, Africa's smallest republic, is located in the Atlantic Ocean, about 370 miles (595 km.) west of Dakar, Senegal off the coast of Africa. The 14-island republic has an area of 1,557 sq. mi. (4,033 sq. km.) and a population of 380,000. Capital: Praia. The refueling of ships and aircraft is the chief economic function of the country. Fishing is important and agriculture is widely practiced, but the Cape Verdes are not self-sufficient in food. Fish products, salt, bananas, coffee, peanuts and shellfish are exported.

The date of discovery of the islands is uncertain. Possibly they were visited by Venetian Captain Alvise Cadamosto in 1456. Portuguese navigator Diogo Gomes claimed them for Portugal in May of 1460. Settlement began two years later. The early importance and wealth of the islands, which caused them to be attacked by Sir Francis Drake and the Dutch, resulted from the monopoly of the Guinea slave trade granted the inhabitants in 1466. Poverty and famine occasioned by frequent periods of severe drought have marked the history of the country since abolition of the slave trade in 1876.

After 500 years of Portuguese rule, the Cape Verdes became independent on July 5, 1975. At the first general election, all seats of the new national assembly were won by the Party for the Independence of Guinea-Bissau and Cape Verde (PAIGC). The PAIGC once had plans to possibly link the two former Portuguese colonies into a common state.

RULERS:
Portuguese to 1975

MONETARY SYSTEM:
1 Escudo = 100 Centavos

PORTUGUESE INFLUENCE

BANCO NACIONAL ULTRAMARINO

CABO VERDE

1958 ISSUE
Decreto Lei 39221

#47-50 portr. Serpa Pinto at r., sailing ship seal at l. Allegorical woman looking out at sailing ships at ctr. on back. Sign. titles: *O-ADMINISTRADOR* and *VICE- GOVERNADOR*. Printer: BWC.

			VG	VF	UNC
47	**20 ESCUDOS**				
	16.6.1958. Green on m/c unpt.		1.50	5.00	27.50
48	**50 ESCUDOS**				
	16.6.1958. Blue on m/c unpt.		5.00	25.00	125.00

			VG	VF	UNC
49	**100 ESCUDOS**				
	16.6.1958. Red on m/c unpt.		3.00	10.00	37.50
50	**500 ESCUDOS**				
	16.6.1958. Brown-violet on m/c unpt.		15.00	50.00	160.00

1971; 1972 ISSUE
Decreto Lei 39221 and 44891

#52 and 53 portr. S. Pinto at r., bank seal at l., arms at lower ctr. W/security thread. Sign. titles: *ADMINISTRADOR* and *VICE-GOVERNADOR*.

		VG	VF	UNC
52	**20 ESCUDOS**			
	4.4.1972. Green on m/c unpt. 2 sign. varieties.	3.00	12.00	30.00

		VG	VF	UNC
53	**50 ESCUDOS**			
	4.4.1972. Blue on m/c unpt.	4.00	16.00	40.00
53A	**500 ESCUDOS**			
	16.6.1971; 29.6.1971. Olive-green on m/c unpt. Infante D. Henrique at r.	15.00	50.00	150.00

REPUBLIC

BANCO DE CABO VERDE

1977 ISSUE

#54-56 A. Cabral w/native hat at r. and as wmk. Printer: BWC.

		VG	VF	UNC
54	**100 ESCUDOS**			
	20.1.1977. Red and m/c. Bow and musical instruments at l. Mountain at l. ctr. on back.	1.50	3.50	8.50

		VG	VF	UNC
55	**500 ESCUDOS**			
	20.1.1977. Blue and m/c. Shark at l. Harbor at Praia on back.	7.00	12.50	25.00

		VG	VF	UNC
56	**1000 ESCUDOS** 20.1.1977. Brown and m/c. Electrical appliance at l. Workers at quarry at l. ctr. on back.	13.50	20.00	40.00

1989 ISSUE

#57-61 A. Cabral at r. and as wmk. Serial # black at l., red at r. Printer: TDLR.

		VG	VF	UNC
57	**100 ESCUDOS** 20.1.1989. Red and brown on m/c unpt. Festival on back.	FV	FV	4.50

		VG	VF	UNC
58	**200 ESCUDOS** 20.1.1989. Green and black on m/c unpt. Modern airport collage vertically at l. on back.	FV	FV	8.00
59	**500 ESCUDOS** 20.1.1989. Blue on m/c unpt. Shipyard on back.		FV	15.00

		VG	VF	UNC
60	**1000 ESCUDOS** 20.1.1989. Brown and red-brown on m/c unpt. Insects on back.	FV	FV	30.00
61	**2500 ESCUDOS** 20.1.1989. Violet on m/c unpt. Palace of National Assembly on back.	FV	FV	75.00

1992 ISSUE

#63-64 wmk: A. Cabral. Printer: TDLR.

		VG	VF	UNC
63	**200 ESCUDOS** 8.8.1992. Black and blue-green on m/c unpt. Sailing ship *Ernestina* at r. Back like #58.	FV	FV	7.00

		VG	VF	UNC
64	**500 ESCUDOS** 23.4.1992. Purple, blue and dk. brown on m/c unpt. Dr. B. Lopes da Silva at r. Back like #59.	FV	FV	14.00

		VG	VF	UNC
65	**1000 ESCUDOS** 5.6.1992. Dk. brown, red-orange and purple on m/c unpt. Bird at ctr. r. Grasshopper on back.	FV	FV	30.00

CAYMAN ISLANDS

The Cayman Islands, a British dependency situated about 180 miles (290 km.) northwest of Jamaica, consists of three islands: Grand Cayman, Little Cayman and Cayman Brac. The islands have an area of 102 sq. mi. (259 sq. km.) and a population of 26,950. Capital: Georgetown. Seafaring, commerce, banking and tourism are the principal industries. Rope, turtle shells and shark skins are exported.

The islands were discovered by Columbus in 1503, and were named by him, Tortugas (Spanish for "turtles") because of the great number of turtles in the nearby waters. The Cayman Islands were colonized from Jamaica by the British and remained dependencies of Jamaica until 1959, when they became a unit territory within the West Indies Federation. They became a separate colony when the Federation was dissolved in 1962.

RULERS:
British

MONETARY SYSTEM:
1 Dollar = 100 Cents

BRITISH INFLUENCE

CAYMAN ISLANDS CURRENCY BOARD

1971 CURRENCY LAW
#1-4 arms at upper ctr., Qn. Elizabeth II at r. Wmk: Tortoise. Printer: TDLR.

		VG	VF	UNC
1	**1 DOLLAR**	1.50	2.00	6.00
	L.1971 (1972). Blue on m/c unpt. Fish, coral at ctr. on back.			

		VG	VF	UNC
2	**5 DOLLARS**	8.00	10.00	20.00
	L.1971 (1972). Green on m/c unpt. Sailboat at ctr. on back.			

		VG	VF	UNC
3	**10 DOLLARS**	14.00	18.00	50.00
	L.1971 (1972). Red on m/c unpt. Beach scene at ctr. on back.			

		VG	VF	UNC
4	**25 DOLLARS**	35.00	45.00	110.00
	L.1971 (1972). Brown on m/c unpt. Compass and map at ctr. on back.			

1974 CURRENCY LAW
#5-11 arms at upper ctr., Qn. Elizabeth II at r. Wmk: Tortoise. Printer: TDLR.

		VG	VF	UNC
5	**1 DOLLAR**			
	L.1974 (1985). Like #1.			
	a. Sign. as #1 illustration.	FV	1.75	5.00
	b. Sign. Jefferson.	FV	1.50	3.00

		VG	VF	UNC
6	**5 DOLLARS**	FV	7.00	12.50
	L.1974. Like #2.			

		VG	VF	UNC
7	**10 DOLLARS**	FV	13.00	22.50
	L.1974. Like #3.			

		VG	VF	UNC
8	**25 DOLLARS**	FV	32.50	50.00
	L.1974. Like #4.			

		VG	VF	UNC
9	**40 DOLLARS**	FV	55.00	95.00
	L.1974 (1981). Purple and m/c. Pirates Week Festival (crowd on beach) at ctr. on back.			

10	**50 DOLLARS**	**VG**	**VF**	**UNC**
	L.1974 (1987). Blue on m/c unpt. Govt. house at ctr. on back.	FV	70.00	90.00

11	**100 DOLLARS**	**VG**	**VF**	**UNC**
	L.1974 (1982). Deep orange and m/c. Seacoast view of George Town at ctr. on back.	FV	135.00	175.00

1991 ISSUE

#12-15 arms at upper ctr., Qn. Elizabeth II at r., treasure chest at lower l. ctr. Red coral at l. on back. Wmk: Tortoise. Printer: TDLR.

12	**5 DOLLARS**	**VG**	**VF**	**UNC**
	1991. Dk. green and olive-brown on m/c unpt. Sailboat in harbor waters at ctr. on back.	FV	FV	10.00

13	**10 DOLLARS**	**VG**	**VF**	**UNC**
	1991. Red and purple on m/c unpt. Open chest, palm tree along coastline at ctr. on back. (2 varieties in color of conch shell at upper ctr. on back.)	FV	FV	20.00

14	**25 DOLLARS**	**VG**	**VF**	**UNC**
	1991. Dk. brown and brown on m/c unpt. Island outlines and compass at ctr. on back.	FV	FV	42.50

15	**100 DOLLARS**	**VG**	**VF**	**UNC**
	1991. Orange and dk. brown on m/c unpt. Harbor view at ctr. on back.	FV	FV	165.00

1996 ISSUE

16	**1 DOLLAR**	**VG**	**VF**	**UNC**
	1996. Purple and blue on m/c unpt. Back similar to #1.	FV	FV	3.00
17	**5 DOLLARS**			
	1996. Dk. green and olive-brown on m/c unpt. Back similar to #12.	FV	FV	9.00
18	**10 DOLLARS**			
	1996. Red and purple on m/c unpt. Back similar to #13.	FV	FV	17.50
19	**25 DOLLARS**			
	1996. Dk. brown and brown on m/c unpt. Back similar to #14.	FV	FV	40.00
20	**100 DOLLARS**			
	1996. Orange and brown on m/c unpt. Back similar to #15.	FV	FV	150.00

COLLECTOR SERIES

CAYMAN ISLANDS CURRENCY BOARD

1974, 1991 ISSUE

NOTE: Estimated availability of #CS1 is 300 sets.

		ISSUE PRICE	**MKT. VALUE**
CS1	**L.1974. 1-100 DOLLARS** #5-11 ovpt: SPECIMEN.	—	125.00
CS2	**1991 5-100 DOLLARS** #12-15 ovpt: SPECIMEN.	61.35	100.00

CENTRAL AFRICAN REPUBLIC

The Central African Republic, a landlocked country in Central Africa, bounded by Chad on the north, Cameroon on the west, Congo (Brazzaville) and Zaire on the south, and The Sudan on the east, has an area of 240,535 sq. mi. (622,984 sq. km.) and a population of 3.13 million. Capital: Bangui. Deposits of uranium, iron ore, manganese and copper remain to be developed. Diamonds, cotton, timber and coffee are exported.

The area that is now the Central African Republic was constituted as the French territory of Ubangi-Shari in 1894. It was united with Chad in 1905 and joined with Middle Congo and Gabon in 1910, becoming one of the four territories of French Equatorial Africa. Upon dissolution of the federation on Dec. 1, 1958, the constituent territories became full autonomous members of the French Community. Ubangi-Shari proclaimed its complete independence as the Central African Republic on Aug. 13, 1960.

On Jan. 1, 1966, Col. Jean-Bedel Bokassa, Chief of Staff of the Armed Forces, overthrew the government of President David Dacko and assumed power as president of the republic. President Bokassa abolished the constitution of 1959 and dissolved the National Assembly. In 1972 the Congress of the sole political party appointed Bokassa president for life. The republic became a constitutional monarchy on Dec. 4, 1976; President Bokassa was named Emperor Bokassa I. Bokassa was ousted as Central African emperor in a bloodless takeover of the government led by former president David Dacko on Sept. 20, 1979, and the African nation proclaimed once again a republic.

See also Central African States, Equatorial African States, and French African States. It is a member of the "Union MOnetaire des Etats de l'Afrique Centrale."

RULERS:
Emperor Bokassa I, 1976-79

MONETARY SYSTEM:
1 Franc = 100 Centimes

SIGNATURE VARIETIES:
Refer to introduction to Central African States.

RÉPUBLIQUE CENTRAFRICAINE

BANQUE DES ÉTATS DE L'AFRIQUE CENTRALE

1974-76 ND ISSUE

		VG	VF	UNC
1	**500 FRANCS** ND (1974). Lilac-brown and m/c. Landscape at ctr. Mask at l., students and chemical testing at ctr., statue at r. on back. Sign. 6.	6.00	25.00	75.00

2	**1000 FRANCS** ND(1974). Blue and m/c. Rhinoceros at l., water buffalo at ctr. Mask at l., trains, planes and bridge at ctr., statue at r. on back. Sign. 6.	VG 10.00	VF 35.00	UNC 100.00

3	**5000 FRANCS** ND(1974). Brown and m/c. Field workers hoeing at l., combine at ctr. Mask at l., bldgs. at ctr., statue at r. on back.	VG	VF	UNC
	a. Sign. 4.	30.00	90.00	275.00
	b. Sign. 6.	25.00	80.00	225.00

4	**10,000 FRANCS** ND(1976). M/c. Sword hilts at l. and ctr. Mask at l., tractor cultivating at ctr., statue at r. on back. Sign. 6.	VG 75.00	VF 185.00	UNC 500.00

EMPIRE CENTRAFRICAIN

BANQUE DES ÉTATS DE L'AFRIQUE CENTRALE

1978-79 ISSUE

#5-8 Emp. Bokassa I at r. Wmk: Antelope's head.

5	**500 FRANCS** 1.4.1978. Similar to #1. Specimen.	VG —	VF —	UNC 1500.
6	**1000 FRANCS** 1.4.1978. Similar to #2. Sign. 9.	50.00	150.00	450.00

7	**5000 FRANCS** ND(1979). Similar to #3. Sign. 9.	VG 50.00	VF 150.00	UNC 450.00

		VG	VF	UNC
8	**10,000 FRANCS** ND(1978). Similar to #4. Sign. 6.	50.00	150.00	350.00

RÉPUBLIQUE CENTRAFRICAINE (RESUMED)

BANQUE DES ÉTATS DE L'AFRIQUE CENTRALE

NOTE: For notes with similar back designs see Cameroon Republic, Chad, Congo (Brazzaville) and Gabon.
#9-10 wmk: Antelope's head.

1980 ISSUE

		VG	VF	UNC
9	**500 FRANCS** 1.1.1980; 1.7.1980; 1.6.1981. Red and m/c. Woman weaving basket at r. Back like #1. Lithographed. Sign. 9.	1.50	3.00	8.00

		VG	VF	UNC
10	**1000 FRANCS** 1.1.1980; 1.7.1980; 1.6.1981; 1.1.1982; 1.6.1984. Blue and m/c. Butterfly at l., waterfalls at ctr., water buffalo at r. Back like #2. Lithographed. Sign. 9.	3.50	6.50	15.00

		VG	VF	UNC
11	**5000 FRANCS** 1.1.1980. Brown and m/c. Girl at l., village scene at ctr. Carving at l., airplane, train crossing bridge and tractor hauling logs at ctr., man smoking a pipe at r. Similar to Equatorial African States #6. Sign. 9.	12.50	30.00	75.00

1983-84 ND ISSUE

		VG	VF	UNC
12	**5000 FRANCS** ND(1984). Brown and m/c. Mask at l., woman w/bundle of fronds at r. Plowing and mine ore conveyor on back. Sign. 9, 14.	FV	FV	35.00

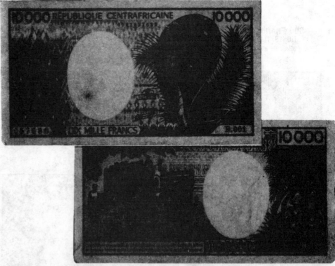

		VG	VF	UNC
13	**10,000 FRANCS** ND(1983). Brown, green and m/c. Stylized antelope heads at l., woman at r. Loading fruit onto truck at l. on back. Sign. 9.	FV	FV	65.00

1985 ISSUE
#14-16 wmk: Carving (as printed on notes). Sign. 9.

14	500 FRANCS	VG	VF	UNC
	1.1.1985; 1.1.1986; 1.1.1987; 1.1.1989; 1.1.1991. Brown on orange and m/c unpt. Carving and jug at ctr. Man carving mark at l. ctr. on back.	FV	FV	6.00

15	1000 FRANCS	VG	VF	UNC
	1.1.1985. Deep blue on m/c unpt. Carving at l., map at ctr., Gen. Kolingba at r. Incomplete map of Chad at top ctr. Elephant at l., animals at ctr., carving at r. on back.	FV	5.00	15.00

1986 ISSUE

16	1000 FRANCS	VG	VF	UNC
	1.1.1986-1.1.1990. Like #15 but complete outline map of Chad at topctr. Wmk: Carving. Sign. 9.	FV	FV	11.00

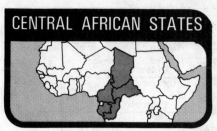
CENTRAL AFRICAN STATES

The Bank of the Central African States (BEAC) is a regional central bank for the monetary and customs union formed by Cameroon, Central African Republic, Chad, Congo (Brazzaville), Gabon, and (since 1985) Equatorial Guinea. It succeeded the Equatorial African States Bank in 1972-73 when the latter was reorganized and renamed to provide greater African control over its operations. The seat of the BEAC was transferred from Paris to Yaounde in 1977 and an African governor assumed responsibility for direction of the bank in 1978. The BEAC is a member of the franc zone with its currency denominated in CFA francs and pegged to the French franc at a rate of 50-1.

BEAC notes carry country names on the face and the central bank name on the back. The 1974-84 series had common back designs but were face-different. A new series begun in 1983-85 uses common designs also on the face except for some 1000 franc notes. The notes carry the signatures of *LE GOUVERNEUR* (*LE DIRECTEUR GENERAL* prior to 1-4-78) and *UN CENSEUR* (since 1972). Cameroon, Gabon, and France each appoint one censeur and one alternate. Cameroon and Congo notes carry the Cameroon censeur signature. Central African Republic, Equatorial Guinea, and Gabon notes carry the Gabon censeur signature. Chad notes have been divided between the two.

Prior to 1978, all BEAC notes were printed by the Bank of France. Since 1978, the 500 and 1000 franc notes have been printed by the private French firm Oberthur. The Bank of France notes are engraved and usually undated. The Oberthur notes are lithographed and most carry dates.

See the individual member countries for specific note listings. Also see Equatorial African States and French Equatorial Africa.

CONTROL LETTER or CODE

Country	1993 onward
Cameroun	E
Central African Republic	F
Chad	P
Congo	C
Equatorial Guinea	N
Gabon	L

SIGNATURE COMBINATIONS

1	Panouillot — Le Directeur-General	Gautier — Le President	1955–72
1A	Panouillot — Le Directeur-General	Duouedi — Un Censeur	1961–72
2.	Panouillot — Le Directeur-General	Koulla — Un Censeur	1972–73
3	Joudiou — Le Directeur-General	Koulla — Un Censeur	1974
4	Joudiou — Le Directeur-General	Renombo — Un Censeur	1974
5	Joudiou — Le Directeur-General	Ntang — Un Censeur	1974–77
6	Joudiou — Le Directeur-General	Ntoutoume — Un Censeur	1974–78
7	Joudiou — Le Directeur-General	Beke Bihege — Un Censeur	1977
8	Joudiou — Le Directeur-General	Kamgueu — Un Censeur	1978
9	Oye Mba — Le Gouverneur	Ntoutoume — Un Censeur	1978–90
10	Oye Mba — Le Gouverneur	Kamgueu — Un Censeur	1978–86
11	Oye Mba — Le Gouverneur	Kamgueu — Un Censeur	1978–80
12	Oye Mba — Le Gouverneur	Tchepannou — Un Censeur	1981–89
13	Oye Mba — Le Gouverneur	Dang — Un Censeur	1990

14	Mamalepot		Ntoutoume		1991
	Le Gouverneur		Un Censeur		
15	Mamalepot		Mebara		1991–93
	Le Gouverneur		Un Censeur		
16	Mamalepot		Ognagna		1994
	Le Gouverneur		Un Censeur		
17	Mamalepot		Kaltjob		1994–
	Le Gouverneur		Un Censeur		

CENTRAL AFRICAN STATES

BANQUE DES ÉTATS DE L'AFRIQUE CENTRALE

1993-94 ISSUE
#1-3 map of Central African States at lower l. ctr.

3 2000 FRANCS

		VG	VF	UNC
(19)93-. Dk. brown and green w/black text on m/c unpt. Woman's head at r. and as wmk. surrounded by tropical fruit. Exchange of passengers and produce w/ship at l. ctr. on back.				
c.	Sign. 15. (19)93; Sign. 16. (19)94.	FV	FV	12.50
e.	Sign. 15. (19)93; Sign. 17. (19)94.	FV	FV	12.50
f.	Sign. 15. (19)94; Sign. 16. (19)94.	FV	FV	15.00
l.	Sign. 15. (19)93. Sign. 16. (19)94.	FV	FV	13.50
n.	Sign. 15. (19)93. Sign. 16. (19)94.	FV	FV	13.50
p.	Sign. 15. (19)93; Sign. 16. (19)94.	FV	FV	15.00

1 500 FRANCS

		VG	VF	UNC
(19)93-. Dk. brown and gray on m/c unpt. Shepherd at r. and as wmk., zebus at ctr. Baobab, antelopes and Kota mask on back.				
c.	Sign. 15. (19)93; Sign. 16. (19)94.	FV	FV	4.50
e.	Sign. 15. (19)93; Sign. 17. (19)94.	FV	FV	4.50
f.	Sign. 15. (19)93; Sign. 16. (19)94.	FV	FV	5.00
l.	Sign. 15. (19)93; Sign. 16. (19)94.	FV	FV	4.50
n.	Sign. 15. (19)93; Sign. 16. (19)94.	FV	FV	6.00
p.	Sign. 15. (19)93; Sign. 16. (19)94.	FV	FV	5.00

4 5000 FRANCS

		VG	VF	UNC
(19)94-. Dk. brown, brown and blue w/violet text on m/c unpt. Laborer wearing hard hat at ctr. r., riggers w/well drill at r. Woman w/head basket at lower l., fisherman along shoreline at ctr. on back.				
c.	Sign. 16. (19)94.	FV	FV	27.50
e.	Sign. 17. (19)94.	FV	FV	27.50
f.	Sign. 16. (19)94.	FV	FV	30.00
l.	Sign. 16. (19)94.	FV	FV	25.00
n.	Sign. 16. (19)94.	FV	FV	25.00
p.	Sign. 16. (19)94.	FV	FV	30.00

2 1000 FRANCS

		VG	VF	UNC
(19)93-. Dk. brown and red w/black text on m/c unpt. Young man at r. and as wmk., harvesting coffee beans at ctr. Forest harvesting, Okoume raft and Bakele wood mask on back.				
c.	Sign. 15. (19)93; Sign. 16. (19)94.	FV	FV	8.00
e.	Sign. 15. (19)93; Sign. 17. (19)94.	FV	FV	8.00
f.	Sign. 15. (19)93; Sign. 16. (19)94; (19)95.	FV	FV	8.00
l.	Sign. 15. (19)93; Sign. 16. (19)94.	FV	FV	8.00
n.	Sign. 15. (19)93; Sign. 16. (19)94.	FV	FV	8.00
p.	Sign. 15. (19)93; Sign. 16. (19)94.	FV	FV	8.00

5 10,000 FRANCS

		VG	VF	UNC
(19)94-. Dk. brown and blue w/blue-black text on m/c unpt. Modern bldg. at ctr., young woman at r. Fisherman, boats and villagers along shoreline at l. ctr. on back.				
c.	Sign. 16. (19)94; (19)95.	FV	FV	45.00
e.	Sign. 17. (19)94.	FV	FV	45.00
f.	Sign. 16. (19)94.	FV	FV	50.00
l.	Sign. 16. (19)94.	FV	FV	47.50
n.	Sign. 16. (19)94.	FV	FV	47.50
p.	Sign. 16. (19)94.	FV	FV	50.00

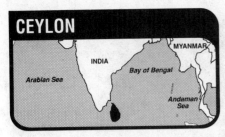

CEYLON

Ceylon (later to become the Democratic Socialist Republic of Sri Lanka), situated in the Indian Ocean 18 miles (29 km.) south-east of India, has an area of 25,332 sq. mi. (65,610 sq. km.) and population of 17.25 million. Capital: Colombo. The economy is chiefly agricultural. Tea, coconut products and rubber are exported.

The earliest known inhabitants of Ceylon, the Veddahs, were subjugated by the Sinhalese from northern India in the 6th century BC. Sinhalese rule was maintained until 1498, after which the island was controlled by China for 30 years. The Portuguese came to Ceylon in 1505 and maintained control of the coastal area for 150 years. They were supplanted by the Dutch in 1658, who were in turn supplanted by the British who seized the Dutch colonies in 1796, and made them a Crown Colony in 1802. In 1815, the British conquered the independent Kingdom of Kandy in the central part of the island. Constitutional changes in 1931 and 1946 granted the Ceylonese a measure of autonomy and a parliamentary form of government. Ceylon became a self-governing dominion of the British Commonwealth on February 4, 1948. On May 22, 1972, the Ceylonese adopted a new constitution which declared Ceylon to be the Republic of Sri Lanka - "Resplendent Island." Sri Lanka is a member of the Commonwealth of Nations. The president is Chief of State. The prime minister is Head of Government.

RULERS:
Dutch to 1796
British 1796-1972

MONETARY SYSTEM:
1 Rix Dollar = 48 Stivers
1 Rupee = 100 Cents, ca.1830-

CEYLON

CENTRAL BANK OF CEYLON

1962-64 ISSUE
#62-66 S. Bandaranaike at r. Back designs like #56-61. Various date and sign. varieties. Wmk: Chinze. Printer: BWC.

		VG	VF	UNC
62 (43)	**2 RUPEES** 8.11.1962-6.4.1965. Brown on lilac, green and blue unpt.	.75	2.50	9.00

		VG	VF	UNC
63 (44)	**5 RUPEES** 8.11.1962; 12.6.1964. Orange on brown and green unpt.	1.00	3.00	12.00

		VG	VF	UNC
64 (45)	**10 RUPEES** 12.6.1964; 28.8.1964; 19.9.1964. Green on purple, orange and blue unpt.	2.00	6.00	20.00

		VG	VF	UNC
65 (46)	**50 RUPEES** 2.11.1961; 5.6.1963; 6.4.1965. Blue and m/c.	6.00	17.50	65.00
66 (47)	**100 RUPEES** 5.6.1963. Brown and m/c.	12.50	30.00	100.00

1965-68 ISSUE
#67-71 statue of Kg. Parakkrama at r. Back designs like #56-61. Various date and sign. varieties. Wmk.: Chinze. Printer: BWC.

		VG	VF	UNC
67 (48)	**2 RUPEES** 9.9.1965; 15.7.1967; 10.1.1968. Brown on lilac, lt. green and blue unpt.	.50	1.50	4.50
68 (49)	**5 RUPEES** 9.9.1965; 15.7.1967; 1.9.1967; 10.1.1968. Orange on brown and green unpt.	.75	2.00	7.00
69 (50)	**10 RUPEES** 10.1.1968. Green on purple, orange and blue unpt.	1.50	4.00	10.00
70 (51)	**50 RUPEES** 7.3.1967; 10.1.1968. Blue and m/c.	6.00	12.50	45.00
71 (52)	**100 RUPEES** 28.5.1966; 22.11.1966; 10.1.1968. Brown and m/c.	12.50	25.00	65.00

1968-69 ISSUE
#72-76 w/bank name in English on both sides. Various date and sign. varieties. Wmk.: Chinze. Printer: BWC.

		VG	VF	UNC
72 (53)	**2 RUPEES** 1969-77. Like #67.			
	a. 10.5.1969-12.5.1972.	.25	.75	1.50
	b. 21.8.1973; 27.8.1974; 26.8.1977.	.25	.75	3.50

		VG	VF	UNC
73	**5 RUPEES**			
(54)	1969-77. Like #68.			
	a. 10.5.1969; 1.6.1970; 1.2.1971.	.40	1.00	5.00
	b. 21.8.1973; 16.7.1974; 27.8.1974; 26.8.1977.	.40	1.00	4.50

		VG	VF	UNC
74	**10 RUPEES**			
(55)	1969-77. Like #69.			
	a. 20.10.1969; 1.6.1970; 1.2.1971; 7.6.1971.	1.00	2.50	8.50
	b. 21.8.1973; 16.7.1974; 6.10.1975; 26.8.1977.	1.00	2.50	7.50
75	**50 RUPEES**			
(56)	20.10.1969. Like #70.	3.50	7.50	37.50

		VG	VF	UNC
76	**100 RUPEES**			
(57)	10.1.1968; 28.5.1968; 10.5.1969. Like #71.	4.00	12.50	50.00

1970 ISSUE

#58-59 Smiling Pres. Bandaranaike w/raised hand. Wmk.: Chinze. Printer: TDLR.

		VG	VF	UNC
77	**50 RUPEES**			
(58)	26.10.1970; 9.12.1970. Blue on lilac, yellow and brown unpt. Monument on back.	3.00	12.50	45.00
78	**100 RUPEES**			
(59)	26.10.1970; 9.12.1970. Purple and m/c. Female dancers on back.	5.50	20.00	65.00

1971-72 ISSUE

#79-80 Pres. Bandaranaike smiling w/o hand raised. Wmk.: Chinze. Printer: BWC.

		VG	VF	UNC
79	**50 RUPEES**			
(60)	28.12.1972; 27.8.1974. Purple and m/c. Landscape on back.	3.00	12.00	40.00

		VG	VF	UNC
80	**100 RUPEES**			
(61)	18.12.1971; 16.7.1974; 27.8.1974; 6.10.1975. Purple, gray and m/c. Ornate stairway on back.	5.00	18.00	60.00

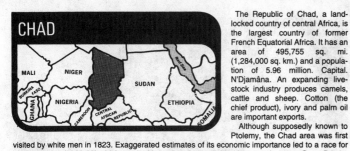

CHAD

The Republic of Chad, a landlocked country of central Africa, is the largest country of former French Equatorial Africa. It has an area of 495,755 sq. mi. (1,284,000 sq. km.) and a population of 5.96 million. Capital. N'Djamâna. An expanding livestock industry produces camels, cattle and sheep. Cotton (the chief product), ivory and palm oil are important exports.

Although supposedly known to Ptolemy, the Chad area was first visited by white men in 1823. Exaggerated estimates of its economic importance led to a race for its possession (1890-93) which resulted in territory being divided by treaty between Great Britain, France and Germany. As a consequence of World War I, the German area was mandated to France in 1919. Chad was absorbed into the colony of French Equatorial Africa, as a part of Ubangi-Shari, in 1910 and became a separate colony in 1920. Upon dissolution of French Equatorial Africa in 1959, the component states became autonomous members of the French Union. Chad became an independent republic on Aug. 11, 1960.

MONETARY SYSTEM:
1 Franc = 100 Centimes

SIGNATURE VARIETIES:
Refer to introduction to Central African States.

NOTE: For later issues see Central African States.

RÉPUBLIQUE DU TCHAD

BANQUE CENTRALE

1971 ISSUE

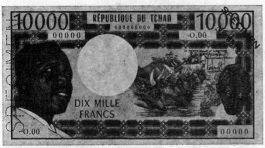

	10,000 FRANCS	VG	VF	UNC
1	ND(1971). M/c. Pres. Tombalbaye at l., cattle watering at ctr. Mask at l., tractor plowing at ctr., statue at r. on back. Sign. 1.	125.00	350.00	900.00

BANQUE DES ÉTATS DEL'AFRIQUE CENTRAL

1974-78; ND ISSUE

	500 FRANCS	VG	VF	UNC
2	ND(1974); 1978. Brown and m/c. Woman at l., birds at ctr. and at r. Mask at l., students and chemical testing at ctr., statue at r. on back.			
	a. Sign. titles and wmk. like #3a. Sign. 6. (1974).	2.50	7.50	20.00
	b. Sign. titles, wmk. and date like #3c. Sign. 10. 1.4.1978.	20.00	75.00	150.00

	1000 FRANCS	VG	VF	UNC
3	ND; 1.4.1978. Blue and m/c. Woman at r. Mask at l., trains, planes and bridge at ctr., statue at r. on back.			
	a. Sign. titles: *LE DIRECTEUR GÉNÉRAL* and *UN CENSEUR*. Engraved. Wmk. Antelope. in half profile. Sign. 5; 7.	4.00	15.00	45.00
	b. Sign. titles: *LE DIRECTEUR GÉNÉRAL* and *UN CENSEUR*. Lithographed. Wmk: Antelope in profile. Sign. 8.	3.00	11.50	30.00
	c. Sign. titles: *LE GOUVERNEUR* and *UN CENSEUR*. Sign. 10. 1.4.1978.	FV	8.00	22.50
4	**5000 FRANCS** ND (1974). Brown-orange and m/c. Pres. Tombalbaye at l. Mask at l., industrial college at ctr., statue at r. on back. Sign. 4.	100.00	250.00	650.00
5	**5000 FRANCS** ND. Brown and m/c. Woman at l. Like #4 on back.			
	a. Sign. 6. (1976).	22.50	40.00	120.00
	b. Sign. 9. (1978).	20.00	35.00	80.00

1980 ISSUE

	500 FRANCS	VG	VF	UNC
6	1.6.1980; 1.6.1984. Red and m/c. Woman weaving basket at r. Sign. 10	FV	3.00	9.00

	1000 FRANCS	VG	VF	UNC
7	1.6.1980; 1.6.1984. Blue and m/c. Water buffalo at r. Back like #3. Sign. 9; 10.	3.00	8.50	20.00

			VG	VF	UNC
8	**5000 FRANCS** 1.1.1980. Brown and m/c. Girl at l., village scene at ctr. Back w/carving, airplane, train, tractor and man smoking pipe. Similar to Central African Republic #11 and others. Sign. 9.		FV	30.00	75.00

			VG	VF	UNC
10A	**1000 FRANCS** 1985-91. Like #10 but complete outline map of Chad at top ctr.				
	a. Sign. 9. 1.1.1985; 1.1.1988; 1 ; 1.1.1989; 1.1.1990.		FV	FV	12.50
	b. Sign. 15. 1.1.1991; 1.1.1992.		FV	FV	11.00

1984-85; ND ISSUE

NOTE: #10 was withdrawn shortly after issue because of the error (incompleteness) at top of the map.

NOTE: For notes with similar back designs see Cameroon Republic, Central African Republic, Congo (Brazzaville) and Gabon.

			VG	VF	UNC
11	**5000 FRANCS** ND(1984-91). Brown and m/c. Mask at l., woman w/bundle of fronds at r. Plowing and mine ore conveyor on back. Sign. 9; 15.		FV	FV	40.00
12	**10,000 FRANCS** ND(1984-91). Brown, green and m/c. Stylized antelope heads at l., woman at r. Loading fruit onto truck at l. on back. Sign. 9; 15.		FV	FV	65.00

			VG	VF	UNC
9	**500 FRANCS** 1985-92. Brown on m/c unpt. Carved statue and jug at ctr. Man carving mask at l. ctr. on back. Wmk: Carving.				
	a. Sign. 10. 1.1.1985; 1.1.1986 6		FV	FV	8.00
	b. Sign. 12. 1.1.1987.		FV	FV	7.00
	c. Sign. 13. 1.1.1990.		FV	FV	7.00
	d. Sign. 15. 1.1.1991; 1.1.1992. 2.		FV	FV	6.00

			VG	VF	UNC
10	**1000 FRANCS** 1.1.1985. Blue and m/c. Animal carving at lower l., map at ctr., starburst at lower r. Incomplete outline map of Chad at top ctr. Elephant at l., statue at r. on back. Wmk: Animal carving. Sign. 9.		10.00	25.00	75.00

CHILE

The Republic of Chile, a ribbon-like country on the Pacific coast of southern South America, has an area of 292,258 sq. mi. (756,945 sq. km.) and a population of 13.3 million. Capital: Santiago. Historically, the economic base of Chile has been the rich mineral deposits of its northern provinces. Copper, of which Chile has 25 percent of the free world's reserves, has accounted for more than 75 per cent of Chile's export earnings in recent years. Other important exports are iron ore, iodine, fruit and nitrate of soda.

Diego de Almargo was the first Spaniard to attempt to wrest Chile from the Incas and Araucanian tribes, 1536. He failed, and was followed by Pedro de Valdivia, a favorite of Pizarro, who founded Santiago in 1541. When the Napoleonic Wars involved Spain, leaving the constituent parts of the Spanish Empire to their own devices, Chilean patriots formed a national government and proclaimed the country's independence, Sept. 18, 1810. Independence, however, was not secured until Feb. 12, 1818, after a bitter struggle led by Bernardo O'Higgins and San Martin.

MONETARY SYSTEM:
1 Escudo = 100 Centesimos, 1960-75
1 Peso = 100 Escudos, 1975-

REPUBLIC

BANCO CENTRAL DE CHILE

1960 PROVISIONAL ISSUE

#124-133 Escudo denominations in red as part of new plates (not ovpt., except #124). on back. Sign. varieties. Printer: CdM- Chile.

		VG	VF	UNC
124	**1/2 CENTESIMO ON 5 PESOS** ND (1960-61). Blue. Ovpt. on #119.	—	—	—

		VG	VF	UNC
125	**1 CENTESIMO ON 10 PESOS** ND (1960-61). Red-brown. Ovpt. on #120.	.50	1.00	6.00

		VG	VF	UNC
126	**5 CENTESIMOS ON 50 PESOS** ND(1960-61). Green ovpt. on #121. Wmk: *L, V* or *X* below portr.			
	a. Imprint 25mm wide.	.50	2.00	5.00
	b. Imprint 22mm wide.	.10	.20	.50

		VG	VF	UNC
127	**10 CENTESIMOS ON 100 PESOS** ND(1960-61). Red on yellow-green unpt. Ovpt. on #122. Wmk: *C, L, V* or *X* below portr.	.10	.25	.75

		VG	VF	UNC
128	**50 CENTESIMOS ON 500 PESOS** ND(1960-61). Blue. Ovpt. on #115.	.50	2.50	10.00

		VG	VF	UNC
129	**1 ESCUDO ON 1000 PESOS** ND(1960-61). Brown. Ovpt. on #116.	.50	1.50	7.50

		VG	VF	UNC
130	**5 ESCUDOS ON 5000 PESOS** ND(1960-61). Brown-violet. Ovpt. on #117.	1.00	3.00	15.00

		VG	VF	UNC
131	**10 ESCUDOS ON 10,000 PESOS** ND(1960-61). Purple on lt. blue unpt. Ovpt. on #118. Dual wmk: Head at l., words *DIEZ MIL* at r.	2.00	10.00	35.00
132	**10 ESCUDOS ON 10,000 PESOS** ND(1960-61). Red-brown. Similar to #131 but w/o wmk. at r.	2.50	15.00	45.00
133	**50 ESCUDOS ON 50,000 PESOS** ND (1960-61). Blue-green and brown on m/c unpt. Ovpt. on #123.	4.50	17.50	60.00

1962-64 ND ISSUE

#134-140 sign. varieties. Wmk: D. Diego Portales P. Printer: CdM-Chile.

134 1/2 ESCUDO
ND(1962). Blue. Portr. B. O'Higgins at ctr. Explorer on horseback at l. ctr. on back.

		VG	VF	UNC
a.	Lt. blue and peach unpt. Red serial #.	.15	.50	1.50
b.	Lt. brown unpt. Black serial #.	.10	.25	1.00

135 1 ESCUDO
ND. Brown-violet w/lilac guilloche on tan unpt. Portr. Prat at ctr. Red-brown arms w/founding of Santiago on back. Engraved. Serial # black (3mm) or brown (4mm).

		VG	VF	UNC
a.	Wmk: 1000 at r.	.50	2.00	7.50
b.	Wmk: 500 at r.	.50	1.50	4.00
c.	W/o wmk. at r. Arms in red-brown on back.	.20	.50	1.00
d.	W/o wmk. at r. Arms in olive on back.	.10	.20	.75

136 1 ESCUDO
ND (1964). Dull violet on tan unpt. Like #135 but arms on back in lt. olive. Lithographed.

VG	VF	UNC
.10	.30	.50

137 5 ESCUDOS
ND. Brown. Portr. Bulnes at ctr. Yellow-orange arms ar l. Battle of Rancagua at ctr. arms at l. on back.

VG	VF	UNC
.75	2.00	5.00

138 5 ESCUDOS
ND (1964). Red. Like #137. Red-brown arms at l. on back.

VG	VF	UNC
.10	.25	1.00

139 10 ESCUDOS
ND. Lilac. Portr. M. Balmaceda at ctr. Dk. or lt. brown arms at l. soldiers meeting at ctr. on back.

VG	VF	UNC
.25	.75	4.00

140 50 ESCUDOS
ND. Green on m/c unpt. Portr. Alessandri at ctr. Back brown and green; Banco Central bldg.

VG	VF	UNC
.10	.25	1.00

141 100 ESCUDOS
ND. Blue and brown on tan unpt. Rengifo at r. Sailing ships at ctr. arms at l. on back.

VG	VF	UNC
.25	.75	3.00

1970-74 ND ISSUES
#142-148 sign. varieties. Wmk: D. Diego Portales P. Printer: CdM-Chile.

142 10 ESCUDOS
ND(1970). Red-brown, blue and green. M. Balmaceda at r.

		VG	VF	UNC
a.	Brown lower margin on back. Engraved.	.20	.50	2.00
b.	Green lower margin on back. Lithographed.	.20	.50	2.00

143 10 ESCUDOS
ND(1973). Brown. Like #142 but lithographed.

VG	VF	UNC
.10	.25	.75

144   500 ESCUDOS

		VG	VF	UNC
ND(1972). Red-brown and m/c. Steel worker at l. Strip mining at ctr. r. on back (mining). W/o 3-line text: *NO DEBEMOS CONSENTIRE* at bottom.		65.00	200.00	—

145   500 ESCUDOS

ND. Like #144 but w/3-line text: *NO DEBEMOS CONSENTIRE* on back at bottom.		.15	.50	2.50

146   1000 ESCUDOS

		VG	VF	UNC
ND(1973). Purple and m/c. Carrera at l. Back like #147.		15.00	.50	3.00

147   5000 ESCUDOS

	VG	VF	UNC
ND(1974). Dk. green and brown on m/c unpt. Carrera at l. Carrera House at ctr. r. on back.			
a. Back w/deep green vignette. Lithographed.	.50	1.50	5.00
b. Back w/dk. olive-green vignette. Partially engraved.	.30	.75	3.00

148   10,000 ESCUDOS

	VG	VF	UNC
ND (1974). Red-brown on m/c unpt. B. O'Higgins at l. Blue serial #. Battle of Rancagua on back.	.50	2.00	6.00

1975-89 ISSUE
#149-153 wmk: D. Diego Portales P. Sign. varieties.
#152-156 printer: CdM-Chile.

149   5 PESOS

	VG	VF	UNC
1975-76. Green on olive unpt. Carrera at r. and as wmk. Back similar to #147.	.40	1.00	3.00

150   10 PESOS

	VG	VF	UNC
1975-76. Red. B. O'Higgins at r. and as wmk. Back similar to #148.			
a. *B. O'HIGGINS* under portr. 1975.	.40	1.00	3.00
b. *LIBERTADOR B. O'HIGGINS* under portr. 1975; 1976.	.25	.75	2.00

151   50 PESOS

	VG	VF	UNC
1975-81. Aqua, purple and green. Portr. Prat at r. Sailing ships at ctr. on back. Wmk: Men in uniforms.			
a. 1975-78.	FV	.50	2.00
b. 1980; 1981.	FV	.25	1.00

152 100 PESOS
1976-84. Purple and m/c unpt. Portales at r. 1837 meeting at ctr. on back.

		VG	VF	UNC
a.	Normal serial #. 1976.	FV	1.00	3.00
b.	Electronic sorting serial #. 1976-84.	FV	FV	2.50

153 500 PESOS
1977-. Dk. brown w/black text on m/c unpt. Valdivia at r. wmk. Founding of Santiago at ctr. on back.

		VG	VF	UNC
a.	1977; 1978.	FV	1.50	6.00
b.	1980-82; 1985-90; 1992.	FV	FV	3.50
c.	1994; 1995.	FV	FV	2.75

154 1000 PESOS
1978-. Dk. blue-green and dk. olive-brown, green and m/c. l. Carrera Pinto at r. and as wmk., military arms at ctr. Monument to Chilean heroes on back.

		VG	VF	UNC
a.	Sign. titles: *PRESIDENTE* and *GERENTE GENERAL*. 1978-80.	FV	2.00	8.00
b.	1982; 1985-87.	FV	FV	6.00
c.	1988; 1989.	FV	FV	5.50
d.	Sign. titles: *PRESIDENTE* and *GERENTE GENERAL INTERINO*. 1990-91.	FV	FV	4.50
e.	Sign. titles like a. 1992-95.	FV	FV	4.00

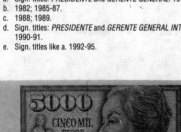

155 5000 PESOS
1981-. Brown and red-violet on m/c unpt. Allegorical woman w/musical instrument, seated male at ctr. Statue of woman w/children at l. ctr., G. Mistral at r. on back. Wmk: G. Mistral.

		VG	VF	UNC
a.	Sign. titles: *PRESIDENTE* and *GERENTE GENERAL*. 1981. Plain security thread.	FV	FV	35.00
b.	1986-90.	FV	FV	23.00
c.	Sign. titles: *PRESIDENTE* and *GERENTE GENERAL INTERINO*. 1991.	FV	FV	25.00
d.	Sign. titles: *PRESIDENTE* and *GERENTE GENERAL*. 1992-93.	FV	FV	20.00
e.	As d but w/segmented foil security thread. 1994-96.	FV	FV	17.50

156 10,000 PESOS
1989-94. Dk. blue and dk. olive-green on m/c unpt. Capt. A. Prat at r. and as wmk. Statue of Liberty at l., Hacienda San Agustin de Punual Cuna at l. ctr. on back. Plain security thread.

	VG	VF	UNC
	FV	FV	42.50

CHINA

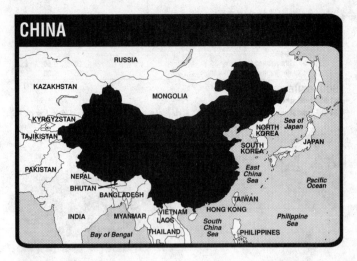

December 1948 by the Peoples Bank of China. Beneficial effects of the centralization were not immediately apparent. The pace of inflation was unslowed and regional note-issuing agencies continued to operate in remote areas for more than a year. Upon the defeat of the Kuomintang and the establishment of the Peoples Republic of China, the Communist government issued a new form of currency, the "Peoples Currency," as a replacement for all other notes in an effort to inject a stabilizing influence into the disorganized economy. Peoples Currency, Foreign Exchange Certificates and certain local or emergency issues are the only forms of paper money permitted to circulate by the Communist government.

MONETARY SYSTEM:
1 Yuan = 10 Chiao
1 Chiao = 10 Fen

MONETARY UNITS	
Yuan	圓 or 圜
Pan Yuan	圓半
5 Jiao	角伍
1 Jiao	角壹
1 Fen	分壹

The Peoples Republic of China, located in eastern Asia, has an area of 3,696,100 sq. mi. (9,572,900 sq. km.), including Manchuria and Tibet, and a population of 1.14 billion. Capital: Beijing (Peking). The economy is based on agriculture, mining and manufacturing. Textiles, clothing, metal ores, tea and rice are exported.

In the fall of 1911, the middle business class of China and Chinese students educated in Western universities started a general uprising against the Manchu dynasty which forced the abdication on Feb. 12, 1912, of the boy emperor Hsuan T'ung (Pu-yi), thus bringing to an end the Manchu dynasty that had ruled China since 1644. Five days later, China formally became a republic with physician and revolutionist Sun Yat-sen as first provisional president.

Dr. Sun and his supporters founded a new party called the Kuomintang, and planned a Chinese republic based upon the Three Principles of Nationalism, Democracy and People's Livelihood. They failed, however, to win control of all China, and Dr. Sun resigned the presidency in favor of Yuan Shih Kai, the most powerful of the Chinese generals. Yuan ignored the constitution of the republic and tried to make himself emperor.

After the death of Yuan in 1917, Sun Yat-sen and the Kuomintang established a republic in Canton. It also failed to achieve the unification of China, and in 1923 Dr. Sun entered into an agreement with the Soviet Union known as the Canton-Moscow Entente. The Kuomintang agreed to admit Chinese communists to the party. The Soviet Union agreed to furnish military advisers to train the army of the Canton Republic. Dr. Sun died in 1925 and was succeeded by one of his supporters, General Chiang Kai-shek.

Chiang Kai-shek launched a vigorous campaign to educate the Chinese and modernize their industries and agriculture. Under his command, the armies of the Kuomintang captured Nanking (1927) and Peking (1928). In 1928, Chiang was made president of the Chinese Republic. His government was recognized by most of the great powers, but he soon began to exercise dictatorial powers. Prodded by the conservative members of the Kuomintang, he initiated a break between the members and the Chinese Communists which, once again, prevented the unification of China.

Persuaded that China would fare better under the leadership of its businessmen in alliance with the capitalist countries than under the guidance of the Chinese Communists and in alliance with the Soviet Union, Chiang expelled all Communists from the Kuomintang, sent the Russian advisers home, and hired German generals to train his army.

The Communists responded by setting up a government and raising an army that during the period of 1930-34 acquired control over large parts of Kiangsi, Fukien, Hunan, Hupeh and other provinces. These early Communist centers issued currency in the form of copper and silver coins and many varieties of notes printed on paper and cloth. A lack of minting facilities limited the issue of coins. Low mintage and the demonetization of silver in China in 1935 have elevated the surviving coinage specimens to the status of highly valued numismatic rarities. The issues of notes, the majority of which bore revolutionary slogans and often cartoon-like vignettes have also suffered a high attrition rate and certain issues command appreciable premiums in today's market.

When his army was sufficiently trained and equipped, Chiang Kai-shek led several military expeditions against the Communist Chinese which, while unable to subdue them, dislodged them south of the Yangtze, forcing them to undertake in 1935 a celebrated "Long March" of 6,000 miles (9,654 km.) from Hunan northwest to a refuge in Shensi province just south of Inner Mongolia from which Chiang was unable to displace them.

The Japanese menace had now assumed warlike proportions. Chiang rejected a Japanese offer of cooperation against the Communists, but agreed to suppress the movement himself. His generals, however, persuaded him to negotiate a truce with the Communists to permit united action against the greater menace of Japanese aggression. Under the terms of the truce, Communists were again admitted to the Kuomintang. They, in turn, promised to dissolve the Soviet Republic of China and to cease issuing their own currency.

The war with Japan all but extinguished the appeal of the Kuomintang, appreciably increased the power of the Communists, and divided China into three parts. The east coast and its principal cities - Peking, Tientsin, Nanking, Shanghai and Canton - were in Japanese-controlled, puppet-ruled states. The Communists controlled the countryside in the north where they were the de facto rulers of 100 million peasants. Chiang and the Kuomintang were driven toward the west, from where they returned with their prestige seriously damaged by their wartime performance.

At the end of World War II, the United States tried to bring the Chinese factions together in a coalition government. American mediation failed, and within weeks the civil war resumed.

By the fall of 1947, most of northeast China was under Communist control. During the following year, the war turned wholly in favor of the Communists. The Kuomintang armies in the northeast surrendered, two provincial capitals in the north were captured, a large Kuomintang army in the Huai river basin surrendered. Four Communist armies converged upon the demoralized Kuomintang forces. The Communists crossed the Yangtse in April 1949. Nanking, the Nationalist capital, fell. The civil war on the mainland was virtually over.

Chiang Kai-shek relinquished the presidency to Li Tsung-jen, his deputy, and after moving to Canton, to Chungking and Chengtu, retreated from the mainland to Taiwan (Formosa) where he resumed the presidency.

The Communist Peoples Republic of China was proclaimed on September 2, 1949. Thereafter relations between the Peoples Republic and the Soviet Union steadily deteriorated. China emerged as independent center of Communist power in 1958.

During and following World War II, the Chinese Communists again established banks at the various Communist centers to issue local currency. Prominent among Communist regional banks were the Bank of Central China, Bank of Peihai, and Bank of Shansi, Chahar and Hopeh.

The complexity of regional banks with their widely varying exchange rates were replaced in

NUMERICAL CHARACTERS

No.	CONVENTIONAL			FORMAL	
1	一	正	元	壹	弌
2	二			弍	貳
3	三			弎	叄
4	四			肆	
5	五			伍	
6	六			陸	
7	七			柒	
8	八			捌	
9	九			玖	
10	十			拾	什
20	十二	廿		拾貳	念
25	五十二	五廿		伍拾貳	
30	十三	卅		拾叄	
100	百一			佰壹	
1,000	千一			仟壹	
10,000	萬一			萬壹	
100,000	萬十	億一		萬拾	億壹
1,000,000	萬百一			萬佰壹	

PEOPLES REPUBLIC OF CHINA

PEOPLES BANK OF CHINA

行銀民人國中
Chung Kuo Jen Min Yin Hang

中國人民銀行
Zhong Guo Ren Min Yin Hang

1962; 1965 ISSUE
#877-879 arms at r. on back.

		VG	VF	UNC
877	**1 JIAO**			
	1962. Brown on m/c unpt. Workers at l.			
	a. Back brown on green and lt. orange unpt. W/ or w/o wmk. *(S/M #C284-30a).*	.75	1.50	5.00
	b. Back brown on lilac and lt. orange unpt. Blue serial #. *(S/M #C284-30b).*	.05	.10	.30
	c. Like #877b but only partially engraved. Red serial #. *(S/M #C284-30c).*	.15	.35	1.25
	d. Lithograph. Red serial #. *(S/M #C284-30d).*	.05	.15	.40

		VG	VF	UNC
878	**2 JIAO**			
	1962. Green. Bridge at l.			
	a. Engraved face. *(S/M #C284-31a).*	.25	1.00	4.00
	b. Lithographed face. *(S/M #C284-31b).*	.05	.15	.40

		VG	VF	UNC
879	**10 YUAN**			
	1965. Black on m/c unpt. Group of people at ctr. Wmk: Great Hall w/rays. *(S/M #C284-40).*	1.50	2.25	5.00

1972 ISSUE

		VG	VF	UNC
880	**5 JIAO**			
	1972. Purple and m/c. Women working in factory. Arms at r. on back. *(S/M #C284-41).*			
	a. Engraved bank title and denomination. Wmk: Lg. star and 4 small stars.	.20	.60	2.00
	b. Lithographed face. W/wmk.	.20	.60	2.00
	c. Lithographed face. W/o wmk.	.05	.20	.50

1980 ISSUE
#881-883 arms at ctr. on back.
#884-889 arms at upper l., stylized birds in unpt. at ctr., dot patterns for poor of sight at lower l. or r.

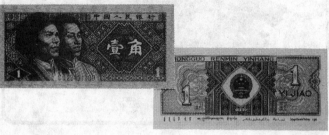

		VG	VF	UNC
881	**1 JIAO**			
	1980. Dk. brown on m/c unpt. 2 men at l. *(S/M #C284-42).*	FV	FV	.25

		VG	VF	UNC
882	**2 JIAO**			
	1980. Grayish olive-green on m/c unpt. 2 youths at l. *(S/M #C284-43).*	FV	FV	.35

		VG	VF	UNC
883	**5 JIAO**			
	1980. Purple on red-violet and lt. blue unpt. 2 children at l. Back: brown-violet on m/c unpt. *(S/M #C284-44).*	FV	FV	.50

		VG	VF	UNC
884	**1 YUAN**			
	1980; 1990. Brown-violet on m/c unpt. 2 youths at r. Great Wall at ctr. on back.			
	a. Blue ser. #. 1980. *(S/M #C284-45a).*	FV	.20	.65
	b. Black ser. #. 1990. *(S/M #C284-45b).*	FV	FV	.50

885   2 YUAN
1980; 1990. Dk. olive-green on m/c unpt. 2 youths at r. Rocky
shoreline on back.

		VG	VF	UNC
a.	1980. *(S/M #C284-46a).*	FV	.50	1.50
b.	1990. *(S/M #C284-46b).*	FV	FV	.85

886   5 YUAN
1980. Dk. brown on m/c unpt. Old man and young woman at r.
Yangtze Gorges on back. Wmk: Ancient *Pu* coin. *(S/M #C284-47).*

	VG	VF	UNC
	FV	FV	3.00

887   10 YUAN
1980; 1990 Black on blue and m/c unpt. Old and young man at r.
Mountains on back. Wmk: Young man.

		VG	VF	UNC
a.	1980. *(S/M #C284-48a).*	FV	FV	7.50
b.	W/Security thread. 1990. *(S/M #C284-48b).*	FV	FV	4.00

888   50 YUAN
1980; 1990. Black on lt. green and m/c unpt. Intellectual, student girl
and industrial male worker at ctr. Waterfalls on back. Wmk: Industrial
male worker.

		VG	VF	UNC
a.	1980. *(S/M #C284-49a).*	FV	7.50	16.50
b.	Security thread at r. 1990. *(S/M #C284-49b).*	FV	FV	15.00

889   100 YUAN
1980; 1990. Black on m/c unpt. 4 great leaders at ctr. Mountains on
back.

		VG	VF	UNC
a.	1980. *(S/M #C284-50a).*	FV	FV	30.00
b.	Security thread at r. 1990. *(S/M #C284-50b).*	FV	FV	27.50

FOREIGN EXCHANGE CERTIFICATES

BANK OF CHINA
This series has been discontinued.

中國銀行
Chung Kuo Yin Hang

1979 ISSUE

FX1   10 FEN
1979. Brown on m/c unpt. waterfalls at ctr. *(S/M #C204-301).*

		VG	VF	UNC
a.	Wmk: Lg. star and 4 small stars.	FV	.25	1.00
b.	Wmk: Star and torch.	FV	FV	3.00

FX2   50 FEN
1979. Purple on m/c unpt. Temple of Heaven at l. ctr. *(S/M #C294-
302).*

VG	VF	UNC
.10	.50	2.00

FX3   1 YUAN
1979. Deep green on m/c unpt. Pleasure boats in lake w/mountains
behind at ctr. *(S/M #294-303).*

VG	VF	UNC
.10	.60	2.50

FX4   5 YUAN   VG   VF   UNC
1979. Deep brown on m/c unpt. Mountain scenery at ctr. (S/M #C294-   .25   1.25   5.00
304).

FX5   10 YUAN   VG   VF   UNC
1979. Deep blue on m/c/ unpt. Yangtze Gorges at ctr. (S/M #C294-   .40   2.00   8.00
305).

FX6   50 YUAN   VG   VF   UNC
1979. Purple and red on m/c unpt. Mountain lake at ctr. (S/M #C294-   2.25 11.50 45.00
306).

FX7   100 YUAN   VG   VF   UNC
1979. Black and blue on m/c unpt. Great Wall at ctr. (S/M #C294-307).   2.50 12.50 50.00

1988 ISSUE

FX8   50 YUAN   VG   VF   UNC
1988. Black, orange-brown and green on m/c unpt. Shoreline rock   1.25   6.00 25.00
formations at ctr. (S/M #C294-308).

FX9   100 YUAN   VG   VF   UNC
1988. Olive-green on m/c unpt. Great Wall at ctr. (S/M #294-309).   1.75   9.00 35.00

PEOPLES REPUBLIC - MILITARY
MILITARY PAYMENT CERTIFICATES

军用代金券
Chn Yung Tai Chin Ch'an

1965 ISSUE
#M44 Held in reserve.

M41   1 FEN   VG   VF   UNC
1965. Greenish brown. Airplane at l. ctr. (S/M #C250.5-11).   2.50   7.50 22.50

M42   5 FEN   VG   VF   UNC
1965. Red. Airplane at ctr. (S/M #C250.5-12).   3.00   9.00 27.50

M43   1 CHIAO   VG   VF   UNC
1965. Purple. Steam passenger train at ctr. r. (S/M #C250.5-13).   3.25 10.00 30.00

M45   1 YUAN   VG   VF   UNC
1965. Green. Truck convoy at l. (S/M #C250.5-15).   4.00 12.50 50.00

M46   5 YUAN   VG   VF   UNC
1965. Truck convoy at l. (S/M #C250.5 -17).   —   —   —

CHINESE ADMINISTRATION OF TAIWAN

The Republic of China, comprising Taiwan (an island located 90 miles off the southeastern coast of mainland China), the islands of Quemoy and Matsu and nearby islets of the Pescadores chain, has an area of 14,000 sq. mi. (35,981 sq. km.). and a population of 20.2 million. Capital: Taipei. In recent years, manufacturing has replaced agriculture in importance. Fruits, vegetables, plywood, textile yarns and fabrics and clothing are exported.

Chinese migration to Taiwan began as early as the sixth century. The Dutch established a base on the island in 1624 and held it until 1661, when they were driven out by supporters of the Ming dynasty who used it as a stage for their unsuccessful attempt to displace the ruling Manchu dynasty on the mainland. Manchu forces occupied the island in 1683 and remained under the syzerainty of China until its cession to Japan in 1895. Following World War II it Taiwan was returned to China, and on December 8, 1949 it became the last remnant of Sun Yat-sen's Republic of China when Chaing Kai-shek moved his army and government from the mainland to the islands following his defeat by the Communist forces of Mao Tse-tung.

BANK OF TAIWAN

行銀灣臺

T'ai Wan Yin Hang

PORTRAIT ABBREVIATIONS

SYS = Sun Yat-sen, 1867–1925
President of Canton Government, 1917–25

CKS = Chaing Kai-shek 1886–1975
President in Nanking, 1927–31
Head of Foromosa Government, Taiwan, 1949–1975

NOTE: Because of the frequency of the above appearing in the following listings their initials are used only in reference to their portraits.

NOTE: S/M # in reference to *CHINESE BANKNOTES* by Ward D. Smith and Brian Matravers.

PRINTERS 1946–

CPF:
廠製印央中
(Central Printing Factory)

CPFT:
廠北台廠製印央中
(Central Printing Factory, Taipei)

FPFT:
廠刷印一第
(First Printing Factory)

PFBT:
所刷印行銀灣臺
(Printing Factory of Taiwan Bank)

1961 ISSUE

#972-975 SYS at I. Printer: CPF.

		VG	VF	UNC
971	**1 YUAN**			
	1961. Dk. blue-green and purple. SYS at I., steep coastline at r. Printer: PFBT.			
	a. Engraved. *(S/M #T73-60)*.	.20	.75	3.50
	b. Lithographed. (1972). *(S/M #T73-60)*.	.10	1.50	2.50

		VG	VF	UNC
972	**5 YUAN**			
	1961. Red on m/c unpt. House w/tower at r. *(S/M #T73-61)*.	.20	.75	3.00

		VG	VF	UNC
973	**5 YUAN**			
	1961. Brown on m/c unpt. Similar to #972. *(S/M #T73-62)*.	.25	1.00	5.50
974	**50 YUAN**			
	1961. Violet on m/c unpt. *(S/M #T73-63)*.	.60	2.50	9.00
975	**100 YUAN**			
	1961. Green on m/c unpt. SYS at I. *(S/M #T73-64)*.	.75	3.00	10.00

1964 ISSUE

#976-977 SYS at I. Printer: CPF.

		VG	VF	UNC
976	**50 YUAN**			
	1964. Violet on m/c unpt. Similar to #974. *(S/M #T73-70)*.	.50	2.00	6.00

		VG	VF	UNC
977	**100 YUAN**			
	1964. Green on m/c unpt. Similar to #975. *(S/M #T73-71)*.	.60	3.00	9.00

REPUBLIC OF CHINA-TAIWAN BANK

行銀灣臺 國民華中

Chung Hua Min Kuo-t'ai Wan Yin Hang

1969 ISSUE

#978 and 979 SYS at I. Printer: CPF.

978 **5 YUAN**
1969. Blue. (S/M #T73-72).

VG	VF	UNC
.15	.35	1.50

979 **10 YUAN**
1969. Red. Similar to #978. (S/M #T73-73).

	VG	VF	UNC
a. W/o plate letter.	.20	.50	2.00
b. Plate letter A at lower r. on face.	.15	.35	1.50

1970 ISSUE
#980-983 SYS at l. Printer: CPF.

980 **50 YUAN**
1970. Violet. (S/M #T73-75).

VG	VF	UNC
FV	2.25	4.00

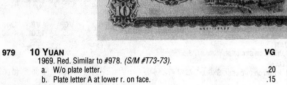

981 **100 YUAN**
1970. Green. (S/M #T73-).

VG	VF	UNC
FV	4.50	8.50

1972 ISSUE

982 **50 YUAN**
1972. Violet, purple and lt. blue. Chungshan bldg. on back. Wide
margin w/guilloche at r. (S/M #T73-76).

VG	VF	UNC
FV	2.00	4.50

983 **100 YUAN**
1972. Dk. green, lt. green and orange. Palace on back. (S/M #T73-77).

VG	VF	UNC
FV	4.00	7.00

1976 ISSUE
#984-986 Printer: CPF.

984 **10 YUAN**
1976. Red and m/c. SYS at l. Bank on back. (S/M #T73-78).

VG	VF	UNC
FV	.50	1.50

985 **500 YUAN**
1976. Olive, purple and m/c. CKS at l. Chungshan bldg. on back. W/o
wmk. at r. (S/M #T73-79).

VG	VF	UNC
FV	20.00	35.00

986 **1000 YUAN**
1976. Blue-black, olive-brown and violet on m/c. unpt. CKS at l.
Presidential Office bldg. on back. W/o wmk. at r. (S/M #T73-80).

VG	VF	UNC
FV	40.00	65.00

1981 Issue
#987 and 988 CKS at l. Printer: CPF.

987 500 YUAN
1981. Brown, red-brown and m/c. Similar to #985 but wmk. of CKS at r. (S/M #T73-81).

	VG	VF	UNC
	FV	FV	30.00

988 1000 YUAN
1981. Blue-black and m/c. Similar to #986 but wmk: CKS at r. (S/M #T73-82).

	VG	VF	UNC
	FV	FV	55.00

1987 Issue

989 100 YUAN
1987 (1988). Red, red-brown and brown-violet on m/c unpt. SYS at l. and as wmk. Chungshan bldg. on back. (S/M #T73-83).

	VG	VF	UNC
	FV	FV	6.00

OFF-SHORE ISLAND CURRENCY

* * * NOTE: This section has been renumbered. * * *

BANK OF TAIWAN

用通門金限   行銀灣臺
Hsien Chin Men T'ung Yung   *Tai Wan Yin Hang*

KINMEN (QUEMOY) BRANCH
Notes of the Bank of Taiwan and later notes of the Republic of China/Bank of Taiwan w/ovpt: 門金

1949 (1963) ISSUES
#R101-R109 portr. SYS at upper ctr. Vertical format.

R101 1 YUAN
(R1001) 1949 (1963). Green. Printer: CPF. (S/M #T74-1).

	VG	VF	UNC
	.25	1.25	5.50

1955-72 ISSUES

R109 5 YUAN
(R1009) 1966. Violet-brown. Printer: CPF. (S/M #T74-50).

	VG	VF	UNC
	.60	3.00	12.00

R110 10 YUAN
(R1010) 1969 (1975). Red ovpt. on #979a. (S/M #T74-60).

	VG	VF	UNC
	.25	1.00	5.00

R111 50 YUAN
(R1011) 1969 (1970). Dk. blue. SYS at r. (S/M #T74-61).

	VG	VF	UNC
	.50	2.00	10.00

R112	100 YUAN		VG	VF	UNC
(R1012)	1972 (1975). Green ovpt. on #983. (S/M #T74-70).		1.00	4.00	20.00

1976; 1981 ISSUES

R112A	10 YUAN		VG	VF	UNC
(R1012A)	1976. Ovpt. on #984. (S/M #T74-).		.20	.50	3.00
R112B	**100 YUAN**				
(R1012B)	1981. Ovpt. on #988. (S/M #T74-).		5.00	7.00	20.00
R112C	**1000 YUAN**				
(R1012C)	1981. Ovpt. on #988. (S/M #T74-).		40.00	50.00	85.00

MATSU BRANCH   限馬祖地區通用

Hsien Ma Tsu Ti Ch'u T'ung Yung

Notes of the Bank of Taiwan and later notes of the Republic of China/Bank of Taiwan w/ovpt: 馬祖

1950-51 (1964; 1967) ISSUES

#R119-R121 portr. SYS at upper ctr. Vertical format.

R117	10 YUAN		VG	VF	UNC
(R1017)	1950 (1964). Blue. Printer: CPF. (S/M #T75-2).		1.00	2.50	12.50

R118	50 YUAN		VG	VF	UNC
(R1018)	1951 (1967). Green. Printer: FPFT. (S/M #T75-10).		3.50	7.50	27.50

1969; 1972 ISSUE

R122	10 YUAN		VG	VF	UNC
(R1022)	1969 (1975). Red. Ovpt. on #979a. Printer: CPF. (S/M #T75-40).		.35	1.00	5.00

R123	50 YUAN		VG	VF	UNC
(R1023)	1969 (1970). Violet on m/c unpt. Printer: CPF. (S/M #T75-45).		1.00	4.00	20.00
R124	**100 YUAN**				
(R1024)	1972 (1975). Green ovpt. on #983. Printer: CPF. (S/M #T75-50).		3.00	10.00	35.00

1976; 1981 ISSUE

R125	10 YUAN		VG	VF	UNC
(R1025)	1976. Ovpt. on #984. (S/M #T75-55).		.25	1.00	4.00
R126	**500 YUAN**				
(R1026)	1981. Ovpt. on #987. (S/M #T75-60).		FV	20.00	45.00
R127	**1000 YUAN**				
(R1027)	1981. Ovpt. on #988. (S/M #T75-61).		FV	35.00	85.00

COLOMBIA

The Republic of Colombia, located in the northwestern corner of South America, has an area of 439,737 sq. mi. (1,138,914 sq. km.) and a population of 33.4 million. Capital: Bogota. The economy is primarily agricultural with a mild, rich coffee the chief crop. Colombia has the world's largest platinum deposits and important reserves of coal, iron ore, petroleum and limestone; precious metals and emeralds are also mined. Coffee, crude oil, bananas, sugar, coal and flowers are exported.

The northern coast of present Colombia was one of the first parts of the American continent to be visited by Spanish navigators, and the site, at Darien in Panama, of the first permanent European settlement on the American mainland in 1510. New Granada, as Colombia was known until 1861, stemmed from the settlement of Santa Maria in 1525. New Granada was established as a Spanish Colony in 1549. Independence was declared in 1813, and secured in 1824. In 1819, Simon Bolivar united Colombia, Venezuela, Panama and Ecuador as the Republic of Greater Colombia. Venezuela withdrew from the Republic in 1829; Ecuador in 1830; and Panama in 1903.

MONETARY SYSTEM:
1 Peso = 100 Centavos

REPUBLIC

BANCO DE LA REPÚBLICA

1941 CERTIFICADOS DE ORO (GOLD CERTIFICATES) ISSUE

		VG	VF	UNC
389	**1 PESO ORO**			
	1941-63. Portr. Gen. A. Nariño at lower r. w/o title: *CAJERO* and sign. on back.			
	a. Series N in red. 20.7.1941.	4.00	20.00	100.00
	b. As a. 20.7.1943.	1.00	5.00	30.00
	c. Series N in violet. 20.7.1944; 1.1.1945; 7.8.1947.	1.50	8.00	40.00
	d. Series N. 12.10.1949.	.25	2.00	25.00
	e. Series EE. 1.1.1950.	.25	2.00	22.50
	f. As e. 2.1.1963.	.20	1.50	20.00

1943 ISSUE

#392 printer: ABNC.

		VG	VF	UNC
392	**20 PESOS ORO**			
(395)	1943-63. Purple and m/c. Bust of Caldas at l., bust of S. Bolívar at r. Liberty at ctr. on back.			
	a. Series U in red. 20.7.1943.	12.50	50.00	200.00
	b. Series U in purple. 20.7.1944; 1.1.1945.	10.00	40.00	150.00
	c. Series U. Prefix A. 7.8.1947.	1.00	4.00	40.00
	d. Series DD. 1.1.1950; 1.1.1951.	1.00	3.00	30.00
	e. Series DD. 2.1.1963.	.50	2.00	20.00

1953 ISSUE

#399-401 printer: TDLR.

		VG	VF	UNC
400	**10 PESOS ORO**			
	1953-61. Blue on m/c unpt. Portr. Gen. A. Nariño at l., palm trees at r. Bank w/Mercury alongside at Cali on back. Series N.			
	a. 1.1.1953.	.25	2.00	25.00
	b. 1.1.1958; 1.1.1960.	.25	1.25	20.00
	c. 2.1.1961.	.25	1.00	17.50

		VG	VF	UNC
401	**20 PESOS ORO**			
	1953-65. Red-brown on m/c unpt. Portr. Caldas and allegory at l. Liberty in frame at r. Newer bank at Barranquilla on back. Series O.			
	a. 1.1.1953.	.25	3.00	25.00
	b. 1.1.1960.	.25	3.00	20.00
	c. 2.1.1961; 2.1.1965.	.20	1.00	17.50

1958 ISSUE

#402-403 printer: ABNC.

		VG	VF	UNC
402	**50 PESOS ORO**			
	1958-67. Lt. brown on m/c unpt. Portr. A. J. de Sucre at lower l. Back olive-green; Liberty at ctr. Series Z.			
	a. 20.7.1958; 7.8.1960.	.50	3.50	22.50
	b. 1.1.1964; 12.10.1967.	.25	2.50	20.00

		VG	VF	UNC
403	**100 PESOS ORO**			
	1958-67. Gray on m/c unpt. Portr. Gen. Santander at r. Back green; Like #402. Series Y.			
	a. 7.8.1958.	.50	3.00	22.50
	b. 1.1.1960; 1.1.1964; 20.7.1965; 20.7.1967.	.50	1.25	10.00

1959-60 Issue

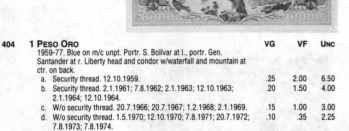

		VG	**VF**	**Unc**
404	**1 Peso Oro**			

1959-77. Blue on m/c unpt. Portr. S. Bolívar at l., portr. Gen. Santander at r. Liberty head and condor w/waterfall and mountain at ctr. on back.

a. Security thread. 12.10.1959.	.25	2.00	6.50
b. Security thread. 2.1.1961; 7.8.1962; 2.1.1963; 12.10.1963; 2.1.1964; 12.10.1964.	.20	1.50	4.00
c. W/o security thread. 20.7.1966; 20.7.1967; 1.2.1968; 2.1.1969.	.15	1.00	3.00
d. W/o security thread. 1.5.1970; 12.10.1970; 7.8.1971; 20.7.1972; 7.8.1973; 7.8.1974.	.10	.35	2.25
e. W/o sercuity thread. 1.1.1977.	1.00	2.75	15.00

1961-64 Issue

		VG	**VF**	**Unc**
406	**5 Pesos Oro**			

1961-81. Deep greenish black and deep brown on m/c unpt. Condor at l., Córdoba at r. Fortress at Cartagena at ctr. on back.

a. Security thread. 2.1.1961; 1.5.1963; 2.1.1964.	1.00	5.00	18.50
b. Security thread. 11.11.1965; 20.7.1966; 12.10.67. 20.7.1968.	.40	2.00	6.50
c. Security thread. 20.7.1971.	.25	1.00	5.00
d. W/o security thread. 1.1.1973; 20.7.1974; 20.7.1975; 20.7.1976; 20.7.1977.	.15	.75	4.00
e. W/o security thread. 1.10.1978; 1.4.1979; 1.1.1980; 1.1.1981.	.10	.50	3.00

		VG	**VF**	**Unc**
407	**10 Pesos Oro**			

1963-80. Lilac and slate blue on green and m/c unpt. Gen. A. Nariño at l., condor at r. Back red-brown and slate blue; archeological site w/monoliths.

a. Security thread. 20.7.1963; 20.7.1964.	1.00	5.00	20.00
b. Security thread. 20.7.1965; 20.7.1967; 2.1.1969.	.50	2.50	8.00
c. Security thread. 12.10.1970; 1.1.1973.	.30	1.50	6.00
d. W/o security thread. 20.7.1974; 1.1.1975; 20.7.1976; 1.1.1978.	.10	.50	3.00
e. W/o security thread. 7.8.1979; 7.8.1980.	.05	.35	2.00
f. Like e., but *SERIE AZ* at l. ctr. and upper r. on face. 7.8.1980.	.10	.50	3.00

		VG	**VF**	**Unc**
408	**500 Pesos Oro**	5.00	17.50	75.00

20.7.1964. Olive-green on m/c unpt. Portr. S. Bolívar at r. Back has no open space under Liberty head. Series AA. Printer: ABNC.

1966-68 Issue

#402-403 printer: ABNC.

		VG	**VF**	**Unc**
409	**20 Pesos Oro**			

1966-83. Brown, gray and green on m/c unpt. Caldas w/globe at r. Back brown and green on m/c unpt.; artifacts from the Gold Museum.

a. Security thread. 12.10.1966; 2.1.1969.	.30	1.00	4.00
b. W/o security thread. 1.5.1972; 1.5.1973; 20.7.1974; 20.7.1975; 20.7.1977.	.20	.40	1.00
c. W/o security thread. 1.4.1979; 1.1.1981; 1.1.1982; 1.1.1983.	.10	.30	1.00

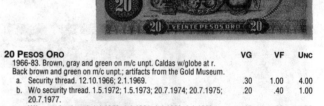

		VG	**VF**	**Unc**
410	**100 Pesos Oro**			

1968-71. Blue on m/c unpt. Gen F. de Paula Santander at r. Capital at Bogotá on back. Series Y.

a. 1.1.1968; 2.1.1969.	.50	2.50	10.00
b. 1.5.1970; 20.7.1971.	.50	1.50	5.00
s. As a. Specimen. 2.1.1969.	—	—	25.00

		VG	**VF**	**Unc**
411	**500 Pesos Oro**			

1968-71. Green on m/c unpt. S. Bolívar at r. Subterranean caves on back. Series A. Printer: ABNC.

a. 1.1.1968.	4.00	10.00	25.00
b. 12.10.1971.	3.50	7.00	17.50
s. As a. Specimen.	—	—	30.00

1969 Issue

412 50 Pesos Oro
1969-70. Brown-violet on m/c unpt. Blue design w/o border at l.,
Torres at r. Arms and flowers on back. Printer: TDLR.

	VG	VF	UNC
a. 2.1.1969.	.25	1.00	5.00
b. 12.10.1970.	.25	.75	3.00

1972-73 Issue

413 2 Pesos Oro
1972-77. Purple on m/c unpt. P. Salavarietta at l. Back brown; *El
Dorado* replica from the Gold Museum.

	VG	VF	UNC
a. Lg. size serial #, and # at r. near upper border. 1.1.1972; 20.7.1972; 1.1.1973.	.15	.75	3.50
b. Sm. size serial #, and # at r. far from upper border. 20.7.1976; 1.1.1977; 20.7.1977.	.10	.50	2.75

414 50 Pesos Oro
20.7.1973; 20.7.1974. Similar to #412 but curved dk. border added at
l. and r., also at r. on back. Printer: TDLR.

VG	VF	UNC
.30	.60	3.00

415 100 Pesos Oro
20.7.1973; 20.7.1974. Similar to #410 but curved dk. border added at
l. and r., also at r. on back. Series Y.

VG	VF	UNC
.50	1.00	7.00

416 500 Pesos Oro
7.8.1973. Red on m/c unpt. Like #411. Series A. Printer: ABNC.

VG	VF	UNC
2.00	5.00	30.00

1974 Issue

417 200 Pesos Oro
20.7.1974; 7.8.1975. Green on m/c unpt. S. Bolívar at ctr. r., church at
r. *BOGOTÁ COLOMBIA* at lower l. ctr. Man picking coffee beans on
back. Printer: TDLR.

VG	VF	UNC
.50	1.75	6.00

1977-79 Issue

418 100 Pesos Oro
1977-80. Violet on m/c unpt. Gen F. de Paula Santander at r. ctr.
Capitol at Bogotá on back. Printer: TDLR.

	VG	VF	UNC
a. 1.1.1977.	.25	.75	3.00
b. Serial # prefix A-C. 1.1.1980.	.15	.60	2.50

419 200 Pesos Oro
(420) 20.7.1978; 1.1.1979; 1.1.1980. Like #417 but w/only *COLOMBIA* at
lower l. ctr.

VG	VF	UNC
FV	.75	3.00

420   **500 P<small>ESOS</small> O<small>RO</small>**

(419)   1977-79. Olive and m/c. Gen. F. de Paula Santander at l. Back gray;
subterranean cave and Liberty head. Printer: ABNC.

		VG	VF	U<small>NC</small>
a.	20.7.1977.	FV	2.00	10.00
b.	1.4.1979.	FV	1.50	8.00

421   **1000 P<small>ESOS</small> O<small>RO</small>**

	VG	VF	U<small>NC</small>
1.4.1979. Black and m/c. J. A. Galan at r. Nariño Palace on back. Printer: ABNC.	FV	2.50	15.00

1980-84 I<small>SSUES</small>

422   **50 P<small>ESOS</small> O<small>RO</small>**

1980-85. Like #414 but *COLOMBIA* added near border at upper l. ctr.
Printer: TDLR (w/o imprint).

		VG	VF	U<small>NC</small>
a.	1.1.1980; 7.8.1981.	FV	.75	1.50
b.	1.1.1983.	FV	.20	1.00

425   **50 P<small>ESOS</small> O<small>RO</small>**

(422A)   1984-86. Like #422, but w/o wmk. Printer: IBB.

a.	12.10.1984; 1.1.1985.	FV	.20	1.00
b.	1.1.1986.	FV	FV	.75

423   **500 P<small>ESOS</small> O<small>RO</small>**

1981-86. Brown, dk. green and red-brown on m/c unpt. Santander at
l., Bogotá on back; screw coinage press at lower r. Wmk: Santander.
Printer: TDLR.

		VG	VF	U<small>NC</small>
a.	20.7.1981.	FV	1.25	5.00
b.	20.7.1984; 20.7.1985.	FV	1.00	4.00
c.	12.10.1985; 20.7.1986.	FV	FV	3.00

424   **1000 P<small>ESOS</small> O<small>RO</small>**

1982-87. Blue and m/c. S. Bolívar at l. Scene honoring 1819 battle
heroes on back. Printer: TDLR.

		VG	VF	U<small>NC</small>
a.	1.1.1982.	FV	2.50	8.00
b.	7.8.1984.	FV	2.00	6.00
c.	1.1.1986; 1.1.1987.	FV	FV	4.50

1983 I<small>SSUE</small>

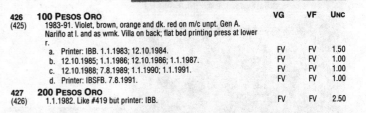

426   **100 P<small>ESOS</small> O<small>RO</small>**

(425)   1983-91. Violet, brown, orange and dk. red on m/c unpt. Gen A.
Nariño at l. and as wmk. Villa on back; flat bed printing press at lower
r.

		VG	VF	U<small>NC</small>
a.	Printer: IBB. 1.1.1983; 12.10.1984.	FV	FV	1.50
b.	12.10.1985; 1.1.1986; 12.10.1986; 1.1.1987.	FV	FV	1.00
c.	12.10.1988; 7.8.1989; 1.1.1990; 1.1.1991.	FV	FV	1.00
d.	Printer: IBSFB. 7.8.1991.	FV	FV	1.00

427   **200 P<small>ESOS</small> O<small>RO</small>**

(426)   1.1.1982. Like #419 but printer: IBB.   FV   FV   2.50

			VG	VF	UNC
428 (426A)	**200 PESOS ORO** 1.4.1983. Green on m/c unpt. Church and Fr. Mutis at l. and as wmk. Cloister in Bogotá on back. Printer: TDLR.		FV	1.50	6.00
429 (426B)	**200 PESOS ORO** 1983-92. Like #428.				
	a. Printer: IBB. 1.4.1983.		FV	.75	4.00
	b. 20.7.1984; 1.11.1984; 1.4.1985.		FV	FV	2.00
	c. 1.11.1985; 1.4.1987.		FV	FV	2.00
	d. Larger stylized and bold serial #. 1.4.1987; 1.4.1988; 1.11.1988; 1.4.1989; 1.11.1989; 1.4.1991.		FV	FV	2.00
	e. Printer: IBSFB. 10.8.1992.		FV	FV	1.25

			VG	VF	UNC
430 (427)	**2000 PESOS ORO** 1983-86. Dk. brown on m/c unpt. S. Bolívar at l. and as wmk. Scene at *Paso dei Paramo de Pisba* at ctr. r. on back. Printer: TDLR.				
	a. 24.7.1983.		FV	2.50	10.00
	b. 24.7.1984.		FV	2.00	9.00
	c. 17.12.1985; 17.12.1986.		FV	FV	7.00

1986-87 ISSUE

			VG	VF	UNC
431 (429)	**500 PESOS ORO** 1986-94. Like #423.				
	a. Printer: IBB. 20.7.1986; 12.10.1987; 20.7.1989; 12.10.1990.		FV	FV	2.50
	b. Printer: IBSFB. 2.3.1992.		FV	FV	2.50
	c. 4.1.1993.		FV	FV	2.00
432 (430)	**1000 PESOS ORO** 1987-94. Like #424.				
	a. Printer: IBB. 1.1.1987; 1.1.1990; 1.1.1991.				
	b. Printer: IBSFB. 31.1.1992; 1.4.1992; 4.1.1993.		FV	FV	3.00
433 (431)	**2000 PESOS ORO** 1986-92. Like #427.				
	a. Printer: IBB. 17.12.1986; 17.12.1988; 17.12.1990.		FV	FV	5.00
	b. Printer: IBSFB. 1.4.1992; 2.3.1992; 3.8.1992.		FV	FV	5.00

1986 COMMEMORATIVE ISSUE
#434, Centennial of the Constitution.

			VG	VF	UNC
434 (432)	**5000 PESOS ORO** 5.8.1986. Deep violet and red-violet on m/c unpt. R. Nuñez at l. and as wmk. Statue at ctr. r. on back. Printer: BDDK.		FV	FV	15.00

1987-90 ISSUES

			VG	VF	UNC
435 (433)	**5000 PESOS ORO** 5.8.1987; 5.8.1988. Similar to #434 but printer: IPS-Roma.		FV	FV	12.50
436 (434)	**5000 PESOS ORO** 1990-93 Like #435.				
	a. Printer: IBB. 1.1.1990.		FV	FV	12.50
	b. Printer: IBSFB. 31.1.1992; 4.1.1993.		FV	FV	12.50

1992 COMMEMORATIVE ISSUE
#437 Quincentennial of Columbus' Voyage, 12.10.1492.

			VG	VF	UNC
437 (435)	**10,000 PESOS ORO** 1992. Deep brown and black on m/c unpt. Early sailing ships at ctr., youthful woman *Major Embera* at ctr. r. and as wmk, native gold statue at r. Native birds around antique world map at l. ctr., Santa Maria sailing ship at lower r. on back. Printer: BDM.		FV	FV	30.00

1993-95 ISSUES
#439-441 printer: IBSFB.

#439-443 portr. as wmk.

			VG	VF	UNC
439 (436)	**2000 PESOS** 1.7.1993; 1.7.1994; 1.11.1994; 17.12.1994. Like #433 but *EL* deleted from title, *ORO* deleted from value.		FV	FV	4.00
440 (437)	**5000 PESOS** 3.1.1994; 4.7.1994; 2.1.1995. Like #434-436 but *EL* deleted the title, *ORO* deleted from value.		FV	FV	9.00
441 (438)	**5000 PESOS** 1.3.1995. Dk. brown, brown and deep blue-green on m/c unpt. Trees at l. and ctr. J. Asuncion Silva and bug at r. Woman, trees and monument at ctr. on back.		FV	FV	9.00
442 (439)	**5000 PESOS** 1.7.1995. Like #441. Printer: TDLR.		FV	FV	9.00
443 (440)	**10,000 PESOS** 1993-94. Like #437, but *EL* deleted from title, *ORO* deleted from value, diff. sign. and titles. Printer: IBSFB.		FV	FV	22.50

1995 COMMEMORATIVE ISSUE
#444, 200th Anniversary of P. Salavarrieta *"La Pola."*

#444 printer: IBSFB.

			VG	VF	UNC
444	**10,000 PESOS** 1.7.1995; 1.8.1995. Red-brown on m/c unpt. P. Salavarrieta at r., Village of Guaduas (ca. 1846) at l. ctr. on back.		FV	FV	22.50

1996 ISSUE
#445-447 printer: IBSFB.

			VG	VF	UNC
445	**2000 PESOS** 2.4.1996. Black, olive-green, red-brown and dk. brown on m/c unpt. Gen. F. de Paula Santandar at r. Casa de Moneda bldg., entrance at l. ctr. on back.		FV	FV	4.50
446	**5000 PESOS** 1.3.1996.		FV	FV	11.00
447 (441)	**20,000 PESOS** 23.7.1996. Black, deep green and dk. blue on m/c unpt. J. Garavito at r. and as wmk. View of the moon at ctr. Satelite view of earth at ctr. r., moon's surface along bottom, geometric forms in unpt. on back.		FV	FV	36.00

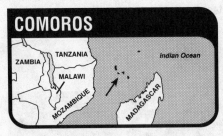

The Federal Islamic Republic of the Comoros, a volcanic archipelago located in the Mozambique Channel of the Indian Ocean 300 miles (483 km.) northwest of Madagascar, has an area of 838 sq. mi. (1,797 sq. km.) and a population of 570,000. Capital: Moroni. The economy of the islands is based on agriculture. There are practically no mineral resources. Vanilla, essence for perfumes, copra and sisal are exported.

Ancient Phoenician traders were probably the first visitors to the Comoros Islands, but the first detailed knowledge of the area was gathered by Arab sailors. Arab dominion and culture were firmly established when the Portuguese, Dutch and French arrived in the 16th century. In 1843 a Malagasy ruler ceded the island of Mayotte to France; the other three principal islands of the archipelago - Anjouan, Moheli and Grand Comore - came under French protection in 1886. The islands were joined administratively with Madagascar in 1912. The Comoros became partially autonomous, with the status of a French overseas territory in 1946 and achieved complete internal autonomy in 1961. On Dec. 31, 1975, after 133 years of French association, the Comoros Islands became the independent Republic of the Comoros.

Mayotte retained the option of determining its future ties and in 1976 voted to remain French. Its present status is that of a French Territorial Collectivity. French coinage and currency also circulates there.

RULERS:
French to 1975

MONETARY SYSTEM:
1 Franc = 100 Centimes

REPUBLIC

BANQUE DE MADAGASCAR ET DES COMORES

1960 ND PROVISIONAL ISSUE

#2-6 additional red ovpt: *COMORES*.

#4-6 dated through 1952 have titles 'A', those dated 1955 or ND have titles 'B'.

2   50 FRANCS
ND (1960-63). Brown and m/c. Woman w/hat at r. Man on back. Ovpt. on Madagascar #45.
   a. Sign. titles: *LE CONTROLEUR GAL.* and *LE DIRECTEUR GAL.* ND (1960).   Reported Not Confirmed
   b. Sign. titles: *LE DIRECTEUR GAL. ADJOINT* and *LE PRESIDENT DIRECTEUR GAL.* ND (1963). 2 sign varieties.   2.00   5.00   20.00

3   100 FRANCS

		VG	VF	UNC

ND (1960-63). M/c. Woman at r., palace of the Qn. of Tananariva in background. Woman, boats and animals on back. Ovpt. on Madagascar #46.
   a. Sign. titles: *LE CONTROLEUR GAL.* and *LE DIRECTEUR GAL.* ND (1960).   6.00 25.00 80.00
   b. Sign. titles: *LE DIRECTEUR GAL. ADJOINT* and *LE PRESIDENT DIRECTEUR GAL.* ND (1963).   1.00 5.00 18.50

4   500 FRANCS

		VG	VF	UNC

ND (1960-63). M/c. Man w/fruit at ctr. Ovpt on Madagascar #47.
   a. Sign. titles: *LE CONTROLEUR GAL* and *LE DIRECTEUR GAL.* - old date 30.6.1950; 9.10.1952 (1960).   30.00 100.00 325.00
   b. Sign. titles: *LE DIRECTEUR GAL. ADJOINT* and *LE PRESIDENT DIRECTEUR GAL.* ND (1963).   15.00 75.00 250.00

5   1000 FRANCS
ND (1960-63). M/c. Woman and man at l. ctr. Ox cart on Back. Ovpt. on Madagascar #48.
   a. Sign. titles: *LE CONTROLEUR GAL.* and *LE DIRECTEUR GAL.* - old date 1950-52; 9.10.1952 (1960).   45.00 125.00 425.00
   b. Sign. titles: *LE DIRECTEUR GAL. ADJOINT* and *LE PRESIDENT DIRECTEUR GAL.* ND (1963).   25.00 90.00 350.00

6   5000 FRANCS

		VG	VF	UNC

ND (1960-63). M/c. Portr. Gallieni at upper l., young woman at r. Huts at l., woman w/baby at r. on back. Ovpt. on Madagascar #49.
   a. Sign. titles: *LE CONTROLEUR GAL.* and *LE DIRECTEUR GAL.* - old date 30.6.1950 (1960).   175.00 425.00 875.00
   b. Sign. titles: *LE DIRECTEUR GAL. ADJOINT* and *LE PRESIDENT DIRECTEUR GAL.* ND (1963).   125.00 325.00 750.00
   c. Sign. titles: *LE DIRECTEUR GÉNÉRAL* and *LE PRÉSIDENT DIRECTEUR GAL.*   150.00 350.00 600.00

INSTITUT D'ÉMISSION DES COMORES

1976 ND ISSUE

#7-9 wmk: Crescent on Maltese cross.

7   500 Francs
ND (1976). Blue-gray, brown and red on m/c unpt. Bldg. at ctr., young woman wearing a hood at r. 2 women at l., boat at r. on back. 2 sign. varieties.

	VG	VF	UNC
	FV	3.00	7.50

11   1000 Francs
ND (1984-). Blue-gray, brown and red on m/c unpt. Woman at r., palm trees at waters edge in background. Women on back.
a. Partially engraved. Sign. titles: *LE DIRECTEUR GÉNÉRAL* and *LE PRÉSIDENT DU CONSEIL D'ADMINISTRATION.* (1986)
b. Offset. Sign. titles: *LE GOUVERNEUR* and *PRÉSIDENT DU....* (1994).

	VG	VF	UNC
a.	FV	4.00	10.00
b.	FV	3.25	8.00

8   1000 Francs
ND (1976). Blue-gray, brown and red on m/c unpt. Woman at r., palm trees at waters edge in background. Women on back.

	VG	VF	UNC
	FV	6.00	15.00

9   5000 Francs
ND (1976). Green on m/c unpt. Man and woman at ctr., boats and bldg. in l. background. Man at ctr. on back.

	VG	VF	UNC
	FV	35.00	75.00

BANQUE CENTRALE DES COMORES

1984-86 ND Issue

#10-12 similar to #7-9 but w/new bank name. Wmk: Maltese cross w/crescent.

12   5000 Francs
ND (1984-). Green on m/c unpt. Man and woman at ctr., boats and bldg. in l. background. Man at ctr. on back. Engraved sign titles: *LE DIRECTEUR GÉNÉRAL* and *LE PRÉSIDENT DU CONSEIL D'ADMINISTRATION*

	VG	VF	UNC
	FV	16.50	40.00

10   500 Francs
ND (1986-). Blue-gray, brown and red on m/c unpt. Bldg. at ctr., young woman wearing a hood at r. 2 women at l., boat at r. on back. 2 sign. varieties.
a. Partially engraved. Sign. titles: *LE DIRECTEUR GÉNÉRAL* and *LE PRÉSIDENT DU CONSEIL D'ADMINISTRATION* (1986). Wmk. is inverted - crescent facing down above stars.
b. Offset. Sign. titles: *LE GOUVERNEUR* and *PRÉSIDENT DU...* (1994). Corrected wmk. crescent facing up under stars.

	VG	VF	UNC
a.	FV	2.25	5.50
b.	FV	FV	4.50

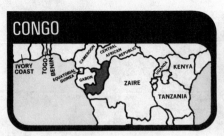

CONGO

The Republic of the Congo (formerly the Peoples Republic of the Congo), located on the equator in west- central Africa, has an area of 132,047 sq. mi. (342,000 sq. km.) and a population of 2.26 million. Capital: Brazzaville. Agriculture forestry, mining, and food processing are the principal industries. Timber, industrial diamonds, potash, peanuts, and cocoa beans are exported.

The Portuguese were the first Europeans to explore the Congo (Brazzaville) area, 14th century. They conducted a slave trade with the tribal kingdoms of Teke, Loango, and Kongo without attempting developmental colonization. French influence was established in 1883 when the King of Teke signed a treaty with Savorgnan de Brazza, thereby placing his kingdom under the protection of France. While a French protectorate, the area was known as Middle Congo. In 1910 Middle Congo became a part of French Equatorial Africa, which also included Gabon, Ubangi-Shari (now the Central African Republic), and Chad. Following World War II, during which it was an important center of Free French activities, the Middle Congo was given a large measure of internal autonomy, and its inhabitants were made French citizens. Upon approval of the constitution of the Fifth French Republic, 1958, it became a member of the new French Community. On Aug. 15, 1960, Middle Congo became the independent Republic of the Congo-Brazzaville. In Jan. 1970 the country's name was changed to Peoples Republic of the Congo. A new constitution which asserts the government's advocacy of socialism was adopted in 1973. In June and July of 1992, a new 125-member National Assembly was elected. Later that year a new president, Pascal Lissouba, was elected. In November, President Lissouba dismissed the previous government and dissolved the National Assembly. A new 23-member government, including members of the opposition, was formed in December 1992 and the name was changed to République du Congo.

RULERS:
French to 1960

MONETARY SYSTEM:
1 Franc = 100 Centimes

NOTE: For later issues and signature chart see Central African States.

RÉPUBLIQUE POPULAIRE DU CONGO

BANQUE CENTRALE

1971 ISSUE

		VG	VF	UNC
1	**10,000 FRANCS** ND (1971). M/c. Young Congolese woman at l., people marching w/sign at ctr. Statue at l. and r., tractor plowing at ctr. on back. Sign. 1.	125.00	350.00	900.00

BANQUE DES ÉTATS DE L'AFRIQUE CENTRALE

1974 ND ISSUE

		VG	VF	UNC
2	**500 FRANCS** ND (1974)-1983. Lilac-brown and m/c. Woman at l., river scene at ctr. Mask at l., students and chemical testing at ctr., statue at r. on back.			
	a. Sign. titles: *LE DIRECTEUR UR GENERAL* and *UN CENSEUR*. Engraved. Sign. 5. ND (1974).	2.00	6.00	15.00
	b. Sign. titles: *LE GOUVERNEUR* and *UN CENSUER*. Lithographed. Sign. 10. 1.4.1978.	4.00	15.00	40.00
	c. Titles as b. Sign. 10; 1.7.1980.	FV	6.00	15.00
	d. Titles as b. Sign. 12. 1.6.1981; 1.1.1982; 1.1.1983; 1.6.1984.	FV	3.00	8.00

		VG	VF	UNC
3	**1000 FRANCS** ND (1974)-1984. Blue and m/c. Industrial plant at ctr., man at r. Mask at l., trains, planes and bridge at ctr., statue at r. on back.			
	a. Sign. titles: *LE DIRECTEUR UR GENERAL* and *UN CENSEUR*. Engraved. Wmk: Antelope head in half profile. Sign. 3. ND (1974).	10.00	25.00	75.00
	b. Like a. Sign. 5.	4.00	10.00	30.00
	c. Sign. titles: *LE DIRECTEUR GENERAL* and *UN CENSEUR*. Lithographed. Wmk: Antelope head in profile. Sign. 8. ND (1978).			
	d. Sign. titles: *LE GOUVEREUR* and *UN CENSEUR*. Lithographed. Wmk: like b. Sign. 10. 1.4.1978.	FV	5.00	22.50
	e. Titles as c. Sign. 12; 1.6.1981; 1.1.1982; 1.1.1983; 1.6.1984.	FV	4.00	15.00

		VG	VF	UNC
4	**5000 FRANCS** ND (1974; 1978). Brown. Woman at l. Mask at l., bldgs. at ctr., statue at r. on back.			
	a. Sign. titles: *LE DIRECTEUR GENERAL* and *UN CENSEUR*. Sign. 3. ND (1974).	30.00	75.00	200.00
	b. Like a. Sign. 5.	15.00	40.00	100.00
	c. Sign. titles: *LE GOUVERNEUR* and *UN CENSEUR*. Sign. 11; 12. ND (1978).	FV	20.00	50.00
5	**10,000 FRANCS** ND (1974-81). M/c. Like #1 except for new bank name on back.			
	a. Sign. titles: *LE DIRECTEUR GENERAL* and *UN CENSEUR*. Sign. 5; 7. ND (1974; 1977).	30.00	60.00	125.00
	b. Sign. titles: *LE GOUVERNEUR* and *UN CENSEUR*. Sign. 11; 12. ND (1978; 1981).	22.50	45.00	100.00

1983-84 ND ISSUE

6	**5000 FRANCS**	VG	VF	UNC
	ND (1984; 1991). Brown and m/c. Mask at l., woman w/bundle of fronds at r. Plowing and mine ore conveyor on back. Sign. 12; 15.	FV	FV	35.00
7	**10,000 FRANCS**			
	ND (1983). Brown, green and m/c. Stylized antelope heads at l., woman at r. Loading fruit onto truck at l. on back. Sign. 12.	FV	FV	65.00

10	**1000 FRANCS**	VG	VF	UNC
	1987-. Like #9 but completed map of Chad at top on face.			
	a. Sign. 12. 1.1.1987; 1.1.1988; 1.1.1989.	FV	FV	13.00
	b. Sign. 13. 1.1.1990.	FV	FV	11.00
	c. Sign. 15. 1.1.1991.	FV	FV	10.00

RÉPUBLIQUE DU CONGO

BANQUE DES ÉTATS DEL'AFRIQUE CENTRALE

1992 ISSUE

1985-87 ISSUES

#8-10 sign. titles: *LE GOUVERNEUR* and *UN CENSEUR*.

NOTE: For issues w/similar back designs see Cameroon Republic, Central African Republic, Chad and Gabon.

8	**500 FRANCS**	VG	VF	UNC
	1985-. Brown on m/c unpt. Statue at l. ctr. and as wmk., jug at ctr. Man carving mask at l. ctr. on back.			
	a. Sign. 12. 1.1.1985; 1.1.1987; 1.1.1988; 1.1.1989.	FV	FV	7.00
	b. Sign. 13. 1.1.1990.	FV	FV	6.00
	c. Sign. 15. 1.1.1991.	FV	FV	5.00

11	**5000 FRANCS**	VG	VF	UNC
	ND (1992). Black text and brown on pale yellow and m/c unpt. African mask at l. and as wmk., woman carrying bundle of cane at r. African string instrument at far l., farm tractor plowing at l. ctr., mineshaft cable ore bucket lift at r. on back. Sign. 15.	FV	FV	35.00

9	**1000 FRANCS**	VG	VF	UNC
	1.1.1985. Blue and m/c. Animal carving at lower l., map of 6 member states at ctr. Unfinished map of Chad at upper ctr. Elephant at l., animals at ctr., carving at r. on back. Wmk: Animal carving. Sign. 12.	FV	4.00	15.00

12	**10,000 FRANCS**	VG	VF	UNC
	ND (1992). Greenish-black text, brown on pale green and m/c unpt. Artistic antelope masks at l., woman's head at r. and as wmk. Loading produce truck w/bananas at l. on back. Sign. 15.	FV	FV	65.00

COOK ISLANDS

Cook Islands, a political dependency of New Zealand consisting of 15 islands located in the South Pacific Ocean about 2,000 miles (3,218 km.) northeast of New Zealand, has an area of 93 sq. mi. (234 sq. km.) and a population of 16,900. Capital: Avarua. The United States claims the islands of Danger, Manahiki, Penrhyn and Rakahanga atolls. Citrus and canned fruits and juices, copra, clothing, jewelry and mother-of-pearl shell are exported.

The islands were first sighted by Spanish navigator Alvaro de Mendada in 1595. Portuguese navigator Pedro Fernandes de Quieros landed on Rakahanga in 1606. English navigator Capt. James Cook sailed to the islands on three occasions: 1773, 1774 and 1777. He named them Hervey Islands, in honor of Augustus John Hervey, a lord of the Admiralty. The islands were declared a British protectorate in 1888, and were annexed to New Zealand in 1901. They were granted internal self-government in 1965. New Zealand provides an annual subsidy and retains responsibility for defense and foreign affairs.

As a territory of New Zealand, the Cook Islands are considered to be within the Commonwealth of Nations.

RULERS:
New Zealand, 1901-

MONETARY SYSTEM:
1 Shilling = 12 Pence
1 Pound = 20 Shillings, to 1967
1 Dollar = 100 Cents, 1967-

NOTE: In June 1995 the Government of the Cook Islands began redeeming all 10, 20 and 50 dollar notes in exchange for New Zealand currency while most coins and their 3 dollar notes will remain in circulation.

NEW ZEALAND INFLUENCE

GOVERNMENT OF THE COOK ISLANDS

1987 ISSUE
#3-5 Ina and the shark at l.

			VG	VF	UNC
3	**3 DOLLARS** ND (1987). Deep green, blue-black and black on m/c. Fishing canoe and statue of the god Te-Rongo on back.		FV	2.75	5.00

			VG	VF	UNC
4	**10 DOLLARS** ND (1987). Violet-brown, blue-black and black on m/c unpt. Pantheon of gods on back.		FV	8.50	12.50

			VG	VF	UNC
5	**20 DOLLARS** ND (1987). Purple, blue-black and black on m/c unpt. Conch shell, turtle shell and drum on back.				
	a. Sign. T. Davis.		FV	16.50	27.50
	b. Sign. M. J. Fleming.		FV	16.00	26.50

1992 COMMEMORATIVE ISSUE
#6, 6th Festival of Pacific Arts, Rarotonga, Oct. 10-27, 1992.

			VG	VF	UNC
6	**3 DOLLARS** Oct. 1992. Black commemorative text ovpt. at l. on back of #3.		FV	3.00	6.50

1992 ISSUE
#7-10 Worshippers at church w/cemetery at ctr. Wmk: Sea turtle.

			VG	VF	UNC
7	**3 DOLLARS** ND (1992). Lilac and green on m/c unpt. Back purple, orange and m/c. *AITUTAKI* at upper ctr., local drummers at l., dancers at ctr., fish at r.		FV	FV	5.00

8   **10 DOLLARS**

		VG	VF	UNC
	ND (1992). Green and olive on m/c unpt. *RAROTONGA* above hillside gathering on back.	FV	FV	11.50

9   **20 DOLLARS**

		VG	VF	UNC
	ND (1992). Brown-orange and olive on m/c unpt. *NGAPUTORU &* *MANGAIA* above 2 islanders w/canoe at ctr. on back.	FV	FV	21.50

10   **50 DOLLARS**

		VG	VF	UNC
	ND (1992). Blue and green on on m/c unpt. *NORTHERN GROUP* above 3 islanders in canoe at l. 2 women seated weaving at ctr. on back.	FV	FV	50.00

COLLECTOR SERIES

GOVERNMENT OF THE COOK ISLANDS

1987 ISSUE

		ISSUE PRICE	MKT. VALUE
CS1	**ND (1987) 3-20 DOLLARS**	55.00	60.00
	#3-5 w/matched serial # in collector pack.		

The Republic of Costa Rica, located in southern Central America between Nicaragua and Panama, has an area of 19,575 sq. mi. (50,700 sq. km.) and a population of 3.03 million. Capital: San Jose. Agriculture predominates; coffee, bananas, beef and sugar contribute heavily to the country's export earnings.

Costa Rica was discovered by Christopher Columbus in 1502, during his last voyage to the new world, and was a colony of Spain from 1522 until independence in 1821. Columbus named the territory Nueva Cartago; the name Costa Rica wasn't generally employed until 1540. Bartholomew Columbus attempted to found the first settlement but was driven off by Indian attacks and the country wasn't pacified until 1530. Costa Rica was absorbed for two years (1821-23) into the Mexican Empire of Agustin de Iturbide. From 1823 to 1848 it was a constituent state of the Central American Republic (q.v.). It was established as a republic in 1848. Today, Costa Rica remains a model of orderly democracy in Latin America.

MONETARY SYSTEM:

1 Peso = 100 Centavos to 1896
1 Colon = 100 Centavos, 1896-

NOTE: Certain listings encompassing issues circulated by various bank and regional authorities are contained in Volume 1.

REPUBLIC

BANCO CENTRAL DE COSTA RICA

1967 PROVISIONAL ISSUE

#214 ovpt: *BANCO CENTRAL DE COSTA RICA/SERIE PROVISIONAL* on Banco Nacional notes.

214   **2 COLONES**

		VG	VF	UNC
	5.12.1967. Black ovpt. on #203. Series F.	2.50	6.00	15.00

1951-70 SERIES A ISSUE

#221-224 printer: W&S.
#225-226 printer: ABNC.

221   **10 COLONES**

		VG	VF	UNC
	1951-62. Blue on m/c unpt. Portr. A. Echeverria at ctr. Back blue; ox-cart at ctr.			
a.	W/*POR* added to sign. title at l. 8.11.1951; 5.12.1951; 29.10.1952.	3.00	10.00	50.00
b.	W/*POR* added to both sign. titles. 28.11.1951.	3.00	10.00	50.00
c.	W/o *POR* title changes. 28.10.1953-27.6.1962.	2.50	8.00	40.00
d.	W/*POR* added to sign. title at r. 24.10.1955.	3.00	10.00	50.00

222 20 COLONES
1952-64. Red on m/c unpt. Portr. C. Picado at ctr. at ctr. Back red, university bldg. at ctr.

		VG	VF	UNC
a.	Date at l. ctr., w/o sign. title changes. 11.6.1952; 10.12.1952; 11.8.1954; 14.10.1955; 13.2.1957.	3.75	15.00	75.00
b.	Sign. title: *SUB-GERENTE* ovpt. at r. 20.4.1955.	3.25	13.50	67.50
c.	Date at lower l. 7.11.1957-9.9.1964.	3.00	12.50	62.50
d.	*POR* added at l. of sign. title at l. 25.3.1953; 25.2.1954.	3.75	15.00	75.00

223 50 COLONES
1957-64. Olive on m/c unpt. Portr. R. F. Guardia at ctr. Back olive; National Library at ctr.

		VG	VF	UNC
a.	3.1.1957-25.11.1959.	6.00	30.00	120.00
b.	7.12.1960-9.9.1964.	5.00	25.00	100.00

225 500 COLONES
7.4.1970; 2.4.1973; 4.5.1974; 4.5.1976; 26.4.1977. Purple on m/c unpt. Portr. M. M. Gutiérrez at r. Back purple; National Theater at ctr.

VG	VF	UNC
50.00	85.00	550.00

226 1000 COLONES
1955-74. Red on m/c unpt. Portr. J. Pena at l. Back: red; Central and National Bank at ctr.

		VG	VF	UNC
a.	17.8.1955-6.10.1958.	100.00	350.00	—
b.	9.6.1965-28.3.1968.	90.00	275.00	500.00
c.	7.4.1970-12.6.1974.	80.00	100.00	350.00

1959-80 SERIES B ISSUE
#228-232 printer: TDLR.

227 5 COLONES
20.5.1959-3.11.1962. Green on m/c unpt. Portr. B. Carrillo at ctr. Back: green; coffee worker at ctr. Printer: W&S.

VG	VF	UNC
4.00	6.25	25.00

228 10 COLONES
19.9.1962-9.10.1967. Blue on m/c unpt. Portr. Echeverria at ctr. Back blue; ox-cart at ctr.

VG	VF	UNC
1.50	5.00	40.00

229 20 COLONES
11.11.1964-30.6.1970. Brown on m/c unpt. Portr. Picado at ctr. Back brown; university bldg. at ctr.

VG	VF	UNC
2.00	7.50	45.00

230 50 COLONES
4.6.1965-30.6.1970. Greenish-brown on m/c unpt. Portr. Guardia at ctr. Back greenish brown; National Library at ctr.

VG	VF	UNC
3.00	12.50	95.00

231 100 COLONES
1961-66. Black on m/c unpt. Portr. J. R. Mora at ctr. Statue of J. Santamaria at ctr. on back.

		VG	VF	UNC
a.	Brown unpt. 18.12.1961-3.12.1964.	5.00	25.00	125.00
b.	Olive unpt. and w/security thread. 9.6.1965; 27.4.1966.	4.50	22.50	110.00

232   500 COLONES

	VG	VF	UNC
1980-85. Purple on m/c unpt. M. M. Gutiérrez at r. National Theatre on back.			
a. Red serial #. 18.12.1980; 12.3.1981.	3.25	6.00	25.00
b. Black serial #. 17.9.1981; 24.12.1981; 18.5.1982; 7.8.1984; 20.3.1985.	FV	5.00	20.00

233   1000 COLONES

	VG	VF	UNC
9.6.1975-7.4.1983; 20.3.1985. Red on m/c unpt. T. Soley Guell at l. National Insurance Institute on back. Printer: ABNC.	FV	8.50	35.00

1963-90 SERIES C ISSUES

NOTE: It is reported that 10,000 pieces of #235b mistakenly reached circulation.

234   5 COLONES

	VG	VF	UNC
3.10.1963-29.5.1967. Green on m/c unpt. Portr. B. Carrillo at ctr. Back green; coffee worker at ctr. Printer: TDLR.	.85	3.75	15.00

235   10 COLONES

	VG	VF	UNC
1969-70; ND. Blue on m/c unpt. Portr. R. Facio Brenes at r. Back blue; Banco Central bldg. at ctr. Printer: ABNC.			
a. 4.3.1969; 17.6.1969.	.75	3.00	15.00
b. 30.6.1970.	.35	1.25	7.50
x. W/o date or sign. (error) 10,000 reportedly released.	—	—	—

236   20 COLONES

	VG	VF	UNC
1972-83. Dk. brown on m/c unpt. C. G. Viquez at l., bldgs. and trees at r. Allegorical scene on back.			
a. *BARBA*- etc. text under bldgs. at ctr. Sign. titles: *EL PRESI-DENTE DE LA JUNTA DIRECTIVA* and *EL GERENTE DEL BANCO* Date at upper r., w/security strip. 10.7.1972; 6.9.1972.	.75	2.50	10.00
b. Text and sign. as a., date position at upper ctr., w/security strip. 13.11.1972-26.4.1977.	.65	2.00	5.00
c. Lt. brown. Sign. titles: *PRESIDENTE EJECUTIVO* and *GERENTE*. W/o security thread. *BARVA*... etc. text under bldgs. at ctr. Date at upper ctr. r. or upper ctr. 1.6.1978-7.4.1983.	FV	.75	3.00

236A   20 COLONES

	VG	VF	UNC
28.6.1983. Design like #236d, but Series Z. Printed on Tyvek (plastic).	.85	2.50	10.00

237   50 COLONES

	VG	VF	UNC
10.9.1973-26.4.1977. Olive on m/c unpt. Meeting scene at at l., M. M. de Peralta y Alfaro at r. Casa *Amarilla* (Yellow House) on back.	1.00	4.00	15.00

238   100 COLONES

	VG	VF	UNC
29.8.1966-27.8.1968. Black on m/c unpt. Portr. Mora at ctr., w/o *C* in corners or at r. Back black; w/statue of J. Santamaria at ctr. Printer: TDLR.	5.00	25.00	100.00

238A 500 Colones
21.1.1987; 21.8.1987; 14.6.1989. Brown-orange and olive-brown on m/c unpt. Similar to #232, but clear wmk. area at l. Printer: TDLR.

	VG	VF	UNC
	FV	FV	13.50

238B 1000 Colones
19.11.1986; 17.6.1987; 6.1.1988; 17.1.1989. Red on m/c unpt. Similar to #233. Printer: ABNC.

	VG	VF	UNC
	FV	7.50	22.50

238C 1000 Colones
1990-. Red on m/c unpt. Similar to #233 and #238B. Printer: USBN.

		VG	VF	UNC
a.	24.4.1990; 3.10.1990; 23.10.1991.	FV	FV	17.50
b.	2.2.1994; 20.4.1994; 15.6.1994; 10.10.1994.	FV	FV	12.50

1968-94 Series D Issue

239 5 Colones
1968-92. Deep green and lilac on m/c unpt. R. Y. Castro at l., flowers at r. Back green m/c; National Theater scene. Printer: TDLR.

		VG	VF	UNC
a.	Date at ctr. w/wmk. and security thread. Error name *T. VILLA* on back. 20.8.1968; 11.12.1968.	1.00	2.50	7.50
b.	Date at ctr. r. w/wmk. and security thread. Error name *T. VILLA* on back. 1.4.1969; 30.6.1970; 8.5.1972.	.15	.75	2.25
c.	Date at ctr. r. wmk. and security thread. Corrected name *J. VILLA* on back. 4.5.1973-4.5.1976.	.25	.50	2.50
d.	W/o wmk. or security thread. C. Changed sign. titles. 28.6.1977-4.10.1989.	.05	.25	1.00
e.	As d. 24.1.1990-15.1.1992.	FV	FV	.50
x.	As d. but w/error date: 7.4.1933 (instead of 1983).	1.00	3.25	10.00

240 10 Colones
1972-87. Blue on m/c unpt. University bldg. at l., R. Facio Brenes at r. Central Bank on back. W/o imprint.

		VG	VF	UNC
a.	Security thread. 6.9.1972-26.4.1977.	.20	1.00	4.00
b.	W/o security thread. 26.4.1977-18.2.1987.	FV	.35	1.50

241 100 Colones
(242) 26.8.1969-26.4.1977. Black on m/c unpt. R. Jimenez O. at l., cows and mountains at ctr. Supreme Court at ctr., figures at r. on back. Printer: TDLR.

	VG	VF	UNC
	1.50	7.50	30.00

241A 500 Colones
6.7.1994. Similar to #238A. Ascending serial # at lower l. Printer: TDLR.

	VG	VF	UNC
	FV	FV	7.50

1978 Commemorative Issue
#241, Centennial of Bank of Costa Rica 1877-1977

242 50 Colones
(241) 1978-86. Olive-green and m/c. Obverse of 1866-dated 50 Centimos coin at l., G. Ortuno y Ors at r. Bank, reverse of 50 Centimos coin and commemorative text: *1877-CENTENARIO...* on back. Printer: TDLR.

		VG	VF	UNC
a.	30.10.1978; 30.4.1979; 18.3.1980; 2.4.1981.	1.00	3.50	7.50
b.	18.5.1982; 22.11.1984; 20.3.1985; 2.4.1986.	.75	1.50	4.50

1987 SERIES E ISSUE
#242A-243 sign. titles: *PRESIDENTE EJECUTIVO* and *GERENTE.*

		VG	VF	UNC
242A	**50 COLONES**	FV	FV	2.75
	15.7.1987; 26.4.1988. Olive green on m/c unpt. Similar to #241 but text: *ANTIGUO EDIFICIO...* on back. Printer: CdM Brazil.			

		VG	VF	UNC
242B	**50 COLONES**	FV	FV	1.50
	19.6.1991; 28.8.1991; 29.7.1992; 2.6.1993; 7.7.1993. Similar to #242A. Printer: TDLR.			

		VG	VF	UNC
243	**100 COLONES**	FV	.75	3.00
	26.4.1977-9.11.1988. M/c. R. Jimenez O. at l. Similar to #241. Printer: TDLR.			

1971 COMMEMORATIVE ISSUE
NOTE: For 20 Colones 1983 printed on Tyvek plastic, see #236A.

#244-249 circular ovpt: *150 AÑOS DE INDEPENDENCIA* 1821-1971.

#250 circular ovpt: *XXV ANIVERSARIO BANCO CENTRAL DE COSTA RICA/1950/1975.*

		VG	VF	UNC
244	**5 COLONES**	1.00	5.00	15.00
	24.5.1971. Ovpt. on #239b. Series D.			

		VG	VF	UNC
245	**10 COLONES**	3.00	15.00	47.50
	24.5.1971. Ovpt. on #235. Series C.			
246	**50 COLONES**	15.00	45.00	175.00
	24.5.1971. Ovpt. on #230. Series B.			

		VG	VF	UNC
247	**100 COLONES**	20.00	65.00	250.00
	24.5.1971; 13.12.1971. Ovpt. on #241. Series D.			

		VG	VF	UNC
248	**500 COLONES**	145.00	375.00	—
	24.5.1971. Ovpt. on #225. Series A.			
249	**1000 COLONES**	175.00	425.00	—
	24.5.1971. Ovpt. on #226. Series A.			

1975 COMMEMORATIVE ISSUE
#250 circular ovpt: *XXV ANIVERSARIO BANCO CENTRAL DE COSTA RICA / 1950 / 1975.*

		VG	VF	UNC
250	**5 COLONES**	1.00	3.50	8.50
	20.3.1975. Ovpt. on #239. Series D.			

1988 SERIES F ISSUE
#251-253 Held in reserve.

			VG	VF	UNC
254	**100 COLONES**		FV	1.00	4.00
	30.11.1988; 4.10.1989; 5.10.1990. Black on m/c unpt. Similar to #241 and 243. Printer: ABNC.				

1992 SERIES G ISSUE

			VG	VF	UNC
255	**100 COLONES**		FV	.85	3.50
	17.9.1992. Like #254 but printer: CdM.				

1993 SERIES H ISSUE

			VG	VF	UNC
256	**100 COLONES**		FV	.75	3.00
	28.9.1993. Like #254. Printer: ABNC.				

1991-92 SERIES A ISSUE

			VG	VF	UNC
257	**5000 COLONES**		FV	FV	65.00
	28.8.1991; 11.3.1992; 29.7.1992; 4.5.1994; 18.1.1995. Dk. blue and dk. brown on m/c unpt. Local sculpture at l. ctr. Bird, leopard, local carving, foliage and sphere on back. Printer: TDLR.				

CROATIA

The Republic of Croatia (Hrvatska), formerly a federal republic of the Socialist Federal Republic of Yugoslavia, has an area of 21,829 sq. mi. (56,538 sq. km.) and a population of about 5 million. Capital: Zagreb.

The country was attached to the Kingdom of Hungary until Dec. 1, 1918, when it joined with Serbia, Slovenia, Bosnia-Herzegovina, Macedonia and Montenegro to form the Kingdom of the Serbs, Croats and Slovenes, which changed its name to the Kingdom of Yugoslavia on Oct. 3, 1929. On April 6, 1941, Hitler, angered by the coup d'etat that overthrew the pro-Nazi regime of regent Prince Paul, sent Nazi forces into Yugoslavia Within a week the army of the Balkan Kingdom was broken. Yugoslavia was dismembered to reward Hitler's Balkan allies. Croatia, reconstituted as a nominal kingdom, was given to the administration of an Italian princeling, who wisely decided to remain in Italy. At the conclusion of World War II, Croatia was one of the 6 Socialist Republics which formed Yugoslavia.

Croatia proclaimed its independence from Yugoslavia on Oct. 8, 1991. Serbian forces had developed a military stronghold in the area around Knin, located in southern Croatia. In Sept. 1995 Croat forces overan this political-military enclave.

MONETARY SYSTEM:
1 Dinar = 100 Para 1918-1941, 1945-
1 Kuna = 100 Banica 1941-1944
1 Kuna = 100 Lipa, 1994-

NOTE: The word "kuna", derived from the Russian "cunica" which means marten, reflects the use of furs for money in medieval eastern Europe.

REPUBLIC

REPUBLIKA HRVATSKA

REPUBLIC OF CROATIA

1991-93 ISSUE

#16-27 R. Boskovic at ctr., geometric calculations at upper r. (Printed in Sweden).

#16-22 vertical back with Zagreb cathedral and artistic rendition of city buildings behind.

#21-26 wmk: Baptismal font.

#23-26 statue of seated Glagolica *Mother Croatia* at ctr. on back.

NOTE: The wmk. paper actually used in the production for #19 was originally prepared for printing Sweden 5 Kroner, #14.

		VG	VF	UNC
16	**1 DINAR** 8.10.1991. Dull orange-brown on m/c unpt. 4.5mm serial #. Wmk: Lozenges.			
	a. Issued note.	—	.05	.10
	s. Specimen.	—	—	20.00

		VG	VF	UNC
17	**5 DINARA** 8.10.1991. Pale violet on m/c unpt. 4mm serial #. Wmk: Lozenges.			
	a. Issued note.	—	.05	.15
	s. Specimen.	—	—	20.00

18   10 DINARA
8.10.1991. Pale red-brown on m/c unpt. 4.5mm serial #. Wmk:
Lozenges.

	VG	VF	UNC
a. Issued note.	.05	.15	.30
s. Specimen.	—	—	20.00

19   25 DINARA
8.10.1991. Dull violet on m/c unpt. Buff paper w/2.8mm serial #.
Wmk: 5's in crossed wavy lines.

	VG	VF	UNC
a. Issued note.	.10	.30	.75
b. Inverted wmk.	6.50	16.00	32.50
s. Specimen.	—	—	30.00

20   100 DINARA
8.10.1991. Pale green on m/c unpt. W/o wmk.

	VG	VF	UNC
a. Issued note.	.10	.40	1.00
s. Specimen.	—	—	40.00

21   500 DINARA
8.10.1991. Lilac on m/c unpt.

	VG	VF	UNC
a. Issued note.	.50	2.00	5.00
s. Specimen.	—	—	30.00

22   1000 DINARA
8.10.1991. Pale blue-violet on m/c unpt.

	VG	VF	UNC
a. Issued note.	.60	2.40	6.00
s. Specimen.	—	—	30.00

23   2000 DINARA
15.1.1992. Deep brown on m/c unpt.

	VG	VF	UNC
a. Issued note.	.35	1.50	3.75
s. Specimen.	—	—	30.00

24   5000 DINARA
15.1.1992. Dark gray on m/c unpt.

	VG	VF	UNC
a. Issued note.	.40	1.60	4.00
s. Specimen.	—	—	30.00

25   10,000 DINARA
15.1.1992. Olive-green on m/c unpt.

	VG	VF	UNC
a. Issued note.	.20	1.00	2.75
s. Specimen.	—	—	30.00

26   50,000 DINARA
30.5.1993. Deep red on m/c unpt.

	VG	VF	UNC
a. Issued note.	.10	.40	1.00
s. Specimen.	—	—	30.00

27   100,000 DINARA
30.5.1993. Dk. blue-green on m/c unpt.

	VG	VF	UNC
a. Issued note.	.10	.50	1.25
s. Specimen.	—	—	30.00

1994 ISSUE
#28-35 shield at upper l. ctr. Printer: G & D.

28   5 KUNA
31.10.1993 (1994). Dk. green and green on m/c unpt. F. K. Frankopan
and P. Zrinski at r. and as wmk. Fortress in Varazdin at l. ctr. on back.

	VG	VF	UNC
a. Issued note.	FV	FV	3.00
x. Error w/o date or sign.	12.00	30.00	60.00
s. Specimen.	—	—	30.00

29	**10 KUNA**	VG	VF	UNC
	31.10.1993 (1994). Purple and violet on m/c unpt. J. Dobrila at r. and as wmk. Pula arena at l. ctr. on back.			
	a. Issued note.	FV	FV	5.50
	s. Specimen.	—	—	30.00

30	**20 KUNA**	VG	VF	UNC
	31.10.1993 (1994). Brown, red and violet on m/c unpt. J. Jelacic at r. and as wmk. Pottery dove and castle of Count Eltz in Vukovar at l. ctr. on back.			
	a. Issued note.	FV	FV	10.00
	s. Specimen.	—	—	30.00

31	**50 KUNA**			
	31.10.1993 (1994). Dk. blue and blue-green on m/c unpt. I. Gunulic at r. and as wmk. Aerial view of old Dubrovnik at l. ctr. on back.			
	a. Issued note.	FV	FV	20.00
	s. Specimen.	—	—	30.00

32	**100 KUNA**	VG	VF	UNC
	31.10.1993 (1994). Red-brown and brown-orange on m/c unpt. I. Mazuranic at r. and as wmk. Plan of and church of St. Vitus in Rijeka at l. ctr. on back.			
	a. Issued note.	FV	FV	35.00
	x. Error w/o serial #.	13.50	32.50	65.00
	s. Specimen.	—	—	30.00

33	**200 KUNA**	VG	VF	UNC
	31.10.1993 (1994). Dk. brown and brown on m/c unpt. S. Radic at r. and as wmk. Town command in Osijek at l. ctr. on back.			
	a. Issued note.	FV	FV	55.00
	s. Specimen.	—	—	30.00

34	**500 KUNA**	VG	VF	UNC
	31.10.1993 (1994). Dk. brown and olive-brown on m/c unpt. M. Marulic at r. and as wmk. Palace of Diocletian in Spit at l. ctr. on back.			
	a. Issued note.	FV	FV	130.00
	s. Specimen.	—	—	30.00

35	**1000 KUNA**			
	31.10.1993 (1994). Dk. brown and purple on m/c unpt. A. Star cevic at r. and as wmk. Equestrian statue of Kg. Tomislav at l. ctr., Zagreb Cathedral at ctr. r. on back.			
	a. Issued note.	FV	FV	240.00
	s. Specimen.	—	—	30.00

1995 ISSUE

36	**10 KUNA**	VG	VF	UNC
	15.1.1995. Black and brown on m/c unpt. Like #29. Printer: G&D.			
	a. Issued note.	FV	FV	5.00
	s. Specimen.	—	—	30.00

REGIONAL

KNIN

РЕПУБЛИКА СРПСКА КРАЈИНА

REPUBLIKA SRPSKA KRAJINA

1992 ISSUE

#R1-R6 arms at l., numerals in heartshaped design below guilloche at r. ctr. Curved artistic design at l. ctr., arms at r. on back. Headings in Serbo-Croatian and Cyrillic.

#R1-R3 wmk: Portr. of a young girl.

#R4 and R5 wmk: Young boy.

Replacement notes: #R1-R34, ZA prefix letters.

NOTE: For notes identical in color and design to #R1-R19 but differing only in text at top, sign. and place of issue Banja Luka, see Bosnia & Herzegovina #33-47.

R1	**10 DINARA**	VG	VF	UNC
	1992. Deep brown on orange and silver unpt. Back with ochre unpt.			
	a. Issued note.	.40	1.60	4.00
	b. Specimen.	—	—	13.50

R2	**50 DINARA**	VG	VF	UNC
	1992. Gray on tan and yellow upt.			
	a. Issued note.	.30	1.25	5.00
	s. Specimen.	—	—	13.50

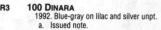

R3   100 DINARA
1992. Blue-gray on lilac and silver unpt.

	VG	VF	UNC
a. Issued note.	.60	2.40	6.00
s. Specimen.	—	—	13.50

R4   500 DINARA
1992. Blue-gray on pink and m/c unpt.

	VG	VF	UNC
a. Issued note.	.80	3.25	13.50
s. Specimen.	—	—	13.50

R5   1000 DINARA
1992. Deep gray on pink and tan unpt.

	VG	VF	UNC
a. Issued note.	1.50	6.00	15.00
s. Specimen.	—	—	13.50

R6   5000 DINARA
1992. Violet on lt. blue, pink and lilac unpt.

	VG	VF	UNC
a. Issued note.	1.50	6.00	15.00
s. Specimen.	—	—	13.50

НАРОДНА БАНКА РЕПУБЛИКЕ СРПСКЕ КРАЈИНЕ

NARODNA BANKA REPUBLIKE SRPSKE KRAJINE

NATIONAL BANK OF THE SERBIAN REPUBLIC - KRAJINA

1992-93 ISSUE
#R7-R8 wmk: Portr. of young boy.
#R7-R16 like #R1-R6.
#R10-R12 wmk: Portr. of young girl.
#R13-R19 wmk: Greek design repeated.
Replacement notes: #R1-R34, ZA prefix letters.

R7   10,000 DINARA
1992. Deep gray-green on lt. blue and tan unpt.

	VG	VF	UNC
a. Issued note.	1.00	4.00	10.00
s. Specimen.	—	—	13.50

R8   50,000 DINARA
1992. Brown on pale orange and pale olive-green unpt.

	VG	VF	UNC
a. Issued note.	1.00	4.00	10.00
s. Specimen.	—	—	13.50

R9   100,000 DINARA
1993. Dull purple and brown on m/c unpt. Wmk: Young women.

	VG	VF	UNC
a. Issued note.	1.00	4.00	10.00
s. Specimen.	—	—	13.50

R10   1 MILLION DINARA
1993. Deep purple on m/c unpt.

	VG	VF	UNC
a. Issued note.	1.25	5.00	12.50
s. Specimen.	—	—	13.50

R11　5 MILLION DINARA
1993. Dk. brown on orange and blue-gray unpt.

	VG	VF	UNC
a. Issued note.	.80	3.25	8.00
s. Specimen.	—	—	13.50

R12　10 MILLION DINARA
1993. Deep blue on pale olive-green and m/c unpt.

	VG	VF	UNC
a. Issued note.	.60	2.40	6.00
s. Specimen.	—	—	13.50

R13　20 MILLION DINARA
1993. Olive-gray on orange and tan unpt.

	VG	VF	UNC
a. Issued note.	1.00	4.00	10.00
s. Specimen.	—	—	13.50

R14　50 MILLION DINARA
1993. Brown-violet on pink and lt. gray unpt.

	VG	VF	UNC
a. Issued note.	1.00	4.00	10.00
s. Specimen.	—	—	13.50

R15　100 MILLION DINARA
1993. Blue-black on lt. blue and gray unpt.

	VG	VF	UNC
a. Issued note.	.50	2.00	5.00
s. Specimen.	—	—	13.50

R16　500 MILLION DINARA
1993. Orange on lilac and yellow unpt.

	VG	VF	UNC
a. Issued note.	.50	2.00	5.00
s. Specimen.	—	—	13.50

R17　1 MILLIARD DINARA
1993. Dull brownish orange on pale blue and lt. orange unpt.

	VG	VF	UNC
a. Issued note.	.80	3.25	8.00
s. Specimen.	—	—	13.50

R18　5 MILLIARD DINARA
1993. Purple on lilac and gray unpt.

	VG	VF	UNC
a. Issued note.	.80	3.25	8.00
s. Specimen.	—	—	13.50

R19 **10 MILLIARD DINARA**

VG VF UNC

1993. Black on orange and pink unpt.

a. Issued note. .80 3.25 8.00

s. Specimen. — — 13.50

1993 ISSUE

Currency Reform, 1993

Dinar = 1,000,000 "old" Dinara

#R20-R27 Knin fortress on hill at l. ctr. Serbian arms at ctr. r. on back. Wmk: Greek design repeated. Replacement notes: #R1-R34, ZA prefix letters.

R20 **5000 DINARA**

VG VF UNC

1993. Red-violet and violet on blue-gray unpt.

a. Issued note. .20 .80 2.00

s. Specimen. — — 13.50

R24 **5 MILLION DINARA**

VG VF UNC

1993. Orange and gray-green on pale orange unpt.

a. Issued note. .20 .80 2.00

s. Specimen. — — 13.50

R21 **50,000 DINARA**

VG VF UNC

1993. Brown, red and red-orange on ochre unpt.

a. Issued note. .20 .80 2.00

s. Specimen. — — 13.50

R25 **100 MILLION DINARA**

VG VF UNC

1993. Olive-brown and gray-green on lt. blue unpt.

a. Issued note. .20 .80 2.00

s. Specimen. — — 13.50

R22 **100,000 DINARA**

VG VF UNC

1993. Violet and blue-gray on pink unpt.

a. Issued note. .20 .80 2.00

s. Specimen. — — 13.50

R26 **500 MILLION DINARA**

VG VF UNC

1993. Chocolate brown and gray-green on pale olvie-green unpt.

a. Issued note. .20 .80 2.00

s. Specimen. — — 13.50

R23 **500,000 DINARA**

VG VF UNC

1993. Brown and gray-green on pale green unpt.

a. Issued note. .20 .80 2.00

s. Specimen. — — 13.50

R27 **5 MILLIARD DINARA**

VG VF UNC

1993. Brown-orange and aqua on gray unpt.

a. Issued note. .30 1.20 3.00

s. Specimen. — — 13.50

R28 **10 MILLIARD DINARA**

VG VF UNC

1993. Purple and red on aqua unpt.

a. Issued note. .40 1.60 4.00

s. Specimen. — — 13.50

R29 50 MILLIARD DINARA
1993. Brown and olive-green on reddish brown unpt.

	VG	VF	UNC
a. Issued note.	.50	2.00	5.00
s. Specimen.	—	—	13.50

1994 ISSUE

Currency Reform, 1994

1 "new" Dinar = 10,000 "old" Dinara

#R30-R34 like #R2-R29. Replacement notes: #R1-R34, ZA prefix letters.

R30 1000 DINARA
1994. Dk. brown and slate-gray on yellow-orange unpt.

	VG	VF	UNC
a. Issued note.	.20	.80	2.00
s. Specimen.	—	—	13.50

R31 10,000 DINARA
1994. Red-brown and dull purple on ochre unpt.

	VG	VF	UNC
a. Issued note.	.20	.80	2.00
s. Specimen.	—	—	13.50

R32 500,000 DINARA
1994. Dk. brown and blue-gray on grayish green unpt.

	VG	VF	UNC
a. Issued note.	.20	.80	2.00
s. Specimen.	—	—	13.50

R33 1 MILLION DINARA
1994. Purple and aqua on lilac unpt.

	VG	VF	UNC
a. Issued note.	.20	.80	2.00
s. Specimen.	—	—	13.50

R34 10 MILLION DINARA
1994. Gray and red-brown on pink unpt.

	VG	VF	UNC
a. Issued note.	.40	1.20	3.00
s. Specimen.	—	—	13.50

CUBA

The Republic of Cuba, situated at the northern edge of the Caribbean Sea about 90 miles (145 km.) south of Florida, has an area of 44,218 sq. mi. (114,524 sq. km.) and a population of 10.7 million. Capital: Havana. The Cuban economy is based on the cultivation and refining of sugar, which provides 80 percent of export earnings.

Discovered by Columbus in 1492 and settled by Diego Velasquez in the early 1500s, Cuba remained a Spanish possession until 1898, except for a brief British occupancy in 1762-63. Cuban attempts to gain freedom were crushed, even while Spain was granting independence to its other American possessions. Ten years of warfare, 1868-78, between Spanish troops and Cuban rebels exacted guarantees of right which were never implemented. The final revolt, begun in 1895, evoked American sympathy, and with the aid of U.S. troops independence was proclaimed on May 20, 1902. Fulgencio Batista seized the government in 1952 and established a dictatorship. Opposition to Batista, led by Fidel Castro, drove him into exile on Jan. 1, 1959. A communist-type, 25-member collective leadership headed by Castro was inaugurated in March 1962.

RULERS:
Spanish to 1898

MONETARY SYSTEMS:
1 Peso = 100 Centavos
1 Peso Convertibles = 1 U.S.A. Dollar, 1995-

REPUBLIC

BANCO NACIONAL DE CUBA

NATIONAL BANK OF CUBA

1961 ISSUE

#94-99 denomination at l. and r. Sign. titles: *PRESIDENTE DEL BANCO* at l., *MINISTRO DE HACIENDA* at r.
Printer: STC-P.

NOTE: Each member of the "Bay of Pigs" invasion force was reportedly issued one hundred each of #97x.

			VG	VF	UNC
94	**1 PESO**				
	1961-65. Olive green on ochre unpt. Portr. J. Martí at ctr. F. Castro w/rebel soldiers entering Havana in 1959 on back.				
	a.	1961.	1.75	3.00	10.00
	b.	1964.	1.25	2.25	8.50
	c.	1965.	FV	2.00	7.00

			VG	VF	UNC
95	**5 PESOS**				
	1961-65. Dull deep green on pink unpt. Portr. A. Maceo at ctr. Invasion of 1958 on back.				
	a.	1961.	FV	5.00	25.00
	b.	1964.	FV	5.00	11.50
	c.	1965.	FV	5.00	10.00

			VG	VF	UNC
96	**10 PESOS**				
	1961-65. Brown on tan and yellow unpt. Portr. M. Gómez at ctr. Castro addressing crowd in 1960 on back.				
	a.	1961.	FV	12.00	35.00
	b.	1964.	FV	10.00	18.50
	c.	1965.	FV	10.00	16.50

			VG	VF	UNC
97	**20 PESOS**				
	1961-65. Blue on pink unpt. Portr. C. Cienfuegos at ctr. Soldiers on the beach in 1956 on back.				
	a.	1961.	FV	22.50	60.00
	b.	1964.	FV	20.00	32.50
	c.	1965.	FV	20.00	30.00
	x.	U.S.A. counterfeit. Series F69; F70, 1961.	3.50	15.00	75.00

			VG	VF	UNC
98	**50 PESOS**				
	1961. Purple on green unpt. Portr. C. García Iniguez at ctr. Nationalization of international industries on back.		30.00	60.00	125.00

99   100 PESOS
1961. Lt. red on orange unpt. Portr. C. M. de Céspedes at ctr. Attack
on Moncada in 1953 on back.

	VG	VF	UNC
	25.00	75.00	200.00

1966 ISSUE
#100 and 101 denomination at. and r. Sign titles: *PRESIDENTE DEL BANCO* at l. and r. Printer: STC-P (w/o
imprint).

		VG	VF	UNC
100	**1 PESO**			
	1966. Like #94.	FV	1.25	10.00
101	**10 PESOS**			
	1966. Like #96.	FV	8.50	35.00

1967; 1971 ISSUE
#102-105 denomination at l. Sign. title: *PRESIDENTE DEL BANCO* at r. Printer: STC-9 (w/o imprint).

		VG	VF	UNC
102	**1 PESO**			
	1967-88. Like #94.			
	a. 1967-70; 1972.	FV	1.00	5.00
	b. 1978-86.	FV	FV	4.00
	c. 1986.	FV	1.50	8.00
	d. 1988.	FV	FV	2.00

 *(img_5 at top right)*

		VG	VF	UNC
104	**10 PESOS**			
	1967-89. Like #96.			
	a. 1967-71.	FV	8.00	35.00
	b. 1978.	FV	FV	25.00
	c. 1983-84; 1986-87.	FV	FV	18.00
	d. 1988-89.	FV	FV	11.00

		VG	VF	UNC
105	**20 PESOS**			
	1971-90. Like #97.			
	a. 1971.	FV	8.00	35.00
	b. 1978.	FV	FV	35.00
	c. 1983.	FV	FV	30.00
	d. 1987-90.	FV	FV	15.00

1975 COMMEMORATIVE ISSUE
#106, 15th Anniversary Nationalization of Banking.

		VG	VF	UNC
106	**1 PESO**	2.50	3.50	7.50
	1975. Olive on violet unpt. Portr. J. Martí at l., arms at r. Ship			
	dockside on back.			

1983 ISSUE

		VG	VF	UNC
103	**5 PESOS**			
	1967-90. Like #95.			
	a. 1967-68.	FV	4.00	20.00
	b. 1970; 1972.	FV	FV	15.00
	c. 1984-87.	FV	FV	10.00
	d. 1988; 1990.	FV	FV	6.00

107 **3 PESOS**
1983-89. Red on m/c unpt. Portr. E. "Che" Guevara at ctr. Back red on
orange unpt.; "Che" cutting sugar cane at ctr.

	VG	VF	UNC
a. 1983-86.	FV	3.00	10.00
b. 1988-89.	FV	FV	4.00

1990-91 ISSUE
Replacement notes: #108-112: EX, DX, CX, BX, AX series #, by denomination.

108 **5 PESOS**
1991. Deep green and deep blue on m/c unpt. A. Maceo at r. Secret
meeting of the rebel military in the woods at l. ctr. on back. Wmk: J.
Marti.

VG	VF	UNC
.25	1.00	2.50

109 **10 PESOS**
1991. Deep brown and deep olive-green on m/c unpt. M. Gómez at r.
"Guerra de todo el Pueblo" at l. ctr. on back. Wmk: J. Marti.

VG	VF	UNC
.50	2.00	5.00

110 **20 PESOS**
1991. Blue-black and purple on m/c unpt. Agricultural scenes at l. ctr.
on back. Wmk: National heroine - Tania.

VG	VF	UNC
1.00	4.00	10.00

111 **50 PESOS**
1990. Deep violet and dk. green on m/c unpt. Arms at ctr. C. García
Iniguez at r. Center of Genetic Engineering and Biotechnology at l. ctr.
on back. Wmk: National heroine - Tania.

VG	VF	UNC
1.25	5.00	15.00

1995 ISSUE
#112 and 113 arms at upper ctr. r.

112 **1 PESO**
1995. Dull olive-green on lt. blue and m/c unpt. J. Martí at l., arms at
upper ctr. r. F. Castro w/rebel soldiers entering Havana in 1959 on
back.

VG	VF	UNC
FV	FV	.75

113 **3 PESOS**
1995. E. "Che" Guevara at rl. "Che" cutting sugar cane on back.

VG	VF	UNC
FV	FV	1.50

FOREIGN EXCHANGE CERTIFICATES
The Banco Nacional de Cuba issued four types of peso certificates in series A, B, C and D. The C and D series
was issued in two designs and orignally required hand issue date and sign. at redemption. Resembling travel-
er's checks.

BANCO NACIONAL DE CUBA

SERIES A
#FX1-FX5 red-violet. Arms at l. Various Colonial Spanish fortresses on back.

FX1 **1 PESO**
ND (1985-). Orange and olive green unpt. Castillo San Salvador de la
Punta on back.

VG	VF	UNC
.30	1.50	3.50

		VG	VF	UNC
FX2	**3 PESOS** ND (1985-). Orange and pink unpt. Castillo San Pedro de la Roca on back.	.60	3.50	7.00
FX3	**5 PESOS** ND (1985-). Orange and blue-green unpt. Castillo de Los Tres Reyes on back.	1.00	5.00	10.00
FX4	**10 PESOS** ND (1985-). Orange and brown unpt. Castillo Nuestra Señora de Los Angeles de Jagua on back.	2.00	9.00	18.00

		VG	VF	UNC
FX5	**20 PESOS** ND (1985-). Orange and blue unpt. Castillo de la Real Fuerza on back.	4.00	20.00	40.00

SERIES B

		VG	VF	UNC
FX6	**1 PESO** ND (1985-). Lt. green and olive-brown unpt. Back like #FX1.	.20	1.00	2.50
FX7	**5 PESOS** ND (1985-). Lt. green and blue-green unpt. Back like #FX3.	1.00	5.00	20.00
FX8	**10 PESOS** ND (1985-). Lt. green and brown unpt. Back like #FX4.	2.00	10.00	30.00
FX9	**20 PESOS** ND (1985-). Lt. green and blue unpt. Back like #FX5.	4.00	20.00	40.00

		VG	VF	UNC
FX10	**50 PESOS** ND (1985-). Lt. green and dull violet unpt. Castillo de la Chorrera on back.	10.00	50.00	100.00

SERIES C FIRST ISSUE

Note: Large quantites were sold into the numismatic market.

#FX11-18 pale blue. Arms at l.

		VG	VF	UNC
FX11	**1 PESO** ND. Lt. blue and lt. red-brown unpt.	.10	.25	1.25

		VG	VF	UNC
FX12	**3 PESOS** ND. Lt. blue and violet unpt.	.10	.30	1.50
FX13	**5 PESOS** ND. Lt. blue and lt. olive unpt.	.10	.35	1.75
FX14	**10 PESOS** ND. Lt. blue and lilac unpt.	.10	.40	2.00
FX15	**20 PESOS** ND. Lt. blue and tan unpt.	.15	.50	2.50
FX16	**50 PESOS** ND. Lt. blue and rose unpt.	.20	.60	3.00
FX17	**100 PESOS** ND. Lt. blue and ochre unpt.	.20	.75	3.00
FX18	**500 PESOS** ND. Lt. blue and tan unpt.	.25	.75	3.75

SERIES C SECOND ISSUE

FX19-FX38 Blue-violet. Similar to FX11-FX18.

		VG	VF	UNC
FX19	**1 PESO** ND		Reported Not Confirmed	
FX20	**3 PESOS** ND. Lt. blue and red unpt.	.15	.60	1.25
FX21	**5 PESOS** ND. Lt. blue and pale olive-green unpt.	.25	1.00	2.00
FX22	**10 PESOS** ND. Lt. blue and brown unpt.	.50	2.00	4.00
FX23	**20 PESOS** ND. Lt. blue and orange-brown unpt.	1.00	4.00	8.00
FX24	**50 PESOS** ND. Lt. blue and violet unpt.	2.00	8.00	16.00
FX25	**100 PESOS** ND. Lt. blue and gray unpt.	3.75	15.00	30.00
FX26	**500 PESOS** ND.		Reported Not Confirmed	

SERIES D FIRST ISSUE

#FX19-23 pale red-brown. Arms at l.

		VG	VF	UNC
FX27	**1 PESO** ND. Lt. orange and orange-brown unpt.	.30	1.50	3.50
FX28	**3 PESOS** ND. Lt. orange and pale blue unpt.	.60	3.00	7.00
FX29	**5 PESOS** ND. Lt. orange and lt. green unpt.	1.00	5.00	10.00
FX30	**10 PESOS** ND. Lt. orange and lilac unpt.	2.00	10.00	18.00
FX31	**20 PESOS** ND. Lt. orange and ochre unpt.	4.00	20.00	32.00

SERIES D SECOND ISSUE

#FX39-FX43 dk. brown. Similar to FX19-FX23. W/ or w/o various *ESPACIO EN BLANCO INUTILIZADO* or *ESPACIO INUTILIZADO* handstamps on back.

		VG	VF	UNC
FX32	**1 PESO** ND. Tan and pale olive-green unpt.	.10	.30	.60
FX33	**3 PESOS** ND. Tan and red unpt.	.15	.60	1.25
FX34	**5 PESOS** ND. Tan and green unpt.	.25	1.00	2.00
FX35	**10 PESOS** ND. Tan and orange unpt.	.50	2.00	4.00
FX36	**20 PESOS** ND. Tan and blue-gray unpt.	1.00	4.00	8.00

1994 ISSUE

#FX24-FX30 arms on back.

FX37	**1 PESO CONVERTIBLE**	**VG**	**VF**	**UNC**
	1994. Orange, brown and olive-green on m/c unpt. J. Martí monument at r. Arms at ctr. on back. Wmk: J. Marti.	FV	FV	2.50
FX38	**3 PESOS CONVERTIBLES**			
	1994. Red-orange and brown on m/c unpt. E. "Che" Guevara monument at r.	FV	FV	6.00
FX39	**5 PESOS CONVERTIBLES**			
	1994. Dk. green, orange and purple on m/c unpt. A. Maceo monument at r.	FV	FV	10.00
FX40	**10 PESOS CONVERTIBLES**			
	1994. Brown, olive-green and purple on m/c unpt. M. Gómez monument at r.	FV	FV	18.50
FX41	**20 PESOS CONVERTIBLES**			
	1994. Red, lt. brown and purple on m/c unpt. C. Cienfuegos monument at r.	FV	FV	35.00
FX42	**50 PESOS CONVERTIBLES**			
	1994. Violet, brown and orange on m/c unpt. C. García monument at r.	FV	FV	80.00
FX43	**100 PESOS CONVERTIBLES**			
	1994. Red, brown-orange and purple on m/c C. Manuel de Céspedes monument at r.	FV	FV	150.00

COLLECTOR SERIES

BANCO NACIONAL DE CUBA

1961-1995 ISSUES

The Banco Nacional de Cuba has been selling specimen notes of the 1961-1989 issues. Specimen notes dated 1961-66 have normal block # and serial # while notes from 1967 to date all have normal block # and all zero srial #.

		ISSUE PRICE	**MKT.**	**VALUE**
CS1	**1961 1-100 PESOS** Ovpt: *SPECIMEN* on #94a-97a, 98, 99.	—		125.00
CS2	**1964 1-20 PESOS** Ovpt: *SPECIMEN* on #94b-97b.	—		16.50
CS3	**1965 1-20 PESOS** Ovpt: *SPECIMAN* on #94c-97c.	—		14.00
CS4	**1966 1, 10 PESOS** Ovpt: *SPECIMEN* on #100, 101.	—		7.00
CS5	**1967 1-10 PESOS** Ovpt: *SPECIMEN* on #102a-104a.	—		10.00
CS6	**1968 1-10 PESOS** Ovpt: *SPECIMEN* on #102a-104a.	—		10.00
CS7	**1969 1, 10 PESOS** Ovpt: *SPECIMEN* on #102a, 104a.	—		7.00
CS8	**1970 1-10 PESOS** Ovpt: *SPECIMEN* on #102a, 103b, 104a.	—		7.00
CS9	**1971 10, 20 PESOS** Ovpt: *SPECIMEN* on #104a, 105a.	—		8.00
CS10	**1972 1, 5 PESOS** Ovpt: *SPECIMEN* on #102a, 103b.	—		7.00
CS11	**1975 1 PESO** Ovpt: *SPECIMEN* on #106.	—		8.00
CS12	**1978 1, 10, 20 PESOS** Ovpt: *SPECIMEN* on #102b, 104b, 105b.	—		11.00
CS13	**1979 1 PESO** Ovpt: *SPECIMEN* on #102b.	—		3.00
CS14	**1980 1 PESO** Ovpt: *SPECIMEN* on #102b.	—		3.00
CS15	**1981 1 PESO** Ovpt: *SPECIMEN* on #102b.	—		3.00
CS16	**1982 1 PESO** Ovpt: *MUESTRA* on #102b.	—		3.00
CS17	**1983 3, 10, 20 PESOS** Ovpt: *MUESTRA* on #104c, 105c, 107a.	—		12.00
CS18	**1984 3, 5, 10 PESOS** Ovpt: *MUESTRA* on #103c, 104c, 107a.	—		12.00
CS19	**1985 1, 3, 5 PESOS** Ovpt: *MUESTRA* on #102b, 103c, 107a.	—		12.00
CS20	**1986 1-10 PESOS** Ovpt: *MUESTRA* on #102b, 103c, 104c, 107a.	—		12.50
CS21	**1987 5, 10, 20 PESOS** Ovpt: *MUESTRA* on #103c-105c.	—		12.00
CS22	**1988 1-20 PESOS** Ovpt: *MUESTRA* on #102c, 103d-105d, 107b.	—		12.50
CS23	**1989 3, 20 PESOS** Ovpt: *MUESTRA* on #105d, 107b.	—		7.00
CS24	**1990 5, 20, 50 PESOS** Ovpt: *MUESTRA* on #103d, 105d, 111	—		10.00
CS25	**1991 5, 10, 20 PESOS** Ovpt: *SPECIMEN* on #108-110.	—		10.00
CS26	**1995 1, 3 PESOS** Ovpt: *MUESTRA* on #112 and 113.	—		5.00

The Republic of Cyprus, a member of the European Commonwealth and Council, lies in the eastern Mediterranean Sea 44 miles (71 km.) south of Turkey and 60 miles (97 km.) west of Syria. It is the third largest island in the Mediterranean Sea, having an area if 3,572 sq. mi. (9,251 sq. km.) and a population of 710,200. Capital: Nicosia. Agriculture and mining are the chief industries. Asbestos, copper, citrus fruit, iron pyrites and potatoes are exported.

The importance of Cyprus dates from the Bronze Age when it was desired as a principal souce of copper (from which the island derived its name) and as a strategic trading center. Its role as an international marketplace made it a prime disseminator of the then prevalent cultures, a role that still influences the civilization of Western man. Because of its fortuitous position and influential role, Cyprus was conquered by a succession of empires; the Assyrian, Egyptian, Persian, Macedonian, Ptolemaic, Roman and Byzantine. It was taken from Isaac Comnenus by Richard the Lion-Hearted in 1191, sold to the Knights Templars, conquered by Venice and Turkey, and made a crown colony of Britain in 1925. Finally on Aug. 16, 1960, it became an independent republic.

In 1964, the ethnic Turks, who favor partition of Cyprus into separate Greek and Turkish states, withdrew from active participation in the government. Turkish forces invaded Cyprus in 1974 and gained control of 40 percent of the island. In 1975, Turkish Cypriots proclaimed their own Federated state in northern Cyprus. The UN held numerous discussions from 1985-92, without any results towards unification.

The president is Chief of State and Head of Government.

* * * NOTE: This section has been renumbered. * * *

RULERS:
British to 1960

MONETARY SYSTEM:
1 Shilling = 9 Piastres
1 Pound = 20 Shillings to 1963
1 Shilling = 50 Mils
1 Pound = 1000 Mils, 1963-83
1 Pound = 100 Cents, 1983-

DEMOCRATIC REPUBLIC

ΚΥΠΡΙΑΚΗ ΔΗΜΟΚΡΑΤΙΑ

KIBRIS CUMHURIYETI

DEMOCRATIC REPUBLIC OF CYPRUS

1961 ISSUE

#37-40 arms at r., map at lower r. Wmk: Eagle's head. Printer: BWC (w/o imprint).

37 (30)	**250 MILS**		**VG**	**VF**	**UNC**
	1.12.1961. Blue on m/c unpt. Fruit at l. Mine on back.		2.25	7.00	27.50
38 (31)	**500 MILS**				
	1.12.1961. Green on m/c unpt. Mountain road lined w/trees on back.		5.50	17.50	55.00

39	1 POUND	VG	VF	UNC
(32)	1.12.1961. Brown on m/c unpt. Viaduct and pillars on back.	5.00	15.00	50.00
40	5 POUNDS			
(33)	1.12.1961. Dk. green on m/c unpt. Embroidery and floral design on back.	12.00	30.00	90.00

ΚΕΝΤΡΙΚΗ ΤΡΑΠΕΖΑ ΤΗΣ ΚΥΠΡΟΥ

KIBRIS MERKEZ BANKASI

CENTRAL BANK OF CYPRUS

1964-66 ISSUE
#41-42 like #37-40. Various date and sign. varieties.

41	250 MILS	VG	VF	UNC
(34)	1964-82. Like #37.			
	a. 1.12.1964-1.12.1969; 1.9.1971. 71.	1.00	2.50	10.00
	b. 1.3.1971; 1.6.1972; 1.5.1973; 3; 1.6.1974.	.50	1.85	7.50
	c. 1.7.1975-1.6.1982.	.40	1.25	5.00

42	500 MILS	VG	VF	UNC
(35)	1964-79. Like #38.			
	a. 1.12.1964-1.6.1972.	1.50	4.00	17.50
	b. 1.5.1973; 1.6.1974; 1.7.1975; 5; 1.8.1976.	1.00	2.50	10.00
	c. 1.6.1979; 1.9.1979.	.75	2.00	7.00

43	1 POUND	VG	VF	UNC
(36)	1966-78. Like #39.			
	a. 1.8.1966-1.6.1972.	1.50	3.50	12.50
	b. 1.11.1972; 1.5.1973; 1.6.1974; 1.8.1976.	1.00	3.00	8.50
	c. 1.7.1975; 1.5.1978.	.75	2.50	6.50

44	5 POUNDS	VG	VF	UNC
(37)	1966-76. Blue on m/c unpt. Like #40.			
	a. 1.8.1966; 1.9.1967; 1.12.1969.	4.00	15.00	45.00
	b. 1.6.1972; 1.11.1972; 1.7.1975.	FV	10.00	30.00
	c. 1.5.1973; 1.6.1974; 1.8.1976.	FV	7.00	25.00

1977-82 ISSUE
#45-48 wmk: Moufflon (ram's) head.

45	500 MILS	VG	VF	UNC
(38)	1.6.1982. Brown and m/c. Woman seated at r., arms at top l. ctr. Dam on back.	FV	1.85	6.00

			VG	VF	UNC
49 (42)	**50 CENTS** 1.10.1983; 1.12.1984. Brown and m/c. Similar to #45.		FV	1.50	4.25

			VG	VF	UNC
46 (39)	**1 POUND** 1.6.1979. Brown and m/c. Nymph at r., arms at top l. ctr. Abbey on back.		FV	2.25	11.00

			VG	VF	UNC
50 (43)	**1 POUND** 1.2.1982; 1.11.1982; 1.3.1984; 1.11.1985. Dk. brown and m/c. Like #46 but bank name in outlined (white) letters by dk. unpt.		FV	2.75	8.00

			VG	VF	UNC
47 (40)	**5 POUNDS** 1.6.1979. Purple and m/c. Limestone head from Hellenistic period at l., arms at upper ctr. r. Theater at Salamis (Roman period) on back.		FV	10.00	40.00

			VG	VF	UNC
51 (44)	**10 POUNDS** 1.4.1987; 1.10.1988. Dk. green and blue-black on m/c unpt. Similar to #48 but w/date above at l. of modified arms on r.		FV	FV	40.00

1987-92 ENHANCED ISSUE
#53-56 w/micro-printing. Wmk: Moufflon (ram's) head.

			VG	VF	UNC
48 (41)	**10 POUNDS** 1977-85; 1993. Dk. green and blue-black on m/c unpt. Archaic bust at l., arms at r. 2 birds on back.				
	a. 1.4.1977; 1.5.1978; 1.6.1979.		FV	25.00	60.00
	b. 1.7.1980; 1.10.1981; 1.6.1982; 1.6.1985.		FV	22.50	50.00

1982-87 ISSUE
Pound/Cent System
#49-51 wmk: Moufflon (ram's) head.

			VG	VF	UNC
52 (45)	**50 CENTS** 1.4.1987; 1.10.1988; 1.11.1989. Like #49 but w/bank name in micro-printing alternately in Greek and Turkish just below upper frame.		FV	FV	2.75

53 (46)	**1 POUND**	VG	VF	UNC
	1987-. Like #50 but w/bank name in unbroken line of micro-printing with Greek at left and Turkish at right just below upper frame.			
	a. W/o lt. beige unpt. color on back. Micro-print line under dark bar at top.1.4.1987; 1.10.1988; 1.11.1989.	FV	FV	6.00
	b. Lt. beige color added to ctr. unpt. on back for security. 1.11.1989; 1.2.1992.	FV	FV	5.00
	c. Dot added near upper l. corner. 1.3.1993.	FV	FV	5.00

54 (47)	**5 POUNDS**	VG	VF	UNC
	1.10.1990. Like #47 but line of micro-printing added.	FV	FV	22.50

55 (48)	**10 POUNDS**	VG	VF	UNC
	1.11.1989; 1.10.1990; 1.2.1992; 1.3.1993. Dk. green and blue-black on m/c unpt. Similar to #51 but w/enhanced security features.	FV	FV	35.00

56 (49)	**20 POUNDS**	VG	VF	UNC
	1.2.1992. Deep blue on m/c unpt. Bust of Aphrodite at l., arms at upper ctr., ancient bird (pottery art) at r. Ancient merchant boat of Kyrenia at ctr., ancient pottery jugs at lower r. on back. Printer: TDLR.			
	a. YIRMI LIRA (error).	FV	FV	70.00
	b. YIRMI LIRA.	FV	FV	70.00

1996 ISSUE

57 (50)	**20 POUNDS**	VG	VF	UNC
	1996.			Expected New Issue

CZECHOSLOVAKIA

The Republic of Czechoslovakia (Ceskoslovenská), located in central Europe, had an area of 49,365 sq. mi. (127,859 sq. km.) and a population of 15.7 million. Capital: Prague. Machinery was the chief export of the highly industrialized economy.

Czechoslovakia proclaimed itself a republic on Oct. 28, 1918. with T. G. Masaryk as president. Hitler provoked Czechoslovakia's German minority in the Sudentenland to agitate for autonomy. At Munich in Sept. of 1938, France and Britain, forced the cession of the Sudentenland to Germany. In March 1939, Germany invaded Czechoslovakia and established the Protectorate of Bohemia and Moravia. Slovakia, a province in southeastern Czechoslovakia, was constituted as a republic under Nazi influence. After the World War II defeat of the Axis powers re-established the physical integrity and independence of Czechoslovakia, while bringing it within the Russian sphere of influence. On Feb. 23-25, 1948, the Communists seized control of the government in a coup d'etat, and adopted a constitution making the country a "people's republic." A new constitution adopted June 11, 1960, converted the country into a "socialist republic" which lasted until 1989. On Nov. 11, 1989, public demonstrations against the communist government began and in Dec. of that same year, communism was overthrown and the Czech and Slovak Federal Republic was formed. On January 1, 1993 this was split to form the Czech Republic and the Republic of Slovakia.

MONETARY SYSTEM:

1 Koruna = 100 Haleru

SPECIMEN NOTES:

Large quantities of specimens were formerly made available to collectors. Most notes issued after 1945 are distinguished by a perforation consisting of a few small holes or letter S. Since the difference in price between original and specimen notes is frequently very great, both types of notes are valued. The earlier issues were recalled from circulation and then perforated: SPECIMEN or NEPLATNE for collectors. Caution should be exercised while examining notes as we have been notified of examples of perforated specimen notes having the holes filled back in.

SOCIALIST REPUBLIC

CESKOSLOVANSKÁ SOCIALISTICKA REPUBLIKA

CZECHOSLOVAK SOCIALIST REPUBLIC

1961 ISSUE

#81 and 82 wmk: Star in circle, repeated.

81	**3 KORUN**	VG	VF	UNC
	1961. Blue-black on blue-green unpt. Similar to #79.			
	a. Issued note.	.20	.50	2.50
	s. Perforated w/3 holes or SPECIMEN.	—	.50	2.00

82	**5 KORUN**	VG	VF	UNC
	1961. Dull black on pale green unpt. Similar to #80.			
	a. Issued note.	.20	.50	2.50
	s. Perforated w/3 holes or SPECIMEN.	—	.50	2.00

STÁTNÍ BANKY CESKOSLOVENSKÉ

CZECHOSLOVAK STATE BANK

1961-64 ISSUE

#88-98 printer: STC-Prague.

NOTE: #91 with an *M-1000* adhesive or printed stamp see Czech Republic; with a Slovakia *1000* stamp see Slovakia.

88	10 KORUN	VG	VF	UNC
	1960. Brown on m/c unpt. 2 girls w/flowers at r. Orava Dam on back.	.10	.50	4.00

89 (90)	25 KORUN	VG	VF	UNC
	1961. Blue. Socialist arms at l. ctr. J. Zizka at r. Tabor town square on back.			
	a. Issued note.	1.00	2.50	10.00
	s. Perforated: *SPECIMEN*.	—	—	5.00

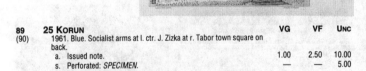

90	50 KORUN	VG	VF	UNC
	1964. Red-brown. Russian soldier and partisan at r. Refinery on back.	1.00	2.50	7.00

91	100 KORUN	VG	VF	UNC
	1961. Deep green on m/c unpt. Factory at lower l., farm couple at r. Charles Bridge and Prague castle on back.			
	a. Wmk: Star within linden leaf, repeated. Series prefix: B, C, D, P, R, T, Z and X01-X24.	1.00	4.50	12.50
	b. Reissue wmk: Multiple stars and linden leaves. Series prefix: X25-. (1990-92).	1.00	2.00	8.00

1970 ISSUE

92	20 KORUN	VG	VF	UNC
	1970. Blue on lt. blue and m/c unpt. Arms at ctr., J. Zizka at r. Medieval procession on back.	1.00	2.00	5.00

1973 ISSUE

NOTE: #93 w/additional *D-500* adhesive stamp, see Czech Republic. With *SLOVENSKA REPUBLIKA* adhesive stamp, see Slovakia.

93	500 KORUN	VG	VF	UNC
	1973. Deep brown-violet and m/c. Soldiers at r. Medieval shield at lower ctr., mountain fortress ruins at Devin at r. on back.	8.00	15.00	50.00

1985-89 ISSUE

NOTE: #95 and 96 w/additional *SLOVENSKA REPUBLIKA* adhesive stamp, see Slovakia.

NOTE: #97 was withdrawn shortly after issue. In circulation only from 1.10.1989 to 31.12.1990.

NOTE: #98 w/additional *M-1000* adhesive stamp or printed, see Czech Republic. With *SLOVENSKA REPUBLIKA* adhesive stamp, see Slovakia.

		VG	VF	UNC
94	**10 KORUN**	.25	1.00	2.25

1986. Deep br View of orava bird at lower l. w/trees and mountains on back.

		VG	VF	UNC
95	**20 KORUN**	.30	1.25	3.50

1988. Blue and m/c. J. Komensky at r., alphabet at l. Tree of life growing from book at ctr., man and woman at l. on back.

		VG	VF	UNC
96	**50 KORUN**	.50	2.00	7.50

1987. Brown-violet and blue on red and orange unpt. L. Sturat r. Bratislava castle on back.

		VG	VF	UNC
97	**100 KORUN**	2.00	5.00	15.00

1989. Dk. green on green and red unpt. K. Gottwald at r. Prague castle on back.

		VG	VF	UNC
98	**1000 KORUN**	15.00	30.00	85.00

1985. Blue black, blue and purple on m/c unpt. B. Smetana at r. Vysehrad Castle at l. on back.

FOREIGN EXCHANGE CERTIFICATES

ODBERNÍ POUKAZ

These certificates were issued by the government-owned company *Tuzex*. Foreign visitors could exchange their hard currency for regular Korun or the Tuzex vouchers. These vouchers were accepted at special stores where imported or exported goods could be bought.

The usual black market rate for Tuzex vouchers was 5-7 regular Korun for 1 Tuzex Koruna.

1970's ND ISSUE

#FX1-FX8 white outer edge. *TUZEX* once in text. Dates of issue up to Dec. 1988. Several text varieties exist. Listings are for type only. Printer: STC-P.

NOITE: #F4-F8 were redeemable 1 year form issue date.

		VG	VF	UNC
FX1	**0.50 KORUNA**	.50	1.00	2.50
	ND. Violet and green.			
FX2	**1 KORUNA**	.50	1.00	2.50
	ND. Green on ochre unpt.			

		VG	VF	UNC
FX3	**5 KORUN**	1.00	2.00	5.00
	ND. Violet on blue and ochre u npt.			
FX4	**10 KORUN**	2.00	4.50	10.00
	ND. Dk. green on green unpt.			
FX5	**20 KORUN**	4.00	8.50	20.00
	ND. Brown on orange and green unpt.			
FX6	**50 KORUN**	8.00	17.50	40.00
	ND. Brown on pink and orange u npt.			
FX7	**100 KORUN**	10.00	25.00	60.00
	ND. Violet on green and violet unpt.			
FX8	**500 KORUN**	20.00	45.00	100.00
	ND. Gray on brown unpt.			

1989 ISSUE

#FX9-16 lg. globe w/*TUZEX* at l. and r. Colors as previous issue but outer edge w/design. Printer STC-P.

NOTE: #FX12-16 were redeemable 1 year from issue date.

		VG	VF	UNC
FX9	**0.50 KORUNA**	.30	.75	2.00
	1989; 1990. Violet edge.			
FX10	**1 KORUNA**	.30	.75	2.00
	1989; 1990. Yellow-brown edge.			
FX11	**5 KORUN**	.60	1.50	4.50
	1989; 1990. Blue and ochre edg e.			
FX12	**10 KORUN**	1.50	4.00	9.00
	1989; 1990. Lt. and dk. green edge.			
FX13	**20 KORUN**	3.00	8.00	18.00
	1989; 1990. Yellow-brown and g reen edge.			
FX14	**50 KORUN**	6.00	15.00	35.00
	1989; 1990. Pink and orange ed ge.			
FX15	**100 KORUN**	8.00	20.00	50.00
	1989; 1990. Violet and green e dge.			
FX16	**500 KORUN**	17.50	40.00	85.00
	1989; 1990. Brown edge.			

CZECH REPUBLIC

The Czech Republic, formerly united with Slovakia in the Czech & Slovak Federal Republic, is bordered in the west by Germany, to the north by Poland, to the east by Slovakia and to the south by Austria. It consists of 3 major regions: Bohemia, Moravia and Silesia. It has an area of 20,431 sq. mi. (78,864 sq. km.) and a population of 10.3 million. Capital: Prague (Praha). Agriculture and livestock are chief occupations while coal deposits are the main mineral resources.

The Czech lands in the western part were united with the Slovaks to form the Czechoslovak Republic, on Oct. 28, 1918 upon the dissolution of Austria-Hungarian Empire. This territory was broken up for the benefit of Germany, Poland and Hungary by the Munich agreement signed by the United Kingdom, France, Germany and Italy on Sept. 29, 1938. In March 1939 the German influenced Slovak government proclaimed Slovakia independent. Germany incorporated the Czech lands into the Third Reich as the "Protectorate of Bohemia and Moravia." A government-in-exile was set up in London in July 1940. The Soviets and USA forces liberated the area by May 1945. Communist influence increased steadily while pressure for liberalization culminated in the overthrow of the Stalinist leader Antonçn Novotny and his associates in 1968. The Communist Party then introduced far reaching reforms which received warnings from Moscow, followed by occupation of Warsaw Pact forces resulting in stationing of Soviet forces. Mass demonstrations for reform began in Nov. 1989 and the Federal Assembly abolished the Communist Party's sole right to govern. New governments followed on Dec. 3. and Dec. 10. The Movement for Democratic Slovakia was apparent in the June 1992 elections with the Slovak National Council adopting a declaration of sovereignty, later a constitution for an independent Slovakia, with the Federal Assembly voting for the dissolvement of the Czech and Slovak Federal Republic. This came into effect on Dec. 31, 1992 and both new republics came into being on Jan. 1, 1993.

MONETARY SYSTEM:
1 Czechoslovak Koruna (Kcs) = 1 Czech Koruna (Kc)
1 Koruna = 100 Haleru

REPUBLIC

CESKÁ NÁRODNÍ BANKA

CZECH NATIONAL BANK

1993 PROVISIONAL ISSUE

#1-3 This issue was released 8.2.1993 having adhesive revalidation stamps affixed (later a printed *1000* was also circulated.) Valid until 31.8.1993 but could be exchanged in deposits until 31.5.1994. Old Czechoslovak notes of 100 Korun and higher denominations became worthless on 7.2.1993. Smaller denominations remained in circulation until 30.11.1993.

		VG	**VF**	**UNC**
1	**100 KORUN** ND (1993-old date 1961). Dk. green *C-100* adhesive stamp affixed to Czechoslovakia #91b.	3.00	7.00	15.00

		VG	**VF**	**UNC**
2	**500 KORUN** ND (1993-old date 1973). Dk. green *D-500* adhesive stamp affixed to Czechoslovakia #93.	15.00	30.00	65.00

		VG	**VF**	**UNC**
3	**1000 KORUN** ND (1993-old date 1985). Deep green *M-1000* revalidation stamp on Czechoslovakia #98.			
	a. Adhesive stamp affixed.	25.00	60.00	150.00
	b. Stamp image printed on note.	30.00	65.00	200.00

1993 ISSUE

#4-9 arms at ctr. r. on back. Serial # prefex *A*.

		VG	**VF**	**UNC**
4	**50 KORUN** 1993. Violet and black on pink and gray unpt. St. A. Ceska at r. and w/crown as wmk. Lg. A within gothic window frame at l. ctr. on back. Printer: STC-P.	FV	FV	5.50

		VG	**VF**	**UNC**
5	**100 KORUN** 1993. Blue-green, green and blue-black on lilac and m/c unpt. Kg. Karel IV at r. and as wmk. Lg. seal of Charles University at l. ctr. on back. Printer: TDLR.	FV	FV	8.50

		VG	**VF**	**UNC**
6	**200 KORUN** 1993. Deep brown on lt. orange and lt. green unpt. J. A. Komensky at r. and as wmk. Hands outreached at l. ctr. on back. Printer: STC-P.			
	a. Security filament w/*200 KCS*.	FV	FV	12.50
	b. Security filament w/*200 KC*.	FV	FV	12.50
	x. Error. Security filament from Zaire note.	—	—	80.00

10	**20 KORUN**	VG	VF	UNC
	1994. Blue-black and gray on lt. blue unpt, Kg. P. Otakar I. and as wmk. Crown with seal above at ctr., stylized crown lower I. on back.			
	a. Series A. Security filament at ctr.	FV	FV	2.00
	b. Series B. Security filament at I. ctr.	FV	FV	2.00

7	**500 KORUN**	VG	VF	UNC
	1993. Dk. brown, brown & brown-violet on pink and tan unpt. Rose in unpt. at upper ctr., Mrs. B. Nemcová at r. and as wmk. Laureate young woman's head at I. ctr. on back. Printer: TDLR.	FV	FV	24.00

11	**50 KORUN**	VG	VF	UNC
	1994. Like #4 but w/o gray in unpt. Stylized heart at lower I. on back. Serial # Prefex B.	FV	FV	5.00

8	**1000 KORUN**	VG	VF	UNC
	1993. Purple and lilac on m/c unpt. F. Palacky at r. and as wmk. Eagle and Kromeriz Castle on back. Printer: STC-P.	FV	FV	45.00

12	**100 KORUN**	VG	VF	UNC
	1995. Like #5, but w/stylized *K* in circle at lower r. on back. Serial # Prefex B.	FV	FV	8.50
13	**200 KORUN**			
	1995. Like #6 but w/stylized open book at lower r. on back. Serial # prefix B.	FV	FV	12.50

9	**5000 KORUN**	VG	VF	UNC
	1993. Black, blue-gray and violet on pink and lt. gray unpt. Pres. T.G. Masaryk at r. Montage of Prague Gothic and Baroque buildings on back. Printer: STC-P.	FV	FV	200.00

1994-95 ISSUE
#10-14 printer: STC-P.

14	**500 KORUN**	VG	VF	UNC
	1995. Like #7, but w/stylized rose at lower r. on back. Serial # Prefex B.	FV	FV	30.00
15	**1000 KORUN**			
	2996. Like #8 but w/ stylized P and tree at lower r. on back.	FV	FV	53.50
16	**2000 KORUN**			
	1996. Dk. olive-green, green and violet on tan unpt. Eva Destinnová at I. Lyre at upper I. in spray. Muse of music and lyric poetry Euterpe, tip I. ctr. Violin and cello and a large *D*. Stylized lyre at lower r. on back.	FV	FV	105.00

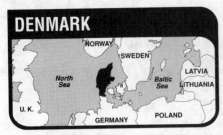

DENMARK

The Kingdom of Denmark, a constitutional monarchy located at the mouth of the Baltic Sea, has an area of 16,633 sq. mi. (43,069 sq. km.) and a population of 5.16 million. Capital: Copenhagen. Most of the country is arable. Agriculture, which employs the majority of the people, is conducted by small farmers served by cooperatives. The largest industries are food processing, iron and metal, and fishing. Machinery, meats (chiefly bacon), dairy products and chemicals are exported.

Denmark, a great power during the Viking period of the 9th-11th centuries, conducted raids on western Europe and England, and in the 11th century united England, Denmark and Norway under the rule of King Canute. Despite a struggle between the crown and the nobility (13th-14th centuries) which forced the King to grant a written constitution, Queen Margaret (1353-1412) succeeded in uniting Denmark, Norway, Sweden, Finland and Greenland under the Danish crown, placing all of Scandinavia under the rule of Denmark. An unwise alliance with Napoleon contributed to the dismembering of the empire and fostered a liberal movement which succeeded in making Denmark a constitutional monarchy in 1849.

RULERS:
Frederik IX, 1947-1972
Margrethe II, 1972-

MONETARY SYSTEM:
1 Krone = 100 Ore (= 1/2 Rigsdaler), 1874-

KINGDOM

DANMARKS NATIONALBANK

1944-46 ISSUE
#35-41 first sign. Svendsen for #35, 36, 37a, 38, 39 - 1944-45. Halberg for #35, 37a, 37b, 38, 40 1945-49. Riim for #35, 37b, 38, 40, 41 - 1948-62.

	500 KRONER	VG	VF	UNC
41	1944-62. Orange. Face like #34. Arms only on back.	110.00	160.00	225.00

1950-63 ISSUE
Law of 7.4.1936

#42-47 first sign. changes. Second sign. Riim, 1952-67 for #42a, 42b, 43, 44, 45a, 45b, 46a, 46b, 47; Valeur from 1970- for #44, 45b, 46b.

	5 KRONER	VG	VF	UNC
42	(19)50-60. Blue-green. Portr. Thorvaldsen at l., 3 Graces at r. Kalundborg city view on back. Wmk: 5 repeated.			
	a. 5 in the wmk. 10.55mm high. W/o dot after 7 in law date. (19)52. Series A0; A1; A2.	2.75	13.50	45.00
	b. As a., but w/dot after 7 in law date. (19)52.	1.85	9.00	30.00
	c. 5 in the wmk. 13mm high. (19)55-60.	1.50	7.50	25.00
	r. Replacement note. (19)50 (sic).	1.50	7.50	25.00

	10 KRONER	VG	VF	UNC
43	(19)50-52. Black and olive-brown. Portr. Andersen at l., birds in nest at r. Green landscape on back. Wmk: 5 repeated.			
	a. Issued note. (19)51-52.	4.00	20.00	65.00
	r. Replacement note. (19)50 (sic).	5.00	25.00	85.00

	10 KRONER	VG	VF	UNC
44	(19)50-74. Black and brown. Portr. Andersen at l. Black landscape on back.			
	a. Top and bottom line in frame commences w/10.	7.50	37.50	125.00
	b. As a., but w/10's in wmk. 14mm high. (19)54-57.	5.50	27.50	90.00
	c. 1957-74. Top and bottom line in frame commences with TI. (19)57-59.	2.00	9.00	30.00
	d. As c. (19)60-69.	2.00	6.00	20.00
	e. As c. (19)70-74.	FV	2.75	5.50
	r. Replacement note. (19)50 (sic).	2.50	4.50	10.00

	50 KRONER	VG	VF	UNC
45	(19)50-70. Blue on green unpt. Portr. O. Romer at l., tower at r. Rock formation on blue back.			
	a. Hand-made paper. Wmk: Crowns and 50 (19)56-61.	15.00	35.00	150.00
	b. Wmk: Rhombuses and 50. (19)62-70.	10.00	15.00	35.00
	r. Replacement note. (19)50 (sic).	12.50	22.50	75.00

	100 KRONER	VG	VF	UNC
46	(19)50-70. Red on red-brown unpt. Portr. H. C. Orsted at l., compass at r. Kronborg city view.			
	a. Handmade paper. Wmk: Close wavy lines. (19)61.	30.00	50.00	125.00
	b. Wmk: 100. (19)61-70.	22.50	35.00	60.00
47	**500 KRONER**			
	(19)63-67. Green. Portr. C. D. F. Reventlow at l., farmer plowing at r. Roskilde city view on back.	100.00	150.00	250.00

1972-79 ISSUE

Issued under *L. 1936*. The year of issue is shown by the 2 middle numerals within the series code at lower l. or r. Sign. varieties.

#48-52 portr. at r. of all notes painted by Danish artist Jens Juel (1745-1802). Wmk: Head of J. Juel and value repeated vertically.

#48-50 printer: BWC (w/o imprint.)

#51-53 printer: TDLR (w/o imprint.)

48	10 KRONER	VG	VF	UNC
	(19)72-78. Black on olive and m/c unpt. Portr. S. Kirchhoff at r. Duck at l. on back.	FV	2.50	5.00

49	20 KRONER	VG	VF	UNC
	(19)79-88. Dk. blue on brown and m/c unpt. Portr. Tutein at r. 2 birds on back.	FV	FV	8.00

50	50 KRONER	VG	VF	UNC
	(19)72-90. Blue. Portr. Ryberg at r. Fish at l. on back.	FV	FV	15.00

51	100 KRONER	VG	VF	UNC
	(19)72-91. Red and m/c. J. Juel's self-portrait at r. Butterfly at l. on back.	FV	FV	28.50

52	500 KRONER	VG	VF	UNC
	(19)72-88. Black on green and m/c unpt. "Unknown lady of Qualen" at r. Reptile on back.	FV	FV	120.00

53	1000 KRONER	VG	VF	UNC
	(19)72-86. Black on gray and m/c unpt. Portr. T. Heiberg at r. Long eared squirrel on back.	FV	FV	235.00

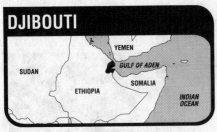

DJIBOUTI

SUDAN | YEMEN | GULF OF ADEN | ETHIOPIA | SOMALIA | INDIAN OCEAN

The Republic of Djibouti (formerly French Somaliland or the French Overseas Territory of Afars and Issas), located in northeast Africa at the Bab el Mandeb Strait connecting the Suez Canal and the Red Sea with the Gulf of Aden and the Indian Ocean, has an area of 8,494 sq. mi. (22,000 sq. km.) and a population of 542,000. Capital: Djibouti. The tiny nation has less than one sq. mi. of arable land, and no natural resources except salt, sand and camels. The commercial activities of the trans-shipment port of Djibouti and the Addis Ababa-Djibouti railroad are the basis of the economy. Salt, fish and hides are exported.

French interest in former French Somaliland began in 1839 with concessions obtained by a French naval lieutenant from the provincial sultans. French Somaliland was made a protectorate in 1884 and its boundaries were delimited by the Franco-British and Ethiopian accords of 1887 and 1897. It became a colony in 1896 and a territory within the French Union in 1946. In 1958, it voted to join the new French Community as an overseas territory, and reaffirmed that choice by a referendum in March 1967. Its name was changed from French Somaliland to the French Territory of Afars and Issas on July 5, 1967.

The French Tricolor, which had flown over the strategically important territory for 115 years, was lowered for the last time on June 27, 1977, when French Afars and Issas became Africa's 49th independent state, under the name of the Republic of Djibouti.

MONETARY SYSTEM:
1 Franc = 100 Centimes

REPUBLIC OF DJIBOUTI

BANQUE NATIONALE

1979; 1984 ND ISSUE

36	**500 FRANCS**	VG	VF	UNC
	ND (1979; 1988). Like #33.			
	a. Blue unpt. W/o sign. (1979).	FV	5.00	10.00
	b. Pale blue unpt. Sign title: *LE GOUVERNEUR* added. (1988).	FV	4.50	8.50

(1979)

(1988)

37	**1000 FRANCS**	VG	VF	UNC
	ND (1979; 1988). Like #34.			
	a. Long Arabic text on back. W/o sign. (1979).	FV	10.00	21.50
	b. Sign. title: *LE GOUVERNEUR* added above *MILLE*. Short Arabic text at top on back. (1988).	FV	8.00	18.50
	c. Long Arabic text on back. (1991).	FV	7.50	16.50
	d. As c but w/ segmented foil over security thread.	FV	FV	14.00

38	**5000 FRANCS**	VG	VF	UNC
	ND (1979). Like #35.			
	a. W/o sign.	FV	50.00	90.00
	b. W/sign.	FV	35.00	55.00
	c. As b but w/segmented foil security thread.	FV	40.00	85.00

39	**10,000 FRANCS**	VG	VF	UNC
	ND (1984). Brown and red on yellow and green. Woman holding baby at l., goats in tree at r. Fish and harbor scene on back.			
	a. Sign. title: *TRÉSORIE*	FV	50.00	120.00
	b. Sign. title: *GOUVERNEUR*. Segmented foil security thread.	FV	FV	100.00

DOMINICAN REP.

The Dominican Republic, which occupies the eastern two-thirds of the island of Hispaniola, has an area of 18,816 sq. mi. (48,734 sq. km.) and a population of 7.3 million. Capital: Santo Domingo. The agricultural economy produces sugar, coffee, tobacco and cocoa. Columbus discovered Hispaniola in 1492, and named it *La Isla Espanola* - "the Spanish Island." Santo Domingo, the oldest white settlement in the Western Hemisphere, was the base from which Spain conducted its exploration of the New World. Later, French buccaneers settled the western third of Hispaniola, which in 1697 was ceded to France by Spain, and in 1804 became the Republic of Haiti - "mountainous country." At this time, the Spanish called their part of Hispaniola Santo Domingo, and the French called their part Saint-Domingue. In 1822, the Haitians conquered the entire island and held it until 1844, when Juan Pablo Duarte, the national hero of the Dominican Republic, drove them out of eastern Hispaniola and established an independent Dominican Republic. The republic returned voluntarily to Spanish dominion - after being rejected by France, Britain and the United States - from 1861 to 1865, when independence was restored.

MONETARY SYSTEM:
1 Peso = 100 Centavos

REPUBLICA DOMINICANA

BANCO CENTRAL DE LA REPÚBLICA DOMINICANA

1956 ISSUE

		VG	VF	UNC
71 (26)	**1 PESO** ND (1957-61). Like #60. Printer: ABNC.	1.50	6.00	27.50

1961 ND ISSUES

		VG	VF	UNC
85	**10 CENTAVOS** ND (1961). Blue and black. Banco de Reservas in round frame at ctr. Back blue. Printer: ABNC.	1.00	3.50	12.50

		VG	VF	UNC
86	**10 CENTAVOS** ND (1961). Black on lt. blue-green safety paper. Banco de Reservas in oval frame at ctr. back green. Local printer.	2.00	6.00	20.00

		VG	VF	UNC
87	**25 CENTAVOS** ND (1961). Red and black. Entrance to the Banco Central in rectangular frame at ctr. Back red. Printer: ABNC.	1.00	4.00	15.00

		VG	VF	UNC
88	**25 CENTAVOS** ND (1961). Black. Entrance to the Banco Central in oval frame at ctr. Back green. Local printer.			
	a. Pink safety paper.	1.75	5.00	20.00
	b. Plain cream paper.	2.50	7.50	22.50

		VG	VF	UNC
89	**50 CENTAVOS** ND (1961). Purple and black. Palacio Nacional in circular frame at ctr. Back purple. Printer: ABNC.	1.75	4.50	17.50

		VG	VF	UNC
90	**50 CENTAVOS** ND (1961). Black on yellow safety paper. Palacio Nacional in oval frame at ctr. Back green. Local printer.	5.50	25.00	60.00

1962 ND ISSUE

#91-98 w/text over seal: *SANTO DOMINGO/DISTRITO NACIONAL/REPUBLICA DOMINICANA.* Medallic portr. Liberty head at l., arms at r. on back. Printer: ABNC.

		VG	VF	UNC
91	**1 PESO** ND (1962-63). Red. Portr. Duarte at ctr.	4.00	16.00	48.00

92 5 PESOS
ND (1962). Red. Portr. Sanchez at ctr. Back purple.

	VG	VF	UNC
	6.00	24.00	72.00

93 10 PESOS
ND (1962). Red. Portr. Mella at ctr. Back brown.

	VG	VF	UNC
	12.50	50.00	150.00

94 20 PESOS
ND (1962). Red. *Puerta del Conde* at ctr. Back olive.

	VG	VF	UNC
	25.00	100.00	300.00

95 50 PESOS
ND (1962). Red. Tomb of Columbus at ctr. Back blue-gray.

	VG	VF	UNC
	50.00	150.00	450.00

96 100 PESOS
ND (1962). Red. Woman w/coffee pot and cup at ctr. Back blue-gray.

	VG	VF	UNC
	75.00	175.00	525.00

97 500 PESOS
ND (1962). "Obelisco de Ciudad Trujillo" at ctr.

	VG	VF	UNC
	—	—	—

98 1000 PESOS
ND (1962). Minor Basilica of Santa Maria at ctr. Unique.

	VG	VF	UNC
	—	—	—

1964 ND ISSUE
#99-106 medallic portr. Liberty head at l., arms at r. on back. Sign. varieties. Printer: TDLR.

99 1 PESO
ND (1964-73). Portr. black on lt. green and pinkish tan unpt. Duarte at ctr. w/eyes looking l., white bow tie. Back black.

	VG	VF	UNC
a. Issued note.	.50	2.50	10.00
s. Specimen.	—	—	20.00

100 5 PESOS
ND (1964-74). Brown on lt. green and lilac unpt. Portr. Sanchez at ctr.

	VG	VF	UNC
a. Issued note.	3.00	10.00	30.00
s. Specimen.	—	—	22.50

101 10 PESOS
ND (1964-74). Green on lt. green and lt. lilac unpt. Portr. Mella at ctr.

	VG	VF	UNC
a. Issued note.	5.00	16.00	48.00
s. Specimen.	—	—	32.50

102 20 PESOS
ND (1964-74). Brown on lt. green and blue unpt. National shrine at ctr.

	VG	VF	UNC
a. Issued note.	8.00	30.00	75.00
s. Specimen.	—	—	50.00

103 50 PESOS
ND (1964-74). Purple. Ox cart at ctr.

	VG	VF	UNC
a. Issued note.	20.00	65.00	130.00
s. Specimen.	—	—	90.00

		VG	VF	UNC
104	**100 PESOS**			
	ND (1964-74). Orange. Banco Central at ctr.			
	a. Issued note.	40.00	125.00	250.00
	s. Specimen.	—	—	175.00

		VG	VF	UNC
105	**500 PESOS**			
	ND (1964-74). Blue. Columbus' tomb and cathedral at ctr.			
	a. Issued note.	100.00	400.00	750.00
	s. Specimen.	—	—	500.00

		VG	VF	UNC
106	**1000 PESOS**			
	ND (1964-74). Red. National Palace at ctr. Medallic portr. Liberty at l. ctr., arms at r. ctr. on back.			
	a. Issued note.	200.00	750.00	1500.
	s. Specimen.	—	—	1000.

1973 ND ISSUE

		VG	VF	UNC
107	**1 PESO**			
	ND (1973-74). Like #99 but Duarte w/eyes looking front, black bow tie.	.50	2.00	8.50

1975 ISSUE

#108-115 dates in upper margin on back.

		VG	VF	UNC
108	**1 PESO**			
	1975-78. Like #107.	.25	1.50	4.50
109	**5 PESOS**			
	1975-76. Like #100.	.50	5.00	15.00
110	**10 PESOS**			
	1975-76. Like #101.	1.50	9.00	27.00
111	**20 PESOS**			
	1975-76. Like #102.	2.50	15.00	45.00
112	**50 PESOS**			
	1975-76. Like #103.	5.50	33.50	100.00
113	**100 PESOS**			
	1975-76. Like #104.	10.00	60.00	180.00
114	**500 PESOS**			
	1975. Like #105.	50.00	250.00	750.00
115	**1000 PESOS**			
	1975-76. Like #106.	95.00	500.00	1500.

1977-80 ISSUES

#116-124 dates in upper margin on back.
#117-124 printer: TDLR.

		VG	VF	UNC
116	**1 PESO**			
	1978-79. Black and m/c. Duarte at r. Sugar factory on back. Printer: ABNC.	.20	1.00	3.50
117	**1 PESO**			
	1980-82. Like #116. Dates very lightly printed.	.75	1.00	3.00

		VG	VF	UNC
118	**5 PESOS**			
	1978-88. Deep brown, red brown brown, red on m/c unpt. Sanchez at r., arms at ctr. Hydroelectric dam on back.			
	a. 1978.	.50	2.50	7.50
	b. 1980-82.	FV	2.00	6.00
	c. 1984; 1985; 1987; 1988.	FV	1.50	4.50

		VG	VF	UNC
119	**10 PESOS**			
	1978-88. Deep green and black on m/c unpt. Mella at r., medallic Liberty head at ctr. Quarry mining scene on back.			
	a. 1978.	1.00	4.00	12.50
	b. 1980-82.	FV	3.00	9.00
	c. 1985; 1987; 1988.	FV	2.50	7.50

120   20 PESOS

	VG	VF	UNC
1978-88. Deep brown and brown on m/c unpt. National shrine at ctr. *Puerta del Conde* on back.			
a. 1978.	2.00	7.00	21.00
b. 1980-82.	FV	5.50	17.50
c. 1985; 1987; 1988.	FV	5.00	15.00

121   50 PESOS

	VG	VF	UNC
1978; 1980. Purple on m/c unpt. Basilica at ctr. First cathedral in America on back.	5.00	22.50	45.00

122   100 PESOS

	VG	VF	UNC
1977-87. Orange and violet on m/c unpt. Entrance to 16th century mint at ctr. Banco Central on back.			
a. Wmk: Indian head. 1977; 1978; 8; 1980; 1981.	10.00	42.50	125.00
b. Wmk: Duarte. 1984; 1987.	FV	50.00	150.00

123   500 PESOS

	VG	VF	UNC
1978; 1980. Deep blue-green, black and brown on m/c unpt. National Theater at ctr. Fort San Felipe on back.	50.00	200.00	400.00

124   1000 PESOS

	VG	VF	UNC
1978-87. Red, purple and violet on m/c unpt. National Palace at ctr. Columbus' fortress on back.			
a. Wmk: Indian head. 1978; 1980.	100.00	275.00	550.00
b. Wmk: Duarte. 1984; 1987.	90.00	225.00	450.00

1982 COMMEMORATIVE ISSUE
#125, 35th Anniversary Banco Central, 1947-1982

125   100 PESOS

	VG	VF	UNC
1982 (- old date 1978). Special commemorative text ovpt. in black below bank on back of #122. Specimen.	—	—	150.00

1984 ISSUE

126   1 PESO

	VG	VF	UNC
1984; 1987; 1988. Black, brown and m/c. New portrait of Duarte at r., otherwise like #117.	FV	FV	.85

1988 ISSUE
#127-130 printer: USBNC.

127   50 PESOS

	VG	VF	UNC
1988. Purple on m/c unpt. Similar to #121.	FV	FV	12.00

128   100 PESOS

	VG	VF	UNC
1988. Orange and violet on m/c unpt. Similar to #122.	FV	FV	18.50

129   500 PESOS

	VG	VF	UNC
1988. Deep blue-green, black and brown on m/c unpt. Similar to #123.	FV	FV	75.00

130   1000 PESOS

	VG	VF	UNC
1988; 1990. Red, purple and violet on m/c unpt. Similar to #124.	FV	FV	135.00

1990 ISSUE
#131-134 w/silver leaf-like underlays at l. and r. on face. Printer: H&S.

131   5 PESOS

	VG	VF	UNC
1990. Deep brown, red-brown, red on m/c unpt. Similar to #118.	FV	FV	1.75

132   10 PESOS

	VG	VF	UNC
1990. Deep green and black on m/c unpt. Similar to #119.	FV	FV	2.75

133   20 PESOS

	VG	VF	UNC
1990. Deep brown and brown on m/c unpt. Similar to #120	FV	FV	5.00

134   500 PESOS

	VG	VF	UNC
1990. Deep blue-green, black and brown on m/c unpt. Similar to #123.	FV	FV	7.00

1991; 1992 ISSUE
#135-138 printer: TDLR.

135   50 PESOS

	VG	VF	UNC
1991; 1994. Purple on m/c unpt. Similar to #127.	FV	FV	11.00

136   100 PESOS

	VG	VF	UNC
1991; 1994. Orange and violet on m/c unpt. Similar to #128.	FV	FV	17.50

137   500 PESOS

	VG	VF	UNC
1991; 1994. Deep blue-green, black and brown on m/c unpt. Similar to #134.	FV	FV	65.00

138   1000 PESOS

	VG	VF	UNC
1992; 1994. Red, purple and violet on m/c unpt. Similar to #130.	FV	FV	125.00

1992 COMMEMORATIVE ISSUE
#139-142, Quincentennial of First Landfall by Christopher Columbus, 1992.

		VG	VF	UNC
139	**20 PESOS** 1992. Similar to #133 but w/brown commemorative text: *1492-1992* *V Centenario...* at l. over seal. Printer: BABNC.	FV	FV	4.00

		VG	VF	UNC
140	**500 PESOS** 1992. Brown and blue-black on m/c unpt. Sailing ships at ctr., C. Columbus at ctr. r. and as wmk. Arms at l., Columbus Lighthouse, placement of Cross of Christianity and map outline at ctr. on back. Printer: CBNC.	FV	FV	65.00

		VG	VF	UNC
141	**500 PESOS** 1992. Black commemorative text ovpt. at r. on #123.	FV	FV	65.00

		VG	VF	UNC
142	**1000 PESOS** 1992. Black commemorative text ovpt. at r. on #124.	FV	FV	125.00

1993 REGULAR ISSUE
#144 and 145 printer: FNMT.

		VG	VF	UNC
143	**5 PESOS** 1993. Deep brown, red-brown, red on m/c unpt. Similar to #131. Printer: USBNC.	FV	FV	1.50
144	**100 PESOS** 1993. Orange and violet on m/c unpt. Similar to #136.	FV	FV	15.00
145	**1000 PESOS** 1993. Red, purple and violet on m/c unpt. Similar to #138.	FV	FV	120.00

1994 ISSUE

		VG	VF	UNC
146	**5 PESOS** 1994. Deep brown, red-brown, red on m/c unpt. Similar to #143. Printer: TDLR.	FV	FV	1.25

1995 ISSUE
#147 and 148 similar to #146 and #132 but w/brighter colored arms. Printer: F-CO.

		VG	VF	UNC
147	**5 PESOS** 1995.	FV	FV	1.35
148	**10 PESOS** 1995.	FV	FV	2.50

COLLECTOR SERIES

BANCO CENTRAL DE LA REPUBLICA DOMINICANA

1974; 1978 ISSUE

		ISSUE PRICE	MKT. VALUE
CS1	**1-1000 PESOS** #99-106. Ovpt: *MUESTRA* twice on face.	—	200.00
CS2	**1-1000 PESOS** #99-106. Ovpt: *MUESTRA* on face and back.	40.00	125.00
CS3	**PESOS** #116, 118-124. Ovpt: *MUESTRA/SIN VALOR* on face, *E SPECIMEN* on back.	40.00	100.00
CS4	**PESOS** #116, 118, 1240. Ovpt: *SPECIMEN* and Maltese cross prefix serial #. #58 is dated 1977.	14.00	60.00

EAST AFRICA

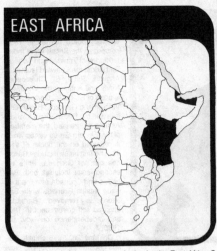

East Africa was an administrative grouping of five separate British territories: Kenya, Tanganyika (now part of Tanzania), the Sultanate of Zanzibar and Pemba (now part of Tanzania), Uganda and British Somaliland (now part of Somalia). See individual entries for specific statistics and history.

The common interest of Kenya, Tanzania and Uganda invited cooperation in economic matters and consideration of political union. The territorial governors, organized as the East Africa High Commission, met periodically to administer such common activities as taxation, industrial development and education. The authority of the Commission did not infringe upon the constitution and internal autonomy of the individual colonies. A common coinage and banknotes, which were also legal tender in Aden, was provided for use of the member colonies by the East Africa Currency Board.

Also see Somaliland Republic, Kenya, Uganda and Tanzania.

RULERS:
British

MONETARY SYSTEM:
1 Shilling = 100 Cents, 1921-

BRITISH INFLUENCE

EAST AFRICAN CURRENCY BOARD, NAIROBI

1961 ND ISSUE

#41-44 portr. Qn. Elizabeth II at upper l. w/3 sign. at l. and 4 at r. Printer: TDLR.

		VG	VF	UNC
41	**5 SHILLINGS**			
	ND (1961-63). Brown on m/c unpt.			
	a. Top l. sign: E. B. David. (1961).	5.00	17.50	150.00
	b. Top l. sign: A. L. Adu. (1962-63).	3.50	15.00	100.00

		VG	VF	UNC
42	**10 SHILLINGS**			
	ND (1961-63). Green on m/c unpt.			
	a. Top l. sign: E. B. David. (1961).	6.00	20.00	175.00
	b. Top l. sign: A. L. Adu. (1962-63).	4.00	15.00	125.00

		VG	VF	UNC
43	**20 SHILLINGS**			
	ND (1961-63). Blue on m/c unpt.			
	a. Top l. sign: E. B. David. (1961).	7.50	35.00	350.00
	b. Top l. sign: A. L. Adu. (1962-63).	5.00	22.50	225.00

		VG	VF	UNC
44	**100 SHILLINGS**			
	ND (1961-63). Red on m/c unpt.			
	a. Top l. sign: E. B. David. (1961).	15.00	90.00	700.00
	b. Top l. sign: A. L. Adu. (1962-63).	10.00	47.50	475.00

1964 ND ISSUE

#45-48 wmk. area at l., sailboat at l. ctr. Various plants on back.

		VG	VF	UNC
45	**5 SHILLINGS**			
	ND (1964). Brown on m/c unpt.	2.50	10.00	50.00

		VG	VF	UNC
46	**10 SHILLINGS**			
	ND (1964). Green on m/c unpt.	4.00	15.00	65.00

47   20 SHILLINGS
ND (1964). Blue on m/c unpt.

	VG	VF	UNC
	5.00	25.00	200.00

48   100 SHILLINGS
ND (1964). Deep red on m/c unpt.

	VG	VF	UNC
	7.50	35.00	160.00

EAST CARIBBEAN STATES

The East Caribbean States, formerly the British Caribbean Territories (Eastern Group), a currency board formed in 1950, comprised the British West Indies territories of Trinidad and Tobago; Barbados; the Leeward Islands of Anguilla, Saba, St, Christopher, Nevis and Antigua; the Windward Islands of St. Lucia, Dominica, St. Vincent and Grenada; British Guiana and the British Virgin Islands. As time progressed, the members of the Eastern Group varied which is reflected on the backs of #13-16. The first issue includes Barbados but not Grenada, while the second issue includes both Barbados and Grenada and the third issue retains Grenada while Barbados is removed. Barbados attained self-government in 1961 and independence on Nov. 30, 1966.

On May 26, 1966 British Guiana became independent as Guyana which later became a cooperative Republic on Feb. 23, 1970.

The British Virgin Islands became a largely self-governing dependent territory of the United Kingdom in 1967. United States currency is the official medioum of exchange.

St. Christopher and Nevis became fully independent on Sept. 19, 1983 but still maintain an *association* with Great Britain.

Trinidad & Tobago became an independent member state of the Commonwealth on August 31, 1962.

RULERS:
British

MONETARY SYSTEM:
1 Dollar = 100 Cents

BRITISH INFLUENCE

EAST CARIBBEAN CURRENCY AUTHORITY

SIGNATURE VARIETIES		
1 Chairman / Director Director Director	**6** Chairman / Director Director Director	
2 Chairman / Director Director Director	**7** Chairman / Director Director Director	
3 Chairman / Director Director Director	**8** Chairman / Director Director Director	
4 Chairman / Director Director Director	**9** Chairman / Director Director Director	
5 Chairman / Director Director Director	**10** Chairman / Director Director Director	

ISLAND PARTICIPATION

Variety I	Variety II	Variety III

VARIETY I: Listing of islands on back includes Barbados but not Grenada.

VARIETY II: Listing includes Barbados and Grenada.

VARIETY III: Listing retains Grenada while Barbados is deleted.

1965 ND ISSUE

#13–16 map al., Qn. Elizabeth II at r. Coastline w/rocks and trees at l. on back. Sign. varieties. Wmk. QE II. Printer: TDLR.

Beginning in 1983, #13–16 were ovpt. with circled letters at l. indicating their particular areas of issue within the Eastern Group. Letters and their respective areas are as follows:

A, Antigua	L, St. Lucia
D, Dominica	M, Montserrat
G, Grenada	U, Anguilla
K, St. Kitts	V, St. Vincentl.

13   1 DOLLAR

ND (1965). Red. Fish at ctr.

		VG	VF	UNC
a.	Sign. 1; 2.	1.00	5.00	27.50
b.	Sign. 3.	.75	3.00	12.50
c.	Sign. 4.	1.00	5.00	55.00
d.	Sign. 5; 6; 7.	.50	2.00	9.50
e.	Sign. 8.	.45	1.50	5.00
f.	Sign. 9; 10. Darker red on back as previous varieties, to Series B77.	—	.65	4.00
g.	Sign. 10. Brighter red on back. Series B83-B91.	—	.65	3.50
h.	Ovpt: A in circle.	—	.50	4.00
i.	Ovpt: D in circle.	—	.50	5.00
j.	Ovpt: G in circle.	—	.50	5.00
k.	Ovpt: K in circle.	—	.50	4.00
l.	Ovpt: L in circle.	—	.50	6.00
m.	Ovpt: M in circle.	—	.50	4.00
n.	Ovpt: V in circle.	—	.50	4.00

14   5 DOLLARS

ND (1965). Green. Flying fish at ctr.

		VG	VF	UNC
a.	Sign. 1.	6.00	25.00	125.00
b.	Sign. 2.	5.50	20.00	125.00
c.	Sign. 3.		Reported Not Confirmed	
d.	Sign. 4.	4.00	10.00	85.00
e.	Sign. 5; 6.	3.50	7.50	45.00
f.	Sign. 7.	4.00	10.00	65.00
g.	Sign. 8.	2.00	5.00	20.00
h.	Sign. 9; 10.	—	3.00	12.00
i.	Ovpt: A in circle.	—	2.50	15.00
j.	Ovpt: D in circle.	—	2.50	15.00
k.	Ovpt: G in circle.	—	2.50	11.00
l.	Ovpt: K in circle.	—	2.50	12.50
m.	Ovpt: L in circle.	—	2.50	75.00
n.	Ovpt: M in circle.	—	2.50	11.00
o.	Ovpt: U in circle.	—	2.50	11.00
p.	Ovpt: V in circle.	—	2.50	11.00

15   20 DOLLARS

ND (1965). Purple. Turtles at ctr.

		VG	VF	UNC
a.	Sign. 1.	—	65.00	500.00
b.	Sign. 2.	20.00	75.00	600.00
c.	Sign. 3.		Reported Not Confirmed	
d.	Sign. 4.	12.50	50.00	300.00
e.	Sign. 5; 6; 7.	10.00	40.00	250.00
f.	Sign. 8.	10.00	12.50	30.00
g.	Sign. 9; 10.	—	10.00	25.00
h.	Ovpt: A in circle.	—	10.00	22.50
i.	Ovpt: D in circle.	—	10.00	27.50
j.	Ovpt: G in circle.	—	10.00	25.00
k.	Ovpt: K in circle.	—	15.00	100.00
l.	Ovpt: L in circle.	—	10.00	22.50
m.	Ovpt: M in circle.	—	10.00	25.00
n.	Ovpt: U in circle.	—	10.00	22.50
o.	Ovpt: V in circle.	—	10.00	22.50

16   100 DOLLARS

ND (1965). Black. Sea horses at ctr.

		VG	VF	UNC
a.	Sign. 1.	150.00	400.00	1250.
b.	Sign. 2.		Reported Not Confirmed	
c.	Sign. 5.	100.00	325.00	1000.
d.	Sign. 3; 4; 6; 7.		Reported Not Confirmed	
e.	Sign. 8.		Reported Not Confirmed	
f.	Sign. 9; 10.	—	60.00	175.00
g.	Ovpt: A in circle.	—	60.00	250.00
h.	Ovpt: D in circle.	50.00	125.00	450.00
i.	Ovpt: G in circle.	—	85.00	275.00
j.	Ovpt: K in circle.	—	95.00	350.00
k.	Ovpt: L in circle.	—	60.00	200.00
l.	Ovpt: M in circle.	—	50.00	185.00
m.	Ovpt: V in circle.	—	55.00	195.00

EASTERN CARIBBEAN CENTRAL BANK

SIGNATURE VARIETIES		
1	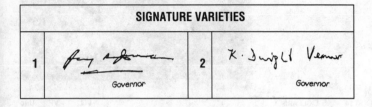Governor	2

1985-87 ND ISSUE

#17-25 have windsurfer at l., Qn. Elizabeth II at r. ctr., map at r. on face. Wmk: QEII. Printer: TDLR.

Notes w/suffix letter of serial # indicating particular areas of issue (as with ovpt. letters on previous issue).

#17-20 do not have name Anguilla at island near top of map at r. Palm tree, swordfish at r. ctr., shoreline in background on back. No $10 without Anguilla was issued. Sign. 1.

17	1 DOLLAR	VG	VF	UNC
	ND (1985-88). Red on m/c unpt.			
	a. Suffix letter A.	—	1.00	3.00
	b. Suffix letter D.	—	1.00	3.00
	c. Suffix letter G.	—	1.00	3.00
	d. Suffix letter K.	—	1.00	3.00
	e. Suffix letter L.	—	1.00	3.00
	f. Suffix letter M.	—	1.00	3.00
	g. Suffix letter V.	—	1.00	3.00
	h. Ovpt: U in circle on suffix letter V issue (1988).	—	1.00	3.00

18	5 DOLLARS	VG	VF	UNC
	ND (1986-88). Deep green on m/c unpt.			
	a. Suffix letter A.	—	—	6.00
	b. Suffix letter D.	—	—	6.00
	c. Suffix letter G.	—	—	6.00
	d. Suffix letter K.	—	—	6.00
	e. Suffix letter L.	—	—	6.00
	f. Suffix letter M.	—	—	5.00
	g. Suffix letter V.	—	—	5.00
	h. Ovpt: U in circle on suffix letter V issue (1988).	—	—	6.00

19	20 DOLLARS	VG	VF	UNC
	ND (1987-88). Purple and brown on m/c unpt.			
	a. Suffix letter A.	—	—	20.00
	b. Suffix letter D.	—	—	22.00
	c. Suffix letter G.	—	—	25.00
	d. Suffix letter K.	—	—	22.00
	e. Suffix letter L.	—	—	200.00
	f. Suffix letter M.	—	12.50	30.00
	g. Suffix letter V.	—	—	20.00
	h. Ovpt: U in circle.	—	—	30.00

20	100 DOLLARS	VG	VF	UNC
	ND (1986-88). Black and orange on m/c unpt.			
	a. Suffix letter A.	—	—	95.00
	b. Suffix letter D.	—	50.00	125.00
	c. Suffix letter G.	—	50.00	110.00
	d. Suffix letter K.	—	—	95.00
	e. Suffix letter L.	—	—	95.00
	f. Suffix letter M.	—	—	95.00
	g. Suffix letter V.	—	—	95.00
	h. Ovpt: U in circle on suffix letter V issue (1988).	—	—	100.00

1985-89 ND ISSUE

#21-25 with *ANGUILLA* island named near top of map at r.

#21, 22, 24 and 25 harbor at St. Lucia on back.

#22-25 have 2 sign. varieites.

21	1 DOLLAR	VG	VF	UNC
	ND (1988-89). Like #17 but Anguilla named. Sign. 1.			
	a. Suffix letter D.	—	1.00	4.00
	b. Suffix letter K.	—	1.00	4.00
	c. Suffix letter L.	—	1.00	4.00
	d. Suffix letter U.	—	1.00	4.00

22	5 DOLLARS	VG	VF	UNC
	ND (1988-93). Like #18 but Anguilla named.			
	a. Suffix letter A. Sign. 1.	—	—	5.00
	b. Like a. Sign. 2.	—	—	5.00
	c. Suffix letter D. Sign. 1.	—	—	5.00
	g. Suffix letter K. Sign. 1.	—	—	5.00
	h. Like g. Sign. 2.	—	—	5.00
	i. Suffix letter L. Sign. 1.	—	—	5.00
	j. Like i. Sign. 2.	—	—	5.00
	k. Suffix letter M. Sign. 1.	—	—	5.00
	m. Suffix letter U. Sign. 1.	—	—	7.00
	p. Suffix letter V. Sign. 2.	—	—	5.00

1993 ND ISSUE

#26-30 Qn. Elizabeth II at ctr. r., and as wmk., turtle at ctr. Island map at ctr. on back. Sign. 2. Printer: TDLR.

23	**10 DOLLARS**	VG	VF	UNC
	ND (1985-93). Blue on m/c unpt. Harbor at Grenada, sailboats at l. and ctr. on back.			
	a. Suffix letter *A*. Sign. 1.	—	—	9.00
	b. Like a. Sign. 2.	—	—	10.00
	c. Suffix letter *D*. Sign. 1.	—	—	9.00
	d. Like c. Sign. 2.	—	—	10.00
	e. Suffix letter *G*. Sign. 1.	—	—	9.00
	g. Suffix letter *K*. Sign. 1.	—	—	9.00
	h. Like g. Sign. 2.	—	—	10.00
	i. Suffix letter *L*. Sign. 1.	—	—	9.00
	j. Like i. Sign. 2.	—	—	9.00
	k. Suffix letter *M*. Sign. 1.	—	—	10.00
	m. Suffix letter *U*. Sign. 1.	—	—	9.00
	o. Suffix letter *V*. Sign. 1.	—	—	9.00
	p. Like o. Sign. 2.	—	—	9.00

24	**20 DOLLARS**			
	ND (1988-93). Purple and brown on m/c unpt. Like #19 but Anguilla named.			
	a. Suffix letter *A*. Sign. 1.	—	—	18.00
	b. Like a. Sign. 2.	—	—	18.00
	c. Suffix letter *D*. Sign. 1.	—	—	20.00
	d. Like c. Sign. 2.	—	—	18.00
	e. Suffix letter *G*. Sign. 1.	—	—	22.50
	g. Suffix letter *K*. Sign. 1.	—	—	20.00
	h. Like g. Sign. 2.	—	—	18.00
	i. Suffix letter *L*. Sign. 1.	—	—	20.00
	j. Like i. Sign. 2.	—	—	18.00
	k. Suffix letter *M*. Sign. 1.	—	—	18.00
	l. Like k. Sign. 2.	—	—	18.00
	m. Suffix letter *U*. Sign. 1.	—	—	20.00
	o. Suffix letter *V*. Sign. 1.	—	—	20.00

26	**5 DOLLARS**	VG	VF	UNC
	ND (1993). Dk. green and black on m/c unpt. Admiral's House in Antigua and Barbuda at l., Trafalgar Falls in Dominica at r. on back.	—	—	6.50

27	**10 DOLLARS**	VG	VF	UNC
	ND (1993). Blue and black on m/c unpt. Admiralty Bay in St. Vincent & the Grenadines at l., Sailing ship *Warspite* at r. ctr. on back.	—	—	11.50

25	**100 DOLLARS**	VG	VF	UNC
	ND (1988-93). Black and orange on m/c unpt. Like #20 but Anguilla named.			
	a. Suffix letter *A*. Sign. 1.	—	—	95.00
	b. Like a. Sign. 2.	—	—	95.00
	c. Suffix letter *D*. Sign. 1.	—	—	95.00
	d. Like c. Sign. 2.	—	—	95.00
	e. Suffix letter *G*. Sign. 1.	—	—	100.00
	g. Suffix letter *K*. Sign. 1.	—	—	100.00
	h. Like g. Sign. 2.	—	—	100.00
	i. Suffix letter *L*. Sign. 1.	—	—	95.00
	j. Like i. Sign. 2.	—	—	100.00
	k. Suffix letter *M*. Sign. 1.	—	—	100.00
	l. Like k. Sign. 2.	—	—	95.00
	m. Suffix letter *U*. Sign. 1.	—	—	100.00
	o. Suffix letter *V*. Sign. 1.	—	—	95.00

28	**20 DOLLARS**	VG	VF	UNC
	ND (1993). Brown-violet and blue on m/c unpt. Govt. House in Montserrat at l., nutmeg in Grenada at r. on back.	—	—	20.00

29   50 DOLLARS

	VG	VF	UNC
ND (1993). Purple and olive-green on m/c unpt. Brimstone Hill in St. Kitts at l., Les Pitons mountains in St. Lucia at r. on back.	—	—	45.00

30   100 DOLLARS

	VG	VF	UNC
ND (1993). Dk. brown, dk. green and m/c. Sir Arthur Lewis at l., E.C.C.B. Central Bank bldg. at r. on back.	—	—	85.00

1995 ND ISSUE

31   5 DOLLARS

	VG	VF	UNC
ND (1995). Dk. green and black on m/c unpt. Like #26 but w/redesigned corner 5's.	—	—	5.50

COLLECTOR SERIES

EASTERN CARIBBEAN CURRENCY AUTHORITY

1983 ISSUE

This set is made from foil thin gold and silver.

CS1   30 DOLLARS

	ISSUE PRICE	MKT. VALUE
ND (1983). 12 Different notes showing various flowers and animals. Notes titled *ANTIGUA & BARBUDA*.	—	300.00

EAST CARIBBEAN CENTRAL BANK

1988 ISSUE

The following set is made with foil thin gold and silver.

CS2   100 DOLLARS

	ISSUE PRICE	MKT. VALUE
ND (1988). 30 Different notes showing various pirate ships.	—	500.00

ECUADOR

The Republic of Ecuador, located astride the equator on the Pacific coast of South America, has an area of 109,484 sq. mi. (283,561 sq. km.) and a population of 9.65 million. Capital: Quito. Agriculture is the mainstay of the economy but there are appreciable deposits of minerals and petroleum. It is the world's largest exporter of bananas and balsa wood. Coffee, cacao and shrimp are also valuable exports.

Ecuador was first sighted, 1526, by Bartolome Ruiz. Conquest was undertaken by Sebastian de Benalcazar who founded Quito in 1534. Ecuador was part of the province, later Vice-royalty, of Peru until 1739 when it became part of the Vice-royalty of New Granada. After two failed attempts to attain independence in 1810 and 1812, it successfully declared its independence in October 1820, and won final victory over Spanish forces May 24, 1822. Incorporated into the Gran Colombia confederacy, it loosened its ties in 1830 and regained full independence in 1835.

MONETARY SYSTEM:
- 1 Peso = 100 Centavos
- 1 Sucre = 10 Decimos = 100 Centavos
- 1 Condor = 25 Sucres
- 1 Nuevo "new" Sucre = 1000 "old" Sucres, 1996-

REPUBLIC

BANCO CENTRAL DEL ECUADOR

1944 ISSUE

#96 and 97 black on m/c unpt. Printer: ABNC.

96   500 SUCRES

1944-1966. Mercury seated at ctr. Back deep orange.

	VG	VF	UNC
a. Sign. title ovpt. *PRESIDENTE* at l. 12.5.1944; 27.6.1944.	175.00	325.00	—
b. Sign. title ovpt. *GERENTE GENERAL* at l., *VOCAL* at r. 31.7.1944; 7.9.1944.	150.00	300.00	—
c. Sign. title ovpt. *GERENTE GENERAL* at r. 12.1.1945-12.7.1947.	125.00	250.00	—
d. As c. 21.4.1961-17.11.1966	100.00	200.00	550.00
s. Specimen. ND.	—	—	400.00

97   1000 SUCRES

1944-67. Woman reclining w/globe and telephone at ctr. Back gray.

	VG	VF	UNC
a. Sign. title ovpt. *PRESIDENTE* at l. 12.5.1944; 7.6.1944.	275.00	—	—
b. Sign. title ovpt. *GERENTE GENERAL* at l., *VOCAL* at r. 31.7.1944; 7.9.1944.	250.00	—	—
c. Sign. title ovpt. *PRESIDENTE* at l., *GERENTE GENERAL* at r. 12.1.1945.	225.00	—	—
d. Sign. title ovpt. *GERENTE GENERAL* at r. 16.10.1945; 12.7.1947.	200.00	—	—
e. As d. 21.4.1961; 27.2.1962; 4.3.1964; 23.7.1964; 17.11.1966; 6.4.1967.	100.00	—	—
s. Specimen. ND.	—	—	400.00

1950 ISSUE

Various dates found w/ or w/o dot after *1* in year.

#98 and 101 sign. title varieties.

#98-101 black on m/c unpt. Many date varieties. Arms at ctr. on back, 31mm wide w/o flagpole stems below. Printer: ABNC.

99 **10 SUCRES**
(101)   1950-74. Black on m/c unpt. Portr. S. de Benalcazar at ctr. Back blue.

		VG	VF	UNC
a.	Plain background. 14.1.1950-28.11.1955.	1.50	5.00	20.00
b.	Ornate background, different background guilloches. 15.6.19566-27.4.1966.	.50	2.00	8.50
c.	24.5.1968-2.1.1974.	.25	1.00	4.00
s.	Specimen. ND.	—	—	25.00

1956 ISSUE

102 **5 SUCRES**
(100)   1956-73. Black on m/c unpt. Portr. A. J. de Sucre at ctr. Back red-violet.

		VG	VF	UNC
a.	19.6.1956; 29.8.1956; 2.4.1957; 2.1.1958.	.50	2.50	10.00
b.	Sign. title: *SUBGERENTE GENERAL.* 24.9.1957.	.25	1.25	5.00
c.	1.1.1966.	.20	.55	3.50
d.	27.2.1970; 3.9.1973. Serial # varieties.	.15	.50	2.00

1962-71 ISSUE
#103, 104, 106 and 107 black on m/c unpt. Printer: ABNC.

103 **20 SUCRES**
1962-73. Church facade at ctr. Back brown.

		VG	VF	UNC
a.	12.12.1962-27.4.1966.	1.00	3.00	10.00
b.	17.11.1966-3.9.1973.	.50	1.50	5.50
s.	Specimen. ND.	—	—	25.00

104 **50 SUCRES**
1968-71. National monument at ctr. Back green.

		VG	VF	UNC
a.	24.5.1968; 5.11.1969.	1.50	3.50	15.00
b.	20.5.1971.	1.00	2.50	8.00
s.	Specimen. ND.	—	—	—

106 **500 SUCRES**
ND (ca.1971). Similar to #96, but w/diff. guilloches and other changes. Back brown. (Not issued). Archive example.
| s. | Specimen. ND. | — | — | — |

107 **1000 SUCRES**
17.11.1966-20.9.1973. Banco Central bldg. at ctr. Back olive-gray.

	VG	VF	UNC
	20.00	50.00	160.00
s. Specimen. ND.	—	—	75.00

1975-80 ISSUE
#108-112 face like #100-105. Arms on back 29mm. Wide, new rendition w/flagpole stems below. Printer: ABNC.

108 **5 SUCRES**
1975-83. Like #100.

		VG	VF	UNC
a.	14.3.1975; 29.4.1977.	.15	.40	1.00
b.	20.8.1982; 20.4.1983.	FV	FV	.50

109 **10 SUCRES**
14.3.1975; 10.8.1976; 29.4.1977; 24.5.1978. Like #101.

VG	VF	UNC
.10	.30	2.00

110	**20 SUCRES**	VG	VF	UNC
	10.8.1976. Like #103.	.50	1.00	3.50

111	**50 SUCRES**	VG	VF	UNC
	10.8.1976. Like #104.	1.00	2.50	5.00

112	**100 SUCRES**	VF	VF	UNC
	24.5.1980. Like #105.	FV	FV	3.00

1957-58 ISSUE

#113 and 116 black on m/c unpt. Several sign. title ovpt. varieties. Security thread used intermittently through 1969. Printer: TDLR.

113	**5 SUCRES**	VG	VF	UNC
	1958-88. Portr. A.J. de Sucre at ctr. Back red-violet; arms at ctr.			
	a. 2.1.1958-7.11.1962.	.60	2.00	7.50
	b. 23.5.1963-27.2.1970.	.25	.50	3.00
	c. 25.7.1979-24.5.1980.	FV	FV	1.00
	d. 22.11.1988.	FV	FV	.50
	s. Specimen. ND; 24.5.1968.	—	—	27.50

114	**10 SUCRES**	VG	VF	UNC
	1968-83. Similar to #109.			
	a. 24.5.1968; 20.5.1971.	.25	.50	3.00
	b. 24.5.1980; 30.9.1982; 20.4.1983.	FV	FV	.50
	s. Specimen. 24.5.1968.	—	—	35.00

115	**20 SUCRES**	VG	VF	UNC
	1961-83. Similar to #110.			
	a. 7.6.1961; 27.2.1962; 6.7.1962.	1.00	3.50	12.50
	b. 1.5.1978; 24.5.1980; 20.4. 1983.	FV	FV	.75
	s. Specimen. ND.	—	—	35.00

116	**50 SUCRES**	VG	VF	UNC
	1957-82. National Monument w/bldgs. in background at ctr. Back green; arms at ctr.			
	a. 2.4.1957; 7.7.1959; 7.4.1960; 7.11.1962; 29.10.1963; 29.1.1965; 6.8.1965.	2.00	8.00	25.00
	b. 1.1.1966; 27.4.1966; 17.11.1966; 4.10.1967; 30.5.1969; 17.7.1974.	.50	2.00	6.00
	c. 24.5.1980; 20.8.1982.	FV	FV	1.50
	s. Specimen. ND; 1.1.1966.	—	—	30.00

116A **100 Sucres**
(105) 1957-80. Like #A105 but w/different guilloches.

		VG	VF	Unc
a.	Sign. title: *SUBGERENTE GENERAL.* 24.9.1957.	10.00	50.00	125.00
b.	6.6.1958; 8.4.1959; 21.4.1961.	4.00	20.00	60.00
c.	1.1.1966-7.7.1970.	2.00	4.00	15.00
d.	1.2.1980.	1.00	2.00	5.00
s.	Specimen. ND.	—	—	32.50

117 **100 Sucres**
29.8.1961; 6.7.1962; 23.7.1964; 6.8.1965. Similar to #112 but crude portr. w/lt. clouds behind.

VG	VF	Unc
4.00	15.00	50.00

118 **100 Sucres**
1965-80. Like #117 but better portr. w/dk. clouds behind.

		VG	VF	Unc
a.	6.8.1965; 20.5.1971; 17.7.1974.	2.00	4.00	15.00
b.	10.8.1976; 10.8.1977; 24.5.1980.	FV	1.50	4.00
s.	Specimen. 20.5.1971.	—	—	35.00

119 **500 Sucres**
1976-82. Black, purple and dk. olive-green on m/c unpt. Dr. E. de Santa Cruz y Espejo at l. Back blue and m/c; arms at ctr. Printer: TDLR.

		VG	VF	Unc
a.	24.5.1976; 10.8.1977; 9.10.1978; 25.1.1979.	1.00	7.50	25.00
b.	20.7.1982.	FV	4.00	10.00
s.	Specimen. ND.	—	—	35.00

120 **1000 Sucres**
1976-82. Dk. green and red-brown on m/c unpt. Ruminahui at r. Back dk. green and m/c; arms at ctr. and as wmk.

		VG	VF	Unc
a.	24.5.1976-25.7.1979.	1.00	9.00	25.00
b.	20.7.1982.	FV	4.00	12.00
s.	Specimen. ND.	—	—	35.00

1984-88 Issues

#121-125 w/o text: *SOCIEDAD ANONIMA* below bank title. Sign. varieties. W/o imprint.

#124-125 wmk: Arms. W/o imprint.

121 **10 Sucres**
29.4.1986; 22.11.1988. Like #114.

VG	VF	Unc
FV	FV	.50

121A **20 Sucres**
29.4.1986; 22.11.1988. Like #115.

VG	VF	Unc
FV	FV	.60

122 **50 Sucres**
5.9.1984; 29.4.1986; 22.11.1988. Like #116.

VG	VF	Unc
FV	FV	.75

125	**1000 SUCRES**	**VG**	**VF**	**UNC**
	1984-. Like #120 but w/o EL in bank title. Serial # style varieties.			
	a. 5.9.1984; 29.9.1986.	FV	FV	3.00
	b. 8.6.1988.	FV	FV	1.50

123	**100 SUCRES**	**VG**	**VF**	**UNC**
	29.4.1986; 20.4.1990. Like #118.	FV	FV	.85

126	**5000 SUCRES**	**VG**	**VF**	**UNC**
	1987-92. Purple on m/c unpt. Juan Montalvo at l., arms at ctr. r. 2 birds and sea tortoise on back.			
	a. 1.12.1987.	FV	FV	8.00
	b. 21.6.1991; 17.3.1992; 22.6.1992.	FV	FV	6.50

123A	**100 SUCRES**	**VG**	**VF**	**UNC**
	1988-. Like #112. Serial # style varieties.			
	a. Blue serial #. 8.6.1988; 21.6.1991.	FV	FV	1.00
	b. 21.2.1992; 9.3.1992; 4.12.1992; 20.8.1993.	FV	FV	.50
	c. Black serial #. 21.2.1994.	FV	FV	.25

1993-96 ISSUE

127	**5000 SUCRES**	**VG**	**VF**	**UNC**
	20.8.1993; 31.1.1995. Like #126 but w/repositioned sign. and both serial # horizontal.	FV	FV	5.00

124	**500 SUCRES**	**VG**	**VF**	**UNC**
	5.9.1984. Like #119.	FV	FV	2.00

128	**10,000 SUCRES**	**VG**	**VF**	**UNC**
	30.7.1988; 21.2.1994; 6.2.1995. Dk.brown and reddish-brown on m/c unpt. Vicente Rocafuerte at l. and as wmk. Arms upper l. ctr., Independence monument in Quito at ctr. r. on back.	FV	FV	9.00

124A	**500 SUCRES**	**VG**	**VF**	**UNC**
	8.6.1988. Similar to #124 but many minor plate differences.	FV	FV	1.25

129	**20,000 SUCRES**	**VG**	**VF**	**UNC**
	31.1.1995. Brown, black and deep blue on m/c unpt. Dr. G. Garcia Moreno at r. and as wmk. Arms at ctr. on back.	FV	FV	17.50

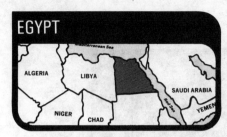

EGYPT

The Arab Republic of Egypt, located on the northeastern corner of Africa, has an area of 386,650 sq. mi. (1,000,000 sq. km.) and a population of 56 million. Capital: Cairo. Although Egypt is an almost rainless expanse of desert, its economy is predominantly agricultural. Cotton, rice and petroleum are exported.

Egyptian history dates back to about 4000 B.C. when the empire was established by uniting the upper and lower kingdoms. Following its 'Golden Age' (16th to 13th centuries B.C.), Egypt was conquered by Persia (525 B.C.) and Alexander the Great (332 B.C.) The Ptolemies ruled until the suicide of Cleopatra (30 B.C.) when Egypt became a Roman colony. Arab caliphs ruled Egypt from 641 to 1517, when the Turks took it for their Ottoman Empire. Turkish rule, interrupted by the occupation of Napoleon (1798-1801), became increasingly casual, permitting Great Britain to inject its influence by purchasing shares in the Suez Canal. British troops occupied Egypt in 1882, becoming the de facto rulers. On Dec. 14, 1914, Egypt was made a protectorate of Britain. British occupation ended on Feb. 28, 1922, when Egypt became a sovereign, independent kingdom. The monarchy was abolished and a republic proclaimed on June 18, 1952.

On Feb. 1, 1958, Egypt and Syria formed the United Arab Republic. Yemen joined on March 8 in an association known as the United Arab States. Syria withdrew from the United Arab Republic on Sept. 29, 1961, and on Dec. 26 Egypt dissolved its ties with Yemen in the United Arab States. On Sept. 2, 1971, Egypt shed the name United Arab Republic in favor of the Arab Republic of Egypt.

* * * This section has been renumbered. * * *

MONETARY SYSTEM:
1 Piastre (Guerche) = 10 Milliemes
1 Pound (Junayh) = 100 Piastres, 1916-

REPUBLIC

CENTRAL BANK OF EGYPT

1961-64 ISSUE
#31-37 sign. and date varieties.

		VG	VF	UNC
35 (31)	**25 PIASTRES** 1.11.1961-18.8.1966. Blue. U. A. R. arms at r.	.50	1.50	6.00

		VG	VF	UNC
36 (32)	**50 PIASTRES** 1.11.1961-14.8.1966. Black. U. A. R. arms at r., also in wmk.	1.00	5.00	15.00

		VG	VF	UNC
37 (33)	**1 POUND** 1.11.1961-23.2.1967. Blue-green and lilac. Tutankhamen's mask at r. Back green.	1.00	2.50	7.00

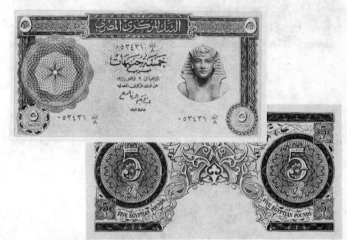

		VG	VF	UNC
38 (34)	**5 POUNDS** 1.11.1961-12.11.1961. Green and brown. Circular guilloche at l., Tutankhamen's mask at r. Wmk: Flower.	7.50	25.00	95.00

		VG	VF	UNC
39 (35)	**5 POUNDS** 13.11.1961-16.6.1964. Green and brown. Similar to #38, but circular area at l. is blank. Guilloche at bottom ctr. on face and back. Wmk: U.A.R. arms.	3.00	10.00	25.00
40 (36)	**5 POUNDS** 17.6.1964-13.2.1965. Lilac and brown. Like #39.	2.50	7.50	22.50

41 **10 POUNDS** | VG | VF | UNC
(37) 1.11.1961-13.2.1965. Dk. green and dk. brown on m/c unpt. | 5.00 | 12.00 | 30.00
Tutankhamen's mask at r. Wmk: U. A. R. arms.

1967-69 ISSUE

#42-46 wmk: Archaic Egyptian scribe.

Replacement notes: Single Arabic letter as prefix.

42 **25 PIASTRES** | VG | VF | UNC
(38) 6.2.1967-4.1.1975. Blue, green and brown on m/c unpt. Sphinx | .25 | 1.00 | 4.50
w/statue at l. ctr. U.A.R. arms at ctr. on back.

43 **50 PIASTRES** | VG | VF | UNC
(39) 2.12.1967-28.1.1978. Red-brown and brown. Al Azhar Mosque at r., | .50 | 1.00 | 3.50
University of Cairo at l. ctr. Ramses II on back.

44 **1 POUND** | VG | VF | UNC
(40) 12.5.1967-19.4.1978. Brown and m/c. Mosque of Sultan Quayet Bey. | 1.00 | 2.00 | 4.00
Ancient statues on back.

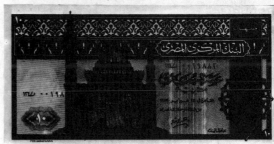

45 **5 POUNDS** | VG | VF | UNC
(41) 1.1.1969-78. Blue, gray and green. Mosque of Ahmad ibn Tulun at | 2.00 | 5.00 | 18.50
Cairo at ctr. Ruins at l., frieze at ctr. r. on back.

46 **10 POUNDS** | VG | VF | UNC
(42) 1.9.1969-78. Red-brown and brown. Sultan Hassan Mosque at Cairo | 4.00 | 7.50 | 22.50
at l. ctr. Pharaoh and pyramids on back.

1976 ISSUE

Replacement notes: Single Arabic letter as prefix.

47 **25 PIASTRES** | VG | VF | UNC
(43) 12.4.1976-28.8.1978. Blue, green and grayish brown on blue and | .25 | .50 | 2.50
orange unpt. Face and wmk. like #42. A. R. E. arms on back.

48 **20 POUNDS**

(44)   5.7.1976; 1978. Green. Mosque of Mohammed Ali at l., Arabic legends at r. Ancient war chariot and frieze on back. Wmk: Egyptian scribe.

	VG	VF	UNC
	8.50	15.00	35.00

1978-79 Issue

#49-62 no longer have conventional reading dates with Arabic day, month and year. In place of this are six Arabic numerals, the first and last making up the year of issue; next 2 digits represent the day and following 2 digits represent the month; i.e. 822119 = 22.11.(19)89. Another example including raised diamonds (= zeroes) 804107 = 4.10.(19)87. Wmk: Tutankhamen's mask.

Replacement notes: #45 single Arabic letter as prefix. #45 onwards Arabic 200 or 300 before single Arabic letter.

49 **25 PIASTRES**

(45)   2.1.-14.3.(19)79. Black on gray, pale blue and m/c unpt. Al-Sayida Aisha Mosque at ctr. Stylized A. R. E. arms, cotton, wheat and corn plants on back.

	VG	VF	UNC
	.25	.50	2.50

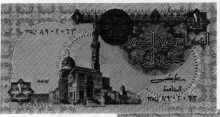

50 **1 POUND**

(46)   29.5.(19)78-. Brown, purple and deep olive-green on m/c unpt. Mosque of Sultan Quayet Bey at ctr. Ancient statues on back.

		VG	VF	UNC
a.	Back deep brown. Solid security thread. 29.5.(19)78-10.4.(19)87.	FV	FV	1.50
b.	Back pale brown. Solid security thread. 19.11.(19)86-24.6.(19)87.	FV	FV	1.50
c.	Back pale brown. Segmented security thread with bank name repeated. 13.8.(19)89-28.2.(19)94.	FV	FV	1.50

51 **10 POUNDS**

(47)   24.6.(19)78-. Brown and brown-violet. Mosque of Ar-Rifai at ctr. Pharaoh on back.

	VG	VF	UNC
	FV	FV	12.00

52 **20 POUNDS**

(48)   6.9.(19)78-. Black, gray-violet and deep green on m/c unpt. Mohammed Ali Mosque at ctr. Ancient sculptures from Chapel of Sesostris I and ancient war chariot on back.

		VG	VF	UNC
a.	Date below wmk. Solid security thread. 6.9.(19)78-22.4.(19)82.	FV	FV	20.00
b.	Date at lower r. of wmk. Solid security thread. 9.12.(19)86; 4.10.(19)87.	FV	FV	18.50
c.	Segmented security thread w/bank name repeated. (19)88-18.3.(19)92.	FV	FV	17.50

53 **100 POUNDS**

(49)   (19)78; (19)92. Blue and m/c. Mosque of Al Sayida Zaynab at ctr. Pharaoh's mask above frieze at ctr. on vertical back.

		VG	VF	UNC
a.	Series 1-6.(19)78.	FV	60.00	120.00
b.	(19)92.	FV		90.00

1980-81 Issue

Replacement notes: Arabic 200 or 300 before single Arabic series letter.

54   **25 PIASTRES**
(50)   17.1.(19)80-84. Dk. green on dk. green and m/c unpt. Like #45.

	VG	VF	UNC
	FV	.25	1.50

55   **50 PIASTRES**
(51)   1.1.(19)81-83. Green, brown and m/c. Al Ahzar Mosque at ctr. Sculptured wall design at l., Ramses II at ctr., ancient seal at r. on back.

	VG	VF	UNC
	FV	.50	2.00

56   **5 POUNDS**
(52)   (19)81-89. Black and blue-black on m/c unpt. Ibn Toulon Mosque at ctr. Design symbolizing bounty of the Nile River on back.

	VG	VF	UNC
a. 1.2.(19)81.	FV	3.00	10.00
b. (19)82-89.	FV	2.50	8.50

1985 ISSUE

Replacement notes: Arabic 200 or 300 before single Arabic series letter.

57   **25 PIASTRES**
(53)   (19)85-. Purple on pale blue, lilac and m/c unpt. Face and wmk. like #49 and #54. Standard A.R.E. arms at l. ctr. on back.

	VG	VF	UNC
a. Solid security thread. 4.4.(19)85-30.1.(19)89.	FV	FV	.85
b. Segmented security thread w/bank name repeated. 17.12.(19)90-8.10.(19)91.	FV	FV	.75

58   **50 PIASTRES**
(54)   (19)85-95. Black on pale orange, pink and m/c unpt. Mosque at r. Back like #55.

	VG	VF	UNC
a. No text line at lower l. on face. Solid security thead. 2.7.(19)85-.	FV	.35	2.00
b. Text line added at lower l. on face. 10.2.(19)87-.	FV	FV	1.25
c. Segmented security thread w/bank name repeated. 8.1.(19)90-95.	FV	FV	1.00

1989-94 ISSUE

Replacement notes: Arabic 200 or 300 before single Arabic series letter.

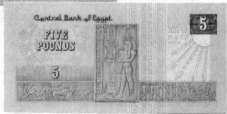

59   **5 POUNDS**
(55)   (19)87-. Black and blue-black on m/c unpt. Like #56 but m/c scrollwork added in unpt. and into wmk. area. Ancient design over wmk. area at r. on back.

	VG	VF	UNC
a. Solid security thread. 4.1.(19)87-.	FV	FV	10.00
b. Segmented security thread w/bank name repeated. 2.4.(19)89-.	FV	FV	5.50

60   **50 POUNDS**
(56)   9.2.(19)93-. Brown, violet and m/c. Mosque at r. Isis above ancient boat, ruins at l. ctr. on back.

	VG	VF	UNC
	FV	FV	37.50

			VG	VF	UNC
61	**100 POUNDS**		FV	FV	70.00
(57)	14.9.(19)94. Dk. brown and brown-violet on m/c unpt. Mosque at lower l. ctr. Sphinx at ctr. on back.				

1995 ISSUE

			VG	VF	UNC
62	**50 PIASTRES**		FV	FV	.75
	6.7.(19)95-. Dull olive-gray on m/c unpt. Like #58.				

CURRENCY NOTES

ARAB REPUBLIC OF EGYPT

Face 5: *ARAB REPUBLIC OF EGYPT* in Arabic.

Back 3: *ARAB REPUBLIC OF EGYPT* in English. Various sign. Imprint: Survey Authority or Postal Printing House.

1958-71 ND ISSUE

			VG	VF	UNC
180	**5 PIASTRES**				
(80)	ND. Lilac. Qn. Nefertiti at r. Wmk: *U A R.*				
	a. Sign. Baghdady w/titles: *VICE-PRESIDENT AND MINISTER OF TREASURY.* Series 15; 16.		1.25	5.00	20.00
	b. Sign. Kaissouni w/titles: *MINISTER OF TREASURY AND PLAN-NING.* Series 16-18.		.25	1.00	6.00
	c. Sign. Daif w/titles: *MINISTER OF TREASURY.* Color lilac to blue. Wmk: 3mm tall. Series 18-22.		.20	.75	4.00
	d. Sign. and titles as c. Wmk: 5mm tall. Series 22-26.		.20	.75	4.00
	e. Sign. Hegazy w/titles as d. Series 26-33.		.20	.75	4.00

1971-91 ND ISSUES

NOTE: As of July 1991, all Egyptian Currency Notes have been demonetized and withdrawn from circulation.

			VG	VF	UNC
180A	**5 PIASTRES**		15.00	50.00	150.00
(80A)	ND. Face like #80. Back w/sign. Kaissouni title: *MINISTER OF TREASURY* (error). Series 16.				

			VG	VF	UNC
181	**5 PIASTRES**				
(82)	ND. Lilac. Similar to #80. Imprint: Survey of Egypt.				
	a. Sign. Hegazy w/title: *MINISTER OF TREASURY.* Wmk: *U A R.* Series 33; 34.		1.00	3.50	15.00
	b. Sign. Hegazy w/title: *MINISTER OF TREASURY.* Wmk: *A R E.* Series 34-36.		.75	3.00	12.00
	c. Sign. Ibrahim w/title: *MINISTER OF FINANCE.* Wmk: *A R E.* Series 36; 37.		.35	1.50	6.00
	d. Sign. El Nashar w/title as c. Series 37.		.60	2.50	10.00
	e. Sign. Ismail. w/title as c. Series 37-40.		.20	.75	3.00
	f. Sign. M. S. Hamed. Series 40-42.		.25	1.00	4.00
	g. Sign. Loutfy. Series 42-47.		.20	.75	3.00
	h. Sign. Meguid. Series 47-50.		.15	.60	2.50
	i. Sign. Hamed. Series. 50.		2.00	6.00	20.00
	j. Like c. Imprint. Postal Printing House. Sign. Hamed. Series 50-72.		.10	.35	1.50
	k. Sign. El Razaz. Series 72.		.25	1.00	5.00

			VG	VF	UNC
182	**10 PIASTRES**				
(81)	ND. Black. Group of militants w/flag having only 2 stars.				
	a. Sign. Baghdady w/titles: *VICE-PRESIDENT AND MINISTER OF TREASURY.* Series 16.		1.50	6.00	22.00
	b. Sign. Kaissouni w/titles: *MINISTER OF TREASURY AND PLAN-NING.* Series 16-18.		.40	1.50	7.50
	c. Sign. Kaissouni w/titles: *MINISTER OF TREASURY.* Series 16.		6.00	25.00	100.00
	d. Sign. Daif w/title as c. Series 18-24.		.25	1.00	5.00
	e. Sign. Hegazy w/title as c. Series 24-29.		.25	1.00	5.00
183	**10 PIASTRES**				
(83)	ND. Black. Similar to #81. Imprint: Survey Authority.				
	a. Sign. Hegazy w/title: *MINISTER OF TREASURY.* Wmk: *U A R.* Series 29; 30.		2.00	8.00	35.00
	b. Sign. Hegazy w/title: *MINISTER OF TREASURY.* Wmk: *A R E.* Series 30; 31.		1.00	4.00	15.00
	c. Sign. Ibrahim w/title: *MINISTER OF FINANCE.* Wmk: *A R E.* Series 31; 32.		.45	1.75	7.00
	d. Sign. El Nashar w/titles as c. Series 32-33.		1.00	4.00	15.00
	e. Sign. Ismail w/titles as c. Series 33-35.		.25	1.00	4.00
	f. Sign. M. S. Hamed w/titles as c. Series 35-38.		.45	1.75	7.00
	g. Sign. Loutfy w/titles as c. Series 38-43.		.25	1.00	4.00
	h. Sign. Meguid w/titles as c. Series 43-46.		.20	.75	3.00
	i. Sign. Hamed w/titles as c. Series 46.		3.00	10.00	30.00
184	**10 PIASTRES**				
(84)	ND. Black. Similar to #83 but new flag w/eagle instead of 2 stars. Sign. title: *MINISTER OF FINANCE.*				
	a. Sign. Hamed. Series 49-69.		.15	.50	2.00
	b. Sign. El Razaz. Series 69-75.		.20	.75	3.00

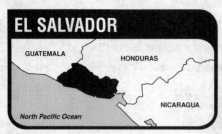

EL SALVADOR

GUATEMALA HONDURAS

North Pacific Ocean NICARAGUA

The Republic of El Salvador, a Central American country bordered by Guatemala, Honduras and the Pacific Ocean, has an area of 8,260 sq. mi. (21,041 sq. km.) and a population of 5.05 million. Capital: San Salvador. This most intensely cultivated country of Latin America produces coffee (the major crop), cotton, sugar and balsam for export. Gold, silver and other metals are largely unexploited.

The first Spanish attempt to subjugate the area was undertaken in 1523 by Pedro de Alvarado, Cortes' lieutenant. He was forced to retreat by superior Indian forces, but returned in 1525 and succeeded in bringing the region under control of the captain generalcy of Guatemala, where it remained until 1821. In 1821, El Salvador and the other Central American provinces declared their independence from Spain. In 1823, the Federal Republic of Central America was formed by the five Central American States. When this federation was dissolved in 1829, El Salvador became an independent republic.

MONETARY SYSTEM:
1 Colon = 100 Centavos 1919-

SUPERINTENDENCIA DE BANCOSE Y OTRAS INSTITUCIONES FINANCIERAS

Juan S. Quinteros	1962-1975	Marco T. Guandique	1977-Feb.1981
Jose A. Mendoza	1968-1975	Rafael T. Carbonell	1981
Jorge A. Dowson	1975-1977	Raul Nolasco	1981-

REPUBLIC

BANCO CENTRAL DE RESERVA DE EL SALVADOR

1962-63 ISSUE
#100-138 backs w/portr. C. Columbus at ctr. l., and later as wmk. also. Various date and sign. ovpts. on back w/different shields and seals.

#100-122, 133, and 138 black on m/c unpt.

#100-104 printer: TDLR.

100	1 COLON	VG	VF	UNC
	12.3.1963; 25.1.1966; 23.8.1966. Central Bank at ctr. Back orange.	.85	3.50	16.50

101	2 COLONES	VG	VF	UNC
	15.2.1962; 9.6.1964. Coffee bush at l. Back red-brown.	1.75	7.00	35.00

102	5 COLONES	VG	VF	UNC
	15.2.1962; 12.3.1963. Woman w/basket of fruit on her head. Back green.	1.75	7.00	35.00

103	10 COLONES	VG	VF	UNC
	15.2.1962; 9.6.1964; 27.12.1966. Portr. M. J. Arce at ctr., serial # at lower l. and upper r. Back brown.	2.50	10.00	47.50

104	25 COLONES	VG	VF	UNC
	12.3.1963; 27.12.1966. Reservoir at ctr. Back dk. blue.	6.50	20.00	80.00

1964-65 ISSUE
#105-107 printer: ABNC.

105	1 COLON	VG	VF	UNC
	8.9.1964. Farmer plowing at ctr., *SAN SALVADOR* at upper l. Black serial # and series letters. Back orange.	2.00	6.00	22.50
106	5 COLONES			
	8.9.1964. Delgado addressing crowd at ctr., *SAN SALVADOR* at upper l. Black serial # at lower l. and upper r. Back green.	2.50	7.50	32.50

107	100 COLONES	VG	VF	UNC
	12.1.1965. Brown and green unpt. Independence monument at ctr. but *SAN SALVADOR* at upper l. Serial # at lower l. and upper r. Back olive-green.	20.00	65.00	200.00

1967 COMMEMORATIVE ISSUE

#108-109 printer: TDLR.

NOTE: #108 and 109 are reportedly a commemorative for the bicentennial of the birth of Jose Cañas.

108   1 COLON

	VG	VF	UNC
20.6.1967. J. Cañas at r., *UN COLON* at ctr. *SAN SALVADOR* and date at r. Back orange.	1.00	2.00	9.00

109   5 COLONES

	VG	VF	UNC
20.6.1967. Pink and green unpt. Scene of J. Cañas freeing the slaves, *31.12.1823* at ctr.	2.00	7.50	25.00

1968-70 ISSUES

#110-114 printer: USBNC.

110   1 COLON

	VG	VF	UNC
1968; 1970. J. Cañas at r., *1 COLON* at ctr. Back orange.			
a. Sign. title: *CAJERO* at r. 13.8.1968.	.75	1.50	6.00
b. Sign. title: *GERENTE* at r. 12.5.1970.	.75	1.50	6.00

111   5 COLONES

	VG	VF	UNC
1968-70. Delgado addressing crowd at ctr., *5 COLONES* at r. Back dk. green; C. Columbus at l. and as wmk.			
a. Sign. title: *CAJERO* at r. 13.8.1968; 4.2.1969.	1.25	3.50	12.50
b. Sign. title: *GERENTE* at r. 12.5.1970.	1.25	3.50	12.50

112   10 COLONES

	VG	VF	UNC
13.8.1968. *10 COLONES* at ctr., M. J. Arce at r. Back black. Wmk: Columbus.	3.00	8.00	30.00

113   25 COLONES

	VG	VF	UNC
12.5.1970. Reservoir at r. Back dk. blue. Wmk: Columbus.	7.00	17.50	50.00

114   100 COLONES

	VG	VF	UNC
12.5.1970. Brown and green unpt. Independence monument at ctr. Back olive-green.	17.50	45.00	145.00

1971-72 ISSUES

#115-119 printer: TDLR.

115 1 COLON
31.8.1971; 24.10.1972. *SAN SALVADOR* and date at l., *UN COLON* at ctr., Jose Cañas at r. Back red.

	VG	VF	UNC
	.50	1.00	3.00

116 2 COLONES
24.10.1972; 15.10.1974. Colonial church of Panchimalco at ctr., *DOS COLONES* at r., w/o wmk. Back red-brown.

	VG	VF	UNC
	.50	1.00	3.50

117 5 COLONES
31.8.1971-24.6.1976. Face like #97 but w/o *5 COLONES* at l., Delgado addressing crowd at ctr. Back green; portr. C. Columbus at l. ctr. and as wmk.

	VG	VF	UNC
	FV	1.50	5.50

118 10 COLONES
13.8.1971-23.12.1976. *DIEZ COLONES* at ctr., M. J. Arce at r. Back black. Wmk: Columbus.

	VG	VF	UNC
	2.50	4.50	15.00

119 25 COLONES
31.8.1971. Reservoir at ctr. Similar to #106 but different design on face and back. Wmk: Columbus.

	VG	VF	UNC
	7.00	12.50	35.00

1974 ISSUE
#120-122 printer: TDLR.

120 1 COLON
15.10.1974. Hydroelectric dam at ctr., w/o *UN COLON* = at l. Back red; like #115.

	VG	VF	UNC
	.30	.75	3.00

121 25 COLONES
15.10.1974; 24.6.1976; 23.12.1976. Acajutla port scene. Back blue. Wmk: Columbus.

	VG	VF	UNC
	FV	8.00	22.50

122 100 COLONES
1974-79. Indian pyramid at Tazumal at ctr. Back olive. Wmk: Columbus.

	VG	VF	UNC
a. Regular serial #. 15.10.1974-11.5.1978.	FV	20.00	80.00
b. Electronic sorting serial #. 3.5.1979.	FV	FV	65.00

1976 ISSUE
#123-124 printer: TDLR.

123 1 COLON
28.10.1976. Similar to #120 but *UN COLON* at l. Back like #125. W/o wmk.

	VG	VF	UNC
	FV	1.50	4.50

124 2 COLONES
24.6.1976. Like #116, w/*DOS COLONES* at l. and r., but m/c unpt. in margins, w/o wmk. Denomination added to face at l. Arms at r. on back.

	VG	VF	UNC
	FV	FV	3.00

1977-79 ISSUES

NOTE: For similar 5 Colones dated 19.6.1980, see #137.

		VG	VF	UNC
125	**1 COLON**			
	1977-82. Like #123 but m/c unpt. on margins. Arms at r. on back. Printer: TDLR.			
	a. Regular style serial #. 7.7.1977; 11.5.1978.	FV	FV	2.00
	b. Electronic sorting serial #. 3.5.1979; 19.6.1980.	FV	FV	1.75
	c. W/o sign. title: *GERENTE* at r. 3.6.1982.	FV	FV	1.50

		VG	VF	UNC
126	**5 COLONES**	FV	FV	3.50
	6.10.1977. Like #117, but *5 COLONES* at l. and r., m/c unpt. in margins, w/o wmk.			

		VG	VF	UNC
127	**10 COLONES**	FV	FV	7.00
	7.7.1977. *DIEZ COLONES* at ctr., M. J. Arce at ctr. r. Back black. Wmk: Columbus. Printer: ABNC.			

		VG	VF	UNC
128	**10 COLONES**	1.50	3.00	9.50
	13.10.1977. Like #127 but blue arms added to face and back. W/o wmk. Printer: ABNC.			

		VG	VF	UNC
129	**10 COLONES**			
	1978-80. Black on m/c unpt. M. J. Arce at r., m/c unpt in margins. Back black. Wmk: Columbus. Printer: TDLR.			
	a. Regular serial #. 11.5.1978.	FV	2.00	6.00
	b. Electronic sorting serial #. 3.5.1979; 21.7.1980.	FV	1.50	5.00

		VG	VF	UNC
130	**25 COLONES**			
	1978-80. Like #121 but m/c unpt. in margins on face.			
	a. Regular serial #. 11.5.1978.	FV	4.00	20.00
	b. Electronic sorting serial #. 3.5.1979; 19.6.1980.	FV	3.00	12.00

		VG	VF	UNC
131	**50 COLONES**			
	1979; 1980. Purple and m/c. Lg. bldg. and statue at l., Capt. Gen. G. Barrios at r. Ships at l. on back. Wmk: Columbus. Printer: TDLR.			
	a. 3.5.1979.	FV	6.00	20.00
	b. 19.6.1980.	FV	5.00	17.50

		VG	VF	UNC
132	**100 COLONES**	FV	FV	55.00
	7.7.1977. Deep olive-green on m/c unpt. Independence monument at r. Wmk: Columbus. Printer: ABNC.			

		VG	VF	UNC
133	**100 COLONES**	FV	FV	35.00
	17.7.1980. Like #122 but w/flag below date at l. Printer: TDLR.			

1983 ISSUE

#134-137 printer: ABNC.

		VG	VF	UNC
134	**5 COLONES**	FV	FV	2.00
	25.8.1983; 17.3.1988. Delgade addressing crowd at ctr. W/o sign. title: *GERENTE* at r. Back green.			
135 (127B)	**10 COLONES**	FV	FV	3.75
	25.8.1983; 17.3.1988. Like #127 but w/o sign., title: *GERENTE* at r.			
136 (135)	**25 COLONES**	FV	FV	7.50
	29.9.1983. Black on m/c unpt. Bridge and reservoir at ctr. w/o sign. title: *GERENTE* at r. Wmk: Columbus.			
137 (132B)	**100 COLONES**	FV	FV	25.00
	29.9.1983; 17.3.1988. Like #132 but w/o sign., title: *GERENTE* at r.			

1990-93 ISSUES

		VG	VF	UNC
138 (136)	**5 COLONES** 16.5.1990. Similar to #126 but w/o sign., title: *GERENTE* at r., w/electronic sorting serial #. Back olive-green and dk. gray. Printer TDLR.	FV	FV	1.75
139 (137)	**5 COLONES** 19.6.1980 (1992). Similar to #109 but w/sign., title: *GERENTE* at r. Printer: ABNC.	FV	FV	2.00
140 (138)	**100 COLONES** 12.3.1993; 22.12.1994. Black on pink, blue and pale green unpt. Like #133 but w/arms at upper l., flag at lower r. on back. Printer: TDLR.	FV	FV	22.50

1995 ISSUE

#141-143 ascending serial #. Wmk: Columbus wearing cap. Printer: TDLR.

		VG	VF	UNC
141	**10 COLONES** 26.5.1995. Like #129.	FV	FV	3.50
142	**25 COLONES** 26.5.1995. Similar to #130 but w/o sign., title: *GERENTE* at r.	FV	FV	7.00
143	**50 COLONES** 26.5.1995. Like #131.	FV	FV	12.50

1996 ISSUE

		VG	VF	UNC
144	**10 COLONES** 9.2.1996. Similar to #141. Printer: CBNC.	FV	FV	3.25

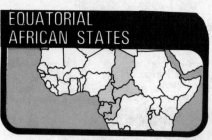

Equatorial African States (Central African States), a monetary union comprising the former French possessions and now independent states of the Republic of Congo (Brazzaville), Gabon, Central African Republic, Chad and Cameroon, issues a common currency for the member states from a common central bank. The monetary unit, the African Financial Community Franc, is tied to and supported by the French franc.

In 1960, an abortive attempt was made to form a union of the newly independent republics of Chad, Congo, Central Africa and Gabon. The proposal was discarded when Chad refused to become a constituent member. The four countries then linked into an Equatorial Customs Unit, to which Cameroon became an associate member in 1961. A more extensive cooperation of the five republics, identified as the Central African Customs and Economic Union, was entered into force at the beginning of 1966.

In 1974 the Central Bank of the Equatorial African States, which had issued coins and paper currency in its own name and with the names of the constituent member nations, changed its name to the Bank of the Central African States.

MONETARY SYSTEM:
1 Franc (C.F.A.) = 100 Centimes

CONTROL LETTER or SYMBOL CODE	
Country	**1961-72**
Cameroun	*
Central African Republic	B
Chad	A
Congo	C
Gabon	D

EQUATORIAL AFRICAN STATES

BANQUE CENTRALE DES ÉTATS DE L'AFRIQUE EQUATORIALE ET DU CAMEROUN

1961 ND ISSUES

		VG	VF	UNC
1	**100 FRANCS** ND (1961-62). Blue and m/c. Woman w/jug at l., portr. Gov. Felix Eboue at ctr., people in canoe at r. Cargo ships at ctr., man at r. on back.			
	a. Code letter *A*.	15.00	60.00	250.00
	b. Code letter *B*.	15.00	65.00	275.00
	c. Code letter *C*.	15.00	60.00	250.00
	d. Code letter *D*.	15.00	60.00	250.00
	e. * for Cameroun.	50.00	150.00	425.00
	f. W/o code letter.	12.50	45.00	200.00
2	**100 FRANCS** ND (1961-62). M/c. Like #1 but denomination also in English. W/* for Cameroun.	50.00	150.00	375.00

1963 ND ISSUES

3   **100 FRANCS**   VG   VF   UNC
ND (1963). Brown and m/c. Musical instrument at l., hut at l. ctr., man at r. Elephant at l., tools at r. on back.

		VG	VF	UNC
a.	Code letter *A*.	8.00	30.00	85.00
b.	Code letter *B*.	8.00	30.00	95.00
c.	Code letter *C*.	8.00	30.00	85.00
d.	Code letter *D*.	8.00	30.00	85.00

4   **500 FRANCS**   VG   VF   UNC
ND (1963). Green and m/c. Girl wearing bandana at r., track mounted crane w/ore bucket in background. Radar unit at l., man on camel at r. on back.

		VG	VF	UNC
a.	Engraved. Code letter *A*. Block #1-4.	15.00	70.00	250.00
b.	As a. Code letter *B*.	15.00	80.00	275.00
c.	As a. Code letter *C*.	18.00	70.00	250.00
d.	As a. Code letter *D*.	15.00	70.00	250.00
e.	Lithographed. Code letter *A*. Block #5-.	10.00	55.00	225.00
f.	As e. Code letter *B*.	10.00	65.00	250.00
g.	As e. Code letter *C*.	12.00	55.00	225.00
h.	As e. Code letter *D*.	10.00	55.00	225.00

7   **10,000 FRANCS**   VG   VF   UNC
ND (1968). M/c. Pres. Bokassa at r., Rock Hotel, Bangui, C.A.R. in   225.00   525.00   1250.
background. Arms of Central African Republic at lower l. on back.

5   **1000 FRANCS**   VG   VF   UNC
ND (1963). M/c. People gathering cotton. Young men logging on back.

		VG	VF	UNC
a.	Engraved. Code letter *A*. Block #1-5.	15.00	80.00	275.00
b.	As a. Code letter *B*.	15.00	90.00	300.00
c.	As a. Code letter *C*.	18.00	80.00	275.00
d.	As a. Code letter *D*.	15.00	80.00	275.00
e.	Lithographed. Code letter *A*. Block #7-.	12.00	70.00	250.00
f.	As e. Code letter *B*.	12.00	80.00	275.00
g.	As e. Code letter *C*.	15.00	70.00	250.00
h.	As e. Code letter *D*.	12.00	70.00	250.00

6   **5000 FRANCS**   VG   VF   UNC
ND (1963). M/c. Girl at l., village scene at ctr. Carving at l., airplane, train crossing bridge and tractor hauling logs at ctr., man smoking a pipe at r. on back.

		VG	VF	UNC
a.	Code letter *A*.	125.00	350.00	650.00
b.	Code letter *B*.	125.00	325.00	650.00
c.	Code letter *C*.	125.00	350.00	650.00
d.	Code letter *D*.	125.00	350.00	650.00

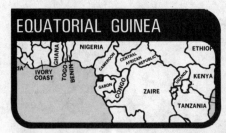

EQUATORIAL GUINEA

The Republic of Equatorial Guinea (formerly Spanish Guinea) consists of Rio Muni, located on the coast of west-central Africa between Cameroon and Gabon, and the offshore islands of Fernando Po, Annobon, Corisco, Elobey Grande and Elobey Chico. The equatorial country has an area of 10,831 sq. mi. (28,051 sq. km.) and a population of 417,000. Capital: Malabo. The economy is based on agriculture and forestry. Cacao, wood and coffee are exported.

Fernando Po was discovered between 1474 and 1496 by Portuguese navigators charting a route to the spice islands of the Far East. Portugal retained control of it and the adjacent islands until 1778 when they, together with trading rights to the African coast between the Ogooue and Niger rivers, were ceded to Spain. Fernando Po was administered, with Spanish consent, by the British from 1827 to 1844 when it was reclaimed by Spain. Mainland Rio Muni was granted to Spain by the Berlin Conference of 1885. The name of the colony was changed from Spanish Guinea to Equatorial Guinea in Dec. of 1963. Independence was attained on Oct. 12, 1968.

MONETARY SYSTEM:
1 Peseta Guineana = 100 Centimos to 1975
1 Ekuele = 100 Centimos, 1975-80
1 Epkwele (pl. Bipkwele) = 100 Centimos, 1980-85
1 Franc (C.F.A.) = 100 Centimes, 1985-
1 Franco (C.F.A.) = 4 Bipkwele

REPUBLIC

BANCO CENTRAL

1969 ISSUE
#1-3 printer: FNMT.

	100 PESETAS GUINEANAS	VG	VF	UNC
1	12.10.1969. Red-brown on lt. tan unpt. Banana tree at l. Shoreline and man w/boat on back. Wmk: Woman's head.	1.00	3.00	9.00

	500 PESETAS GUINEANAS	VG	VF	UNC
2	12.10.1969. Green. Derrick loading logs at l., shoreline at ctr. Woman w/bundle on head at r. on back. Wmk: Man's head.	2.00	6.00	20.00

	1000 PESETAS GUINEANAS	VG	VF	UNC
3	12.10.1969. Blue. Pres. M. Nguema Biyogo at ctr. Tree at l., arms at ctr. on back. Wmk: King and queen.	2.75	7.50	22.50

BANCO POPULAR

1975 FIRST DATED ISSUE
#4-8 w/portr. Pres. M. N. Biyogo at r. and as wmk. Name under portrait: *MACIAS NGUEMA BIYOGO*. Printer: TDLR.

#6-8 arms at ctr.

	25 EKUELE	VG	VF	UNC
4	7.7.1975. Purple on lt. orange and green unpt. Trees at ctr. Arms at l., bridge at ctr. on back. Name underneath: *PUENTE MACIAS NGUEMA BIYOGO*.	.65	1.60	3.75

	50 EKUELE	VG	VF	UNC
5	7.7.1975. Brown on green and pink unpt. Plants at ctr. Arms at l., logging at ctr. on back.	.65	1.60	4.00

6   **100 EKUELE**

7.7.1975. Green on pink and m/c unpt. Bridge and boats on back.

	VG	VF	UNC
	.65	1.60	4.50

7   **500 EKUELE**

7.7.1975. Blue on m/c unpt. National Palace on back.

	VG	VF	UNC
	1.25	4.00	12.50

8   **1000 EKUELE**

7.7.1975. Red on m/c unpt. Bank on back.

	VG	VF	UNC
	2.00	4.00	10.00

1975 SECOND DATED ISSUE

#4A-8A like #4-8 but name under portrait: *MASIE NGUEMA BIYOGO NEGUE NDONG.* Different sign. also.

4A   **25 EKUELE**

7.7.1975. Like #4 except for name change on both sides.

	VG	VF	UNC
	1.00	2.00	6.00

5A   **50 EKUELE**

7.7.1975. Like #5 except for name change.

	VG	VF	UNC
	1.00	2.50	6.00

6A   **100 EKUELE**

7.7.1975. Like #6 except for name change on both sides.

1.00	2.50	6.00

7A   **500 EKUELE**

7.7.1975. Like #7 except for name change.

1.50	4.00	10.00

8A   **1000 EKUELE**

7.7.1975. Like #8 except for name change.

1.50	3.50	8.50

BANCO DE GUINEA ECUATORIAL

1979 ISSUE

#9-12 wmk: T.E. Nkogo. Printer: FNMT.

9   **100 BIPKWELE**

3.8.1979. Dk. olive-green and m/c. Arms at ctr., T. E. Nkogo at r. Boats along pier of Puerto de Bata on back.

	VG	VF	UNC
	1.75	4.00	10.00

10   **500 BIPKWELE**

3.8.1979. Black on green and pink unpt. Arms at ctr., R. Uganda at r. Back brown and black; sailboat, shoreline and trees.

	VG	VF	UNC
	3.00	8.00	20.00

11   **1000 BIPKWELE**

3.8.1979. Brown, black and m/c. Arms at ctr., R. Bioko at r. Back maroon and brown; men cutting food plants.

	VG	VF	UNC
	5.00	12.50	35.00

12 **5000 BIPKWELE**
3.8.1979. Blue-gray on m/c unpt. Arms at ctr., E. N. Okenve at r. Back blue-gray and blue; logging scene at ctr.

	VG	VF	UNC
	3.00	7.50	22.50

1980 PROVISIONAL ISSUE

13 **1000 BIPKWELE**
21.10.1980. Black ovpt. of new denomination and date on #1. (Not issued).

	VG	VF	UNC
	—	3.50	15.00

14 **5000 BIPKWELE**
21.10.1980. Similar red ovpt. on #2. (Not issued).

	VG	VF	UNC
	—	6.00	22.50

BANQUE DES ÉTATS DE L'AFRIQUE CENTRALE

1985 ISSUE

#15-17 wmk: Carving (as printed on notes). Sign. 9. For signature see listings at Central Africa States.
#18 *Deleted*.

15 **500 FRANCOS**
1.1.1985. Brown on m/c unpt. Carving and jug at ctr. Man carving mask at l. ctr. on back.

	VG	VF	UNC
	FV	3.00	6.00

16 **1000 FRANCOS**
1.1.1985. Dk. blue on m/c unpt. Animal carving at lower l., map at ctr., starburst at lower r. Incomplete map of Chad at upper ctr. Elephant at l., statue at r. on back.

	VG	VF	UNC
	FV	6.00	10.00

17 **5000 FRANCOS**
1.1.1985; 1.1.1986. Brown, yellow and m/c. Carved mask at l., woman carrying bundle at r. Farmer plowing w/tractor at l., ore lift at r. on back.

	VG	VF	UNC
	FV	20.00	35.00

ESTONIA

The Republic of Estonia (formerly the Estonian Soviet Socialist Republic of the U.S.S.R.) is the northernmost of the three Baltic states in eastern Europe. It has an area of 17,413 sq. mi. (45,100 sq. km.) and a population of 1.6 million. Capital: Tallinn. Agriculture and dairy farming are the principal industries. Butter, eggs, bacon, timber and petroleum are exported.

This small and ancient Baltic state has enjoyed but two decades of independence since the 13th century. After having been conquered by the Danes, the Livonian Knights, the Teutonic Knights of Germany (who reduced the people to serfdom), the Swedes, the Poles and Russia, Estonia declared itself an independent republic on Nov. 15, 1917, but was not freed until Feb. 1919. The peace treaty was signed Feb. 2, 1920. Shortly after the start of World War II, it was again occupied by Russia and incorporated as the 16th state of the U.S.S.R. Germany occupied the tiny state from 1941 to 1944, after which it was retaken by Russia. Some of the nations of the world, including the United States and Great Britain, did not recognize Estonia's incorporation as an S.S.R. into the Soviet Union.

On August 20, 1991, the Parliament of the Estonian S.S.R. voted to reassert the republic's independence.

MONETARY SYSTEM

1 Kroon = 100 Senti, 1928-1941, 1991-
The U.S.S.R. ruble circulated in the early days of WW II and again from 1944-91.

REPUBLIC

EESTI PANK

BANK OF ESTONIA

1991-92 ISSUE

		VG	VF	UNC
69	**1 KROON**	FV	FV	.50

1992. Brownish black on yellow-orange and dull violet-brown unpt. K. Raud at l. Toampea castle w/Tall Hermann (national landmarks) on back.

		VG	VF	UNC
70	**2 KROONI**	FV	FV	.75

1992. Black on lt. blue-violet and grayish green unpt. K. E. von Baer at l. Tartu University bldg. at ctr. on back.

		VG	VF	UNC
71	**5 KROONI**	FV	FV	1.50

1991 (1993). Black and tan on m/c unpt. P. Keres at ctr., chessboard and arms at upper r. Teutonic Fortress along Narva River, church on back.

		VG	VF	UNC
72	**10 KROONI**	FV	FV	2.50

1991 (1993). Purple and red-violet on m/c unpt. J. Hurt at l. ctr. Tamme-lauri oak tree at Urvaste at r. on back.

		VG	VF	UNC
73	**25 KROONI**	FV	FV	6.00

1991 (1993). Deep olive-green on m/c unpt. A. Hanse-Tammsaare at l. ctr., wilderness in background at r. Early rural log construction farm; view of Vargamäe on back.

74 **100 KROONI**
1991 (1993); 1992. Black and deep blue on lt. blue and m/c unpt. L. Koidula at l. ctr., cuckoo bird at lower r. Waves breaking against rocky cliffs of Northcoast at ctr. to r. on back.

	VG	VF	UNC
	FV	FV	22.50

75 **500 KROONI**
1991 (1993). Blue-black and purple on m/c unpt. C. R. Jakobson at l. ctr., harvest between 2 farmers with Sakala above at r. Barn swallow in flight over rural pond at r. on back.

	VG	VF	UNC
	FV	FV	80.00

1995-96 ISSUE

76 **5 KROONI**
(199x)

	VG	VF	UNC
			Expected New Issue

77 **10 KROONI**
(199x)

	VG	VF	UNC
			Expected New Issue

78 **50 KROONI**
1994. Green and black on m/c unpt. R. Tobias at l. ctr., gates at lower ctr. r. Opera House in Tallinn at ctr. r. on back.

	VG	VF	UNC
	FV	FV	11.00

79 **100 KROONI**
1994. Black and dk. blue on m/c unpt. Like #74 but w/gray seal at upper r.

	VG	VF	UNC
	FV	FV	20.00

80 **500 KROONI**
1994. Blue-black and purple on m/c unpt. Like #75 but w/dk. gray bank seal at upper r.

	VG	VF	UNC
	FV	FV	75.00

ETHIOPIA

The Peoples Democratic Republic of Ethiopia, faces on the Red Sea in east-central Africa. The country has an area of 424,214 sq. mi. (1.099,900 sq. km.) and a population of 55 million people who are divided among 40 tribes and speak 270 languages and dialects. Capital: Addis Ababa. The economy is predominantly agricultural and pastoral. Gold and platinum are mined and petroleum fields are being developed. Coffee, oilseeds, hides and cereals are exported.

Legend claims that Menelik I, the son born to Solomon, King of Israel, by the Queen of Sheba, settled in Axum in Northern Ethiopia to establish the dynasty which then reigned - with only brief interruptions - until 1974. Modern Ethiopian history began with the reign of Emperor Menelik II (1889-1913) under whose guidance the country emerged from medieval isolation. Ethiopia was invaded by Mussolini in 1935, and together with Italian Somaliland and Eritrea became part of Italian East Africa until liberated by British and Ethiopian troops in 1941. Haile Selassie I, 225th consecutive Solomonic ruler, was deposed by a military committee on Sept. 12, 1974. In July 1976, Ethiopia's military provisional government referred to the country as Socialist Ethiopia.

Eritrea, a former Ethiopian province fronting on the Red Sea, was an Italian colony from 1890 until its incorporation into Italian East Africa in 1936. It was under British military administration from 1941 to Sept. 15, 1952, when the United Nations designated it an autonomous unit within the federation of Ethiopia and Eritrea. On Nov. 14, 1962, it was fully integrated with Ethiopia. On May 24, 1993, Eritrea became an independent nation.

RULERS:
Haile Selassie I, 1930-1936, 1941-1974

MONETARY SYSTEM:
1 Birr (Dollar) = 100 Canteems (Cents), 1941-

KINGDOM

STATE BANK OF ETHIOPIA

1961 ND ISSUE
Dollar System
#18-24 Haile Selassie at r. Arms at ctr. on back. Printer: BWC.

18 **1 DOLLAR**
ND (1961). Green on lilac and lt. orange unpt. Coffee bushes at l.

	VG	VF	UNC
	3.00	15.00	45.00

19 **5 DOLLARS**
ND (1961). Orange on green and m/c unpt. University (old palace) at l.

	VG	VF	UNC
	7.50	35.00	125.00

20 **10 DOLLARS**
ND (1961). Red on m/c unpt. Harbor at Massawa at l.

	20.00	65.00	250.00

21	**20 DOLLARS**	**VG**	**VF**	**UNC**
	ND (1961). Brown on m/c unpt. Ancient stone monument (Axum) at l.	30.00	125.00	385.00
22	**50 DOLLARS**			
	ND (1961). Blue on m/c unpt. Bridge over Blue Nile at l.	90.00	250.00	700.00
23	**100 DOLLARS**			
	ND (1961). Purple on m/c unpt. Trinity Church at Addis Ababa at l.			
	a. Sign. title: *GOVERNOR*.	100.00	250.00	700.00
	b. Sign. title: *ACTING GOVERNOR*.	70.00	200.00	550.00
24	**500 DOLLARS**			
	ND (1961). Dk. green on m/c unpt. Castle at Gondar at l.	250.00	600.00	1500.

NATIONAL BANK OF ETHIOPIA

1966 ISSUE

#25-29 Emperor Haile Selassie at r. Arms at ctr. on back. Printer: TDLR.

25	**1 DOLLAR**	**VG**	**VF**	**UNC**
	ND (1966). Green on m/c unpt. Aerial view of Massawa harbor, city at l.	2.00	6.00	20.00

26	**5 DOLLARS**	**VG**	**VF**	**UNC**
	ND (1966). Brown on m/c unpt. Bole-Airport Addis Ababa at l. Back orange.	5.00	20.00	85.00

27	**10 DOLLARS**	**VG**	**VF**	**UNC**
	ND (1966). Dk. red on m/c unpt. National Bank at Addis Ababa at l.	3.00	10.00	40.00

28	**50 DOLLARS**	**VG**	**VF**	**UNC**
	ND (1966). Blue on m/c unpt. Koka High Dam at l.	20.00	75.00	275.00

29	**100 DOLLARS**	**VG**	**VF**	**UNC**
	ND (1966). Purple on green and m/c unpt. Bet Giorgis in Lalibela (rock church) at l.	15.00	55.00	175.00

REPUBLIC

ARMS VARIETIES

Type A — Type B — Type C — Type D

SIGNATURE VARIETIES

1	T. Deguefe, 1974–76 CHAIRMAN OF THE BOARD	**3**	B. Tamirat, 1987–91 ADMINISTRATOR
2	T. G. Kidan, 1978–87 ADMINISTRATOR	**4**	L. Berhann, 1991– GOVERNOR

NATIONAL BANK OF ETHIOPIA

1976 ND ISSUE

Birr System

Law EE 1969 (1976 AD)

#30-34 have map at l., lion head in unpt. at l. ctr.

30	**1 BIRR**	**VG**	**VF**	**UNC**
	L.EE1969 (1976). Black on green on lt. brown and green unpt. Young man at ctr. r., longhorns at r. Back black on m/c unpt; birds and Tisisat waterfalls of Blue Nile on back.			
	a. Sign. 1.	.50	2.00	5.00
	b. Sign. 2.	.25	1.50	2.50

31	**5 BIRR**	**VG**	**VF**	**UNC**
	L.EE1969 (1976). Black and brown-orange on m/c unpt. Man picking coffee beans at ctr. r., plant at r. Kudu, leopard and Semien Mountains on back.			
	a. Sign. 1.	1.00	4.00	8.00
	b. Sign. 2.	1.25	3.50	7.00

32 10 BIRR
L.EE1969 (1976). Brown violet and red on m/c unpt. Woman weaving basket at ctr. r., basket w/lid at r. Plowing w/tractor on back.

	VG	VF	UNC
a. Sign. 1.	3.00	8.00	15.00
b. Sign. 2.	2.50	5.00	10.00

33 50 BIRR
L.EE1969 (1976). Blue-black and dk. brown on lilac and m/c unpt. Science students at ctr. r., musical instrument at r. Fasilides Castle on back.

	VG	VF	UNC
a. Sign. 1.	12.50	22.50	50.00
b. Sign. 2.	11.50	20.00	40.00

34 100 BIRR
L.EE1969 (1976). Purple, violet and dk. brown on m/c unpt. Warrior standing at ctr. r., flowers at r. Young man w/microscope on back.

	VG	VF	UNC
a. Sign. 1.	25.00	45.00	75.00
b. Sign. 2.	20.00	35.00	65.00

1987 ND ISSUE

#36-40 similar to #30-34 but w/ornate tan design at l. and r. edges on back. Sign. 3.

			VG	VF	UNC
36	**1 BIRR**	*L.EE1969* (1987). Like #30.	.20	1.00	1.75
37	**5 BIRR**	*L.EE1969* (1987). Like #31.	.85	2.50	5.00
38	**10 BIRR**	*L.EE1969* (1987). Like #32.	1.50	3.50	7.50
39	**50 BIRR**	*L.EE1969* (1987). Like #33.	10.00	17.50	35.00
40	**100 BIRR**	*L.EE1969* (1976). Like #34 but w/flowers and dark shield at r.	20.00	32.50	55.00

1991 ISSUE

#41-45 like #36-40 but w/new arms Type B, C or D at r. on back.

41 1 BIRR
L.EE1969 (1991). Like #36. Arms Type D.

	VG	VF	UNC
a. Sign. 3 w/title in Amharic script.	FV	FV	1.50
b. Sign. 4 w/title: IGOVERNOR and also in Amharic script.	FV	FV	1.25

42 5 BIRR
L.EE1969 (1991). Like #37.

	VG	VF	UNC
a. Sign 3 w/title in Amharic script. Arms Type B.	FV	FV	4.50
b. Sign. 4 w/title GOVERNOR and also in Amheric script. Arms Type C.	FV	FV	4.00

43 10 BIRR
L.EE1969 (1991). Like #38. Arms Type D.

	VG	VF	UNC
a. Sign. 3 w/title in Amharic script.	FV	FV	7.50
b. Sign. 4 w/title: GOVERNOR and also in Amharic script. Sign. 4	FV	FV	6.00

44 50 BIRR
L.EE1969 (1991). Like #39.

	VG	VF	UNC
a. Sign. 3 w/title in Amharic script. Arms Type B.	FV	FV	40.00
b. Sign. 4 w/title: GOVERNOR and also in Amharic script. Arms Type C.	FV	FV	35.00
c. As b. Arms Type D.	FV	FV	30.00

45 100 BIRR
L.EE1969 (1991). Like #40. Arms Type D.

	VG	VF	UNC
a. Sign. 3 w/title in Amharic script.	FV	FV	50.00
b. Sign. 4 w/title: GOVERNOR and also in Amharic script.	FV	FV	45.00

FAEROE ISLANDS

The Faeroe Islands, a self-governing community within the kingdom of Denmark, are situated in the North Atlantic between Iceland and the Shetland Islands. The 17 inhabited islets and reefs have an area of 540 sq. mi. (1,399 sq. km.) and a population of 48,000. Capital: Thorshavn. The principal industries are fishing and grazing. Fish and fish products are exported.

While it is thought that Irish hermits lived on the islands in the 7th and 8th centuries, the present inhabitants are descended from the 6th century Norse settlers. The Faeroe Islands became a Norwegian fief in 1035 and became Danish in 1380 when Norway and Denmark were united. They have ever since remained in Danish possession and were granted self-government (except for an appointed governor-general) with their own legislature, executive and flag in 1948.

The islands were occupied by British troops during World War II, after the German occupation of Denmark.

RULERS:
Danish

MONETARY SYSTEM:
1 Króne = 100 Øre

DANISH INFLUENCE

FØROYAR

1964-74 ISSUE
#16-23 have coded year dates in the l. series # (the 2 middle digits). Wmk: Anchor chain.

16	10 KRÓNER	VG	VF	UNC
	L.1949 (19)74. Green. Shield w/ram at l. Rural scene on back. Sign. of L. Groth and A. P. Dam.	FV	FV	5.00
17	50 KRÓNER	VG	VF	UNC
	L.1949 (19)67. Black lt. blue and blue-green unpt. N. Pall at l. Back blue on green unpt. Drawing of homes and church across ctr. Sign. M. Wahl and P. M. Dam.	11.50	17.50	27.50

18	100 KRÓNER			
	L.1949 (19)64; 69; 72; 75. Black on pink and gold unpt. V. U. Hammershaimb at l. Back blue on tan unpt. Drawing of house and mountains on back.			
	a. Sign. M. Wahl and H. Djurhuus. (19)64.	20.00	32.50	60.00
	b. Sign. M. Wahl and Kr. Djurhuus (19)69; 72.	20.00	32.50	60.00
	c. Sign. L. Groth and A. P. Dam. (19)75.	20.00	30.00	50.00

1976-86 ISSUE

19	20 KRÓNOR	VG	VF	UNC
	L.1949 (19)86; 88. Deep purple on pink and aqua unpt. Man w/ice tool at r. Back red and black; drawing of animals at ctr.			
	a. Sign. N. Bentsen and A. P. Dam. (19)86.	FV	FV	5.50
	b. Sign. B. Klinte and A. P. Dam. (19)88.	FV	FV	5.50

20	50 KRÓNER	VG	VF	UNC
	L.1949 (19)78; 87. Black on lt. blue and gray unpt. Similar to #17 but reduced size. 140 x 72mm. Back black on gray unpt. Wmk: Chain links.			
	a. Sign. L. Groth and A. P. Dam. (19)78.	FV	FV	15.00
	b. Sign. N. Bentsen and A. P. Dam. (19)87.	FV	FV	14.00

21	100 KRÓNER	VG	VF	UNC
	L.1949 (19)78; 83; 87; 88; 90. Black on tan unpt. Similar to #16 but reduced size. Back black and green on ochre unpt. Wmk: Chain links.			
	a. Sign. L. Groth and A. P. Dam. (19)78.	FV	FV	35.00
	b. Sign. N. Bentsen and P. Ellefsen. (19)83.	FV	FV	32.50
	c. Sign. N. Bentsen and A. P. Dam. (19)87.	FV	FV	30.00
	d. Sign. B. Klinte and A. P. Dam. (19)88.	FV	FV	28.50
	e. Sign. B. Klinte and J. Sundstestein. (19)90.	—	—	27.50

		VG	VF	UNC
22	**500 KRÓNER**			
	L.1949 (19)78-. Black on green and dull purple unpt. Fisherman at r. Fishermen in boat at sea on back. Sign. L. Groth and A. P. Dam.	FV	FV	135.00

		VG	VF	UNC
23	**1000 KRÓNER**			
	L.1949 (19)78; 83; 87; 89. Blue-green, black and green. H. O. Djurhuus at l. Street scene on back.			
	a. Sign. L. Groth and A. P. Dam. (19)78.	FV	FV	250.00
	b. Sign. N. Bentsen and P. Ellefsen. (19)83.	FV	FV	225.00
	c. Sign. N. Bentsen and A. P. Dam. (19)87.	FV	FV	210.00
	d. Sign. B. Klinte and A. P. Dam. (19)89.	FV	FV	200.00

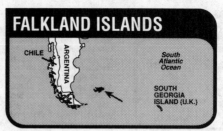

FALKLAND ISLANDS

The Colony of the Falkland Islands and Dependencies, a British colony located in the South Atlantic about 500 miles northeast of Cape Horn, has an area of 4,700 sq. mi. (12,173 sq. km.) and a population of 2,100. East Falkland, West Falkland, South Georgia, and South Sandwich are the largest of the 200 islands. Capital: Stanley. Sheep grazing is the main industry. Wool, whale oil, and seal oil are exported.

The Falklands were discovered by British navigator John Davis (Davys) in 1592, and named by Capt. John Strong - for Viscount Falkland, treasurer of the British navy - in 1690. French navigator Louis De Bougainville established the first settlement, at Port Louis, in 1764. The following year Capt. John Byron claimed the islands for Britain and left a small party at Saunders Island. Spain later forced the French and British to abandon their settlements but did not implement its claim to the islands. In 1829 the Republic of Buenos Aires, which claimed to have inherited the Spanish rights, sent Louis Vernet to develop a colony on the islands. In 1831 he seized three American sailing vessels, whereupon the men of the corvette, *U.S.S. Lexington,* destroyed his settlement and proclaimed the Falklands to be "free of all governance." Britain, which had never renounced its claim, then re-established its settlement in 1833.

RULERS:
British

MONETARY SYSTEM:
1 Shilling = 12 Pence
1 Pound = 20 Shillings to 1966
1 Pound = 100 Pence, 1966-

BRITISH INFLUENCE

GOVERNMENT OF THE FALKLAND ISLANDS

1960-67 ISSUE
#7-9 portr. On. Elizabeth II at r. Printer: TDLR.

		VG	VF	UNC
8	**1 POUND**			
	1967-82. Blue on gray-green and lilac unpt.			
	a. 2.1.1967.	2.00	5.00	27.50
	b. 20.2.1974.	1.75	3.50	20.00
	c. 1.12.1977.	2.50	10.00	40.00
	d. 1.1.1982.	2.00	6.00	28.50
	e. 15.6.1982.	1.75	3.00	20.00

		VG	VF	UNC
9	**5 POUNDS**			
	1960; 1975. Red on green unpt.			
	a. Sign. L. Gleadell: 10.4.1960.	9.00	20.00	95.00
	b. Sign. H. T. Rowlands: 30.1.1975.	7.50	15.00	75.00

1969; 1975 ISSUE
#10 and 11 portr. Qn. Elizabeth II at r. Printer: TDLR.

10	50 PENCE	VG	VF	UNC
	1969; 1974. Brown on gray unpt.			
	a. Sign: L. Gleadell. 25.9.1969.	1.50	3.50	18.00
	b. Sign: H. T. Rowlands. 20.2.1974.	1.25	3.00	15.00

11	10 POUNDS	VG	VF	UNC
	1975-82. Green on lt. orange and yellow-green unpt. Sign. H. T. Rowlands.			
	a. 5.6.1975.	17.50	25.00	100.00
	b. 1.1.1982.	18.50	30.00	150.00
	c. 15.6.1982.	16.50	20.00	90.00

1983 COMMEMORATIVE ISSUE
#13, 150th Anniversary of English rule, 1833-1983.

12	5 POUNDS	VG	VF	UNC
(13)	14.6.1983. Red on m/c unpt. Like #12. Commemorative legend at lower ctr.	FV	FV	15.00

1984-90 ISSUE
#13-16 Qn. Elizabeth II at r.

13	1 POUND	VG	VF	UNC
(12)	1.10.1984. Blue on brown and yellow unpt. Penguins and shield at l., seals at r. Governor's home and church on back.	FV	2.50	15.00

14	10 POUNDS	VG	VF	UNC
	1.9.1986. Gray-green on m/c unpt. Like #12.	FV	FV	27.00

15	20 POUNDS	VG	VF	UNC
	1.10.1984. Brown on m/c unpt. Like #12.	FV	FV	50.00

16	50 POUNDS	VG	VF	UNC
	1.7.1990. Blue on m/c unpt. Like #12.	FV	FV	115.00

FIJI

The Dominion of Fiji, an independent member of the British Commonwealth, consists of about 320 islands located in the southwestern Pacific 1,100 miles (1,770 km.) north of New Zealand. The islands have a combined area of 7,056 sq. mi. (18,274 sq. km.) and a population of 747,000. Capital: Suva on the island of Biti Levu. Fiji's economy is based on agriculture and mining. Sugar, coconut products, manganese and gold are exported.

The Fiji Islands were discovered by Dutch navigator Abel Tasman in 1643 and visited by British naval captain James Cook in 1774. The first complete survey of the island was conducted by the United States in 1840. Settlement by missionaries from Tonga and traders attracted by the sandalwood trade began in 1835. Following a lengthy period of intertribal warfare, the islands were unconditionally and voluntarily ceded to Great Britain in 1874 by King Thakombau. The trading center was Levuka on the island of Ovalau which was also the capital under the British from 1874-82. Fiji became a sovereign and independent nation on Oct 10, 1970, the 96th anniversary of the cession of the islands to Queen Victoria. It is a member of the Commonwealth of Nations. The Queen of England is Chief of State.

MONETARY SYSTEM:
1 Shilling = 12 Pence
1 Pound = 20 Shillings to 1969
1 Dollar = 100 Cents, 1969-

BRITISH INFLUENCE

GOVERNMENT OF FIJI

1954-57 ISSUE
Pound System
#43-47 arms at upper ctr., portr. Qn. Elizabeth II at r. Printer: BWC.

43 (30)	5 SHILLINGS	VG	VF	UNC
	1957-65. Green and blue on lilac and green unpt.			
	a. 1.6.1957; 28.4.1961; 1.12.1962.	2.00	7.50	65.00
	b. 1.9.1964; 1.12.1964; 1.10.1965.	1.50	6.00	50.00

44 (31)	10 SHILLINGS	VG	VF	UNC
	1957-65. Brown on lilac and green unpt.			
	a. 1.6.1957; 28.4.1961; 1.12.1962.	3.00	22.50	275.00
	b. 1.9.1964; 1.10.1965.	2.50	17.50	250.00

45 (32)	1 POUND	VG	VF	UNC
	1954-67. Green on yellow and blue unpt.			
	a. 1.7.1954; 1.6.1957; 1.9.1959.	8.00	25.00	300.00
	b. 1.12.1961-1.1.1967.	3.00	20.00	250.00

46 (33)	5 POUNDS	VG	VF	UNC
	1954-67. Purple on lt. orange and green unpt.			
	a. 1.7.1954; 1.9.1959; 1.10.1960.	40.00	225.00	1000.
	b. 1.12.1962; 20.1.1964; 1.12.1964; 1.1.1967.	30.00	200.00	750.00

47 (34)	10 POUNDS	VG	VF	UNC
	1954-64. Blue.			
	a. 1.7.1954.	75.00	375.00	1500.
	b. 1.9.1959; 1.10.1960; 20.1.1964; 11.6.1964.	50.00	285.00	700.00

48 (35)	20 POUNDS			
	1.1.1953. Black and violet. Title: *GOVERNMENT OF FIJI* at top on back.	350.00	1500.	3750.

49 (36)	20 POUNDS			
	1.1.1953; 1.7.1954; 1.11.1958. Red. Titles: *GOVERNMENT OF FIJI* at top on back.	350.00	1500.	4000.

1968 ND ISSUE
Dollar System
#50-55 Qn. Elizabeth at r. Arms and heading: *GOVERNMENT OF FIJI* at upper ctr. 2 sign. Ritchie and Barnes. Wmk: Fijian male's head. Printer: TDLR.

#52-55 w/o pictorial designs on back.

50 (37)	50 CENTS	VG	VF	UNC
	ND (1968). Green on m/c unpt. Thatched roof house and palms on back.	1.00	2.50	15.00

51 (38)	1 DOLLAR	VG	VF	UNC
	ND (1968). Brown on lilac and lt. green unpt. Scene of Yanuca in the Mamanuca Group of Islands, South Yasewas on back.	1.00	5.00	20.00

52 (39)	2 DOLLARS			
	ND (1968). Green on yellow and lt. blue unpt.	3.00	10.00	55.00

53 (40)	5 DOLLARS			
	ND (1968). Orange on lilac and gray unpt.	7.00	25.00	185.00

54 (41)	10 DOLLARS			
	ND (1968). Purple on lt. orange and lilac unpt.	15.00	40.00	265.00

55 (42)	20 DOLLARS			
	ND (1968). Blue on lt. green and orange unpt.	27.50	85.00	500.00

1971 ND Issue

#56-61 like #50-55 but w/only 1 sign.

			VG	VF	UNC
56 (43)	**50 Cents** ND (1971). Green on m/c unpt. Like #50.				
	a. Sign. Wesley Barrett.		1.00	2.50	12.00
	b. Sign. C. A. Stinson.		1.00	2.00	10.00
57 (44)	**1 Dollar** ND (1971). Brown on lilac and lt. green unpt. Like #51.				
	a. Sign. Wesley Barrett.		1.50	3.50	32.50
	b. Sign. C. A. Stinson.		1.50	5.00	45.00
58 (45)	**2 Dollars** ND (1971). Green on yellow and lt. blue unpt. Like #52.				
	a. Sign. Wesley Barrett.		2.50	7.50	85.00
	b. Sign. C. A. Stinson.		Reported Not Confirmed		

			VG	VF	UNC
59 (46)	**5 Dollars** ND (1971). Like #53.				
	a. Sign. Wesley Barrett.		5.00	20.00	165.00
	b. Sign. C. A. Stinson.		5.00	25.00	250.00
60 (47)	**10 Dollars** ND (1971). Like #54.				
	a. Sign. Wesley Barrett.		12.00	37.50	250.00
	b. Sign. C. A. Stinson.		12.50	45.00	350.00
61 (48)	**20 Dollars** ND (1971). Like #55.				
	a. Sign. Wesley Barrett.		25.00	65.00	400.00
	b. Sign. C. A. Stinson.		25.00	75.00	450.00

Central Monetary Authority of Fiji

1974 ND Issue

#62-67 like #50-55 but w/new heading: *FIJI* at top, and issuing authority name across lower ctr. 2 sign. Printer: TDLR.

			VG	VF	UNC
62 (48A)	**50 Cents** ND (1974). Like #50. Sign. D. J. Barnes and R. J. A. Earland. (Not issued).		—	—	—
63 (49)	**1 Dollar** ND (1974). Like #51.				
	a. Sign. D. J. Barnes and R. J. Earland.		1.00	2.00	9.00
	b. Sign. D. J. Barnes and H. J. Tomkins.		1.00	2.00	9.00

			VG	VF	UNC
64 (50)	**2 Dollars** ND (1974). Like #52.				
	a. Sign. D. J. Barnes and I. A. Craik.		3.00	12.00	75.00
	b. Sign. D. J. Barnes and R. J. Earland.		1.50	3.00	22.50
	c. Sign. D. J. Barnes and H. J. Tomkins.		1.50	3.00	25.00
65 (51)	**5 Dollars** ND (1974). Like #53.				
	a. Sign. D. J. Barnes and I. A. Craik.		7.50	25.00	185.00
	b. Sign. D. J. Barnes and R. J. Earland.		3.50	10.00	65.00
	c. Sign. D. J. Barnes and H. J. Tomkins.		3.50	8.50	57.50
66 (52)	**10 Dollars** ND (1974). Like #54.				
	a. Sign. D. J. Barnes and I. A. Craik.		17.50	50.00	375.00
	b. Sign. D. J. Barnes and R. J. Earland.		8.50	17.50	135.00
	c. Sign. D. J. Barnes and H. J. Tomkins.		7.50	15.00	100.00
67 (53)	**20 Dollars** ND (1974). Like #55.				
	a. Sign. D. J. Barnes and I. A. Craik.		30.00	75.00	525.00
	b. Sign. D. J. Barnes and R. J. Earland.		15.00	30.00	150.00
	c. Sign. D. J. Barnes and H. J. Tomkins.		15.00	55.00	200.00

1980 ND Issue

#68-72 Qn. Elizabeth II at r. ctr., arms at ctr., artifact at r. Sign. D.J. Barnes and H.J. Tomkins. Printer: TDLR.

			VG	VF	UNC
68 (54)	**1 Dollar** ND (1980). Brown on m/c unpt. Open air fruit market on back.		FV	1.00	7.50

			VG	VF	UNC
69 (55)	**2 Dollars** ND (1980). Green on m/c unpt. Harvesting sugar cane on back.		FV	2.50	17.50

			VG	VF	UNC
70 (56)	**5 Dollars** ND (1980). Orange on m/c unpt. Circle of fishermen w/net on back.		FV	7.00	37.50

			VG	VF	UNC
71 (57)	**10 Dollars** ND (1980). Purple on m/c unpt. Men doing a dance on back.		FV	15.00	90.00

			VG	VF	UNC
72 (58)	**20 Dollars** ND (1980). Blue on m/c unpt. Native hut on back.		FV	35.00	200.00

1983 ISSUE

#73-74 like #54-58. Backs retouched and lithographed. Sign. D. J. Barnes and S. Siwatibaku.

73	**1 DOLLAR**	VG	VF	UNC
(59)	ND (1983). Black on m/c unpt. Like #54.	FV	FV	5.50

74	**2 DOLLARS**	VG	VF	UNC
(60)	ND (1983). Green on m/c unpt. Like #55.	FV	FV	12.50

75	**5 DOLLARS**	VG	VF	UNC
(61)	ND (1986). Orange on m/c unpt. Like #56.	FV	FV	15.00

76	**10 DOLLARS**	VG	VF	UNC
(62)	ND (1986). Purple on m/c unpt. Like #57.	FV	FV	27.50

77	**20 DOLLARS**	VG	VF	UNC
(63)	ND (1986). Blue on m/c unpt. Like #58.	FV	FV	60.00

RESERVE BANK OF FIJI

1987-91 ND ISSUE

#78-82 modified portr. of Qn. Elizabeth II at r., and new banking authority. Similar to #73-77. Sign. S. Siwatibau.

#78, 79, and 82 printer: BWC.

78	**1 DOLLAR**	VG	VF	UNC
(64)	ND (1987). Dk. gray on m/c unpt. Similar to #73.	FV	FV	4.00

79	**2 DOLLARS**	VG	VF	UNC
(65)	ND (1988). Deep green on m/c unpt. Similar to #74.	FV	FV	6.50

80	**5 DOLLARS**	VG	VF	UNC
(66)	ND. (ca.1991). Brown-orange and violet on m/c unpt. Similar to #75. Printer: TDLR.	FV	FV	15.00

81	**10 DOLLARS**	VG	VF	UNC
(67)	ND (1989). Similar to Purple, violet and brown on m/c unpt. Similar to #76. Printer: TDLR.	FV	FV	25.00

82	**20 DOLLARS**	VG	VF	UNC
(68)	ND (1988). Dk. blue, blue-green and black on m/c unpt. Similar to #77.	FV	FV	45.00

1992-95 ND Issue

#83-87 similar to #79-82 but w/slightly redesigned portr. Sign. Kubuabola. Printer: TDLR.
#84-87 vertical serial # at l., segmented foil over security thread.

83 **1 Dollar**
(69)   ND (1993). Dk. gray on m/c unpt. Similar to #78. W/o segmented
security thread.

	VG	VF	UNC
	FV	FV	3.00

84 **2 Dollars**
(70)   ND (1995). Deep green on m/c unpt. Similar to #79.

	VG	VF	UNC
	FV	FV	5.50

85 **5 Dollars**
(71)   ND (1992). Brown-orange and violet on m/c unpt. Similar to #80.

	VG	VF	UNC
	FV	FV	11.00

86 **10 Dollars**
(72)   ND (1992). Purple, violet and brown on m/c unpt. Similar to #81.

	VG	VF	UNC
	FV	FV	16.00

87 **20 Dollars**
(73)   ND (1992). Dk. blue on m/c unpt. Similar to #82.

	VG	VF	UNC
	FV	FV	30.00

1995-96 ND Issue

#88-92 mature bust of Qn. Elizabeth II at r., arms at upper r. Segmented foil over security thread. Wmk:
Fijian male's head. Printer: TDLR.

88 **2 Dollars**
(74)   ND (1996). Dk. green, blue and olive-brown on m/c unpt. Kaka bird at
lower l. Fijian family of 5 at l. ctr. on back.

	VG	VF	UNC
	FV	FV	4.50

89 **5 Dollars**
(75)   ND (1995). Brown-orange and violet on m/c unpt. Bunedamu bird at
lower l. Nadi international Airport at l. ctr., ferry boat at lower ctr. r. on
back.

	VG	VF	UNC
	FV	FV	9.00

90 **10 Dollars**
(76)   ND (1996). Purple, violet and brown on m/c unpt. Kaka bird at lower l.
Children swimming, family in boat constructed of reeds with thatched
roof shelter at l. ctr. on back.

	VG	VF	UNC
	FV	FV	17.50

91 **20 Dollars**
(77)   ND.

Expected New Issue

92 **50 Dollars**
(78)   ND (1996). Black, red, orange and violet on m/c unpt. Kaka bird at
lower l. Ascending vertical serial # at l. Flag raising ceremony at l.,
signing of Deed of Cession over Cession Stone at ctr. on back.

	VG	VF	UNC
	FV	FV	75.00

FINLAND

The Republic of Finland, the second most northerly state of the European continent, has an area of 130,120 sq. mi. (337,009 sq. km.) and a population of 5 million. Capital: Helsinki. Lumbering, shipbuilding, metal and woodworking are the leading industries. Paper, timber, woodpulp, plywood and metal products are exported.

The Finns, who probably originated in the Volga region of Russia, took Finland from the Lapps late in the 7th century. They were conquered in the 12th century by Eric IX of Sweden, and brought into contact with Western Christendom. In 1809, Sweden was conquered by Alexander I of Russia, and the peace terms gave Finland to Russia which became a grand duchy within the Russian Empire until Dec. 6, 1917, when, shortly after the Bolshevik revolution, it declared its independence. After a brief but bitter civil war between the Russian sympathizers and Finnish nationalists in which the Whites (nationalists) were victorious, a new constitution was adopted, and on Dec. 6, 1917 Finland was established as a republic. In 1939 Soviet troops invaded Finland over disputed territorial concessions which were later granted in the peace treaty of 1940. When the Germans invaded Russia, Finland also became involved and in the Armistice of 1944 lost the Petsamo area also to the Soviets.

MONETARY SYSTEM:
1 Markka = 100 Pennia 1860-1963
1 Markka = 100 'Old' Markkaa 1963-

REPUBLIC

SUOMEN PANKKI - FINLANDS BANK

1963 DATED ISSUES
#98-102 w/o *Litt.* designation. Replacements notes: * suffix.

98	1 MARKKA	VG	VF	UNC
	1963. Lilac-brown on olive unpt. Wheat ears.			
	a. Issued note.	FV	.50	1.25
	s. Specimen.	—	—	100.00

99	5 MARKKAA	VG	VF	UNC
	1963. Blue. Conifer branch.			
	a. Issued note.	FV	1.50	3.00
	s. Specimen.	—	—	125.00

100	10 MARKKAA	VG	VF	UNC
	1963. Dk. green. Paasikivi at l. (Wmk. direction varies.)			
	a. Issued note.	FV	3.00	6.00
	s. Specimen.	—	—	150.00

101	50 MARKKAA	VG	VF	UNC
	1963. Brown. K. J. Stahlberg at l.			
	a. Issued note.	FV	FV	20.00
	s. Specimen.	—	—	175.00

102	100 MARKKAA	VG	VF	UNC
	1963. Violet. J. V. Snellman at l.			
	a. Issued note.	FV	FV	35.00
	s. Specimen.	—	—	200.00

1963 DATED ISSUE, LITT. A
#103-106 *Litt. A.* Replacement notes: * suffix.

103	5 MARKKAA	VG	VF	UNC
	1963. Blue. Similar to #99, but border and date designs are more detailed.	FV	FV	3.00

104   10 MARKKAA
    1963. Dk. green. Like #100. (Wmk. direction varies.)

	VG	VF	UNC
	FV	3.00	5.00

105   50 MARKKAA
    1963. Brown. Like #101.

	VG	VF	UNC
	FV	15.00	30.00

106   100 MARKKAA
    1963. Violet. Like #102.

	VG	VF	UNC
	FV	FV	35.00

1963 DATED ISSUE, LITT. B

#106A and 107 *Litt. B*. Replacement notes: * suffix.

106A   5 MARKKAA
    1963. Blue. Like #99.

	VG	VF	UNC
	FV	FV	2.00

107   50 MARKKAA
    1963. Brown. Like #101 and #105. (Wmk. direction varies.)

	VG	VF	UNC
	FV	FV	20.00

1975-77 ISSUE

#108-110 replacement notes: * suffix.

108   50 MARKKAA
    1977. Brown and m/c. K. J. Stahlberg at l. and as wmk. (Wmk.
    position and direction varies.)
    a.   Issued note.
    s.   Specimen.

	VG	VF	UNC
a.	FV	FV	150.00
s.	—	—	250.00

109   100 MARKKAA
    1976. Violet. J. V. Snellman at l. and as wmk.

	VG	VF	UNC
	FV	FV	33.00

110   500 MARKKAA
    1975. Blue and violet. Urho Kekkonen at l. and as wmk. Arms and 9
    small shields on back.
    a.   Thin metallic security thread.
    b.   Broad yellow plastic security thread.

	VG	VF	UNC
a.	FV	FV	150.00
b.	FV	FV	150.00

1980 ISSUES

#111 replacement notes: * suffix.

#112 replacement notes: w/99 as 2nd and 3rd digits in serial #.

111   10 MARKKAA
    1980. Green on brown and orange unpt. Like #100 except for color
    and addition of 4 raised discs at r. ctr. for denomination identification
    by the blind. Back green and purple. Wmk: Paasikivi.

	VG	VF	UNC
	FV	FV	5.00

112 **10 MARKKAA**
    1980. Similar to #111 but date under portr., and 5 small circles at bottom. *Litt. A.*

	VG	VF	UNC
	FV	FV	5.00

1986 ISSUE
#113-117 wmk as portr. Circles above lower r. serial #. #113-115, 117 replacement notes: w/99 as 2nd and 3rd digits in serial #.

113 **10 MARKKAA**
    1986. Deep blue on blue and green unpt. P. Nurmi at l. and as wmk. Helsinki Olympic Stadium on back.

	VG	VF	UNC
	FV	FV	4.50

114 **50 MARKKAA**
    1986. Black on red-brown and m/c unpt. A. Aalto at l. and as wmk. 4 raised circles at lower r. for the blind. Finlandia Hall on back.

	VG	VF	UNC
	FV	FV	18.50

115 **100 MARKKAA**
    1986. Black on green and m/c unpt. J. Sibelius at l. and as wmk. 3 raised circles at lower r. for the blind. Swans on back.

	VG	VF	UNC
	FV	FV	35.00

116 **500 MARKKAA**
    1986. Black on red, brown and yellow unpt. E. Lonnrot at l. and as wmk. Punkaharjuesker on back.

	VG	VF	UNC
	FV	FV	140.00

117 **1000 MARKKAA**
    1986. Blue and purple on m/c unpt. D'Anders Chydenium at l. and as wmk. King's gate, sea fortress of Suomenlinna in Helsinki harbor, seagulls on back.

	VG	VF	UNC
	FV	FV	275.00

1991-93 ISSUE
#118-122 wmk as portr.
#119-122 like #114-117 but w/*Litt. A* above denomination added to lower l. and variable optical device (VOD) added at upper r. to higher denominations. Circles above bank name.

118 **20 MARKKAA**
    1993. Black on blue and gold unpt. V. Linna at l. and as wmk. Optical variable device at upper r. Tampere street scene on back.

	VG	VF	UNC
	FV	FV	6.50

119 50 MARKKAA
1986 (1991). Similar to #114.

	VG	VF	UNC
	FV	FV	16.00

120 100 MARKKAA
1986 (1991). Similar to #115.

	VG	VF	UNC
	FV	FV	30.00

121 500 MARKKAA
1986 (1991). Similar to #116.

	VG	VF	UNC
	FV	FV	120.00

122 1000 MARKKAA
1986 (1991). Similar to #117.

	VG	VF	UNC
	FV	FV	235.00

FRANCE

The French Republic, largest of the West European nations, has an area of 220,668 sq. mi. (547,026 sq. km.) and a population of 57.5 million. Capital: Paris. Agriculture, mining and manufacturing are the most important elements of France's diversified economy. Textiles and clothing, iron and steel products, machinery and transportation equipment, agricultural products and wine are exported.

France, the Gaul of ancient times, emerged from the Renaissance as a modern centralized national state which reached its zenith during the reign of Louis XIV (1643-1715) when it became an absolute monarchy and the foremost power in Europe. Although his reign marks the golden age of French culture, the domestic abuses and extravagance of Louis XIV plunged France into a series of costly wars. This, along with a system of special privileges granted the nobility and other favored groups, weakened the monarchy, brought France to bankruptcy - and laid the way for the French Revolution of 1789-94 that shook Europe and affected the whole world.

The monarchy was abolished and the First Republic formed in 1793. The new government fell in 1799 to a coup led by Napoleon Bonaparte who, after declaring himself First Consul for life, had himself proclaimed emperor of France and king of Italy. Napoleon's military victories made him master of much of Europe, but his disastrous Russian campaign of 1812 initiated a series of defeats that led to his abdication in 1814 and exile to the island of Elba. The monarchy was briefly restored under Louis XVIII. Napoleon returned to France in March 1815, but his efforts to regain power were totally crushed at the Battle of Waterloo. He was exiled to the island of St. Helena where he died in 1821.

The monarchy under Louis XVIII was again restored in 1815, but the ultrareactionary regime of Charles X (1824-30) was overthrown by a liberal revolution and Louis Philippe of Orleans replaced him as monarch. The monarchy was ousted by the Revolution of 1848 and the Second Republic proclaimed. Louis Napoleon Bonaparte (nephew of Napoleon I) was elected president of the Second Republic. He was proclaimed emperor in 1852. As Napoleon III, he gave France two decades of prosperity under a stable, autocratic regime, but led it to defeat in the Franco-Prussian War of 1870, after which the Third Republic was established.

The Third Republic endured until 1940 and ended by the capitulation of France to the swiftly maneuvering German forces. Marshal Henri Petain formed a puppet government that sued for peace and ruled unoccupied France from Vichy. Meanwhile, General Charles de Gaulle escaped to London where he formed a wartime government in exile and the Free French army. De Gaulle's provisional exile government was officially recognized by the Allies after the liberation of Paris in 1944, and De Gaulle, who had been serving as head of the provisional government, was formally elected to that position. In October 1945, the people overwhelmingly rejected a return to the prewar government, thus paving the way for the formation of the Fourth Republic.

De Gaulle was unanimously elected president of the Fourth Republic, but resigned in January 1946 when leftists withdrew their support. In actual operation, the Fourth Republic was remarkably like the Third, with the National Assembly the focus of power. The later years of the Fourth Republic were marked by a burst of industrial expansion unmatched in modern French history. The growth rate, however, was marred by a nagging inflationary trend that weakened the franc and undermined the competitive posture of France's export trade. This and the Algerian conflict led to the recall of De Gaulle to power, the adoption of a new constitution vesting strong powers in the executive, and establishment in 1958 of the current Fifth Republic.

* * * This section has been reorganized by issue, and renumbered. * * *

MONETARY SYSTEM
1 Franc = 10 Decimes = 100 Centimes, 1794-1960
1 Nouveaux Franc = 100 "old" Francs, 1960-

FRENCH DENOMINATIONS

1 Un	13 Treize	125 Cent Vingt-Cinq
2 Deux	14 Quatorze	200 Deux Cents
3 Trois	15 Quinze	250 Deux Cent Cinquante
4 Quatre	16 Seize	300 Trois Cents
5 Cinq	20 Vingt	400 Quatre Cents
6 Six	25 Vingt-Cinq	500 Cinq Cents
7 Sept	30 Trente	750 Sept Cent Cinquante
8 Huit	40 Quarante	1000 Mille
9 Neuf	10 Cinquante	2000 Deux Mille
10 Dix	80 Quatre-Vingts	5000 Cinq Mille
11 Onze	90 Quatre-Vingt-Dix	10,000 Quatre-Vingt-Dix
12 Douze	100 Cent	

REPUBLIC

BANQUE DE FRANCE

1959 ISSUE
#141-145 denomination: *NOVEAUX FRANCS* (NF).

141	**5 NOUVEAUX FRANCS**	**VG**	**VF**	**UNC**
(73)	5.3.1959-5.11.1965. Blue, orange and m/c. Pantheon in Paris at l., V. Hugo at r. Village at r., V. Hugo at l. on back.	1.50	9.00	30.00
142	**10 NOUVEAUX FRANCS**			
(74)	5.3.1959-4.1.1963. M/c. Skyline across, Richelieu at r. Similar scene on back, Richelieu at l.	2.50	15.00	35.00
143	**50 NOUVEAUX FRANCS**			
(75)	5.3.1959-5.4.1962. M/c. Henry IV at ctr., bridge in in background. Henry IV at ctr., castle at l. on back.	12.50	37.50	125.00
144	**100 NOUVEAUX FRANCS**			
(76)	5.3.1959-6.5.1964. M/c. Arch at l. Bonaparte at r. Capital bldg. at r., Bonaparte at l. on back.	20.00	33.50	110.00

145	**500 NOUVEAUX FRANCS**	**VF**	**VF**	**UNC**
(77)	1959-66. M/c. Moliere at ctr.			
	a. Sign. G. Gouin d'Ambrieres, R. Tondu and P. Gargam. 2.7.1959-8.1.1965.	FV	200.00	300.00
	b. Sign. H. Morant, R. Tondu and P. Gargam. 6.1.1966-1.9.1966.	200.00	250.00	350.00

1962-66 ISSUE

146	**5 FRANCS**	**VG**	**VF**	**UNC**
(78)	1966-70. Brown, purple and m/c. L. Pasteur at l., bldg. Laboratory implements, Pasteur at r. on back.			
	a. Sign. R. Tondu, P. Gargam and H. Morant. 5.5.1966-4.11.1966.	1.00	5.00	20.00
	b. Sign. R. Tondu, H. Morant and G. Bouchet. 5.5.1967-8.1.1970.	1.00	6.00	22.50

148	**50 FRANCS**	**VG**	**VF**	**UNC**
(80)	1962-76. M/c. Bldgs. w/courtyard at ctr., Racine at r. Racine at l., bldgs across on back.			
	a. Sign. G. Gouin d'Ambrieres, R. Tondu and P. Gargam. 7.6.1962-4.3.1965.	FV	15.00	45.00
	b. Sign. H. Morant, R. Tondu and P. Gargam. 7.12.1967-5.11.1970.	20.00	30.00	50.00
	c. Sign. G. Bouchet, R. Tondu and H. Morant. 7.12.1967-5.11.1970.	FV	15.00	35.00
	d. Sign. G. Bouchet, P. Vergnes and H. Morant. 3.6.1971-3.10.1974.	FV	15.00	35.00
	e. Sign. G. Bouchet, Tronche and H. Morant. 6.2.1975-2.10.1975.	FV	15.00	35.00
	f. Sign. P.A. Strohl, G. Bouchet and J. Tronche. 2.1.1976-3.6.1976.	FV	15.00	35.00

149	**100 FRANCS**	**VG**	**VF**	**UNC**
(81)	1964-79. M/c. P. Corneille at ctr. surrounded by arches.			
	a. Sign. R. Tondu. G. Gouin d'Ambrieres and P. Gargam. 2.4.1964-2.12.1965.	FV	25.00	75.00
	b. Sign. R. Tondu, H. Morant and P. Gargam. 3.2.1966-6.4.1967.	FV	25.00	50.00
	c. Sign. R. Tondu, G. Bouchet and H. Morant. 5.10.1967-1.4.1971.	FV	25.00	40.00
	d. Sign. P. Vergnes, G. Bouchet and H. Morant. 1.7.1971-3.10.1974.	FV	25.00	37.50
	e. Sign. J. Tronche, G. Bouchet and H. Morant. 6.2.1975-6.11.1975.	FV	25.00	37.50
	f. Sign. P. A. Strohl, G. Bouchet and J. Tronche. 2.1.1976-1.2.1979.	FV	25.00	37.50

1968-81 ISSUE

147	**10 FRANCS**	**VG**	**VF**	**UNC**
(79)	1963-73. Red and m/c. Bldg. at ctr., Voltaire at r. Similar scene w/Voltaire at l. on back.			
	a. Sign. G. Gouin d'Ambrieres, P. Gargam and R. Tondu. 4.1.1963-2.12.1965.	FV	5.00	17.50
	b. Sign. H. Morant, P. Gargam and R. Tondu. 6.1.1966-6.4.1967.	FV	5.00	15.00
	c. Sign. G. Bouchet, H. Morant and R. Tondu. 6.7.1967-4.2.1971.	FV	5.00	15.50
	d. Sign. G. Bouchet, H. Morant and P. Vergnes. 3.6.1971-6.12.1973.	FV	5.00	12.50

150 **10 FRANCS**
(82)

		VG	VF	UNC
	1972-79. Red, brown and olive. H. Berlioz conducting at r. Berlioz at l., musical instrument at r. on back.			
a.	Sign. H. Morant, G. Bouchet and P. Vergnes. 23.11.1972-3.11.1974.	FV	2.50	6.00
b.	Sign. H. Morant, G. Bouchet and J. Tronche. 6.2.1975-4.12.1975.	FV	2.50	5.00
c.	Sign. P. Strohl, G. Bouchet and J. Tronche. 2.1.1976-31.1.1979.	FV	2.25	4.00

151 **20 FRANCS**
(83)

		VG	VF	UNC
	1980-. Dull violet, brown and m/c. C. Debussy at r., sea scene in background (La Mer) Similar but w/lake scene on back.			
a.	Sign. P. A. Strohl, J. Tronche and B. Dentaud. 1980-86.	FV	FV	6.50
b.	Sign. P. A. Strohl, D. Ferman and B. Dentaud. 1987.	FV	FV	6.00
c.	W/security thread. Sign. D. Ferman, B. Dentaud and A. Charriau. 1990.	FV	FV	6.00
d.	Sign. D. Burneel, B. Dentaud and A. Charriau. 1991.	FV	FV	6.00
e.	Sign. D. Burneel, J. Bonnardin and A. Charriau. 1992; 1993.	FV	FV	5.50
f.	Sign. D. Burneel, J. Bonnardin and C. Vigier. 1994.	FV	FV	5.50

152 **50 FRANCS**
(84)

		VG	VF	UNC
	1976-92. Deep blue-black on m/c unpt. M. Quentin de la Tour at r. ctr. Similar scene reversed on back.			
a.	Sign. P. Strohl, G. Bouchet and J. Tronche. 1976-79.	FV	FV	16.50
b.	Sign. P. Strohl, J. Tronche and B. Dentaud. 1979-86.	FV	FV	15.00
c.	Sign. P. Strohl, D. Ferman and B. Dentaud. 1987.	FV	FV	14.00
d.	Sign. D. Ferman, B. Dentaud and A. Charriau. 1988-90.	FV	FV	13.50
e.	Sign. D. Burneel, B. Dentaud and A. Charriau. 1991.	FV	FV	13.50
f.	Sign. D. Burneel, J. Bonnardin and A. Charriau. 1992.	FV	FV	13.50

153 **100 FRANCS**
(85)

		VG	VF	UNC
	1978. Brown. E. Delacroix at l. ctr., woman holding tricolor at r. Sign. P. Strhol, G. Bouchet and J. Tronche.	FV	FV	37.50

154 **100 FRANCS**
(86)

		VG	VF	UNC
	1978-. Brown. Like #85 but retouched _100 CENT FRANCS_ w/heavier diagonal lines at upper l.			
a.	Sign. P. Strohl, G. Bouchet and J. Tronche. 1978-79.	FV	FV	32.50
b.	Sign. P. Strohl, J. Tronche and B. Dentaud. 1979-86.	FV	FV	30.00
c.	Sign. P. Strohl, D. Ferman and B. Dentaud. 1987.	FV	FV	27.50
d.	Sign. D. Ferman, B. Dentaud and A. Charriau. 1988-90.	FV	FV	26.50
e.	Sign. D. Burneel, B. Dentaud and A. Charriau. 1991.	FV	FV	25.00
f.	Sign. D. Burneel, J. Bonnardin and A. Charriau. 1992; 1993.	FV	FV	22.50
g.	Sign. D. Burneel, J. Bonnardin and C. Vigier. 1994.	FV	FV	23.50

155 **200 FRANCS**
(87)

		VG	VF	UNC
	1981-. Blue-green, yellow and m/c. Figure w/staff at l., Baron de Montesquieu at r. Similar but w/town view on back.			
a.	Sign. P. Strohl, J. Tronche and B. Dentaud. 1981-86.	FV	FV	57.50
b.	Sign. P. Strohl, D. Ferman and B. Dentaud. 1987.	FV	FV	55.00
c.	Sign. D. Ferman, B. Dentaud and A. Charriau. 1988-90.	FV	FV	52.50
d.	Sign. D. Burneel, B. Dentaud and A. Charriau. 1991.	FV	FV	50.00
e.	Sign. D. Burneel, J. Bonnardin and A. Charriau. 1992; 1993.	FV	FV	47.50
f.	Sign. D. Burneel, J. Bonnardin and C. Vigier. 1994.	FV	FV	45.00

156 (88)	**500 FRANCS**		VG	VF	UNC
	1968-. Yellow-brown and dk. brown. Tower of St. Jacques Church in Paris at l., B. Pascal at ctr., B. Pascal at l., abbey of Port Royal on back.				
	a.	Sign. G. Bouchet, R. Tondu and H. Morant. 4.1.1968-8.1.1970.	FV	115.00	160.00
	b.	Sign. G. Bouchet, P. Vergnes and H. Morant. 5.8.1971-5.9.1974.	FV	110.00	150.00
	c.	Sign. G. Bouchet, J. Tronche and H. Morant. 5.12.1974-6.11.1975.	FV	FV	135.00
	d.	Sign. P. Strohl, G. Bouchet and J. Tronche. 1.4.1976-7.6.1979.	FV	FV	130.00
	e.	Sign. P. Strohl, J. Tronche and B. Dentaud. 7.6.1979-6.2.1986.	FV	FV	130.00
	f.	Sign. P. Strohl, D. Ferman and B. Dentaud. 8.1.1987; 22.1.1987; 5.11.1987.	FV	FV	125.00
	g.	Sign. of D. Ferman, B. Dentaud and A. Charriau. 3.3.1988; 2.2.1989.	FV	FV	125.00
	h.	Sign. D. Burneel, B. Dentaud and A. Charriau. 1991.	FV	FV	125.00
	i.	Sign. D. Burneel, J. Bonnardin and A. Charriau. 1992; 1993.	FV	FV	125.00
	j.	Sign. D. Burneel, J. Bonnardin and C. Vigier. 1994.	FV	FV	125.00

1993-97 ISSUE

157 (89)	**50 FRANCS**		VG	VF	UNC
	1992 (1993-). Purple and dk. blue on blue, green and m/c unpt. Drawing of small child at l. Old airplane at upper border, topographical map of Africa at ctr., A. de Saint-Exupéry at r. and as wmk. Biplane on back. Many technical anti-counterfeiting techniques used.				
	a.	Sign. D. Burneel, J. Bonnardin and A. Charriau. 1993.	FV	FV	13.50
	b.	Sign. D. Burneel, J. Bonnardin and C. Vigier. 1994.	FV	FV	13.50
158 (90)	**100 FRANCS**				Expected New Issue
	(1997).				
159 (91)	**200 FRANCS**		VG	VF	UNC
	(1996). Red on m/c unpt. G. Eiffel.		FV	FV	47.50

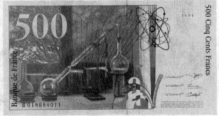

160 (92)	**500 FRANCS**	VG	VF	UNC
	1994 (1995). Dk. green and black on m/c unpt. M. and P. Curie at ctr. r. Segmented foil strip at l. Laboratory utencils at l. ctr. on back. Wmk: M. Curie. Sign. as #89b.	FV	FV	125.00

The French Overseas Territory of Afars and Iassas (Formerly French Somaliland, later to be independent as Dijbouti) is located in northeast Africa at the Bab el Mandeb Strait connecting the Suez Canal and the Red Sea with the Gulf of Aden and the Indian Ocean, has an area of 8,494 sq. mi. (22,000 sq. km.) and a population of 542,000. Capital: Djibouti. The tiny nation has less than one sq. mi. of arable land, and no natural resources except salt, sand and camels. The commercial activities of the trans-shipment port of Djibouti and the Addis Ababa-Djibouti railroad are the basis of the economy. Salt, fish and hides are exported.

French interest in former French Somaliland began in 1839 with concessions obtained by a French naval lieutenant from the provincial sultans. French Somaliland was made a protectorate in 1884 and its boundaries were delimited by the Franco-British and Ethiopian accords of 1887 and 1897. It became a colony in 1896 and a territory within the French Union in 1946. In 1958, it voted to join the new French Community as an overseas territory, and reaffirmed that choice by a referendum in March 1967. Its name was changed from French Somaliland to the French Territory of Afars and Issas on July 5, 1967.

The French Tricolor, which had flown over the strategically important territory for 115 years, was lowered for the last time on June 27, 1977, when French Afars and Issas became Africa's 49th independent state, Dijbouti.

RULERS:
French to 1977

MONETARY SYSTEM:
1 Franc = 100 Centimes

FRENCH AFARS AND ISSAS

TRÉSOR PUBLIC, TERRITOIRE FRANÇAIS DES AFARS ET DES ISSAS

1969 ND ISSUE

30	ND (1969). M/c. Aerial view of Djibouti harbor at ctr.	VG 55.00	VF 175.00	UNC 350.00

1973-74 ND ISSUE

31	ND (1973). M/c. Ships at l. ctr.	VG 8.50	VF 20.00	UNC 80.00

Three French overseas departments, Guiana, Guadeloupe and Martinique which issued a common currency from 1961-1975. Since 1975 Bank of France notes have circulated.

RULERS:
French

MONETARY SYSTEM:
1 Nouveau Franc = 100 "old" Francs
1 Franc = 100 Centimes

FRENCH INFLUENCE

INSTITUT D'EMISSION DES DÉPARTEMENTS D'OUTRE-MER

1961 PROVISIONAL ISSUE
Nouveaux Franc System
#1-3 ovpt: *GUADELOUPE, GUYANE, MARTINIQUE.*

		VG	VF	UNC
32	ND (1974). M/c. Woman holding jug at l. ctr. on face and back.	15.00	50.00	200.00

1975 ND ISSUE

		VG	VF	UNC
33	ND (1975). M/c. Man at l., rocks in sea and storks at r. Stern of ship at r. on back.	5.00	15.00	60.00

		VG	VF	UNC
34	ND (1975). M/c. Woman at l., people by trains at ctr. Camels and driver on back.	8.00	17.50	85.00

		VG	VF	UNC
1	**1 NOUVEAUX FRANC ON 100 FRANCS**			
	ND (1961). M/c. La Bourdonnais at l. Woman at r. on back.	10.00	40.00	175.00
2	**10 NOUVEAUX FRANCS ON 1000 FRANCS**			
	ND (1961). M/c. Fishermen from the Antilles.	35.00	175.00	565.00

		VG	VF	UNC
35	ND (1975). M/c. Man at r., forest scene at ctr. Aeriel view at ctr. on back.	35.00	65.00	165.00

		VG	VF	UNC
3	**50 NOUVEAUX FRANCS ON 5000 FRANCS**			
	ND (1961). M/c. Woman w/fruit bowl.	125.00	450.00	1300.

SECOND 1961 PROVISIONAL ISSUE
#4, ovpt: *DÉPARTEMENT DE LA GUADELOUPE - DÉPARTEMENT DE LA GUYANE - DÉPARTEMENT DE LA MARTINIQUE.*

4 **5 NOUVEAUX FRANC ON 500 FRANCS**

		VG	VF	UNC
ND (1961). Brown on m/c unpt. Sailboat at l., 2 native women at r. Men w/carts containing plants and wood on back.		35.00	150.00	475.00

INSTITUT D'EMISSION DES DÉPARTEMENTS D'OUTRE-MER RÉPUBLIQUE FRANCAISE

1963 ISSUE

#5-10 ovpt: *DÉPARTEMENT DE LA GUADELOUPE - DÉPARTEMENT DE LA GUYANE - DÉPARTEMENT DE LA MARTINIQUE.*

5 **10 NOUVEAUX FRANCS**

		VG	VF	UNC
ND (1963). Brown and green on m/c unpt. Girl at r., coastal scenery in background. People cutting sugar cane on back.		3.00	12.50	80.00

6 **50 NOUVEAUX FRANCS**

		VG	VF	UNC
ND (1963). Green on m/c unpt. Banana harvest. Shoreline w/houses at l., man and woman at r. on back.		12.50	45.00	135.00

1964 ISSUE

#7-10 w/2 sign. varieties.

7 **5 FRANCS**

		VG	VF	UNC
ND (1964). Like #4, but smaller size.		7.50	20.00	120.00

8 **10 FRANCS**

		VG	VF	UNC
ND (1964). Like #5.		3.00	12.50	55.00

9 **50 FRANCS**

		VG	VF	UNC
ND (1964). Like #6.		7.50	22.00	125.00

10 **100 FRANCS**

		VG	VF	UNC
ND (1964). Brown and m/c. Gen. Schoelcher at ctr. r. Schoelcher at l. ctr., various arms and galleon around on back.		25.00	50.00	200.00

FRENCH GUIANA

The French Overseas Department of French Guiana, located on the northeast coast of South America, bordered by Surinam and Brazil, has an area of 32,252 sq. mi. (91,000 sq. km.) and a population of 114,800. Capital: Cayenne. Placer gold mining and shrimp processing are the chief industries. Shrimp, lumber, gold, cocoa and bananas are exported.

The coast of Guiana was sighted by Columbus in 1498 and explored by Amerigo Vespucci in 1499. The French established the first successful trading stations and settlements, and placed the area under direct control of the French Crown in 1674. Portuguese and British forces occupied French Guiana for five years during the Napoleonic Wars. Devil's Island, the notorious penal colony in French Guiana where Capt. Alfred Dreyfus was imprisoned, was established in 1852 - and finally closed in 1947. When France adopted a new constitution in 1946, French Guiana voted to remain within the French Union as an overseas department.

RULERS:
French

MONETARY SYSTEM:
1 Nouveaux (new) Franc = 100 "old" Francs, 1961-

FRENCH INFLUENCE

CAISSE CENTRALE DE LA FRANCE D'OUTRE-MER

1961 ND ISSUE

Nouveaux Franc System

#29-33 ovpt: *GUYANE* and nouveaux franc denominations.

29 **1 NOUVEAUX FRANC ON 100 FRANCS**

		VG	VF	UNC
ND (1961). Ovpt. on #23. M/c. B. d'Esnambuc at l., sailing ship at r.		15.00	45.00	275.00

30 **5 NOUVEAUX FRANCS ON 500 FRANCS**

		VG	VF	UNC
ND (1961). Ovpt. on #24. M/c. La Bourdeonnais at l., women at r.		50.00	150.00	500.00

31 **10 NOUVEAUX FRANCS ON 1000 FRANCS**

		VG	VF	UNC
ND (1961). Ovpt. on #27. M/c. Fishermen.		125.00	400.00	1100.

32 **10 NOUVEAUX FRANCS ON 1000 FRANCS**

		VG	VF	UNC
ND. Ovpt. on #25. M/c. 2 woman at r.		110.00	300.00	725.00

33 **50 NOUVEAUX FRANCS ON 5000 FRANCS**

		VG	VF	UNC
ND. Ovpt. on #28. Woman w/fruit bowl.		375.00	800.00	1500.

FRENCH PACIFIC TERRITORIES

The French Pacific Territories include French Polynesia, New Caledonia and formerly the New Hebrides Condominium. For earlier issues also refer to French Oceania and Tahiti.

FRENCH INFLUENCE

INSTITUT D'EMISSION D'OUTRE-MER

1985-96 ISSUE

NOTE: For #1 w/ovpt: *NOUMEA* **on back see New Caledonia #45.**

			VG	VF	UNC
1	**500 FRANCS**				
	ND (1992). M/c. Sailboat at ctr., fisherman at r., Man at l., objects at r. on back.				
	a. 2 sign. W/o security thread.		FV	FV	15.00
	b. 3 sign. W/security thread.		FV	FV	12.50
2	**1000 FRANCS**				
	ND (1996). M/c. Hut in palm trees at l., girl at r.		FV	FV	22.50
3	**5000 FRANCS**				
	ND (1996). M/c. Bouganville at l., sailing ships at ctr.		FV	FV	92.50

		VG	VF	UNC
4	**10,000 FRANCS**	FV	FV	180.00
	ND (1985). M/c. Tahitian girl w/headdress at l., touristic bungalows at ctr. Fish at ctr., Melanesian girl wearing flower at r. on back. Wmk: 2 ethnic heads.			

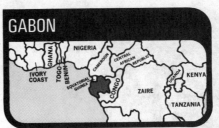

GABON 255

GABON

The Gabonese Republic, a member of the French Community, straddles the equator on the west coast of Africa. The hot and humid rain forest country has an area of 103,347 sq. mi. (267,667 sq. km.) and a population of 1.1 million, almost all of Bantu origin. Capital: Libreville. Extravagantly rich in resources, Gabon exports crude oil, manganese ore, gold and timbers.

Gabon was first visited by Portuguese navigator Diego Cam in the 15th century. Dutch, French and British traders, lured by the rich stands of hard woods and oil palms, quickly followed. The French founded their first settlement on the left bank of the Gabon River in 1839 and established their presence by signing treaties with the tribal chiefs. After gradually extending their influence into the interior during the last half of the 19th century, France occupied Gabon in 1885 and, in 1910, organized it as one of the four territories of French Equatorial Africa. It became an autonomous republic within the French Union in 1946, and on Aug. 17, 1960, became a completely independent republic within the new French Community.

RULERS:
French to 1960

MONETARY SYSTEM:
1 Franc = 100 Centimes

NOTE: For related currency see the Equatorial African States.

SIGNATURE VARIETIES:
Refer to introduction to Central African States.

REPUBLIC

BANQUE CENTRALE

1971 ISSUE

		VG	VF	UNC
1	**10,000 FRANCS**	30.00	85.00	250.00
	ND (1971). M/c. Mask at l., Pres. O. Bongo at r., mine elevator at ctr. Statue at l. and r., tractor plowing at ctr. on back. Sign. 1.			

BANQUE DES ÉTATS DE L'AFRIQUE CENTRALE

1974 ISSUE

2 **500 FRANCS**
ND (1974); 1978. Lilac-brown and m/c. Woman wearing kerchief at l., logging at ctr. Mask at l., students and chemical testing at ctr., statue at r. on back.

	VG	VF	UNC
a. Engraved. Sign. 6. ND (1974).	2.50	5.00	15.00
b. Lithographed. Sign. 9. 1.4.1978.	2.00	4.00	8.00

3 **1000 FRANCS**
ND (1974; 1978); 1978-84. Red, blue and m/c. Ship and oil refinery at ctr., Pres. O. Bongo at r. Mask at l., trains, planes and bridge at ctr., statue at r. on back.

	VG	VF	UNC
a. Sign. titles: *LE DIRECTEUR GÉNÉRAL* and *UN CENSEUR.* Engraved. Wmk: Antelope head in half profile. Sign. 4. ND (1974).	45.00	125.00	210.00
b. Like a. Sign. 6.	FV	10.00	23.50
c. Sign. titles: *LE DIRECTEUR GÉNÉRAL* and *UN CENSEUR.* Lithographed. Wmk. Antelope head in profile. Sign. 6. ND (1978).	FV	9.00	20.00
d. Sign titles: *LE GOUVERNEUR* and *UN CENSEUR.* Lithographed. Wmk. like b. Sign. 9. 1.4.1978; 1.1.1983; 1.6.1984.	FV	8.00	17.50

4 **5000 FRANCS**
ND (1974; 1978). Brown. Oil refinery at l., open pit mining and Pres. O. Bongo at r. Mask at l., bldgs. at ctr., statue at r. on back.

	VG	VF	UNC
a. Sign. titles: *LE DIRECTEUR UR GENERAL* and *UN CENSEUR.* Sign. 4. ND (1974).	35.00	85.00	200.00
b. Like a. Sign. 6.	20.00	40.00	100.00
c. Sign. titles: *LE GOUVERNEUR* and *UN CENSEUR.* Sign. 9. ND (1978).	FV	25.00	65.00

5 **10,000 FRANCS**
ND (1974; 1978). M/c. Similar to #1 except for new bank name on back.

	VG	VF	UNC
a. Sign. titles: *LE DIRECTEUR GÉNÉRAL* and *UN CENSEUR.* Sign. 6. ND (1974).	40.00	65.00	125.00
b. Sign. titles: *LE GOUVENEUR* and *UN CENSEUR.* Sign. 9. ND (1978).	40.00	50.00	90.00

1983-84 ISSUE

6 **5000 FRANCS**
ND (1984-). Brown and m/c. Mask at l., woman w/fronds at r. Plowing and mine ore conveyor on back. Sign. 9; 14.

	VG	VF	UNC
	FV	15.00	32.50

7   10,000 FRANCS
ND (1983-91). Brown, green and m/c. Stylized antelope heads at l., woman at r. Loading fruit onto truck at l. on back. Sign. 9; 14.

	VG	VF	UNC
	FV	25.00	65.00

1985 ISSUE
#8-10 Wmk: carving (same as printed on notes).

8   500 FRANCS
1.1.1985. Brown on orange and m/c unpt. Carving and jug at ctr. Man carving mask at l. ctr. on back.

	VG	VF	UNC
	FV	2.25	5.50

9   1000 FRANCS
1.1.1985. Deep blue on m/c unpt. Carving at l., map at ctr., Pres. O. Bongo at r. Incomplete outline map of Chad at top ctr. Elephant at l., animals at ctr., man carving at r. on back.

	VG	VF	UNC
	FV	FV	16.50

10   1000 FRANCS
1986-91. Like #9 but w/outline map of Chad at top completed.
a. Sign. 9. 1.1.1986; 1.1.1987; 1; 1.1.1990.
b. Sign. 14. 1.1.1991.

	VG	VF	UNC
a.	FV	FV	12.50
b.	FV	FV	11.50

GAMBIA

The Republic of The Gambia, an independent member of the British Commonwealth, occupies a strip of land 7 miles (11 km.) to 20 miles (32 km.) wide and 200 miles (322 km.) long encompassing both sides of West Africa's Gambia River, and completely surrounded by Senegal. The republic, one of Africa's smallest countries, has an area of 4,361 sq. mi. (11,295 sq. km.) and a population of 840,000. Capital: Banjul. Agriculture and tourism are the principal industries. Peanuts constitute 95 per cent of export earnings.

The Gambia was once part of the great empires of Ghana and Songhay. When Portuguese gold seekers and slave traders visited The Gambia in the 15th century, it was part of the Kingdom of Mali. In 1588 the territory became, through purchase, the first British colony in Africa. English slavers established Fort James, the first settlement, on a small island a dozen miles up the Gambia River in 1664. After alternate periods of union with Sierra Leone and existence as a separate colony, The Gambia became a British colony in 1888. On Feb. 18, 1965, The Gambia achieved independence as a constitutional monarchy within the Commonwealth of Nations, with the Queen of England as Chief of State. It became a republic on April 24, 1970, remaining a member of the Commonwealth, but with the president as Chief of State and Head of Government.

RULERS:
British to 1970

MONETARY SYSTEM:
1 Shilling = 12 Pence
1 Pound = 20 Shillings to 1970
1 Dalasi = 100 Bututs 1970-

SIGNATURE VARIETIES

1	CHAIRMAN / DIRECTOR	7
2	GENERAL MANAGER / GOVERNOR	8
3	/ S.S. Sisay	9 — GENERAL MANAGER / ACTING GOVERNOR
4	/ S.S. Sisay	10 — GENERAL MANAGER / GOVERNOR
5	/ S.S. Sisay	11
6	/ S.S. Sisay	12

REPUBLIC

GAMBIA CURRENCY BOARD

1965-70 ND ISSUE
Pound Sterling System
#1-3 sailboat at l. Wmk: Crocodile's head. Sign. 1.

1 10 SHILLINGS
ND (1965-70). Green and brown on m/c unpt. Workers in field on back.

	VG	VF	UNC
	3.00	9.00	28.50

2 1 POUND
ND (1965-70). Red and brown on m/c unpt. Loading sacks at dockside on back.

	VG	VF	UNC
	5.00	15.00	50.00

3 5 POUNDS
ND (1965-70). Blue and green on m/c unpt. Back blue; man and woman operating agricultural machine at ctr. r.

	VG	VF	UNC
	15.00	35.00	80.00

CENTRAL BANK OF THE GAMBIA

1971-72 ND ISSUE

Dalasi System
#4-8 sailboat at l., Pres. D. Kairaba Jawara at r. Sign. varieties. Wmk: Crocodile's head.

4 1 DALASI
ND (1971-87). Purple on m/c unpt. Back like #1.

	VG	VF	UNC
a. Sign. 2.	3.00	10.00	25.00
b. Sign. 3.	1.25	4.00	10.00
c. Sign. 4.	1.00	3.00	7.00
d. Sign. 5.	.50	2.00	5.00
e. Sign. 6.	.25	.75	2.50
f. Sign. 7.	.25	.75	2.50
g. Sign. 8.	.50	2.00	4.50

5 5 DALASIS
ND (1972-86). Red on m/c unpt. Back like #2.

	VG	VF	UNC
a. Sign. 2.	12.50	30.00	70.00
b. Sign. 4.	2.00	6.00	15.00
c. Sign. 6.	1.50	4.00	7.50
d. Sign. 7.	FV	2.00	5.00

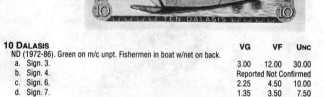

6 10 DALASIS
ND (1972-86). Green on m/c unpt. Fishermen in boat w/net on back.

	VG	VF	UNC
a. Sign. 3.	3.00	12.00	30.00
b. Sign. 4.	Reported Not Confirmed		
c. Sign. 6.	2.25	4.50	10.00
d. Sign. 7.	1.35	3.50	7.50

7 25 DALASIS
ND (1972-83). Blue on m/c unpt. Back similar to #3 but design is at l. ctr.

	VG	VF	UNC
a. Sign. 2.	35.00	80.00	190.00
b. Sign. 6.	17.50	40.00	90.00

1978 COMMEMORATIVE ISSUE
#8, Opening of Central Bank on 18.2.1978.

8   1 DALASI

ND (1978). Purple on m/c unpt. Central bank bldg. on back; commemorative legend beneath. Sign. 5.

	VG	VF	UNC
	4.00	10.00	25.00

1987 ISSUE

#9-11 w/line of micro printing under text: *PROMISE TO PAY....* Wmk: Crocodile's head.

9   5 DALASIS

ND (1987-90). Like #5 but back red and orange.

	VG	VF	UNC
a. Sign. 8.	.75	2.00	5.50
b. Sign. 10.	.65	1.50	5.00

10   10 DALASIS

ND (1987-90). Like #6 but back green and lt. olive.

	VG	VF	UNC
a. Sign. title: *GOVERNOR* at r. Sign. 8.	1.50	4.00	11.00
b. Sign. title: *ACTING GOVERNOR* at r. Sign. 9.	1.25	3.00	8.00

11   25 DALASIS

ND (1987-90). Like #7 but back blue, black and aqua.

	VG	VF	UNC
a. Sign. title: *GOVERNOR* at r. Sign. 8.	4.00	10.00	27.50
b. Sign. title: *ACTING GOVERNOR* at r. Sign. 9.	3.00	8.00	22.50
c. Sign. 10.	2.75	6.00	16.50

1989-91 ISSUE

#12-15 Pres. Jawara at r. Micro printing of bank name above and below title. Wmk: Crocodile's head.

12   5 DALASIS

ND (1991-95). Red and orange on m/c unpt. Giant Kingfisher at ctr. Herding cattle on back.

	VG	VF	UNC
a. Sign. 10.	FV	FV	2.50
b. Sign. 11.	FV	FV	2.25

13   10 DALASIS

ND (1991-95). Dk. green, green and olive-green on m/c unpt. Sacred Ibis at ctr. Lg. dish antenna, communications station at l. ctr. on back.

	VG	VF	UNC
a. Sign. 10.	FV	FV	5.00
b. Sign. 11.	FV	FV	4.50

14   25 DALASIS

ND (1991-95). Dk. blue-violet, black and blue on m/c unpt. Carmine Bee Eater at ctr. Govt. house at l. ctr. on back. Sign. 10.

	VG	VF	UNC
	FV	FV	9.00

15   50 DALASIS

ND (1989-95). Purple and violet on m/c unpt. Crested birds ctr. Stones in a circle on back. Sign. 10.

	VG	VF	UNC
	FV	FV	18.50

1996 ND ISSUE
#16-19 similar to #12-15. Wmk: Crocodile's head. W/o imprint. Sign. 12.

			VG	VF	UNC
16	**5 DALASIS**		FV	FV	2.00
	ND (1996). Red, orange and dk. brown on m/c unpt. Giant Kingfisher at ctr., young girl at r. Back like #12.				

			VG	VF	UNC
17	**10 DALASIS**		FV	FV	3.50
	ND (1996). Dk. green, bright green and olive-green on m/c unpt. Sacred Ibis at ctr., young boy at r. Back like #13.				

			VG	VF	UNC
18	**25 DALASIS**		FV	FV	8.00
	ND (1996). Deep blue-violet, black and blue on m/c unpt. Carmine Bee Eater at ctr., man at r. Back like #14.				

			VG	VF	UNC
19	**50 DALASIS**		FV	FV	15.00
	ND (1996). Purple and violet on m/c unpt. Crested bird at ctr., woman at r. Back like #15.				

GEORGIA

Georgia (formerly the Georgian Social Democratic Republic under the U.S.S.R.), is bounded by the Black Sea to the west and by Turkey, Armenia and Azerbaijan. It occupies the western part of Transcaucasia covering an area of 26,900 sq. mi. (69,700 sq. km.) Capital: Tbilisi. Hydro-electricity, minerals, forestry and agriculture are the chief industries.

The Georgian dynasty first emerged after the Macedonian victory over the Achaemenid Persian empire in the 4th century B.C. Roman "friendship" was imposed in 65 B.C. after Pompey's victory over Mithradates. The Georgians embraced Christianity in the 4th century A.D. During the next three centuries Georgia was involved in the ongoing conflicts between the Byzantine and Persian empires. The latter developed control until Georgia regained its independence in 450-503 A.D. but then it reverted to a Persian province in 533 A.D., Then restored as a kingdom by the Byzantines in 562 A.D. It was established as an Arab emirate in the 8th century. The Seljuk Turks invaded but the crusades thwarted their interests. Over the following centuries Turkish and Persian rivalries along with civil strife divided the area under the two influences.

Czarist Russian interests increased and a treaty of alliance was signed on July 24, 1773 whereby Russia guaranteed Georgian independence and it acknowledged Russian suzerainty. Persia invaded again in 1795 leaving Tiflis in ruins. Russia slowly took over annexing piece by piece and soon developed total domination. After the Russian Revolution the Georgians, Armenians and Azerbaijanis formed the short- lived Transcaucasian Federal Republic on Sept. 20, 1917 which broke up into three independent republics on May 26, 1918. A Germano-Georgian treaty was signed on May 28, 1918, followed by a Turko- Georgian peace treaty on June 4. The end of WW I and the collapse of the central powers allowed free elections.

On May 20, 1920, Soviet Russia concluded a peace treaty, recognizing its independence, but later invaded on Feb. 11, 1921 and a soviet republic was proclaimed. On March 12, 1922 Stalin included Georgia in a newly formed Transcaucasian Soviet Federated Socialist Republic. On Dec. 5, 1936 the T.S.F.S.R. was dissolved and Georgia became a direct member of the U.S.S.R. The collapse of the U.S.S.R. allowed full transition to independence and on April 9, 1991 a unanimous vote declared the republic an independent state based on its original treaty of independence of May 1918.

MONETARY SYSTEM:
1 Lari = 100 Thetri
1 Lari = 1,000,000 'old' Laris, 1995-

REPUBLIC

GEORGIAN NATIONAL BANK

FIRST 1993 *KUPONI* ISSUE
#23-32, view of Tbilisi at ctr. r. w/equestrian statue of Kg. V. Gorgosal in foreground, Mt. Tatzminda in background. Cave dwellings at l. ctr. on back. Fractional serial # prefix w/1 as denominator. Wmk: Hexagonal design repeated.

#23-28 w/o ornate triangular design at l. and r. of lg. value in box at l. ctr. on face, or at sides of value at r. on back.

23	**1 (LARIS)**			Reported Not Confirmed
	ND (1993).			
24	**3 (LARIS)**			Reported Not Confirmed
	ND (1993).			

			VG	VF	UNC
25	**5 (LARIS)**		.05	.20	1.00
	ND (1993). Dull brown on lilac unpt. W/rosettes at sides of value on face and back.				

			VG	VF	UNC
26	**10 (LARIS)**		.05	.30	1.50
	ND (1993). Yellow-brown on lilac unpt.				

			VG	VF	UNC
27	**50 (LARIS)**		.10	.50	2.50
	ND (1993). Lt. blue on lilac unpt.				
28	**100 (LARIS)**		.15	.75	4.00
	ND (1993). Greenish gray and lt. brown on lilac unpt.				

29   **500 (LARIS)**   VG   VF   UNC
ND (1993). Purple on lilac unpt.   .20   1.00   4.50

30   **1000 (LARIS)**   VG   VF   UNC
ND (1993). Blue-gray and brown on lilac unpt.   .30   1.50   8.00

31   **5000 (LARIS)**   VG   VF   UNC
ND (1993). Green and brown on lilac unpt. Back green on pale brown-orange.   .25   1.25   6.00

32   **10,000 (LARIS)**
ND (1993). Violet on lilac and brown unpt.   .60   3.00   15.00

SECOND 1993 ISSUE

#33-38 like #25-28 but w/ornate triangular design at l. and r. of lg. value in box at l. ctr. on face, and at sides of value at r. on back. Fractional serial # prefix w/2 as denominator. Wmk: Hexagonal design repeated.

33   **1 (LARIS)**   VG   VF   UNC
ND (1993). Red-orange and lt. brown on lilac unpt. Like #25.   —   .05   .25

34   **3 (LARIS)**   VG   VF   UNC
ND (1993). Purple and lt. brown on lilac unpt. Like #25.   .05   .10   .50

35   **5 (LARIS)**   VG   VF   UNC
ND (1993). Like #25.   .05   .10   .60

36   **10 (LARIS)**   VG   VF   UNC
ND (1993). Like #26.   .05   .15   .75

37   **50 (LARIS)**   VG   VF   UNC
ND (1993). Like #27.   .05   .20   1.00

38   **100 (LARIS)**   VG   VF   UNC
ND (1993). Like #28.   .10   .50   2.50

THIRD 1993 ISSUE

#39-42 similar to first 1993 issue but fractional serial # prefix w/3 as denominator.

39   **10,000 (LARIS)**   VG   VF   UNC
1993. Violet on lilac and brown unpt.   .15   .75   3.50

40   **25,000 (LARIS)**   VG   VF   UNC
1993. Orange and dull brown on lilac unpt   .20   1.00   4.50

41   **50,000 (LARIS)**   VG   VF   UNC
1993. Pale red-brown and tan on lilac unpt. Back dull red-brown on pale brown-orange unpt.   .20   1.00   4.50

42	**100,000 (LARIS)**	**VG**	**VF**	**UNC**
	1993. Olive-green and brown on lilac unpt. Back pale olive-green on dull brown-orange unpt.	.20	1.00	5.00

FOURTH 1993 ISSUE

#43-46 griffin at l. and r. of ornate round design at ctr. on face. 2 bunches of grapes w/vine above and below value on back. Wmk: Isometric rectangular design.

43	**250 (LARIS)**	**VG**	**VF**	**UNC**
	1993. Dk. blue on green, lilac and lt. blue unpt.			
	a. W/security thread.	.05	.15	.75
	b. W/o security thread.	—	—	—

44	**2000 (LARIS)**	**VG**	**VF**	**UNC**
	1993. Green and blue on gold and green unpt.	.10	.50	2.50

45	**3000 (LARIS)**	**VG**	**VF**	**UNC**
	1993. Brown and yellow on lt. brown unpt.	.10	.45	2.25

46	**20,000 (LARIS)**	**VG**	**VF**	**UNC**
	1993-. Purple on lt. red and blue unpt.			
	a. Lg. wmk. 1993.	.10	.50	2.50
	b. W/security printing at l. edge of design. Sm. wmk. 1994.	.10	.50	2.50

1994 ISSUE

#47-52 similar to #43-46. Wmk: Geometric rectangular pattern repeated.

47	**30,000 (LARIS)**	**VG**	**VF**	**UNC**
	1994. Dull red-brown on pale orange and lt. gray unpt.	.10	.55	2.75

48	**50,000 (LARIS)**	**VG**	**VF**	**UNC**
	1994. Dk. olive-green and dull black on pale olive-green and tan unpt.	.15	.75	3.50

48A	**100,000 (LARIS)**	**VG**	**VF**	**UNC**
	1994. Dk. gray on lt. blue and lt. gray unpt.			
	a. Lg. wmk.	.20	1.00	4.50
	b. Sm. wmk.	.20	1.00	4.50

49	**150,000 (LARIS)**	**VG**	**VF**	**UNC**
	1994. Dk. blue-green on pale blue, lt. gray and lilac unpt.	.20	1.00	4.50

50	**250,000 (LARIS)**	**VG**	**VF**	**UNC**
	1994. Brown-orange on pale orange and lt. green unpt.	.20	1.00	5.00

51	**500,000 (LARIS)**	**VG**	**VF**	**UNC**
	1994. Deep violet on pale purple and pink unpt.	.20	1.00	5.50

52	**1 MILLION (LARIS)**	**VG**	**VF**	**UNC**
	1994. Red on pink and pale yellow-brown unpt.	.50	2.25	11.00

1995 ISSUE

#57-59 wmk: Griffin.

#53-59 arms at l. to ctr.

53   1 Lari
1995. Deep purple on m/c unpt. N. Pirosmani between branches at ctr. View of Tbilisi, painting of deer at ctr. r. on back.

VG FV   VF FV   Unc 3.50

54   2 Lari
1995 Deep olive-green on m/c unpt. Bars of music at l., Z. Paliashvili at ctr. r. Opera House in Tbilisi at ctr. r. on back.

VG FV   VF FV   Unc 6.00

55   5 Lari
1995. Brown on m/c unpt. I. Javakhishvili at ctr., map above ornate lion statue at l. ctr., Tbilisi State University above open book at r.

VG FV   VF FV   Unc 12.50

56   10 Lari
1995. Blue-black on m/c unpt. Flowers at l., A. Tsereteli and swallow at ctr. r. Woman seated on stump while spinning yarn with a crop spindle between ornamental branches at ctr. r. on back. Wmk: Arms repeated vertically.

VG FV   VF FV   Unc 18.50

57   20 Lari
1995. Dk. brown on m/c unpt. Open book and newspaper at upper l., I. Chavchavadze at ctr. Statue of Kg. V. Gorgosal between views of Tbilisi at ctr. r. on back.

VG FV   VF FV   Unc 35.00

58   50 Lari
1995. Dk. brown and deep blue-green on m/c unpt. Griffin at l., Princess Tamara at ctr. r. Mythical figure at ctr. r. on back.

VG FV   VF FV   Unc 65.00

59   100 Lari
1995. Dk. brown, purple and black on m/c unpt. Carved bust of S. Rustaveli at ctr. r., Frieze at upper ctr. r. on back.

VG FV   VF FV   Unc 125.00

60   500 Laris
1995. Deep purple on m/c unpt. Kg. David "The Builder" w/bldg. at ctr. Early Georgian inscriptions, cross on back. (Not issued.)

—   —   —

GERMANY-FEDERAL REP.

The Federal Republic of Germany (formerly West Germany), located in north-central Europe, since 1990 with the unification of East Germany, has an area of 137.82 sq. mi. (356,854 sq. km.) and a population of 81.30 million. Capital: Bonn. The economy centers about one of the world's foremost industrial establishments. Machinery, motor vehicles, iron, steel, yarns and fabrics are exported.

During the post-Normandy phase of World War II, Allied troops occupied the western German provinces of Schleswig-Holstein, Hamburg, Lower Saxony, Bremen, North Rhine-Westphalia, Hesse, Rhineland- Palatinate, Baden-Wurttemberg, Bavaria and Saarland. The conquered provinces were divided into American, British and French occupation zones. Five eastern German provinces were occupied and administered by the forces of the Soviet Union.

The western occupation forces restored the civil status of their zones on Sept. 21, 1949, and resumed diplomatic relations with the provinces on July 2, 1951. On May 5, 1955, nine of the ten western provinces, organized as the Federal Republic of Germany, became fully independent. The tenth province, Saarland, was restored to the republic on Jan. 1, 1957.

The post-WW II division of Germany ended on Oct. 3, 1990, when the German Democratic Republic (East Germany) ceased to exist and its five constituent provinces were formally admitted to the Federal Republic of Germany. An election Dec. 2, 1990, chose representatives to the united federal parliament (Bundestag), which then conducted its opening session in Berlin in the old Reichstag building. Although Berlin technically is the capital of the reunited Germany, the actual seat of government remains for the time being in Bonn.

MONETARY SYSTEM:
1 Deutsche Mark (DM) = 100 Pfennig

FEDERAL REPUBLIC

DEUTSCHE BUNDESBANK

1960 ISSUE
#18-43 portr. as wmk.
#19-21 and 23 w/ or w/o ultraviolet senstive features.

		VG	VF	UNC
18	**5 DEUTSCHE MARK** 2.1.1960. Green on m/c unpt. Young Venetian woman by A. Durer at r. Sprig on back.	FV	5.00	13.00
19	**10 DEUTSCHE MARK** 2.1.1960. Blue on m/c unpt. Young man at r. Sailing ship *Gorch Fock* on back.	FV	20.00	45.00
20	**20 DEUTSCHE MARK** 2.1.1960. Black and green on m/c unpt. E. Tucher by A. Durer ar r. Violin, bow and clarinet on back.	FV	35.00	80.00

		VG	VF	UNC
21	**50 DEUTSCHE MARK** 2.1.1960. Brown and olive-green on m/c unpt. Chamberlain H. Urmiller at r. Lubecker Holsten-Tor gate on back.	FV	45.00	95.00
22	**100 DEUTSCHE MARK** 2.1.1960. Blue on m/c unpt. *Master Seb. Munster* by C. Amberger at r. Eagle on back.	FV	80.00	175.00

		VG	VF	UNC
23	**500 DEUTSCHE MARK** 2.1.1960. Brown-lilac on m/c unpt. Male portrait by Hans Maler zu Schwaz. Eltz Castle on back.	FV	FV	650.00
24	**1000 DEUTSCHE MARK** 2.1.1960. Dk. brown on m/c unpt. Astronomer Schoner (by Lucas Cranach the Elder) at r. and as wmk. Cathedral of Limburg on the Lahn on back.	FV	FV	1500.

1970 ISSUE
#25-30 like #18-24 but different sign. and legal penalty.
#26-29 letters of serial # either 2.8 or 3.3 mm.

		VG	VF	UNC
25	**5 DEUTSCHE MARK** 2.1.1970. Green on m/c unpt. Young Venetian woman by A. Dürer at r. Oak sprig on l. ctr. on back.	FV	10.00	25.00

		VG	VF	UNC
26	**10 DEUTSCHE MARK** 2.1.1970. Blue on m/c unpt. Young man by A. Dürer at r. Sailing ship *Gorch Fock* on back.	FV	FV	32.50

		VG	VF	UNC
27	**20 DEUTSCHE MARK** 2.1.1970. Black and green on m/c unpt. E. Tucher by A. Dürer at r. Violin, bow and clarinet on back.	FV	FV	50.00
28	**50 DEUTSCHE MARK** 2.1.1970. Brown and olive-green on m/c unpt. Chamberlain H. Urmiller at r. Turreted bldg. Holsten-Tor (in Lubeck) on back.	FV	FV	80.00

		VG	VF	UNC
29	**100 DEUTSCHE MARK** 2.1.1970. Blue on m/c unpt. Master Seb. Münster at r. Eagles on back.	FV	FV	130.00
30	**500 DEUTSCHE MARK** 2.1.1970. Brown-lilac on m/c unpt. Male portr. by H. Malerzu Schwaz at r. Castle Eltz on back.	FV	FV	500.00

1977 ISSUE
#31-36 like #26-30 but different date and sign.

		VG	VF	UNC
31	**10 DEUTSCHE MARK** 1.6.1977. Blue. Like #26.	FV	FV	12.00

		VG	VF	UNC
32	**20 DEUTSCHE MARK** 1.6.1977. Green. Like #27.	FV	FV	30.00
33	**50 DEUTSCHE MARK** 1.6.1977. Brown and green. Like #28.	FV	FV	50.00
34	**100 DEUTSCHE MARK** 1.6.1977. Blue. Like #29.	FV	FV	90.00
35	**500 DEUTSCHE MARK** 1.6.1977. Like #30.	FV	FV	425.00
36	**1000 DEUTSCHE MARK** 1.6.1977. Dk. brown on m/c unpt. Astronomer Schöner by L. Cranach "the elder" at r. and as wmk. Cathedral of Limburg on the Lahn on back.	FV	FV	800.00

1980 ISSUE
#38-41 like #25-30 but different date, w/ or w/o copyright notice at lower l. margin on back.

		VG	VF	UNC
37	**5 DEUTSCHE MARK** 2.1.1980. Like #25 but w/© *DEUTSCHE BUNDESBANK 1963* on back.	FV	FV	5.00

		VG	VF	UNC
38	**10 DEUTSCHE MARK** 2.1.1980. Like #26.			
	a. W/o copyright notice.	FV	FV	17.50
	b. W/©*DEUTSCHE BUNDESBANK 1 K 1963* on back.	FV	FV	11.00
39	**20 DEUTSCHE MARK** 2.1.1980. Like #27.			
	a. W/o copyright notice.	FV	FV	60.00
	b. W/©*DEUTSCHE BUNDESBANK 1K 1961* on back.	FV	FV	20.00
40	**50 DEUTSCHE MARK** 2.1.1980. Like #28.			
	a. W/o copyright notice.	FV	FV	62.50
	b. W/©*DEUTSCHE BUNDESBANK 1K 1962* on back.	FV	FV	45.00

		VG	VF	UNC
41	**100 DEUTSCHE MARK** 2.1.1980. Like #29.			
	a. W/o copyright notice.	FV	FV	95.00
	b. W/©*DEUTSCHE BUNDESBANK 1K 1962* on back.	FV	FV	90.00
42	**500 DEUTSCHE MARK** 2.1.1980. Like #30.	FV	FV	400.00

		VG	VF	UNC
43	**1000 DEUTSCHE MARK** 2.1.1980. Like #36.	FV	FV	800.00

1989-91 ISSUE
#44-51 portr. as wmk.

		VG	VF	UNC
44	**5 DEUTSCHE MARK** 1.8.1991. Green and olive-green on m/c unpt. B. von Arnim at r. Bank seal and Brandenburg Gate at l. ctr. on back. Sign. Schlesinger-Tietmeyer.	FV	FV	5.00

45	**10 DEUTSCHE MARK**	**VG**	**VF**	**UNC**
	1989-93. Bluish purple and blue. C. F. Gauss at r. Sextant on back.			
	a. Sign. Pöhl-Schlesinger. 2.1.1989.	FV	FV	20.00
	b. Sign. Schlesinger-Tietmeyer. 1.8.1991.	FV	FV	15.00
	c. Sign. Tietmeyer-Gaddom. 1.10.1993.	FV	FV	9.00

46	**20 DEUTSCHE MARK**	**VG**	**VF**	**UNC**
	1991; 1993. Green, black and red-violet on m/c unpt. A. von Droste-Hülshoff at r. Quill pen and tree at l. ctr., open book at lower r. on back.			
	a. Sign. Schlesinger-Tietmeyer. 1.8.1991.	FV	FV	16.50
	b. Sign. Tietmeyer-Gaddom. 1.10.1993.	FV	FV	16.50

47	**50 DEUTSCHE MARK**	**VG**	**VF**	**UNC**
	1989-93. Dark brown on m/c unpt. B. Neuman at r. Architectural drawing on back.			
	a. Sign. Pöhl-Schlesinger. 2.1.1989.	FV	FV	75.00
	b. Sign. Schlesinger-Tietmeyer. 1.8.1991.	FV	FV	40.00
	c. Sign. Tietmeyer-Gaddom. 1.10.1993.	FV	FV	37.50

48	**100 DEUTSCHE MARK**	**VG**	**VF**	**UNC**
	1989-93. Blue and m/c. C. Schumann at r. Building, grand piano on back. Multiple tuning forks in wmk. area.			
	a. Sign. Pöhl-Schlesinger. 2.1.1989.	FV	FV	200.00
	b. Sign. Schlesinger-Tietmeyer. 1.8.1991.	FV	FV	80.00
	c. Sign. Tietmeyer-Gaddom. 1.10.1993.	FV	FV	165.00

49	**200 DEUTSCHE MARK**	**VG**	**VF**	**UNC**
	2.1.1989. Red-orange and m/c. P. Ehrlich at r. Microscope on back. Sign. Pöhl-Schlesinger.	FV	FV	160.00

50	**500 DEUTSCHE MARK**	**VG**	**VF**	**UNC**
	1991; 1993. Reddish purple and m/c. M. S. Merian at r. Dandelion w/butterfly and caterpillar on back.			
	a. Sign. Schlesinger-Tietmeyer. 1.8.1991.	FV	FV	375.00
	b. Sign. Tietmeyer-Gaddom. 1.10.1993.	FV	FV	375.00

51	**1000 DEUTSCHE MARK**	**VG**	**VF**	**UNC**
	1.8.1991; 1.10.1993. Deep violet brown and blue-green on m/c unpt. City drawing at ctr., Wilhelm and Jacob Grimm at ctr. r. Bank seal at l., book frontispice of "Deutches Wörterbuch" over entry for freedom. Child collecting falling stars in wmk. area at ctr. on back.			
	a. Sign. Schlesinger-Tietmeyer. 1.8.1991.	FV	FV	750.00
	b. Sign. Tietmeyer-Gaddom. 1.10.1993.	FV	FV	750.00

GERMAN DEM REP.

The German Democratic Republic (East Germany), located on the great north European plain ceased to exist in 1990. During the closing days of World War II in Europe, Soviet troops advancing into Germany from the east occupied the German provinces of Mecklenburg, Brandenburg, Saxony-Anhalt, Saxony and Thuringia. These five provinces comprised the occupation zone administered by the Soviet Union after the cessation of hostilities. The other three zones were administered by the U.S., Great Britain and France. Under the Potsdam agreement, questions affecting Germany as a whole were to be settled by the commanders in chief of the occupation zones acting jointly and by unanimous decision. When Soviet intransigence rendered the quadripartite commission inoperable, the three western zones were united to form the Federal Republic of Germany, May 23, 1949. Thereupon the Soviet Union dissolved its occupation zone and established it as the Democratic Republic of Germany, Oct. 7, 1949. East and West Germany became reunited as one country on Oct. 3, 1990.

MONETARY SYSTEM:
1 Mark = 100 Pfennig

SOVIET OCCUPATION

DEUTSCHE NOTENBANK

1964 ISSUE
#22 and 25 arms at l. on back.
#23, 24 and 26 arms at upper r. ctr.
#24-26 portr. as wmk.

		VG	VF	UNC
22	**5 MARK**			
	1964. Brown on m/c unpt. A. von Humboldt at r. Humboldt University in Berlin at l. ctr. on back.	1.25	3.00	8.00

		VG	VF	UNC
23	**10 MARK**			
	1964. Green on m/c unpt. F. von Schiller at r. Zeiss Factory in Jena at l. ctr. on back.	3.00	6.00	15.00

		VG	VF	UNC
24	**20 MARK**			
	1964. Red-brown on m/c unpt. J.W. von Goethe at r. National Theater in Weimar at l. ctr. on back.	2.00	8.50	18.00
25	**50 MARK**			
	1964. Blue-green on m/c unpt. F. Engels at r. Wheat threshing at l. ctr. on back.	5.00	10.00	40.00

		VG	VF	UNC
26	**100 MARK**			
	1964. Blue on m/c unpt. K. Marx at r. Brandenburg Gate in Berlin at l. ctr. on back.	4.00	12.00	50.00

STAATSBANK DER DDR

1971; 1975 ISSUE
#27-31 arms at upper l. on face. Arms at l. on back. Portr. as wmk.

		VG	VF	UNC
27	**5 MARK**			
	1975. Purple on m/c unpt. T. Müntzer at r. Harvesting on back.			
	a. 6 digit lg. serial #.	.50	1.00	3.50
	b. 6 digit sm. serial #. (1987).	.10	.50	1.75
	x. Error. Mismatched serial #.	30.00	70.00	120.00

		VG	VF	UNC
28	**10 MARK**			
	1971. Brown on m/c unpt. C. Zetkin at r. Woman at radio station on back.			
	a. 6 digit lg. serial #.	.50	2.00	6.00
	b. 7 digit sm. serial #. (1985).	.25	1.00	3.00

		VG	VF	UNC
29	**20 MARKS**			
	1975. Green on m/c unpt. Goethe at r. Children leaving school on back.			
	a. 6 digit lg. serial #.	.85	2.50	10.00
	b. 7 digit sm. serial #. (1986).	.40	1.25	5.00

		VG	VF	UNC
30	**50 MARK**			
	1971. Red on m/c unpt. F. Engels at r. Oil refinery on back.			
	a. 7 digit lg. serial #.	2.00	7.00	15.00
	b. 7 digit sm. serial #. (1986).	1.00	3.50	7.50

31   100 MARK

		VG	VF	UNC
	1975. Blue on m/c unpt. K. Marx at r. Street scene in East Berlin on back.			
a.	7 digit lg. serial #.	4.00	10.00	20.00
b.	7 digit sm. serial #. (1986).	2.00	5.00	10.00

1985 ISSUE

32   200 MARK

	VG	VF	UNC
1985. Dk. olive-green and dk. brown on m/c unpt. Family at r. Teacher dancing w/children in front of modern school bldg. at ctr. on back. Wmk: Dove. (Not issued.)	—	—	75.00

33   500 MARK

	VG	VF	UNC
1985. Dk. brown on m/c unpt. Arms at r. and as wmk. Govt. bldg. Staatsrat (in Berlin) at ctr. on back. (Not issued.)	—	—	90.00

1989 ISSUE

34   20 MARK

	VG	VF	UNC
22.12.1989. Black and purple on m/c unpt. Brandenburg Gate in Berlin at ctr. (Not issued.)	—	Unc	100.00

FOREIGN EXCHANGE CERTIFICATES

FORUM-AUSSENHANDELSGESELLSCHAFT M.B.H.

1979 ISSUE

Certificates issued by state-owned export-import company. These were in the form of checks for specified amounts for purchase of goods.

1 Mark = 1 DM (West German Mark)

FX1   50 PFENNIG

	VG	VF	UNC
1979. Violet and orange.	1.00	2.00	4.00

FX2   1 MARK

	VG	VF	UNC
1979. Brown and rose.	1.00	2.00	4.00

FX3   5 MARK

1979. Green and rose.	1.50	3.00	6.00

FX4   10 MARK

1979. Blue and lt. green.	2.00	4.50	10.00

FX5   50 MARK

1979. Red and orange.	3.00	7.00	15.00

FX6   100 MARK

1979. Olive and yellow.	4.00	10.00	30.00

FX7   500 MARK

1979. Gray-brown, violet and lt. blue.	8.00	20.00	85.00

GHANA

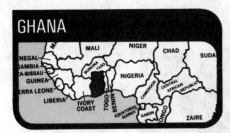

The Republic of Ghana, a member of the British Commonwealth situated on the West Coast of Africa between the Ivory Coast and Togo, has an area of 92,098 sq. mi. (238,537 sq. km.) and a population of 15.6 million, almost entirely African. Capital: Accra. Cocoa (the major crop), coconuts, palm kernels and coffee are exported. Mining, second in importance to agriculture, is concentrated on gold, manganese and industrial diamonds.

Ghana was first visited by Portuguese traders in 1470, and through the 17th century was used by various European powers - England, Denmark, Holland, Germany - as a center for their slave trade. Britain achieved control of the Gold Coast in 1821, and established the colony of Gold Coast in 1874. In 1901, Britain annexed the neighboring Ashanti Kingdom; the same year a northern region known as the Northern Territories became a British protectorate. Part of the former German colony of Togoland was mandated to Britain by the League of Nations and administered as part of the Gold Coast. The state of Ghana, comprising the Gold Coast and British Togoland, obtained independence on March 6, 1957, becoming the first black African colony to do so. On July 1, 1960, Ghana adopted a republican constitution, changing from a ministerial to a presidential form of government. The government was overthrown, the constitution suspended and the National Assembly dissolved by the Ghanaian Army and police on Feb. 24, 1966. The government was returned to civilian authority in Oct. 1969, but was again seized by military officers in a bloodless coup on Jan. 13, 1972. Ghana remains a member of the Commonwealth of Nations, with executive authority vested in the Supreme Military Council.

Ghana's monetary denomination of "cedi" is derived from the word "sedie" meaning cowrie, a shell money commonly employed by coastal tribes.

MONETARY SYSTEM:
1 Shilling = 12 Pence
1 Pound = 20 Shillings to 1965
1 Cedi = 100 Pesewas, 1965-

REPUBLIC

BANK OF GHANA

1958-63 ISSUE
#1-3 various date and sign. varieties. Wmk: *GHANA* in star.
NOTE: #4 was used in interbank transactions.

1	10 SHILLINGS	VG	VF	UNC
	1958-63. Green and brown. Bank of Ghana bldg. in Accra at ctr r. Star on back.			
	a. 2 sign. Printer: TDLR. 1.7.1958.	2.00	5.00	20.00
	b. W/o imprint. 1.7.1961; 1.7.1962.	1.00	3.00	12.00
	c. 1 sign. 1.7.1963.	.75	2.50	10.00

2	1 POUND	VG	VF	UNC
	1958-62. Red-brown and blue. Bank of Ghana bldg. in Accra at ctr. Cocoa pods in 2 heaps on back.			
	a. Printer: TDLR. 1.7.1958; 1.4.1959.	1.00	3.00	12.00
	b. W/o imprint. 1.7.1961; 1.7.1962.	1.00	2.50	10.00

3	5 POUNDS	VG	VF	UNC
	1.7.1958-1.7.1962. Purple and orange. Bank of Ghana bldg. in Accra at ctr. Cargo ships, logs in water on back.	5.00	15.00	45.00

4	1000 POUNDS	VG	VF	UNC
	1.7.1958. Black-brown. Bank of Ghana bldg. in Accra at lower r. Used in inter-bank transactions.	—	75.00	250.00

1965 ISSUE
#5-9 portr. Kwame Nkrumah and as wmk.

5	1 CEDI	VG	VF	UNC
	ND (1965). Blue on m/c unpt. K. Nkrumah at r. Bank on back.	.50	2.00	4.00
6	5 CEDIS			
	ND (1965). Dk. brown on m/c unpt. K. Nkrumah at r. Paliament House on back.	1.00	3.00	7.50

7	10 CEDIS	VG	VF	UNC
	ND (1965). Green on m/c unpt. K. Nkrumah at l. Island and palm trees on back.	2.00	5.00	15.00

8 **50 Cedis**
ND (1965). Red on m/c unpt. K. Nkrumah at l. Island and palm trees on back.

VG	VF	UNC
6.00	12.50	35.00

9 **100 Cedis**
ND (1965). Purple on m/c unpt. K. Nkrumah at r. Hospital on back.

VG	VF	UNC
10.00	25.00	60.00

9A **1000 Cedis**
ND(1965). Black. Lg. star at upper l. Bank of Ghana bldg. in Accra at r. on back.

VG	VF	UNC
—	—	—

1967 Issue
Various date and sign. varieties.
#10-16 wmk: Arms.

10 **1 Cedi**
23.2.1967; 8.1.1969; 1.10.1970; 1.10.1971. Blue on m/c unpt. Cocoa tree with pods at r. Shield and ceremonial sword on back.

VG	VF	UNC
.25	1.00	3.50

11 **5 Cedis**
23.2.1967; 8.1.1969. Dk. brown on m/c unpt. Wood carving of a bird at r. Animal carvings on back.

VG	VF	UNC
2.00	8.00	30.00

12 **10 Cedis**
23.2.1967; 8.1.1969; 1.10.1970. Red on m/c unpt. Art products at r. Small statuettes on back.

VG	VF	UNC
1.00	5.00	17.50

1972-73 Issue
NOTE: Date 2.1.1976 has 2 minor varieties in length of *"2nd"* as part of date.

13 **1 Cedi**
1973-78. Blue-black on deep green, deep purple and m/c unpt. Young boy w/slingshot at r. Man cutting cocoa pods from tree on back.

	VG	VF	UNC
a. 2.1.1973.	.20	.50	1.50
b. 2.1.1975; 2.1.1976.	.10	.20	.50

14 **2 CEDIS**
1972-78. Green on m/c unpt. Young man w/hoe at r. Workers in field on back.

	VG	VF	UNC
a. 21.6.1972. Sign. 1. J. J. Ansah.	.25	.60	2.00
b. 21.6.1972. Sign. 2. G. Rikes.	.25	.60	2.00
c. 2.1.1977; 2.1.1978.	.10	.25	.65

15 **5 CEDIS**
1973-78. Brown on m/c unpt. Woman wearing lg. hat at r. Huts on back.

	VG	VF	UNC
a. 2.1.1973; 2.1.1975.	.25	.60	2.00
b. 2.1.1977; 4.7.1977; 2.1.1978.	.20	.50	1.00

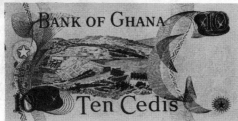

16 **10 CEDIS**
1973-78. Red, violet and dk. brown on m/c unpt. Elderly man smoking a pipe at r. Dam on back.

	VG	VF	UNC
a. 2.1.1973. Sign. 1. Serial # prefix A/1.	.35	1.25	4.50
b. 2.1.1973. Sign. 2. Serial # prefix B/1-.	.35	1.25	4.50
c. 2.1.1975.	.35	1.25	4.50
d. 2.1.1976; 2.1.1977; 2.1.1978.	.10	.20	.40

1979 ISSUE
#17-21, 2 serial # varieties.

#17-22 wmk: Arms.

NOTE: Date 2.1.1980 is reported for #22, not confirmed.

17 **1 CEDI**
7.2.1979; 6.3.1982. Green and m/c. Young man at r. Man weaving on back.

	VG	VF	UNC
	.10	.20	1.00

18 **2 CEDIS**
7.2.1979; 2.1.1980; 2.7.1980; 6.3.1982. Blue and m/c. School girl at r. Workers w/plants in field on back.

	VG	VF	UNC
	.10	.25	.75

19 **5 CEDIS**
7.2.1979; 2.1.1980; 6.3.1982. Red and m/c. Elderly man at r. Men cutting log on back.

	VG	VF	UNC
	.15	.35	1.25

20 **10 CEDIS**
7.2.1979; 2.1.1980; 6.3.1982. Purple and m/c. Young woman at r. Fishermen w/long net on back.

	VG	VF	UNC
	.25	1.50	7.00

21 20 CEDIS
7.2.1979; 2.7.1980; 6.3.1982. Green and m/c. Miner at r. Man weaving on back.

VG	VF	UNC
.35	1.00	10.00

22 50 CEDIS
7.2.1979; 2.7.1980. Brown and m/c. Old man at r. Men splitting cocoa pods on back.

VG	VF	UNC
.20	.60	3.50

1983-91 ISSUE
#24-28 wmk: Eagle's head above star.
#29-31 arms at lower l. and as wmk. Sign. G. K. Agama.

23 10 CEDIS
15.5.1984. Purple and m/c. W. Larbi, F. Otoo, E. Nukpor at l. People going to rural bank on back.

VG	VF	UNC
FV	.25	.75

24 20 CEDIS
15.5.1984; 15.7.1986. Shades of green and aqua. Qn. Mother Yaa Asantewa at l. Workers and flag procession on back.

VG	VF	UNC
FV	.50	1.75

25 50 CEDIS
1.4.1983; 15.5.1984; 15.7.1986. Brown, violet and m/c. Boy w/hat at l. ctr. Drying grain at ctr. on back.

VG	VF	UNC
FV	.60	2.00

26 100 CEDIS
1983-. Purple, blue and m/c. Woman at l. ctr. Loading produce onto truck at ctr. on back.

	VG	VF	UNC
a. Sign. J. S. Addo. 1.4.1983; 15.5.1984; 15.7.1986.	FV	.75	3.50
b. Sign. G. K. Agama. 19.7.1990; 19.9.1991.	FV	FV	2.50

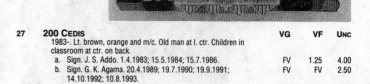

27 200 CEDIS
1983-. Lt. brown, orange and m/c. Old man at l. ctr. Children in classroom at ctr. on back.

	VG	VF	UNC
a. Sign. J. S. Addo. 1.4.1983; 15.5.1984; 15.7.1986.	FV	1.25	4.00
b. Sign. G. K. Agama. 20.4.1989; 19.7.1990; 19.9.1991; 14.10.1992; 10.8.1993.	FV	FV	2.50

28   500 CEDIS

	VG	VF	UNC
1986-. Purple and blue-green on m/c unpt. Arms at r. Coaca trees w/coaca pods and miner at ctr. on back.			
a. Sign. J. S. Addo. 31.12.1986.	FV	2.00	7.00
b. Sign. G. K. Agama. 20.4.1989; 19.7.1990; 19.9.1991; 14.10.1992; 10.8.1993; 10.6.1994.	FV	FV	3.75

31   5000 CEDIS

	VG	VF	UNC
29.6.1994; 6.1.1995. Lg. stars in unpt. at ctr., supported shield of arms at upper r. Red-brown and green on m/c unpt. Map at l., freighter in harbor, log flow in foreground on back.	FV	FV	22.00

COLLECTOR SERIES

BANK OF GHANA

1977 ISSUE

		ISSUE PRICE	MKT. VALUE
CS1 1977 1-10 CEDIS			
#13-16 w/ovpt: *SPECIMEN* and Maltese cross prefix serial #.		14.00	25.00

29   1000 CEDIS

	VG	VF	UNC
1991-. Dk. brown, dk. blue and dk. green on m/c unpt. Jewels at r. Harvesting, splitting cocoa pods at ctr. on back.			
a. 22.2.1991.	FV	2.00	7.00
b. Segmented foil security thread. 22.7.1993; 10.6.1994; 6.1.1995.	FV	FV	4.50

30   2000 CEDIS

	VG	VF	UNC
15.6.1994; 6.1.1995. Red-brown, violet and black on m/c unpt. Suspension bridge at r. Fisherman loading nets into boat at l. ctr. on back.	FV	FV	9.00

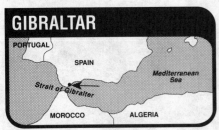

The British Colony of Gibraltar, located at the southernmost point of the Iberian Peninsula, has an area of 2.25 sq. mi. (5.8 sq. km.) and a population of 29,048 Capital (and only town): Gibraltar. Aside from its strategic importance as guardian of the western entrance to the Mediterranean Sea, Gibraltar is also a free port, British naval base, and coaling station.

Gibraltar, rooted in Greek mythology as one of the Pillars of Hercules, has long been a coveted stronghold. Moslems took it from Spain and fortified it in 711. Spain retook it in 1309, lost it again to the Moors in 1333, and retook it in 1462. After Barbarossa sacked Gibraltar in 1540, Spain strengthened its defenses and held it until the War of the Spanish Succession when it was captured by a combined British and Dutch force, 1704. Britain held it against the Franco-Spanish attacks of 1704-05 and through the historic "Great Siege" of 1779-83. Recently Spain has attempted to discourage British occupancy by harassment and economic devices. In 1967, Gibraltar's inhabitants voted 12,138 to 44 to remain under British rule.

RULERS:
British

MONETARY SYSTEM:
1 Shilling = 12 Pence
1 Pound = 20 Shillings to 1971
1 Pound = 100 New Pence, 1971-

BRITISH INFLUENCE

GOVERNMENT OF GIBRALTAR

1958 ISSUE
#17-19 printer: TDLR.

	17	10 SHILLINGS	VG	VF	UNC
		3.10.1958; 1.5.1965. Blue on yellow-brown unpt. Rock of Gibraltar at l.	2.50	15.00	95.00

18	1 POUND	VG	VF	UNC
	1958-75. Green on yellow-brown unpt. Rock of Gibraltar at bottom ctr.			
	a. Sign. title: *FINANCIAL SECRETARY.* 3.10.1958; 1.5.1965.	2.50	8.50	37.50
	b. Sign. title: *FINANCIAL AND DEVELOPMENT SECRETARY.* 20.11.1971.	2.00	5.00	17.00
	c. 20.11.1975.	3.00	15.00	85.00

19	5 POUNDS	VG	VF	UNC
	1958-75. Brown. Rock of Gibraltar at bottom ctr.			
	a. Sign. title: *FINANCIAL SECRETARY.* 3.10.1958; 1.5.1965.	12.50	35.00	165.00
	b. Sign. title: *FINANCIAL AND DEVELOPMENT SECRETARY.* 1.5.1965; 20.11.1971; 20.11.1975.	10.00	27.50	125.00

1975 ISSUE
#20-24 Qn. Elizabeth II at ctr. and as wmk. Sign. varieties. Printer: TDLR.

20	1 POUND	VG	VF	UNC
	1975-. Brown and red on m/c unpt. Bldg. w/flag on back. 3 sign. varieties.			
	a. 20.11.1975 (1978).	FV	FV	6.00
	b. 15.9.1979.	FV	FV	5.50
	c. 10.11.1983; 21.10.1986; 4.8.1988.	FV	FV	4.50

21	5 POUNDS	VG	VF	UNC
	1975; 1988. Green on m/c unpt. Back like #20. 2 sign. varieties.			
	a. 20.11.1975.	FV	FV	20.00
	b. 4.8.1988.	FV	FV	15.00
22	10 POUNDS			
	20.11.1975 (1977). Blue on m/c unpt. Lg. bldg. on back.	FV	FV	25.00

23	20 POUNDS	VG	VF	UNC
	1975-. Lt. brown on m/c unpt. Back similar to #22. 3 sign. varieties.			
	a. 20.11.1975 (1978).	FV	50.00	195.00
	b. 15.9.1979.	FV	40.00	140.00
	c. 1.7.1986.	FV	FV	48.50

1986 ISSUE

			VG	VF	UNC
24	**50 POUNDS**		FV	FV	115.00

27.11.1986. Purple and m/c. Rock of Gibraltar on back.

1995 ISSUE

#25-28 Qn. Elizabeth at r. and as wmk., shield of arms at l.

			VG	VF	UNC
25	**5 POUNDS**		FV	FV	13.50

1.7.1995. Green and purple on m/c unpt. Urn above gateway at l. ctr. Tavik ibn Zeyad w/sword at r., Moorish castle at upper l. on back.

			VG	VF	UNC
26	**10 POUNDS**		FV	FV	25.00

1.7.1995. Orange-brown and violet on m/c unpt. Lighthouse above cannon at l. ctr. Portr. Gen. Eliott at r., scene of "The Great Siege, 1779-85" at upper l. ctr. on back.

			VG	VF	UNC
27	**20 POUNDS**		FV	FV	47.50

1.7.1995. Purple and violet on m/c unpt. Bird above cannon at l. ctr. Portr. Admiral Nelson at r., H.M.S. Victory at upper l. ctr. on back.

			VG	VF	UNC
28	**50 POUNDS**		FV	FV	110.00

1.7.1995. Red and violet on m/c unpt. Gibraltar monkey above horse and carriage at l. ctr. Portr. W. Churchill at r., spitfire airplanes at the North Front, 1942 at upper l. ctr. on back.

COLLECTOR SERIES

GOVERNMENT OF GIBRALTAR

1975 ISSUE

			ISSUE PRICE	MKT. VALUE
CS1	**1975 1-20 POUNDS.**		14.00	35.00

#20-23 w/ovpt: SPECIMEN and Maltese cross prefix serial #.

GREAT BRITAIN

Great Britain, also known as the United Kingdom, is located off the northwest coast of the European continent, has an area of 94,227 sq. mi. (244,046 sq. km.) and a population of 57.7 million. Capital: London. The economy is based on industrial activity and trading. Machinery, motor vehicles, chemicals, and textile yarns and fabrics are exported.

After the departure of the Romans, who brought Britain into an active relationship with Europe, Britain fell prey to invaders from Scandinavia and the Low Countries who drove the original Britons into Scotland and Wales, and established a profusion of kingdoms that finally united in the 11th century under the Danish King Canute. Norman rule, following the conquest of 1066, stimulated the development of those institutions which have since distinguished British life. Henry VIII (1509-47) turned Britain from continental adventuring and faced it to the sea - a decision that made Britain a world power during the reign of Elizabeth I (1558-1603). Strengthened by the Industrial Revolution and the defeat of Napoleon, 19th century Britain turned to the remote parts of the world and established a colonial empire of such extent and prosperity that the world has never seen its like. World Wars I and II sealed the fate of the Empire and relegated Britain to a lesser role in world affairs by draining her resources and inaugurating a worldwide movement toward national self-determination in her former colonies.

By the mid-20th century, most of the territories formerly comprising the British Empire had gained independence, and the empire had evolved into the Commonwealth of Nations, an association of equal and autonomous states which enjoy special trade interests. The Commonwealth is presently (1995) composed of 53 member nations, including the United Kingdom. All recognize the British monarch as head of the Commonwealth. Fourteen continue to recognize the British monarch as Chief of State. They are: United Kingdom, Australia, New Zealand, Bahamas, Barbados, Canada, Fiji, Jamaica, Mauritius, Papua New Guinea, Solomon Islands, St. Lucia, Kiribati and Tuvalu.

RULERS:
Elizabeth II, 1952-

MONETARY SYSTEM:
1 Shilling = 12 Pence
1 Pound = 20 Shillings to 1971
1 Pound = 100 New Pence, 1971-
1 Guinea = 21 Shillings

KINGDOM

BANK OF ENGLAND

1957 ISSUE

			VG	VF	UNC
371	**5 POUNDS**				
	ND (1957-67). Blue and m/c. Helmeted Britannia hd. at l., St. George and dragon at lower ctr., denomination £5 in blue print on back. Sign. L. K. O'Brien.		10.00	30.00	50.00
372	**5 POUNDS**				
	ND (1961-63). Blue and m/c. Like #371 but denomination £5 recessed in white on back.		10.00	30.00	50.00

1960 ISSUE

#373 and 374 portr. Qn. Elizabeth II at r.

		VG	VF	UNC
373	**10 SHILLINGS**			
	ND (1960-70). Brown on m/c unpt.			
a.	Sign. L. K. O'Brien. (1960-61).	2.00	4.00	12.00
b.	Sign. J. Q. Hollom. (1962-66).	1.50	3.00	10.00
c.	Sign. J. S. Fforde. (1966-70).	1.50	2.50	7.00

		VG	VF	UNC
374	**1 POUND**			
	ND (1960-77). Deep green on m/c unpt.			
a.	Sign. L. K. O'Brien. (1960-61).	2.00	4.00	12.00
b.	Sign. J. Q. Hollom. (1962-66).	2.00	4.00	9.00
c.	Sign. J. S. Fforde. (1966-70).	2.00	4.00	8.00
d.	Sign. J. B. Page. (1970-77).	2.00	4.00	7.00

		VG	VF	UNC
375	**5 POUNDS**			
	ND (1963-72). Deep blue on m/c unpt.			
a.	Sign. J. Q. Hollom. (1962-66).	9.00	17.50	32.50
b.	Sign. J. S. Fforde. (1966-70).	9.00	15.00	30.00
c.	Sign. J. B. Page. (1970-71).	9.00	15.00	30.00

376	**10 POUNDS**	VG	VF	UNC
	ND (1964). Deep brown on m/c unpt.			
	a. Sign. J. Q. Hollom. (1964-66).	18.00	25.00	50.00
	b. Sign. J. S. Fforde. (1966-70).	18.00	22.50	45.00
	c. Sign. J. B. Page. (1970-77).	18.00	22.50	45.00

1971-82 ISSUE

#135-138 Qn. Elizabeth II in robes on r.

377	**1 POUND**	VG	VF	UNC
	ND (1978-82). Deep green on m/c unpt. Back guilloches gray at lower l. and r. Corners. Sir I. Newton at ctr. r. on back and in wmk.			
	a. Green sign. J. B. Page. (1978-82).	2.00	3.00	6.00
	b. Back guilloches lt. green at lower l. and r. Black sign. D. H. F. Somerset. (1982-84).	2.00	3.00	5.00

378	**5 POUNDS**	VG	VF	UNC
	ND (1971-90). Blue-black on m/c unpt. Duke of Wellington on back and in wmk.			
	a. Blue-gray sign. J. B. Page. (1971-72).	FV	FV	30.00
	b. Black sign. J. B. Page. Litho back w/small *L* at lower l. (1973-82).	FV	FV	22.50
	c. Black sign. D. H. F. Somerset. (1982-88). Thin security thread.	FV	FV	20.00
	d. Sign. D. H. F. Somerset. Thick security thread.	FV	FV	35.00
	e. Sign. G. M. Gill (1988-91).	FV	FV	20.00

379	**10 POUNDS**	VG	VF	UNC
	ND (1975-91). Deep brown on m/c unpt. F. Nightingale on back and as wmk.			
	a. Brown sign. J. B. Page. (1978-82).	FV	20.00	50.00
	b. Black sign. D. H. F. Somerset (1982-88).	FV	FV	50.00
	c. Black sign. D. H. F. Somerset. W/segmented security thread. (1982-88).	FV	FV	50.00
	d. Sign. G. M. Gill (1988-91).	FV	FV	40.00
	e. Sign. G. E. A. Kentfield (1991).	FV	FV	40.00

380	**20 POUNDS**	VG	VF	UNC
	ND (1970-91). Purple on m/c unpt. Shakespeare statue on back. Wmk: Qn. Elizabeth.			
	a. Wmk: Qn. Sign. J. S. Fforde. (1970).	35.00	70.00	175.00
	b. Wmk: Qn. Sign. J. B. Page. (1970-82).	35.00	50.00	90.00
	c. Wmk: Qn. Sign. D. H. F. Somerset. (1982-84).	FV	FV	85.00
	d. Wmk: Shakespeare. Modified background colors. Segmented security thread. D. H. F. Somerset. (1984-88).	FV	FV	80.00
	e. Sign. G. M. Gill (1988-91).	FV	FV	80.00

381 50 POUNDS

		VG	VF	UNC
ND (1981-93). Olive-green and brown on m/c unpt. Wmk: Qn. Elizabeth II at l., w/o imprint. View and plan of St. Paul's Cathedral at l., Sir C. Wren at ctr. r. on back.				
a. Black sign. D. H .F. Somerset (1981-88).		FV	FV	200.00
b. Modified background and guilloche colors. Segmented foil on security thread on surface. Sign. G. M. Gill (1988-91).		FV	FV	165.00
c. Sign. G. E. A. Kentfield (1991-93).		FV	FV	165.00

1990-92 ISSUE
#382-384 Qn. Elizabeth II at r., and as wmk.

382 5 POUNDS

		VG	VF	UNC
©1990 (1990-93). Dk. brown and deep blue-green on m/c unpt. Britannia seated at upper l.; Rocket locomotive at l.; G. Stephenson at r. on back.				
a. Lt. blue-gray sign. of G. M. Gill (1990-91).		FV	FV	20.00
b. Blue-black sign. of G. M. Gill, darker brownish-black portr. of Qn. Elizabeth II (1991).		FV	FV	16.00
c. Like b. Sign. G. E. A. Kentfield (1991).		FV	FV	15.00

383 10 POUNDS

		VG	VF	UNC
©1992 (1992-93). Black, brown and red on m/c unpt. Arms at l. Cricket match at l., Charles Dickens at r. on back. Sign. G. E. A. Kentfield (1992).		FV	FV	26.50

384 20 POUNDS

		VG	VF	UNC
©1991 (1991-93). Black, teal-violet and purple on m/c unpt. Britannia arms at l. Broken vertical foil strip and purple optical device at l. ctr. M. Faraday w/students at l., portr. at r. on back. Serial # olive-green to maroon at upper l. and dk. blue at r.				
a. Sign. G. M. Gill (1990-91).		FV	FV	55.00
b. Sign. G. E. A. Kentfield (1991).		FV	FV	52.50

1993 MODIFIED ISSUE
#385-388 Qn. Elizabeth II at r. and as wmk. Sign. G. E. A. Kentfield.

385 5 POUNDS

		VG	VF	UNC
©1990 (1993-). Like #382 but w/dk. value symbol at upper l. corner, also darker shading on back.		FV	FV	15.00

386 10 POUNDS

		VG	VF	UNC
©1993 (1993-). Like #383 but w/enhanced symbols for value and substitution of value £10 for crown at upper r. on face. Additional value system at top r. on back.		FV	FV	20.00

387 20 POUNDS
©1993 (1993-). Like #384 but w/dk. value symbol at upper l. corner
and substitution of value symbol for crown at upper r. corner on face.
Additional value symbol at top r. on back.

	VG	VF	UNC
	FV	FV	37.50

388 50 POUNDS
©1994 (1994-). Brownish-black, red and violet on m/c unpt. Allegory
in oval in unpt. at l. Bank gatekeeper at lower l., his house at l. and Sir
J. Houblon at r. on back.

	VG	VF	UNC
	FV	FV	100.00

MILITARY

BRITISH ARMED FORCES, SPECIAL VOUCHERS

NOTE: The Ministry of Defense sold large quantities of remainders #M20c, M26a, M27a, M28a, M32 and
M35 2-hole punch cancelled w/normal serial # a few years ago. Original specimens of #M20c, M27a,
M28 and M35 have one punched hole and special serial # 123456 and larger denominations some-
times have an additional serial # 789012.

1962 ND FOURTH SERIES
#M30-M36 w/o imprint. (Not issued).

M30 3 PENCE
ND (1962). Slate, violet and lt. green. Specimen.

	VG	VF	UNC
	—	Rare	—

M31 6 PENCE
ND (1962). Blue, violet and lt. green. Specimen.

	VG	VF	UNC
	—	Rare	—

M32 1 SHILLING
ND. Dk. brown, olive and orange.
a. Normal serial #, but w/o punch cancellations.
b. Cancelled remainder w/2 punched holes.
c. Specimen w/1 punched hole.

	VG	VF	UNC
a.	6.00	25.00	100.00
b.	—	Rare	—
c.	—	Rare	—

M33 2 SHILLINGS - 6 PENCE
ND (1962). Red-orange, violet and lt. green. Specimen.

	—	Rare	—

M34 5 SHILLINGS
ND. Green and lt. brown. Specimen only.

	VG	VF	UNC
	—	Rare	—

M35 10 SHILLINGS
ND. Violet, blue and green.
a. Normal serial # but w/o punch cancellations.
b. Cancelled remainder w/normal serial # and 2 punched holes.
c. Specimen w/special serial # and 1 punched hole.

	VG	VF	UNC
a.	5.00	20.00	80.00
b.	—	—	5.00
c.	—	Rare	—

M36 1 POUND
ND. Lilac and green.
a. Normal serial #, w/o punch cancellations.
b. Specimen w/special serial # and 1 punched hole.

	VG	VF	UNC
a.	—	—	4.00
b.	—	Rare	—

1960's FIFTH SERIES
#M37-M43 only known as specimens.

M37 3 PENCE
ND. Red-brown, purple and green. Specimen.

	VG	VF	UNC
	—	Rare	—

M38 6 PENCE
ND. Green, turquoise and lt. brown. Specimen.

	—	Rare	—

M39 1 SHILLING
ND. Lilac and green. Specimen.

	—	Rare	—

M40 2 SHILLINGS - 6 PENCE
ND. Purple, turquoise and lt. brown. Specimen.

	—	Rare	—

M41 5 SHILLINGS
ND. Blue, red and turquoise. Specimen.

	—	Rare	—

M42 10 SHILLINGS
ND. Orange, green and slate. Specimen.

	—	Rare	—

M43 1 POUND
ND. Olive and red-brown. Specimen.

	—	Rare	—

SIXTH SERIES (1972)
#M44-M46 printer: DLR.
#M47-M49 printer: BWC.

M44 5 NEW PENCE
ND (1972). Brown and green.

	VG	VF	UNC
	—	—	2.00

M45 10 NEW PENCE
ND (1972). Violet and green.

	VG	VF	UNC
	—	—	3.00

		VG	VF	UNC
M46	**50 NEW PENCE** ND (1972). Green.	—	—	4.00

SIXTH SERIES, SECOND ISSUE

		VG	VF	UNC
M47	**5 NEW PENCE** ND (1972). Like #M44.	—	—	1.50
M48	**10 NEW PENCE** ND (1972). Like #M45.	—	—	2.00
M49	**50 NEW PENCE** ND (1972). Like #M46.	—	—	3.00

COLLECTOR SERIES

BANK OF ENGLAND

1995 ISSUE

#CS1 and CS2 commemorate the 200th Anniversary of the first 5 Pound note.

		ISSUE PRICE	MKT. VALUE
CS1	**5 POUNDS** Uncut sheet of 3 notes #385 in folder. Serial #AB16-AB18. Last web printing.	68.00	70.00
CS2	**5 POUNDS** Uncut sheet of 3 notes #385 in folder. Serial #AC01-AC03. First sheet printing.	68.00	70.00

GREECE

The Hellenic Republic of Greece is situated in southeastern Europe on the southern tip of the Balkan Peninsula. The republic includes many islands, the most important of which are Crete and the Ionian Islands. Greece (including islands) has an area of 51,146 sq. mi. (131,944 sq. km.) and a population of 10.3 million. Capital: Athens. Greece is still largely agricultural. Tobacco, cotton, fruit and wool are exported.

Greece, the Mother of Western civilization, attained the peak of its culture in the 5th century BC, when it contributed more to government, drama, art and architecture than any other people to this time. Greece fell under Roman domination in the 2nd and 1st centuries BC, becoming part of the Byzantine Empire until Constantinople fell to the Crusaders in 1202. With the fall of Constantinople to the Turks in 1453, Greece became part of the Ottoman Empire. Independence from Turkey was won with the revolution of 1821-27. In 1833, Greece was established as a monarchy, with sovereignty guaranteed by Britain, France and Russia. After a lengthy power struggle between the monarchist forces and democratic factions, Greece was proclaimed a republic in 1925. The monarchy was restored in 1935 and reconfirmed by a plebiscite in 1946. The Italians invaded Greece via Albania on Oct. 28,1940 but were driven back well within the Albanian border. Germany began its invasion on April 6, 1941 and quickly overran the entire country, driving off a British Expeditionary force by the end of April. King George II and his new government went into exile. The German - Italian occupation of Greece lasted until Oct. 1944. On April 21, 1967, a military junta took control of the government and suspended the constitution. King Constantine II made an unsuccessful attempt against the junta in the fall of 1968 and consequently fled to Italy. The monarchy was formally abolished by plebiscite, Dec. 8, 1974, and Greece established as the "Hellenic Republic," the third republic in Greek history.

The island of Crete (Kreti), located 60 miles southeast of the Peloponnesus, was the center of a brilliant civilization that flourished before the advent of Greek culture. After being conquered by the Romans, Byzantines, Moslems and Venetians, Crete became part of the Turkish Empire in 1669. As a consequence of the Greek Revolution of the 1820s, it was ceded to Egypt. Egypt returned the island to the Turks in 1840, and they ceded it to Greece in 1913, after the Second Balkan War.

The Ionian Islands, situated in the Ionian Sea to the west of Greece, is the collective name for the islands of Corfu, Cephalonia, Zante, Santa Maura, Ithaca, Cthera and Paxo, with their minor dependencies. Before Britain acquired the islands, 1809-1814, they were at various times subject to the authority of Venice, France, Russia and Turkey. They remained under British control until their cession to Greece on March 29, 1864.

RULERS:
Paul I, 1947-1964
Constantine II, 1964-1973

MONETARY SYSTEM:
1 Drachma = 100 Lepta, 1831-

GREEK ALPHABET

A	α	Alpha	(ä)	I	ι	Iota	(ē)	P	ρ	Rho	(r)
B	β	Beta	(b)	K	κ	Kappa	(k)	Σ	σ	Sigma	(s)6
Γ	γ	Gamma	(g)	Λ	λ	Lambda	(l)	T	τ	Tau	(t)
Δ	δ	Delta	(d)	M	μ	Mu	(m)	Y	υ	Upsilon	(oo)
E	ε	Epsilon	(e)	N	ν	Nu	(n)	Φ	φ	Phi	(f)
Z	ζ	Zeta	(z)	Ξ	ξ	Xi	(ks)	X	χ	Chi	(H)
H	η	Eta	(ā)	O	o	Omicron	(o)	Ψ	ψ	Psi	(ps)
Θ	θ	Theta	(th)	Π	π	Pi	(p)	Ω	ω	Omega	(ō)

KINGDOM

ΤΡΑΠΕΖΑ ΤΗΣ ΕΛΛΑΔΟΣ

BANK OF GREECE

1964-70 ISSUE

195 50 DRACHMAI
  1.10.1964. Blue on m/c unpt. Arethusa at l., galley at bottom r. Shipyard on back.

VG	VF	UNC
.45	.85	2.00

196 100 DRACHMAI
  1966-67. Red-brown on m/c unpt. Demokritos at l., bldg. and atomic symbol at r. University at ctr. on back.

	VG	VF	UNC
a. Sign. Zolotas as Bank President. 1.7.1966.	8.00	20.00	65.00
b. Sign. Galanis as Bank President. 1.10.1967.	.90	1.50	4.00

197 500 DRACHMAI
  1.11.1968. Olive on m/c unpt. Relief of Elusis at ctr. Relief of animals at bottom l., fruit at bottom ctr. on back.

VG	VF	UNC
FV	FV	9.00

198 1000 DRACHMAI
  1.11.1970. Brown on m/c unpt. Zeus at l., stadium at bottom ctr. Back brown and green; woman at l. and view of city Hydra on the Isle of Hydra.

	VG	VF	UNC
a. Wmk: Head of Aphrodite of Knidnidus in 3/4 profile (1970).	FV	20.00	50.00
b. Wmk: Head of Ephebus of Anticyicythera in profile (1972).	FV	FV	15.00

REPUBLIC - 1970s

ΤΡΑΠΕΖΑ ΤΗΣ ΕΛΛΑΔΟΣ

BANK OF GREECE

1978 ISSUE
#199 and 200 wmk: man's head from Delphi.

199 50 DRACHMAI
  8.12.1978. Blue on m/c unpt. Poseidon at l. Sailing ship at ctr., man and woman at r. on back.

VG	VF	UNC
FV	FV	1.00

200 100 DRACHMAI
  8.12.1978. Brown and violet on m/c unpt. Athena at l. Back maroon, green and orange; A. Korans at l., church at bottom r.

VG	VF	UNC
FV	FV	1.75

1983-87 ISSUE
#201-203 wmk: man's head from Delphi.

201 500 DRACHMAI
  1.2.1983. Deep green on m/c unpt. I. Capodistrias at l. ctr., his birthplace at lower r. Fortress overlooking Corfu on back.

VG	VF	UNC
FV	FV	4.50

202   1000 DRACHMAI
  1.7.1987. Brown on m/c unpt. Ancient coin at lower ctr., Apollo at ctr.
  r. Discus thrower and Hera Temple ruins on back.

	VG	VF	UNC
	FV	FV	8.00

203   5000 DRACHMAI
  23.3.1984. Deep blue on m/c unpt. T. Kolokotronis at l. Landscape
  and view of town of Karytaina at ctr. r. on back.

	VG	VF	UNC
	FV	FV	35.00

205   10,000 DRACHMAI
  16.1.1995. Deep purple purple on m/c unpt. Dr. G. Papanikolaou at l.
  ctr., microscope at lower ctr. r. Medical care frieze at bottom ctr.,
  statue of Asklā)pios at ctr. r.

	VG	VF	UNC
	FV	FV	65.00

1995-96 ISSUE
#204 and 205 wmk: Man's head from Delphi.

204   200 DRACHMAI
  2.9.1996. Brown-orange on m/c unpt. R. Velestinlis Ferios at l. Secret
  school of Greek priests (during Ottoman occupation) at ctr. r. on back.

	VG	VF	UNC
	FV	FV	3.25

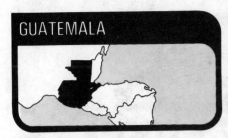

GUATEMALA

The Republic of Guatemala, the northernmost of the five Central American republics, has an area of 42,042 sq. mi. (108,889 sq. km.) and a population of 9.4 million. Capital: Guatemala City. The economy of Guatemala is heavily dependent on resources which are being developed. Coffee, cotton and bananas are exported.

Guatemala, once the site of the ancient Mayan civilization, was conquered by Pedro de Alvarado, the lieutenant of Cortes who undertook the conquest from Mexico. Skilled in strategy and cruelty, he progressed rapidly along the Pacific coastal lowlands to the highland plain of Quezaltenango where the decisive battle for Guatemala was fought. After routing the Mayan forces, he established the first capital of Guatemala in 1524.

Guatemala of the colonial period included all of Central America but Panama. Guatemala declared its independence of Spain in 1821 and was absorbed into the short-lived Mexican empire of Augustin Iturbide, 1822-23. From 1823 to 1839 Guatemala was a constituent state of the Central American Republic. Upon dissolution of the federation, Guatemala became an independent republic.

* * * NOTE: This section has been renumbered * * *

MONETARY SYSTEM:
    1 Peso = 100 Centavos to 1924
    1 Quetzal = 100 Centavos, 1924-

REPUBLIC

BANCO DE GUATEMALA

1958 ISSUE
#38 and 39 printer: ABNC.

		VG	VF	UNC
35 (91A)	**1/2 QUETZAL** 22.1.1958. Brown. Hermitage of Cerro del Carmen at l. 2 Guatemalans on back.	2.00	7.50	40.00
36 (92A)	**1 QUETZAL** 16.1.1957; 22.1.1958. Green. Palace of the Captains General at l. Lake Atitlan on back.	2.00	6.00	32.50

		VG	VF	UNC
37 (93A)	**5 QUETZALES** 22.1.1958. Purple vase (Vasija de Uaxactum) at l. Mayan-Spanish battle scene on back.	8.00	30.00	100.00
38 (94A)	**10 QUETZALES** 22.1.1958; 12.1.1962; 9.1.1963; 8.1.1964. Like #26.	10.00	50.00	145.00

		VG	VF	UNC
39 (95A)	**20 QUETZALES** 1958(?); 9.1.1963; 8.1.1964; 15.1.1965. Like #27.	20.00	75.00	235.00

1959-60 ISSUES
#41, 43, 45, 47, 48 and 50 sign. varieties. Printer: W&S.

		VG	VF	UNC
40 (A97A)	**1/2 QUETZAL** 18.2.1959. Like #29. Lighter brown shadings around value guilloche at l. Printed area 2mm smaller than #41. 6-digit serial #.	2.00	7.00	40.00
41 (97A)	**1/2 QUETZAL** 18.2.1959; 13.1.1960; 18.1.1961. Similar to #40 but darker brown shadings around value guilloche at l. 7-digit serial #.	1.00	3.00	25.00
42 (A98A)	**1 QUETZAL** 18.2.1959. Green palace. Like #30. Dull green back. 6-digit serial #.	2.00	6.00	45.00
43 (98A)	**1 QUETZAL**	VG	VF	UNC
	18.2.1959-8.1.1964. Black and green. Like #42, but black palace. Back bright green. 7-digit serial #.	1.00	4.50	22.50

		VG	VF	UNC
44 (99A)	**5 QUETZALES** 18.2.1959. Like #31. Vase in purple.	8.00	25.00	90.00
45 (99B)	**5 QUETZALES** 18.2.1959-8.1.1964. Similar to #44 but redesigned guilloche. Vase in brown.	5.00	20.00	80.00
47 (100B)	**10 QUETZALES** 18.2.1959; 13.1.1960; 18.1.1961. Similar to #46 but redesigned guilloche. Stone in brown.	12.50	30.00	110.00

		VG	VF	UNC
48 (101A)	**20 QUETZALES** 13.1.1960-15.1.1965. Blue. Similar to #33, but portr. R. Landivar at r.	20.00	65.00	180.00

		VG	VF	UNC
50 (102A)	**100 QUETZALES** 13.1.1960-15.1.1965. Dk. blue. Indio de Nahuala in brown at r.	115.00	250.00	450.00

1964-67 ISSUE
#51-57 sign. varieties. Printer: TDLR.

#53-57, 2 wmk. varieties.

		VG	VF	UNC
51 (103)	**1/2 QUETZAL** 8.1.1964-5.1.1972. Like #41.	1.00	2.00	12.50

52	1 QUETZAL	VG	VF	UNC
(104)	8.1.1964-5.1.1972. Like #43.	1.50	3.00	15.00
53	5 QUETZALES			
(105)	8.1.1964-6.1.1971. Like #45.	3.00	7.50	27.50
54	10 QUETZALES			
(106)	15.1.1965-7.1.1970. Similar to #47.	8.00	25.00	85.00
55	20 QUETZALES			
(107)	15.1.1965-6.1.1971. Like #48.	17.50	45.00	165.00

56	50 QUETZALES	VG	VF	UNC
(108)	13.1.1967-5.1.1973. Orange and blue. Gen. J. M. Orellana at r. Back orange; bank at ctr.	60.00	120.00	275.00
57	100 QUETZALES			
(109)	21.1.1966-7.1.1970. Dk. blue and brown. Face like #50. City and mountain on back.	75.00	140.00	300.00

60	5 QUETZALES	VG	VF	UNC
(112)	1969-83. Purple and m/c. Gen. (later Pres.) J. R. Barrios at r. Classroom scene on back.			
	a. 3.1.1969; 6.1.1971; 5.1.1972; 5.1.1973.	FV	3.75	15.00
	b. 2.1.1974; 3.1.1975; 7.1.1976; 20.4.1977.	FV	2.50	10.00
	c. Date at r. 4.1.1978; 3.1.1979; 7.1.1981; 6.1.1982; 6.1.1983.	FV	2.00	8.00

1969-74 ISSUE

#58-64 various date and sign. varieties. Printer: TDLR.

#60-64 wmk: Tecun Uman.

58	1/2 QUETZAL	VG	VF	UNC
(110)	1972-83. Brown and m/c. Tecun Uman (National Hero) at r. Tikal Temple on back.			
	a. W/o security (flourescent) imprint. 5.1.1972; 5.1.1973.	FV	1.50	4.50
	b. Security (flourescent) imprint on back. 2.1.1974; 3.1.1975; 7.1.1976; 20.4.1977.	FV	.60	2.50
	c. Date at r. 4.1.1978; 3.1.1979; 2.1.1980; 7.1.1981; 6.1.1982; 6.1.1983.	FV	.50	2.50

61	10 QUETZALES	VG	VF	UNC
(113)	1971-79; 1983. Red and m/c. Gen. M. G. Granados at r. National Assembly session of 1872 on back.			
	a. 6.1.1971; 5.1.1972.	2.25	5.00	28.50
	b. 3.1.1975; 7.1.1976; 5.1.1977; 20.4.1977.	FV	4.50	18.50
	c. 3.1.1979-6.1.1983.	FV	3.75	15.00

59	1 QUETZAL	VG	VF	UNC
(111)	1972-83. Green and m/c. Gen. J. M. Orellana at r. Banco de Guatemala on back.			
	a. Security (flourescent) imprint on face. Date at lower r. 5.1.1972; 5.1.1973.	FV	1.50	5.50
	b. Security imprint as a. on face and back. 2.1.1974; 3.1.1975; 7.1.1976.	FV	1.00	4.50
	c. Date at r. 5.1.1977; 20.4.1977; 4.1.1978; 2.1.1980; 7.1.1981.	FV	.50	2.50

62	20 QUETZALES	VG	VF	UNC
(114)	1972-74; 1983; 1988. Blue and m/c. Dr. M. Galvez at r. Granting of Independence to Central America on back.			
	a. 5.1.1972; 5,1,1973; 2.1.1974.	FV	7.50	30.00
	b. 6.1.1983.	FV	6.00	25.00
	c. 6.1.1988.	FV	5.00	20.00

63	**50 QUETZALES**	VG	VF	UNC
(115)	1974; 1981-83. Orange and m/c. C. O. Zachrisson at r. Crop workers on back.			
	a. 2.1.1974.	10.00	18.50	75.00
	b. 7.1.1981; 6.1.1982; 6.1.1983.	9.00	15.00	60.00

68	**10 QUETZALES**	VG	VF	UNC
(120)	30.12.1983-6.1.1988. Red-violet, red-brown and m/c. Gen. M. G. Granados at r. Similar to #61. National Assembly session of 1872 on back.	FV	3.50	10.00
69	**20 QUETZALES**			
(121)	6.1.1983-7.1.1987. Blue and m/c. Dr. M. Galvez at r. Similar to #62.	FV	3.00	16.50

64	**100 QUETZALES**	VG	VF	UNC
(116)	1975-82. Brown and m/c. F. Marroquin at r. University of San Carlos de Borromeo on back.			
	a. 5.1.1972.	25.00	37.50	125.00
	b. 3.1.1975; 7.1.1976; 3.1.1979.	20.00	32.50	110.00
	c. 6.1.1982; 6.1.1983.	FV	30.00	100.00

1983 ISSUE

#65-71 similar to #58-64. Wmk: Tecun Uman. Printer: G&D.

70	**50 QUETZALES**	VG	VF	UNC
(122)	30.12.1983-7.1.1987. Orange, yellow-orange and m/c. C. O. Zachrisson at r. Similar to #63. Crop workers on back.	FV	16.50	32.50
71	**100 QUETZALES**			
(123)	30.12.1983-7.1.1987. Brown and m/c. F. Marroquin at r. Similar to #64.	FV	25.00	55.00

1989-90 ISSUE

#72-74 printer: CBN. Sign. varieties.

#75-78 similar to #68-71. Vertical serial # at I. Printer: TDLR. Sign. varieties.

65	**1/2 QUETZAL**	VG	VF	UNC
(117)	6.1.1983-4.1.1989. Brown and m/c. Tecun Uman at r. Tikal Temple on back. Similar to #58.	FV	FV	1.25
66	**1 QUETZAL**			
(118)	30.12.1983-4.1.1989. Blue-green and m/c. Gen. J. Orellana at r. Banco de Guatemala bldg. on back. Similar to #59.	FV	FV	2.50
67	**5 QUETZALES**			
(119)	6.1.1983-6.1.1988. Purple and m/c. J. R. Barrios at r. Similar to #60. Classroom scene on back.	FV	FV	7.00

72	**1/2 QUETZAL**	VG	VF	UNC
(124)	4.1.1989; 14.2.1992. Similar to #65. W/o wmk.	FV	FV	.75

73	**1 QUETZAL**		VG	VF	UNC
(125)	3.1.1990; 6.3.1991; 22.1.1992; 14.2.1992; 6.9.1995. Similar to #66. W/o wmk.		FV	FV	1.00

74	**5 QUETZALES**		VG	VF	UNC
(126)	3.1.1990; 6.3.1991; 22.1.1992. Similar to #67.		FV	FV	3.00

75	**10 QUETZALES**		VG	VF	UNC
(127)	4.1.1989; 3.1.1990. 22.1.1992. Brown-violet, red and m/c. Similar to #68.		FV	FV	5.50

76	**20 QUETZALES**		VG	VF	UNC
(128)	4.1.1989; 3.1.1990; 22.1.1992. Blue-black, purple and blue on m/c unpt. Similar to #69.		FV	FV	10.00

77	**50 QUETZALES**		VG	VF	UNC
(129)	4.1.1989; 3.1.1990. Orange and green on m/c unpt. Similar to #70.		FV	FV	23.50

78	**100 QUETZALES**		VG	VF	UNC
(130)	4.1.1989; 3.1.1990; 22.1.1992. Brown and red-brown on m/c unpt. Similar to #71. Back lilac and m/c.		FV	FV	35.00

1992 ISSUE

#79-82 similar to #65-68 but more colorful backs. Printer: Oberthur F-CO.

#83-85 similar to #69-71 but more colorful backs. Printer: BABN.

79	**1/2 QUETZAL**		VG	VF	UNC
(131)	16.7.1992. Similar to #65.		FV	FV	.75
80	**1 QUETZAL**				
(132)	16.7.1992. Similar to #66.		FV	FV	1.00

81	**5 QUETZALES**		VG	VF	UNC
(133)	16.7.1992. Similar to #67.		FV	FV	3.00
82	**10 QUETZALES**				
(134)	16.7.1992. Similar to #68.		FV	FV	5.50
83	**20 QUETZALES**				
(135)	12.8.1992. Similar to #69.		FV	FV	10.00
84	**50 QUETZALES**				
(136)	12.8.1992. Similar to #70.		FV	FV	18.00

85	100 QUETZALES		VG	VF	UNC
(137)	27.5.1992. Similar to #71. Date at lower l., gold colored device at r. Back lt. brown and m/c.		FV	FV	35.00

1993-95 ISSUE
#86-89 printer: CBNC.

86	1/2 QUETZAL		VG	VF	UNC
	27.10.1993; 27.9.1994. Similar to #79 but w/colorful back.		FV	FV	.40
87	1 QUETZAL				
	27.10.1993; 6.9.1994; 6.9.1995. Similar to #80 but w/colorful back.		FV	FV	.75
88	5 QUETZALES				
(138)	27.10.1993; 16.6.1995. Similar to #81 but w/colorful back.		FV	FV	2.75
89	10 QUETZALES				
	16.6.1995. Similar to #82 but w/colorful back.		FV	FV	5.25

1994 ISSUE
#90 and 91 printer: F-CO.

90	1 QUETZAL		VG	VF	UNC
	27.9.1994. Like #72 but w/colorful back.		FV	FV	.60
91	10 QUETZALES				
	29.6.1994. Like #75 but w/colorful back.		FV	FV	4.00

1994; 1995 ISSUE
#92-94 similar to #74, 77 and 78. Printer: TDLR.

92	5 QUETZALES		VG	VF	UNC
	29.6.1994. Similar to #74 but w/colorful back.		FV	FV	2.25
93	50 QUETZALES				
	16.6.1995. Similar to #77 but w/colorful back.		FV	FV	17.50
94	100 QUETZALES				
	29.6.1994; 16.6.1995. Similar to #78 but w/colorful back.		FV	FV	32.50

1995 ISSUE

95	20 QUETZALES		VG	VF	UNC
	16.6.1995. Similar to #69 but w/colorful back. Printer: G&D.		FV	FV	7.50

GUERNSEY

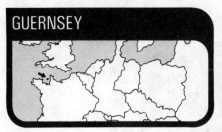

The Bailiwick of Guernsey, a British crown dependency located in the English Channel 30 miles (48 km.) west of Normandy, France, has an area of 30 sq. mi. (78 sq. km.), including the Isles of Alderney, Jethou, Herm, Brechou and Sark, and a population of 53,794. Capital: St. Peter Port. Agriculture and cattle breeding are the main occupations.

Militant monks from the Duchy of Normandy established the first permanent settlements on Guernsey prior to the Norman invasion of England, but the prevalence of prehistoric monuments suggests an earlier occupancy. The island, the only part of the Duchy of Normandy belonging to the British crown, has been a possession of Britain since the Norman Conquest of 1066. During the Anglo-French Wars, the harbors of Guernsey were employed in the building and outfitting of ships for the English privateers preying on French shipping. Guernsey is administered by its own laws and customs. Acts passed by the British Parliament are not applicable to Guernsey unless the island is specifically mentioned. During World War II, German troops occupied the island from June 30, 1940 to June 6, 1944.

RULERS:
British to 1940, 1944-

MONETARY SYSTEM:
1 Shilling = 12 Pence
1 Pound = 20 Shillings to 1971
1 Pound = 100 New Pence 1971-

BRITISH INFLUENCE - POST WW II

STATES OF GUERNSEY

1945; 1956 ISSUE
#42-44 printer: PBC.

42	10 SHILLINGS	VG	VF	UNC
	1945-66. Lilac on lt. green un pt. Back purple.			
	a. 1.8.1945-1.9.1957.	18.00	65.00	250.00
	b. 1.7.1958-1.3.1965.	5.00	45.00	90.00
	c. 1.7.1966.	8.00	20.00	60.00

43	1 POUND	VG	VF	UNC
	1945-66. Purple on green unpt. Harbor entrance across ctr. Back: green.			
	a. 1.8.1945-1.3.1957.	7.50	50.00	180.00
	b. 1.9.1957-1.3.1962; 1.6.1963; 1 ; 1.3.1965.	5.00	20.00	65.00
	c. 1.7.1966.	3.50	15.00	65.00

44	5 POUNDS	VG	VF	UNC
	1.12.1956; 1.3.1965; 1.7.1966. Green and blue. Flowers at l.	60.00	200.00	500.00

1969; 1975 ND ISSUE
#45-47 printer: BWC.

45	**1 POUND**	VG	VF	UNC
	ND (1969-75). Olive on pink and yellow unpt. Arms at ctr. Castle Cornet on back.			
	a. Sign. Guillemette.	2.00	5.00	25.00
	b. Sign. Hodder.	2.00	4.50	20.00
	c. Sign. Bull.	2.00	4.50	15.00

46	**5 POUNDS**	VG	VF	UNC
	ND (1969-75). Purple on lt. brown unpt. Arms at r. City view and harbor wall on back.			
	a. Sign. Guillemette.	9.00	20.00	85.00
	b. Sign. Hodder.	9.00	15.00	50.00
	c. Sign. Bull.	9.00	17.50	57.50

47	**10 POUNDS**	VG	VF	UNC
	ND (1975-80). Blue, green and m/c. Britannia w/lion and shield at l. Sir I. Brock and Battle of Queenston Hgts. on blue back. Sign. Hodder.	20.00	45.00	165.00

1980 ND ISSUE
#48-51 Guersey States seal at lower l. on face and as wmk. Printer: BWC.

48	**1 POUND**	VG	VF	UNC
	ND (1980). Dk. green and black on m/c unpt. Market square scene of 1822 at lower ctr. in unpt. D. De Lisle Brock and Royal Court of St. Peter Port on back. 135 x 67mm.			
	a. Black sign. W. C. Bull.	FV	FV	7.00
	b. Sign. M. J. Brown.	FV	FV	6.00

49	**5 POUNDS**	VG	VF	UNC
	ND (1980). Purple, dk. brown and olive-brown on m/c unpt. Fort Grey at lower ctr. in unpt. T. De La Rue and Fountain St. at ctr., workers at envelope making machine at lower r. on back. Black sign. W. C. Bull. 146 x 78 mm.	FV	FV	18.50

50	**10 POUNDS**	VG	VF	UNC
	ND (1980). Purple, blue and blue-black on m/c unpt. Castle Cornet at lower ctr. Maj. Sir Isaac Brock and battle of Queenston Hgts. on back. 151 x 85mm.			
	a. Black sign. W. C. Bull.	FV	FV	35.00
	b. Sign. M. J. Brown.	FV	FV	32.50

51	**20 POUNDS**	VG	VF	UNC
	ND (1980). Red, red-violet, brown and orange on m/c unpt. 1815 scene of Saumarez Park at lower ctr. in unpt. Adm. Lord de Saumarez and ships on back. 161 x 90mm.			
	a. Black sign. W. C. Bull.	FV	FV	65.00
	b. Sign. M. J. Brown.	FV	FV	60.00

1990-91 ND ISSUE

#52-55 similar to #48-51 but reduced size. Wmk: Guersey States seal. Printer: DLR.

52	1 POUND	VG	VF	UNC
	ND (ca.1991-). Similar to #48. 128 x 65mm.			
	a. Green sign. M. J. Brown.	FV	FV	4.50
	b. Sign. D. P. Trestain.	FV	FV	4.00

53	5 POUNDS	VG	VF	UNC
	ND (1990-95). Similar to #49. 136 x 70mm.			
	a. Brown sign. M. J. Brown.	FV	FV	15.00
	b. Sign. D. P. Trestain.	FV	FV	13.50
54	10 POUNDS			
	ND (ca.1991-95). Similar to #50. 142 x 75mm.			
	a. Blue sign. M. J. Brown.	FV	FV	28.50
	b. Sign. D. P. Trestain.	FV	FV	26.50

55	20 POUNDS	VG	VF	UNC
	ND (ca.1991-95). Similar to #51. 149 x 80mm.			
	a. Red-orange sign. M. J. Brown.	FV	FV	52.50
	b. Sign. D. P. Trestain.	FV	FV	50.00

1994-96 ND ISSUE

#56-59 Qn. Elizabeth II at r. and as wmk. Guersey States seal at lower ctr. r. Sign. D. P. Trestain. Printer: TDLR.

56	5 POUNDS	VG	VF	UNC
	ND (1996). Purple and brown on m/c unpt. St. Peter Port Town Church at lower l. Saumarez Park, Les Niaux Watermill and Le Trepied Dolmen on back.	FV	FV	12.50

57	10 POUNDS	VG	VF	UNC
	ND (1995). Violet, blue and dk. blue on m/c unpt. Elizabeth College at lower l. Saumarez Park above Le Niaux Watermill and Le Trepid Dolmen at l. ctr. on back.	FV	FV	25.00

58	20 POUNDS	VG	VF	UNC
	ND (1996). Pink, dk. brown and orange on m/c unpt. St. James Concert Hall at lower l. Flowers at lower l., St. Sampson's Church at l. ctr., sailboats below Vale Castle at ctr. r., ship at upper r.	FV	FV	47.50

59	50 POUNDS	VG	VF	UNC
	ND (1994). Dk. brown, dk. green and blue-black on m/c unpt. Royal Court House at lower l. Stone carving, letter of Marque at lower l., St. Andrew's Church at ctr. r. on back.	FV	FV	115.00

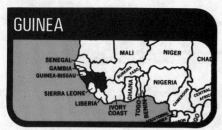

GUINEA

The Republic of Guinea (formerly French Guinea), situated on the Atlantic coast of Africa between Sierra Leone and Guinea-Bissau, has an area of 94,964 sq. mi. (245,957 sq. km.) and a population of 6.1 million. Capital: Conakry. Although Guinea contains one-third of the world's reserves of bauxite and significant deposits of iron ore, gold and diamonds, the economy is still dependent on agriculture. Aluminum, bananas, copra and coffee are exported.

The coast of Guinea was known to Portuguese navigators of the 15th century but was seldom visited by European traders of the 16th-18th centuries because of its dangerous coastal waters. French penetration of the area began in the mid-19th century with the entering into of protectorate treaties with several of the coastal chiefs. After a long struggle with Guinea's native leader Samory Toure, France secured the area and until 1890 administered it as a part of Senegal. In 1895 the colony (Guinee Francaise) became an autonomous part of the federation of French West Africa. The inhabitants were extended French citizenship in 1946 when the colony became an overseas territory of the French Union. Guinea became an independent republic on Oct. 2, 1958, when it declined to enter the new French Community.

RULERS:
French to 1958

MONETARY SYSTEM:
1 Franc = 100 Centimes to 1971
1 Syli = 10 Francs, 1971-1980
Franc System 1985-

REPUBLIC

BANQUE CENTRALE DE LA RÉPUBLIQUE DE GUINÉE

1960 ISSUE
#12-15 Pres. Sekou Toure at l. Wmk: Dove.

		VG	VF	UNC
12	**50 FRANCS**			
	1.3.1960. Brown and m/c. Heavy machinery on back.	1.00	3.00	12.50

		VG	VF	UNC
13	**100 FRANCS**			
	1.3.1960. Brown-violet and m/c. Pineapple harvesting on back.	1.00	3.00	15.00
14	**500 FRANCS**			
	1.3.1960. Blue and m/c. Men pulling long boats ashore on back.	3.00	10.00	65.00

		VG	VF	UNC
15	**1000 FRANCS**			
	1.3.1960. Green and m/c. Banana harvesting on back.	2.50	8.00	40.00

1971 ISSUE
#16-19 wmk: Dove.

		VG	VF	UNC
16	**10 SYLIS**			
	1971. Brown and m/c. Patrice Lumbumba at r. People w/bananas on back.	.20	.60	1.75

		VG	VF	UNC
17	**25 SYLIS**			
	1971. Dk. brown and m/c. Man smoking a pipe at r. Man and cows on back.	.30	.85	3.00

		VG	VF	UNC
18	**50 SYLIS**			
	1971. Green and m/c. Bearded man at l. Landscape w/large dam and reservoir on back.	1.00	3.00	10.00

19	100 SYLIS	VG	VF	UNC
	1971. Purple and m/c. A. S. Toure at l. Steam shovel and 2 dump trucks on back.	.75	2.25	8.00

1980; 1981 ISSUE
Law of 1.3.1960

#20-27 wmk: Multiple stars and design.

NOTE: #27 is purported to commemorate Marshal Tito's visit to Guinea.

20	1 SYLI	VG	VF	UNC
	1981. Olive on green unpt. Mafori Bangoura at r.			
	a. Issued note.	.05	.15	.50
	s. Specimen.	—	—	5.00

21	2 SYLIS	VG	VF	UNC
	1981. Black and brown on orange unpt. Green guilloche at ctr. Kg. Mohammed V of Morocco at l.			
	a. Issued note.	.05	.25	.75
	s. Specimen.	—	—	5.00

22	5 SYLIS	VG	VF	UNC
	1980. Blue on pink unpt. Kwame Nkrumah at r. Back like #16.			
	a. Issued note.	.20	.65	2.00
	s. Specimen.	—	—	7.00

23	10 SYLIS	VG	VF	UNC
	1980. Red-violet and red-orange on m/c unpt. Like #16.			
	a. Issued note.	.25	.75	2.50
	s. Specimen.	—	—	8.50

24	25 SYLIS	VG	VF	UNC
	1980. Dk. green and m/c. Like #17. Back green and m/c.			
	a. Issued note.	.40	1.20	4.00
	s. Specimen.	—	—	9.00

25	50 SYLIS	VG	VF	UNC
	1980. Dk. red, brown and m/c. Like #18.			
	a. Issued note.	.65	2.00	7.00
	s. Specimen.	—	—	10.00

26	100 SYLIS			
	1980. Blue and m/c. Like #19.			
	a. Issued note.	1.75	6.00	15.00
	s. Specimen.	—	—	12.50

27	500 SYLIS	VG	VF	UNC
	1980. Dk. brown and m/c. J. Broz Tito at l. Modern bldg. on back.			
	a. Issued note.	.85	2.50	12.50
	s. Specimen.	—	—	15.00

1985 ISSUE
Law of 1.3.1960

#28-33 arms at ctr.

			VG	VF	UNC
28	**25 FRANCS**				
	1985. Blue and m/c. Young boy at l. Girl by huts at ctr. r. on back.				
	a. Issued note.		FV	.20	2.25
	s. Specimen.		—	—	2.50

			VG	VF	UNC
29	**50 FRANCS**				
	1985. Dk. red and m/c. Bearded man at l. Plowing w/water buffalo at ctr. on back.				
	a. Issued note.		FV	.75	1.00
	s. Specimen.		—	—	4.50
30	**100 FRANCS**				
	1985. Purple and m/c. Young woman at l. Harvesting bananas at ctr. on back.				
	a. Issued note.		FV	.50	2.00
	s. Specimen.		—	—	6.50

			VG	VF	UNC
31	**500 FRANCS**				
	1985. Green and m/c. Woman at l. Minehead at ctr. on back.				
	a. Issued note.		FV	1.25	4.50
	s. Specimen.		—	—	7.50

			VG	VF	UNC
32	**1000 FRANCS**				
	1985. Blue, brown and m/c. Girl at l. Shovel loading ore into open end dump trucks at ctr., mask at r. on back.				
	a. Issued note.		FV	1.85	6.50
	s. Specimen.		—	—	9.00
33	**5000 FRANCS**				
	1985. Blue, brown and m/c. woman at l. Dam at ctr., mask at r. on back.				
	a. Issued note.		FV	6.00	20.00
	s. Specimen.		—	—	13.50

The Republic of Guinea-Bissau, a former Portuguese overseas province on the west coast of Africa between Senegal and Guinea, has an area of 13,948 sq. mi. (36,125 sq. km.) and a population of 929,000. Capital: Bissau. The country has undeveloped deposits of oil and bauxite. Peanuts, oil-palm kernels and hides are exported.

The African Party for the Independence of Guinea-Bissau was founded in 1956, and several years later began a guerrilla warfare that grew in effectiveness until 1974, when the rebels controlled most of the colony. Portugal's costly overseas wars in her African territories resulted in a military coup in Portugal in April 1974, that appreciably brightened the prospects for freedom for Guinea-Bissau. In August 1974, the Lisbon government signed an agreement granting independence to Portuguese Guinea effective Sept. 10, 1974. The new republic took the name of Guinea-Bissau.

On Jan. 1, 1997, Guinea-Bissau became a member of the West Affrican States, and as such are expected to soon issue CFA currency notes.

RULERS:
Portuguese until 1974

MONETARY SYSTEM:
1 Peso = 100 Centavos, 1975-

REPUBLIC

BANCO NACIONAL DA GUINÉ-BISSAU

1975 ISSUE
#1-4 wmk: A. Cabral.
#4 *Deleted.* See #8.

			VG	VF	UNC
1	**50 PESOS**				
	24.9.1975. Blue. P. Nalsna at l. Field workers at ctr. woman at r. on back.		1.00	2.50	7.50

			VG	VF	UNC
2	**100 PESOS**				
	24.9.1975. Brown. D. Ramos at l. Objects and woman on back.		1.50	3.50	10.00

3   **500 PESOS**   VG   VF   UNC
24.9.1975. Green and brown. Pres. A. Cabral at l. Carving and 2   8.00   20.00   47.50
youths on back.

1978-83 ISSUES

#5-9 arms at lower r. on face. Wmk: A. Cabral.

5   **50 PESOS**   VG   VF   UNC
28.2.1983. Orange on m/c unpt. Artifact at l. ctr., P. Nalsna at r. Local   FV   1.00   3.00
scene on back. Printer: BWC.

6   **100 PESOS**   VG   VF   UNC
28.2.1983. Red on m/c unpt. Carving at l., D. Ramos at r. Bldg. on   FV   1.25   4.00
back. W/o imprint.

7   **500 PESOS**   VG   VF   UNC
28.2.1983. Deep blue on m/c unpt. Carving at l., F. Mendes at r. Slave   FV   2.00   5.00
trade scene on back. W/o imprint.

8   **1000 PESOS**   VG   VF   UNC
24.9.1978. Green on brown and m/c unpt. Weaver and loom at lower l.
ctr., Pres. A. Cabral at r. Allegory w/title: *Apoteose ao Triunfo* on back.
Printer: BWC.
    a.   Sign. titles: *COMISSARIO PRINCIPAL, COMISSARIO DE ESTADO*   7.50   20.00   62.50
         DES FINANCAS and *GOVERNADOR.*
    b.   Sign. titles: *PRIMEIRO MINISTRO, MINISTRO DE ECONOMIA E*   FV   3.00   7.00
         FINANCAS and *GOVERNADOR.*

9   **5000 PESOS**   VG   VF   UNC
12.9.1984. Brown-orange and m/c unpt. Map at ctr., Pres. A. Cabral at   FV   4.00   10.00
r. Harvesting grain at ctr. on back. W/o imprint.

1990 ISSUE

#10-15 sign. titles: *MINISTRO-GOVERNADOR* and *VICE-GOVERNADOR.* Printer: TDLR.

#10-12 wmk: *BCG.*

#13-15 wmk: Portr. A. Cabral.

10   **50 PESOS**   VG   VF   UNC
1.3.1990. Red on m/c unpt. Similar to #5 but reduced size w/o wmk.   FV   FV   1.00
area.

11   100 PESOS
  1.3.1990. Olive-gray on m/c unpt. Similar to #6 but reduced size w/o
  wmk. area.

VG	VF	UNC
FV	FV	.75

12   500 PESOS
  1.3.1990. Deep blue on m/c unpt. Similar to #7 but reduced size w/o
  wmk. area.

VG	VF	UNC
FV	FV	2.50

13   1000 PESOS
  1990; 1993. Dk. brown, brown-violet and orange on m/c unpt. Similar
  to #8.

	VG	VF	UNC
a. Sign. titles: *MINISTRO-GOVERNADOR* and *VICE-GOVERNADOR*. 1.3.1990.	FV	FV	3.00
b. Sign. titles: *GOVERNADOR* and *VICE-GOVERNADOR*. 1.3.1993.	FV	FV	2.00

14   5000 PESOS
  1990; 1993. Purple, violet and brown on m/c unpt. Similar to #9.

	VG	VF	UNC
a. Sign. titles: *MINISTRO-GOVERNADOR* and *VICE-GOVERNADOR*. 1.3.1990.	FV	FV	4.25
b. Sign. titles: *GOVERNADOR* and *VICE-GOVERNADOR*. 1.3.1993.	FV	FV	3.75

15   10,000 PESOS
  1990; 1993. Green, olive-brown and blue on m/c unpt. Statue at lower
  l. ctr., outline map at ctr., A. Cabral at r. Local people fishing w/nets in
  river at ctr. on back.

	VG	VF	UNC
a. Sign titles: *MINISTRO-GOVERNADOR* and *VICE-GOVERNADOR*. 1.3.1990.	FV	FV	8.00
b. Sign. titles: *GOVERNADOR* and *VICE-GOVERNADOR*. 1.3.1993.	FV	FV	7.00

The Cooperative Republic of Guyana, (formerly British Guiana) an independent member of the British Commonwealth situated on the northeast coast of South America, has an area of 83,000 sq. mi. (214,969 sq. km.) and a population of 779,000. Capital: Georgetown. The economy is basically agrarian. Sugar, rice and bauxite are exported.

The original area of Guyana, which included present-day Surinam, French Guiana, and parts of Brazil and Venezuela, was sighted by Columbus in 1498. The first European settlement was made late in the 16th century by the Dutch. For the next 150 years, possession alternated between the Dutch and the British, with a short interval of French control. The British exercised de facto control after 1796, although the area, which included the Dutch colonies of Essequebo, Demerary and Berbice, wasn't ceded to them by the Dutch until 1814. From 1803 to 1831, Essequebo and Demerary were administered separately from Berbice. The three colonies were united in the British Crown Colony of British Guiana in 1831. British Guiana won internal self-government in 1952 and full independence, under the traditional name of Guyana, on May 26, 1966.

Notes of the British Caribbean Currency Board circulated from 1950-1965.

RULERS:
British to 1966

MONETARY SYSTEM:
1 Dollar = 4 Shillings 2 Pence, 1837-1965
1 Dollar = 100 Cents, 1966-

SIGNATURE VARIETIES

1	Horst Bockelmann / signature GOVERNOR — MINISTER OF FINANCE	**5**	signature / F S Hope GOVERNOR — MINISTER OF FINANCE
2	signature / P A Reid GOVERNOR — MINISTER OF FINANCE	**6**	signature / H V Nagle GOVERNOR — VICE PRESIDENT ECONOMIC PLANNING AND FINANCE
3	signature / H V Nagle GOVERNOR — MINISTER OF FINANCE	**7**	signature / Carl B Greenidge GOVERNOR (a.g.) — MINISTER OF FINANCE
4	signature / F S Hope GOVERNOR — MINISTER OF FINANCE	**8**	Ah Meredith / Carl B Greenidge GOVERNOR — MINISTER OF FINANCE
4A	signature / signature GOVERNOR — MINISTER OF FINANCE	**9**	Ah Meredith / signature GOVERNOR — MINISTER OF FINANCE

REPUBLIC

BANK OF GUYANA

1966 ISSUE
#21-29 wmk: Macaw's (parrot) head. Printer: TDLR
#21-27 Kaieteur Falls at r.
#25 and 26 held in reserve.

21	**1 DOLLAR**	VG	VF	UNC
	ND (1966-). Red on m/c unpt. Black bush polder at l., rice harvesting at r. on back.			
	a. Sign. 1; 2.	.60	3.00	15.00
	b. Sign. 3; 4.	1.25	6.00	30.00
	c. Sign. 4A.	.05	.30	1.50
	d. Sign. 5.	.20	1.00	4.00
	e. Sign. 6 (1983).	.10	.40	1.50
	f. Serial # prefix B/1 or higher. Sign. 7 (1989).	FV	FV	.75
	g. Sign. 8 (1992).	FV	FV	.50

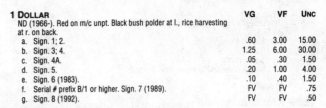

22	**5 DOLLARS**	VG	VF	UNC
	ND (1966-). Dk. green on m/c unpt. Cane sugar harvesting at l., conveyor at r. on back.			
	a. Sign. 1; 2.	1.65	8.00	40.00
	b. Sign. 3.	2.00	10.00	50.00
	c. Sign. 5.	.20	1.00	5.00
	d. Sign. 6 (1983).	.15	.60	3.00
	e. Serial # prefix A/27 or higher. Sign. 7 (1989).	FV	FV	1.00
	f. Sign. 8 (1992); 9.	FV	FV	.75

23	**10 DOLLARS**	VG	VF	UNC
	ND (1966-). Dk. brown on m/c unpt. Bauxite mining at l., aluminum plant at r. on back.			
	a. Sign. 1; 2; 3.	2.00	10.00	50.00
	b. Sign. 5.	.50	2.50	12.50
	c. Sign. 6 (1983).	.30	1.25	6.00
	d. Serial # prefix A/16 or higher. Sign. 7 (1989).	FV	FV	1.00
	e. Sign. 8 (1992); 9.	FV	FV	1.00

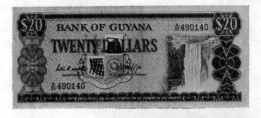

24 20 DOLLARS
ND (1966-88). Purple on m/c unpt. Shipbuilding at l., ferry vessel at r. on back.

	VG	VF	UNC
a. Sign. 1; 4A.	2.00	10.00	50.00
b. Sign. 5.	FV	3.00	15.00
c. Sign. 6 (1983).	FV	2.50	12.50
d. Serial # prefix A/42 or higher. Sign. 7 (1989).	FV	FV	2.50

1989-92 ISSUE

27 20 DOLLARS
ND (1989). Brown on m/c unpt. Similar to #24, but design element at l. and r. Sign. 7; 9.

VG	VF	UNC
FV	FV	2.50

28 100 DOLLARS
ND (1989). Blue on m/c unpt. Arms at ctr., map at r. Cathedral at ctr. on back. Sign 7; 8.

VG	VF	UNC
FV	FV	6.00

29 500 DOLLARS
ND (ca. 1992). Lilac-brown and purple on m/c unpt. Map of Guyana at r. Public bldgs. in Georgetown on back.

	VG	VF	UNC
a. Sign. 8.	FV	FV	20.00
b. Sign. 9.	FV	FV	7.50

30 1000 DOLLARS
ND.

Expected New Issue

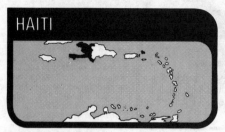

HAITI

The Republic of Haiti, which occupies the western one third of the island of Hispañola in the Caribbean Sea between Puerto Rico and Cuba, has an area of 10,714 sq. mi. (27,750 sq. km.) and a population of 6.2 million. Capital: Port-au-Prince. The economy is based on agriculture, light manufacturing and tourism which is becoming increasingly important. Coffee, bauxite, sugar, essential oils and handicrafts are exported.

Columbus discovered Hispañola in 1492. Spain colonized the island, making Santo Domingo the base for exploration of the Western Hemisphere. Later French buccaneers settled the western third of Hispañola which was ceded to France by Spain in 1697. Slaves brought over from Africa to work the coffee and sugar cane plantations made it one of the richest colonies of the French Empire. The Republic of Haiti was established in 1804 by the slave revolt of the 1790's, making it the oldest black republic in the world and the second oldest republic (after the United States) in the Western Hemisphere.

MONETARY SYSTEM:
1 Gourde = 100 Centimes
1 Piastre = 300 Gourdes, 1873
5 Gourdes = 1 U.S. Dollar, 1919-89

REPUBLIC

BANQUE NATIONALE DE LA RÉPUBLIQUE D'HAITI

CONVENTION DU 12 AVRIL 1919

SIXTH ISSUE (CA.1951-64)

#178-181, 183 and 184 arms at ctr. on back. First sign. title: *Le President.* Printer: ABNC.

178 1 GOURDE
L.1919. Dk. brown on lt. blue and m/c. unpt. Citadel rampart at ctr. Prefix letters AS-BM. 5 sign. varieties.

VG	VF	UNC
.75	2.00	17.50

179 2 GOURDES
L.1919. Blue and m/c. lt. green in unpt. Like #178. Prefix letters Z-AF. 6 sign. varieties.

VG	VF	UNC
1.00	3.00	22.00

180 5 GOURDES
L.1919. Orange on green unpt. Woman harvesting coffee beans at l. Prefix letters G-M. 3 sign. varieties.

VG	VF	UNC
1.50	4.50	20.00

181 10 GOURDES
L.1919. Green on m/c unpt. Coffee plant at ctr. Prefix letters B-D. 2 sign. varieties.

VG	VF	UNC
3.00	10.00	50.00

183 50 GOURDES
L.1919. Olive-green on m/c unpt. Cotton bolls at ctr. Specimen.

VG	VF	UNC
—	—	225.00

184 100 GOURDES
L.1919. Purple on m/c unpt. Field workers at l. Back purple. Prefix letter A.

	VG	VF	UNC
a. Issued note.	20.00	50.00	200.00
s. Specimen, punched hole cancelled.	—	—	175.00

CONVENTION DU 12 AVRIL 1919

SEVENTH ISSUE (CA.1964)

#185-189 like #178-180 but new guilloche patterns, w/o green in unpt. Arms at ctr. on back. Printer: ABNC.

185 1 GOURDE
L.1919. Dk. blue on lt. blue and m/c unpt. Like #178. Prefix letters BK-BT.

VG	VF	UNC
.50	1.50	8.50

186 2 GOURDES
L.1919. Blue on lt. blue and m/c unpt. Like #179. Prefix letters AF-AJ.

VG	VF	UNC
.75	2.50	15.00

187 5 GOURDES
L.1919. Orange on lt. pale blue and m/c unpt. Like #180. Prefix letter N.

VG	VF	UNC
.50	1.00	7.00

188 50 GOURDES
L.1919. Olive-green on blue and magenta unpt. Similar to #183. (Not issued). Archive example.

VG	VF	UNC
—	—	—

189 100 GOURDES
L.1919. Purple on m/c unpt. Similar to #184. (Not issued). Archive example.

VG	VF	UNC
—	—	—

CONVENTION DU 12 AVRIL 1919

EIGHTH ISSUE (CA.1967)
#190-195 arms at ctr. on back. Printer: TDLR.
#190-193 second sign. title: *LE DIRECTEUR.*

190 1 GOURDE
L.1919. Brown on m/c unpt. Similar to #185. Prefix letters DA-DL.

VG	VF	UNC
.30	1.00	7.50

191 2 GOURDES
L.1919. Grayish blue on m/c unpt. Similar to #186. Prefix letters DA-DF.

VG	VF	UNC
.50	1.50	9.00

192 5 GOURDES
L.1919. Similar to #187. Prefix letters DA-DK.

VG	VF	UNC
1.00	4.00	13.50

193 10 GOURDES
L.1919. Similar to #181. Prefix letters DA.

VG	VF	UNC
3.00	8.00	30.00

194 50 GOURDES
L.1919. Similar to #183. Prefix letters DA. Second sign. title: *UN DIRECTEUR.*

VG	VF	UNC
10.00	17.50	80.00

195 100 GOURDES
L.1919. Similar to #205. Prefix letters DA.

VG	VF	UNC
20.00	35.00	150.00

CONVENTION DU 12 AVRIL 1919

NINTH ISSUE
#196-198 Pres. Dr. F. Duvalier at ctr. or l. Arms at ctr. on back. Printer: TDLR.

196 1 GOURDE
L.1919. Dk. brown on m/c unpt. Prefix letters DK-DT.

VG	VF	UNC
.25	.60	3.50

197 2 GOURDES
L.1919. Grayish blue on m/c unpt. Like #196. Prefix letters DG-DJ.

VG	VF	UNC
.50	1.25	4.50

198 5 GOURDES
L.1919. Orange on m/c unpt. Portr. Pres. Duvalier at l. Prefix letters DJ-DK.

	VG	VF	UNC
	1.00	2.50	7.50

CONVENTION DU 13 AVRIL 1919

TENTH ISSUE
#201-207 w/4 lines of text on back (like previous issues).
#200-203 arms at ctr. on back. Printer: ABNC.
#208 and 209 held in reserve.

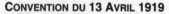

200 1 GOURDE
L.1919. Dk. brown on m/c unpt. Portr. Pres. F. Duvalier at ctr. Prefix letters A-Z; AA-CR. 3 sign. varieties.

	VG	VF	UNC
	.25	.60	2.00

201 2 GOURDES
L.1919. Blue on m/c unpt. Like #200. First issued w/o prefix, then letters A-Q.

	.50	1.25	3.50

202 5 GOURDES
L.1919. Orange on m/c unpt. Portr. Pres. F. Duvalier at l. First issued w/o prefix then letters A-Z; AA-AP. 3 sign. varieties.

	VG	VF	UNC
	1.00	2.00	4.50

203 10 GOURDES
L.1919. Dk. green on m/c unpt. Portr. Pres. F. Duvalier at ctr. First issued w/o prefix, then letter A.

	2.50	5.00	12.50

204 50 GOURDES
L.1919. Dk. gray on m/c unpt. Portr. Pres. L. F. Salomon Jeune at ctr. First issued w/o prefix, then letters A-C. 2 sign. varieties.

	VG	VF	UNC
	10.00	17.50	30.00

205 100 GOURDES
L.1919. Purple on m/c unpt. Portr. H. Christophe (Pres., later Kg.) at l. W/o prefix letter. 2 sign. varieties.

	VG	VF	UNC
	20.00	40.00	70.00

206 250 GOURDES
L.1919. Dk. yellow-green on m/c unpt. J. J. Dessalines at r. W/o prefix letter.

	VG	VF	UNC
	55.00	110.00	200.00

207 500 GOURDES
L.1919. Red on m/c unpt. Similar to #203. W/o prefix letter.

	VG	VF	UNC
	82.50	165.00	300.00

ELEVENTH ISSUE (CA.1973)
Lois des 21 Mai 1935 et 15 Mai 1953 et au Décret du 22 Novembre 1973 (issued 1979)
#210-214 arms at ctr. on back. Printer: ABNC.
#211-214 w/3 lines of text on back.
#215-217 held in reserve.

210 1 GOURDE
L.1973, etc Like #200. Prefix letters A-Z; AA-AC.

	VG	VF	UNC
	.30	.60	2.00

211 2 GOURDES
L.1973, ect. Like #201. Prefix letters A-J.

	.60	1.25	3.00

212 5 GOURDES
L.1973, etc. Like #202. Prefix letters A-AA.

	1.00	2.00	4.00

213 50 GOURDES
L.1973, etc. Like #204. Prefix letter A.

	VG	VF	UNC
	10.00	17.50	27.50

214 100 GOURDES
L.1973, etc. Like #205. W/o prefix letter. 2 serial # varieties.

	20.00	35.00	70.00

TWELFTH ISSUE
Lois des 21 Mai 1935 et 15 Mai 1953 et au Décret du 22 Novembre 1973
#219-229 held in reserve.

218 **25 GOURDES**
L.1973, etc. Dk. blue, and brown-violet on m/c unpt. Pres. Jean-Claude Duvalier at l., antenna at r. Prefix letters DA-DD. National Palace on back. Printer: TDLR.

	VG	VF	UNC
	3.00	7.50	15.00

BANQUE DE LA RÉPUBLIQUE D'HAITI

1980-82 ISSUE

Loi du 17 Aout 1979

#230-232, 235-238 sign. titles: *LE GOUVERNEUR, LE GOUVERNEUR ADJOINT* and *LE DIRECTEUR.* Arms at ctr. on back. Printer: ABNC.

#233 and 234 held in reserve.

230 **1 GOURDE**
L.1979. Like #210. W/ or w/o prefix letter.

	VG	VF	UNC
a. Printed on paper w/planchettes. Smaller size numerals in serial #.	FV	.20	.75
b. Printed on Tyvek. Larger size numerals in serial #.	FV	.50	1.50

231 **2 GOURDES**
L.1979. W/o or w/ prefix letter.

	VG	VF	UNC
a. Printed on paper w/planchettes. Smaller size numerals in serial #.	FV	.50	1.50
b. Printed on Tyvek. Larger size numerals in serial #.	FV	.75	2.00

232 **5 GOURDES**
L.1979. Like #212. Prefix letters A-T, AA-.

	FV	1.00	3.00

235 **50 GOURDES**
L.1979. Like #213.

	VG	VF	UNC
a. Printed on dull white paper w/ w/planchettes. W/o prefix letter or letter A; B; G.	FV	12.00	25.00
b. Printed on Tyvek. Prefix letter C. Wmk: American bald eagle symbol of ABNC.	FV	12.00	27.50
c. Printed on Tyvek but w/o wmk. Prefix letter D; F.	FV	12.00	25.00

236 **100 GOURDES**
L.1979. Like #205.

	VG	VF	UNC
a. Printed on paper w/planchettes Prefix letters A; B.	FV	16.00	40.00
b. Printed on Tyvek. Prefix letter C; D.	FV	16.00	40.00

237 **250 GOURDES**
L.1979. Similar to #206. Printed on Tyvek.

	FV	45.00	100.00

238 **500 GOURDES**
L.1979. Similar to #207. Printed on Tyvek.

	FV	90.00	200.00

1984-85 ISSUE

#239-240 arms at ctr. on back. Printer: TDLR.

#241-243 sign. title at r: *LE DIRECTEUR GENERAL.* Arms at ctr. on back.

#244 *Deleted.* See #240.

239 **1 GOURDE**
L.1979 (1984). Brown. Like #196. Double prefix letters. Sign. titles like #230.

	VG	VF	UNC
	FV	.20	.60

240 **2 GOURDES**
L.1979 (1985). Similar to #191.

	VG	VF	UNC
a. Sign. titles like #239.	FV	.50	1.50
b. Sign. titles like #241.	FV	.35	1.25

241 **5 GOURDES**
L.1979 (1985). Orange on m/c unpt. Portr. Pres. Jean-Claude Duvalier at l. Arms at ctr. on back. Printer: G&D.

	VG	VF	UNC
	FV	1.00	4.00

242 **10 GOURDES**
L.1979 (1984). Similar to #203, but portr. Jean-Claude Duvalier at ctr. Printer: ABNC.

	VG	VF	UNC
	FV	2.00	6.00

243   25 GOURDES
L.1979 (1985). Blue-violet on pink and m/c unpt. Like #241. Printer: G&D.

	VG	VF	UNC
	FV	4.50	15.00

1986-88 ISSUE
#245-252 sign. title at r: *LE DIRECTEUR GENERAL*. Arms at ctr. on back.

245   1 GOURDE
1987. Dk. brown and brown-black on m/c unpt. Toussaint L'Oouerture at ctr. Printer: G&D.

	VG	VF	UNC
	FV	FV	.50

246   5 GOURDES
1987. Orange and brown on m/c unpt. Statue of Combat de Vertiéres at upper ctr. Wmk: Palm tree. Printer: G&D.

	VG	VF	UNC
	FV	FV	2.50

247   10 GOURDES
1988. Green, red and blue on m/c unpt. Catherine Flon Arcahaie seated sewing the first flag of the Republic at r. Back green. Printer: ABNC.

	VG	VF	UNC
	FV	FV	4.50

248   25 GOURDES
1988. Purple and dk. blue on m/c unpt. Palace of Justice at ctr. Wmk: Palm tree. Printer: G&D.

	VG	VF	UNC
	FV	FV	9.00

249   50 GOURDES
1986. Green and m/c. Design and sign. titles like #235. Printer: ABNC.

	VG	VF	UNC
	FV	FV	30.00

250   100 GOURDES
1986. Similar to #236 but printer: TDLR.

	VG	VF	UNC
	FV	FV	45.00

251   250 GOURDES
1988. Tan on m/c unpt. Similar to #237. Printer: ABNC.

	VG	VF	UNC
	FV	FV	80.00

252   500 GOURDES
1988. Red. Pres. A. Pétion at r. Printer: ABNC.

	VG	VF	UNC
	FV	FV	150.00

1989-91 ISSUE
#253-255 arms at ctr. on back. Printer: USBC.

#256-258 legal clause on face and back w/o reference to the United States. Arms at ctr. on back. Wmk: Palm tree. Printer: G&D.

253   1 GOURDE
1989. Dk. brown and brown-black on m/c unpt. Toussaint L'Ouverture w/short hair at ctr.

	VG	VF	UNC
	FV	FV	.60

254   2 GOURDES
    1990. Blue-black on m/c unpt. Citadel rampart. Shortened legal clause
    w/o reference to United States on face and back.

	VG	VF	UNC
	FV	2.00	10.00

255   5 GOURDES
    1989. Orange and brown on m/c unpt. Like #246. Wmk: Palm tree.

	VG	VF	UNC
	FV	FV	1.75

256   10 GOURDES
    1991. Green, red and blue on m/c unpt. Similar to #247.

	VG	VF	UNC
	FV	FV	4.00

257   50 GOURDES
    1991. Dk. olive-green and black-green on m/c unpt. Portr. Pres. L. F.
    Salomon Jeune at ctr.

	VG	VF	UNC
	FV	FV	10.00

258   100 GOURDES
    1991. Purple on m/c unpt. Portr. H. Christophe at l.

	VG	VF	UNC
	FV	FV	20.00

1992-94 ISSUE

#259-261 printer: TDLR.

#259-263 w/o laws. Shortened clause on face and back: *CE BILLET EST EMIS CONFORMEMENT... Arms at
    ctr. on back.*

259   1 GOURDE
    1992. Like #245.

	VG	VF	UNC
	FV	FV	.35

260   2 GOURDES
    1992. Like #254.

	VG	VF	UNC
	FV	FV	.75

261   5 GOURDES
    1992. Like #246.

	VG	VF	UNC
	FV	FV	1.50

262   250 GOURDES
    1994. Olive-brown and dk. brown on m/c unpt. Portr. J. J. Dessalines
    at l.

	VG	VF	UNC
	FV	FV	33.50

263   500 GOURDES
    1993. Violet on m/c unpt. Portr. Pres. Pétion at l.

	VG	VF	UNC
	FV	FV	60.00

The Republic of Honduras, situated in Central America between Nicaragua and Guatemala, has an area of 43,277 sq. mi. (112,088 sq. km.) and a population of 5.1 million. Capital: Tegucigalpa. Agriculture, mining (gold and silver), and logging are the chief industries. Bananas, timber and coffee are exported.

Honduras, a site of the ancient Mayan Empire, was claimed for Spain by Columbus in 1502, during his last voyage to the Americas. The first settlement was made by Cristobal de Olid under orders of Hernan Cortes, then in Mexico. The area, regarded as one of the most promising sources of gold and silver in the new world, was a part of the Captaincy General of Guatemala throughout the colonial period. After declaring its independence from Spain, in 1821, Honduras fell briefly to the Mexican empire of Agustin de Iturbide, and then joined the Central American Federation (1823-39). Upon dissolution of the federation, Honduras became an independent republic.

MONETARY SYSTEM:
 l Peso = 100 Centavos, 1871-1926
 1 Lempira = 100 Centavos, 1926-

RÉPUBLICA DE HONDURAS

BANCO CENTRAL DE HONDURAS
Established 1950 by merger of Banco Atlantida and Banco de Honduras. Various date and sign. varieties.

1950-51 ISSUE

		VG	VF	UNC
49	**100 LEMPIRAS**			
	1951-72. Yellow on m/c unpt. Valle at l., arms at r. Village and bridge on back.			
	a. W/o security thread, lilac-pink unpt. Printer: W&S. 16.3.1951; 8.3.1957.	85.00	225.00	—
	b. W/o security thread, w/fibers at r. ctr., lt. green and lt. orange unpt. Printer: W&S. 5.2.1964; 22.3.1968; 10.12.1969.	65.00	150.00	—
	c. W/security thread, yellow unpt. 13.10.1972; 23.3.1973.	55.00	125.00	225.00
	s. Specimen, punched hole cancelled.	—	—	200.00

1953-56 ISSUE

		VG	VF	UNC
50	**1 LEMPIRA**			
	10.2.1961; 30.7.1965. Red on m/c unpt. Lempira at l., modified design of #45 w/black serial #. Dios del Maiz/Idolo Maya and Mayan artifacts on back. 2 sign. varieties. Printer: TDLR.	1.00	4.00	15.00

		VG	VF	UNC
51	**5 LEMPIRAS**			
	1953-67. Gray on m/c unpt. Morazan at l., arms at r. Serial # at upper l. and upper r. Battle of Trinidad on back. Printer: ABNC.			
	a. Date horizontal. 17.3.1953; 19.3.1954; 7.5.1954.	6.00	27.50	100.00
	b. As a. 21.2.1958-7.1.1966.	4.00	20.00	75.00
	c. Date vertical. 15.4.1966; 29.9.1967; 22.3.1968.	3.50	17.50	60.00

		VG	VF	UNC
52	**10 LEMPIRAS**			
	1954-70. Brown on m/c unpt. Cabanas at l., arms at r. Old bank on back. Date and sign. Style varieties. Printer: TDLR.			
	a. R. sign. title: *MINISTRO DE HACIENDA...* 19.11.1954.	15.00	60.00	125.00
	b. R. sign. title: *MINISTRO DE ECONOMIA...* 19.2.1960-10.1.1969.	10.00	25.00	75.00

		VG	VF	UNC
53	**20 LEMPIRAS**			
	1954-72. Green. D. Herrera at l., arms at r. Waterfalls on back. Printer: TDLR.			
	a. 4.6.1954; 6.3.1959.	21.50	52.50	175.00
	b. 27.4.1962-6.3.1964.	18.00	45.00	150.00
	c. 7.1.1966-18.2.1972.	15.00	37.50	125.00

1968-70 ISSUE

		VG	VF	UNC
55	**1 LEMPIRA**			
	1968-72. Red on green and pink unpt. Lempira at l., design different from #50 and 45. *Rinas de Copan Juego de Pelota* on back. Printer: TDLR.			
	a. R. sign. title: *MINISTRO DE ECONOMIA...* 25.10.1968.	.80	2.50	8.00
	b. R. sign. title: *MINISTRO DE HACIENDA...* 21.1.1972.	.75	1.00	3.50

		VG	VF	UNC
56	**5 LEMPIRAS**			
	1968-74. Gray on m/c unpt. Like #51. Serial # at lower l. and upper r. Printer: ABNC.			
	a. Date horizontal. 29.11.1968; 11.4.1969.	3.00	15.00	55.00
	b. Date vertical. 11.4.1969-24.8.1974.	2.50	8.00	30.00

57 **10 LEMPIRAS**
18.12.1970-13.11.1975. Brown on m/c unpt. Cabanas at l., arms at r.
Ruins and new bank on back. Printer: ABNC.

VG	VF	UNC
3.50	12.50	35.00

1973-74 ISSUE

58 **1 LEMPIRA**
11.3.1974. Red on green and lilac unpt. Lempira w/o feather at l.,
arms at r. Different view of Ruinas de Copan on back. Printer: TDLR.

VG	VF	UNC
.50	.70	1.50

59 **5 LEMPIRAS**
1974-78. Gray on m/c unpt. Morazan at l., arms at r. Battle of Trinidad
at l. on back. Printer: ABNC.
  a. Date vertical. 24.10.1974.
  b. Date horizontal. 12.12.1975-13.2.1978.

	VG	VF	UNC
a.	2.50	7.50	27.50
b.	2.00	4.00	18.00

60 **20 LEMPIRAS**
2.3.1973-3.6.1977. Green on m/c unpt. D. Herrera at l., arms at r.
Presidential residence on back. Date placement varieties. Printer:
TDLR.

VG	VF	UNC
8.50	25.00	75.00

1976 COMMEMORATIVE ISSUE

61 **2 LEMPIRAS**
23.9.1976. Purple on m/c unpt. Arms at l., M. A. Soto at r. Island and
Port of Amapala on back. Printer: TDLR.

VG	VF	UNC
FV	.60	2.00

1975-78 REGULAR ISSUE

62 **1 LEMPIRA**
30.6.1978. Red. Like #58 but Indian symbols added below bank name
on back. Printer: TDLR.

VG	VF	UNC
FV	.35	1.50

63 **5 LEMPIRAS**
1978-. Black, dk. blue, and deep green on m/c unpt. Arms at l.,
Morazan at r. Battle of Trinidad Nov. 11, 1827 on back. Printer: TDLR.
  a. 4.10.1978; 8.5.1980.
  b. 8.12.1985; 30.3.1989.
  c. Red serial # at upper l. in ascending size. 14.1.1993.

	VG	VF	UNC
a.	FV	1.25	3.50
b.	FV	1.00	2.50
c.	FV	FV	1.75

64 **10 LEMPIRAS**
1976-89. Brown on m/c unpt. Cabanas at l. Scene of City University
on back. Printer: ABNC.
  a. 18.3.1976-10.5.1979.
  b. 8.9.1983; 5.10.1989.

	VG	VF	UNC
a.	FV	2.50	6.50
b.	FV	2.00	5.50

65 **20 LEMPIRAS**
1978-93. Deep green on m/c unpt. D. de Herrera at r. Port of Cortes
on back. Date placement varieties. Printer: ABNC.
  a. 2.11.1978.
  b. Vertical date at r. 23.6.1982; 5.1.1984; 9.4.1987.
  c. Horizontal date at upper l. 5.10.1989; 24.1.1991; 9.5.1991;
    29.8.1991.
  d. 10.12.1992; 1.7.1993.

	VG	VF	UNC
a.	FV	5.00	10.00
b.	FV	4.00	8.50
c.	FV	3.50	7.00
d.	FV	FV	5.50

66 **50 LEMPIRAS**
29.1.1976-1.7.1993. Deep blue on m/c unpt. J. M. Galvez D. at l.
National Development Bank on back. Wmk: tree. Printer: ABNC
  a. Vertcal date at r. 29.1.1976-10.9.1979.
  b. 3.7.1986-24.9.1987; 10.11.1989.
  c. Horizontal date at upper l. 13.12.1990-29.8.1991.
  d. 18.3.1993; 1.7.1993.

	VG	VF	UNC
a.	FV	12.50	20.00
b.	FV	8.00	16.50
c.	FV	7.00	13.50
d.	FV	FV	9.00

67 **100 LEMPIRAS**
16.1.1975; 29.1.1976; 18.3.1976; 13.1.1977; 12.1.1978; 10.9.1979.
Brown-orange on m/c unpt. Valle at l. Signatepeque school of forestry
on back. Printer: TDLR.

VG	VF	UNC
FV	20.00	45.00

1980-81 ISSUE

			VG	VF	UNC
68	**1 LEMPIRA**				
	1980; 1984; 1989. Red on m/c unpt. Arms at l., Lempira at r. Ruins of Copan on back. Printer: TDLR.				
	a.	W/o security thread. 29.5.1980; 16.10.1984.	FV	.30	1.00
	b.	W/security thread. 30.3.1989.	FV	FV	.75

			VG	VF	UNC
69	**100 LEMPIRAS**				
	1981-93. Brown-orange, dk. olive-green, and dp. purple m/c unpt. Valle at r. and as wmk. Different view of forestry school on back. Printer: TDLR.				
	a.	Regular serial #. 8.1.1981; 23.6.1982; 8.9.1983.	FV	15.00	28.50
	b.	3.7.1986; 10.12.1987; 21.12.1989.	FV	12.50	25.00
	c.	13.12.1989-12.5.1994.	FV	FV	22.50

1989 ISSUE

		VG	VF	UNC
70	**10 LEMPIRAS**			
	21.9.1989. Dk. brown and red on m/c unpt. Arms at l. Cabanas at r. City University on back. Printer: TDLR.	FV	1.50	3.75

1992-93 ISSUE
#72-75 printer: TDLR.

			VG	VF	UNC
71	**1 LEMPIRA**				
	10.9.1992. Dk. red on m/c unpt. Similar to #47a but back in paler colors. Printer: CBNC.		FV	FV	.65
72	**2 LEMPIRA**				
	14.1.1993; 25.2.1993. Like #61 but w/lt. blue unpt. at l. Serial # at upper l. in ascending size.		FV	FV	1.00

		VG	VF	UNC
73	**20 LEMPIRAS**			
	14.1.1993 (1994); 25.2.1993 (1995); 12.5.1994. Deep green and dk. brown on m/c unpt. D. de Herrera at r. and as wmk. Back vertical, Presidential House at ctr. Wmk: tree.	FV	FV	5.00

			VG	VF	UNC
74	**50 LEMPIRAS**				
	14.1.1993 (1994); 25.2.1993 (1995); 12.5.1994. Blue-black and dk. brown on m/c unpt. J. M. Galvez D. at r. and as wmk. Back vertical, Central Bank Annex at ctr.		FV	FV	11.00
75	**100 LEMPIRAS**				
	1993-94. Like #69 but w/engraved date. Serial # at upper l. in ascending size. Enchanced unpt. in wmk. area on back.				
	a.	Black sign. Red serial #. 14.1.1993.	FV	FV	20.00
	b.	Dk. brown sign. Brown serial #. 12.5.1994.	FV	FV	18.50
76	**500 LEMPIRAS**				
	(1996).				Expected New Issue

1994 ISSUE

		VG	VF	UNC
77	**1 LEMPIRA**			
	Like #71 but printer: TDLR.	FV	FV	.50

HONG KONG

Hong Kong, a British colony situated at the mouth of the Canton or Pearl River 90 miles (145 km.) southeast of Canton, has an area of 409 sq. mi. (1,045 sq. km.) and a population of 5.6 million. Capital: Victoria. The free port of Hong Kong, the commercial center of the Far East, is a transshipment point for goods destined for China and the countries of the Western Pacific. Light manufacturing and tourism are important components of the economy.

Long a haven for fishermen-pirates and opium smugglers, the island of Hong Kong was ceded to Britain at the conclusion of the first Opium War (1839-1842). At the time, the acquisition of "a barren rock" was ridiculed by both London and English merchants operating in the Far East. The Kowloon Peninsula and Stonecutter's Island were ceded in 1860 and the so-called New Territories, comprising most of the mainland of the colony, were leased to Britain for 99 years in 1898. They will return to mainland China's rule on Dec. 20, 1997.

RULERS:
British (1845-1997)

MONETARY SYSTEM:
1 Dollar = 100 Cents

COMMERCIAL BANKS:
Chartered Bank - #68-81
Hong Kong & Shanghai Banking Corporation - #181-205
Mercantile Bank Limited - #244-245
Standard Chartered Bank - #278-289
Government of Hong Kong - #325-327
Bank of China - #329-333

BRITISH INFLUENCE

CHARTERED BANK

行銀打渣[1]

Cha Ta Yin Hang

香港渣打銀行

Hong Kong Cha Ta Yin Hang

Prior to the 1950's was known as The Chartered Bank of India, Australia & China. In the 1980's it became the Standard Bank. Later became the Standard Chartered Bank.

1961; 1967 ND ISSUES

#68-72 wmk: Helmeted warrior's head. Printer: TDLR.

		VG	VF	UNC
68	**5 DOLLARS**			
	1961-62; ND. Black and green on m/c unpt. Arms at lower l. Chinese junk and sampan at ctr. on back.			
	a. 1.7.1961.	12.00	60.00	300.00
	b. 3.3.1962.	15.00	80.00	400.00
	c. ND (1962-70).	4.00	30.00	150.00

		VG	VF	UNC
69	**5 DOLLARS**			
	ND (1967). Black and yellow-brown on m/c unpt. Like #68.	3.50	25.00	125.00
70	**10 DOLLARS**			
	1961-62; ND. Black and red-violet on red unpt. Arms at l. Chartered Bank bldg. at ctr. on back.			
	a. 1.7.1961; 3.3.1962.	16.50	45.00	225.00
	b. ND (1962-70).	2.50	20.00	100.00

		VG	VF	UNC
71	**100 DOLLARS**			
	1961; ND. Dk. green and brown on m/c unpt. Arms at ctr. Harbor view on back.			
	a. 1.7.1961.	60.00	240.00	1200.
	b. ND (1961-70).	32.00	160.00	800.00

		VG	VF	UNC
72	**500 DOLLARS**			
	1961-77. Black and dk. brown on m/c unpt. Male portr. at l., boat, harbor view at ctr. on back.			
	a. Sign. titles: *ACCOUNTANT* and *MANAGER*. 1.7.1961.	160.00	500.00	2500.
	b. Sign. titles as a. ND (1962-?).	FV	200.00	1000.
	c. Sign. titles: *ACCOUNTANT* and *CHIEF MANAGER IN HONG KONG*. ND (?-1975).	FV	200.00	1000.
	d. Sign. titles as c. 11.1.1977.	FV	160.00	800.00

1970-77 ISSUE

#73-76 bank bldg. at l., bank crest at ctr. Wmk: Helmeted warrior's head. Printer: TDLR.

		VG	VF	UNC
73	**5 DOLLARS**			
	ND (1970-75); 1975. Dk. brown on m/c unpt. City Hall at ctr. r. on back.			
	a. Sign. title: *MANAGER* at r. ND (1970-75).	.85	2.00	10.00
	b. Sign. title: *CHIEF MANAGER IN HONG KONG* at r. ND; 1.6.1975.	1.25	2.75	13.50

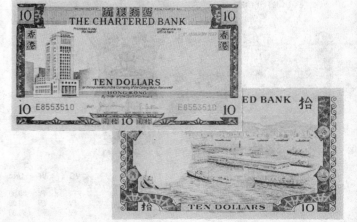

74	**10 DOLLARS**	VG	VF	UNC
	ND; 1975; 1977. Dk. green on m/c unpt. Ocean terminal at ctr. r.			
	a. Sign. titles: *ACCOUNTANT* and *MANAGER.* ND (1970-75).	FV	5.00	25.00
	b. Sign. titles: *ACCOUNTANT* and *CHIEF MANAGER IN HONG KONG.* ND; 1.6.1975.	FV	4.00	20.00
	c. Sign. titles as b. 1.1.1977.	FV	2.50	10.00

75	**50 DOLLARS**	VG	VF	UNC
	ND (1970-75). Blue on m/c unpt. City Hall at ctr. r. on back.	FV	70.00	350.00

76	**100 DOLLARS**			
	ND; 1977. Red on m/c unpt.			
	a. ND (1970-75).	FV	50.00	250.00
	b. 1.1.1977.	FV	40.00	200.00

1979-80 ISSUE
#77-81 bank bldg. at l., arms at ctr. on back. Wmk: Helmeted warrior's head. Printer: TDLR (w/o imprint).

77	**10 DOLLARS**	VG	VF	UNC
	1.1.1980; 1.1.1981. Green. Stylistic carp at r.	FV	FV	8.00

78	**50 DOLLARS**	VG	VF	UNC
	1979-82. Blue on m/c unpt. Chinze at r.			
	a. 1.1.1979.	FV	FV	80.00
	b. 1.1.1981; 1.1.1982.	FV	FV	50.00

79	**100 DOLLARS**	VG	VF	UNC
	1979-82. Red on m/c unpt. Mythical horse *Qilin* at r.			
	a. 1.1.1979.	FV	FV	80.00
	b. 1.1.1980.	FV	FV	60.00
	c. 1.1.1982.	FV	FV	50.00

80	**500 DOLLARS**	VG	VF	UNC
	1979; 1982. Brown on m/c unpt. Mythical phoenix at r.			
	a. 1.1.1979.	FV	FV	150.00
	b. 1.1.1982.	FV	FV	120.00

81	**1000 DOLLARS**	VG	VF	UNC
	1979; 1982. Yellow-orange on m/c unpt. Dragon at r.			
	a. 1.1.1979.	FV	FV	350.00
	b. 1.1.1982.	FV	FV	225.00

HONG KONG & SHANGHAI BANKING CORPORATION

行銀理滙海上港香

Hsiang K'ang Shang Hai Hui Li Yin Hang

Formerly The Hong Kong and Shanghai Banking Company, Limited. Hong Kong Branch

1932-35 ISSUE

179 500 DOLLARS

1935-69. Brown and blue. Arms at top ctr., Sir T. Jackson at r. Back blue; allegorical female head at l., bank bldg. at ctr.

	VG	VF	UNC
a. Handsigned. 1.6.1935-1.7.1937.	250.00	700.00	2850.
b. Printed sign. 1.4.1941-1.8.1952.	170.00	275.00	850.00
c. 11.7.1960-1.8.1966.	FV	250.00	750.00
d. 31.7.1967.	FV	225.00	650.00
e. 11.2.1968; 27.3.1969.	FV	135.00	350.00

1959 ISSUE

181 5 DOLLARS
(C21)

1959-75. Brown. Similar to #173 and 180 but smaller size. New bank bldg. at ctr. on back.

	VG	VF	UNC
a. Sign. titles: *CHIEF ACCOUNTANT* and *CHIEF MANAGER.* 2.5.1959-29.6.1960.	1.75	7.00	35.00
b. 1.5.1963.	5.50	27.50	140.00
c. 1.5.1964-27.3.1969.	1.50	4.00	18.00
d. Sign. titles: *CHIEF ACCOUNTANT* and *GENERAL MANAGER.* 1.4.1970-18.3.1971.	.60	2.25	12.00
e. 13.3.1972; 31.10.1972.	.50	1.40	7.00
f. Sm. serial #. 31.10.1973; 31.3.1975.	FV	1.00	5.00

182 10 DOLLARS

1959-83. Dk. green on m/c unpt. Woman w/sheaf of grain at upper l., arms below. Back similar to #184.

	VG	VF	UNC
a. Sign. titles: *CHIEF ACCOUNTANT* and *CHIEF MANAGER.* 21.5.1959-12.2.1960.	FV	7.00	35.00
b. 1.5.1963; 1.9.1963.	1.85	10.00	50.00
c. 1.5.1964; 1.9.1964.	FV	7.00	35.00
d. 1.10.1964.	8.00	40.00	200.00
e. 1.2.1965; 1.8.1966; 31.7.1967.	FV	5.00	25.00
f. 20.3.1968; 23.11.1968; 27.3.1969; 18.3.1971.	FV	3.00	15.00
g. Sign. titles: *CHIEF ACCOUNTANT* and *GENERAL MANAGER.* 1.4.1970-31.3.1977.	FV	2.00	10.00
h. Sign. titles: *CHIEF ACCOUNTANT* and *EXECUTIVE DIRECTOR.* 31.3.1978; 31.3.1979.	FV	2.00	10.00
i. Sign. titles: *CHIEF ACCOUNTANT* and *GENERAL MANAGER.* 31.3.1980; 31.3.1981.	FV	FV	6.00
j. Sign. titles: *MANAGER* and *GENERAL MANAGER.* 31.3.1982; 31.3.1983.	FV	FV	6.00

183 100 DOLLARS

1959-72. Red on m/c unpt. Woman seated at l. w/open book, arms at upper ctr. Wmk: Helmeted warrior's head and denomination.

	VG	VF	UNC
a. Sign. titles: *CHIEF ACCOUNTANT* and *CHIEF MANAGER.* 21.8.1959-1.10.1964.	18.00	50.00	250.00
b. 1.2.1965-27.3.1969.	14.00	40.00	200.00
c. Sign. titles: *CHIEF ACCOUNTANT* and *GENERAL MANAGER.* 1.4.1970; 18.3.1971; 13.3.1972.	14.00	33.50	170.00

1968-73 ISSUE
#184-186 printer: BWC.

184 50 DOLLARS

1968-83. Dk. blue on m/c unpt. Arms at r. New bank bldg. at l. ctr. on back. Wmk: Helmeted warriors head and denomination.

	VG	VF	UNC
a. Sign. titles: *CHIEF ACCOUNTANT* and *CHIEF MANAGER.* 31.5.1968; 27.3.1969.	FV	15.00	75.00
b. Sign. titles: *CHIEF ACCOUNTANT* and *GENERAL MANAGER.* 31.10.1973; 31.3.1975; 31.3.1978.	FV	13.50	5.00
c. Sign. titles as b. 31.3.1977.	FV	17.50	85.00
d. Sign. titles: *CHIEF ACCOUNTANT* and *EXECUTIVE DIRECTOR.* 31.3.1979.	FV	18.00	90.00
e. Sign. titles: *CHIEF ACCOUNTANT* and *GENERAL MANAGER.* 31.3.1980.	FV	FV	25.00
f. 31.3.1981.	FV	FV	22.50
g. Sign. titles: *MANAGER* and *GENERAL MANAGER.* 31.3.1982; 31.3.1983.	FV	FV	20.00

185 100 DOLLARS
(186)

1972-76. Red on m/c unpt. Arms at l. Facing lions at lower l. and r.; bank bldg. at ctr., dragon in medallion at r.

	VG	VF	UNC
a. W/4 lg. serial # on back. 13.3 3.3.1972; 31.10.1972.	FV	32.50	160.00
b. Smaller electronic sorting ser serial # on face. W/o serial # on back. 31.10.1972.	FV	40.00	200.00
c. 31.10.1973.	FV	18.50	80.00
d. 31.3.1975; 31.3.1976.	FV	17.50	75.00

186 500 DOLLARS
(188)

31.10.1973; 31.3.1975; 31.3.1976. Brown on m/c unpt. Arms at l. Bank bldg. at l., lion's head at r. on back.

	VG	VF	UNC
	FV	FV	250.00

1977; 1978 ISSUE

#187, 189 and 190 wmk: Lion's head. Printer: BWC.

#188 *Deleted.* See #186.

187	100 DOLLARS	VG	VF	UNC
	1977-83. Red on lighter m/c unpt. Similar to #186.			
	a. Sign. titles: *CHIEF ACCOUNTANT* and *EXECUTIVE DIRECTOR.* 31.3.1977; 31.3.1978.	FV	16.00	80.00
	b. Sign. titles as a. 31.3.1979; 9; 31.3.1980; 31.3.1981.	FV	FV	40.00
	c. Sign. titles: *MANAGER* a and *GENERAL MANAGER.* 31.3.1982; 31.3.1983.	FV	FV	30.00
189	500 DOLLARS			
	1978-83. Brown and black on m/c unpt. Similar to #188 but w/modified frame designs.			
	a. 31.3.1978; 31.3.1980; 31.3.198 1981.	FV	FV	200.00
	b. 31.3.1982; 31.3.1983.	FV	FV	150.00

190	1000 DOLLARS	VG	VF	UNC
	1977-83. Gold and black on m/c unpt. Arms at r. Lion at l., bank bldg. at ctr. r. on back.			
	a. 31.3.1977.	FV	FV	300.00
	b. 31.3.1979; 31.3.1980; 31.3.198 1981; 31.3.1983.	FV	FV	225.00

1985-87 ISSUE

#191-196 arms at l. Facing lions at lower l. and r. w/new bank bldg. at ctr. on back. Sign. varieties. Wmk: Lion's head. Printer: TDLR.

191	10 DOLLARS	VG	VF	UNC
	1985-92. Deep green on m/c unpt. Sampan and ship at r. at r. on back.			
	a. Sign. title: *GENERAL MANAGER.* 1.1.1985; 1.1.1986; 1.1.1987.	FV	FV	4.50
	b. Sign. title: *EXECUTIVE DIRECTOR.* 1.1.1988.	FV	FV	4.00
	c. Sign. title: *GENERAL MANAGER.* 1.1.1989; 1.1.1990; 1.1.1992.	FV	FV	3.50

192	20 DOLLARS	VG	VF	UNC
	1986-89. Deep gray-green and brown on m/c unpt. Clock tower, ferry in harbor view at r. on back.			
	a. Sign. title: *GENERAL MANAGER.* 1.1.1986; 1.1.1987.	FV	FV	8.50
	b. Sign. title: *EXECUTIVE DIRECTOR.* 1.1.1988.	FV	FV	7.50
	c. Sign. title: *GENERAL MANAGER.* 1.1.1989.	FV	FV	6.50

193	50 DOLLARS	VG	VF	UNC
	1985-92. Violet on m/c unpt. Men in boats at r. on back.			
	a. Sign. title: *GENERAL MANAGER.* 1.1.1985; 1.1.1986; 1.1.1987.	FV	FV	17.50
	b. Sign. title: *EXECUTIVE DIRECTOR.* 1.1.1988.	FV	FV	15.00
	c. Sign. title: *GENERAL MANAGER.* 1.1.1989; 1.1.1989; 1.1.1991; 1.1.1992.	FV	FV	12.50
194	100 DOLLARS			
	1985-88. Red on m/c unpt. Tiger Balm Garden pagoda at r.			
	a. Sign. title: *GENERAL MANAGER.* 1.1.1985; 1.1.1986; 1.1.1987.	FV	FV	27.50
	b. Sign. title: *EXECUTIVE DIRECTOR.* 1.1.1988.	FV	FV	25.00

		VG	VF	UNC
195	**500 DOLLARS**			
	1987-92. Brown on m/c unpt. Old tower at r. on back.			
	a. Sign. title: *GENERAL MANAGER*. 1.1.1987.	FV	FV	100.00
	b. Sign. title: *EXECUTIVE DIRECTOR*. 1.1.1988.	FV	FV	95.00
	c. Sign. title: *GENERAL MANAGER*. 1.1.1989; 1.1.1990; 1.1.1991; 1.1.1992.	FV	FV	90.00
196	**1000 DOLLARS**			
	1.1.1985; 1.1.1986; 1.1.1987. Red, brown and orange on m/c unpt. Old Supreme Court bldg. at r. on back.	FV	FV	175.00

1988-90 ISSUE

		VG	VF	UNC
197	**20 DOLLARS**			
	1.1.1990; 1.1.1991; 1.1.1992. Like #192 but gray on orange, pink and m/c unpt. Sign. title: *GENERAL MANAGER*.	FV	FV	6.00
198	**100 DOLLARS**			
	1.1.1989; 1.1.1990; 1.1.1991; 1.1.1992. Similar to #194 Sign. title: *GENERAL MANAGER*. Back red and black on m/c unpt.	FV	FV	22.50
199	**1000 DOLLARS**			
	1988-1991. Similar to #196. Back orange, brown and olive-brown on m/c unpt.			
	a. Sign. title: *EXECUTIVE DIRECTOR*. 1.1.1988.	FV	FV	175.00
	b. Sign title: *GENERAL MANAGER*. 1.1.1989; 1.1.1990; 1.1.1991.	FV	FV	170.00

1993; 1995 ISSUE

#201-205 lion's head at l. and as wmk., city view in unpt. at ctr. New bank bldg. at ctr. between facing lions on back. Sign. title: *EXECUTIVE DIRECTOR*. Printer: TDLR.

#200 Held in Reserve.

Replacement notes: Serial # prefix *ZZ*.

		VG	VF	UNC
201	**20 DOLLARS**			
	1.1.1993; 1.1.1994; 1.1.1995. Gray on m/c unpt.	FV	FV	5.00

		VG	VF	UNC
202	**50 DOLLARS**			
	1.1.1993; 1.1.1994; 1.1.1995. Purple and violet on m/c unpt.	FV	FV	11.00

		VG	VF	UNC
203	**100 DOLLARS**			
	1.1.1993; 1.1.1994; 1.1.1995. Red, orange and black on m/c unpt. Ten Thousand Buddha Pagoda at Shatin at r. on back.	FV	FV	20.00
204	**500 DOLLARS**			
	1.1.1993; 1.1.1994; 1.1.1995. Brown and red-orange on m/c unpt. Government house at upper r. on back.	FV	FV	85.00
205	**1000 DOLLARS**			
	1.1.1993; 1.1.1994; 1.1.1995. Orange, red-brown and olive-green on pink and m/c unpt. Legislative Council bldg. at r. on back.	FV	FV	165.00

MERCANTILE BANK LIMITED

行銀利有港香

Hsiang K'ang Yu Li Yin Hang

Formerly The Mercantile Bank of India Limited. In 1978 this bank was absorbed by the Hong Kong & Shanghai Banking Corp. and its note issuing right ended.

1964 ISSUE

244-245 wmk: Dragon. Printer: TDLR.

		VG	VF	UNC
244	**100 DOLLARS**			
	1964-73. Red-brown on m/c unpt. Aerial view of coastline. Woman standing w/pennant and shield at ctr. on back.			
	a. 28.7.1964.	35.00	85.00	500.00
	b. 5.10.1965; 27.7.1968.	15.00	37.50	325.00
	c. 16.4.1970; 1.11.1973.	FV	32.50	275.00

1974 ISSUE

		VG	VF	UNC
245	**100 DOLLARS**			
	4.11.1974. Red, purple and brown on m/c unpt. Woman standing w/pennant and shield at l. Back red on m/c unpt., city view at ctr.	FV	16.50	100.00

STANDARD CHARTERED BANK

香港渣打銀行

Hong Kong Cha Ta Yin Hang

1985; 1988 ISSUE

#278 -283 bank bldg. at l., bank arms at ctr. on back. Sign. titles: *FINANCIAL CONTROLLER* and *AREA GEN-ERAL MANAGER*. Wmk: Helmeted warrior's head.

		VG	VF	UNC
283	**1000 DOLLARS** 1.1.1985-. Yellow-orange on m/c unpt. Similar to #81.	FV	FV	185.00

1993 ISSUE

#284-289 Bauhinia flower blossom replaces bank arms at ctr. on back. Sign. titles: *CHIEF FINANCIAL OF-FICER* and *AREA GENERAL MANAGER*. Wmk: *SCB* above helmeted warrior's head.

		VG	VF	UNC
278	**10 DOLLARS** 1.1.1985. Dk. green on yellow-green unpt. Similar to #77.	FV	FV	3.50

		VG	VF	UNC
279	**20 DOLLARS** 1.1.1985; 1.1.1992. Dk. gray, orange and brown on m/c unpt. Turtle at r.	FV	FV	6.00

		VG	VF	UNC
284	**10 DOLLARS** 1993-. Dk. green on yellow-green unpt. Face like #278.			
	a. Sign. titles: *CHIEF FINANCIAL OFFICER* and *AREA GENERAL MANAGER*. 1.1.1993.	FV	FV	3.50
	b. Sign. titles: *HEAD OF OFFICE* and *GENERAL MANAGER*. 1.1.1994; 1.1.1995.	FV	FV	2.75

		VG	VF	UNC
280	**50 DOLLARS** 1.1.1985-1.1.1992. Purple, violet and dk. gray on m/c unpt. Similar to #78.	FV	FV	13.50

		VG	VF	UNC
285	**20 DOLLARS** 1993-. Dk. gray, orange and brown on m/c unpt. Face like #279.			
	a. Sign. titles: *CHIEF FINANCIAL OFFICER* and *AREA GENERAL MANAGER*. 1.1.1993.	FV	FV	6.00
	b. Sign. titles: *HEAD OF OFFICE* and *GENERAL MANAGER*. 1.1.1994; 1.1.1995.	FV	FV	5.00

		VG	VF	UNC
281	**100 DOLLARS** 1.1.1985-1.1.1992. Red on m/c unpt. Similar to #79.	FV	FV	22.50
282	**500 DOLLARS** 1.1.1988-1.1.1992. Maroon, gray and green on m/c unpt. Similar to #80.	FV	FV	90.00

		VG	VF	UNC
286	**50 DOLLARS** 1993-. Purple, violet and dk. gray on m/c unpt. Face like #280.			
	a. Sign. titles: *CHIEF FINANCIAL OFFICER* and *AREA GENERAL MANAGER*. 1.1.1993.	FV	FV	13.50
	b. Sign. titles: *HEAD OF OFFICE* and *GENERAL MANAGER*. 1.1.1994; 1.1.1995.	FV	FV	12.50

287 100 DOLLARS
1993-. Red and purple on m/c unpt. Face like #281.

		VG	VF	UNC
a.	Sign. titles: *CHIEF FINANCIAL OFFICER* and *AREA GENERAL MANAGER.* 1.1.1993.	FV	FV	23.50
b.	Sign. titles: *HEAD OF OFFICE* and *GENERAL MANAGER.* 1.1.1994; 1.1.1995.	FV	FV	22.50

288 500 DOLLARS
1993-. Brown and blue-green on m/c unpt. Face like #282.

		VG	VF	UNC
a.	Sign. titles: *CHIEF FINANCIAL OFFICER* and *AREA GENERAL MANAGER.* 1.1.1993.	FV	FV	92.50
b.	Sign. titles: *HEAD OF OFFICE* and *GENERAL MANAGER.* 1.1.1994; 1.1.1995.	FV	FV	90.00

289 1000 DOLLARS
1993-. Yellow-orange on m/c unpt. Face like #283.

		VG	VF	UNC
a.	Sign. titles: *CHIEF FINANCIAL OFFICER* and *AREA GENERAL MANAGER.* 1.1.1993.	FV	FV	180.00
b.	Sign. titles: *HEAD OF OFFICE* and *GENERAL MANAGER.* 1.1.1994; 1.1.1995.	FV	FV	175.00

GOVERNMENT OF HONG KONG

府政港香
Hsiang K'ang Cheng Fu

FINANCIAL SECRETARY: SIGNATURE VARIETIES

1	J.J. Cowperthwaite, 1961–71	4	Sir Piers Jacobs, 1986–92
2	C. P. Haddon-Cave, 1971–81	5	Sir Hamish Macleod, 1992–
3	Sir J. H. Bremridge, 1981–86	6	

1952; 1961 (ND) ISSUE

#325-328 Qn. Elizabeth II at r.
#325-327 uniface.

325 1 CENT
ND (1961-). Brown on lt. blue unpt.

		VG	VF	UNC
a.	Sign. 1.	—	.05	.20
b.	Sign. 2.	—	.10	.65
c.	Sign. 3.	.10	.65	3.00
d.	Sign. 4.	—	.05	.20
d.	Sign. 5.	—	FV	.10

326 5 CENTS
ND (1961-65). Green on lilac unpt.

VG	VF	UNC
.20	.50	2.50

327 10 CENTS
ND (1961-65). Red on grayish unpt.

VG	VF	UNC
.15	.35	1.50

BANK OF CHINA

中國銀行
Chung Kuo Yin Hang

HONG KONG BRANCH

1994 ISSUE

#329-333 Bank of China Tower at l. Wmk: Stone lion statue. Printer: TDLR (HK) Ltd. (W/o imprint).

329 20 DOLLARS
1.5.1994; 1.1.1996. Blue-black, blue and violet on m/c unpt. Narcissus flowers at lower ctr. r. Aerial view of Wanchai and Central Hong Kong at ctr. r. on back.

VG	VF	UNC
FV	FV	4.50

330 50 DOLLARS
1.5.1994; 1.1.1996. Purple and blue on violet and m/c unpt. Chrysanthemum flowers at lower ctr. r. Aerial view of cross-harbor tunnel at ctr. r. on back.

VG	VF	UNC
FV	FV	10.00

331 100 DOLLARS   VG   VF   UNC
1.5.1994; 1.1.1996. Red-violet, orange and red on m/c unpt. Lotus   FV   FV   18.00
flowers at lower ctr. r. Aerial view of Tsimshatsui, Kowloon Peninsula
at ctr. r. on back.

332 500 DOLLARS   VG   VF   UNC
1.5.1994; 1.1.1996. Dk. brown and blue on m/c unpt. Peony flowers at   FV   FV   80.00
lower ctr. r. Hong Kong Container Terminal in Kwai Chung at ctr. r. on
back.

333 1000 DOLLARS   VG   VF   UNC
1.5.1994; 1.1.1996. Reddish brown, orange and pale olive-green on   FV   FV   155.00
m/c unpt. Bauhinia flowers at lower ctr. r. Aerial view overlooking the
Central district at ctr. r. on back.

HUNGARY

The Hungarian Republic, located in central Europe, has an area of 35,919 sq. mi. (93,030 sq. km.) and a population of 10.3 million. Capital: Budapest. The economy is based on agriculture and a rapidly expanding industrial sector. Machinery, chemicals, iron and steel, and fruits and vegetables are exported.

The ancient kingdom of Hungary, founded by the Magyars in the 9th century, expanded its greatest power and authority in the mid-14th century. After suffering repeated Turkish invasions, Hungary accepted Habsburg rule to escape Turkish occupation, regaining independence in 1867 with the Emperor of Austria as king of a dual Austro-Hungarian Empire. Sharing the defeat of the Central Powers in World War I, Hungary lost the greater part of its territory and population and underwent a period of drastic political revision. The short-lived republic of 1918 was followed by a chaotic interval of communist rule, 1919, and the restoration of the monarchy in 1920 with Admiral Horthy as regent of a kingdom without a king. Although a German ally in World War II, Hungary was occupied by German troops who imposed a pro-Nazi dictatorship, 1944. Soviet armies drove out the Germans in 1945 and assisted the communist minority in seizing power. A revised constitution published on Aug. 20, 1949, had established Hungary as a "People's Republic" of the Soviet type, but it is once again a republic as of Oct. 23, 1989.

RULERS:
Austrian to 1918

MONETARY SYSTEM:
1 Korona = 100 Fillér to 1926
1 Pengö = 100 Fillér to 1946
1 Milpengö = 1 Million Pengö
1 B(illió) Pengö = 1 Billion Pengö
1 Adopengö = 1 Tax Pengö
1 Forint = 100 Fillér 1946-
1 Forint (florin) = 60 Krajczar

DENOMINATIONS
Egy = 1   Ötven = 50
Két = Kettö = 2   Száz = 100
Öt = 5   Ezer = 1000
Tíz = 10   Millió = Million
Húsz = 20   Milliárd = 1,000 Million
Huszonöt = 25

These words used separately or in combination give denomination.

REPUBLIC

MAGYAR NEMZETI BANK

HUNGARIAN NATIONAL BANK

1957-83 ISSUE
#168-173 arms of 3-bar shield w/star in grain spray.

168 10 FORINT   VG   VF   UNC
1957-75. Deep olive-green and blue-black on m/c unpt. Value at l.,
portr. S. Petöfi at r. Trees and river, "Birth of (Hungarian) Song" by
János Jankó at ctr. on back.
a. 23.5.1957.   .75   3.00   10.00
b. 24.8.1960.   .50   2.00   7.00
c. 12.10.1962.   .50   1.50   5.00
d. 30.6.1969.   .25   1.00   3.00
e. 28.10.1975.   .10   .35   2.00
s. As d. Specimen w/red ovpt. and perforated: MINTA.   —   —   25.00

169   20 Forint
1957-80. Deep blue on m/c unpt. Value at l., portr. G. Dózsa at r. Nude
penthathlete male Csaba Hegedüs with hammer and wheat at ctr. on
back.

		VG	VF	Unc
a.	23.5.1957.	.75	5.00	20.00
b.	24.8.1960.	2.00	6.00	30.00
c.	12.10.1962.	.75	2.00	7.50
d.	3.9.1965.	.50	1.00	6.00
e.	30.6.1969.	.20	.65	4.00
f.	28.10.1975.	.50	1.00	2.00
g.	30.9.1980.	.25	.50	1.50
s.	As e. Specimen w/red ovpt. and perforated: *MINTA*.	—	—	25.00

170   50 Forint
1965-89. Deep brown and brown on m/c unpt. Value at l., portr.
Prince F. Rákóczi II at r. Battle of the Hungarian insurrectionists
"kuruc" against pro-Austrian soldiers "labanc" scene at ctr. on back.

		VG	VF	Unc
a.	3.9.1965.	1.50	3.00	10.00
b.	30.6.1969.	1.50	2.50	8.00
c.	28.10.1975.	1.50	2.50	5.00
d.	30.9.1980. Serial # prefix D.	FV	FV	3.00
e.	30.9.1989. Serial # prefix H.	FV	FV	25.00
f.	10.11.1983.	FV	FV	2.75
g.	4.11.1986.	FV	FV	2.50
h.	10.1.1989.	FV	FV	1.50

171   100 Forint
1957-89. Violet and deep brown on m/c unpt. Value at l., portr. L.
Kossuth at r. Horse drawn wagon in "Took Refuge from the Storm" by
L. Károly at ctr. on back.

		VG	VF	Unc
a.	23.5.1957.	4.00	8.00	15.00
b.	24.8.1960.	4.00	8.00	15.00
c.	12.10.1962.	2.00	4.00	10.00
d.	24.10.1968.	FV	3.00	10.00
e.	28.10.1975. Serial # varieties.	FV	2.00	8.50
f.	30.9.1980.	FV	FV	6.50
g.	30.10.1984.	FV	FV	4.00
h.	10.1.1989.	FV	FV	2.50
s.	As b. Specimen w/red ovpt. and perforted: *MINTA*.	—	—	25.00

172   500 Forint
1969-80. Purple on m/c unpt. Portr. E. Ady at r. Aerial view of
Budapest and Danube river on back.

		VG	VF	Unc
a.	30.6.1969.	FV	8.00	30.00
b.	28.10.1975.	FV	6.00	20.00
c.	30.9.1980.	FV	4.00	15.00
d.	25.3.1983.	FV	FV	13.50

173   1000 Forint
1983. Deep green on m/c unpt. Portr. B. Bartók at r. Back green on
m/c unpt. Mother nursing baby statue by Medgyessy Ferenc at ctr. on
back.

		VG	VF	Unc
a.	25.3.1983.	FV	FV	30.00
b.	10.11.1983.	FV	FV	25.00

1990; 1992 Issue
#174-177 St. Stephan's Crown over Hungarian Arms replaces 3-bar shield.

174   100 Forint
1992-. Like #171 but w/new arms.

		VG	VF	Unc
a.	15.1.1992.	FV	FV	2.50
b.	16.12.1993.	FV	FV	2.00
c.	20.12.1995.	FV	FV	1.75

175	**500 FORINT**	**VG**	**VF**	**UNC**
	31.7.1990. Like #172 but w/new arms.	FV	FV	8.50
176	**1000 FORINT**			
	1992; 1993. Like #173 but w/new arms.			
	a. 30.10.1992.	FV	FV	16.50
	b. 16.12.1993.	FV	FV	15.00
	c. 31.8.1995.	FV	FV	13.50
	d. 15.1.1996.	FV	FV	11.50

177	**5000 FORINT**	**VG**	**VF**	**UNC**
	1990-93. Deep brown and brown on orange and m/c unpt. Portr. I. Széchenyi at r. Academy of Science at ctr. on back.			
	a. 31.7.1990.	FV	FV	70.00
	b. 30.10.1992.	FV	FV	60.00
	c. 16.12.1993.	FV	FV	50.00
	d. 31.8.1995.	FV	FV	45.00

1997 ISSUE

178	**100 FORINT**	**VG**	**VF**	**UNC**
	1997. L. Kossuth.		Expected New Issue	
179	**200 FORINT**			
	1997. K. Róbert.		Expected New Issue	
180	**500 FORINT**			
	1997. F. Rákó II.		Expected New Issue	
181	**1000 FORINT**			
	1997. Kg. Mátyas.		Expected New Issue	
182	**2000 FORINT**			
	1997. G. Bethlen.		Expected New Issue	
183	**5000 FORINT**			
	1997. Count I. Széchenyi.		Expected New Issue	
184	**10,000 FORINT**			
	1997. St. Stephan.		Expected New Issue	

ICELAND

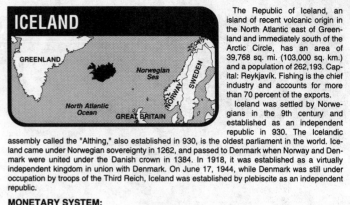

The Republic of Iceland, an island of recent volcanic origin in the North Atlantic east of Greenland and immediately south of the Arctic Circle, has an area of 39,768 sq. mi. (103,000 sq. km.) and a population of 262,193. Capital: Reykjavík. Fishing is the chief industry and accounts for more than 70 percent of the exports.

Iceland was settled by Norwegians in the 9th century and established as an independent republic in 930. The Icelandic assembly called the "Althing," also established in 930, is the oldest parliament in the world. Iceland came under Norwegian sovereignty in 1262, and passed to Denmark when Norway and Denmark were united under the Danish crown in 1384. In 1918, it was established as a virtually independent kingdom in union with Denmark. On June 17, 1944, while Denmark was still under occupation by troops of the Third Reich, Iceland was established by plebiscite as an independent republic.

MONETARY SYSTEM:
1 Krona = 100 Aurar, 1874-

SIGNATURE VARIETIES

31	V. Thor – J. G. Mariasson, 1961–1964	44	G. Hjartarson – T. Arnason, 1984
32	J. Nordal – V. Thor, 1961–64	45	T. Arnason – J. Nordal, 1984–93
33	J. G. Mariasson – J. Nordal, 1961–67	46	T. Arnason – D. Olafsson, 1984–93
34	J. Nordal – J. G. Mariasson, 1961–67	47	J. Nordal – T. Arnason, 1984–93
35	S. Klemenzson – J. G. Mariasson, 1966–67	48	G. Hallgrimsson – T. Arnason, 1986–90
36	J. Nordal – S. Klemenzson, 1966–67	49	J. Nordal – G. Hallgrimsson, 1986–90
37	J. Nordal – D. Olafsson, 1967–86	50	B. I. Gunnarsson – T. Arnason, 1991–93
38	D. Olafsson – J. Nordal, 1967–86	51	J. Nordal – B. I. Gunnarsson, 1991–93
39	S. Klemenzson – D. Olafsson, 1967–71	52	J. Sigurthsson – B.I. Gunnarsson,1944
40	S. Frimannsson – D. Olafsson, 1971–73	53	B. I. Gunnarsson – J. Sigurthsson, 1994
41	J. Nordal – S. Frimannsson, 1971–73	54	E. Gufnason – S. Hermansson, 1994–
42	G. Hjartarson – D. Olafsson, 1974–84	55	S. Hermansson – E. Gudnason, 1994–
43	J. Nordal – G.Hjartarson, 1974–84		

REPUBLIC

SEDLABANKI ÍSLANDS

CENTRAL BANK OF ICELAND

LAW OF 29.3.1961
#42-47 sign. varieties. Printer: BWC (w/o imprint).
#43-47 wmk: Portr. S. Bjornsson.

42	10 KRÓNUR	VG	VF	UNC
	L.1961. Brown-violet on green and orange unpt. J. Eiriksson at l. Ship in harbor lower ctr. Dock scene on back. Sign. 33; 34.	1.00	2.00	4.00

43	25 KRÓNUR	VG	VF	UNC
	L.1961. Purple on m/c unpt. M. Stephensen-Logmadur at l. Fjord at ctr. Fishing boats near large rock formation on back. Sign. 34.	1.00	2.00	5.00

44	100 KRÓNUR	VG	VF	UNC
	L.1961. Dk. blue-green on m/c unpt. T. Gunnarsson at l. Sheepherders, horseback, sheep w/mountains in background on back. Sign. 31-33; 35; 36; 38-43.	.30	1.00	2.50

45	500 KRÓNUR	VG	VF	UNC
	L.1961. Green on lilac and m/c unpt. H. Hafstein at l. Sailors on back. Sign. 36; 38-43.	1.00	2.00	6.00

46	1000 KRÓNUR	VG	VF	UNC
	L.1961. Blue on m/c unpt. J. Sigurdsson at r., bldg. at lower ctr. Rock formations on back. Sign. 31-34; 36; 38-43.	2.50	4.00	7.00

47	5000 KRÓNUR	VG	VF	UNC
	L.1961. Brown on m/c unpt. Similar to #41. E. Benediktsson at l., dam at lower ctr. Man overlooking waterfalls on back. Sign. 36; 38-43.	5.00	12.00	25.00

LAW 29 MARCH 1961 (1981-86 ISSUE)
#48-52 Printer: BWC (w/o imprint), then later by TDLR (w/o imprint). These made after takeover of BWC by TDLR.
#48-53 sign. varieties. Wmk: J. Sigurdsson.

48	10 KRÓNUR	VG	VF	UNC
	L.1961. (1981). Blue on m/c unpt. A. Jónsson at r. Old Icelandic household scene on back. Sign. 37; 38; 42; 43.	FV	FV	1.00

52   1000 Krónur
L.1961 (1984). Purple on m/c unpt. Bishop B. Sveinsson w/book at r. Church at ctr. on back. Sign. 37; 38; 43; 45; 48-51.

	VG	VF	UNC
	FV	FV	25.00

49   50 Krónur
L.1961 (1981). Brown on m/c unpt. Bishop Guobrandur Porlaksson at l. 2 printers on back. Sign. 37; 38; 42; 43.

	VG	VF	UNC
	FV	FV	2.00

53   5000 Krónur
L.1961 (1986). Blue on m/c unpt. R. Jónsdór at ctr. Bishop G. Porláksson w/two previous wives at r. Jónsdór and two girls examining embroidery on back. Sign. 38; 46; 47.

	VG	VF	UNC
	FV	FV	125.00

LAW 5 MAI 1986 (1994- ISSUE)
#54-56 like #50-52 but w/new sign. and law date.

50   100 Krónur
L.1961 (1981). Dk. green and m/c Prof. Magnússon at r. Monk w/illuminated manuscript on back. Sign. 37; 38; 42; 43; 45-49; 51-53.

	VG	VF	UNC
	FV	FV	4.00

54   100 Krónur
L.1986 (1994). Sign 52; 53.

	VG	VF	UNC
	FV	FV	3.00

55   500 Krónur
L.1986 (1994). Sign. 45; 50; 51.

	VG	VF	UNC
	FV	FV	13.50

51   500 Krónur
L.1961 (1981). Red on m/c unpt. J. Sigurdsson at l. ctr. Sigurdsson working at his desk on back. Sign. 37; 38; 43; 45.

	VG	VF	UNC
	FV	FV	15.00

56   1000 Krónur
L.1986 (1994). Sign. 45; 50; 51.

	VG	VF	UNC
	FV	FV	22.50

57   2000 Krónur
L.1986 (1995). Brown and blue-violet on m/c unpt. Painting "Inside, outside" at ctr. J. S. Kajarval at r. Painting "Yearning for Flight" (Leda and the Swan) and "Woman with Flower" on back. Sign. 53-55.

	VG	VF	UNC
	FV	FV	45.00

58   5000 Krónur
L.1986 (199x). Like #53.

Expected New Issue

INDIA

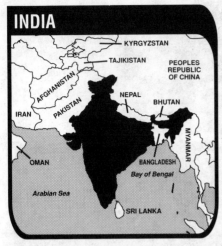

The Republic of India, a subcontinent jutting southward from the mainland of Asia, has an area of 1,266,595 sq. mi. (3,287,590 sq. km.) and a population of 833.4 million, second only to that of the Peoples Republic of China. Capital: New Delhi. India's economy is based on agriculture and industrial activity. Engineering goods, cotton apparel and fabrics, handicrafts, tea, iron and steel are exported.

The people of India have had a continuous civilization based since about 2500 BC, when an urban culture based on commerce and trade, and to a lesser extent, agriculture, was developed by the inhabitants of the Indus River Valley. The origins of this civilization are uncertain, but it declined about 1500 B.C., when the region was conquered by the Aryans. Over the following 2,000 years, the Aryans developed a Brahmanic civilization and introduced the caste system. Several successive empires flourished in India over the following centuries, notably those of the Mauryans, Guptas and Mughals. In the 7th and 8th centuries AD, the Arabs expanded into western India, bringing with them the Islamic faith. A Muslim dynasty (the Mughal Empire) controlled virtually the entire subcontinent during the period preceding the arrival of the Europeans; an Indo-Islamic style of art and architecture evolved, of which the Taj Mahal is a splendid example.

The Portuguese were the first to arrive, off Calicut in May 1498. It wasn't until 1612, after Portuguese and Spanish power began to wane, that the English East India Company established its initial settlement at Surat. By the end of the century, English traders were firmly established in Bombay, Madras and Calcutta, as well as in some parts of the interior, and Britain was implementing a policy to create the civil and military institutions that would insure British dominion over the country. By 1757, following the successful conclusion of a war of colonial rivalry with France, the British were firmly established in India as not only traders, but as conquerors. During the next 60 years, the English East India Company acquired dominion over most of India by bribery and force, and ruled directly, or through puppet princelings.

The Indian Mutiny (also called Sepoy Mutiny) of 1857-59, begun by Indian troops in the service of the British East India Company, revealed the intensity of the growing resentment against British domination. The widespread rebellion against British rule was unsuccessful, but resulted in the transfer of government from the company to the British crown, and was a source of inspiration to later Indian nationalists. Agitation for representation in the government continued.

Following World War I, in which India sent six million troops to fight at the side of the Allies, Indian nationalism intensified under the banner of the Indian National Congress and the leadership of Mohandas Karamchand Gandhi, who called the non-violent revolt against British authority. The Government of India Act of 1935 proposed a federal status linking the British India provinces with the many princely states; in addition, provincial legislatures were to be created. The federal status was never implemented, but the legislatures were created after the election of 1937, with the National Congress winning majorities in most of the provinces.

When Britain declared war on Germany in Sept., 1939, the viceroy declared India also to be at war with a common enemy. The Congress, however, demanded independence as a condition for cooperation. Britain refused. But as the Japanese advanced into Asia, Britain offered to transfer to Indians power over all but military affairs during the war, and set forth a plan for postwar independence. Congress was willing to accept the wartime transfer of power, but both Congress and the Muslim League rejected Britain's plan for independence; Congress because it did not sufficiently safeguard Indian unity, the Muslims (who wanted a separate Muslim state) because of fears of what would happen to Muslims within a united India.

Early in 1947, Prime Minister Clement Attlee announced that Britain would leave India "by a date not later than June 1948," even though the Hindus and Muslims could not agree among themselves on a plan for self-government. The National Congress, aware that the Muslim League would revolt rather than accept an all-India government, reluctantly agreed to the formation of a separate Muslim state. The Muslim-populated provinces of the northwest frontier, Sindh and West Punjab in the west, and East Bengal in the east were separated from India to form the Muslim state of Pakistan, which became independent on August 14, 1947. India became independent on the following day. Initially, Pakistan consisted of East and West Pakistan, two areas separated by 1,000 miles of Indian territory. East Pakistan seceded from Pakistan on March 26, 1971, and with the support of India established itself as the independent Peoples Republic of Bangladesh.

The Republic of India is a member of the Commonwealth of Nations. The president is the Chief of State. The prime minister is the Head of Government.

NOTE: Since 1994, 1, 2 and 5 Rupee notes are no longer issued. They have been replaced by coins.

MONETARY SYSTEM:
1 Rupee = 100 Naye Paise, 1957-1964
1 Rupee = 100 Paise, 1964-

STAPLE HOLES AND CONDITION
Perfect uncirculated notes are rarely encountered without having at least two tiny holes made by staples, stick pins or stitching having been done during age old accounting practices before and after a note is released to circulation.

SIGNATURE VARIETIES

Governors, Reserve Bank of India (all except 1 Rupee notes)

1	C. D. Deshmukh February 1943–June 1949	10	K. R Puri August 1975–May 1977
2	B. Rama Rau July 1949–January 1957	11	M. Narasimham May 1977–November 1977

3	K.G. Ambegaokar January 1957–February 1957	12	I. G. Patel December 1977–1981
4	H.V.R. Iengar March 1957–February 1962	13	Manmohan Singh, 1981–1983
5	P.C. Bhattacharyya March 1962–June 1967	14	R. N. Malhotra, 1983–1984
6	L.K. Jha July 1967–May 1970	15	Abhitam Ghosh, 1984 (in office 20 days)
7	B.N. Adarkar May 1970–June 1970	16	S. Venkitaramanan, 1984–
8	S. Jagannathan June 1970–May 1975	17	C. Rangarajan
9	N. C. Sen Gupta May 1975–August 1975		

REPUBLIC OF INDIA
RESERVE BANK OF INDIA
FIRST SERIES
#29-31, 35, 36, 39, 40, 43-45 and 47 Asoka column at r. Lg. letters in unpt. beneath serial #. Wmk: Asoka column.

NOTE: For similar notes but in different colors, please see Haj Pilgrim and Persian Gulf listings at the end of this country listing.

29	2 RUPEES	VG	VF	UNC

ND. Red-brown on violet and green unpt. Tiger head at l. on back. Value in English and corrected Hindi on both sides. Third value text line on back 24mm long. Tiger's head to l.
a. Sign. 2. — 1.25 / 5.00 / 20.00
b. Sign. 4. — .65 / 2.50 / 10.00

30	2 RUPEES	VG	VF	UNC

ND. Red-brown on green unpt. Face like #29. Tiger head at l. looking to r., w/13 value text lines at ctr. on back. Sign. 5. — 1.00 / 4.00 / 16.50

31	**2 RUPEES** ND. Olive on tan unpt. Like #30. Sign. 5.	**VG** .50	**VF** 2.25	**UNC** 9.00

34	**5 RUPEES** ND. Fourth value text line on back 26mm long. Sign. 2.	**VG** .75	**VF** 3.00	**UNC** 9.00

40	**10 RUPEES** ND. Like #39 but sign. title: *GOVERNOR* centered. 13 value text lines on back.	**VG**	**VF**	**UNC**
	a. Letter A. Sign. 5.	1.50	4.00	12.50
	b. Letter B. Sign. 5.	1.50	4.00	12.50

42	**100 RUPEES**			
	a. Black serial #. Sign. B. Rama Rau.	15.00	40.00	85.00
	b. Red serial #. Sign. B. Rama Rau.	15.00	40.00	85.00

35	**5 RUPEES** ND. Green on brown unpt. Value in English and correct Hinki. *Rs. S* and antelope on back, but redesigned panels at l. and r.	**VG**	**VF**	**UNC**
	a. W/o letter. Sign. 4.	.75	3.00	12.00
	b. Letter A. Sign. 4.	.50	2.00	8.00

36	**5 RUPEES** Like #35 but sign. title: *GOVERNOR* centered. 13 value text lines on back.	**VG**	**VF**	**UNC**
	a. Letter A. Sign. 5.	1.25	5.00	20.00
	b. Letter B. Sign. 5.	1.00	4.00	12.50

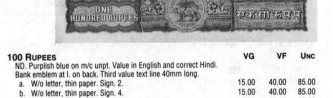

43	**100 RUPEES** ND. Purplish blue on m/c unpt. Value in English and correct Hindi. Bank emblem at l. on back. Third value text line 40mm long.	**VG**	**VF**	**UNC**
	a. W/o letter, thin paper. Sign. 2.	15.00	40.00	85.00
	b. W/o letter, thin paper. Sign. 4.	15.00	40.00	85.00
	c. Letter A, thick paper. Sign. 4.	15.00	40.00	85.00

39	**10 RUPEES** ND. Violet on m/c unpt. English and correct Hindi value. Dhow at ctr. on back. Third value text line on back 29mm long.	**VG**	**VF**	**UNC**
	a. W/o letter. Sign. 2.	1.00	4.50	13.50
	b. W/o letter. Sign. 4.	1.00	4.00	12.00
	c. Letter A. Sign. 4.	1.00	4.00	12.00

	52	**2 RUPEES**	**VG**	**VF**	**UNC**
		ND. Deep pink and m/c. Numeral *2* at ctr. 15mm high. Tiger at ctr. on back. Sign. B.	.35	1.50	6.00
	53	**2 RUPEES**			
		ND. Like #52 but corrected Urdu at bottom l. on back. English text at l. on face.			
	a.	W/o letter. Sign. 8.	.30	.85	3.00
	b.	W/o letter. Sign. 10.	.30	.85	3.00
	c.	Letter A. Sign. 10.	.30	.85	3.00
	d.	Letter A. Sign. 11.	Reported Not Confirmed		
	e.	Letter A. Sign.12.	.25	.75	2.00
	f.	Letter B. Sign. 12.	.20	.75	2.00
	g.	Letter C. Sign. 12.	.20	.75	2.00
	h.	Letter C. Sign. 13.	.15	.60	1.25

	44	**100 RUPEES**	**VG**	**VF**	**UNC**
		ND. Violet and m/c. Heading in rectangle at top, serial # at upper l. and lower r. title: *GOVERNOR* at ctr. r. Dam at ctr. w/13 value text lines at l. on back. Sign. 4.	12.50	25.00	65.00
	45	**100 RUPEES**			
		ND. Like #44 but sign. title: *GOVERNOR* is centered. Sign. 5.	12.50	25.00	65.00
	47	**1000 RUPEES**			
		ND. Brown on green and blue unpt. Value in English and correct Hindi. Tanjore Temple at ctr. 13 value lines on back. BOMBAY. Sign. 5.	50.00	110.00	—
	49	**5000 RUPEES**			
		ND. Green, violet and brown. Asoka column at l. Value in English and correct Hindi. Gateway of India on back. BOMBAY. Sign. 4.	200.00	325.00	800.00

	53A	**2 RUPEES**	**VG**	**VF**	**UNC**
		ND. Similar to #53 but English text at r. on face.			
	a.	W/o letter. Sign. 13.	.30	1.00	3.00
	b.	Letter A. Sign. 14.	.30	1.00	3.00
	c.	Letter B. Sign. 14.	.30	1.00	3.00
	d.	W/o letter. Sign. 15.	.30	1.25	5.00
	e.	Letter B. Sign. 16.	.15	.50	1.50

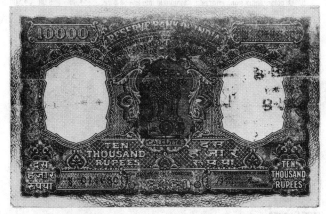

	50	**10,000 RUPEES**	**VG**	**VF**	**UNC**
		ND. Blue, violet and brown. Asoka column at ctr. Value in English and in error Hindi on face and back.			
	a.	BOMBAY. Sign. 2.	400.00	650.00	1250.
	b.	CALCUTTA. Sign. 2.	400.00	650.00	1250.
	c.	MADRAS. Sign. 4.	400.00	650.00	1250.
	50A	**10,000 RUPEES**			
		ND. Like #50 but Hindi corrected. BOMBAY. Sign. 4.	400.00	650.00	1250.

	54	**5 RUPEES**	**VG**	**VF**	**UNC**
		ND. Green and m/c. Numeral *5* at ctr. 11mm high. Antelope at ctr. on back.			
	a.	Sign. title: *GOVERNOR* centered at bottom. Sign. 5.	.40	1.75	7.00
	b.	Sign. title: *GOVERNOR* at ctr. r. Sign. 6.	.30	1.25	5.00

SECOND SERIES

Most notes of reduced size. Large letters found in unpt. beneath serial #.

#51-65 Asoka column at r.

Urdu Incorrect (actually Persian)	Corrected to Urdu

VARIETIES: #51-52, 54-55, 57-59, 62-63, 67-70 have bottom value line on back in Urdu expressed incorrectly ending in Persian (Farsi) at l.

	55	**5 RUPEES**	**VG**	**VF**	**UNC**
		ND. Dk. green on m/c unpt. numeral *5* at ctr. 17mm high. Antelope at ctr. on back. Sign. 8.	.30	1.25	5.00
	56	**5 RUPEES**			
		ND. Like #55 but corrected Urdu at bottom l. on back.			
	a.	W/o letter. Sign. 8.	.40	1.00	3.00
	b.	Letter A. Sign. 8.	.40	1.00	3.00
	c.	Letter A. Sign. 10.	Reported Not Confirmed		
	d.	Letter A. Sign. 11.	Reported Not Confirmed		

	51	**2 RUPEES**	**VG**	**VF**	**UNC**
		ND. Brown and m/c. Numeral *2* at ctr. 7mm high. Tiger at ctr. on back.			
	a.	Sign. title: *GOVERNOR* centered at bottom. Sign. 5.	.35	1.50	6.00
	b.	Sign. title: *GOVERNOR* at ctr. r. Sign. 6.	.35	1.50	6.00

57 10 RUPEES
ND. Purple and m/c. Numeral *10* at ctr. 30mm broad. Dhow at ctr. on back.

		VG	VF	UNC
a.	Sign. title: *GOVERNOR* centered at bottom. Sign. 5.	1.00	2.50	7.50
b.	Sign. title: *GOVERNOR* at ctr. r. Sign. 6.	1.00	2.50	7.50

58 10 RUPEES
ND. Brown and m/c. Numeral *10* at ctr. 18mm broad. Heading in English and Hindi on back. Sign. 6.

VG	VF	UNC
2.50	10.00	25.00

59 10 RUPEES
ND. Dk. brown on m/c unpt. Like #58. Heading only in Hindi on back.

		VG	VF	UNC
a.	W/o letter. Sign. 8.	.75	2.00	7.00
b.	Letter A. Sign. 8.	.75	2.00	7.00

60 10 RUPEES
ND. Like #59 but corrected Urdu at bottom l. on back.

		VG	VF	UNC
a.	Letter A. Sign. 8.	.75	2.00	7.50
b.	Letter B. Sign. 8.	1.00	4.00	12.00
c.	Letter B. Sign. 10.	.75	2.00	7.50
d.	Letter B. Sign. 11.	1.00	4.00	12.00
e.	Letter C. Sign. 11.	.75	2.00	7.50
f.	Letter C. Sign. 12	.75	1.50	6.00
g.	Letter D. Sign. 12.	.75	1.50	6.00
h.	Letter D. Sign.13.	.50	1.00	4.00
i.	Letter E. Sign. 13.	.50	1.00	4.00
j.	Letter E. Sign. 14.	.50	1.00	4.00
k.	Letter F. Sign. 14.	.50	1.00	4.00
l.	Letter G. Sign. 14.	.50	1.00	4.00
m.	W/o letter. Sign. 14.	.60	1.50	10.00
n.	Sign. 15.	.60	1.50	10.00

60A 10 RUPEES
ND. Similar to #60 but w/Hindi title above *RESERVE BANK OF INDIA* and Hindi text at l. of *10* and *I PROMISE...* at r. Sanskrit title added under Asoka column at r. Sign. 16.

VG	VF	UNC
FV	FV	2.00

**Incorrect Kashmiri
(actually Persian)**

Corrected Kashmiri

61 20 RUPEES
ND. Orange and m/c. Parliament House at ctr. on back. Sign. 8.

		VG	VF	UNC
a.	Dk. colors under sign., error or in Kashmiri in fifth line on back.	2.00	6.00	17.50
b.	Lt. colors under sign., error or in Kashmiri in fifth line on back.	1.50	5.00	12.00
c.	Lt. colors under sign., corrected Kashmiri line on back.	1.50	5.00	12.00

62 100 RUPEES
ND. Blue and m/c. Numeral *100* at ctr. 43mm broad. Dam at ctr. w/only English heading on back.

		VG	VF	UNC
a.	Sign. 5.	6.00	15.00	45.00
b.	Sign. 6.	6.00	15.00	45.00

63 100 RUPEES
ND. Blue and m/c. Numeral *100* at ctr. 28mm broad. Dam at ctr. w/only Hindi heading on back. Sign. 8.

VG	VF	UNC
6.00	14.00	35.00

64 100 RUPEES
ND. Like #63 but corrected Urdu value line on back.

		VG	VF	UNC
a.	W/o letter. Sign. 8.	5.00	14.00	35.00
b.	W/o letter. Sign. 10.	5.00	14.00	35.00
c.	W/o letter. Sign. 11.	5.00	14.00	35.00
d.	Letter A. Sign. 12.	5.00	12.00	30.00

65   1000 RUPEES
ND. Brown on m/c unpt. Text in English and Hindi on face. Temple at
ctr. on back. BOMBAY.

	VG	VF	UNC
a. Sign. 9.	30.00	50.00	100.00
b. Sign. 10.	30.00	50.00	100.00

GOVERNMENT OF INDIA

1969 COMMEMORATIVE ISSUE
#66, Centennial of Birth of Gandhi.

66   1 RUPEE
ND (1969-70). Violet and m/c. Coin w/Gandhi and *1869-1948* at r.
Reverse of Gandhi coin on back at l. Sign. 12.

	VG	VF	UNC
	.25	1.00	4.00

RESERVE BANK OF INDIA

1969 COMMEMORATIVE ISSUE
##67-70, Centennial of Birth of Ghandi.

67   2 RUPEES
ND (1969-70). Red-violet and m/c. Face like #52. Gandhi seated at ctr.
on back.

	VG	VF	UNC
a. Sign. 6.	.40	1.75	7.50
b. Sign. 7.	.40	1.75	7.50

68   5 RUPEES
ND (1969-70). Dk. green on m/c unpt. Face like #55. Back like #67.

	VG	VF	UNC
a. Sign. 6.	.40	1.75	7.50
b. Sign. 7.	.40	1.75	7.50

69   10 RUPEES
ND (1969-70). Brown and m/c. Face like #59. Back like #68.

	VG	VF	UNC
a. Sign. 6.	.50	1.75	7.50
b. Sign. 7.	.50	1.75	7.50

70   100 RUPEES
ND (1969-70). Blue and m/c. Face like #63. Back like #68.

	VG	VF	UNC
a. Sign. 6.	5.50	22.00	65.00
b. Sign. 7.	5.50	22.00	65.00

GOVERNMENT OF INDIA

SIGNATURE VARIETIES			
Various Secretaries, (1 Rupee notes only)			
33	H. M. Patel, 1951–1957	35	L. K. Jha, 1957–1963
34	A. K. Roy, 1957	36	S. Boothalingam, 1964–1966
NOTE: The sign. H. M. Patel is often misread as "Mehta." There was never any such individual serving as Secretary. Do not confuse H. M. Patel with I. G. Patel who served later.			
37	S. Jagannathan, 1967–1968	43	Pratap Kishen Kaul, 1983–1985
38	I. G. Patel, 1968–1972	44	S. Venkitaramanan, 1985–88

39	 M. G. Kaul, 1973–1976	**45**	 Gopi Arora, 1989
40	 Manomohan Singh, 1976–1980	**46**	 Bimal Jalan, 1990
41	 R. N. Malhotra, 1980–1981	**47**	 Montek Singh Ahluwalia, 1991–
42	M. Narasimham, 1981–85	**48**	

1957; 63 ISSUE
#75-78A wmk: Asoka column.

75	**1 RUPEE**	VG	VF	UNC
	1957. Violet and m/c. Redesigned coin w/Asoka column at r. Coin dated 1957 *100 Naye Paise* in Hindi, 7 value lines on back.			
	a. W/o letter. Sign. 33 w/sign. title: *SECRETARY...* (1956).	Reported Not Confirmed		
	b. Letter A. Sign. 33 w/sign. title: *SECRETARY...*	.35	1.50	6.00
	c. Letter A. Sign. 33 w/sign. title: *PRINCIPAL SECRETARY...*	.20	.85	3.50
	d. Letter B. Sign. 34 w/sign. title: *SECRETARY...*	.30	1.25	5.00
	e. Letter B. Sign. 35.	1.50	6.00	25.00
	f. Letter C. Sign. 35.	.20	.75	3.00
	g. Letter D. Sign. 35.	.20	.75	3.00

76	**1 RUPEE**	VG	VF	UNC
	1963-65. Violet on m/c unpt. Redesigned note. Coin w/various dates and *1 Rupee* in Hindi, 13 value lines on back.			
	a. Letter A. Sign. 35. 1963.	.20	7.50	3.00
	b. Letter B. Sign. 36. 1964.	1.75	7.50	30.00
	c. Letter B. Sign. 36. 1965.	.20	.75	3.00

77	**1 RUPEE**	VG	VF	UNC
	1966-80. Violet on m/c unpt. Redesigned note, serial # at l. Coin w/various dates on back.			
	a. W/o letter. Sign. 36. 1966.	.15	.60	2.50
	b. Letter A. Sign. 37. 1967.	.20	.75	3.00
	c. Letter A. Sign. 37. 1968.	.20	.75	3.00
	d. Letter B. Sign. 38 w/sign. title: *SPECIAL SECRETARY...* 1968.	.20	.75	3.00
	e. Letter B. Sign. 38 w/sign. title: *SPECIAL SECRETARY...* 1969.	.50	2.00	8.00
	f. Letter C. Sign. 38 w/title: *SPECIAL SECRETARY...* 1969.	.15	.60	2.50
	g. Letter C. Sign. 38. 1970.	.15	.60	2.50
	h. Letter C. Sign. 38. 1971.	.15	.60	2.50
	i. Letter D. Sign. 38. 1971.	.15	.60	2.50
	j. Letter D. Sign. 38. 1972.	.15	.60	2.50
	k. Letter E. Sign. 38. 1972.	.15	.60	2.50
	l. Letter E. Sign. 39. 1973.	.15	.60	2.50
	m. Letter F. Sign. 39. 1973.	.15	.60	2.50
	n. Letter F. Sign. 39. 1974.	.15	.60	2.50
	o. Letter G. Sign. 39. 1974.	.15	.60	2.50
	p. Letter G. Sign. 39. 1975.	.15	.60	2.50
	q. Letter H. Sign. 39. 1975.	.15	.60	2.50
	r. Letter H. Sign. 39. 1976.	.15	.60	2.50
	s. Letter I. Sign. 39. 1976.	.15	.60	2.50

		VG	VF	UNC
	t. W/o letter. Sm. serial #. Sign. 40. 1976.	.15	.60	2.50
	u. Sm. serial #. Sign. 40. 1977.	.10	.50	2.00
	v. Letter A. Sign. 40. 1978.	.10	.50	2.00
	w. Letter A. Sign. 40. 1979.	.10	.50	2.00
	x. Letter A. Sign. 40. 1980.	.10	.50	2.00
	y. W/o letter. Sign. 41. 1980.	.10	.50	2.00
	z. Letter A. Sign. 41. 1980.	.10	.50	2.00
	aa. Letter B. Sign. 41. 1980.	.10	.50	2.00

78	**1 RUPEE**	VG	VF	UNC
	1981-82. Purple and violet on lt. blue, brown and m/c unpt. Coin w/Asoka column at upper r. Offshore oil drilling platform and reverse of coin w/date on back.			
	a. Sign. 41. 1981.	FV	.15	.50
	b. Sign. 42. 1981.	FV	.15	.50
	c. Sign. 42. 1982.	FV	.15	.50

78A	**1 RUPEE**	VG	VF	UNC
	1983-. Similar to #78 but w/new coin design.			
	a. Sign. 43 w/title: *SECRETARY...* 1983-85.	FV	.15	.50
	b. Sign. 44 w/title: *FINANCE SECRETARY...* 1985-86.	FV	.15	.50
	c. Letter A. Sign. 44. 1986-88.	FV	.15	.50
	d. Letter B. Sign. 45. 1989.	FV	.15	.50
	e. Letter B. Sign. 46. 1990.	FV	.15	.50
	f. Letter B. Sign. 47 w/title: *SECRETARY...* 1991.	FV	.15	.50
	g. Letter B. Sign. 47. 1992.	FV	.15	.50
	h. Letter B. Sign. 47 w/title: *FINANCE SECRETARY...* 1993.	FV	.15	.50
	i. Letter B. Sign. 47. 1994.	FV	.15	.50

RESERVE BANK OF INDIA

THIRD SERIES
Lg. letters in unpt. beneath serial #.
#79-88 Asoka column at r. and as wmk.

79	**2 RUPEES**	VG	VF	UNC
	ND. Orange on m/c unpt. Space craft at ctr. on back.			
	a. Sign. 10.	.10	.35	1.50
	b. Sign. 11.	.10	.35	1.50
	c. W/o letter. Sign. 12.	.10	.35	1.50
	d. Letter A. Sign. 12.	.10	.35	1.50
	e. W/o letter. Sign. 13.	.10	.35	1.50
	f. Letter A. Sign. 13.	.10	.35	1.50
	g. W/o letter. Sign. 14.	.10	.35	1.50
	h. Letter A. Sign. 14.	.10	.25	1.00
	i. Letter B. Sign. 14.	.10	.25	1.00
	j. Letter A. Sign. 15.	.50	2.00	8.00
	k. Letter B. Sign. 16.	.10	.20	.80
	l. Letter B. Sign. 17.	.10	.20	.80

82 20 RUPEES

ND. Red and purple on m/c unpt. Back orange on m/c unpt. Buddhist
Wheel of Life at lower ctr. on back.

		VG	VF	UNC
a.	Sign. 8.	FV	1.25	4.00
b.	Sign. 10.	FV	1.25	4.00
c.	Sign. 11.	FV	1.25	4.00
d.	W/o letter. Sign. 12	FV	1.25	4.00
e.	Letter A. Sign. 12.	FV	1.25	4.00
f.	Letter A. Sign. 13.	FV	1.25	4.00
g.	Letter A. Sign. 14.	FV	1.25	4.00
h.	Letter B. Sign. 14.	FV	1.25	4.00
i.	Sign. 15.	Reported Not Confirmed		
j.	Sign. 17.	FV	FV	2.00
k.	Letter B. Sign. 17.	FV	FV	2.00

80 5 RUPEES

ND. Gray-green on m/c unpt. Farmer plowing w/tractor at ctr. on back.

		VG	VF	UNC
a.	W/o letter. Sign. 8.	FV	.50	2.00
b.	W/o letter. Sign. 10.	FV	.50	2.00
c.	Letter A. Sign. 10.	FV	.50	2.00
d.	Letter A. Sign. 11.	FV	.50	2.00
e.	Letter A. Sign. 12.	FV	.50	2.00
f.	Letter B. Sign. 12.	FV	.50	2.00
g.	Letter C. Sign. 12.	FV	.50	2.00
h.	Letter D. Sign. 13.	FV	.50	2.00
i.	W/o letter. New seal in Hindi and English. Sign. 14.	FV	.50	2.00
j.	Letter A. New seal. Sign. 14.	FV	.50	2.00
k.	Letter E. Sign. 14.	FV	.50	2.00
l.	Letter F. Sign. 14.	FV	.50	2.00
m.	Letter G. Sign. 14.	FV	.50	2.00
n.	Letter D. Sign. 15.	.50	2.50	10.00
o.	W/o letter. Sign. 16.	FV	.40	1.50
p.	Letter B. Sign. 16.	FV	.40	1.50
q.	Letter B. Sign. 17.	FV	.30	1.25
r.	Letter B. Sign. 17.	FV	.30	1.25

83 50 RUPEES

ND. Black and purple on lilac and m/c unpt. Parliament House at ctr.
on back. W/o flag at top of flagpole.

		VG	VF	UNC
a.	Sign. 8.	FV	2.25	8.00
b.	Sign. 10.	FV	2.25	8.00
c.	Sign. 11.	FV	2.50	10.00
d.	Sign. 12.	FV	2.25	8.00

81 10 RUPEES

ND. Lilac and brown on m/c unpt. Tree w/peacocks at ctr. on back.

		VG	VF	UNC
a.	W/o letter. Sign. 8.	FV	.85	3.00
b.	W/o letter. Sign. 10.	FV	.85	3.00
c.	W/o letter. Sign. 11.	FV	.85	3.00
d.	Letter A. Sign. 12.	FV	.85	3.00
e.	W/o letter. Sign.12.	FV	.85	3.00
f.	W/o letter. Sign. 13.	FV	.85	3.00
g.	Letter A. Sign. 13.	FV	.85	3.00
h.	Sign. 14.	FV	.75	2.00
i.	Letter B. Sign. 14.	FV	.75	2.00
j.	Letter C. Sign. 14.	FV	.75	2.00
k.	Sign. 15.	.75	3.00	12.50

84 50 RUPEES

ND. Black and purple on orange, lilac and m/c unpt. Similar to #83 but
w/flag at top of flagpole.

		VG	VF	UNC
a.	Sign. 12.	FV	2.25	7.00
b.	Sign. 13.	FV	2.25	7.00
c.	Sign. 14.	FV	2.25	6.00
d.	Letter A. Sign. 14.	FV	2.25	6.00
e.	Letter B. Sign. 14.	FV	2.25	6.00
f.	W/o letter. Sign. 15.	Reported Not Confirmed		
g.	Sign. 16.	FV	2.00	6.00
h.	Sign. 17.	FV	1.75	3.50
i.	Letter A. Sign. 17.	FV	FV	3.50
j.	Letter B. Sign. 17.	FV	FV	3.50
k.	Letter C. Sign. 17.	FV	FV	3.50

85	100 RUPEES	VG	VF	UNC
	ND. Black, brown-violet and dk. green on blue-violet on brown and m/c unpt. (tan at ctr.), Dam, agricultural work at ctr. on back. Denomination above bar at lower r. Black sign.			
a.	Sign. 8.	FV	5.00	20.00
b.	Sign. 10.	FV	4.00	17.50
c.	Sign. 11.	FV	4.00	17.50
d.	Sign. 12	Reported Not Confirmed		
e.	Sign. 14.	FV	3.50	15.00
f.	Sign. 15.	4.00	10.00	25.00

87	500 RUPEES	VG	VF	UNC
	ND (1987). Brown, deep blue-green and deep blue on m/c unpt. M. K. Gandhi at ctr. r. Electronic sorting marks at lower l. Gandhi leading followers across back. Wmk: Asoka column.			
a.	Sign. 14.	FV	20.00	35.00
b.	Sign. 16.	FV	FV	32.50
c.	Sign. 17.	FV	FV	30.00

1992 ISSUE

85A	100 RUPEES	VG	VF	UNC
	ND. Like #85 but w/o bar under denomination at lower r. Sign. 14.	FV	3.50	10.00

88	10 RUPEES	VG	VF	UNC
	ND (1992).Dull brown-violet on orange, green and m/c unpt. Rural temple at l. ctr. on back.			
a.	Sign. 16.	FV	.50	2.00
b.	Sign. 17.	FV	.35	1.50
c.	Letter A. Sign. 17.	FV	FV	1.25
d.	Letter B. Sign. 17.	FV	FV	1.25
e.	Letter C. Sign. 17.	FV	FV	1.00
f.	Letter D. Sign. 17.	FV	FV	1.00
g.	Letter E. Sign. 17.	FV	FV	1.00

1996 ND ISSUE

#89 and 90 M. K. Gandhi at r. and as wmk. Reserve Bank seal at lower r.

86	100 RUPEES	VG	VF	UNC
	ND. Black, deep red and purple on m/c unpt. (pink at ctr.). Like #85A. Deep red sign.			
a.	Sign. 12.	FV	3.50	15.00
b.	Sign. 13.	FV	3.50	15.00
c.	Sign. 14.	FV	3.50	7.50
d.	Sign. 16.	FV	3.50	6.50
e.	Letter A. Sign. 16.	FV	3.50	8.00
f.	W/o letter. Sign. 17.	FV	FV	6.00
g.	Letter A. Sign. 17.	FV	FV	6.00
h.	Letter B. Sign. 17.	FV	FV	6.00

89   **10 RUPEES**   **VG**   **VF**   **UNC**
      ND (1996). Pale brown-violet on m/c unpt. Ornamented rhinoceros   FV   FV   1.25
      and elephant heads behind tiger at l. ctr. on back. Sign. 17.

90   **100 RUPEES**   **VG**   **VF**   **UNC**
      ND (1996). Black, purple and dk. olive-green on pale blue-green and   FV   FV   6.50
      m/c unpt. Himalaya mountains at l. ctr. on back. Sign. 17.

PERSIAN GULF

Intended for circulation in area of Oman, Bahrain, Qatar and Trucial States during 1950s and early 1960s. Z prefix in serial #. Known as "Gulf Rupees."

RESERVE BANK OF INDIA

(ND) ISSUE

R2   **5 RUPEES**   **VG**   **VF**   **UNC**
      ND. Like #35a but orange. Sign. 4.   5.00   15.00   90.00

R3   **10 RUPEES**   **VG**   **VF**   **UNC**
      ND. Like #39c but red. Sign. 4.   7.00   20.00   130.00

R4   **100 RUPEES**   **VG**   **VF**   **UNC**
      ND. Like #43b but green. Sign. 4.   40.00   150.00   500.00

HAJ PILGRIM

RESERVE BANK OF INDIA

(ND) ISSUE

#R5-R6, for use by Moslem pilgrims in Mecca, Saudi Arabia. Letters HA near serial #, and HAJ l. and r. of bank title at top.

R5   **10 RUPEES**   **VG**   **VF**   **UNC**
      ND. Like #39c but blue. Sign. 4.   25.00   75.00   400.00
R6   **100 RUPEES**
      ND. Like #43b but red. Sign. 4.   85.00   250.00   725.00

The Republic of Indonesia, the world's largest archipelago, extends for more than 3,000 miles (4,827 km.) along the equator from the mainland of southeast Asia to Australia. The more than 13,500 islands comprising the archipelago have a combined area of 735,268 sq. mi. (2,042,005 sq. km.) and a population of 187.7 million, including East Timor. Capital: Jakarta. Petroleum, timber, rubber and coffee are exported.

Had Columbus succeeded in reaching the fabled Spice Islands, he would have found advanced civilizations a millennium old, and temples still ranked among the finest examples of ancient art. During the opening centuries of the Christian era, the islands were influenced by Hindu priests and traders who spread their culture and religion. Moslem invasions began in the 13th century, fragmenting the island kingdoms into small states which were unable to resist Western colonial infiltration. Portuguese traders established posts in the 16th century, but they were soon outnumbered by the Dutch who arrived in 1602 and gradually asserted control over the islands comprising present-day Indonesia, Dutch dominance, interrupted by British incursions during the Napoleonic Wars, established the Netherlands East Indies as one of the richest colonial possessions in the world.

The Indonesian independence movement, which began between the two world wars, was encouraged by the Japanese during their 3-year occupation during World War II. Indonesia proclaimed its independence on Aug. 17, 1945, three days after the surrender of Japan, and established it on Dec. 28, 1949, after four years of Dutch military efforts to reassert control. West Irian, formerly Netherlands New Guinea, came under the administration of Indonesia on May 1, 1963.

MONETARY SYSTEM:
1 Rupiah = 100 Sen, 1945-

REPUBLIC

REPUBLIK INDONESIA

1961 ISSUE

		VG	VF	UNC
78	**1 RUPIAH** 1961. Dk. green. Rice field workers at l. Farm produce on back.	.10	.25	.75

		VG	VF	UNC
79	**2 1/2 RUPIAH** 1961. Black, dk. blue and brown on blue-green unpt. Corn field work at l.	.10	.25	.75

1961 BORNEO ISSUE

#79A and 79B Pres. Sukarno at l. Javanese dancer at r. on back.

		VG	VF	UNC
79A	**1 RUPIAH** 1961. Green on orange unpt.	1.00	2.00	6.00

		VG	VF	UNC
79B	**2 1/2 RUPIAH** 1961. Blue on gray-brown unpt.	1.00	2.00	6.00

1964 ISSUE

#80 and 81 Pres. Sukarno at l.

		VG	VF	UNC
80	**1 RUPIAH** 1964. Red and brown.			
	a. Imprint: *Pertjetakan Kebajoran* at bottom ctr. on face.	.75	2.00	5.00
	b. W/o imprint.	.25	.50	2.00

		VG	VF	UNC
81	**2 1/2 RUPIAH** 1964. Blue and brown.			
	a. Imprint like #80a.	1.00	2.50	6.00
	b. W/o imprint.	1.00	2.50	6.00

BANK INDONESIA

1963 ISSUE

		VG	VF	UNC
89	**10 RUPIAH** 1963. Blue and brown. Wood carver at l. Huts, shrine at ctr., mythical figure at r. on back.	.10	.25	1.00

1964 ISSUE

#95-96, 98 and 101 have printed Indonesian arms in wmk. area at r.

		VG	VF	UNC
90	**1 SEN** 1964. Green-blue. Man w/straw hat at r.	—	—	.10

91   **5 SEN**   VG   VF   UNC
1964. Lilac-brown. Girl in uniform at r.   —   —   .10

92   **10 SEN**
1964. Blue-black on yellow-green unpt. Like #91.   —   —   .10

93   **25 SEN**   VG   VF   UNC
1964. Red. Man in uniform at r.   —   —   .15

94   **50 SEN**   VG   VF   UNC
1964. Purple. Like #93.   —   .10   .30

95   **25 RUPIAH**
1964. Green. Woman weaver at l.   .15   .50   1.50

96   **50 RUPIAH**   VG   VF   UNC
1964. Dk. brown and green. Woman spinner at l.   .15   .50   1.75

97   **100 RUPIAH**   VG   VF   UNC
1964. Brown and red. Worker on rubber plantation at l.
   a.   Printer's name: *P. T. Pertjetakan Kebajoran Imp.* 16mm. long at   1.00   2.50   5.00
      r. on back.
   b.   Printer's name: *PN Pertjetakan Kebajoran Imp.* 22mm. long at r.   .25   .75   3.00
      on back.

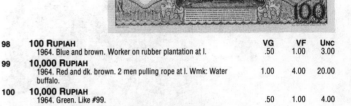

98   **100 RUPIAH**   VG   VF   UNC
1964. Blue and brown. Worker on rubber plantation at l.   .50   1.00   3.00

99   **10,000 RUPIAH**
1964. Red and dk. brown. 2 men pulling rope at l. Wmk: Water   1.00   4.00   20.00
buffalo.

100   **10,000 RUPIAH**
1964. Green. Like #99.   .50   1.00   4.00

101   **10,000 RUPIAH**   VG   VF   UNC
1964. Green. Like #100, but w/wmk. arms.
   a.   Wmk. at ctr.   .35   2.00   6.00
   b.   Wmk. at l. and r.   .25   1.00   4.00

1968 ISSUE
#102 and 103 wmk: Arms at ctr.
#102-112 Gen. Sudirman at l.
#104-110 wmk: Arms at r.

102   **1 RUPIAH**   VG   VF   UNC
1968. Red. Woman shelling coconut at l. on back.   .10   .25   1.50

103	2 1/2 RUPIAH	VG	VF	UNC
	1968. Dk. blue. Arms at r. Woman holding rice stalks at l. on back.	.10	.25	1.50
104	5 RUPIAH			
	1968. Dull violet on m/c unpt. Dam construction scene on back.	.10	.25	2.00

108	100 RUPIAH	VG	VF	UNC
	1968. Deep red on m/c unpt. Rail coalyard on back.	.50	1.50	4.00

105	10 RUPIAH	VG	VF	UNC
	1968. Lt. brown. Oil refinery on back.	.25	.50	2.00

109	500 RUPIAH	VG	VF	UNC
	1968. Dk. green. Yarn spinning on back.	.50	1.75	7.50

106	25 RUPIAH	VG	VF	UNC
	1968. Green and brown. Bridge over Musi River at ctr. r. on back.	.25	.75	3.00

110	1000 RUPIAH	VG	VF	UNC
	1968. Orange and dk. brown. Petro-chemical plant on back.	.65	1.50	6.00
111	5000 RUPIAH			
	1968. Blue-green. Industrial plant on back.	3.00	12.50	50.00
112	10,000 RUPIAH			
	1968. Red-brown and violet. Industrial scene on back.	5.00	25.00	60.00

1975 ISSUE

107	50 RUPIAH	VG	VF	UNC
	1968. Violet and dk. blue. Airplanes on back.	.35	1.00	6.00

112A	500 RUPIAH	VG	VF	UNC
	ND. Prince Diponegoro at l. Terraced fields on back. (Not issued.)	—	—	—

113   1000 RUPIAH

	VG	VF	UNC
1975. Blue-green. Princ Diponegoro at l. Farm scene on back. Wmk: Man's head.	.60	1.50	5.00

113A   5000 RUPIAH

	VG	VF	UNC
ND. Brown. Prince Diponegoro at r. Back like #114. (Not issued.)	—	—	—

114   5000 RUPIAH

	VG	VF	UNC
1975. Brown and m/c. Fisherman w/net at r. 3 men sailing ships on back. Wmk: Tjut Njak Din's head.	2.50	5.00	20.00

114A   10,000 RUPIAH

	VG	VF	UNC
ND. Green and red. Like #113A. Peasants at ctr. on back. (Not issued.)	—	—	—

115   10,000 RUPIAH

	VG	VF	UNC
1975. Brown and m/c. Stone relief at Borobudur Temple. Large mask from Bali at l. on back. Wmk: Gen. Soedirman.	5.00	12.00	50.00

1977 ISSUE

116   100 RUPIAH

	VG	VF	UNC
1977. Red and m/c. Rhinoceros at l. Rhinoceros in jungle scene at ctr. r. on back. Wmk: Arms.	.10	.20	1.25

117   500 RUPIAH

	VG	VF	UNC
1977. Green and m/c. Woman w/2 orchids at l. Bank of Indonesia at ctr. on back and as wmk.	.35	.75	3.00

1979 ISSUE

118 **10,000 RUPIAH**

	VG	VF	UNC
1979. M/c. Musicians playing the "Gamelan" at ctr. Prambanan Temple on back. Wmk: Dr. Soetomo.	4.50	9.00	22.50

1980 ISSUE

119 **1000 RUPIAH**

	VG	VF	UNC
1980. Blue and m/c. Dr. Soetomo at ctr. r. Mountain scene in Sianok Valley on back. Wmk: Sultan Hasanudin.	.45	.65	2.00

120 **5000 RUPIAH**

	VG	VF	UNC
1980. Brown and m/c. Diamond cutter at ctr. Back brown, green and m/c. 3 Torajan houses from Celebes at ctr. Wmk: D. Sartika.	2.25	6.00	17.50

1982 ISSUE

121 **500 RUPIAH**

	VG	VF	UNC
1982. Dk. green and m/c. Man standing by Amorphophallus Titanum flower at I. Bank of Indonesia on back. Wmk: Gen. A. Yani.	.35	1.00	2.25

1984-88 ISSUE

122 **100 RUPIAH**

	VG	VF	UNC
1984. Red on m/c unpt. Goura Victoria at I. Asahan Dam on back. Wmk: Arms.			
a. Engraved.	FV	FV	.75
b. Litho.	FV	FV	.50

123 **500 RUPIAH**

	VG	VF	UNC
1988. Brown and dk. green on m/c unpt. Stag at I. Branch Bank of Indonesia at Cirebon at r. on back. Wmk: Gen. A. Yani.	FV	FV	1.50

124 **1000 RUPIAH**

	VG	VF	UNC
1987. Blue-black on m/c unpt. Arms at I.; Raja Sisingamangaraja XII at ctr. Yogyakarta Palace at ctr. on back. Wmk: Sultan Hasanuddin.	FV	FV	2.00

125 **5000 RUPIAH**
1986. Dk. brown on m/c unpt. Teuku Umar at ctr. Minaret of Kudus
mosque at r. on back. Wmk: C. M. Tijahahu.

	VG	VF	UNC
	FV	FV	10.00

126 **10,000 RUPIAH**
1985. Purple and m/c. R. A. Kartini at l. Temple at ctr. Female graduate
at ctr. r. on back. Wmk: Dr. T. Mangoenkoesoemo.

	VG	VF	UNC
	FV	FV	20.00

1992 ISSUE
#127-132 arms at upper r. area. Printer: PPU.

127 **100 RUPIAH**
1992-. Red on orange and m/c unpt. Sailboat *Pinisi* at l. Volcano *Anak
Krakatau* at r. on back. Wmk: K. H. Dewantara.

	VG	VF	UNC
a. 1992.	FV	FV	.65
b. 1992/1995.	FV	FV	.55

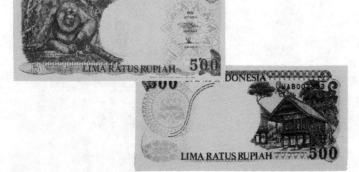

128 **500 RUPIAH**
1992-. Dk. gray and deep brown on green and m/c unpt. Orangutan
resting on limb at l. Native huts at E. Kalimanoan at r. on back. Wmk:
H. O. S. Tjokroaminoto.

	VG	VF	UNC
a. 1992.	FV	FV	1.25
b. 1992/1994.	FV	FV	1.10
c. 1992/1995.	FV	FV	1.00

129 **1000 RUPIAH**
1992. Deep blue on lt. blue and m/c unpt. Aerial view of Lake Toba at l.
ctr. Native huts, stone monument at Nias Island at ctr. on back. Wmk:
Tjut Njak Meutia.

	VG	VF	UNC
	FV	FV	2.00

130 **5000 RUPIAH**
1992. Black, brown and dk. brown on m/c unpt. Musical instrument,
tapestry at ctr. Volcano w/3-color Lake Kelimutu at ctr. on back. Wmk:
Tjut Njak Din.

	VG	VF	UNC
	FV	FV	6.00

131 **10,000 RUPIAH**
1992. Rose and purple on m/c unpt. Sri Sultan Hamengku Buwono IX
at l., girl scouts at ctr. r. Borobudur Temple on hillside on back. Wmk:
W. R. Soepratman.

	VG	VF	UNC
	FV	FV	11.00

132 **20,000 RUPIAH**
1992. Black, dark grayish green and red on m/c unpt. Red
Cendrawasih bird at ctr. Cloves flower at ctr., map of Indonesian
Archipeligo at r. Wmk: K. H. Dewantara.

	VG	VF	UNC
	FV	FV	20.00

1993 COMMEMORATIVE ISSUE
#133 and 134, 25 Years of Economic Development.

133 **50,000 RUPIAH**
1993-. Greenish blue, tan and gray. Pres. Soeharto at l. ctr.,
surrounded by various scenes of development. Anti-counterfeiting
design at r. Jet plane over Soekarno-Hatta International Airport at ctr.
on back. Wmk: W. R. Soepratman.

	VG	VF	UNC
a. W/security thread. 1993.	FV	FV	50.00
b. W/segmented foil over security thread.	FV	FV	42.50

134	50,000 RUPIAH	VG	VF	UNC
(133A)	1993. Design like #133, but pale gray plastic. Soeharto in OVD at r.	—	—	95.00

REGIONAL - IRIAN BARAT

REPUBLIC INDONESIA

1963 ND PROVISIONAL ISSUE
#R1 and R2 Pres. Sukarno at l. w/ovpt: *IRIAN BARAT* on Republik Indonesia issue.

R1	1 RUPIAH	VG	VF	UNC
	ND (1963 - old date 1961). Orange.	2.50	7.50	20.00

R2	2 1/2 RUPIAH	VG	VF	UNC
	ND (1963 - old date 1961). Violet.	3.50	8.50	25.00

BANK INDONESIA

1963 ND PROVISIONAL ISSUE
#R3-R5 Pres. Sukarno at l. w/ovpt: *IRIAN BARAT* on Bank Indonesia issue.

R3	5 RUPIAH	VG	VF	UNC
	ND (1963 - old date 1960). Gray-olive.	4.00	15.00	40.00
R4	10 RUPIAH			
	ND (1963 - old date 1960). Red.	6.00	17.50	35.00
R5	100 RUPIAH			
	ND (1963 - old date 1960). Green.	10.00	25.00	60.00

REGIONAL - RIAU

REPUBLIC INDONESIA

1963 ND PROVISIONAL ISSUE
#R6 and R7 Pres. Sukarno at l. w/ovpt: *RIAU* on Republik Indonesia issue.

R6	1 RUPIAH	VG	VF	UNC
	ND (1963 - old date 1961). Orange.	4.00	15.00	40.00

R7	2 1/2 RUPIAH	VG	VF	UNC
	ND (1963 - old date 1961). Blue.	6.00	20.00	50.00

BANK INDONESIA

1963 ND PROVISIONAL ISSUE
#R8-R10 Pres. Sukarno at l. w/ovpt: *RIAU* on Bank Indonesia issue.

NOTE: Counterfeits on #82a but w/o prefix X on serial # exist.

R8	5 RUPIAH	VG	VF	UNC
	ND (1963 - old date 1960). Violet. Ovpt. on #82a, w/prefix *X* in serial #.	4.00	15.00	40.00

R9	10 RUPIAH	VG	VF	UNC
	ND (1963 - old date 1960). Red.	4.00	10.00	30.00
R10	100 RUPIAH			
	ND (1963 - old date 1960). Green.	20.00	45.00	100.00

IRAN

The Islamic Republic of Iran, located between the Caspian Sea and the Persian Gulf in southwestern Asia, has an area of 636,296 sq. mi. (1,648,000 sq. km.) and a population of 51 million. Capital: Tehran. Although predominantly an agricultural state, Iran depends heavily on oil for foreign exchange. Crude oil, carpets and agricultural products are exported.

Iran (historically known as Persia) is one of the world's most ancient and resilient nations. Strategically astride the lower land gate to Asia, it has been conqueror and conquered, sovereign nation and vassal state, ever emerging from its periods of glory or travail with its culture and political individuality intact. Iran (Persia) was a powerful empire under Cyrus the Great (600-529 B.C.), its borders extending from the Indus to the Nile. It has also been conquered by the predatory empires of antique and recent times - Assyrian, Medean, Macedonia, Seljuq, Turk, Mongol - and more recently been coveted by Russia, Germany and Great Britain. Revolts against the absolute power of the Shahs resulted in the establishment of a constitutional monarchy in 1906. In 1931 the Kingdom of Persia became known as the Kingdom of Iran. In 1979, the monarchy was toppled and an Islamic Republic proclaimed.

RULERS:
Mohammad Reza Pahlavi, SH1320-58/1941-79AD

MONETARY SYSTEM:
1 Toman = 10 Rials SH1310- (1932-)
1 Pahlavi = 10 Tomans

SIGNATURE/TITLE VARIETIES

Kingdom: Mohammad Reza Pahlavi

	GENERAL DIRECTOR	MINISTER OF FINANCE
7	Ebrahim Kashani	Abdolbagi Shoaii
8	Dr. Ali Asghar Pourhomayoun	Abdul Hossein Behnia
9	Mehdi Samii	Abdul Hossein Behnia
10	Mehdi Samii	Amir Abbas Hoveyda
11	Mehdi Samii	Dr. Jamshid Amouzegar
12	Khodadad Farmanfarmaian	Dr. Jamshid Amouzegar
13	Abdol Ali Jahanshahi	Dr. Jamshid Amouzegar
14	Mohammad Yeganeh	Dr. Jamshid Amouzegar
	GENERAL DIRECTOR	MINISTER OF ECONOMIC AND FINANCIAL AFFAIR
15	Mohammad Yeganeh	Hushang Ansary
16	Hassan Ali Mehran	Hushang Ansary
17	Hassan Ali Mehran	Mohammad Yeganeh

NOTE: Some signers used more than one signature (Jamshid Amouzegar), some held more than one term of office (Mehdi Samii) and others held the office of both General Director and Minister of Finance (Mohammad Yeganeh) at different times.

Shah Mohammad Reza Pahlavi, SH1323–58/1944–79 AD

Type V. Imperial Iranian Army (IIA). Uniform. Full face. SH1337–40.

Type VI. Imperial Iranian Air Force (IIAF) Uniform. Three quarter face. SH1341–44.

Type VII. Imperial Iranian Army (IIA) Uniform. Full face. SH1347–48.

Type VIII. Commander in Chief of Iran's Armed Forces. Three quarter face. Large portrait. MS2535 to SH1358.

Type IX. Shaf Pahlavi in CinC Uniform and his father Shah Reza in Imperial Iranian Army (IIA) Uniform. MS2535.

KINGDOM OF IRAN

BANK MARKAZI IRAN

1961; 1962 ISSUE

#71 and 72 fifth portr. of Shah Pahlavi in army uniform at r. Wmk: Young Shah Pahlavi. Yellow security thread runs vertically. Sign. 7. Printer: Harrison (w/o imprint).

#73-75 sixth portr. of Shah Pahlavi in air force uniform. Wmk: Young Shah Pahlavi. Yellow security thread runs vertically. Sign. 8. Printer: Harrison (w/o imprint).

		VG	VF	UNC
71	**10 RIALS** SH1340 (1961). Blue, green and orange. Geometric design and ctr. Amir Kabir dam near Karaj on back.	.50	1.00	2.75

		VG	VF	UNC
72	**20 RIALS** SH1340 (1961). Dk. brown, lt. brown and orange. Geometric design at ctr. Statue of Shah and Ramsar Hotel on back.	.60	1.50	3.50

73 50 RIALS
SH1341 (1962). Green, orange and blue. Shah Pahlavi at r. Koohrang
dam and tunnel on back.

	VG	VF	UNC
a. Sm. date 2.5mm high.	1.00	2.00	5.00
b. Lg. date 4.0mm high.	1.00	2.00	5.00

74 500 RIALS
SH1341 (1962). Black, pink and purple. Shah Pahlavi at ctr. Winged
horses on back.

VG	VF	UNC
7.50	20.00	70.00

75 1000 RIALS
SH1341 (1962). Brown, red and blue. Shah Pahlavi at ctr. Tomb of
Hafez in Shiraz on back.

VG	VF	UNC
12.00	45.00	145.00

1963; 1964 ISSUE

#76 and 77 sixth portr. of Shah Pahlavi in armed forces uniform at r. Wmk: Young Shah Pahlavi. Yellow
security thread. Printer: Harrison (w/o imprint).

76 50 RIALS
(77) SH1343 (1964). Dk. green, orange and blue. Ornate design at ctr.
Koohrang dam and tunnel on back. Sign. 9.

VG	VF	UNC
1.00	3.50	9.00

77 100 RIALS
(76) SH1342 (1963). Maroon and lt. green. Ornate design on back. Oil
refinery at Abadan on back. Sign. 9.

1.00	3.00	8.00

1965 ND ISSUE

#78-82 sixth portr. of Shah Pahlavi in armed forces uniform at r. Wmk: Young Shah Pahlavi. Yellow security
thread. Printer: Harrison (w/o imprint).

78 20 RIALS
ND (1965). Dk. brown, pink and green. Ornate design at ctr. Oriental
hunters on horseback on back.

	VG	VF	UNC
a. Sign. 9.	.35	.85	2.25
b. Sign. 10.	.50	1.50	4.00

79 50 RIALS
ND (1965). Dk. green, orange and blue. Ornate design at ctr.
Koohrang dam and tunnel on back.

a. Sign. 9.	1.75	5.00	15.00
b. Sign. 10.	1.75	5.00	15.00

80 100 RIALS
(83) ND (1965). Maroon and olive-green. M/c ornate design. Oil refinery at
Abadan on back. Sign. 10.

1.50	4.50	12.50

81 200 RIALS
(80) ND (1965). Dk. blue, orange and lavender. M/c ornate design at ctr.
Railroad bridge on back. Sign. 9.

2.00	8.00	25.00

82 500 RIALS
(81) ND (1965). Black, pink and purple. Shat at ctr. Winged horses on
back. Sign. 9.

6.00	20.00	70.00

83 1000 RIALS
(82) ND (1965). Brown, red and blue. Shah at ctr. Tomb of Hafez at Shiraz
on back. Sign. 9.

10.00	35.00	115.00

1969 ND ISSUE

#84-87 seventh portr. of Shah Pahlavi in army uniform at r. Wmk: Young Shah Pahlavi. Yellow security
thread runs vertically. Sign. 11 or 12. Printer: Harrison (w/o imprint).

#84-89 are called "Dark Panel" notes. The bank name is located on a contrasting dk. ornamental panel at
the top ctr.

#88- 89A seventh portr. of Shah Pahlavi in army uniform at ctr. Sign. 11.

84 20 RIALS
ND (1969). Dk. brown, pink and green. Ornate design at ctr. Oriental
hunters on horseback on back.

VG	VF	UNC
.35	.85	2.25

85 50 RIALS
ND (1969-71). Green, orange and blue. Ornate design at ctr. Koohrang
dam and tunnel on back.

a. Sign. 11.	.35	.85	2.25
b. Sign. 12.	.75	1.50	4.00

86 100 RIALS
ND (1969-71). Maroon and lt. green. Ornate design at ctr. Oil refinery
at Abadan on back.

a. Sign. 11.	1.00	2.00	5.00
b. Sign. 12.	1.00	2.00	5.00

87 200 RIALS
ND (1969-71). Dk. blue, orange and purple. M/c ornate design.
Railroad bridge on on back.

a. Sign. 11.	3.00	8.00	20.00
b. Sign. 12.	4.00	11.00	25.00

88 500 RIALS
ND (1969). Black, pink and purple. Ornate frame at ctr. Winged horses
on back.

4.00	12.00	40.00

89	**1000 Rials**	**VG**	**VF**	**Unc**
	ND (1969). Brown, red and blue. Ornate frame at ctr. Tomb of Hafez at Shiraz on back.	6.00	18.00	60.00
89A	**5000 Rials**			
	ND (1969). Purple. Ornate frame at ctr. Golestan Palace in Tehran on back. Printed in Pakistan.	90.00	450.00	1000.

1971 ND Issue

#90-92 seventh portr. of Shah Pahlavi in army uniform at #93-96 seventh portr. of Shah Pahlavi in army uniform at r. Wmk: Young Shah Pahlavi. Yellow security ctr. Wmk: Young Shah Pahlavi. thread runs vertically. Printer: Harrison w/o imprint).

#90-96 are called "Light Panel" notes. The bank name is located on a contrasting lt. ornamental background panel at the top ctr.

90	**50 Rials**	**VG**	**VF**	**Unc**
	ND (1971). Dk. green, orange and blue. Ornamental design at ctr. Koohrang dam and tunnel on back. Sign. 13.	1.00	2.75	7.00

91	**100 Rials**	**VG**	**VF**	**Unc**
	ND (1971-73). Maroon and lt. green. Ornate design at ctr. Oil refinery at Abadan on back.			
	a. Sign. 11.	1.00	2.50	6.00
	b. Sign. 12.	1.00	4.00	9.00
	c. Sign. 13.	1.00	2.50	6.00

92	**200 Rials**	**VG**	**VF**	**Unc**
	ND (1971-73). Blue, orange and purple. Ornate design at ctr. Railroad bridge on back.			
	a. Sign. 11.	2.00	8.00	20.00
	b. Sign. 12.	3.00	10.00	30.00
	c. Sign. 13.	1.50	4.00	10.00

93	**500 Rials**	**VG**	**VF**	**Unc**
	ND (1971-73). Black, pink and purple. Ornate frame at ctr. Winged horses on back.			
	a. Sign. 11.	3.00	10.00	30.00
	b. Sign. 12.	6.00	15.00	60.00
	c. Sign. 13.	5.00	15.00	40.00

94	**1000 Rials**	**VG**	**VF**	**Unc**
	ND (1971-73). Brown, red and blue. Ornate design at ctr. Tomb of Hafez at Shiraz on back.			
	a. Sign. 11.	7.50	20.00	70.00
	b. Sign. 12.	6.50	17.50	65.00
	c. Sign. 13.	5.00	15.00	40.00

95	**5000 Rials**	**VG**	**VF**	**Unc**
	ND (1971-72). Purple and red. Ornate frame at ctr. Golestan Palace in Tehran on back.			
	a. Sign. 12.	20.00	60.00	200.00
	b. Sign. 13.	15.00	50.00	150.00

96   10,000 RIALS

		VG	VF	UNC
ND (1972-73). Dk. green and brown. Ornate frame at ctr. National Council of Ministries in Tehran on back.
a.	Sign. 11.	75.00	150.00	400.00
b.	Sign. 13.	60.00	125.00	350.00

1971 ND COMMEMORATIVE ISSUE

2,500th Anniversary of the Persian Empire

#97 and 98 lg. eighth portr. of Shah Pahlavi in the "Commander in Chief" of Iranian armed forces uniform at r. Wmk: Young Shah Pahlavi. Yellow security thread runs vertically. Sign. 11 or 12. Printer: TDLR.

#99 *Deleted*. See #101a.

97   50 RIALS

		VG	VF	UNC
SH1350 (1971). Green, blue and brown. M/c. Floral design. Shah Pahlavi giving land deeds to villager on back.
a.	Sign. 11.	1.00	2.50	6.00
b.	Sign. 13.	1.00	2.50	6.00

98   100 RIALS

	VG	VF	UNC
	.50	1.50	4.50

SH1350 (1971). Dk. red, purple and orange. M/c geometric and floral design. 3 vignettes labeled: *HEALTH, AGRICULTURE* and *EDUCATION* on back.

1974 ND ISSUE

#100-107 lg. eighth portr. of Shah Pahlavi at r. Wmk: Young Shah Pahlavi. Yellow security thread runs vertically. Printer: TDLR.

100   20 RIALS

		VG	VF	UNC
ND (1974-79). Brown, orange amd pink. Persian carpet design, shepherd and ram. Amir Kabir Dam near Karaj on back.
a.	Sign. 16.	.50	1.00	2.50
b.	Sign. 17.	.50	1.00	3.00
c.	Sign. 18.	.50	1.00	2.50

101   50 RIALS

		VG	VF	UNC
ND (1974-79). Green, brown and blue. Persian carpet design Tomb of Cyrus the Great at Persepolis on back.
a.	Yellow security thread. Sign. 14.	.50	1.00	2.50
b.	Yellow security thread. 15.	.20	.50	1.25
c.	Yellow security thread. Sign. 16.	.50	1.00	2.50
d.	Black security thread. Sign: 17.	.50	1.00	3.00
e.	Black security thread. Sign. 18.	.50	1.00	3.00

102   100 RIALS

		VG	VF	UNC
ND (1974-79). Maroon, purple and orange. Persian carpet design. Marmar Palace on back.
a.	Yellow security thread. Sign. 15.	1.00	2.50	6.50
b.	Yellow security thread. Sign. 16.	.50	1.25	3.00
c.	Black security thread. Sign. 17.	.50	1.25	3.00
d.	Black security thread. Sign. 18.	.50	1.25	3.00

103 200 RIALS

	VG	VF	UNC
ND (1974-79). Blue and green. Persian carpet design. Shahyad Square in Tehran on back.			
a. 6 point star in design on back. Yellow security thread. Monument name as Maidane Shahyad at lower l. on back. Sign. 1.	2.50	6.00	15.00
b. 12 point star in design on back. Yellow security thread. Monument name as Maidane Shahyad. Sign. 16.	1.00	4.00	9.00

	VG	VF	UNC
c. 12 point star in design on back. Yellow security thread. Monument name changed to Shahyad Aryamer. Sign. 16.	1.00	3.50	8.00
d. 12 point star in design on back. Black security thread and Shahyad Aryamer monument. Sign. 17.	1.00	4.00	9.00
e. 12 point star in design on back. Black security thread and Shahyad Aryamer monument. Sign. 18.	1.00	2.00	5.00

104 500 RIALS

	VG	VF	UNC
ND (1974-79). Black, green amd orange. Persian carpet design. Winged horses on back.			
a. 6 point star in design below Shah Pahlavi. Yellow security thread. Sign. 15.	1.50	4.00	15.00
b. 6 point star in design below Shah Pahlavi. Yellow security thread. Sign. 16.	1.00	3.00	10.00
c. Diamond design below Shah Pahlavi. Black security thread. Sign. 17.	1.00	3.50	10.00
d. Diamond design below Shah Pahlavi. Black security thread. Sign. 18.	1.00	3.00	10.00

105 1000 RIALS

	VG	VF	UNC
ND (1974-79). Brown, green and yellow. Persian carpet design. Tomb of Hafez in Shiraz on back.			
a. Yellow security thread. Sign. 15.	4.00	11.00	30.00
b. Yellow security thread. Sign. 16.	1.00	3.00	10.00
c. Black security thread. Sign. 17.	1.00	3.00	9.00
d. Black security thread. Sign. 18.	1.50	4.00	13.50

106 5000 RIALS

	VG	VF	UNC
ND (1974-79). Purple, pink and green. Persian carpet design. Golestan Palace in Tehran on back.			
a. Yellow security thread. Sign. 15.	12.00	45.00	145.00
b. Yellow security thread. Sign. 16.	1.50	6.50	25.00
c. Black security thread. Sign. 17.	1.50	6.00	23.50
d. Black security thread. Sign. 18.	7.50	20.00	75.00

107 10,000 RIALS

	VG	VF	UNC
ND (1974-79). Green and brown. Persian carpet design. National Council of Ministries in Tehran on back.			
a. Yellow security thread. Sign. 15.	30.00	90.00	300.00
b. Yellow security thread. Sign. 16.	7.50	20.00	75.00
c. Black security thread. Sign. 17.	20.00	60.00	200.00
d. Black security thread. Sign. 18.	12.50	40.00	100.00

1976 ND COMMEMORATIVE ISSUE

50th Anniversary of the founding of the Pahlavi Dynasty

#108, ninth portr. of Shah Pahlavi w/Shah Reza at r. Wmk: Young Shah Pahlavi. Yellow security thread runs vertically. Sign. 16. Printer: TDLR.

108 100 RIALS
ND (1976). Maroon, orange and green. Persian carpet design w/old
Bank Melli at bottom ctr. 50th anniversary design in purple and
lavender consisting of 50 suns surrounding Pahlavi Crown on back.

	VG	VF	UNC
108	.50	1.50	4.50

ISLAMIC REPUBLIC

REVOLUTIONARY OVERPRINTS

After the Islamic Revolution of 1978-79, the Iranian government used numerous overprints on existing stocks
of unissued paper money to obliterate Shah Pahlavi's portrait. There were numerous unauthorized and illegal
crude stampings and hand obliterations used by zealous citizens which circulated freely, but only three major
types of official overprints were used by the government.

PROVISIONAL ISSUES

All provisional government ovpt. were placed on existing notes of Shah Pahlavi already printed. Overprinting
was an interim action meant to discredit and disgrace the deposed Shah as well as to publicize and give cre-
dence to the new Islamic Republic. The overprints themselves gave way to more appropriate seals and em-
blems, changes of watermarks and finally to a complete redesigning of all denominations of notes.

In all cases the Shah's portr. was covered by an arabesque design. Eight different styles and varieties of this
ovpt. were used. Watermark ovpt., when used, are either the former Iranian national emblem of Lion and Sun
or the calligraphic Persian text *JUMHURI-YE-ISLAMI-YE-IRAN* (Islamic Republic of Iran) taken from the obverse of the country's new emblem. All ovpt. colors are very dark and require careful scrutiny to distinguish
colors other than black.

Three major types of official ovpt. were used by the government.

Measurements of ovpt. in mm.

At times there are variances in size of the ovpt. on the Shah's portr. The place to measure for the correct mm.
size is across the widest part of the top of the ovpt., approximately a position from "ear to ear".

GOVERNMENT

TYPE 1 PROVISIONAL ISSUE

#110-116 Type I ovpt: Arabesque design over portr. Wmk. area w/o ovpt.

#109 *Deleted.*

		VG	VF	UNC
110	**20 RIALS** ND. Black 27mm ovpt. on #100a.	.75	2.50	7.50
111	**50 RIALS** ND. Ovpt. on #101b.			
	a. Black 27mm ovpt.	.75	2.00	5.00
	b. Green 27mm ovpt.	1.00	2.50	7.00
112	**100 RIALS** ND. Ovpt. on #102c.			
	a. Black 27mm ovpt.	1.00	3.00	10.00
	b. Maroon 27mm ovpt.	2.50	10.00	25.00

		VG	VF	UNC
113	**200 RIALS** ND. Ovpt. on #103.			
	a. Black 28mm. ovpt. on #103a.	2.50	10.00	30.00
	b. Black 28mm. ovpt. on #103b.	2.50	10.00	30.00
	c. Black 28mm. ovpt on #103d.	1.50	8.00	20.00
	d. Black 32mm. ovpt on #103d.	2.50	10.00	30.00

		VG	VF	UNC
114	**500 RIALS** ND. Ovpt. on #104.			
	a. Black 28mm. ovpt. on #104b.	4.00	12.00	40.00
	b. Black 28mm. ovpt. on #104d.	4.00	11.00	35.00
115	**1000 RIALS** ND. Ovpt. on #105.			
	a. Black 32mm ovpt. on #105b.	4.00	12.00	45.00
	b. Black 32mm. ovpt. on #105d.	7.00	20.00	65.00
	c. Brown 32mm ovpt. on #105d.	7.00	20.00	65.00
116	**5000 RIALS** ND. Ovpt. on #106.			
	a. Black 32mm. ovpt. on #106b.	17.50	60.00	175.00
	b. Black 32mm. ovpt. on #106c.	17.50	60.00	175.00
	c. Black 32mm. ovpt. on #106d.	15.00	50.00	160.00

TYPE 2 PROVISIONAL ISSUE

#117-122 Type II ovpt: Arabesque design over portr. and lion and sun national emblem over wmk. area.

		VG	VF	UNC
117	**50 RIALS** ND. Ovpt. on #101.			
	a. Black 27mm ovpt. on #101b.	1.50	5.00	15.00
	b. Black 27mm ovpt. on #101c.	2.50	7.00	20.00
118	**100 RIALS** ND. Ovpt. on #102.			
	a. Black 28mm ovpt. on #102c.	2.00	5.00	15.00
	b. Black 33mm ovpt. on #102d.	.35	1.00	3.00
119	**200 RIALS** ND. Ovpt. on #103.			
	a. Black 28mm ovpt. on #103d.	4.00	12.00	35.00
	b. Black 33mm ovpt. on #103d.	5.00	15.00	40.00
120	**500 RIALS** ND. Ovpt. on #104.			
	a. Black 28mm ovpt. on #104d.	7.00	20.00	65.00
	b. Black 22mm ovpt. on #104d.	7.00	20.00	70.00
121	**1000 RIALS** ND. Ovpt. on #105.			
	a. Black 32mm ovpt. on #105b.	5.00	15.00	50.00
	b. Black 32mm ovpt. on #105d.	4.00	12.50	45.00
122	**5000 RIALS** ND. Ovpt. on #106.			
	a. Black 32mm. ovpt. on #106b.	25.00	70.00	200.00
	b. Black 32mm. ovpt. on #106d.	25.00	70.00	200.00

TYPE 3 PROVISONAL ISSUE

#123-126 Type III ovpt: Arabesque design over portr. and the calligraphic Persian text *JUMHURI-YE ISLA-
MI-YE- IRAN* (Islamic Republic of Iran) over wmk. area.

NOTE: Some notes w/Shah portr. are found w/unofficial ovpts., i.e. large purple or black stamped *X* on portr. and wmk. area.

		VG	VF	UNC
123	**50 RIALS** ND. Black arabesque ovpt. over portr. on #101.			
	a. 28mm ovpt., dk. green script on #101b.	2.00	6.00	20.00
	b. 33mm ovpt., black script on #101d.	.35	1.00	3.00
124	**500 RIALS** ND. Black arabesque and script ovpt. on #104.			
	a. 28mm ovpt. on #104b.	3.00	10.00	35.00
	b. 33mm ovpt. on #104d.	2.50	7.50	22.50
125	**1000 RIALS** ND. Ovpt. on #105.			
	a. Black 32mm ovpt., black script on #105b.	5.00	15.00	50.00
	b. Black 32mm ovpt., black script on #105d.	4.50	14.00	45.00
	c. Brown 32mm ovpt., violet script on #105b.	7.50	20.00	75.00

126   5000 RIALS

		VG	VF	UNC
	ND. Ovpt. on #106.			
a.	Purple 32mm. ovpt., purple script on #106b.	20.00	60.00	200.00
b.	Black 32mm. ovpt., purple script on #106d.	20.00	60.00	200.00

1980 EMERGENCY CIRCULATING CHECK ISSUE

126A   10,000 RIALS

	VG	VF	UNC
ND (1980). Dk. blue w/black text on green unpt. Drawings of modern bldgs. at l. and ctr. Wmk: Bank name repeated. Uniface.	20.00	55.00	120.00

BANK MARKAZI IRAN

	Notes of the Islamic Republic of Iran	
18	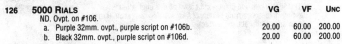 Yousef Khoshkish (on ovpt.)	Mohammad Yeganeh (on ovpt.)
19	Mohammad Ali Mowlavi	Ali Ardalan
20	Ali Reza Nobari	Abol Hassan Bani-Sadr
21	Dr. Mohsen Nourbakhsh	Hossein Nemazi
22	Dr. Mohsen Nourbakhsh	Iravani
23	Ghasemi	Iravani
24	Ghasemi	Dr. Mohsen Nourbakhsh
25	Mohammad Hossein Adeli	Dr. Mohsen Nourbakhsh

1981 ND FIRST ISSUE

#127-131 calligraphic Persian (Farsi) text from republic seal at l., Iman Reza mosque at r. W/o wmk. Yellow security thread w/*BANK MARKAZI IRAN* in black runs through vertically. Sign.19. Printer: TDLR (w/o imprint).

#127 and #130 have calligraphic seal printed in the same color as the note (blue and lavender, respectively) and with no variation. #128, 129 and 131 had the calligraphic seal applied locally after notes were printed. Numerous color varieties, misplacement or total omission can be seen on face or back, or both.

127   200 RIALS

		VG	VF	UNC
	ND (1981). Blue and green. To,b of Ibn-E-Sina in Hamadan at l. on back.			
a.	Ovpt. lion and sun on face.	.75	2.00	5.50
b.	Ovpt. dk. brown seal.	—	—	—

128   500 RIALS

	VG	VF	UNC
ND (1981). Brown, orange and green. Winged horses on back.	.30	1.50	4.50

129   1000 RIALS

	VG	VF	UNC
ND (1981). Rust, brown and green. Tomb of Hafez in Shiraz on back.	2.00	6.00	15.00

130 **5000 RIALS**
ND (1981). Lavender and green. Oil refinery at Tehran on back.

	VG	VF	UNC
a. Security thread.	4.00	15.00	50.00
b. W/o security thread.	10.00	35.00	100.00

131 **10,000 RIALS**
ND (1981). Green and brown. National Council of Ministries in Tehran on back.

	VG	VF	UNC
a. Dk. brown circular seal on wmk.	8.00	25.00	80.00
b. No dk. brown seal, exposing lion and sun ovpt.	10.00	35.00	100.00
c. No lion and sun ovpt.	10.00	35.00	100.00

1981 ND SECOND ISSUE

#132-134 Islamic motifs. Wmk.: Islamic Republic seal. White security thread w/*BANK MARKAZI IRAN* in black Persian script runs vertically. Sign. 20 unless 21 noted. Printer: TDLR (w/o imprint).

132 **100 RIALS**
ND (1981). Maroon and brown. Imam Reza shrine at Mashad at r. Madressa Chahr-Bagh in Isfahan on back.

	VG	VF	UNC
	.50	1.00	3.50

133 **5000 RIALS**
ND (1981). Violet, red-orange and brown on m/c unpt. Mullahs leading marchers carrying posters of Ayatollah Khomeini at ctr. Hazrat Masoumeh shrine at l. ctr. on back.

	VG	VF	UNC
	5.00	12.00	30.00

134 **10,000 RIALS**
ND (1981). Deep blue-green on yellow and m/c unpt. Face like #133. Imam Reza shrine in Mashad at ctr. on back. Wmk.: Arms.

	VG	VF	UNC
a. Sign. 20. Wmk: Republic seal.	6.00	15.00	50.00
b. Sign. 21. Wmk: Arms.	6.00	15.00	50.00

1982; 1983 ND ISSUE

#135-139 Islamic motifs. Wmk: Upraised broadsword in 2 curved arcs (arms) at l. White security thread w/black *BANK MARKAZI IRAN* in Persian letters repeatedly runs vertically. Printer: TDLR.

NOTE: #139 exists w/2diff. sign. 21 style of Nemazi.

135 **100 RIALS**
ND (1982). Maroon and brown. Imam Reza shrine. at r. Madressa Chahr-Bagh on back. Like #132.

	VG	VF	UNC
	.40	1.00	2.00

136 **200 RIALS**
ND (1982). Grayish blue and m/c. Mosque. Farmers and tractor on back.

	VG	VF	UNC
a. Sign. 21.	.30	.75	2.25
b. Sign. 23.	FV	FV	2.00

CENTRAL BANK OF THE ISLAMIC REPUBLIC OF IRAN

1985; 1986 ND ISSUE

137	**500 RIALS**	VG	VF	UNC
	ND (1982). Gray and olive. Feyzieh Madressa seminary at lower l., lg. prayer gathering at ctr. Tehran University on back.			
a.	Sign. 21. Wmk: Arms.	FV	FV	7.50
b.	Sign. 22.	FV	5.00	25.00
c.	Sign. 23.	FV		7.00
d.	Sign. 23. Wmk: Mohd. H. Fahmideh (youth).	FV		3.75
e.	Sign. 24.	FV	FV	3.50
f.	Sign. 25.	FV	FV	3.50

140	**100 RIALS**	VG	VF	UNC
	ND (1985). Purple and m/c. Ayatollah Moddaress at r. Parliament at l. on back. Wmk: Arms. Printer: TDLR.			
a.	Sign. 21.	FV	FV	3.00
b.	Sign. 22.	FV	FV	2.50
c.	Sign. 23.	FV	FV	2.25
d.	Sign. 23. Wmk: Mohd. M. Fahmid mideh (youth).	FV	FV	2.00
e.	Sign. 24.	FV	FV	2.00
f.	Sign. 25.	FV	FV	1.75

Wmk: ☾

138	**1000 RIALS**	VG	VF	UNC
	ND (1982; 1986). Lt. green, red-brown and brown. Feyzieh Madressa seminary at ctr. Mosque of Omar (Dome of the Rock) in Jerusalem on back.			
a.	Sign. 21. Additional short line of text under bldg. on back. Wmk: Arms.	FV	FV	12.50
b.	Sign. like a. No line of text under bldg. on back.	FV	FV	30.00
c.	Sign. 22.	FV	FV	15.00
d.	Sign. 23.	FV	FV	10.00
e.	Sign. 23. Wmk: Mohd. H. Fahmideh (youth).	FV	FV	7.00
f.	Sign. 24.	FV	FV	6.00
g.	Sign. 25.	FV	FV	5.00

141	**2000 RIALS**	VG	VF	UNC
	ND(1986). Violet, dk. brown ad m/c. Revolutionists before mosque at ctr. r. Kaabain Mecca on back.			
a.	Sign. 21.Wmk: Arms.	FV	FV	7.50
b.	Sign. 22.	FV	FV	7.50
c.	Sign. 23.	FV	FV	10.00
d.	Sign.23. Wmk: Mohd. H. Fahmideh (youth).	FV	FV	7.50
e.	Sign. 24.	FV	FV	7.50
f.	Sign. 25.	FV	FV	7.50

1992; 1993 ND ISSUE

#143-146 Khomeini at r. Sign. 25.

#145 and 146 wmk: Khomeini.

#142 and 144 Held in Reserve.

139	**5000 RIALS**	VG	VF	UNC
	ND (1983). Red and m/c. Similar to #133; reduced crown. Radiant sun removed from upper l. on face. 2 small placards of Khomeini added to crowd.	FV	FV	24.00

143 1000 RIALS
ND (1992). Brown and deep olive-green on m/c unpt. Mosque of Omar (Dome of the Rock) in Jerusalem at ctr. on back. Wmk: Youthful revolutionary male portrait.

VG	VF	UNC
FV	FV	4.00

145 5000 RIALS
ND (1993). Dk. brown and olive-green on m/c unpt. Flowers and birds at ctr. r. on back.

VG	VF	UNC
FV	FV	14.50

146 10,000 RIALS
ND (1992). Deep blue-green, blue and olive-green on m/c unpt. Mount Damavand at ctr. r. on back.

VG	VF	UNC
FV	FV	25.00

The Republic of Iraq, historically known as Mesopotamia, is located in the Near East and is bordered by Kuwait, Iran, Turkey, Syria, Jordan and Saudi Arabia. It has an area of 167,925 sq. mi. (434,924 sq. km.) and a population of 17.6 million. Capital: Baghdad. The economy of Iraq is based on agriculture and petroleum. Crude oil accounts for 94 percent of the exports before the war with Iran began in 1980.

Iraq was the site of a number of flourishing civilizations of antiquity - Sumerian, Assyrian, Babylonian, Parthian, Persian - and of the Biblical cities of Ur, Nineveh and Babylon. Desired because of its favored location which embraced the fertile alluvial plains of the Tigris and Euphrates Rivers, Mesopotamia - "land between the rivers" - was conquered by Cyrus the Great of Persia, Alexander of Macedonia and by Arabs who made the legendary city of Baghdad the capital of the ruling caliphate. Suleiman the Great conquered Mesopotamia for Turkey in 1534, and it formed part of the Ottoman Empire until 1623, and from 1638 to 1917. Great Britain, given a League of Nations mandate over the territory in 1920, recognized Iraq as a kingdom in 1922. Iraq became an independent constitutional monarchy presided over by the Hashemite family, direct descendants of the prophet Mohammed, in 1932. In 1958, the army-led revolution of July 14 overthrew the monarchy and proclaimed a republic.

MONETARY SYSTEM:
1 Dinar (Pound) = 1000 Fils

REPUBLIC

CENTRAL BANK OF IRAQ

1958 ISSUE
#51-55 new Republic arms w/1958 at r. and as wmk. Sign. varieties.

51 1/4 DINAR
1958. Green on m/c unpt. Palm tree at ctr. on back.

VG	VF	UNC
1.00	5.00	15.00

52 1/2 DINAR
1958. Brown on m/c unpt.

VG	VF	UNC
2.00	8.00	30.00

53 1 DINAR
1958. Blue on m/c unpt. Ornate harp-like piece w/strings on back.

VG	VF	UNC
1.50	6.50	20.00

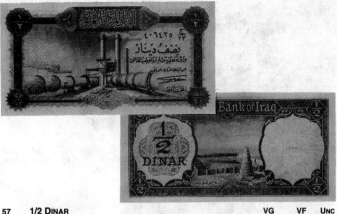

57 1/2 DINAR
ND (1971). Brown on m/c unpt. Oil refinery. Walled fort and minaret at ctr. *1/2 Dinar* at l. on back.

	VG	VF	UNC
	2.50	8.00	25.00

54 5 DINARS
1958. Lt. purple on m/c unpt.

	VG	VF	UNC
	2.50	12.50	35.00

58 1 DINAR
ND (1971). Blue and brown on m/c unpt. Factory at ctr. Doorway at ctr., *1 Dinar* at l. on back.

	VG	VF	UNC
	2.00	6.00	18.50

55 10 DINARS
1958. Dk. blue on m/c unpt.

	VG	VF	UNC
	6.00	30.00	90.00

1971 ND ISSUE
#56-60 wmk: Falcon's head. Sign. varieties.

59 5 DINARS
ND (1971). Lilac on brown and m/c unpt. Parliament bldg. across face. 2 ancient figures at ctr., *5 Dinars* at l. on back.

	VG	VF	UNC
	5.00	15.00	45.00

56 1/4 DINAR
ND (1971). Green and brown on m/c unpt. Harbor at ctr. Back like #51. *1/4 Dinar* at l. on back.

	VG	VF	UNC
	1.00	3.00	9.00

60	**10 DINARS**	**VG**	**VF**	**UNC**
	ND (1971). Purple, blue and brown on m/c unpt. Coffer dam at ctr. Ancient carvings of winged creatures at ctr., *10 Dinars* at l. on back.	5.00	15.00	45.00

1973 ND; 1978 ISSUE

#61-66 wmk: Falcon's head. Sign. varieties.

61	**1/4 DINAR**	**VG**	**VF**	**UNC**
	ND (1973). Green and black on m/c unpt. Similar to #56. *Quarter Dinar* at bottom r. on back.	.50	1.50	5.00

62	**1/2 DINAR**	**VG**	**VF**	**UNC**
	ND (1973). Brown on m/c unpt. Face design similar to #57. *Half Dinar* below Minaret of the Great Mosque at Samarra at ctr. on back.	1.25	4.00	12.50

63	**1 DINAR**			
	ND (1973). Blue on green m/c unpt. Similar to #58. *One Dinar* at bottom r. on back.			
	a. W/o line of Arabic inscription below factory.	1.00	3.25	10.00
	b. 1 line of Arabic inscription below factory.	1.00	4.50	20.00

64	**5 DINARS**	**VG**	**VF**	**UNC**
	ND (1973). Lilac on m/c unpt. Similar to #59. *Five Dinars* at bottom on back.	.75	2.50	7.50

65	**10 DINARS**	**VG**	**VF**	**UNC**
	ND (1973). Purple on m/c unpt. Coffer dam at r. Back similar to #60, but *Ten Dinars* at bottom.	1.50	4.50	13.50

66	**25 DINARS**	**VG**	**VF**	**UNC**
	1978-AH1398; 1980-AH1400. Green and brown on m/c unpt. 3 Arabian horses at ctr., date below sign. at lower r. Abbaside Palace on back. 182 x 88mm.	2.50	7.50	22.50

1979-86 ISSUE

#67-72 wmk: Arabian horse's head. Sign. varieties.

NOTE: In a sudden economic move during summer of 1993, it was announced that all previous 25 Dinar notes issued before #74 had become worthless.

67 **1/4 Dinar**

1979/AH1399. Green and m/c. Palm trees at ctr. Bldg. on back.

VG	VF	Unc
.15	.50	1.50

71 **10 Dinars**

1980/AH1400; 1981/AH1401; 1982/AH1402; 1983/AH1403. Purple and m/c. A. Abulhasan ibn al Hisham at r. Tower on back.

VG	VF	Unc
.65	2.00	6.50

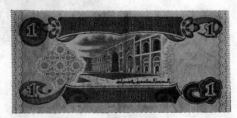

68 **1/2 Dinar**

1980/AH1400; 1985/AH1405. Brown and m/c. Astrolabe at r. Minaret of Samarra on back.

VG	VF	Unc
.15	.50	1.50

72 **25 Dinars**

1981/AH1401; 1982/AH1402. Green and brown. Similar to #66 but date below horses. Reduced size, 175 x 80mm.

VG	VF	Unc
.75	2.50	7.50

69 **1 Dinar**

1979/AH1399; 1980/AH1400; 1984/AH1404; 1984 AH1405. Olive-green and deep blue on m/c unpt. Coin design at ctr. Musanteriah School in Baghdad on back.

VG	VF	Unc
.25	.75	2.25

70 **5 Dinars**

1980/AH1400; 1981/AH1401; 1982/AH1402. Brown-violet on deep blue and m/c unpt. Waterfalls at ctr. Walled city on back.

VG	VF	Unc
.30	1.00	3.00

73 **25 Dinars**

1986. Brown and black on green, blue and m/c unpt. Medieval horsemen charging at ctr., S. Hussein at r. City gate at l., monument at ctr. on back. Wmk: Hussein.

VG	VF	Unc
.75	2.50	7.50

1990; 1991 EMERGENCY GULF WAR ISSUE
#74-76 local printing.

74   25 DINARS

	VG	VF	UNC
1990/AH1411; 1991/AH1411. Similar to #72 but green and gray on lt. green unpt. Litho.	FV	FV	5.00

75   50 DINARS

	VG	VF	UNC
1991/AH1411. Brown and blue-green on m/c unpt. S. Hussein at r. Minaret of the Great Mosque at Samarra at ctr. r. on back.	.75	2.50	7.50

76   100 DINARS

	VG	VF	UNC
1991/AH1411. Dk. blue-green on lilac and m/c unpt. S. Hussein at r. Crossed swords below Iraqi flag at ctr. on back.	1.00	3.00	9.00

1992-93 EMERGENCY ISSUE
#77-79 dull lithograph printing. W/o wmk.
#80 and 81 S. Hussein at r. Printed in China.
#82 Held in Reserve.

77   1/4 DINAR

	VG	VF	UNC
1993/AH1413. Green on m/c unpt. Like #67.	FV	FV	.75

78   1/2 DINAR

	VG	VF	UNC
1993/AH1413. Brown on m/c unpt. Like #68.	FV	FV	1.00

79   1 DINAR

	VG	VF	UNC
1992/AH1412. Green and blue-black on m/c unpt. Like #69.	FV	FV	1.25

80   5 DINARS

	VG	VF	UNC
1992/AH1412. Red-brown on pale orange, lilac and m/c unpt. Temple at l. ctr. Monument at ctr., ancient stone carvings at l. on back. Shade varieties.			
a. W/border around embossed text at ctr.	FV	FV	3.50
b. W/o border around embossed text at ctr.	FV	FV	3.50

81   10 DINARS
    1992/AH1412. Violet, blue-green and m/c. Winged lion sculpture at l.
on back.

	VG	VF	UNC
	FV	FV	5.50

1994-95 ISSUE
#83-85 S. Hussein at r.

NOTE: Shade varieties exist.

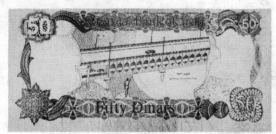

83   50 DINARS
    1994/AH1414. Brown and pale green on m/c unpt. Ancient statuette,
monument at l. ctr. Modern Saddam bridge at ctr. on back.

	VG	VF	UNC
	FV	FV	4.00

84   100 DINARS
    1994/AH1414. Blue-black on lt. blue and pale ochre unpt. Walled
compound at ctr. Modern bldg. at ctr. on back. Printed wmk: Falcon's
head.

	VG	VF	UNC
	FV	FV	4.00

85   250 DINARS
    1995/AH1415. Purple on m/c unpt. Hydro-electric dam at l. ctr.,
Archaic frieze across back.

	VG	VF	UNC
	FV	FV	5.00

IRELAND REPUBLIC

The Republic of Ireland which occupies five-sixths of the island of Ireland located in the Atlantic Ocean west of Great Britain, has an area of 27,136 sq. mi. (70,283 sq. km.) and a population of 3.5 million. Capital: Dublin. Agriculture and dairy farming are the principal industries. Meat, livestock, dairy products and textiles are exported.

The Irish Free State was established as a dominion on Dec. 6, 1921. Ireland withdrew from the Commonwealth and proclaimed itself a republic on April 18, 1949. The government, however, does not use the term "Republic if Ireland," which tacitly acknowledges the partitioning of the island into Ireland and Northern Ireland, but refers to the country simply as "Ireland".

RULERS:
British to 1949

MONETARY SYSTEM:
1 Dollar = 100 Cents
1 Shilling = 12 Pence
1 Pound = 20 Shillings to 1971
1 Pound = 100 New Pence, 1971-

REPUBLIC

CENTRAL BANK OF IRELAND

1961-63 ISSUE
#63-65 portr. Lady Hazel Lavery at l., denomination at bottom ctr.
#66-69 Lady Hazel Lavery in Irish national costume w/chin resting on her hand and leaning on an Irish harp.

		VG	VF	UNC
63	**10 SHILLINGS**			
	3.1.1962-6.6.1968. Orange. Sign. M. O. Muimhneachain and T. K. Whitaker.	1.25	5.00	18.00

		VG	VF	UNC
64	**1 POUND**			
	1962-76. Green.			
	a. Sign. M. O. Muimhneachain and T. K. Whitaker. 16.3.1962-8.10.1968.	2.75	6.00	25.00
	b. Sign. T. K. Whitaker and C. H. Murray. 1.3.1969-17.9.1970.	2.50	5.00	19.00
	c. Sign. like b, but metallic security thread at l. of ctr. 8.7.1971-21.4.1975.	2.25	4.00	15.00
	d. Sign. C. H. Murray and M. O. Murchu. 30.9.1976.	2.00	3.00	12.00

		VG	VF	UNC
65	**5 POUNDS**			
	1961-75. Brown.			
	a. Sign. M. O. Muimhneachain and T. K. Whitaker. 15.8.1961-12.8.1968.	12.50	25.00	85.00
	b. Sign. T. K. Whitaker and C. H. Murray. 12.5.1969; 27.2.1970.	11.50	20.00	70.00
	c. Sign. like b., but metallic security thread at l. of ctr. 18.1.1971-5.9.1975.	10.00	12.50	50.00

		VG	VF	UNC
66	**10 POUNDS**			
	1962-76. Blue.			
	a. Sign. M. O. Muimhneachain and T. K. Whitaker. 2.5.1962-16.7.1968.	21.50	45.00	120.00
	b. Sign. T. K. Whitaker and C. H. Murray. 5.5.1969; 9.3.1970.	20.00	35.00	100.00
	c. Sign. like b, but metallic security thread at l. of ctr. 19.5.1971-10.2.1975.	18.50	25.00	85.00
	d. Sign. C. H. Murray and M. O. Murchu. 2.12.1976.	17.50	22.50	80.00
67	**20 POUNDS**			
	1961-76. Red.			
	a. Sign. M. O. Muimhneachain and T. K. Whitaker. 1.6.1961-15.6.1965.	40.00	85.00	250.00
	b. Sign. T. K. Whitaker and C. H. Murray. 3.3.1969-6.1.1975.	37.50	60.00	185.00
	c. Sign. C. H. Murray and M. O. Murchu. 24.3.1976.	35.00	50.00	150.00
68	**50 POUNDS**			
	1962-77. Purple.			
	a. Sign. M. O. Muimhneachain and T. K. Whitaker. 1.2.1962-6.9.1968.	95.00	150.00	325.00
	b. Sign. T. K. Whitaker and C. H. Murray. 4.11.1970-16.4.1975.	90.00	125.00	275.00
	c. Sign. C. H. Murray and M. O. Murchu. 4.4.1977.	87.50	100.00	250.00

69	**100 POUNDS**	VG	VF	UNC
	1963-77. Green.			
	a. Sign. M. O. Muimhneachain and T. K. Whitaker. 16.1.1963-9.9.1968.	185.00	275.00	525.00
	b. Sign. T. K. Whitaker and C. H. Murray. 26.10.1970; 4.5.1972; 26.2.1973.	180.00	225.00	475.00
	c. Sign. C. H. Murray and M. O. Murchu. 4.4.1977.	175.00	200.00	425.00

1976-82 ISSUE

70	**1 POUND**	VG	VF	UNC
	1977-89. Dk. olive-green and green on m/c unpt. Qn. Medb at r. Old writing on back. Wmk: Lady Lavery.			
	a. Sign. C. H. Murray and M. O. M. Murchu. 10.6.1977-29.11.1977	2.00	3.00	10.00
	b. Sign. C. H. Murray and T. O'Co 'Cofaigh. 30.8.1978-30.10.1981.	FV	2.50	8.00
	c. Sign. T. O'Cofaigh and M. F. D. Doyle. 30.6.1982-22.4.1987.	FV	2.00	7.00
	d. Sign. M. F. Doyle and S. P. Cr Cromien. 23.3.1988-17.7.1989.	FV	2.00	6.50

71	**5 POUNDS**	VG	VF	UNC
	1976-93. Brown and red. J. S. Eriugena at r. Old writing on back.			
	a. Sign. T. K. Whitaker and C. H. Murray. 26.2.1976.	FV	FV	30.00
	b. Sign. C. H. Murray and M. O. Murchu. 18.5.1976-17.10.1977.	FV	FV	27.50
	c. Sign. C. H. Murray and T. O'Cofaigh. 25.4.1979-13.10.1981	FV	FV	25.00
	d. Sign. T. O'Cofaigh and M. F. Doyle. 1982; 7.10.1983-22.4.1987.	FV	FV	22.50
	e. Sign. M. F. Doyle and S. P. Cromien. 12.8.1988-7.5.1993.	FV	FV	20.00

72	**10 POUNDS**	VG	VF	UNC
	1978-92. Violet and purple. J. Swift at r. Old street map on back.			
	a. Sign. C. H. Murray and T. O'Cofaigh. 1.6.1978-20.10.1981.	FV	FV	50.00
	b. Sign. T. O'Cofaigh and M. F. Doyle. 1982; 25.2.1983-4.4.1986.	FV	FV	42.50
	c. Sign. M. F. Doyle and S. P. Cromien. 1.2.1988-14.4.1992.	FV	FV	37.50

73	**20 POUNDS**	VG	VF	UNC
	1980-92. Blue and m/c. W. B. Yeats at r., Abbey Theatre symbol at ctr. Map on back.			
	a. Sign. C. H. Murray and T. O'Cofaigh. 7.1.1980-28.10.1981.	FV	FV	75.00
	b. Sign. T. O'Cofaigh and M. F. Doyle. 11.7.1983-28.8.1986.	FV	FV	65.00
	c. Sign. M. F. Doyle and S. P. Cromien. 5.7.1988-21.1.1992.	FV	FV	60.00

74	**50 POUNDS**	VG	VF	UNC
	1982; 1991. Red and brown. Carolan playing harp in front of group. Musical instruments on back.			
	a. Sign. T. O'Cofaigh and M. F. Doyle. 1.11.1982.	FV	FV	150.00
	b. Sign. M. F. Doyle and S. P. Cromien. 5.11.1991.	FV	FV	120.00

1992-95 ISSUE
#75-78 wmk: Lady Lavery and value.

75   5 POUNDS
1994-. Dk. brown, reddish brown, and grayish purple on m/c unpt.
Mater Misericordiae Hospital at bottom l. ctr., C. McAuley at r. School
children at ctr. on back.

		VG	VF	UNC
a.	Sign. M. F. Doyle and S. P. Cromien. 15.3.1994.	FV	FV	16.50
b.	Sign. O'Connell and Mullarkey. 27.4.1994.	FV	FV	13.50

76   10 POUNDS
14.7.1993-. Dk. green, brown, blue and m/c. Aerial iew of Diblin at
ctr., J. Joyce at r. Sculpted head representing Liffey River at l., map in
unpt. on back. Sign. M. F. Doyle and S. P. Cromien.

VG	VF	UNC
FV	FV	25.00

77   20 POUNDS
21.9.1992-. Violet, brown and dk. grayish blue on m/c unpt.
Derryname Abbey at l. ctr., D. O'Connell at r. Writings and bldg. on
back. Sign. M. F. Doyle and S. P. Cromien.

VG	VF	UNC
FV	FV	45.00

78   50 POUNDS
6.10.1995; 14.2.1996. Dk. blue and violet on m/c unpt. D. Hyde at r.,
Áras an Uachtaráin bldg. in background at ctr. Back dk. gray and deep
olive-green on m/c unpt; seated piper at l., crest of Conradhna Gaeilge
at upper ctr. r.

VG	VF	UNC
FV	FV	110.00

NORTHERN IRELAND

From 1800 to 1921 Ireland was
an integral part of the United
Kingdom. The Anglo-Irish treaty
of 1921 established the Irish Free
State of 26 counties within the
Commonwealth of Nations and
recognized the partition of Ireland. The six predominantly Protestant counties of northeast
Ulster chose to remain a part of
the United Kingdom with a limited
self-government.

Up to 1928 the notes of the private or commerical banks were
circulating in the whole of Ireland. After the establishment of the Irish Free
State, the private or commercial notes were valid only in Northern Ireland.

NOTE: For notes of the Irish Republic see Ireland/Éire.

RULERS:
British

MONETARY SYSTEM:
1 Shilling = 12 Pence
1 Pound = 20 Shillings to 1971
1 Pound = 100 New Pence, 1971-

BRITISH INFLUENCE

ALLIED IRISH BANKS LTD.

Formerly Provincial Bank of Ireland Ltd., later became First Trust Bank.

1982 ISSUE

#1-5 designs similar to Provincial Bank of Ireland Ltd. (#247-251) except for bank title and sign. Printer: TDLR.

1   1 POUND
1.1.1982; 1.7.1983; 1.12.1984. Green on m/c unpt. Young girl at r.
Sailing ship *Girona* at ctr. on back.

VG	VF	UNC
FV	6.00	15.00

2   5 POUNDS
1.1.1982. Blue and purple on m/c unpt. Young woman at r. Dunluce
Castle at ctr. on back.

VG	VF	UNC
FV	12.50	30.00

3	**10 POUNDS**	VG	VF	UNC
	1.1.1982; 1.12.1984. Brown and gray-green on m/c unpt. Young man at r. Wreck of the *Girona* at ctr. on back.	FV	22.50	50.00
4	**20 POUNDS**			
	1.1.1982. Purple and green. Elderly woman at r. Chimney at Lacada Pt. at ctr. on back.	FV	42.50	95.00
5	**100 POUNDS**			
	1.1.1982. Black, olive and green. Elderly man at r. The *Armada* at ctr. on back.	FV	185.00	325.00

ALLIED IRISH BANKS PUBLIC LIMITED COMPANY
Formerly Allied Irish Banks Ltd., later became First Trust Bank.

1987-88 ISSUE
#6-9 like #2-5 except for bank title and sign. Printer: TDLR.

6	**5 POUNDS**	VG	VF	UNC
	1.1.1987; 1.1.1990. Similar to #2.	FV	FV	22.50

7	**10 POUNDS**			
	1.3.1988; 1.1.1990; 18.5.1993. Similar to #3.	FV	FV	43.50
8	**20 POUNDS**			
	1.4.1987. Similar to #4.	FV	FV	80.00

9	**100 POUNDS**	VG	VF	UNC
	1.12.1988. Similar to #5.	FV	FV	300.00

BANK OF IRELAND

BELFAST BRANCH

1967 ND ISSUE
#56-64 Mercury at l., woman w/harp at r. Airplane, bank bldg. and boat on back. Sign. title as Agent.
#59 and 60 *Deleted*.

56	**1 POUND**	VG	VF	UNC
	ND (1967). Green-lilac. 151 x 72mm. Sign. W. E. Guthrie.	2.00	5.00	22.50
57	**5 POUNDS**			
	ND (1967-68). Brown-violet.			
	a. Sign. W. E. Guthrie. (1967). .	9.00	17.50	65.00
	b. Sign. H. H. M. Chestnutt. (196 1968).	8.00	15.00	55.00
58	**10 POUNDS**			
	ND (1967). Brown and yellow. Sign. W. E. Guthrie.	18.00	35.00	120.00

1971-74 ND ISSUES

61	**1 POUND**	VG	VF	UNC
	ND (1972-77). Black on lt. green and lilac unpt. Like #56 but smaller size. 134 x 66mm.			
	a. W/o signs in corners. Sign. H. H. M. Chestnutt. (1972).	FV	3.00	20.00
	b. Corners as a. Sign. A. S. J. O'Neill. (1977).	FV	FV	12.00
62	**5 POUNDS**			
	ND (1971-77). Blue on lt. green and lilac unpt. 146 x 78mm.			
	a. W/o £ signs in corners. Sign. of H. H. M. Chestnutt. (1971).	FV	13.50	37.50
	b. Corners as a. Sign. of A. S. J. O'Neill. (1977).	FV	12.50	27.50
63	**10 POUNDS**			
	ND (1971-77). Brown on lt. green and lt. orange unpt.			
	a. Sign. of H. H. M. Chestnutt. (1971).	FV	25.00	75.00
	b. Sign. of A. S. J. O'Neill. (1977).	FV	20.00	45.00
64	**100 POUNDS**			
	ND (1974-78). Red on m/c unpt.			
	a. Sign. of H. H. M. Chestnutt. (1974).	FV	FV	375.00
	b. Sign. of A. S. J. O'Neill. (1978).	FV	FV	300.00

1980s ND ISSUE

65	**1 POUND**	VG	VF	UNC
	ND. Like #61 but w/*STERLING* added.	FV	FV	6.00
66	**5 POUNDS**			
	ND. £ signs added in corners.			
	a. Sign. A. S. J. O'Neill.	FV	11.00	25.00
	b. Sign. D. F. Harrison.	FV	13.50	30.00
67	**10 POUNDS**			
	ND (1984). Dk. green on m/c unpt.	FV	18.50	60.00
	a. Sign. A. S. J. O'Neill.	FV	35.00	60.00
	b. Sign. D. F. Harrison.	FV	37.50	75.00

68	**100 POUNDS**	VG	VF	UNC
	ND. Similar to #64 but w/£ sign at upper r. and lower l. corners on face and back. *Sterling* added at lower ctr. on face.			
	a. Sign. A. S. J. O'Neill.	FV	FV	285.00
	b. Sign. D. F. Harrison.	FV	FV	210.00

1983 COMMEMORATIVE ISSUE
#66, Bank of Ireland Bicentenary, 1783-1983

69	**20 POUNDS**	VG	VF	UNC
	1983. Dk. green on m/c unpt. Like #67 but commemorative text below bank title.	75.00	150.00	400.00

1990-95 ISSUE
#70-74 bank seal (Hibernia seated) at l. Queen's University in Belfast on back. Sign. D. F. Harrison. Wmk: Medusa head.

NOTE: 120 specimens in 3-subject sheets were sold to collectors. Low numbers were also available in special folders.

70	**5 POUNDS**	VG	VF	UNC
	28.8.1990. Blue and purple on m/c unpt.	FV	FV	15.00
71	**10 POUNDS**			
	14.5.1991. Purple and maroon on m/c unpt.	FV	FV	27.50
72	**20 POUNDS**			
	9.5.1991. Green and brown on m/c unpt.	FV	FV	52.50
73	**50 POUNDS**			
	1.7.1995. Brown, olive and m/c. The Queen's University in Belfast on back.	FV	FV	110.00
74 (73)	**100 POUNDS**			
	28.8.1992. Red on m/c unpt.	FV	FV	225.00

BELFAST BANKING COMPANY LIMITED

NOTE: See also Ireland.

BELFAST BRANCH

1922-23 ISSUE
#126-131 arms at top or upper ctr. w/payable text: . . . at our Head Office, Belfast.

127	**5 POUNDS**	VG	VF	UNC
	1923-66. Black on red unpt.			
	a. Black serial #. 3.1.1923; 3.5.1923; 7.9.1927.	17.50	45.00	150.00
	b. Red serial #. 8.3.1928-2.10.1942.	12.50	35.00	80.00
	c. Red serial #. 6.1.1966.	10.00	20.00	50.00

128	**10 POUNDS**	VG	VF	UNC
	1923-65. Black on green unpt.			
	a. Black serial #. 3.1.1923.	40.00	65.00	225.00
	b. Green serial #. 9.1.1929-1.1.1943.	30.00	55.00	150.00
	c. Green serial #. 3.12.1963; 5.6.1965.	18.00	30.00	75.00
129	**20 POUNDS**			
	1923-65. Black on purple unpt.			
	a. Black serial #. 3.1.1923.	45.00	100.00	300.00
	b. Mauve serial #. 9.11.1939; 10.8.1940.	40.00	90.00	250.00
	c. Black serial #. 3.2.1943	37.50	65.00	180.00
	d. Black serial #. 5.6.1965.	35.00	50.00	150.00

130	**50 POUNDS**	VG	VF	UNC
	1923-63. Black on orange unpt.			
	a. Black serial #. 3.1.1923; 3.5.1923.	150.00	275.00	500.00
	b. Yellow serial #. 9.11.1939; 10.8.1940.	125.00	150.00	375.00
	c. Black serial #. 3.2.1943.	95.00	125.00	300.00
	d. Black serial #. 3.12.1963.	85.00	125.00	250.00

131 100 POUNDS

1923-68. Black on red unpt.

	VG	VF	UNC
a. 3.1.1923; 3.5.1923.	170.00	350.00	600.00
b. 9.11.1939; 3.2.1943.	FV	200.00	450.00
c. 3.12.1963.	FV	185.00	350.00
d. 8.5.1968.	FV	175.00	300.00

FIRST TRUST BANK

Formerly Allied Irish Banks PLC, which acquired the Trustee Savings Bank. Member AIB Group Northern Ireland PLC.

1994 ISSUE

#132-135 five shields at bottom ctr. Printer: TDLR. Sign. title: GROUP MANAGING DIRECTOR. Wmk: Young woman.

132 10 POUNDS

10.1.1994. Dk. brown and violet. Face similar to #3. Sailing ship Girona at ctr. on back.

VG	VF	UNC
FV	FV	25.00

133 20 POUNDS

10.1.1994. Violet, dk. brown and red-brown on m/c unpt. Face similar to #4. Chimney at Lacada Pt. at ctr. on back.

VG	VF	UNC
FV	FV	50.00

134 50 POUNDS

10.1.1994. Black, dk. olive-green and blue on m/c unpt. Face similar to #5. Cherubs holding armada medallion at ctr. on back.

VG	VF	UNC
FV	FV	110.00

135 100 POUNDS

10.1.1994. Black and olive-brown on m/c unpt. Elderly couple at r. The *Armada* at ctr. on back.

VG	VF	UNC
FV	FV	200.00

NORTHERN BANK LIMITED

1929 REGULAR ISSUE

#178 sailing ship, plow and man at grindstone at upper ctr.

178 1 POUND

1929-68. Black. Blue guilloche.

	VG	VF	UNC
a. Red serial #. 6.5.1929; 1.7.1929; 1.8.1929.	15.00	35.00	90.00

		VG	VF	UNC
b.	Black prefix letters and serial #. 1.1.1940.	6.00	15.00	45.00
c.	1.10.1968.	3.00	12.00	35.00

1930-43 ISSUE
#181 sailing ship, plow and man at grindstone at upper ctr.

		VG	VF	UNC
181	**10 POUNDS**			
	1930-68. Black on red unpt.			
	a. Red serial #. 1.1.1930-1.1.1940.	40.00	80.00	150.00
	b. Black serial #. 1.8.1940; 1.9.1940.	30.00	70.00	120.00
	c. Red serial #. 1.1.1942-1.11.1943.	25.00	50.00	100.00
	d. Imprint on back below central design. 1.10.1968.	FV	25.00	60.00

1968 ISSUE

		VG	VF	UNC
184	**5 POUNDS**			
	1.10.1968. Black on green unpt.	10.00	20.00	47.50
185	**50 POUNDS**			
	1.10.1968. Black on dk. blue unpt. *NBLD* monogram on back.	85.00	150.00	300.00
186	**100 POUNDS**			
	1.10.1968. Black on dk. blue unpt. *NBLD* monogram on back.	175.00	300.00	500.00

1970 ISSUE
#187-192 cows at l., ship yard at bottom ctr., loom at r. Sign. varieties.

		VG	VF	UNC
187	**1 POUND**			
	1970-82. Green on pink unpt. Printer: BWC.			
	a. 1.7.1970; 1.10.1971.	FV	2.50	12.50
	b. 1.8.1978; 1.7.1979; 1.4.1982.	FV	2.25	10.00
188	**5 POUNDS**			
	1.7.1970-1.4.1982. Lt. blue.	FV	11.00	27.50
189	**10 POUNDS**			
	1.7.1970; 1.10.1971; 1.1.1975; 15.6.1988. Brown.	FV	20.00	45.00
190	**20 POUNDS**			
	1.7.1970; 15.6.1988. Purple.	FV	37.50	85.00
191	**50 POUNDS**			
	1.7.1970. Orange.	FV	87.50	200.00
192	**100 POUNDS**			
	1.7.1970; 1.10.1971; 1.1.1975. Red.	FV	175.00	350.00

1988-90 ISSUE
#193-197 dish antenna at l., stylized *N* at ctr. and computer on back. Printer: TDLR.

		VG	VF	UNC
193	**5 POUNDS**	VG	VF	UNC
	24.8.1988; 24.8.1989; 24.8.1990. Blue and m/c. Station above trolley car at ctr., W. A. Traill at r.	FV	FV	22.50

		VG	VF	UNC
194	**10 POUNDS**	VG	VF	UNC
	24.8.1988; 14.5.1991. Red and brown on m/c unpt. Early automobile above bicyclist at ctr., J. B. Dunlop at r.	FV	FV	32.50

		VG	VF	UNC
195	**20 POUNDS**	VG	VF	UNC
	24.8.1988; 24.8.1989; 9.5.1991; 30.3.1992. Purple brown, red and m/c. Airplane at ctr., H. G. Ferguson at r., tractor at bottom r.	FV	FV	60.00

		VG	VF	UNC
196	**50 POUNDS**	VG	VF	UNC
	1.11.1990. Bluish green, black and m/c. Tea dryer, centrifugal machine at ctr, Sir S. Davidson at r.	FV	FV	150.00

197	**100 POUNDS**	VG	VF	UNC
	1.11.1990. Lilac, black, blue and m/c. Airplanes and ejection seat at ctr., Sir J. Martin at r.	FV	FV	300.00

PROVINCIAL BANK OF IRELAND LIMITED

See also Ireland-Republic and Northern - Allied Irish Banks Ltd

BELFAST BRANCH

1954 ISSUE

#242 and 242A printer: W&S.

242	**5 POUNDS**	VG	VF	UNC
	5.10.1954-5.7.1961. Brown. Woman at ctr.	15.00	45.00	100.00
242A	**5 POUNDS**			
	5.10.1954-5.7.1961. Brown. Woman at ctr. Printer: W&S.	15.00	30.00	65.00

1965 ISSUE

243	**1 POUND**	VG	VF	UNC
	1.12.1965. Green. Woman at ctr. Printer: TDLR.	6.00	15.00	40.00
244	**5 POUNDS**			
	6.12.1965. Similar to #242A but printer: TDLR.	11.00	25.00	60.00

1968 ISSUE

245	**1 POUND**	VG	VF	UNC
	1.1.1968-1.1.1972. Green. Like #241. 150 x 71mm.	4.00	10.00	30.00
246	**5 POUNDS**			
	5.1.1968; 5.1.1970; 5.1.1972. Brown. Like #243. 139 x 84mm.	10.00	15.00	45.00

1977-81 ISSUE

#247-251, designs similar to Allied Irish Banks Ltd. issues except for bank title and sign. Printer: TDLR.

247	**1 POUND**	VG	VF	UNC
	1977; 1979. Green on m/c unpt. Young girl at r. Sailing ship *Girona* at ctr. on back.			
	a. Sign. J. G. McClay. 1.1.1977.	2.00	7.00	17.50
	b. Sign. F. H. Hollway. 1.1.1979.	FV	6.00	15.00

248	**5 POUNDS**	VG	VF	UNC
	1977; 1979. Blue and purple on m/c unpt. Young woman at r. Dunluce Castle at ctr. on back.			
	a. Sign. J. G. McClay. 1.1.1977.	10.00	18.50	37.50
	b. Sign. F. H. Hollway. 1.1.1979.	10.00	13.50	35.00
249	**10 POUNDS**			
	1977; 1979. Brown and gray-green on m/c unpt. Young man at r. Wreck of the *Girona* at ctr. on back.			
	a. Sign. J. G. McClay. 1.1.1977.	20.00	30.00	65.00
	b. Sign. F. H. Hollway. 1.1.1979.	20.00	25.00	60.00

250	**20 POUNDS**	VG	VF	UNC
	1.3.1981. Purple and green. Elderly woman at r. Chimney at Lacada Pt. at ctr. on back.	FV	50.00	110.00
251	**100 POUNDS**			
	1.3.1981. Black, olive and green. Elderly man at r. The *Armada* at ctr. on back.	FV	175.00	385.00

ULSTER BANK LIMITED

BELFAST BRANCH

1966-70 ISSUE

#321-324 view of Belfast at lower l. and r., port w/bridge at lower ctr. below sign., date to r. Arms at ctr. on back. Sign. Jno. J. A. Leitch. Printer: BWC.

321	**1 POUND**	VG	VF	UNC
	4.10.1966. Dk. blue on m/c unpt. 151 x 72 mm.	4.00	8.50	21.50
322	**5 POUNDS**			
	4.10.1966. Brown on m/c unpt. 140 x 85 mm.	10.00	25.00	65.00
323	**10 POUNDS**			
	4.10.1966. Green on m/c unpt. 151 x 93 mm.	20.00	40.00	100.00
324	**20 POUNDS**			
	1.7.1970. Lilac on m/c unpt. 161 x 90 mm. Specimen.	—	—	—

1971-82 ISSUE
#325-330 similar to #321-324 but date at l., sign. at ctr. r. Printer: BWC.

			VG	VF	UNC
325	**1 POUND**				
	1971-76. 135 x 67 mm.				
	a. Sign. H. E. O'B. Traill. 15.2.1971.		4.00	8.50	17.50
	b. Sign. R. W. Hamilton. 1.3.1973; 1.3.1976.		3.00	4.50	12.50
326	**5 POUNDS**				
	1971-83. 146 x 78 mm.				
	a. Sign. H. E. O'B. Traill. 15.2.1971.		9.00	20.00	60.00
	b. Sign R. W. Hamilton. 1.3.1973; 1.3.1976.		8.50	13.50	40.00
	c. Sign. V. Chambers. 1.10.1982; 1.10.1983; 1.9.1986.		FV	10.00	30.00

			VG	VF	UNC
327	**10 POUNDS**				
	1971-88. 151 x 86 mm.				
	a. Sign. H. E. O'B. Traill. 15.2. .2.1971.		18.50	35.00	90.00
	b. Sign. R. W. Hamilton. 1.3.1973; 1.3.1976; 2.6.1980.		17.50	25.00	75.00
	c. Sign. V. Chambers. 1.10.1982; 1.10.1983; 1.2.1988.		FV	22.50	55.00
328	**20 POUNDS**				
	1.10.1982; 1.10.1983. Sign. V. Chambers.		FV	47.50	85.00
329	**50 POUNDS**				
	1.10.1982. Brown on m/c unpt. Sign. V. Chambers.		FV	90.00	135.00
330	**100 POUNDS**				
	1.3.1973. Red on m/c unpt. Sign. R. W. Hamilton.		FV	FV	350.00

1989-90 ISSUE
#331-334 similar to previous issue but smaller size notes. Sign. J. Wead. Printer: TDLR.

NOTE: The Bank of Ireland sold to collectors matched serial # sets of £5-10-20 notes as well as 100 sets of replacement serial II, Z perfix.

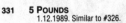

			VG	VF	UNC
331	**5 POUNDS**				
	1.12.1989. Similar to #326.		FV	FV	16.50

			VG	VF	UNC
332	**10 POUNDS**				
	1.12.1990. Similar to #327. Printer: TDLR.		FV	FV	30.00
333	**20 POUNDS**				
	1.11.1990. Similar to #32.		FV	FV	55.00
334	**100 POUNDS**				
	1.12.1990. Similar to #330.		FV	FV	250.00

COLLECTOR SERIES

BANK OF IRELAND

1978 ISSUE

		ISSUE PRICE	MKT. VALUE
CS1	**ND (1978) 1, 5, 10, 100 POUNDS**		
	#61b, #63b, #65b and #68b ovpt: *SPECIMEN* and Maltese cross prefix serial #.	7.00	75.00

PROVINCIAL BANK OF IRELAND LIMITED

1978 ISSUE

		ISSUE PRICE	MKT. VALUE
CS2	**1978 1, 5, 10 POUNDS**		
	#247a-249a dated 1.1.1977. Ovpt: *SPECIMEN* and Maltese cross prefix serial #.	7.00	45.00

ISLE OF MAN

The Isle of Man, a dependency of the British Crown located in the Irish Sea equidistant from Ireland, Scotland and England, has an area of 227 sq. mi. (588 sq. km.) and a population of 61,000. Capital: Douglas. Agriculture, dairy farming, fishing and tourism are the chief industries.

The prevalence of prehistoric artifacts and monuments on the island give evidence that its mild, almost sub-tropical climate was enjoyed by mankind before the dawn of history. Vikings came to the Isle of Man during the 9th century and remained until ejected by Scotland in 1266. The island came under the protection of the British Crown in 1288, and in 1406 was granted, in perpetuity, to the Earls of Derby, from whom it was inherited, 1736, by the Duke of Atholl. Rights and title were purchased from the Duke of Atholl in 1765 by the British Crown; the remaining privileges of the Atholl family were transferred to the crown in 1829. The Isle of Man is ruled by its own legislative council and the House of Keys, one of the oldest legislative assemblies in the world. Acts of Parliament passed in London do not affect the island unless it is specifically mentioned.

RULERS:
British

MONETARY SYSTEM:
1 Pound = 20 Shillings to 1971 1 Pound = 100 New Pence, 1971-

BRITISH INFLUENCE

LLOYDS BANK LIMITED

1955 ISSUE

13	1 POUND	GOOD	FINE	XF
	21.1.1955-14.3.1961. Black on green unpt. Bank arms at upper ctr.			
	a. Issued note.	75.00	150.00	300.00
	r. Unsigned remainder. ND.	—	—	100.00

WESTMINSTER BANK LIMITED
Formerly the London County Westminster and Parr's Bank Limited.

1955 ISSUE
#23A, various date and sign. varieties.

23A	1 POUND	GOOD	FINE	XF
	1955-61. Black on lt. yellow unpt. Crowned Triskele supported by lion and unicorn at upper ctr. W/text: *INCORPORATED IN ENGLAND* added below bank name. Printer: W&S.			
	a. 23.11.1955.	125.00	250.00	500.00
	b. 4.4.1956-10.3.1961.	50.00	120.00	250.00

GOVERNMENT

SIGNATURE VARIETIES			
1 Garvey		**5** Dawson	
2 Stallard		**6** Cashen	
3 Paul (26mm)			
4 Paul (20mm)			

1961 ND ISSUE
#24-27 Triskele arms at lower ctr., young portr. of Qn. Elizabeth II at r. Printer: BWC.

24	10 SHILLINGS	VG	VF	UNC
	ND (1961). Red on m/c unpt. Old sailing boat on back.			
	a. Sign. 1.	5.00	15.00	37.50
	b. Sign. 2.	5.00	15.00	37.50
	s. Sign. 1. Specimen.	—	—	45.00

25	1 POUND	VG	VF	UNC
	ND (1961). Purple on m/c unpt. Tynwald Hill on back.			
	a. Sign. 1.	5.00	15.00	45.00
	b. Sign. 2.	5.00	15.00	37.50
	s. Sign. 1. Specimen.	—	—	55.00

26	5 POUNDS	VG	VF	UNC
	ND (1961). Green and blue. Castle Rushen on back.			
	a. Sign. 1.	30.00	100.00	400.00
	b. Sign. 2.	30.00	90.00	350.00
	s. Sign. 1. Specimen w/normal serial # blocked out.	—	—	125.00

1969 ND ISSUE

30	5 POUNDS	VG	VF	UNC
	ND (1972). Blue and lilac-brown. Back similar to #26.			
	a. Sign. 2.	15.00	35.00	200.00
	b. Sign. 3.	8.00	15.00	85.00

27	50 NEW PENCE	VG	VF	UNC
	ND (1969). Blue on m/c unpt. Back like #24. 139 x 66mm. Sign. 2.	3.00	8.00	25.00

1972 ND ISSUE

#28-31 Triskele arms at ctr., mature portr. Qn. Elizabeth II at r. Sign. title: *LIEUTENANT GOVERNOR*. Printer: BWC.

31	10 POUNDS	VG	VF	UNC
	ND (1972). Brown and green. Peel Castle ca.1830 on back. Sign. 3.			
	a. Sign. 2.	150.00	350.00	1000.
	b. Sign. 3.	50.00	150.00	400.00
	s. Sign. 2. Specimen.	—	—	165.00

1979 COMMEMORATIVE ISSUE

#32, Millennium Year 1979

28	50 NEW PENCE	VG	VF	UNC
	ND (1972). Blue on m/c unpt. Back like #24. 126 x 62 mm.			
	a. Sign. 2.	1.00	5.00	30.00
	b. Sign. 3.	1.00	2.50	18.00
	c. Sign. 4.	1.00	2.00	12.00

29	1 POUND	VG	VF	UNC
	ND (1972). Purple on m/c unpt. Back similar to #25.			
	a. Sign. 2.	4.00	15.00	65.00
	b. Sign. 3.	2.00	10.00	75.00
	c. Sign. 4.	1.50	3.00	18.50

32	20 POUNDS	VG	VF	UNC
	1979. Red-orange, orange and dk. brown on m/c unpt. Triskele at ctr. Qn. Elizabeth II at r. Island outline at upper r. Commemorative text at lower r. of triskele. Laxey wheel ca. 1854, crowd of people and hills in background on back. Printer: BWC.	50.00	120.00	350.00

1979; 1983 ND ISSUES

#33-37 new sign. title: *TREASURER OF THE ISLE OF MAN.* Wmk: Triskele arms. Printer: BWC.

			VG	VF	UNC
33	**50 PENCE**				
	ND. Like #28. Sign. 5.		FV	FV	6.00
34	**1 POUND**				
	ND. Like #29. Sign. 5.		FV	FV	7.00
35	**5 POUNDS**				
	ND. Like #30.				
	a. Sign. 5. Series A-C.		FV	15.00	65.00
	b. Sign. 5. Series D, guilloche variety.		FV	12.00	40.00
36	**10 POUNDS**				
	ND. Like #31.		FV	22.50	40.00
37	**20 POUNDS**				
	ND (1979). Like #32 but w/o commemorative text.		FV	38.50	100.00
38	**50 POUNDS**				
	ND (1983). Lt. blue and green. Qn. Elizabeth II at r. Douglas Bay on back.		FV	90.00	150.00

			VG	VF	UNC
39	**1 POUND**				
	ND (1983). Green on m/c unpt. Like #25 but printed on Bradvek, a special plastic.		FV	5.00	10.00

1983 ND REDUCED SIZE ISSUE

#40-44 smaller format. Qn. Elizabeth II at r. Wmk: Triskele. Printer: TDLR.

			VG	VF	UNC
40	**1 POUND**				
	ND. Purple and m/c. Back like #25.				
	a. Sign. 5.		FV	FV	6.00
	b. Sign. 6.		FV	FV	4.50

			VG	VF	UNC
41	**5 POUNDS**				
	ND. Greenish blue, lilac brown and m/c. Back like #30.				
	a. Sign. 5.		FV	FV	20.00
	b. Sign. 6.		FV	FV	17.50

			VG	VF	UNC
42	**10 POUNDS**				
	ND. Brown, green and m/c. Back brown, orange and m/c. like #31. Sign. 6.		FV	FV	22.50
	a. Sign. 5.			Reported Not Confirmed	
	b. Sign. 6.		FV	FV	22.50

			VG	VF	UNC
43	**20 POUNDS**				
	ND. Brown, red-orange and m/c. Back like #32.				
	a. Sign. 5.		FV	FV	100.00
	b. Sign. 6.		FV	FV	67.50
44	**50 POUNDS**				
	ND. Blue-gray, bright green and olive on m/c unpt. Back like #38.		FV	FV	125.00

ISRAEL

The State of Israel, at the eastern end of the Mediterranean Sea, bounded by Lebanon on the north, Syria on the northeast, Jordan on the east, and Egypt on the southwest, has an area of 7,847 sq. mi. (23,309 sq. km.) and a population of 4.5 million. Capital: Jerusalem. Diamonds, chemicals, citrus, textiles, and minerals are exported.

Palestine, which corresponds to Canaan of the Bible, was settled by the Philistines about the 12th century B.C. and shortly thereafter was invaded by the Jews who established the kingdoms of Israel and Judah. Because of its position as part of the land bridge connecting Asia and Africa, Palestine was invaded and conquered by nearly all of the historic empires of ancient Europe and Asia. In the 16th century it became a Turkish satrap. After falling to the British in World War I, it, together with Transjordan, was mandated to Great Britain by the League of Nations, 1922.

For more than half a century prior to the termination of the British mandate over Palestine, 1948, Zionist leaders had sought to create a Jewish homeland for Jews dispersed throughout the world. For almost as long, Jews fleeing persecution had immigrated to Palestine. The Nazi persecutions of the 1930s and 1940s increased the Jewish movement to Palestine and generated international support for the creation of a Jewish state, first promulgated by the Balfour Declaration of 1917 which asserted British support for the endeavor. The dream of a Jewish homeland was realized on May 14, 1948 when Palestine was proclaimed the State of Israel.

MONETARY SYSTEM:

1 Lira = 100 Agorot, 1958-1980
1 Sheqel = 10 "old" Lirot, 1980-85
1 Sheqel = 100 New Agorot, 1980-1985
1 New Sheqel = 1000 "old" Sheqalim, 1985-
1 New Sheqel = 100 Agorot, 1985-

STATE OF ISRAEL

BANK OF ISRAEL

1958-60 / 5718-20 ISSUE

#29 and 30 printer: JEZ (w/o imprint).
#31 and 32 printer: TDLR (w/o imprint).

29	1/2 LIRA	VG	VF	UNC
	1958/5718. Green. Woman soldier w/basket full of oranges at l. and as wmk. Tombs of the Sanhedrin on back. Printer: JEZ.	.50	1.25	5.00

30	1 LIRA	VG	VF	UNC
	1958/5718. Blue and m/c. Fisherman w/net and anchor at l. and as wmk. Wreath on back. Printer: JEZ.			
a.	Paper w/security thread at l. Black serial #.	.25	.75	3.00
b.	Red serial #.	.25	.75	3.00
c.	Paper w/security thread and morse tape, brown serial #.	.15	.50	2.00

31	5 LIROT	VG	VF	UNC
	1958/5718. Brown and m/c. Worker w/hammer in front of factory at l. and as wmk. Seal of Shema on back. Printer: TDLR (w/o imprint).	.40	1.25	5.00

32	10 LIROT	VG	VF	UNC
	1958/5718. Lilac and violet. Scientist w/microscope and test tube at l. and as wmk. Dead Sea scroll and vases on back. Printer: TDLR (w/o imprint).			
a.	Paper w/security thread. Black serial #.	.35	1.00	4.00
b.	Paper w/security thread and morse tape. Red serial #.	.35	1.00	4.00
c.	Paper w/security thread and morse tape. Blue serial #.	.35	1.00	4.00
d.	Paper w/security thread and morse tape. Brown serial #.	.25	.75	3.00

33	50 LIROT	VG	VF	UNC
	1960/5720. Brown and m/c. Boy and girl at l. and as wmk. Mosaic of menorah on back. Printer: JEZ (w/o imprint).			
a.	Paper w/security thread. Black serial #.	1.00	3.00	15.00
b.	Paper w/security thread. Red serial #.	1.00	3.00	15.00
c.	Paper w/security thread and morse tape. Blue serial #.	.85	2.50	10.00
d.	Paper w/security thread and morse tape. Green serial #.	.85	2.50	10.00
e.	Paper w/security thread and morse tape. Brown serial #.	.60	1.75	7.00

1968 / 5728 ISSUE

#34-37 printer: JEZ (w/o imprint).

34	**5 LIROT**	VG	VF	UNC
	1968/5728. Gray-green and blue on m/c unpt. A. Einstein at r. and as wmk. Bldg. on back.			
	a. Black serial #.	.40	1.25	5.00
	b. Red serial #.	.40	1.25	5.00
35	**10 LIROT**			
	1968/5728. Brown, violet and m/c. C. Nachman Bialik at r. and as wmk. House on back.			
	a. Black serial #.	.25	.75	3.00
	b. Green serial #.	.25	.75	3.00
	c. Blue serial #.	.25	.75	3.00

38	**5 LIROT**	VG	VF	UNC
	1973/5733. Lt. and dk. brown. H. Szold at r. Lion's Gate on back.	.15	.50	2.00

36	**50 LIROT**	VG	VF	UNC
	1968/5728. Lt. brown and green on m/c unpt. Pres. C. Weizmann at r. and as wmk. Knesset bldg. on back.			
	a. Black serial #.	1.00	3.00	6.50
	b. Blue serial #.	1.00	2.50	5.50

39	**10 LIROT**	VG	VF	UNC
	1973/5733. Purple on lilac unpt. Sir M. Montefiore at r. Jaffa Gate on back.	.15	.50	2.00

37	**100 LIROT**	VG	VF	UNC
	1968/5728. Blue and green on m/c unpt. Dr. T. Herzl at r. and as wmk. Menorah and surrounding objects on back.			
	a. Wmk: Profile. Black serial #. 3.5mm.	2.00	5.00	12.50
	b. Wmk: 3/4 profile r. Red serial #.	2.00	5.00	12.50
	c. Wmk: Profile. Black serial #. 2.8mm. W/o series letter.	1.00	4.00	9.00
	d. Wmk: Profile. Brown serial #.	1.00	3.00	8.00

1973-75 / 5733-35 ISSUE

#38-51 printer: JEZ (w/o imprint).

All the following notes except #41 and 45 have marks for the blind on the face. #38-46 have barely discernible bar code strips at lower l. and upper r. on back. All have portr. as wmk. Various gates in Jerusalem on backs.

40	**50 LIROT**	VG	VF	UNC
	1973/5733. Green on olive unpt. C. Weizmann at r. Sichem Gate on back.	.35	1.00	4.00

41 100 LIROT
1973/5733. Blue on blue and brown unpt. Dr. T. Herzl at r. Zion Gate on back.

VG	VF	UNC
.35	1.00	4.00

42 500 LIROT
1975/5735. Black on tan and brown unpt. D. Ben-Gurion at r. Golden Gate on back.

VG	VF	UNC
1.65	5.00	20.00

1978-84 / 5738-44 ISSUE

NOTE: Colored bars on #46 and 47 wee used to identify various surfaced coataed papers, used experimentally.

43 1 SHEQEL
1978/5738 (1980). Purple. Like #39.

VG	VF	UNC
.15	.40	1.50

44 5 SHEQALIM
1978/5738 (1980). Green. Like #40.

VG	VF	UNC
.40	1.25	5.00

45 10 SHEQALIM
1978/5738 (1980). Blue. Like #41.

VG	VF	UNC
.25	.75	3.00

46 50 SHEQALIM
1978/5738 (1980). Black on tan and brown unpt. Like #42.

	VG	VF	UNC
a. W/o small bars below serial # # or barely discernible bar code strips on back.	.15	.50	2.00
b. W/o small bars below serial #, but w/bar code strips on back.	.50	1.50	6.00
c. 2 green bars below serial # on back.	3.00	15.00	75.00
d. 4 black bars below serial # on back.	3.00	15.00	75.00
e. 12-subject sheet.	—		15.00

47 100 SHEQALIM
1979/5739. Red-brown. Ze'ev Jabotinsky at r. Herod's Gate on back.

	VG	VF	UNC
a. W/o bars below serial # on back.	.15	.50	2.00

b. 2 bars below serial # on back. 2.00 10.00 50.00

50	5000 SHEQALIM	VG	VF	UNC
	1984/5744. Blue and m/c. City view at ctr., L. Eshkol at r. Water pipe and modern design on back.			
	a. Issued note.	.65	2.00	8.00
	b. Uncut sheet of 3.	—	—	27.50

48	500 SHEQALIM	VG	VF	UNC
	1982/5742. Red and m/c. Farm workers at ctr., Baron E. de Rothschild at r. Vine leaves on back.	.50	1.50	6.00

51	10,000 SHEQALIM	VG	VF	UNC
	1984/5744. Brown, black, orange and dk. green on m/c unpt. Stylized tree at ctr., G. Meir at r. and as wmk. Gathering in front of Moscow synagogue on back.			
	a. Issued note.	1.65	5.00	20.00
	b. Uncut sheet of 3.	—	—	70.00

1985-92 / 5745-52 ISSUE
#51A-56 portr. as wmk. Printer: JEZ (w/o imprint). All with marks for the blind.

SIGNATURE VARIETIES			
5	Mandelbaum, 1986	7	Lorincz and Bruno, 1987–91
6	Shapira and Mandelbaum, 1985	8	Lorincz and Frankel, 1992

49	1000 SHEQALIM	VG	VF	UNC
	1983/5743. Green and m/c. Rabbi M. B. Maimon-Maimonides at r. View of Tiberias at l. on back.			
	a. Error in first letter *he* of second word at r. in vertical text (right to left), partly completed letter resembling 7.	.85	2.50	10.00
	b. Corrected letter resembling *17*.	.65	2.00	8.00
	c. As a. Uncut sheet of 3.	—	—	35.00
	d. As b. Uncut sheet of 3.	—	—	27.50

51A	1 NEW SHEKEL	VG	VF	UNC
	1986/5746. Like #49 except for denomination. Sign. 5.			
	a. Issued note.	FV	.35	2.00
	b. Uncut sheet of 3.	—	—	7.00
	c. Uncut sheet of 12.	—	—	27.50
	d. Uncut sheet of 18.	—	—	42.50

		VG	VF	UNC
52	**5 NEW SHEQALIM**			
	1985/5745; 1987/5747. Like #50 except for denomination.			
	a. Sign. 6. 1985/5745.	FV	FV	10.00
	b. Sign. 7. 1987/5747.	FV	FV	8.00
	c. Uncut sheet of 3.	—	—	27.50

		VG	VF	UNC
53	**10 NEW SHEQALIM**			
	1985/5745; 1987/5747; 1992/5752. Like #51 except for denomination.			
	a. Sign. 6. 1985/5745.	FV	FV	20.00
	b. Sign. 7. 1987/5747.	FV	FV	12.50
	c. Sign. 8. 1992/5752.	FV	FV	10.00
	d. Uncut sheet of 3.	—	—	35.00

		VG	VF	UNC
54	**20 NEW SHEQALIM**			
	1987/5747; 1993/5753. Dk. gray on m/c unpt. M. Sharett standing holding flag at ctr., his bust at r. and as wmk. Herzlya High School at ctr. on back.			
	a. W/o sm. double circle w/dot in wmk. area face and back. Sign. 7. 1987/5747.	FV	FV	25.00
	b. W/sm. double circle w/dot in wmk. area face and back. Sign. 7. 1987/5747.	FV	FV	20.00
	c. Sign. 8. 1993/5753.	FV	FV	16.50

		VG	VF	UNC
55	**50 NEW SHEQALIM**			
	1985/5745-1992/5752. Purple on m/c unpt. S. J. Agnon at r. and as wmk. Various bldgs. and book titles on back.			
	a. Sign. 6. 1985/5745.	FV	FV	50.00
	b. Sign. 7. Slight color variations. 1988/5748.	FV	FV	45.00
	c. Sign 8. 1992/5752.	FV	FV	42.50

		VG	VF	UNC
56	**100 NEW SHEQALIM**			
	1986/5746; 1989/5749; 1995/5755. Brown on m/c unpt. Y. Ben-Zvi at r. and as wmk. Stylized village and carob tree on back.			
	a. Sign. 5. Plain security thread and plain white paper. 1986/5746.	FV	FV	75.00
	b. Sign. 6. W/security thread inscribed: *Bank Israel,* paper w/colored threads. 1989/5749.	FV	FV	60.00
	c. Sign. 8. 1995/5755.	FV	FV	75.00

		VG	VF	UNC
57	**200 NEW SHEQALIM**			
	1991/5751-. Deep red, purple and blue-green on m/c unpt. Z. Shazar at r. and as wmk. School girl writing at ctr. on back.			
	a. Sign. 7. 1991/5721.	FV	FV	125.00
	b. Sign. 8. 1994/5724/	FV	FV	110.00

ITALY

The Italian Republic, a 700-mile-long peninsula extending into the heart of the Mediterranean Sea, has an area of 116,304 sq. mi. (301,255 sq. km.) and a population of 57.4 million. Captal: Rome. The economy centers about agriculture, manufacturing, forestry and fishing. Machinery, textiles, clothing and motor vehicles are exported.

From the fall of Rome until modern times, "Italy" was little more than a geographical expression. Although nominally included in the Empire of Charlemagne and the Holy Roman Empire, it was in reality divided into a number of independent states and kingdoms presided over by wealthy families, soldiers of fortune or hereditary rulers. The 19th century unification movement fostered by Mazzini, Garibaldi and Cavor attained fruition in 1860-1870 with the creation of the Kingdom of Italy and the installation of Victor Emanuele, King of Italy. Benito Mussolini came to power during the post-World War I period of economic and political unrest, installed a Fascist dictatorship with a figurehead king as titular Head of State.

Mussolini entered Italy into the German-Japanese anti-Comintern pact (Tri-Partite Pact) and withdrew from the League of Nations. The war did not go well for Italy and Germany was forced to assist Italy in its failed invasion of Greece. The Allied invasion of Sicily on July 10, 1943 and bombing of Rome brought the Fascist councl to a no vote of confidence on July 24, 1943. Mussolini was arrested but soon escaped and set up a government in Saló. Rome fell to the Allied forces in June 1944 and the country was allowed the status of co-belligerent against Germany. The Germans held northern Italy for another year. Mussolini was eventually captured and executed by partisans. Following the defeat of the Axis powers the Italian monarchy was dissolved by plesbiscite, and the Italian Republic proclaimed on June 10, 1946.

* * * This section has been renumbered. * * *

MONETARY SYSTEM:
1 Lira = 100 Centesimi

DECREES:
There are many different dates found on the following notes of the Banca d'Italia. These include ART. DELLA LEGGE (law date) and the more important DECRETO MINISTERI-ALE (D. M. date). The earliest D.M. date is usually found on the back of the note while later D.M. dates are found grouped together. The actual latest date (of issue) is referred to in the following listings.

FACE SEAL VARIETIES

Type B
Facing head of Medusa

Type C
Winged lion of St. Mark of Venice above 3 shields of Genoa, Pisa and Amalfi

REPUBLIC

REPUBBLICA ITALIANA - BIGLIETTO DI STATO

1966 ISSUE

			VG	VF	UNC
93	**500 LIRE**				
(64)	1966-75. Dk. gray on m/c unpt. Eagle w/snake at l., Arethusa at r. 3 sign. varieties.				
	a. 20.6.1966; 20.10.1967; 23.2.1970.		1.00	2.00	10.00
	b. 23.4.1975.		10.00	30.00	240.00

DECRETO MINISTERIALE 14.2.1974

			VG	VF	UNC
94	**500 LIRE**				
(64A)	14.2.1974; 2.4.1979. Green-blue. Mercury at r. 3 sign. varieties.		.50	1.00	2.00

DECRETO MINISTERIALE 6.8.1976

			VG	VF	UNC
95	**500 LIRE**				
(64B)	20.12.1976. Like #64A.		.50	1.50	3.50

BANCA D'ITALIA

BANK OF ITALY

1947 ISSUES

			VG	VF	UNC
80	**500 LIRE**				
(29)	1947-61. Purple on lt. brown unpt. "Italia" at l. Back purple on gray unpt. Seal: Type B. Wmk: Head of "Italia".				
	a. Sign. Einaudi and Urbini. 20.3.1947; 10.2.1948.		3.00	15.00	120.00
	b. Sign. Carli and Ripa. 23.3.1961.		3.00	17.50	130.00
85	**5000 LIRE**				
(42)	1947-63. Green and brown. 2 women seated at ctr. (Venezia and Genova). Seals: Type A/F. Wmk: Dante at l., "Italia" at r.				
	a. Sign. Einaudi and Urbini. 7.1.1947; 27.10.1947; 23.4.1948.		200.00	500.00	1600.
	b. Sign. Menichella and Urbini. 10.2.1949; 5.5.1952; 7.2.1953.		40.00	100.00	500.00
	c. Sign. Menichella and Boggione. 23.3.1961; 7.1.1963.		40.00	100.00	500.00
	d. Sign. Carli and Ripa. 23.3.1961; 7.1.1963.		40.00	100.00	500.00

1948 ISSUE

			VG	VF	UNC
88	**1000 LIRE**				
(39)	1948-61. Purple and brown. Portr. "Italia" at l. and as wmk. Back blue on gray unpt. Seal: Type B.				
	a. Sign. Einaudi and Urbini. 10.2.1948.		2.00	10.00	140.00
	b. Sign. Menichella and Urbini. 11.2.1949.		2.00	10.00	140.00
	c. Blue-gray. Sign. Menichella and Boggione. 15.9.1959.		3.00	20.00	200.00
	d. Color like c. Sign. Carli and Ripa. 25.9.1961.		2.00	10.00	140.00
89	**10,000 LIRE**				
(46)	1948-62. Brown, orange and m/c. 2 women seated at ctr. (Venezia and Genova). Seal: Type B. Wmk: Verdi at l., Galilei at r.				
	a. Sign. Einaudi and Urbini. 8.5.1948.		25.00	50.00	300.00
	b. Sign. Menichella and Urbini. 10.2.1949-7.2.1953.		20.00	45.00	280.00
	c. Sign. Menichella and Boggione. 27.10.1953-12.5.1960.		20.00	45.00	280.00
	d. Sign. Carli and Ripa. 23.3.1961-24.3.1962.		20.00	40.00	250.00

1962 ISSUE
Decreto Ministeriale 12.4. 1962; Decreto Ministeriale 28.6.1962.

			VG	VF	UNC
96	**1000 LIRE**				
(71)	1962-68. Blue on red and brown unpt. G. Verdi at r.				
	a. Sign. Carli and Ripa. 14.7.1962; 14.1.1964.		FV	1.50	25.00
	b. Sign. Carli and Ripa. 5.7.1963; 25.7.1964.		FV	4.00	65.00
	c. Sign. Carli and Febbraio. 10.8.1965; 20.5.1966.		FV	1.50	30.00
	d. Sign. Carli and Pacini. 4.1.1968.		FV	4.00	80.00

97 **10,000 LIRE**
(70)   1962-73. Brown, purple, orange and red-brown w/dk. brown text on
       m/c unpt. Michaelangelo at r. Piazzadel Campidoglio in Rome.

	VG	VF	UNC
a. Sign. Carli and Ripa. 3.7.1962; 14.1.1964; 27.7.1964.	FV	10.00	30.00
b. Sign. Carli and Febbraio. 20.5.1966.	FV	10.00	30.00
c. Sign. Carli and Pacini. 4.1.1968.	FV	10.00	35.00
d. Sign. Carli and Lombardo. 8.6.1970.	FV	10.00	30.00
e. Sign. Carli and Barbarito. 15.2.1973; 27.11.1973.	FV	FV	30.00

1964 ISSUE
Decreto Ministeriale 20.8.1964.

98 **5000 LIRE**
(72)   1964-70. Green on pink unpt. Columbus at r. Ship on back.

	VG	VF	UNC
a. Sign. Carli and Ripa. 3.9.1964.	4.00	10.00	140.00
b. Sign. Carli and Pacini. 4.1.1968.	4.00	10.00	140.00
c. Sign. Carli and Lombardo. 20.1.1970.	4.00	10.00	140.00

1967 ISSUE
Decreto Ministeriale 27.6.1967.

99 **50,000 LIRE**
(73)   1967-74. Brownish black, dk. brown and reddish brown w/black text
       on m/c unpt. Leonardo da Vinci at r. Bldgs. on back. Wmk: bust of
       Madonna.

	VG	VF	UNC
a. Sign. Carli and Febbraio. 4.12.1967.	FV	80.00	350.00
b. Sign. Carli and Lombardo. 19.7.1970.	FV	50.00	280.00
c. Sign. Carli and Barbarito. 16.5.1972; 4.2.1974.	FV	50.00	280.00

100 **100,000 LIRE**
(74)   1967-74. Brownish black, brown and deep olive-green on m/c unpt. A.
       Manzoni at r. Mountains on back. Wmk: Archaic female bust. Seal:
       Type B.

	VG	VF	UNC
a. Sign. Carli and Febbraio. 3.7.1967.	FV	100.00	400.00
b. Sign. Carli and Lombardo. 19.7.1970.	FV	90.00	300.00
c. Sign. Carli and Barbarito. 6.2.1974.	FV	90.00	300.00

1969; 1971 ISSUE
Decreto Ministeriale 26.2.1969; Decreto Ministeriale 15.5.1971.

101 **1000 LIRE**
(75)   1969-81. Blue and lilac. Harp at l. ctr., G. Verdi at r. Paper w/security
       thread. La Scala opera house on back. Seal: Type B.

	VG	VF	UNC
a. Sign. Carli and Lombardo. 25.3.1969; 11.3.1971.	FV	1.00	4.00
b. Sign. Carli and Barbarito. 15.2.1973.	FV	1.25	7.00
c. Sign. Carli and Barbarito. 5.8.1975.	FV	1.00	4.00
d. Sign. Baffi and Stevani. 10.1.1977; 10.5.1979.	FV	1.00	7.00
e. Sign. Ciampi and Stevani. 20.2.1980; 6.9.1980; 30.5.1981.	FV	1.00	4.00

102 **5000 LIRE**
(76)   1971-77. Olive. Mythical seahorse at ctr., Columbus at r. 3 sailing
       ships of Columbus on back. Seal: Type C.

	VG	VF	UNC
a. Sign. Carli and Lombardo. 20.5.1971.	FV	4.00	20.00
b. Sign. Carli and Barbarito. 11.4.1973.	FV	5.00	30.00
c. Sign. Baffi and Stevani. 10.11.1977.	FV	5.00	30.00

1973; 1974 ISSUE
Decreto Ministeriale 10.9.1973; Decreto Ministeriale 20.12.1974.

103	2000 LIRE	VG	VF	UNC
(77)	1973; 1976; 1983. Brown and green. Galileo at ctr. Zodiac signs on back. Seal: Type C.			
	a. Sign. Carli and Barbarito. 8.10.1973.	FV	2.50	15.00
	b. Sign. Baffi and Stevani. 20.10.1976.	FV	2.00	10.00
	c. Sign. Ciampi and Stevani. 24.10.1983.	FV	FV	4.00

104	20,000 LIRE	VG	VF	UNC
(78)	21.2.1975. Brownish-black and dk. brown on red-brown and pale olive-green unpt. Titian at ctr. Painting at l. ctr. on back. Wmk: Woman's head. Seal: Type C. Sign. Carli and Barbarito.	FV	30.00	90.00

1976-79 ISSUE
Decreto Ministeriale 2.3.1979; Decreto Ministeriale 25.8.1976; Decreto Ministeriale 20.6.1977; Decreto Ministeriale 16.6.1978.

107	50,000 LIRE	VG	VF	UNC
(81)	1977-82. Blue, red and green. Young women and lion of St. Mark at l. Modern design of arches on back. Seal: Type C.			
	a. Sign. Baffi and Stevani. 20.6.1977; 12.6.1978; 23.10.1978.	FV	30.00	40.00
	b. Sign. Ciampi and Stevani. 11.4.1980.	FV	30.00	40.00
	c. Sign. Ciampi and Stevani. 2.11 .11.1982.	FV	35.00	100.00

108	100,000 LIRE	VG	VF	UNC
(82)	D.1978. Red-violet and black on m/c unpt. Woman's bust at l. and as wmk. Modern bldg. design at r. on back. Seal: Type C.			
	a. Sign. Ciampi and Stevani. 20.6.1978.	FV	65.00	100.00
	b. Sign. Ciampi and Stevani. 1.7.1980-10.5.1982.	FV	65.00	135.00

105	5000 LIRE	VG	VF	UNC
(79)	1979-83. Brown and green. Man at l. Bldg. and statuary on back. Seal: Type C.			
	a. Sign. Baffi and Stevani. 9.3.1979.	FV	5.50	10.00
	b. Sign. Ciampi and Stevani. 1.7.1980; 3.11.1982; 19.10.1983.	FV	5.00	10.00

106	10,000 LIRE	VG	VF	UNC
(80)	1976-84. Black and m/c. Man at l. Column at r. on back. Seal: Type C.			
	a. Sign. Baffi and Stevani. 30.10.1976; 29.12.1978.	FV	11.00	18.50
	b. Sign. Ciampi and Stevani. 6.9.1980; 3.11.1982; 8.3.1984.	FV	10.00	16.50

1982; 1983 ISSUE
Decreto Ministeriale 6.1.1982; Decreto Ministeriale 1.9.1983.

110 **100,000 LIRE**
(84)   *D.1983.* Dk. brown and brown on green and olive-green unpt. Couple at ctr., Caravaggio at r. and as wmk. Fruit basket at l., castle at upper ctr. on back. Seal: Type C.

		VG	VF	UNC
a.	Sign. Ciampi and Stevani. 1.9.1983.	FV	FV	125.00
b.	Sign. Ciampi and Speziali. 1.9.1983.	FV	FV	110.00

109 **1000 LIRE**
(83)   *D.1982.* Dk. green, tan and m/c. Marco Polo at r. and as wmk. Bldg. on vertical back. Printer: ODBI. Seal: Type C.

		VG	VF	UNC
a.	Sign. Ciampi and Stevani. 6.1.1982.	FV	FV	2.00
b.	Sign. Ciampi and Speziali. 6.1.1982.	FV	FV	2.00

1984; 1985 ISSUE
Decreto Ministeriale 4.1.1985; Decreto Ministeriale 3.9.1984; Decreto Ministeriale 6.2.1984.

113 **50,000 LIRE**
(87)   *D.1984.* Red-violet and m/c. Figurine at ctr., G.L. Bernini at r. and as wmk. Equestrian statue on back. Seal: Type C.

		VG	VF	UNC
a.	Sign. Ciampi and Stevani. 5.12.1984; 28.10.1985; 1.12.1986.	FV	FV	55.00
b.	Sign. Ciampi and Speziali. 25.1.1990.	FV	FV	50.00

111 **5,000 LIRE**
(85)   *ND (1985).* Olive green and m/c unpt. Coliseum at ctr., V. Bellini at r. and as wmk. Scene from opera *Norma* on back. Seal: Type C.

		VG	VF	UNC
a.	Sign. Ciampi and Stevani. 4.1.1985.	FV	FV	7.50
b.	Sign. Ciampi and Speziali. 4.1.1985.	FV	FV	7.50

112 **10,000 LIRE**
(86)   *D.1984.* Dk. blue on m/c unpt. Lab instrument at ctr. A. Volta at r. and as wmk. Mausoleum on back. Seal: Type C.

		VG	VF	UNC
a.	Sign. Ciampi and Stevani. 3.9.1984.	FV	FV	14.00
b.	Sign. Ciampi and Speziali. 3.9.1984.	FV	FV	14.00

1990-94 ISSUE
Decreto Ministeriale 3.10.1990; Decreto Ministeriale 27.5.1992; Decreto Ministeriale 6.5.1994.

114 **1000 LIRE**
(88)   *D.1990.* Red-violet and m/c. M. Montessori at r. and as wmk. Teacher and student on back. Seal: Type C.

		VG	VF	UNC
a.	Sign. Clampi and Speziali.	FV	FV	2.00
b.	Sign. Fazio and Speziali.	FV	FV	1.75

115 **2000 LIRE**
(89)   *D.1990.* Dk. brown on m/c unpt. Arms at l. ctr.; G. Marconi at r. and as wmk. Ship, radio tower and early radio set on back. Seal: Type C. Sign. Ciampi and Speziali.

	VG	VF	UNC
	FV	FV	3.00

116 (90)	**50,000 LIRE**	VG	VF	UNC

D.1992. Violet and dull green on m/c unpt. Similar to #113. Seal: Type C. Sign. Ciampi and Speziali.

FV FV 50.00

117 (91)	**100,00 LIRE**	VG	VF	UNC

D.1994. Dk. brown, reddish brown and pale green on m/c unpt. Similar to #110. Seal: Type C.
  a. Sign. Fazio and Speziali. 6.5.1994. FV FV 90.00
  b. Sign. Fazio and Amici. 6.5.1994. FV FV 87.50

JAMAICA

Jamaica, a member of the British Commonwealth situated in the Caribbean Sea 90 miles south of Cuba, has an area of 4,232 sq. mi. (10,991 sq. km.) and a population of 2.4 million. Capital: Kingston. The economy is founded chiefly on mining, tourism and agriculture. Alumina, bauxite, sugar, rum and molasses are exported.

Jamaica was discovered by Columbus on May 3, 1494, and settled by Spain in 1509. The island was captured in 1655 by a British naval force under the command of Admiral William Penn, and ceded to Britain by the Treaty of Madrid, 1670. For more than 150 years, the Jamaican economy of sugar, slaves and piracy was one of the most prosperous in the new world. Dissension between the property-oriented island legislature and the home government prompted parliament to establish a crown colony government for Jamaica in 1866. From 1958 to 1961 Jamaica was a member of the West Indies Federation, withdrawing when Jamaican voters rejected the association. The colony attained independence on Aug. 6, 1962. Jamaica is a member of the Commonwealth of Nations. The Queen of England is Chief of State.

A decimal standard currency system was adopted on Sept. 8, 1969.

RULERS:
  British

MONETARY SYSTEM:
  1 Shilling = 12 Pence
  1 Pound = 20 Shillings to 1969
  1 Dollar = 100 Cents, 1969-

BRITISH INFLUENCE

BANK OF JAMAICA

SIGNATURE VARIETIES			
1	Stanley W. Payton, 1960–64	**7**	Horace G. Barber, 1983–86
2	Richard T. P. Hall, **Acting Governor** – 1964–66	**8**	Headley A. Brown, 1986–89
3	Richard T. P. Hall **Governor** – 1966–67	**9**	Dr. Owen C. Jefferson, **Acting Governor** – 1989-90
4	G. Arthur Brown, 1967–77	**10**	G. A. Brown, 1990–93
5	Herbert Samuel Walker, 1977–81	**11**	R. Rainsford, 1993
6	Dr. Owen C. Jefferson, **Acting Governor** – 1981–83	**12**	J. Bussieres, 1994–

LAW 1960

FIRST ND ISSUE
Pound System
Law 1960
#49-51 Qn. Elizabeth II at l. Latin motto below arms. Sign. S. W. Payton. Printer: TDLR.

49	**5 SHILLINGS**	**VG**	**VF**	**UNC**
	L.1960. Red on m/c unpt. River rapids on back.	3.00	12.50	60.00
50	**10 SHILLINGS**			
	L.1960. Purple on m/c unpt. Men w/bananas on back.	5.00	17.50	170.00

52	**5 POUNDS**	**VG**	**VF**	**UNC**
	L.1960. Blue on m/c unpt. Storage plant at ctr., woman w/fruit basket at r. on back.			
	a. Sign. 1. 2 serial # varieties, Gothic and Roman.	30.00	150.00	600.00
	b. Sign. 3.	27.50	135.00	550.00
	c. Sign. 4.	25.00	125.00	500.00

LAW 1960

FIRST ND ISSUE

51	**1 POUND**	**VG**	**VF**	**UNC**
	L.1960. Green on m/c unpt. Harvesting on back.	5.00	20.00	170.00

SECOND ND ISSUE

#49A-51A like previous issue, but English motto below arms. Printer: TDLR.

53	**50 CENTS**	**VG**	**VF**	**UNC**
	L.1960 (1970). Red and m/c. M. Garvey at l. National shrine on back.	.50	1.00	4.50

49A	**5 SHILLINGS**	**VG**	**VF**	**UNC**
	L.1960. Red on m/c unpt.			
	a. Sign. 1. 2 serial # varieties.	2.00	7.00	55.00
	b. Sign. 2.	2.50	8.00	75.00
	c. Sign. 4.	1.50	5.00	50.00
50A	**10 SHILLINGS**			
	L.1960. Purple on m/c unpt.			
	a. Sign. 1. 2 serial # varieties.	3.00	7.50	110.00
	b. Sign. 2.	3.00	8.50	125.00
	c. Sign. 3.	3.50	12.50	150.00
	d. Sign. 4.	2.00	6.00	100.00

54	**1 DOLLAR**	**VG**	**VF**	**UNC**
	L.1960 (1970). Purple and m/c. Sir A. Bustamante at l. Tropical harbor on back.	.50	1.50	5.50

51A	**1 POUND**	**VG**	**VF**	**UNC**
	L.1960. Green on m/c unpt.			
	a. Sign. 1. 2 serial # varieties, Gothic and Roman.	5.00	17.50	150.00
	b. Sign. 2.	5.00	17.50	165.00
	c. Sign. 3.	7.50	25.00	200.00
	d. Sign. 4.	4.00	15.00	140.00

55	**2 DOLLARS**	**VG**	**VF**	**UNC**
	L.1960 (1970). Dk. green and m/c. P. Bogle at l., bird at ctr. Group of people on back.	.85	2.50	10.00

56   5 DOLLARS
L.1960 (1970). Dk. brown, green and blue-gray on m/c unpt. N. Manley at I. Old Parliament on back.

	VG	VF	UNC
	2.50	7.50	22.50

57   10 DOLLARS
L.1960 (1970). Blue-black and black on m/c unpt G.W. Gordon at I. Bauxite industry on back.

	VG	VF	UNC
	5.00	15.00	50.00

1973 FAO COMMEMORATIVE ISSUE
#58, 25th Anniversary Declaration of Human Rights 1948-73.

58   2 DOLLARS
1973. Like #55 but *Universal Declaration of Human Rights/1948 - 10 December - 1973. Toward Food Education Employment for All/Articles 23-26* added on back. Serial # double prefix FA-O.

	VG	VF	UNC
	1.00	3.25	13.50

1970 SECOND ISSUE
#59-63 new guilloches in corners and some larger denomination numerals on face and back. Printer: TDLR.

Replacement notes: Serial # prefix *ZY* or *ZZ*.

59   1 DOLLAR
L.1960. Like #54 but w/corner design modifications.

	VG	VF	UNC
a. Sign. 4.	.35	1.50	6.00
b. Sign. 5.	.25	1.00	3.00

60   2 DOLLARS
L.1960. Like #55 but w/corner design modifications.

	VG	VF	UNC
a. Sign. 4.	.50	2.00	8.50
b. Sign. 5.	.50	2.00	5.50

61   5 DOLLARS
L.1960. Like #57 but w/corner design modifications.

	VG	VF	UNC
a. Sign. 4.	1.25	5.00	17.50
b. Sign. 5.	.85	3.50	12.00

62   10 DOLLARS
L.1960. Like #58 but w/corner design modifications. Sign. 4.

	VG	VF	UNC
	3.00	12.50	40.00

63   20 DOLLARS
L.1960 (1977). Maroon and m/c. N. Nethersole at I., flag at ctr. Bank of Jamaica on back. Sign. 4.

	VG	VF	UNC
	4.00	15.00	65.00

1978-84 ISSUE
Bank of Jamaica Act
#64-68 wmk: Pineapple. Printer: TDLR.
Replacement notes: Serial # prefix *ZY* or *ZZ*.

64	**1 DOLLAR**	VG	VF	UNC
	ND (1982-86). Like #59.			
	a. Sign. 6.	.15	.50	2.50
	b. Sign. 7.	.10	.35	1.50
65	**2 DOLLARS**			
	ND (1982-86). Like #60.			
	a. Sign. 6.	.20	.65	5.00
	b. Sign. 7.	.10	.30	4.00
66	**5 DOLLARS**			
	ND (1984). Similar to #61. Sign. 7.	.15	.60	6.00

67	**10 DOLLARS**	VG	VF	UNC
	1978-81. Bluish purple on m/c unpt. Like #62.			
	a. Sign. 5. 1.10.1978; 1.10.1979.	.50	1.50	17.50
	b. Sign. 9. 1.12.1981.	.40	1.00	7.50

69	**2 DOLLARS**	VG	VF	UNC
	1985-. Dk. green and violet on m/c unpt. Similar to #65 but lithographed. Horizontal sorting bar at r.			
	a. Sign. 7. 1.1.1985.	FV	FV	2.50
	b. Sign. 8. 1.3.1986; 1.2.1987; 1.9.1987.	FV	FV	2.00
	c. Sign. 9. 1.7.1989.	FV	FV	1.75
	d. Sign. 11. 1.1.1990; 29.5.1992.	FV	FV	1.00
	e. Sign. 11. 1.2.1993.	FV	FV	.50

68	**20 DOLLARS**	VG	VF	UNC
	1978-83. Red and m/c. Like #63.			
	a. Sign. 5. 1.10.1978; 1.10.1979; 1.10.1981.	1.00	2.50	25.00
	b. Sign. 6. 1.12.1981.	.85	2.00	20.00
	c. Sign. 7. 1.12.1983.	.75	1.25	12.50

1985 REDUCED SIZE ISSUE

#68A-76 note size: 144 x 68mm. Wmk: Pineapple. Printer: TDLR.

#70-76 arms at bottom ctr.

Replacement notes: Serial # prefix ZY or ZZ.

70	**5 DOLLARS**	VG	VF	UNC
	1985-. Similar to #66 but w/2 horizontal blue-green sorting bars at l. and r.			
	a. Sign. 7. 1.1.1985.	FV	FV	4.00
	b. Sign. 8. 1.9.1987.	FV	FV	3.00
	c. Sign. 9. 1.5.1989.	FV	FV	2.00
	d. Sign. 10. 1.7.1991; 1.8.1992.	FV	FV	.85

68A	**1 DOLLAR**	VG	VF	UNC
	1985-90. Similar to #64; lower corner guilloches modified.			
	a. Sign. 7. 1.1.1985.	FV	FV	1.50
	b. Sign. 8. 1.3.1986; 1.2.1987; 1.9.1987.	FV	FV	1.00
	c. Sign. 9. 1.7.1989.	FV	FV	1.00
	d. Sign. 10. 1.1.1990.	FV	FV	.75

71	**10 DOLLARS**	VG	VF	UNC
	1985-. Similar to #67 but 3 horizontal sorting bars at l. and r.			
	a. Sign. 7. 1.1.1985.	FV	FV	6.00
	b. Sign. 8. 1.9.1987.	FV	FV	5.00
	c. Sign. 9. 1.8.1989.	FV	FV	4.00
	d. Sign. 10. 1.5.1991; 1.8.1992.	FV	FV	1.50
	e. Sign. 12. 1.3.1994.	FV	FV	1.25

72	**20 DOLLARS**	VG	VF	UNC
	1985-. Red-orange, violet and black on m/c unpt. Similar to #68 but circular electronic sorting mark at l.			
	a. Sign. 7. 1.1.1985.	FV	FV	8.00
	b. Sign. 8. 1.3.1986; 1.2.1987; 1.9.1987.	FV	FV	6.00
	c. Sign. 9. 1.9.1989.	FV	FV	4.00
	d. Sign. 10. 1.10.1991.	FV	FV	3.00
	e. Sign. 12. 1.2.1995.	FV	FV	2.00

1986-91 ISSUE

#73-75 printer: TDLR.

Replacement notes: Serial # prefix *ZY* or *ZZ.*

73	**50 DOLLARS**	VG	VF	UNC
	1988-. Brown, purple, red-violet on m/c unpt. S. Sharpe at l. Doctor's Cave on back.			
	a. Sign. 8. 1.8.1988.	FV	FV	4.50
	b. Sign. 11. 1.2.1993.	FV	FV	4.00
	c. Sign. 12. 1.2.1995.	FV	FV	3.75

74	**100 DOLLARS**	VG	VF	UNC
	1.12.1986; 1.9.1987. Black and purple on m/c unpt. Sir D. Sangster at l. Dunn's River Falls at r. on back. Sign. 8.	FV	5.00	12.00

75	**100 DOLLARS**	VG	VF	UNC
	1991-93. Like #74 but w/lilac unpt. and 2 circles at r., w/vertical orange bar. More silver waves added to both *$100* on back.			
	a. Sign. 10. 1.7.1991.	FV	FV	7.50
	b. 1.6.1992.	FV	FV	7.00
	c. 1.2.1993.	FV	FV	6.50

1994 ISSUE

#76-78 printer: TDLR.

Replacement notes: Serial # prefix *ZY* or *ZZ.*

76	**100 DOLLARS**	VG	VF	UNC
	1.3.1994. Like #75 but w/ascending serial # and segmented foil over security thread.	FV	FV	6.00

77	**500 DOLLARS**	VG	VF	UNC
(76)	1.5.1994. Purple, violet and brown on m/c unpt. Nanny of the Maroons at l. Map of islands above Fort Royal at ctr. r. on back. Sign. 12.	FV	FV	25.00

COLLECTOR SERIES

BANK OF JAMAICA

1978 ISSUE

			ISSUE PRICE	MKT. VALUE
CS1	**1976 1-10 DOLLARS**		30.00	20.00
	#54-57 w/matching red star prefix serial # and *SERIES 1976*. (5000 sets issued).			
CS2	**1977 1-10 DOLLARS**		29.50	15.00
	#54-57 w/matching red star prefix serial # and *SERIES 1977*. (7500 sets issued).			

			ISSUE PRICE	MKT. VALUE
CS3	**1978 1-10 DOLLARS**		61.00	30.00
	#54-57 in double set. One is like #CS1-2 w/ *SERIES 1978* and the other w/additional ovpt: *Twenty-fifth Anniversary of the Coronation June 2, 1953* and *SERIES 1978* at r. All w/matching red star prefix serial #. (6250 sets issued).			

JAPAN

Japan, a constitutional monarchy situated off the east coast of Asia, has an area of 145,856 sq. mi. (377,644 sq. km.) and a population of 123.2 million. Capital: Tokyo. Japan, one of the three major industrial nations of the free world, exports machinery, motor vehicles, textiles and chemicals.

Japan, founded (so legend holds) in 660 BC by a direct descendant of the Sun Goddess, was first brought into contact with the west by a storm-blown Portuguese ship in 1542. European traders and missionaries proceeded to enlarge the contact until the Shogunate, sensing a military threat in the foreign presence, expelled all foreigners and severed relations with the outside world in the 17th century. After contact was reestablished by Commodore Perry of the U.S. Navy in 1854, Japan rapidly industrialized, abolished the Shogunate and established a parliamentary form of government, and by the end of the 19th century achieved the status of a modern economic and military power. A series of wars with China and Russia, and participation with the Allies in World War I, enlarged Japan territorially but brought its interests into conflict with the Far Eastern interests of the United States and Britain, causing it to align with the Axis powers for the pursuit of World War II. After its defeat in World War II, Japan renounced military aggression as a political instrument, established democratic self-government, and quickly reasserted its position as an economic world power.

RULERS:
Hirohito (Showa), 1926-1989
Akihito (Heisei), 1989-

MONETARY SYSTEM:
1 Sen = 10 Rin
1 Yen = 100 Sen

CONSTITUTIONAL MONARCHY

BANK OF JAPAN

日 本 銀 行 券
Nip-pon Gin-ko Ken

1950-58 ND ISSUE

90	**100 YEN**	VG	VF	UNC
	ND (1953). Brown-violet on green unpt. Portr. I. Taisuke at r. 12 varieties exist. Diet Bldg. at r. on back.			
	a. Single letter serial # prefix.	6.00	20.00	65.00
	b. Double letter serial # prefix. Lt. brown paper.	1.50	5.00	15.00
	c. As b., but white paper.	FV	1.50	2.50
	s. As a. Specimen w/red ovpt. and perforated: *Mi-hon*.	—		1000.

91 500 YEN

		VG	VF	UNC
ND (1951). Blue. Portr. I. Tomomi at r. Back gray and pale green; Mt. Fuji at r.
a.	Single letter serial # prefix.	8.00	25.00	80.00
b.	Double letter serial # prefix. Cream paper.	5.50	7.00	30.00
c.	As b., but white paper.	FV	5.50	11.50
s.	As a. Specimen w/red ovpt. and perforated: *Mi-hon*.	—	—	1000.

92 1000 YEN

		VG	VF	UNC
ND (1950). Black on green unpt. Portr. Shotoku-Taishi at r. Back brown and blue; Yumedono Pavilion at l.
a.	Single letter serial # prefix.	15.00	40.00	125.00
b.	Double letter serial # prefix.	FV	15.00	50.00

93 5000 YEN

		VG	VF	UNC
ND (1957). Green and m/c. Portr. Shotoku-Taishi at ctr. and as wmk. Back green; Bank of Japan at ctr.
a.	Single letter serial # prefix.	FV	65.00	125.00
b.	Double letter serial # prefix.	FV	FV	70.00

94 10,000 YEN

		VG	VF	UNC
ND (1958). Dk. brown and dk. green. Portr. Shotohu-Taishi at r. Back brown; phoenix at l. and r. in unpt. within ornate frame. Wmk: Yumedono Pavilion.
a.	Single letter serial # prefix.	FV	125.00	200.00
b.	Double letter serial # prefix.	FV	FV	130.00

1963-69 ND ISSUE

95 500 YEN

		VG	VF	UNC
ND (1969). Blue. Portr. Iwakura Tomomi at r. Back steel blue; Mt. Fuji at l. ctr.
a.	Single letter serial # prefix	FV	7.50	20.00
b.	Double letter serial # prefix.	FV	5.50	7.50

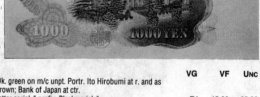

96 1000 YEN

		VG	VF	UNC
ND (1963). Dk. green on m/c unpt. Portr. Ito Hirobumi at r. and as wmk. Back brown; Bank of Japan at ctr.
a.	Single letter serial # prefix. Black serial #.	FV	15.00	65.00
b.	As a., but w/double letter serial # prefix.	FV	FV	15.00
c.	Single letter serial # prefix. Blue serial #.	FV	12.00	37.50
d.	As c., but w/double letter serial # prefix.	FV	FV	13.00

1984 ND ISSUE

#97-99 wmk. same as portr.

97 1000 YEN

		VG	VF	UNC
ND (1984-93). Blue and m/c. Natsume Soseki at r. Crane at l. and r. on back.				
a.	Single letter serial # prefix. Black serial #	FV	12.00	25.00
b.	As a., but w/double letter serial # prefix.	FV	FV	13.50
c.	Single letter serial # prefix. Blue serial #.	FV	FV	20.00
d.	As c., but w/double letter serial # prefix.	FV	FV	15.00

98 5000 YEN

		VG	VF	UNC
ND (1984-93). Violet and m/c. Nitobe Inazo at r. Lake and Mt. Fuji at ctr. on back.				
a.	Single letter serial # prefix. Black serial #.	FV	50.00	75.00
b.	As a., but w/double letter serial # prefix.	FV	FV	70.00

99 10,000 YEN

		VG	VF	UNC
ND (1984-93). Lt. brown and m/c. Fukuzawa Yukichi at r. Pheasant at l. and r. on back.				
a.	Single letter serial # prefix.	FV	110.00	140.00
b.	As a., but w/double letter serial # prefix.	FV	FV	130.00

1993 ND ISSUE

#100-102 microprinting added. Wmk: Same as portr.

100 1000 YEN

		VG	VF	UNC
ND (1993-). Blue and m/c. Like #97				
a.	Single letter serial # prefix. Brown serial # (1993).	FV	FV	15.00
b.	As a., but w/double letter serial # prefix.	FV	FV	12.50

101 5000 YEN

		VG	VF	UNC
ND (1993-). Violet and m/c. Like #98.				
a.	Single letter serial # prefix. Brown serial # (1993).	FV	FV	65.00
b.	As a., but w/double letter serial # prefix.	FV	FV	60.00

102 10,000 YEN

		VG	VF	UNC
ND (1993-). Lt. brown and m/c. Like #99.				
a.	Single letter serial # prefix. Brown serial # (1993).	FV	FV	125.00
b.	As a., but w/double letter serial # prefix.	FV	FV	120.00

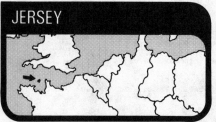

JERSEY

The Bailiwick of Jersey, a British Crown dependency located in the English Channel 12 miles (19 km.) west of Normandy, France, has an area of 45 sq. mi. (117 sq. km.) and a population of 72,691. Capital: St. Helier. The economy is based on agriculture and cattle breeding - the importation of cattle is prohibited to protect the purity of the island's world-famous strain of milk cows.

Jersey was occupied by Neanderthal man 100,000 years B.C., and by Iberians of 2000 B.C. who left their chamber tombs in the island's granite cliffs. Roman legions almost certainly visited the island although they left no evidence of settlement. The country folk of Jersey still speak an archaic form of Norman-French, lingering evidence of the Norman annexation of the island in 933 B.C. Jersey was annexed to England in 1206, 140 years after the Norman Conquest. The dependency is administered by its own laws and customs; laws enacted by the British Parliament do not apply to Jersey unless it is specifically mentioned. During World War II, German troops occupied the island from July 1, 1940 until June 6, 1944.

RULERS:
British

MONETARY SYSTEM:
1 Shilling = 12 Pence
1 Pound = 20 Shillings, 1877-1971
1 Pound = 100 New Pence, 1971-

BRITISH INFLUENCE

STATES OF JERSEY, TREASURY

	SIGNATURE VARIETIES		
1	F.N. Padgham, 1963–72	4	Baird, 1993-
2	J. Clennett, 1972–83	5	
3	Leslie May, 1983–93	6	

1963 (ND) ISSUE
#7-10 Qn. Elizabeth II at r. looking l., wearing cape. Printer: TDLR.

7 10 SHILLINGS

	VG	VF	UNC
ND (1963). Brown on m/c unpt. St. Ouen's Manor on back.	2.00	6.00	12.00

8 **1 POUND**
ND (1963). Green. Mont Orgueil Castle on back. 2 sign. varieties.

		VG	VF	UNC
a.	Sign. 1.	3.00	8.50	35.00
b.	Sign. 2.	3.00	6.00	22.50
c.	W/o sign.	15.00	30.00	75.00
s.	Specimen.	—	—	20.00

9 **5 POUNDS**
ND (1963). Dk. red. St. Aubin's Fort on back.

		VG	VF	UNC
a.	Sign. 1.	10.00	25.00	125.00
b.	Sign. 2.	8.50	12.00	30.00
s.	Specimen.	—	—	35.00

10 **10 POUNDS**
ND (1972). Purple and m/c. Back similar to #7.

		VG	VF	UNC
a.	Sign. 2.	18.00	25.00	55.00
s.	Specimen.	—	—	40.00

1976 (ND) ISSUE

#11-13 sign. varieties. Printer: TDLR.
#11-14 Qn. Elizabeth at ctr. r. looking l., wearing a tiara.

11 **1 POUND**
ND (1976-88). Blue. Battle of Jersey scene on back.

		VG	VF	UNC
a.	Sign. 2.	FV	2.00	9.00
b.	Sign. 3.	FV	1.75	7.50
s.	Specimen.	—	—	5.00

12 **5 POUNDS**
ND (1976-88). Brown. Sailing ships, Elizabeth Castle on back.

		VG	VF	UNC
a.	Sign. 2.	FV	10.00	30.00
b.	Sign. 3.	FV	9.00	22.50
s.	Specimen.	—	—	15.00

13 **10 POUNDS**
ND (1976-88). Green. Victoria College on back.

		VG	VF	UNC
a.	Sign. 2.	FV	20.00	45.00
b.	Sign. 3.	FV	18.00	37.50
s.	Specimen.	—	—	25.00

14 **20 POUNDS**
ND (1976-88). Red-brown. Sailing ship, Gorey Castle on back.

		VG	VF	UNC
a.	Sign. 2.	FV	42.50	90.00
b.	Sign. 3.	FV	35.00	85.00
s.	Specimen.	—	—	35.00

1989 (ND) ISSUE

#15-19 birds at l. corner, arms at ctr., Qn. Elizabeth II at r. facing, wearing cape. Wmk: Cow's head.

15 **1 POUND**
ND (1989). Dk. green and violet on m/c unpt. Church at l. ctr. on back.

		VG	VF	UNC
a.	Sign. 3.	FV	FV	5.00
s.	Specimen.	—	—	5.00

16   5 POUNDS
ND (1989). Rose on m/c unpt. La Corbiere lighthouse on back.

	VG	VF	UNC
a. Sign. 3.	FV	FV	20.00
s. Specimen.	—	—	10.00

17   10 POUNDS
ND (1989). Orange-brown on m/c unpt. Battle of Jersey on back.

	VG	VF	UNC
a. Sign. 3.	FV	FV	35.00
s. Specimen.	—	—	15.00

18   20 POUNDS
ND (1989). Blue on m/c unpt. St. Ouen's Manor on back.

	VG	VF	UNC
a. Sign. 3.	FV	FV	67.50
s. Specimen.	—	—	25.00

19   50 POUNDS
ND (1989). Dk. gray on m/c unpt. Government House on back.

	VG	VF	UNC
a. Sign. 3.	FV	FV	135.00
s. Specimen.	—	—	50.00

1993 (ND) ISSUE

#20-24 like #15-19 but w/solid color denomination at upper r. Wmk: Cow's head.

20   1 POUND
ND (1993). Like #15.

	VG	VF	UNC
a. Sign. 4.	FV	FV	3.75
s. Specimen.	—	—	10.00

21   5 POUNDS
ND (1993). Like #16.

	VG	VF	UNC
a. Sign. 4.	FV	FV	12.50
s. Specimen.	—	—	12.50

22   10 POUNDS
ND (1993). Like #17.

	VG	VF	UNC
a. Sign. 4.	FV	FV	23.50
s. Specimen.	—	—	15.00

23   20 POUNDS
ND (1993). Like #18.

	VG	VF	UNC
a. Sign. 4.	FV	FV	45.00
s. Specimen.	—	—	25.00

24   50 POUNDS
ND (1993). Like #19.

	VG	VF	UNC
a. Sign. 4.	FV	FV	110.00
s. Specimen.			

1995 COMMEMORATIVE ISSUE

#25, 50th Anniversary Liberation of Jersey.

			VG	VF	UNC
25	**1 POUND**		FV	FV	3.50

9.5.1995. Face like #15 w/text: *50th Anniversary...* at l. in wmk. area. Face and back of German Occupation 1 Pound #6 on back. Wmk: Cow's head. Sign. 4. Printer: TDLR.

COLLECTOR SERIES

STATES OF JERSEY, TREASURY

1978 ISSUE

		ISSUE PRICE	MKT. VALUE
CS1	**ND (1978) 1-20 POUNDS**	14.00	45.00

#11a-14a w/ovpt: *SPECIMEN* and Maltese cross prefix serial #.

JORDAN

The Hashemite Kingdom of Jordan, a constitutional monarchy in southwest Asia, has an area of 37,738 sq. mi. (97,740 sq. km.) and a population of 3 million. Capital: Amman. Agriculture and tourism comprise Jordan's economic base. Chief exports are phosphates, tomatoes and oranges.

Jordan is the Edom and Moab of the time of Moses. It became part of the Roman province of Arabia in 106 AD, was conquered by the Arabs in 633-36, and was part of the Ottoman Empire from the 16th century until World War I. At that time, the regions presently known as Jordan and Israel were mandated to Great Britain by the League of Nations as Transjordan and Palestine. In 1922 Transjordan was established as the semi-autonomous Emirate of Transjordan, ruled by the Hashemite Prince Abdullah but still nominally a part of the British mandate. The mandate over Transjordan was terminated in 1946, the country becoming the independent Hashemite Kingdom of Transjordan. The kingdom was renamed The Hashemite Kingdom of The Jordan in 1950.

RULERS:
Hussein I, 1952-

MONETARY SYSTEM:
1 Dirham = 100 Fils
1 Dinar = 10 Dirhams, until 1993
1 Dinar = 10 Piastres, 1993-

KINGDOM

CENTRAL BANK OF JORDAN

SIGNATURE VARIETIES					
10			**16**		
11			**17**		
12			**18**		
13			**19**		
14			**20**		
15			**21**		

1959 FIRST ISSUE

Law 1959

#9-12 Kg. Hussein at l. Wmk: Kg. Hussein wearing turban.

		VG	VF	UNC
9	**500 FILS**	3.50	15.00	42.50

L.1959. Brown on m/c unpt. Forum Jerash on back. w/*FIVE HUNDRED FILS* at bottom margin on back. Sign. 10-12.

		VG	VF	UNC
10	**1 DINAR**	3.00	10.00	40.00

L.1959. Green on m/c unpt. al-Aqsa Mosque "Dome of the Rock" at ctr. w/columns at r. on back. Sign. 10-12.

11   5 DINARS

	VG	VF	UNC
L.1959. Red-brown on m/c unpt. al-Hazne, Treasury of Pharaoh at Petra at ctr. r. on back. Sign. 10-12.	10.00	25.00	90.00

12   10 DINARS

	VG	VF	UNC
L.1959. Blue-gray on m/c unpt. Baptismal site on River Jordan on back. Sign. 10; 11.	25.00	65.00	175.00

1959 SECOND ISSUE

#13-16 Kg. Hussein I at l., w/o law date 1959. Wmk: Kg. Hussein wearing turban.

13   1/2 DINAR

	VG	VF	UNC
ND. Like #9, but w/HALF DINAR at bottom margin on back. Sign. 12-15.	1.00	3.00	13.50

14   1 DINAR

	VG	VF	UNC
ND. Like #10. Sign. 12-15.	1.75	5.00	21.00

15   5 DINARS

	VG	VF	UNC
ND. Like #11. Sign. 12-15.	2.25	9.00	37.50

16   10 DINARS

	VG	VF	UNC
ND. Like #12. Sign. 12-15.	4.00	16.50	65.00

1975; 1977 ISSUE

#17-21 Kg. Hussein at l. Wmk: Kg. Hussein wearing turban.

17   1/2 DINAR

	VG	VF	UNC
ND (1975-92). Brown on m/c unpt. Jerash at r. on back. Sign. 15-18.	FV	.60	3.00

18   1 DINAR

ND (1975-92). Dk. green on m/c unpt. al-Aqsa Mosque "Dome of the Rock" behind columns at r. on back. Sign. 15-18.

	VG	VF	UNC
a. Sign. 15.	FV	FV	10.00
b. Sign. 16.	FV	FV	8.50
c. Sign. 17.	FV	FV	7.50
d. Sign. 18.	FV	FV	6.50
e. Sign. 19.	FV	FV	4.50

19   5 DINARS

ND (1975-92). Red on m/c unpt. El Hazne, Treasury of the Pharaoh at Petra at r. on back.

	VG	VF	UNC
a. Sign. 15.	FV	FV	30.00
b. Sign. 16.	FV	FV	27.50
c. Sign. 17.	FV	FV	25.00
d. Sign. 18.	FV	FV	22.50
e. Sign. 19.	FV	FV	20.00

1992 ISSUE
#23-27 Kg. Hussein wearing headdress at ctr. r. and as wmk. Sign. 19.

20   10 DINARS

		VG	VF	UNC
ND (1975-92). Blue on m/c unpt. Cultural palace above and amphitheater at ctr. r. on back. Sign. 15-18.				
	a. Sign. 15.	FV	FV	85.00
	b. Sign. 16.	FV	FV	65.00
	c. Sign. 17.	FV	FV	50.00
	d. Sign. 18.	FV	FV	45.00
	e. Sign. 19.	FV	FV	35.00

23 1/2 DINAR	VG	VF	UNC
AH 1412/1992. Lilac-brown and dk. brown on m/c unpt. Qusayr Amra fortress at r. on back.	FV	FV	2.50

24 1 DINAR	VG	VF	UNC
AH 1412/1992. Green on olive and m/c unpt. Ruins of Jerash at ctr. r. on back.	FV	FV	4.50

21   20 DINARS

	VG	VF	UNC
1977; 1981; 1985; 1987; 1988. Deep brown on m/c unpt. Electric power station of Zerga on back. Sign. 16-18.	FV	FV	57.50

1991 ISSUE

25 5 DINARS	VG	VF	UNC
AH 1412/1992. Red and violet-brown on m/c unpt. Treasury at Petra on back.	FV	FV	15.00

22   20 DINARS

	VG	VF	UNC
1977 (1991); 1982 (1991); 1985 (1992). Blue on m/c unpt. Like #21. (Sign. 16; 15; 17, respectively.)	FV	FV	65.00

26	10 DINARS	VG	VF	UNC
	AH1412/1992. Blue, gray-violet and green on m/c unpt. al-Rabadh Castle on back.	FV	FV	27.50

27	20 DINARS	VG	VF	UNC
	AH 1412/1992. Dk. brown, green and red-brown on m/c unpt. Dome of the Rock at l. ctr. on back.	FV	FV	50.00

1995-96 ISSUE

#27-32 w/title: *THE HASHEMITE KINGDOM KINGDOM OF JORDAN* on back.

28	1/2 DINAR	VG	VF	UNC
	(1996). Lilac-brown and dk. brown on m/c unpt. Like #23.	FV	FV	2.50
29	1 DINAR			
	AH 1415/1995. Green and olive on m/c unpt. Like #25.	FV	FV	4.00
30	5 DINARS			
	(1996). Red and violet-brown on m/c unpt.	FV	FV	13.50
31	10 DINARS			
	(1996). Blue, gray-violet and green on m/c unpt. Like #26.	FV	FV	25.00
32	20 DINARS			
	(1996). Dk. brown, green and red-brown on m/c unpt. Like #27.	FV	FV	47.50

KATANGA

Katanga, the southern province of Zaire (formerly Belgian Congo) extends northeast to Lake Tanganyika, east and south to Zambia, and west to Angola. It was inhabited by Luba and Bantu peoples, and was one of Africa's richest mining areas.

In 1960, Katanga, under the leadership of provincial president Moise Tshombe and supported by foreign mining interests, seceded from newly independent Republic of the Congo. A period of political confusion and bloody fighting involving Congolese, Belgian and United Nations forces ensued. At the end of the rebellion in 1962, Katanga was reintegrated into the republic, and is known as the Shaba region.

For additional history, see Zaïre.

MONETARY SYSTEM:
1 Franc = 100 Centimes

INDEPENDENT

GOVERNMENT

1961 ND PROVISIONAL ISSUE

#1-4 w/red ovpt: *GOUVERNEMENT KATANGA* on face and back of Banque D'Emission du Rwanda et du Burundi notes.

1	5 FRANCS			
	ND (- old date 15.5.1961). Ovpt. on Rwanda & Burundi #1.	—	Rare	—
2	10 FRANCS			
	ND (- old date 15.9.1960; 5.10.1960). Ovpt. on Rwanda & Burundi #2.	—	Rare	—

3	20 FRANCS			
	ND (- old date 5.9.1960; 5.10.1960). Ovpt. on Rwanda & Burundi #3.	—	Rare	—

4	50 FRANCS			
	ND (- old date 1.10.1960). Ovpt. on Rwanda & Burundi #4.	—	Rare	—

BANQUE NATIONALE DU KATANGA

1960 ISSUE
#5-10 Moise Tsjombe at r. Various dates.

5	**10 FRANCS**	VG	VF	UNC
	1.12.1960; 15.12.1960. Lilac and yellow.			
	a. Issued note.	10.00	15.00	30.00
	b. Remainder, no serial #.	—	—	40.00

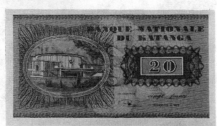

6	**20 FRANCS**	VG	VF	UNC
	1960. Blue-green.			
	a. 2.11.1960.	12.00	30.00	60.00
	b. 1.12.1960.	25.00	60.00	120.00
	c. Remainder, w/o serial #.	—	—	80.00
7	**50 FRANCS**			
	10.11.1960. Brown and salmon.			
	a. Issued note.	13.50	40.00	80.00
	b. Remainder, w/o serial #.	—	—	125.00

8	**100 FRANCS**	VG	VF	UNC
	31.10.1960. Brown, green and yellow.			
	a. Issued note.	20.00	60.00	100.00
	b. Remainder, w/o serial #.	—	—	150.00
9	**500 FRANCS**			
	31.10.1960. Green, violet and olive.			
	a. Issued note.	60.00	150.00	200.00
	b. Remainder, w/o serial #.	—	—	200.00
10	**1000 FRANCS**			
	31.10.1960. Blue and brown.			
	a. Issued note.	100.00	200.00	350.00
	b. Remainder, w/o serial #.	—	—	300.00

1961 (ND) ISSUE

11	**10 FRANCS**	VG	VF	UNC
	ND. Green, brown and red. Moise Tshombe at l., flag at r. Foundry on back. Printer: W&S. (Not issued).	—	—	500.00

1962 ISSUE
#12-14 wheel of masks and spears on back. Wmk: elephant. Various dates.

12	**100 FRANCS**	VG	VF	UNC
	18.5.1962; 15.8.1962; 15.9.1962; 14.1.1963. Dk. green and bown on m/c unpt. Woman carrying ears of corn at r.			
	a. Issued note.	8.00	20.00	50.00
	s. Specimen.	—	—	75.00
13	**500 FRANCS**			
	17.4.1962. Purple and m/c. Man w/fire at r.			
	a. Issued note.	80.00	200.00	350.00
	s. Specimen.	—	—	400.00

14	**1000 FRANCS**	VG	VF	UNC
	26.2.1962. Dk. blue, red and brown on m/c unpt. Woman carrying child on back and picking cotton at r.			
	a. Issued note.	40.00	100.00	200.00
	s. Specimen.	—	—	250.00

KAZAKHSTAN

The Republic of Kazakhstan (formerly Kazakhstan S.S.R.) is bordered to the west by the Caspian Sea and Russia, to the north by Russia, in the east by the Peoples Republic of China and in the south by Uzbekistan and Kirghizia and has an area of 1,049,155 sq. mi. (2,717,300 sq. km.) and a population of 16.7 million. Capital: Alma-Ata (formerly Verny). Rich in mineral resources including coal, tungsten, copper, lead, zinc and manganese with huge oil and natural gas reserves; while agriculture is important, as it was at once, 20 percent of the total acreage of the combined U.S.S.R. Non-ferrous metallurgy, heavy engineering and chemical industries are leaders in its economy.

The Kazakhs are a branch of the Turkic peoples which led the nomadic life of herdsman until WW I. In the 13th century they come under Genghis Khan's eldest son Juji and later became a part of the Golden Horde, a western Mongol empire. Around the beginning of the 16th century they were divided into 3 confederacies, known as zhuz or hordes, in the steppes of Turkistan. At the end of the 17th century an incursion by the Kalmucks, a remnant of the Oirat Mongol confederacy, resulted in heavy losses on both sides which facilitated Russian penetration. Resistance to Russian settlements varied throughout the 1800's, but by 1900 over 100 million acres was declared Czarist state property and used for a planned peasant colonization. After a revolution in 1905 Kazakh deputies were elected. In 1916 the tsarist government ordered mobilization of all males, between 19 and 43, for auxilary service. The Kazakhs rose in defiance which led the governor general of Turkistan to send troops against the rebels. Shortly after the Russian revolution Kazakh Nationalists asked for full autonomy. The Communist coup d'état of Nov. 1917 led to civil war. In 1919-20 the Red army defeated the "White" Russian forces and occuped Kazakhstan and fought against the Nationalist government formed on Nov. 17, 1917 by Ali Khan Bukey Khan. The Kazakh Autonomous Soviet Socialist Republic was proclaimed on Aug. 26, 1920 within the R.S.F.S.R. Russian and Ukrainian colonization continued while 2 purges in 1927 and 1935 quelled any Kazakh feelings of priority in the matters of their country. On Dec. 5, 1936 Kazakhstan qualified for full status as an S.S.R. and held its first congress in 1937. Independence was declared on Dec. 16, 1991 and Kazakhstan joined the C.I.S.

MONETARY SYSTEM:
1 Tenge = 100 Tyin = 500 Rubles (Russian), 1993 -

REPUBLIC

КАЗАКСТАН УЛТТЫК БАНКI

KAZAKHSTAN NATIONAL BANK

1993-94 ISSUE

Tenge System
#1-6 ornate denomination in circle at r. Circular arms at l. on back. Serial # at l. or lower l. for each. Wmk. paper.
#7-9 wmk: symetrical design repeated
#7-15 arms at upper ctr. r. on back.
#14-16 al-Farabi at r. and as wmk.

1	1 TYIN		VG	VF	UNC
	1993. Violet and blue-violet on m/c unpt. 2 wmk. varieties.		FV	FV	.15

2	2 TYIN	VG	VF	UNC
	1993. Blue-violet on lt. blue and m/c unpt.			
	a. 2 wmk. varieties.	FV	FV	.25
	b. W/o wmk.	FV	FV	.20

3	5 TYIN		VG	VF	UNC
	1993. Violet on lt. blue and m/c unpt.		FV	FV	.35

4	10 TYIN		VG	VF	UNC
	1993. Deep red on pink and m/c unpt.		FV	FV	.50

5	20 TYIN		VG	VF	UNC
	1993. Black and blue-gray on m/c unpt.		FV	FV	.65

6	50 TYIN		VG	VF	UNC
	1993. Dk. brown and black on m/c unpt.		FV	FV	.75

7	1 TENGE		VG	VF	UNC
	1993. Blue-black on m/c unpt. al-Farabi at ctr. r. Back lt. blue on m/c unpt; architectural drawings of mosque at l. ctr., arms at upper r.		FV	FV	.45

8   **3 TENGE**   **VG**   **VF**   **UNC**
       1993. Dk. green on m/c unpt. Suinbai at ctr. r. Mountains, forest, and   FV   FV   .85
       river at l. ctr. on back.

9   **5 TENGE**   **VG**   **VF**   **UNC**
       1993. Dk. brown-violet on m/c unpt. Kurmangazy at ctr. r. Cemetary at   FV   FV   1.25
       l. ctr. on back.

10   **10 TENGE**   **VG**   **VF**   **UNC**
       1993. Dk. green on m/c unpt. Shoqan Valikhanov at ctr. r. and as   FV   FV   2.00
       wmk. Mountains, forest, and lake at l. ctr. on back.

11   **20 TENGE**   **VG**   **VF**   **UNC**
       1993. Brown on m/c unpt. A. Kunanbrev at ctr. r. and as wmk.   FV   FV   2.50
       Equestrian hunter at l. ctr. on back.

12   **50 TENGE**   **VG**   **VF**   **UNC**
       1993. Red-brown and deep violet on m/c unpt. Abilkhair Khan at ctr. r.   FV   FV   3.50
       and as wmk. Native artwork at l. ctr. on back.

13   **100 TENGE**   **VG**   **VF**   **UNC**
       1993. Purple and dk. blue on m/c unpt. Abylai Khan at ctr. r. and as   FV   FV   6.00
       wmk. Domed bldg. at l. ctr. on back.

14   **200 TENGE**
       1993. Red and brown on m/c unpt. Domes of bldg. at l. on back.   FV   FV   10.00

15   **500 TENGE**
       1994. Blue-black and violet on m/c unpt. Ancient bldg. on back.   FV   FV   22.50

16   **1000 TENGE**
       1994. Deep green, red and orange on m/c unpt. Ancient bldg. on back.   FV   FV   40.00

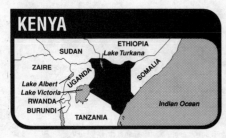

KENYA

SUDAN
ETHIOPIA
Lake Turkana
ZAIRE
UGANDA
SOMALIA
Lake Albert
Lake Victoria
RWANDA
BURUNDI
TANZANIA
Indian Ocean

The Republic of Kenya, located on the east coast of Central Africa, has an area of 224,961 sq. mi. (582,646 sq. km.) and a population of 25.9 million. Capital: Nairobi. The predominantly agricultural country exports coffee, tea and petroleum products.

The Arabs came to the coast of Kenya in the 8th century and established posts to conduct an ivory and slave trade. The Portuguese, the inveterate wanderers of the Age of Exploration, followed in the 16th century. After a lengthy and bitter struggle with the sultans of Zanzibar who controlled much of the southeastern coast of Africa, the Portuguese were driven away (late 17th century) and for many years Kenya was simply a port of call on the route to India. German and British interests in the 19th century produced agreements defining their respective spheres of influence. The British sphere was administrated by the Imperial East Africa Co. until 1895, when the British government purchased the company's rights in the East Africa Protectorate which in 1920, was designated as Kenya Colony and protectorate - the latter being a 10-mile wide coastal strip together with Mombasa, Lamu and other small islands nominally retained by the Sultan of Zanzibar. Kenya achieved self-government in June of 1963 as a consequence of the 1952-60 Mau Mau terrorist campaign to secure land reforms and political rights for Africans. Independence was attained on Dec. 12, 1963. Kenya became a republic in 1964. It is a member of the Commonwealth of Nations. The president is Chief of State and Head of Government.

Notes of the East African Currency Board were in use during the first years.

RULERS:
British to 1964

MONETARY SYSTEM:
1 Shilling (Shilingi) = 100 Cents

REPUBLIC

CENTRAL BANK OF KENYA

1966 ISSUE
#1-5 M. Jomo Kenyatta at l. Values also in Arabic numerals and letters. Various dates. Wmk: Lion's head.

1	5 SHILLINGS	VG	VF	UNC
	1966-68. Brown on m/c unpt. Woman picking coffee beans at r. on back.			
	a. 1.7.1966.	2.50	8.00	45.00
	b. 1.7.1967; 1.7.1968.	2.50	8.00	45.00

2	10 SHILLINGS	VG	VF	UNC
	1966-68. Green on m/c unpt. Tea pickers in field on back.			
	a. 1.7.1966.	3.00	15.00	85.00
	b. 1.7.1967; 1.7.1968.	4.00	17.50	90.00

3	20 SHILLINGS	VG	VF	UNC
	1966-68. Blue on m/c unpt. Plants and train w/sisal on back.			
	a. 1.7.1966.	6.00	35.00	150.00
	b. 1.7.1967; 1.7.1968.	6.00	35.00	150.00

4	50 SHILLINGS	VG	VF	UNC
	1966-68. Dk. brown on m/c unpt. Cotton picking below Mt. Kenya on back.			
	a. 1.7.1966.	90.00	300.00	650.00
	b. 1.7.1967; 1.7.1968.	95.00	325.00	700.00

5	100 SHILLINGS	VG	VF	UNC
	1966; 1968. Purple on m/c unpt. Workers at pineapple plantation on back.			
	a. 1.7.1966.	25.00	85.00	400.00
	b. 1.7.1968.	25.00	90.00	450.00

1969 ISSUE
#6-10 M. Jomo Kenyatta at l., values w/o Arabic numerals and letters. Different text at lower ctr. Sign. varieties. Wmk: Lion's head.

6	**5 SHILLINGS**	VG	VF	UNC
	1.7.1969-1.7.1973. Brown. Similar to #1.	1.00	4.00	15.00
7	**10 SHILLINGS**			
	1.7.1969-1.7.1974. Green. Similar to #2.	2.00	6.00	32.50
8	**20 SHILLINGS**			
	1.7.1969-1.7.1973. Blue. Similar to #3.	3.00	20.00	135.00
9	**50 SHILLINGS**			
	1.7.1969; 1.7.1971. Dk. brown. Similar to #4.	90.00	300.00	675.00
10	**100 SHILLINGS**			
	1.7.1969-1.7.1973. Purple. Similar to #5.	10.00	55.00	225.00

1974 ISSUE

#11-14 M. Jomo Kenyatta at l., values indistinct or barely visible at bottom l. corners. Various date and sign. varieties. Wmk: Lion's head.

11	**5 SHILLINGS**	VG	VF	UNC
	12.12.1974; 1.1.1975; 1.7.1976; 1.7.1977. Brown-orange on m/c unpt. Woman picking coffee beans on back.	.50	1.75	5.00

12	**10 SHILLINGS**	VG	VF	UNC
	1.1.1975; 1.7.1976; 1.7.1977. Dk. green and dk. brown on m/c unpt. Cattle on back.	1.00	3.00	9.00

13	**20 SHILLINGS**	VG	VF	UNC
	12.12.1974; 1.1.1975; 1.7.1976; 1.7.1977. Blue-black and blue on m/c unpt. Lions on back.	2.00	6.00	22.50

14	**100 SHILLINGS**	VG	VF	UNC
	12.12.1974; 1.1.1975; 1.7.1976; 1.7.1977. Violet, dk. brown and dk. blue on m/c unpt. Kenyatta statue and tower on back. 153 x 79mm.	7.50	25.00	60.00

1978 ISSUE

#15-18 M. Jomo Kenyatta at l., w/English value in 3rd line only on face. Wmk: Lion's head.

NOTE: #15-18 were withdrawn soon after Kenyatta's death. A shortage of currency resulted in a limited re-issue during Dec. 1993 - Jan. 1994 of mostly circulated notes.

15	**5 SHILLINGS**	VG	VF	UNC
	1.7.1978. Brown-orange on m/c unpt. Similar to #11. W/English value on face in third line only.	.50	2.00	4.00
16	**10 SHILLINGS**			
	1.7.1978. Dk. green and dk. brown on m/c unpt. Similar to #12.	1.00	3.00	7.50
17	**20 SHILLINGS**			
	1.7.1978. Blue-black and blue on m/c unpt. Similar to #13.	1.50	5.00	15.00
18	**100 SHILLINGS**			
	1.7.1978. Violet, dk. brown and dk. blue on m/c unpt. Similar to #14 but w/different colors in guilloches. 157 x 81mm.	3.50	12.50	30.00

1980-81 ISSUE

#19-23 arms at ctr., Pres. Daniel T.A. Moi at r. Wmk: Lion's head.

19	**5 SHILLINGS**	VG	VF	UNC
	1.1.1981; 1.1.1982; 1.7.1984. Brown and m/c. 3 rams w/giraffes and mountain in background on back.	FV	.75	3.00

20	**10 SHILLINGS**	VG	VF	UNC
	1.1.1981-1.7.1988. Green and m/c. 2 cows at l., 2 school children drinking milk at ctr. on back.	FV	.75	3.00

21 20 SHILLINGS
1.1.1981-1.7.1987. Blue and m/c. 4 women reading newspaper at ctr. on back.

	VG	VF	UNC
	FV	1.50	5.50

22 50 SHILLINGS
1.6.1980; 1.7.1985; 14.9.1986; 1.7.1987; 1.7.1988. Dk. red and m/c. Back olive; jet aircraft flying over Jomo Kenyata airport.

	VG	VF	UNC
	FV	3.50	10.00

23 100 SHILLINGS
1.6.1980-1.7.1988. Purple and m/c. Kenyatta statue, tower and mountains on back.

	VG	VF	UNC
	2.50	10.00	22.50

1986-90 ISSUES
#24-30 arms at l. ctr., Pres. D. T. A. Moi at r. Wmk: Lion's head.

24 10 SHILLINGS
1989-. Dk. green, dk. blue and brown on m/c unpt. University at l. ctr. on back.

	VG	VF	UNC
a. 14.10.1989; 1.7.1990.	.25	.75	2.00
b. 1.7.1991; 2.1.1992.	FV	.50	1.50
c. 1.7.1993; 1.1.1994.	FV	FV	1.25

25 20 SHILLINGS
1988-92. Dk. blue, violet and dk. green on m/c unpt. Moi International Sports Complex on back.

	VG	VF	UNC
a. 12.12.1988.	1.35	4.00	12.50
b. 1.7.1989; 1.7.1990.	.50	1.60	4.00
c. 1.7.1991; 2.1.1992.	FV	1.00	3.00

26 50 SHILLINGS
10.10.1990; 1.7.1992. Red-brown on m/c unpt. Back green; modern bldgs. at l.

	VG	VF	UNC
	1.25	4.00	10.00

27 100 SHILLINGS
1989-. Purple, dk. green and red on m/c unpt. Monument to 25th anniversary of independence w/Mt. Kenya on back.

	VG	VF	UNC
a. 14.10.1989; 1.7.1990; 1.7.1991.	2.75	5.00	11.50
b. 2.1.1992.	FV	4.00	10.00
c. 2.7.1992; 1.1.1994; 1.1.1995.	FV	4.00	10.00

28   200 SHILLINGS

	VG	VF	UNC
14.9.1986; 1.7.1987; 1.7.1988. Dk. brown on m/c unpt. Triangle in lower l. border. No silvering on value at upper r. Fountain at ctr. on back.	FV	6.50	23.50

29   200 SHILLINGS

	VG	VF	UNC
1989-. Similar to #28 but rose rose replaces colored triangle to r. of *200* at lower l. Additional silver diamond design under 200 at upper r. Vertical serial # at l.			
a. 1.7.1989; 1.7.1990.	FV	5.50	13.50
b. 2.1.1992.	FV	4.50	12.50
c. 1.7.1992; 14.9.1993; 1.1.1994.	FV	4.00	11.50

30   500 SHILLINGS

	VG	VF	UNC
1988-. Black, deep green and red on m/c unpt. Roses at l. Modern bldg., Mt. Kenya on back.			
a. 14.10.1988.	FV	25.00	90.00
b. 1.7.1990-1.1.1995.	FV	FV	30.00

1993 ISSUE

#31 and 32 Pres. D. T. A. Moi at r.

31   20 SHILLINGS

	VG	VF	UNC
14.9.1993; 1.1.1994. Similar to #25 but w/roses added to l. border, vertical red serial #, engraved date and m/c symmetrical design below upper border. Male runner and other artistic enhancements on back.	FV	FV	2.25

1995; 1996 ISSUE

#32-37 Pres. D. T. A. Moi at ctr. r., arms at l. ctr. Ascending serial #. Wmk: Lion's head.

32   20 SHILLINGS

	VG	VF	UNC
1.7.1995. Dk. blue and olive-green on m/c unpt.	FV	FV	1.50

33   50 SHILLINGS

	VG	VF	UNC
1.1.1996. M/c. Camel caravan on back.	FV	FV	2.75

34   100 SHILLINGS

	VG	VF	UNC
1.7.1996. M/c.	FV	FV	5.00

35   200 SHILLINGS

	VG	VF	UNC
1.7.1996. Dk. brown on m/c unpt.	FV	FV	9.00

36   500 SHILLINGS

	VG	VF	UNC
1.7.1995. Black and red on m/c unpt.	FV	FV	21.50

37   1000 SHILLINGS
(32)

	VG	VF	UNC
12.12.1994; 1.7.1995. Brown and violet on m/c unpt. Pres. D. T. A. Moi at l. ctr., arms at upper r. Water buffalo, elephants and bird on back. Wmk: Lion's head.	FV	FV	40.00

The Democratic Peoples Republic of Korea, situated in northeastern Asia on the northern half of the Korean peninsula between the Peoples Republic of China and the Republic of Korea, has an area of 46,540 sq. mi. (120,538 sq. km.) and a population of 22.4 million. Capital: Pyongyang. The economy is based on heavy industry and agriculture. Metals, minerals and farm produce are exported.

Japan replaced China as the predominant foreign influence in Korea in 1895 and annexed the peninsular country in 1910. Defeat in World War II brought an end to Japanese rule. U.S. troops entered Korea from the south and Soviet forces entered from the north. The Cairo conference (1943) had established that Korea should be "free and independent." The Potsdam conference (1945) set the 38th parallel as the line dividing the occupation forces of the United States and Russia. When Russia refused to permit a U.N. commission designated to supervise reunification elections to enter North Korea, an election was held in South Korea which established the Republic of Korea on Aug. 15, 1948. North Korea held an unsupervised election on Aug. 25, 1948, and on the following day proclaimed the establishment of the Democratic Peoples Republic of Korea.

MONETARY SYSTEM:
1 Won = 100 Chon

DEMOCRATIC PEOPLES REPUBLIC

KOREAN CENTRAL BANK

1959 ISSUE

12	50 CHON		VG	VF	UNC
	1959. Blue. Arms at upper l.		.15	.50	2.00

13	1 WON		VG	VF	UNC
	1959. Red-brown. Fishing boat at ctr.		.15	.50	2.00

14	5 WON		VG	VF	UNC
	1959. Green and m/c. Lg. bldg. at ctr.		.15	.40	2.00

15	10 WON		VG	VF	UNC
	1959. Red and m/c. Pagoda at ctr. r. Woman picking fruit on back.		.20	.50	2.00

16	50 WON		VG	VF	UNC
	1959. Purple and m/c. Arms at l., bridge and city at ctr. Woman w/wheat on back.		.20	.50	2.00

17	100 WON		VG	VF	UNC
	1959. Green and m/c. Arms at l., steam freight train in factory area at ctr. River w/cliffs on back.		.25	.75	3.00

1978 ISSUE

#18-22, arms.

NOTE: Circulation of varieties #18-21: a., for general circulation; b., for Socialist visitors; c., for non-Socialist visitors; d., replaced a.; e., not known.

18	1 WON	VG	VF	UNC
	1978. Green and m/c. 2 adults and 2 children at ctr. Back purple and m/c. Soldier at l., woman w/flowers at ctr., woman at r.			
	a. Red and black serial #. No seal on back.	.25	.75	3.00
	b. Black serial #. Green seal on back.	.20	.60	2.50
	c. Red serial #. Red seal at l. on back.	.20	.60	2.50
	d. Red serial #. Lg. numeral 1 in red guilloche on back.	.20	.60	2.50
	e. Black serial #. Lg. numeral 1 in blue guilloche on back.	.20	.60	2.50

21	50 WON	VG	VF	UNC
	1978. Olive and m/c. Soldier w/man holding torch, woman w/wheat, man w/book at ctr. Lake scene on back.			
	a. Red and black serial #. No seal on back.	.50	1.50	6.00
	b. Black serial #. Green seal at lower r. on back.	.35	1.10	4.50
	c. Red serial #. Red seal at lower r. on back.	.35	1.10	4.50
	d. Red serial #. Lg. numeral 50 in red guilloche on back.	.50	1.10	4.50
	e. Black serial #. Lg. numeral 50 in blue guilloche on back.	.50	1.10	4.50

19	5 WON	VG	VF	UNC
	1978. Blue-gray and m/c. Worker w/book and gear, and woman w/wheat at ctr. Mt. Gumgang on back.			
	a. Red and black serial #. No seal on back.	.25	.75	3.00
	b. Black serial #. Green seal at l. on back.	.25	.85	3.50
	c. Red serial #. Red seal at l. on back.	.25	.85	3.50
	d. Red serial #. Lg. numeral 5 in red guilloche on back.	.25	.85	3.50
	e. Black serial #. Lg. numeral 5 in blue guilloche on back.	.25	.85	3.50

22	100 WON	VG	VF	UNC
	1978. Purple and m/c. Kim Il Sung at ctr. r. House w/trees on back. Red and black serial #. No seal on back.	.75	2.50	10.00

1988 'CAPITALIST VISITOR' ISSUE

#23-26 have arms at upper l. on face; red serial #. 'Value' backs.

#27-30, dk. green on blue and pink unpt. w/winged equestrian statue. "Chonllima" at ctr., arms at upper r. Red serial #.

20	10 WON	VG	VF	UNC
	1978. Brown and m/c. Winged equestrian statue 'Chonllima' at ctr. Waterfront factory on back.			
	a. Red and black serial #. No seal on back.	.40	1.25	5.00
	b. Black serial #. Green seal at upper r. on back.	.30	1.00	4.00
	c. Red serial #. Red seal at upper r. on back.	.30	1.00	4.00
	d. Red serial #. Lg. numeral 10 in red guilloche on back.	.30	1.00	4.00
	e. Black serial #. Lg. numeral 10 in blue guilloche on back.	.30	1.00	4.00

23	1 CHON	VG	VF	UNC
	1988. Blue on purple unpt.	.10	.20	.40
24	5 CHON			
	1988. Blue on pink unpt.	.15	.25	.50
25	10 CHON			
	1988. Blue and black on green-yellow unpt.	.20	.40	.75
26	50 CHON			
	1988. Blue on yellow unpt.	.25	.50	1.00
27	1 WON			
	1988.	.30	.75	2.50

40	5 WON		VG	VF	UNC
	1992. Blue-black and deep purple on m/c unpt. Students at ctr. r. w/modern bldg. and factory in background. Palace on back.		FV	FV	4.00

28	5 WON	VG	VF	UNC
	1988.	.40	1.50	7.50
29	10 WON			
	1988.	.75	3.00	12.50
30	50 WON			
	1988.	1.50	8.00	40.00

1988 'SOCIALIST VISITOR' ISSUE

#31-38, arms at upper r. Denomination on back. Black serial #.
#35-38 red on blue and ochre unpt. Temple at ctr., olive sprig on globe at r. Olive sprig on globe on back.

31	1 CHON	VG	VF	UNC
	1988. Red-brown on pink and blue unpt.	FV	FV	1.25

32	5 CHON	VG	VF	UNC
	1988. Purple on pink and blue unpt.	FV	FV	1.75
33	10 CHON			
	1988. Olive-green on pink and blue unpt.	FV	FV	2.50
34	50 CHON			
	1988. Brown-violet on pink and blue unpt.	FV	FV	3.00

41	10 WON		VG	VF	UNC
	1992. Deep brown and red-brown on m/c unpt. Factory worker, winged equestrian statue "Chonllima" at ctr., factories in background at r. Flood gates on back.		FV	FV	7.50

35	1 WON	VG	VF	UNC
	1988.	FV	FV	3.50
36	5 WON			
	1988.	FV	FV	12.50
37	10 WON			
	1988.	FV	FV	25.00
38	50 WON			
	1988.	FV	FV	100.00

42	50 WON		VG	VF	UNC
	1992. Deep brown and deep olive-brown on m/c unpt. Monument to 5 year plan at l. and as wmk., young professionals at ctr. r., arms at upper r. Landscape of pine trees and mountains on back.		FV	FV	35.00

1992 ISSUE

#39-42 arms at upper l. Wmk: Winged Equestrian statue "Chonllima".

39	1 WON	VG	VF	UNC
	1992. Grayish olive-green and olive-brown on m/c unpt. Young woman w/flower basket at ctr. r. Mt. Gumgang on back.	FV	FV	1.50

43	100 WON		VG	VF	XF
	1992. Deep brown and brown-violet on m/c unpt. Arms at lower l. ctr., Kim Il Sung at r. Rural home at ctr. on back. Wmk: Arched gateway.		FV	FV	65.00

COLLECTOR SERIES

KOREAN CENTRAL BANK

1978 ISSUE

CS1	1978 1-100 WON.		ISSUE PRICE	MKT. VALUE
	Red ovpt. Korean characters for specimen on #18a-22a (w/all zero serial #).		—	30.00

1992 ISSUE

CS2	1992 1-100 WON.		ISSUE PRICE	MKT. VALUE
	Red, rectangular ovpt. Korean characters for specimen on #39-43. (39, 42 and 43 all zero serial #, 40-41 w/normal serial #).		—	20.00

KOREA-SOUTH

The Republic of Korea, situated in northeastern Asia on the southern half of the Korean peninsula between North Korea and the Korean Strait, has an area of 38,025 sq. mi. (98,484 sq. km.) and a population of 43.27 million. Capital: Seoul. The economy is based on agriculture and textiles. Clothing, plywood and textile products are exported. Japan replaced China as the predominant foreign influence in Korea in 1895 and annexed the peninsular country in 1910. Defeat in World War II brought an end to Japanese rule. U.S. troops entered Korea from the south and Soviet forces entered from the north. The Cairo Conference (1943) had established that Korea should be "free and independent." The Potsdam Conference (1954) set the 38th parallel as the line dividing the occupation forces of the United States and Russia. When Russia refused to permit a U.N. commission designated to supervise reunification elections to enter North Korea, an election was held in South Korea on May 10, 1948. By its determination, the Republic of Korea was inaugurated on Aug. 15, 1948.

NOTE: For Bank of Chosen notes issued in South Korea under the Allied Occupation during the post WWII period 1945 to 1948 refer to Korea listings.

MONETARY SYSTEM:
  1 Won (Hwan) = 100 Chon
  1 new Won = 10 old Hwan, 1962-

DATING:

The modern notes of Korea are dated according to the founding of the first Korean dynasty, that of the house of Tangun, in 2333 BC.

REPUBLIC

BANK OF KOREA

1958-60 ISSUE

25	1000 HWAN	VG	VF	UNC
	4293 (1960); 4294 (1961); 1962. Black on olive unpt. Kg. Sejong the Great at r. Back blue-green and lt. brown; flaming torch at ctr.	1.50	10.00	75.00

1961-62 ISSUE
Hwan System.

26	500 HWAN	VG	VF	UNC
	4294 (1961). Blue-green on m/c unpt. Kg. Sejong the Great at r. Back green; bldg. at r. 8-character imprint.	10.00	60.00	300.00

27   100 HWAN

	VG	VF	UNC
1962. Green on orange and m/c unpt. Woman reading to child at r. Archway at l., date at bottom r. margin on back.	12.50	50.00	250.00

1962 ND ISSUES
Won System.

28   10 JEON

	VG	VF	UNC
1962. Deep blue on pale blue and pink unpt.	.05	.10	.50

29   50 JEON

	VG	VF	UNC
1962. Black on pale green and ochre unpt.	.05	.10	.50

30   1 WON

	VG	VF	UNC
ND (1962). Violet on brown unpt.	.05	.10	1.00

31   5 WON

	VG	VF	UNC
ND (1962). Black on gray-green unpt.	.10	.25	2.00

32   10 WON

	VG	VF	UNC
ND (1962). Brown on green unpt.	.35	1.00	6.00

33   10 WON

	VG	VF	UNC
1962-65; ND. Brown on lilac and green unpt. Tower at l. Medieval tortoise warship at ctr. on back.			
a. Date at lower r. on back.	1.65	5.50	47.50
b. W/o date at lower r. on back.	.15	.75	3.50

34   50 WON

	VG	VF	UNC
ND (1962). Red-brown on blue and lilac unpt. Rock in the sea at l. Torch at ctr. on back.	2.00	7.00	45.00

35   100 WON

	VG	VF	UNC
1962-65. Green on olive unpt. Archway at l. Unpt: *100* Won at ctr. Pagoda and date on back.	1.00	6.00	50.00

36   100 WON

	VG	VF	UNC
ND (1962). Green on blue and gold unpt. Archway similar to #35 at l. Unpt. 5-petaled blossom at ctr. Back like #34.	2.00	10.00	55.00

37   500 WON

	VG	VF	UNC
ND (1962). Blue on lilac and green unpt. Pagoda portal at l. Back like #34.	4.00	17.50	85.00

1965; 1966 ND ISSUE

38   100 WON
ND (1965). Dk. green. Bank name and denomination in red. Kg.
Sejong the Great at r. Bldg. on back.

VG	VF	UNC
.65	1.75	7.50

38A   100 WON
ND (1965). Dk. blue-green. Bank name and denomination in maroon.
Like #38.

VG	VF	UNC
.75	2.25	10.00

39   500 WON
ND (1966). Gray on m/c unpt. City gate at l. Medieval tortoise
warships on back.

VG	VF	UNC
.75	1.50	6.00

1969-73 ND ISSUE

40   50 WON
ND (1969). Black on green and brown unpt. Pavilion at l. Back blue;
torch at ctr.

VG	VF	UNC
.25	1.00	4.00

41   5000 WON
ND (1972). Brown on green and m/c unpt. Yi I at r. Lg. bldg. on back.

VG	VF	UNC
7.50	12.50	40.00

42   10,000 WON
ND (1973). Dk. brown and m/c. Kg. Sejong the Great at l. ctr. Bldgs.
and pavilion on back.

VG	VF	UNC
15.00	25.00	60.00

1973-79 ND ISSUE

43   500 WON
ND (1973). Blue and m/c. Adm. Yi Sun-shin at l., medieval tortoise
warship at ctr. Bldg. w/steps on back.

VG	VF	UNC
FV	1.00	3.50

44   1000 WON
ND (1975). Purple and m/c. Yi Hwang at r. Do-San Academy in black
on back.

VG	VF	UNC
FV	2.00	6.00

45   5000 WON
ND (1977). Brown on m/c unpt. Yi I at r. Sm. bldg. w/steps on back.

	VG	VF	UNC
	FV	8.50	20.00

49   10,000 WON

	VG	VF	UNC
	FV	FV	24.00

ND (1983). Dk. green on m/c unpt. Monument at l; Kg. Sejong at r. Three raised colored dots for blind at lower l. Pavilion at ctr. on back.

46   10,000 WON

	VG	VF	UNC
	FV	20.00	40.00

ND (1979). Black, dk. green and m/c. Monument at l., Kg. Sejong at r. Pavilion at ctr. on back.

1983 ND ISSUE

47   1000 WON

	VG	VF	UNC
	FV	FV	4.50

ND (1983). Purple on m/c unpt. Yi Hwang at r. One raised colored dot for blind at lower l. Bldgs. in courtyard on back.

48   5000 WON

	VG	VF	UNC
	FV	FV	13.00

ND (1983). Brown on m/c unpt. Yi I at r. Two raised colored dots for blind at lower l. Sm. bldg. w/steps on back.

AUXILIARY MILITARY PAYMENT CERTIFICATE COUPONS

Issued to Korean troops in Vietnam to facilitate their use of United States MPC. These coupons could not be used as currency by themselves.

SERIES I

#M1-M8 were issued on Dec. 29, 1969, and were valid only until June or Oct. 7, 1970. Anchor on glove crest. Validation stamp on back. Uniface.

		VG	VF	UNC
M1	**5 CENTS**	90.00	225.00	—
	ND (1969). Maroon, red-brown and yellow ctr. Flowering branch at l., lg. *5* at r.			
M2	**10 CENTS**	90.00	225.00	—
	ND (1969). Dk. blue w/lt. blue-green ctr. Flowers at l., lg. *10* at. r.			
M3	**25 CENTS**	—	—	—
	ND (1969). Brown and yellow ctr. Flower at l., lg. *25* at r.			
M4	**50 CENTS**	—	—	—
	ND (1969). Green and yellow ctr. Flower at l., lg. *50* at r.			
M5	**1 DOLLAR**	—	—	—
	ND (1969). Brown and yellow ctr. Korean flag at l., lg. *1* at r.			
M6	**5 DOLLARS**	—	—	—
	ND (1969). Blue and turquoise ctr. Flowers at l., lg. *5* at r.			
M7	**10 DOLLARS**	—	—	—
	ND (1969). Brown and yellow ctr. Flowers at l.			
M8	**20 DOLLARS**	—	—	—
	ND (1969). Green and yellow ctr. Flowers at l.			

SERIES II

#M9-M16 were issued June (or Oct.) 1970. Anchor symbol ctr., 702 at l., lg. denomination numerals r. Fact and back similar.

		VG	VF	UNC
M9	**5 CENTS**	20.00	65.00	200.00
	ND (1970). Maroon and violet on ochre unpt. Space capsule at l.			

		VG	VF	UNC
M10	**10 CENTS**	30.00	90.00	275.00
	ND (1970). Red and yellow on green paper. Flowers at l. Back red.			

M11 **25 CENTS**
ND (1970). Green and blue. Crown at l.

	VG	VF	UNC
	90.00	225.00	—

M12 **50 CENTS**
ND (1970). Blue and green. Pottery w/legs at l.

	VG	VF	UNC
	90.00	225.00	—

M13 **1 DOLLAR**
ND (1970). Maroon and red on lt. green paper. Torch at l.

	VG	VF	UNC
	—	—	—

M14 **5 DOLLARS**
ND (1970). Red, ochre and yellow on lt. blue paper. Holed coin at l.

| | — | — | — |

M15 **10 DOLLARS**
ND (1970). Blue on yellow paper. Pagoda at l.

| | — | — | — |

M16 **20 DOLLARS**
ND (1970). Green on pink paper. Vignette at l.

| | — | — | — |

SERIES III
#M17-M24, military symbol in circle at ctr. on face.

M17 **5 CENTS**
ND. Brown and maroon on yellow paper. "5" at l., clam shell and pearl at ctr. Kettle on back.

	VG	VF	UNC
	20.00	65.00	200.00

M18 **10 CENTS**
ND. Blue w/green tint. "10" at l., snail at ctr. Candle holder on back.

| | 30.00 | 75.00 | 275.00 |

M19 **25 CENTS**
ND. Red, lilac and ochre. "25" at l., crest seal on turtle at r. Back pink; archway at ctr.

	VG	VF	UNC
	90.00	225.00	—

M20 **50 CENTS**
ND. Green and blue. "50" at l., tiger at ctr. Balancing rock on back.

| | — | — | — |

M21 **1 DOLLAR**
ND. Brown and maroon. Flowers at l. Shrine on back.

	VG	VF	UNC
	—	—	—

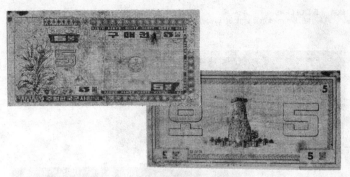

M22 **5 DOLLARS**
ND. Blue and lt. blue on yellow paper. Bush at l., crest seal on rayed cloud at r. Tower at ctr. on back.

	VG	VF	UNC
	—	—	—

M23 **10 DOLLARS**
ND. Yellow and maroon. Pagoda on face. Turtle boat on back.

| | — | — | — |

M24 **20 DOLLARS**
ND. 2 dragons at ctr. Korean house on back.

| | — | — | — |

SERIES IV
#M25-M32, Korean warrior at ctr. on face.

M25 **5 CENTS**
ND. Pink, deep green and lt. blue. Beams and steel mill at ctr. on back.

	VG	VF	UNC
	20.00	40.00	185.00

M26 **10 CENTS**
ND. Deep green on yellow-green. Modern city complex on back. Thick or thin paper.

	VG	VF	UNC
	20.00	40.00	185.00

M27 **25 CENTS**
ND. Yellow and maroon. 2 bridges on back.

| | 60.00 | 200.00 | — |

M28 **50 CENTS**
ND. Blue-green and maroon. Back blue-green and red; dam.

| | 90.00 | 225.00 | — |

M29 **1 DOLLAR**
ND. Green on lt. green unpt. Oil refinery on back.

	VG	VF	UNC
	35.00	100.00	250.00

M30   5 DOLLARS
ND. Brown on gold unpt. Back red-orange; natural gas tank.

	VG	VF	UNC
	350.00	700.00	—

M31   10 DOLLARS
ND. Pink and green. Back pink and blue; loading area at docks.

	VG	VF	UNC
	60.00	200.00	—

M32   20 DOLLARS
ND. Blue and purple. Back green; 4-lane superhighway.

	VG	VF	UNC
	—	—	—

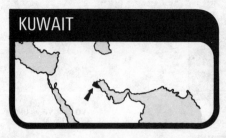

KUWAIT

The State of Kuwait, a constitutional monarchy located on the Arabian Peninsula at the northwestern corner of the Persian Gulf, has an area of 6,880 sq. mi. (17,818 sq. km.) and a population of 2.1 million. Capital: Kuwait. Petroleum, the basis of the economy, provides 95 per cent of the exports.

The modern history of Kuwait began with the founding of the men who wandered northward from the region of the Qatar Peninsula of eastern Arabia. Fearing that the Turks would take over the sheikhdom, Shaikh Mubarak entered into an agreement with Great Britain, 1899, placing Kuwait under the protection of Britain and empowering Britain to conduct its foreign affairs. Britain terminated the protectorate on June 19, 1961, giving Kuwait its independence (by a simple exchange of notes) but agreeing to furnish military aid on request.

The Kuwait dinar, one of the world's strongest currencies, is backed 100 percent by gold and foreign exchange holdings.

On Aug. 2, 1990 Iraqi forces invaded and rapidly overran Kuwaiti forces. Annexation by Iraq was declared on Aug. 8. The Kuwaiti government established itself in exile in Saudi Arabia. The United Nations forces attacked on Feb. 24, 1991 and Kuwait City was liberated on Feb. 26. Iraq quickly withdrew remaining forces.

RULERS:
British to 1961
Abdullah, 1961-1965
Sabah Ibn Salim Al Sabah, 1965-1977
Jabir Ibn Ahmad Al Sabah, 1977-

MONETARY SYSTEM:
1 Dinar = 1000 Fils

SIGNATURE VARIETIES

#	Signature			#	Signature	
1	Amir H. Sheik Jaber Al-Ahmad					
	BANK GOVERNOR	**FINANCE MINISTER**			**BANK GOVERNOR**	**FINANCE MINISTER**
2	Hamza Abbas	Abdul Rehman Al Atiquei		6	Salem Abdul Aziz Al Sabah	Jassem Mohammad Al Kharafi
3	Hamza Abbas	Abdul Latif Al Hamad		7	Salem Abul Aziz Al Sabah	
4	Abdul Wahab Al Tammar	Ali Khalifa Al Sabah		8		
5	Abdul Wahab Al Tammar	Jassem Mohammad Al Kharafi		9		

STATE

KUWAIT CURRENCY BOARD

LAW OF 1960
#1-5 Amir Shaikh Abdullah at r. and as wmk. Sign. 1.

1   1/4 DINAR
L.1960. Brown on m/c unpt. Aerial view, Port of Kuwait at ctr. on back.

VG	VF	UNC
4.00	15.00	35.00

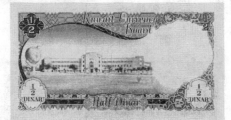

2   1/2 DINAR
L.1960. Purple on m/c unpt. School at ctr. on back.

VG	VF	UNC
4.50	17.50	50.00

3   1 DINAR
L.1960. Red-brown on m/c unpt. Cement plant at ctr. on back.

VG	VF	UNC
7.50	20.00	110.00

4   5 DINARS
L.1960. Blue on m/c unpt. Street scene on back.

VG	VF	UNC
50.00	150.00	400.00

5   10 DINARS
L.1960. Green on m/c unpt. Dhow on back.

VG	VF	UNC
60.00	200.00	450.00

CENTRAL BANK OF KUWAIT

LAW OF 1968, FIRST ISSUE
#6-10 Amir Shaikh Sabah at r. Sign. #2.

6   1/4 DINAR
L.1968. Brown on m/c unpt. Back like #1.

VG	VF	UNC
1.00	3.00	12.00

7   1/2 DINAR
L.1968. Purple on m/c unpt. Back like #2.

VG	VF	UNC
1.75	3.50	13.50

8   1 DINAR
L.1968. Red-brown on m/c unpt. Oil refinery on back.

VG	VF	UNC
3.50	6.00	30.00

12 1/2 DINAR
		VG	VF	UNC
L.1968 (1980). Purple on m/c unpt. Tower at l. Harbor scene on back.				
	a. Sign. 2-4.	.60	1.25	6.00
	b. Sign. 6.	.50	1.00	5.00

13 1 DINAR
		VG	VF	UNC
L.1968 (1980-91). Brown-violet, purple and black on m/c unpt. Modern bldg. at l. Old fortress on back.				
	a. Overall ornate unpt. Sign. 2-4.	1.00	2.50	12.50
	b. Plain colored unpt. at top and and bottom. Sign. 6.	.75	2.00	7.50

9 5 DINARS
	VG	VF	UNC
L.1968. Blue on m/c unpt. View of Kuwait on back.	12.50	30.00	80.00

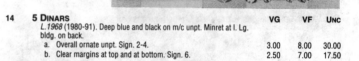

10 10 DINARS
	VG	VF	UNC
L.1968. Green on m/c unpt. Back similar to #5.	20.00	50.00	120.00

LAW OF 1968, SECOND ISSUE

#11-16 arms at r. Black serial #. #11-15 wmk.: Dhow.

NOTE: During the 1991 war with Iraq, their forces stole the following groups of notes:

#11 - 1/4 Dinar, Prefix denominators 54-68.

. #12 - 1/2 Dinar, #30-37.

#13 - 1 Dinar, #47-53.

#14 - 5 Dinar, #18-20.

#15 - 10 Dinar, #70-87.

#16 - 20 Dinar, #9-13.

14 5 DINARS
		VG	VF	UNC
L.1968 (1980-91). Deep blue and black on m/c unpt. Minret at l. Lg. bldg. on back.				
	a. Overall ornate unpt. Sign. 2-4.	3.00	8.00	30.00
	b. Clear margins at top and at bottom. Sign. 6.	2.50	7.00	17.50

15 10 DINARS
		VG	VF	UNC
L.1968 (1980-91). Green on m/c unpt. Falcon at l. Sailing boat on back. Sign. 2-4.				
	a. Overall ornate unpt. Sign. 2-4.	4.00	10.00	40.00
	b. Clear margins at top and at bottom. Sign. 6.	4.00	10.00	400.00

11 1/4 DINAR
		VG	VF	UNC
L.1968 (1980-91). Brown and purple on m/c unpt. Oil rig at l. Oil refinery on back.				
	a. Sign. 2-4.	.50	1.00	3.00
	b. Sign. 6.	.40	.75	2.50

16	**20 DINARS**	**VG**	**VF**	**UNC**
	L.1968 (1986-91). Brown and olive-green on m/c unpt. Bldg. at l. Central Bank at l. ctr. on back. Wmk: Eagle's head. Sign. 5; 6.	12.50	35.00	125.00

1992 POST LIBERATION ISSUE

After the 1991 Gulf War, Kuwait declared all previous note issues worthless.

#17-22 like previous issue. Red serial # at top r. Sign. 7.

17	**1/4 DINAR**	**VG**	**VF**	**UNC**
	L.1968 (1992). Violet and black on silver and m/c unpt. Like #11.	FV	1.00	2.75

18	**1/2 DINAR**	**VG**	**VF**	**UNC**
	L.1968 (1992). Deep blue, blue-green and deep violet on silver and m/c unpt. Like #12.	FV	2.00	5.00

19	**1 DINAR**	**VG**	**VF**	**UNC**
	L.1968 (1992). Deep olive-green, green and deep blue on silver and m/c unpt. Like #13.	FV	FV	7.50

20	**5 DINARS**	**VG**	**VF**	**UNC**
	L.1968 (1992). Olive-brown, pink, green and m/c. Like #14.	FV	FV	35.00

21	**10 DINARS**	**VG**	**VF**	**UNC**
	L.1968 (1992). Orange-red, brown-olive and m/c. Like #15.	FV	FV	65.00
22	**20 DINARS**	**VG**	**VF**	**UNC**
	L.1968 (1992). Violet-brown and m/c. Like #16.	FV	FV	120.00

1994 ND ISSUE

#23-28 outline of falcon's head above arms at l., segmented silver vertical thread at ctr. r. Wmk: Falcon's head. Sign. 8.

#26-28 silver foiling of falcon's head at l. ctr.

NOTE: #23-27 were reported as withdrawn in early 1995 due to the word *Allah* being present.

23	**1/4 DINAR**	**VG**	**VF**	**UNC**
	L.1968 (1994). Brown, grayish purple and red-orange on m/c unpt. Ship at bottom ctr. r. Girls playing game on back.	FV	FV	3.50

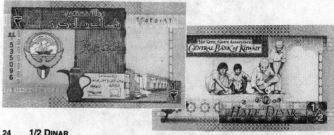

24	**1/2 DINAR**			
	L.1968 (1994). Brown and dk. grayish green on m/c unpt. Souk shops at lower r. Boys playing game on back.	FV	FV	5.00

25 **1 DINAR**
L.1968 (1994). Deep brown, purple and dk. gray on m/c unpt. Pinnacles at ctr. r. Aerial view of harbor docks on back.

VG	VF	UNC
FV	FV	9.00

26 **5 DINARS**
L.1968 (1994). Grayish green and red-violet on m/c unpt. Pinnacle at r. Oil refinery at ctr. on back.

VG	VF	UNC
FV	FV	35.00

27 **10 DINARS**
L.1968 (1994). Purple, violet and dk. brown on m/c unpt. Mosque at lower r. Pearl fisherman at l. ctr., dhow at r. on back.

VG	VF	UNC
FV	FV	60.00

28 **20 DINARS**
L.1968 (1994). Dk. olive-green, orange and olive-brown on m/c unpt. Fortress at low er r. Central bank at bottom l. ctr., old fortress gate, pinnacle at r. on back.

VG	VF	UNC
FV	FV	110.00

COLLECTOR SERIES

CENTRAL BANK OF KUWAIT

1993 ISSUE

CS1 **26.2.1993 1 DINAR**
Orange-red, violet-blue and blue. Plastic w/silver on window. Issued in special folder for "Second Anniversary of Liberation of Kuwait." Text on back includes: "THIS IS NOT LEGAL TENDER."

ISSUE PRICE	MKT. VALUE
—	12.50

KYRGYZSTAN

The Republic of Kyrgyzstan, (formerly Kirghiz S.S.R., a Union Republic of the U.S.S.R.), independent state since Aug. 31, 1991, member of the UN and of the C.I.S. It was the last state of the Union Republics to declare its sovereignty. Capital: Bishkek (formerly Frunze).

Originally part of the Autonomous Turkestan S.S.R. founded on May 1, 1918, the Kyrgyz ethnic area was established on October 14, 1924 as the Kara-Kirghiz Autonomous Region within the R.S.F.S.R. Then on May 25, 1925 the name Kara (black) was dropped. It became an A.S.S.R. on Feb. 1, 1926 and a Union Republic of the U.S.S.R. in 1936. On Dec. 12, 1990, the name was then changed to the Republic of Kyrgyzstan.

MONETARY SYSTEM:
  1 COM = 100 ТЫЙЫН
  1 SOM = 100 Tyiyn

REPUBLIC

КЫРГЫЗ РЕСПУБЛИКАСЫ

KYRGYZ REPUBLIC

1993 ISSUE
#1-3 bald eagle at ctr. Ornate design at ctr. on back. Wmk: Eagle in repeating pattern.

			VG	VF	UNC
1	**1 TYIYN** ND (1993). Dk. brown on pink and brown-orange unpt.		FV	FV	.20

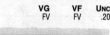

			VG	VF	UNC
2	**10 TYIYN** ND (1993). Brown on pale green and brown-orange unpt.		FV	FV	1.00

			VG	VF	UNC
3	**50 TYIYN** ND (1993). Gray on blue and brown-orange unpt.		FV	FV	1.75

КЫРГЫЗСТАН БАНКЫ

KYRGYZSTAN BANK

1993 ISSUE
#4-6 Equestrian statue of Manas the Noble at r. Manas' mausoleum at l. on back. Wmk: Eagle in repeating pattern.

			VG	VF	UNC
4	**1 SOM** ND (1993). Red on m/c unpt.		FV	FV	1.50

			VG	VF	UNC
5	**5 SOM** ND (1993). Deep grayish green on m/c unpt.		FV	FV	7.50

			VG	VF	UNC
6	**20 SOM** ND (1993). Purple on m/c unpt.		FV	FV	25.00

1994 ISSUE

			VG	VF	UNC
7	**1 SOM** ND (1994). Yellow-brown A. Maldubayer at r. String musical instruments, modern bldg. on back.		FV	FV	1.25

8	**5 SOM**	VG	VF	UNC
	ND (1994). Blue and yellow on m/c unpt. B. Beishenalieva at r. Classical bldg. on back.	FV	FV	3.00

9	**10 SOM**	VG	VF	UNC
	ND (1994). Green and brown on m/c unpt. Kassim at r. Mountains on back.	FV	FV	5.50
10	**20 SOM**			
	ND (1994). Red-orange on m/c unpt. T. Moldo at r.	FV	FV	7.50
11	**50 SOM**			
	ND (1994). Reddish brown on m/c unpt. K. Datka at r. Mausoleum and minaret on back.	FV	FV	15.00
12	**100 SOM**			
	ND (1995). M/c. Toktogul at r. Hydroelectric dam at l. ctr. on back.	FV	FV	22.50

LAOS

The Lao People's Democratic Republic, located on the Indo-Chinese Peninsula between the Socialist Republic of Vietnam and the Kingdom of Thailand, has an area of 91,429 sq. mi. (236,800 sq. km.) and a population of 4.2 million. Captial: Vientiane. Agriculture employs 95 percent of the people. Tin, lumber and coffee are exported.

The first United Kingdom of Laos was established in the mid-14th century by King Fa Ngum who ruled an area including present Laos, northeastern Thailand, and the southern part of China's Yunnan province from his capital at Luang Prabang. Thailand and Vietnam obtained control over much of the present Lao territory in the 18th century and remained dominant until France established a protectorate over the area in 1893 and incorporated it into the Union of Indo-China. The Independence of Laos was proclaimed in March of 1945, during the last days of the Japanese occupation of World War II. France reoccupied Laos in 1946, and established it as a constitutional monarchy within the French Union in 1949. In 1953, war erupted between the government and the Pathet Lao, a Communist movement supported by the Vietnamese Communist forces. Peace was declared in 1954 with Laos becoming fully independent in 1955 and the Pathet Lao being permitted to occupy two northern provinces. Civil war broke out again in 1960 with the United States supporting the government of the Kingdom of Laos and the North Vietnamese helping the Communist Pathet Lao, and continued, with intervals of truce and political compromise, until the formation of the Lao People's Democratic Republic on Dec. 2, 1975.

RULERS:
Sisavang Vong, 1949-1959
Savang Vatthana, 1959-1975

MONETARY SYSTEM:
1 Kip = 100 At, 1955-1978
1 new Kip = 100 old Kip, 1979-

KINGDOM

BANQUE NATIONALE DU LAOS

SIGNATURE VARIETIES		
	LE GOUVERNEUR ຜູ້ອຳນວຍການ	UN CENSEUR ຜູ້ກວດການຜູ້ນຶ່ງ
1	*Rhon Panya*	*H. Wuidos*
2	*Rhon Panya*	*Reinly*
3	*Rhon Panya*	*Sava*
4	*mony buvannany*	*Sava*
5	*mony buvannany*	*H.B*
6	*mony buvannany*	*G.*

1962-63 REGULAR ISSUE
#9-14 wmk: Tricephalic elephant arms.
#11-14 Kg. Savang Vatthana at l.

8	**1 KIP**	VG	VF	UNC
	ND (1962). Brown on pink and bue unpt. Stylized figure at l. Tricephalic elephant arms at ctr. on back.			
	a. Sign. 3; 4.	.10	.20	.75
	s. Sign. 3. Specimen.	—	—	30.00

12 50 KIP
ND (1963). Purple on brown and blue unpt. Pagoda at ctr. back purple; bldg. at r.

		VG	VF	UNC
a.	Sign. 5; 6.	.10	.25	1.00
s.	Sign. 5. Specimen.	—	—	150.00

9 5 KIP
ND (1962). Green on m/c unpt. S. Vong at r. Temple at l., man on elephant at ctr. on back.

		VG	VF	UNC
a.	Sign. 2.	4.50	17.50	42.50
b.	Sign. 5.	.15	.35	1.35
s.	Sign. 2. Specimen.	—	—	150.00

13 200 KIP
ND (1963). Blue on green and gold unpt. Temple of That Luang at ctr. Waterfalls on back.

		VG	VF	UNC
a.	Sign. 4.	.40	1.25	5.00
b.	Sign. 6.	.20	.50	2.00
s.	As a. Specimen.	—	—	150.00

10 10 KIP
ND (1962). Blue on yellow and green unpt. Woman at l. (like back of Fr. Indochina #102). Stylized sunburst on back (like face of #102).

		VG	VF	UNC
a.	Sign. 1.	12.50	50.00	—
b.	Sign. 5.	.15	.35	1.50
s.	As a. Specimen.	—	—	150.00

11 20 KIP
ND (1963). Brown on tan and blue unpt. Bldg. at ctr. Pagoda at ctr. r. on back.

		VG	VF	UNC
a.	Sign 5.	.15	.35	1.50
b.	Sign 6.	.10	.30	1.25
s.	As a. Specimen.	—	—	150.00

14 1000 KIP
ND (1963). Brown on blue and gold unpt. Temple at ctr. 3 long canoes on back.

		VG	VF	UNC
a.	Sign. 5.	.40	1.00	5.00
b.	Sign. 6.	.25	.75	3.00
s.	As a. Specimen.	—	—	150.00

1974; 1975 ND ISSUE
#16-19 Kg. Savang Vatthana at l. Wmk: Tricephalic elephant arms. Sign. 6.

15	**10 KIP**	VG	VF	UNC
	ND (1974). Blue on m/c unpt. Kg. Savang Vatthana at ctr. r. Back blue and brown; ox cart. Sign. 6.			
	a. Issued note.	—	200.00	600.00
	s. Specimen.	—	—	1000.

16	**100 KIP**	VG	VF	UNC
	ND (1974). Brown on blue, green and pink unpt. Pagoda at ctr. Ox cart on back.			
	a. Issued note.	.15	.35	1.50
	s. Specimen.	—	—	150.00

17	**500 KIP**	VG	VF	UNC
	ND (1974). Red on m/c unpt. Pagoda at ctr. Dam on back.			
	a. Issued note.	.20	.40	1.75
	s. Specimen.	—	—	150.00

18	**1000 KIP**	VG	VF	UNC
	ND. Black on m/c unpt. Elephant on back.			
	a. Issued note.	—	300.00	800.00
	s. Specimen.	—	600.00	1500.

19	**5000 KIP**	VG	VF	UNC
	ND (1975). Blue-gray on m/c unpt. Pagoda at ctr. Musicians w/instruments on back.			
	a. Issued note.	.75	2.50	10.00
	s. Specimen.	—	—	125.00

STATE OF LAOS

PATHET LAO GOVERNMENT

ND ISSUE
#A20-24 printed in Peoples Republic of China and circulated in areas under control of Pathet Lao insurgents. Later these same notes became the accepted legal tender for the entire country.

A20	**1 KIP**	VG	VF	UNC
	ND. Green on yellow and blue unpt. Threshing grain at ctr. Medical clinic scene on back. (Not issued).	—	—	50.00

20   10 KIP
ND. Lilac and red on m/c unpt. Medical examination scene. Fighters in the brush on back.

		VG	VF	UNC
a.	Wmk: Temples.	.10	.25	.75
b.	Wmk: 5-pointed stars.	.05	.15	.50
s.	As b. Specimen.	—	—	50.00

21   20 KIP
ND. Brown on green unpt. Rice distribution. Forge workers on back.

		VG	VF	UNC
a.	Wmk: Temples.	.10	.25	1.00
b.	Wmk: 5-pointed stars.	.10	.25	1.00
s.	As b. Specimen.	—	—	50.00

22   50 KIP
ND. Purple on m/c unpt. Factory workers. Plowing ox on back.

		VG	VF	UNC
a.	Wmk: Temples.	.05	.35	1.50
b.	Wmk: 5-pointed stars.	.10	.25	1.25
s.	As b. Specimen.	—	—	50.00

23   100 KIP
ND. Blue on m/c unpt. Long boats on lake. Scene in textile store on back. Wmk: Temples.

		VG	VF	UNC
a.	Issued note.	.10	.25	1.50
s.	Specimen.	—	—	50.00

23A   200 KIP
ND. Green on m/c unpt. Road and trail convoys. Factory scene on back. Wmk: Temples.

		VG	VF	UNC
a.	Issued note.	.15	.40	1.75
s.	Specimen.	—	—	50.00
x.	Lithograph counterfeit (1974) on plain paper, w/o serial #. Ho Chi Minh at r. on back.	12.00	40.00	100.00

24   500 KIP
ND. Brown on m/c unpt. Armed field workers in farm scene. Soldiers shooting down planes on back. Wmk: Temples.

		VG	VF	UNC
a.	Issued note.	.15	.35	1.50
s.	Specimen.	—	—	50.00

PEOPLES DEMOCRATIC REPUBLIC

GOVERNMENT

1972 PROVISIONAL ISSUE
Currency Reform
1 "new" Kip = 100 "old" Kip

24A	50 KIP ON 500 KIP	VG	VF	UNC
	ND. New legends and denomination ovpt. on #24. (Not issued).	15.00	100.00	300.00

1979-92 ISSUE
#25-32 wmk: Lg. stars.

25	1 KIP	VG	VF	UNC
	ND (1979). Blue-gray. Militia unit at l., arms at r. Schoolroom scene on back.			
	a. Issued note.	.05	.10	.20
	s. Specimen.	—		30.00

26	5 KIP	VG	VF	UNC
	ND (1979). Green. Shoppers at a store, arms at r. Logging elephants on back.			
	a. Issued note.	.05	.15	.40
	s. Specimen.	—		30.00

27	10 KIP	VG	VF	UNC
	ND (1979). Brown on green and yellow unpt. Lumber mill at l., arms at r. Medical scenes on back.			
	a. Issued note.	.10	.20	.50
	s. Specimen.	—	—	30.00

28	20 KIP	VG	VF	UNC
	ND (1979). Brown on green and pink unpt. Arms at l., tank w/troop column at ctr. Back brown and maroon; textile mill at ctr.			
	a. Issued note.	.10	.20	.75
	s. Specimen.	—	—	50.00

29	50 KIP	VG	VF	UNC
	ND (1979). Brownish red on green unpt. Rice planting at l. ctr., arms at r. Back red and brown; hydroelectric dam.			
	a. Issued note.	.15	.35	1.25
	s. Specimen.	—		50.00

30	100 KIP	VG	VF	UNC
	ND. Deep blue-green and deep blue on yellow and pink unpt. Grain harvesting at l., arms at r. Bridge, storage tanks, and soldier on back.	FV	FV	1.50

31	500 KIP	VG	VF	UNC
	1988. Brown and deep blue on m/c unpt. Modern irrigation systems at ctr. below arms. Harvesting fruit at ctr. on back.	FV	FV	2.00

32	1000 KIP	VG	VF	UNC
	1992. Blue-black and green on m/c unpt. 3 women at l., temple at ctr. r., arms at r. Cattle at ctr. on back.	FV	FV	3.50

LATVIA

The Republic of Latvia, the central Baltic state in east Europe, has an area of 24,595 sq. mi. (43,601 sq. km.) and a population of *2.6 million. Capital: Riga. Livestock raising and manufacturing are the chief industries. Butter, bacon, fertilizers and telephone equipment are exported.

The Latvians, of Aryan descent, were nomadic tribesmen who settled along the Baltic prior to the 13th century. Lacking a central government, they were easily conquered by the German Teutonic knights, Russia, Sweden and Poland. Following the third partition of Poland by Austria, Prussia and Russia in 1795, Latvia came under Russian domination and did not experience autonomy until the Russian Revolution of 1917 provided an opportunity for freedom. The Latvian republic was established on Nov. 18, 1918. It was occupied by Soviet troops in 1939 and annexed to the Soviet Union in 1940. Following the German occupation of 1941-44, it was retaken by Russia and reestablished as a member S.S. Republic of the Soviet Union. Western countries, including the United States, did not recognize Latvia's incorporation into the Soviet Union. Latvia declared Its independence from the former U.S.S.R. on Aug. 22, 1991.

MONETARY SYSTEM:
1 Lats = 100 Santimu, 1923-40; 1992
1 Lats = 200 Rublu, 1993
1 Rublis = 1 Russian Ruble, 1992

REPUBLIC

GOVERNMENT

1992 ISSUE
#35-40 wmk: Symmetrical design.

			VG	**VF**	**UNC**
35	**1 RUBLIS**	1992. Violet on yellow and ochre unpt. Back violet-brown on lt. green and yellow unpt.	—	.10	.25

			VG	**VF**	**UNC**
36	**2 RUBLI**	1992. Purple on brown-orange and yellow unpt.	—	.10	.25

			VG	**VF**	**UNC**
37	**5 RUBLI**	1992. Deep blue on lt. blue and lt. yellow-orange unpt. Back blue-black on blue and lt. blue unpt.	—	.15	.50

			VG	**VF**	**UNC**
38	**10 RUBLU**	1992. Purple on red-orange and pale orange unpt.	.10	.25	.75

			VG	**VF**	**UNC**
39	**20 RUBLU**	1992. Violet on lilac and pink unpt.	.15	.60	1.75

			VG	**VF**	**UNC**
40	**50 RUBLU**	1992. Gray-green on lt. blue and pink unpt.	.20	.85	2.75

			VG	**VF**	**UNC**
41	**200 RUBLU**	1992. Greenish black on yellow and blue-green unpt. Back greenish black on lt. blue and pink unpt.	.50	2.00	5.00

			VG	**VF**	**UNC**
42	**500 RUBLU**	1992. Violet-brown on gray and dull orange unpt.	1.35	4.00	10.00

1993-94 ISSUE
#43-48 Lielvarde belt vertically at r. Metalized belt at l., arms at lower r. on back. Wmk: Young woman in national costume.

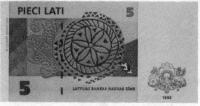

			VG	**VF**	**UNC**
43	**5 LATI**	1992 (1993). Varied shades of green on tan and pale green unpt. Oak tree at ctr. r. Local art at ctr. on back.	FV	FV	13.50

44 10 LATU
1992 (1993). Violet and purple on m/c unpt. Landscape of Daugava
River at ctr. National bow broach at ctr. on back.

	VG	VF	UNC
	FV	FV	25.00

45 20 LATU
1992 (1993). Brown and dk. brown on m/c unpt. Rural house at r.
National ornamented woven linen at l. ctr. on back.

	VG	VF	UNC
	FV	FV	47.50

46 50 LATU
1992 (1994). Deep blue on m/c unpt. Sailing ship at r. Two crossed
kegs and a cross on back.

	VG	VF	UNC
	FV	FV	115.00

47 100 LATU
1992 (1994). Red and dk. brown on m/c unpt. K. Barons at r.
Ornaments of the woven national belt on back.

	VG	VF	UNC
	FV	FV	225.00

48 500 LATU
1992. Purple on m/c unpt. Young woman in national costume at r.
Small ornamental brass crowns on back. (Not released).

	VG	VF	UNC
	—	—	—

LEBANON

The Republic of Lebanon, situated on the eastern shore of the Mediterranean Sea between Syria and Israel, has an area of 4,015 sq. mi. (10,400 sq. km.) and a population of 2.8 million. Capital: Beirut. The economy is based on agriculture, trade and tourism. Fruit, other foodstuffs and textiles are exported.

Almost at the beginning of recorded history, Lebanon appeared as the well-wooded hinterland of the Phoenicians who exploited its famous forests of cedar. The mountains were a Christian refuge and a Crusader stronghold. Lebanon, the history of which is essentially the same as that of Syria, came under control of the Ottoman Turks early in the 16th century. Following the collapse of the Ottoman Empire after World War I, Lebanon, along with Syria, became a French mandate. The French drew a border around the predominantly Christian Lebanon Sanjak or administrative subdivision and on Sept. 1, 1920 proclaimed the area the State of Grand Lebanon (Etat du Grand Liban), a republic under French control. France announced the independence of Lebanon during WWII after Vichy control was deposed on Nov. 26, 1941. It became fully independent on Jan. 1, 1944, but the last British and French troops did not leave until the end of Aug. 1946.

RULERS
French to 1943

MONETARY SYSTEM
1 Livre (Pound) = 100 Piastres

RÉPUBLIQUE LIBANAISE

BANQUE DE SYRIE ET DU LIBAN

1952; 1956 ISSUE
#55-60 all dated 1 January. Sign. varieties. Printer: TDLR.

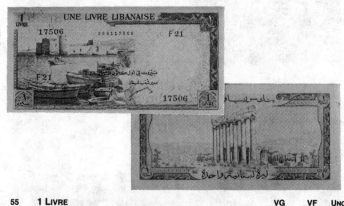

55 1 LIVRE
1.1.1952-64. Brown and m/c. Boats at dockside (Saida) at l. Columns
of Baalbek on back. W/ or w/o security strip.

	VG	VF	UNC
	.50	5.00	20.00

56 5 LIVRES
1.1.1952-64. Blue and m/c. Courtyard of the Palais de Beit-Eddine.
Snowy mountains w/trees on back. W/ or w/o security strip.

	VG	VF	UNC
	2.00	17.50	90.00

57   **10 LIVRES**
1.1.1956; 1.1.1961; 1.1.1963. Green and m/c. Ruins of pillared temple. Shoreline w/city on hills on back.

	VG	VF	UNC
	6.00	30.00	135.00

59   **50 LIVRES**
1.1.1952; 1.1.1953; 1.1.1964. Deep brown on m/c unpt. Coast landscape. Lg. rock formations in water on back. Wmk: Lion's head.

	VG	VF	UNC
	45.00	115.00	450.00

60   **100 LIVRES**
1.1.1952; 1.1.1953; 1.1.1958; 1.1.1963. Blue. View of Beyrouth. Cedar tree at ctr. on back and as wmk.

	VG	VF	UNC
	12.50	35.00	125.00

REPUBLIC

BANQUE DU LIBAN

1964; 1978 ISSUE
#61-69 printer: TDLR.

61   **1 LIVRE**
1964-80. Brown on blue unpt. Columns of Baalbek. Cavern on back. Wmk: 2 eagles.

		VG	VF	UNC
a.	1964; 1968.	.85	2.50	10.00
b.	1971; 1972; 1974.	.65	2.00	6.50
c.	1978; 1980.	.50	1.50	5.00

62   **5 LIVRES**
1964-88. Green on blue and lt. yellow unpt. Bldgs. Footbridge on back. Wmk: Ancient galley.

		VG	VF	UNC
a.	1964.	1.65	5.00	15.00
b.	1967; 1968.	1.00	3.00	11.50
c.	1972; 1974; 1978.	.85	2.50	8.50
d.	1986; 1988.	.10	.15	.35

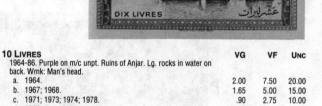

63   **10 LIVRES**
1964-86. Purple on m/c unpt. Ruins of Anjar. Lg. rocks in water on back. Wmk: Man's head.

		VG	VF	UNC
a.	1964.	2.00	7.50	20.00
b.	1967; 1968.	1.65	5.00	15.00
c.	1971; 1973; 1974; 1978.	.90	2.75	10.00
d.	1986.	.10	.20	.50

64   **25 LIVRES**
1964-83. Brown on gold unpt. Citadel on the sea (Saida). Ruin on rocks on back. Wmk: Lion's head.

		VG	VF	UNC
a.	1964; 1967; 1968.	4.00	12.50	35.00
b.	1972; 1973; 1974; 1978.	2.50	8.50	27.50
c.	1983.	.15	.30	1.00

65	50 LIVRES	VG	VF	UNC
	1964-88. Dk. gray, purple and dk. olive-green on m/c unpt. Ruins of Temple of Bacchus on face. Bldg. on back. Wmk: Cedar tree.			
	a. 1964; 1967; 1968.	4.50	15.00	45.00
	b. 1972; 1973; 1974; 1978.	3.50	10.00	30.00
	c. Guilloche added above temple ruins w/10-petaled rosette at l. in unpt. 1983; 1985.	.25	.30	1.50
	d. W/o control # above ruins on face. 1988.	FV	FV	1.00

66	100 LIVRES	VG	VF	UNC
	1964-88. Blue-black on lt. pink and l. blue unpt. Palais Beit-Eddine w/inner courtyard. Snowy trees in mountains on back. Wmk: bearded male elder.			
	a. 1964; 1967; 1968.	5.50	13.50	40.00
	b. 1973; 1974; 1977; 1978; 1980.	4.00	8.50	25.00
	c. Guilloche added under bank name on back. 1983; 1985.	.15	.60	2.50
	d. Guilloche added under title on face. 1988.	.10	.30	1.00

67	250 LIVRES	VG	VF	UNC
	1978-88. Deep gray-green and blue-black on m/c unpt. Ruins on face and back. Wmk: Ancient circular sculpture w/head at ctr. from the Grand Temple Podium.			
	a. 1978.	3.00	16.50	50.00
	b. 1983. Control # at top ctr.	1.50	7.50	40.00
	c. 1985-87.	.20	1.00	5.00
	d. W/o control # above sign. at at archway on face. 1988.	.15	.50	2.25

1988; 1993 ISSUE
Law of 1988

68	500 LIVRES	VG	VF	UNC
	1988. Brown and olive-green on m/c unpt. City scene at ctr. Ruins at l. ctr. on back. Wmk: Lion's head.	.50	.85	1.75

69	1000 LIVRES	VG	VF	UNC
	1988; 1990; 1991. Dk. blue, blue-black and green on m/c unpt. Map at r. Ruins at ctr., modern bldg. at ctr. back. Wmk: Cedar tree.	.85	1.50	3.00

70   10,000 LIVRES

    1993. Violet, olive-brown and purple on m/c unpt. Ancient ruins at ctr.
City ruins w/5 archaic statues on back. Wmk: Ancient circular
sculpture w/head at ctr. from of the Grand Temple Podium.

	VG	VF	UNC
	FV	FV	12.50

1994 ISSUE

#71-74 ornate block designs and as unpt. Arabic serial # and matching bar code, #. Wmk: Cedar tree. Printer: BABN.

71   5000 LIVRES

    1994. Red and purple on pink and m/c unpt. Geometric designs on
back.

	VG	VF	UNC
	FV	FV	8.00

72   20,000 LIVRES

    1994. Red-brown and orange on yellow and m/c unpt. Geometric
designs w/lg. *LIBAN* l. ctr. on back.

	VG	VF	UNC
	FV	FV	25.00

73   50,000 LIVRES

    1994. Blue-black and brown-violet on m/c unpt. Cedar tree at upper l.,
artistic boats at lower l. ctr. Lg. diamond w/BDL at l. ctr., cedar tree at
lower l. on back.

	VG	VF	UNC
	FV	FV	60.00

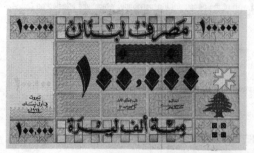

74   100,000 LIVRES

    1994. Dk. blue-green and dk. green on m/c unpt. Cedar tree at lower r.
Artistic bunch of grapes and grain stalks at l. ctr. on back.

	VG	VF	UNC
	FV	FV	115.00

LESOTHO

The Kingdom of Lesotho, a constitutional monarchy located within the east-central part of the Republic of Africa, has an area of 11,716 sq. mi. (30,355 sq. km.) and a population of 1.7 million. Capital: Maseru. The economy is based on subsistence agriculture and livestock raising. Wool, mohair, and cattle are exported. Lesotho (formerly Basutoland) was sparsely populated until the end of the 16th century. Between the 16th and 19th centuries an influx of refugees from tribal wars led to the development of a distinct Basotho group. During the reign of tribal chief Moshesh I (1823-70), a series of wars with the Orange Free State resulted in the loss of large areas of territory to South Africa. Moshesh appealed to the British for help, and Basutoland was constituted a native state under British protection. In 1871 it was annexed to Cape Colony, but was restored to direct control by the Crown in 1884. From 1884 to 1959 legislative and executive authority was vested in a British High Commissioner. The constitution of 1959 recognized the expressed wish of the people for independence, which was attained on Oct. 4, 1966. Lesotho is a member of the Commonwealth of Nations. The king of Lesotho is Chief of State.

RULERS:
King Motlotlehi Moshoeshoe II, 1966-

MONETARY SYSTEM:
1 Loti = 100 Lisente

DATING: Partial date given in the 2 numbers of the serial # prefix for #1-8.

KINGDOM

LESOTHO MONETARY AUTHORITY

1979 ISSUE
#1-3A arms at ctr., military bust of Kg. Moshoeshoe II at r. Wmk: Basotho hat. Sign. 1.

			VG	VF	UNC
1	**2 MALOTI**				
	(19)79. Dk. brown on m/c unpt. Bldg. and Lesotho flag at l. on back.				
	a. Blue and brown unpt. at r. of of Kg.		1.00	2.00	6.00
	b. Brown unpt. at r. of Kg.		Reported Not Confirmed		

			VG	VF	UNC
2	**5 MALOTI**				
	(19)79. Deep blue on m/c unpt. Craftsmen weaving at l. ctr. on back.		2.00	5.00	15.00

		VG	VF	UNC
3	**10 MALOTI**			
	(19)79. Red and purple on m/c unpt. Basotho horseman in maize field at ctr. on back.	5.00	12.00	45.00

		VG	VF	UNC
3A	**20 MALOTI**			
	(19)79. Herdsmen w/cattle at l. ctr. on back. Specimen.	—	—	—

CENTRAL BANK OF LESOTHO

SIGNATURE VARIETIES		
	Minister of Finance	Governor
1	*[signature]*	*[signature]*
2	*[signature]*	*[signature]*
3	*[signature]*	*[signature]*
4	*[signature]*	*[signature]*
5	*[signature]* Governor	

1981; 1984 ISSUE
#4-8 arms at ctr., military bust of Kg. Moshoeshoe II at r. Partial year date given as the denominator of the serial # prefix. Wmk: Basotho hat.

		VG	VF	UNC
4	**2 MALOTI**			
	(19)81; 84. Like #1.			
	a. Sign. 1 (19)81.	1.00	2.00	6.00
	b. Sign. 2 (19)84.	.75	1.25	4.50

5 **5 MALOTI**
(19)81. Face like #2. Waterfalls at ctr. on back. Sign 1.

	VG	VF	UNC
	FV	2.50	6.50

6 **10 MALOTI**
(19)81. Like #3.

		VG	VF	UNC
a.	Sign. 1 (19)81.	FV	4.50	15.00
b.	Sign. 2 (19)81 (issued 1984).	FV	4.25	13.50

7 **20 MALOTI**
(19)81; 84. Dk. green and olive-green on m/c unpt. Mosotho Herdsboy w/cattle at l. ctr. on back.

		VG	VF	UNC
a.	Sign. 1 (19)81.	FV	10.00	35.00
b.	Sign. 2 (19)84.	FV	8.50	25.00

8 **50 MALOTI**
(19)81. Purple and deep blue on m/c unpt. "Qiloane" mountain at l. on back. Sign. 1.

	VG	VF	UNC
	FV	25.00	65.00

1989 ISSUE
#9-13 arms at ctr., civilian bust of Kg. Moshoeshoe II in new portr. at r. Designs similar to #4-8 but w/Kg. also as wmk. Sign. 3.

9 **2 MALOTI**
1989. Similar to #4.

	VG	VF	UNC
	FV	FV	1.85

10 **5 MALOTI**
1989. Similar to #5.

	VG	VF	UNC
	FV	FV	3.50

11 **10 MALOTI**
1989; 1990. Similar to #6.

	VG	VF	UNC
	FV	FV	6.50

			VG	VF	UNC
12	**20 MALOTI** 1989; 1990. Dk. green and blue-black on m/c unpt. Similar to #7.		FV	FV	11.50
13	**50 MALOTI** 1989. Similar to #8.		FV	FV	45.00

1992 ISSUE

			VG	VF	UNC
14	**50 MALOTI** 1992. Purple, dk. olive, green and dk. blue on m/c unpt. Seated Kg. Moshoeshoe I at r. "Qiloane" mountain on back. Sign. 4.		FV	FV	27.50

1994 ISSUE

#15-18 seated Kg. Moshoeshoe I at l., arms at ctr. and as wmk. Sign. 5.

			VG	VF	UNC
15	**20 MALOTI** 1994. Deep olive-green and blue-black on m/c unpt. Mosotho herdsboy w/cattle near huts at ctr. r. on back.		FV	FV	10.00

			VG	VF	UNC
16	**50 MALOTI** 1994. Purple, olive-green and dk. blue on m/c unpt. Herdsman horseback w/packmule at ctr., "Qiloane" mountain at r. on back.		FV	FV	22.50

			VG	VF	UNC
17	**100 MALOTI** 1994. Dk. olive-green, orange and brown on m/c unpt. Sheep by shed and home at ctr. r. on back.		FV	FV	33.50
18	**200 MALOTI** 1994. Purple, brown and orange on m/c unpt. Herdsman and sheep on back.		FV	FV	65.00

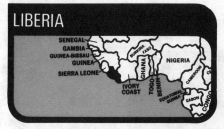

LIBERIA

The Republic of Liberia, located on the southern side of the west African bulge between Sierra Leone and the Ivory Coast, has an area of 38,250 sq. mi. (111,369 sq. km.) and a population of 2.5 million. Capital: Monrovia. The major industries are agriculture, mining and lumbering. Iron ore, diamonds, rubber, coffee and cocoa are exported.

The Liberian coast was explored and chartered by Portuguese navigator Pedro de Cintra in 1461. For the following three centuries Portuguese traders visited the area regularly to trade for gold, slaves and pepper. The modern country of Liberia, Africa's first republic, was settled in 1822 by the American Colonization Society as a homeland for American freed slaves, with the U.S. government furnishing funds and assisting in negotiations for procurement of land from the native chiefs. The various settlements united in 1839 to form the Commonwealth of Liberia, and in 1847 established the country as a republic with a constitution modeled after that of the United States.

Notes were issued from 1857 through 1880; thereafter the introduction of dollar notes of the United States took place. U.S. money was declared legal tender in Liberia in 1943, replacing British West African currencies. Not until 1989 was a distinctive Liberian currency again issued.

MONETARY SYSTEM:
1 Dollar = 100 Cents

REPUBLIC

NATIONAL BANK OF LIBERIA
#19-20 printer: TDLR.

1989 ISSUE

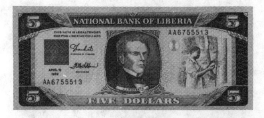

		VG	**VF**	**UNC**
19	**5 DOLLARS**	FV	FV	6.50
	12.4.1989. Black and deep green on m/c unpt. Portr. J. J. Roberts at ctr., tapping trees at r. Back: deep green on m/c unpt.; National Bank bldg. at ctr.			

1991 ISSUE

		VG	**VF**	**VF**
20	**5 DOLLARS**	FV	FV	3.25
	6.4.1991. Similar to #19 but w/arms at ctr.			

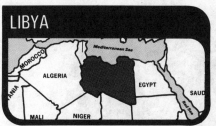

LIBYA

The Socialist People's Libyan Arab Jamahiriya, located on the north central coast of Africa between Tunisia and Egypt, has an area of 679,359 sq. mi. (1,759,540 sq. km.) and a population of 4 million. Capital: Tripoli. Crude oil, which accounts for 90 per cent of the export earnings, is the mainstay of the economy.

Libya has been subjected to foreign rule throughout most of its history, various parts of it having been ruled by the Phoenicians. Carthaginians, Vandals, Byzantines, Greeks, Romans, Egyptians, and in the following centuries the Arab's language, culture and religion were adopted by the indigenous population. Libya was conquered by the Ottoman Turks in 1553, and remained under Turkish domination, becoming a Turkish vilayet in 1835, until it was conquered by Italy and made into a colony in 1911. The name "Libya", the ancient Greek name for North Africa exclusive of Egypt, was given to the colony by Italy in 1934. Libya came under Allied administration after the fall of Tripoli on Jan. 23, 1943 and was divided into zones of British and French control. On Dec. 24, 1951, in accordance with a United Nations resolution, Libya proclaimed its independence as a constitutional monarchy, thereby becoming the first country to achieve independence through the United Nations. The monarchy was overthrown by a coup d'etat on Sept. 1, 1969, and Libya was established as a republic.

RULERS:
Idris I, 1951-1969

MONETARY SYSTEM:
1 Piastre = 10 Milliemes
1 Pound = 100 Piastres = 1000 Milliemes, 1951-1971
1 Dinar = 1000 Dirhams, 1971-

CONSTITUTIONAL MONARCHY

BANK OF LIBYA

LAW OF 5.2.1963 - FIRST ISSUE
#23-27 crowded arms at l. Wmk: Arms.

		VG	**VF**	**UNC**
23	**1/4 POUND**	3.50	15.00	85.00
	L.1963/AH1382. Red on m/c unpt.			
24	**1/2 POUND**	5.00	25.00	145.00
	L.1963/AH1382. Purple on m/c unpt.			
25	**1 POUND**	8.00	35.00	200.00
	L.1963/AH1382. Blue on m/c unpt.			

		VG	**VF**	**UNC**
26	**5 POUNDS**	15.00	85.00	350.00
	L.1963/AH1382. Green on m/c unpt.			

27	**10 Pounds**		VG	VF	UNC
	L.1963/AH1382. Brown on m/c unpt.		20.00	120.00	500.00

LAW OF 5.2.1963 - SECOND ISSUE

#28-32 crowned arms at l. Reduced size notes. Wmk: Arms.

28	**1/4 Pound**		VG	VF	UNC
	L.1963/AH1382. Red on m/c unpt.		4.00	17.50	125.00
29	**1/2 Pound**				
	L.1963/AH1832. Purple on m/c unpt.		5.00	27.50	150.00
30	**1 Pound**				
	L.1963/AH1382. Blue on m/c unpt.		7.00	35.00	200.00

31	**5 Pounds**		VG	VF	UNC
	L.1963/AH1382. Green on m/c unpt.		15.00	65.00	300.00
32	**10 Pounds**				
	L.1963/AH1382. Brown on m/c unpt.		25.00	100.00	500.00

SOCIALIST PEOPLES REPUBLIC

CENTRAL BANK OF LIBYA

SIGNATURE VARIETIES			
1		3	
2		4	

1971 ISSUE

#33-37 w/ or w/o Arabic inscription at lower r. on face.
38-42 *Deleted*. See #33b-37b.

33	**1/4 Dinar**		VG	VF	UNC
	ND. Orange-brown on m/c unpt. Heraldic eagle at l. Doorway on back.				
	a. W/o inscription (1971).		5.00	20.00	100.00
	b. W/ inscription (1972).		1.00	3.50	40.00

34	**1/2 Dinar**		VG	VF	UNC
	ND. Purple on m/c unpt. Heraldic eagle at l. Oil refinery on back.				
	a. W/o inscription (1971).		7.50	35.00	150.00
	b. W/inscription (1972).		2.00	10.00	35.00

35	**1 Dinar**		VG	VF	UNC
	ND. Blue on m/c unpt. Gate and minaret at l. Hilltop for on back.				
	a. W/o inscription (1971).		10.00	40.00	250.00
	b. W/ inscription (1972).		3.00	7.50	50.00

36   5 DINARS
ND. Olive on m/c unpt. Arms at l. Fortress on back.

		VG	VF	UNC
a.	W/o inscription (1971).	20.00	65.00	300.00
b.	W/ inscription (1972).	8.00	27.50	100.00

37   10 DINARS
ND. Blue-gray on m/c unpt. Omar El Mukhtar at l. 3 horsemen at ctr. on back.

		VG	VF	UNC
a.	W/o inscription (1971).	35.00	100.00	475.00
b.	W/ inscription (1972).	8.50	28.50	90.00

1980-81 ISSUE

42A   1/4 DINAR
ND (1981). Green on m/c unpt. Ruins at l. Fortress and palms on back. 2 sign. varieties.

		VG	VF	UNC
a.	Sign. 1.	.45	1.75	5.50
b.	Sign. 2.	.40	1.50	4.50

43   1/2 DINAR
ND (1981). Green on m/c unpt. Petroleum refinery at l. Irrigation system above wheat field on back.

		VG	VF	UNC
a.	Sign. 1.	.75	3.00	9.00
b.	Sign. 2.	.50	2.25	6.00

44   1 DINAR
ND (1981). Green on m/c unpt. Mosque at l. Interior of mosque on back. Sign. 1.

VG	VF	UNC
2.00	4.00	12.00

45   5 DINARS
ND (1980). Green on m/c unpt. Camels at l. Crowd around monument on back. 2 sign. varieties.

		VG	VF	UNC
a.	Sign. 1.	2.50	10.00	32.50
b.	Sign. 2.	2.25	9.00	22.50

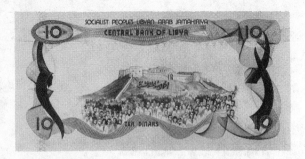

46   10 DINARS
ND (1980). Green on m/c unpt. Omar El Mukhtar at l. Lg. crowd below
hilltop fortress at ctr. on back.

		VG	VF	UNC
a.	Sign. 1.	5.50	22.00	75.00
b.	Sign. 2.	5.00	20.00	40.00

1984 ISSUE
#47-51 designs generally similar to previous issue. Sign. 2.

47   1/4 DINAR
ND (1984). Green and brown on m/c unpt. Similar to #42A.

	VG	VF	UNC
	FV	1.50	4.50

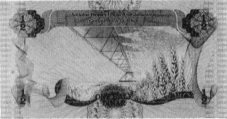

48   1/2 DINAR
ND (1984). Green and purple on m/c unpt. Similar to #43.

	VG	VF	UNC
	FV	2.25	6.00

49   1 DINAR
ND (1984). Green and dk. blue on m/c unpt. Similar to #44.

	VG	VF	UNC
	FV	4.00	11.50

50   5 DINARS
ND (1984). Dk. green and lt. green on m/c unpt. Similar to #45.

	VG	VF	UNC
	FV	8.50	22.50

51   10 DINARS
ND (1984). Dk. green on m/c unpt. Similar to #46.

	VG	VF	UNC
	FV	15.00	43.50

1988-90 ISSUE
#52-58 wmk: Heraldic falcon.

52   1/4 Dinar
ND (ca.1990). Black on m/c unpt. Ruins at ctr. Back brown; English text at top. Design features similar to #47. Sign. 3. Wmk: Heraldic Falcon.

VG	VF	Unc
FV	FV	4.00

57   1/4 Dinar
ND (ca.1991). Like #52, but w/all Arabic text on back. More pink in unpt. on face.

	VG	VF	Unc
a. Sign. 3.	FV	FV	3.00
b. Sign. 4.	FV	FV	2.00

53   1/2 Dinar
ND (ca.1990). Dk. purple, blue and m/c. Oil refinery at l. ctr. Back: purple; English text at top. Similar to #48. Sign. 3.

VG	VF	Unc
FV	FV	4.00

58   1/2 Dinar
ND (ca. 1991). Like #53, but w/all Arabic text on back. More pinkish unpt. at upper corners.

	VG	VF	Unc
a. Sign. 3.	FV	FV	3.75
b. Sign. 4.	FV	FV	3.50

59   1 Dinar
ND (1993). Like #54 but w/modfied green and pink unpt. Sign. 4.

VG	VF	Unc
FV	FV	6.50

54   1 Dinar
ND (1988). Blue and m/c. M. Kadaffy at l. ctr. Temple at lower ctr. on back. Sign. 3.

VG	VF	Unc
FV	FV	8.00

55   5 Dinars
ND (ca.1991). Gray and violet on m/c unpt. Camel at ctr. Bac Back similar to #50 but w/English text. Sign. 3.

VG	VF	Unc
FV	FV	21.50

56   10 Dinars
ND (1989). Green on m/c unpt. Omar el-Mukhtar at l. Arabic text; lg. crowd before hilltop fortress at ctr., Octagonal frame w/o unpt. at upper r. on back. Sign. 3.

VG	VF	Unc
FV	FV	40.00

1991-93 Issue

60   5 Dinars
ND (ca. 1991). Gray and violet on m/c unpt. Like #55 but w/all Arabic text on back.

	VG	VF	Unc
a. Sign. 3.	FV	FV	17.50
b. Sign. 4.	FV	FV	17.50

		VG	**VF**	**UNC**
61	**10 DINARS** ND (1991). Green on m/c unpt. Like #56 but w/unpt. in octagonal frame at upper r. on back. Sign. 4.	FV	FV	32.50

LITHUANIA

The Republic of Lithuania (formally the Lithuanian Soviet Federated Socialist Republic), southernmost of the Baltic states in east Europe, has an area of 26,173 sq. mi. (65,201 sq. km.) and a population of 3.72 million. Capital: Vilnius. The economy is based on livestock raising and manufacturing. Hogs, cattle, hides and electric motors are exported.

Lithuania emerged as a grand duchy joined to Poland through the Lublin Union in 1569. In the 15th century it was a major power of central Europe, stretching from the Baltic to the Black Sea. Following the third partition of Poland by Austria, Prussia and Russia, 1795, Lithuania came under Russian domination and did not regain its independence until shortly before the end of World War I when it declared itself a sovereign republic. The republic was occupied by Soviet troops in June of 1940 and annexed to the U.S.S.R. Following the German occupation of 1940-44, it was retaken by Russia and reestablished as a member republic of the Soviet Union. Western countries, including the United States, did not recognize Lithuania's incorporation into the Soviet Union.

Lithuania declared its independence March 11, 1990, and it was recognized by the United States on Sept. 2, 1991, followed by the Soviet government in Moscow on Sept. 6. They were seated in the UN General Assembly on Sept. 17, 1991.

MONETARY SYSTEM:
 1 Litas = 100 Centu

REPUBLIC

LIETUVOS BANKAS

BANK OF LITHUANIA

1991 ISSUE

Talonas System

#29-31 plants on face, arms at ctr. in gray on back. W/ and w/o counterfeiting clause at bottom.

#32-38 value w/plants at ctr., arms in gray at r. Animals or birds on back. Wmk: Lg. squarish diamond w/symbol of the republic throughout paper. W/ and w/o counterfeiting clause at bottom of face.

		VG	**VF**	**UNC**
29	**0.10 TALONAS** 1991. Brown on green and yellow unpt.			
	a. W/o 3 lines of black text at ctr.	.05	.15	.35
	b. W/3 lines of black text at ctr.	.05	.10	.25
	x. Error. As b. but w/"PAGAL ISTATYMA" repeated.	3.00	9.00	15.00

		VG	**VF**	**UNC**
30	**0.20 TALONAS** 1991. Lilac on green and yellow unpt. W/3 lines of black text at ctr.	.05	.10	.25

		VG	**VF**	**UNC**
31	**0.50 TALONAS** 1991. Blue-green on green and yellow unpt.			
	a. W/o 3 lines of black text at ctr.	.10	.20	.50
	b. W/3 lines of black text at ctr.	.05	.15	.25
	x. Error. As b. but first word of text *VALSTYBINIS*.	3.00	9.00	15.00

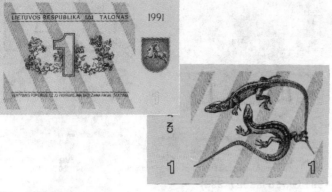

32 1 (TALONAS)
1991. Brown on yellow-gold unpt. Numeral w/cranberry branch at ctr.
2 lizards on back.

		VG	VF	UNC
a.	W/o text.	.10	.20	.50
b.	W/ text.	.10	.20	.50

33 3 (TALONU)
1991. Dk. green and gray on blue-green, ochre and brown unpt.
Numeral w/juniper branch at ctr. 2 birds (pewits) on back.

		VG	VF	UNC
a.	W/o text.	.25	.75	.50
b.	W/ text.	.10	.20	.50

34 5 (TALONU)
1991. Dk. purple and gray on blue-green, green and gray unpt.
Numeral w/oak tree branch at ctr. Hawk at ctr. on back.

		VG	VF	UNC
a.	W/o text.	1.00	3.00	9.00
b.	W/ text.	.50	.75	1.00

35 10 (TALONU)
1991. Brown on pinkish unpt. Numerals w/walnut tree branch at ctr. 2
martens on back.

		VG	VF	UNC
a.	W/o text.	.50	1.35	4.00
b.	W/ text.	.50	1.00	2.00

36 25 (TALONU)
1991. Purplish gray on blue and orange unpt. Numerals w/pine tree
branch at ctr. Lynx on back.

		VG	VF	UNC
a.	W/o text.	2.50	7.50	15.00
b.	W/ text.	.40	1.00	3.00

37 50 (TALONU)
1991. Green and orange on orange unpt. Numerals w/seashore plant
at ctr. Elk on back.

		VG	VF	UNC
a.	W/o text.	1.50	4.50	10.00
b.	W/ text.	.50	1.35	4.00

38 100 (TALONU)
1991. Green and brown on brown unpt. Numerals and dandelions at
ctr. European bison on back.

		VG	VF	UNC
a.	W/o text.	1.50	4.50	10.00
b.	W/ text.	.85	2.50	7.50

1992 ISSUE
#39-44 value on plant at ctr., shield of arms at r. on face. Wmk. as #32-38. Smaller size than #32-38.

39 1 (TALONAS)
1992. Brown on orange and ochre unpt., dk. brown shield. 2 brids on
back.

	VG	VF	UNC
	.05	.10	.20

40   10 (TALONU)
1992. Brown on tan and ochre unpt., gray shield. Nest w/birds on back.

	VG	VF	UNC
	.10	.25	.75

41   50 (TALONU)
1992. Dk. grayish green on lt. green and gray unpt., dk. gray-green shield. 2 birds on back.

	VG	VF	UNC
	.15	.35	1.00

42   100 (TALONU)
1992. Grayish purple on blue and red-orange unpt., gray shield. 2 martens on back.

	VG	VF	UNC
	.25	.65	2.00

43   200 (TALONU)
1992. Dk. brown on red and brown unpt., gray shield. 2 deer on back.

	VG	VF	UNC
	.40	1.00	3.00

44   500 (TALONU)
1992. Brown-violet on blue unpt., brown shield. Bear on back.

	VG	VF	UNC
	1.25	3.00	8.00

1993 ISSUE

#45 and 46 arms in brown at l., value w/branches at ctr. Animals on back. Wmk: Pattern repeated, circle w/design inside.

45   200 TALONU
1993. Brown and red on blue unpt. 2 deer on back.

	VG	VF	UNC
	.65	1.65	5.00

46   500 TALONU
1993. Brown on blue and brown unpt. 2 wolves on back.

	VG	VF	UNC
	.50	1.35	4.00

1991 DATED ISSUE (1993)

Litu System

#47-50 arms "Vytis" at upper r. on back. Printer: USBNC (w/o imprint).

47   10 LITU
1991 (1993). Brownish black and dk. brown on tan unpt. Aviators S. Darius and S. Girénas at ctr. Monoplane 'Lituanica' at upper ctr. on back.

	VG	VF	UNC
a. GIRENAS name w/o accent on E (error).	FV	3.00	10.00
b. GIRÉNAS name w/accent on E.	FV	2.50	8.00

48   20 LITU
1991 (1993). Dk. brown and green on violet and tan unpt. J. Maironis at r., Liberty at l. Museum of History in Kaunas at ctr. on back.

	VG	VF	UNC
	FV	5.00	15.00

49   50 LITU
1991 (1993). Yellowish black and brown on ochre and tan unpt. J. Basanavicius at r. Catheral at Vilnius at l. on back.

	VG	VF	UNC
	FV	12.50	30.00

50 100 LITU
1991 (1993). Deep green, blue and brown on m/c unpt. Arms "Vytis" at ctr., S. Daukantas at r. Aerial view of University of Vilnius at l. ctr. on back.

VG	VF	UNC
FV	25.00	45.00

51 500 LITU
1991. Arms "Vytis" at ctr. V. Kudirka at r. Liberty bell on back. (Not issued).

—	—	80.00

52 1000 LITU
1991. Arms "Vytis" at ctr. M. Ciurlionis at r. 2 people on back. (Not issued).

—	—	140.00

1993-94 ISSUE
#53-58 wmk: Arms "Vytis." Shield w/"Vytis" at ctr. r. on back. Printer: TDLR (w/o imprint).

53 1 LITAS
1994. Black and dk. brown on orange and m/c unpt. J. Zemaite at r.

VG	VF	UNC
FV	FV	1.00

54 2 LITAI
1993. Black and dk. green on pale green and m/c unpt. Samogitian Bishop M. Valancius at r. Trakai castle at l. on back.

VG	VF	UNC
FV	FV	2.00

55 5 LITAI
1993. Purple, violet and dk. blue-green on m/c unpt. J. Jablonskis at ctr. r. Mother and daughter at spinning wheel at l. on back.

VG	VF	UNC
FV	FV	2.75

56 10 LITU
1993. Dk. blue, dk. green, and brown-violet on m/c unpt. Similar to #47 but pilots at r.

VG	VF	UNC
FV	FV	5.00

57 20 LITU
1993. Dk. brown-violet and dk. green on m/c unpt. Similar to #48.

VG	VF	UNC
FV	FV	9.00

58 50 LITU
1993. Dk. brown, red-brown and blue-black on m/c unpt. Similar to #49.

VG	VF	UNC
FV	FV	17.50

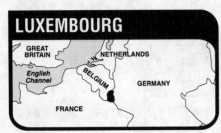

The Grand Duchy of Luxembourg is located in western Europe between Belgium, Germany and France, has an area of 998 sq. mi. (2,586 sq. km.) and a population of 390,000. Capital: Luxembourg. The economy is based on steel - Luxembourg's per capita production of 16 tons is the highest in the world.

Founded about 963, Luxembourg was a prominent country of the Holy Roman Empire; one of its sovereigns became Holy Roman Emperor as Henry VII, 1308. After being made a duchy by Emperor Charles IV, 1534, Luxembourg passed under the domination of Burgundy, Spain, Austria and France in 1443-1815. It regained autonomy under the Treaty of Vienna, 1815, as a grand duchy in union with the Netherlands, though ostensibly a member of the German Confederation. When Belgium seceded from the Kingdom of the Netherlands, in 1830, Luxembourg was forced to cede its greater western section to Belgium. The tiny duchy left the German Confederation in 1867 when the Treaty of London recognized it as an independent state and guaranteed its perpetual neutrality. Luxembourg was occupied by Germany and liberated by American troops in both World Wars.

RULERS:
Charlotte, 1919-1964
Jean, 1964-

MONETARY SYSTEM:
1 Franc = 100 Centimes

GRAND DUCHY

BANQUE INTERNATIONALE A LUXEMBOURG

INTERNATIONAL BANK IN LUXEMBOURG

1968 ISSUE

			VG	VF	UNC
14	**100 FRANCS**		2.00	4.00	15.00
	1.5.1968. Green-blue and blue on m/c unpt. Tower at l., Portr. Grand Duke Jean at r. Steelworks and dam on back. Wmk: *BIL*.				

1981 ISSUE

			VG	VF	UNC
14A	**100 FRANCS**		FV	3.50	7.50
	8.3.1981. Brown and purple on m/c unpt. Bridge to Luxembourg City at l., Grand Duke Jean at r., Henry in background. Two stylized female figures swirling around wmk. area on back. Wmk: *BIL*.				

GRAND DUCHÉ DE LUXEMBOURG

1961-63 ISSUE

		VG	VF	UNC
51	**50 FRANCS**			
	6.2.1961. Brown on m/c unpt. Grand Duchess Charlotte at r. landscape w/combine harvester on back.			
	a. Issued note.	2.00	4.00	10.00
	s. Specimen, punched hole cancelled.	—	—	45.00
52	**100 FRANCS**			
	18.9.1963. Red-brown on m/c unpt. Grand Duchess Charlotte at r. Hydroelectric dam on back.			
	a. Issued note.	5.00	10.00	30.00
	s. Specimen, punched hole cancelled.	—	—	65.00

1966-70 ISSUE

		VG	VF	UNC
53	**10 FRANCS**			
	20.3.1967. Green on m/c unpt. Grand Duchess Charlotte Bridge in city on back.			
	a. Issued note.	.50	1.25	3.50
	s. Specimen, punched hole cancelled.	—	—	25.00

54 20 FRANCS
7.3.1966. Blue on m/c unpt. Moselle River w/dam and lock on back.

	VG	VF	UNC
a. Issued note.	FV	1.75	4.50
s. Specimen, punched hole cancelled.	—	—	35.00

55 100 FRANCS
15.7.1970. Red on m/c unpt. View of Adolphe Bridge on back.

	VG	VF	UNC
a. Issued note.	FV	4.00	8.50
s. Specimen, punched hole cancelled.	—	—	50.00

1972; 1980 ISSUE

56 50 FRANCS
25.8.1972. Dk. brown on m/c unpt. Guilloche unpt at l. Factory on back.

	VG	VF	UNC
a. Sign. title: *LE MINISTRE DES FINANCES.*	FV	FV	8.50
b. Sign. title: *LE MINISTRE D'ETAT.*	FV	FV	7.00
s. Specimen, punched hole cancelled.	—	—	40.00

57 100 FRANCS
14.8.1980. Red on m/c unpt. Grand Duke Jean at ctr. r., bldg. at l. Back gold and red; city of Luxembourg scene. Sign. varieties.

	VG	VF	UNC
	FV	FV	6.50

INSTITUT MONETAIRE LUXEMBOURGEOIS

1986-93 ISSUE

SIGNATURE VARIETIES	
MINISTRE DU TRESOR	
1 J. Poos	2 J. Santer

#68-60, Grand Duke Jean at ctr. r. and as wmk.

58 100 FRANCS
ND (1986). Red on m/c unpt. Like #57 but w/new issuer's name.

	VG	VF	UNC
a. W/o © symbol. Sign. 1. Series A-K.	FV	FV	6.50
b. W/© symbol. Sign. 2. Series L-.	FV	FV	4.50

59 1000 FRANCS
ND (1985). Brown on m/c unpt. Castle of Vianden at l., Grand Duke Jean at ctr. Bldg. sketches at r. ctr. on back.

	VG	VF	UNC
	FV	FV	45.00

60 5000 FRANCS
ND (1993). Green, orange and olive-green on brown and m/c unpt. Chateau de Clevaux at l. 17th century map, European Center at Luxembourg-Kirchberg at ctr. r. on back.

	VG	VF	UNC
	FV	FV	200.00

The Province of Macao, a Portuguese overseas province located in the South China Sea 35 miles southwest of Hong Kong, consists of the peninsula and the islands of Taipa and Coloane. It has an area of 6 sq. mi. (16. sq. km.) and a population of 433,000. Capital: Macao. Macao's economy is based on light industry, commerce, tourism, fishing and gold trading - Macao is one of the few entirely free markets for gold in the world. Cement, textiles, firecrackers, vegetable oils and metal products are exported.

Established by the Portuguese in 1557, Macao is the oldest European settlement in the Far East. The Chinese, while agreeing to Portuguese settlement, did not recognize Portuguese sovereign rights and the Portuguese remained largely under control of the Chinese until 1849, when the Portuguese abolished the Chinese custom house and declared the independence of the port. The Manchu government formally recognized the Portuguese right to "perpetual occupation" of Macao in 1887, but its boundaries are still not delimited. In Mar. 1940 the Japanese army demanded recognition of the nearby "puppet" government at Changshan. in Sept. 1943 they demanded installation of their "advisors" in lieu of a military occupation.

Macao is scheduled to become a special administrative area under The Peoples Republic of China in 1999.

* * * This section has been partially renumbered. * * *

RULERS:
Portuguese

MONETARY SYSTEM:
1 Pataca = 100 Avos

PORTUGUESE INFLUENCE

BANCO NACIONAL ULTRAMARINO

行銀理滙外海國洋西大
Ta Hsi Yang Kuo Hai Wai Hui Li Yin Hang

1963-68 ISSUE

#49, 50, and 52 portr. Bishop D. Belchior Carneiro at r. and as wmk. Sailing ship seal at l. on back. Printer: BWC.

		VG	VF	UNC
49	**5 PATACAS**			
(52)	21.3.1968. Brown on m/c unpt. Sign. varieties.	2.00	6.00	15.00

		VG	VF	UNC
50	**10 PATACAS**			
(49)	8.4.1963. Deep blue on m/c unpt. Sign. varieties.	2.50	8.00	20.00

		VG	VF	UNC
51	**100 PATACAS**			
	1.8.1966. Brown on m/c unpt portr. M. de Arriaga Brum da Silveira a t r. Flag atop archway at ctr. on back. Printer: TDLR.	20.00	40.00	100.00
52	**500 PATACAS**			
(50)	8.4.1963. Green on m/c unpt.	75.00	150.00	250.00

1973 ISSUE

		VG	VF	UNC
53	**100 PATACAS**			
	13.12.1973. Blue on m/c unpt. Ruin of S. Paulo Cathedral at r. and as wmk. Sailing ship at l. on back. Sign. titles: *GOVERNADOR* and *ADMINISTRADOR* above signs.	15.00	35.00	100.00

1976-79 ISSUE

#54-57 w/text: *CONSELHO DE GESTAO* at ctr.

		VG	VF	UNC
54	**5 PATACAS**			
	18.11.1976. Brown on m/c unpt. Portr. Bishop D. Belchior Carneiro at r. Sign. varietes.	.75	2.50	7.50
55	**10 PATACAS**			
	7.12.1977. Blue on m/c unpt. Portr. Bishop D. Belchior Carneiro at r.	1.50	4.50	13.50

		VG	VF	UNC
59	**10 PATACAS** 8.8.1981; 12.5.1984. Brown and m/c. Lighthouse w/flag at r.			
	a. W/sign. title: *PRESIDENTE* at l.	FV	4.50	13.50
	b. W/sign. title: *VICE-PRESIDENTE* at l.	FV	3.00	9.00
	c. W/o sign. title at l. 2 sign. varieties.	FV	2.50	7.50
	d. 3 decrees at upper l. 12.5.1984.	FV	2.00	6.00

| **56** | **50 PATACAS**
 1.9.1976. Greenish-gray on m/c unpt. Portr. L. de Camoes at r. | 8.00 | 25.00 | 75.00 |

| **60** | **50 PATACAS**
 8.8.1981. Purple on m/c unpt. Portr. L. de Camoes at r. | FV | 8.00 | 18.50 |

| **57** | **100 PATACAS**
 8.6.1979. Blue on m/c unpt. Like #53. Sign. title: *PRESIDENTE* at l. sign. | 12.50 | 25.00 | 50.00 |
| **57A** | **500 PATACAS**
 24.4.1979. Green on m/c unpt. Like #50. | 70.00 | 140.00 | 240.00 |

1981; 1988 ISSUE
#58-62 19th century harbor scene on back.

61	**100 PATACAS** 1981; 1984. Blue, purple and m/c. Portr. C. Pessanha at r.			
	a. W/sign. title: *PRESIDENTE* at l. 8.8.1981; 12.5.1984.	FV	15.00	32.50
	b. W/o sign. title: *PRESIDENTE PRESIDENTE* at l. 12.5.1984.	FV	13.50	28.50

58	**5 PATACAS** 8.8.1981. Green and m/c. Temple at r.			
	a. W/sign. title: *PRESIDENTE* at l.	FV	2.50	7.50
	b. W/o sign. title: *PRESIDENTE* at l. 2 sign. varieties.	FV	1.50	4.50

| **62** | **500 PATACAS**
 8.8.1981; 12.5.1984. Olive and m/c. Portr. V. de Morais at r. Peninsula on back. | FV | 75.00 | 120.00 |
| **63** | **1000 PATACAS**
 8.8.1988. Brown and yellow-orange on m/c unpt. Stylized dragon at r. Modern view of bridge to Macao on back. | FV | 145.00 | 200.00 |

1988 COMMEMORATIVE ISSUE
#64, 35th Anniversary Grand Prix.

			VG	VF	UNC
64	**10 PATACAS**		—	—	40.00
	11.26-27.1988 (-old date 1984). Black ovpt. at l. on face, at ctr. on back of #59a.				

1990-96 ISSUE
#65-70, bridge and city view on back. Wmk: Junk.

			VG	VF	UNC
65	**10 PATACAS**		FV	FV	4.00
	8.7.1991. Brown, olive and m/c. Bldg. at r.				
66	**20 PATACAS**		FV	FV	5.50
	1.9.1996. Green on m/c unpt. B.N.U. bldg. at r., facing facing dragons in border at l. and r.				
67 (66)	**50 PATACAS**		FV	FV	13.50
	13.7.1992. Olive-brown and m/c. Holiday marcher w/dragon costume at ctr. r., man at r.				

			VG	VF	UNC
68 (67)	**100 PATACAS**		FV	FV	25.00
	13.7.1992. Black and m/c. Early painting of settlement at ctr., junk at r.				
69 (68)	**500 PATACAS**		FV	FV	90.00
	3.9.1990. Olive and m/c. Bldg. at r.				
70 (69)	**1000 PATACAS**		FV	FV	175.00
	8.7.1991. Orange and m/c. Dragon at r.				

BANCO DA CHINA

中國銀行

Chung Kuo Yin Hang

1995; 1996 ISSUE
#90-95 Bank of China-Macao bldg. at l., lotus blossom at lower ctr. on back. Wmk: Lotus blossom(s).

			VG	VF	UNC
90 (70)	**10 PATACAS**		FV	FV	4.00
	16.10.1995. Dk. brown and deep green on m/c unpt. unpt. Farel de Guia lighthouse at r.				
91	**20 PATACAS**		FV	FV	5.50
	1.9.1996. M/c. Ama Temple at r.				

			VG	VF	UNC
92 (71)	**50 PATACAS**		FV	FV	13.50
	16.10.1995. Black, dk. brown and brown on m/c unpt. University of Macao at r.				

			VG	VF	UNC
93 (72)	**100 PATACAS**		FV	FV	25.00
	16.10.1995. Black, brown and purple on m/c unpt. New terminal of Port Exterior at r.				

94 **500 PATACAS**
(73)   16.10.1995. Dk. green and dk. blue on m/c unpt. Ponte de Amizade bridge at r.

	VG	VF	UNC
	FV	FV	90.00

95 **1000 PATACAS**
(74)   16.10.1995. Brown, orange and red on m/c unpt. Aerial view of Praia Oeste.

	VG	VF	UNC
	FV	FV	175.00

The Republic of Macedonia is land-locked, and is bordered in the north by Yugoslavia, to the east by Bulgaria, in the south by Greece and to the west by Albania. It has an area of 9,923 sq. mi. (25,713 sq. km.) and a population at the 1991 census was 2,038,847, of which the predominating ethnic groups were Macedonians. The capital is Skopje.

The Slavs, settled in Macedonia since the 6th century, who had been Christianized by Byzantium, were conquered by the non-Slav Bulgars in the 7th century and in the 9th century formed a Macedo-Bulgarian empire, the western part of which survived until Byzantine conquest in 1014. In the 14th century it fell to Serbia, and in 1355 to the Ottomans. After the Balkan Wars of 1912-13 Turkey was ousted, and Serbia received the greater part of the territory, the balance going to Bulgaria and Greece. In 1918, Yugoslav Macedonia was incorporated into Serbia as 'South Serbia,' becoming a republic in the S.F.R. of Yugoslavia. Claims to the historical Macedonian territory have long been a source of contention between Bulgaria and Greece.

On Nov. 20, 1991 parliament promulgated a new constitution, and declared its independence on Nov. 20, 1992, but failed to secure EC and US recognition owing to Greek objections to its use of the name "Macedonia."

On Dec. 11, 1992, the UN Security Council authorized the expedition of a small peacekeeping force to prevent hostilities spreading to Macedonia.

There is a 120-member single-chamber National Assembly.

MONETARY SYSTEM:
   1 Denar = 100 Deni

REPUBLIC

НАРОДНА БАНКА НА МАКЕДОНИЈА

NATIONAL BANK OF MACEDONIA

1992 ISSUE
#1-6 farmers harvesting at l. Ilenden monument in Krushevo at l. on back. Wmk. paper.

1 **10 (DENAR)**
   1992. Blue-black on lilac unpt .

	VG	VF	UNC
	.05	.10	.25

2 **25 (DENAR)**
   1992. Red on lilac unpt.

	VG	VF	UNC
	.10	.20	.35

3 **50 (DENAR)**
1992. Brown on ochre unpt.

	VG	VF	UNC
	.10	.25	.75

4 **100 (DENAR)**
1992. Blue-black on lt. blue unpt.

	VG	VF	UNC
	.15	.35	1.00

5 **500 (DENAR)**
1992. Bright green on ochre unpt.

	VG	VF	UNC
	.35	.80	2.50

6 **1000 (DENAR)**
1992. Dull blue-violet on pink unpt.

	VG	VF	UNC
	.50	1.65	4.50

7 **5000 (DENAR)**
1992. Deep brown and dull red on m/c unpt. Woman at desk top
computer at ctr. Ilenden monument at l. on back. Wmk. paper.

	VG	VF	UNC
	2.00	3.00	7.50

8 **10,000 (DENAR)**
1992. Blue-black on pink and gray unpt. Bldgs. at ctr. r. Musicians at l.
of Ilenden monument at ctr. r. on back. Wmk. paper.

	VG	VF	UNC
	3.00	6.00	15.00

НАРОДНА БАНКА НА РЕПУБЛИКА МАКЕДОНИЈА

NATIONAL BANK OF THE REPUBLIC OF MACEDONIA

1993 ISSUE
Currency Reform
1 "New" Denar = 100 "Old' Denari
#9-12 wmk: Ilenden monument at Krushero.

9 **10 DENARI**
1993. Lt. blue on m/c unpt. Ilenden monument at l. Houses on
mountainside in Krushevo on back.

	VG	VF	UNC
	FV	FV	1.00

10 20 Denari

1993. Wine-red on m/c unpt. Turkish bath in Skopje at l. Tower in Skopje vertically on back.

		VG	VF	UNC
10	20 Denari	FV	FV	2.25

11 50 Denari

1993. Lt. red on m/c unpt. Church of St. Pantaleimon at l. Bldg. of National Bank in Skopje on back.

		VG	VF	UNC
11	50 Denari	FV	FV	4.50

12 100 Denari

1993. Brown on m/c unpt. St. Sophia church in Ohrid at l. National Museum in Ohrid on back.

		VG	VF	UNC
12	100 Denari	FV	FV	8.00

		VG	VF	UNC
13	**500 Denari** 1993. Greenish gray on m/c unpt. Orthodox church at l. and as wmk. City Wall across upper back.	FV	FV	35.00

1996 Issue

		VG	VF	UNC
14	**10 Denari** 8.9.1996. Red-violet and olive-green w/black text on m/c unpt. Torso of statue of Goddess Isida at ctr. r. and as wmk. Back blue-gray and tan on m/c unpt. Mosaic of branch over peacock and duck.	FV	FV	1.50
15	**50 Denari** 8.9.1996. Brown on m/c unpt. Byzantine copper follis of Anastasia at ctr. r. and as wmk. Archangel Gabriel at l. ctr. on back.	FV	FV	3.75
16	**100 Denari** 8.9.1996. Brown and violet on m/c unpt. Lg. baroque wooden ceiling rosette in Debar town house at ctr. r. and as wmk. J. Harevin's engraving of Skopje "seen" thru town house window frame at l. ctr.	FV	FV	6.00
17	**500 Denari** 8.9.1996. Black and violet on m/c unpt. 6th century golden death mask, Trebenista, Ohrid at r. and as wmk. Violet poppy flower and plant at l. ctr. on back.	FV	FV	22.50
18	**1000 Denari** 8.9.1996. Brown and orange on m/c unpt. 14th century icon of Madonna Episkepsis and Christ Child, church of St. Vrach-Mali, Ohrid at ctr. r. Partial view of the St. Sophia church in Ohrid at l. ctr. Wmk: Madonna.	FV	FV	40.00
19	**5000 Denari** 8.9.1996. Black and violet on olive-green and m/c unpt. 6th century bronze figurine of Tetovo Maenad VI (horizontally) at ctr. r. and as wmk. 6th century mosaic of Cerberus the Dog tied to a fig tree, representing the watcher of Heaven (horizontally) at l. ctr. on back.	FV	FV	175.00

The Democratic Republic of Madagascar, an independent member of the French Community located in the Indian Ocean 250 miles (402 km.) off the southeast coast of Africa, has an area of 226,658 sq. mi. (587,041 sq. km.) and a population of 12.4 million. Capital: Antananarivo. The economy is primarily agricultural; large bauxite deposits are presently being developed. Coffee, vanilla, graphite and rice are exported.

Diago Diaz, a Portuguese navigator, sighted the island of Madagascar on Aug. 10, 1500, when his ship became separated from an India-bound fleet. Attempts at settlement by the British during the reign of Charles I and by the French during the 17th and 18th centuries were of no avail, and the island became a refuge and supply base for Indian Ocean pirates. Despite considerable influence on the island, the British accepted the imposition of a French protectorate in 1886 in return for French recognition of Britain's sphere of influence in Zanzibar. Madagascar was made a French colony in 1896 after absolute control had been established by military force. Britain occupied the island after the fall of France in 1942, to prevent its seizure by the Japanese, and gave it to the Free French in 1943. On Oct. 14, 1958, following a decade of intermittent but bitter warfare, Madagascar, as the Malagasy Republic, became an autonomous state within the French Community. On June 27, 1960, it became a sovereign independent nation, though remaining nominally within the French Community. The Malagasy Republic was renamed the Democratic Republic of Madagascar in 1976.

MONETARY SYSTEM:
1 CFA Franc = 0.02 French Franc, 1959-1961
5 Malagasy Francs (F.M.G.) = 1 Ariary, 1961-

MALAGASY

INSTITUT D'EMISSION MALGACHE

1961 ND PROVISIONAL ISSUE

#51-55 new bank name and new Ariary denominations ovpt. on previous issue of Banque de Madagascar et des Comores.

51	**50 FRANCS = 10 ARIARY**	VG	VF	UNC
	ND (1961). M/c. Woman w/hat at r. Man on back. Ovpt. on #45.			
	a. Sign. title: *LE CONTROLEUR GENERAL.*	3.00	12.50	50.00
	b. Sign. title: *LE DIRECTEUR GENERAL ADJOINT.*	3.00	15.00	60.00

52	**100 FRANCS = 20 ARIARY**	VG	VF	UNC
	ND (1961). M/c. Woman at r., palace of the Qn. of Tananariva in background. Woman, boats nd animals on back. Ovpt. on #46b.	4.00	20.00	65.00

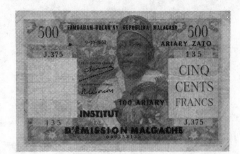

53	**500 FRANCS = 100 ARIARY**	VG	VF	UNC
	ND (1961). M/c. Man w/fruit at ctr. Ovpt. on #47.	15.00	65.00	200.00

54	**1000 FRANCS = 200 ARIARY**	VG	VF	UNC
	ND (1961 -old date 9.10.1952). M/c. Man and woman at l. ctr. Ox cart on back. Ovpt. on #48.	20.00	125.00	325.00
55	**5000 FRANCS = 1000 ARIARY**			
	ND (1961). M/c. Gallieni at upper l., woman at r. Woman and baby on back. Ovpt. on #49.	50.00	275.00	650.00

1963 ND REGULAR ISSUE

56	**1000 FRANCS = 200 ARIARY**	VG	VF	UNC
	ND (1963). M/c. People in canoes at l., president at ctr. Wmk: Woman's head.			
	a. W/o sign. and title.	50.00	375.00	600.00
	b. W/sign. and title.	40.00	250.00	550.00

1966 ND ISSUE
#57-60 wmk: Woman's head.

57	**100 FRANCS = 20 ARIARY**	VG	VF	UNC
	ND (1966). M/c. 3 women spinning. Trees on back. 2 sign. varieties.	2.50	10.00	30.00

58 **500 FRANCS = 100 ARIARY**
ND (1966). M/c. Woman at l., Landscape in background. River scene
on back. 2 sign varieties.

VG	VF	UNC
5.00	35.00	165.00

59 **1000 FRANCS = 200 ARIARY**
ND (1966). M/c. Woman and man at l. Similar to #48 and #54 bt size
150 x 80mm.

VG	VF	UNC
7.50	40.00	175.00

60 **5000 FRANCS = 1000 ARIARY**
ND (1966). M/c. President at l., workers in rice field at r. Women and
boy on back.

VG	VF	UNC
12.50	45.00	200.00

1969 ISSUE

61 **50 FRANCS = 10 ARIARY**
ND (1969). M/c. Like #45 and #51. Different sign. title.

VG	VF	UNC
2.25	7.50	25.00

MADAGASCAR DEMOCRATIC REPUBLIC

BANKY FOIBEN'NY REPOBLIKA MALAGASY

BANQUE CENTRALE DE LA RÉPUBLIQUE MALGACHE

1974 (ND) ISSUE
#64-66 wmk: Zebu's head.

62 **50 FRANCS = 10 ARIARY**
ND (1974-75). Violet and m/c. Young man at r. Fruit market on back.

VG	VF	UNC
1.50	4.00	10.00

63 **100 FRANCS = 20 ARIARY**
ND. Brown and m/c. Old man at r. Rice planting on back.

VG	VF	UNC
1.50	4.00	12.00

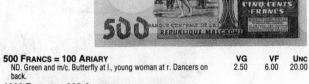

64 **500 FRANCS = 100 ARIARY**
ND. Green and m/c. Butterfly at l., young woman at r. Dancers on
back.

VG	VF	UNC
2.50	6.00	20.00

65 **1000 FRANCS = 200 ARIARY**
ND. Blue and m/c. Lemurs at l., man in straw hat at r. Trees and
designs on back.

VG	VF	UNC
3.50	8.00	37.50

66 **5000 FRANCS = 1000 ARIARY**
ND. Red, violet and m/c. Oxen at l., young woman at r. Back violet and
orange; tropical plants and African carving at ctr.

VG	VF	UNC
15.00	30.00	70.00

BANKY FOIBEN'I MADAGASIKARA

1983 (ND) ISSUE
#67-70 wmk: Zebu's head. Sign. varieties.

67	500 FRANCS = 100 ARIARY	VG	VF	UNC
	ND (1983-87). Brown, gray and m/c. Boy w/fish in net at ctr. Aerial view of port at r. on back.	FV	1.50	5.00

68	1000 FRANCS = 200 ARIARY	VG	VF	UNC
	ND (1983-87). Violet and m/c. Man w/hat playing flute at ctr. Fruits and vegetables at r. on back.	FV	2.00	7.50

69	5000 FRANCS = 1000 ARIARY	VG	VF	UNC
	ND (1983-87). Blue and m/c. Woman and child at ctr. School, book and monument at r. on back.	FV	9.00	32.50

70	10,000 FRANCS = 2000 ARIARY	VG	VF	UNC
	ND (1983-87). Green on m/c unpt. Young girl w/sheaf at ctr. Harvesting rice at r. on back.	FV	20.00	65.00

1988 (ND) ISSUE
#71-76 vertical serial # at r. Sign. varieties. Wmk: Zebu's head.

71	500 FRANCS = 100 ARIARY	VG	VF	UNC
	ND (1988-93). Similar to #67, but modified unpt.	FV	1.50	4.00

72	1000 FRANCS = 200 ARIARY	VG	VF	UNC
	ND (1988-93). Similar to #68, but modified unpt.	FV	2.50	7.50

73	**5000 Francs = 1000 Ariary**	**VG**	**VF**	**UNC**
	ND (1988-94). Similar to #69, but modified unpt.	FV	7.00	20.00

76	**1000 Francs = 200 Ariary**	**VG**	**VF**	**UNC**
	ND (1994). Dk. brown and dk. bllue on m/c unpt. Young man at r., boats in background. Young woman w/basket of shellfish, fisherman w/net at l. ctr. on back.	FV	FV	3.00
77	**2500 Francs = 500 Ariary**			
	ND (1993). Red, green, blue and black on m/c unpt. Older woman at ctr. Heron, tortoise, lemur, and butterfly in foliage on back.	FV	FV	4.50
78	**5000 Francs = 1000 Ariary**			
	ND (1995). Dk. brown and violet on lilac and m/c unpt. Young male head at r., ox cart, cane cutters at ctr. Animals, birds and seashells on back.	FV	FV	5.00
79	**10,000 Francs = 2000 Ariary**			
	ND (1995). Dk. brown on tan and m/c unpt. Old man at r., statuette, local artifacts at ctr. artisans at work on back.	FV	FV	8.50

74	**10,000 Francs = 2000 Ariary**	**VG**	**VF**	**UNC**
	ND (1988-94). Similar to #70, but modified unpt.	FV	10.00	30.00

1993-95 (ND) Issue
#75-78 wmk: Zebu's head.

80	**25,000 Francs = 5000 Ariary**	**VG**	**VF**	**UNC**
	ND (1993) Olive-green and green on m/c unpt. Old man at ctr., island outline at l. Scene of traditional bullfighting at r. on back.	FV	FV	20.00

75	**500 Francs = 100 Ariary**	**VG**	**VF**	**UNC**
	ND (1994). Dk. brown and dk. green on m/c unpt. Girl at r., village in unpt. at upper ctr. Herdsmen w/Zebus, village in background at l. ctr. on back.	FV	FV	2.00

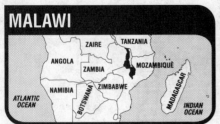

MALAWI

The Republic of Malawi (formerly Nyasaland), located in southeastern Africa to the west of Lake Malawi (Nyasa), has an area of 45,747 sq. mi. (118,484 sq. km.) and a population of 8.6 million. Capital: Lilongwe. The economy is predominantly agricultural. Tobacco, tea, peanuts and cotton are exported.

Although the Portuguese, heirs to the restless spirit of Prince Henry, were the first Europeans to reach the Malawi area, the first meaningful contact was made by missionary-explorer Dr. David Livingstone who arrived at Lake Malawi on Sept. 16, 1859, and remained to make extensive explorations in the 1860s. Subsequent clashes between settlements of Scottish missionaries and Arab slave traders, and the procurement of development rights by Cecil Rhodes, 1884, stimulated British interest and brought about the establishment of the Nyasaland protectorate in 1891. In 1953, Nyasaland reluctantly joined the Federation of Rhodesia and Nyasaland and, after prolonged protest, was granted self-government within the federation. Nyasaland became the independent nation of Malawi on July 6, 1964, and became a republic two years later. Malawi is a member of the Commonwealth of Nations. The president is the Chief of State and Head of Government.

Also see Rhodesia, Rhodesia and Nyasaland.

RULERS:
British to 1964

MONETARY SYSTEM:
1 Pound = 20 Shillings to 1971
1 Kwacha = 100 Tambala 1971-

REPUBLIC

RESERVE BANK OF MALAWI

1964 RESERVE BANK ACT; FIRST ISSUE
Pound System

#1-4 portr. Dr. H. K. Banda at l., sunrise, fishermen in boat on Lake Malawi at ctr. Sign. title: *GOVERNOR* only. Wmk: Rooster.

			VG	VF	UNC
1	**5 SHILLINGS**				
	L.1964. Blue-gray. Arms w/bird on back.		4.00	14.00	75.00
2	**10 SHILLINGS**				
	L.1964. Brown. Workers in tobacco field on back.		7.50	55.00	250.00

			VG	VF	UNC
3	**1 POUND**				
	L.1964. Green. Workers picking cotton on back.		7.50	62.50	300.00

			VG	VF	UNC
4	**5 POUNDS**				
	L.1964. Blue and brown. Tea pickers below Mt. Mulanje on back.		20.00	100.00	800.00

1964 RESERVE BANK ACT; SECOND ISSUE
#1A-3A portr. Dr. H. K. Banda at l., fishermen at ctr. Sign. titles: *GOVERNOR* and *GENERAL MANAGER*.

			VG	VF	UNC
1A	**5 SHILLINGS**				
	L.1964. Like #1.		2.50	10.00	50.00

			VG	VF	UNC
2A	**10 SHILLINGS**				
	L.1964. Like #2.		3.50	14.50	75.00
3A	**1 POUND**				
	L.1964. Like #3.		5.50	22.50	90.00

1964 RESERVE BANK ACT; 1971 ISSUE
Kwacha System

			VG	VF	UNC
5	**50 TAMBALA**				
	L.1964 (1971). Blue-gray. Face like #1A. Independence Arch in Blantyre at r. on back.		5.50	22.50	125.00
6	**1 KWACHA**				
	L.1964 (1971). Brown. Like #2A.		12.00	48.50	185.00
7	**2 KWACHA**				
	L.1964 (1971). Green. Like #3A.		14.00	55.00	225.00

			VG	VF	UNC
8	**10 KWACHA**				
	L.1964 (1971). Blue and brown. Like #4 but 2 signs.		22.00	87.50	400.00

1973-74 ISSUE
#9-12 portr. Dr. H. K. Banda as Prime Minister at r. W/ or w/o dates. Wmk: Rooster.

9	**50 TAMBALA**		VG	VF	UNC
	L.1964 (ND); 1974-75. Gray-green. Sugar cane harvesting on back.				
	a. ND (1973).		3.75	15.00	100.00
	b. 30.6.1974.		1.50	6.50	40.00
	c. 31.1.1975.		.85	3.50	30.00
10	**1 KWACHA**				
	L.1964 (ND); 1974-75. Brown. Plantation worker, hill in background on back.				
	a. ND (1973).		4.00	16.50	110.00
	b. 30.6.1974.		3.00	12.00	75.00
	c. 31.1.1975.		1.25	5.00	40.00
11	**5 KWACHA**				
	L.1964 (ND); 1974-75. Red. Worker w/basket at ctr., *K5* at upper l. on back.				
	a. ND (1973).		11.00	45.00	300.00
	b. 30.6.1974.		8.50	35.00	225.00
	c. 31.1.1975.		6.50	26.50	175.00
12	**10 KWACHA**				
	L.1964 (ND); 1974-75. Blue. Plantation workers, w/mountains in background on back.				
	a. ND (1973).		12.50	50.00	325.00
	b. 30.6.1974.		13.50	53.50	350.00
	c. 31.1.1975.		7.50	30.00	210.00

1976; 1983 ISSUE
#13-17 portr. Dr. H. K. Banda as President at r. Wmk: Rooster. Sign. varieties.

13	**50 TAMBALA**		VG	VF	UNC
	1976-84. Gray-blue. Cotton harvest on back.				
	a. 31.1.1976; 1.7.1978.		.75	3.00	20.00
	b. 1.5.1982.		.50	2.00	12.00
	c. 1.1.1983.		.75	3.00	20.00
	d. 1.11.1984.		1.00	4.50	30.00
	s. Specimen. 31.1.1976.		—	—	35.00

14	**1 KWACHA**		VG	VF	UNC
	1976-84. Violet-brown on m/c unpt. Workers harvesting, mountains in background on back.				
	a. 31.1.1976; 1.7.1978; 30.6.1979.		.75	3.00	22.00
	b. 1.1.1981; 1.5.1982; 1.1.1983; 1.4.1984.		.50	2.00	15.00
	c. 1.11.1984.		.50	2.00	15.00
	s. Specimen. 31.1.1976.		—	—	40.00

15	**5 KWACHA**		VG	VF	UNC
	1976-84. Red. Field workers, *K5* at upper r. on back.				
	a. 31.1.1976; 1.7.1978; 30.6.1979.		2.75	11.00	60.00
	b. 1.1.1981-1.1.1983.		1.75	7.00	40.00
	c. 1.11.1984.		2.00	8.00	55.00
	s. Specimen. 31.1.1976.		—	—	50.00

16	**10 KWACHA**		VG	VF	UNC
	1976-84. Deep blue and brown on m/c unpt. Capital bldg. at Lilongwe on back.				
	a. 31.1.1976; 1.7.1978; 30.6.1979.		5.00	20.00	110.00
	b. 1.1.1981; 1.1.1983.		3.75	15.00	85.00
	c. 1.11.1984; 1.8.1985.		5.00	20.00	125.00
	s. Specimen. 31.1.1976.		—	—	45.00

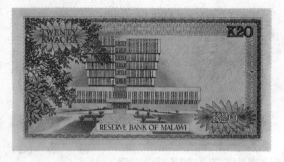

17   20 KWACHA

		VG	VF	UNC
1983; 1984. Green, brown-violet and m/c. Back green and m/c. Bank at ctr.				
a. 1.7.1983.		3.75	15.00	85.00
b. 1.11.1984.		8.75	35.00	175.00

1986 ISSUE
#18-22 portr. Pres. Banda at r. Wmk: Rooster.

18   50 TAMBALA

	VG	VF	UNC
1.3.1986. Dk. brown on m/c unpt. Picking corn on back.	.15	.75	6.00

19   1 KWACHA

	VG	VF	UNC
1986; 1988. Brown-violet on m/c unpt. Cultivating tobacco on back.			
a. 1.3.1986.	.45	1.75	9.00
b. 1.4.1988.	.15	.75	5.00

20   5 KWACHA

	VG	VF	UNC
1986; 1988. Red-orange on m/c unpt. University of Malawi on back.			
a. 1.3.1986.	1.85	7.50	32.50
b. 1.4.1988.	.90	3.75	18.50

21   10 KWACHA

	VG	VF	UNC
1986; 1988. Blue-black on m/c unpt. Lilongwe, capital city, on back.			
a. 1.3.1986.	3.00	12.50	55.00
b. 1.4.1988.	2.00	8.50	42.50

22   20 KWACHA

	VG	VF	UNC
1986; 1988. Deep green on m/c unpt. Kamuzu International Airport on back.			
a. 1.3.1986.	6.00	25.00	120.00
b. 1.4.1988.	3.00	13.00	65.00

1989 ACT; 1990-93 ISSUES
#23-28 palm tree, man in dugout canoe, and rayed silver circle at ctr., portr. Dr. H. K. Banda as President at r. Ascending vertical serial # at l. Wmk: Rooster.

23   1 KWACHA

	VG	VF	UNC
1990; 1992. Brown-violet on m/c unpt. Back like #19.			
a. 1.12.1990.	FV	FV	3.50
b. 1.5.1992.	FV	FV	2.50

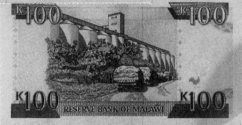

	24	**5 KWACHA**	**VG**	**VF**	**UNC**
		1990; 1994. Red-orange and olive-green on m/c unpt. University of Malawi at l. ctr. on back.			
		a. 1.12.1990.	FV	FV	8.00
		b. 1.1.1994.	FV	FV	5.00

	29	**100 KWACHA**	**VG**	**VF**	**UNC**
		1993; 1994. Blue-black, dp. brown, violet and bright green on m/c unpt. Trucks hauling maize to storage facility at ctr. on back.			
		a. 1.4.1993.	FV	15.00	70.00
		b. 1.1.1994.	FV	FV	22.50

1995 ISSUE

#30-35 Pres. Muluzi at r., sunrise above fisherman in boat on Lake Malawi at ctr., silver segmented sunburst at l. Wmk: Fish.

	25	**10 KWACHA**	**VG**	**VF**	**UNC**
		1990-94. Blue-gray, blue-violet and dk. brown on m/c unpt. Lilongwe City municipal bldg. at l. ctr. on back.			
		a. 1.12.1990.	FV	FV	15.00
		b. 1.9.1992.	FV	FV	13.00
		c. Smaller sign. as b. 1.1.1994.	FV	FV	6.00
	26	**20 KWACHA**			
		1.9.1990. Green, orange and blue on m/c unpt. Kamazu International Airport at l. ctr. on back.	FV	FV	15.00
	27	**20 KWACHA**			
		1.7.1993. Like #26 but w/larger airplane on back.	FV	FV	7.50

	30	**5 KWACHA**	**VG**	**VF**	**UNC**
		1.6.1995. Red and orange-brown on m/c unpt. Zebras at l. on back.	FV	FV	1.75

	31	**10 KWACHA**	**VG**	**VF**	**UNC**
		1.6.1995. Black, dk. blue and dk. brown on m/c unpt. Capital City bldg., Lilongwe at l. ctr. on back.	FV	FV	3.00

	28	**50 KWACHA**	**VG**	**VF**	**UNC**
		1990; 1994. Pale purple, violet and blue on m/c unpt. Independence Arch at Blantyre at ctr. on back.			
		a. 1.6.1990.	FV	11.00	52.50
		b. 1.1.1994.	—	—	28.50

32   20 KWACHA
1.6.1995. Deep green and dk. brown on m/c unpt. Harvesting tea
leaves at l. ctr. on back.

	VG	VF	UNC
	FV	FV	4.50

33   50 KWACHA
1.6.1995. Purple and violet on m/c unpt. Independence Arch in
Blantyre at l. ctr. on back.

	VG	VF	UNC
	FV	FV	9.00

34   100 KWACHA
1.6.1995. Purple and deep ultramarine on m/c unpt. Trucks hauling
grain to maize storage facility at l. ctr. on back.

	VG	VF	UNC
	FV	FV	16.50

35 **200 KWACHA**
(30)   1.6.1995. Brown-violet and blue-green and silver on m/c unpt. Bird at
upper l. Elephants on back.

	VG	VF	UNC
	FV	FV	32.50

MALAYA & BRITISH BORNEO

Malaya and British Borneo, a
Currency Commission named
the Board of Commissioners of
Currency, Malaya and British
North Borneo, was initiated on
Jan. 1, 1952, for the purpose of
providing a common currency for
use in Johore, Kelantan, Kedah,
Perlis, Trengganu, Negri Sembi-
lan, Pahang, Perak, Salangor,
Penang, Malacca, Singapore,
North Borneo, Sarawak and Bru-
nei.

For later issues see Brunei, Malaysia and Singapore.

RULERS:
British

MONETARY SYSTEM:
1 Dollar = 100 Cents

BRITISH INFLUENCE

BOARD OF COMMISSIONERS OF CURRENCY

1959 ISSUE

8   1 DOLLAR
1.3.1959. Blue on m/c unpt. Sailing boat at l. Men w/boat and arms of
5 states on back. Wmk: Tiger's head.

		VG	VF	UNC
a.	Printer: W&S.	6.00	16.00	60.00
b.	Printer: TDLR.	3.00	8.00	30.00

1961 ISSUE

9   10 DOLLARS
1.3.1961. Red and dk. brown on m/c unpt. Farmer plowing w/ox at r.
Printer: TDLR.

		VG	VF	UNC
a.	Sm. serial #. Series A.	16.50	50.00	150.00
b.	Lg. serial #. Series A.	17.50	52.50	160.00
c.	Lg. serial #. Series B.	18.50	55.00	165.00

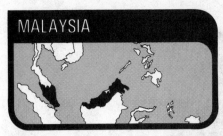

MALAYSIA

Malaysia, an independent federation of southeast Asia consisting of 11 states of West Malaysia on the Malay Peninsula and two states of East Malaysia on the island of Borneo, has an area of 127,316 sq. mi. (329,747 sq. km.) and a population of 18.6 million. Capital: Kuala Lumpur. The federation came into being on Sept. 16, 1963. Rubber, timber, tin, iron ore and bauxite are exported.

The constituent states of Malaysia are Johore, Kedah, Kelantan, Malacca, Negri Sembilan, Pahang, Penang, Perak, Perlis, Selangor and Trengganu of West Malaysia; and Sabah and Sarawak of East Malaysia. Singapore joined the federation in 1963, but broke away on Aug. 9, 1965, to become an independent republic. Malaysia is a member of the Commonwealth of Nations. The "Paramount Ruler" is Chief of State. The prime minister is Head of Government.

MONETARY SYSTEM:
1 Ringgit (Dollar) = 100 Sen

FEDERATION

BANK NEGARA MALAYSIA

All notes w/Yang Di-Pertuan Agong, Tunku Abdul Rahman, first Head of State of Malaysia (died 1960).

1967 ND ISSUE
#1-6 old spelling of *DI-PERLAKUAN*. Arms on back. Wmk: Tiger's head. Sign. of Ismail Md. Ali w/title: *GABENOR*.
#1-2 printer: BWC.
#3-5 printer: TDLR.

		VG	VF	UNC
1	**1 RINGGIT**			
	ND (1967-72). Blue on m/c unpt.			
	a. Solid security thread.	.50	2.00	6.00
	b. Segmented foil over security thread.	.50	2.25	7.00

		VG	VF	UNC
2	**5 RINGGIT**			
	ND (1967-72). Green on m/c unpt.			
	a. Solid security thread.	2.50	6.00	30.00
	b. Segmented foil security thread.	2.50	7.00	23.50
3	**10 RINGGIT**			
	ND (1967-72). Red-orange on m/c unpt. *(SAPULOH)*.			
	a. Solid security thread.	5.00	7.50	37.50
	b. Segmented foil security thread.	5.00	8.00	40.00
4	**50 RINGGIT**			
	ND (1967-72). Blue on m/c unpt. *(LIMA PULOH)*.			
	a. Solid security thread.	22.50	30.00	75.00
	b. Segmented foil security thread.	22.50	30.00	75.00

		VG	VF	UNC
5	**100 RINGGIT**			
	ND (1967-72). Violet on m/c unpt. *(SARATUS)*.			
	a. Solid security thread.	FV	55.00	165.00
	b. Segmented foil security thread.	FV	55.00	175.00
6	**1000 RINGGIT**			
	ND (1967-72). Brown-violet on m/c unpt. *(SARIBU)*. Printer: BWC.	FV	550.00	1000.

1972; 1976 ND ISSUE
#7-12 new spelling *DIPERLAKUKAN*. Arms on back. Wmk: Tiger's head. Sign. of of Ismail Md. Ali w/title: *GABENUR*.
#7-8 printer: BWC.
#9 and 10 printer: TDLR.
#11 and 12 printer: BWC.

		VG	VF	UNC
7	**1 RINGGIT**			
	ND (1972-76). Blue on m/c unpt.	FV	1.00	3.25

		VG	VF	UNC
8	**5 RINGGIT**			
	ND (1976). Green on m/c unpt.	FV	3.00	9.00

		VG	VF	UNC
9	**10 RINGGIT**			
	ND (1972-76). Red-orange and brown on m/c unpt. *(SEPULUH)*. Printer: TDLR.			
	a. Solid security thread.	FV	5.00	15.00
	b. Segmented foil security thread.	FV	5.00	17.50

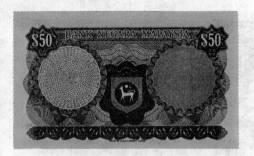

10	**50 RINGGIT**	**VG**	**VF**	**UNC**
	ND (1972-76). Blue on m/c unpt.*(LIMA PULUH)*.			
	a. Solid security thread.	FV	22.50	50.00
	b. Segmented foil security thread.	FV	22.50	57.50
11	**100 RINGGIT**			
	ND (1972-76). Violet on m/c unpt. *(SERATUS)*.	FV	50.00	120.00
12	**1000 RINGGIT**			
	ND (1972-76). Brown-violet on m/c unpt. *(SERIBU)*.	FV	FV	750.00

1976; 1981 ND ISSUES

#13-18 arms on back. Wmk: Tiger's head.

#13-16 different guilloche w/latent image numeral at lower l.

#13-15 printer: BWC.

13	**1 RINGGIT**	**VG**	**VF**	**UNC**
	ND (1976-83). Blue on m/c unpt. Like #7.			
	a. Sign. Ismail Md. Ali. (1976).	FV	.75	2.00
	b. Sign. Abdul Aziz Taha. (1981).	FV	.70	1.50
14	**5 RINGGIT**			
	ND (1976-83). Green on m/c unpt. Like #8.			
	a. Sign. Ismail Md. Ali. (1976).	FV	3.00	6.00
	b. Sign. Abdul Aziz Taha. (1981).	FV	2.50	5.00
15	**10 RINGGIT**			
	ND (1976-81). Red-orange and brown on m/c unpt. Like #9. Sign. Ismail Md. Ali. (1976).	FV	6.00	9.00
15A	**10 RINGGIT**			
	ND (1981-83). Like #15 but printer: TDLR. Sign. Abdul Aziz Taha.	FV	5.00	8.00

16	**50 RINGGIT**	**VG**	**VF**	**UNC**
	ND (1976-83). Blue on m/c unpt. Like #10.			
	a. Sign. Ismail Md. Ali. (1976). Printer: BWC.	FV	30.00	40.00
	b. Sign. Abdul Aziz Taha. (1981). Printer: TDLR.	FV	30.00	40.00
17	**100 RINGGIT**			
	ND (1976-83). Purple on m/c unpt. Like #11. Printer: TDLR.			
	a. Sign. Ismail Md. Ali. (1976).	FV	50.00	70.00
	b. Sign. Abdul Aziz Taha. (1981).	FV	FV	65.00
18	**1000 RINGGIT**			
	ND (1976-81). Purple and green on m/c unpt. Like #12. Sign. Ismail Md. Ali. Printer: BWC.	FV	FV	650.00

1981-83 ND ISSUES

#19A-21 printer: TDLR.

#19-26 new design w/marks for the blind. Sign. of Abdul Aziz Taha. Wmk: T. A. Rahman.

19	**1 RINGGIT**	**VG**	**VF**	**UNC**
	ND (1982-84). Blue and brown on pink and m/c unpt. National Monument Kuala Lumpurate at ctr. on back. Printer: BWC.	FV	.50	1.25
19A	**1 RINGGIT**			
	ND (1981-83). Like #19.	FV	.50	1.00

20	**5 RINGGIT**	**VG**	**VF**	**UNC**
	ND (1983-84). Dk. green and blue on m/c unpt. King's Palace at Kuala Lumpur on back.	FV	2.50	4.00

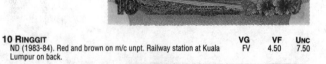

21	**10 RINGGIT**	**VG**	**VF**	**UNC**
	ND (1983-84). Red and brown on m/c unpt. Railway station at Kuala Lumpur on back.	FV	4.50	7.50

22   20 RINGGIT
ND (1982-84). Deep. brown and dk. blue on m/c unpt. Bank Negara
Malaysia bldg. in Kuala Lumpur on back. Printer: BWC.

	VG	VF	UNC
	FV	9.00	15.00

23   50 RINGGIT
ND (1983-84). Black and blue-gray on m/c unpt. National Museum at
Kuala Lumpur on back. Printer: TDLR.

	VG	VF	UNC
	FV	22.50	32.00

24   100 RINGGIT
ND (1983-84). Red-brown and violet on m/c unpt. National Mosque in
Kuala Lumpur on back. Printer: TDLR.

	VG	VF	UNC
	FV	45.00	65.00

25   500 RINGGIT
ND (1982-84). Dk. red and purple on m/c unpt. High Court Bldg. in
Kuala Lumpur on back. Printer: BWC.

	VG	VF	UNC
	FV	225.00	300.00

26   1000 RINGGIT
ND (1983-84). Gray-green on m/c unpt. Parliament bldg. in Kuala
Lumpur on back. Printer: TDLR.

	VG	VF	UNC
	FV	425.00	575.00

1986-95 ND ISSUES

**#27-34 similar to #19-26 but no mark for the blind, white space for wmk. (both sides), and vertical serial
#. Sign. Datuk Jaafar Hussein. Wmk: T. A. Rahman.**

#27-31 printer: TDLR.

#33-34 printer: TDLR.

27   1 RINGGIT
ND (1986; 1989). Blue on m/c unpt.
  a.   Usual security thread (1986).
  b.   Segmented foil security thread (1989).

	VG	VF	UNC
a.	FV	FV	1.00
b.	FV	FV	.85

28   5 RINGGIT
ND (1986; 1989). Dk. olive-green and green on m/c unpt.
  a.   Usual security thread (1986).
  b.   Segmented foil security thread (1989).
  c.   Flagpole w/o cross bar at top of back (1991).

	VG	VF	UNC
a.	FV	FV	4.00
b.	FV	FV	3.75
c.	FV	FV	3.50

29   10 RINGGIT
ND (1989). Brown, red-orange and violet on m/c unpt. Segmented foil
security thread (1989).

	VG	VF	UNC
	FV	FV	7.50

30   20 RINGGIT
ND (1989). Deep brown, olive and m/c.

	VG	VF	UNC
	FV	FV	12.50

31   50 RINGGIT
ND (1989). Blue and m/c. Segmented silver foil over security thread.

	VG	VF	UNC
	FV	FV	27.50

31A   50 RINGGIT
ND (1991-92). Like #31, but printer: BABN.

	VG	VF	UNC
	FV	FV	25.00

---

32   100 RINGGIT
ND (1989). Purple and m/c. Segmented silver foil over security thread. Printer: TDLR.

	VG	VF	UNC
	FV	FV	55.00

32A   100 RINGGIT
ND (1991-93). Like #32, but printer: USBNC.

	FV	FV	50.00

33   500 RINGGIT
ND (1989). Red, brown and yellow. Segmented foil security thread.

	FV	FV	240.00

34   1000 RINGGIT
ND (1989). Blue, green and purple. Segmented foil security thread.

	FV	FV	475.00

1995 ND ISSUES
#35-38 sign. Ahmed Mohd. Don. Wmk. portr. T.A. Rahman.

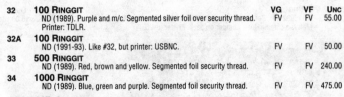

35   5 RINGGIT
ND (1995). Like #28 but printer: TDLR.

	VG	VF	UNC
	FV	FV	3.50

36   10 RINGGIT
ND (1995). Like #29 but printer: F-CO.

	VG	VF	UNC
	FV	FV	6.50

37   10 RINGGIT
ND (1995). Dk. brown, red-orange and violet on m/c unpt. Like #29 but printer: BABN.

	FV	FV	10.00

38   10 RINGGIT
ND (1995). Like #29 but printer: G&D.

	FV	FV	6.50

1996 ND ISSUE

39   2 RINGGIT
ND (1996). Purple and red-violet on m/c unpt. T. A. Rahman at r. and as wmk. Modern tower at l., communications satellite at upper ctr. Printer: NBM (w/o imprint).

	VG	VF	UNC
	FV	FV	1.50

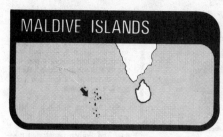

MALDIVE ISLANDS

The Republic of Maldives, an archipelago of 2,000 coral islets in the northern Indian Ocean 417 miles (671 km.) southwest of Ceylon, has an area of 115 sq. mi. (298 sq. km.) and a population of 213,200. Capital: Malá. Fishing employs 95 percent of the work force. Dried fish, copra and coir yarn are exported.

The Maldive Islands were visited by Arab traders and converted to Islam in 1153. After being harassed in the 16th and 17th centuries by Mopla pirates of the Malabar coast and Portuguese raiders, the Maldivians voluntarily placed themselves under the suzerainty of Ceylon. In 1887, the islands became an internally self-governing British protectorate and a nominal dependency of Ceylon. Traditionally a sultanate, the Maldives became a republic in 1953 but restored the sultanate in 1954. The Sultanate of the Maldive Islands attained complete internal and external autonomy on July 26, 1965, and on Nov. 11, 1968 again became a republic.

RULERS:
British to 1965

MONETARY SYSTEM:
1 Rupee = 100 Lari

REPUBLIC

MALDIVIAN STATE, GOVERNMENT TREASURER

1951-80 ISSUE

7	**50 RUPEES**	VG	VF	UNC
(6)	1951-80. Blue on m/c unpt. Waterfront bldg. at ctr. on back.			
	a. 1951/AH1371.	35.00	90.00	250.00
	b. 4.6.1960/AH1379.	5.00	15.00	35.00
	c. Litho. 1.8.1980/AH17.7.1400.	6.00	17.50	40.00

MALDIVES MONETARY AUTHORITY

1983 ISSUE

#9-14 dhow at r. Wmk: Arms. Printer: BWC.

9	**2 RUFIYAA**	VG	VF	UNC
	7.10.1983/AH1404. Black on olive-brown and m/c unpt. Shoreline village on back.	FV	FV	1.50

10	**5 RUFIYAA**	VG	VF	UNC
	7.10.1983/AH1404. Deep purple on green and m/c unpt. Fishing boats at ctr. on back.	FV	FV	2.25

11	**10 RUFIYAA**	VG	VF	UNC
	7.10.1983/AH1404. Brown on m/c unpt. Villagers working at ctr. on back.	FV	FV	3.50

12	**20 RUFIYAA**	VG	VF	UNC
	7.10.1983/AH1404. Red-violet on m/c unpt. Fishing boats at dockside in Malé Harbour on back.			
	a. 7.10.1983/AH1404.	FV	FV	6.50
	b. 1987/AH1408.	FV	FV	5.50

13	**50 RUFIYAA**	VG	VF	UNC
	1983; 1987. Blue on m/c unpt. Village market in Malé at ctr. on back.			
	a. Imprint at bottom ctr. on back ack. 7.10.1983/AH1404.	FV	FV	13.50
	b. W/o imprint. 1987/AH1408.	FV	FV	11.50

14	**100 RUFIYAA**	VG	VF	UNC
	1983; 1987. Green on m/c unpt. Tomb of Medhuziyaarath at ctr. on back.			
	a. Imprint at bottom ctr. on back ack. 7.10.1983/AH1404.	FV	FV	25.00
	b. W/o imprint. 1987/AH1408.	FV	FV	22.00

1990 ISSUE

#15, 16, 20 and 21 Printer: TDLR.
17-19 Held in reserve.

		VG	VF	UNC
15	**2 RUFIYAA** 1990/AH1411. Like #9, but darker dhow and trees, also slightly diff. unpt. colors.	FV	FV	1.00
16	**5 RUFIYAA** 1990/AH1411. Like #10, but brown unpt. at ctr., also darker boats on back.	FV	FV	2.00
20	**100 RUFIYAA** 1995.	FV	FV	20.00
21	**500 RUFIYAA** 1990/AH1411. Orange and green on m/c unpt. Grand Friday Mosque and Islamic Ctr. on back.	FV	FV	80.00

MALI

The Republic of Mali, formerly the French Sudan, a landlocked country in the interior of West Africa southwest of Algeria, has an area of 478,764 sq. mi. (1,240,000 sq. km.) and a population of 9.36 million. Capital: Bamako. Livestock, fish, cotton and peanuts are exported.

Malians are descendants of the ancient Malinke Kingdom of Mali that controlled the middle Niger from the 11th to the 17th centuries. The French penetrated the Sudan (now Mali) about 1880, and established their rule in 1898 after subduing fierce native resistance. In 1904 the area became the colony of Upper Senegal-Niger (changed to French Sudan in 1920), and became part of the French Union in 1946. In 1958 French Sudan became the Sudanese Republic with complete internal autonomy. Senegal joined with the Sudanese Republic in 1959 to form the Mali Federation which, in 1960, became a fully independent member of the French Community. Upon Senegal's subsequent withdrawal from the Federation, the Sudanese, on Sept. 22, 1960, proclaimed their nation the fully independent Republic of Mali and severed all ties with France.

Mali seceded from the African Financial Community in 1962, then rejoined in 1984. Issues specially marked with letter *D* for Mali were made by the Banque des Etats de l'Afrique de l'Ouest. See also French West Africa, and West African States.

MONETARY SYSTEM:
1 Franc = 100 Centimes

SIGNATURE VARIETIES

1	Ministre Des Finances	Gouverneur de La Banque
2	Ministre d'Etat Ministre Des Finances	Gouverneur de La Banque
3	Le Président du Counseil d'Administration	Le Directeur Général
4	Le Président du Counseil d'Administration	Le Directeur Général
5	Le Président du Counseil d'Administration	Le Directeur Général
6	Le Président du Counseil d'Administration	Le Directeur Général
7	Le Président du Counseil d'Administration	Le Directeur Général
8	Le Président du Counseil d'Administration	Le Directeur Général
9	Le Président du Counseil d'Administration	Le Directeur Général

REPUBLIC

BANQUE DE LA RÉPUBLIQUE DU MALI

FIRST 1960 (1962) ISSUE

NOTE: Postdated on Day of Independence.
#1-5 Pres. Modibo Keita at l. Sign. 1.

		VG	VF	UNC
1	**50 FRANCS** 22.9.1960. Purple on m/c unpt. Village on back.	5.00	25.00	115.00

		VG	VF	UNC
2	**100 FRANCS** 22.9.1960. Brown on yellow unpt. Cattle on back.	5.00	28.00	135.00
3	**500 FRANCS** 22.9.1960. Red on lt. blue and orange unpt. Woman and tent on back.	55.00	175.00	500.00

		VG	VF	UNC
4	**1000 FRANCS** 22.9.1960. Blue on lt. green and orange unpt. Farmers w/oxen at lower r. Back blue; man and huts.	20.00	85.00	275.00
5	**5000 FRANCS** 22.9.1960. Green on m/c unpt. 2 farmers plowing w/oxen at r. Market scene and bldg. on back.	150.00	350.00	850.00

SECOND 1960 (1967) ISSUE
NOTE: Postdated on Day of Independence.
#6-10 Modibo Keita at r. Sign 2. Printer: TDLR.

		VG	VF	UNC
6	**50 FRANCS** 22.9.1960 (1967). Purple on blue and lt. green unpt. Dam at lower l. Back purple; woman and village.	17.50	50.00	185.00

		VG	VF	UNC
7	**100 FRANCS** 22.9.1960 (1967). Brown on green and lilac unpt. Tractors at lower l. Back brown; old man at r., canoes at ctr., city view behind.	12.50	40.00	175.00
8	**500 FRANCS** 22.9.1960 (1967). Green on yellow, blue and red unpt. Bldg. at lower l. Longhorn cattle on back.	30.00	125.00	350.00

		VG	VF	UNC
9	**1000 FRANCS** 22.9.1960 (1967). Blue on lilac and brown unpt. Bank at lower l. Back blue; people and Djenne mosque.	25.00	135.00	300.00
10	**5000 FRANCS** 22.9.1960 (1967). Dk. red on green unpt. Farmers at ctr. Market scene and bldgs. on back.	65.00	250.00	525.00

BANQUE CENTRALE DU MALI

1970-73 ND ISSUES
#12-15 sign. varieties.

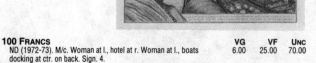

		VG	VF	UNC
11	**100 FRANCS** ND (1972-73). M/c. Woman at l., hotel at r. Woman at l., boats docking at ctr. on back. Sign. 4.	6.00	25.00	70.00

12   500 FRANCS
ND (1973-84). M/c. Soldier at l., tractors at r. Men and camels on back.

		VG	VF	UNC
a.	Sign. 4.	1.50	5.00	13.50
b.	Sign. 5.	1.50	5.00	13.50
c.	Sign. 6.	1.50	5.00	13.50
d.	Sign. 7.	1.50	5.00	13.50
e.	Sign. 8.	1.50	5.00	13.50
f.	Sign. 9.	5.00	15.00	40.00

13   1000 FRANCS
ND (1970-84). M/c. Bldg. at l., older man at r. Carvings at l., mountain village at ctr. on back.

		VG	VF	UNC
a.	Sign. 4.	2.50	6.00	15.00
b.	Sign. 5.	2.50	6.00	15.00
c.	Sign. 6.	2.50	6.00	15.00
d.	Sign. 7.	2.50	6.00	15.00
e.	Sign. 8.	2.50	6.00	15.00

15   10,000 FRANCS
ND (1970-84). M/c. Man w/fez at l., factory at lower r. Weaver at l., young woman w/coin headband at r. on back. 6 sign. varieties.

		VG	VF	UNC
a.	Sign. 3.	20.00	50.00	110.00
b.	Sign. 4.	15.00	35.00	70.00
c.	Sign. 5.	15.00	35.00	70.00
d.	Sign. 6.	15.00	35.00	70.00
e.	Sign. 7.	15.00	35.00	70.00
f.	Sign. 8.	15.00	35.00	70.00
g.	Sign. 9.	15.00	35.00	70.00

14   5000 FRANCS
ND (1972-84). M/c. Cattle at lower l., man w/turban at r. Woman and flowers at l., woman w/machinery at r. on back. 5 sign. varieties.

		VG	VF	UNC
a.	Sign. 4.	8.50	25.00	50.00
b.	Sign. 5.	8.50	25.00	50.00
c.	Sign. 6.	8.50	25.00	50.00
d.	Sign. 7.	8.50	25.00	50.00
e.	Sign. 8.	8.50	25.00	50.00

MALTA

The Republic of Malta, an independent parliamentary democracy within the British Commonwealth, is situated in the Mediterranean Sea between Sicily and North Africa. With the islands of Gozo and Comino, Malta has an area of 122 sq. mi. (316 sq. km.) and a population of 359,900. Capital: Valletta. Malta has no proven mineral resources, an agriculture insufficient to its needs and a small but expanding, manufacturing facility. Clothing, textile yarns and fabrics, and knitted wear are exported.

For more than 3,500 years Malta was ruled, in succession, by Phoenicians, Carthaginians, Romans, Arabs, Normans, the Knights of Malta, France and Britain. Napoleon seized Malta by treachery in 1798. The French were ousted by a Maltese insurrection assisted by Britain, and in 1814 Malta, of its own free will, became part of the British Empire. Malta obtained full independence in Sept., 1964; electing to remain within the Commonwealth with the British monarch as the nominal head of state.

Malta became a republic on Dec. 13, 1974, but remained a member of the Commonwealth of Nations. The president is Chief of State, while the prime minister is the Head of Government.

RULERS:
British to 1974

MONETARY SYSTEM:
1 Shilling = 12 Pence
1 Pound = 20 Shillings to 1971
1 Cent = 10 Mils
1 Lira (Pound) = 100 Cents, 1971-

REPUBLIC

GOVERNMENT OF MALTA

1949 ORDINANCE; 1963 ND ISSUE
#25-27 Qn. Elizabeth II at r. Printer: BWC.

		VG	VF	UNC
25	**10 SHILLINGS**	4.00	10.00	75.00
	L.1949 (1963). Green, blue and m/c. Cross at ctr. Mgarr Harbour, Gozo on back.			

		VG	VF	UNC
26	**1 POUND**	5.00	20.00	87.50
	L.1949 (1963). Brown. Violet and m/c. Cross at ctr. Industrial Estate, Marsa on back.			

		VG	VF	UNC
27	**5 POUNDS**			
	L.1949 (1961). Blue and m/c. Cross at ctr. Grand Harbour on back.			
	a. Sign. D. A. Shepherd (1961).	30.00	150.00	600.00
	b. Sign. R. Soler (1963).	30.00	150.00	550.00

BANK CENTRALI TA'MALTA

CENTRAL BANK OF MALTA

1967 CENTRAL BANK ACT; 1968-69 ND ISSUE
#28-30 designs similar to #25-27. Printer: BWC.

		VG	VF	UNC
28	**10 SHILLINGS**	3.50	10.00	42.50
	L.1967 (1968). Red and m/c. Similar to #25.			

		VG	VF	UNC
29	**1 POUND**	3.00	12.50	75.00
	L.1967 (1969). Olive and m/c. Similar to #26.			

		VG	VF	UNC
30	**5 POUNDS**	10.00	35.00	200.00
	L.1967 (1968). Brown, violet and m/c. Similar to #27.			

1967 CENTRAL BANK ACT; 1973 ND ISSUE

#31-33 arms at r., map at ctr. Printer: TDLR.
Replacement notes: Serial # prefix *X/1, Y/1* or *Z/1* (by denomination).

31	**1 LIRA**		VG	VF	UNC
	L.1967 (1973). Green and m/c. War Memorial at l. Prehistoric Temple in Tarxien at l., old capital city of Medina at ctr. on back.				
	a.	Sign J. Sammut and A. Camilleri.	FV	4.00	22.50
	b.	Sign. H. de Gabriele and J. Laspina.	FV	4.00	22.50
	c.	Sign. H. de Gabriele and A. Camilleri.	FV	4.00	22.50
	d.	Sign. J. Laspina and J. Sammut.	FV	4.00	22.50
	e.	Sign. A. Camilleri and J. Laspina.	FV	4.00	22.50
	f.	Sign. J. Sammut and H. de Gabriele.	FV	4.00	22.50

32	**5 LIRI**		VG	VF	UNC
	L.1967 (1973). Blue and m/c. Neptune at l. Yacht marina and boats on back.				
	a.	Sign. H. de Gabriele and J. Laspina.	FV	15.00	65.00
	b.	Sign. H. de Gabriele and A. Camilleri.	FV	15.00	65.00
	c.	Sign. J. Laspina and J. Sammut.	FV	15.00	65.00
	d.	Sign. A. Camilleri and J. Laspina.	FV	15.00	65.00
	e.	Sign. J. Sammut and H. de Gabriele.	FV	15.00	65.00
	f.	Sign J. Sammut and A. Camilleri.	FV	15.00	65.00

33	**10 LIRI**		VG	VF	UNC
	L.1967 (1973). Brown and m/c. Like #32. View of Grand Harbour and boats on back.				
	a.	Sign. of H. de Gabriele and A. Camilleri.	FV	30.00	125.00
	b.	Sign. of J. Laspina and J. Sammut.	FV	35.00	165.00
	c.	Sign of A. Camilleri and J. Laspina.	FV	35.00	165.00
	d.	Sign. of J. Sammut and H. de Gabriele.	FV	35.00	165.00
	e.	Sign. of L. Spiteri w/title: *DEPUTAT GOVERNATUR*.	FV	35.00	125.00

1979 ND ISSUE

Central Bank Act, 1967 #34-36 map at upper l. Wmk: Allegorical head of Malta. Printer: TDLR.
Replacement notes: Serial # prefix *X/2, Y/2* or *Z/2* (by denomination).

34	**1 LIRA**		VG	VF	UNC
	L.1967 (1979). Brown and m/c. Watch tower "Gardjola" at ctr. New University on back.				
	a.	W/o dot.	FV	3.50	11.50
	b.	W/1 dot added for poor of sight at upper r.	FV	3.00	8.50

35	**5 LIRI**		VG	VF	UNC
	L.1967 (1979). Violet and m/c. Statue of "Culture" at ctr. Marsa Industrial Estate on back.				
	a.	W/o 2 dots.	FV	14.00	42.50
	b.	W/2 dots added for poor of sight at upper r.	FV	13.00	37.50

36	**10 LIRI**		VG	VF	UNC
	L.1967 (1979). Gray, pink and m/c. Statue of "Justice" at ctr. Part of Malta Drydocks on back.				
	a.	W/o 3 dots.	FV	28.00	60.00
	b.	W/3 dots added for poor of sight at upper r.	FV	28.00	65.00

1986 ND Issue

#37-40 sailing craft and map of Malta at ctr., A. Barbara at r.
Replacement notes: Serial # prefix W/2, X/2, Y/2 or Z/2 (by denomination).

37	**2 Liri**	VG	VF	Unc
	L.1967 (1986). Red-orange on m/c unpt. Dockside crane at l., aerial harbor view at r. on back.	FV	FV	16.50

38	**5 Liri**	VG	VF	Unc
	L.1967 (1986). Gray-green and blue; 2 black horizontal accounting bars at lower r. Sailboats in harbor and repairing of fishing nets on back.	FV	FV	30.00

39	**10 Liri**	VG	VF	Unc
	L.1967 (1986). Olive and dk. green on m/c unpt. 3 dk. green horizontal accounting bars at lower r. Shipbuilding on back.	FV	FV	60.00

40	**20 Lira**	VG	VF	Unc
	L.1967 (1986). Brown on m/c unpt. 4 brown horizontal accounting bars at lower r. Statue and govt. bldg. at ctr. on back.	FV	FV	120.00

1989 ND Issue

#41-44 doves at l., Malta standing w/rudder at ctr. r. Wmk: Turreted head of Malta. Printer: TDLR.
Replacement notes: Serial # prefix W/2, X/2, Y/2 or Z/2 (by denomination).

41	**2 Liri**	VG	VF	Unc
	L.1967 (1989). Violet on m/c unpt. Bldgs. in Malta and Gozo on back.	FV	FV	13.50
42	**5 Liri**			
	L.1967 (1989). Blue on m/c unpt. Historical tower on back.	FV	FV	26.50
43	**10 Liri**			
	L.1967 (1989). Green on m/c unpt. Wounded people being brought into National Assembly on back.	FV	FV	50.00
44	**20 Lira**			
	L.1967 (1989). Brown on m/c unpt. Prime Minister Dr. G. B. Olivier on back.	FV	FV	95.00

1994 ND Issue

#45-48 like 41-44 but w/enhanced colors and segmented foil over security threads.

45	**2 Liri**	VG	VF	Unc
	L.1967 (1994).	FV	FV	12.00
46	**5 Liri**			
	L.1967 (1994).	FV	FV	23.50
47	**10 Liri**			
	L.1967 (1994).	FV	FV	45.00
48	**20 Lira**			
	L.1967 (1994).	FV	FV	87.50

COLLECTOR SERIES

BANK CENTRALI TA'MALTA

1979 Issue

CS1	**ND (1979) 1-10 Liri**	Issue Price	Mkt. Value
	#34-36 w/ovpt: SPECIMEN and Maltese cross prefix serial #.	14.00	27.50

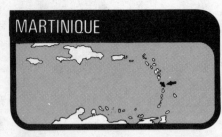

The French Overseas Department of Martinique, located in the Lesser Antilles of the West Indies between Dominica and Saint Lucia, has an area of 425 sq. mi. (1,101 sq. km.) and a population of 329,000. Capital: Fort-de-France. Agriculture and tourism are the major sources of income. Bananas, sugar and rum are exported.

Christopher Columbus discovered Martinique, probably on June 15, 1502. France took possession on June 25, 1635, and has maintained possession since that time except for three short periods of British occupation during the Napoleonic Wars. A French department since 1946, Martinique voted a reaffirmation of that status in 1958, remaining within the new French Community. Martinique was the birthplace of Napoleon's Empress Josephine, and the site of the eruption of Mt. Pelee in 1902 that claimed over 40,000 lives.

RULERS:
French

MONETARY SYSTEM:
1 Franc = 100 Centimes

FRENCH INFLUENCE

NOTE: For later issues see French Antilles.

CAISSE CENTRALE DE LA FRANCE D'OUTRE-MER

1961 ND PROVISIONAL ISSUE

#37-39B ovpt: *MARTINIQUE* and new denominations on previous "old" Franc issues.

		VG	VF	UNC
37	**1 NOUVEAUX FRANC ON 100 FRANCS** ND (1961). M/c. La Bourdonnais at l., native coupe at r.	9.00	65.00	225.00

		VG	VF	UNC
38	**5 NOUVEAUX FRANCS ON 500 FRANCS** ND (1961). M/c. 2 women at r., sailboat at l. Farmers w/ox carts on back.	20.00	160.00	375.00

		VG	VF	UNC
39	**10 NOUVEAUX FRANCS ON 1000 FRANCS** ND (1961). M/c. Fisherman. Woman w/box of produce on her head at l. ctr. on back.	35.00	185.00	575.00
40	**50 NOUVEAUX FRANCS ON 5000 FRANCS** ND (1961). M/c. Woman holding fruit bowl at ctr. Harvesting scene on back.	150.00	650.00	—
41	**50 NOUVEAUX FRANCS ON 5000 FRANCS** ND (1961). M/c. Gen. Schoelcher. Specimen.	—	—	—

MAURITANIA

The Islamic Republic of Mauritania, located in northwest Africa bounded by Spanish Sahara, Mali, Algeria, Senegal and the Atlantic Ocean, has an area of 397,955 sq. mi. (1,030,700 sq. km.) and a population of 2.11 million. Capital: Nouakchott. The economy centers about herding, agriculture, fishing and mining. Iron ore, copper concentrates and fish products are exported.

The indigenous Negroid inhabitants were driven out of Mauritania by Berber invaders of the Islamic faith in the 11th century. The Berbers in turn were conquered by Arab invaders, the Beni Hassan, in the 16th century. Arab traders carried on a gainful trade in gum arabic, gold and slaves with Portuguese, Dutch, English and French traders until late in the 19th century when France took control of the area, and in 1920 made it a part of French West Africa. Mauritania became a part of the French Union in 1946 and was made an autonomous republic within the new French Community in 1958, when the Islamic Republic of Mauritania was proclaimed. The republic became independent on November 28, 1960, and withdrew from the French Community in 1966.

On June 28, 1973, in a move designed to emphasize its non-alignment with France, Mauritania converted its currency from the old French-supported CFA franc unit to a new unit called the Ouguiya.

MONETARY SYSTEM:
    1 Ouguiya = 5 Khoum
    100 Ouguiya = 500 CFA Francs, 1973-

NOTE: Issues specially marked with letter *E* for Mauritania were made by the Banque Centrale des Etats de l'Afrique de l'Ouest. These issues were used before Mauritania seceded from the French Community of the West African States in 1973. For listing see West African States.

REPUBLIC

BANQUE CENTRALE DE MAURITANIE

1973 ISSUE

1	**100 OUGUIYA**	**VG**	**VF**	**UNC**
	20.6.1973. Blue. Mauritanian girl at ctr. Men loading boat on back.			
	a. Issued note.	10.00	20.00	60.00
	s. Specimen.	—	—	17.50

2	**200 OUGUIYA**	**VG**	**VF**	**UNC**
	20.6.1973. Brown. Bedouin woman at l., tents in background. Camels and huts on back.			
	a. Issued note.	11.00	22.00	65.00
	s. Specimen.	—	—	15.00

3	**1000 OUGUIYA**	**VG**	**VF**	**UNC**
	20.6.1973. Green. Woman weaving on loom at l., metal worker at r. ctr. Local musicians and scenes on back.			
	a. Issued note.	15.00	35.00	100.00
	s. Specimen.	—	—	25.00

1974-79 ISSUE
#4-7 wmk: Old man w/beard. Sign. varieties.

4	**100 OUGUIYA**	**VG**	**VF**	**UNC**
	1974-89. Purple, violet and brown on m/c unpt. Musical instruments at l., cow and tower at r. on back.			
	a. 28.11.1974. Thin security thread.	4.00	10.00	25.00
	b. 28.11.1983.	7.50	15.00	35.00
	c. 28.11.1985.	2.00	7.50	13.50
	d. 28.11.1989. Thick security thread.	FV	3.25	10.00
	e. 28.11.1992.	FV	3.00	9.00
	f. 28.11.1993.	FV	FV	9.00

5	**200 OUGUIYA**	**VG**	**VF**	**UNC**
	1974-89. Brown, dk. olive-green and brown-orange on m/c unpt. Bowl, dugout canoe and palm tree on back.			
	a. 28.11.1974. Thin security thread.	6.00	15.00	30.00
	b. 28.11.1985.	4.00	10.00	22.50
	c. 28.11.1989. Thick security thread.	FV	6.00	18.00
	d. 28.11.1992.	FV	5.00	15.00
	e. 28.11.1993.	FV	FV	12.50

6	**500 OUGUIYA**	VG	VF	UNC
	1979-1985. Green, brown and dk. green on m/c unpt. Back brown, green and black; field workers at l., factory at r.			
	a. 28.11.1979. Thin security thread.	18.00	40.00	100.00
	b. 28.11.1983.	16.00	35.00	90.00
	c. 28.11.1985.	8.50	15.00	40.00
	d. 28.11.1989. Thick security thread.	FV	12.00	36.00
	e. 28.11.1991.	FV	10.00	30.00
	f. 28.11.1992.	FV	8.00	24.00
	g. 28.11.1993.	FV	FV	24.00

7	**1000 OUGUIYA**	VG	VF	UNC
	1974-1991. Blue, violet and blue-black on m/c unpt. Bowl of fish, camel, hut and tower back.			
	a. 28.11.1974. Thin security thread.	18.00	40.00	100.00
	b. 28.11.1985.	10.00	22.50	60.00
	c. 28.11.1989	FV	20.00	45.00
	d. 28.10.1991. Thick security thread.	FV	15.00	40.00
	e. 28.11.1992.	FV	12.00	40.00
	f. 28.11.1993.	FV	12.00	35.00

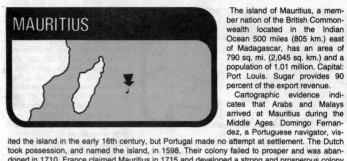

MAURITIUS

The island of Mauritius, a member nation of the British Commonwealth located in the Indian Ocean 500 miles (805 km.) east of Madagascar, has an area of 790 sq. mi. (2,045 sq. km.) and a population of 1.01 million. Capital: Port Louis. Sugar provides 90 percent of the export revenue.

Cartographic evidence indicates that Arabs and Malays arrived at Mauritius during the Middle Ages. Domingo Fernandez, a Portuguese navigator, visited the island in the early 16th century, but Portugal made no attempt at settlement. The Dutch took possession, and named the island, in 1598. Their colony failed to prosper and was abandoned in 1710. France claimed Mauritius in 1715 and developed a strong and prosperous colony that endured until the island was captured by the British in 1810, during the Napoleonic Wars. British possession was confirmed by the Treaty of Paris, 1814. Mauritius became independent on March 12, 1968. It is a member of the Commonwealth of Nations. The Queen of England is Chief of State.

RULERS:
British

MONETARY SYSTEM:
1 Rupee = 100 Cents, 1848-

BRITISH INFLUENCE

BANK OF MAURITIUS

SIGNATURE VARIETIES						
	GOVERNOR OF THE BANK	MANAGING DIRECTOR			GOVERNOR OF THE BANK	MANAGING DIRECTOR
1				4		
2				5	GOVERNOR	
3				6		

1967 ND ISSUE
#30-33 Qn. Elizabeth II at r. Wmk: Dodo bird. Printer: TDLR.
Replacement notes: Serial # prefix Z/#.

30	**5 RUPEES**	VG	VF	UNC
	ND (1967). Blue on m/c unpt. Sailboat on back.			
	a. Sign. 1.	.75	1.75	7.00
	b. Sign. 3.	1.00	3.00	22.50
	c. Sign. 4.	.50	1.25	4.00

35 10 RUPEES
ND (1985). Green on m/c unpt. Arms at lower l. ctr., bldg. w/flag at
ctr. r. Bridge on back.

	VG	VF	UNC
a. Dk. green printing.	FV	FV	3.00
b. Lt. green printing.	FV	FV	1.75

31 10 RUPEES
ND (1967). Red on m/c unpt. Government bldg. on back.

	VG	VF	UNC
a. Sign. 1.	.85	2.00	11.50
b. Sign. 2.	1.00	3.00	15.00
c. Sign. 4.	.75	1.25	8.50

32 25 RUPEES
ND (1967). Green on m/c unpt. Ox-cart on back.

	VG	VF	UNC
a. Sign. 1.	2.50	4.50	25.00
b. Sign. 4.	2.00	3.50	22.50

36 20 RUPEES
ND. Bluish purple, blue-green, blue and orange on m/c unpt. Lady
Jugnauth at l., arms at ctr. bldg. w/flag at lower r. Satellite dishes at
ctr. on back.

	VG	VF	UNC
	FV	FV	3.50

33 50 RUPEES
ND (1967). Purple on m/c unpt. Ships docked at Port Louis harbor on
back.

	VG	VF	UNC
a. Sign. 1.	5.00	12.00	55.00
b. Sign. 2.	7.50	20.00	85.00
c. Sign. 4.	4.00	10.00	40.00

1985-91 ND ISSUE
#34-36 outline of Mauritius map on back. Wmk: Dodo bird. Printer: TDLR. Sign. 5.
#37-41 arms at lower l. to lower ctr., bldg. w/flag at r. Wmk: Dodo bird. Printer: BWC.

37 50 RUPEES
ND (1986). Dk. blue on m/c unpt. 2 deer and butterfly on back.

	VG	VF	UNC
	FV	FV	7.00

34 5 RUPEES
ND (1985). Brown on m/c unpt. Arms at lower l. ctr., bldg. w/flag at r.
Bank on back.

	VG	VF	UNC
	FV	FV	1.25

38 100 RUPEES
ND (1986). Red on m/c unpt. Landscape on back.

	VG	VF	UNC
	FV	FV	12.50

39   200 RUPEES   **VG   VF   UNC**
ND (1985). Blue on m/c unpt. Sir Seewoodsagur Ramgoolam at l. Lg.   FV   FV   22.50
home (Le Réduit) on back. Printer: TDLR.

40   500 RUPEES   **VG   VF   UNC**
ND (1988). Brown and orange on m/c unpt. Bldg. w/flag at ctr., arms   FV   FV   57.50
below, Sir A. Jugnaurh (Prime Minister) at r. Sugar cane field workers
loading wagon w/mountains in background on back.

41   1000 RUPEES   **VG   VF   UNC**
ND (1991). Blue and purple on m/c unpt. Sir V. Ringadoo at l., palm   FV   FV   110.00
trees and bldg. w/flag at ctr. Port Louis harbor on back.

COLLECTOR SERIES

BANK OF MAURITIUS

1978 ND ISSUE

CS1   ND (1978) 5-50 RUPEES   **ISSUE PRICE   MKT. VALUE**
#30-33 w/ovpt.: *SPECIMEN* and Maltese cross prefix serial #.   14.00   30.00

The United Mexican States located immediately south of the United States has an area of 759,529 sq. mi. (1,967,183 sq. km.) and a population of 84.4 million. Capital: Mexico City. The economy is based on agriculture, manufacturing and mining. Cotton, sugar, coffee and shrimp are exported.

Mexico was the site of highly advanced Indian civilizations 1,500 years before conquistador Hernando Cortes conquered the wealthy Aztec empire of Montezuma. 1519-1521, and founded a Spanish colony which lasted for nearly 300 years. During the Spanish period, Mexico, then called New Spain, stretched from Guatemala to the present states of Wyoming and California, its present northern boundary having been established by the secession of Texas during (1836) and the war of 1846-1848 with the United States.

Independence from Spain was declared by Father Miguel Hidalgo on Sept. 16, 1810, (Mexican Independence Day) and was achieved by General Agustin de Iturbide in 1821. Iturbide became emperor in 1822 but was deposed when a republic was established a year later. For more than half a century following the birth of the republic, the political scene of Mexico was characterized by turmoil which saw two emperors (including the unfortunate Maximilian), several dictators and an average of one new government every nine months passing swiftly from obscurity to oblivion. The land, social, economic and labor reforms promulgated by the Reform Constitution of Feb. 5, 1917 established the basis for a sustained economic development and participative democracy that have made Mexico one of the most politically stable countries of modern Latin America.

* * * This section has been renumbered. * * *

MONETARY SYSTEM:
1 Peso = 100 Centavos
1 Nuevo Peso = 1000 "old" Pesos, 1992-1996
1 Peso = 1 Nuevo Peso, 1996-

ESTADOS UNIDAS DE MEXICO

UNITED STATES OF MEXICO

BANCO DE MEXICO, S.A.

1948 ISSUE
#49, 51 and 52 sign. varieties. Printer: ABNC.

		VG	VF	UNC
49	**50 PESOS**			
(718A)	1948-72. Deep blue on m/c unpt. Portr. I. de Allende at l. Middle sign. title: *INTERVENTOR DE LA COM. NAC. BONCARIA.* Engraved dates. Back blue; Independence Monument at ctr.			
	a. 22.12.1948. Black series letters. Series: BM-BD.	3.00	6.00	15.00
	b. 23.11.1949. Series: BU-BX.	3.00	6.00	15.00
	c. 26.7.1950. Series: BY-CF.	3.00	5.00	12.50
	d. 27.12.1950. Series: CS-DH.	3.00	5.00	12.50
	e. 19.1.1953. Series: DK-DV.	2.00	4.00	11.00
	f. 10.2.1954. Series: DW-EH.	2.00	4.00	10.00
	g. 8.9.1954. Series: EI-FF.	2.00	4.00	10.00
	h. 11.1.1956. Series: FK-FV.	2.00	4.00	10.00
	i. 19.6.1957. Series: FW-GP.	2.00	4.00	10.00
	j. 20.8.1958. Series: HC-HR.	2.00	4.00	10.00
	k. 18.3.1959. Red series letters. Series: HS-IP.	2.00	4.00	10.00
	l. 20.5.1959. Series: IQ-JN.	2.00	4.00	10.00
	m. 25.1.1961. Series: JO-LB.	1.50	3.00	8.00
	n. 8.11.1961. Series: LC-AID.	1.50	3.00	8.00
	o. 24.4.1963. Series: AIE-BAP.	1.50	3.00	8.00
	p. 17.2.1965. Series: BAQ-BCD.	1.00	2.50	5.50
	q. 10.5.1967. Series: BCY-BEG.	1.00	2.50	5.00
	r. 19.11.1969 Series: BGK-BIC.	1.00	2.50	4.50
	s. 22.7.1970. Series: BIG-BKN.	1.00	2.50	4.50
	t. 27.6.1972. Series: BLI-BMG.	1.00	2.50	4.50
	u. 29.12.1972. Series: BNG-BRB.	1.00	2.00	4.00
	v. Specimen, punched hole cancelled.	—	—	125.00

51
(720B)
500 Pesos
1948-78. Black on m/c unpt. Portr. J. M. Morelos y Pavon at r. W/o "No" above serial #. Middle sign. title: *INTERVENTOR DE LA COM. NAC. BANCARIO*. Back green; Palace of Mining at ctr.

	VG	VF	UNC
a. 22.12.1948. Series: BA.	15.00	40.00	150.00
b. 27.12.1950. Series: CS-CT.	15.00	40.00	150.00
c. 3.12.1951. Series: DI-DJ.	15.00	40.00	150.00
d. 19.1.1953. Series: DK-DN.	12.00	25.00	60.00
e. 31.8.1955. Series: FG-FJ.	12.00	20.00	50.00
f. 11.1.1956. Series: FK-FL.	12.00	20.00	50.00
g. 19.6.1957. Series: FW-GB.	12.00	20.00	50.00
h. 20.8.1958. Series: HC-HH.	10.00	20.00	40.00
i. 18.3.1959. Series: HS-HX.	10.00	20.00	40.00
j. 20.5.1959. Series: IQ-IV.	10.00	20.00	40.00
k. 25.1.1961. Series: JO-JT.	10.00	20.00	40.00
l. 8.11.1961. Series: LC-MP.	10.00	20.00	40.00
m. 17.2.1965. Series: BAQ-BCN.	6.00	12.00	25.00
n. 24.3.1971. Series: BKD-BKT.	2.50	5.00	12.50
o. 27.6.1972. Series: BLI-BLT.	2.50	5.00	12.50
p. 29.12.1972. Series: BNG-BNP.	2.50	5.00	12.50
q. 18.7.1973. Series: BUY-BWB.	1.75	5.00	12.50
r. 2.8.1974. Series: BXV-BZI.	1.75	3.50	8.00
s. 18.2.1977. Series: BZJ-CCK.	1.00	3.50	7.50
t. 18.1.1978. Series: CCL-CDY.	1.00	3.50	7.50

52
(721B)
1000 Pesos
1948-77. Black on m/c unpt. Cuauhtemoc at r. Middle sign. title: *INTERVENTOR DE LA COM. NAC. BANCARIO*. Back brown; Chichen Itzfl pyramid at ctr.

	VG	VF	UNC
a. 22.12.1948. Series: BA.	25.00	45.00	150.00
b. 23.11.1949. Series: BU.	25.00	45.00	150.00
c. 27.12.1950. Series: CS.	25.00	45.00	125.00
d. 3.12.1951. Series: DI-DJ.	25.00	45.00	125.00
e. 19.1.1953. Series: DK-DL.	25.00	45.00	125.00
f. 31.8.1955. Series: FG-FH.	20.00	40.00	75.00
g. 11.1.1956. Series: FK; FL.	20.00	40.00	75.00
h. 19.6.1957. Series: FN-FX.	20.00	35.00	60.00
i. 20.8.1958. Series: HC-HE.	20.00	35.00	60.00
j. 18.3.1959. Series: HS-HU.	18.00	30.00	50.00
k. 20.5.1959. Series: IQ-IS.	18.00	30.00	50.00
l. 25.1.1961. Series: JO-JQ.	18.00	30.00	45.00
m. 8.11.1961. Series: LC-LV.	18.00	30.00	45.00
n. 17.2.1965. Series: BAQ-BCN.	7.00	15.00	30.00
o. 24.3.1971. Series: BKO-BKT.	2.00	4.00	10.00
p. 27.6.1972. Series: BLI-BLM.	2.00	4.50	12.00
q. 29.12.1972. Series: BNG-BNK.	2.00	4.50	12.00
r. 18.7.1973. Series: BUY-BWB.	2.00	4.50	12.00
s. 2.8.1974. Series: BXV-BYY.	2.00	4.50	12.00
t. 18.2.1977. Series: BZL-CBQ.	2.00	4.00	10.00

1950 Issue
#54 and 55 sign. varieties. Printer: ABNC.

54
(717C)
20 Pesos
1950-70. Black on m/c unpt. Portr. J. Ortiz de Dominguez at l. W/o "No" above serial #. Back olive-green; Federal Palace courtyard at ctr.

	VG	VF	UNC
a. 27.12.1950. Black series letters. Series: CS-CT.	1.10	3.00	9.00
b. 19.1.1953. Series: DK.	1.10	3.00	9.00
c. 10.2.1954. Red series letters. Series: DW.	1.10	2.50	8.50
d. 11.1.1956. Series: FK.	1.10	2.50	8.50
e. 19.6.1957. Series: FW.	1.10	2.50	8.00
f. 20.8.1958. Series: HC, HD.	1.10	2.50	8.00
g. 18.3.1959. Series: HS, HT.	1.10	2.00	7.00
h. 20.5.1959. Series: IQ, IR.	1.10	2.00	7.00
i. 25.1.1961. Series: JO, JP.	.75	1.50	6.00
j. 8.11.1961. Series: LC-LG.	.75	1.50	6.00
k. 24.4.1963. Series: AIE-AIH.	.50	1.25	5.00
l. 17.2.1965. Series: BAQ-BAV.	.50	1.25	5.00
m. 10.5.1967. Series: BCY-BDB.	.50	1.25	5.00
n. 27.8.1969. Series: BGA-BGB.	.50	1.25	5.00
o. 18.3.1970. Series: BID-BIF.	.50	1.25	5.00
p. 22.7.1970. Series: BIG-BIK.	.50	1.25	5.00
s. Specimen, punched hole cancelled.	—	—	125.00

55
(719A)
100 Pesos
1950-61. Brown on m/c unpt. Portr. M. Hidalgo at l. Middle sign. title: *INTERVENTOR DE LA COM. NAC. BANCARIA*. Engraved dates. Back olive-green; coin w/national seal at ctr.

	VG	VF	UNC
a. 27.12.1950. Black series letters. Series: CS-CZ.	6.00	10.00	25.00
b. 19.1.1953. Series: DK-DP.	3.50	7.00	15.00
c. 10.2.1954. Series: DW-DZ.	3.50	7.00	15.00
d. 8.9.1954. Series: EI-ET.	3.50	7.00	15.00
e. 11.1.1956. Series: FK-FV.	3.50	7.00	12.00
f. 19.6.1957. Series: FW-GH.	3.50	7.00	12.00
g. 20.8.1958. Series: HC-HR.	3.50	7.00	12.00
h. 18.3.1959. Series: HS-IH.	3.50	7.00	12.00
i. 20.5.1959. Series: IQ-JF.	3.50	7.00	12.00
j. 25.1.1961. Series: JO-KL.	3.50	7.00	12.00

1954 Issue

58
(716)
10 Pesos
1954-67. Black on m/c unpt. Portr. E. Ruiz de Valezquez at r. Text: *MEXICO D.F.* above series letters. Back brown; road to Guanajuato at ctr. Printer: ABNC.

	VG	VF	UNC
a. 10.2.1954. Series: DW, DX.	.50	1.00	7.00
b. 8.9.1954. Series: EI-EN.	.25	1.00	4.00
c. 19.6.1957. Series: FW, FX.	.60	2.50	8.00
d. 24.7.1957. Series: GQ.	.60	2.50	8.00
e. 20.8.1958. Series: HC-HF.	.25	1.50	5.00
f. 18.3.1959. Series: HS-HU.	.25	1.50	5.00
g. 20.5.1959. Series: IQ-IS.	.25	1.50	5.00
h. 25.1.1961. Series: JO-JT.	.25	1.00	4.00
i. 8.11.1961. Series: LC-LV.	.25	1.00	4.00
j. 24.4.1963. Series: AIE-AIT.	.25	1.00	4.00
k. 17.2.1965. Series: BAQ-BAX.	.25	1.00	4.00
l. 10.5.1967. Series: BCY-BDA.	.25	1.00	3.00
s. Specimen, punched hole cancelled.	—	—	150.00

1961 Issue

59
(712)
1 Peso
1957-70. Black on m/c unpt. Aztec calendar stone at ctr. Text: *MEXICO D.F.* added above date at lower l. Back red. Independence monument at ctr.

	VG	VF	UNC
a. 19.6.1957. Series: FW-GF.	.10	1.00	3.00
b. 24.7.1957. Series: GH-GR. (Do not exist).	—	—	—
c. 4.12.1957. Series: GS-HB.	.10	.75	2.50
d. 20.8.1958. Series: HC-HL.	.10	.75	2.50
e. 18.3.1959. Series: HS-IB.	.10	.50	2.00
f. 20.5.1959. Series: IQ-IZ.	.10	.50	2.00
g. 25.1.1961. Series: JO-KC.	.10	.25	1.50
h. 8.11.1961. Series: LC-LD.	.10	.25	1.50
i. 9.6.1965. Series: BCO-BCX.	.10	.25	1.75
j. 10.5.1967. Series: BCY-BEB.	.10	.25	1.25
k. 27.8.1969. Series: BGA-BGJ.	.10	.25	1.25
l. 22.7.1970. Series: BIG-BIP.	.10	.20	1.00

60
(714A)
5 Pesos
1957-70. Black on m/c unpt. Portr. G. Faure at ctr. Text: *MEXICO D.F.* before date. Back gray; Independence Monument at ctr.

	VG	VF	UNC
a. 19.6.1957. Series: FW, FX.	.40	2.00	6.00
b. 24.7.1957. Series: GQ, GR.	.40	2.00	6.00
c. 20.8.1958. Series: HC-HJ.	.25	1.50	5.00
d. 18.3.1959. Series: HS-HV.	.25	1.50	5.00
e. 20.5.1959. Series: IQ-IT.	.25	1.50	5.00
f. 25.1.1961. Series: JO-JV.	.15	.75	3.00
g. 8.11.1961. Series: LC-MP.	.15	.75	3.00
h. 24.4.1963. Series: AIE-AJJ.	.15	.50	2.00
i. 19.11.1969. Series: BGK-BGT.	.15	.50	2.00
j. 22.7.1970. Series: BIG-BII.	.15	.50	2.00

61 **100 PESOS**
(719B)   1961-73. Brown on m/c unpt. Like #55 but series letters below serial #. Printer: ABNC.

		VG	VF	UNC
a.	8.11.1961. Red series letters. Series: LN-YL, AAP-ADW.	2.00	5.00	10.00
b.	24.4.1963. Series: AIS-ASX.	2.00	5.00	10.00
c.	17.2.1965. Series: BAQ-BBU.	2.00	5.00	10.00
d.	10.5.1967. Series: BDE-BFI.	2.00	5.00	10.00
e.	22.7.1970. Series: BIG-BKO.	1.00	3.00	7.50
f.	24.3.1971. Series: BKP-BLH.	1.00	3.00	7.50
g.	27.6.1972. Series: BLP-BMO.	2.00	5.00	10.00
h.	29.12.1972. Series: BPI-BUM.	1.00	2.00	7.50
i.	18.7.1973. Series: BVG-BXS.	1.00	2.00	7.50

1969-74 ISSUE
#62-66 bank title w/*S.A.* Sign. varieties. Printer: BdM.

62 **5 PESOS**
(723)   1969-72. Black on m/c unpt. J. Ortiz de Dominguez at r. Yucca plant, aqueduct, village of Queretaro and national arms on back.

		VG	VF	UNC
a.	3.12.1969.	.15	.25	2.00
b.	27.10.1971.	.15	.25	1.00
c.	27.6.1972.	.15	.25	.75

63 **10 PESOS**
(724)   1969-77. Dk. green and m/c. Bell at l., M. Hidalgo y Castilla at r. National arms and Dolores Cathedral on back.

		VG	VF	UNC
a.	16.9.1969.	.25	.50	4,00
b.	3.12.1969.	.15	.25	1.50
c.	22.7.1970.	.15	.25	1.00
d.	3.2.1971.	.15	.25	1.00
e.	29.12.1972.	.15	.25	1.00
f.	18.7.1973.	.10	.20	.50
g.	16.10.1974.	.10	.20	.50
h.	15.5.1975.	.10	.20	.50
i.	18.2.1977.	.10	.20	.50

64 **20 PESOS**
(725)   1972-77. Red and black on m/c unpt. J. Morelos y Pavon at r. w/bldg. in background. Pyramid of Quetzalcoatl on back.

		VG	VF	UNC
a.	29.12.1972.	.25	.50	2.00
b.	18.7.1973.	.10	.20	.50
c.	8.7.1976.	.10	.20	.50
d.	8.7.1977.	.10	.20	.50

65 **50 PESOS**
(726)   1973; 1976. Blue on m/c unpt. Gov't palace at l., B. Juárez at r. Red and black series letters and serial #. Temple and Aztec god on back.

		VG	VF	UNC
a.	18.7.1973.	.30	1.00	4.00
b.	8.7.1976.	.30	1.00	2.00

66 **100 PESOS**
(727)   30.5.1974. Purple on m/c unpt. V. Carranza at l., "La Trinchera" painting at ctr. Red and black series letters and serial #. Stone figure on back.

	VG	VF	UNC
	.30	1.00	3.00

1978-80 ISSUE
#67-71 bank title w/*S.A.* Printer: BdM.

67 **50 PESOS**
(726A)   1978; 1979. Blue on m/c unpt. Like #65 but only red series letters and a black serial #.

		VG	VF	UNC
a.	5.7.1978.	.30	1.00	2.00
b.	17.5.1979.	.20	.40	1.00

68 **100 PESOS**
(727A)   1978; 1979. Purple on m/c unpt. Like #66 but only red series letters and a black serial #.

		VG	VF	UNC
a.	5.7.1978.	.20	.60	2.00
b.	17.5.1979.	.20	.40	1.00

69
(728) **500 Pesos**
29.6.1979. Black on dk. olive-green and m/c unpt. F. I. Madero at l. and as wmk. Aztec calendar stone on back.

	VG	VF	UNC
	1.00	3.00	9.00

70
(729) **1000 Pesos**
1978-79. Dk. brown and brown on m/c unpt. J. de Asbaje at r. and as wmk. Santo Domingo plaza at l. ctr. on back.

	VG	VF	UNC
a. 5.7.1978.	2.00	4.50	15.00
b. 17.5.1979.	1.00	4.00	10.00
c. 29.6.1979.	1.00	3.00	9.00

71
(730) **5000 Pesos**
25.3.1980. Red and m/c unpt. on blue paper. Cadets at l. ctr., one of them as wmk. Chapultepec castle on back.

	VG	VF	UNC
	4.00	10.00	35.00

72
(730A) **10,000 Pesos**
18.1.1978. Purple on m/c unpt. Portr. M. Romero at l. Back green; National palace at ctr. Printer: ABNC. Series CCL-CES.

	VG	VF	UNC
	5.00	20.00	60.00

1981 ISSUE
#73-78 bank title w/*S.A.* W/4 sign. and sign. varieties. Printer: BdM.

73
(731) **50 Pesos**
27.1.1981. Blue on m/c unpt. Similar to #67 but 4 sign.

	VG	VF	UNC
	.10	.20	.50

74
(732) **100 Pesos**
1981-82. Purple on m/c unpt. Similar to #68 but 4 sign.

	VG	VF	UNC
a. 27.1.1981.	.10	.20	.50
b. 3.9.1981.	.10	.20	.50
c. 25.3.1982.	.10	.20	.50

75
(733) **500 Pesos**
1981-82. Green on m/c unpt. Similar to #69 but 4 sign. and narrower serial #.

	VG	VF	UNC
a. 27.1.1981.	.25	1.00	4.50
b. 25.3.1982.	.25	1.00	4.00

76
(734) **1000 Pesos**
1981-82. Dk. brown and brown on m/c unpt. Similar to #70 but 4 sign. and narrower serial #.

	VG	VF	UNC
a. Engraved bldgs. on back. 27.1.1981.	.50	2.00	8.00
b. Litho. bldgs. on back. 27.1.1981.	.50	2.00	8.00
c. 3.9.1981.	.50	2.00	8.00
d. 25.3.1982.	.50	2.00	8.00

77
(735) **5000 Pesos**
1981-82. Red and black on m/c unpt., lt. blue paper. Similar to #71 but 4 sign. and narrower serial #.

	VG	VF	UNC
a. 27.1.1981.	1.00	5.00	25.00
b. 25.3.1982.	1.00	5.00	25.00

78 **10,000 PESOS**
(736)
1981-82. Blue-black, brown and deep blue-green on grayish green
and m/c unpt. Gen. Lazaro Cardenas at r. and as wmk. Back dk. green,
red and blue; Coyolxauhqui stone carving at ctr.

		VG	VF	UNC
a.	8.12.1981.	2.50	7.50	40.00
b.	25.3.1982.	2.00	10.00	30.00
c.	30.9.1982.	2.00	6.00	30.00

1983-84 ISSUES
#79-84 *S.A.* removed from bank title. W/4 sign. Printer: BdM.

79 **500 PESOS**
(737)
1983-84. Similar to #75 but silk threads and w/o wmk. Design
continued over wmk. area on both sides.

		VG	VF	UNC
a.	14.3.1983.	.20	.50	2.50
b.	7.8.1984.	.20	.50	2.50

80 **1000 PESOS**
(738)
13.5.1983; 7.8.1984. Like #76 but *S.A.* removed from title.

VG	VF	UNC
1.00	2.50	6.00

81 **1000 PESOS**
(739)
30.10.1984. Similar to #80 but rayed quill pen printed over wmk. area
at l.

	VG	VF	UNC
	.35	.85	2.50

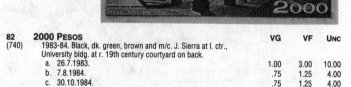

82 **2000 PESOS**
(740)
1983-84. Black, dk. green, brown and m/c. J. Sierra at l. ctr.,
University bldg. at r. 19th century courtyard on back.

		VG	VF	UNC
a.	26.7.1983.	1.00	3.00	10.00
b.	7.8.1984.	.75	1.25	4.00
c.	30.10.1984.	.75	1.25	4.00

83 **5000 PESOS**
(741)
13.5.1983; 26.7.1983; 5.12.1983. Like #77 but *S.A.* removed from
title.

VG	VF	UNC
3.00	5.00	9.00

84 **10,000 PESOS**
(742)
1983-85. Similar to #78 but *S.A.* removed from bank title.

		VG	VF	UNC
a.	13.5.1983.	2.00	4.50	12.50
b.	5.12.1983.	2.00	4.50	12.50
c.	Red and dk. blue serial #. 26.7.1983.	2.00	4.50	12.50
d.	Green and blue serial #. 26.7.1983.	2.00	4.00	10.00
e.	19.7.1985.	2.00	4.00	10.00

1985 ISSUES
#85-94 w/3 sign. *S.A.* removed from bank title. Printer: BdM.

85 **1000 PESOS**
(743)
19.7.1985, Like #81.

VG	VF	UNC
.35	.65	2.00

86   **2000 Pesos**
(744)   1985-89. Like #82.

		VG	VF	UNC
a.	W/*SANTANA* at lower l. 19.7.1985; 24.2.1987.	.75	1.25	3.00
b.	W/o *SANTANA*. 28.3.1989.	.75	1.25	1.50

87   **5000 Pesos**
(745)   19.7.1985. Red on m/c unpt. Blue tint paper. Like #83.

VG	VF	UNC
1.75	2.25	7.50

88   **5000 Pesos**
(746)   1985-89. Purple and brown-orange on m/c unpt. Like #87 but design continued over wmk. area. W/o wmk.

		VG	VF	UNC
a.	W/*SANTANA* vertically at lower l. 19.7.1985; 24.2.1987.	1.75	2.50	5.00
b.	W/o *SANTANA*. 28.3.1989.	1.75	2.50	3.00

89   **10,000 Pesos**
(747)   19.7.1985; 24.2.1987. Like #84.

VG	VF	UNC
2.00	5.00	12.00

90   **10,000 Pesos**
(748)   1987-91. Deep blue-black on brown and blue-green unpt. Similar to #89 but wmk. area filled in.

		VG	VF	UNC
a.	W/*SANTANA* at lower l. under refinery design. 24.2.1987.	1.50	3.00	9.00
b.	W/o *SANTANA* 1.2.1988	1.50	2.50	7.00
c.	28.3.1989; 16.5.1991	1.50	2.50	7.00

91   **20,000 Pesos**
(749)   1.2.1988; 28.3.1989. Blue-black on blue and pink unpt. Similar to #90 but design continued over wmk. area.

VF	VF	UNC
3.50	5.00	10.00

92   **20,000 Pesos**
(750)   19.7.1985; 24.2.1987; 27.8.1987. Deep blue on blue and m/c unpt. Fortress above coastal cliffs at ctr. Don A. Quintana Roo at r. and as wmk. Artwork on back.

VG	VF	UNC
4.00	7.00	20.00

93   **50,000 Pesos**
(751)   1986-90. Purple and m/c. Cuauhtémoc at r. and as wmk. Aztec and Spaniard fighting at l. ctr. on back.

		VF	VF	UNC
a.	12.5.1986; 24.2.1987; 27.8.1987; 1.2.1988.	7.50	13.50	30.00
b.	28.3.1989; 10.1.1990; 20.12.1990.	7.00	12.50	25.00

94   **100,000 Pesos**
(752)   1988-1991. Black and maroon on m/c unpt. P. E. Calles at l. and as wmk. Banco de Mexico at ctr. Deer, cactus lake and mountain on back.

		VG	VF	UNC
a.	4.1.1988.	15.00	22.50	55.00
b.	2.9.1991.	13.50	20.00	45.00

1992 FIRST ISSUE

Nuevos Pesos System
#95-98 similar to #91-94. 3 sign. and sign. varieties. Printer: BdM.

95	10 NUEVOS PESOS	VG	VF	UNC
(753)	31.7.1992. Similar to #91. Series A-Y.	FV	FV	5.00

96	20 NUEVOS PESOS	VG	VF	UNC
(754)	31.7.1992. Similar to #92. Series A-Q.	FV	FV	10.00

97	50 NUEVOS PESOS	VG	VF	UNC
(755)	31.7.1992. Similar to #93. Series A-P.	FV	FV	22.50

98	100 NUEVOS PESOS	VG	VF	UNC
(756)	31.7.1992. Similar to #94. Series A-Q.	FV	FV	45.00

1992 (1994) SECOND ISSUE

#99-104 printer: BdM.

99	10 NUEVOS PESOS	VG	VF	UNC
(757)	10.12.1992 (1994). Deep blue-green and blue-black on m/c unpt. E. Zapata at r., hands holding of corn at ctr. Machinery at lower l., statue of Zapata horseback by peasant at ctr. r., bldg. in background. Series A-T.	FV	FV	3.50

100	20 NUEVOS PESOS	VG	VF	UNC
(758)	10.12.1992 (1994). Purple, blue and violet on m/c unpt. B. Juárez at r., heraldic eagle at ctr. Monument, statues "Hemicicio a Juárez" on back. Series A-T.	FV	FV	6.50

101	50 NUEVOS PESOS	VG	VF	UNC
(759)	10.12.1992 (1994). Violet, red, and black on m/c unpt. J. M. Morelos at r., crossed cannons on outlined bow and arrow below his flag at l. ctr. Butterflies at l., boat fishermen at ctr. on back. Series A-AF.	FV	FV	15.00

102
(760) **100 Nuevos Pesos**
10.12.1992 (1994). Red and brown on m/c unpt. Nezahualcóyoti at r., and as wmk., Aztec figure at ctr. Xochipilli on back. Series A-V.

VG	VF	Unc
FV	FV	25.00

103
(761) **200 Nuevos Pesos**
10.12.1992 (1994). Dk. olive-green, dk. brown and olive-brown on m/c unpt. J. de Asbaje at r., and as wmk., open book and quill pen at ctr. Temple de San Jerónimo on back. Series A-E.

VG	VF	Unc
FV	FV	45.00

104
(762) **500 Nuevos Pesos**
10.12.1992 (1994). Red-brown, deep purple and dk. brown-violet on m/c unpt. I. Zaragoza at ctr. r. and as wmk., Battle of Puebla at l. ctr. Cathedral at Puebla at ctr. on back. Series A-C.

VG	VF	Unc
FV	FV	110.00

1994; 1995 (1996) Issue

#105-116 similar to #99-104 except *NUEVOS* and *PAGARA A LA VISTA AL PORTADOR* are omitted. 2 sign. Printer: BdM.

105
(763) **10 Pesos**
6.5.1994 (1996). Deep blue-green and blue-black on m/c unpt. Similar to #99.

VG	VF	Unc
FV	FV	3.50

106
(764) **20 Pesos**
6.5.1994 (1996). Purple, violet and blue on m/c unpt. Similarr to #100.

VG	VF	Unc
FV	FV	6.50

107
(765) **50 Pesos**
6.5.1994 (1996). Violet and red-violet on m/c unpt. Similar to #101.

VG	VF	Unc
FV	FV	15.00

108
(766) **100 Pesos**
6.5.1994 (1996). Red and brown-orange on m/c unpt. Similar to #102.

VG	VF	Unc
FV	FV	28.50

109
(767) **200 Pesos**
7.2.1995 (1996). Dk. olive-green, dk. brown and olive-brown on m/c unpt. Similar to #103. Series A-.

VG	VF	Unc
FV	FV	50.00

110
(768) **500 Pesos**
7.2.1995 (1996). Red-brown, deep purple and dk. brown-violet on m/c unpt. Similar to #104. Series A-.

VG	VF	Unc
FV	FV	120.00

MOLDOVA

UKRAINE
TRANSDNIESTRA
ROMANIA
Black Sea

Romanian, until 1940 The Republic of Moldova (formerly the Moldavian S.S.R.) is bordered in the east and south by the Ukraine and on the west by Romania. It has an area of 13,000 sq. mi. (33,700 sq. km.) and a population of 4.4 million. (This includes the area and people of Transdniestria, an area in dispute.) Fish, agricultural products including canned goods, steel, concrete and dairy products are leading industries.

The Moldavian A.S.S.R. was created on Oct. 12, 1924, as part of the Ukrainian S.S.R., a Soviet protest against the recovery of Bessarabia by Romania. In 1940 Romania yielded to a Soviet ultimatum and ceded Bessarabia to the U.S.S.R. and the Soviet government formed a Moldavian S.S.R. comprised of the major part of Bessarabia. In June 1941, the Romanians allied with Germany reincorporated the whole of Bessarabia into Romania. Soviet armies reconquered it late in 1944 restoring the Moldavian S.S.R. A new constitution was adopted in April 1978. A declaration of republican sovereignty was adopted in June 1990 and the area was renamed Moldova, an independent republic, declared in Aug. 1991. In Dec. 1991 Moldova became a member of the Commonwealth of Independent States. Separatists and government forces clashed in 1992. A joint declaration by Russian and Moldavian presidents on July 3, 1992 envisaged a demarcation line held by neutral forces and withdrawal of the Russian army from Transdniestria, which had developed into a self-styled republic.

REPUBLIC

TREASURY

RUBLE CONTROL COUPONS

			VG	VF	UNC
A11	**20 RUBLE**				
	1992.				
	a. Full sheet.		—	.50	1.00
	b. Coupon.		—	—	.10

BANCA NATIONALA A MOLDOVEI

1992; 1993 "CUPON" ISSUE
#1-4 arms at l. Castle at r. on back. Wmk: Wavy lines.

			VG	VF	UNC
1	**50 CUPON**				
	1992. Gray-green on gray unpt.		.10	.40	2.00

			VG	VF	UNC
2	**200 CUPON**				
	1992. Blue-black on gray unpt. Back purple on lilac unpt.		.20	.65	5.00

			VG	VF	UNC
3	**1000 CUPON**				
	1993. Brown on pale blue-green and ochre unpt. Bank monogram at upper l.		.25	.75	3.00

			VG	VF	UNC
4	**5000 CUPON**				
	1993. Pale brown-violet, orange and pale olive-green unpt. Bank monogram at upper l. Back pale brown-violet on pale brown-orange unpt.		.45	1.35	6.00

1992 (1993) ISSUE
Currency Reform
1 Leu = 1000 Cupon, 1993-
#5-7 Kg. Stefan at l., arms at upper ctr. r. Cetatea Soroca Castle at ctr. r. on back.

			VG	VF	UNC
5	**1 LEU**				
	1992 (1993). Brown and dk. olive-green on ochre unpt.		FV	.45	2.00

			VG	VF	UNC
6	**5 LEI**				
	1992 (1993). Purple on lt. blue and ochre unpt.		FV	1.00	5.50

			VG	VF	UNC
7	**10 LEI**				
	1992 (1993). Red brown and olive-green on pale orange unpt.		FV	1.75	8.00

1992; 1994 ISSUE

#8-16 Kg. Stefan at l. and as wmk., arms at upper ctr. r.
#8-14 bank monogram at upper r.

8	**1 LEU**	VG	VF	UNC
	1994; 1995. Brown on ochre and pale yellow-green on m/c unpt. Monastary at Capriana at ctr. r. on back. Monastary at Hërbovet at ctr. r. on back.	FV	FV	1.50

9	**5 LEI**	VG	VF	UNC
	1994; 1995. Grayish blue-green on lilac and pale aqua. Basillica of St. Dumitrudin Orhei at ctr. r. on back.	FV	FV	3.00

10	**10 LEI**	VG	VF	UNC
	1994; 1995. Red-brown on pale blue and m/c unpt. Monastary at Hîrjauca at ctr. r. on back.	FV	FV	5.50

13	**20 LEI**	VG	VF	UNC
	1992 (1993); 1994; 1995. Blue-green on lt. green, aqua and ochre. Back dk. green and blue-green on lt. green unpt.	FV	2.75	10.00
14	**50 LEI**			
	1992 (1994); 1994. Red violet on lilac and m/c unpt. Monastary at Hîrbovet at ctr. r. on back.	FV	FV	18.50
15	**100 LEI**			
	1992 (1995).	FV	FV	35.00
16	**200 LEI**			
	1992 (1995).	FV	FV	65.00

MONGOLIA

The State of Mongolia (formerly the Mongolian Peoples Republic), a landlocked country in central Asia between the Soviet Union and the Peoples Republic of China, has an area of 604,247 sq. mi. (1,565,000 060 km.) and a population of 2.26 million. Capital: Ulan Bator. Animal herds and flocks are the chief economic asset. Wool, cattle, butter, meat and hides are exported.

Mongolia (often referred to as Outer Mongolia), one of the world's oldest countries, attained its greatest power in the 13th century when Genghis Khan and his successors conquered all of China and extended their influence westward as far as Hungary and Poland. The empire dissolved in later centuries and in 1691 was brought under suzerainty of the Manchus, who had conquered China in 1644. After the Chinese republican movement led by Sun Yat-sen overthrew the Manchus and set up the Chinese Republic in 1911. Mongolia, with the support of Russia, proclaimed its independence from China, on March 13, 1921, when the Provisional Peoples Government was established. Later, on Nov. 26, 1924, the government proclaimed the Mongolian Peoples Republic. Opposition to the communist party developed in late 1989 and after demonstrations and hunger strikes the Politburo resigned on Mar. 12, 1990 and the new State of Mongolia was organized.

RULERS:

Chinese to 1921

MONETARY SYSTEM:

1 Tugrik (Tukhrik) = 100 Mongo

STATE

УЛСЫН БАНК

STATE BANK

1966 ISSUE

#35-41 Socialist arms at upper l.
#36-41 portr. Sukhe-Bataar at r.

35	**1 TUGRIK**	VG	VF	UNC
	1966. Brown. No portr.	.20	.50	1.00
36	**3 TUGRIK**			
	1966. Green.	.25	.60	1.25
37	**5 TUGRIK**			
	1966. Blue.	.25	.60	1.25
38	**10 TUGRIK**			
	1966. Red-brown.	.25	.75	1.35
39	**25 TUGRIK**			
	1966. Brown-violet.	.50	1.00	1.50
40	**50 TUGRIK**			
	1966. Green. Govt. bldg. and Ulan-Bataar on back.	1.00	2.50	3.00

41	**100 TUGRIK**	VG	VF	UNC
	1966. Brown. Back like #40.	2.00	4.00	7.50

1981-83 ISSUE

#42-45 and 47-48 like #36-41.
#43-45, #47-48 portr. Sukhe-Bataar at r.

42	1 TUGRIK		VG	VF	UNC
	1983. Brown.		FV	FV	.65

43	3 TUGRIK		VG	VF	UNC
	1983. Green.		FV	FV	.85

44	5 TUGRIK		VG	VF	UNC
	1981. Blue-green on blue-gray and pale green unpt.		FV	FV	1.00

45	10 TUGRIK		VG	VF	UNC
	1981. Red-brown on pale orange and blue-green unpt.		FV	FV	1.75

46	20 TUGRIK		VG	VF	UNC
	1981. Yellow-green. Sukhe-Bataar at ctr. Power station at Ulan-Bataar at ctr on back.		FV	FV	2.00

47	50 TUGRIK		VG	VF	UNC
	1981. Dk. green.		FV	FV	4.00

48	100 TUGRIK		VF	VF	UNC
	1981. Dk. brown on ochre and blue-green unpt.		FV	FV	8.00

МОНГОЛ БАНК

MONGOL BANK

1993 ND ISSUE

#49-51 "Soemba" arms at upper ctr.
#52-60 wmk: Genghis Khan.
#53-57 youthful portr. Suhe-Bator at l., "Soemba" arms at ctr. Horses grazing in mountainous landscape at ctr. r. on back.
#58-61 Genghis Khan at l., "Soemba" arms at ctr. Ox drawn yurte, village at ctr. r. on back.

#49   #50   #51

49   10 MONGO
ND (1993). Red-violet on pale red orange. 2 archers at lower ctr. on face and back.

VG	VF	UNC
FV	FV	.50

50   20 MONGO
ND (1993). Brown on ochre and yellow-brown unpt. 2 atheletes at lower ctr. on face and back.

VG	VF	UNC
FV	FV	.50

51   50 MONGO
ND (1993). Greenish-black on blue and pale green unpt. 2 horseman at lower ctr. on face and back.

VG	VF	UNC
FV	FV	.50

52   1 TUGRIK
ND (1993). Dull olive-green andd brown-orange on ochre unpt. Chinze at l. "Soemba" arms at ctr. r. on back.

VG	VF	UNC
FV	FV	.85

53   5 TUGRIK
ND (1993). Red-orange, ochre and brown on m/c unpt.

VG	VF	UNC
FV	FV	1.00

54   10 TUGRIK
ND (1993). Green, blue and lt. green on m/c unpt.

VG	VF	UNC
FV	FV	1.00

55   20 TUGRIK
ND (1993). Violet, orange and red on m/c unpt.

VG	VF	UNC
FV	FV	1.25

56   50 TUGRIK
ND (1993). Dk. brown on m/c unpt.

VG	VF	UNC
FV	FV	1.25

57   100 TUGRIK
ND (1993). Purple, red-brown and dk. blue on m/c unpt.

VG	VF	UNC
FV	FV	1.75

58   500 TUGRIK
ND (1993). Dk. green, brown and yellow-green on m/c unpt.

VG	VF	UNC
FV	FV	4.50

59   1000 TUGRIK
ND (1993). Blue-gray, brown and blue on m/c unpt.

VG	VF	UNC
FV	FV	8.50

60   5000 TUGRIK
ND (1994). Purple, brown and red on m/c unpt. Bldg., fountain on back.

	VG	VF	UNC
	FV	FV	16.50

61   10,000 TUGRIK
ND (1996). Dk. olive-green and orange on m/c unpt. Lg. bldg., tree, people on back.

	VG	VF	UNC
	FV	FV	32.50

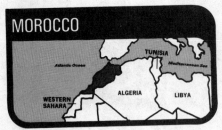

The Kingdom of Morocco situated on the northwest corner of Africa south of Spain, has an area of 172,413 sq. mi. (712,550 sq. km.) and a population of 25.7 million. Capital: Rabat. The economy is essentially agricultural. Phosphates, fresh and preserved vegetables, canned fish, and raw material are exported.

Morocco's strategic position at the gateway to western Europe has been the principal determinant of its violent, frequently unfortunate history. Time and again the fertile plain between the rugged Atlas Mountains and the sea has echoed the battle's trumpet as Phoenicians, Romans, Vandals, Visigoths, Byzantine Greeks and Islamic Arabs successively conquered and occupied the land. Modern Morocco is a remnant of an early empire formed by the Arabs at the close of the 7th century which encompassed all of northwest Africa and most of the Iberian Peninsula. During the 17th and 18th centuries, while under the control of native dynasties, it was the headquarters of the famous Sale pirates. Morocco's strategic position involved it in the competition of 19th century European powers for political influence in Africa, and resulted in the division of Morocco into French and Spanish spheres of interest which were established as protectorates in 1912. Morocco became independent on March 2, 1956, after France agreed to end its protectorate. Spain signed similar agreements on April 7 of the same year.

RULERS:
Muhammad V, AH1346-1380/1927-1961AD
Hassan II, AH1380- /1961- AD

MONETARY SYSTEM:
1 Dirham = 100 Francs, 1921-1974
1 Dirham = 100 Santimat, 1974-

KINGDOM

BANQUE DU MAROC
Established June 30, 1959

1960 (ND); 1965 ISSUE
#53-55 wmk: Lion's head.

		VG	VF	UNC
53	**5 DIRHAMS**			
	ND; 1965-69. M/c. Kg. Muhammad V wearing a fez at r. Harvesting on back. 6 sign. varieties.			
	a. ND(1960).	2.50	8.00	35.00
	b. 1965/AH1384; 1966/AH1386.	1.50	6.00	30.00
	c. 1968/AH1387; 1969/AH1389.	1.50	5.00	27.50

		VG	VF	UNC
54	**10 DIRHAMS**			
	ND; 1965-69. M/c. Kg. Muhammad V wearing a fez at l. Orange picking on back. 5 sign. varieties.			
	a. ND.	3.00	10.00	45.00
	b. 1965/AH1384.	2.00	7.50	35.00
	c. 1968/AH1387; 1969/AH1389.	2.00	6.00	30.00

		VG	VF	UNC
55	**50 DIRHAMS**			
	1965-69. M/c. Kg. Hassan II at r. Miners st work on back. 4 sign. varieties.			
	a. 1965/AH1385; 1966/AH1386.	15.00	60.00	300.00
	b. 1968/AH1387; 1969/AH1389.	13.50	50.00	250.00

1970 ISSUE
#56-59 Kg. Hassan II at l. and as wmk. Printer: TDLR.

		VG	VF	UNC
56	**5 DIRHAMS**			
	1970/AH1390. Purple. Castle at ctr. Industrial processing on back.	FV	1.50	5.00

		VG	VF	UNC
57	**10 DIRHAMS**			
	1970/AH1390; 1985/AH1405. Brown. Villa at ctr. Processing oranges on back.	FV	2.00	5.50
58	**50 DIRHAMS**			
	1970/AH1390; 1985/AH1405. Green. City at ctr. Dam on back.	FV	12.00	20.00

59 100 DIRHAMS
1970/AH1390; 1985/AH1405. Brown, blue and m/c. Bldg. at ctr. Oil
refinery on back.

	VG	VF	UNC
	FV	20.00	30.00

BANK AL-MAGHRIB

1987 ISSUE
#60-62 Kg. Hassan II facing at r. and as wmk. 2 sign. varieties.

60 10 DIRHAMS
1987/AH1407. Red-brown, red and m/c. Musical instrument and pillar
at l. ctr. on back.

	VG	VF	UNC
	FV	FV	6.50

61 50 DIRHAMS
1987/AH1407. Green and m/c. Mounted militia charging, flowers at
ctr. on back.

	VG	VF	UNC
	FV	10.00	20.00

62 100 DIRHAMS
1987/AH1407. Brown and m/c. Demonstration on back.

	VG	VF	UNC
	FV	FV	27.50

1991 ISSUE
#63-66 older bust of Kg. Hassan II at r. facing half l. Wmk: Kg. facing. 2 sign. varieties.

63 10 DIRHAMS
1987/AH407 (ca.1991). Brown-violet and purple on m/c unpt. Back
like #60, but diff. colors of unpt.

	VG	VF	UNC
	FV	FV	3.00

64 50 DIRHAMS
1987/AH1407 (ca.1991). Green and m/c. Back like #61.

	FV	FV	10.00

65 100 DIRHAMS
1987/AH1407 (ca.1991). Brown, blue and m/c. Back like #62.

	FV	FV	18.50

66 200 DIRHAMS
1987/AH1407 (ca.1991). Blue-violet, blue and m/c. Mausoleum of Kg.
Muhammad V at ctr. sailboat, shell and coral on back.

	VG	VF	UNC
	FV	FV	35.00

1996 ISSUE
67 20 DIRHAMS
1996. M/c. Kg. Hassan II at l., mosque at ctr. Fountain on back.

	VG	VF	UNC
	FV	FV	5.50

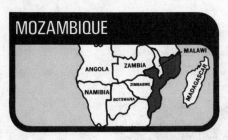

The People's Republic of Mozambique, a former overseas province of Portugal stretching for 1,430 miles (2,301 km.) along the southeast coast of Africa, has an area of 309,494 sq. mi. (783,030 sq. km.) and a population of 16.1 million, 99 percent of whom are native Africans of the Bantu tribes. Capital: Maputo. Agriculture is the chief industry. Cashew nuts, cotton, sugar, copra and tea are exported.

Vasco da Gama explored all the coast of Mozambique in 1498 and found Arab trading posts already along the coast. Portuguese settlement dates from the establishment of the trading post of Mozambique in 1505. Within five years Portugal absorbed all the former Arab sultanates along the east African coast. The area was organized as a colony in 1907 and became an overseas province in 1952. In Sept. of 1974, after more than a decade of guerrilla warfare with the forces of the Mozambique Liberation Front, Portugal agreed to the independence of Mozambique, effective June 25, 1975.

RULERS:
Portuguese to 1975

MONETARY SYSTEM:
1 Escudo = 100 Centavos, 1907-1975

PORTUGUESE INFLUENCE

BANCO NACIONAL ULTRAMARINO

MOZAMBIQUE BRANCH

1961-67 ISSUE
Escudo System
#109 and 110 printer: BWC.

109	100 ESCUDOS	VG	VF	UNC
	27.3.1961. Green on m/c unpt. Portr. A. de Ornelas at r., arms at upper ctr. Bank steamship seal at l. on back.			
	a. Wmk: Arms.	1.50	3.50	8.00
	b. W/o wmk.	1.00	3.00	7.00

110	500 ESCUDOS	VG	VF	UNC
	22.3.1967. Brown-violet on m/c unpt. Portr. C. Xavier at r., arms at upper ctr.	4.00	12.00	30.00

1970 ISSUE
Sign. varieties.

111	50 ESCUDOS	VG	VF	UNC
	27.10.1970. Black on m/c unpt. J. de Azevedo Coutinho at l. ctr., arms at upper ctr. r. Bank green; bank steamship seal at l. Wmk: Arms.	1.00	3.00	5.00

FIRST 1972 ISSUE

112	1000 ESCUDOS	VG	VF	UNC
	16.5.1972. Black-blue on m/c unpt. Kg. Afonso V at r., arms at upper ctr. Allegorical woman w/ships at l. on back, bank steamship seal at upper ctr. 3 sign. varieties.	10.00	20.00	75.00

SECOND 1972 ISSUE

113	100 ESCUDOS	VG	VF	UNC
	23.5.1972. Blue on m/c unpt. G. Coutinho and S. Cabral at l. ctr. Surveyor at ctr. on back. Wmk: Coutinho.	2.00	4.00	10.00

114	500 ESCUDOS	VG	VF	UNC
	23.5.1972. Violet on m/c unpt. G. Coutinho at l. ctr. and as wmk. Cabral and airplane on back.	5.00	15.00	40.00

115 1000 ESCUDOS

	VG	VF	UNC
23.5.1972. Green on m/c unpt. Like #114. 2 men in cockpit of airplane on back.	10.00	20.00	60.00

PEOPLES REPUBLIC

BANCO DE MOÇAMBIQUE

1976 PROVISIONAL ISSUE
#116-119 black ovpt. of new bank name.

116 50 ESCUDOS

	VG	VF	UNC
ND (1976 - old date 27.10.1970). Black on m/c unpt. Ovpt. on #111.	.10	.20	.50

117 100 ESCUDOS

	VG	VF	UNC
ND (1976 - old date 27.3.1961). Green on m/c unpt. Ovpt. on #109.	.10	.20	.50

118 500 ESCUDOS

	VG	VF	UNC
ND (1976 - old date 22.3.1967). Brown-violet on m/c unpt. Ovpt. on #110.	.15	.40	1.00

119 1000 ESCUDOS

	VG	VF	UNC
ND (1976 - old date 23.5.1972). Green on m/c unpt. Ovpt. on #115.	.25	1.00	3.00

1976 ISSUE
Metica System
#120-124 Pres. S. Machel at l. ctr. Printer: TDLR.
NOTE: #120-124 appear to be unadopted designs.

120 5 METICAS

	VG	VF	UNC
25.6.1976. Brown and m/c. Kudo on back. Specimen.	—	—	—

121 10 METICAS

25.6.1976. Blue on m/c. Lions on back. Specimen.	—	—	—

122 20 METICAS

25.6.1976. Red and m/c. Giraffes on back. Specimen.	—	—	—

123 50 METICAS

25.6.1976. Purple and m/c. Cape buffalo on back. Specimen.	—	—	—

124 100 METICAS

	VG	VF	UNC
25.6.1976. Green and m/c. Elephants on back. Specimen.	—	—	—

REPÚBLICA POPULAR DE MOÇAMBIQUE

1980 ISSUE
#125-128 arms at ctr.

			VG	VF	UNC
125	**50 METICAIS**		.15	.40	1.25

16.6.1980. Dk. brown and brown on m/c unpt. Soldiers at l., flag ceremony at r. Soldiers in training on back.

			VG	VF	UNC
129	**50 METICAIS**		.10	.35	1.00

16.6.1983; 16.6.1986. Similar to #125 except for arms.

			VG	VF	UNC
126	**100 METICAIS**		.20	.50	1.50

16.6.1980. Green on m/c unpt. Soldiers at flagpole at l., E. Mondlane at r. Public ceremony on back.

			VG	VF	UNC
130	**100 METICAIS**		.10	.35	1.00

16.6.1983; 16.6.1986; 16.61989. Similar to #126 except for arms.

			VG	VF	UNC
127	**500 METICAIS**		.40	1.00	3.50

16.6.1980. Deep blue-violet and dk. blue-green on m/c unpt. Government assembly at l., chanting crowd at r. Chemists and school scene on back.

			VG	VF	UNC
131	**500 METICAIS**		.25	1.00	2.50

16.6.1983; 16.6.1986; 16.6.1989. Similar to #127 except for arms.

			VG	VF	UNC
128	**1000 METICAIS**		.75	2.00	5.00

16.6.1980. Red on m/c unpt. Pres. S. Machel w/3 young boys at r., revolutionary monument l. Mining and harvesting scenes on back.

1983-88 ISSUE

#129-132 modified arms at ctr. Smaller size serial #.

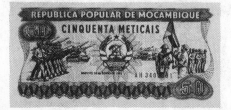

			VG	VF	UNC
132	**1000 METICAIS**		.60	1.75	4.00

16.6.1983; 16.6.1986; 16.6.1989. Similar to #128 except for arms.

133   5000 METICAIS
   3.2.1988; 3.2.1989. Purple, brown and violet on m/c unpt. Carved
   statues at l., painting at r. Dancers and musicians on back. Wmk:
   Pres. Machel.

	VG	VF	UNC
	.60	1.75	4.00

1991-93 ISSUE
#134-137 arms at upper ctr. r. printed on silver or gold underlay. Bank seal at lower l. on back. Wmk: J.
   Chissano. Printer: TDLR.
#138 and 139 Bank of Mozambique bldg. at l. ctr., arms at upper r. Cabora Bassa hydroelectric dam on
   back.

134   500 METICAIS
   16.6.1991. Brown and grayish blue on m/c unpt. Native statue of
   couple in grief at l. ctr., native art at r. Back blue; dancing warriors at
   ctr.

	VG	VF	UNC
	FV	.35	1.50

135   1000 METICAIS
   16.6.1991. Brown and red on m/c unpt. E. Mondlane at l. ctr., military
   flag raising ceremony at r. Back red; monument at l. ctr.

	VG	VF	UNC
	FV	.50	2.25

136   5000 METICAIS
   16.6.1991. Purple, red and orange-brown on m/c unpt. S. Machel at l.
   ctr., monument to the Socialist vanguard at r. Foundry workers at ctr.
   on back.

	VG	VF	UNC
	FV	1.00	4.00

137   10,000 METICAIS
   16.6.1991. Blue-green, brown and orange on m/c unpt. J. Chissano at
   l. ctr., high tension electrical towers at r. w/farm tractor in field and
   high-rise city view in background at r. Plowing with oxen at ctr on
   back.

	VG	VF	UNC
	FV	1.50	6.50

138   50,000 METICAIS
   16.6.1993 (1994). Red-brown and brown on m/c unpt.

	VG	VF	UNC
	FV	6.50	15.00

139   100,000 METICAIS
   16.6.1993 (1994). Red and black on m/c unpt.

	VG	VF	UNC
	FV	12.50	28.50

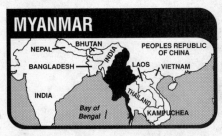

MYANMAR

The Socialist Republic of the Union of Myanmar (formally called Burma), a country of Southeast Asia fronting on the Bay of Bengal and the Andaman Sea, has an area of 261,789 sq. mi. (676,552 sq. km.) and a population of 41.5 million. Capital: Rangoon. Myanmar is an agricultural country heavily dependent on its leading product (rice) which embodies two-thirds of the cultivated area and accounts for 40 per cent of the value of exports. Petroleum, lead, tin, silver, zinc, nickel, cobalt and precious stones are exported.

The first European to reach Burma, about 1435, was Nicolo Di Conti, a merchant of Venice. During the beginning of the reign of Bodawpaya (1782-1819AD) the kingdom comprised most of the same area as it does today including Arakan which was taken over in 1784-85. The British East India Company, while unsuccessful in its 1612 effort to establish posts along the Bay of Bengal, was enabled by the Anglo-Burmese Wars of 1824-86 to expand to the whole of Burma and to secure its annexation to British India. In 1937, Burma was separated from India, becoming a separate British colony with limited self-government. The Japanese occupied Burma in 1942, and on Aug. 1, 1943 Burma became an "independent and sovereign state" under Dr. Ba Maw who was appointed the Adipadi (head of state) which collpased with the surrender of Japanese forces. Burma became an independent nation outside the British Commonwealth on Jan. 4, 1948, the constitution of 1948 providing for a parliamentary democracy and the nationalization of certain industries. However, political and economic problems persisted, and on March 2, 1962, Gen. Ne Win took over the government, suspended the constitution, installed himself as chief of state, and pursued a socialistic program with nationalization of nearly all industry and trade. On Jan. 4, 1974, a new constitution adopted by referendum established Burma as a "socialist republic" under one-party rule. The country name was changed to Union of Myanmar in 1989.

* * * NOTE: This section has been renumbered. * * *

MONETARY SYSTEM:
1 Kyat = 100 Pya, 1943-1945, 1952-

CENTRAL BANK OF MYANMAR

1990 ND ISSUE

67	1 KYAT		VG	VF	UNC
	ND (1990). Pale brown, orange and m/c. Gen. Aung San at l. and as wmk. Dragon carving at l. on back.		FV	FV	.35

1991-96 ND ISSUE
#68 and 69 Held in reserve.

68	50 PYA	VG	VF	UNC
(66A)	ND (1994). Dull purple and dull brown on gray and tan unpt. Musical string instrument at ctr. Wmk: OM.	FV	FV	.20
69	1 KYAT			
	ND (1996). M/c.	FV	FV	.30
70	5 KYATS			
	ND (1996). Dk. brown and blue-green on m/c unpt. Chinze at l. Ball game scene on back.	FV	FV	.45
71	10 KYATS			
	ND (1996). Deep purple and violet on m/c unpt. Chinze at r. Elaborate barge on back.	FV	FV	.85

72	20 KYATS		VG	VF	UNC
(70)	ND (1994). Deep olive-green, brown and blue-green on m/c unpt. Chinze at l. Fountain of elephants in park at ctr. r. on back. Wmk: Chinze over value.		FV	FV	1.25

73	50 KYATS		VG	VF	UNC
(71)	ND (1994). Red-brown, tan and dk. brown on m/c unpt. Chinze at r. and as wmk. Coppersmith at l. ctr. on back.		FV	FV	2.25

74	100 KYATS		VG	VF	UNC
(72)	ND (1994). Blue-violet, blue-green and dk. brown on m/c unpt. Chinze at l. Workers restoring temple and grounds at ctr. r. on back. Wmk: Chinze over value.		FV	FV	3.50

75
(73) **200 KYATS**
ND (ca.1991). Dk. blue and green on m/c unpt. Chinze at r., his head as wmk. Elephant pulling log at ctr. r. on back.

VG	VF	UNC
FV	FV	7.50

76
(74) **500 KYATS**
ND (1994). Purple, brown-violet and brown-orange on m/c unpt. Chinze at l. Workers restoring medieval statue, craftsman and water hauler at ctr. r. on back. Wmk: Chinze over value.

VG	VF	UNC
FV	FV	12.50

FOREIGN EXCHANGE CERTIFICATES

CENTRAL BANK

1993 ND ISSUE

FX1 **1 DOLLAR (USA)**
ND (1993). Blue, brown, yellow and green

VG	VF	UNC
—	—	3.00

FX2 **5 DOLLARS (USA)**
ND (1993). Maroon, yellow and blue.

VG	VF	UNC
—	VF	13.50

FX3 **10 DOLLARS (USA)**
ND (1993). Blue, green and gray.

VG	VF	UNC
—	—	25.00

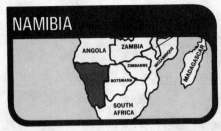

NAMIBIA

The Republic of Namibia (formerly the international territory of Namibia), once the German colonial territory of German South West Africa, is situated on the Atlantic coast of southern Africa, bounded on the north by Angola, on the east by Botswana, and on the south by South Africa. It has an area of 318,261 sq. mi. (824,290 sq. km.) and a population of #1.4 million. Capital: Windhoek. Diamonds, copper, lead, zinc and cattle are exported.

South Africa undertook the administration of South West Africa under the terms of a League of Nations mandate on Dec. 17, 1920. When the League of Nations was dissolved in 1946, its supervisory authority for South West Africa was inherited by the United Nations. In 1946 the UN denied South Africa's request to annex South West Africa. South Africa responded by refusing to place the territory under a UN trusteeship. In 1950 the International Court of Justice ruled that South Africa could not unilaterally modify the international status of South West Africa. A 1966 UN resolution declaring the mandate terminated was rejected by South Africa, and the status of the area remained in dispute. In June 1968 the UN General Assembly voted to rename the territory Namibia. In 1971 the International Court of Justice ruled that South Africa's presence in Namibia was illegal. In Dec. 1973 the UN appointed a UN Commissioner, and a multi-racial Advisory Council was also appointed. An interim government was formed in 1977 and independence was to be declared by Dec. 31, 1978. This resolution was rejected by major UN powers. In April 1978 South Africa accepted a plan for UN-supervised elections which led to political abstention by the South West Africa People's Organization (SWAPO) party. The result was the dissolution of the Minister's Council and National Assembly in Jan. 1983. A Multi-Party Conference (MPC) was formed in May 1984 which held talks with SWAPO. The MPC petitioned South Africa for Namibian self-government and on June 17, 1984 the Transitional Government of National Unity was installed. Negotiations were held in 1988 between Angola, Cuba and South Africa reaching a peaceful settlement on Aug. 5, 1988. By April 1, 1989, Cuban troops were to withdraw from Angola and South African troops from Namibia. The Transitional Government resigned on Feb. 28, 1988 for the upcoming elections of the constituent assembly in Nov. 1989. Independence was finally achieved on March 21, 1990.

MONETARY SYSTEM:
1 Namibia Dollar = 100 Cents

NOTE: For notes of the 3 commercial banks that circulated until 1963 see South West Africa listings in Vol. I.

REPUBLIC

BANK OF NAMIBIA

1993 ND ISSUE
#1-3 Capt. H. Wittbooi at l. ctr. Printer: TB.

			VG	VF	UNC
1	**10 NAMIBIA DOLLARS**		FV	FV	5.50
	ND (1993). Blue-black on m/c unpt. Arms at upper l. Springbok at r. on back.				

			VG	VF	UNC
2	**50 NAMIBIA DOLLARS**		FV	FV	21.50
	ND (1993). Blue-green and dk. brown on m/c unpt. Arms at upper ctr. Kudu at r. on back.				

			VG	VF	UNC
3	**100 NAMIBIA DOLLARS**		FV	FV	45.00
	ND (1993). Red, brown and red-brown on m/c unpt. Arms at upper ctr. r. Oryx at r. on back.				

1996 ND ISSUE
#5 and 9 Capt. H. Wittbooi at l. ctr., arms at upper ctr. Segmented foil over security thread and ascending serial #. Sign. J. B. Ahmad.
#4 Held in Reserve.
#6-8 Held in Reserve.

			VG	VF	UNC
5	**20 NAMIBIA DOLLARS**		FV	FV	10.00
	ND (1996). Orange and violet on m/c unpt. Red hartebeest at ctr. r. on back.				

			VG	VF	UNC
9	**200 NAMIBIA DOLLARS**		FV	FV	75.00
	ND (1996). Purple and violet on m/c unpt. Roan antelope at ctr. r. on back.				

COLLECTOR SERIES

BANK OF NAMIBIA

1993 ISSUE

			ISSUE PRICE	MKT. VALUE
CS1	**10-100 DOLLARS**		150.00	150.00
	ND (1993). #1-3 w/matched serial # mounted in a special plexiglass frame.			

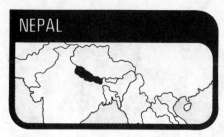

NEPAL

The Kingdom of Nepal, the world's only Hindu kingdom, is a landlocked country located in central Asia along the southern slopes of the Himalayan Mountains. It has an area of 56,136 sq. mi. (140,797 sq. km.) and a population of 19.4 million. Capital: Kathmandu. Nepal has substantial deposits of coal, copper, iron and cobalt but they are largely unexploited. Agriculture is the principal economic activity. Livestock, rice, timber and jute are exported.

Prithvi Narayan Shah, ruler of the principality of Gurkha, formed Nepal from a number of independent mountain states in the latter half of the 18th century. After his death a period of political instability ensued which lasted until the 1840's when the Rana family reduced the monarch to a figurehead and established itself as hereditary Prime Ministers. A popular revolution (1950-51) toppled the Rana family and reconstituted the power in the throne. In 1959 King Mahendra declared Nepal a constitutional monarchy. A new constitution promulgated in 1962 instituted a system of panchayat (village council) democracy from the village to the national levels.

RULERS:
Tribhuvana Vira Vikrama Shahi Deva, 1911-1950; 1951-1955
Jnanendra Vira Vikrama Shahi Deva, 1950-1951
Mahendra Vira Vikrama Shahi Deva, 1955-1972
Birendra Bir Bikram Shahi Deva, 1972-

MONETARY SYSTEM:
1 Mohru = 100 Paisa to 1961
1 Rupee = 100 Paisa, 1961-

SIGNATURE VARIETIES

1	Janak Raj	7	Bekh Bahadur Thapa
2	Bharat Raj	8	Yadav Prasad Pant
3	Narendra Raj	9	Kul Shekhar Sharma
4	Himalaya Shamsher (J. B. Rama)	10	Kalyan Dikram Adhikary
5	Lakshmi Nath Gautam	11	Ganesh Bahadur Thapa
6	Pradhumna Lal (Rajbhandari)	12	Harishankar Tripathi

KINGDOM

STATE BANK OF NEPAL

1961; 1965 ND ISSUE
Rupee System

#12-15 like previous issue. Denominations in Nepalese language changed from "Mohru" to "Rupees" on both face and back.

		VG	VF	UNC
12	**1 RUPEE**			
	ND (1965). Violet and olive. Coin at l., temple at ctr. Back lilac and green; arms at ctr., coin at r. Sign. 6; 8.	.20	.85	3.50

		VG	VF	UNC
13	**5 RUPEES**			
	ND (1961). Violet and aqua. Stupa at ctr. Back violet; Himalayas. Sign. 5; 7; 8.	.50	1.35	4.00

		VG	VF	UNC
14	**10 RUPEES**			
	ND (1961). Dk. brown and red. Temple at ctr. Arms at ctr. on back. Sign. 5; 6; 7; 8.	.90	2.75	8.00

		VG	VF	UNC
15	**100 RUPEES**			
	ND (1961). Green and brown. Temple at Lalitpor at ctr. Rhinoceros on back. Sign. 6; 7; 8.	3.00	10.00	35.00

1972 ND ISSUE
Rupee System

#16-21 Kg. Mahendra Vira Vikrama wearing military uniform w/white cap at l. Sign. 8. Wmk: Crown.

		VG	VF	UNC
16	**1 RUPEE**			
	ND (1972). Brown and blue. Back brown and purple; 4-chair rotary swing; arms on back.	.20	.65	1.75

17 **5 RUPEES**
ND (1972). Green and lilac. Back green and blue. Terraces
w/Himalayas in background on back.

	VG	VF	UNC
	.30	.85	2.50

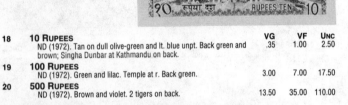

18 **10 RUPEES**
ND (1972). Tan on dull olive-green and lt. blue unpt. Back green and
brown; Singha Dunbar at Kathmandu on back.

	VG	VF	UNC
	.35	1.00	2.50

19 **100 RUPEES**
ND (1972). Green and lilac. Temple at r. Back green.

3.00 7.00 17.50

20 **500 RUPEES**
ND (1972). Brown and violet. 2 tigers on back.

13.50 35.00 110.00

21 **1000 RUPEES**
ND (1972). Blue and m/c. Great Stupa at Bodhnath. House and
mountains on back.

	VG	VF	UNC
	26.50	70.00	200.00

1974 ND ISSUE
#22-28 Kg. Birendra Bir Bikram in military uniform w/dk. cap at l. Wmk: Crown.

22 **1 RUPEE**
ND (1974). Blue, purple and gold. Temple at ctr. Back blue and brown;
2 musk deer at ctr. Sign. 9; 10; 11; 12.

	VG	VF	UNC
	.05	.20	.80

23 **5 RUPEES**
ND (1974). Red, brown and green. Temple at ctr. Back red and brown;
2 yaks. Sign. 9; 10; 11.

	VG	VF	UNC
	.15	.40	2.50

24 **10 RUPEES**
ND (1974). M/c. Vishnu on Garnda at ctr. Back brown amd green; 2
antelopes at ctr. Sign. 9; 10.

	VG	VF	UNC
	.30	.85	2.75

25 **50 RUPEES**
ND (1974). Purple and green. Bldg. at ctr. Back blue and brown;
mountain goat standing l. at ctr. Sign. 9.

	VG	VF	UNC
	1.50	3.50	10.00

26 **100 RUPEES**
ND (1974). Green and purple. Mountains at ctr., temple at r. Back
green; rhinoceros walking l., "eye" at upper l. corner. Sign. 9.

	VG	VF	UNC
	3.00	7.00	20.00

27 **500 RUPEES**
ND (1974). Brown. Monastery at ctr. Back brown and gold; 2 tigers.
Sign. 9; 10.

12.50 30.00 100.00

28 **1000 RUPEES**
ND (1974). Blue and m/c. Temple and Great Stupa at ctr. Elephant on
back. Sign. 9.

25.00 55.00 225.00

1981-87 ND Issue

#29-36 Kg. Birendra Bir Bikram wearing plumed crown at l. Wmk: Crown.

29   2 RUPEES

		VG	VF	UNC
ND (1981). Green, blue and lilac. Temple at ctr. Back m/c; leopard at ctr.				
a.	Line from king's lower lip extending downward. Sign. 10.	FV	FV	2.00
b.	No line from king's lower lip. Sign. 10; 11; 12.	FV	FV	.50

30   5 RUPEES

	VG	VF	UNC
ND (1987). Brown on red and m/c unpt. Temple at ctr. Back similar to #23. 2 serial # varieties. Sign. 11; 12.	FV	FV	1.25

31   10 RUPEES

	VG	VF	UNC
ND (1985). Dk. brown, orange, lilac and m/c. Vishnu on Garnda at ctr. Antelopes at ctr. on back. Sign. 11; 12.	FV	FV	1.75

32   20 RUPEES

	VG	VF	UNC
ND (1982-87). Orange on m/c unpt. Janakpur Temple at ctr. Back orange and m/c; deer at ctr. Sign. 10; 11.	FV	FV	5.00

33   50 RUPEES

		VG	VF	UNC
ND (1983-). Blue on m/c unpt. Palace at ctr. Mountain goat at ctr. on back.				
a.	Sign. 10 w/title at r. (1983).	FV	FV	5.00
b.	Sign. 11; 12 w/title at ctr. (1988).	FV	FV	3.00

34   100 RUPEES

		VG	VF	UNC
ND (1981). Green on pale purple and tan unpt. Temple at r. Back green; rhinoceros walking l. Similar to #26, but w/o "eye" at upper l. Sign. 10; 11.				
a.	Line from king's lower lip extending downward. W/security thread. Sign. 10.	FV	FV	6.50
b.	No line from king's lower lip. Sign. 10; 11.	FV	FV	5.50
c.	Segmented foil over security thread. Sign. 12.	FV	FV	4.50

35   500 RUPEES

		VG	VF	UNC
ND (1981). Brown and blue-violet on m/c unpt. Temple at ctr. Back brown and gold; 2 tigers. Sign. 10; 11.				
a.	As #34a. Sign. 10.	FV	FV	45.00
b.	As #34b. Sign. 10; 11.	FV	FV	20.00
c.	As #34c. Sign. 12.	FV	FV	18.00

36	1000 RUPEES	VG	VF	UNC
	ND (1981). Blue and brown on m/c unpt. Stupa and temple on face, elephant at ctr. on back. Sign. 10; 11.			
	a. As #34a. Sign. 10.	FV	FV	85.00
	b. As #34b. Sign. 10; 11.	FV	FV	37.50
	c. As #34c. Sign. 12.	FV	FV	35.00

1988; 1991 ND ISSUE

37 (28A)	1 RUPEE	VG	VF	UNC
	ND (1991). Blue on m/c unpt. Back similar to #22. Sign. 12.	FV	FV	.40

38 (32A)	20 RUPEES	VG	VF	UNC
	ND (1988). Orange on m/c unpt. Like #32, but m/c border. M/c borders on back. Sign. 11; 12.	FV	FV	2.00

NETHERLANDS

The Kingdom of the Netherlands, a country of western Europe fronting on the North Sea and bordered by Belgium and Germany, has an area of 15,770 sq. mi. (40,844 sq. km.) and a population of 15.1 million. Capital: Amsterdam, but the seat of government is at The Hague. The economy is based on dairy farming and a variety of industrial activities. Chemicals, yarns and fabrics, and meat products are exported.

After being a part of Charlemagne's empire in the 8th and 9th centuries, the Netherlands came under the control of Burgundy and the Austrian Hapsburgs, and finally was subjected to Spanish domination in the 16th century. Lead by William of Orange, the Dutch revolted against Spain in 1568 the seven northern provinces formed the Union of Utrecht and declared their independence in 1581, becoming the Republic of the United Netherlands. In the following century, the 'Golden Age' of Dutch history, the Netherlands became a great sea and colonial power, a patron of the arts and a refuge for the persecuted. In 1814, all the provinces of Holland and Belgium were merged into the Kingdom of the United Netherlands under William I. The Belgians withdrew in 1830 to form their own Kingdom, the last substantial change in the configuration of European Netherlands. German forces invaded in 1940 and the royal family soon fled with cargos of wealth to England where a government in exile was formed. German High Commissioner, Arthur Seyss-Inquart, was placed in command until 1945 and the arrival of Allied military forces.

RULERS:
Juliana I, 1948-1981
Beatrix, 1981-

MONETARY SYSTEM:
1 Gulden = 100 Cents

KONINKRIJK - KINGDOM
DE NEDERLANDSCHE BANK
NETHERLANDS BANK
1966-72 ISSUE

90	5 GULDEN	VG	VF	UNC
	26.4.1966. Green. Vondel at r. Modern bldg. design on back. Wmk: Inkwell, quill pen and scroll.			
	a. Serial # at upper l. and lower r. Gray paper w/clear wmk.	FV	FV	10.00
	b. Serial # at upper l. and lower r. White paper w/vague wmk. Series XA/XM.	FV	FV	12.50
	c. Serial # at upper l. and ctr. r. in smaller type. (Experimental issue only; circulated in the province of Utrecht.) Series 6AA.			

91	10 GULDEN	VG	VF	UNC
	25.4.1968. Dk. blue on violet and m/c unpt. Stylized self-portrait of F. Hals at r. Wmk: Cornucopia.			
	a. *0* in "bullseye" at upper l. on back.	FV	6.00	12.00
	b. Plain "bullseye" at upper l. on back.	FV	FV	10.00

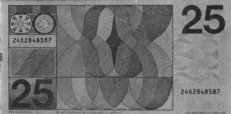

92   **25 GULDEN**
10.2.1971. Red. J. Pietersz Sweelinck at r. Wmk: Rectangular wave
design.

	VG	VF	UNC
	FV	FV	22.50

93   **100 GULDEN**
14.5.1970. Dk. brown. Adm. M. Adriaensz de Ruyter at r.

	VG	VF	UNC
	FV	FV	90.00

94   **1000 GULDEN**
30.3.1972. Black on dk. blue-green unpt. B. d' Espinoza at r. Wmk:
Pyramid.

	VG	VF	UNC
	FV	FV	700.00

1973-85 ISSUE

95   **5 GULDEN**
28.3.1973. Dk. green on green and m/c unpt. J. Vondel at r. Wmk. like
#90.

	VG	VF	UNC
	FV	FV	7.50

96   **50 GULDEN**
4.1.1982. Orange on m/c unpt. Sunflower w/bee at lower ctr. Vertical
format. Map and flowers on back. Wmk: Bee.

	VG	VF	UNC
	FV	FV	40.00

97   **100 GULDEN**
28.7.1977 (1981). Dk. brown on m/c unpt. Water-snipe bird at r. Head
of great snipe bird on back and as wmk.

	VG	VF	UNC
	FV	FV	80.00

98   **250 GULDEN**
25.7.1985 (1986). Violet on m/c unpt. Lighthouse. Vertical format.
Lighthouse and map on back. Wmk: Rabbit and *VHP*.

	VG	VF	UNC
	FV	FV	185.00

1989-94 ISSUE
#101 and 103 Held in reserve.

99   **10 GULDEN**

	VG	VF	UNC
			Expected New Issue

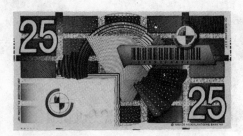

100 **25 GULDEN**
5.4.1989. Red on m/c unpt. Value and geometric designs on face and back. Wmk: Robin.

	VG	VF	UNC
	FV	FV	20.00

102 **100 GULDEN**
9.1.1992 (7.9.1993). Dk. and lt. brown, gray and gold on m/c unpt. Value and geometric designs on face and back. Wmk: Little owl.

	VG	VF	UNC
	FV	FV	77.50

104 **1000 GULDEN**
2.6.1994. Dk. gray and green. Geometrical designs. Geometrical designs on back. Wmk: Lapwing's head.

	FV	FV	675.00

NETHERLANDS ANTILLES

The Netherlands Antilles, part of the Netherlands realm, comprise two groups of islands in the West Indies: Bonaire and Curacao near the Venezuelan coast; and St. Eustatius, Saba and the southern part of St. Martin (St. Maarten) southeast of Puerto Rico. The island group has an area of 385 sq. mi. (961 sq. km.) and a population of 191,000. Capital: Willemstad. Chief industries are the refining of crude oil, and tourism Petroleum products and phosphates are exported.

On Dec. 15, 1954, the Netherlands Antilles were given complete domestic autonomy and granted equality within the Kingdom with Surinam and the Netherlands.

The island of Aruba gained independence in 1986.

RULERS:
Dutch

MONETARY SYSTEM:
1 Gulden = 100 Cents

DUTCH INFLUENCE

BANK VAN DE NEDERLANDSE ANTILLEN

1962 ISSUE

#1-7 woman seated w/scroll and flag in oval at l. Printer: JEZ.

		VG	VF	UNC
1	**5 GULDEN** 2.1.1962. Blue. View of Curacao at ctr.	4.00	10.00	40.00
2	**10 GULDEN** 2.1.1962. Green. Highrise bldg. (Aruba) at ctr.	7.50	18.00	75.00
3	**25 GULDEN** 2.1.1962. Black-gray. View of Bonaire at ctr.	20.00	40.00	115.00

		VG	VF	UNC
4	**50 GULDEN** 2.1.1962. Brown. City by the seaside (St. Maarten) at ctr.	35.00	85.00	225.00
5	**100 GULDEN** 2.1.1962. Violet. Monument (St. Eustatius) at ctr.	70.00	125.00	300.00
6	**250 GULDEN** 2.1.1962. Olive. Boats on the beach (Saba) at ctr.	175.00	350.00	600.00

		VG	VF	UNC
7	**500 GULDEN** 2.1.1962. Red. Oil refinery (Curacao) at ctr.	350.00	425.00	700.00

1967 ISSUE

#8-13 monument *Steunend op eigen Kracht...* at l. Printer: JEZ.

		VG	VF	UNC
8	**5 GULDEN** 1967; 1972. Dk. blue and green. View of Curacao at ctr.			
	a. 28.8.1967.	3.50	6.00	20.00
	b. 1.6.1972.	3.50	5.00	15.00

9	**10 Gulden**	VG	VF	UNC
	1967; 1972. Green. View of Aruba at ctr.			
	a. 28.8.1967.	7.00	10.00	30.00
	b. 1.6.1972.	6.50	6.50	25.00
10	**25 Gulden**			
	1967; 1972. Black-gray. View of Bonaire at ctr.			
	a. 28.8.1967.	14.00	27.50	75.00
	b. 1.6.1972.	13.00	20.00	50.00
11	**50 Gulden**			
	1967; 1972. Brown. Beach (St. Maarten) at ctr.			
	a. 28.8.1967.	28.00	65.00	150.00
	b. 1.6.1972.	26.00	45.00	95.00

16	**2 1/2 Gulden**	VG	VF	UNC
	8.9.1970. Blue. Jetliner.	FV	3.00	5.00

1979-80 Issue
#13A-13E like #8-13. Printer: JEZ.

13A	**5 Gulden**	VG	VF	UNC
	23.12.1980; 1.6.1984. Blue. Like #8.	FV	4.00	20.00

12	**100 Gulden**	VG	VF	UNC
	1967; 1972. Violet. Boats and fishermen on the beach (St. Eustatius) at ctr.			
	a. 28.8.1967.	75.00	100.00	250.00
	b. 1.6.1972.	70.00	85.00	150.00
13	**250 Gulden**			
	28.8.1967. Olive. Mountains (Saba) at ctr.	175.00	200.00	425.00

1955 MUNTBILJETTEN CURRENCY NOTES ISSUE

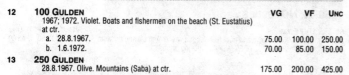

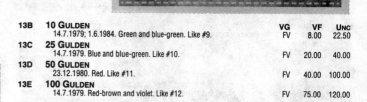

13B	**10 Gulden**	VG	VF	UNC
	14.7.1979; 1.6.1984. Green and blue-green. Like #9.	FV	8.00	22.50
13C	**25 Gulden**			
	14.7.1979. Blue and blue-green. Like #10.	FV	20.00	40.00
13D	**50 Gulden**			
	23.12.1980. Red. Like #11.	FV	40.00	100.00
13E	**100 Gulden**			
	14.7.1979. Red-brown and violet. Like #12.	FV	75.00	120.00

14	**2 1/2 Gulden**	VG	VF	UNC
	1955; 1964. Blue. Ship in dry dock at ctr. Crowned supported arms at ctr. on back. Printer: ABNC.			
	a. 1955.	5.00	22.50	100.00
	b. 1964.	5.00	25.00	120.00

1986 Issue
#17-22 back and wmk: Shield-like bank logo. Sign. and sign. title varieties. Printer: JEZ.

1970 Issue
#15-16 arms at r. on back. Printer: JEZ.

15	**1 Gulden**	VG	VF	UNC
	8.9.1970. Red and orange. Aerial view of harbor at l. ctr.	FV	1.00	2.00

17	**5 Gulden**	VG	VF	UNC
	1986; 1990; 1994. Dk. blue and m/c. Tropical bird at ctr.			
	a. 31.3.1986.	FV	FV	8.00
	b. 1.1.1990.	FV	FV	7.00
	c. 1.5.1994.	FV	FV	6.50

18	**10 GULDEN**	VG	VF	UNC
	1986; 1990; 1994. Dk. green and m/c. Colibri (hummingbird) at ctr.			
	a. 31.3.1986.	FV	FV	15.00
	b. 1.1.1990.	FV	FV	13.50
	c. 1.5.1994.	FV	FV	12.00

19	**25 GULDEN**	VG	VF	UNC
	1986; 1990; 1994. Red and m/c. Flamingo at ctr.			
	a. 31.3.1986.	FV	FV	35.00
	b. 1.1.1990.	FV	FV	32.50
	c. 1.5.1994.	FV	FV	26.50

20	**50 GULDEN**	VG	VF	UNC
	1986; 1990; 1994. Brown-orange and m/c. Rufous (collard sparrow) at ctr.			
	a. 31.3.1986.	FV	FV	67.50
	b. 1.1.1990.	FV	FV	62.50
	c. 1.5.1994.	FV	FV	52.50

21	**100 GULDEN**	VG	VF	UNC
	1986; 1990; 1994. Brown and m/c. Bananaquit at ctr.			
	a. 31.3.1986.	FV	FV	100.00
	b. 1.1.1990.	FV	FV	90.00
	c. 1.5.1994.	FV	FV	85.00

22	**250 GULDEN**	VG	VF	UNC
	1986; 1990. Purple, red-violet and m/c. Caribbean mockingbird at ctr.			
	a. 31.3.1986.	FV	FV	240.00
	b. 1.1.1990.	FV	FV	210.00

NEW CALEDONIA

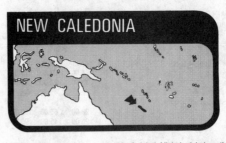

The French Overseas Territory of New Caledonia, a group of about 25 islands in the South Pacific, is situated about 750 miles (1,207 km.) east of Australia. The territory, which includes the dependencies of Ile des Pins, Loyalty Islands, Ile Huon, Isles Belep, Isles Chesterfield, and Ile Walpole, has a total land area of 6,530 sq. mi. (19,058 sq. km.) and a population of 152,000. Capital: Noumea. The islands are rich in minerals; New Caledonia has the world's largest known deposit of nickel. Nickel, nickel castings, coffee and copra are exported.

British navigator Capt. James Cook discovered New Caledonia in 1774. The French took possession in 1853, and established a penal colony on the island in 1854. The European population of the colony remained disproportionately convict until 1894. New Caledonia became an overseas territory within the French Community in 1946, and in 1958 and 1972 chose to remain affiliated with France.

* * * NOTE: This section has been renumbered. * * *

RULERS:
French

MONETARY SYSTEM:
1 Franc = 100 Centimes

FRENCH INFLUENCE

INSTITUT D'EMISSION D'OUTRE-MER

NOUMÉA BRANCH

1969-92 ND ISSUES

59 (43)	**100 FRANCS**	VG	VF	UNC
	ND (1969). Brown and m/c. Girl wearing wreath and playing guitar at r. W/o *REPUBLIQUE FRANÇAISE*, Intaglio printing.	3.00	12.50	45.00

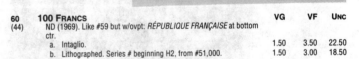

60 (44)	**100 FRANCS**	VG	VF	UNC
	ND (1969). Like #59 but w/ovpt: *RÉPUBLIQUE FRANÇAISE* at bottom ctr.			
	a. Intaglio.	1.50	3.50	22.50
	b. Lithographed. Series # beginning H2, from #51,000.	1.50	3.00	18.50

61	**500 FRANCS**	**VG**	**VF**	**UNC**
(45)	ND (1969-92). M/c. Fisherman at r. Man at l. on back. Sign. varieties.	6.00	8.50	13.50
62	**1000 FRANCS**			
(46)	ND (1969). M/c. Hut under palm tree at l., girl at r. W/o ovpt: *RÉPUBLIQUE FRANIÇAISE*.	10.00	25.00	75.00
63	**1000 FRANCS**			
(47)	ND (1978). M/c. Like #46 but w/ovpt: *RÉPUBLIQUE FRANÇAISE* ovpt. at lower l. Sign. varieties.	FV	FV	23.50

64	**5000 FRANCS**	**VG**	**VF**	**UNC**
(48)	ND (1969). M/c. Bougainville at l., sailing ships at ctr. Ovpt: *RÉPUBLIQUE FRANÇAISE*.	FV	FV	125.00

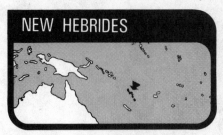

New Hebrides Condominium, a group of islands located in the South Pacific 500 miles (800 km.) west of Fiji, were under the joint sovereignty of Great Britain and France. The islands have an area of 5,700 sq. mi. (14,763 sq. km.) and a population of mainly Melanesians of mixed blood. Capital: Port-Vila. The volcanic and coral islands, while material and subject to frequent earthquakes, are extremely fertile, and produce copra, coffee, tropical fruits and timber for export.

The New Hebrides were discovered by Portuguese navigator Pedro de Quiros in 1606, visited by French explorer Bougainville in 1768, and named by British navigator Capt. James Cook in 1774. Ships of all nations converged on the islands to trade for sandalwood, prompting France and Britain to relinquish their individual claims and declare the islands a neutral zone in 1878. The New Hebrides were placed under the control of a mixed Anglo-French commission of naval officers during the native uprisings of 1887, and established as a condominium under the joint sovereignty of France and Great Britain in 1906.

RULERS:
British and French to 1980

MONETARY SYSTEM:
1 Franc = 100 Centimes

BRITISH AND FRENCH INFLUENCE

INSTITUT D'EMISSION D'OUTRE-MER, NOUVELLES HÉBRIDES

1965; 1967 ND ISSUE

16	**100 FRANCS**	**VG**	**VF**	**UNC**
	ND (1965-71). M/c. Black on yellow and green unpt. Girl w/guitar at r. *NOUVELLES-HÉBRIDES* in capital letters on back. Sign. varieties.	5.00	25.00	75.00

17	**1000 FRANCS**	**VG**	**VF**	**UNC**
	ND (1967-71). Red. Hut w/palms at l., girl at r. *NOUVELLES HÉBRIDES* in capital letters on back.	15.00	50.00	175.00

1972 ND ISSUE

18	**100 FRANCS**	**VG**	**VF**	**UNC**
	ND (1972). M/c. Like #16, but red and blue unpt. *Nouvelles Hébrides* in script on face and back.			
	a. Intaglio plates.	1.50	5.50	22.50
	b. Lithographed Series beginning E1, from no. 51,000.	1.35	5.00	20.00

19	**500 FRANCS**	**VG**	**VF**	**UNC**
	ND (1972). Blue, green and m/c. Fisherman at r.	6.50	10.00	28.50

20	**1000 FRANCS**	**VG**	**VF**	**UNC**
	ND (1972). Orange and brown. Like #17. *Nouvelles Hébrides* in script on face and back.	12.50	18.50	55.00

NEW ZEALAND

New Zealand, a parliamentary state located in the southwestern Pacific 1,250 miles (2,011 km.) east of Australia, has an area of 103,736 sq. mi. (269,056 sq. km.) and a population of 3.46 million. Capital: Wellington. Wool, meat, dairy products and some manufactured items are exported.

New Zealand was discovered and named by Dutch navigator Abel Tasman in 1642, and explored by British navigator Capt. James Cook who surveyed it in 1769 and annexed the land to Great Britain. The British government disavowed the annexation and for the next 70 years the only white settlers to arrive were adventurers attracted by the prospects of lumbering, sealing and whaling. Great Britain annexed the land in 1840 by treaty with the native chiefs and made it a dependency of New South Wales. The colony was granted self-government in 1852, a ministerial form of government in 1856, and full dominion status on Sept. 26, 1907. Full internal and external autonomy, which New Zealand had in effect possessed for many years, was formally extended in 1947. New Zealand is a member of the Commonwealth of Nations. The Queen of England is Chief of State.

RULERS:
British

MONETARY SYSTEM:
1 Shilling = 12 Pence
1 Pound = 20 Shillings (also 2 Dollars) to 1967
1 Dollar = 100 Cents, 1967-

BRITISH INFLUENCE

RESERVE BANK OF NEW ZEALAND

1940 ND ISSUE
#158-162 portr. Capt. J. Cook at lower r. Sign. title: *CHIEF CASHIER*. Wmk: Maori chief. Printer: TDLR.

158	**10 SHILLINGS**	**VG**	**VF**	**UNC**
	ND (1940-67). Brown on m/c unpt. Arms at upper ctr. Kiwi at l., treaty signing at ctr. on back.			
	a. Sign. T. P. Hanna. (1940-55).	2.50	15.00	100.00
	b. Sign. G. Wilson. (1955-56).	4.50	30.00	195.00
	c. Sign. R. N. Fleming. W/o security thread. (1956-67).	1.50	5.00	55.00
	d. Sign. as c. W/security thread. (1967).	1.50	4.00	27.50

159 1 POUND
ND (1940-67). Purple on m/c unpt. Arms at upper ctr. Sailing ship on
sea at l. on back.

	VG	VF	UNC
a. Sign. T. P. Hanna. (1940-55).	3.00	9.00	110.00
b. Sign. G. Wilson. (1955-56).	4.00	15.00	120.00
c. Sign. R. N. Fleming. W/o security thread. (1956-67).	3.00	7.00	70.00
d. Sign. as c. W/security thread. (1967).	2.00	5.00	35.00

160 5 POUNDS
ND (1940-67). Blue on m/c unpt. Crowned arms at upper ctr. Island,
water and mountains on back.

	VG	VF	UNC
a. Sign. T. P. Hanna. (1940-55).	9.00	20.00	135.00
b. Sign. G. Wilson. (1955-56).	9.00	25.00	175.00
c. Sign. R. N. Fleming. W/o security thread. (1956-67).	9.00	17.50	120.00
d. Sign. as c. W/security thread. (1967).	6.50	10.00	50.00

161 10 POUNDS
ND (1940-67). Green on m/c unpt. Crowned arms, sailing ship at l.
Herd of animals on back.

	VG	VF	UNC
a. Sign. T. P. Hanna. (1940-55).	30.00	55.00	360.00
b. Sign. G. Wilson. (1955-56).	35.00	70.00	400.00
c. Sign. R. N. Fleming. (1956-67).	17.50	30.00	90.00
d. Sign. as c. W/security thread. (1967).	10.00	18.50	70.00

162 50 POUNDS
ND (1940-67). Red on m/c unpt. Crowned arms, sailing ship at l. Dairy
farm and mountain on back.

	VG	VF	UNC
a. Sign. T. P. Hanna. (1940-55).	220.00	450.00	1750.
b. Sign. G. Wilson. (1955-56).	220.00	450.00	2000.
c. Sign. R. N. Fleming. (1956-67).	125.00	400.00	850.00

1967 ND ISSUE

#163-168 Qn. Elizabeth II on face. Birds and plants on back. Wmk: Capt. J. Cook. Printer: TDLR.

163 1 DOLLAR
ND (1967-81). Brown.

	VG	VF	UNC
a. Sign. R. N. Fleming. (1967-68).	1.50	5.00	40.00
b. Sign. D. L. Wilks. (1968-75).	1.50	3.00	15.00
c. Sign. R. L. Knight. (1975-77).	1.00	1.50	6.00
d. Sign. H. R. Hardie. (1977-81).	1.00	1.50	5.50

164 2 DOLLARS
ND (1967-81). Purple.

	VG	VF	UNC
a. Sign. R. N. Fleming. (1967-68).	2.00	5.00	30.00
b. Sign. D. L. Wilks. (1968-75).	2.00	4.00	22.50
c. Sign. R. L. Knight. (1975-77).	1.50	2.50	11.50
d. Sign. H. R. Hardie. (1977-81).	1.50	2.50	10.00

165 5 DOLLARS
ND (1967-81). Orange.

	VG	VF	UNC
a. Sign. R. N. Fleming. (1967-68).	4.00	8.00	55.00
b. Sign. D. L. Wilks. (1968-75).	10.00	20.00	90.00
c. Sign. R. L. Knight. (1975-77).	3.00	5.00	25.00
d. Sign. H. R. Hardie. (1977-81).	3.00	5.00	25.00

166 10 DOLLARS

	VG	VF	UNC
ND (1967-81). Blue.			
a. Sign. R. N. Fleming. (1967-68).	7.00	12.50	80.00
b. Sign. D. L. Wilks. (1968-75.)	8.00	15.00	135.00
c. Sign. R. L. Knight. (1975-77).	7.00	10.00	75.00
d. Sign. H. R. Hardie. (1977-81).	6.00	9.00	55.00

167 20 DOLLARS

	VG	VF	UNC
ND (1967-81). Green.			
a. Sign. R. N. Fleming. (1967-68).	15.00	22.50	100.00
b. Sign. D. L. Wilks. (1968-75).	15.00	25.00	225.00
c. Sign. R. L. Knight. (1975-77).	12.00	17.50	100.00
d. Sign. H. R. Hardie. (1977-81).	12.00	15.00	75.00

168 100 DOLLARS

	VG	VF	UNC
ND (1967-77). Red.			
a. Sign. R. N. Fleming. (1967-68).	85.00	150.00	650.00
b. Sign. R. L. Knight. (1975-77).	65.00	100.00	425.00

1981-83 ND ISSUE

#169-175 new portr. of Qn. Elizabeth II on face. Birds and plants on back. Wmk: Capt. J. Cook. Printer: BWC.

169 1 DOLLAR

	VG	VF	UNC
ND (1981-). Dk. brown and m/c.			
a. Sign. H. R. Hardie w/title: *CHIEF CASHIER*. (1981-85).	FV	1.00	3.50
b. Sign. S. T. Russell w/title: *GOVERNOR*. (1985-89).	FV	1.00	3.00
c. Sign. D. T. Brash. (1989-92).	FV	1.00	2.00

170 2 DOLLARS

	VG	VF	UNC
ND (1981-). Purple and m/c.			
a. Sign. H. R. Hardie w/title: *CHIEF CASHIER*. (1981-85).	FV	1.75	5.00
b. Sign. S.T. Russell w/title: *GOVERNOR*. (1985-89).	FV	1.50	4.50
c. Sign. D. T. Brash. (1989-92).	FV	1.50	4.00

171 5 DOLLARS

	VG	VF	UNC
ND (1981-92). Orange and m/c.			
a. Sign. H. R. Hardie w/title: *CHIEF CASHIER*. (1981-85).	FV	4.50	10.00
b. Sign. S.T. Russell w/title: *GOVERNOR*. (1985-89).	FV	3.75	7.50
c. Sign. D. T. Brash. (1989-92).	FV	3.75	7.50

172 10 DOLLARS

	VG	VF	UNC
ND (1981-92). Blue and m/c.			
a. Sign. H. R. Hardie w/title: *CHIEF CASHIER*. (1981-85).	FV	8.50	18.50
b. Sign. S.T. Russell w/title: *GOVERNOR*. (1985-89).	FV	7.50	15.00
c. Sign. D. T. Brash. (1989-92).	FV	7.50	13.50

173 20 DOLLARS

	VG	VF	UNC
ND (1981-92). Green on m/c unpt.			
a. Sign. H. R. Hardie w/title: *CHIEF CASHIER*. (1981-85).	FV	16.50	28.50
b. Sign. S.T. Russell w/title: *GOVERNOR*. (1985-89).	FV	15.00	28.50
c. Sign. D. T. Brash. (1989-92).	FV	15.00	25.00

1992-93 ND Issue
#177-181 wmk: Qn. Elizabeth II. Sign. D.T. Brash. Printer: TDLR.

174	**50 Dollars**	VG	VF	UNC
	ND (1983-92). Yellow-orange on m/c unpt.			
a.	Sign. H. R. Hardie. (1981-85).	FV	35.00	70.00
b.	Sign. D. T. Brash. (1989-92).	FV	35.00	65.00

177	**5 Dollars**	VG	VF	UNC
	ND (1992-). Red-brown, brown and brown-orange on m/c unpt. Mt. Everest at l., Sir Ed. Hillary at ctr. Flora w/penguin at ctr. r. on back.			
a.	Issued note.	FV	FV	5.50
b.	Uncut pair in special folder.	FV	FV	8.50
c.	Uncut block of 4 in special folder.	FV	FV	16.00

175	**100 Dollars**	VG	VF	UNC
	ND (1981-). Red on m/c unpt.			
a.	Sign. H. R. Hardie w/title: *CHIEF CASHIER*. (1981-85).	FV	70.00	140.00
b.	Sign. S.T. Russell w/title: *GOVERNOR*. (1985-89).	FV	70.00	135.00

1990 Commemorative Issue
#176, 150th Anniversary of Treaty of Waitangi, 1840-1990
NOTE: #176 w/prefix letters *AAA* was issued in 2, 4, 8, 16 and 32 subject panes.

178	**10 Dollars**	VG	VF	UNC
	ND (1993-94). Blue and purple on m/c unpt. Flowers at l., K. Sheppard at ctr. r. Pair of Whio ducks at ctr. r. on back.			
a.	Issued note.	FV	FV	11.00
b.	Uncut pair in special folder.	FV	FV	16.50
c.	Uncut block of 4 in special folder.	FV	FV	30.00

176	**10 Dollars**	VG	VF	UNC
	1990. Blue on m/c unpt. Face design like #172, w/addition of 1990 Commission logo, the White Heron (in red and white w/date 1990) at r. of Qn. Special inscription and scene of treaty signing on back. Wmk: Capt. J. Cook. Printer: BWC.			
a.	Regular issue. Prefix letters *CCC; DDD.*	FV	FV	10.00
b.	Prefix letters *CWB* for County Wide Bank.	—	—	10.00
c.	Prefix letter *FTC* for Farmers Trading Co.	—	—	10.00
d.	Prefix letters *MBL* for Mobil Oil Co.	—	—	10.00
e.	Prefix letters *RNZ* for Radio New Zealand.	—	—	10.00
f.	Prefix letters *RXX* for Rank Xerox Co.	—	—	10.00
g.	Prefix letters *TNZ* for Toyota New Zealand.	—	—	10.00
h.	Special folder w/explanatory text and enclosing a single note. Prefix letters *BBB.*	—	—	10.00

179	**20 Dollars**	VG	VF	UNC
	ND (1993-94). Green on m/c unpt. Qn. Elizabeth II at r., bldg. at l. in unpt. Back pale green and blue; Karearea falcons at ctr.			
a.	Issued note.	FV	FV	20.00
b.	Uncut block of 4 in special folder.	FV	FV	60.00

180 50 DOLLARS
ND (1993-). Purple, violet and deep blue on m/c unpt. Sir A. Ngata at r., early school house at l., in unpt. Kokako crow at r. on back.

	VG	VF	UNC
a. Issued note.	FV	FV	42.50
b. Red serial #. (3000 were issued w/$50 phone card).	FV	FV	65.00
c. Uncut block of 4 in special folder.	FV	FV	150.00

181 100 DOLLARS
ND (1993-). Violet-brown and red on m/c unpt. Lord Rutherford of Nelson at ctr., gold medallion in unpt. at l. Mohua yellowhead bird on tree trunk at ctr. r., moth at lower l. on back.

	VG	VF	UNC
a. Issued note.	FV	FV	80.00
b. Uncut block of 4 in special folder.	FV	FV	300.00

1994 ND ISSUE

182 10 DOLLARS
ND (1994). Like #178 but bright blue at ctr. behind Whio ducks on back.

VG	VF	UNC
FV	FV	10.00

183 20 DOLLARS
ND (1994). Like #179 but bright green at ctr. behind Karearea falcon on back.

VG	VF	UNC
FV	FV	18.00

1996 COMMEMORATIVE ISSUE

#184, 70th Birthday Qn. Elizabeth II.

NOTE: Issued in a special folder w/a $5 Commemorative coin (3000).

184 20 DOLLARS
ND (1996). Green on m/c unpt. Commemorative ovpt. on #183. Serial # prefix *ER*.

VG	VF	UNC
FV	FV	30.00

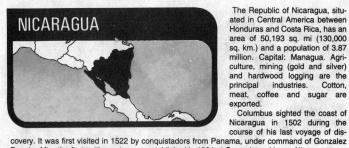

NICARAGUA

The Republic of Nicaragua, situated in Central America between Honduras and Costa Rica, has an area of 50,193 sq. mi (130,000 sq. km.) and a population of 3.87 million. Capital: Managua. Agriculture, mining (gold and silver) and hardwood logging are the principal industries. Cotton, meat, coffee and sugar are exported.

Columbus sighted the coast of Nicaragua in 1502 during the course of his last voyage of discovery. It was first visited in 1522 by conquistadors from Panama, under command of Gonzalez Davola. After the first settlements were established in 1524 at Granada and Leon, Nicaragua was incorporated, for administrative purpose, in the Captaincy General of Guatemala, which included every Central American state but Panama. The Captaincy General declared its independence from Spain on Sept. 15, 1821. The next year Nicaragua united with the Mexican Empire of Agustin de Iturbide, then in 1823 with the Central American Republic. When the federation was dissolved, Nicaragua declared itself an independent republic in 1838.

MONETARY SYSTEM:
- 1 Córdoba = 100 Centavos, 1912-1987
- 1 New Córdoba = 1000 Old Córdobas, 1988-90
- 1 Córdoba Oro = 100 Centavos = 1 U.S.A. Dollar, 1990-

REPUBLIC

BANCO CENTRAL DE NICARAGUA

DECRETO 26.4.1962

SERIES A

#107-114 portr. F. Hernandez Córdoba at ctr. on back. Printer: ABNC.

107 1 CÓRDOBA
D.1962. Blue on m/c unpt. Banco Central at upper ctr.

VG	VF	UNC
.15	.75	4.00

108 5 CÓRDOBAS
D.1962. Green on m/c unpt. Portr. C. Nicarao at upper ctr. Similar to #100.

VG	VF	UNC
.75	2.50	10.00

			VG	VF	UNC
109	**10 CÓRDOBAS**				
	D.1962. Red on m/c unpt. Portr. M. de Larreynaga at upper ctr.		1.50	4.50	20.00

			VG	VF	UNC
110	**20 CÓRDOBAS**				
	D.1962. Orange-brown on m/c unpt. Portr. T. Martinez at upper ctr.		3.00	10.00	40.00

			VG	VF	UNC
111	**50 CÓRDOBAS**				
	D.1962. Purple and m/c. Portr. M. Jerez at upper ctr.		6.00	25.00	75.00

			VG	VF	UNC
112	**100 CÓRDOBAS**				
	D.1962. Red-brown and m/c. Portr. J. D. Estrada at upper ctr.		4.00	20.00	40.00
113	**500 CÓRDOBAS**				
	D.1962. Black and m/c. Portr. R. Dario at upper ctr.		50.00	175.00	400.00
114	**1000 CÓRDOBAS**				
	D.1962. Brown and m/c. Portr. A. Somoza at upper ctr.		60.00	200.00	450.00

DECRETO 25.5.1968
SERIES B
#115-120 F. Hernandez Córdoba on back. Printer: TDLR.

NOTE: Some of #118-120 were apparently released w/o r.h. sign. after the Managua earthquake of 1972 damaged the Central Bank building.

			VG	VF	UNC
115	**1 CÓRDOBA**				
	ND. Blue on m/c unpt. Like #107.				
	a. W/3 sign.		.10	.35	1.00
	b. Pres. A. Somoza hand sign. at l.		—	—	—

			VG	VF	UNC
116	**5 CÓRDOBAS**				
	D.1968. Green on m/c unpt. Like #108.		.50	1.50	4.00
117	**10 CÓRDOBAS**				
	D.1968. Red on m/c unpt. Like #109.		.75	2.00	6.00
118	**20 CÓRDOBAS**				
	D.1968. Orange-brown on m/c unpt. Like #110.				
	a. W/3 sign.		1.00	3.00	10.00
	b. W/o r.h. sign.		—	—	—
119	**50 CÓRDOBAS**				
	D.1968. Purple on m/c unpt. Like #111.				
	a. W/3 sign.		4.00	7.50	27.50
	b. W/o r.h. sign.		—	—	—
120	**100 CÓRDOBAS**				
	D.1968. Red-brown on m/c unpt. Like #112.				
	a. W/3 sign.		3.00	6.00	17.50
	b. W/o r.h. sign.		—	—	—

DECRETO 27.4.1972
SERIES C
#121-128 printer: TDLR.

			VG	VF	UNC
121	**2 CÓRDOBAS**				
	D.1972. Olive-green on m/c unpt. Banco Central at r. Furrows at l. on back.				
	a. W/3 sign.		.10	.25	2.00
	b. W/o l.h. sign.		—	—	350.00

122 **5 Córdobas**
D.1972. Dk. green on m/c unpt. C. Nicarao standing at r. w/bow. Fruitseller at l. on back.

	VG	VF	Unc
	.25	.75	2.50

123 **10 Córdobas**
D.1972. Red on m/c unpt. A. Castro standing at r. atop rocks. Hacienda at l. on back.

	VG	VF	Unc
	.30	.85	2.50

124 **20 Córdobas**
D.1972. Orange-brown on m/c unpt. R. Herrera igniting cannon at r. Signing ceremony of abrogation of Chamorro-Bryan Treaty of 1912, Somoza at ctr.

	VG	VF	Unc
	.50	1.25	3.50

125 **50 Córdobas**
D.1972. Purple on m/c unpt. M. Jerez at r. Cows at l. on back.

	VG	VF	Unc
	8.00	20.00	50.00

126 **100 Córdobas**
D.1972. Violet on m/c unpt. J. Dolores Estrada at r. Flower at l. on back.

	VG	VF	Unc
	.50	1.50	4.00

127 **500 Córdobas**
D.1972. Black on m/c unpt. R. Dario at r. National Theater at l. on back.

	VG	VF	Unc
	10.00	25.00	100.00

128 **1000 Córdobas**
D.1972. Brown on m/c unpt. A. Somoza G. at r. View of Managua at l. on back.

	VG	VF	Unc
	12.00	30.00	120.00

Decreto of 20.2.1978
SERIES D
#129-130 printer: TDLR.

129 **20 Córdobas**
D.1978. Like #124.

	VG	VF	Unc
	.30	1.00	8.00

130 **50 Córdobas**
D.1978. Like #125.

	VG	VF	Unc
	.30	1.00	10.00

DECRETO 16.8.1979
SERIES E
FIRST ISSUE
#131-133 w/frame. Printer: TDLR.

				VG	VF	UNC
131	**50 CÓRDOBAS**					
	D.1979. Purple on m/c unpt. Comdt. C. F. Amador at r. Liberation of 19.7.1979 on back.			.50	1.50	4.00

				VG	VF	UNC
132	**100 CÓRDOBAS**					
	D.1979. Dk. brown on m/c unpt. Like #126.			.50	1.50	4.00

				VG	VF	UNC
133	**500 CÓRDOBAS**					
	D.1979. Deep blue on m/c unpt. Like #127.			.50	1.25	5.00

1979 ND SECOND ISSUE
#134-139 w/o frame. Wmk: Sandino. Printer: TDLR.

				VG	VF	UNC
134	**10 CÓRDOBAS**					
	D.1979. Red on m/c unpt. A. Castro standing atop rocks at r. Miners on back.			.25	.60	2.50

				VG	VF	UNC
135	**20 CÓRDOBAS**					
	D.1979. Orange-brown on m/c unpt. Comdt. G. P. Ordonez at r. Marching troops on back.			.30	.75	3.00

				VG	VF	UNC
136	**50 CÓRDOBAS**					
	D.1979. Purple on m/c unpt. Comdt. C. F. Amador at r. Liberation of 19.7.1979 on back.			.35	.85	3.50

				VG	VF	UNC
137	**100 CÓRDOBAS**					
	D.1979. Brown on m/c unpt. J. D. Estrada at r. Flower on back. Sign. varieties.			.50	1.25	5.00

				VG	VF	UNC
138	**500 CÓRDOBAS**					
	D.1979. Dk. olive-green on m/c unpt. R. Dario at r. Teatro Popular at l. on back. Sign. varieties. 3 sign. varieties.			.65	1.65	6.50

139 **1000 CÓRDOBAS**
D.1979. Blue-gray on m/c unpt. Gen. A. C. Sandino at r. Hut
(Sandino's birthplace) on back. Sign. varieties.

	VG	VF	UNC
	1.50	6.00	25.00

RESOLUTION OF 6.8.1984

SERIES F

#140-143 wmk: Sandino. Printer: TDLR.

		VG	VF	UNC
140	**50 CÓRDOBAS** *L.1984* (1985). Like #136.	.20	.50	2.00
141	**100 CÓRDOBAS** *L.1984* (1985). Like #137.	.20	.50	2.00
142	**500 CÓRDOBAS** *L.1984* (1985). Like #138.	.20	.50	5.00
143	**1000 CÓRDOBAS** *L.1984* (1985). Like #139.	.50	2.00	12.50

RESOLUTION OF 11.6.1985

SERIES G

#144-146 wmk: Sandino. Printer: TDLR.

144 **500 CÓRDOBAS**
L.1985 (1987). Like #142. Lithographed.

	VG	VF	UNC
	.20	.50	3.00

145 **1000 CÓRDOBAS**
L.1985 (1987). Like #143 but dk. gray on m/c unpt.

		VG	VF	UNC
a.	Engraved.	.35	1.00	4.00
b.	Lithographed.	.15	.50	2.75

146 **5000 CÓRDOBAS**
L.1985 (1987). Brown, black and m/c. Map at upper ctr., Gen. B.
Zeledon at r. National Assembly bldg. on back.

	VG	VF	UNC
	.15	.50	2.50

1987 ND PROVISIONAL ISSUE

#147-149 black ovpt. new denomination on face and back of old Series F and G notes printed by TDLR.

147 **20,000 CÓRDOBAS ON 20 CÓRDOBAS**
ND (1987). Ovpt. on unissued 20 Cordobas Series F. Colors and
design like #135.

	VG	VF	UNC
	.20	.50	2.25

148 **50,000 CÓRDOBAS ON 1000 CÓRDOBAS**
ND (1987). Ovpt. on #140.

	VG	VF	UNC
	.25	.60	2.50

		VG	VF	UNC
149	**100,000 CÓRDOBAS ON 500 CÓRDOBAS**	.30	.75	3.00
	ND (1987). Ovpt. on #144b.			

		VG	VF	UNC
153	**50 CÓRDOBAS**	.10	.35	1.00
	1985 (1988). Brown and dk. red on m/c unpt. Gen. J. D. Estrada at r. Medical clinic scene at l. on back.			

		VG	VF	UNC
150	**500,000 CÓRDOBAS ON 1000 CÓRDOBAS**	.50	1.25	5.00
	ND (1987). Ovpt. on #145b.			

1985 (1988) ISSUE
#151-156 wmk: Sandino. (W/o imprint.)

		VG	VF	UNC
154	**100 CÓRDOBAS**	.20	.50	2.00
	1985 (1988). Deep blue, blue and gray on m/c unpt. R. Lopez Perez at r. State council bldg. at l. on back.			

		VG	VF	UNC
151	**10 CÓRDOBAS**	.10	.35	1.25
	1985 (1988). Green and olive on m/c unpt. Comdt. C. F. Amador at r. Troop formation marching at l. on back.			

		VG	VF	UNC
155	**500 CÓRDOBAS**	.25	.60	2.50
	1985 (1988). Purple, blue and brown on m/c unpt. R. Dario at r. Classroom w/students at l. on back.			

		VG	VF	UNC
152	**20 CÓRDOBAS**	.10	.35	1.25
	1985 (1988). Blue-black and blue on m/c unpt. Comdt. G. P. Ordonez at r. Demonstration for agrarian reform at l. on back.			

		VG	VF	UNC
156	**1000 CÓRDOBAS**			
	1985 (1988). Brown on m/c unpt. Gen. A. C. Sandino at r. Liberation of 19.7.1979 on back.			
	a. Engraved w/wmk. at l. Serial # prefix FA.	.25	.60	2.00
	b. Lithographed w/o wmk. at l. Serial # prefix FC.	.25	.50	1.25

1988-89 ND PROVISIONAL ISSUE

#158 and 159 black ovpt. new denominations on face and back of earlier notes.

NOTE: Ovpt. errors exist and are rather common.

157 5000 CÓRDOBAS

ND (1988). Ovpt. elements in black on face and back of #146. Face ovpt.: sign. and title: *PRIMER VICE PRESIDENTE BANCO CENTRAL DE NICARAGUA* at l., 2 lines of text at lower ctr., blocked out guilloche added at r. Back ovpt., guilloche at l. and r., same sign. title as on face at r.

	VG	VF	UNC
	.25	.60	1.75

158 10,000 CÓRDOBAS ON 10 CÓRDOBAS

ND (1989). Ovpt. on #151.

	VG	VF	UNC
	.25	.75	2.25

159 100,000 CÓRDOBAS ON 100 CÓRDOBAS

ND (1989). Black ovpt. on face and back of #154.

	VG	VF	UNC
	.40	1.00	3.50

1989 ND EMERGENCY ISSUE

#160 and 161 grid map of Nicaragua at ctr. on face and back. Wmk: Sandino.

160 20,000 CÓRDOBAS

ND (1989). Black on blue, yellow and m/c unpt. Comdt. G. P. Ordonez at r. Church of San Francisco Granada at l. on back.

	VG	VF	UNC
	.35	.85	3.50

161 50,000 CÓRDOBAS

ND (1989). Brown on purple, orange and m/c unpt. Gen. J. D. Estrada at r. Hacienda San Jacinto on back.

	VG	VF	UNC
	.25	.60	2.50

1990 ND PROVISIONAL ISSUE

#162-164, black ovpt. new denomination on face and back of earlier notes.

NOTE: Ovpt. errors exist and are rather common.

162 200,000 CÓRDOBAS ON 1000 CÓRDOBAS

ND (1990). Ovpt. on #156b.

	VG	VF	UNC
	.15	.40	1.75

163 500,000 CÓRDOBAS ON 20 CÓRDOBAS

ND (1990). Ovpt. on #152.

	VG	VF	UNC
	.40	1.00	3.50

164 1 MILLION CÓRDOBAS ON 1000 CÓRDOBAS

ND (1990). Ovpt. on #156b.

	VG	VF	UNC
	.40	1.00	3.50

1990 ND Emergency Issue
#165 and 166 wmk: Sandino head, repeated.

165   5 MILLION CÓRDOBAS
ND (1990). Purple and orange on red and m/c unpt. C. Ordonez at r. Church of San Francisco Granada at l., map at ctr. on back.

	VG	VF	UNC
	.20	.50	2.00

166   10 MILLION CÓRDOBAS
ND (1990). Purple and lilac on blue and m/c unpt. Gen. J. D. Estrada at r. Hacienda San Jacinto at l., map at ctr. on back.

	VG	VF	UNC
	.25	.60	2.50

1990; 1991-92 ND Issues
#173-177, 2 sign. varieties.

Córdoba Oro System

#167-170, F. H. Córdoba at r. Arms at l., flower at r. on back. Printer: Harrison.

#171, 172, 176 and 177 printer: CBNC.

#173-177, 2 sign. varieties.

NOTE: Although originally issued on par with the U.S.A. Dollar, the rate of exchange has fallen to 8 Córdoba (Oro) to 1 U.S.A. Dollar.

167   1 CENTAVO
ND (1991). Purple on pale green and m/c unpt.

	VG	VF	UNC
	FV	.05	.15

168   5 CENTAVOS
ND (1991). Red-violet on pale green and m/c unpt. 2 sign. varieties.

	VG	VF	UNC
	FV	.05	.20

169   10 CENTAVOS
ND (1991). Olive-green on lt. green and m/c unpt. 2 sign. varieties.

	VG	VF	UNC
	FV	.10	.25

170   25 CENTAVOS
ND (1991). Blue-gray on pale green and m/c unpt. 2 sign. varieties.

	VG	VF	UNC
	FV	.15	.35

171   1/2 CÓRDOBA
ND (1991). Brown and green on m/c unpt. F. H. Córdoba at l., plant at r. Arms at ctr. on green back.

	VG	VF	UNC
	FV	FV	.50

172   1/2 CÓRDOBA
ND (1992). Face like #171. Arms at l., national flower at r. on green back.

	VG	VF	UNC
	FV	FV	.65

173 1 CÓRDOBA

	VG	VF	UNC
1990. Blue on purple and m/c unpt. Sunrise over field of maize at l., F. H. Córdoba at r. Back green and m/c; arms at ctr. Printer: TDLR. 2 sign. varieties.	FV	FV	.75

174 5 CÓRDOBAS

	VG	VF	UNC
ND (1991). Red-violet and dk. olive-green on m/c unpt. Indian Chief Diriangén at l., sorghum plants at r. R. Herrera firing cannon at British warship on green back. Printer: CBNC. 2 sign. varieties.	FV	FV	2.00

175 10 CÓRDOBAS

	VG	VF	UNC
1990. Green on blue and m/c unpt. Sunrise over rice field at l., M. de Larreynaga at r. Back dk. green and m/c; arms at ctr. Printer: TDLR.	FV	FV	3.50

176 20 CÓRDOBAS

	VG	VF	UNC
ND (1990). Pale red-orange and dk. brown on m/c unpt. Sandino at l., coffee plant at r. E. Mongalo at l., fire in the Mesón de Rivas (1854) at ctr. on green back. 2 sign. varieties.	FV	FV	6.00

177 50 CÓRDOBAS

	VG	VF	UNC
ND (1991). Purple and violet on m/c unpt. Dr. P. J. Chamorro at l., banana plants at r. Toppling of Somoza's statue and scene at polling place on green back. 2 sign. varieties.	FV	FV	12.50

178 100 CÓRDOBAS

	VG	VF	UNC
1990. Blue and red on m/c unpt. Sunrise over cotton field at l., R. Darío at r. Back green and m/c; arms at ctr. Printer: TDLR.	FV	FV	22.50

1995-96 ISSUE

		VG	VF	UNC
179	**1 CÓRDOBA**			
	1995. Similar to #173 but printer: BABN. Series B.	FV	FV	.65
180	**5 CÓRDOBAS**			
	1995. Similar to #174 but printer: F-CO.	FV	FV	1.75
181	**10 CÓRDOBAS**			
	1996. Similar to #175 but printer: GD. Series B.	FV	FV	3.00
182	**20 CÓRDOBAS**			
	1995. Similar to #176 but printer: F-CO.	FV	FV	5.50

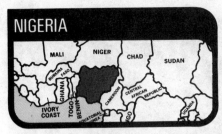

NIGERIA

The Federal Republic of Nigeria, situated on the Atlantic coast of Africa between Benin and Cameroon, has an area of 356,667 sq. mi. (923,768 sq. km.) and a population of 88.5 million. Capital: Lagos. The economy is based on petroleum and agriculture. Crude oil, cocoa, tobacco and tin are exported.

Following the Napoleonic Wars, the British expanded their trade with the interior of Nigeria. British claims to a sphere of influence in that area were recognized by the Berlin Conference of 1885, and in the following year the Royal Niger Company was chartered. Direct British control of the territory was initiated in 1900, and in 1914 the amalgamation of northern and southern Nigeria into the Colony and Protectorate of Nigeria was effected. In 1960, following a number of territorial and constitutional changes, Nigeria was granted independence within the British Commonwealth as a federation of the northern, western and eastern regions. Nigeria altered its political relationship with Great Britain on Oct. 1, 1963, by proclaiming itself a republic. It did, however, elect to remain a member of the Commonwealth of Nations. The Supreme Commander of Armed Forces is the Head of the Federal Military Government.

On May 30, 1967, the Eastern Region of the republic - an area occupied principally by the proud and resourceful Ibo tribe - seceded from Nigeria and proclaimed itself the independent Republic of Biafra. Civil war erupted and raged for 31 months. Casualties, including civilian, were about two million, the majority succumbing to malnutrition and disease. Biafra surrendered to the federal government on January 15, 1970. After military coups in 1983 and 1985 the government was assumed by an Armed Forces Ruling Council. A transitional civilian council was formed in 1993.

RULERS:
British to 1963

MONETARY SYSTEM:
1 Shilling = 12 Pence
1 Pound = 20 Shillings to 1973
1 Naira (10 Shillings) = 100 Kobo, 1973-

SIGNATURE/TITLE VARIETIES

1	*GOVERNOR* *CHIEF OF BANKING OPERATIONS*	**6**	
2		**7**	*GOVERNOR* *DIRECTOR OF CURRENCY OPERATIONS*
3		**8**	
4	*GOVERNOR* *DIRECTOR OF DOMESTIC OPERATIONS*	**9**	
5		**10**	

FEDERAL REPUBLIC OF NIGERIA

CENTRAL BANK OF NIGERIA

1967 ND ISSUE

Pound System
#6-13 bank bldg. at l. Wmk: Lion's head.

			VG	VF	UNC
6	**5 SHILLINGS** ND (1967). Lilac and blue. Back lilac; log cutting.		3.00	15.00	125.00
7	**10 SHILLINGS** ND (1967). Green and brown. Back green; stacking grain sacks.		6.50	32.50	250.00
8	**1 POUND** ND (1967). Red and dk. brown. Back red; beating plant at r.		.50	1.00	5.00
9	**5 POUNDS** ND (1967). Blue-gray and blue-green on m/c unpt. Back blue-gray; food preparation.		10.00	40.00	325.00

1968 ND ISSUE

#10-13 designs similar to previous issue. Wmk: Lion's head.

			VG	VF	UNC
10	**5 SHILLINGS** ND (1968). Green and orange. Back green.				
	a. R. sign. title: *GENERAL MANAGER*.		4.00	20.00	150.00
	b. R. sign. title: *CHIEF OF BANKING OPERATIONS*.		5.00	25.00	175.00

			VG	VF	UNC
11	**10 SHILLINGS** ND (1968). Blue on m/c unpt.				
	a. R. sign. title: *GENERAL MANAGER*.		6.50	32.50	225.00
	b. R. sign. title: *CHIEF OF BANKING OPERATIONS*.		8.50	42.50	275.00
12	**1 POUND** ND (1968). Olive-brown a.. violet. Back olive-brown.				
	a. R. sign. title: *GENERAL MANAGER*.		6.50	32.50	225.00
	b. R. sign. title: *CHIEF OF BANKING OPERATIONS*.		10.00	50.00	325.00
13	**5 POUNDS** ND (1968). Red-brown and blue. Back red-brown.				
	a. R. sign. title: *GENERAL MANAGER*.		20.00	65.00	425.00
	b. R. sign. title: *CHIEF OF BANKING OPERATIONS*.		25.00	95.00	475.00

1973; 1977 ND ISSUE

Naira System
#14-17 bank bldg. at l. ctr. Wmk: Heraldic eagle.

		VG	VF	UNC
14	**50 KOBO** ND (1973-78). Blue and violet on m/c unpt. Back brown; logging at r.			
	a. Sign. 1.	1.00	4.00	8.00
	b. Sign. 2.	1.50	5.00	32.50
	c. Sign. 3.	.50	2.00	13.50
	d. Sign. 4.	.65	2.50	16.50
	e. Sign. 5.	.50	2.00	13.50
	f. Sign. 6.	.25	1.75	11.00
	g. Sign. 7; 8; 9.	FV	FV	.85

15	1 NAIRA	VG	VF	UNC
	ND (1973-78). Red and brown on m/c unpt. Back red; stacking grain sacks.			
	a. Sign. 1.	2.00	5.00	11.00
	b. Sign. 2.	1.50	4.00	11.00
	c. Sign. 3.	1.50	4.00	11.00
	d. Sign. 4.	4.00	16.50	45.00

16	5 NAIRA	VG	VF	UNC
	ND (1973-). Blue-gray and olive-green on m/c unpt. Back blue-gray; beating plant.			
	a. Sign. 1.	7.00	15.00	65.00
	b. Sign. 2.	4.00	10.00	45.00
	c. Sign. 3.	15.00	60.00	275.00
	d. Sign. 4.	20.00	75.00	325.00

17	10 NAIRA	VG	VF	UNC
	ND (1973-78). Carmine and dk. blue on m/c unpt. Back carmine; dam at ctr.			
	a. Sign. 1.	15.00	35.00	110.00
	b. Sign. 2.	7.00	22.50	75.00
	c. Sign. 3.	35.00	125.00	400.00
	d. Sign. 4.	40.00	150.00	485.00

18	20 NAIRA			
	ND (1977-84). Yellow-green on m/c unpt. Gen M. Muhammed at l. Arms at ctr. r. on back.			
	a. Sign. 2.	30.00	100.00	325.00
	b. Sign. 3.	20.00	60.00	200.00
	c. Sign. 4.	8.00	20.00	65.00
	d. Sign. 5.	6.00	15.00	45.00
	e. Sign. 6.	4.00	10.00	33.50

1979 ND ISSUE

#19-22 sign. titles: *GOVERNOR* and *DIRECTOR OF DOMESTIC OPERATIONS*. Wmk: Heraldic eagle.

19	1 NAIRA	VG	VF	UNC
	ND (1979-84). Red on m/c unpt. H. Macauley at l. Mask at ctr. r. on back.			
	a. Sign. 4.	.50	1.50	5.00
	b. Sign. 5.	.30	1.00	3.00
	c. Sign. 6.	.25	.75	1.50

20	5 NAIRA	VG	VF	UNC
	ND (1979-84). Green on m/c unpt. Alhaji Sir Abubaker Tafawa Balewa at l. Dancers at ctr. on back.			
	a. Sign. 4.	2.00	5.00	13.50
	b. Sign. 5.	1.50	4.00	10.00
	c. Sign. 6.	1.00	3.00	8.50

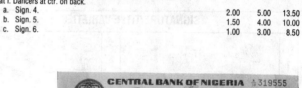

21	10 NAIRA	VG	VF	UNC
	ND (1979-84). Brown, purple and violet on m/c unpt. A. Ikoku at l. 2 women w/bowls on heads at ctr. r. on back.			
	a. Sign. 4.	4.00	12.00	27.50
	b. Sign. 5.	3.00	8.00	22.50
	c. Sign. 6.	7.00	20.00	—

1984; 1991 ND ISSUE

#23-27 new colors and sign. Like #18-21 but smaller. Wmk: Heraldic eagle.

23	1 NAIRA	VG	VF	UNC
	ND (1984-). Red, violet and green. Like #19. Back olive and lt. violet.			
	a. Sign. title at r.: *DIRECTOR OF DOMESTIC OPERATIONS*. Sign. 6.	FV	1.00	2.50
	b. Sign. title at r.: *DIRECTOR OF CURRENCY OPERATIONS*. Sign. 7.	FV	.50	1.75
	c. Titles as b. Sign. 8.	FV	FV	1.25
	d. Titles as b. Sign. 9.	FV	FV	1.25

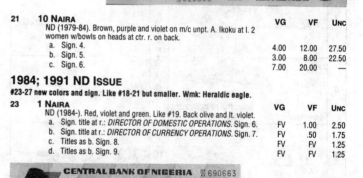

24   5 NAIRA
ND (1984-). Purple and brown-violet on m/c unpt. Like #20.

	VG	VF	UNC
a. Sign. title at r.: *DIRECTOR OF DOMESTIC OPERATIONS.* Sign. 6.	FV	2.00	5.00
b. Sign. title at r.: *DIRECTOR OF CURRENCY OPERATIONS.* Sign. 7.	FV	1.00	2.25
c. Titles as b. Sign. 8.	FV	FV	1.75
d. Titles as b. Sign. 9.	FV	FV	1.50

25   10 NAIRA
ND (1984-). Red-violet and orange on m/c unpt. Back red. Like #21.

	VG	VF	UNC
a. Sign. title at r.: *DIRECTOR OF DOMESTIC OPERATIONS.* Sign. 6.	FV	2.50	7.50
b. Sign. title at r.: *DIRECTOR OF CURRENCY OPERATIONS.* Sign. 7.	FV	2.50	5.00
c. Titles as b. Sign. 8.	FV	FV	2.25
d. Titles as b. Sign. 9.	FV	FV	2.00
e. Titles as b. Sign. 10.	FV	FV	2.00

26   20 NAIRA
ND (1984-). Dk. blue-green, dk. green and green on m/c unpt. Like #18.

	VG	VF	UNC
a. Sign. title at r.: *DIRECTOR OF DOMESTIC OPERATIONS.* Sign. 6.	FV	5.00	17.50
b. Sign. title at r.: *DIRECTOR OF CURRENCY OPERATIONS.* Sign. 7.	FV	FV	4.50
c. Titles as b. Sign. 8.	FV	FV	3.50
d. Titles as b. Sign. 9.	FV	FV	3.00
e. Titles as b. Sign. 10.	FV	FV	2.00

27   50 NAIRA
ND (1991-). Dk. blue, black and gray on m/c unpt. Four busts reflecting varied citizenry at l. ctr. Three farmers in field at ctr. r., arms at lower r. on back.

	VG	VF	UNC
a. Sign. 8.	FV	3.50	11.50
b. Sign. 9.	FV	FV	6.50
c. Sign. 10.	FV	FV	5.50

NORWAY

The Kingdom of Norway, a constitutional monarchy located in northwestern Europe, has an area of 150,000 sq. mi. (388,500 sq. km.) including the island territories of Spitzbergen (Svalbard) and Jan Mayen, and a population of 4.27 million. Capital: Oslo (Christiania until 1924). The diversified economic base of Norway includes shipping, fishing, forestry, agriculture, and manufacturing. Nonferrous metals, paper and paperboard, paper pulp, iron, steel and oil are exported.

A United Norwegian kingdom was established in the 9th century, the era of the indomitable Norse Vikings who ranged far and wide, visiting the coasts of northwestern Europe, the Mediterranean, Greenland and North America. In the 13th century, the Norse kingdom was united briefly with Sweden, then passed, through the Union of Kalmar, 1397, to the rule of Denmark which was maintained until 1814. In 1814, Norway fell again under the rule of Sweden. The union lasted until 1905 when the Norwegian Parliament arranged a peaceful separation and invited a Danish prince (King Haakon VII) to occupy the throne of an independent Kingdom of Norway.

RULERS:
   Olav V, 1957-1991
   Harald V, 1991-

MONETARY SYSTEM:
   1 Krone = 100 Øre, 1873-

KINGDOM

NORGES BANK

1948-55 ISSUE
#30-33 Replacement notes: Serial # prefix *Z.*
#31 Replacement notes: Serial # prefix *X.*
#34 and 35 Replacement notes: Serial # prefix *G.*

30   5 KRONER
1955-63. Blue. Portr. F. Nansen at l. Fishing scene on back.

	VG	VF	UNC
a. Sign. Brofoss - Thorp. 1955-57.	5.00	20.00	50.00
b. Sign. Brofoss - Ottesen. 1959-63.	3.00	10.00	40.00

31   10 KRONER
1954-73. Yellow-brown. Portr. C. Michelsen at l. Mercury w/ships on back.

	VG	VF	UNC
a. Sign. Jahn - Thorp. 1954. Series A-D.	3.00	8.00	40.00
b. Sign. Brofoss - Thorp. 1954 Series D-1958 Series N.	3.00	8.00	30.00
c. Sign. Brofoss - Ottesen. 1959-1965 Series A.	FV	3.00	20.00
d. Sign. Brofoss - Petersen. 1965 Series F-1969.	FV	2.50	12.00
e. Sign. Brofoss - Odegaard. 1970.	FV	2.50	11.00
f. Sign. Wold - Odegaard. 1971-73.	FV	FV	8.00

34   500 Kroner
1948-76. Dk. green. Portr. N. Henrik Abel at upper l. and as wmk.,
crowned supported arms at upper ctr. Factory workers on back.

		VG	VF	UNC
a.	Sign. Jahn - Thorp. 1948; 1951.	115.00	225.00	—
b.	Sign. Brofoss and Thorp. 1954; 1956; 1958.	90.00	200.00	—
c.	Sign. Brofoss - Ottesen. 1960-64.	FV	165.00	—
d.	Sign. Brofoss - Petersen. 1966-69.	FV	140.00	—
e.	Sign. Brofoss - Odegaard. 1970.	FV	125.00	—
f.	Sign. Wold - Odegaard. 1971-76.	FV	115.00	200.00
s.	Specimen.	—	—	—

32   50 Kroner
1950-65. Dk. green. Portr. B. Bjornson at upper l. and as wmk.,
crowned arms at upper ctr. Harvesting on back.

		VG	VF	UNC
a.	Sign. Jahn - Thorp. 1950-54 Series A; B.	15.00	50.00	200.00
b.	Sign. Brofoss - Thorp. 1954 Series B-1958.	13.50	30.00	125.00
c.	Sign. Brofoss - Ottesen. 1959-65.	10.00	28.50	100.00

33   100 Kroner
1949-62. Red. Portr. H. Wergel at upper l. and as wmk., crowned
arms at upper ctr. Logging on back.

		VG	VF	UNC
a.	Sign. Jahn - Thorp. 1949-54 Series C.	22.50	50.00	200.00
b.	Sign. Brofoss - Thorp. 1954-58.	20.00	30.00	125.00
c.	Sign. Brofoss - Ottesen. 1959-62.	20.00	30.00	100.00

35   1000 Kroner
1949-74. Red-brown. Portr. H. Ibsen at l. and as wmk., crowned
supported arms at upper ctr. Old man and child on back.

		VG	VF	UNC
a.	Sign. Jahn - Thorp. 1949; 1951; 1953.	175.00	250.00	—
b.	Sign. Brofoss - Thorp. 1955; 1958.	175.00	250.00	—
c.	Sign. Brofoss - Ottesen. 1961; 1962.	170.00	225.00	—
d.	Sign. Brofoss - Petersen. 1965-70.	FV	200.00	—
e.	Sign. Brofoss - Odegaard. 1971-74.	FV	175.00	300.00

1962-78 Issue
#36 and 41 Replacement notes: Serial # prefix *H* or *Q*.
#37-40 Replacement notes: Serial # prefix *X* or *Z*.

36 10 KRONER

	VG	VF	UNC
1972-84. Blue-black on m/c unpt. F. Nansen at l. Fisherman and cargo ship on back.			
a. Replacement note. Sign. Wold and Odegaard. Serial # prefix *Q*.	2.25	6.75	15.00
b. Sign. Wold and Odegaard. 1973-76.	1.50	4.50	10.00
c. Sign. Wold and Sagård. 1977.	FV	2.00	5.00

37 50 KRONER

	VG	VF	UNC
1966-83. Green. B. Bjornson at l. and as wmk. Old church on back.			
a. Sign. Brofoss and Petersen. 1966-67; 1969.	13.50	20.00	37.50
b. Sign. Wold and Odegaard. 1971-73.	12.50	18.50	32.50
c. As b. W/security thread. 1974-75.	FV	16.50	27.50
d. Sign. Wold and Sagård. 1976-83.	FV	15.00	25.00

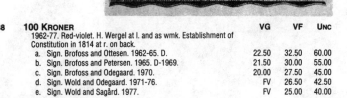

38 100 KRONER

	VG	VF	UNC
1962-77. Red-violet. H. Wergel at l. and as wmk. Establishment of Constitution in 1814 at r. on back.			
a. Sign. Brofoss and Ottesen. 1962-65. D.	22.50	32.50	60.00
b. Sign. Brofoss and Petersen. 1965. D-1969.	21.50	30.00	55.00
c. Sign. Brofoss and Odegaard. 1970.	20.00	27.50	45.00
d. Sign. Wold and Odegaard. 1971-76.	FV	26.50	42.50
e. Sign. Wold and Sagård. 1977.	FV	25.00	40.00

39 500 KRONER

	VG	VF	UNC
1978-85. Green on brown unpt. N. Henrik Abel at l. and as wmk. University of Oslo at r. on back.			
a. Sign. Skånland and Sagård. 1978; 1982.	FV	100.00	150.00
b. Sign. Wold and Sagård. 1985.	FV	90.00	125.00

40 1000 KRONER

	VG	VF	UNC
1975-87. Brown and violet. H. Ibsen at l. and as wmk. Scenery on back.			
a. Sign. Wold and Odegaard. 1975.	FV	200.00	275.00
b. Sign. Wold and Sagård. 1978-85. C.	FV	FV	250.00
c. Sign. Skånland and Sagård. C-1987.	FV	FV	225.00

1977 ISSUE

41 100 KRONER

	VG	VF	UNC
1977-82. Purple on pink and m/c unpt. C. Collett at l. and as wmk. Date at top l. ctr. Filigree design on back. Sign. Wold and Sagård.			
a. Brown serial #. 1977.	FV	18.50	45.00
b. Black serial #. 1979; 1980.	FV	18.50	40.00
c. 1981; 1982.	FV	FV	37.50

1983-91 ISSUE

45	1000 KRONER	VG	VF	UNC
	1989; 1990. Purple and dk. blue on m/c unpt. C. M. Falsen at l. 1668 royal seal on back. Sign. Skånland and Johansen.	FV	FV	185.00

1994; 1997 ISSUE

46	50 KRONER	VG	VF	UNC
	1997.			Expected New Issue
47	100 KRONER			
	1997.			Expected New Issue
49	500 KRONER			
				Expected New Issue

42	50 KRONER	VG	VF	UNC
	1984-95. Green on m/c unpt. A. O. Vinje at l. Stone carving w/soldier slaying dragon on back. Wmk: 50 repeated within diagonal bars.			
	a. Sign. Wold and Sagård. 1984.	FV	10.00	25.00
	b. Sign. Skånland and Sagård. 1985-87.	FV	FV	20.00
	c. Sign. Skånland and Johansen. 1989-90; 1993.	FV	FV	12.50
	d. Sign. Moland and Johansen. 1995.	FV	FV	11.50

43	100 KRONER	VG	VF	UNC
	1983-. Red-violet on pink and m/c unpt. Similar to #41 but smaller printing size, and date at lower r.			
	a. Wold and Sagård. 1983.	FV	20.00	45.00
	b. Lg. date. 1984.	FV	FV	32.50
	c. Sign. Skånland and Sagård. 1985-87.	FV	FV	27.50
	d. Sign. Skånland and Johansen. 1988-93.	FV	FV	25.00
	e. Sign. Moland and Johansen. 1994.	FV	FV	23.50

48	200 KRONER	VG	VF	UNC
	1994. Blue-black and dk. blue on m/c unpt. K. Birkeland at r. and as repeated vertical wmk. Map of the North Pole; North America and Northern Europe at l. ctr. on back. Sign. Moland and Johansen.	FV	FV	45.00
50	1000 KRONER			
				Expected New Issue

44	500 KRONER	VG	VF	UNC
	1991; 1994; 1996. Violet-blue and m/c unpt. E. Grieg at l. Floral mosaic at ctr. on back. Wmk: Multiple portr. of Grieg vertically.			
	a. Sign. Skånland and Johansen. 1991.	FV	FV	100.00
	b. Sign. Moland and Johansen. 1994.	FV	FV	95.00
	c. Sign. Storvik and Johansen. 1996.	FV	FV	90.00

OMAN

The Sultanate of Oman (formerly Muscat and Oman), an independent monarchy located in the southeastern part of the Arabian Peninsula, has an area of 82,030 sq. mi. (212,457 sq. km.) and a population of 2.07 million. Capital: Muscat. The economy is based on agriculture, herding and petroleum. Petroleum products, dates, fish and hides are exported.

The first European contact with Muscat and Oman was made by the Portuguese who captured Muscat, the capital and chief port, in 1508. They occupied the city, utilizing it as a naval base and factory and holding it against land and sea attacks by Arabs and Persians until finally ejected by local Arabs in 1650. It was next occupied by the Persians who maintained control until 1741, when it was taken by Ahmed ibn Sa'id of the present ruling family. Muscat and Oman was the most powerful state in Arabia during the first half of the 19th century, until weakened by the persistent attack of interior nomadic tribes. British influence, initiated by the signing of a treaty of friendship with the Sultanate in 1798, remains a dominant fact of the civil and military phases of the government, although Britain recognizes the Sultanate as a sovereign state and there is no colonial relationship between them.

Sultan Sa'id bin Taimur was overthrown by his son, Qabus bin Sa'id, on July 23, 1970. He changed the nation's name to Sultanate of Oman.

RULERS:
Sa'id bin Taimur, AH1351-1390/1932-1970 AD
Qaboos bin Sa'id, AH1390-/1970 AD-

MONETARY SYSTEM:
1 Rial Omani = 1000 Baiza (Baisa)
1 Rial Saidi = 1000 Baiza (Baisa)

MUSCAT AND OMAN

SULTANATE OF MUSCAT AND OMAN

1970 ND ISSUE
#1-6 arms at r. and as wmk.
#2-6 different fortresses on back.

			VG	VF	UNC
1	**100 BAIZA**				
	ND (1970). Brown and green on m/c unpt.		.30	.80	2.50

			VG	VF	UNC
2	**1/4 RIAL SAIDI**				
	ND (1970). Blue and brown on m/c unpt.		.70	1.00	3.25

			VG	VF	UNC
3	**1/2 RIAL SAIDI**				
	ND (1970). Green and violet on m/c unpt.		1.25	2.00	6.00

			VG	VF	UNC
4	**1 RIAL SAIDI**				
	ND (1970). Red and olive on m/c unpt.		2.50	4.00	10.00

			VG	VF	UNC
5	**5 RIALS SAIDI**				
	ND (1970). Purple and blue on m/c unpt. Fort Nizwa on back.		12.50	20.00	45.00

			VG	VF	UNC
6	**10 RIALS SAIDI**				
	ND (1970). Dk. brown and blue on m/c unpt.		20.00	45.00	75.00

OMAN

OMAN CURRENCY BOARD

1973 ND ISSUE
#7-12 arms at r. and as wmk.
#8-12 different fortresses on back.

7	**100 BAIZA**	VG	VF	UNC
	ND (1973). Dk. brown on pale blue-green and m/c unpt.	.50	1.00	2.00

8	**1/4 RIAL OMANI**	VG	VF	UNC
	ND (1973). Blue and brown on m/c unpt.	.40	1.00	3.75

9	**1/2 RIAL OMANI**	VG	VF	UNC
	ND (1973). Green and violet on m/c unpt.	1.75	2.75	6.00

10	**1 RIAL OMANI**	VG	VF	UNC
	ND (1973). Red and olive on m/c unpt.	2.75	6.50	10.00

11	**5 RIALS OMANI**	VG	VF	UNC
	ND (1973). Purple and blue on m/c unpt.	15.00	25.00	45.00

12	**10 RIALS OMANI**	VG	VF	UNC
	ND (1973). Dk. brown and blue on m/c unpt.	30.00	45.00	70.00

CENTRAL BANK OF OMAN

1977; 1985 ISSUE
#13-21 arms at r. and as wmk.

13	**100 BAISA**	VG	VF	UNC
	ND (1977). Lt. brown on m/c unpt. Port of Qaboos on back.	FV	FV	1.50

14 **200 BAISA**   VG   VF   UNC
ND (1985). Purple on m/c unpt. Rustaq Fortress on back.   FV   FV   2.25

15 **1/4 RIAL**   VG   VF   UNC
ND (1977). Blue and brown on m/c unpt. Back like #8.   FV   FV   2.50

16 **1/2 RIAL**   VG   VF   UNC
ND (1977). Green and violet on m/c unpt. Back like #9.   FV   FV   4.00

17 **1 RIAL**   VG   VF   UNC
ND (1977). Red and brown on m/c unpt. Back like #10.   FV   FV   7.00

18 **5 RIALS**   VG   VF   UNC
ND (1977). Lilac and blue on m/c unpt. Back like #11.   FV   FV   26.50

19 **10 RIALS**   VG   VF   UNC
ND (1977). Brown on m/c unpt. Back like #12.   FV   FV   50.00

20 **20 RIALS**   VG   VF   UNC
ND (1977). Gray-blue and orange on m/c unpt. Sultan Qaboos bin   FV   60.00   100.00
Sa'id at r. Central Bank at l. ctr. on back. Wmk: Arms.

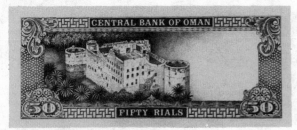

21   50 RIALS
　　ND. Olive-brown, blue and dk. brown on m/c unpt. Jabreen Fort at l.
　　ctr. on back.

	VG	VF	UNC
	FV	145.00	225.00

1985-90 ISSUE
#22-30 Sultan Qaboos bin Sa'id at r. and as wmk.

22   100 BAISA
　　1987/AH1408-. Lt. brown on m/c unpt. Port of Qaboos on back.

	VG	VF	UNC
a. 1987/AH1408.	FV	FV	1.25
b. 1989/AH1409.	FV	FV	1.00
c. 1994/AH1414.	FV	FV	.85

23   200 BAISA
　　1987/AH1407-. Purple on m/c unpt. Rustaq Fort on back.

	VG	VF	UNC
a. 1987/AH1407.	FV	FV	2.00
b. 1993/AH1413.	FV	FV	1.75
c. 1994/AH1414.	FV	FV	1.50

24   1/4 RIAL
　　1989/AH1409. Blue on m/c unpt. Modern fishing industry on back.

	VG	VF	UNC
	FV	FV	2.00

25   1/2 RIAL
　　1987/AH1408. Green on m/c unpt. Aerial view of Sultan Qaboos
　　University on back.

	VG	VF	UNC
	FV	FV	3.00

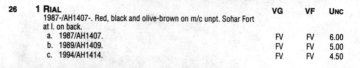

26   1 RIAL
　　1987-/AH1407-. Red, black and olive-brown on m/c unpt. Sohar Fort
　　at l. on back.

	VG	VF	UNC
a. 1987/AH1407.	FV	FV	6.00
b. 1989/AH1409.	FV	FV	5.00
c. 1994/AH1414.	FV	FV	4.50

27   5 RIALS
　　1990/AH1411. Dk. rose, brown-violet and m/c. Fort Nizwa on back.

	VG	VF	UNC
	FV	FV	22.50

28   10 RIALS
1987-/AH1408-. Dk. brown, red-brown and blue on m/c unpt. Fort
Mirani at l. ctr. on back.

	VG	VF	UNC
a. 1987/AH1408.	FV	FV	45.00
b. 1993/AH1413.	FV	FV	42.50

29   20 RIALS
1987-/AH1407-. Brown, dk. olive-brown and blue-gray on m/c unpt.
Central Bank at l. ctr. on back.

	VG	VF	UNC
a. 1987/AH1408.	FV	FV	85.00
b. 1994/AH1414.	FV	FV	80.00

30   50 RIALS
1985-/AH1405-. Olive-brown, blue and dk. brown on m/c unpt. Like
#21 but w/*Jabreen Fort* added at lower r. on back.

	VG	VF	UNC
a. 1985/AH1405.	FV	FV	210.00
b. 1992/AH1413.	FV	FV	200.00

1995 ISSUE
#31-38 Sultan Qaboos at r. and as wmk., arms at upper l.

31   100 BAISA
1995/AH1416. Deep olive-green, dk. green-blue and purple on m/c
unpt. Irrigation canal at ctr. Birds and animals at l. ctr. on back.

	VG	VF	UNC
	FV	FV	.65

32   200 BAISA
1995/AH1416. Black, deep blue and green on m/c unpt. Airport at l.
ctr. Marine Science and Fisheries Centre at lower l., aerial view of port
at ctr. on back.

	VG	VF	UNC
	FV	FV	1.25

33   1/2 RIAL
1995/AH1416. Dk. brown and gray on m/c unpt. Fortress at ctr., al-
Hazm fortress at lower l., Nakhl fortress at ctr. on back.

	VG	VF	UNC
	FV	FV	2.25

34   1 RIAL
1995/AH1416. Deep purple, purple and blue-green on m/c unpt.
Monument and stadium at ctr. Dagger, bracelets and ornaments
w/boats in background unpt. on back.

	VG	VF	UNC
	FV	FV	4.00

35   5 RIALS
1995/AH1416. Red on pale blue and m/c unpt. Bldg. w/clock tower at
ctr. View of city at l. ctr. on back.

	VG	VF	UNC
	FV	FV	18.50

36   10 RIALS
  1995/AH1416. Dk. brown on pale blue and m/c unpt. Tower at ctr.,
  Jabreen fortress, city at l. ctr. on back.

VG	VF	UNC
FV	FV	36.50

37   20 RIALS
  1995/AH1416. Dk. blue-green and olive-green on m/c unpt. Bldg. at
  ctr., minaret at r., govt. bldg. at l., aerial view of industrial park at ctr.,
  Chamber of Commerce and Industry bldg. at upper r.

VG	VF	UNC
FV	FV	70.00

38   50 RIALS
  1995/AH1416. Purple and violet on m/c unpt. Bldgs. at l. and ctr. r. on
  back.

VG	VF	UNC
FV	FV	165.00

PAKISTAN

The Islamic Republic of Pakistan, located on the Indian subcontinent between India and Afghanistan, has an area of 310,404 sq. mi. (803,943 sq. m.) and a population of 114 million. Capital: Islamabad. Pakistan is mainly an agricultural land. Yarn, cotton, rice and leather are exported.

Afghan and Turkish intrusions into northern India between the 11th and 18th centuries resulted in large numbers of indians being converted to Islam. The idea of a separate Moslem state indepenent of Hindu India developed in the 1930's and was agreed to by Britain in 1946. The Islamic majority areas of india, consisting of the separate geographic entities known as East and West Pakistan, achieved self-government as Pakistan, with dominion status in the British Commonwealth, when the British withdrew from India on Aug. 14, 1947. Pakistan became a republic in 1956. When a basic constitutional crisis initiated by the election of Dec. 1, 1970 - the first direct general election in Pakistani history - could not be resolved by the leaders of East and West Pakistan, the East Pakistanis seceded from the Islamic Republic of Pakistan (March 26, 1971) and formed the independent People's Republic of Bangladesh.

MONETARY SYSTEM:
  1 Rupee = 16 Annas to 1961
  1 Rupee = 100 Paisa (Pice), 1961-

REPUBLIC

GOVERNMENT OF PAKISTAN

1969 ND ISSUE

9   1 RUPEE
  ND (1969). Blue on m/c unpt. Back violet.

VG	VF	UNC
.25	.75	2.50

1973 ND ISSUE

10   1 RUPEE
  ND (1973). Brown on m/c unpt. Arms at r. and as wmk. Archway at l.
  ctr. on back. 2 sign. varieties.

VG	VF	UNC
.35	1.25	3.50

STATE BANK OF PAKISTAN

CITY OVERPRINT VARIETIES

ঢাকা ঢাকা করাচী کراچی লাহোর لاہور

Dacca   Karachi   Lahore

Some notes exist w/Arabic and some w/Sanskrit ovpt. denoting city of issue, Dacca, Karachi or Lahore. These are much scarcer than the regular issues. Sign. varieties.

1957 ISSUE

19	**500 RUPEES**	VG	VF	UNC
	ND (1964). Red on gold and lt. green unpt. Jinnah at ctr. Bank on back. Sign. in Urdu or Latin letters. 2 sign. varieties.			
	a. Ovpt: *Dacca*.	3.50	10.00	55.00
	b. Ovpt: *Karachi*.	4.00	12.00	60.00
	c. Ovpt: *Lahore*.	4.00	12.00	60.00

1973 ND ISSUE
#20-23 portr. of M. Ali Jinnah and as wmk.

20	**5 RUPEES**	VG	VF	UNC
	ND (1973). Red-brown on blue and green unpt. Jinnah at ctr. terraces on back. 3 sign. varieties.	.50	2.00	3.50

21	**10 RUPEES**	VG	VF	UNC
	ND (1973). Green on m/c unpt. Like #16. 2 sign. varieties.	.75	3.00	7.50
22	**50 RUPEES**			
	ND (1973). Blue on m/c unpt. Like #17. 3 sign. varieties.	2.00	8.00	15.00

23	**100 RUPEES**	VG	VF	UNC
	ND (1973). Dk. blue on m/c unpt. Jinnah at l. Mosque on back. 2 sign. varieties	4.00	10.00	30.00

GOVERNMENT OF PAKISTAN

SIGNATURE VARIETIES			
1	Abdur Rauf	6	Rafiq Akhind
2	Aftab Ahmed Khan	7	Qazi Alimullah Marfi
3	Habibullah Baig	8	Khalid Javed
4	Izhar ul-Hag	9	Javed Talat
5	Saeed Ahmad Qureshi	10	

1975 ND ISSUES

24	**1 RUPEE**	VG	VF	UNC
	ND (1975). Blue on lt. green and lilac unpt. Arms at r. and as wmk. Archway at l. ctr., plain panel above lower border. Sign. 1.	.30	1.25	3.00

24A (24)	**1 RUPEE**	VG	VF	UNC
	ND (1975-81). Blue on lt. green and lilac unpt. Arms at r. and as wmk. Like #24 but w/deeper ornate panel above lower border. Tower on back. Sign. 1-3.	.25	1.00	2.50

1981-83 ND ISSUE

URDU TEXT LINE A

URDU TEXT LINE B

25	**1 RUPEE**	VG	VF	UNC
	ND (1981-82). Brown and m/c. Arms at r. and as wmk. Tomb of Allama Iqbal on back. No Urdu text line at bottom on back. Serial # at upper ctr. Sign. 3.	FV	.40	1.00

26	**1 RUPEE**	VG	VF	UNC
	ND (1982). Like #24A, but w/Urdu text line A at bottom on back.			
	a. Serial # at upper ctr. Sign. 3.	FV	.15	.75
	b. Serial # at lower r. Sign. 3.	FV	.10	.40

27   1 RUPEE

	VG	VF	UNC
ND (1983-). Like #24B, but w/Urdu text line B at bottom on back.			
a. Serial # at ctr. Sign. 3.	FV	.10	.35
b. Serial # at lower r. Sign. 3.	FV	FV	.30
c. As a., but sign. 4.	FV	FV	.25
d. As b., but sign. 4.	FV	FV	.25
e. As a., but sign. 5.	FV	FV	.25
f. As b., but sign. 5.	FV	FV	.25
g. As a., but sign. 6.	FV	FV	.25
h. As b., but sign. 6.	FV	FV	.20
i. As b., but sign. 7.	FV	FV	.20
j. Serial # at upper ctr. Sign. 7.	FV	FV	.20
k. As b., but sign. 8.	FV	FV	.20
l. As b., but sign. 9.	FV	FV	.15
m. As b., but sign. 10.	FV	FV	.10

STATE BANK OF PAKISTAN

1975-78 ND ISSUE
#28-31 portr. of M. Ali Jinnah at r. and as wmk. Serial # and sign. varieties.

28   5 RUPEES

	VG	VF	UNC
ND (1975-84). Brown on tan and pink unpt. The Khajak railroad tunnel on back. No Urdu text line beneath upper title on back. 2 sign. varieties.	FV	.40	1.50

29   10 RUPEES

	VG	VF	UNC
ND (1975-84). Green and m/c. View of Mohanjodaro on back. No Urdu text line beneath upper title on back. 2 sign. varieties.	FV	.75	1.75

30   50 RUPEES

	VG	VF	UNC
ND (1978-84). Purple and m/c. Gate of Lahore fort on back. No Urdu text line beneath upper title on back. 2 sign. varieties.	FV	3.00	10.00

31   100 RUPEES

	VG	VF	UNC
ND (1975-84). Red, orange and m/c. Islamic College, Peshawar, on back. No Urdu text line beneath upper title on back. 2 sign. varieties.	FV	7.50	20.00

1985 ND ISSUE
#33-36 portr. of M. Ali Jinnah at r. and as wmk.

#32 *Deleted*.

33   5 RUPEES

	VG	VF	UNC
ND (1985). Like #28, but w/Urdu text line A beneath upper title on back.	FV	.75	2.00

34   10 RUPEES

	VG	VF	UNC
ND (1985). Like #29, but w/Urdu text line A beneath upper title on back.	FV	.85	2.25

35   50 RUPEES

	VG	VF	UNC
ND (1985). Like #30, but w/Urdu text line A beneath upper title on back.	FV	3.25	12.00

36   100 RUPEES

	VG	VF	UNC
ND (1985). Like #31, but w/Urdu text line A beneath upper title on back.	FV	8.50	25.00

1986-87 ND ISSUE
#37-43 portr. of M. Ali Jinnah at r. and as wmk.

NOTE: #37 shade varieties exist.

37   2 RUPEES

	VG	VF	UNC
ND (1986-). Pale purple on m/c unpt. Arms at r. and as wmk. Badshahi mosque on back. Urdu text line B beneath upper title on back. 5 sign. varieties.	FV	FV	.50

38   5 RUPEES

	VG	VF	UNC
ND (1986). Like #28, but w/Urdu text line B beneath uppper title on back. 5 sign. varieties.	FV	FV	1.00

39   10 RUPEES

	VG	VF	UNC
ND (1986). Like #29, but w/Urdu text line B beneath upper title on back. 5 sign. varieties.	FV	FV	1.50

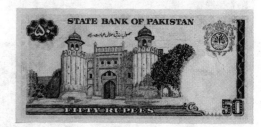

40   50 RUPEES

	VG	VF	UNC
ND (1986). Like #30, but w/Urdu text line B beneath upper title on back. 5 sign. varieties.	FV	FV	5.00

41   100 RUPEES

	VG	VF	UNC
ND (1986). Like #31, but w/Urdu text line B beneath upper title on back. 5 sign. varieties.	FV	FV	10.00

42   500 RUPEES

	VG	VF	UNC
ND (1986-). Deep blue-green and olive on m/c unpt. State Bank of Pakistan bldg. at ctr. on back. 5 sign. varieties.	FV	FV	35.00

		VG	VF	UNC
43	**1000 RUPEES** ND (1987-). Deep purple and blue-black on m/c unpt. Tomb of Jahangir on back. 3 sign. varieties.	FV	FV	70.00

		VG	VF	UNC
R7 (R6)	**100 RUPEES** ND. Gold and m/c. Like #31; dk. brown ovpt. 2 sign. varieties.	10.00	20.00	55.00

REGIONAL

STATE BANK OF PAKISTAN

CA. 1960s ND ISSUES

#R3-R5 ovpt: *FOR HAJ PILGRIMS FROM PAKISTAN/FOR USE IN SAUDI ARABIA ONLY.*

NOTE: All Haj Pilgrim notes were discontinued or destroyed in 1994.

		VG	VF	UNC
R3	**10 RUPEES** ND. Green and m/c. Ovpt. on #21. 2 sign. varieties.	7.50	16.50	50.00
R4	**10 RUPEES** ND. Purple and m/c. Like #16 but w/ovpt.	1.50	3.50	5.50

		VG	VF	UNC
R5	**100 RUPEES** ND. Brown and m/c. Like #23; black ovpt.	25.00	100.00	225.00

CA. 1970s ND ISSUE

#R6 and R7 ovpt: *FOR HAJ PILGRIMS FROM PAKISTAN/FOR USE IN SAUDI ARABIA ONLY* and Arabic for "Haj Pilgrim."

		VG	VF	UNC
R6 (R7)	**10 RUPEES** ND. Blue-black on m/c unpt. Like #34; black ovpt.	.50	1.25	4.00

PAPUA NEW GUINEA

Papua New Guinea, an independent member of the British Commonwealth, occupies the eastern half of the island of New Guinea. It lies north of Australia near the equator and borders on West Irian. The country, which includes nearby Bismarck archipelago, Buka and Bougainville, has an area of 176,280 sq. mi. (461,691 sq. km.) and a population of 3.7 million who are divided into more than 1,000 separate tribes speaking more than 700 mutually unintelligible languages. Capital: Port Moresby. The economy is agricultural, and exports include copra, rubber, cocoa, coffee, tea, gold and copper.

New Guinea, the world's largest island after Greenland, was discovered by Spanish navigator Jorge de Menezes, who landed on the northwest shore in 1527. European interests, attracted by exaggerated estimates of the resources of the area, resulted in the island being claimed in whole or part by Spain, the Netherlands, Great Britain and Germany.

Papua (formerly British New Guinea), situated in the southeastern part of the island of New Guinea, has an area of 90,540 sq. mi. (234,499 sq. km.) and a population of 740,000. It was temporarily annexed by Queensland in 1883 and by the British Crown in 1888. Papua came under control of the Australian Commonwealth in 1901 and became the Territory of Papua in 1906. Japan invaded New Guinea and Papua early in 1942, but Australian control was restored before the end of the year in Papua and in 1945 in New Guinea.

In 1884 Germany annexed the area known as German New Guinea (also Neu-Guinea or Kaiser Wilhelmsland) comprising the northern section of eastern New Guinea, and granted its administration and development to the New-Guinea Compagnie. Administration reverted to Germany in 1889 following the failure of the company to exercise adequate administration. While a German protectorate, German New Guinea had an area of 92,159 sq. mi. (238,692 sq. km.) and a population of about 250,000. Capital: Herbertshohe, later named Rabaul. Copra was the chief crop. Australian troops occupied German New Guinea in Aug. 1914, shortly after Great Britain declared war on Germany. It was mandated to Australia by the League of Nations in 1920 and known as the Territory of New Guinea. The territory was invaded and occupied by Japan in 1942. Following the Japanese surrender, it came under U.N. trusteeship, Dec. 13, 1946, with Australia as the administering power.

The Papua and New Guinea Act, 1949, provided for the government of Papua and New Guinea as one administrative unit. On Dec. 1, 1973, Papua New Guinea became self-governing with Australia retaining responsibility for defense and foreign affairs. Full independence was achieved on Sept. 16, 1975 and Papua New Guinea is now a member of the Commonwealth of Nations. The Queen of England is Chief of State.

RULERS:
British

MONETARY SYSTEM:
1 Kina = 100 Toea, 1975-

BRITISH INFLUENCE

BANK OF PAPUA NEW GUINEA

SIGNATURE VARIETIES					
1	*Ohens* *Mooranta*		4	*Ohens* *signature*	
2	*Ohens* *signature*		5	*signature* *signature*	
3	*Ohens* *signature*		6		

1975 ISSUE
#1-4 stylized Bird of Paradise at l. ctr. and as wmk.

			VG	VF	UNC
1	**2 KINA** ND (1975). Black on green and m/c unpt. Artifacts on back. Sign. 1.		FV	3.75	15.00

			VG	VF	UNC
2	**5 KINA** ND (1975). Violet on m/c unpt. Mask at ctr. r. on back. Sign. 1.		FV	7.00	30.00

			VG	VF	UNC
3	**10 KINA** ND (1975). Blue on m/c unpt. Bowl, ring and other artifacts on back. Sign. 1.		FV	14.00	55.00

			VG	VF	UNC
4	**20 KINA** ND (1977). Red and m/c. Boar's head at r. on back. Sign. 1.		FV	22.00	85.00

1981-85 ISSUE
#8 Held in reserve.

			VG	VF	UNC
5	**2 KINA** ND (1981). Like #1. Green unpt. w/white strip 16mm wide.				
	a. Sign. 1.		FV	FV	10.00
	b. Sign. 2.		FV	FV	7.00
	c. Sign. 3.		FV	FV	6.00
6	**5 KINA** ND (1981). Like #2. Pink unpt. w/white strip 22mm wide.				
	a. Sign. 1.		FV	6.50	22.50
	b. Sign. 2.		FV	7.00	25.00
7	**10 KINA** ND (1985). Like #3. Blue unpt. w/white strip 18mm. wide. Sign. 1.		FV	10.00	45.00

		VG	VF	UNC
9	**10 KINA** ND (1988). Similar to #7 but different design elements in unpt. representing a modern bldg. Ornate corner designs omitted on face and back.			
	a. Sign. 2.	FV	15.00	75.00
	b. Sign. 3.	FV	FV	25.00
10	**20 KINA** ND. Similar to #4 but different design elements in unpt. Sign. 3.	FV	FV	45.00

		VG	VF	UNC
11	**50 KINA** ND (1989). Orange, yellow and m/c. National Parliament bldg. at ctr. Foreign Affairs Minister M. Somare at l. ctr., ceremonial masks at r. on back. Wmk: Central Bank logo. Sign. 3.	FV	FV	75.00

1991 COMMEMORATIVE ISSUE
#12, 9th South Pacific Games 1991

		VG	VF	UNC
12	**2 KINA** 1991. Black and dk. green on lt. green and m/c unpt. Similar to #5 but w/stylized Bird of Paradise in clear circle at lower r. Polymer. Printer: NPA (w/o imprint).	FV	FV	6.00

1992 REGULAR ISSUES
#13 and 14 wmk: Stylized Bird of Paradise.

		VG	VF	UNC
13	**5 KINA** ND (1992). Like #6 but most design elements much lighter. Serial # darker and heavier. Sign. 3.	FV	FV	15.00

		VG	VF	UNC
14	**5 KINA** ND (1993). Like #13 but w/segmented security thread and new sign. title: *Secretary for Finance and Planning.* Sign. 4.	FV	FV	12.50

1996 COMMEMORATIVE ISSUE
#15, 20th Anniversary Bank of Papua New Guinea

		VG	VF	UNC
15	**2 KINA** ND (1995). Similar to #12 but w/ornate *20 ANNIVERSARY* logo at l. Sign 4. Polymer. Printer: NPA (w/o imprint).	FV	FV	5.00

PARAGUAY

The Republic of Paraguay, a landlocked country in the heart of South America surrounded by Argentina, Bolivia and Brazil, has an area of 157,048 sq. mi. (406,752 sq. km.) and a population of 4.4 million, 95 percent of whom are of mixed Spanish and Indian descent. Capital: Asuncion. The country is predominantly agrarian, with no important mineral deposits or oil reserves. Meat, timber, oilseeds, tobacco and cotton account for 70 percent of Paraguay's export revenue.

Paraguay was first visited by Alejo Garcia, a shipwrecked Spaniard, in 1520. The interior was explored by Sebastian Cabot in 1526 and 1529, when he sailed up the Parana and Paraguay Rivers. Asuncion, which would become the center of a province embracing much of southern South America, was established by the Spanish explorer Juan de Salazar on Aug. 15, 1537. For a century and a half the history of Paraguay was largely the history of the agricultural colonies established by the Jesuits in the south and east to Christianize the Indians. In 1811, following the outbreak of the South American wars of independence, Paraguayan patriots overthrew the local Spanish authorities and proclaimed their country's independence.

MONETARY SYSTEM:
1 Guarani = 100 Centimos, 1944-

REPUBLIC

BANCO CENTRAL DEL PARAGUAY

DECRETO LEY DE NO. 18 DEL 25 DE MARZO DE 1952 (FROM AUG. 1963)

#192-201 arms at l. Sign. size and name varieties. Printer: TDLR

NOTE: Do not confuse green #198 w/later issue #205 also in green. #198 w/value: *CIEN GUARANIES* at bottom on back.

Replacement notes: Serial # prefix *Z*.

		VG	VF	UNC
192	**1 GUARANI**			
	L.1952. Green on m/c unpt. Soldier at r. Black serial # at lower l. and lower r. Banco Central on back.	.25	1.00	4.00

		VG	VF	UNC
193	**1 GUARANI**			
	L.1952. Green on m/c unpt. Soldier at r. Palacio Legislativo on back.			
	a. Black serial # at lower l. and lower r.	.10	.35	1.75
	b. Black serial # at upper l. and lower r.	.10	.25	1.25
194	**5 GUARANIES**			
	L.1952. Blue on m/c unpt. Girl holding jug at r., black serial # at lower l. and lower r. Hotel Guarani on back.	.25	1.50	6.00

		VG	VF	UNC
195	**5 GUARANIES**			
	L.1952. Black on m/c unpt. Like #194.			
	a. Red serial # at lower l. and lower r.	.10	.30	1.50
	b. Red serial # at upper l. and lower r.	.10	.30	1.25

		VG	VF	UNC
196	**10 GUARANIES**			
	L.1952. Deep red on m/c unpt. Gen. E. A. Garay at r. International bridge on back.			
	a. Black serial # at lower l. and lower r.	.15	.40	2.25
	b. Black serial # at upper l. and lower r.	.15	.40	2.00

		VG	VF	UNC
197	**50 GUARANIES**			
	L.1952. Brown on m/c unpt. M. J. F. Estigarribia at r. Country road on back.			
	a. Black serial # at lower l. and lower r.	.75	1.75	7.00
	b. Black serial # at upper l. and lower r.	.20	.75	4.00

198   100 GUARANIES

		VG	VF	UNC
L.1952. Blue-green on m/c unpt. Gen. J. E. Diaz at r. Black serial # at lower l. and lower r. Ruins of Humaita on back.		.75	3.00	15.00

199   100 GUARANIES

		VG	VF	UNC
L.1952. Orange on m/c unpt. Like #198.				
a.	Black serial # at lower l. and lower r.	1.25	1.75	4.00
b.	Black serial # at upper l. and lower r.	.50	1.00	3.00

200   500 GUARANIES

		VG	VF	UNC
L.1952. Blue-green on m/c unpt. Gen. B. Caballero at r. Federal merchant ship on back.				
a.	Black serial # at lower l. and lower r.	1.50	4.00	10.00
b.	Black serial # at upper l. and lower r.	1.00	2.00	6.00

201   1000 GUARANIES

		VG	VF	UNC
L.1952. Violet on m/c unpt. Mariscal F. S. Lopez at r. National shrine on back.				
a.	Black serial # at lower l. and lower r.	4.00	8.00	20.00
b.	Black serial # at upper l. and lower r.	2.00	6.00	15.00
x.	As b. but w/mismatched serial al #.	—	—	10.00

202   5000 GUARANIES

		VG	VF	UNC
L.1952. Red-orange on m/c unpt. Arms at ctr., D. C. A. Lopez at r. Lopez Palace on back.				
a.	Black serial # at lower l. and lower r.	7.50	20.00	60.00
b.	Black serial # at upper l. and lower r.	5.00	15.00	45.00

203   10,000 GUARANIES

		VG	VF	UNC
L.1952. Brown on m/c unpt. Arms at ctr., Dr. J. Caspar Rodriguez de Francia at r., black serial # at lower l. and lower r. Historical scene from 14.5.1811 on back.		9.00	30.00	80.00

204   10,000 GUARANIES

		VG	VF	UNC
L.1952. Like #203 but CASPAR changed to GASPAR below Francia.				
a.	Black serial # at lower l. and lower r.	9.00	30.00	80.00
b.	Black serial # at upper l. and lower r.	FV	20.00	50.00

1982; 1990 ND ISSUE

#205-210 printer: TDLR. Replacement notes: Serial # prefix Z.

205   100 GUARANIES

		VG	VF	UNC
L.1952 (1982). Green on m/c unpt. Similar to #198 and 199 but value on back stated: SA GUARANI. 4 sign. varieties.		FV	FV	1.25

206   500 GUARANIES

		VG	VF	UNC
L.1952 (1982). Similar to #200 but value on back stated: PO SA GUARANI. 5 sign varieties.		FV	FV	1.85

207   1000 GUARANIES

	VG	VF	UNC
L.1952 (1982). Similar to #201 but value on back stated: *SU GUARANI.* 5 sign. varieties.	FV	FV	2.00

208   5000 GUARANIES

	VG	VF	UNC
L.1952 (1982). Similar to #202 but value on back stated: *PO SU GUARANI.* 6 sign. varieties.	FV	FV	6.50

209   10,000 GUARANIES

	VG	VF	UNC
L.1952 (1982). Similar to #203 but value on back stated: *PA SU GUARANI.* 4 sign. varieties.	FV	FV	11.00

210   50,000 GUARANIES

	VG	VF	UNC
L.1952 (1990). Purple and lt. blue on m/c unpt. Soldier at r., outline map of Paraguay at ctr. Back purple and olive-green on m/c unpt. House of Independence at ctr. Wmk: Face of soldier. 3 sign. varieties.	FV	FV	45.00

1994 ND ISSUE

211   50,000 GUARANIES

	VG	VF	UNC
L.1952 (1994). Like #210 but w/segmented foil over security thread and other enhanced security features. 3 sign. varieties.	FV	FV	40.00

212   100,000 GUARANIES

L.1952.	Expected New Issue

1995 ND ISSUE

#213 and 214 printer: F-CO.

213   500 GUARANIES

	VG	VF	UNC
L.1952 (1995). Similar to #206 but w/modified portr.	FV	FV	1.10

214   1000 GUARANIES

	VG	VF	UNC
L.1952 (1995). Similar to #207 but w/modified portr.	FV	FV	2.00

COLLECTOR SERIES

BANCO CENTRAL DEL PARAGUAY

1979 ISSUE

CS1   100-10,000 GUARANIES

	ISSUE PRICE	MKT. VALUE
1979. 199b-202b, 204b ovpt: *SPECIMEN* and w/Maltese cross prefix serial #.	14.00	25.00

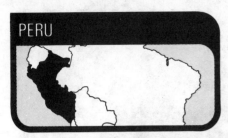

PERU

The Republic of Peru, located on the Pacific coast of South America, has an area of 496,222 sq. mi. (1,285,216 sq. km.) and a population of 21.6 million. Capital: Lima. The diversified economy includes mining, fishing and agriculture. Fish meal, copper, sugar, zinc and iron ore are exported.

Once part of a great Inca Empire that reached from northern Ecuador to Central Chile, Peru was conquered in 1531-33 by Francisco Pizarro. Desirable as the richest of the Spanish viceroyalties, it was torn by warfare between avaricious Spaniards until the arrival in 1569 of Francisco de Toledo, who initiated 2 1/2 centuries of efficient colonial rule which made Lima the most aristocratic colonial capital and the stronghold of Spain's American possessions. Jose de San Martin of Argentina proclaimed Peru's independence on July 28, 1821; Simon Bolívar of Venezuela secured it in Dec. of 1824 when he defeated the last Spanish army in South America. After several futile attempts to re-establish its South American empire, Spain recognized Peru's independence in 1879.

MONETARY SYSTEM:
- 1 Sol = 1 Sol de Oro = 100 Centavos, 1879-1985
- 1 Inti = 1000 Soles de Oro, 1986-1991
- 1 Nuevo Sol = 1 Million Intis, 1991-

REPUBLIC

BANCO CENTRAL DE RESERVA DEL PERU

1962; 1964 ISSUE

#83-87 Liberty seated holding shield and staff at ctr. Arms at ctr. on back. Printer: TDLR.

		VG	VF	UNC
83	**5 SOLES DE ORO**			
	9.2.1962; 20.9.1963; 18.6.1965; 18.11.1966; 23.2.1968. Green. Serial # at lower l. and upper r.	.30	1.00	3.00

		VG	VF	UNC
84	**10 SOLES DE ORO**			
	8.6.1962; 20.9.1963; 20.5.1966; 25.5.1967; 23.2.1968. Orange.	.30	1.00	3.00
85	**50 SOLES DE ORO**			
	9.2.1962; 20.9.1963; 23.2.1968. Blue. Like #78 but serial # at lower l. and upper r.	.75	3.00	10.00
86	**100 SOLES DE ORO**			
	13.3.1964; 23.2.1968. Black on lt. blue unpt. Like #80c.	2.00	6.00	18.00

		VG	VF	UNC
87	**500 SOLES DE ORO**			
	9.2.1962; 20.9.1963; 20.5.1966; 23.3.1968. Brown on lt. brown. Like #82b.	2.75	8.00	25.00

1962; 1965 REDUCED SIZE ISSUE

#88-91 like #83-87 but reduced size. Printer: ABNC.

		VG	VF	UNC
88	**10 SOLES DE ORO**			
	26.2.1965. Red-orange on lt. green unpt. Similar to #84.	.50	1.50	4.00

		VG	VF	UNC
89	**50 SOLES DE ORO**			
	20.8.1965. Blue. Similar to #86.	1.00	5.00	15.00
90	**100 SOLES DE ORO**			
	12.9.1962; 20.8.1965. Black on lt. blue unpt. Similar to #88.	2.00	6.00	18.00
91	**500 SOLES DE ORO**			
	26.2.1965. Brown. Similar to #90.	8.00	25.00	60.00

1968 ISSUE

#92-98 arms at ctr. 3 sign. Printer: TDLR.

Replacement notes: Serial # Z999 . . .

		VG	VF	UNC
92	**5 SOLES DE ORO**			
	23.2.1968. Green on m/c unpt. Artifacts at l., Inca Pachacutec at r. Back green; Fortaleza de Sacsahuaman.	.25	.50	2.50
93	**10 SOLES DE ORO**			
	23.2.1968. Red-orange on m/c unpt. Bldg. at l., G. Inca de la Vega at r. Back red-orange; Lake Titicaca and boats.	.20	.65	1.75
94	**50 SOLES DE ORO**			
	23.2.1968. Blue-gray on m/c unpt. Workers at l., Tupac Amaru II at r. Back blue-gray; scene of historic town of Tinta.	.25	.75	4.50
95	**100 SOLES DE ORO**			
	23.2.1968. Black on m/c unpt. Dock workers at l., H. Unanue at r. Back black; church.	.50	1.50	6.00

96	**200 S<small>OLES DE</small> O<small>RO</small>**			
	23.2.1968. Purple on m/c unpt. Fishermen at l., R. Castilla at r. Frigate Amazonas on back.	1.00	3.50	10.00
97	**500 S<small>OLES DE</small> O<small>RO</small>**			
	23.2.1968. Brown on m/c unpt., tan near ctr. Builders at l., N. de Pierola at r. National mint on back.	2.00	5.00	15.00
98	**1000 S<small>OLES DE</small> O<small>RO</small>**			
	23.2.1968. Lilac on m/c unpt. M. Grau at l., Francisco Bolognesi (misspelled BOLOG-ÑESI) at r. Scene of Machu Picchu on back.	4.00	12.00	25.00

1969 I<small>SSUE</small>

#99-105 like #92-98. 2 sign. Printer: TDLR.

Replacement notes: Serial # *Z999* . . .

99	**5 S<small>OLES DE</small> O<small>RO</small>**	VG	VF	U<small>NC</small>
	1969-74. Like #92.			
	a. 20.6.1969.	.10	.30	1.50
	b. 16.10.1970; 9.9.1971; 4.5.1972.	.10	.30	1.25
	c. 24.5.1973; 16.5.1974; 15.8. 15.8.1974.	.10	.25	1.00

100	**10 S<small>OLES DE</small> O<small>RO</small>**	VG	VF	U<small>NC</small>
	1969-74. Like #93.			
	a. 20.6.1969.	.10	.30	1.50
	b. 16.10.1970; 9.9.1971.	.10	.30	1.25
	c. 4.5.1972; 24.5.1973; 16.5.1974.	.10	.25	1.00
101	**50 S<small>OLES DE</small> O<small>RO</small>**			
	1969-74. Like #94.			
	a. 20.6.1969.	.25	.75	4.00
	b. 16.10.1970; 9.9.1971; 4.5.1972.	.20	.60	3.00
	c. 24.5.1973; 16.5.1974; 15.8.1974.	.20	.50	2.00

102	**100 S<small>OLES DE</small> O<small>RO</small>**	VG	VF	U<small>NC</small>
	1969-74. Like #95.			
	a. 20.6.1969.	.25	.75	4.00
	b. 16.10.1970; 9.9.1971; 4.5.1972.	.20	.60	3.00
	c. 24.5.1973; 16.5.1974; 15.8.1974.	.20	.50	2.50
103	**200 S<small>OLES DE</small> O<small>RO</small>**			
	1969-74. Like #96.			
	a. 20.6.1969.	.60	2.50	8.00
	b. 24.5.1973; 16.5.1974; 15.8.1974.	.50	1.75	6.50

104	**500 S<small>OLES DE</small> O<small>RO</small>**	VG	VF	U<small>NC</small>
	1969-74. Like #97.			
	a. 20.6.1969.	1.25	4.00	15.00
	b. 20.6.1969; 16.10.1970; 9.9.1971; 4.5.1972; 24.5.1973.	1.00	3.50	12.00
	c. 16.5.1974; 15.8.1974.	.60	2.50	8.00

105	**1000 S<small>OLES DE</small> O<small>RO</small>**	VG	VF	U<small>NC</small>
	1969-73. Like #98 but *BOLOGNESI* correctly spelled at r.			
	a. 20.6.1969; 16.10.1970.	1.75	6.00	25.00
	b. 9.9.1971; 4.5.1972; 24.5.1973.	1.50	5.00	22.50

1975 I<small>SSUE</small>

#106-111 3 sign. Printer: TDLR.

Replacement notes: Serial # *Z999* . . .

#109 *Deleted.*

106	**10 S<small>OLES DE</small> O<small>RO</small>**	VG	VF	U<small>NC</small>
	2.10.1975. Like #93.	.10	.25	1.00
107	**50 S<small>OLES DE</small> O<small>RO</small>**			
	2.10.1975. Like #94.	.10	.30	1.25
108	**100 S<small>OLES DE</small> O<small>RO</small>**			
	2.10.1975. Like #95.	.20	.50	2.00
110	**500 S<small>OLES DE</small> O<small>RO</small>**			
	2.10.1975. Like #97. Pale green unpt. near ctr.	1.00	3.00	10.00
111	**1000 S<small>OLES DE</small> O<small>RO</small>**			
	2.10.1975. Like #98. Name correctly spelled.	2.00	5.00	22.50

1976-77 I<small>SSUE</small>

#112 and 113 w/o *Pagara al Portador* at top. 3 sign. Replacement notes: Serial # *Z999* . . .

112	10 Soles de Oro	VG	VF	UNC
	17.11.1976. Like #106. Printer: TDLR.	.10	.25	.85

113	50 Soles de Oro	VG	VF	UNC
	15.12.1977. Like #107. Printer: TDLR.	.10	.30	1.00

114	100 Soles de Oro	VG	VF	UNC
	22.7.1976. Green, brown and m/c. Arms at l., Tupac Amaru II at r. Machu Picchu on back. Printer: IPS-Roma.	.10	.30	1.25
115	500 Soles de Oro			
	22.7.1976. Green, blue and yellow. Arms at ctr., J. Quinones at r. Logging scene on back. Printer: IPS-Roma.	.05	.15	.85

116	1000 Soles de Oro	VG	VF	UNC
	22.7.1976. Green and m/c. Arms at ctr., M. Grau at r. Fishermen on back. Printer: BDDK.	.50	2.00	6.00

117	5000 Soles de Oro	VG	VF	UNC
	1976-85. Brown and maroon on m/c unpt. Arms at ctr., Col. Bolognesi at r. and as wmk. 2 miners in mine on back. Printer: BDDK.			
	a. 22.7.1976.	1.00	2.50	7.00
	b. 5.11.1981.	.15	.50	1.50
	c. 21.6.1985.	.05	.15	.65

1979 Issue

#118-120 portr. as wmk. Printer: TDLR.
#117A *Deleted*. See #125A.
#121 *Deleted*. See #125B.

118	1000 Soles de Oro	VG	VF	UNC
	1.2.1979; 3.5.1979. Black, green and m/c. Arms at ctr., Adm. Grau at r. Fishermen and boats on back.	.50	1.00	3.00

119	5000 Soles de Oro	VG	VF	UNC
	1.2.1979. Brown-violet and m/c. Similar to #117 but *CINCO MIL* added at bottom on face. Miners on back.	.50	1.50	5.00

120	10,000 Soles de Oro	VG	VF	UNC
	1.2.1979; 5.11.1981. Blue, purple and m/c. Garcilaso Inca de la Vega at r. Indian digging and woman w/flowers on back.	.65	2.00	10.00

1981 ISSUE

#122-125 portr. as wmk. Printer: ABNC.

			VG	VF	UNC
122	1000 SOLES DE ORO	5.11.1981. Black, green and m/c. Similar to #118 but modified guilloche in unpt. at ctr.	.05	.15	.65

			VG	VF	UNC
123	5000 SOLES DE ORO	5.11.1981. Black and red-brown on m/c unpt. Similar to #119 but denomination is above signs. at ctr.	.35	1.00	4.00
124	10,000 SOLES DE ORO	5.11.1981. Similar to #120.	.50	1.50	6.00

			VG	VF	UNC
125	50,000 SOLES DE ORO	5.11.1981; 2.11.1984. Like #121.	1.00	3.00	12.50

1982; 1985 ISSUE

			VG	VF	UNC
125A (117A)	500 SOLES DE ORO	18.3.1982. Like #115 but printer: DLR.	.25	.50	3.00
125B (121)	50,000 SOLES DE ORO	23.8.1985. Black, orange and m/c. N. de Pierola at r. Drilling rig at l. on back, helicopter approaching.	.75	2.25	6.50

1985 PROVISIONAL ISSUE

#127 Held in reserve.

			VG	VF	UNC
126	100,000 SOLES DE ORO	ND (ca.1985). Ovpt. bank name and new denomination in red on #122.	30.00	90.00	225.00

1985-91 ISSUES

During the period from around 1984 and extending into 1990, Peru suffered from a hyperinflation that saw the inti depreciate in value dramatically and drastically. A sudden need for banknotes caused the government to approach a number of different security printers in order to satisfy the demand for new notes of increasingly higher denominations.

#128-150 involve six different printers: BDDK, CdM-B, FNMT, G&D, IPS-Roma and TDLR. Listings proceed by denomination and in chronological order. All portr. appear also as wmk., and all notes have arms at ctr. on face.

#144-150 arms at ctr. Various printers.

Replacement notes: BDDK - Serial # prefix *Y;* IPS-Roma - Serial # prefix *Y;* TDLR - Serial # prefix and suffix *Z.*

			VG	VF	UNC
128	10 INTIS	3.4.1985; 17.1.1986. Black, dk. blue and purple on m/c unpt. R. Palma at r. Back aqua and purple; Indian farmer digging at l. and another picking cotton at ctr. Printer: TDLR.	.05	15.00	.40

			VG	VF	UNC
129	10 INTIS	26.6.1987. Like #128. Printer: IPS-Roma.	.05	.10	.25
130	50 INTIS	3.4.1985. Black, red-orange and green on m/c unpt. N. de Pierola at r. Drilling rig at l. on back, helicopter approaching. Printer: TDLR.	.15	.30	1.00

131 50 INTIS
1986-87. Like #130. Printer: CdM-Brazil.

		VG	VF	UNC
a.	6.3.1986.	.10	.20	.60
b.	26.6.1987.	.05	.10	.35

132 100 INTIS
1985-86. Black and dk. brown on m/c unpt. R. Castilla at r. Women workers by cotton spinning frame at l. ctr. on back. Printer: CdM-Brazil.

		VG	VF	UNC
a.	1.3.1985.	1.00	2.00	10.00
b.	6.3.1986. Add'l red and green vertical unpt. at r.	.15	.30	1.00

136 1000 INTIS
1986-88. Deep green, olive-brown and red on m/c unpt. Mariscal A. Avelino C. at r. Ruins off Chan Chan on back. Printer: TDLR.

		VG	VF	UNC
a.	6.3.1986.	.15	.30	1.00
b.	26.6.1987; 28.6.1988.	.05	.10	.35

133 100 INTIS
26.6.1987. Like #132. Printer: BDDK.

	VG	VF	UNC
	.05	.10	.35

137 5000 INTIS
28.6.1988. Purple, deep brown and red-orange on m/c unpt. Adm. M. Grau at r. Fishermen repairing nets on back. Printer: G&D.

	VG	VF	UNC
	.05	.15	.50

138 5000 INTIS
28.6.1988. Like #137. Printer: IPS-Roma.

	VG	VF	UNC
	.25	.80	2.50

139 5000 INTIS
9.9.1988. Like #137. W/o wmk. Printer: TDLR.

	VG	VF	UNC
	.25	.80	2.50

134 500 INTIS
1985; 1987. Deep brown-violet and olive-brown on m/c unpt. J. G. Condorcanqui Tupac Amaru II at r. Mountains and climber at ctr. on back. Printer: BDDK.

		VG	VF	UNC
a.	1.3.1985.	.15	.30	1.00
b.	26.6.1987. Ornate red-orange vertical strip at l. end of design w/added security thread underneath.	.05	.10	.35

135 500 INTIS
6.3.1986. Similar to #134b. Printer: FNMT.

	VG	VF	UNC
	1.50	4.00	10.00

140 10,000 INTIS
28.6.1988. Dk. blue, and orange on lt. green and m/c unpt. C. Vallejo at r. Black and red increasing size serial # (anti-counterfeiting device). Santiago de Chuco street scene on back. Printer IPS-Roma.

	VG	VF	UNC
	.05	.25	.65

141 **10,000 INTIS**   VG   VF   UNC
28.6.1988. Like #140 but w/broken silver security thread. Printer: TDLR.   .25   .75   2.75

142	**50,000 INTIS**	VG	VF	UNC
	28.6.1988. Red, violet and dk. blue on m/c unpt. Victor Raul Haya de la Torre at r. Chamber of National Congress on back. Printer: IPS-Roma.	.15	.50	1.50
143	**50,000 INTIS**			
	28.6.1988. Like #142 but w/segmented foil security thread. Printer: TDLR.	.50	2.00	5.00

144	**100,000 INTIS**	VG	VF	UNC
	1988. Brown and black on m/c unpt. F. Bolognesi at r. Local boats in Lake Titicaca on back. Printer: TDLR.			
	a. Bolognesi's printed image on wmk. area at l. 21.11.1988.	.25	.75	2.25
	b. Segmented foil security thread, also w/Bolognesi as regular wmk. 21.12.1988.	.50	1.65	5.00
145	**100,000 INTIS**			
	21.12.1989. Like #144b, but w/black security thread at r. of arms. Printer: BdeM.	.25	.75	2.25

146	**500,000 INTIS**	VG	VF	UNC
	1988. Blue and blue-violet on m/c unpt. Face like #128. Church of *La Caridad* (charity), site of first National Congress, on back. Printer: TDLR.			
	a. R. Palma's printed image on wmk. area at l. 21.11.1988.	.30	1.50	4.50
	b. Segemented foil security thread, also w/Palma as wmk. 21.12.1988.	.35	1.65	5.00

147	**500,000 INTIS**	VG	VF	UNC
	21.12.1989. Like #146b, but w/black security thread at r. Printer: BdeM.	.20	.60	1.75

148	**1 MILLION INTIS**	VG	VF	UNC
	5.1.1990. Dk. red, green and m/c. H. Unanue at r. and as wmk. Medical college at San Fernando at l. ctr. on back. Printer: TDLR.	.25	.75	3.00
149	**5 MILLION INTIS**			
	5.1.1990. Brown, red and m/c. A. Raimondi at r. and as wmk. Indian comforting Raimundi on back. Printer: BdeM.	2.25	7.00	20.00
150	**5 MILLION INTIS**			
	16.1.1991. Similar to #149 but plants printed on wmk. area at l. on face, old bldg. at r. on back. Printer: IPS-Roma.	.65	2.00	6.00

1991-92 ISSUE

#151and 152 arms at upper r.

#153-155 arms at upper r. Printer: IPS-Roma.

151	**10 NUEVOS SOLES**	VG	VF	UNC
	1.2.1991. Dk. green and blue-green on m/c unpt. WW II era fighter plane as monument at upper ctr., J. Abelardo Quiñones at r. and as wmk. Biplane inverted at l. ctr. on back. Printer: TDLR.	FV	FV	8.50
151A (152A)	**10 NUEVOS SOLES**			
	10.9.1992. Like #151 but printer: IPS-Roma.	FV	FV	8.50

152 **20 Nuevos Soles**

	VG	VF	Unc
1.2.1991. Black and orange on m/c unpt. Archway to fountain at ctr., R. Porras B. at r. and as wmk. Palace of Torre Tagle at l. ctr. on back. Printer: TDLR.	FV	FV	20.00

153 **20 Nuevos Soles**

	VG	VF	Unc
25.6.1992. Like #152 but printer: IPS-Roma.	FV	FV	16.00

154 **50 Nuevos Soles**

	VG	VF	Unc
1.2.1991; 25.6.1992; 16.6.1994. Brown, deep blue and black on m/c unpt. Bldg. at ctr., A. Valdelomar at r. and as wmk., arms at upper r. Laguna de Huacachina at l. ctr. on back.	FV	FV	40.00

155 **100 Nuevos Soles**

	VG	VF	Unc
1.2.1991 (1992); 25.6.1992; 10.9.1992. Black, blue-black, red-violet and deep green on m/c unpt. Arch monument at ctr., J. Basadre at r. and as wmk., arms at upper r. National Library at l. on back.	FV	FV	70.00

1994 Issue
#156 and 157 printer: TDLR.

156 **10 Nuevos Soles**

	VG	VF	Unc
16.6.1994. Similar to #151 but w/o wmk.	FV	FV	7.50

157 **20 Nuevos Soles**

	VG	VF	Unc
16.6.1994. Similar to #152.	FV	FV	14.00

158 **50 Nuevos Soles**

Expected New Issue

159 **100 Nuevos Soles**

Expected New Issue

1995 Issue
#160 and 161 printer: G&D.

160 **10 Nuevos Soles**

	VG	VF	Unc
20.4.1995. Similar to #156.	FV	FV	7.00

161 **20 Nuevos Soles**

	VG	VF	Unc
20.4.1995. Similar to #157.	FV	FV	13.50

Banco de Credito del Peru/Banco Central de Reserva del Peru

Monetary Emergency, 1985

R2 **100,000 Soles**

	VG	VF	Unc
2.9.1985. Black text on lt. blue text unpt. 2 sign. varieties.	25.00	65.00	—

Banco de la Nación/Banco Central de Reserva del Peru

Cheques Circulares De Gerencia Issue

R6 **50,000 Soles**

	VG	VF	Unc
9.9.1985; 16.9.1985. Black text on tan unpt. Bank at ctr.	FV	65.00	—

R7 **100,000 Soles**

	VG	VF	Unc
2.9.1985. Black text on lt. blue unpt. Like #R6.	25.00	65.00	—

R8 **200,000 Soles**

	VG	VF	Unc
2.9.1985. Black text on pink unpt. Like #R6.	25.00	65.00	—

PHILIPPINES

The Republic of the Philippines, an archipelago in the western Pacific 500 miles (805 km.) from the southeast coast of Asia, has an area of 115,830 sq. mi. (300,000 sq. km.) and a population of 60.9 million. Capital: Manila. The economy of the 7,000-island group is based on agriculture, forestry and fishing. Timber, coconut products, sugar and hemp are exported.

Migration to the Philippines began about 30,000 years ago when land bridges connected the islands with Borneo and Sumatra. Ferdinand Magellan claimed the islands for Spain in 1521. The first permanent settlement was established by Miguel de Legazpi at Cebu in April of 1565; Manila was established in 1572. A British expedition captured Manila and occupied the Spanish colony in Oct. of 1762, but it was returned to Spain by the treaty of Paris, 1763. Spain held the Philippines amid a growing movement of Filipino nationalism until 1898 when they were ceded to the United States at the end of the Spanish-American War. The Filipinos then fought unsuccessfully against the United States to maintain their independent Republic proclaimed by Emilio Aguinaldo. The country became a self-governing commonwealth of the United States in 1935, and attained independence as the Republic of the Philippines on July 4, 1946. During World War II the Japanese had set up a puppet republic, but this quasi-government failed to achieve worldwide recognition. The occupation lasted from late 1941 to 1945. Ferdinand Marcos lost to Corazón Aquino in elections of 1986. Marcos then fled the country. In 1992 Fidel Ranos was elected President.

MONETARY SYSTEM:
1 Peso = 100 Centavos to 1967
1 Piso = 100 Sentimos, 1967-

REPUBLIC

CENTRAL BANK OF THE PHILIPPINES

1949 ND "ENGLISH" ISSUES
#125, 127, and 129 sign. E. Quirino and M. Cuaderno. Printer: SBNC.
#130-141 printer: TDLR.
#133-141 bank seal at lower r.

		VG	VF	UNC
125	**5 CENTAVOS** ND. Red on tan unpt. Back red.	.25	.50	1.50
126 (128)	**5 CENTAVOS** ND. Like #125. Sign. R. Magsaysay and M. Cuaderno. Printer: W&S.	.10	.25	1.00
127 (126)	**10 CENTAVOS** ND. Brownish purple on tan unpt. Back brownish purple.			
	a. Issued note.	.25	.50	2.50
	r. Remainder w/o serial #.	—	100.00	250.00
128 (129)	**10 CENTAVOS** ND. Like #126. Sign. R. Magsaysay and M. Cuaderno. Printer: W&S.	.25	.50	1.25
129 (127)	**20 CENTAVOS** ND. Green on lt. green unpt. Back green.			
	a. Issued note.	.30	.60	3.50
	r. Remainder w/o serial # (error).	—	100.00	250.00
130	**20 CENTAVOS** ND. Green on lt. green unpt. Back green.			
	a. Sign. R. Magsaysay and M. Cuaderno.	.20	.50	2.00
	b. Sign. C. Garcia and M. Cuaderno.	.20	.50	1.50
131	**50 CENTAVOS** ND. Blue on lt. blue unpt. Back blue. Sign. R. Magsaysay and M. Cuaderno.	.20	.50	2.25

		VG	VF	UNC
132	**1/2 PESO** ND. Green on yellow and blue unpt. Ox-cart w/Mt. Mayon in background at ctr. Back green. Sign. C. Garcia and M. Cuaderno.	.20	.75	2.25

		VG	VF	UNC
133	**1 PESO** ND. Black on lt. gold and blue unpt. A. Mabini at l. Back black; Barasoain Church at ctr.			
	a. Sign. E. Quirino and M. Cuaderno. *GENUINE* in very lt. tan letters just beneath top heading on face.	7.00	22.00	85.00
	b. Sign. E. Quirino and M. Cuaderno w/o *GENUINE* on face.	.50	1.50	5.00
	c. Sign. R. Magsaysay and M. Cuaderno.	.25	.75	3.00
	d. Sign. C. Garcia and M. Cuaderno.	.25	.75	2.00
	e. Sign. C. Garcia and A. Castillo w/title: *Acting Governor.*	.50	1.00	3.50
	f. Sign. D. Macapagal and A. Castillo w/title: *Governor.*			
	g. Sign. F. Marcos and A. Castillo.	.25	.75	2.00
	h. Sign. F. Marcos and A. Calalang.	.10	.30	1.00
	s. Sign. as f. Specimen.	—	—	55.00
134	**2 PESOS** ND. Black on blue and gold unpt. Portr. J. Rizal at l. Back blue; landing of Magellan in the Philippines.			
	a. Sign. E. Quirino and M. Cuaderno.	1.00	4.00	15.00
	b. Sign. R. Magsaysay and M. Cuaderno.	.75	2.00	5.00
	c. Sign. C. Garcia and A. Castillo w/title: *Acting Governor.*	.75	1.50	4.00
	d. Sign. D. Macapagal and A. Castillo w/title: *GOVERNOR.*	.15	.75	1.50
	s. Sign. as b. Specimen.	—	—	60.00
	s. Sign. as d. Specimen.	—	—	60.00

		VG	VF	UNC
135	**5 PESOS** ND. Black on yellow and gold unpt. Portr. M. H. del Pilar at l., Lopez Jaena at r. Back gold; newspaper "La Solidaridad".			
	a. Sign. E. Quirino and M. Cuaderno.	2.00	7.50	25.00
	b. Sign. R. Magsaysay and M. Cuaderno.	1.00	3.50	10.00
	c. Sign. C. Garcia and M. Cuaderno.	1.50	4.00	15.00
	d. Sign. C. Garcia and A. Castillo w/title: *Acting Governor.*	1.25	3.00	12.00
	e. Sign. D. Macapagal and A. Castillo w/title: *Governor.*	.20	.40	1.50
	f. Sign. F. Marcos and G. Licaros.	.20	.40	1.50
	s. Sign. as e. Specimen.	—	—	65.00

		VG	VF	UNC
136	**10 PESOS** ND. Black on tan and lt. red unpt. Fathers Burgos, Gomez and Zamora at l. Back brown; monument.			
	6. Sign. E. Quirino and M. Cuaderno.	8.00	25.00	75.00
	b. Sign. R. Magsaysay and M. Cuaderno.	2.50	7.00	20.00
	c. Sign. C. Garcia and M. Cuaderno.	3.00	7.50	22.50
	d. Sign. C. Garcia and A. Castillo w/title: *Acting Governor.*	2.50	7.00	17.50
	e. Sign. D. Macapagal and A. Castillo w/title: *Governor.*	.25	.75	2.25
	f. Sign. F. Marcos and G. Licaros.	1.00	2.50	7.50
	s. Sign. as b. Specimen.	—	—	70.00
	s. Sign. as d. Specimen.	—	—	70.00

		VG	VF	UNC
137	**20 PESOS** ND. Black on yellow unpt. Portr. A. Bonifacio at l., E. Jacinto at r. Back brownish orange; flag and monument.			
	a. Sign. E. Quirino and M. Cuaderno.	10.00	30.00	85.00
	b. Sign. R. Magsaysay and M. Cuaderno.	2.75	8.00	25.00
	c. Sign. C. Garcia and A. Castillo w/title: *Acting Governor.*	2.25	7.00	20.00
	d. Sign. D. Macapagal and A. Castillo w/title: *Governor.*	.50	1.50	4.50
	e. Sign. F. Marcos and G. Licaros.	.35	1.00	3.00
	s. Sign. as a. Specimen.	—	—	100.00
	s. Sign. as d. Specimen.	—	—	75.00

138 50 PESOS
ND. Black on pink and lt. tan unpt. Portr. A. Luna at l. Back red; scene of blood compact of Sikatuna and Legaspi.

	VG	VF	UNC
a. Sign. E. Quirino and M. Cuaderno.	50.00	170.00	—
b. Sign. R. Magsaysay and M. Cuaderno.	20.00	45.00	90.00
c. Sign. C. Garcia and M. Cuaderno.	8.00	20.00	40.00
d. Sign. D. Macapagal and A. Castillo.	.65	3.00	7.50
s. Sign. as d. Specimen.	—	—	85.00

143 5 PISO
ND (1969). Green and brown on m/c unpt. A. Bonifacio at l. in brown. Scene of the Katipunan organization on back.

	VG	VF	UNC
a. Sign. F. Marcos and A. Calalang.	.50	1.50	4.50
b. Sign. F. Marcos and G. Licaros.	.20	1.00	2.50
s. Sign. as b. Specimen.	—	—	15.00

139 100 PESOS
ND. Black on gold unpt. T. Sora at l. Back yellow; regimental flags. Sign. E. Quirino and M. Cuaderno.

VG	VF	UNC
3.00	7.50	20.00

140 200 PESOS
ND. Green on pink and lt. blue unpt. Pres. Manuel Quezon at l. Back green; Legislative bldg. Sign. E. Quirino and M. Cuaderno.

VG	VF	UNC
5.00	12.50	30.00

144 10 PISO
ND (1969). Brown on m/c unpt. A. Mabini at l. Barasoain Church on back.

	VG	VF	UNC
a. Sign. F. Marcos and A. Calalang.	.50	1.65	5.00
b. Sign. F. Marcos and G. Licaros.	.50	1.65	5.00
s. Sign. as b. Specimen.	—	—	20.00

141 500 PESOS
ND. Black on purple and lt. tan unpt. Pres. Manuel Roxas at l. Back purple; Central Bank. Sign. E. Quirino and M. Cuaderno.

VG	VF	UNC
10.00	30.00	75.00

BANGKO SENTRAL NG PILIPINAS

1969 ND "PILIPINO" ISSUE

#142-147 heading at top in double outline. Wmk. as portr.
#143-145 printer: G&D (w/o imprint).

142 1 PISO
ND (1969). Blue and m/c. J. Rizal at l. Scene of Agui-naldo's Independence Declaration of June 12, 1898 on back.

	VG	VF	UNC
a. Sign. F. Marcos and A. Calalang.	.20	.60	1.75
b. Sign. F. Marcos and A. Licaros.	.15	.50	1.50

145 20 PISO
ND (1969). Orange and brown on m/c unpt. M. L. Quezon at l. in brown. Malakanyang Palace on back.

	VG	VF	UNC
a. Sign. F. Marcos and A. Calalang.	.80	2.50	7.50
b. Sign. F. Marcos and G. Licaros.	.80	2.50	7.50
s. Sign. as b. Specimen.	—	—	25.00

146 50 PISO
ND (1969). Red on m/c unpt. S. Osmeña at l. Legislative bldg. on back.

	VG	VF	UNC
a. Sign. F. Marcos and A. Calalang.	1.35	4.00	12.00
b. Sign. F. Marcos and G. Licaros.	1.35	4.00	12.00
s. Sign. as b. Specimen.	—	—	30.00

147 100 PISO
ND (1969). Purple on m/c unpt. M. Roxas at l. Old Central Bank on back.

	VG	VF	UNC
a. Sign. F. Marcos and A. Calalang.	2.50	7.50	21.50
b. Sign. F. Marcos and G. Licaros.	2.50	7.50	21.50

FIRST 1970S ND ISSUE
#148-151 heading at top in single outline. Sign. F. Marcos and G. Licaros.

148 5 PISO
ND. Green on m/c unpt. Like #143 but A. Bonifacio in green.

	VG	VF	UNC
a. Issued note.	.25	.75	2.25
s. Specimen.	—	—	20.00

149 10 PISO
ND. Brown on m/c unpt. Like #144 but w/o white paper showing at sides on face or back.

	VG	VF	UNC
a. Issued note.	.50	1.65	5.00
s. Specimen.	—	—	30.00

150 20 PISO
ND. Orange and blue on m/c unpt. Like #145 but M. L. Quezon in orange.

	VG	VF	UNC
a. Issued note.	.25	.75	2.25
s. Specimen.	—	—	40.00

151 50 PISO
ND. Red on m/c unpt. Similar to #146. Seal under denomination instead of over, sign. closer, *LIMAMPUNG PISO* in one line, and other modifications.

	VG	VF	UNC
a. Issued note.	3.00	8.00	25.00
s. Specimen.	—	—	50.00

SECOND 1970S ND ISSUE
#152-158 light, fully detailed bank seal w/ovpt: *ANG BAGONG LIPUNAN* (New Society) on wmk. area, 1974-85.

152 2 PISO
ND. Blue on m/c unpt. J. Rizal at l., his wmk. at r. Scene of Aguinaldo's Independence Declaration of 1898 on back. Sign. F. Marcos and G. Licaros.

	VG	VF	UNC
a. Issued note.	.20	.40	1.25

153 5 PISO
ND. Green on m/c unpt. Like #148. Sign. F. Marcos and G. Licaros.

	VG	VF	UNC
a. Issued note.	.50	1.00	2.00
s. Specimen.	—	—	15.00

154 10 PISO
ND. Brown on m/c unpt. Like #149. Sign. F. Marcos and G. Licaros.

	VG	VF	UNC
a. Issued note.	.30	.90	1.75
s. Specimen.	—	—	25.00

155 20 PISO
ND. Orange on m/c unpt. Like #150. Sign. F. Marcos and G. Licaros.

	VG	VF	UNC
a. Issued note.	1.50	3.00	6.00
s. Specimen.	—	—	35.00

156 50 PISO
ND. Red on m/c unpt. Like #151. Sign. F. Marcos and G. Licaros.

	VG	VF	UNC
a. Issued note.	5.00	10.00	30.00
s. Specimen.	—	—	45.00

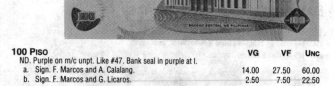

157 100 PISO
ND. Purple on m/c unpt. Like #47. Bank seal in purple at l.

	VG	VF	UNC
a. Sign. F. Marcos and A. Calalang.	14.00	27.50	60.00
b. Sign. F. Marcos and G. Licaros.	2.50	7.50	22.50

158	100 Piso	VG	VF	UNC
	ND. Purple on m/c unpt. Face resembling #157 but heading at top in single outline, green bank seal at lower r., and denomination near upper r. Back similar to #157 but denomination at bottom. Sign. F. Marcos and G. Licaros.			
	a. Issued note.	12.00	25.00	55.00
	s. Specimen.	—	—	100.00

THIRD 1970s ND ISSUE
#159-167 w/dk. silhouette bank seal.

159	2 Piso	VG	VF	UNC
	ND. Blue on m/c unpt. Like #152.			
	a. Sign. F. Marcos and G. Licaros.	.10	.30	1.00
	b. Sign. F. Marcos and J. Laya, w/black serial #.	.10	.30	1.00
	c. Sign. F. Marcos and J. Laya, w/red serial #.	.10	.30	1.00
	d. Sign. as b. Uncut sheet of 4.	—	—	15.00
	s. Sign. as b. Specimen.	—	—	15.00
160	5 Piso			
	ND. Green on m/c unpt. Like #153.			
	a. Sign. F. Marcos and G. Licaros.	.15	.40	1.50
	b. Sign. F. Marcos and J. Laya, w/black serial #.	.15	.40	1.50
	c. Sign. F. Marcos and J. Laya, w/red serial #.	.15	.40	1.50
	d. Sign. F. Marcos and J. Fernandez.	.15	.50	2.00
	e. Sign. as b. Uncut sheet of 4.	—	—	30.00
	f. Sign. as d. Uncut sheet of 4.	—	—	30.00
	s. Sign. as b. Specimen.	—	—	20.00

161	10 Piso	VG	VF	UNC
	ND. Brown on m/c unpt. Like #154.			
	a. Sign. F. Marcos and G. Licaros.	.30	1.00	2.50
	b. Sign. F. Marcos and J. Laya.	.25	.75	2.50
	c. Sign. F. Marcos and J. Fernandez, w/black serial #.	.20	.50	2.00
	d. Sign. F. Marcos and J. Fernandez, w/red serial #.	.20	.50	2.00
	e. Sign. as b. Uncut sheet of 4.	—	—	37.50
	f. Sign. as c. Uncut sheet of 4.	—	—	37.50
	s. Sign. as b. Specimen.	—	—	25.00
162	20 Piso			
	ND. Orange and blue on m/c unpt. Like #155.			
	a. Sign. F. Marcos and G. Licaros.	.30	1.00	3.00
	b. Sign. F. Marcos and J. Laya.	.30	1.00	3.00
	c. Sign. F. Marcos and J. Fernandez.	.30	1.00	3.00
	d. Sign. as b. Uncut sheet of 4.	—	—	40.00
	e. Sign. as d. Uncut sheet of 4.	—	—	40.00
	s. Sign. as b. Specimen.	—	—	30.00
163	50 Piso			
	ND. Red on m/c unpt. Like #156.			
	a. Sign. F. Marcos and G. Licaros.	.50	1.50	4.50
	b. Sign. F. Marcos and J. Laya.	.50	1.50	4.50
	c. Sign. F. Marcos and J. Fernandez.	.50	1.50	4.50
	s. Sign. as b. Specimen.	—	—	35.00

164	100 Piso	VG	VF	UNC
	ND. Purple on m/c unpt. Face like #158. New Central Bank complex, w/ships behind on back.			
	a. Sign. F. Marcos and G. Licaros.	3.00	8.00	20.00
	b. Sign. F. Marcos and J. Laya.	2.50	7.00	18.00
	c. Sign. F. Marcos and J. Fernandez, w/black serial #.	.80	2.50	7.50
	s. Sign. as b. Specimen.	—	—	40.00

1978 COMMEMORATIVE ISSUE
#165, Centennial Birth of Pres. Osmeña, 1978

165	50 Piso	VG	VF	UNC
	1978. Like #163a but w/black circular commemorative ovpt. at l.	2.25	7.00	15.00

1981 COMMEMORATIVE ISSUE
#166, Papal Visit of John Paul II, 1981

#167, Inauguration of Pres. Marcos, 1981

166	2 Piso	VG	VF	UNC
	1981. Like #159b but w/black commemorative ovpt. at ctr. r.			
	a. Regular prefix letters before serial #.	.10	.35	1.00
	b. Special JP prefix letters and all zero numbers (presentation).	—	—	

167	10 Piso	VG	VF	UNC
	1981. Like #161b but w/black commemorative ovpt. at ctr. r.			
	a. Regular prefix letters before serial #.	.25	.75	2.25
	b. Special F M prefix letters and all zero numbers (presentation).	—	—	20.00

1985-87 ND ISSUE
#168-173 portr. as wmk.

168	5 Piso	VG	VF	UNC
	ND (1985-). Deep green on m/c unpt. Agui-naldo at l. ctr., plaque w/cannon at r. Declaration of Independence (1898) on back.			
	a. Sign. F. Marcos and J. Fernandez.	FV	.65	2.00
	b. Sign. C. Aquino and J. Fernandez, w/black serial #.	FV	FV	1.00
	c. Sign. as b. w/red serial # (1990).	FV	FV	.75
	d. Sign. C. Aquino and J. Cuisia Jr. (1990-).	FV	FV	.75
	e. Sign. Ramos and J. Cuisia Jr.	FV	FV	.65
	f. Sign. as b. Uncut sheet of 4.	—	—	30.00
	g. Sign. as d. Uncut sheet of 4.	—	—	30.00
	h. Sign. as e. Uncut sheet of 4.	—	—	15.00
	s1. Sign. as b. Specimen.	—	—	15.00
	s2. Sign. as b. Specimen.	—	—	15.00
	s3. Sign. as d. Specimen.	—	—	20.00

169 **10 PISO**
ND (1985-). Dk. brown and blue-gray on m/c unpt. Mabini at l. ctr.,
handwritten scroll at r. Barasoain church on back.

		VG	VF	UNC
a.	Sign. F. Marcos and J. Fernandez.	FV	1.00	2.50
b.	Sign. C. Aquino and J. Fernandez.	FV	FV	1.25
c.	Sign. C. Aquino and J. Cuisia Jr. w/black serial #.			
d.	Sign. Ramos and J. Cuisia Jr.	FV	FV	1.25
e.	Sign. as c. w/red serial #.	FV	FV	1.25
f.	Sign. as b. Uncut sheet of 4.	—	—	38.50
g.	Sign. as b. Uncut sheet of 32.			
s.	Sign. as b. Specimen.	—	—	25.00

170 **20 PISO**
ND (1986-). Orange and blue on m/c unpt. Pres. M. Quezon at l. ctr.,
arms at r. Malakanyang Palace on back.

		VG	VF	UNC
a.	Sign. F. Marcos and J. Fernandez.	FV	FV	3.00
b.	Sign. C. Aquino and J. Fernandez.	FV	FV	2.75
c.	Sign. C. Aquino and J. Cuisia Jr. w/black serial #.	FV	FV	2.50
d.	Sign. as c. w/red serial #.	FV	FV	2.25
e.	Sign. Ramos and J. Cuisia Jr.	FV	FV	2.00
f.	Sign. as b. Uncut sheet of 4.	—	—	45.00
s.	Sign. as b. Specimen.	—	—	35.00

171 **50 PISO**
ND (1987-). Red on m/c unpt. Pres. S. Osmeña at l. ctr., and gavel at
r. Legislative bldg. on back.

		VG	VF	UNC
a.	Sign. C. Aquino and J. Fernandez.	FV	FV	4.00
b.	Sign. C. Aquino and J. Cuisia Jr.	FV	FV	3.25
c.	Sign. Ramos and J. Cuisia Jr.	FV	FV	3.00
s1.	Sign. as a. Specimen.	—	—	45.00
s2.	Sign. as b. Specimen.	—	—	9.00
s3.	Sign. as b. Specimen. Uncut sheet of 4.	—	—	30.00
s4.	Sign. as a. Specimen.	—	—	45.00

172 **100 PISO**
ND (1987-). Purple on m/c unpt. Pres. M. Roxas at l. ctr., US and
Philippine flags at r. New Central Bank complex on back.

		VG	VF	UNC
a.	Sign. C. Aquino and J. Fernandez.	FV	FV	9.00
b.	Sign. C. Aquino and J. Cuisia Jr. w/black serial #.	FV	FV	7.50
c.	Sign. as b. w/red serial #.	FV	FV	6.50
d.	Sign. Ramos and J. Cursia Jr.	FV	FV	6.00
s1.	Sign. as a. Specimen.	—	—	15.00
s2.	Sign. as b. Specimen.	—	—	13.50
s3.	Sign. as c. Specimen.	—	—	15.00
s4.	Sign. as d. Specimen.	—	—	25.00
s5.	Sign. as d. Uncut sheet of 4. Specimen.	—	—	25.00
s6.	Sign. as b. Specimen. Uncut sheet of 4.	—	—	47.50
s7.	Sign. as b. Specimen. Uncut sheet of 32.	—	—	350.00

173 **500 PISO**
ND (1987-94). Black on m/c impt. Benigno Aquino and flag at ctr.,
typewriter at lower r. Various scenes and gatherings of Aquino's
career on back.

		VG	VF	UNC
a.	Sign. C. Aquino and J. Fernandez.	FV	FV	35.00
b.	Sign. C. Aquino and J. Cuisia Jr.	FV	FV	32.50
c.	Sign. Ramos and J. Cuisia Jr.	FV	FV	30.00
s1.	Sign. as a. Specimen.	—	—	55.00
s2.	Sign. as b. Specimen.	—	—	25.00
s3.	Sign. as b. Specimen. Uncut sheet of 4.	—	—	90.00

174 **1000 PISO**
ND (1991-94). Dk. blue on m/c unpt. J. A. Santos, Josefa L. Escoda
and V. Lim at l. ctr. and as wmk. Flaming torch at r. Banawe rice
terraces at l. to ctr., local carving and hut at ctr. r. on back.

		VG	VF	UNC
a.	Sign. C. Aquino and J. Cuisia Jr.	FV	FV	62.50
b.	Sign. Ramos and J. Cuisia Jr.	FV	FV	50.00

COMMEMORATIVE ISSUES

NOTE: Commemorative ovpt. not listed are currently being produced privately in the Philippines.

#175-179 uncut sheets of 4 or 8 subjects exist for certain commemorative issues.

#175, visit of Pres. Aquino to the United States

#176, Canonization of San Lorenzo Ruiz.

#177, 40th Anniversary of Central Bank.

#178, Women's Rights 1990.

#179, II Plenary Council, 1991.

179	**5 Piso**	VG	VF	UNC
	1991. Like #168 but w/black commemorative design and date on wmk. area.	FV	FV	1.00

1995 ND ISSUE
#180-186 like #168 but w/redesigned Central Bank seal at r. Sign. Ramos and G. Singson.

180	**5 Piso**	VG	VF	UNC
	ND (1995-). Dk. brown on m/c unpt.	FV	FV	1.00
181	**10 Piso**			
	ND (1995-). Dk. brown and blue-gray on m/c unpt.	FV	FV	1.85
182	**20 Piso**			
	ND (1995-). Orange and blue on m/c unpt.			
	a. Issued note.	FV	FV	3.50
	s. Specimen. Uncut sheet of 4.	FV	FV	100.00
183	**50 Piso**			
	ND (1995-). Red on m/c unpt.	FV	FV	8.00
184	**100 Piso**			
	ND (1995-). Purple on m/c unpt.	FV	FV	15.00
185	**500 Piso**			
	ND (1995-). Black on m/c unpt.	FV	FV	28.50
186	**1000 Piso**			
	ND (1995-). Dk. blue on m/c unpt.	FV	FV	57.50

COLLECTOR SERIES

BANGKA SENTRAL NG PILIPINAS

1978 ISSUE

CS1	**1978 2-100 Piso**	ISSUE PRICE	MKT. VALUE
	#159-164 ovpt: *SPECIMEN* and w/Maltese cross prefix serial #.	14.00	30.00

175	**5 Piso**	VG	VF	UNC
	1986. Deep green on m/c unpt. Like #168 but w/commemorative text, seal and visit dates on wmk. area. Prefix letters CA. Sign. C. Aquino and J. Cuisia Jr.			
	a. Serial #1-20,000 in folder.	FV	FV	10.00
	b. Serial # above 20,000.	FV	FV	1.25
	c. Uncut sheet of 4.	—	—	37.50

176	**5 Piso**	VG	VF	UNC
	18.10.1987. Deep green on m/c unpt. Like #168 but w/commemorative design, text and date on wmk. area.			
	a. Issued note.	FV	FV	1.25
	c. Uncut sheet of 8.	FV	FV	16.00

177	**5 Piso**	VG	VF	UNC
	1989. Deep green on m/c unpt. Like #168 but w/red commemorative design, text and date on wmk. area.			
	a. Issued note.	FV	FV	1.00
	b. Uncut sheet of 8 in folder.	FV	FV	20.00

178	**5 Piso**	VG	VF	UNC
	1990. Like #168 but w/black commemorative design on wmk. area.	FV	FV	1.00

POLAND

The Republic of Poland, formerly the Polish Peoples Republic, located in central Europe, has an area of 120,725 sq. mi. (312,677 sq. km.) and a population of 38 million. Capital: Warsaw. The economy is essentially agricultural, but industrial activity provides the products for foreign trade. Machinery, coal, coke, iron, steel and transport equipment are exported.

Poland, which began as a Slavic duchy in the 10th century and reached its peak of power between the 14th and 16th centuries, has had a turbulent history of invasion, occupation or partition by Mongols, Turkey, Hungary, Sweden, Austria, Prussia and Russia.

The first partition took place in 1772. Prussia took Polish Pomerania. Russia took part of the eastern provinces. Austria took Galicia, in which lay the fortress city of Krakow (Cracow). The second partition occurred in 1793 when Russia took another slice of the eastern provinces and Prussia took what remained of western Poland. The third partition, 1795, literally removed Poland from the map. Russia took what was left of the eastern provinces. Prussia seized most of central Poland, including Warsaw. Austria took what was left of the south. Napoleon restored to Poland much of the territory lost to Prussia and Austria, but after his defeat another partition returned the Duchy of Warsaw to Prussia, made Kracow into a tiny republic, and declared what remained to be the Kingdom of Poland under the czar and in permanent union with Russia.

Poland re-emerged as an independent state recognized by the Treaty of Versailles on June 28, 1919, and maintained its independence until 1939 when it was invaded by, and partitioned between Germany and Russia. Poland's present boundaries were determined by the U.S.-British-Russian agreement of Aug. 16, 1945. The Government of National Unity was replaced when the Polish Communist-Socialist faction won a decisive victory at the polls in 1947 and established a "People's Democratic Republic" of the Soviet type. In Dec. 1989, Poland became a republic once again.

MONETARY SYSTEM:
1 Zloty = 100 Groszy, 1919-

PEOPLES REPUBLIC

NARODOWY BANK POLSKI

POLISH NATIONAL BANK

1965 ISSUE

140A	20 ZLOTYCH	VG	VF	UNC
	2.1.1965. M/c. Man at r., arms at upper l. ctr. (Not issued).	—	—	—

141	1000 ZLOTYCH	VG	VF	UNC
	1962; 1965. M/c. Copernicus at ctr. r. and as wmk., arms at upper r. Zodiac signs in ornate sphere on back.			
	a. Issued note. 29.10.1965.	.85	3.00	12.50
	s1. Specimen ovpt: *WZOR.* 24.5.1962. (Not issued).	—	—	120.00
	s2. Specimen ovpt: *WZOR* w/regular serial #. 29.10.1965.	—	—	20.00

1974-77 ISSUE

#142-147 eagle arms at lower ctr. or lower r. and as wmk. Sign. varieties.

142	50 ZLOTYCH	VG	VF	UNC
	1975-88. Olive-green on m/c unpt. K. Swierczewski at ctr. Cross at l. on back.			
	a. 9.5.1975.	.15	.50	2.50
	b. 1.6.1979; 1.6.1982.	.10	.30	1.00
	c. 1.6.1986; 1.12.1988.	.10	.25	.75
	s1. Specimen ovpt: *WZOR.* 1975; 1986; 1988.	—	—	8.50
	s2. Specimen ovpt: *WZOR.* 1979.	—	—	7.00
	s3. Specimen ovpt: *WZOR.* 1982.	—	—	11.50

143	100 ZLOTYCH	VG	VF	UNC
	1975-86. Brown on lilac and m/c unpt. L. Warynski at r. Old paper on back.			
	a. 15.1.1975; 17.5.1976.	.15	.50	3.00
	b. 1.6.1979; 1.6.1982.	.10	.30	1.00
	c. 1.6.1986; 1.12.1988.	.10	.25	.75
	s1. Specimen ovpt: *WZOR.* 1975; 1982.	—	—	8.50
	s2. Specimen ovpt: *WZOR.* 1976.	—	—	7.00
	s3. Specimen ovpt: *WZOR.* 1979.	—	—	11.50

144	200 ZLOTYCH	VG	VF	UNC
	1976-88. Purple on orange and m/c unpt. J. Dabrowski at r. standing woman at wall on back.			
	a. 25.5.1976.	.20	.75	3.00
	b. 1.6.1979; 1.6.1982.	.10	.30	1.00
	c. 1.6.1986; 1.12.1988.	.10	.25	.75
	s1. Specimen ovpt: *WZOR.* 1976; 1986.	—	—	8.50
	s2. Specimen ovpt: *WZOR.* 1979.	—	—	7.00
	s3. Specimen ovpt: *WZOR.* 1982.	—	—	11.50

145 500 ZLOTYCH
1974-82. Brown on tan and m/c unpt. T. Kosciuszko at ctr. Arms and flag on back.

	VG	VF	UNC
a. 16.12.1974; 15.6.1976.	.75	2.25	8.50
b. 1.6.1979.	.20	.65	2.00
c. 1.6.1982.	.10	.25	.85
s1. Specimen ovpt. *WZOR.* 1974; 1976.	—	—	8.50
s2. Specimen ovpt. *WZOR.* 1979.	—	—	7.00
s3. Specimen ovpt. *WZOR.* 1982.	—	—	11.50

146 1000 ZLOTYCH
1975-82. Blue on olive and m/c unpt. Copernicus at r. Atomic symbols on back.

	VG	VF	UNC
a. 2.7.1975.	.75	2.25	8.50
b. 1.6.1979.	.40	1.35	4.00
c. 1.6.1982.	.15	.40	1.50
s1. Specimen ovpt. *WZOR.* 1975; 1982.	—	—	11.50
s2. Specimen ovpt. *WZOR.* 1979.	—	—	7.00

POLSKA RZECZPOSPOLITA LUDOWA

PEOPLES REPUBLIC OF POLAND

NARODOWY BANK POLSKI

POLISH NATIONAL BANK

1977-82 ISSUE

147 2000 ZLOTYCH
1977-82. Dk. green and dk. brown. Mieszko I at r. B. Chrobry on back.

	VG	VF	UNC
a. 1.5.1977.	.75	2.25	8.00
b. 1.6.1979.	.30	1.00	3.00
c. 1.6.1982.	.20	.65	2.00
s1. Specimen ovpt. *WZOR.* 1977.	—	—	11.50
s2. Specimen ovpt. *WZOR.* 1979.	—	—	7.00
s3. Specimen ovpt. *WZOR.* 1982.	—	—	15.00

1982 ISSUE
#148-149 wmk. pattern in paper.

148 10 ZLOTYCH
1.6.1982. Blue, green and m/c. J. Bem at l. ctr.

	VG	VF	UNC
a. Issued note.	.10	.25	.75
s. Specimen ovpt. *WZOR.*	—	—	11.50

149 20 ZLOTYCH
1.6.1982. Brown, purple and m/c. R. Traugutt at l. ctr.

	VG	VF	UNC
a. Issued note.	.10	.25	.75
s. Specimen ovpt. *WZOR.*	—	—	11.50

150 5000 ZLOTYCH
1982-88. Black, purple and dk. green on m/c unpt. F. Chopin at r. Arms at lower ctr. and as wmk. *Polonaise* music score on back.

	VG	VF	UNC
a. 1.6.1982.	.25	1.00	4.00
b. 1.6.1986.	FV	.75	3.00
c. 1.12.1988.	FV	FV	2.50
s. Specimen ovpt. *WZOR.*	—	—	13.50

1987-90 ISSUE
#151-158 arms at lower ctr. or lower r. and as wmk.

151 **10,000 ZLOTYCH**
1.2.1987; 1.12.1988. Black and red on m/c unpt. S. Wyspianski at l. ctr. Trees and city scene on back.

	VG	VF	UNC
a. Issued note.	FV	.50	3.00
s. Specimen ovpt. *WZOR*.	—	—	8.50

152 **20,000 ZLOTYCH**
1.2.1989. Dk. brown on tan and gold unpt. M. Curie at r. Scentific instrument on back.

	VG	VF	UNC
a. Issued note.	FV	1.35	4.00
s. Specimen ovpt. *WZOR*.	—	—	7.00

153 **50,000 ZLOTYCH**
1.12.1989. Dk. brown and greenish black on m/c unpt. S. Staszic at l. ctr. Staszic Palace in Warsaw on back.

	VG	VF	UNC
a. Issued note.	FV	2.50	4.50
s. Specimen ovpt. *WZOR*.	—	—	8.50

154 **100,000 ZLOTYCH**
1.2.1990. Black and grayish purple on m/c unpt. S. Moniuszko at r. Warsaw Theatre at l. on back.

	VG	VF	UNC
a. Issued note.	FV	5.50	7.50
s. Specimen ovpt. *WZOR*.	—	—	11.50

155 **200,000 ZLOTYCH**
1.12.1989. Dk. purple and red on tan and m/c unpt. Coin of Sigismund III at lower ctr., arms at r. Back purple on brown unpt.; Warsaw shield at l., view of Warsaw.

	VG	VF	UNC
a. Issued note.	1.50	11.00	30.00
s. Specimen ovpt. *WZOR*.	—	—	15.00

RZECZPOSPOLITA POLSKA

REPUBLIC OF POLAND

NARODOWY BANK PLOSKI

POLISH NATIONAL BANK

1990-92 ISSUE

156 **500,000 ZLOTYCH**
20.4.1990. Dk. blue-green and black on m/c unpt. H. Sienkiewicz at l. ctr. Shield w/3 books, also 2 flags, on back.

	VG	VF	UNC
a. Issued note.	FV	25.00	35.00
s. Specimen ovpt. *WZOR*.	—	—	37.50

157 **1 MILLION ZLOTYCH**
15.2.1991. Brown-violet, purple and red on m/c unpt. W. Reymont at r. Tree w/rural landscape in background on back.

	VG	VF	UNC
a. Issued note.	FV	45.00	65.00
s. Specimen ovpt. *WZOR*.	—	—	70.00

158 **2 MILLION ZLOTYCH**
14.8.1992. Black and deep brown-violet on m/c unpt. I. Paderewski at l. ctr. Imperial eagle at l. on back.

	VG	VF	UNC
a. Issued note, misspelling *KONSTYTUCYJY* on back. Series A.	—	—	200.00
b. As a., but corrected spelling *KONSTYTUCYJNY* on back. Series B.	FV	90.00	110.00
s. Specimen ovpt. *WZOR*.	—	—	135.00

1993 ISSUE

#159-163 similar to #153, 154, 156-158 but modified w/color in wmk. area, eagle w/crown at lower ctr. Wmk: Eagle's head.

159 **50,000 ZLOTYCH**
16.11.1993. Dk. blue-green and black on m/c unpt. Similar to #156.

	VG	VF	UNC
a. Issued note.	FV	3.00	6.50
s. Specimen ovpt. *WZOR*.	—	—	8.50

160 **100,000 ZLOTYCH**
16.11.1993. Black and grayish purple on m/c unpt. Similar to #154.

	VG	VF	UNC
a. Issued note.	FV	6.50	10.00
s. Specimen ovpt. *WZOR*.	—	—	11.50

161 **500,000 ZLOTYCH**
16.11.1993. Dk. blue-green and black on m/c unpt. Similar to #156.

	VG	VF	UNC
a. Issued note.	FV	27.50	40.00
s. Specimen ovpt. *WZOR*.	—	—	37.50

162	**1 MILLION ZLOTYCH**	VG	VF	UNC
	16.11.1993. Brown-violet, purple and red on m/c unpt. Similar to #157.			
	a. Issued note.	FV	47.50	70.00
	s. Specimen ovpt. *WZOR.*	—	—	70.00
163	**2 MILLION ZLOTYCH**			
	16.11.1993. Black and deep brown on m/c unpt. Similar to #158.			
	a. Issued note.	FV	95.00	125.00
	s. Specimen ovpt: *WZOR.*	—	—	135.00

1990 (1996) "CANCELLED" ISSUE

Currency Reform

1 "new" Zlotych = 10,000 "old" Zlotych

#164-172 arms at l. and as wmk.

NOTE: #164-172 were printed in Germany (w/o imprint). Before their release, it was decided a more sophisticated issue of notes should be prepared and these notes were later ovpt: *NIEOBIEGOWY* (non-negotiable) and released to the public. Specimens also have been reported.

164	**1 ZLOTY**	VG	VF	UNC
	1.3.1990. Blue-gray and brown on m/c unpt. Bldg. in Gdynia at r. Sailing ship at l. on back.	—	—	3.00

165	**2 ZLOTE**	VG	VF	UNC
	1.3.1990. Dk. brown and brown on m/c unpt. Mining conveyor tower at Katowice at r. Battle of Upper Silesia (1921) monument at l. on back.	—	—	3.00

166	**5 ZLOTYCH**	VG	VF	UNC
	1.3.1990. Deep green on m/c unpt. Bldg. in Zamosc at r. Order of Grunwald at l. on back.	—	—	3.00

167	**10 ZLOTYCH**	VG	VF	UNC
	1.3.1990. M/c. Bldg. in Warszawa at r. Statue of Warszawa at l.	—	—	3.00

168	**20 ZLOTYCH**	VG	VF	UNC
	1.3.1990. Brownish black and deep violet on m/c unpt. Grain storage facility in Gdansk at r. Male statue at l. on back.	—	—	3.00

169	**50 ZLOTYCH**	VG	VF	UNC
	1.3.1990. Purple on m/c unpt. Church in Wroclaw at r. Medallion at l. on back.	—	—	3.00

170	**100 ZLOTYCH**	VG	VF	UNC
	1.3.1990. Dk. brown and black on m/c unpt. Bldg. in Poznan at r. Medieval seal at l. on back.	—	—	3.00

171	200 ZLOTYCH	VG	VF	UNC
	1.3.1990. Black and deep purple on m/c unpt. Bldgs. in Krakow at r. Medieval coin at l. on back.	—	—	3.00

172	500 ZLOTYCH	VG	VF	UNC
	1.3.1990. Black on m/c unpt. Church in Gniezno at r. Medieval seal at l. on back.	—	—	3.00

175	50 ZLOTYCH	VG	VF	UNC
(166)	25.3.1994. Blue-violet and deep blue and green on m/c unpt. Portr. Kg. Kazimierz III at ctr. r. Medallion, orb and sceptre at l. ctr. on back.			
	a. Issued note.	FV	FV	27.50
	s. Specimen.	—	—	35.00
176	100 ZLOTYCH			
(167)	1994. Olive-green on m/c unpt. Wladyslaw II Jagie 110. Teutonic Knights' castle in Malbork on back.			
	a. Issued note.	FV	FV	52.50
	s. Specimen ovpt. *WZOR*.	—	—	67.50
177	200 ZLOTYCH			
(168)	1994. Brown on m/c unpt. Kg. Zygmunt. Eagle in hexagon from the Zygmunt's chapel in the Wawel Cathedral and Wawel's court on back.			
	a. Issued note.	FV	FV	100.00
	s. Specimen ovpt. *WZOR*.	—	—	130.00

1994 SERIES

173	10 ZLOTYCH	VG	VF	UNC
(164)	25.3.1994. Dk. brown, brown and olive-green on m/c unpt. Prince Mieszko I at ctr. r. Medieval coin at l. ctr. on back.			
	a. Issued note.	FV	FV	6.50
	s.Specimen ovpt. *WZOR*.	—	—	7.50

COLLECTOR SERIES

NARODOWY BANK POLSKI

1978 ISSUE

CS2	1978 20,100 ZLOTYCH	ISSUE PRICE	MKT. VALUE
	#137, 139a w/dk. blue ovpt: *150 LAT BANKU POLSKIEGO 1828-1978* on face.	—	25.00

1979-92 ISSUE

NOTE: Originally #CS3 was sold in a special booklet by Pekao Trading Company at its New York City, NY, and Warsaw offices. Currently available only from the Polish Numismatic Society.

174	20 ZLOTYCH	VG	VF	UNC
(165)	25.3.1994. Purple and deep blue on m/c unpt. Kg. Boleslaw I at ctr. r. Medieval coin at l. ctr. on back.			
	a. Issued note.	FV	FV	12.00
	s. Specimen.	—	—	13.50

CS3	1979-92; 20-2 MILLION ZLOTYCH	ISSUE PRICE	MKT. VALUE
	#142-157a, 148a w/red ovpt: *WZOR* on face; all zero serial # and additional black specimen # w/star suffix. Red ovpt: *SPECIMEN* on back.		300.00

PORTUGAL

The Portuguese Republic, located in the western part of the Iberian Peninsula in southwestern Europe, has an area of 35,553 sq. mi. (92,080 sq. km.) and a population of 9.86 million. Capital: Lisbon. Portugal's economy is based on agriculture and a small but expanding industrial sector. Textiles, machinery, chemicals, wine and cork are exported.

After centuries of domination by Romans, Visigoths and Moors, Portugal emerged in the 12th century as an independent kingdom financially and philosophically prepared for the great period of exploration that would follow. Attuned to the inspiration of Prince Henry the Navigator (1394-1460), Portugal's daring explorers of the 14th and 15th centuries roamed the world's oceans from Brazil to Japan in an unprecedented burst of energy and endeavor that culminated in 1494 with Portugal laying claim to half the transoceanic world. Unfortunately for the fortunes of the tiny kingdom, the Portuguese proved to be inept colonizers. Less than a century after Portugal laid claim to half the world, English, French and Dutch trading companies had seized the lion's share of the world's colonies and commerce, and Portugal's place as an imperial power was lost forever. The monarchy was overthrown in 1910 and a republic established.

On April 25, 1974, the government of Portugal was seized by a military junta which reached agreements providing for independence for the Portuguese overseas provinces of Portuguese Guinea (Guinea-Bissau), Mozambique, Cape Verde Islands, Angola, and St. Thomas and Prince Islands (Sao Tome Principe).

MONETARY SYSTEM:
1 Escudo = 100 Centavos, 1910-

COLONIAL ISSUE OVERPRINTS

AÇÔRES, see Azores and Madeira
BOLAMA, see Portuguese Guinea
CABO VERDE, see Cape Verde
GUINÉ, see Portuguese Guinea
LOANDA, see Angola

LOURENÇO MARQUES, see Mozambique
MOEDA INSULANA, see Azores and Madeira
NOVA GOA, see Portuguese India
S. TIAGO or S. THIAGO, see Cape Verde
S. TOMÉ, see St. Thomas and Prince

REPUBLIC

BANCO DE PORTUGAL

1960 ISSUE, CHAPA 6A AND 7A

163 (69)	20 ESCUDOS	VG	VF	UNC
	26.7.1960. Ch. 6A. Dk. green and purple. Portr. of D. Antonio Luiz de Menezes at r. and as wmk. Back purple and m/c; bank arms at l.	2.50	7.50	30.00

164 (79)	50 ESCUDOS	VG	VF	UNC
	24.6.1960. Ch. 7A. Blue on m/c unpt. Arms at upper ctr. F. Pereira de Mello at r. and as wmk. Back dk. green and m/c; statue "The Thinker" at l.	4.00	8.00	15.00

165	100 ESCUDOS	VG	VF	UNC
	19.12.1961. Ch. 6A. Black and deep violet on pink and m/c unpt. P. Nunes at r. and as wmk. Back: lilac; fountain and arches at l. 3 sign. varieties.	4.50	13.50	40.00

166	1000 ESCUDOS	VG	VF	UNC
	30.5.1961. Ch. 8A. Purple on m/c unpt. Qn. at r. and as wmk. Basic design similar to to #107 but many stylistic changes. Back: blue. Printer: BWC (w/o imprint).	10.00	30.00	100.00

1964-66 ISSUE

167	20 ESCUDOS	VG	VF	UNC
	26.5.1964. Ch. 7. Olive and purple on m/c unpt. S. Antonio at r. and as wmk. Back: olive; Church of Santo Antonio de Lisboa at l.			
	a. Olive brown unpt. at l. and r. r.	.35	1.00	4.50
	b. Green unpt. at l. and r.	.35	1.00	2.50

168   50 ESCUDOS

	VG	VF	UNC
28.2.1964. Ch. 9. Brown-violet on pink and m/c unpt. qn. Isabella at r. and as wmk. Old city Conimbria on back. Sign. title varieties.	.50	1.50	4.50

169   100 ESCUDOS

	VG	VF	UNC
30.11.1965; 20.9.1978. Ch. 7. Blue and m/c. C. Castello Branco at r. and as wmk. City of Porto in 19th century at l. on back. Sign. title varieties.	1.00	1.50	6.00

170   500 ESCUDOS

	VG	VF	UNC
25.1.1966; 6.9.1979. Ch. 10. Brown and m/c. Old map at ctr., Joãl at r. and as wmk. Ornate round design and double statue on back: Sign. title varieties. Printer: JEZ (w/o imprint).			
a. 25.1.1966.	5.00	8.00	20.00
b. 6.9.1979.	4.00	7.00	15.00

171   1000 ESCUDOS

	VG	VF	UNC
2.4.1965. Ch. 9. Gray-blue on red-brown and m/c unpt. Pillar at l., arms at upper ctr., D. Diniz at r. and as wmk. Scene of founding of University of Lisbon in 1290 on back. Printer: JEZ (w/o imprint).	110.00	165.00	300.00

1967 ISSUE

172   1000 ESCUDOS

	VG	VF	UNC
19.5.1967. Ch. 10. Blue and violet on m/c unpt. Flowers at l., Qn. Maria II at r. and as wmk. Her medallion portr. at l., Banco de Portugal in 1846 bldg. at lower r. on back. Sign. and sign. title varieties. Printer: JEZ (w/o imprint).	8.00	15.00	30.00

1968; 1971 DATED ISSUE

173   20 ESCUDOS

	VG	VF	UNC
27.7.1971. Ch. 8. Gray, green (shades) and lt. brown. D. de Orta at r. and as wmk. Back: dk. green and m/c; 16th century market in Goa. Sign. and sign. title varieties.	FV	10.00	20.00

174   50 ESCUDOS

	VG	VF	UNC
28.5.1968; 1.2.1980. Ch. 9. Brown and m/c. Arms at l., D. Maria at r. and as wmk. Sintra in 1507 on back. Sign. varieties.	FV	1.00	3.75

175   1000 ESCUDOS
1968-82. Ch. 11. Blue and m/c Don Pedro V at ctr. and as wmk.
Conjoined busts at l., procession and old train at bottom ctr. and r. on
back. Sign. and sign. title varieties. Printer: BWC (w/o imrint).

	VG	VF	UNC
a. 28.5.1968.	FV	10.00	22.50
b. 16.9.1980; 3.12.1981; 21.9.1982; 26.10.1982.	FV	8.00	20.00

1978; 1979 DATED ISSUE

176   20 ESCUDOS
13.9.1978; 4.10.1978. Green and m/c. Adm. Coutinho at r. and as
wmk. Airplane on back. Lg. or sm. size numerals in serial #. Sign. and
title varieties.

VG	VF	UNC
FV	.50	2.00

177   500 ESCUDOS
4.10.1979 (1982). Ch. 11. Brown and m/c. Old street layout of part of
Braga at ctr., F. Sanches at r. and as wmk. 17th century street scene in
Braga on back. Printer: JEZ (w/o imprint).

VG	VF	UNC
FV	5.00	9.00

1980-87 DATED ISSUES

178   100 ESCUDOS
2.9.1980; 24.2.1981; 31.1.1954; 12.3.1985; 4.6.1985. Ch. 8. Dk. blue
and m/c. Manuel M. B. du Bocage seated at r. and as wmk. Early 19th
century scene of Rossio Square in Lisbon on back.

VG	VF	UNC
FV	1.25	4.50

179   100 ESCUDOS
16.10.1986; 12.2.1987; 3.12.1987; 26.5.1988; 24.11.1988. Ch. 9.
Blue and purple on m/c unpt. F. Pessoa at ctr. r. and as wmk. Rosebud
on back. Sign. title varieties.

	VG	VF	UNC
a. Regular issue.	FV	1.00	3.50
b. Prefix letters *FIL*. 12. 12.2.1987.	—	—	10.00

180   500 ESCUDOS
1987-92. Ch. 12. Brown and m/c. M. de Silveira at ctr. r. and wmk.
Sheaf on back. Sign. title varieties.

	VG	VF	UNC
a. 20.11.1987.		FV	8.00
b. 4.8.1988.		FV	7.00
c. 4.10.1989.		FV	6.50
d. 13.2.1992; 18.3.1993; 29.4.1994.		FV	6.00

		VG	VF	UNC
181	**1000 ESCUDOS** 1983-90. Ch. 12. Purple and dk. brown on m/c unpt. T. Braga at ctr. r. and as wmk. Museum artifacts on back. Sign. title varieties.			
	a. 2.8.1983.	FV	FV	15.00
	b. 12.6.1986; 26.2.1987; 3.9.1987; 22.12.1988; 9.11.1989.	FV	FV	13.00
	c. 26.7.1990; 20.12.1990; 6.2.1992; 17.6.1993; 3.3.1994.	FV	FV	11.50
183	**5000 ESCUDOS** 10.9.1980; 27.1.1981; 24.5.1983; 4.6.1985; 7.1.1986. Ch. 1. Brown and m/c. Antonio Sergio at l. ctr. and as wmk. A. Sergio walking at ctr. on back. Printer: TDLR (w/o imprint).	FV	40.00	70.00

		VG	VF	UNC
184	**5000 ESCUDOS** 1987-93. Ch. 2; 2A. Olive-green, brown and m/c. A. de Quental at ctr. r. and as wmk. Six hands w/rope and chain at ctr. on back.			
	a. Ch. 2. 12.2.1987; 3.12.1987.	FV	FV	55.00
	b. Ch. 2A. 28.10.1988; 6.7.1989; 19.10.1989; 31.10.1991; 18.3.1993; 2.9.1993.	FV	FV	52.50
185	**10,000 ESCUDOS** 12.1.1989; 14.12.1989; 16.5.1991. Ch. 1. Orange, lt. brown and yellow. Dr. E. Moniz by human brain at ctr. and as wmk. Nobel Prize medal, snakes, tree at ctr. on back.	FV	FV	97.50

1991 DATED ISSUE

		VG	VF	UNC
186	**2000 ESCUDOS** 23.5.1991; 29.8.1991; 16.7.1992; 21.10.1993. Ch. 1. Dk. brown and blue on m/c unpt. B. Dias at l. and as wmk., astrolabe at ctr. Sailing ship at ctr., arms at r. on back. Sign. title varieties.	FV	FV	22.50

1995; 1996 ISSUE

		VG	VF	UNC
187	**1000 ESCUDOS** 18.4.1996. Ch. 13. Purple and brown on m/c unpt. P. Alvares Cabral wearing helmet at r. Brazilian arms at ctr. Old sailing ship at ctr., birds and animals of Brazilian jungle in unpt. on back.	FV	FV	11.00
188	**2000 ESCUDOS** 21.9.1995; 1.2.1996. Ch. 2. Purple on m/c unpt. B. Dias at r. and as wmk., cruzado coin of D. João II at upper ctr., sailing instrument below. Old sailing ship at ctr. r., compass, map at l. ctr. on back.	FV	FV	21.50
189	**5000 ESCUDOS** 5.1.1995. Ch. 3. Deep olive-green on m/c unpt. V. da Gama at r. and as wmk., medallion at upper ctr. Old sailing ship at ctr. r., V. da Gama w/kg. and court at l.	FV	FV	50.00

		VG	VF	UNC
190	**10,000 ESCUDOS** 2.5.1996. Ch. 2. Violet and dk. brown on m/c unpt. Infante D. Henrique at r. and as wmk., arms at ctr. Old sailing ship at ctr. on back.	FV	FV	95.00

PORTUGUESE GUINEA

Portuguese Guinea (now Guinea-Bissau), a former Portuguese province of the west coast of Africa bounded on the north by Senegal and on the east and southeast by Guinea, had an area of 13,948 sq. mi. (36,125 sq. km.). Capital: Bissau. The province exported peanuts, timber and beeswax. Portuguese Guinea was discovered by Portuguese navigator Nuno Tristao in 1446. Trading rights in the area were granted to Cape Verde islanders but few prominent posts were established before 1851, and they were principally coastal installations. The chief export of this colony's early period was slaves for South America, a practice that adversely affected trade with the native people and retarded subjection of the interior. Territorial disputes with France delayed final demarcation of the colony's frontiers until 1905.

The African Party for the Independence of Guinea-Bissau was founded in 1956, and several years later began a guerrilla warfare that grew in effectiveness until 1974, when the rebels controlled most of the colony. Portugal's costly overseas wars in her African territories resulted in a military coup in Portugal in April 1974, that appreciably brightened the prospects for freedom for Guinea-Bissau. In August, 1974, the Lisbon government signed an agreement granting independence to Portuguese Guinea effective Sept. 10, 1974. The new republic took the name of Guinea-Bissau.

RULERS:
Portuguese to 1974

MONETARY SYSTEM:
1 Escudo = 100 Centavos 1910-1975

NOTE: For later issues see Guinea-Bissau.

PORTUGUESE INFLUENCE

BANCO NACIONAL ULTRAMARINO, GUINÉ

1964 ISSUE

		VG	VF	UNC
40	**50 ESCUDOS** 30.6.1964. Dk. green on lilac and m/c unpt.	4.00	15.00	45.00

		VG	VF	UNC
41	**100 ESCUDOS** 30.6.1964. Blue-green on m/c unpt.	7.50	30.00	90.00
42	**500 ESCUDOS** 30.6.1964. Brown on m/c unpt.	12.50	50.00	150.00

		VG	VF	UNC
43	**1000 ESCUDOS** 30.4.1964. Red-orange on m/c unpt. Portr. H. Barreto at r. Printer: BWC.	22.50	65.00	200.00

1971 ISSUE

		VG	VF	UNC
44	**50 ESCUDOS** 17.12.1971. Olive-green on m/c unpt. Portr. N. Tristao at r.	3.00	10.00	35.00
45	**100 ESCUDOS** 17.12.1971. Blue on m/c unpt. Portr. N. Tristao at r.	3.00	12.50	55.00
46	**500 ESCUDOS** 27.7.1971. Purple on m/c unpt. Portr. H. Barreto at r.	10.00	40.00	135.00

QATAR

The State of Qatar, an emirate in the Persian Gulf between Bahrain and Trucial Oman, has an area of 4,247 sq. mi. (11,000 sq. km.) and a population of 382,000. Capital: Doha. Oil is the chief industry and export.

Qatar was under Turkish control from 1872 until the beginning of World War I when the Ottoman Turks evacuated the Qatar Peninsula. In 1916 Sheikh Abdullah placed Qatar under the protection of Great Britain and gave Britain responsibility for its defense and foreign relations. Qatar joined with Dubai in a Monetary Union and issued coins and paper money in 1966 and 1969. When Britain announced in 1968 that it would end treaty relationships with the Persian Gulf sheikhdoms in 1971, this union was dissolved. Qatar joined Bahrain and the seven trucial sheikhdoms (the latter now called the United Arab Emirates) in an effort to form a union of Arab emirates. However, the nine sheikhdoms were unable to agree on terms of union, and Qatar declared its independence as the State of Qatar on Sept. 3, 1971.

Also see Qatar and Dubai.

MONETARY SYSTEM:
1 Riyal = 100 Dirhem

EMIRATE

QATAR MONETARY AGENCY

1973 ND ISSUE

#1-6 arms in circle at r. Wmk: Falcon's head.

		VG	VF	UNC
1	**1 RIYAL** ND (1973). Lilac-red on m/c unpt. Harbor at l. on back.	1.00	2.50	10.00

		VG	VF	UNC
2	**5 RIYALS** ND (1973). Lilac-brown on m/c unpt. Bldg. at l. on back.	2.00	4.50	15.00

		VG	VF	UNC
3	**10 RIYALS** ND (1973). Green on m/c unpt. Qatar Monetary Agency bldg. at l. on back.	4.00	7.50	25.00

		VG	VF	U<small>NC</small>
4	**50 R<small>IYALS</small>** ND (1976). Blue on m/c unpt. Offshore oil drilling platform at l. on back.	55.00	175.00	400.00

		VG	VF	U<small>NC</small>
5	**100 R<small>IYALS</small>** ND (1973). Olive-green and lt. brown on m/c unpt. Modern bldg. at l. on back.	37.50	70.00	180.00

		VG	VF	U<small>NC</small>
6	**500 R<small>IYALS</small>** ND (1973). Blue-green on m/c unpt. Mosque and minaret at l. on back.	180.00	300.00	750.00

1980s ND I<small>SSUE</small>

#7-13 arms at r. Wmk: Falcon's head.

		VG	VF	U<small>NC</small>
7	**1 R<small>IYAL</small>** ND. Brown on m/c unpt. City street scene in Doha at l. ctr. on back.	FV	.65	2.00

		VG	VF	U<small>NC</small>
8	**5 R<small>IYALS</small>** ND. Red and purple on m/c unpt. Back red-brown; sheep and plants at l. ctr.	FV	2.25	3.50

		VG	VF	U<small>NC</small>
9	**10 R<small>IYALS</small>** ND. Green and blue on m/c unpt. National Museum at l. ctr. on back.	FV	4.00	7.00
10	**50 R<small>IYALS</small>** ND (1989). Blue on m/c unpt. Face similar to #7. Industrial scene on back.	FV	18.50	25.00

		VG	VF	U<small>NC</small>
11	**100 R<small>IYALS</small>** ND. Green on m/c unpt. Qatar Monetary Agency bldg. at l. ctr. on back.	FV	36.50	45.00

12	**500 RIYALS**	**VG**	**VF**	**UNC**
	ND. Blue and green on m/c unpt. Offshore oil drilling platform on back.	FV	170.00	210.00

1985 ND ISSUE

13	**1 RIYAL**	**VG**	**VF**	**UNC**
	ND (1985). Brown on m/c unpt. Face like #7. Boat beached at l. on back.	FV	FV	1.25

QATAR CENTRAL BANK

1996 ND ISSUE
#14-19 similar to #8-13. Wmk: Falcon's head.

14	**1 RIYAL**	**VG**	**VF**	**UNC**
	ND (1996). M/c. Similar to #13.	FV	FV	1.50
15	**5 RIYALS**			
	ND (1996). M/c. Similar to #8.	FV	FV	3.25
16	**10 RIYALS**			
	ND (1996). M/c. Similar to #9.	FV	FV	6.00
17	**50 RIYALS**			
	ND (1996). M/c. Similar to #10.	FV	FV	23.50
18	**100 RIYALS**			
	ND (1996). M/c. Similar to #11.	FV	FV	43.50
19	**500 RIYALS**			
	ND (1996). M/c. Similar to #12.	FV	FV	200.00

The State of Qatar, which occupies the Qatar Peninsula jutting into the Persian Gulf from eastern Saudi Arabia, has an area of 4,247 sq. mi. (11,000 sq. km.) and a population of 382,000. Capital: Doha. The traditional occupations of pearling, fishing and herding have been replaced in economics by petroleum- related industries. Crude oil, petroleum products, and tomatoes are exported.

Dubai is one of the seven sheikhdoms comprising the United Arab Emirates (formerly Trucial States) located along the southern shore of the Persian Gulf. It has a population of about 60,000. Capital (of the United Arab Emirates): Abu Dhabi.

Qatar, which initiated protective treaty relations with Great Britain in 1820, achieved independence on Sept. 3, 1971, upon withdrawal of the British military presence from the Persian Gulf, and replaced its special treaty arrangement with Britain with a treaty of general friendship. Dubai attended independence on Dec. 1, 1971, upon termination of Britain's protective treaty with the trucial sheikhdoms, and on Dec. 2, 1971, entered into the union of the United Arab Emirates.

Despite the fact that the sultanate of Qatar and the sheikhdom of Dubai were merged under a monetary union, the two territories were governed independently from each other. Qatar now uses its own currency while Dubai uses the United Arab Emirates currency and coins.

MONETARY SYSTEM:
1 Riyal = 100 Dirhem

QATAR AND DUBAI CURRENCY BOARD

1960s ND ISSUE
#1-6 dhow, derrick and palm tree at l. Wmk: Falcon's head.

1	**1 RIYAL**	**VG**	**VF**	**UNC**
	ND. Dk. green on m/c unpt.	3.00	15.00	45.00

2	**5 RIYALS**	**VG**	**VF**	**UNC**
	ND. Purple on m/c unpt.	8.00	40.00	135.00
3	**10 RIYALS**			
	ND. Gray-green on m/c unpt.	20.00	75.00	285.00
4	**25 RIYALS**			
	ND. Blue on m/c unpt.	85.00	450.00	1500.

5	**50 RIYALS**	**VG**	**VF**	**UNC**
	ND. Red on m/c unpt.	125.00	550.00	1500.

6	**100 RIYALS**	**VG**	**VF**	**UNC**
	ND. Olive on m/c unpt.	125.00	450.00	1250.

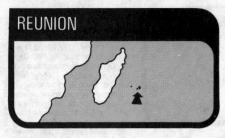

The Department of Reunion, an overseas department of France located in the Indian Ocean 400 miles (640 km.) east of Madagascar, has an area of 969 sq. mi. (2,510 sq. km.) and a population of 556,000. Capital: Saint-Denis. The island's volcanic soil is extremely fertile. Sugar, vanilla, coffee and rum are exported.

Although first visited by Portuguese navigators in the 16th century, Reunion was uninhabited when claimed for France by Capt. Goubert in 1638. It was first colonized as Isle de Bourbon by the French in 1662 as a layover station for ships rounding the Cape of Good Hope to India. It was renamed Reunion in 1793. The island remained in French possession except for the period of 1810-15, when it was occupied by the British. Reunion became an overseas department of France in 1946, and in 1958 voted to continue that status within the new French Union. Bauque du France notes were introduced 1.1.1973.

RULERS:
French, 1638-1810, 1815
British, 1810-1815

MONETARY SYSTEM:
1 Franc = 100 Centimes
1 Nouveau Franc = 100 Old Francs, 1960

FRENCH INFLUENCE

INSTITUT D'EMISSION DES DÉPARTEMENTS D'OUTRE-MER, RÉPUBLIQUE FRANÇAISE

1964; 1965 ND PROVISIONAL ISSUE

		VG	VF	UNC
51	**500 FRANCS**			
	ND (1964). M/c. 2 girls at r.			
	a. Issued note.	8.50	40.00	200.00
	s. Specimen.	—	—	175.00
52	**1000 FRANCS**			
	ND (1964). M/c. 2 women (symbol of the "Union Française") at r.			
	a. Issued note.	15.00	60.00	300.00
	s. Specimen.	—	—	250.00
53	**5000 FRANCS**			
	ND (1965). Brown on m/c unpt. Gen. Schoelcher at ctr. r.			
	a. Issued note.	35.00	130.00	550.00
	s. Specimen.	—	—	450.00

1967 ND PROVISIONAL ISSUE

		VG	VF	UNC
54	**10 NOUVEAUX FRANCS ON 500 FRANCS**			
	ND (1967). M/c. Ovpt. on #51.			
	a. Sign. A. Postel Vinay and P. Calvet. (1967).	5.00	27.50	85.00
	b. Sign. A. Postel Vinay and B. Clappier. (1971).	5.00	27.50	85.00

		VG	VF	UNC
55	**20 NOUVEAUX FRANCS ON 1000 FRANCS**			
	ND (1967). M/c. Ovpt. on #52.			
	a. Sign. A. Postel Vinay and P. Calvet. (1967).	7.50	32.50	95.00
	b. Sign. A. Postel Vinay and B. Clappier. (1971).	7.50	32.50	95.00
56	**100 NOUVEAUX FRANCS ON 5000 FRANCS**			
	ND (1967). M/c. Ovpt. on #53.			
	a. Sign. A. Postel Vinay and P. Calvet. (1967).	22.50	75.00	225.00
	b. Sign. A. Postel Vinay and B. Clappier. (1971).	22.50	75.00	225.00

The "Republic of" Rhodesia (never recognized by the British Government and was referred to as "Southern Rhodesia") (now Zimbabwe) located in the east-central part of southern Africa, has an area of 150,804 sq. mi. (390,580 sq. km.) and a population of 9.9 million. Capital: Salisbury. The economy is based on agriculture and mining. Tobacco, sugar, asbestos, copper and chrome ore and coal are exported.

The Rhodesian area, the habitat of paleolithic man, contains extensive evidence of earlier civilizations, notably the world-famous ruins of Zimbabwe, a gold-trading center that flourished about the 14th or 15th century AD. The Portuguese of the 16th century were the first Europeans to attempt to develop south-central Africa, but it remained for Cecil Rhodes and the British South Africa Co. to open the hinterlands. Rhodes obtained a concession for mineral rights from local chiefs in 1888 and administered his African empire (named Southern Rhodesia in 1895) through the British South Africa Co. until 1923, when the British government annexed the area after the white settlers voted for existence as a separate entity, rather than for incorporation into the Union of South Africa. From Sept. of 1953 through 1963 Southern Rhodesia was joined with the British protectorates of Northern Rhodesia and Nyasaland into a multiracial federation. When the federation was dissolved at the end of 1963, Northern Rhodesia and Nyasaland became the independent states of Zambia and Malawi.

Britain was prepared to grant independence to Southern Rhodesia but declined to do so when the politically dominant white Rhodesians refused to give assurances of representative government. In November 1965, the white minority government of Southern Rhodesia unilaterally declared Southern Rhodesia an independent dominion. The United Nations and the British Parliament both proclaimed this unilateral declaration of independence null and void. Following a conference in London in December 1979, the opposition government conceded and it was agreed that the British Government should resume control. In 1970, the government proclaimed a republic, but this too received no recognition. In 1979, the government purported to change the name of the Colony to Zimbabwe Rhodesia, but again this was never recognized. A British Governor soon returned to Southern Rhodesia. One of his first acts was to affirm the nullification of the purported declaration of independence. On April 18, 1980, pursuant to an act of the British Parliament, the Colony of Southern Rhodesia became independent within the commonwealth as the Republic of Zimbabwe.

RULERS:
British to 1970 (1980)

MONETARY SYSTEM:
1 Shilling = 12 Pence
1 Pound = 20 Shillings to 1970
1 Dollar = 100 Cents, 1970-80

NOTE: For later issues see Zimbabwe.

BRITISH INFLUENCE

RESERVE BANK OF RHODESIA

1964 ISSUE

Pound System

#24-26 arms at upper ctr., Qn. Elizabeth II at r. Various date and sign. varieties. Wmk. C. Rhodes. Printer: BWC. Printed in England from engraved plates.

		VG	VF	UNC
24	**10 SHILLINGS**			
	30.9.1964-16.11.1964. Blue on m/c unpt. Blue portr. w/black serial #. Tobacco field on back.	7.50	30.00	165.00

25 1 POUND
(26)

		VG	VF	UNC
3.9.1964-16.11.1964. Red on m/c unpt. Red portr., w/black serial #. Victoria Falls at l. on back.		5.00	25.00	100.00

26 5 POUNDS
(28)

	VG	VF	UNC
10.11.1964; 12.11.1964; 16.11.1964. Blue-green on m/c unpt. Lilac portr., black serial #. Zimbabwe ruins at ctr. on back.	10.00	35.00	90.00

1966 ISSUE
#27-29 arms at upper ctr., Qn. Elizabeth II at r. Various date and sign. varieties. Wmk: C. Rhodes. Printed in Rhodesia (w/o imprint). Lithographed.

27 10 SHILLINGS
(25)

	VG	VF	UNC
1.6.1966; 10.9.1968. Blue on m/c unpt. Similar to #24 but black portr., red serial #.	2.50	10.00	45.00

28 1 POUND
(27)

	VG	VF	UNC
15.6.1966-14.10.1968. Pale red on m/c unpt. Similar to #25 but brown portr. and w/red serial #.	3.00	10.00	65.00

29 5 POUNDS

	VG	VF	UNC
1.7.1966. Blue-green on m/c unpt. Similar to #26 but purple portr. and w/red serial #.	15.00	60.00	235.00

REPUBLIC

RESERVE BANK OF RHODESIA

1970-72 ISSUE
Dollar System
#30-33 bank logo at upper ctr., arms at r. Replacement notes: W/1, X/1, Y/1, Z/1 respectively.

30 1 DOLLAR

	VG	VF	UNC
1970-79. Blue on m/c unpt. Back like #27. 2 sign. varieties.			
a. Wmk: C. Rhodes. 17.2.1970-18.8.1971.	1.50	3.50	11.50
b. Wmk: as a. 14.2.1973-18.4.1978.	1.00	2.50	7.50
c. Wmk: Zimbabwe bird. 2.8.1979.	.50	1.50	6.50

31 2 DOLLARS

	VG	VF	UNC
1970-79. Red on m/c unpt. Back like #28. 2 sign. varieties.			
a. Wmk: C. Rhodes. 17.2.1970-4.1.1972.	2.00	5.00	17.50
b. Wmk: as a. 29.6.1973-5.8.1977.	1.50	3.00	12.50
c. Wmk: as a. 10.4.1979.	10.00	40.00	135.00
d. Wmk: Zimbabwe bird. 10.4.1979; 24.5.1979.	1.00	2.50	10.00

32	**5 DOLLARS**	**VG**	**VF**	**UNC**
	1972-79. Brown on m/c unpt. Giraffe at lower l. 2 lions on back. 2 sign. varieties.			
	a. Wmk: C. Rhodes. 16.10.1972.	3.00	7.00	25.00
	b. Wmk. as a. 1.3.1976; 20.10.1978.	3.00	6.00	22.50
	c. Wmk: Zimbabwe bird. 15.5.1979. (1980).	3.00	7.00	25.00

33	**10 DOLLARS**	**VG**	**VF**	**UNC**
	1970-79. Blue-green on m/c unpt. Antelope at lower l. Back like #29. 2 sign. varieties.			
	a. Wmk: C. Rhodes. 17.2.1970-8.5.1972.	7.00	15.00	50.00
	b. Wmk. as a. 20.11.1973-1.3.1976.	5.00	10.00	27.50
	c. Wmk: Zimbabwe bird. 2.1.1979.	5.00	10.00	27.50

RHODESIA & NYASALAND

Rhodesia and Nyasaland (now the Republic of Zimbabwe) located in the east-central part of southern Africa, has an area of 150,804 sq. mi. (390,580 sq. km.) and a population of 6.9 million. Capital: Salisbury. The economy is based on agriculture and mining. Tobacco, sugar, asbestos, copper and chrome ore and coal are exported.

The Rhodesian area, the habitat of paleolithic man, contains extensive evidence of earlier civilizations, notably the world-famous ruins of Zimbabwe, a gold-trading center that flourished about the 14th or 15th century AD. The Portuguese of the 16th century were the first Europeans to attempt to develop south-central Africa, but it remained for Cecil Rhodes and the British South Africa Co. to open the hinterlands. Rhodes obtained a concession for mineral rights from local chiefs in 1888 and administered his African empire (named Southern Rhodesia in 1895) through the British South Africa Co. until 1923, when the British government annexed the area after the white settlers voted for existence as a separate entity, rather than for incorporation into the Union of South Africa. From Sept. of 1953 through 1963 Southern Rhodesia was joined with the British protectorates of Northern Rhodesia and Nyasaland into a multiracial federation. When the federation was dissolved at the end of 1963, Northern Rhodesia and Nyasaland became the independent states of Zambia and Malawi.

Britain was prepared to grant independence to Southern Rhodesia but declined to do so when the politically dominant white Rhodesians refused to give assurances of representative government. On May 11, 1965, following two years of unsuccessful negotiation with the British government, Prime Minister Ian Smith issued an unilateral declaration of independence. Britain responded with economic sanctions supported by the United Nations. After further futile attempts to effect an accommodation, the Rhodesian Parliament severed all ties with Britain, and on March 2, 1970, established the Republic of Rhodesia.

On March 3, 1978, Prime Minister Ian Smith and three moderate black nationalist leaders signed an agreement providing for black majority rule. The name of the country was changed to Zimbabwe Rhodesia.

After the election of March 3, 1980, the country again changed its name to the Republic of Zimbabwe. The Federation of Rhodesia and Nyasaland (or the Central African Federation), comprising the British protectorates of Northern Rhodesia and Nyasaland and the self-governing colony of Southern Rhodesia, was located in the east-central part of southern Africa. The multiracial federation had an area of about 487,000 sq. mi. (1,261,330 sq. km.) and a population of 6.8 million. Capital: Salsbury, in Southern Rhodesia. The geographical unity of the three British possessions suggested the desirability of political and economic union as early as 1924. Despite objections by the African constituency of Northern Rhodesia and Nyasaland, who by the dominant influence of prosperous and self governing Southern Rhodesia, the Central African Federation was established in Sept. of 1953. As feared, the Federation was effectively and profitably dominated by the European consituency of Southern Rhodesia despite the fact that the three component countries largely retained their prefederation political structure. It was dissolved at the end of 1963, largely because of the effective opposition of the Nyasaland African Congress. Northern Rhodesia and Nyasaland became independent states of Zambia and Malawi in 1964. Southern Rhodesia unilaterally decalred its independence as Rhodesia the following year which was not recognized by the British Government.

For earlier issues refer to Southern Rhodesia Volume 2. For later issues refer to Malawi, Zambia, Rhodesia and Zimbabwe.

RULERS:
British to 1963

MONETARY SYSTEM:
1 Shilling = 12 Pence
1 Pound = 20 Shillings to 1963

BRITISH INFLUENCE

BANK OF RHODESIA AND NYASALAND

1956 ISSUE
#20-23 portr. Qn. Elizabeth II at r. Various date and sign. varieties. Wmk: C. Rhodes. Printer: BWC.

20	**10 SHILLINGS**	**VG**	**VF**	**UNC**
	1956-61. Reddish brown on m/c unpt. River scene on back.			
	a. Sign. Graffery-Smith. 3.4.1956-6.5.1960.	10.00	50.00	250.00
	b. Sign. H. J. Richards. 30.12.1960-30.1.1961.	8.00	40.00	200.00

		VG	VF	UNC
21	**1 POUND**			
	1956-61. Green on m/c unpt. Zimbabwe ruins at ctr. on back.			
	a. Sign. Graffery-Smith. 22.5.1956-17.6.1960.	7.50	50.00	350.00
	b. Sign. H. J. Richards. 23.11.1960-23.1.1961.	6.00	47.50	325.00

		VG	VF	UNC
22	**5 POUNDS**			
	1956-61. Blue on m/c unpt. Victoria Falls on back.			
	a. Sign. Graffery-Smith. 3.4.1956-19.6.1959.	15.00	90.00	450.00
	b. Sign. H. J. Richards. 30.1.1961; 1.2.1961.	13.50	85.00	400.00
23	**10 POUNDS**			
	1956-61. Brown on m/c unpt. Back gray-green; elephants at ctr.			
	a. Sign. Graffery-Smith. 3.4.1956; 15.4.1957; 3.7.1959; 3.6.1960.	150.00	500.00	1750.
	b. Sign. H. J. Richards. 1.2.1961.	125.00	450.00	1500.

ROMANIA

The Republic of Romania (formerly the Socialist Republic of Romania), a Balkan country in southeast Europe, has an area of 91,699 sq. mi. (237,500 sq. km.) and a population of 23.2 million. Capital: Bucharest. The economy is predominantly agricultural; heavy industry and oil have become increasingly important since 1959. Machinery, foodstuffs, raw minerals and petroleum products are exported.

Romania, the ancient Roman province of Dacia, endured wave after wave of barbarian conquest, until the late 13th century. The Vlach tribes of south of the Danube river moved north, mixing in with the Slavs and Tatars developing the two principalities of Walachia and Moldavia.

The early years of the principality of Walachia were involved in struggles with Hungary. Soon afterwards they found themselves at war with the Turks. Final capitulation to Turkey came in 1417.

Moldavia first appeared as an independent state in 1349. Polish overlordship came about at the end of the 14th century. Stephen the Great (1457-1504) was a champion of Christendom against the Turks. When Peter Rares (1527-38 and 1541-46) came to the throne, he allied himself with the Turks as he made war on the imperial forces in Transylvania and Poland. Later he allied himself with the emperor against Poland and the sultan, but was defeated and deposed in 1538. In 1541 he returned to the throne with Turkish help.

The treaty of Kuchuk Kainarji, which ended the Russo-Turkish war in 1774, resulted in Moldavia losing its northern tip, Bukovina, to Austria. As a result of Russia's continuing interests in the area and the peace of Bucharest in 1812, southeastern Moldavia, known as Bessarabia, ceded.

Peasant uprisings in 1848 were put down by the Turks and a Russo-Turkish military intervention returned things back to normal. Russian troops did not evacuate the principalities until 1851 and during the Crimean War were occupied in turn by Russia and Austria. The treaty of Paris (1856) placed the principalities with their existing privileges, ending the Russian protectorate.

Union of the principalities was voted for unanimously in 1848 and the two assemblies elected a single Prince in the person of Alexander Cuza on Jan. 17, 1859, accomplishing the *defacto* union of Romania. The prince through lack of agrarian reform was compelled to abdicate in Feb. 1866, and was succeeded by Prince Carol I who later became king in 1881. Later, in 1888 it changed to a constitutional monarchy with a bicameral legislation in 1888.

The First Balkan War in 1912 gave birth to the claim for Silistra, awarded in May 1917. The intervention and deployment of Romanian troops into Bulgaria in the Second Balkan War of 1913 resulted in the acquisition of southern Dobruja.

Crossing into Transylvania, Romania declared war on Austro-Hungary on Aug. 22, 1916. They were soon expelled and the Central Powers occupied Bucharest by Dec. 6, 1916. The Treaty of Bucharest was signed on May 7, 1918, and the Central Powers disorganized the finance of the Kingdom, ensuring financial ruin. On Nov. 9, 1918, when the defeat of the Central Powers was eminent, war was declared again. The king re-entered Bucharest on Nov. 30, 1918, after the German troops had evacuated Romania under the terms of the Armistice. Bessarabia was incorporated along with Transylvania and the old frontier borders were recognized by the treaties of St. Germain and Trianon.

The government was reorganized along Fascist lines between September 14, 1940 and January 23, 1941 following a military dictatorship. Marshal Ion Antonescu installed himself as chief of state. When the Germans invaded the Soviet Union, Romania also become involved for recovering the region of Bessarabia annexed by Stalin in 1940.

On August 23, 1944, King Mihai I proclaimed the armistice with Allied Forces. The Romanian army drove out the Germans and Hungarians in North Transylvania, but the country had been subsequently occupied by the Soviet Army. That monarchy was abolished on December 30, 1947, and Romania became a "Peoples Republic" on the Soviet pattern, which was later proclaimed a "Socialist Republic" in 1965. With the accession of N. Ceausescu to power (1965) a repressive and impoverished domestic scene worsened.

On December 22, 1989 the Communist government was overthrown by organized freedom fighters in Bucharest. Ceausescu and his wife were later executed. The new government has established the republic, the official and constitutional name being Romania.

MONETARY SYSTEM:
   1 Leu = 100 Bani

SOCIALIST REPUBLIC

BANCA NATIONALA A REPUBLICII SOCIALISTE ROMANIA

1966 ISSUE
#86-89 arms at ctr.
#90-92 arms at ctr. r.

		VG	VF	UNC
91	**1 LEU**			
(86)	1966. Olive-brown and tan.	.05	.10	.25

92	3 LEI	VG	VF	UNC
(87)	1966. Blue-gray and m/c.	.10	.20	.50

93	5 LEI	VG	VF	UNC
(88)	1966. Dk. brown and blue-black on m/c unpt. Cargo ships at dockside on back.	.15	.30	.75

94	10 LEI	VG	VF	UNC
(89)	1966. Violet, grayish green and gray. Harvesting on back.	.20	.40	1.00

95	25 LEI	VG	VF	UNC
(90)	1966. Dk. green and m/c. Portr. T. Vladimirescu at l. Large refinery on back.	.30	.60	2.00

96	50 LEI	VG	VF	UNC
(91)	1966. Dk. green and m/c. A. I. Cuza at l. Ornate bldg. on back.	.30	.60	2.50

97	100 LEI	VG	VF	UNC
(92)	1966. Dk. blue and m/c. Portr. N. Balcescu at l. Romanesque bldg. on back.	.35	.75	3.00

REPUBLIC

BANCA NATIONALA A ROMANIEI

1991 ISSUE

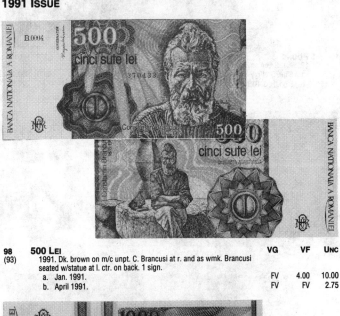

98	500 LEI	VG	VF	UNC
(93)	1991. Dk. brown on m/c unpt. C. Brancusi at r. and as wmk. Brancusi seated w/statue at l. ctr. on back. 1 sign.			
	a. Jan. 1991.	FV	4.00	10.00
	b. April 1991.	FV	FV	2.75

99	1000 LEI	VG	VF	UNC
(94)	1991; 1993. Red-brown, blue-green and brown-orange on m/c unpt. Circular shield at l. ctr., sails of sailing ships at lower ctr., M. Eminescu at r. and as wmk. Putna monastery on back. 2 sign.			
	a. Sept. 1991.	FV	FV	4.50
	b. May 1993.	FV	FV	3.75

1992-93 ISSUE

100 **200 LEI**
(95)

	VG	VF	UNC
Dec. 1992. Dull deep brown and brown-violet on m/c unpt. Square toped shield at l. ctr., steamboat "Tudor Vadimirescu" above heron and Sulina Lighthouse at ctr., G. Antipa at r. Herons, fish, and net on outline of Danube Delta at l. ctr. on back. Wmk: Bank monogram repeated.	FV	FV	.50

101 **500 LEI**
(96)

	VG	VF	UNC
Dec. 1992. Dull deep green, reddish-brown and violet on m/c unpt. Square topped shield at l. ctr., sculptures at ctr., C. Brincusi at r. Sculptures at l. and ctr. on back.			
a. Wmk: Bust facing.	FV	FV	2.25
b. Wmk: Bust to r.	FV	FV	1.75

102 **1000 LEI**
(97)

	VG	VF	UNC
May 1993. Similar to #94 but square topped shield.	FV	FV	3.00

103 **5000 LEI**
(98)

	VG	VF	UNC
March 1992. Pale purple on m/c unpt. Seal at l. ctr., chruch ctr., A. Iancu at r. and as wmk. Church at l., "Poarta Cetatii Alba Julia" at l. ctr., seal at ctr. r. on back.	FV	4.00	13.50

104 **5000 LEI**
(99)

	VG	VF	UNC
May 1993. Similar to #98 but square topped shield.	FV	FV	5.50

105 **10,000 LEI**
(100)

	VG	VF	UNC
Feb. 1994. Brown-violet and reddish brown on m/c unpt. N. Lorga at r., snake god Glycon at ctr. Historical Museum in Bucharest, statue of Fortuna and the Thinking Man of Hamangia on back.	FV	FV	10.00

106 **50,000 LEI**

	VG	VF	UNC
1996. Blue-violet on m/c unpt. G. Enescu at r. and as wmk., floral ornament, musical notes at ctr., arms at upper l. Sphinx of Carpathian mountains at l. ctr., musical chord above.	FV	FV	18.50

RUSSIA

Russia, (formerly the central power of the Union of Soviet Socialist Republics and now of the Commonwealth of Independent States) which occupies the northern part of Asia and the far eastern part of Europe, in 1991 had an area of 8,649,538 sq. mi. (22,402,200 sq. km.) and a population of *288.7 million. Capital: Moscow. Exports include machinery, iron and steel, crude oil, timber and nonferrous metals.

The first Russian dynasty was founded in Novgorod by the Viking Rurik in 862 AD. Under Yaroslav the Wise (1019-54) the subsequent Kievan state became one of the great commercial and cultural centers of Europe before falling to the Mongols of the Batu Khan, 13th century, who ruled Russia until late in the 15th century when Ivan III threw off the Mongol yoke. The Russian Empire was enlarged, solidified and Westernized during the reigns of Ivan the Terrible, Peter the Great and Catherine the Great, and by 1881 extended to the Pacific and into Central Asia.

Assignats, the first government paper money of the Russian Empire, were introduced in 1769, and gave way to State Credit Notes in 1843. Russia was put on the gold standard in 1897 through the efforts of Finance Minister Count Sergei Witte, and Russia reformed her currency at that time.

All pre-1898 notes were destroyed as they were turned in to the Treasury, accounting for their uniform scarcity today.

The last Russian Czar, Nicholas II (1894-1917), was deposed by the provisional government under Prince Lvov and later Alexander Kerensky during the military defeat in World War I. This government rapidly lost ground to the Bolshevik wing of the Socialist Democratic Labor Party which attained power following the Bolshevik Revolution. During the Russian Civil War (1917-1922) many regional governments, national states and armies in the field were formed which issued their own paper money.

After the victory of the Red armies, these areas became federal republics of the Russian Socialist Federal Soviet Republic (RSFSR), or autonomous soviet republics which united on Dec. 30, 1922, to form the Union of Soviet Socialist Republics (USSR) under the premiership of Lenin.

Beginning with the downfall of the communist government in Poland, other European countries occupied since WW II began democratic elections which spread into Russia itself, leaving the remaining states united in a newly founded Commonwealth of Independent States (C.I.S.) developed after Mikhail Gorbachev resigned on Dec. 25, 1991. The USSR Supreme Soviet voted a formal end to the treaty of union signed in 1992 and dissolved itself.

MONETARY SYSTEM:
1 Ruble = 100 Kopeks

CYRILLIC ALPHABET

А	а	𝒜	𝒶	A	С	с	𝒞	𝒸	S
Б	б	𝒯𝒪	𝒷	B	Т	т	𝒯	𝓉	T
В	в	𝐵	𝓋	V	У	у	𝒰	𝓎	U
Г	г	𝒯	𝑔	G	Ф	ф	𝒳	𝒻	F
Д	д	𝒟	𝒹	D	Х	х	𝒳	𝓍	Kh
Е	е	𝐸	𝑒	ye	Ц	ц	𝒰	𝒸	C
Ё	ё	𝐸	𝑒	yo	Ч	ч	𝒰	𝒸	ch
Ж	ж	𝒲	𝒿	zh	Ш	ш	𝒰𝒰	𝓌	sh
З	з	𝒵	𝓏	Z	Щ	щ	𝒰𝒰	𝓌	shch
И	и	𝐼	𝒾	I	Ъ	ъ	ъ*)	ъ*)	'
Й	й	𝐼	𝒾̆	J	Ы	ы	ы	ы	'
К	к	𝒦	𝓀.𝓀	K	Ь	ь**)	ь**)	ь	'
Л	л	𝐿	𝓁	L	Э	э	𝒺	𝑒	E
М	м	𝑀	𝓂	M	Ю	ю	𝒥𝒪	𝓎	yu
Н	н	𝐻	𝓃	N	Я	я	𝒦	𝓎	ya
О	о	𝒪	𝑜	O			𝒴	𝒾	I
П	п	𝒯	𝓃	P			𝒴	𝓅	yo
Р	р	𝒫	𝓅	R					

*) "hard", and **) "soft" signs; both soundless. Г and Ѣ were dropped in 1918.

C.C.C.P. - СОЮЗ СОВЕТСКИХ СОЦИАЛИС ТИЧЕСКИХ РЕСОУБЛІК

U.S.S.R. - UNION OF SOVIET SOCIALIST REPUBLIC

ГОСУДАРСТВЕННЫЙ КАЗНАЧЕЙСКИЙ БИЛЕТ

STATE TREASURY NOTES

1961 ISSUE
#222-224 arms at upper l.

		VG	VF	UNC
222	**1 RUBLE** 1961. Brown on pale green unpt. Back red on m/c unpt.	.05	.10	.20

		VG	VF	UNC
223	**3 RUBLES** 1961. Greenish black on m/c unpt. View of Kremlin. Back lt. blue on green and m/c unpt.	.05	.10	.50

		VG	VF	UNC
224	**5 RUBLES** 1961. Blue on peach unpt. Kremlin Spasski tower at l. Back blue and m/c.	.05	.15	.50

БИЛЕТ ГОСУДАРСТВЕННОГО БАНКА C.C.C.P.

STATE BANK NOTE U.S.S.R.

1961 ISSUE
#234-236 portr. V. I. Lenin at upper l., arms at upper ctr.

		VG	VF	UNC
233	**10 RUBLES** 1961. Red-brown on pale gold unpt. Portr. Lenin at r. Wmk: Stars.	.10	.25	.75

		VG	VF	UNC
234	**25 RUBLES** 1961. Purple on pale lt. green unpt. Wmk: Stars.	.15	.35	1.00

		VG	VF	UNC
235	**50 RUBLES** 1961. Dk. green and green on green and pink unpt. Kremlin at upper ctr. on back.	.10	.25	1.00

		VG	VF	UNC
236	**100 RUBLES** 1961. Brown on lt. blue unpt. Kremlin tower at ctr. on back.	.40	.75	2.00

1991 ISSUE
#237-243 similar to #222-236.

#237-239 wmk: Star in circle repeated.

#244-246 portr. V. I. Lenin at upper l. and as wmk., arms at upper ctr. Different views of the Kremlin on back.

		VG	VF	UNC
237	**1 RUBLE** 1991. Dk. green and red-brown on tan unpt. Similar to #222.	.05	.10	.20

238 **3 RUBLES**
1991. Green on blue and m/c unpt. Kremlin at ctr. Similar to #223.

VG	VF	UNC
.20	.65	2.00

239 **5 RUBLES**
1991. Blue-gray on lt. blue, pale green and pink unpt. Tower at l. similar to #224.

VG	VF	UNC
.05	.15	.50

240 **10 RUBLES**
1991. Red-brown and green on m/c unpt. Similar to #233.

VG	VF	UNC
.15	.25	.75

241 **50 RUBLES**
1991. Dk. brown, green and red on m/c unpt. Similar to #235.

VG	VF	UNC
.20	.60	1.75

242 **100 RUBLES**
1991. Deep red-brown and blue on m/c unpt. Similar to #236.

VG	VF	UNC
.35	1.00	3.00

243 **100 RUBLES**
1991. Like #242 but w/added pink and green guilloche at r. in wmk. area, blue guilloche at l. on back. Wmk: Stars.

VG	VF	UNC
.35	1.00	3.00

244 **200 RUBLES**
1991. Green and brown on m/c unpt.

VG	VF	UNC
.30	1.00	3.00

245 **500 RUBLES**
1991. Red and green on m/c unpt.

VG	VF	UNC
.50	2.50	6.50

246 **1000 RUBLES**
1991. Brown and blue on green and m/c unpt.

VG	VF	UNC
1.00	3.50	10.00

1992 ISSUE

247   50 RUBLES

	VG	VF	UNC
1992. Brown and gray on green and m/c unpt. Similar to #241. Wmk: Star in circle repeated.	.15	.35	1.00

248   200 RUBLES

	VG	VF	UNC
1992. Green and brown on m/c unpt. Similar to #244, but guilloche added in wmk. area on back. Wmk. as #247.	.30	.90	2.50

249   500 RUBLES

	VG	VF	UNC
1992. Red, violet and dk. green on m/c unpt. Similar to #245, but guilloche added in wmk. area on back. Wmk: Stars.	.25	.75	3.00

250   1000 RUBLES

	VG	VF	UNC
1992. Dk. brown and deep green on m/c unpt. Similar to #246, but guilloche added in wmk. area on back. Wmk: Stars.	.40	1.25	3.50

C.I.S. - COMMONWEALTH OF INDEPENDENT STATES
РОССИЙСКАЯ ФЕДЕРАЦИЯ
RUSSIAN FEDERATION
1992 GOVERNMENT PRIVATIZATION CHECK ISSUE

251   10,000 RUBLES
(253)

	VG	VF	UNC
1992. Dk. brown on m/c unpt. Scene from walkway along the Neva River is St. Petersburg at ctr. Text indicating method of redemption into shares of govt.-owned property on back. Handstamp from bank added at bottom. Valid until Dec. 31, 1993.	5.00	15.00	35.00

БАНК РОССИИ
BANK OF RUSSIA
1992 ISSUE

252   5000 RUBLES
(251)

	VG	VF	UNC
1992. Blue-green and maroon on m/c unpt. St. Basil's Cathedral at l. Kremlin on back. Wmk: Stars.	.45	1.35	3.50

253   10,000 RUBLES
(252)

	VG	VF	UNC
1992. Brown, black and red on m/c unpt. Kremlin w/new tricolor flag at l. ctr. and as wmk. Kremlin towers at ctr. r. on back.	.90	2.75	5.50

1993 ISSUE

#254-260 new tricolor flag over stylized Kremlin at l., monogram at or near upper r. at or near ctr. on back.

#254-256 wmk: Stars within wavy lines repeated.

#258-260 new flag over Kremlin at l. and as wmk. Kremlin at or near ctr. on back.

254	100 RUBLES	VG	VF	UNC
	1993. Blue-black on pink and lt. blue unpt. Kremlin, Spasaki tower at ctr. r. on back.	.05	.10	.50

255	200 RUBLES	VG	VF	UNC
	1993. Brown on pink and m/c unpt. Kremlin gate at ctr. on back.	.05	.15	.75

256	500 RUBLES	VG	VF	UNC
	1993. Green, blue and violet on m/c unpt. Kremlin at l. ctr. on back.	.05	.15	1.00

257	1000 RUBLES	VG	VF	UNC
	1993. Green, olive-green and brown on m/c unpt. Kremlin at ctr. on back. Wmk: Stars.	.10	.25	1.50

258	5000 RUBLES	VG	VF	UNC
	1993; 1993/94. Blue-black, brown and violet on m/c unpt.			
	a. 1993.	FV	FV	4.00
	b. 1993//94.	FV	FV	16.00

259	10,000 RUBLES	VG	VF	UNC
	1993; 1993//94. Violet, greenish blue, brownish purple and m/c.			
	a. 1993.	FV	FV	3.50
	b. 1993//94.	FV	FV	25.00

260	50,000 RUBLES	VG	VF	UNC
	1993; 1993//94. Olive-green, black and reddish brown on m/c unpt.			
	a. 1993.	FV	FV	13.50
	b. 1993//94.	FV	FV	50.00

1995 ISSUE

261	1000 RUBLES	VG	VF	UNC
	1995. Dk. brown and brown on m/c unpt. Seaport of Vladivostok at l. ctr., memorial column at ctr. r. and as wmk. Entrance to Vladivostok Bay at ctr. on back. Wmk: 1000 and memorial column.	FV	FV	1.00

262 5000 RUBLES

	VG	VF	UNC
1995. Deep blue-green and dk. olive-green on m/c unpt. Monument of the Russian Millennium in Novgorod at l. ctr. Cathedral of St. Sophia at l. ctr. and as wmk. Old towered city wall at upper l. ctr. on back.	FV	FV	2.50

263 10,000 RUBLES

	VG	VF	UNC
1995. Dk. brown and dk. gray on m/c unpt. Arch bridge over Yenisei River in Krasnoyarsk at l. ctr., steeple at ctr. r. and as. wmk. Hydroelectric dam at ctr. on back.	FV	FV	4.50

264 50,000 RUBLES

	VG	VF	UNC
1995. Dk. brown, grayish purple and black on m/c unpt. Monument at ctr. Fountain in St. Petersburg at upper ctr. on back. Wmk: Bldg. w/steeple.	FV	FV	20.00

265 100,000 RUBLES

	VG	VF	UNC
1995. Purple and brown on m/c unpt. Chariot monument at ctr. Bolshoy (Great) Theatre in Moscow on back. Wmk: Bldg. over value.	FV	FV	36.50

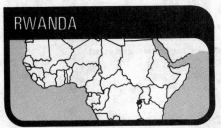

RWANDA

The Republic of Rwanda, located in central Africa between the Republic of the Congo and Tanzania, has an area of 10,169 sq. mi. (26,340 sq. km.) and a population of *7.3 million. Capital: Kigali. The economy is based on agriculture and mining. Coffee and tin are exported.

German lieutenant Count von Goetzen was the first European to visit Rwanda, 1894. Four years later the court of the Mwami (the Tutsi king of Rwanda) willingly permitted the kingdom to become a protectorate of Germany. In 1916, during the African campaigns of World War I, Belgian troops from the Congo occupied Rwanda. After the war it, together with Burundi, became a Belgian League of Nations mandate under the name of the Territory of Ruanda-Urundi. Following World War II, Ruanda-Urundi became a Belgian administered U.N. trust territory. The Tutsi monarchy was deposed by the U.N. supervised election of 1961, after which Belgium granted Rwanda internal autonomy. On July 1, 1962, the U.N. terminated the Belgian trusteeship and granted full independence to both Rwanda and Burundi. Banknotes were used in common with the Belgian Congo, and later with Burundi.

Also see Belgian Congo, Rwanda-Burundi.

MONETARY SYSTEM:
1 Franc (Amafranga, Amafaranga) = 100 Centimes

REPUBLIC

BANQUE NATIONALE DU RWANDA

BANKI NASIYONALI Y'U RWANDA

1962 PROVISIONAL ISSUE
#1-5 ovpt: *BANQUE NATIONALE DU RWANDA* and sign. title: *LE GOUVERNEUR* on Banque d'Emission du Rwanda et du Burundi notes.

#1-3 stamped ovpt.

1 20 FRANCS

	GOOD	FINE	XF
ND (1962-old date 5.10.1960). Green on tan and pink unpt. Maroon or black ovpt. on Rwanda-Burundi #3.	70.00	175.00	400.00

2 50 FRANCS

	GOOD	FINE	XF
ND (1962-old dates 15.9.1960; 1.10.1960). Red on m/c unpt. Maroon ovpt. on Rwanda-Burundi #4.	75.00	225.00	500.00

3 100 FRANCS

	VG	VF	UNC
ND (1962-old dates 15.9.1960; 1.10.1960; 31.7.1962). Blue on lt. green and tan unpt. Ovpt. on Rwanda-Burundi #5.			
a. Black ovpt.	75.00	135.00	300.00
b. Purple ovpt.	75.00	135.00	300.00

4 500 FRANCS

	GOOD	FINE	XF
ND (1962-old dates 15.9.1960; 15.9.1961). Lilac-brown on m/c unpt. Embossed ovpt. and embossed facsimile sign. on Rwanda-Burundi #6.	300.00	800.00	1200.

5 1000 FRANCS

	GOOD	FINE	XF
ND (1962-old dates 15.5.1961; 1.7.1962). Green on m/c unpt. Embossed ovpt. and embossed facsimile sign. on Rwanda-Burundi #7.	250.00	750.00	1100.

1964 ISSUE
Various date and sign. title varieties.

6	**20 FRANCS**	**VG**	**VF**	**UNC**
	1964-76. Brown and m/c. Flag of Rwanda at l. 4 young boys w/pipeline on back.			
	a. Sign. titles: *VICE GOUVERNEUR* and *GOUVERNEUR*, w/security thread. 1.7.1964; 31.3.1966; 15.3.1969; 1.9.1969.	2.50	7.50	15.00
	b. Sign. titles: *VICE GOUVERNEUR* and *ADMINISTRATEUR*, w/security thread. 1.7.1965.	3.50	8.50	20.00
	c. Sign. titles: *GOUVERNEUR* and *ADMINISTRATEUR*, w/security thread. 1.7.1971.	1.25	3.00	7.50
	d. Sign. titles: *ADMINISTRATEUR* and *ADMINISTRATEUR*, w/security thread. 30.10.1974.	.50	1.50	6.00
	e. Sign. titles: *ADMINISTRATEUR* and *GOUVERNEUR*, w/o security thread. 1.1.1976.	.50	.75	1.35
	s1. As a. Specimen. 1.7.1964; 31.3.1966; 15.3.1969	—	—	5.00
	s2. As b. Specimen. 1.7.1965.	—	—	3.50
	s3. As c. Specimen. 1.7.1971.	—	—	3.50
	s4. As d. Specimen. 30.10.1974.	—	—	6.00

7	**50 FRANCS**	**VG**	**VF**	**UNC**
	1964-76. Blue and m/c. Map of Rwanda at l. Miners on back.			
	a. Sign. titles: *VICE GOUVERNEUR* and *GOUVERNEUR*, w/security thread. 1.7.1964; 31.1.1966; 1.9.1969.	3.00	10.00	20.00
	b. Sign. titles: *ADMINISTRATEUR* and *GOUVERNEUR*, w/security thread. 1.7.1971; 30.10.1974.	.75	2.00	7.00
	c. Sign. titles: *ADMINISTRATEUR* and *GOUVERNEUR*, w/o security thread. 1.1.1976.	.50	1.00	2.00
	s1. As a. Specimen. 1.7.1964; 31.1.1966; 1.9.1969.	—	—	4.00
	s2. As b. Specimen. 1.7.1971; 30.10.1974.	—	—	4.00

8	**100 FRANCS**	**VG**	**VF**	**UNC**
	1964-76. Purple and m/c. Map of Rwanda at l. Woman w/basket at l; banana trees at ctr. on back.			
	a. Sign. titles: *VICE GOUVERNEUR* and *GOUVERNEUR*, w/security thread. 1.7.1964; 31.3.1966; 31.10.1969.	1.00	3.00	9.00
	b. Sign. titles: *VICE GOUVERNEUR* and *ADMINISTRATEUR*, w/security thread. 1.7.1965.	5.00	12.00	20.00
	c. Sign. titles: *ADMINISTRATEUR* and *GOUVERNEUR*, w/security thread. 1.7.1971; 30.10.1974.	1.25	2.50	8.50
	d. Sign. titles: *ADMINISTRATEUR* and *GOUVERNEUR*, w/o security thread. 1.1.1976.	.75	1.50	3.00
	s1. As a. Specimen. 1.7.1964; 31.10.1969.	—	—	6.00
	s2. As c. Specimen. 1.7.1971; 30.10.1974.	—	—	6.00

9	**500 FRANCS**	**VG**	**VF**	**UNC**
	1964-76. Dk. green and m/c. Arms of Rwanda at l. Man w/basket at l., rows of plants behind on back.			
	a. Sign. titles: *VICE GOUVERNEUR* and *GOUVERNEUR*. 1.7.1964; 31.3.1966; 31.10.1969.	5.00	10.00	40.00
	b. Sign. titles: *ADMINISTRATUER* and *GOUVERNEUR*. 1.7.1971; 30.10.1974; 1.1.1976.	3.00	7.50	25.00
	s1. As a. Specimen. 1.7.1964; 31.3.1966.	—	—	12.50
	s2. As b. Specimen. 1.7.1971; 30.10.1974	—	—	12.50

10	**1000 FRANCS**	**VG**	**VF**	**UNC**
	1964-76. Red and m/c. Arms of Rwanda at l. Man and terraced hills on back.			
	a. Sign. titles: *VICE GOUVERNEUR* and *GOUVERNEUR*. 1.7.1964; 31.3.1966; 15.3.1969.	12.50	25.00	65.00
	b. Sign. titles: *ADMINISTRATEURNI* and *GOUVERNEUR*. 1.7.1971; 30.10.1974.	10.00	20.00	45.00
	c. Printed sign. titles like b. 1.1.1976.	7.50	15.00	30.00
	s1. As a. Specimen. 31.3.1966; 15.3.1969.	—	—	17.50
	s2. As b. Specimen. 1.7.1971.	—	—	17.50

1974 ISSUE

11	**500 FRANCS**	**VG**	**VF**	**UNC**
	19.4.1974. Green and m/c. Gen. Habyarimana at l. Back like #9.			
	a. Issued note.	7.50	15.00	40.00
	s. Specimen.	—	—	10.00

1978 ISSUE

12   100 FRANCS

	VG	VF	UNC
1.1.1978. Lt. blue and m/c. Zebras. Woman and child, natural scenery on back.			
a. Issued note.	1.00	2.50	6.00
s. Specimen.	—	—	12.50

13   500 FRANCS

	VG	VF	UNC
1.1.1978. Orange and m/c. Impalas. 8 drummers at l., strip mining at r. on back.			
a. Wmk: Impala's head.	5.00	7.50	15.00
b. W/o wmk.	30.00	65.00	150.00
s. As a. Specimen.	—	—	20.00

14   1000 FRANCS

	VG	VF	UNC
1.1.1978. Green and m/c. Boy picking tea leaves. Dancer on back. Wmk: Impala's head.			
a. Issued note.	9.00	15.00	27.50
s. Specimen.	—	—	25.00

15   5000 FRANCS

	VG	VF	UNC
1.1.1978. Green, blue and m/c. Female w/basket on her head at l., field workers at ctr. Lake and mountains on back. Wmk: Impala's head.			
a. Issued note.	45.00	65.00	125.00
s. Specimen.	—	—	100.00

1981 ISSUE

16   500 FRANCS

	VG	VF	UNC
1.7.1981. Brown and m/c. Arms at l., 3 gazelle at r. Men working in field at l. on back. Wmk: Crowned crane's head.			
a. Issued note.	FV	10.00	20.00
s. Specimen.	—	—	20.00

17   1000 FRANCS

	VG	VF	UNC
1.7.1981. Green, brown and m/c. 2 Watusi warriors at r. 2 gorillas at l., canoe in lake at r. on back. Wmk: Crowned crane's head.			
a. Issued note.	FV	20.00	30.00
s. Specimen.	—	—	32.50

1982 ISSUE

18   100 FRANCS

	VG	VF	UNC
1.8.1982. Black on lilac and m/c unpt. Zebras at ctr. and r. Back purple and m/c; woman carrying baby at l., view of mountains at ctr. on back. Wmk: Impala's head.	FV	2.00	6.00

1988-89 ISSUE

#19, 21 and 22 similar to #18, #17 and #15, but new spelling *AMAFARANGA* on back. Slight color differences and new sign. titles: *2E VICE-GOUVERNEUR* and *LE GOUVERNEUR*.

#20 *Deleted.*

| 19 | **100 FRANCS** | | **VG** | **VF** | **UNC** |
| | 24.4.1989. Similar to #18. | | FV | FV | 3.00 |

21	**1000 FRANCS**		**VG**	**VF**	**UNC**
	1.1.1988; 24.4.1989. Similar to #17.		FV	FV	15.00
22	**5000 FRANCS**				
	1.1.1988; 24.4.1989. Similar to #15.		FV	FV	62.50

1994 ISSUE

#23-25 mountainous landscape at r. Wmk: Impala's head. Printer: G&D (w/o imprint).

23	**500 FRANCS**		**VG**	**VF**	**UNC**
	1.12.1994. Blue-black, black and dk. blue-green on m/c unpt.		FV	FV	5.00
	Antelope at l. ctr. on back.				

24	**1000 FRANCS**		**VG**	**VF**	**UNC**
	1.12.1994. Purple, red-brown and dk. brown on m/c unpt. Vegetation		FV	FV	10.00
	at l., water buffalo at ctr. on back.				

25	**5000 FRANCS**		**VG**	**VF**	**UNC**
	1.12.1994. Dk. brown, violet and purple on m/c unpt. Reclining lion at		FV	FV	40.00
	l. ctr. on back.				

RWANDA-BURUNDI

Rwanda-Burundi, a Belgian League of Nations mandate and United Nations trust territory comprising the provinces of Rwanda and Burundi of the former colony of German East Africa, was located in central Africa between the present Republic of the Congo, Uganda and mainland Tanzania. The mandate-trust territory had an area of 20,916 sq. mi. (54,272 sq. km.) and a population of 4.3 million.

For specific statistics and history of Rwanda and Burundi see individual entries.

When Rwanda and Burundi were formed into a mandate for administration by Belgium, their names were changed to Ruanda and Urundi and they were organized as an integral part of the Belgian Congo, during which time they used a common banknote issue with the Belgian Congo. After the Belgian Congo acquired independence as the Republic of the Congo, the provinces of Ruanda and Urundi reverted to their former names of Rwanda and Burundi and issued notes with both names on them. In 1962, both Rwandi and Burundi became separate independent states.

Also see Belgian Congo, Burundi and Rwanda.

MONETARY SYSTEM:

1 Franc = 100 Centimes

INDEPENDENT

BANQUE D'EMISSION DU RWANDA ET DU BURUNDI

1960 ISSUE

1	**5 FRANCS**		**VG**	**VF**	**UNC**
	1960-63. Lt. brown on green unpt. Antelope at l.				
	a. 15.9.1960; 15.5.1961.		12.50	20.00	40.00
	b. 15.4.1963.		25.00	40.00	80.00

| 5 | **100 FRANCS** | | **GOOD** | **FINE** | **XF** |
| | 15.9.1960; 1.10.1960; 31.7.1962. Blue on lt. and tan unpt. Zebu at l. | | 17.50 | 40.00 | 100.00 |

6	**500 FRANCS**		**GOOD**	**FINE**	**XF**
	15.9.1960; 15.5.1961; 15.9.1961. Lilac-brown on m/c unpt.		185.00	450.00	—
	Rhinoceros at ctr. r.				

| 7 | **1000 FRANCS** | | **GOOD** | **FINE** | **XF** |
| | 15.9.1960; 15.5.1961; 31.7.1962. Green on m/c unpt. Zebra at r. | | 165.00 | 425.00 | — |

The Colony of St. Helena, a British colony located about 1,150 miles (1,850 km.) from the west coast of Africa, has an area of 47 sq. mi. (122 sq. km.) and a population of 5,700. Capital: Jamestown. Flax, lace and rope are produced for export. Ascension and Tristan da Cunha are dependencies of St. Helena.

The island was discovered and named by the Portuguese navigator Joao de Nova Castella in 1502. The Portuguese imported livestock, fruit trees and vegetables but established no permanent settlement. The Dutch occupied the island temporarily, 1645-1651. The original European settlement was founded by representatives of the British East India Company sent to annex the island after the departure of the Dutch. The Dutch returned and captured St. Helena from the British on New Year's Day, 1673, but were in turn ejected by a British force under Sir Richard Munden. Thereafter St. Helena was the undisputed possession of Great Britian. The island served as the place of exile for Napoleon, several Zulu chiefs, and an ex-sultan of Zanzibar.

RULERS:
British

MONETARY SYSTEM:
1 Pound = 20 Shillings to 1971
1 Pound = 100 New Pence, 1971

BRITISH INFLUENCE

GOVERNMENT OF ST. HELENA

1976; 1979 ND ISSUE
#5-8 views of the island at l., Qn. Elizabeth II at r.
#5-7 Royal arms w/motto at l., shield w/ship at ctr. r. on back.
NOTE: #5 w/serial #170,001-200,000 are non-redeemable.

		VG	VF	UNC
5	**50 PENCE**			
	ND (1979). Purple on pink and pale yellow-green unpt. correctly spelled *ANGLIAENI* in motto.	1.00	1.50	3.50

		VG	VF	UNC
6	**1 POUND**			
	ND (1976). Deep olive-green on pale orange and ochre unpt. Incorrect spelling *ANGLAE* in motto. 153 x 7mm.	2.50	6.00	20.00

		VG	VF	UNC
7	**5 POUNDS**			
	ND (1976). Blue.			
	a. Incorrect spelling *ANGLIAE* in motto.	FV	10.00	25.00
	b. Corrected spelling *ANGLIAE* in motto.	FV	FV	15.00

		VG	VF	UNC
8	**10 POUNDS**			
	ND (1979). Lt. red. Arms on back, correctly spelled *ANGLIAE* in motto. Sign. varieties.			
	a. Issued note.	FV	FV	28.50
	b. As b. Uncut sheet of 3.	—	—	275.00
	r. Remainder w/o sign. or serial #.	—	—	100.00

1982; 1986 ND ISSUE
#9, 10 Qn. Elizabeth II at r. Royal arms w/motto at l., shield w/sailing ship at ctr. r. on back.
NOTE: #9 w/serial #A/1 350,000 - A/1 400,000 are non-redeemable.

		VG	VF	UNC
9	**1 POUND**			
	ND (1982). Deep olive-green on pale orange and ochre unpt. Like #6 but corrected spelling *ANGLIAE* in motto. Reduced size. 147 x 66mm.	FV	FV	5.00

		VG	VF	UNC
10	**20 POUNDS**			
	ND (1986). Dk. brown on m/c unpt. Harbor view at l. ctr. Back lt. green.	FV	FV	55.00

The Territorial Collectivity of St. Pierre and Miquelon, a French overseas territory located 10 miles (16 km.) off the south coast of Newfoundland, has an area of 93 sq. mi. (242 sq. km.) and a population of *6,000. Capital: St. Pierre. The economy of the barren archipelago is based on cod fishing and fur farming. Fish and fish products, and mink and silver fox pelts are exported.

The islands, occupied by the French in 1604, were captured by the British in 1702 and held until 1763 when they were returned to the possession of France and employed as a fishing station. They passed between France and England on six more occasions between 1778 and 1814 when they were awarded permanently to France by the Treaty of Paris. The rugged, soil-poor granite islands, which will support only evergreen shrubs, are all that remain to France of her extensive colonies in North America. In 1958 St. Pierre and Miquelon voted in favor of the new constitution of the Fifth Republic of France, thereby choosing to remain within the French Community.

Notes of the Banque de France circulated 1937-1942; afterwards notes of the Caisse Centrale de la France Libre and the Caisse Centrale de la France d'Outre-Mer.

RULERS:
French

MONETARY SYSTEM:
1 Franc = 100 Centimes
5 Francs 40 Centimes = 1 Canada Dollar
1 Nouveaux Franc = 100 'old', 1960-

FRENCH INFLUENCE

CAISSE CENTRALE DE LA FRANCE D'OUTRE-MER

SAINT PIERRE ET MIQUELON

1960 ND PROVISIONAL ISSUE
#30-35 ovpt: *SAINT-PIERRE-ET-MIQUELON* and new denomination.

		VG	VF	UNC
30	**1 NOUVEAUX FRANC ON 50 FRANCS**			
	ND (1960). M/c. Ovpt. on Reunion #25.	3.00	8.00	32.50

		VG	VF	UNC
31	**1 NOUVEAUX FRANC ON 50 FRANCS**			
	ND (1960). M/c. B. d'Esnambuc at l., ship at r. Woman on back.	35.00	150.00	350.00
32	**2 NOUVEAUX FRANC ON 100 FRANCS**			
	ND (1963). M/c. La Bourdonnais at l., 2 women at r. Woman looking at mountains on back.	4.00	15.00	45.00
33	**10 NOUVEAUX FRANC ON 500 FRANCS**			
	ND (1964). M/c. Bldgs. and sailboat at l., 2 women at r. Ox-carts w/wood and plants on back.	12.00	35.00	185.00

		VG	VF	UNC
34	**20 NOUVEAUX FRANC ON 1000 FRANCS**			
	ND (1964). M/c. 2 women at r. Women at r., 2 men in small boat on back.	35.00	100.00	325.00

		VG	VF	UNC
35	**100 NOUVEAUX FRANC ON 5000 FRANCS**			
	ND (1960). M/c. Gen. Schwelcher at ctr. r. Family on back.	85.00	275.00	700.00

ST. THOMAS & PRINCE

The Democratic Republic of Sao Tomé and Príncipe (formerly the Portuguese overseas province of St. Thomas and Prince Islands) is located in the Gulf of Guinea 150 miles (241 km.) off the west African coast. It has an area of 372 sq. mi. (960 sq. km.) and a population of *121,000. Capital: Sao Tomé. The economy of the islands is based on cocoa, copra and coffee.

St. Thomas and St. Prince were uninhabited when discovered by Portuguese navigators Joao de Santarem and Pedro de Escobar in 1470. After the failure of their initial settlement, 1485, the Portuguese successfully colonized St. Thomas with a colony of prisoners and exiled Jews, 1493. An initial prosperity based on the sugar trade gave way to a time of misfortune, 1567-1709, that saw the colony attacked and occupied or plundered by the French and Dutch; ravaged by the slave revolt of 1595; and finally rendered destitute by the transfer of the world sugar trade to Brazil. In the late 1800s, the colony turned from the production of sugar to cocoa, the basis of its present prosperity.

The islands were designated a Portuguese overseas province in 1951. On April 25, 1974, the government of Portugal was seized by a military junta which reached agreements providing for independence for the Portuguese overseas provinces of Portuguese Guinea (Guinea-Bissau), Mozambique, Cape Verde Islands, Angola, and St. Thomas and Prince Islands. The Democratic Republic of Sao Tomé and Príncipe was declared on July 12, 1975.

RULERS:
Portuguese to 1975

MONETARY SYSTEM:
1 Escudo = 100 Centavos, 1914-1976
1 Dobra = 100 Centimos, 1977-

PORTUGUESE INFLUENCE

BANCO NACIONAL ULTRAMARINO

ST. TOMÉ E PRINCIPE BRANCH

1964 ISSUE
#36-38 bank seal at l., Portuguese arms at lower ctr., D. Afonso V at lower r.

			VG	VF	UNC
40	**1000 ESCUDOS**				
	11.5.1964. Green on m/c unpt. J. de Santarem at r.		25.00	60.00	125.00
	a. Issued note.		—	—	100.00
	s. Specimen.				

1974 CIRCULATING BEARER CHECK ISSUE

			VG	VF	UNC
41	**100 ESCUDOS**				
	31.3.1974.		—	—	—
42	**500 ESCUDOS**				
	28.4.1974.		—	—	—
43	**500 ESCUDOS**				
	31.12.1974		20.00	50.00	125.00

			VG	VF	UNC
49	**1000 ESCUDOS**		45.00	85.00	150.00
	23.12.1974; 31.12.1974.				

DEMOCRATIC REPUBLIC

BANCO NACIONAL DE S. TOMÉ E PRINCIPE

1976 PROVISIONAL ISSUE
#44-46 bank seal at l., Portuguese arms at lower ctr., Kg. D. Afonso V at r. Printer: BWC.
#44-48 red. New bank name ovpt. on both sides of Banco Nacional Ultramarino notes.

			VG	VF	UNC
44	**20 ESCUDOS**		2.00	5.00	10.00
	1.6.1976 (- old date 20.11.1958). Brown on m/c unpt.				

			VG	VF	UNC
45	**50 ESCUDOS**		2.50	6.00	15.00
	1.6.1976 (- old date 21.11.1958). Brown-violet on m/c unpt.				

			VG	VF	UNC
46	**100 ESCUDOS**		4.00	10.00	20.00
	1.6.1976 (- old date 20.11.1958). Purple on m/c unpt.				

47	**500 ESCUDOS**	**VG**	**VF**	**UNC**
	1.6.1976 (- old date 18.4.1956). Blue on m/c unpt. Kg. D. Afonso V at r., bank seal at l., Portuguese arms at lower r.	15.00	37.50	100.00
48	**1000 ESCUDOS**			
	1.6.1976 (- old date 11.5.1964). Green on m/c unpt. J. de Santarem at r. Woman, sailing ships at l. ctr. on back.	1.50	40.00	120.00

1976 CIRCULATING BEARER CHECK ISSUE

50	**500 ESCUDOS**	**VG**	**VF**	**UNC**
	21.6.1976. 167 x 75mm.	10.00	27.50	85.00
51	**1000 ESCUDOS**			
	21.6.1976. 167 x 75mm.	13.50	33.00	100.00

DECRETO-LEI NO. 50/76; 1977 ISSUE

#52-53 Rei Amador at r. and as wmk. Sign. titles: *O MINISTRO DA COORDENACÃO ECONOMICA* and *O GOVERNADOR*. Printer: BWC.

52	**50 DOBRAS**	**VG**	**VF**	**UNC**
	12.7.1977. Red and m/c. Parrot at ctr. Scene w/2 fishermen in boats on back.	.65	2.00	5.50

53	**100 DOBRAS**	**VG**	**VF**	**UNC**
	12.7.1977. Green and m/c. Flower at ctr. Group of people preparing food on back.	1.50	4.00	7.50

54	**500 DOBRAS**	**VG**	**VF**	**UNC**
	12.7.1977. Purple and m/c. Turtle at ctr. Waterfall on back.	3.00	10.00	22.50

55	**1000 DOBRAS**	**VG**	**VF**	**UNC**
	12.7.1977. Blue and m/c. Bananas at ctr. Fruit gatherer on back.	7.00	20.00	75.00

DECRETO-LEI NO. 6/82

#56-55 like #52-54 except sign. titles: *O MINISTRO DO PLANO* and *O GOVERNADOR*.

56	**50 DOBRAS**	**VG**	**VF**	**UNC**
	30.9.1982. Like #52.	.40	1.25	5.00
57	**100 DOBRAS**			
	30.9.1982. Like #53.	.50	1.50	7.00
58	**500 DOBRAS**			
	30.9.1982. Like #54.	1.75	5.50	20.00

59	**1000 DOBRAS**	**VG**	**VF**	**UNC**
	30.9.1982. Like #55.	3.00	10.00	30.00

DECRETO-LEI NO. 1/88

#60-62 designs like #56-59 except sign. title at l.: *O MINISTRO DA ECONOMIA E FINANCAS*. Printer: TDLR.

60	**100 DOBRAS**	**VG**	**VF**	**UNC**
	4.1.1989. Green and m/c. Like #56.	.40	1.25	4.00
61	**500 DOBRAS**			
	4.1.1989. Red, purple and m/c. Like #58.	.90	2.00	6.00
62	**1000 DOBRAS**			
	4.1.1989. Blue, green and m/c. Like #59.	1.75	5.00	15.00

BANCO CENTRAL DE S.TOMÉ E PRINCIPE

1993; 1996 ISSUE

63	**1000 DOBRAS**	**VG**	**VF**	**UNC**
	26.8.1993. Violet and blue on m/c unpt. Similar to #62.	FV	FV	8.50
64	**2000 DOBRAS**			
	1996.			Expected New Issue
65	**5000 DOBRAS**			
	1996.			Expected New Issue
66	**10,000 DOBRAS**			
	1996.			Expected New Issue

SAUDI ARABIA

The Kingdom of Saudi Arabia, an independent and absolute hereditary monarchy comprising the former sultanate of Nejd, the old kingdom of Hejaz, Asir and El Jasa, occupies four-fifths of the Arabian peninsula. The kingdom has an area of 830,000 sq. mi. (2,149,690 sq. km.) and a population of 15.4 million. Capital: Riyadh. The economy is based on oil, which provides 85 percent of Saudi Arabia's revenue.

Mohammed united the Arabs in the 7th century and his followers founded a great empire with its capital at Medina. The Turks established nominal rule over much of Arabia in the 16th and 17th centuries, and in the 18th century divided it into principalities.

The Kingdom of Saudi Arabia was created by King Ibn-Saud (1882-1953), a descendant of earlier Wahabi rulers of the Arabian peninsula. In 1901 he seized Riyadh, capital of the Sultanate of Nejd, and in 1905 established himself as Sultan. In 1913 he captured the Turkish province of Hasa; took the Hejaz in 1925 and by 1926 most of Asir. In 1932 he combined Nejd and Hejaz into the single kingdom of Saudi Arabia. Asir was incorporated into the kingdom a year later.

One of the principal cities, Mecca, is the Holy center of Islam and is the scene of an annual Pilgrimage from the entire Moslem world.

RULERS:
Sa'ud Ibn Abdul Aziz, AH1373-1383/1953-1964AD
Faisal, AH1383-1395/1964-1975AD
Khaled, AH1395-1402/1975-1982AD
Fahd, AH1402-/1982AD-

MONETARY SYSTEM:
1 Riyal = 20 Ghirsh

KINGDOM

SAUDI ARABIAN MONETARY AGENCY

SIGNATURE VARIETIES			
1		3	
2		4	

1961 ND ISSUE
Law of 1.7.AH1379 (1961)
#6-10 Saudi arms (palm tree and crossed swords) on back.

6	1 RIYAL	VG	VF	UNC
	L. AH1379 (1961). Brown on lt. blue and green unpt. Hill of Light at ctr. Back violet-brown and green. Sign. #1.	2.00	10.00	35.00

7	5 RIYALS	VG	VF	UNC
	L. AH1379 (1961). Blue and green on m/c unpt. City wall at ctr.			
	a. Sign. #1.	15.00	60.00	225.00
	b. Sign. #2.	20.00	75.00	275.00

8	10 RIYALS	VG	VF	UNC
	L. AH1379 (1961). Green on pink and m/c unpt. Dhows in harbor of Jedda.			
	a. Sign. #1.	15.00	65.00	250.00
	b. Sign. #2.	20.00	100.00	350.00
9	50 RIYALS			
	L. AH1379 (1961). Violet and olive on m/c unpt. Derrick.			
	a. Sign. #1.	60.00	200.00	750.00
	b. Sign. #2.	60.00	200.00	750.00

10	100 RIYALS	VG	VF	UNC
	L. AH1379 (1961). Red on m/c unpt. Bldg. at l., archway on background at ctr., bldg. at r.			
	a. Sign. #1.	200.00	650.00	1750.
	b. Sign. #2.	175.00	550.00	1500.

1966 ND ISSUE
Law of 1.7.AH1379

11	1 RIYAL	VG	VF	UNC
	L. AH1379 (1966). Purple on m/c unpt. Gov't. bldg. at r. Saudi arms on back.			
	a. Sign. #2.	.50	2.50	10.00
	b. Sign. #3.	.50	2.50	10.00

12	5 RIYALS	VG	VF	UNC
	L. AH1379 (1966). Green on m/c unpt. Airport. Oil loading on ships at dockside on back.			
	a. Sign. #2.	2.00	7.50	35.00
	b. Sign. #3.	5.00	25.00	65.00

13   10 RIYALS
L. AH1379 (1966). Gray-blue on m/c unpt. Mosque. Al-Masa Wall w/arches on back. Sign. #2.

	VG	VF	UNC
	2.50	9.00	35.00

14   50 RIYALS
L. AH1379 (1966). Brown on m/c unpt. Courtyard of mosque at r. Saudi arms at l., row of palms at ctr. on back.

	VG	VF	UNC
a. Sign. #2.	20.00	60.00	250.00
b. Sign. #3.	18.00	55.00	225.00

15   100 RIYALS
L. AH1379 (1966). Red on m/c unpt. Gov't. bldg. at r. Derricks on back.

	VG	VF	UNC
a. Sign. #2.	30.00	100.00	350.00
b. Sign. #3.	25.00	90.00	300.00

1976; 1977 ND ISSUE
Law of 1.7.AH1379
#16-19 portr. Kg. Faisal at r. Sign. 4.

16   1 RIYAL
L. AH1379 (1977). Red-brown on m/c unpt. Mountain at ctr. Airport on back.

	VG	VF	UNC
	.25	.50	2.00

INCORRECT   CORRECTED

17   5 RIYALS
L. AH1379 (1977). Green and brown on m/c unpt. Irrigation canal at ctr. Dam on back.

	VG	VF	UNC
a. Incorrect Khamsa (five) in lower ctr. panel of text.	1.50	5.00	15.00
b. Corrected Khamsa (five) in lower ctr. panel of text.	1.00	2.00	6.50

18   10 RIYALS
L. AH1379 (1977). Magenta and brown on m/c unpt. Oil drilling platform at ctr. Oil refinery on back.

	VG	VF	UNC
	FV	4.00	15.00

19   50 RIYALS
L. AH1379 (1976). Green, purple and brown on m/c unpt. Arches of mosque at ctr. Courtyard of mosque on back.

	VG	VF	UNC
	FV	16.00	40.00

20   100 RIYALS
L. AH1379 (1976). Blue and turquoise on m/c unpt. Mosque at ctr.,
Kg. 'Abd al-'Aziz Ibn Saud at r. Long bldg. w/arches on back.

	VG	VF	UNC
	FV	30.00	70.00

1983; 1984 ND ISSUE
Law of 1.7.AH1379
#25-26 Saudi arms in latent image area at l. ctr.
#21-24 upper l. panel also exists w/unnecessary upper accent mark in "Monetary."

INCORRECT   CORRECTED

21   1 RIYAL
L. AH1379 (1984). Dk. brown on m/c unpt. 7th century gold dinar at l.,
Portr. Kg. Fahd at ctr. r. Flowers and landscape on back. 2 sign.
varieties.

	VG	VF	UNC
a. Incorrect text. Sign. 5.	FV	1.00	2.00
b. Corrected "Monetary." Sign. 5; 6.	FV	FV	1.25

22   5 RIYALS
L. AH1379 (1983). Purple, brown, and blue-green on m/c unpt.
Dhows at l., portr. Kg. Fahd at ctr. r. Oil refinery at ctr. r. on back.

	VG	VF	UNC
a. Incorrect text. Sign. 5.	FV	1.50	4.50
b. Corrected "Monetary." Sign. 5.	FV	FV	3.25

23   10 RIYALS
L. AH1379 (1983). Black, brown and purple on m/c unpt. Fortress at
l., portr. Kg. Jahd at ctr. r. Palm trees at ctr. r. on back.

	VG	VF	UNC
a. Incorrect text. Sign. 5.	FV	4.00	9.00
b. Corrected "Monetary." Sign. 5.	FV	FV	7.00

24   50 RIYALS
L. AH1379 (1983). Dk. green and dk. brown on m/c unpt. Mosque of
Omar (Dome of the Rock) in Jerusalem at l., portr. Kg. Fahd at ctr. r.
Mosque at ctr. on back.

	VG	VF	UNC
a. Incorrect text. Sign. 5.	FV	FV	30.00
b. Corrected "Monetary." Sign. 5.	FV	FV	25.00

25   100 RIYALS
L. AH1379 (1984). Brown-violet and olive-green on m/c unpt. Mosque
at l., portr. Kg. Fahd at ctr. r. Mosque at ctr. on back. Sign. 5.

	VG	VF	UNC
	FV	FV	45.00

INCORRECT   CORRECTED

26   500 RIYALS
L. AH1379 (1983). Purple and green on m/c unpt. Courtyard at l.,
portr. Kg. 'Abd al-'Aziz Ibn Saud at ctr. r. Courtyard of Great Mosque
at ctr. on back.

	VG	VF	UNC
a. Incorrect "Five Hundred Riyals" in lower ctr. panel of text. Sign. 5.	FV	FV	225.00
b. Corrected "Five Hundred Riyals" in lower ctr. panel of text. Sign. 5.	FV	FV	185.00

SCOTLAND

Scotland, a part of the United Kingdom of Great Britain and Northern Scotland, consists of the northern part of the island of Great Britain. It has an area of 30,414 sq. mi. (78,772 sq. km.). Capital: Edinburgh. Principal industries are agriculture, fishing, manufacturing and ship-building.

In the 5th century, Scotland consisted of four kingdoms; that of the Picts, the Scots, Strathclyde, and Northumbria. The Scottish kingdom was united by Malcolm II (1005-34), but its ruler was forced to do homage to the English crown in 1174. Scotland won independence under Robert Bruce at Bannockburn in 1314 and was ruled by the house of Stuart from 1371 to 1688. The personal union of the kingdoms of England and Scotland was achieved in 1603 by the accession of King James VI of Scotland as James I of England. Scotland was united with England by Parliamentary act in 1707.

RULERS:
British

MONETARY SYSTEM:
1 Shilling = 12 Pence
1 Pound = 20 Shillings to 1971
1 Pound = 100 New Pence, 1971-1981
1 Pound = 100 Pence, 1982-

BRITISH INFLUENCE

BANK OF SCOTLAND

1961 ISSUE

102	**1 POUND**	VG	VF	UNC
	10.5.1961-11.5.1965. Lt. brown and lt. blue. Medallion at ctr. Date below.			
	a. Imprint end: *LD*. Sign. Lord Bilsland and Sir Wm. Watson. 10.5.1961-13.2.1964.	3.00	9.00	22.50
	b. Imprint ends: *LTD*. Sign. Lord Bilsland and Sir Wm. Watson. 7.2.1964-11.5.1965.	2.50	8.00	20.00

103	**5 POUNDS**	VG	VF	UNC
	14.9.1961-22.9.1961. Like #99 but reduced size. Sign. Lord Bilsland and Sir Wm. Watson.	10.00	20.00	37.50

1962; 1965 ISSUE

105	**1 POUND**	VG	VF	UNC
	1.6.1966; 3.3.1967. Lt. brown and lt. blue. Similar to #102 but *EDINBURGH* and date at r. Sign. Lord Polwarth and J. Letham w/titles: *GOVERNOR* and *TREASURER & GENERAL MANAGER* 2 wmk. varieties.			
	a. W/o electronic sorting marks on back. 1.6.1966.	2.50	8.00	22.50
	b. W/electronic sorting marks on back. 3.3.1967.	2.50	7.50	20.00

106	**5 POUNDS**	VG	VF	UNC
	1962-67. Blue and lt. brown. Medallion of fortune at ctr. Arms and ship on back, numeral of value filled in at base.			
	a. Sign. Lord Bilsland and Sir Wm. Watson w/titles: *GOVERNOR* and *TREASURER*. 25.9.1961-12.1.1965.	11.00	22.50	50.00
	b. Sign. Lord Polwarth and Sir Wm. Watson. 7.3.1966-8.3.1966.	10.00	20.00	45.00
	c. Lighter shades of printing. Sign. Lord Polwarth and J. Letham w/titles: *GOVERNOR* and *TREASURER & GENERAL MANAGER*. 2.1.1967; 2.21967.	10.00	20.00	45.00
	d. Sign. titles as b. W/electronic sorting marks on back. 1.11.1967.	9.00	18.50	42.50

1968; 1969 ISSUE

109	**1 POUND**	VG	VF	UNC
	17.7.1968; 18.8.1969. Ochre and m/c. Arms at ctr. (2 women).			
	a. *EDINBURGH* 19mm in length. 17.7.1968.	2.50	10.00	25.00
	b. *EDINBURGH* 24mm in length. 18.8.1969.	2.50	10.00	25.00

112	**5 POUNDS**	**VG**	**VF**	**UNC**
	1970-88. Blue and m/c. Back similar to #111.			
	a. Sign. Lord Polwarth and T. W. Walker. 10.8.197; 2.9.1971.	10.00	30.00	50.00
	b. Sign. Lord Clydesmuir and T. W. Walker. 4.12.1972; 5.9.1973.	10.00	30.00	50.00
	c. Sign. Lord Clydesmuir and A. M. Russell. 4.11.1974; 1.12.1975; 21.11.1977; 19.10.1978.	8.00	10.00	40.00
	d. Sign. Lord Clydesmuir and D. B. Pattullo. 28.9.1979; 28.11.1980.	FV	10.00	30.00
	e. Sign. T. N. Risk and D. B. Pattullo. 27.7.1981; 25.6.1982.	FV	10.00	30.00
	f. W/o encoding marks. 13.10.1983; 29.2.1988.	FV	8.00	20.00

110	**5 POUNDS**	**VG**	**VF**	**UNC**
	1968-69. Green and m/c. Arms at ctr. (2 women).			
	a. *EDINBURGH* 19mm in length. 1.11.1968.	10.00	30.00	75.00
	b. *EDINBURGH* 24mm in length. 8.12.1969.	10.00	30.00	75.00

110A	**20 POUNDS**	**VG**	**VF**	**UNC**
	5.5.1969. Scottish arms in panel at l., medallion of Goddess of Fortune below arms at ctr. r. Bank bldg. on back. Lord Polwarth and J. Letham. W/security thread. Wmk: Thistle.	40.00	80.00	—

1970; 1974 ISSUE
#111-115 Sir W. Scott at r.

Replacement notes: #111 - Serial # prefix *Z/1, Z/2* or *Z/3;* #112 - Serial # prefix *ZA* or *ZB;* #113 - Serial # prefix *ZB.*

113	**10 POUNDS**	**VG**	**VF**	**UNC**
	1974-90. Brown. Medallions of sailing ship at lower l., Pallas seated at upper l. ctr., arms at r. on back.			
	a. Sign. Lord Clydesmuir and A. M. Russell. 1.5.1974-10.10.1979.	16.00	22.50	60.00
	b. Sign. Lord Clydesmuir and D. B. Pattullo. 5.2.1981.	16.00	20.00	50.00
	c. Sign. T. N. Risk and D. B. Pattullo. 22.7.1981; 16.6.1982; 14.10.1983; 17.9.1984; 20.10.1986; 6.8.1987.	FV	FV	40.00
	d. Sign. T.N. Risk and P. Burt. 1.9.1989; 31.10.1990.	FV	FV	27.50

111	**1 POUND**	**VG**	**VF**	**UNC**
	1970-88. Green and m/c. Sailing ship at l., arms at upper ctr., medallion of Pallas seated at r. on back.			
	a. Sign. Lord Polwarth and T. W. Walker. 10.8.1970; 31.8.1971.	4.00	8.00	30.00
	b. Sign. Lord Clydesmuir and T. W. Walker. 1.11.1972; 30.8.1973.	5.00	10.00	40.00
	c. Sign. Lord Clydesmuir and A. M. Russell. 28.10.1974-3.10.1978.	3.00	5.00	15.00
	d. Sign. Lord Clydesmuir and D. B. Pattullo. 15.10.1979; 4.11.1980.	FV	4.00	10.00
	e. Sign. T. N. Risk and D. B. Pattullo. 30.7.1981.	FV	5.00	12.00
	f. W/o sorting marks on back. Sign. like e. 7.10.1983; 9.11.1984; 12.12.1985; 18.11.1986.	FV	2.25	7.50
	g. Sign. T. N. Risk and L. P. Burt. 19.8.1988.	FV	2.00	6.50

114	**20 POUNDS**	**VG**	**VF**	**UNC**
	1970-87. Purple. Arms at upper l. above sailing ship w/medallion of Pallas seated below, head office bldg. at ctr. on back.			
	a. Sign. Lord Polwarth and T. W. Walker. 1.10.1970.	40.00	90.00	140.00
	b. Sign. Lord Clydesmuir and T. W. Walker. 3.1.1973.	37.50	45.00	95.00
	c. Sign. Lord Clydesmuir and A. M. Russell. 8.11.1974; 14.1.1977.	35.00	45.00	90.00
	d. Sign. Lord Clydesmuir and D. B. Pattullo. 16.7.1979; 2.2.1981.	FV	42.50	85.00
	e. Sign. T. N. Risk and D. B. Pattullo. 4.8.1981-5.12.1987.	FV	35.00	75.00

115	**100 POUNDS**	**VG**	**VF**	**UNC**
	1971-92. Red. Arms at upper l., medallions of sailing ship at lower l., Pallas seated at lower r., head office bldg. at ctr. on back.			
	a. Sign. Lord Clydesmuir and T. W. Walker. 6.12.1971; 6.9.1973.	FV	175.00	300.00
	b. Sign. D. B. Pattullo and P. Burt. 22.1.1992.	FV	FV	225.00

1990-92 ISSUE
#116-118 similar to previous issue. Smaller size notes.

116 5 POUNDS
1990-. Similar to #112, but 135 x 70mm.

	VG	VF	UNC
a. Sign. T. N. Risk and P. Burt. 20.6.1990.	FV	FV	16.50
b. Sign. D. B. Pattullo and P. Burt. 6.11.1981; 18.1.1993; 7.1.1994.	FV	FV	14.00

117 10 POUNDS
7.5.1992; 9.3.1993; 13.4.1994. Deep brown on m/c unpt. Similar to #113, but 142 x 75mm. Sign. of D. B. Pattullo and P. Burt.

VG	VF	UNC
FV	FV	27.00

118 20 POUNDS
1.7.1991; 3.2.1992; 12.1.1993. Similar to #114 but 148 x 81mm, and *STERLING* added above sign. of D. B. Pattullo and P. Burt.

VG	VF	UNC
FV	FV	50.00

1995 COMMEMORATIVE ISSUE
#119-122, Bank of Scotland's Tercentenary

#119-123 Sir W. Scott at l. and as wmk., bank arms at ctr. Bank head office bldg. at lower l., medallion of Pallas seated, arms and medallion of sailing ships at r. on back. Sign. D. B. Pattullo and P. Burt. Printer: TDLR. (W/o imprint).

119 5 POUNDS
4.1.1995. Dk. blue and purple on m/c unpt. Oil well riggers working w/drill at ctr. on back.

VG	VF	UNC
FV	FV	12.50

120 10 POUNDS
1.2.1995. Dk. brown and deep olive-green on m/c unpt. Workers by distilling equipment at ctr. on back.

VG	VF	UNC
FV	FV	22.50

121 20 POUNDS
1.5.1995. Violet and brown on m/c unpt. Woman researcher at laboratory station at ctr. on back.

VG	VF	UNC
FV	FV	45.00

122 50 POUNDS
1.5.1995. Dk. green and olive-brown on m/c unpt. Music director and violinists at ctr. on back.

VG	VF	UNC
FV	FV	110.00

123 100 POUNDS
17.7.1995. Red-violet and red-orange on m/c unpt. Golf outing at ctr. on back.

VG	VF	UNC
FV	FV	200.00

BRITISH LINEN BANK
NOTE: Formerly the British Linen Company. See Vol. 1.

1961; 1962 ISSUE
#162-170 printer: TDLR.

				VG	VF	UNC
162 (S197)	**1 POUND** 30.9.1961. Similar to #157.			6.00	12.00	25.00
163 (S198)	**5 POUNDS** 2.1.1961; 3.2.1961. Blue and red. Similar to #158.			45.00	100.00	150.00
164 (S199)	**20 POUNDS** 4.4.1962. Blue and red. Similar to #159.			40.00	75.00	120.00

				VG	VF	UNC
165 (S200)	**100 POUNDS** 1961-62 (3.5.1962 confirmed). Blue and red. Similar to #160.			200.00	275.00	375.00

1962 ISSUE

				VG	VF	UNC
166 (S201)	**1 POUND** 31.3.1962-13.6.1967. Similar to #162 but 150 x 72mm.					
		a.	Sign. A. P. Anderson. 31.3.1962.	5.00	10.00	25.00
		b.	Test note w/lines for electronic sorting on back. 31.3.1962.	16.00	32.00	80.00
		c.	Sign. T. W. Walker. 1.7.1963-13.6.1967.	4.00	8.00	20.00
167 (S202)	**5 POUNDS** 21.9.1962-18.8.1964. Blue and red. Sir Walter Scott at r. 140 x 85mm.			10.00	22.50	35.00

1967 ISSUE

				VG	VF	UNC
168 (S203)	**1 POUND** 13.6.1967. Blue and red. Like #166 but modified design and w/lines for electronic sorting on back.			2.50	5.00	15.00

1968 ISSUE

				VG	VF	UNC
169 (S204)	**1 POUND** 1968. Blue and red. Sir Walter Scott at r., supported arms at top ctr.					
		a.	29.2.1968; 5.11.1969.	2.50	5.00	10.00
		b.	20.7.1970.	—	—	—

				VG	VF	UNC
170 (S205)	**5 POUNDS** 3.2.1968-20.7.1970. Blue and red. Similar to #167, but different size, and many plate changes. 146 x 78 mm.			10.00	20.00	30.00

CLYDESDALE AND NORTH OF SCOTLAND BANK LTD.
Formerly, and later to become the Clydesdale Bank Ltd. again.

1961 ISSUE

				VG	VF	UNC
195	**1 POUND** 1.3.1961; 2.5.1962; 1.2.1963. Green. Arms at r. Ship and tug on back.			5.00	10.00	40.00

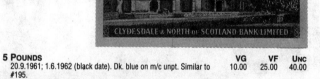

				VG	VF	UNC
196	**5 POUNDS** 20.9.1961; 1.6.1962 (black date). Dk. blue on m/c unpt. Similar to #195.			10.00	25.00	40.00

CLYDESDALE BANK LIMITED
Formerly the Clydesdale and North of Scotland Bank Ltd. Later became Clydesdale Bank PLC.

1963-64 ISSUE

				VG	VF	UNC
197	**1 POUND** 2.9.1963-3.4.1967. Green. Like #195.			5.00	12.00	45.00
198	**5 POUNDS** 1963-66. Blue and violet. Like #196.			10.00	22.50	50.00
199	**10 POUNDS** 1964-70. Brown. Arms at r.			20.00	45.00	90.00
200	**20 POUNDS** 1964-70. Carmine. Arms at r.			37.50	65.00	120.00
201	**100 POUNDS** 1964-70. Violet.			175.00	250.00	425.00

1967 ISSUE

				VG	VF	UNC
202	**1 POUND** 3.4.1967; 1.10.1968; 1.9.1969. Green. Like #197 but lines for electronic sorting on back.			5.00	12.00	45.00

			VG	**VF**	**UNC**
203	**5 POUNDS**				
	1967-69. Blue and violet. Like #198 but lines for eletronic sorting on back.		10.00	20.00	50.00

1971-81 ISSUES
#206 *Deleted.* See #205.

			VG	**VF**	**UNC**
204	**1 POUND**				
	1971-81. Greenish black on m/c unpt. Robert the Bruce at l. Scene of Battle of Bannockburn, 1314 on back.				
	a.	Sign. R. D. Fairbairn, w/title: *GENERAL MANAGER.* 1.3.1971.	5.00	12.00	30.00
	b.	Sign. A. R. Macmillan, w/title: *GENERAL MANAGER.* 1.5.1972; 1.8.1973.	8.00	15.00	40.00
	c.	Sign. A. R. Macmillan, w/title: *CHIEF GENERAL MANAGER.* 1.3.1974-27.2.1981.	FV	5.00	12.00

			VG	**VF**	**UNC**
205	**5 POUNDS**				
	1.3.1971; 1.5.1972; 1.2.1980. Blue on m/c unpt. R. Burns at l. Mouse and rose from Burn's poems on back.		9.00	20.00	45.00

			VG	**VF**	**UNC**
207	**10 POUNDS**				
	1.3.1972; 1.3.1977; 31.1.1979. Brown and pale purple. D. Livingstone at l.		FV	25.00	80.00
208	**20 POUNDS**				
	1.3.1972; 1.2.1978. Lilac. Lord Kelvin at l.		FV	50.00	120.00

			VG	**VF**	**UNC**
209	**50 POUNDS**				
	1.9.1981. Olive and m/c. A. Smith at l. Sailing ships, blacksmith implements and farm on back.		FV	90.00	200.00
210	**100 POUNDS**				
	1.3.1972. Red and m/c. Lord Kelvin at l. Lecture Hall at Glasgow University on back.		FV	175.00	300.00

CLYDESDALE BANK PLC
Formerly the Clydesdale Bank Limited.

1982-89 "STERLING" ISSUES
#211-220 wmk: Old sailing ships.
#216 *Deleted.* See #221.

			VG	**VF**	**UNC**
211	**1 POUND**				
	1982-88. Greenish black on m/c unpt. Like #204.				
	a.	W/sorting marks. Sign. A. R. M. Macmillan. 29.3.1982.	FV	5.00	15.00
	b.	Like a. Sign. Cole-Hamilton. 5.1.1983.	FV	5.00	15.00
	c.	W/o sorting marks. Sign. Cole-Hamilton. 8.4.1985; 25.11.1985.	FV	2.50	8.00
	d.	Sign. title: *CHIEF EXECUTIV TIVE.* 18.9.1987; 9.11.1988 .	FV	3.00	9.00

			VG	**VF**	**UNC**
212	**5 POUNDS**				
	1982-89. Blue on m/c unpt. Like #205.				
	a.	Sign. A. R. Macmillan. 29.3.1982.	FV	14.00	35.00
	b.	Sign. Cole-Hamilton. 5.1.1983.	FV	12.00	30.00
	c.	W/o sorting marks. Sign. Cole-Hamilton. 8.4.1958-25.11.1986.	FV	15.00	30.00
	d.	Sign. title: *CHIEF EXECUTIVE.* 18.9.1987; 2.8.1988; 28.6.1989.	FV	12.00	20.00

213	10 POUNDS		VG	VF	UNC
	1982-87. Brown and pale purple. Like #207.				
	a.	Sign. A. R. Macmillan. 29.3.1982.	FV	30.00	60.00
	b.	Sign. Cole-Hamilton. 5.1.1983; 8.4.1985; 18.9.1986.	FV	25.00	50.00
	c.	Sign. title: *CHIEF EXECUTIVE*. 18.9.1987.	FV	20.00	40.00

214	10 POUNDS	VG	VF	UNC
	7.5.1988; 3.9.1989. Dk. brown on m/c unpt. D. Livingstone in front of map at I. Blantyre (Livingstone's birthplace) on back. Wmk: Sailing ships.	FV	FV	40.00

215	20 POUNDS		VG	VF	UNC
	1982-87. Lilac. Like #208.				
	a.	Sign. A. R. Macmillan. 29.3.1982.	FV	45.00	100.00
	b.	Sign. Cole-Hamilton. 5.1.1983; 8.4.1985.	FV	40.00	75.00
	c.	Sign. title: *CHIEF EXECUTIVE*. 18.9.1987.	FV	37.50	65.00

217	100 POUNDS	VG	VF	UNC
	8.4.1985. Red on m/c unpt. Similar to #210.	FV	FV	250.00

1990-92 "STERLING" ISSUE
#218-221 smaller size notes.

218	5 POUNDS		VG	VF	UNC
	1990-. Blue on m/c unpt. Similar to #205, but 135 x 70mm.				
	a.	Sign. Cole-Hamilton. 2.4.1990.	FV	FV	15.00
	b.	Sign. Goodwin. 1.1.1994.	FV	FV	13.50

219	10 POUNDS		VG	VF	UNC
	1992-. Deep brown and green on m/c unpt. Similar to #215 with modified sailing ship outlines at r. 142 x 75mm.				
	a.	Sign. Cole-Hamilton. 3.9.1992.	FV	FV	32.50
	b.	Sign. Charles-Love. 5.1.1993.	FV	FV	22.50
220	20 POUNDS				
	1990-. Violet, purple, brown and brown-orange on m/c unpt. Robert the Bruce at l. His equestrian statue, Monymusk reliquary, Stirling castle and Wallace Monument on back. 148 x 80mm.				
	a.	Sign. Cole-Hamilton. 30.11.1990; 2.8.1991; 3.9.1992.	FV	FV	55.00
	b.	Sign. Charles Love. 5.1.1993.	FV	FV	70.00
	c.	Sign. Goodwin. 22.3.1996.	FV	FV	50.00
221 (216)	50 POUNDS				
	3.9.1989. Olive-green on m/c unpt. Similar to #209.		FV	FV	120.00
222	100 POUNDS				
	9.11.1991. Red on m/c unpt. Similar to #217, but reduced size.		FV	FV	175.00

1994 "STERLING" ISSUE

223	20 POUNDS	VG	VF	UNC
	1.9.1994. Like #220. Purple, dk. brown and deep orange on m/c unpt. Sign. F. Cicutto.	FV	FV	45.00

1996 COMMEMORATIVE ISSUE
#224, Robert Burns

224	50 POUNDS	VG	VF	UNC
	21.7.1996. Ovpt. on #218.			
	a. "A man's a man for a'that - Then let us..."	FV	FV	13.00
	b. "Tam O'Shanter - Now, wha this..."	FV	FV	13.00
	c. "Ae Fond Kiss - But to see..."	FV	FV	13.00
	d. "Scots wha hae - By oppressions woes..."	FV	FV	13.00

NATIONAL COMMERCIAL BANK OF SCOTLAND LIMITED
Formed by an amalgamation of The Commercial Bank of Scotland Ltd. and The National Bank of Scotland Ltd. in 1959. In 1969 it amalgamated with The Royal Bank of Scotland.

1961 ISSUE

269 (S595)	1 POUND	VG	VF	UNC
	1.11.1961-4.1.1966. Green on m/c unpt. Forth Railway bridge. Reduced size. 151 x 72mm.	2.50	6.00	15.00

270 (S596)	5 POUNDS	VG	VF	UNC
	3.1.1961. Green and m/c. Arms at bottom ctr. r. Forth Railway bridge on back. Reduced size: 159 x 90 mm.	10.00	20.00	45.00

1963-67 ISSUE

271 (S600)	1 POUND	VG	VF	UNC
	4.1.1967; 4.6.1967. Green. Like #269, but lines for electronic sorting on back. 150 x 72mm.	2.50	6.00	12.00
272 (S597)	5 POUNDS			
	2.1.1963; 1.8.1963; 1.10.1964; 4.1.1966; 1.8.1966. Blue, red and green. Arms at lower ctr. Landscape w/bldgs. on back. 180 x 97mm.	9.00	15.00	35.00
273 (S599)	10 POUNDS			
	18.8.1966. Brown. Arms at lower ctr. Forth Railway bridge on back. 151 x 94mm.	20.00	30.00	60.00

1968 ISSUE

274 (S601)	1 POUND	VG	VF	UNC
	4.1.1968. Green. Similar to #271, but some minor plate changes and reduced size. 136 x 67mm.	2.50	6.00	12.00
275 (S598)	5 POUNDS			
	4.1.1968. Like #272 but electronic sorting marks on back.	9.00	15.00	35.00

ROYAL BANK OF SCOTLAND
Later became the Royal Bank of Scotland Limited.

1964 ISSUE

325	1 POUND	VG	VF	UNC
	1.8.1964-1.11.1967. Black and brown on yellow unpt. Like #322, but 150 x 71mm.			
	a. Sign. W. R. Ballantyne. 1.8.1964-1.6.1965.	3.00	8.00	20.00
	b. Sign. G. P. Robertson. 2.8.1965-1.11.1967.	3.00	8.00	20.00

326	5 POUNDS			
	2.11.1964; 2.8.1965. Dk. blue, orange-brown and yellow. Uniface. Like #323, but 140 x 85mm.	12.00	25.00	50.00

1966; 1967 ISSUE

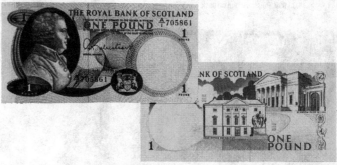

327	1 POUND	VG	VF	UNC
	1.9.1967. Green and m/c. D. Dale at l.	2.50	8.00	20.00

328	5 POUNDS	VG	VF	UNC
	1.1.1966; 1.3.1967. Blue and m/c. D. Dale at l.	15.00	25.00	50.00

ROYAL BANK OF SCOTLAND LIMITED
Formerly the Royal Bank of Scotland. Later became the Royal Bank of Scotland plc.

1969 ISSUE

329	1 POUND	VG	VF	UNC
	19.3.1969. Green. Bridge.	3.00	5.00	18.50

		VG	VF	UNC
330	**5 POUNDS** 19.3.1969. Blue. Arms at l.	9.00	13.50	40.00
331	**10 POUNDS** 19.3.1969. Brown. Arms at ctr. Bridge on back.	20.00	37.50	85.00
332	**20 POUNDS** 19.3.1969. Purple. Bridge on back.	40.00	65.00	200.00

		VG	VF	UNC
333	**100 POUNDS** 19.3.1969. Red. Bridge on back.	180.00	250.00	400.00

1970 ISSUE

		VG	VF	UNC
334	**1 POUND** 15.7.1970. Like #329 but only 1 sign.	3.00	10.00	25.00
335	**5 POUNDS** 15.7.1970. Like #330 but only 1 sign.	8.50	20.00	40.00

1972 ISSUE
#336-340 arms at r. Printer: BWC.

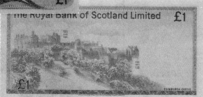

		VG	VF	UNC
336	**1 POUND** 5.1.1972-1.5.1981. Dk. green on m/c unpt. Edinburgh Castle on back. Wmk: A. Smith.	FV	4.00	10.00

		VG	VF	UNC
337	**5 POUNDS** 5.1.1972-2.4.1973; 1.5.1975; 1.5.1979; 1.5.1981. Blue and m/c. Culzean Castle on back.	FV	20.00	45.00

		VG	VF	UNC
338	**10 POUNDS** 5.1.1972; 2.5.1978; 10.1.981. Brown and m/c. Glamis Castle on back.	FV	35.00	75.00
339	**20 POUNDS** 5.1.1972; 1.5.1981. Purple and m/c. Brodick Castle on back.	FV	60.00	140.00

		VG	VF	UNC
340	**100 POUNDS** 5.1.1972; 1.5.1981. Red and m/c. Balmoral Castle on back.	FV	225.00	375.00

ROYAL BANK OF SCOTLAND PLC
Formerly the Royal Bank of Scotland Limited.

1982-86 ISSUES
REPLACEMENT NOTE #341-345 arms at r. Sign. title varieties.
Replacement note: #341-356 Z/1 prefix.

		VG	VF	UNC
341	**1 POUND** 1982-85. Like #336. Sign. C. Winter. Printer: BWC.			
	a. W/sorting marks. 3.5.1982.	2.50	5.00	25.00
	b. W/o sorting marks. 1.10.1983; 4.1.1984; 3.1.1985.	FV	4.00	8.00

341A 1 POUND
1986. Like #341. Printer: TDLR.

	VG	VF	UNC
a. Sign. C. Winters. 1.5.1986.	FV	5.00	10.00
b. Sign. R. M. Maiden. 17.12.1986.	FV	5.00	12.00

342 5 POUNDS
1982-85. Like #337. Printer: BWC.

	VG	VF	UNC
a. W/sorting marks. 3.5.1982; 5.1.1983.	FV	15.00	45.00
b. W/o sorting marks. 4.1.1984.	FV	13.50	40.00
c. Sign. title larger size. 3.1.1985.	FV	12.50	45.00

342A 5 POUNDS
17.12.1986. Like #342. Printer: BWC.

	VG	VF	UNC
	FV	15.00	30.00

343 10 POUNDS
3.5.1982; 4.1.1984; 17.12.1986. Like #338. Printer: BWC.

	VG	VF	UNC
	FV	25.00	40.00

343A 10 POUNDS
17.12.1986. Like #343. Printer: TDLR.

	VG	VF	UNC
	FV	22.50	35.00

344 20 POUNDS
3.5.1982; 3.1.1985. Like #339. Printer: BWC.

	VG	VF	UNC
	FV	37.50	85.00

345 100 POUNDS
3.5.1982. Like #340. Printer: BWC.

	VG	VF	UNC
	FV	175.00	250.00

1987 ISSUE
#346-350 Lord Ilay at r. and as wmk. Printer: TDLR.

346 1 POUND
25.3.1987. Dk. green on m/c unpt. Edinburgh castle on back.

	VG	VF	UNC
	FV	FV	6.50

347 5 POUNDS
25.3.1987; 22.6.1988. Black and blue-black on m/c unpt. Culzean castle on back.

	VG	VF	UNC
	FV	10.00	20.00

348 10 POUNDS
25.3.1987; 24.2.1988; 22.2.1989; 24.1.1990. Deep brown and brown on m/c unpt. Glamis castle on back.

	VG	VF	UNC
	FV	20.00	40.00

		VG	VF	UNC
349	**20 POUNDS**	FV	35.00	75.00
	25.3.1987; 24.1.1990. Black and purple on m/c unpt. Brodick castle on back.			
350	**100 POUNDS**	FV	FV	235.00
	25.3.1987; 24.1.1990. Red on m/c unpt. Balmoral castle on back.			

1988-92 ISSUE
#351-356 designs similar to #346-350, but reduced size notes.

		VG	VF	UNC
351	**1 POUND**			
	1988-. Similar to #346, but 127 x 65mm. Printer: TDLR.			
	a. Sign.A. Maiden w/title: *MANAGING DIRECTOR.* 13.12.1988; 26.7.1989; 19.12.1990.	FV	FV	5.00
	b. Sign. C. Winter w/title: *CHIEF EXECUTIVE.* 24.7.1991.	FV	FV	4.50
	c. Sign. G. R. Mathewson w/title: *CHIEF EXECUTIVE.* 24.3.1992; 24.2.1993; 24.1.1996.	FV	FV	4.00
	d. W/o wmk. Printer: BABN. 23.3.1994.	FV	6.50	32.50

1992 COMMEMORATIVE ISSUE
#352, European summit at Edinburgh, Dec. 1992.

		VG	VF	UNC
352	**1 POUND**	FV	FV	5.00
	8.12.1992. Like #351c. Additional blue-violet ovpt. containing commemorative inscription at l.			

1988-92 REGULAR ISSUE

		VG	VF	UNC
353	**5 POUNDS**			
	1988-. Similar to #347, but 135 x 70mm. Sign. title: *MANAGING DIRECTOR.*			
	a. Sign. R. M. Maiden. 13.12.1988; 24.1.1990.	FV	FV	15.00
	b. Sign. G. R. Mathewson.	FV	FV	13.50
354	**10 POUNDS**	FV	FV	22.50
	28.1.1992; 7.5.1992; 24.2.1993. Similar to #348, but 142 x 75mm. Sign. G. R. Mathewson, w/title: *CHIEF EXECUTIVE.*			
355	**20 POUNDS**			
	27.3.1991. Similiar to #349 but 150 x 81mm.			
	a. Sign. C. Winter w/title: *CHIEF EXECUTIVE.* 27.3.1991.	FV	FV	50.00
	b. Sign. G. R. Mathewson. 28.1.1992.	FV	FV	42.50
356	**100 POUNDS**	FV	FV	225.00
	23.3.1994. Red on m/c unpt. Similar to #350. Sign. G. R. Mathewson.			

1994 COMMEMORATIVE
#357, Robert Louis Stevenson Death Centennial

		VG	VF	UNC
357	**1 POUND**	FV	FV	4.00
	3.12.1994. Like 351c. Commemorative ovpt. in wmk area. Back portr. R. L. Stevenson and images of his life and works.			

COLLECTOR SERIES

CLYDESDALE BANK PLC

1996 ISSUE

		ISSUE PRICE	MKT. VALUE
CS1	**1996 5 POUNDS**	60.00	60.00
	Matched serial # (prefix R/B 0 - R/B 3) set #224a-d. (4000 sealed sets, also unsealed sets).		

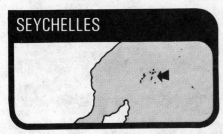

SEYCHELLES

The Republic of Seychelles, an archipelago of 85 granite and coral islands situated in the Indian Ocean 600 miles (965 km.) northeast of Madagascar, has an area of 156 sq. mi. (455 sq. km.) and a population of 70,400. Among these islands are the Aldabra Islands, the Farquhar Group, and Ile Desroches, which the United Kingdom ceded to the Seychelles upon its independence. Capital: Victoria, on Mahe. The economy is based on fishing, a plantation system of agriculture and tourism. Copra, cinnamon and vanilla are exported.

Although the Seychelles are marked on Portuguese charts of the early 16th century, the first recorded visit to the islands, by an English ship, occurred in 1609. The Seychelles were annexed to France by Captain Lazare Picault in 1743 and permanently settled in 1768, with the intention of establishing spice plantations to compete with the Dutch monopoly of the spice trade. British troops seized the islands in 1810, during the Napoleonic Wars; they were formally ceded to Britain by the Treaty of Paris, 1814. The Seychelles were a dependency of Mauritius until Aug. 31, 1903, when they became a separate British Crown Colony. The colony was granted limited internal self-government in 1970, and attained independence on June 28, 1976, becoming Britain's last African possession to do so. Seychelles is a member of the Commonwealth of Nations. The president is the Head of State and of Government.

RULERS:
   British to 1976

MONETARY SYSTEM:
   1 Rupee = 100 Cents

BRITISH INFLUENCE

GOVERNMENT OF SEYCHELLES

1954 ISSUE
#12 and 13 portr. Qn. Elizabeth II in profile at r. Denominations on back. Various date and sign. varieties. Printer: TDLR.

11	**5 RUPEES**	VG	VF	UNC
	1954; 1960. Lilac and green.			
	a. 1.8.1954.	8.50	35.00	130.00
	b. 1.8.1960.	7.00	20.00	120.00

12	**10 RUPEES**	VG	VF	UNC
	1954-67. Green and red. Like #11.			
	a. 1.8.1954.	12.50	45.00	425.00
	b. 1.8.1960.	10.00	40.00	400.00
	c. 1.5.1963.	10.00	35.00	400.00
	d. 1.1.1967.	10.00	35.00	375.00

13	**50 RUPEES**	VG	VF	UNC
	1954-67. Black. Like #11.			
	a. 1.8.1954.	30.00	100.00	750.00
	b. 1.8.1960.	25.00	90.00	700.00
	c. 1.5.1963.	25.00	85.00	700.00
	d. 1.1.1967.	25.00	85.00	700.00

1968 ISSUE
#14-18 Qn. Elizabeth II at r. Wmk: Black parrot's head. Various date and sign. varieties.

14	**5 RUPEES**	VG	VF	UNC
	1.1.1968. Dk. brown on m/c unpt. Parrot at l.	1.00	4.00	25.00

15	**10 RUPEES**	VG	VF	UNC
	1968; 1974. Lt. blue on m/c unpt. Sea tortoise at l. ctr.			
	a. 1.1.1968.	3.00	12.00	110.00
	b. 1.1.1974.	2.50	10.00	100.00

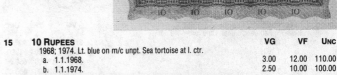

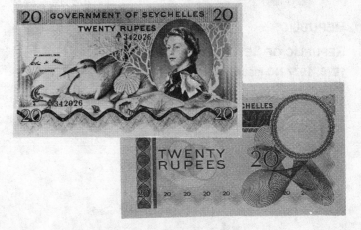

16	**20 RUPEES**	VG	VF	UNC
	1968-74. Purple on m/c unpt. Nesting bird at l.			
	a. 1.1.1968.	6.00	20.00	250.00
	b. 1.1.1971.	5.00	12.50	120.00
	c. 1.1.1974.	4.00	10.00	110.00

17	**50 RUPEES**	VG	VF	UNC
	1968-73. Olive on m/c unpt. Sailing ship at l. Word *SEX* descernible in trees at r.			
	a. 1.1.1968.	12.50	50.00	350.00
	b. 1.1.1969.	15.00	65.00	400.00
	c. 1.10.1970.	12.00	55.00	650.00
	d. 1.1.1972.	7.50	35.00	300.00
	e. 1.8.1973.	7.50	35.00	300.00

18	**100 RUPEES**	VG	VF	UNC
	1968-75. Red on m/c unpt. Land turtles at l. ctr.			
	a. 1.1.1968.	37.50	150.00	900.00
	b. 1.1.1969.	75.00	350.00	1200.
	c. 1.1.1972.	50.00	135.00	650.00
	d. 1.8.1973.	45.00	125.00	650.00
	e. 1.6.1975.	45.00	125.00	650.00

REPUBLIC

REPUBLIC OF SEYCHELLES

1976; 1977 ND ISSUE
#19-22 Pres. J. R. Mancham at r. Wmk: Black parrot's head.

19	**10 RUPEES**	VG	VF	UNC
	ND (1976). Dk. blue and blue on m/c unpt. Seashell at lower l. Hut w/boats and cliffs on back.	1.00	2.25	8.50

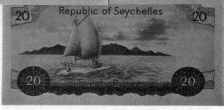

20	**20 RUPEES**	VG	VF	UNC
	ND (1977). Purple on m/c unpt. Sea tortoise at lower l. Sailboat on back.	2.00	4.50	15.00

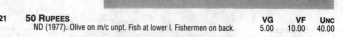

21	**50 RUPEES**	VG	VF	UNC
	ND (1977). Olive on m/c unpt. Fish at lower l. Fishermen on back.	5.00	10.00	40.00

22	**100 RUPEES**	VG	VF	UNC
	ND (1977). Red and m/c. 2 birds at lower l. Dock area and islands on back.	10.00	20.00	70.00

SEYCHELLES MONETARY AUTHORITY

1980s ND ISSUE
#23-27 vertical format on back. Wmk: Black parrot's head.

23   10 RUPEES
ND. Blue, green and pink on m/c unpt. Nesting bird at ctr. Girl picking
flowers on back.

	VG	VF	UNC
	FV	1.75	4.00

26   100 RUPEES
ND. Red and lt. blue on m/c unpt. Tropical fish at ctr. Man w/tools,
swordfish on back.

	VG	VF	UNC
	22.50	55.00	200.00

24   25 RUPEES
ND. Brown, purple and gold on m/c unpt. Coconuts at ctr. green and
brown back; man and basket.

	VG	VF	UNC
	FV	4.00	12.00

27   100 RUPEES
ND. Brown and lt. blue on m/c unpt. Like #26.

	VG	VF	UNC
	FV	22.50	60.00

CENTRAL BANK OF SEYCHELLES

1983 ND ISSUE
#28-31 like previous issue except for new bank name and sign. title. Wmk: Black parrot's head.

25   50 RUPEES
ND. Olive, brown and lilac on m/c unpt. Turtle at ctr. Bldgs. and palm
trees on back.

	VG	VF	UNC
	FV	8.00	30.00

28   10 RUPEES
ND (1983). Like #23.

	VG	VF	UNC
	FV	FV	5.00

29   25 RUPEES
ND (1983). Like #24.

	VG	VF	UNC
	FV	FV	9.00

30   50 RUPEES
ND (1983). Like #25.

	VG	VF	UNC
	FV	FV	23.50

31   100 RUPEES
ND (1983). Like #27.

	VG	VF	UNC
	FV	FV	42.50

LABANK SANTRAL SESEL
CENTRAL BANK OF SEYCHELLES

1989 ND ISSUE

#32-35 bank at ctr., flying fish at l. and ctr. r. Wmk: Black parrot's head.

32	10 RUPEES	VG	VF	UNC
	ND (1989). Blue-black and deep blue-green on m/c unpt. Boy scouts at lower l., image of man w/flags and broken chain at r. Local people dancing to drummer at ctr. on back.	FV	FV	4.00

33	25 RUPEES	VG	VF	UNC
	ND (1989). Purple on m/c unpt. 2 men w/coconuts at lower l., boy near palms at upper r. Primitive ox drawn farm equipment on back.	FV	FV	10.00

34	50 RUPEES	VG	VF	UNC
	ND (1989). Dk. green and brown on m/c unpt. 2 men in boat, Seychelles man at lower l., prow of boat in geometric outline at upper r. Seagulls, fishermen w/nets, modern ships on back.	FV	FV	18.50

35	100 RUPEES	VG	VF	UNC
	ND (1989). Red and brown on m/c unpt. Men in ox-cart at lower l., girl w/shell at upper r. Bldg. at ctr. on back.	FV	FV	35.00

The Republic of Sierra Leone, a British Commonwealth nation located in western Africa between Guinea and Liberia, has an area of 27,699 sq. mi. (71,740 sq. km.) and a population of *4.1 million. Capital: Freetown. The economy is predominantly agricultural but mining contributes significantly to export revenues. Diamonds, iron ore, palm kernels, cocoa, and coffee are exported.

The coast of Sierra Leone was first visited by Portuguese and British slavers in the 15th and 16th centuries. The first settlement, at Freetown, 1787, was established as a refuge for freed slaves within the British Empire, runaway slaves from the United States and blacks discharged from the British armed forces. The first settlers were virtually wiped out by tribal attacks and disease. The colony was reestablished under the auspices of the Sierra Leone Company and transferred to the British Crown in 1907. The interior region was secured and established as a protectorate in 1896. Sierra Leone became independent within the Commonwealth on April 27, 1961, and adopted a republican constitution ten years later. It is a member of the Commonwealth of Nations. The president is Chief of State and Head of Government.

RULERS:
British to 1971

MONETARY SYSTEM:
1 Leone = 100 Cents
1 Pound = 20 Shillings

REPUBLIC

BANK OF SIERRA LEONE

1964 ND ISSUE

#1-3 w/300-year-old cotton tree and court bldg. on face. Sign. varieties. Wmk: Lion's head. Printer: TDLR.

1	1 LEONE	VG	VF	UNC
	ND (1964-70). Green and m/c. Diamond mining on back.			
	a. ND (1964). Prefix A/1-A/6.	4.50	13.50	55.00
	b. ND (1969). Prefix A/7-A/8.	6.00	18.50	75.00
	c. ND (1970). Prefix A/9-A/12.	2.75	8.00	45.00

2	2 LEONES	VG	VF	UNC
	ND (1964-70). Red and m/c. Village scene on back.			
	a. ND (1964). Prefix B/1-B/21.	5.00	15.00	60.00
	b. ND (1967). Prefix B/22-B/25.	12.50	35.00	140.00
	c. ND (1969). Prefix B/26-B/30.	6.00	18.50	75.00
	d. ND (1970). Prefix B/31-B/41.	5.00	16.00	65.00

3   5 LEONES

	VG	VF	UNC
ND (1964). Purple and m/c. Dockside and boats on back. Prefix C/1.	25.00	150.00	575.00

1974-80 ISSUE

#4-8 Pres. S. Stevens at l. Wmk: Lion's head. Printer: TDLR.
Replacement notes: Serial # prefix *Z/1.*

4   50 CENTS

	VG	VF	UNC
ND; 1979-84. Brown and m/c. Bank on back.			
a. ND (1972). Prefix D/1-D/2.	.75	2.00	5.50
b. ND (1974). Prefix D/3-D/5.	.75	2.00	5.50
c. 1.7.1979.	.50	1.00	3.00
d. 1.7.1981.	.15	.50	1.50
e. 4.8.1984.	.10	.25	.75

5   1 LEONE

	VG	VF	UNC
1974-84. Green and m/c. Bank on back.			
a. 19.4.1974.	.75	3.00	7.50
b. 1.1.1978.	1.00	4.00	10.00
c. 1.3.1980.	.25	1.00	4.00
d. 1.7.1981.	.25	.50	2.00
e. 4.8.1984.	.25	.50	1.00

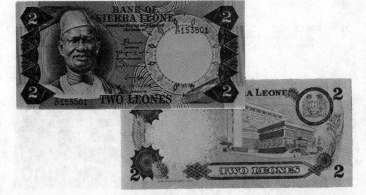

6   2 LEONES

	VG	VF	UNC
1974-85. Red-orange and m/c. Bank on back.			
a. 19.4.1974.	1.25	3.75	11.50
b. 1.1.1978.	6.00	15.00	45.00
c. 1.7.1978.	1.00	4.00	12.50
d. 1.7.1979.	.75	2.00	7.50
e. 1.5.1980.	.75	2.00	7.00
f. 1.7.1983.	.35	.75	3.00
g. 4.8.1984; 4.8.1985.	.20	.45	1.25

7   5 LEONES

	VG	VF	UNC
1975-85. Purple, dk. blue and m/c. Plant leaves at ctr. Parliament bldg. on back.			
a. 4.8.1975. Prefix C/1.	3.00	10.00	32.50
b. 1.7.1978. Prefix C/2.	2.00	7.00	25.00
c. 1.3.1980. Prefix C/3.	1.00	4.00	12.50
d. 1.7.1981.	.75	3.00	7.50
e. 19.4.1984; 4.8.1984; 4.8.1985.	.50	1.00	3.50

8   10 LEONES

	VG	VF	UNC
1980; 1984. Blue-gray and m/c. Dredging operation on back.			
a. 1.7.1980.	1.00	4.00	12.00
b. 19.4.1984; 4.8.1984.	.40	1.00	3.00

1980 COMMEMORATIVE ISSUE

#9-13 red ovpt: *COMMEMORATING THE ORGANISATION OF AFRICAN UNITY CONFERENCE / FREETOWN 1980.*

#10-13 ovpt. in circle around wmk. area at r., date below.

NOTE: #9-13 were prepared in special booklets.

9   50 CENTS

	VG	VF	UNC
1.7.1980. Ovpt. in 4 lines at upper l. ctr., date twice on face. Ovpt. on #4.	—	—	25.00

10   1 LEONE

	VG	VF	UNC
1.7.1980. Ovpt. on #5.	—	—	30.00

11   2 LEONES

1.7.1980. Ovpt. on #6.	—	—	40.00

12   5 LEONES

1.7.1980. Ovpt. on #7.	—	—	50.00

13   10 LEONES

1.7.1980. Ovpt. on #8.	—	—	60.00

1982 ISSUE

14	20 LEONES	VG	VF	UNC
	1982; 1984. Brown and m/c. Tree at ctr., Pres. S. Stevens at r. 2 youths pan mining (gold or diamonds) on back. Printer: BWC. Wmk: Lion's head.			
	a. 24.8.1982.	1.00	2.50	10.00
	b. 24.8.1984.	.40	1.10	4.50

1988-93 ISSUE

#15-21 arms at upper ctr. Wmk: Lion's head.

#15-19 Pres. Dr. Joseph Saidu Momoh at r.

#20-21 arms at upper ctr. Printer: TDLR.

Replacement notes: Serial # prefix Z/1.

15	10 LEONES	VG	VF	UNC
	27.4.1988. Dk. green and purple on m/c unpt. Steer at l., farmer harvesting at ctr. on back.	FV	.50	2.00

16	20 LEONES	VG	VF	UNC
	27.4.1988. Brown, red and green on m/c unpt. Like #14, but new president at r.	FV	.65	2.50

17	50 LEONES	VG	VF	UNC
	1988-89. Purple, blue and black on m/c unpt. Sports stadium at ctr. Dancers on back.			
	a. W/o imprint. 27.4.1988.	FV	1.50	3.00
	b. Printer: TDLR. 27.4.1989.	FV	.75	2.00

18	100 LEONES	VG	VF	UNC
	1988-90. Blue and black on m/c unpt. Bldg. and ship at ctr. Local designs at l. and r., modern bldg. at l. ctr. on back.			
	a. W/o imprint. 27.4.1988.	FV	1.00	4.50
	b. Printer: TDLR. 27.4.1989; 26.9.1990.	FV	.65	2.50

19	500 LEONES	VG	VF	UNC
	27.4.1991. Red-brown and dark green on m/c unpt. Modern bldg. below arms at l. ctr. 2 boats on back.	FV	1.00	4.00

20 **1000 LEONES**
    4.8.1993. Red and yellow on m/c unpt. B. Bureh at r., carving at lower ctr. Dish antenna at l. ctr. on back.

	VG	VF	UNC
	FV	1.50	5.50

21 **5000 LEONES**
    4.8.1993. Blue and violet on m/c unpt. S. Pieh at r., bldg. at lower ctr. Dam at l. ctr. on back.

	VG	VF	UNC
	FV	6.50	20.00

1995 ISSUE
#22 and 23 Held in Reserve.

24 **500 LEONES**
    27.4.1995. Blue-green, brown and green on m/c unpt. K. Londo at r., arms at upper ctr., spearhead at l., bldg. at lower ctr. Fishing boats at l. ctr., artistic carp at r. Wmk: Lion's head. Printer: TDLR.

	VG	VF	UNC
	FV	FV	2.50

COLLECTOR SERIES

BANK OF SIERRA LEONE

ND ISSUE

CS1 **ND 50 CENTS - 5 LEONES**
    #4-7 w/ovpt: *SPECIMEN* and Maltese cross prefix serial #.

	ISSUE PRICE	MKT. VALUE
	14.00	20.00

The Republic of Singapore, a British Commonwealth nation situated at the southern tip of the Malay peninsula, has an area of 224 sq. mi. (633 sq. km.) and a population of *2.7 million. Capital: Singapore. The economy is based on entrepot trade, manufacturing and oil. Rubber, petroleum products, machinery and spices are exported.

Singapore's modern history - it was an important shipping center in the 14th century before the rise of Malacca and Penang - began in 1819 when Sir Thomas Stamford Raffles, an agent for the British East India Company, founded the town of Singapore. By 1825 its trade exceeded that of Malaca and Penang combined. The opening of the Suez Canal (1869) and the demand for rubber and tin created by the automobile and packaging industries combined to make Singapore one of the major ports of the world. In 1826 Singapore, Penang and Malacca were combined to form the Straits Settlements, which was made a Crown Colony in 1867. Singapore became a separate Crown Colony in 1946 when the Straits Settlements was dissolved. It joined in the formation of Malaysia in 1963, but broke away on Aug. 9, 1956, to become an independent republic. Singapore is a member of the Commonwealth of Nations. The president is Chief of State. The prime minister is Head of Government.

MONETARY SYSTEM:
    1 Dollar = 100 Cents

REPUBLIC

SINGAPORE

SIGNATURE SEAL VARIETIES	
Type I: Dragon, seal script, lion	Type II: Sealscript w/symbol

1967-73 ND ISSUE
#1-2, 6 wmk: Lion's head. Sign. varieties. Printer: BWC.
#3-5, 7-8A wmk: Lion's head. Printer: TDLR.

1 **1 DOLLAR**
    ND (1967-72) Blue on m/c unpt. Lt. red flowers at ctr., arms at r. Apartment bldgs. on back.

		VG	VF	UNC
a.	W/o red seal. Sign. Lim Kim San (1967).	.85	1.50	10.00
b.	Red sign. seal Type I at center. Sign. Dr. Goh Keng Swee (1970).	1.00	2.50	15.00
c.	W/o red seal. Sign. Hon Sui Sen (1971).	.75	2.00	12.00
d.	Red sign. seal Type II at ctr. Sign. Hon Sui Sen (1972).	.75	1.00	6.00

2   5 DOLLARS
ND (1967-73). Green on m/c unpt. Lt. orange flowers at ctr., arms at upper r. Small boats at moorings on back.

	VG	VF	UNC
a. W/o red seal. Sign. Lim Kim San (1967).	3.75	10.00	50.00
b. Red sign. Type I at ctr. Sign. Dr. Goh Keng Swee (1970).	20.00	100.00	300.00
c. W/o red seal. Sign. Hon Sui Sen (1972).	6.00	12.50	80.00
d. Red sign. seal Type II at ctr. Sign. Hon Sui Sen (1973).	3.75	5.50	40.00

3   10 DOLLARS
ND (1967-73). Red on m/c unpt. Lilac flowers at ctr., arms at lower r. 4 hands clasping wrists over map on back.

	VG	VF	UNC
a. W/o red seal. Sign. Lim Kim San (1967).	7.50	10.00	50.00
b. Red sign. seal Type I at ctr. Sign. Dr. Goh Keng Swee (1970).	9.00	18.50	110.00
c. W/o red seal. Sign. Hon Sui Sen (1972).	8.00	11.50	60.00
d. Red sign. seal Type II at ctr. Sign. Hon Sui Sen (1973).	7.50	10.00	40.00

4   25 DOLLARS
ND (1972). Dk. brown on m/c unpt. Yellow flowers at ctr., arms at upper r. Capitol on back.

	VG	VF	UNC
	18.50	30.00	75.00

5   50 DOLLARS
ND (1967-73). Blue on m/c unpt. Violet flowers at ctr., arms at lower r. Bldgs. and boats on back.

	VG	VF	UNC
a. W/o red seal. Sign. Lim Kim San (1967).	37.50	60.00	140.00
b. Red sign. seal Type I at ctr. Sign. Dr. Goh Keng Swee (1970).	40.00	65.00	160.00
c. W/o red seal. Sign. Hon Sui Se Sen (1972).	37.50	60.00	150.00
d. Red sign. seal Type II at ctr. Sign. Hon Sui Sen (1973).	35.00	50.00	100.00

6   100 DOLLARS
ND (1967-73). Blue and violet on m/c unpt. Red flowers at ctr., arms at r. Sailing vessels in harbor on back.

	VG	VF	UNC
a. W/o red seal. Sign. Lim Kim San (1967).	75.00	90.00	225.00
b. Red sign. seal Type I at ctr. Sign. Dr. Goh Keng Swee (1970).	85.00	300.00	725.00
c. W/o red seal. Sign. Hon Sui Sen (1972).	77.50	100.00	240.00
d. Red sign. seal Type II at ctr. Sign. Hon Sui Sen (1973).	72.50	90.00	200.00

7   500 DOLLARS
ND (1972). Dk. green. Lilac colored flowers at ctr. Government bldg. on back.

	VG	VF	UNC
	375.00	400.00	675.00

8   1000 DOLLARS
ND (1967-75). Purple. Lilac-brown colored flowers at ctr., arms at r. City scene on back.

	VG	VF	UNC
a. W/o red seal. Sign. Lim Kim San (1967).	FV	700.00	1200.
b. W/o red seal. Sign. Dr. Goh Keng Swee (1970).	FV	750.00	1600.
c. Red sign. seal Type I at ctr. Sign. Dr. Goh Keng Swee (1970).	FV	750.00	1400.
d. W/o red seal. Sign. Hon Sui Sen (1973).	FV	725.00	1325.
e. Red sign. seal Type II at ctr. Sign. Hon Sui Sen (1975).	FV	700.00	1100.

8A   10,000 DOLLARS
ND (1973). Green. Orchids at ctr., arms at r. Bldg. on back. Sign. Hon Sui Sen.

	VG	VF	UNC
	FV	FV	9000.

1976-80 ND ISSUE
#9-17 city skyline along bottom, arms at upper r. Wmk: Lion's head.

9   1 DOLLAR
ND (1976). Blue-black on m/c unpt. Tern at l. Parade on back. Printer: BWC.

	VG	VF	UNC
	FV	FV	3.00

10   5 DOLLARS
ND (1976). Green and m/c. Bulbul at l. Skylift above river w/ships on back. Printer: BWC.

	VG	VF	UNC
	FV	FV	7.00

11   10 DOLLARS
ND (1976). Dk. brown, deep green and purple on m/c unpt. Kingfisher at l. Modern bldgs. on back. Printer: TDLR.

	VG	VF	UNC
a. Continuous security thread (1979).	FV	7.50	40.00
b. Segmented security thread (1980).	FV	FV	22.50

			VG	VF	Unc
15	**500 DOLLARS**				
	ND (1977). Green and m/c. Oriole at l. Back green; view of island and refinery. Printer: TDLR.		FV	FV	500.00
16	**1000 DOLLARS**				
	ND (1978). Violet and brown. Brahminy Kite bird at l. Ship on back. Printer: TDLR.		FV	FV	950.00

			VG	VF	Unc
12	**20 DOLLARS**				
	ND (1979). Brown, yellow and m/c. Yellow breasted sunbird at l. Back brown; dancer at l., Concorde and airport at ctr. Printer: BWC.		FV	15.00	25.00

			VG	VF	Unc
13	**50 DOLLARS**				
	ND (1976). Dk. blue and m/c. Bird of Paradise at l. High school band playing in formation on back. Printer: TDLR.				
	a. Continuous security thread.		FV	FV	60.00
	b. Segmented security thread.		FV	FV	55.00

			VG	VF	Unc
17	**10,000 DOLLARS**				
	ND (1980). Green. White bellied sea eagle at l. 19th century Singapore River scene above, modern view below on back. Printer: TDLR.		FV	FV	8000.

1984-89 ND ISSUE

#18-25 wmk: Lion's head. Printer: TDLR.

#21 Held in Reserve.

			VG	VF	Unc
14	**100 DOLLARS**				
	ND (1977). Blue. Blue-throated bee eater. Dancers on back. Printer: BWC.		FV	FV	110.00

			VG	VF	Unc
18	**1 DOLLAR**				
	ND (1987). Deep blue and green. Sailing ship at l. Back deep blue; flowers and satellite tracking station at ctr.				
	a. Sign. Goh Ken Swee.		FV	FV	1.50
	b. Sign. Hu Tsu Tau.		FV	FV	1.50

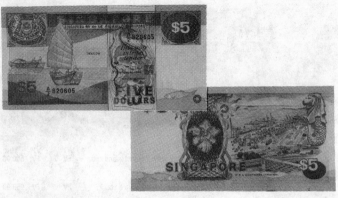

25	**1000 DOLLARS**	**VG**	**VF**	**UNC**
	ND (1984). Purple and m/c. Arms at upper l. ctr., container ship at l. ctr. Repair ship on back.	FV	FV	775.00
26	**10,000 DOLLARS**			
	ND (1987). Red and m/c. Arms at upper l., bulk carrier at l., statuary at ctr. r. 1987 National Day parade on back.	FV	FV	7750.

19	**5 DOLLARS**	**VG**	**VF**	**UNC**
	ND (1989). Green and red-violet on m/c unpt. 2 local boats at l. PSA Container Terminal at r. on back.	FV	FV	5.50

1990 ND ISSUE

20	**10 DOLLARS**	**VG**	**VF**	**UNC**
	ND (1988). Red-orange and violet on m/c unpt. Sailboat at l. Stylized map at ctr., public housing at r. on back.	FV	FV	10.00
22	**50 DOLLARS**			
	ND (1987; 1994). Blue and m/c. Coaster vessel at l. 2 raised area in circles at lower r. for the blind. Bridge and city view on back.			
	a. Thin continuous security thread. (1987).	FV	FV	55.00
	b. Deeper blue w/silver security thread containing inscription. (1994).	FV	FV	52.00

27	**2 DOLLARS**	**VG**	**VF**	**UNC**
	ND (ca.1990). Orange and red on yellow-green unpt. Arms at upper l., 3 boats at ctr. Chingay procession on back. Wmk: Lion's head.	FV	FV	2.50

23	**100 DOLLARS**	**VG**	**VF**	**UNC**
	ND (1985; 1995). Dk. brown, violet and orange-brown on m/c unpt. Ship at l. ctr. Airplane above Changi air terminal at ctr. r. on back.			
	a. Security thread. (1985).	FV	FV	95.00
	b. Segmented foil over security thread. (1995).	FV	FV	90.00
24	**500 DOLLARS**			
	ND (1988). Green on m/c unpt. Arms at upper l. Cargo vessel at l. National defense members on back.	FV	FV	425.00

28	**2 DOLLARS**	**VG**	**VF**	**UNC**
	ND (1992). Purple and brown-violet on m/c unpt. Like #27, but w/progressively larger serial #, one of which is vertical.	FV	FV	2.50

1990, 1992 COMMEMORATIVE ISSUE

#29, 25th Anniversary of Board of Commissioners of Currency, Singapore

#30 and 31, 25th Anniversary of Independence

NOTE: Sheets of 25 subjects w/red BCCS logo at upper r. were offered at about $150.

29	**2 DOLLARS**	**VG**	**VF**	**UNC**
	ND (1992). Logo of the Board ovpt. in red at l. beneath arms.	FV	FV	5.00

30   50 DOLLARS
   9.8.1990. Red, purple and m/c. Silver hologram of Yusof bin Ishak at
   ctr. Old harbor scene at l., modern bldgs. at r. First parliament and
   group of people below flag and arms on back. Plastic.

	VG	VF	UNC
	FV	FV	50.00

31   50 DOLLARS
   ND (1990). Like #30 but w/o date.

	VG	VF	UNC
	FV	FV	47.50

COLLECTOR SERIES

SINGAPORE

ND ISSUE

		ISSUE PRICE	MKT. VALUE
CS1	**ND 1 DOLLAR - 100 DOLLARS** #1a-3a, 5a and 6a ovpt: *SPECIMEN.* (77 sets).	—	1800.
CS2	**ND 1 DOLLAR - 100 DOLLARS** #1c-3c, 5c and 6c ovpt: *SPECIMEN.* (89 sets).	—	1700.
CS3	**ND 1 DOLLAR - 100 DOLLARS** #1d-3d, 4, 5d and 6d ovpt: *SPECIMEN.* (82 sets).	—	2400.
CS4	**ND (1989) 1-100 DOLLARS** #9-11, 13 and 14 ovpt: *SPECIMEN.* (311 sets).	—	1200.

SLOVAKIA

Slovakia as a republic has an area of 18,923 sq. mi. (49,011 sq. km.) and a population of almost 5.3 million. Capital: Bratislava. Textiles, steel, and wood products are exported.

Slovakia was settled by Slavic Slovaks in the 6th or 7th century and was incorporated into Greater Moravia in the 9th century. After the Moravian state was destroyed early in the 10th century, Slovakia was conquered by the Magyars and remained a land of the Hungarian crown until 1918, when it joined the Czechs in forming Czechoslovakia. In 1938, the Slovaks declared themselves an autonomous state within a federal Czecho-Slovak state. After the German occupation, Slovakia became nominally independent under the protection of Germany, March 16, 1939. Father Jozef Tiso was appointed President. Slovakia was liberated from German control in Oct. 1944, but in May 1945 ceased to be an independent Slovak state. In 1968 it became a constituent state of Czechoslovakia as Slovak Socialist Republic. In January 1991 the Czech and Slovak Federal Republic was formed, and after June 1992 elections, it was decided to split the federation into the Czech Republic and Slovakia on 1 January, 1993.

MONETARY SYSTEM:
   1 Korun = 100 Halierov, 1939-1945, 1993-

REPUBLIC

SLOVENSKA REPUBLIKA

REPUBLIC OF SLOVAKIA

1993 ND PROVISIONAL ISSUE
#15-17 Czechoslovakian issue w/adhesive stamps affixed w/*SLOVENSKA* over arms.

15   20 KORUN
   ND (1993- old date 1988). Black and lt. blue adhesive stamp on
   Czechoslovakia #95.

	VG	VF	UNC
	1.00	2.50	4.00

16   50 KORUN
   ND (1993- old date 1987). Black and yellow adhesive stamp on
   Czechoslovakia #96.

	VG	VF	UNC
	2.25	3.50	6.50

17   100 KORUN
   ND (1993- old date 1961). Black and orange adhesive stamp on
   Czechoslovakia #91b. Series G37.

	VG	VF	UNC
	4.00	5.00	9.00

18   500 KORUN
   ND (1993- old date 1973). Adhesive stamp on Czechoslovakia #93.

| | 18.50 | 25.00 | 50.00 |

19   1000 KORUN
   ND (1993- old date 1985). Adhesive stamp on Czechoslovakia #98.

| | 35.00 | 45.00 | 90.00 |

NÁRODNÁ BANKA SLOVENSKA

SLOVAK NATIONAL BANK

1993 ISSUE
#20-26 shield of arms at lower ctr. on back. Sign. varieties.

#20 and 21 printer: BABN.

#22-24 printer: TDLR.

NOTE: Security thread position is moved closer to ctr. on 1995 dated notes.

20	20 K<small>ORUN</small>	VG	VF	U<small>NC</small>
	1993-. Black and green on m/c unpt. Prince Pribina at r. and as wmk. Nitra Castle at l. on back.			
	a. Pale green unpt. 1.9.1993.	FV	FV	2.00
	b. As a. but w/green unpt. at r. 1.6.1995.	FV	FV	1.75
	c. As a. Serial # prefix A. Uncut sheet of 60 (6000).	—	—	60.00

23 (24)	500 K<small>ORUN</small>	VG	VF	U<small>NC</small>
	1.10.1993. Dk. gray and brown on m/c unpt. L. Stúr at r. and as wmk. Bratislava Castle and St. Nicholas' Church on back.			
	a. Serial # prefix E.	FV	FV	30.00
	b. Serial # prefix A. Uncut sheet of 28 (2500).	—	—	525.00

21	50 K<small>ORUN</small>	VG	VF	U<small>NC</small>
	1993-. Black, blue and aqua on m/c unpt. St. Cyril and St. Metod at r. and as wmk. Medieval Church at Drazovce and first 7 letters of Slavonic alphabet on back.			
	a. 1.8.1993.	FV	FV	4.50
	b. 1.6.1995.	FV	FV	4.00
	c. As a. Serial # prefix A. Uncut sheet of 45 (4000).	—	—	100.00

24 (25)	1000 K<small>ORUN</small>	VG	VF	U<small>NC</small>
	1993-. Dk. gray and purple on red-violet and m/c unpt. A. Hlinka at r. and as wmk. Madonna of the church of Liptovké Sliace near Ruzomberok and church of St. Andrew in Ruzomberok on back.			
	a. 1.10.1993.	FV	FV	55.00
	b. 1.6.1995.	FV	FV	52.50
	c. As a. Serial # prefix A. Uncut sheet of 28 (1500).	—	—	1050.

1995-96 I<small>SSUE</small>

22	100 K<small>ORUN</small>	VG	VF	U<small>NC</small>
	1.9.1993. Red and black on orange and m/c unpt. Madonna (by master woodcarver Pavel) from the altar of the Birth in St. Jacob's Church in Levoca. Levoca town view on back.			
	a. Serial # prefix D.	FV	FV	8.00
	b. Serial # prefix A. Uncut sheet of 35 (4000).	—	—	165.00

25 (27)	100 K<small>ORUN</small>	VG	VF	U<small>NC</small>
	1.7.1996. Like #22 but red-orange replaces dull orange in corners on back.	FV	FV	6.50

SLOVENIA

The Republic of Slovenia (formerly a part of the Kingdom of the Serbs, Croats and Slovenes which became Yugoslavia) is bounded in the north by Austria, northeast by Hungary, southeast by Croatia and to the west by Italy. It has an area of 5,246 sq. mi. (20,251 sq. km.) and a population of almost 2.0 million. Capital: Ljubljana. The economy is based on electricity, minerals, forestry, agriculture and fishing. Small industries are being developed during privatization.

The lands originally settled by Slovenes in the 6th century were steadily encroached upon by Germans. Slovenia developed as part of Austri-Hungary after the defeat of the latter in World War I, becoming part of the Kingdom of the Serbs, Croats and Slovenes (Yugoslavia) on December 1, 1918. A legal opposition group, the Slovene League of Social Democrats, was formed in Jan. 1989. In Oct. 1989 the Slovene Assembly voted a constitutional amendment giving it the right to secede from Yugoslavia. On July 2, 1990 the Assembly adopted a 'declaration of sovereignty' and in Sept. proclaimed its control over the territorial defense force on its soil. A referendum on Dec. 23 resulted in a majority vote for independence, which was formally declared on Dec. 26. In Feb. 1991 parliament ruled that henceforth Slovenian law took precedence over federal. On June 25, Slovenia declared independence, but agreed to suspend this for 3 months at peace talks sponsored by the EC. The moratorium having expired, Slovenia (and Croatia) declared their complete independence of the Yugoslav federation on Oct. 8, 1991.

MONETARY SYSTEM:
1 (Tolar) = 1 Yugoslavian Dinar

26 (23)	**200 KORUN** 1.8.1995. Dk. gray and blue-green on m/c unpt. A. Bernolák at r. and as wmk. Trnava town view at l. ctr. on back. Printer: G&D.	FV	FV	15.00

REPUBLIC

REPUBLIKA SLOVENIJA

1990-92 ISSUE
#1-10 column pedestal at lower l., denomination numeral in guilloche over a fly in unpt. at ctr. r. Date given as first 2 numerals of serial #. Mountain ridge at l. ctr. on back. Wmk: Repeated symmetrical designs.

27 (28)	**500 KORUN** 31.10.1996. Like #24 but blue replaces tan unpt. at l. ctr. and in corners on face and in upper l. ctr. and in corners on back. Dk. brown replaces dk. gray at ctr. on back.	FV	FV	27.50

29 (26)	**5000 KORUN** 3.4.1995. Brown-violet and pale yellow-brown on m/c unpt. M. R. Stefánik at r., Sun and moon at ctr. Stefánik's grave at Bradlo Hill, part of *Ursa Major* constellation and a pasque flower on back. Printer: G&D.	FV	FV	200.00

		VG	VF	UNC
1	**1 (TOLAR)** (19)90. Dk. olive-green on lt. gray and lt. olive-green unpt.			
	a. Issued note.	.05	.10	.25
	s. Specimen.	—	—	2.50
2	**2 (TOLARJEV)** (19)90. Dk. brown and brown on tan and ochre unpt.			
	a. Issued note.	.05	.10	.35
	s. Specimen.	—	—	2.50
3	**5 (TOLARJEV)** (19)90. Maroon on lt. gray violet, lt. maroon and pink unpt.			
	a. Issued note.	.05	.15	.55
	s. Specimen.	—	—	2.50
4	**10 (TOLARJEV)** (19)90. Dk. blue-green and grayish purple on lt. blue-green and lt. gray unpt.			
	a. Issued note.	FV	FV	.65
	s. Specimen.	—	—	2.50
5	**50 (TOLARJEV)** (19)90. Dk. gray on tan and lt. gray unpt.			
	a. Issued note.	FV	FV	5.00
	s. Specimen.	FV	FV	2.50
6	**100 (TOLARJEV)** (19)90. Reddish brown and violet on orange and lt. violet unpt.			
	a. Issued note.	FV	FV	4.00
	s. Specimen.	—	—	2.50
7	**200 (TOLARJEV)** (19)90. Greenish black and dk. brown on lt. gray and lt. green unpt.			
	a. Issued note.	FV	FV	25.00
	s. Specimen.	—	—	2.50

8   500 (TOLARJEV)

		VG	VF	UNC
	(19)90; (19)92. Lilac and red on pink unpt.			
a.	Issued note.	FV	FV	25.00
s.	Specimen.	—	—	2.50

9   1000 (TOLARJEV)

		VG	VF	UNC
	(19)91; (19)92. Dk. blue-gray and gray on lt. gray and pale blue unpt.			
a.	Issued note.	FV	FV	35.00
s.	Specimen.	—	—	3.00

10   5000 (TOLARJEV)

		VG	VF	UNC
	(19)92. Purple and lilac on pink unpt.			
a.	Issued note.	FV	FV	130.00
s.	Specimen.	—	—	3.50

BANKA SLOVENIJE

1992-93 ISSUE
#11-20 portr. as wmk.

11   10 TOLARJEV

		VG	VF	UNC
	15.1.1992. Black, brown-violet and brown-orange on m/c unpt. Quill pen at l. ctr., P. Trubar at r. Ursuline church in Ljubljana on back.			
a.	Issued note.	FV	FV	.40
s.	Specimen.	FV	FV	8.50

12   20 TOLARJEV

		VG	VF	UNC
	15.1.1992. Brownish black, deep brown and brown-orange on m/c unpt. Topographical outlines at l. ctr., cherub arms at r. Compass at l., J. Vajkard Valvasor at r. and topographical outlines on back.			
a.	Issued note.	FV	FV	.50
s.	Specimen.	—	—	10.00

13   50 TOLARJEV

		VG	VF	UNC
	15.1.1992. Black, purple and brown-orange on m/c unpt. J. Vega at r., geometric design and calculations at ctr. Academy at upper l., planets and geometric design at ctr.			
a.	Issued note.	FV	FV	1.50
s.	Specimen.	—	—	12.50

14   100 TOLARJEV

		VG	VF	UNC
	15.1.1992. Black, blue-black and brown-orange on m/c unpt. R. Jakopic at r. Outline of the Jarkopicev Pavilion at ctr. r. on back.			
a.	Issued note.	FV	FV	2.75
s.	Specimen.	—	—	15.00

18   1000 TOLARJEV
1.6.1993. Black, deep blue-green and brown-orange on m/c unpt. Like
#17 but modified portrait and other incidental changes including
color.

		VG	VF	UNC
a.	Issued note.	FV	FV	17.50
s.	Specimen.	—	—	25.00

15   200 TOLARJEV
15.1.1992. Black, violet-brown and brown-orange on m/c unpt.
Musical facade at l., I Gallus at r. Drawing of Slovenia's Philharmonic
bldg. at upper l., music scores at upper ctr. on back.

		VG	VF	UNC
a.	Issued note.	FV	FV	5.00
s.	Specimen.	—	—	17.50

16   500 TOLARJEV
15.1.1992. Black, red and brown-orange on m/c unpt. J. Plecnik at r.
Drawing of the National and University Library of Ljubljana at l. ctr. on
back.

		VG	VF	UNC
a.	Issued note.	FV	FV	12.50
s.	Specimen.	—	—	20.00

19   5000 TOLARJEV
1.6.1993. Brownish-black, dk. brown and brown-orange on m/c unpt.
I. Kobika at r. National Galery in Ljubljana at upper l.

		VG	VF	UNC
a.	Issued note.	FV	FV	65.00
s.	Specimen.	—	—	30.00

17   1000 TOLARJEV
15.1.1992. Brownish black, deep green and brown-orange on m/c
unpt. F. Preseren at r. and as wmk. The poem "Drinking Toast" at ctr.
on back.

		VG	VF	UNC
a.	Issued note.	FV	FV	18.50
s.	Specimen.	—	—	25.00

20   10,000 TOLARJEV
28.6.1994. Black, purple and brown-orange on m/c unpt. I. Cankar at
r. Chrysanthemum blossom at l. on back.

		VG	VF	UNC
a.	Issued note.	FV	FV	110.00
s.	Specimen.	—	—	35.00

The Solomon Islands, located in the Southwest Pacific east of Papua New Guinea, has an area of 10,983 sq. mi. (28,450 sq. km.) and an estimated population of 349,500. Capital: Honiara. The most important islands of the Solomon chain are Guadalcanal (scene of some of the fiercest fighting of World War II), Malaitia, New Georgia, Florida, Vella Lavella, Choiseul, Rendova, San Cristobal, the Lord Howe group, the Santa Cruz islands, and the Duff group. Copra is the only important cash crop but it is hoped that timber will become an economic factor.

The Solomon Islands were discovered by Spanish navigator Alvaro de Mendana in 1567, and in 1569 he made an unsuccessful attempt to colonize them. European knowledge of the group would not be completed until the end of the 18th century. Germany declared a protectorate over the northern Solomons in 1885. The British protectorate over the southern Solomons was established in 1893. In 1899 Germany transferred its claim to all Solomon Islands except Buka and Bougainville to Great Britain in exchange for recognition of German claims in western Samoa. Australia occupied the two German islands in 1914, and administered them after 1920.

The Japanese invaded the Solomons during 1942-43, but were driven out by an American counteroffensive after a series of bloody clashes.

Following World War II, the islands returned to the status of a British protectorate. In 1976 the protectorate was abolished, and the Solomons became a self-governing dependency. Full independence was achieved on July 7, 1978. Solomon Islands is a member of the Commonwealth of Nations. The Queen of England is Chief of State.

RULERS:
British

MONETARY SYSTEM:
1 Shilling = 12 Pence
1 Pound = 20 Shillings to 1966
1 Dollar = 100 Cents, 1966-

SIGNATURE/TITLE VARIETIES

1	Chairman		Member	4	Governor		Director
2				5			
3				6			

BRITISH INFLUENCE

SOLOMON ISLANDS MONETARY AUTHORITY

1977; 1981 ND ISSUE
Dollar System
#5-8 Qn. Elizabeth II at r. Wmk: Falcon. Printer: TDLR (w/o imprint).

			VG	VF	UNC
5	**2 DOLLARS** ND (1977). Dk. green on pink and pale green unpt. Fisherman on back. Sign. 1.		1.00	2.00	6.00

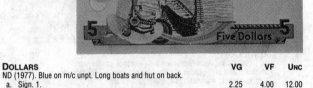

			VG	VF	UNC
6	**5 DOLLARS** ND (1977). Blue on m/c unpt. Long boats and hut on back.				
	a. Sign. 1.		2.25	4.00	12.00
	b. Sign. 2.		2.25	5.00	15.00

			VG	VF	UNC
7	**10 DOLLARS** ND (1977). Purple on gray and violet unpt. Weaver on back.				
	a. Sign. 1.		4.00	7.50	22.50
	b. Sign. 2.		4.00	8.00	25.00

			VG	VF	UNC
8	**20 DOLLARS** ND (1981). Brown and purple on m/c unpt. Line of people on back. Sign. 3.		7.00	15.00	40.00

CENTRAL BANK OF SOLOMON ISLANDS

1984 ND ISSUE
#11 and 12 like #7 and 8 except for new bank name. Wmk: Falcon. Sign. 4.

			VG	VF	UNC
11	**10 DOLLARS** ND (1984). Purple on gray and violet unpt.		FV	FV	20.00

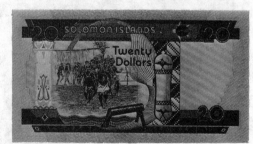

12	**20 DOLLARS**	**VG**	**VF**	**UNC**
	ND (1984). Brown and purple on m/c unpt.	FV	FV	37.50

1986 ND ISSUE

#13-17 arms at r. Wmk: Falcon. Sign. 5.

#13-16 backs like #5-8.

13	**2 DOLLARS**	**VG**	**VF**	**UNC**
	ND (1986). Green on m/c unpt.	FV	FV	2.75

14	**5 DOLLARS**	**VG**	**VF**	**UNC**
	ND (1986). Dk. blue, deep purple and violet on m/c unpt.	FV	FV	6.50

15	**10 DOLLARS**	**VG**	**VF**	**UNC**
	ND (1986). Purple and red-violet on m/c unpt.	FV	FV	10.00
16	**20 DOLLARS**			
	ND (1986). Brown on m/c unpt.	FV	FV	18.00

17	**50 DOLLARS**	**VG**	**VF**	**UNC**
	ND (1986). Blue-green and purple on m/c unpt. Butterflies and reptiles on back.	FV	FV	42.50

1996; 1997 ND ISSUE

#18-22 similar to #13-17 but w/added security devices.

18	**2 DOLLARS**	**VG**	**VF**	**UNC**
	ND (1997). Green on m/c unpt.			Expected New Issue
19	**5 DOLLARS**			
	ND (1997). Dk. blue, deep purple and violet on m/c unpt.			Expected New Issue
20	**10 DOLLARS**			
	ND (1996). Purple and red-violet on m/c unpt.			Expected New Issue
21	**20 DOLLARS**			
	ND (1996). Brown on m/c unpt.			Expected New Issue
22	**50 DOLLARS**			
	ND (1996). Blue-green and purple on m/c unpt.			Expected New Issue

COLLECTOR SERIES

SOLOMON ISLAND MONETARY AUTHORITY

1979 ISSUE

CS1	**1979 2-10 DOLLARS**	**ISSUE PRICE**	**MKT. VALUE**
	#5-7 w/ovpt: *SPECIMEN* and Maltese cross prefix serial #.	14.00	25.00

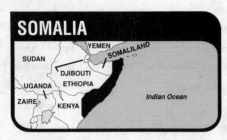

SOMALIA

Somalia, the Somali Democratic Republic, comprising of the former Italian Somaliland, is located on the coast of the eastern projection of the African continent commonly referred to as the "Horn". It has an area of 178,201 sq. mi. (461,657 sq. km.). Capital: Mogadishu. The economy is pastoral and agricultural. Livestock, bananas and hides are exported. The area of the British Somaliland Protectorate was known to the Egyptians at least 1,500 years B.C., and was occupied by the Arabs and Portuguese before British sea captains obtained trading and anchorage rights in 1827. The land of sandy clay and sporadic rainfall acquired a strategic importance with the opening of the Suez Canal in 1869. After negotiating treaties with the tribes, Britain declared the area a protectorate in 1888. Italy acquired Italian Somaliland in 1895 by purchase from the sultan of Zanzibar. Britain occupied Italian Somaliland in 1941 and administered it until April 1, 1950, when it was returned to Italy as a U.N. trusteeship. The British Somaliland protectorate became independent on June 26, 1960. Five days later it joined with Italian Somaliland to form the Somali Republic. The country was presently under a revolutionary military regime installed Oct. 21, 1969. After 11 years of civil war rebel forces fought their way into the capital. A. M. Muhammad became president in Aug. 1991 but interfactional fighting continued. A UN-sponsored truce was signed in March 1992 and a peace plan and pact was signed Jan. 15, 1993. The northern Somali National Movements (SNM) declared a secession of the northwestern Somaliland Republic on May 17, 1991 which is not recognized by the Somali Democratic Republic.

MONETARY SYSTEM:
1 Scellino = 1 Shilling = 100 Centesimi

REPUBLIC

BANCA NAZIONALE SOMALA

1962 ISSUE
#1-16 w/dual denomination of Scellini and Shilling. Wmk: Leopard's head.
#1-4 sign. title: *PRESIDENTE* at l. Printer: OCV.

		VG	VF	UNC
1	**5 SCELLINI** 1962. Red on green and orange unpt. Antelope at l. Back orange-brown; small sailing vessel.	15.00	35.00	140.00

		VG	VF	UNC
2	**10 SCELLINI** 1962. Green on red-brown and green unpt. Flower at l. Back brown and green; river scene.	20.00	55.00	235.00

		VG	VF	UNC
3	**20 SCELLINI** 1962. Brown on blue and gold unpt. Banana plant at l. Back brown and blue; bank bldg.	25.00	75.00	425.00

		VG	VF	UNC
4	**100 SCELLINI** 1962. Blue on green and orange unpt. Artcraft at l. Back blue and red; bldg.	35.00	125.00	500.00

1966 ISSUE
#5-8 slight changes in colors and design elements; (w/o imprint).

		VG	VF	UNC
5	**5 SCELLINI** 1966. Similar to #1 but different guilloche in unpt. Back w/blue unpt.	10.00	30.00	125.00
6	**10 SCELLINI** 1966. Similar to #2 but different guilloche in unpt. Back green w/lt. tan unpt.	15.00	50.00	285.00
7	**20 SCELLINI** 1966. Similar to #3 but unpt. is pink, blue and green. Brown bank bldg. on back.	25.00	65.00	400.00
8	**100 SCELLINI** 1966. Similar to #4 but unpt. is green, purple and tan.	35.00	120.00	550.00

1968 ISSUE
#9-12 sign. title: *Governatore* at l.

		VG	VF	UNC
9	**5 SCELLINI** 1968. Red on green and orange unpt. Like #5.	12.50	35.00	175.00
10	**10 SCELLINI** 1968. Green on red-brown and green unpt. Like #6.	20.00	55.00	375.00
11	**20 SCELLINI** 1968. Brown on blue and gold unpt. Like #7.	27.50	85.00	475.00
12	**100 SCELLINI** 1968. Blue on green and orange unpt. Like #8.	37.50	125.00	650.00

DEMOCRATIC REPUBLIC

BANCA NAZINALE SOMALA

1971 ISSUE
#13-16 sign. titles: *GOVERNATORE* at l. and *CASSIERE* at r.

		VG	VF	UNC
13	**5 SCELLINI** 1971. Purple-brown on blue, green and gold unpt. Like #9.	8.00	22.50	135.00
14	**10 SCELLINI** 1971. Green on red-brown and green unpt. Like #10.	10.00	27.50	220.00
15	**20 SCELLINI** 1971. Brown on blue and gold unpt. Like #11.	15.00	40.00	350.00
16	**100 SCELLINI** 1971. Blue on green and orange unpt. Like #12.	17.50	60.00	475.00

BANKIGA QARANKA SOOMAALIYEED

SOMALI NATIONAL BANK

LAW OF 11.12.1974
#17-20 w/dual denominations of Scellini and Shilling. Wmk: Hassan.
#17-20 arms at l.

17 5 SHILIN

	VG	VF	UNC
L.1974. 1975. Violet on gold and m/c unpt. Gnus and zebras at bottom ctr. Banana harvesting on back.	1.50	5.00	20.00

18 10 SHILIN

	VG	VF	UNC
L.1974. 1975. Dk. green on pink and m/c unpt. Lighthouse at l. ctr. Shipbuilders at work on back.	2.00	6.50	32.50
19 20 SHILIN *L.1974*. 1975. Brown on m/c unpt. Bank bldg. at ctr. Cattle on back.	2.25	6.50	75.00
20 100 SHILIN *L.1974*. 1975. Blue on gold and m/c unpt. Woman w/baby, rifle and farm tools at l. ctr. Dagathur monument at ctr. r. Workers in factory on back.	7.00	20.00	100.00

BANKIGA DHEXE EE SOOMAALIYA

CENTRAL BANK OF SOMALIA

LAW OF 6.12.1977

#20A-24 arms at l. Black series and serial #. W/dual denominations of Shilin and Shilling. Wmk: Hassan.

20A 5 SHILIN

	VG	VF	UNC
L.1977. 1978. Violet on gold and m/c unpt. Like #17.	4.00	10.00	35.00

21 5 SHILIN

	VG	VF	UNC
L.1977. 1978. Violet on gold and m/c unpt. Similar to #20A but Cape Buffalo herd at bottom ctr.	.50	2.00	8.50

22 10 SHILIN

L.1977. 1978. Dk. green on pink and m/c unpt. Similar to #18.	1.00	4.00	20.00

23 20 SHILIN

	VG	VF	UNC
L.1977. 1978. Brown on m/c unpt. Similar to #19.	1.75	7.00	35.00
24 100 SHILIN *L.1977*. 1978. Blue on gold and m/c unpt. Similar to #20.	2.25	9.00	45.00

LAW OF 5.4.1980

#26-28 arms at l. Red series and serial #. Different sign. title at l. Wmk: Hassan.

#25 *Deleted*.

26 10 SHILIN

	VG	VF	UNC
L.1980. 1980. Dk. green on pink and m/c unpt. Like #22.	.60	2.50	10.00

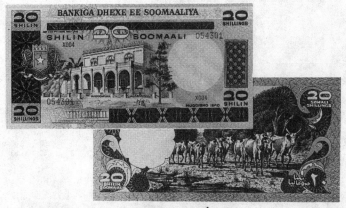

27 20 SHILIN

	VG	VF	UNC
L.1980. 1980. Brown on m/c unpt. Like #23.	1.00	5.00	20.00

28	100 SHILIN	VG	VF	UNC
	L.1980. 1980. Blue on gold and m/c unpt. Like #24.	2.25	9.00	35.00

LAW OF 9.12.1981
#29-30 wmk: Hassan.

29	20 SHILIN	VG	VF	UNC
	L.1981. 1981. Brown on m/c unpt. Like #27.	1.00	5.50	40.00

30	100 SHILIN	VG	VF	UNC
	L.1981. 1981. Blue on gold and m/c unpt. Like #28.	4.00	12.00	35.00

LAW OF 30.12.1982
#31-35 arms at upper l., star at or near lower ctr.
#32-35 wmk: Hassan.
Reduced size notes.

33	20 SHILIN	VG	VF	UNC
	L.1982. 1983-89. Brown and m/c. Bank at l. Back similar to #19.			
	a. 1983.	.35	1.50	6.00
	b. 1986-87; 1989.	.25	1.00	4.00

34	50 SHILIN	VG	VF	UNC
	1983-89. Red-brown and m/c. Walled city at l. and ctr. Watering animals at ctr. on back.			
	a. 1983.	.50	1.50	6.00
	b. 1986; 1987. 2 sign. varieties.	.15	.40	2.00
	c. 1988; 1989.	.10	.30	1.25

31	5 SHILIN	VG	VF	UNC
	L.1982. 1983-87. Brown-violet. Cape Buffalo herd at l. ctr. Harvesting bananas on back.			
	a. 1983.	.10	.50	2.00
	b. 1986-87.	.10	.40	1.50

35	100 SHILIN	VG	VF	UNC
	1983-89. Blue-black, dk. blue and dk. green on m/c unpt. Woman w/baby, rifle and farm tools at l. Dagathur monument at l. ctr. Back purple and m/c; similar to #20.			
	a. 1983.	.60	2.50	7.50
	b. 1986; 1987. 2 sign. varieties.	.30	1.00	4.00
	c. 1988; 1989.	.15	.40	2.00

LAW OF 1.1.1989

32	10 SHILIN	VG	VF	UNC
	L.1982. 1983-87. Green and m/c. Lighthouse at l. Shipbuilders on back.			
	a. 1983.	.25	.75	3.00
	b. 1986-87.	.20	.60	1.50

36 500 SHILIN
   L.1989. 1989; 1990. Green and blue on m/c unpt. Fishermen mending
   net at l. and ctr. Mosque on back. 2 sign. varieties.

	VG	VF	UNC
	.20	1.00	3.00

37 1000 SHILIN
   L.1989. 1990. Violet and orange on m/c unpt. Women seated weaving
   baskets at l. ctr.; arms above. Bldgs., Port. of Mogadishu on back.

	VG	VF	UNC
	.15	.75	2.00

REGIONAL

In Mogadishu-North, forces loyal to warlord Ali Mahdi Mohammed have issued currency valued in "N" Shilin. The notes may have originally been part of a plan to replace older currency.

MOGADISHU-NORTH FORCES

1991 ISSUE
#R1 and R2 arms at top l. ctr.

R1 20 N SHILIN
   1991. Violet, red-brown, brown-orange and olive-green on m/c unpt.
   Trader leading camel in unpt. at l. ctr. Picking cotton at ctr. on back.
   Wmk: Hassan.

	VG	VF	UNC
	1.00	4.00	12.00

R2 50 N SHILIN
   1991. Man working at loom on face. Young person leading a donkey
   w/3 children on back.

	VG	VF	UNC
	1.25	5.00	15.00

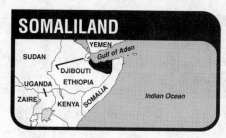

The Somaliland Republic, comprising of the former British Somaliland Protectorate is located on the coast of the northeastern projection of the African continent commonly referred to as the "Horn" on the southwestern end of the Gulf of Aden.

Bordered by Eritrea to the west, Ethiopia to west and south and Somalia to the east. It has an area of 68,000* sq. mi. (176,000* sq. km). Capital: Hargeysa. It is mostly arid and mountainous except for the gulf shoreline.

The Protectorate of British Somaliland was established in 1888 and from 1905 the territory was administered by a commissioner under the British Colonial Office. Italian Somaliland was administered as a colony from 1893 to 1941, when the territory was occupied by British forces. In 1950 the United Nations allowed Italy to resume control of Italian Somaliland under a trusteeship. In 1960 British and Italian Somaliland were united as Somalia, an independent republic outside the Commonwealth.

Civil War erupted in the late 1970's and continued until the capital of Somalia was taken in 1990. The United Nations provided aid and peacekeeptes. A UN sponsored truce was signed in March 1992 and a peace plan and pact was signed Jan. 15, 1993. The northern Somali National Movement (SMN) declared a secession of the Somaliland Republic on May 17, 1991 which is not recognized by the Somali Democratic Republic.

The currency issued by the East African Currency Board was used in British Somaliland from 1945 to 1961, Somali currency was used later until 1995.

REPUBLIC

BAANKA SOMALILAND

1994 ISSUE
#1-4 bldg. at ctr. Greater Kudu at r. Traders w/camels on back.
#5 and 6 bldg. at ctr. Ship dockside, herdsmen w/sheep at ctr. on back.

1 5 SOMALILAND SHILLINGS
   1994. Bright green, olive-green and red-brown on m/c unpt.

	VG	VF	UNC
	FV	FV	1.50

2 10 SOMALILAND SHILLINGS
   1994. Violet, purple and red-brown on m/c unpt.

	VG	VF	UNC
	FV	FV	1.50

3 20 SOMALILAND SHILLINGS
   1994. Brown and red-brown on m/c unpt.

	VG	VF	UNC
	FV	FV	2.50

4   50 SOMALILAND SHILLINGS
1994. Blue-violet, blue-gray and red-brown on m/c unpt.

	VG	VF	UNC
	FV	FV	3.50

5   100 SOMALILAND SHILLINGS
1994. Brownish black and red-violet on m/c unpt.

	VG	VF	UNC
	FV	FV	6.50

6   500 SOMALILAND SHILLINGS
1994. Purple, blue-black and blue-green on m/c unpt.

	VG	VF	UNC
	FV	FV	20.00

1996 ISSUE

7   50 SOMALILAND SHILLINGS
1996. Blue-violet, blue-gray and violet on m/c unpt. Like #4 but increased size. 130 x 58mm.

	VG	VF	UNC
	FV	FV	2.00

1996 "BRONZE" COMMEMORATIVE ISSUE

#8-13, 5th Anniversary of Independence

#8-13 bronze ovpt: *5th Anniversary of Independence 18 May 1996 - Sanad Gurada 5ee Gobanjmadda 18 May 1996.*

8   5 SOMALILAND SHILLINGS
18.5.1996 (- old date 1994). Bronze ovpt. on #1.

	VG	VF	UNC
	FV	FV	1.75

9   10 SOMALILAND SHILLINGS
18.5.1996 (- old date 1994). Bronze ovpt. on #2.

	VG	VF	UNC
	FV	FV	2.00

10   20 SOMALILAND SHILLINGS
18.5.1996 (- old date 1994). Bronze ovpt. on #3.

	VG	VF	UNC
	FV	FV	3.00

11   50 SOMALILAND SHILLINGS
18.5.1996 (- old date 1994). Bronze ovpt. on #4.

	VG	VF	UNC
	FV	FV	4.25

12   100 SOMALILAND SHILLINGS
18.5.1996 (- old date 1994). Bronze ovpt. on #5.

	VG	VF	UNC
	FV	FV	7.50

13   500 SOMALILAND SHILLINGS
18.5.1996 (- old date 1994). Bronze ovpt. on #6.

	VG	VF	UNC
	FV	FV	26.50

1996 "SILVER" COMMEMORATIVE ISSUE

#14-19, 5th Anniversary of Independence

#14-19 silver ovpt: *Sanad Gurada 5ee Gobanjmadda 18 May 1996.*

14   5 SOMALILAND SHILLINGS
18.5.1996 (- old date 1994). Silver ovpt. on #1.

	VG	VF	UNC
	FV	FV	1.75

15   10 SOMALILAND SHILLINGS
18.5.1996 (- old date 1994). Silver ovpt. on #2.

	VG	VF	UNC
	FV	FV	2.00

16   20 SOMALILAND SHILLINGS
18.5.1996 (- old date 1994). Silver ovpt. on #3.

	VG	VF	UNC
	FV	FV	3.00

17   50 SOMALILAND SHILLINGS
18.5.1996 (- old date 1994). Silver ovpt. on #4.

	VG	VF	UNC
	FV	FV	4.25

18   100 SOMALILAND SHILLINGS
18.5.1996 (- old date 1994). Silver ovpt. on #5.

	VG	VF	UNC
	FV	FV	7.50

19   500 SOMALILAND SHILLINGS
18.5.1996 (- old date 1994). Silver ovpt. on #6.

	VG	VF	UNC
	FV	FV	26.50

The Republic of South Africa, located at the southern tip of Africa, has an area, including the enclave of Walvis Bay, of 472,359 sq. mi. (1,221,040 sq. km.) and a population of 33.14 million. Capital: Administrative, Pretoria; Legislative, Cape Town; Judicial, Bloemfontein. Manufacturing, mining and agriculture are the principal industries. Exports include wool, diamonds, gold and metallic ores.

Portuguese navigator Bartholomeu Diaz became the first European to sight the region of South Africa when he rounded the Cape of Good Hope in 1488, but throughout the 16th century the only white men to come ashore were the survivors of ships wrecked while attempting the stormy Cape passage. The first permanent settlement was established by Jan van Riebeeck of the Dutch East India Company in 1652. In subsequent decades additional Dutch and Germans and Huguenot refugees from France settled in the Cape area to form the Afrikaner segment of today's population.

Great Britain captured the Cape colony in 1795, and again in 1806, receiving permanent title in 1814. To escape British political rule and cultural dominance, many Afrikaner farmers (Boers) migrated northward (the Great Trek) beginning in 1836, and established the independent Boer republics of the Transvaal (the South African Republic, Zuid Afrikaansche Republic) in 1852, and the Orange Free State in 1854. British political intrigues against the two republics, coupled with the discovery of diamonds and gold in the Boer- settled regions, led to the bitter Boer Wars (1880-1881, 1899-1902) and the incorporation of the Boer republics into the British Empire.

On May 31, 1910, the two former Boer republics (Transvaal and Orange Free State) were joined with the British colonies of Cape of Good Hope and Natal to form the Union of South Africa, a dominion of the British Empire. In 1934 the Union achieved status as a sovereign state within the British Empire. Political integration of the various colonies did not still the conflict between the Afrikaners and the English-speaking groups, which continued to have a significant impact on political developments. A resurgence of Afrikaner nationalism in the 1940s and 1950s led to a referendum in the white community authorizing the relinquishment of dominion status and the establishment of a republic. The decision took effect on May 31, 1961. The Republic of South Africa withdrew from the British Commonwealth in Oct., 1961. The apartheid era ended on April 27, 1994 with the first democratic election for all people of South Africa. Nelson Mandela was inaugurated as president on May 10, 1994. South Africa was readmitted to the Commonwealth of Nations.

South African currency carries inscriptions in both Afrikaans and English.

RULERS:
British to 1961

MONETARY SYSTEM:
1 Shilling = 12 Pence
1 Pound = 20 Shillings to 1961
1 Rand = 100 Cents (= 10 Shillings), 1961-

REPUBLIC OF SOUTH AFRICA

SOUTH AFRICAN RESERVE BANK

1961 ND ISSUE

Rand System

#102-122 portr. Jan van Riebeeck at I. and as wmk.

102	1 RAND	VG	VF	UNC
	ND (1961-62). Rust brown. First line of bank name and value in English. 135 x 77mm.			
	a. Sign. Dr. M. H. de Kock (1961).	2.50	7.50	30.00
	b. Sign. Dr. G. Rissik (1962).	2.00	6.00	25.00
103	1 RAND			
	ND (1961-62). Rust brown. Like #102 but first line of bank name and value in Afrikaans. 137 x 78mm.			
	a. Sign. Dr. M. H. de Kock (1961).	2.50	7.50	30.00
	b. Sign. Dr. G. Rissik (1962).	2.00	6.00	25.00
104	2 RAND			
	ND (1961-62). Blue. Similar to #83. First line of bank name and value in English. 150 x 85mm.			
	a. Sign. Dr. M. H. de Kock (1961).	1.50	5.75	22.50
	b. Sign. Dr. G. Rissik (1962).	1.50	3.00	12.00

105	**2 RAND**	VG	VF	UNC
	ND (1961-62). Like #104 but first line of bank name and value in Afrikaans. 150 x 85mm.			
	a. Sign. Dr. M. H. de Kock (1961).	1.50	5.75	22.50
	b. Sign. Dr. G. Rissik (1962).	1.50	3.00	12.00
106	**10 RAND**			
	ND (1961-62). Green and brown on m/c unpt. Similar to #91. First line of bank name and value in English. Sailing ship on back. 170 x 97mm.			
	a. Sign. Dr. M. H. de Kock (1961).	5.00	13.50	60.00
	b. Sign. Dr. G. Rissik (1962).	3.50	10.00	40.00
107	**10 RAND**			
	ND (1961-62). Green and brown on m/c unpt. Like #106 but first line of bank name and value in Afrikaans. 170 x 97mm.			
	a. Sign. Dr. M. H. de Kock (1961).	5.00	13.50	60.00
	b. Sign. Dr. G. Rissik (1962).	3.50	10.00	40.00
108	**20 RAND**			
	ND (1961-62). Brown-violet. First line of bank name and value in English. Machinery on back. Sign. Dr. M. H. de Kock.	8.50	25.00	100.00

108A	**20 RAND**	VG	VF	UNC
	ND (1962). Like #108 but first line of bank name in Afrikaans. Sign. Dr. G. Rissik.	9.00	25.00	110.00

1966 ND ISSUE
#109-114 J. van Riebeeck at l. and as wmk.

109	**1 RAND**	VG	VF	UNC
	ND (1966-72). Dk. reddish brown on m/c unpt. First line of bank name and value in English. Rams in field on back. 126 x 64mm.			
	a. Sign. Dr. G. Rissik (1966).	.75	2.25	11.00
	b. Sign. Dr. T. W. de Jongh (1967).	.50	1.50	8.00

110	**1 RAND**	VG	VF	UNC
	ND (1966-72). Dk. reddish brown on m/c unpt. Like #109 but first line on bank name and value in Afrikaans. 126 x 64mm.			
	a. Sign. Dr. G. Rissik (1966).	.75	2.25	11.00
	b. Sign. Dr. T. W. de Jongh (1967).	.50	1.50	8.00

111	**5 RAND**	VG	VF	UNC
	ND (1966-76). Purple. Covered wagons on trail at r. corner. First line of bank name and value in English. Factory w/train on back. 133 x 70mm.			
	a. Sign. Dr. G. Rissik (1966).	4.00	12.00	45.00
	b. Sign. Dr. T. W. de Jongh. Wmk: Springbok (1967-74).	2.50	5.00	20.00
	c. Sign. Dr. T. W. de Jongh. Wmk: J. van Riebeeck (1975).	2.00	4.50	20.00

112	**5 RAND**	VG	VF	UNC
	ND (1966-76). Purple. Like #111 but first line of bank name and value in Afrikaans.			
	a. Sign. Dr. G. Rissik (1966).	4.00	12.00	45.00
	b. Sign. Dr. T. W. de Jongh. Wmk: Springbok (1967-74).	2.25	5.00	20.00
	c. Sign. Dr. T. W. de Jongh. Wmk: J. van Riebeeck (1975).	2.00	4.50	20.00

113	**10 RAND**	VG	VF	UNC
	ND (1966-76). Dk. green and brown. Capitol bldg. at ctr. First line on bank name and value in English. Old sailing ships on back. 140 x 76mm.			
	a. Sign. Dr. G. Rissik (1966).	7.00	12.00	35.00
	b. Sign. Dr. T. W. de Jongh. Wmk: Springbok (1967-74).	5.00	7.50	20.00
	c. Sign. Dr. T. W. de Jongh. Wmk: J. van Riebeeck (1975).	3.75	5.50	16.00
114	**10 RAND**			
	ND (1966-76). Dk. green and brown. Like #113 but first line of bank name and value in Afrikaans. 140 x 76mm.			
	a. Sign. Dr. G. Rissik (1966).	7.00	12.00	35.00
	b. Sign. Dr. T. W. de Jongh. Wmk: Springbok (1967-74).	5.00	7.50	20.00
	c. Sign. Dr. T. W. de Jongh. Wmk: J. van Riebeeck (1975).	3.75	5.50	16.00

1973-84 ISSUE
#115-122 J. van Riebeeck at l. and as wmk.

115	**1 RAND**	VG	VF	UNC
	ND (1973-75). Brown. Like #109 but 120 x 57mm.			
	a. Sign. Dr. T. W. de Jongh. Wmk: Springbok (1973).	.65	1.00	5.00
	b. Sign. Dr. T. W. de Jongh. Wmk: J. van Riebeeck (1975).	.65	1.00	5.00
116	**1 RAND**			
	ND (1973-75). Brown. Like #110 but 120 x 57mm.			
	a. Sign. Dr. T. W. de Jongh. Wmk: Springbok (1973).	.65	1.00	5.00
	b. Sign. Dr. T. W. de Jongh. Wmk: J. van Riebeeck (1975).	.65	1.00	5.00

117	**2 RAND**	VG	VF	UNC
	ND (1973-76). Blue. First line of bank name and value in Afrikaans. Hydroelectric dam on back. 127 x 62mm.			
	a. Sign. Dr. T. W. de Jongh. Wmk: Springbok (1974).	1.25	3.00	12.00
	b. Sign. Dr. T. W. de Jongh. Wmk: J. van Riebeeck (1976).	1.00	2.50	9.00

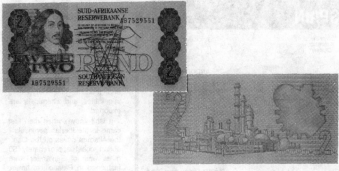

118   2 RAND

		VG	VF	UNC
ND (1978-90). Blue and m/c. Electrical tower at ctr. Refinery on back. 120 x 57mm.				
a.	Sign. Dr. T. W. de Jongh (1978-81).	FV	1.50	5.00
b.	Sign. G. P. C de Kock. W/o security thread. (1981).	1.60	4.00	12.00
c.	As b. Fractional numbering system. (1981-83).	FV	1.00	3.50
d.	As b. Alphanumeric system. (1983-90).	FV	FV	2.50
e.	Sign. Dr. C. L. Stals. (1990).	FV	2.50	10.00

119   5 RAND

		VG	VF	UNC
ND (1978-90). Purple and m/c. First line of bank name and value in English. Diamond at ctr. Grain storage on back. 127 x 63mm.				
a.	Sign. Dr. T. W. de Jongh (1978-81).	FV	3.00	11.00
b.	Sign. G. P. C. de Kock. W/o security thread. (1981).	7.00	20.00	100.00
c.	As b. Fractional numbering system. (1981-89).	FV	2.00	7.50
d.	As b. Alphanumeric system. (1989-90).	FV	3.00	9.50
e.	Sign. Dr. C. L. Stals. (1990-94).	FV	1.50	6.00

120   10 RAND

		VG	VF	UNC
ND (1978-90). Green and m/c. Flower at ctr. Bull and ram on back. 134 x 70mm.				
a.	Sign. Dr. T. W. de Jongh (1978-81).	FV	3.00	13.00
b.	Sign. G. P. C. de Kock. W/o security thread. (1981).	3.00	7.00	25.00
c.	As b. Fractional numbering system. (1982-85).	FV	4.00	14.00
d.	As b. Alphanumeric system. (1985-90).	FV	3.50	10.50
e.	Sign. Dr. C. L. Stals. (1990-93).	FV	3.00	9.00

121   20 RAND

		VG	VF	UNC
ND (1984-90). Brown and m/c. Bldg. at ctr. 3 sailing ships and arms on back. 144 x 77mm.				
a.	Sign. Dr. T. W. de Jongh (1978-81).	FV	6.50	23.00
b.	Sign. G. P. C. de Kock. W/o security thread. (1981).	6.00	12.00	37.00
c.	As b. Fractional numbering system. (1982-85).	FV	6.00	18.00
d.	As b. Alphanumeric system. (1985-90).	FV	8.00	22.50
e.	Sign. Dr. C. L. Stals. (1990-93).	FV	FV	13.50

122   50 RAND

		VG	VF	UNC
ND (1984-90). Red on m/c unpt. Lion at ctr. First line of bank name and value in Afrikaans. Local animals at lower l., mountains at ctr., plants at r. on back. 147 x 83mm.				
a.	Sign. G. de Kock (1984).	15.00	25.00	50.00
b.	Sign. Dr. C. L. Stals (1990).	13.75	20.00	40.00
x.	Error. Wmk. sideways. Serial # prefix BP.	16.50	27.50	60.00

1992-94 ISSUE
#123-127 sign. Dr. C. L. Stals.

123   10 RAND

	VG	VF	UNC
ND (1993). Dk. green and dk. blue on brown and m/c unpt. White rhinoceros at ctr., lg. white rhino at r. and as wmk. Ram's head over sheep at l. on back.	FV	FV	5.00

124 20 RAND
ND (1993). Dp. brown, brown and red-brown on m/c unpt. Elephants at ctr., lg. elephant head at r. and as wmk. Open pit mining at l. ctr. on back.

	VG	VF	UNC
	FV	FV	9.00

125 50 RAND
ND (1992). Maroon and deep blue-green on m/c unpt. Lions w/cub drinking water at ctr., male lion head at r. and as wmk. Refinery at l. ctr. on back.

	VG	VF	UNC
	FV	FV	21.50

126 100 RAND
ND (1994). Blue-violet and dk. gray on m/c unpt. Water buffalo at ctr. and lg. water buffalo head at r. and as wmk. Zebras along bottom from l. to ctr. on back.

	VG	VF	UNC
	FV	FV	38.50

127 200 RAND
ND (1994). Orange on m/c unpt. Leopard at ctr., leopard's head at r. Dish antenna at upper l., modern bridge at lower l. on back.

	VG	VF	UNC
	FV	FV	70.00

SPAIN

The Spanish State, forming the greater part of the Iberian Peninsula of southwest Europe, has an area of 195,988 sq. mi. (504,714 sq. km.) and a population of *39.4 million including the Balearic and the Canary Islands. Capital: Madrid. The economy is based on agriculture, industry and tourism. Machinery, fruit, vegetables and chemicals are exported.

It isn't known when man first came to the Iberian peninsula - the Altamira caves off the Cantabrian coast approximately 50 miles west of Santander were fashioned in Palaeolithic times. Spain was a battleground for centuries before it became a united nation, fought for by Phoenicians, Carthaginians, Greeks, Celts, Romans, Vandals, Visigoths and Moors. Ferdinand and Isabella destroyed the last Moorish stronghold in 1492, freeing the national energy and resources for the era of discovery and colonization that would make Spain the most powerful country in Europe during the 16th century. After the destruction of the Spanish Armada, 1588, Spain never again played a major role in European politics. Napoleonic France ruled Spain between 1808 and 1814. The monarchy was restored in 1814 and continued, interrupted by the short-lived republic of 1873–74, until the exile of Alfonso XIII in 1931, when the Second Republic was established.

The monarchy was reconstituted in 1947 under the regency of General Francisco Franco, the king designated to be crowned after Franco's death. Franco died on Nov. 30, 1975. Two days after his passing, Juan Carlos de Borbon, the grandson of Alfonso XIII, was proclaimed King of Spain.

RULERS:
Francisco Franco, 1937-1975
Juan Carlos I, 1975-

MONETARY SYSTEM:
1 Peseta = 100 Centimos 1874-

REPUBLIC

BANCO DE ESPAÑA

1965 (1970; 1971) ISSUE
#150-151 printer: FNMT.

150 100 PESETAS
19.11.1965 (1970). Brown on m/c unpt. G.A. Bécquer at r. ctr. Woman w/parasol and cathedral of Sevilla on back. Wmk: Woman's head.

	VG	VF	UNC
	FV	2.00	6.00

151   1000 PESETAS
19.11.1965 (1971). Green on m/c unpt. S. Isidoro at l. Imaginary figure w/basilica behind on back.

	VG	VF	UNC
	FV	18.00	35.00

1970-71 ISSUE
152 and 153 printer: FNMT.

152   100 PESETAS
17.11.1970 (1974). Brown on lt. orange unpt. M. de Falla at r. and as wmk. Patio scene of the Generalife of Granada on back.

	VG	VF	UNC
	FV	1.00	3.00

153   500 PESETAS
23.7.1971 (1973). Blue-gray, black and m/c. J. Verdaguer at r. and as wmk. View of Mt. Canigó w/village of Vignolas d'Oris on back.

	VG	VF	UNC
	FV	8.00	20.00

1974 COMMEMORATIVE ISSUE
#154, Centennial of the Banco de España's becoming the sole issuing bank, 1874-1974. Printer: FNMT.

154   1000 PESETAS
17.9.1971 (1974). Green. J. Echegaray at r. Bank of Spain in Madrid and commemorative legend on back.

	VG	VF	UNC
	FV	10.00	20.00

1976 ISSUE

155   5000 PESETAS
6.2.1976 (1978). Purple and brown on m/c unpt. Carlos III at r. Museum of Prado on back.

	VG	VF	UNC
	FV	45.00	75.00

1982-87 ISSUE
#156-161 wmk. as portr. Printer: FNMT.

156   200 PESETAS
16.9.1980 (1984). Brown, orange and m/c. Cross at ctr., L. Alas (Clarín) at r. and as wmk. Tree at l. on back.

	VG	VF	UNC
	FV	3.00	6.00

157   500 PESETAS
23.10.1979 (1983). Dk. blue and black on m/c unpt. R. de Castro at r. and as wmk. Villa on back.

	VG	VF	UNC
	FV	5.00	10.00

158   1000 PESETAS
  23.10.1979 (1982). Gray-blue and green on m/c unpt. Tree at ctr., B.
  Perez Galdos at r. and as wmk. Rock formations, mountains and map
  of Canary Islands on back.

VG	VF	UNC
FV	9.00	14.00

159   2000 PESETAS
  22.7.1980 (1983). Deep red, orange and m/c. Rose at ctr., J. R.
  Jimenez at r. and as wmk. Villa de la Rosa at l. on back.

VG	VF	UNC
FV	17.50	30.00

160   5000 PESETAS
  23.10.1979 (1982). Brown, violet and m/c. Fleur-de-lis at ctr., Kg.
  Juan Carlos I at r. and as wmk. Royal Palace on back.

VG	VF	UNC
FV	42.50	62.50

161   10,000 PESETAS
  24.9.1985 (1987). Gray-black on m/c unpt. Arms at ctr., Kg. Juan
  Carlos I at r. Back blue-gray on m/c unpt. Prince of Asturias at l.

VG	VF	UNC
FV	85.00	130.00

1992 ISSUE

162   2000 PESETAS
(163)   24.4.1992. Red-violet and orange on m/c unpt. J. C. Mutis observing
  flower at r. and as wmk. Royal Botanical Garden and title page of
  Mutis' work on back. 2 serial #.

VG	VF	UNC
FV	FV	27.50

1992 (1996) ISSUE
#163-166 w/blurred *BANCO DE ESPAÑA* at r. margin.

163   1000 PESETAS
(162)   12.10.1992. Dk. green, purple and red-brown on m/c unpt. H. Cortes
  at r. F. Pizarro on back and as wmk.

VG	VF	UNC
FV	FV	13.50

164   2000 PESETAS
(166)   24.4.1992. Red-violet and orange on m/c unpt. Like #163 but w/title:
  BANCO DE ESPAÑA added to r. edge. 1 serial #.

	VF	UNC
FV	FV	26.50

165   5000 PESETAS
(164)   12.10.1992. Violet-brown, brown and red-brown on m/c unpt. C.
  Columbus at r. and as wmk. Back vertical; astrolob at lower ctr.

	VF	UNC
FV	FV	57.50

166   10,000 PESETAS
(165)   12.10.1992. Slate blue on m/c unpt. Kg. J. Carlos at r. Casa de
  America in Madrid at lower ctr. Back vertical; A. de Ulloa y de Jorge
  Juan above astronomical navigation diagram and as wmk.

	VF	UNC
FV	FV	120.00

1997 ISSUE

167   20,000 PESETAS

VG	VF	UNC
		Expected New Issue

SRI (SHRI) LANKA

The Democratic Socialist Republic of Sri (Shri) Lanka (formerly
Ceylon), situated in the Indian
Ocean 18 miles (29 km.) southeast of India, has an area of
25,332 sq. mi. (65,610 sq. km.)
and a population of 17.25 million.
Capital: Colombo. The economy
is chiefly agricultural. Tea, coconut products and rubber are
exported.

The earliest known inhabitants
of Ceylon, the Veddahs, were
subjugated by the Sinhalese from
northern India in the 6th century BC. Sinhalese rule was maintained until 1408, after which the
island was controlled by China for 30 years. The Portuguese came to Ceylon in 1505 and maintained control of the coastal area for 150 years. They were supplanted by the Dutch in 1658, who
were in turn supplanted by the British who seized the Dutch colonies in 1796, and made them a
Crown Colony in 1802. In 1815, the British conquered the independent Kingdom of Kandy in the
central part of the island. Constitutional changes in 1931 and 1946 granted the Ceylonese a measure of autonomy and a parliamentary form of government. Ceylon became a self-governing
dominion of the British Commonwealth on February 4, 1948. On May 22, 1972, the Ceylonese
adopted a new constitution which declared Ceylon to be the Republic of Sri Lanka - 'Resplendent
Island'. Shri Lanka is a member of the Commonwealth of Nations. The president is Chief of State.
The prime minister is Head of Government.

RULERS:
Dutch to 1796
British, 1796-1972

MONETARY SYSTEM:
1 Rupee = 100 Cents, ca. 1830-

SRI LANKA

CENTRAL BANK OF CEYLON

1977 ISSUE
#62-63 Sri Lanka arms at r. Wmk: Chinze. Printer: BWC.

62	50 RUPEES	VG	VF	UNC
	26.8.1977. Purple, green and m/c. Back like #60.	2.50	6.00	22.50

63	100 RUPEES	VG	VF	UNC
	26.8.1977. Purple, black and m/c. Back like #61.	4.00	10.00	35.00

1979 ISSUE
#64-69 backs vertical format. Wmk: Chinze.

64	2 RUPEES	VG	VF	UNC
	26.3.1979. Red and m/c. Fish at r. Butterfly and lizard on back.	.30	.75	2.50

65	5 RUPEES	VG	VF	UNC
	26.3.1979. Gray and m/c. Butterfly and lizard at r. Flying squirrel and bird on back.	.50	1.75	5.00

66	10 RUPEES	VG	VF	UNC
	26.3.1979. Green and m/c. Bird in tree at ctr. Flowers and animals on back.	.60	2.00	8.50

67 **20 RUPEES**
26.3.1979. Brown, green and m/c. Bird at ctr., monkey at r. Bird, tree and animals on back.

	VG	VF	UNC
	1.35	2.75	14.50

68 **50 RUPEES**
26.3.1979. Blue, brown and m/c. Butterfly at ctr., bird at r. Lizard and birds on back.

	VG	VF	UNC
	3.50	8.50	30.00

71 **1000 RUPEES**
1.1.1981. Green and m/c. Dam at r. Peacock and mountains on back.

	VG	VF	UNC
	40.00	90.00	150.00

1982 ISSUE
#72-76 backs vertical format. Wmk: Chinze. Printer: BWC.

69 **100 RUPEES**
26.3.1979. Gold, green and m/c. Snakes and tree at ctr., birds at r. Bird in tree, butterfly below on back.

	VG	VF	UNC
	5.00	12.50	55.00

72 **5 RUPEES**
1.1.1982. Lt. red on m/c unpt. Ruins at r. Stone carving of deity and child on back.

	VG	VF	UNC
	FV	.35	3.00

1981 ISSUE
#70-71 backs vertical format. Wmk: Chinze.

73 **10 RUPEES**
1.1.1982; 1.1.1985. Olive-green on m/c unpt. Temple of the Tooth at r. Shrine on back.

	VG	VF	UNC
	FV	.50	5.00

70 **500 RUPEES**
1.1.1981; 1.1.1985. Brown, purple and m/c. Elephant w/rider at r. Abhayagiri Stupa, Anuradhapura temple on hill on back.

	VG	VF	UNC
	15.00	35.00	85.00

74 20 RUPEES
1.1.1982; 1.1.1985. Violet on m/c unpt. Moonstone Anuradhapura at
r. Shrine on back.

VG	VF	UNC
FV	.75	7.00

75 50 RUPEES
1.1.1982. Dk. blue and dk. brown on m/c unpt. Tomb at r. Back dk.
blue and m/c; ruins at ctr.

VG	VF	UNC
FV	3.00	12.50

76 100 RUPEES
1.1.1982. Brown and orange on m/c unpt. Stone carving of lion at
lower r. Parliament bldg. on back.

VG	VF	UNC
FV	3.50	13.50

SRÍ LANKÁ MAHA BÄNKUVA

CENTRAL BANK OF SRI LANKA

1987-89 ISSUE
#77-82 wmk: Chinze.

#77-81 similar to #70, 72-76 but w/old bank name now changed in English from *CEYLON* to *Sri Lanka.* Printer:
BWC.

77 10 RUPEES
1.1.1987; 21.11.1988; 21.2.1989; 5.4.1990. Green and m/c. Similar to
#73 but bank name changed in English text.

VG	VF	UNC
FV	.40	2.50

78 20 RUPEES
1988-90. Purple on m/c unpt. Similar to #74 but bank name changed
in English text.
a. 21.11.1988.
b. 21.2.1989; 5.4.1990.

	VG	VF	UNC
a.	FV	1.50	10.00
b.	FV	.75	3.75

79 50 RUPEES
21.2.1989. Blue and brown on m/c unpt. Similar to #75 but bank
name changed in English text.

VG	VF	UNC
FV	1.75	7.00

80 100 RUPEES
1.1.1987; 1.2.1988; 21.2.1989; 21.2.1989; 5.4.1990. Brown and
orange on m/c unpt. Similar to #76 but bank name changed in English
text.

VG	VF	UNC
FV	2.75	9.00

81 500 RUPEES
1.1.1987; 21.11.1988; 21.2.1989; 5.4.1990. M/c. Similar to #70 but
w/ clearer wmk. area, vertical silver security markings, bird and
borders deeper red brown. Hill and temple in violet on back.

VG	VF	UNC
FV	13.50	35.00

82 1000 RUPEES
1.1.1987; 21.2.1989; 5.4.1990. Deep green on m/c unpt. Victoria dam
at r. Peacock and University of Ruhuna on back.

VG	VF	UNC
FV	25.00	65.00

1991 ISSUE
#83-88 backs vertical format. Wmk: Chinze. Printer: TDLR.
Replacement notes: Serial # prefix *Z/1.*

83 10 RUPEES
1.1.1991; 19.8.1994; 15.11.1995. Deep brown and green on m/c unpt.
Sinhalese Chinze at r. Crane above Presidential Secretariat bldg. in
Colombo, flowers in lower foreground on back.

VG	VF	UNC
FV	.25	1.35

84   20 RUPEES
1.1.1991; 19.8.1994. Purple and red on m/c unpt. Native bird mask at
r. Two youths fishing, sea shells on back.

VG	VF	UNC
FV	.30	2.25

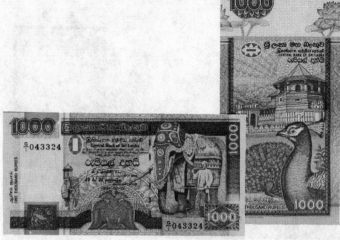

85   50 RUPEES
1.1.1991; 19.8.1994; 15.11.1995. Brown-violet, deep blue and blue-
green on m/c unpt. Male dancer w/local headdress at r. Butterflies
above temple ruins, w/shield and ornamental sword hilt in lower
foreground on back.

VG	VF	UNC
FV	.35	4.00

88   1000 RUPEES
1.1.1991; 1.7.1992; 15.11.1995. Brown, dk. green and purple on m/c
unpt. Chinze at lower l., two-headed bird at bottom ctr. and elephant
w/trainer at r. Peacocks on palace lawn; lotus flowers above and
Octagon of the Temple of Tooth in Kandy on back.

VG	VF	UNC
FV	FV	50.00

1992 ISSUE

89   100 RUPEES
1.7.1992; 15.11.1995. Dk. brown and orange on m/c unpt. Like #86
but back orange on m/c. Printer: TDLR.

VG	VF	UNC
FV	FV	5.50

86   100 RUPEES
1991-92. Dk. brown and orange on m/c unpt. Decorative urn at r. Back
dk. brown and orange on m/c unpt.; tea leaf pickers, 2 parrots on
back.

	VG	VF	UNC
a. W/o dot on value in Tamil at l. 1.1.1991.	FV	FV	10.00
b. W/dot on value in Tamil at l. 1.1.1991; 1.7.1992.	FV	FV	6.00

87   500 RUPEES
1.1.1991. Dk. brown, violet and brown-orange on m/c unpt. Musicians
at r., dancer at l. ctr. Kingfisher above temple and orchids on back.

VG	VF	UNC
FV	FV	32.50

SUDAN

The Democratic Republic of the Sudan, located in northeast Africa on the Red Sea between Egypt and Ethiopia, has an area of 967,500 sq. mi. (2,505,810 sq. km.) and a population of 29.97 million. Capital: Khartoum. Agriculture and livestock raising are the chief occupations. Cotton, gum arabic and peanuts are exported.

The Sudan, site of the powerful Nubian kingdom of Roman times, was a collection of small independent states from the 14th century until 1820-22 when it was conquered and united by Mohammed Ali, Pasha of Egypt. Egyptain forces were driven from the area during the Mahdist revolt, 1881-98, but the Sudan was retaken by Anglo-Egyptian expeditions, 1896-98, and established as an Anglo-Egyptian condominium in 1899. Britain supplied the administrative apparatus and personnel, but the appearance of joint Anglo-Egyptian administration was continued until Jan. 9, 1954, when the first Sudanese self-government parliament was inaugurated. The Sudan achieved independence on Jan. 1, 1956 with the consent of the British and Egyptian governments. On June 30, 1989 Gen. Omar Hassan Ahmad al-Bashir overthrew the civilian government in a military coup. The rebel guerrilla PLA forces are active in the south. Notes of Egypt were in use before 1956.

MONETARY SYSTEM:
1 Ghirsh (Piastre) = 10 Millim (Milliemes)
1 Sudanese Pound = 100 Piastres to 1992
1 Dinar = 10 Old Sudanese Pounds, 1992

REPUBLIC

BANK OF SUDAN

1961-64 ISSUE
#6-10 various date and sign. varieties. Arms (desert camel rider) on back.

6   25 PIASTRES
1964-68. Red on m/c unpt. Soldiers in formation at l.

	VG	VF	UNC
a. 6.3.1964; 25.1.1967.	6.00	15.00	85.00
b. W/o Arabic text al-Khartoum. 7.2.1968.	5.00	12.00	70.00

7   50 PIASTRES
1964-68. Green on m/c unpt. Elephants at l.

	VG	VF	UNC
a. 6.3.1964; 25.1.1967.	15.00	55.00	300.00
b. W/o Arabic text al-Khartoum. 7.2.1968.	12.00	45.00	250.00

8   1 POUND
1961-68. Blue on yellow and m/c unpt. Dam at l.

	VG	VF	UNC
a. 8.4.1961.	8.00	25.00	125.00
b. 2.3.1965; 20.1.1966; 25.1.1967.	6.00	17.50	100.00
c. W/o Arabic text al-Khartoum. 7.2.1968.	5.00	14.00	80.00

9   5 POUNDS
1962-68. Lilac-brown on m/c unpt. Dhow at l.

	VG	VF	UNC
a. 1.7.1962.	20.00	50.00	400.00
b. 2.3.1965; 20.1.1966; 25.1.1967.	10.00	40.00	300.00
c. W/o Arabic text al-Khartoum.7.2.1968.	8.00	37.50	250.00

10   10 POUNDS
1964-68. Gray-black on m/c unpt. Bank of Sudan bldg. at l.

	VG	VF	UNC
a. 6.3.1964; 20.1.1966; 25.1.1967.	20.00	50.00	425.00
b. W/o Arabic text al-Khartoum. 7.2.1968.	16.00	40.00	350.00

1970 ISSUE
#11-15 Bank of Sudan at l. on face. Various date and sign. varieties. Printer: TDLR.

11   25 PIASTRES
1970-80. Red. Textile industry on back.

	VG	VF	UNC
a. Jan. 1970; Jan. 1971; Jan. 1972.	1.50	7.50	25.00
b. 1.4.1973-28.5.1978.	.75	2.50	10.00
c. 2.1.1980.	.50	1.00	4.50

12   50 PIASTRES
1970-80. Green. University of Khartoum on back.

	VG	VF	UNC
a. Jan. 1970; Jan. 1971; Jan. 1972.	3.00	9.00	35.00
b. 1.4.1973-28.5.1978.	1.00	2.50	10.00
c. 2.1.1980.	.75	1.50	7.50

13   1 POUND
1970-80. Blue and m/c. Ancient temple on back.

	VG	VF	UNC
a. Wmk: Rhinoceros head. Jan. 1970; Jan. 1971.	7.00	20.00	85.00
b. Wmk: Arms (secretary bird). Jan. 1972-28.5.1978.	2.50	5.00	15.00
c. 2.1.1980.	2.00	5.00	15.00

14 5 POUNDS
1970-80. Brown, lilac and m/c. Domestic and wild animals on back.

	VG	VF	UNC
a. Wmk: Rhinoceros head. Jan. 1970.	17.50	50.00	185.00
b. Wmk: Arms. Jan. 1971-28.5.1978.	7.00	15.00	75.00
c. 2.1.1980.	7.00	15.00	60.00

15 10 POUNDS
1970-80. Purple, green and m/c. Transportation elements (ship, plane, etc.) on back.

	VG	VF	UNC
a. Wmk: Rhinoceros head. Jan. 1970.	27.50	75.00	300.00
b. Wmk: Arms. Jan. 1 1971-28.5.1978.	7.50	20.00	60.00
c. 2.1.1980.	5.00	15.00	45.00

1981 ISSUE
#16-21 Pres. J. Nimeiri wearing national headdress at l., arms at ctr.
#18-21 wmk: Arms.

16 25 PIASTRES
1.1.1981. Brown and m/c. Kosti bridge on back.

VG	VF	UNC
.40	1.00	2.75

17 50 PIASTRES
1.1.1981. Purple on brown unpt. Bank of Sudan on back.

VG	VF	UNC
.60	1.25	3.75

18 1 POUND
1.1.1981. Blue and m/c. People's Assembly on back.

VG	VF	UNC
1.00	3.50	12.00

19 5 POUNDS
1.1.1981. Green and m/c. Back green, w/Islamic Centre Mosque at Khartoum at r.

VG	VF	UNC
2.00	5.00	12.50

20 10 POUNDS
1.1.1981. Blue, brown and m/c. Kenana sugar factory on back.

VG	VF	UNC
7.50	15.00	75.00

21 20 POUNDS
1.1.1981. Green and m/c. Like #22 but w/o commemorative text.

VG	VF	UNC
10.00	20.00	85.00

1981 COMMEMORATIVE ISSUE
#22, 25th Anniversary of Independence

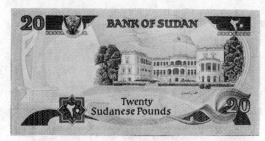

22	**20 POUNDS**	VG	VF	UNC
	1.1.1981. Green and m/c. Map at ctr., commemorative legend in circle at r. around wmk., monument at r. Unity Monument at l., People's Palace at r. on back.	15.00	35.00	90.00

1983-84 ISSUE

#23-29 like previous issue but some in different colors.

23	**25 PIASTRES**	VG	VF	UNC
	1.1.1983. Red-orange on yellow unpt. Like #16.	.25	.50	1.75
24	**50 PIASTRES**			
	1.1.1983. Like #17.	.60	1.25	2.25
25	**1 POUND**			
	1.1.1983. Like #18 but bldg. on back is blue.	.50	1.25	3.00
26	**5 POUNDS**			
	1.1.1983. Like #19.	2.00	5.00	12.50
27	**10 POUNDS**			
	1.1.1983. Purple and red-brown on m/c unpt. Like #20.	4.50	10.00	22.50
28	**20 POUNDS**			
	1.1.1983. Like #21.	7.00	15.00	35.00

29	**50 POUNDS**	VG	VF	UNC
	25.5.1984. Brown-orange and blue on m/c unpt. Pres. Nimeiri at l. Back blue on m/c unpt.; sailing ship at ctr., modern oil tanker at r.	12.50	25.00	60.00

LAW OF 30.6.1985/AH1405

#30-36 outline map of Sudan at ctr. Bank of Sudan at ctr. on back. Wmk: Arms. Sign. title w/2 lines of Arabic text (Acting Governor).

Replacement notes: Serial # prefix Z/...

30	**25 PIASTRES**	VG	VF	UNC
	L.1985. Purple. Camels at l.	.10	.40	2.00

31	**50 PIASTRES**	VG	VF	UNC
	L.1985. Red on lilac and peach unpt. Lyre and drum at l., peanut plant at r.	.15	.50	3.00

32	**1 POUND**	VG	VF	UNC
	L.1985. Green on m/c unpt. Cotton boll at l. Back blue on m/c unpt.	.20	.75	4.00

33	**5 POUNDS**	VG	VF	UNC
	L.1985. Olive and brown on m/c unpt. Cattle at l.	.50	3.00	15.00

34	**10 POUNDS**	VG	VF	UNC
	L.1985. Brown on m/c unpt. City gateway at l.	2.00	6.00	27.50

35	**20 POUNDS**	VG	VF	UNC
	L.1985. Green and purple on m/c unpt. Dhow at l.	10.00	25.00	100.00

36	**50 POUNDS**	VG	VF	UNC
	L.1985. Brown, purple and red-orange on m/c unpt. Columns along pool below National Museum at l., spear at r. Back red.	7.50	22.50	90.00

612 SUDAN

1987-90 ISSUE
#37-43 sign. title in 1 line of Arabic text (Governor). #40-43 wmk: Arms.

			VG	VF	UNC
37	**25 PIASTRES**				
	1987. Like #30.		.05	.15	.35

			VG	VF	UNC
38	**50 PIASTRES**				
	1987. Like #31.		.05	.25	.50

			VG	VF	UNC
39	**1 POUND**				
	1987. Like #32.		.10	.50	1.00

			VG	VF	UNC
40	**5 POUNDS**				
	1987; 1989; 1990. Like #33.		.25	.75	5.00

			VG	VF	UNC
41	**10 POUNDS**				
	1987; 1989; 1990. Like #34.		.50	1.50	7.50

			VG	VF	UNC
42	**20 POUNDS**				
	1987; 1989; 1990. Like #35.		.65	2.00	12.00

			VG	VF	UNC
43	**50 POUNDS**				
	1987; 1989. Like #36.		1.00	3.00	13.50

			VG	VF	UNC
44	**100 POUNDS**				
	1988-90. Brown, purple and deep green on m/c unpt. Bldg. at l., book at r. Bank of Sudan and coin on back. Wmk: Arms.				
	a. 1988.		.40	1.25	4.00
	b. 1989; 1990.		2.00	5.50	22.50

1991/AH1411 ISSUE
#45-50 wmk: Arms.

			VG	VF	UNC
45	**5 POUNDS**				
	1991/AH1411. Similar to #40 but red, orange and violet on m/c unpt. Back red-orange on m/c unpt.		.20	.60	2.75

			VG	VF	UNC
46	**10 POUNDS**				
	1991/AH1411. Similar to #41 but black and deep green on m/c unpt. Back black on m/c unpt.		.30	.90	3.75

47   20 POUNDS

	VG	VF	UNC
1991/AH1411. Similar to #42 but purple and violet on m/c unpt. Back violet on m/c unpt.	.25	.75	4.00

48   50 POUNDS

	VG	VF	UNC
1991/AH1411. Similar to #43 but yellow-orange, brownish black and dk. brown on m/c unpt. Back dk. brown on m/c unpt.	.35	1.00	4.50

49   100 POUNDS

	VG	VF	UNC
1991/AH1411. Similar to #44 but ultramarine and blue-green on m/c unpt. Ultramarine shield at l., lt. blue-green map image at ctr. Shiny lt. green coin design at r. on back (partially engraved).	.60	1.75	7.00

50   100 POUNDS

	VG	VF	UNC
1991/AH1411; 1992/AH1412. Similar to #45 but colors rearranged. Blue-green shield at l., darker details on bldg. and ultramarine map image at ctr. Pink coin design at r. on back. (litho)	.60	1.75	7.00

1992-94 ISSUE
Currency Reform, 1992
1 Dinar = 10 Pounds
#51-55 People's Palace at ctr. or lower r. Wmk: Domed bldg. w/tower.
NOTE: First issues w/fractional serial # prefix, replaced w/local printings w/double letter serial # prefix.

51   5 DINARS

	VG	VF	UNC
1993/AH1413. Dk. brown and red-orange on m/c unpt. Plants including sunflowers on back.	FV	FV	2.75

52   10 DINARS

	VG	VF	UNC
1993/AH1413. Deep red and dk. brown on m/c unpt. Domed bldg. w/tower at l. ctr. on back.	FV	FV	3.50

53   25 DINARS

	VG	VF	UNC
1992/AH1412. Brownish black and green on m/c unpt. Circular design at l. on back.			
a. W/artist's name *DOSOUGI* at lower r.	FV	FV	12.50
b. W/o artist's name.	FV	FV	2.00

54   50 DINARS

	VG	VF	UNC
1992/AH1412. Dk. blue-green, black and purple on m/c unpt. 2 sign varieties.			
a. W/artist's name *DOSOUGI* at lower r. below palace.	FV	FV	20.00
b. W/o artist's name. 2 sign. varieties.	FV	FV	3.50

55   100 DINARS

	VG	VF	UNC
1994/AH1414. Black and deep brown-violet on m/c unpt. Double doorway at ctr. Bldg. at l. ctr. on back.	FV	FV	5.50

56   500 DINARS
199x.   Expected New Issue

57   1000 DINARS
199x.   Expected New Issue

SURINAM

The Republic of Surinam, formerly known as Dutch Guiana, located on the north central coast of South America between Guyana and French Guiana, has an area of 63,037 sq. mi. (163,270 sq. km.) and a population of 404,300. Capital: Paramaribo. The country is rich in minerals and forests, and self-sufficient in rice, the staple food crop. The mining, processing and exporting of bauxite is the principal economic activity.

Lieutenants of Amerigo Vespucci sighted the Guiana coast in 1499. Spanish explorers of the 16th century, disappointed at finding no gold, departed leaving the area to be settled by the British in 1652. The colony prospered and the Netherlands acquired it in 1667 in exchange for the Dutch rights in Nieuw Nederland (state of New York). During the European wars of the 18th and 19th centuries, which were fought in part in the New World, Surinam was occupied by the British from 1799-1814. Surinam became an autonomous part of the Kingdom of the Netherlands on Dec. 15, 1954. Full independence was achieved on Nov. 25, 1975.

RULERS:
Dutch to 1975

MONETARY SYSTEM:
1 Gulden = 1 Florin = 100 Cents

DUTCH INFLUENCE

MUNTBILJETTEN

LAW 8.4.1960
#23-24 various date and sign. varieties. Printer: JEZ.

23	1 GULDEN		VG	VF	UNC
	1961-86. Dk. green w/black text on pale olive-green and brown unpt. Bldg. w/tower and flag at l. Back brown and green.				
	a.	Sign. title: *De Minister van Financien* in facsimile only. 1.8.1961-1.4.1969.	.75	3.00	9.00
	b.	Sign. in facsimile w/printed name below. 1.4.1971.	.50	2.00	6.00
	c.	Similar to b., but name of signer at r. 1.11.1974.	.50	2.00	5.50
	d.	Similar to a., but shorter text, and sign. title centered. 1.11.1974; 25.6.1979.	.40	1.50	7.00
	e.	Similar to d., but sign. title: *De Minister van Financien en Planning*. 1.9.1982; 2.1.1984; 1.12.1984; 1.10.1986.	.15	.50	1.50

24	2 1/2 GULDEN	VG	VF	UNC
	2.1.1961; 2.7.1967. Red-brown. Girl wearing hat at l.	.85	2.50	7.50

24A	2 1/2 GULDEN		VG	VF	UNC
	1973; 1978. Red-brown, lt. blue and m/c. Bird on branch at l. 3 lines of text above sign. title at ctr. Lizard and Afobaka Dam on back. Printer: BWC.				
	a.	Sign. title: *De Minister van Financien*. Printed name below sign. 1.9.1973.	.50	2.25	9.00
	b.	W/o printed name below sign. 1.8.1978.	.20	.65	2.50

24B	2 1/2 GULDEN	VG	VF	UNC
	1.11.1985. Like #24A but 4 lines of text above sign. W/sign. title: *De Minister Financien en Planning* at ctr.	.20	.55	2.25

CENTRALE BANK VAN SURINAME

1963 ISSUE
#30-34 different arms on back. Wmk: Toucan's head. Printer: JEZ.

NOTE: #34 was recently sold in quantity by the Central Bank to the numismatic community. See #39.

30	5 GULDEN	VG	VF	UNC
	1.9.1963. Blue on m/c unpt. Similar to #25. 2 serial # varieties.	.10	.25	.85

31   10 GULDEN
1.9.1963. Orange on m/c unpt. Similar to #26.

	VG	VF	UNC
	.10	.25	1.00

35   5 GULDEN
1.4.1982. Dk. blue on m/c unpt.

	VG	VF	UNC
	.15	.35	1.00

36   10 GULDEN
1.4.1982. Red on m/c unpt.

	VG	VF	UNC
	.15	.40	1.25

32   25 GULDEN
1.9.1963. Green on m/c unpt. Similar to #27.

	VG	VF	UNC
	2.50	7.50	20.00

37   25 GULDEN
1982; 1985. Green on m/c unpt.

	VG	VF	UNC
a. 1.4.1982.	1.00	3.00	10.00
b. 1.11.1985.	.10	.25	.85

33   100 GULDEN
1.9.1963. Purple on m/c unpt. Similar to #28.

	VG	VF	UNC
	8.00	20.00	65.00

38   100 GULDEN
1982; 1985. Purple on m/c unpt.

	VG	VF	UNC
a. 1.4.1982.	5.00	15.00	45.00
b. 1.11.1985.	.30	1.25	3.50

34   1000 GULDEN
1.9.1963. Brown on m/c unpt. Similar to #29.

	VG	VF	UNC
	.15	1.50	5.50

REPUBLIC

CENTRAL BANK VAN SURINAME

1982 ISSUE

#35-39 soldiers and woman at r. Bldg. w/flag on back. Wmk: Toucan's head. Sign. varieties. Printer: JEZ.

NOTE: 1000 new notes of #39 were sold by the Central Bank to the numismatic community for USA $2.00 each.

39   500 GULDEN
1.4.1982. Brown on m/c unpt.

	VG	VF	UNC
	.30	1.25	4.50

1986-88 ISSUE

#40-44 Anton DeKom at l., militia at r., row of bldgs. across bottom. Toucan at l., speaker w/people at r. on back. Wmk: Toucan. Printer: TDLR.

		VG	VF	UNC
40	**5 GULDEN** 1.7.1986; 9.1.1988. Blue on m/c unpt.	FV	1.00	3.25

		VG	VF	UNC
41	**10 GULDEN** 1.7.1986. Orange and red on m/c unpt.	FV	1.25	4.00
42	**25 GULDEN** 1.7.1986. Green on m/c unpt.	FV	2.00	8.00
43	**100 GULDEN** 1.7.1986. Purple on m/c unpt. 2 serial # varieties.	FV	6.00	20.00
44	**250 GULDEN** 9.1.1988. Blue-gray on m/c unpt.	FV	7.50	35.00

		VG	VF	UNC
45	**500 GULDEN** 1.7.1986. Brown on m/c unpt.	FV	15.00	75.00

1991-93 ISSUE

#46-50 Central Bank bldg., Paramaribo at ctr. Toucan at l. ctr. and as wmk., arms at upper r. on back. Printer: TDLR.

		VG	VF	UNC
46	**5 GULDEN** 9.7.1991; 1.6.1995. Deep blue and green on m/c unpt. Log trucks at upper l. Logging at ctr. r. on back.	FV	FV	.10

		VG	VF	UNC
47	**10 GULDEN** 9.7.1991. Red and green on m/c unpt. Bananas at upper l. Banana harvesting at ctr. r. on back.	FV	FV	.20

		VG	VF	UNC
48	**25 GULDEN** 9.7.1991. Green and brown-orange on m/c unpt. Track participants at upper l. Competition swimmer in breaststroke at ctr. r. on back.	FV	FV	.35

		VG	VF	UNC
49	**100 GULDEN** 9.7.1991. Violet and purple on m/c unpt. Factory at upper l. Strip mining at ctr. r. on back.	FV	FV	1.00

		VG	VF	UNC
50	**500 GULDEN** 9.7.1991. Brown and red-orange on m/c unpt. Crude oil pump at upper l. Drilling for crude oil at ctr. r. on back.	FV	FV	3.50

		VG	VF	UNC
51	**1000 GULDEN** 1.7.1993. Black on m/c unpt. Combine at upper l. Combining grain at ctr. r. on back.	FV	FV	6.50

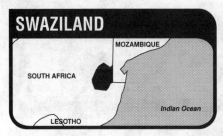

SWAZILAND

The Kingdom of Swaziland, located in southeastern Africa, has an area of 6,704 sq. mi. (17,360 sq. km.) and a population of 681,000. Capital: Mbabane (administrative); Lobamba (legislative). The diversified economy includes mining, agriculture and light industry. Asbestos, iron ore, wood pulp and sugar are exported.

The people of the present Swazi nation established themselves in an area including what is now Swaziland in the early 1800s. The first Swazi contact with the British came early in the reign of the extremely able Swazi leader Mswati when he asked the British for aid against Zulu raids into Swaziland. The British and Transvaal responded by guaranteeing the independence of Swaziland, 1881. South Africa assumed the power of protection and administration in 1894 and Swaziland continued under this administration until the conquest of the Transvaal during the Anglo-Boer War, when administration was transferred to the British government. After World War II, Britain began to prepare Swaziland for independence, which was achieved on Sept. 6, 1968. The kingdom is a member of the Commonwealth of Nations. The king of Swaziland is Chief of State. The prime minister is Head of Government.

RULERS:
British to 1968
Sobhuza II, 1968-82
Queen Ntombi, as regent, 1982-86
King Mswati III, 1986-

MONETARY SYSTEM:
1 Lilangeni = 100 Cents

SIGNATURE VARIETIES

	MINISTER FOR FINANCE	GOVERNOR		MINISTER FOR FINANCE	GOVERNOR
1	*R.P.Steph*	*Hayaela*	5	*B.Dlamini*	*Sajees Nxumalo*
2	*Himelane*	*HBOlimmi*	6	*Bedway*	*Sajees Nxumalo*
3	*Dnalo*	*HBOlimmi*	7	*Al*	*Sajees Nxumalo*
4	*B.Dlamini*	*HBOlimmi*			

KINGDOM

MONETARY AUTHORITY OF SWAZILAND

1974-78 ISSUE

#1-5 Kg. Sobhuza II at l., Parliament House at bottom ctr. r. Sign. 1. Wmk: Shield and spears. Printer: TDLR.

1	1 LILANGENI	VG	VF	UNC
	ND (1974). Red-brown on m/c unpt. Sobhuza's wives dancing on back.	.60	.85	2.50

2	2 EMALANGENI	VG	VF	UNC
	ND (1974). Dk. brown on pink and m/c unpt. Sugar mill on back.	1.00	2.50	5.50
3	5 EMALANGENI			
	ND (1974). Dk. green on yellow-green and m/c unpt. Mantenga Falls and landscape on back.	2.00	6.00	10.00

4	10 EMALANGENI	VG	VF	UNC
	ND (1974). Blue-black on blue and m/c unpt. Asbestos mine on back.	7.50	17.50	45.00

5	20 EMALANGENI	VG	VF	UNC
	ND (1978). Violet and dk. brown on m/c unpt. Agricultural products and cows on back.	15.00	40.00	115.00

CENTRAL BANK OF SWAZILAND

1985 ISSUE

#6 and 7 wmk: Shield and spears.

6	2 EMALANGENI	VG	VF	UNC
	ND (1985). Dk. brown on pink and m/c unpt. Similar to #2 but new issuer's name at top.			
	a. Sign. 2.	1.75	3.75	7.50
	b. Sign. 4.	.75	1.50	3.00

7   5 EMALANGENI

		VG	VF	UNC
ND (1982). Dk. green on yellow-green and m/c unpt. Similar to #3 but new issuer's name at top.				
a. Sign. 2.		2.50	6.00	12.50
b. Sign. 4.		1.75	3.00	6.00

10   10 EMALANGENI

		VG	VF	UNC
ND (1983). Blue-black on blue and m/c unpt. Like #8 but w/o commemorative inscription on face.				
a. Sign. 2.		7.50	12.50	40.00
b. Sign. 3.		FV	7.50	25.00
c. Sign. 4.		FV	4.00	9.00

1981 COMMEMORATIVE ISSUE

#8 and 9, Diamond Jubilee of Kg. Sobhuza II. Wmk: Shield and spears. Sign. 2.

8   10 EMALANGENI

		VG	VF	UNC
1981. Blue-black on blue and m/c unpt. Black commemorative text on wmk. area. Back like #4.		20.00	75.00	225.00

11   20 EMALANGENI

		VG	VF	UNC
ND (1983). Violet and dk. brown on m/c unpt. Like #9 but w/o commemorative inscription on face.				
a. Sign. 3.		FV	15.00	37.50
b. Sign. 4.		FV	8.50	17.50

9   20 EMALANGENI

		VG	VF	UNC
1981. Violet and dk. brown on m/c unpt. Like #8. Back like #5.		15.00	65.00	200.00

1983 ISSUE

#10 and 11 wmk: Shield and spears.

12   20 EMALANGENI

		VG	VF	UNC
ND (1986). Violet and dk. brown on m/c unpt. Kg. Mswati III at l., otherwise like #11. Printer: TDLR. Sign. 4.		5.50	8.50	25.00

1986-88 ISSUES

#13-16 Facing portr. of young Kg. Mswati III at l., arms at lower ctr. Wmk: Shield and spears. Sign. 4. Printer: TDLR

13   2 EMALANGENI

		VG	VF	UNC
ND (1986). Dk. brown on m/c unpt. Wildlife on back.		FV	FV	2.50

	5 EMALANGENI		VG	VF	UNC
14	ND (1986). Dk. green, dk. brown and bright green on m/c unpt. Warriors on back.		FV	FV	4.50

			VG	VF	UNC
15	**10 EMALANGENI** ND (1986). Dk. blue and black on m/c unpt. Hydroelectric plant at Luphohlo and bird on back.		FV	FV	12.50
16	**20 EMALANGENI** ND (1988). Violet, brown and purple on m/c unpt. Cattle and truck on back.		FV	FV	22.50

1989 COMMEMORATIVE ISSUE
#17, 21st Birthday of Kg. Mswati III

			VG	VF	UNC
17	**20 EMALANGENI** 19.4.1989. Like #16, w/silver commemorative text and dates ovpt. on wmk. area.		FV	8.50	18.00

1992 ISSUE
#18-22 similar to #13-16 but w/older portr. of Kg. Mswati III at l. facing half r. Backs like #13-16. Wmk: Shield and spears.

#18-21 similar to #13-16.

	2 EMALANGENI		VG	VF	UNC
18	ND (1992-).				
	a. Sign. 4.		FV	FV	2.00
	b. Sign. 6.		FV	FV	2.00

	5 EMALANGENI		VG	VF	UNC
19	ND (1992-95).				
	a. Sign. 4.		FV	FV	5.00
	b. Sign. 6.		FV	FV	5.00

	10 EMALANGENI		VG	VF	UNC
20	ND (1992-95).				
	a. Sign. 4.		FV	FV	9.00
	b. Sign. 5.		FV	FV	11.00

	20 EMALANGENI		VG	VF	UNC
21	ND (1992-95).				
	a. Sign. 4.		FV	FV	18.00
	b. Sign. 5.		FV	FV	21.50

22	**50 EMALANGENI**	VG	VF	UNC
	ND (1992-). Sign. 4.	FV	FV	40.00

1995 ISSUE

#23-25 similar to #18-20 w/segmented foil over security thread. Sign. 7.
#24 and 25 ascending serial #. Printer: F-CO.

23	**5 EMALENGENI**	VG	VF	UNC
	ND (1995). Similar to #19 but natives on back in dk. brown. Printer: H&S.	FV	FV	5.00
24	**10 EMALENGENI**			
	ND (1995).	FV	FV	9.00

25	**20 EMALENGENI**			
	ND (1995).	FV	FV	18.00

COLLECTOR SERIES

CENTRAL BANK OF SWAZILAND

1974 ISSUE

CS1	**ND (1974). 1-20 EMALANGENI**	ISSUE PRICE	MKT. VALUE
	#1-5 w/ovpt: *SPECIMEN* and Maltese cross prefix serial #.	14.00	23.50

SWEDEN

The Kingdom of Sweden, a limited constitutional monarchy located in northern Europe between Norway and Finland, has an area of 173,732 sq. mi. (449,960 sq. km.) and a population of 8.6 million. Capital: Stockholm. Mining, lumbering and a specialized machine industry dominate the economy. Machinery, paper, iron and steel, motor vehicles and wood pulp are exported.

Sweden was founded as a Christian stronghold by Olaf Skottkonung late in the 10th century. After conquering Finland late in the 13th century, Sweden, together with Norway, came under the rule of Denmark, 1397-1523, in an association known as the Union of Kalmar. Modern Sweden had its beginning in 1523 when Gustavus Vasa drove the Danes out of Sweden and was himself chosen king. Under Gustavus Adolphus II and Charles XII, Sweden was one of the great powers of the 17th century Europe - until Charles invaded Russia, 1708, and was defeated at the Battle of Pultowa in June 1709. Early in the 18th century, a coalition of Russia, Poland and Denmark took away Sweden's Baltic empire and in 1809 Sweden was forced to cede Finland to Russia. Norway was ceded to Sweden by the Treaty of Kiel in January 1814. The Norwegians resisted for a time but later signed the Act of Union at the Convention of Moss in August 1814. The Union was dissolved in 1905 and Norway became independent. A new constitution which took effect on Jan. 1, 1975, restricts the function of the king to a ceremonial role.

* * * This section has been renumbered. * * *

RULERS:
   Gustaf VI Adolf, 1950-1973
   Carl XVI Gustaf, 1973-

MONETARY SYSTEM:
   1 Korona = 100 Öre (= 1 Riksdaler Riksmynt), 1873

KINGDOM

SW(V)ERIGES RIKSBANK

1952-55 ISSUE
#42 and 43 replacement notes: Serial # star suffix.

		VG	VF	UNC
42 (12)	**5 KRONOR** 1954-61. Dk. brown on red and blue unpt. Beige paper. Portr. Kg. Gustaf VI Adolf at r. ctr. and as wmk. Svea standing w/shield on back.			
	a. W/2 safety letters at lower l. 1954-56.	1.00	3.00	6.00
	b. W/o safety letters. 1959-61.	1.00	3.00	6.00
	c. W/star. 1956; 1959-61.	10.00	40.00	150.00

		VG	VF	UNC
43 (22)	**10 KRONOR** 1953-62. Gray-blue. Portr. G. Vasa at l. and as wmk. Blue date and serial #.			
	a. 1953-54.	1.65	2.25	6.00
	b. 1955-56.	1.65	2.25	6.00
	c. 1957-59.	1.65	2.25	6.00
	d. 1960.	2.00	4.00	10.00
	e. 1962.	1.65	2.25	6.00
	f. W/star. 1956-60; 1962.	15.00	40.00	160.00

		VG	VF	UNC
46 (53)	**1000 KRONOR** 1952-73. Brown and m/c. Svea standing (modelled by Greta Hoffstrom). Kg. Gustav V on back and as wmk.			
	a. Blue and red safety fibers. 1952.	165.00	250.00	500.00
	b. 1957.	165.00	250.00	500.00
	c. 1962.	165.00	250.00	450.00
	d. 1965.	165.00	250.00	450.00
	e. One vertical filament. 1971.	165.00	200.00	400.00
	f. 1973.	165.00	200.00	400.00

1958; 1959 ISSUE
#47 and 48 replacement notes: Serial # star suffix.

		VG	VF	UNC
47 (33)	**50 KRONOR** 1959-62. Like #44. Second sign. at l. Sm. serial #.			
	a. 1959-62.	10.00	20.00	60.00
	b. W/star. 1959-62.	20.00	50.00	120.00
48 (43)	**100 KRONOR** 1959-63. Like #45. Second sign. at l. Sm. date and serial #.			
	a. 1959-63.	17.50	30.00	60.00
	b. W/star. 1959-63.	20.00	60.00	120.00

1962 ISSUE

		VG	VF	UNC
50 (13)	**5 KRONOR** 1962-63. Dk. brown. Like #42 but wmk: E. Tegner. Paper w/security thread.			
	a. 1962-63.	1.00	2.00	4.00
	b. W/star. 1962-63.	5.00	15.00	40.00

1963-76 ISSUE

		VG	VF	UNC
51 (14)	**5 KRONOR** 1965-81. Violet, green and orange. G. Vasa at r. Back blue and reddish brown. Abstract design of rooster crowing. Wmk: Square w/5 repeated.			
	a. W/year in dk. red letter press. 1965-69.	FV	1.25	3.50
	b. W/year in deep red offset. 1970.	FV	FV	3.00
	c. As a. 1972-74; 1976-77.	FV	FV	2.50
	d. W/year in pale red offset. 1977-79; 1981.	FV	FV	2.25
	e. W/star.	2.00	4.00	12.00

52 (23)	**10 KRONOR**	VG	VF	UNC
	1963-90. Dk. green blue and red. Arms at ctr., Kg. Gustaf Adolf at r. Norhtern lights and snowflakes on back. Wmk: A. Strindberg (repeated).			
	a. W/year in dk. red letter press. 1963.	FV	FV	6.50
	b. As a. 1966; 1968.	FV	FV	5.50
	c. As a. 1971-72; 1975.	FV	FV	4.50
	d. W/year in pale red offset. Engraved sign. 1976-77; 1979; 1983; 1985.	FV	FV	4.00
	e. As d. but w/offset sign. 1980-81; 1983-84; 1987-90.	FV	FV	3.50
	f. W/star.	5.50	16.50	32.50

53 (34)	**50 KRONOR**	VG	VF	UNC
	1965-90. Blue, green and brown. Beige paper. Kg. Gustaf III at r. C. von Linné (Linnaeus) on back Wmk: Anna Maria Lenngren.			
	a. Sm. wmk. 1965; 1967; 1970.	FV	10.00	22.50
	b. Lg. wmk. w/year in dk. red letter press. 1974; 1976.	FV	FV	20.00
	c. Lg. wmk. as b. w/year in red-brown offset. 1978-79; 1981.	FV	FV	18.50
	d. As c. Black serial #. 1982; 1984; 1986; 1989-90.	FV	FV	17.50
	e. W/star.	8.50	16.50	32.50

54 (44)	**100 KRONOR**	VG	VF	UNC
	1965-85. Red-brown and blue on lt. blue paper. Kg. Gustav II Adolf at r. Royal Man-o-War *Vasa* and wood carvings on back. Wmk: A. Oxenstierna.			
	a. Sm. wmk. 22mm. 1965; 1968; 1970.	FV	20.00	35.00
	b. Lg. wmk. 27mm. w/year in dk. blue letter press. 1971-72; 1974; 1976.	FV	FV	32.50
	c. Lg. wmk. as b. W/year in blue-green offset. 1978; 1980-83; 1985.	FV	FV	30.00
	d. W/star.	20.00	30.00	50.00

55 (54)	**1000 KRONOR**	VG	VF	UNC
	1976-88. Red-brown on green and violet unpt. Carl XIV Johan at r. Bessemer steel process on back. Wmk: J. Berzelius.			
	a. 1976-78.	FV	FV	235.00
	b. 1980; 1981; 1983-86; 1988.	FV	FV	210.00
	c. W/star.	FV	250.00	400.00

1968 COMMEMORATIVE ISSUE

56 (24)	**10 KRONOR**	VG	VF	UNC
	1968. Blue violet and m/c. Svea standing w/ornaments at r. Back violet-brown; old Riksbank bldg. at ctr. Wmk: Crowned monogram Kg. Charles XI.			
	a. Issued note.	FV	2.00	5.00
	b. In banquet program folder "SVERIGES RIGSBANK/1668-1968."	—	—	65.00

1985-89 REGULAR ISSUES
#57-60 replacement notes: Serial # star suffix.

57	**100 KRONOR**	VG	VF	UNC
	(198)6-(198)8; (199)2. Blue-green and brown-violet on m/c unpt. C. von Linnä (Linnaeus) at r. and as wmk., plants at l. ctr. Bee polinating flowers at ctr. on back.			
	a. Issued note.	FV	FV	26.50
	b. W/star.	FV	25.00	40.00

58	**500 KRONOR**	VG	VF	UNC
	(198)5-(198)6. Gray-blue and red-brown. Kg. Carl XI at r. and as wmk. C. Polhem seated on back.			
	a. (198)5.	FV	120.00	210.00
	b. (198)6.	FV	120.00	170.00
	c. W/star. (198)5.	FV	150.00	300.00

59 **500 KRONOR**
(198)9; (199)1; 2; 4; 5. Red and m/c. Similar to #58 but w/o white margin on face, also other slight changes.

		VG	VF	UNC
a.	Issued note.	FV	FV	110.00
b.	W/star. (198)9.	FV	120.00	150.00

60 **1000 KRONOR**
(198)9-(199)2. Brownish black on m/c unpt. Kg G. Vasa at r. and as wmk. Medieval harvest and threshing scene on back.

		VG	VF	UNC
a.	Issued note.	FV	FV	200.00
b.	W/star. (198)9.	FV	220.00	250.00

1991; 1996 ISSUE
#63 *Deleted.* See #57.
#64 *Deleted.* See #59.
#65 *Deleted.* See #60.

61 **20 KRONOR**
(199)1-2; (199)4-5. Deep purple on m/c unpt. Horse-drawn carriage at lower ctr., Selma Lagerlöf at r. and as wmk. Story scene w/small lad riding a goose in flight on back.

		VG	VF	UNC
a.	Issued note.	FV	FV	5.50
b.	W/star. (199)1.	FV	7.00	10.00

62 **50 KRONOR**
(199)6. Dk. brown on m/c unpt. J. Lind at ctr. and as wmk. (repeated), music scores at l., stage at r. Violin, abstract musical design on back.
FV FV 13.50

SWITZERLAND

The Swiss Confederation, located in central Europe north of Italy and south of Germany, has an area of 15,941 sq. mi. (41,290 sq. km.) and a population of 6.9 million. Capital: Bern. The economy centers about a well developed manufacturing industry. Machinery, chemicals, watches and clocks, and textiles are exported.

Switzerland, the habitat of lake dwellers in prehistoric times, was peopled by the Celtic Helvetians when Julius Caesar made it a part of the Roman Empire in 58 BC. After the decline of Rome, Switzerland was invaded by Teutonic tribes, who established small temporal holdings which, in the Middle Ages, became a federation of fiefs of the Holy Roman Empire. As a nation, Switzerland originated in 1291 when the districts of Nidwalden, Schwyz and Uri united to defeat Austria and attain independence as the Swiss Confederation. After acquiring new cantons in the 14th century, Switzerland was made independent from the Holy Roman Empire by the 1648 Treaty of Westphalia. The revolutionary armies of Napoleonic France occupied Switzerland and set up the Helvetian Republic, 1798-1803. After the fall of Napoleon, the Congress of Vienna, 1815, recognized the independence of Switzerland and guaranteed its neutrality. The Swiss Constitutions of 1848 and 1874 established a union modeled upon that of the United States.

MONETARY SYSTEM:
1 Franc (Franken) = 10 Batzen = 100 Centimes (Rappen)

CONFEDERATION

SCHWEIZERISCHE NATIONALBANK

SWISS NATIONAL BANK

The Presidents of the Bank Council Der Präsident des Bankrates Le Président du Conseil		The Chief Cashiers Der Hauptkassier Le caissier principal	
Dr. Alfred Müller 1947-59	*(signature)*	Otto Kunz 1954-66	*(signature)*
Dr. Brenno Galli 1959-78	*(signature)*	Rudolf Aebersold 1966-1981	*(signature)*
Dr. Edmund Wyss 1978-86	*(signature)*		
Prof. Dr. François Schaller 1986-89	*(signature)*		
Peter Gerber 1989-93	*(signature)*		
Dr. Jakob Schönenberger 1993-	*(signature)*		

The Members of the Board of Directors Ein Mitglied des Direktoriums Un membre de la direction générale		Dr. Dr. h. c. Fritz Leutwiler 1968-84	*(signature)*
Dr. h. c. Paul Rossy 1937-55	*(signature)*	Prof. Dr. Dr. h. c. Leo Schürmann 1974-80	*(signature)*
Prof. Dr. Paul Keller 1947-56	*(signature)*	Dr. h. c. Pierre Languetin 1976-88	*(signature)*
Dr. Walter Schwegler 1954-66	*(signature)*	Dr. Markus Lusser 1981-96	*(signature)*
Dr. Riccardo Motta 1955-66	*(signature)*	Dr. Hans Meyer 1985-	*(signature)*
Dr. Max Iklé 1956-68	*(signature)*	Jean Zwahlen 1988-96	*(signature)*
Alexandre Hay 1966-75	*(signature)*	Dr. Jean-Pierre Roth 1996-	no notes with Mr Roth's signature have appeared so far
Dr. Dr. h. c. Edwin Stopper 1966-74	*(signature)*	Prof. Dr. Bruno Gehrig 1996-	no notes with Mr Gehrig's signature have appeared so far

1954-57 ISSUE
#174-175 printer: OFZ.

174	10 FRANKEN	VG	VF	UNC
	1955-77. Red-brown and purple. Gottfried Keller at r. Carnation flower across back.			
	a. 25.8.1955; 20.10.1955.	10.00	18.00	35.00
	b. 29.11.1956; 18.12.1958; 23.12.1959.	FV	FV	25.00
	c. 22.12.1960-15.1.1969.	FV	FV	17.50
	d. 5.1.1970-6.1.1977.	FV	FV	12.50

175	20 FRANKEN	VG	VF	UNC
	1954-76. Blue and m/c. Gen. G. H. Dufour at r. Silver Thistle at l. ctr. on back.			
	a. 1.7.1954.	15.00	32.50	85.00
	b. 7.7.1955; 20.10.1955; 5.7.1956; 4.10.1957	FV	25.00	60.00
	c. 18.12.1958; 23.12.1959.	FV	17.50	32.50
	d. 22.12.1960-15.1.1969.	FV	FV	30.00
	e. 5.1.1970-9.4.1976.	FV	FV	27.50

176	50 FRANKEN	VG	VF	UNC
	7.7.1955; 4.10.1957; 18.12.1958. Green and red on m/c unpt. Girl at r. Apple harvesting scene on back (symbolizing fertility). Printer: W&S.			
	a. 7.7.1955.	FV	60.00	125.00
	b. 4.10.1957; 18.12.1958.	FV	50.00	85.00
176A	50 FRANKEN			
	4.5.1961-7.2.1974. Like #176 but printer: TDLR.			
	a. 4.5.1961-15.1.1969.	FV	FV	75.00
	b. 5.1.1970-7.2.1974.	FV	FV	60.00

177	100 FRANKEN	VG	VF	UNC
	1956-73. Blue and brown on m/c unpt. Boy's head at r. St. Martin sharing his cape on back. Printer: TDLR.			
	a. 25.10.1956.	FV	90.00	200.00
	b. 1.10.1957; 18.12.1958.	FV	80.00	165.00
	c. 21.12.1961-15.1.1969.	FV	FV	150.00
	d. 5.1.1970-7.3.1973.	FV	FV	125.00

178	500 FRANKEN	VG	VF	UNC
	31.1.1957; 4.10.1957; 18.12.1958. Brown-orange and olive m/c unpt. Woman looking in mirror at r. Elders w/4 girls bathing at ctr. r. on back (Fountain of Youth). Printer: W&S.	FV	450.00	750.00
178A	500 FRANKEN			
	21.12.1961-7.2.1974. Like #176 but printer: TDLR.			
	a. 21.12.1961-15.1.1969.	FV	525.00	665.00
	b. 5.1.1970-7.2.1974.	FV	FV	575.00

182	50 FRANKEN		VG	VF	UNC
	(19)78; 80; 81; 83; 85; 87; 88. Green and m/c. K. Gessner at r. Eagle owl, *Primula auricu-la* plant and stars on back.				
	a. 1978.		FV	FV	65.00
	b. 1979-81.		FV	FV	57.50
	c. 1983; 1985.		FV	FV	55.00
	d. 1987; 1988.		FV	FV	52.50

179	1000 FRANKEN		VG	VF	UNC
	1954-74. Purple and blue on m/c unpt. Female head at r. Allegorical scene "dance macabre" on back.				
	a. 30.9.1954.		FV	900.00	1500.
	b. 4.10.1957; 18.12.1958; 22.12.1960.		FV	850.00	1250.
	c. 21.12.1961-1.1.1967.		FV	FV	1175.
	d. 5.1.1970-7.2.1974.		FV	FV	1100.

1976-79 ISSUE

#180-185 series of notes printed in 4 languages - the traditional German, French and Italian plus Romansch; (Rhaeto - Romanisch), the language of the mountainous areas of Graubunden Canton. Wmk. as portr. Sign. varieties. The first 2 numerals before the serial # prefix letter are date (year) indicators. Printer: OFZ.

180	10 FRANKEN		VG	VF	UNC
	(19)79; 80; 81; 82; 83; 86; 87; 90. Orange-brown and m/c. L. Euler at r. Water turbine, light rays through lenses and Solar System on back.				
	a. 1979-81.		FV	FV	16.50
	b. 1982; 1983; 1986.		FV	FV	13.50
	c. 1987.		FV	FV	12.50
	d. Sign. 62. 1990.		FV	FV	15.00
	e. Sign. 61; 63; 64. 1990; 1991.		FV	FV	14.50

183	100 FRANKEN		VG	VF	UNC
	(19)75; 77; 80; 81; 82; 83; 84; 86; 88; 89; 91; 92; 93. Blue and m/c. F. Borromini at r. Bldg. w/towers on back. Baroque architectural drawing and view of S. Ivo alla Sapienza.				
	a. Sign. 49. 1975.		FV	FV	135.00
	b. 1975.		FV	FV	110.00
	c. 1977; 1980.		FV	FV	105.00
	d. 1981-84.		FV	FV	97.50
	e. 1986; 1988; 1989.		FV	FV	95.00
	f. 1991-93.		FV	FV	93.50

181	20 FRANKEN		VG	VF	UNC
	(19)78; 80; 81; 82; 83; 86; 87; 89; 90; 92. Blue and m/c. H-B. de Saussure at r. Fossel and early mountain expedition team hiking on back.				
	a. 1978; 1980.		FV	FV	28.00
	b. 1981-83.		FV	FV	25.00
	c. 1986; 1987.		FV	FV	23.50
	d. 1989; 1990; 1992.		FV	FV	22.50

184	500 FRANKEN		VG	VF	UNC
	(19)76; 86; 92. Brown and m/c. A. von Haller at r. Anatomical muscles of the back, schematic blood circulation and a purple orchid flower.				
	a. 1976.		FV	FV	450.00
	b. 1986.		FV	FV	440.00
	c. 1992.		FV	FV	435.00

185	1000 FRANKEN	VG	VF	UNC
	(19)77; 80; 84; 87; 88; 93. Violet and m/c. A. Forel at r. Ants and ant hill on back.			
a.	1977.	FV	FV	865.00
b.	1980; 1984.	FV	FV	850.00
c.	1987; 1988.	FV	FV	845.00
d.	1993.	FV	FV	840.00

188	50 FRANKEN	VG	VF	UNC
	(19)94. Deep olive-green and purple on m/c unpt. S. Taeuber-Arp at upper l. and bottom and as wmk. Examples of her abstract art works on back.	FV	FV	50.00
189	100 FRANKEN			
	(1997). Blue. A. Giacometti. Artist A. Giacometti.			Expected New Issue
190	200 FRANKEN			
	(1997). Brown. Author C. F. Ramuz.			Expected New Issue
191	1000 FRANKEN			
	(1998). Purple. Art Historian J. Burckhardt.			Expected New Issue

1994-98 ISSUE

#186-191 reduced size. Excessive security features added.

186	10 FRANKEN	VG	VF	UNC
	(1997). Orange on m/c unpt. Architect Le Corbusier, (aka. C. E. Jeanneret-Gris).			Expected New Issue

187	20 FRANKEN	VG	VF	UNC
	(19)94. Red and green on m/c unpt. A. Honegger at bottom ctr. Music score, steam locomotive wheel, trumpet valves on back.	FV	FV	21.50

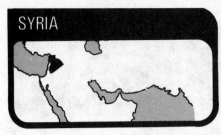

SYRIA

The Syrian Arab Republic, located in the Near East at the eastern end of the Mediterranean Sea, has an area of 71,498 sq. mi. (185,180 sq. km.) and a population of 12.6 million. Capital: Greater Damascus. Agriculture and animal breeding are the chief industries. Cotton, crude oil and livestock are exported.

Ancient Syria, a land bridge connecting Europe, Africa and Asia, has spent much of its history in thrall to the conqueror's whim. Its subjection by Egypt about 1500 BC was followed by successive conquests by the Hebrews, Phoenicians, Babylonians, Assyrians, Persians, Macedonians, Romans, Byzantines and finally, in 636 AD, by the Moslems. The Arabs made Damascus, one of the oldest continuously inhabited cities of the world, the trade center and capital of an empire stretching from India to Spain. In 1517, following the total destruction of Damascus by the Mongols of Tamerlane, Syria fell to the Ottoman Turks and remained a Turkish province until World War I. The League of Nations gave France a mandate to the Levant states of Syria and Lebanon in 1920. In 1930, following a series of uprisings, France recognized Syria as an independent republic, but still subject to the mandate. Lebanon became fully independent on Nov. 22, 1943, and Syria on Jan. 1, 1944.

On Feb. 1, 1958, Egypt and Syria formed the United Arab Republic. Yemen joined on March 8 in an association known as the United Arab States. Syria withdrew from the United Arab Republic on Sept. 29, 1961, and on Dec. 26 Egypt dissolved its ties with Yemen in the United Arab States.

RULERS:
French, 1920-1944

MONETARY SYSTEM:
1 Pound (Livre) = 100 Piastres

REPUBLIC

BANQUE CENTRALE DE SYRIE

CENTRAL BANK OF SYRIA

1958 ISSUE

#86-92 bank name in English on back.

#86-88 wmk: Arabian horse's head. Printer: The Pakistan Security Printing Corporation, Ltd., Karachi (w/o imprint).

#89-92 wmk: Arabian horse's head. Printer: JEZ.

86	**1 POUND**	VG	VF	UNC
	1958. Brown on m/c unpt. Worker at r. Water wheel of Hama on back.			
	a. Issued note.	1.50	5.00	20.00
	s. Specimen.	—	—	25.00
87	**5 POUNDS**			
	1958. Green on m/c unpt. Like #86. Citadel of Aleppo on back.			
	a. Issued note.	3.00	15.00	65.00
	s. Specimen.	—	—	45.00

88	**10 POUNDS**	VG	VF	UNC
	1958. Purple on m/c unpt. Like #86. Courtyard of Omayad Mosque on back.			
	a. Issued note.	5.00	25.00	100.00
	s. Specimen.	—	—	90.00

89	**25 POUNDS**	VG	VF	UNC
	1958. Blue on m/c unpt. Girl w/ basket at r. Interior view of El-Azm Palace in Damascus on back.			
	a. Issued note.	12.50	65.00	200.00
	s. Specimen.	—	—	165.00
90	**50 POUNDS**			
	1958. Red and brown on m/c unpt. Like #89. Mosque of Sultan Selim on back.			
	a. Issued note.	17.50	75.00	225.00
	s. Specimen.	—	—	200.00
91	**100 POUNDS**			
	1958;1962 Olive on m/c unpt. Like #89. Old ruins of Palmyra on back.			
	a. 1958.	25.00	125.00	350.00
	b. 1962.	15.00	75.00	200.00
	s. Specimen.	—	—	225.00
92	**500 POUNDS**			
	1958. Brown and purple on m/c unpt. Motifs from ruins of Kingdom of Ugarit, head at r. Ancient religious wheel and cuneiform clay tablet on back.			
	a. Issued note.	100.00	400.00	—
	s. Specimen.	—	—	500.00

1963-66 ISSUE

#93-98 wmk: Arabian horse's head. W/o imprint.

93	**1 POUND**	VG	VF	UNC
	1963-82. Brown on m/c unpt. Like #86.			
	a. W/o security thread. 1963.	1.00	3.00	10.00
	b. 1967.	.60	2.00	6.00
	c. 1973.	.25	.75	2.00
	d. Security thread w/ *Central Bank of Syria* in sm. letters. 1978; 1982.	.15	.45	2.00
94	**5 POUNDS**			
	1963-73. Green on m/c unpt. Like #87.			
	a. 1963.	2.50	10.00	40.00
	b. 1967.	1.75	6.00	30.00
	c. 1970.	1.00	4.00	25.00
	d. 1973.	.50	2.50	12.50
95	**10 POUNDS**			
	1965-73. Purple on m/c unpt. Like #88.			
	a. 1965.	3.00	8.50	50.00
	b. 1968.	2.00	6.00	40.00
	c. 1973.	1.00	3.50	20.00

96	**25 POUNDS**	VG	VF	UNC
	1966-73. Blue on m/c unpt. Worker at the loom. Ancient amphitheater on back.			
	a. 1966.	6.00	27.50	140.00
	b. 1970.	4.00	20.00	110.00
	c. 1973.	3.00	17.50	85.00

97	**50 POUNDS**	VG	VF	UNC
	1966-73. Brown and olive on m/c unpt. Arab w/agricultural machine. Fortress on back.			
	a. 1966; 1970.	10.00	30.00	150.00
	b. 1973.	5.00	25.00	135.00

98	**100 POUNDS**	VG	VF	UNC
	1966-74. Green and blue on m/c unpt. Port installation at l. Back purple; dam at ctr.			
	a. 1966; 1968.	15.00	55.00	300.00
	b. 1971.	12.50	40.00	200.00
	c. 1974.	10.00	30.00	150.00

1976-77 ISSUE

#99-105 wmk: Arabian horse's head. Shades vary between early and late printings.

99	**1 POUND**	VG	VF	UNC
	1977. Orange on m/c unpt. Lg. bldg. at ctr., craftsman at r. Back red-brown; cutting wheat at ctr.	1.00	5.00	22.50

100	**5 POUNDS**	VG	VF	UNC
	1977-91. Dk. green on m/c unpt. Ancient ruins and statue of female warrior at r. Cotton picking and spinning frame on back.			
	a. Security thread. 1977.	.75	2.50	7.50
	b. Security thread. W/Central Bank of Syria in sm. letters. 1978; 1982.	FV	FV	2.00
	c. 1988; 1991.	FV	FV	1.00

101	**10 POUNDS**	VG	VF	UNC
	1977-82. Purple and violet on m/c unpt. Palace courtyard at ctr., dancing woman at r. Water treatment plant on back.			
	a. Like #100a. 1977.	1.50	4.00	10.00
	b. Like #100b. 1978; 1982.	FV	FV	2.50
	c. 1988;1991.	FV	FV	1.50

102	**25 POUNDS**	VG	VF	UNC
	1977-91. Dk. blue and dk. green on m/c unpt. Fortress at ctr., old Sultan at r. Central Bank bldg. on back.			
	a. Llke #100a. 1977.	3.00	8.00	20.00
	b. Like #100b. 1978; 1982.	FV	.85	4.00
	c. 1988; 1991.	FV	FV	2.50

103	**50 POUNDS**	**VG**	**VF**	**UNC**

1977-82. Brown, black and green on m/c unpt. Dam at ctr., ancient statue at r. Fortress at Aleppo on back.

		VG	VF	UNC
a.	Like #100a. 1977.	4.50	10.00	25.00
b.	Like #100b. 1978; 1982.	FV	3.00	12.00
c.	1988.	FV	FV	4.00
d.	1991.	FV	FV	9.50

104	**100 POUNDS**	**VG**	**VF**	**UNC**

1977-82. Dk. blue and dk. green on dk. brown on m/c unpt. Ancient ruins at ctr., archaic bust at r. Grain silos at Lattakia on back.

		VG	VF	UNC
a.	Like #100a. 1977.	5.00	15.00	50.00
b.	Like #100b. 1978.	FV	6.50	25.00
c.	1982.	FV	FV	12.50
d.	1990.	FV	FV	7.50

105	**500 POUNDS**	**VG**	**VF**	**UNC**

1976-90. Dk. violet-brown and brown on m/c unpt. Motifs from ruins of Kingdom of Ugarit, head at r. Ancient religious wheel and cuneiform clay tablet on back.

		VG	VF	UNC
a.	1976.	12.50	15.00	60.00
b.	1979.	37.50	50.00	180.00
c.	1982.	FV	FV	50.00
d.	1986.	FV	FV	40.00
e.	1990.	FV	FV	30.00

TAHITI

Tahiti, the largest island of the central South Pacific French overseas territory of French Polynesia, has an area of 402 sq. mi. (1,042 sq. km.) and a population of 79,500. Papeete on the northwest coast is the capital and administrative center of French Polynesia. Copra, sugar cane, vanilla and coffee are exported. Tourism is an important industry. MCapt. Samuel Wallis of the British Navy discovered Tahiti in 1768 and named it King George III Island. Louis-Antoine de Bougainville arrived in the following year and claimed it for France. Subsequent English visits were by James Cook in 1769 and William Bligh in the HMS "Bounty" in 1788.

Members of the Protestant London Missionary Society established the first European settlement in 1797, and with the aid of the local Pomare family gained control of the entire island and established a "missionary kingdom" with a scriptural code of law. Nevertheless, Tahiti was subsequently declared a French protectorate (1842) and a colony (1880), and since 1958 is part of the overseas territory of French Polynesia.

* * * This section has been partially renumbered. * * *

RULERS:
French

MONETARY SYSTEM:
1 Franc = 100 Centimes

FRENCH INFLUENCE
BANQUE DE L'INDOCHINE
PAPEETE BRANCH
1939-40 ND ISSUE

14 (16)	**100 FRANCS**	**GOOD**	**FINE**	**XF**

ND (1939-65). Brown and m/c. woman wearing wreath and holding sm. figure of Athena at ctr. Angkor statue on back.

		GOOD	FINE	XF
a.	Sign. M. Borduge and P. Baudouin w/titles: *LE PRÉSIDENT* and *LE ADMINISTRATEUR DIRECTEUR GÉNÉRAL*.	6.00	20.00	60.00
b.	Sign. titles: *LE PRÉSIDENT* and *LE ADMINISTRATEUR DIRECTEUR GÉNÉRAL*.	5.00	17.50	50.00
c.	Sign. titles: *LE PRÉSIDENT* and *LE VICE-PRÉSIDENT DIRECTEUR GÉNÉRAL*.	4.00	15.00	35.00
d.	Sign. titles: *LE PRÉSIDENT* and *LE DIRECTEUR GÉNÉRAL*.	3.00	12.50	27.50

1951 ND ISSUE

21 (15)	**20 FRANCS**	**VG**	**VF**	**UNC**

ND (1951-63). M/c. Youth at l., flute player at r. Fruit at l., woman at r. on back. Wmk: Man w/hat.

		VG	VF	UNC
a.	Sign. titles: *LE PRÉSIDENT* and *LE DIRECTEUR GAL.* (1951).	3.50	9.00	35.00
b.	Sign. titles: *LE PRÉSIDENT* and *LE VICE-PRÉSIDENT DIRECTEUR GÉNÉRAL* (1954-1958).	1.50	6.00	20.00
c.	Sign. titles: *LE PRÉSIDENT* and *LE DIRECTEUR GÉNÉRAL*. (1963).	1.25	5.00	15.00

1963 ND PROVISIONAL ISSUE

22A	100 FRANCS	GOOD	FINE	XF
(17)	ND (1963). Brown and m/c. Red ovpt: *PAPEETE* on New Caledonia #27d.	35.00	120.00	260.00

INSTITUT D'EMISSION D'OUTRE-MER

PAPEETE BRANCH

1969-92 ND ISSUES

28	5000 FRANCS	VG	VF	UNC
	ND (1969). M/c. Bougainville at l., sailing ship at ctr. 4 sign. varieties.	FV	60.00	100.00

23	100 FRANCS	VG	VF	UNC
	ND (1969). Brown and m/c. Girl wearing wreath holding guitar at r., w/o *REPUBLIQUE FRANCAISE* near bottom ctr. Girl at l., town scene at ctr. on back. Printed from engraved copper plates.	3.00	10.00	35.00

24	100 FRANCS	VG	VF	UNC
	ND. M/c. Like #23, but w/*REPUBLIQUE FRANCAISE* at bottom ctr.			
	a. Printed from engraved copper plates.	1.00	4.50	17.50
	b. Offset printing.	1.00	4.00	15.00

25	500 FRANCS	VG	VF	UNC
	ND (1969-92). Blue and m/c. Fisherman at r. Man at l., objects at r. on back. 4 sign. varieties.	FV	7.00	12.50
26	1000 FRANCS			
	ND (1969). M/c. Hut under palms at l., girl at r. W/o *REPUBLIQUE FRANCAISE* ovpt. at bottom ctr.	12.00	35.00	90.00
27	1000 FRANCS			
	ND (1969). M/c. Like #26 but w/*REPUBLIQUE FRANCAISE* at bottom ctr. 5 sign. varieties.	FV	12.50	22.50

TAJIKISTAN

The Republic of Tajikistan, (Tadjiquistan, formerly the Tajik Soviet Socialist Republic) was formed from those regions of Bukhara and Turkestan where the population consisted mainly of Tajiks. It is bordered in the north and west by Uzbekistan and Kyrgyzstan; in the east by China and in the south by Afghanistan. It has an area of 55,240 sq. miles. (143,100 sq. km.) It includes 2 provinces of Khudzand and Khatlon together with the Gorno-Badakhshan Autonomous Region with a population of 5,092,603. Capital: Dushanbe. Tajikistan was admitted as a constituent republic of the Soviet Union on Dec. 5, 1929. In Aug. 1990 the Tajik Supreme Soviet adopted a declaration of republican sovereignty, and in Dec. 1991 the republic became a member of the CIS. After demonstrations and fighting the Communist government was replaces by a Revolutionary Coalition Council on May 7, 1992. Following further demonstrations President Nabiev was ousted on Sept. 7, 1992. Civil war broke out, and the government resigned on Nov. 10, 1992. On Nov. 30, 1992 it was announced that a CIS peacekeeping force would be sent to Tajikistan. A state of emergency was imposed in Jan. 1993.

MONETARY SYSTEM:
1 Ruble = 100 Tanga

REPUBLIC

БОНКИ МИЛЛИИ ЧУМХУРИИ ТОЧИКИСТОН

NATIONAL BANK OF THE REPUBLIC OF TAJIKISTAN

1994 ISSUE
#1-8 arms at upper l. or l. Bldg. w/flag at ctr. r. on back. Wmk: Multiple stars.

		VG	VF	UNC
1	**1 RUBLE** 1994. Brown on m/c unpt.	FV	FV	.40

		VG	VF	UNC
2	**5 RUBLES** 1994. Deep purple on m/c unpt.	FV	FV	.90

		VG	VF	UNC
3	**10 RUBLES** 1994. Deep red on m/c unpt.	FV	FV	1.25
4	**20 RUBLES** 1994. Deep violet on m/c unpt.	FV	FV	2.00
5	**50 RUBLES** 1994. Dk. olive-green on m/c unpt.	FV	FV	3.00
6	**100 RUBLES** 1994. Blue-black and brown on m/c unpt.	FV	FV	4.50
7	**200 RUBLES** 1994. Deep olive-green and pale violet on m/c unpt.	FV	FV	8.50
8	**500 RUBLES** 1994. Brown-violet on m/c unpt.	FV	FV	20.00

TANZANIA

The United Republic of Tanzania, located on the east coast of Africa between Kenya and Mozambique, consists of Tanganyika and the islands of Zanzibar and Pemba. It has an area of 364,900 sq. mi. (945,090 sq. km.) and a population of 25.1 million. Capital: Dar es Salaam (Haven of Peace). The chief exports are cotton, coffee, diamonds, sisal, cloves, petroleum products and cashew nuts.

German East Africa (Tanganyika), located on the coast of east-central Africa between British East Africa (now Kenya) and Portuguese East Africa (now Mozambique), had an area of 362,284 sq. mi. (938,216 sq. km.) and a population of about 6 million. Capital: Dar es Salaam. Chief products prior to German control were ivory and slaves; after German control, sisal, coffee and rubber. Germany acquired control of the area by treaties with coastal chiefs in 1884, established it as a protectorate in 1891, and proclaimed it the Colony of German East Africa in 1897. After World War I, Tanganyika was entrusted to Great Britain as a League of Nations mandate, and after World War II as a United Nations trust territory. Tanganyika became an independent nation within the British Commonwealth on Dec. 9, 1961.

The British Protectorate of Zanzibar and Pemba, and adjacent small islands, located in the Indian Ocean 22 miles (35 km.) off the coast of Tanganyika, comprised a portion of British East Africa. Zanzibar was also the name of a sultanate which included the Zanzibar and Kenya protectorates. Zanzibar has an area of 637 sq. mi. (1,651 sq. km.). Chief city: Zanzibar. Pemba has an area of 380 sq. mi. (984 sq. km.). Chief city: Chake Chake. The islands are noted for their cloves, of which Zanzibar is the world's foremost producer.

Zanzibar and Pemba share a common history. Zanzibar came under Portuguese control in 1503, was conquered by the Omani Arabs in 1698, became independent of Oman in 1860, and (with Pemba) came under British control in 1890. Britain granted the protectorate self-government in 1961, and independence within the British Commonwealth on Dec. 19, 1963. On April 26, 1964, Tanganyika and Zanzibar (with Pemba) united to form the United Republic of Tanganyika and Zanzibar. The name of the country, which remained within the British Commonwealth, was changed to Tanzania on Oct. 29, 1964.

Tanzania is a member of the Commonwealth of Nations. The president is Chief of State. Also see East Africa and Zanzibar.

MONETARY SYSTEM:
1 Shilingi (Shilling) = 100 Senti

REPUBLIC

BANK OF TANZANIA

SIGNATURE VARIETIES							
1	*Aniifun* MINISTER FOR FINANCE	*Ruante* GOVERNOR	6	*Aunta.* WAZIRI WA FEDHA	*signature* GAVANA
2	*Shaga*	*Ruante*	7	*Shauya*	*G.Rutlind*
3	*Shaga*	*signature*	8	*Sorcilone*	*G.Rutlind*
4	*Aunt*	*signature*	9	*signature*	*G.Rutlind*
5	*Rumti*	*signature*	10		

1966 ND ISSUE
NOTE: Sign. 3-5 w/English titles on #2 and 3, changed to Swahili titles for later issues.
#1-5 arms at ctr., Pres. J. Nyerere at r. Wmk: Giraffe's head.

		VG	VF	UNC
1	**5 SHILLINGS** ND (1966). Brown and m/c. Sign. 1. Mountain view on back.	1.00	3.00	10.00

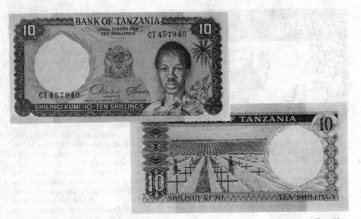

2 **10 Shillings**
ND (1966). Green and m/c. Sisal drying on back.

		VG	VF	Unc
a.	Sign. 1.	1.50	3.00	7.50
b.	Sign. 2.	2.00	4.00	10.00
c.	Sign. 3.	7.50	30.00	120.00
d.	Sign. 4.	1.00	2.00	7.50
e.	Sign. 5.	1.00	2.00	6.00

5 **100 Shillings**
ND (1966). Red and m/c. Various animals on back.

		VG	VF	Unc
a.	Sign. 1.	20.00	75.00	200.00
b.	Sign. 3.	12.50	45.00	135.00

Benki Kuu Ya Tanzania

1977-78 ND Issue

#6-8 arms at top ctr., Pres. J. Nyerere at r. Wmk: Giraffe's head.

NOTE: For #6-8, sign. are shown in chronological order of appearance. It seems sign. 3 was used again following several later combinations.

3 **20 Shillings**
ND (1966). Blue and m/c. Work bldgs. on back.

		VG	VF	Unc
a.	Sign. 1.	2.00	5.00	12.50
b.	Sign. 2.	2.00	5.00	12.50
c.	Sign. 3.	3.00	7.00	17.50
d.	Sign. 4.	2.00	5.00	12.50
e.	Sign. 5.	1.50	3.00	10.00

6 **10 Shilingi**
ND (1978). Green and m/c. Monument and mountain at ctr. on back.

		VG	VF	Unc
a.	Sign. 5.	.25	1.50	4.00
b.	Sign. 6.	.25	1.00	3.00
c.	Sign. 3.	.25	.75	2.00

7 **20 Shilingi**
ND (1978). Blue and m/c. Cotton knitting machine on back.

		VG	VF	Unc
a.	Sign. 5.	1.00	2.50	6.50
b.	Sign. 6.	1.00	2.25	5.50
c.	Sign. 3.	1.00	2.25	5.50

4 **100 Shillings**
ND (1966). Red and m/c. Sign. 1. Masai herdsman w/animals on back.

VG	VF	Unc
20.00	60.00	200.00

8   100 SHILINGI
ND (1977). Purple and m/c. Teacher and students at l., farmers at ctr.
on back.

		VG	VF	UNC
a.	Sign. 4.	4.00	8.00	22.50
b.	Sign. 5.	4.00	7.00	20.00
c.	Sign. 6.	3.00	6.50	17.50
d.	Sign. 3.	2.50	6.00	15.00

1985 ND ISSUE

#9-11 new portr. of Pres. J. Nyerere at r., torch at l., arms at ctr. Islands of Mafia, Pemba and Zanzibar
are omitted from map on back. Sign. 3. Wmk: Giraffe's head.

9   20 SHILINGI
ND (1985). Purple, brown and m/c. Tire factory scene on back.

VG	VF	UNC
.15	.50	2.00

10   50 SHILINGI
ND (1985). Red-orange, lt. brown and m/c. Brick making on back.

VG	VF	UNC
.30	1.25	5.00

11   100 SHILINGI
ND (1985). Blue, purple and m/c. Graduation procession on back.

VG	VF	UNC
.50	2.75	9.00

1986 ND ISSUE

#12-14 same as #9-11 but islands of Mafia, Pemba and Zanzibar now included in map on back.

12   20 SHILINGI
ND (1986). Like #9 but w/islands in map.

VG	VF	UNC
.15	.60	2.50

13   50 SHILINGI
ND (1986). Like #10 but w/islands in map.

VG	VF	UNC
.25	1.00	4.50

14   100 SHILINGI
ND (1986). Like #11 but w/islands in map.

		VG	VF	UNC
a.	Sign. 3.	.50	2.00	5.00
b.	Sign. 8.	.20	.75	3.00

1986-90 ND ISSUE

#15-19 arms at ctr., Pres. Mwinyi at r. Wmk: Giraffe's head.

15   20 SHILINGI
ND (1987). Purple, red-brown and m/c. Back like #12.

VG	VF	UNC
.10	.40	1.50

16   50 SHILINGI
ND (1986). Red-orange, lt. brown and m/c. Back like #13.

		VG	VF	UNC
a.	Sign. 3.	.30	1.00	3.50
b.	Sign. 7.	.20	.75	2.75

		VG	VF	UNC
21	**50 SHILINGI** ND (1992). Red-orange and lt. brown on m/c unpt.	.10	.50	1.75

18 **200 SHILINGI**
ND (1986). Black, orange and ochre on m/c unpt. 2 fishermen on back.

		VG	VF	UNC
a.	Sign. 3.	.50	2.00	6.00
b.	Sign. 7.	.65	2.25	7.00

		VG	VF	UNC
22	**200 SHILINGI** ND (1992). Black and tan on m/c unpt.	.50	1.50	6.00

1993; 1995 ND ISSUE
#23, 25-27 arms at ctr., Pres. Mwinyi at r. Wmk: Giraffe's head. Reduced size.

19 **500 SHILINGI**
ND (1989). Dk. blue and m/c. Zebra at l. Harvesting on back.

		VG	VF	UNC
a.	Sign. 3.	2.50	10.00	30.00
b.	Sign. 7.	1.50	5.00	12.50
c.	Sign. 8.	1.25	3.00	10.00

		VG	VF	UNC
23	**50 SHILINGI** ND (1993). Red-orange, brown and m/c. Animal grazing at l. Men making brick on back. Sign. 9.	FV	FV	1.00

20 **1000 SHILINGI**
ND (1990). Green, brown and m/c. Elephants at l. Kiwira Coal Mine at l. ctr., door to the Peoples Bank of Zanzibar at lower r. on back.

VG	VF	UNC
2.50	6.00	18.50

1992 ND ISSUE
#21-22 similar to #16 and #18 but w/modified portr. Wmk: Giraffe's head.

		VG	VF	UNC
24	**100 SHILINGI** ND (1993). Blue, aqua and m/c. Kudu at l., arms at ctr., J. Nyerere at r. Graduation procession on back. Sign. 9.	FV	FV	1.75

			VG	VF	UNC
25	**200 SHILINGI** ND (1993). Black and orange on m/c unpt. Leopards at l. Back similar to #18. Sign. 9.		FV	FV	3.00

			VG	VF	UNC
26	**500 SHILINGI** ND (1993). Purple, blue-green and violet on m/c unpt. Zebra at lower l. Back similar to #19 w/arms at lower r.				
	a.	Sign. 9.	FV	FV	6.50
	b.	Sign. 10.	FV	FV	5.50
	c.	Sign. 11.	FV	FV	5.00

			VG	VF	UNC
27	**1000 SHILINGI** ND (1993). Dk. green, brown and orange-brown on m/c unpt. Similar to #20.				
	a.	Sign. 10.	FV	FV	10.00
	b.	Sign. 11.	FV	FV	9.00
28	**5000 SHILINGI** ND (1995). M/c. Rhino at lower l. Giraffe on back.				
	a.	Sign. 10.	FV	FV	25.00
	b.	Sign. 11.	FV	FV	22.50
29	**10,000 SHILINGI** ND (1995). M/c. Lion at lower l.				
	a.	Sign. 10.	FV	FV	47.50
	b.	Sign. 11.	FV	FV	42.50

Tatarstan, an autonomous republic in the Russian Federation, is situated between the middle of the Volga river and its tributary Kama, extends east to the Ural mountains, covering 26,500 sq. mi. (68,000 sq. km.) and as of the 1970 census has a population of 3,743,600. Captial: Kazan. Tatarstan's economy combines its ancient traditions in the craftsmanship of wood, leather, cloth and ceramics with modern engineering, chemical, and food industries.

Colonized by the Bulgars in the 5th century, the territory of the Volga-Kama Bulgar State was inhabited by Turks. In the 13th century, Ghengis Khan conquered the area and established control until the 15th century when residual Mongol influence left Tatarstan as the Tatar Khanate, seat of the Kazar (Tatar) Khans. In 1552, under Ivan IV (the Terrible), Russia conquered, absorbed and controlled Tatarstan until the dissolution of the U.S.S.R. in the late 20th century.

Constituted as an autonomous republic on May 27, 1990, and as a sovereign state equal with Russia in April, 1992, Tatarstan, with Russia's president, signed a treaty in February, 1994, defining Tatarstan as a state united with Russia (Commonwealth of Independent States), but this has yet to be ratified by Russia's parliament.

MONETARY SYSTEM:
1 Ruble = 100 Kopeks

ТАТАРСКАЯ С.С.Р.

REPUBLIC OF TATARSTAN

TREASURY

1996 ND КУПОН - RUBLE CONTROL COUPON ISSUES
#1-3 red and green stripes w/black ТАТАРСКА repeated on back.

ТССР КУПОН НА 1 руб. ЯНВАРЬ	ТССР КУПОН НА 1 руб. ЯНВАРЬ	ТССР КУПОН НА 1 руб. ЯНВАРЬ	ТССР КУПОН НА 3 руб. ЯНВАРЬ
ТССР КУПОН НА 1 руб. ЯНВАРЬ	ТССР КУПОН НА 1 руб. ЯНВАРЬ	ТССР КУПОН НА 1 руб. ЯНВАРЬ	ТССР КУПОН НА 3 руб. ЯНВАРЬ
ТССР КУПОН НА 1 руб. ЯНВАРЬ	ТССР КУПОН НА 1 руб. ЯНВАРЬ	ТССР КУПОН НА 1 руб. ЯНВАРЬ	ТССР КУПОН НА 3 руб. ЯНВАРЬ
ТССР КУПОН НА 3 руб. ЯНВАРЬ	ТАТАРСКАЯ ССР КАРТОЧКА ПОТРЕБИТЕЛЯ на 50 рублей. ЯНВАРЬ		ТССР КУПОН НА 1 руб. ЯНВАРЬ
ТССР КУПОН НА 1 руб. ЯНВАРЬ	Название организации _____ Фамилия _____ Руководитель _____ Главный бухгалтер _____ мп		ТССР КУПОН НА 3 руб. ЯНВАРЬ
ТССР КУПОН НА 1 руб. ЯНВАРЬ	ТССР КУПОН НА 1 руб. ЯНВАРЬ	ТССР КУПОН НА 1 руб. ЯНВАРЬ	ТССР КУПОН НА 5 руб. ЯНВАРЬ
ТССР КУПОН НА 15 руб. ЯНВАРЬ	ТССР КУПОН НА 1 руб. ЯНВАРЬ	ТССР КУПОН НА 1 руб. ЯНВАРЬ	ТССР КУПОН НА 5 руб. ЯНВАРЬ
ТССР КУПОН НА 1 руб. ЯНВАРЬ	ТССР КУПОН НА 1 руб. ЯНВАРЬ	ТССР КУПОН НА 1 руб. ЯНВАРЬ	ТССР КУПОН НА 5 руб. ЯНВАРЬ

			VG	VF	UNC
1	**50 RUBLES** ND (1996). Black text on green unpt. w/month: ЯНВАРЬ (January).				
	a.	Full sheet.	—	4.75	8.00
	b.	Coupon.	—	.20	.50
2	**50 RUBLES** ND (1996). Black text on pink unpt. w/month: ФЕВЯАЛЬ (February).				
	a.	Full sheet.	—	5.00	9.00
	b.	Coupon.	—	.20	.50

ТССР КУПОН НА 1 руб. МАРТ	ТССР КУПОН НА 1 руб. МАРТ	ТССР КУПОН НА 1 руб. МАРТ	ТССР КУПОН НА 3 руб. МАРТ
ТССР КУПОН НА 1 руб. МАРТ	ТССР КУПОН НА 1 руб. МАРТ	ТССР КУПОН НА 1 руб. МАРТ	ТССР КУПОН НА 3 руб. МАРТ
ТССР КУПОН НА 1 руб. МАРТ	ТССР КУПОН НА 1 руб. МАРТ	ТССР КУПОН НА 1 руб. МАРТ	ТССР КУПОН НА 3 руб. МАРТ
ТССР КУПОН НА 3 руб. МАРТ	ТАТАРСКАЯ ССР КАРТОЧКА ПОТРЕБИТЕЛЯ на 50 рублей. МАРТ		ТССР КУПОН НА 1 руб. МАРТ
ТССР КУПОН НА 1 руб. МАРТ			ТССР КУПОН НА 1 руб. МАРТ
ТССР КУПОН НА 1 руб. МАРТ	ТССР КУПОН НА 1 руб. МАРТ	ТССР КУПОН НА 1 руб. МАРТ	ТССР КУПОН НА 3 руб. МАРТ
ТССР КУПОН НА 1 руб. МАРТ	ТССР КУПОН НА 1 руб. МАРТ	ТССР КУПОН НА 1 руб. МАРТ	ТССР КУПОН НА 5 руб. МАРТ
ТССР КУПОН НА 1 руб. МАРТ	ТССР КУПОН НА 1 руб. МАРТ	ТССР КУПОН НА 1 руб. МАРТ	ТССР КУПОН НА 5 руб. МАРТ

3 **50 RUBLES**
ND (1996). Black text on blue unpt. w/month: MAPT (March).

		VG	VF	UNC
a.	Full sheet.	—	5.00	9.00
b.	Coupon.	—	.20	.50

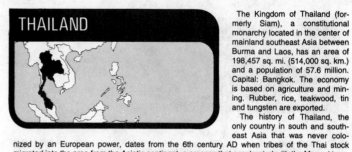

THAILAND

The Kingdom of Thailand (formerly Siam), a constitutional monarchy located in the center of mainland southeast Asia between Burma and Laos, has an area of 198,457 sq. mi. (514,000 sq. km.) and a population of 57.6 million. Capital: Bangkok. The economy is based on agriculture and mining. Rubber, rice, teakwood, tin and tungsten are exported.

The history of Thailand, the only country in south and southeast Asia that was never colonized by an European power, dates from the 6th century AD when tribes of the Thai stock migrated into the area from the Asiatic continent, a process that accelerated with the Mongol invasion of China in the 13th century. After 400 years of sporadic warfare with the neighboring Burmese, King Taksin won the last battle in 1767. He founded a new capital, Dhonburi, on the west bank of Chao Praya River. King Rama I moved the capital to Bangkok in 1782.

The Thai were introduced to the Western world by the Portuguese, who were followed by the Dutch, British and French. Rama III of the present ruling dynasty negotiated a treaty of friendship and commerce with Britain in 1826, and in 1896 the independence of the kingdom was guaranteed by an Anglo-French accord. The absolute monarchy was changed into a constitutional monarchy in 1932.

In 1909 Siam ceded to Great Britain its suzerain rights over the dependencies of Kedah, Kelantan, Trengganu and Perlis, Malay states situated in southern Siam just north of British Malaya. This eliminated any British jurisdiction in Siam proper.

On Dec. 8, 1941, after five hours of fighting, Thailand agreed to permit Japanese troops passage through the country to invade northern British Malaya. This eventually led to increased Japanese intervention and finally occupation of the country. On Jan. 25, 1942, Thailand declared war on Great Britain and the United States. A free Thai guerrilla movement was soon organized to counteract the Japanese. In July 1943, Japan transferred the four northern Malay States back to Thailand. These were returned to Great Britain after peace treaties were signed in 1946.

RULERS:
Rama IX (Bhumiphol Adulyadej), 1946-

MONETARY SYSTEM:
1 Baht (Tical) = 100 Satang

SIGNATURE VARIETIES

	MINISTER OF FINANCE รัฐมนตรีว่าการกระทรวงการคลัง	GOVERNOR OF THE BANK OF THAILAND ผู้ว่าการธนาคารแห่งประเทศไทย
34		
35		
36		
37		
38		
39		
40		
41		
42		
43		

**signed as Undersecretary/Deputy Finance Minister
ปลัดกระทรวงการคลังผู้ใช้อำนาจของ

44		
45		
46		
47		
48		
49		
50		

	MINISTER OF FINANCE รัฐมนตรีว่าการกระทรวงการคลัง	GOVERNOR OF THE BANK OF THAILAND ผู้ว่าการธนาคารแห่งประเทศไทย
51		
52		
53		
54		
55		
56		
57		
58		
59		
60		

KINGDOM

GOVERNMENT OF THAILAND

1953-56 ND ISSUE

#74-78 slightly modified Kg. in Field Marshall's uniform w/collar insignia and 3 decorations. Black serial #. Printer: TDLR.

Small letters in 2-line text on back.

Large letters in 2-line text on back.

74   1 BAHT

		VG	VF	UNC
ND (1955). Blue on m/c unpt. Like #69.				
a.	Wmk: Constitution. Red and blue security threads. Sign. 34.	.25	1.00	6.00
b.	Wmk: Constitution. Metal security strip. Sign. 34; 35 (lg. size).	.25	1.00	5.00
c.	Wmk: Kg. profile. Sm. letters in 2-line text on back. Sign. 35.	.25	1.00	5.00
d.	Wmk: Kg. profile. Larger letters in 2-line text on back. Sign. 36; 37; 38; 39; 40; 4l.	.20	.60	4.00

75   5 BAHT

		VG	VF	UNC
ND (1956). Purple on m/c unpt. Like #70.				
a.	Wmk: Constitution. Red and blue security threads. Sign. 34.	.50	2.00	4.00
b.	Wmk: Constitution. Metal security strip. Sign. 34; 35 (lg. size).	.50	1.50	3.50
c.	Wmk: Kg. profile. Sm. letters in 2-line text on back. Sign. 35; 36.	.50	1.50	3.50
d.	Wmk: Kg. profile. Larger letters in 2-line text on back. Sign. 38; 39; 40; 41.	.25	1.00	2.00

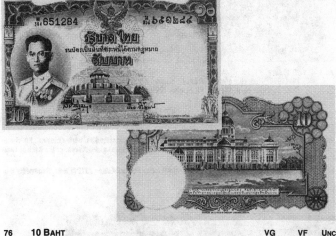

76   10 BAHT

		VG	VF	UNC
ND (1953). Brown on m/c unpt. Like #71.				
a.	Wmk: Constitution. Red and blue security threads. Sign. 34.	.50	2.00	6.00
b.	Wmk: Constitution. Metal security strip. Sign. 34; 35 (lg. size).	.50	2.00	4.50
c.	Wmk: Kg. profile. Sm. letters in 2-line text on back. Sign. 35; 36; 37; 38.	.50	1.00	2.50
d.	Wmk: Kg. profile. Larger letters in 2-line text on back. Sign. 39; 40; 41; 42; 44.	.50	1.00	2.25

77   20 BAHT

		VG	VF	UNC
ND (1953). Olive-green on m/c unpt. Like #72.				
a.	Wmk: Constitution. Red and blue security threads. Sign. 34.	1.00	3.50	11.50
b.	Wmk: Constitution. Metal security strip. Sign. 34; 35 (lg. size).	1.00	2.50	6.00
c.	Wmk: Kg. profile. Sm. letters in 2-line text on back. Sign. 35; 37- 42; 44.	FV	1.25	3.00
d.	Wmk: Kg. profile. Larger letters in 2-line text on back. Sign. 35; 37-42; 44.	FV	1.25	3.00

78   100 BAHT

		VG	VF	UNC
ND (1955). Red on m/c unpt. Like #73.				
a.	Wmk: Constitution. Red and blue security threads. Sign. 34.	4.50	10.00	25.00
b.	Wmk: Constitution. Metal security strip. Sign. 34; 35; 37; 38.	4.25	8.50	20.00
c.	Wmk: Kg. profile. Sm. letters in 2-line text on back. Sign. 38-41.	FV	6.00	15.00
d.	Wmk: Kg. profile. Larger letters in 2-line text on back. Sign. 38-41.	FV	6.00	15.00

BANK OF THAILAND

1968 ISSUE; SERIES 10

79	**100 BAHT**	**VG**	**VF**	**UNC**
	ND (1968). Red, blue and m/c. Rama IX in uniform at r. and as wmk. Royal barge on back. Sign. 41; 42. Printer: TDLR.	4.50	7.00	15.00

1969 COMMEMORATIVE ISSUE
SERIES 11

Printed in Thailand by the Thai Banknote Printing Works. Officially described as "Series Eleven". Kg. Rama IX wearing traditional robes at r., sign. of Finance Minister (above) and Governor of the Bank of Thailand (below) at ctr. Wmk: Rama IX.

#80-81 text at bottom: *opening of the Thai Banknote Printing Works 24 June 2512* (1969). Reportedly 6 or 7,000 sets issued.

80	**5 BAHT**	**VG**	**VF**	**UNC**
	24.6.1969. Purple and m/c. Abhorn Pimoke Throne Hall on back. Serial # prefix 00A. Sign. 41.	5.00	25.00	250.00

81	**10 BAHT**	**VG**	**VF**	**UNC**
	24.6.1969. Brown on m/c unpt. Similar to #80. Wat Benchamabophitr temple on back. Serial # and sign. like #80.	5.00	25.00	250.00

1969-75 ND ISSUE; SERIES 11

82	**5 BAHT**	**VG**	**VF**	**UNC**
	ND (1969). Purple on m/c unpt. Like #80 but w/o commemorative line at bottom. Sign. 41; 42.	.25	.40	1.25

83	**10 BAHT**	**VG**	**VF**	**UNC**
	ND (1969). Brown on m/c unpt. Like #81 but w/o commemorative line at bottom. Sign. 41; 42; 43; 44; 45; 46; 47; 48; 49; 50; 51; 52; 53.	.50	.75	2.00

84	**20 BAHT**	**VG**	**VF**	**UNC**
	ND (1971). Dk. green, olive-green and brown-violet on m/c unpt. Royal barge on back. Sign. 41; 42; 43; 44; 45; 46; 47; 48; 49; 50; 51; 52; 53.	1.00	1.50	3.00

85	**100 BAHT**	**VG**	**VF**	**UNC**
	ND (1972). Red-brown on m/c unpt. Emerald Buddha section of Grand Palace on back.			
a.	W/o black Thai ovpt. on face. Sign. 42; 43; 44; 45; 46; 47; 48; 49.	4.50	6.50	12.50
b.	Black Thai ovpt. line just below upper sign. for change of title. Sign. 43.	4.50	7.00	27.50

86	**500 Baht**	**VG**	**VF**	**UNC**
	ND (1975). Purple on m/c unpt. Pra Prang Sam Yod Lopburi (3 towers) on back. Sign. 47; 49; 50; 51; 52; 53; 54; 55.	22.50	28.50	60.00

1978-81 ND Issue; Series 12

#87-89 Kg. Rama IX wearing dk. Field Marshall's uniform at r. and as wmk. Sign. of Finance Minister (upper) and Governor of the Bank of Thailand (lower) at ctr.

87	**10 Baht**	**VG**	**VF**	**UNC**
	ND (1980). Dk. brown on m/c unpt. Mounted statue of Kg. Chulalongkorn on back. Sign. 52; 53; 54; 56; 59.	FV	.50	1.50

88	**20 Baht**	**VG**	**VF**	**UNC**
	ND (1981). Dk. green and black on m/c unpt. Kg. Taksin's statue at Chantaburi w/3 armed men on back. Sign. 52; 55; 56; 59; 61; 65.	FV	1.00	2.50

89	**100 Baht**	**VG**	**VF**	**UNC**
	ND (1978). Violet, red and orange on m/c unpt. Kg. Narasuan the Great on elephant's back on back. Sign. 49; 50; 52; 53; 54; 56; 57.	FV	5.00	10.00

1985-92 ND Issue; Series 12

90	**50 Baht**	**VG**	**VF**	**UNC**
	ND (1985). Dk. blue and purple on m/c unpt. Kg. Rama IX facing r., wearing traditional robe and as wmk. Palace at l., statue of Kg. Rama VII at ctr., his arms and sign. at upper l. on back.			
a.	Kg. w/pointed eartips. Sign. 54.	FV	2.50	5.50
b.	Darker blue color obscuring pointed eartips. Sign. 55; 56; 57; 60.	FV	2.50	5.00

91	**500 Baht**	**VG**	**VF**	**UNC**
	ND(1988). Purple and violet on m/c unpt. Kg. Rama IX at r. in Field Marshall's uniform and as wmk. Statue on back. Sign. 54; 55; 56; 58; 59; 60.	FV	22.50	30.00
92	**1000 Baht**			
	ND (1992). Gray, brown, orange and m/c. Kg. at ctr. r. and as wmk. Kg. and Qn. greeting children at l. ctr., viewing map at ctr. r. on back. Sign. 58.	FV	45.00	65.00

1987 Commemorative Issue
#93, King's 60th Birthday

93	**60 Baht**	**VG**	**VF**	**UNC**
	BE2530 (5.12.1987). Dk. brown on m/c unpt. Kg. Rama IX seated on throne at ctr. Victory crown at l., Royal Regalia at r. Royal family seated w/subjects on back. Sign. 55.			
a.	Issued note.	—	—	7.00
s.	Specimen in blue folder.	—	—	100.00

1992 COMMEMORATIVE ISSUES

#94 and 95, 90th Birthday of Princess Mother
#96, Qn. Sirikit's 60th Birthday

			VG	VF	UNC
94	**50 BAHT**		FV	FV	4.50
	ND (1992). Blue on m/c unpt. Similar to #90. 2 lines of text added under Princess Mother's wmk. on face. Sign. 57.				
95	**500 BAHT**		FV	FV	37.50
	ND (1992). Purple and m/c. Similar to #91. 2 lines of text added under Princess Mother's wmk. on face. Sign. 57.				
96	**1000 BAHT**		FV	FV	65.00
	ND (1992). Black, deep olive-green and yellow-brown on m/c unpt. Like #92 but w/commemorative text in 3 lines under Qn. Sirikit's wmk. on face and back. Sign. 62.				

1994 ND ISSUE

			VG	VF	UNC
97	**100 BAHT**		FV	FV	8.50
	ND (1994). Violet, red and brown-orange on m/c unpt. Kg. Rama IX at r. Statue of Kg. and prince at ctr. r. between children on back. Sign. 63.				

1995 COMMEMORATIVE ISSUE

#98, 120th Anniversary of the Ministry of Finance

			VG	VF	UNC
98	**10 BAHT**		FV	FV	1.25
	ND (1995). Grayish brown on m/c unpt. Like #87 but w/Commemorative text in lower margin. Sign. 63.				

1996 COMMEMORATIVE ISSUES

#99 and 100, 50th Anniversary of Reign

			VG	VF	UNC
99	**50 BAHT**		FV	FV	5.00
	ND (1996). Purple on lt. blue and m/c unpt. Kg. Rama IX wearing Field Marshall's uniform at r. and as a shadow design in clear area at l., royal seal of kingdom at upper r. Back like #94. Polymer plastic. Sign. 64. Printer: NPA (w/o imprint).				
100	**500 BAHT**		FV	FV	37.50
	ND (1996). Purple and red-violet on m/c unpt. Similar to #101 but w/Crowned Royal seal w/50 at ctr. r., arms above dancers at r. replacing crowned radiant Chakra at l. ctr. Sign. 64.				

1996 ND REGULAR ISSUE

			VG	VF	UNC
101	**500 BAHT**		FV	FV	35.00
	ND (1996). Purple and red-violet on m/c unpt. Kg. Rama IX at r. and as wmk. Arms at upper l., radiant crowned Chakra seal on platform at l. ctr. Palace at l. ctr., 2 statues on back. Sign. 64.				

MILITARY - VIET NAM WAR

AUXILIARY MILITARY PAYMENT CERTIFICATE COUPONS

Issued to Thai troops in Vietnam to facilitate their use of United States MPC. These coupons could not be used as currency by themselves.

FIRST SERIES

#M1-M8 issued probably from January to April or May, 1970. Larger shield at ctr. on face and back. Words *Coupon* below shield or at r., *Non Negotiable* at r. Small Thai symbol only at upper l. corner; denomination at 3 corners. Black print on check-type security paper.

			GOOD	FINE	XF
M1	**5 CENTS**		110.00	275.00	—
	ND (1970). Yellow paper. Seahorse shield design.				
M2	**10 CENTS**		110.00	275.00	—
	ND (1970). Lt. gray paper. Shield w/leaping panther and *RTAVF. Non Negotiable* under shield; *Coupon* deleted.				
M3	**25 CENTS**		—	—	—
	ND (1970). Pink paper. Shield w/*Victory Vietnam. Coupon* at r.				
M4	**50 CENTS**		—	—	—
	ND (1970). Lt. blue paper. Circle w/shaking hands and *Royal Thai Forces Vietnam.*				

			GOOD	FINE	XF
M5	**1 DOLLAR**		—	—	—
	ND (1970). Yellow paper. Inscription *Victory Vietnam. Coupon* at r.				
M6	**5 DOLLARS**		—	—	—
	ND (1970). Lt. gray paper. Seahorse in shield.				
M7	**10 DOLLARS**		—	—	—
	ND (1970). Yellow paper. Shield w/leaping panther.				
M8	**20 DOLLARS**		—	—	—
	ND (1970). Lt. green paper. Circle w/hands shaking.				

SECOND SERIES

#M9-M16 issued April or May, 1970 to possibly Oct. 7, 1970. Shield desgns similar to previous issue, but paper colors are different. Larger shield outline around each shield at l. ctr. *Coupon* in margin at lower ctr., denomination at all 4 corners.

			GOOD	FINE	XF
M9	**5 CENTS**		35.00	150.00	425.00
	ND (1970). Yellow paper. Shield similar to #M1.				

			GOOD	FINE	XF
M10	**10 CENTS**		40.00	175.00	450.00
	ND (1970). Lt. green paper. Shield similar to #M2.				

			GOOD	FINE	XF
M11	**25 CENTS**		—	—	—
	ND (1970). Yellow paper. Shield similar to #M3.				
M12	**50 CENTS**		—	—	—
	ND (1970). Lt. gray paper. Shield similar to #M4.				
M13	**1 DOLLAR**		—	—	—
	ND (1970). Pink paper. Shield similar to #M5.				
M14	**5 DOLLARS**		—	—	—
	ND (1970). Lt. green paper. Shield similar to #M6.				
M15	**10 DOLLARS**		—	—	—
	ND (1970). Pale yellow paper. Shield similar to #M7.				

			GOOD	FINE	XF
M16	**20 DOLLARS**		—	—	—
	ND (1970). Lt. green paper. Shield similar to #M8.				

THIRD SERIES

#M17-M23 date of issue not known (Oct., 1970?). All notes w/hands shaking in shield at lower r. on face. Different shield designs at upper l. on back. More elaborate design across face and back.

			GOOD	FINE	XF
M17	**5 CENTS**		35.00	150.00	275.00
	ND. Lt. gray, maroon and green.				

M18 10 CENTS
ND. Lt. yellow and green.

	GOOD	FINE	XF
	35.00	150.00	275.00

M19 25 CENTS
ND. Green, pink and maroon.

	GOOD	FINE	XF
	35.00	150.00	275.00

M20 50 CENTS
ND. Yellow, green, blue and red.

	GOOD	FINE	XF
	35.00	150.00	275.00

M21 1 DOLLAR
ND. Pink, blue and green.

	GOOD	FINE	XF
	65.00	175.00	325.00

M22 5 DOLLARS
ND. Yellow, green, blue and red.

	GOOD	FINE	XF
	100.00	250.00	475.00

M23 10 DOLLARS
ND. Green, maroon and dk. red.

	GOOD	FINE	XF
	85.00	225.00	450.00

TIMOR

INDONESIA

AUSTRALIA

Timor, an island of Indonesia between the Savu and Timor Seas, has an area, including the former colony of Portuguese Timor, of 11,883 sq. mi. (30,775 sq. km.) and a population of 1.5 million. Western Timor is administered as part of Nusa Tenggara Timur (East Nusa Tenggara) province. Capital: Kupang. The eastern half of the island, the former Portuguese colony, forms a single province, Timor Timur (East Timor). Capital: Dili. Timor exports sandalwood, coffee, tea, hides, rubber and copra.

Portuguese traders reached Timor about 1520, and moved to the north and east when the Dutch established themselves in Kupang, a sheltered bay at the southwestern tip, in 1613. Treaties effective in 1860 and 1914 established the boundaries between the two colonies. Japan occupied the entire island during World War II. The former Dutch colony in the western part of the island became part of Indonesia in 1950.

At the end of Nov., 1975, the Portuguese Province of Timor attained independence as the People's Democratic Republic of East Timur. In Dec., 1975 or early in 1976 the government of the People's Democratic Republic was seized by a guerrilla faction sympathetic to the Indonesian territorial claim to East Timur which ousted the constitutional government and replaced it with the Provisional Government of East Timur. On July 17, 1976, the Provisional Government enacted a law which dissolved the free republic and made East Timur the 24th province of Indonesia.

NOTE: For later issues see Indonesia listing.

MONETARY SYSTEM:
1 Pataca = 100 Avos to 1958
1 Escudo = 100 Centavos, 1958-1975

PORTUGUESE INFLUENCE

BANCO NACIONAL ULTRAMARINO

1959 ISSUE

#22-25 portr. J. Celestino da Silva at. r. Bank seal and crowned arms on back. Printer: BWC.

		VG	VF	UNC
22	**30 ESCUDOS**			
	2.1.1959. Blue on m/c unpt.			
	a. Issued note.	5.00	20.00	125.00
	s. Specimen.	—	—	100.00
23	**60 ESCUDOS**			
	2.1.1959. Red on m/c unpt.			
	a. Issued note.	5.00	25.00	170.00
	s. Specimen.	—	—	135.00
24	**100 ESCUDOS**			
	2.1.1959. Brown on m/c unpt.			
	a. Issued note.	7.50	37.50	225.00
	s. Specimen.	—	—	175.00
25	**500 ESCUDOS**			
	2.1.1959. Dk. brown and black on m/c unpt.			
	a. Issued note.	40.00	170.00	475.00
	s. Specimen.	—	—	375.00

1963-68 ISSUE

#26-30 Portr. R. D. Aleixo at r. Bank seal and crowned arms on back. Sign. varieties. Printer: BWC.

26	**20 ESCUDOS**	**VG**	**VF**	**UNC**
	24.10.1967. Olive-brown on m/c unpt.	1.50	5.00	15.00
27	**50 ESCUDOS**			
	24.10.1967. Blue on m/c unpt.	2.50	6.00	20.00
28	**100 ESCUDOS**			
	25.4.1963. Brown on m/c unpt. 2 sign. varieties.	3.00	10.00	25.00
29	**500 ESCUDOS**			
	25.4.1963. Dk. brown on m/c unpt.	10.00	25.00	100.00
30	**1000 ESCUDOS**			
	21.3.1968. Green on m/c unpt.	20.00	42.50	135.00

1969 ND PROVISIONAL ISSUE

31 (32)	**20 ESCUDOS**	**VG**	**VF**	**UNC**
	ND Green and m/c. Rugula Jose Nunes at l. Bank seal at ctr., local huts on pilings at r. on back. Specimen.	—	—	—
32 (31)	**500 ESCUDOS**			
	ND (1969 - old date 22.3.1967). Brown and violet on m/c unpt. Ovpt: *PAGAVEL EM TIMOR* on Mozambique #110, face and back.	125.00	300.00	500.00

The Kingdom of Tonga (or Friendly Islands), a member of the British Commonwealth, is an archipelago situated in the southern Pacific Ocean south of Western Samoa and east of Fiji comprising 150 islands. Tonga has an area of 270 sq. mi. (748 sq. km.) and a population of 103,000. Capital: Nuku'alofa. Primarily agricultural, the kingdom exports bananas and copra.

Dutch navigators Willem Schouten and Jacob Lemaire were the first Europeans to visit Tonga in 1616. They were followed by the noted Dutch explorer Abel Tasman who visited the Tongatapu group in 1643. No further European contact was made until 1773 when British navigator Capt. James Cook arrived and, impressed by the peaceful deportment of the natives, named the islands the Friendly Islands. Within a few years of Cook's visit, Tonga was embroiled in a civil war that lasted until the great chief Taufa'ahau, who reigned as George Tubou I (1845-93), was converted to Christianity and brought unity and peace to the islands. Tonga became a self-governing protectorate of Great Britain in 1900 and a fully independent state on June 4, 1970. The monarchy is a member of the Commonwealth of Nations. The monarch is Chief of State and Head of Government.

RULERS:
Queen Salote, 1918-1965
King Taufa'ahau, 1965-

MONETARY SYSTEM:
1 Shilling = 12 Pence
1 Pound = 20 Shillings to 1967
1 Pa'anga = 100 Seniti, 1967-

KINGDOM

GOVERNMENT OF TONGA

1940-42 ISSUE
#9-12 w/denomination spelled out on both sides of arms at ctr. Printer: TDLR.

9	**4 SHILLINGS**	**VG**	**VF**	**UNC**
	1941-66. Brown on m/c unpt. *FOUR SHILLINGS* at l. and r.			
	a. 1.12.1941-22.10.1946. 3 sign.	25.00	100.00	—
	b. 7.2.1949; 15.2.1951; 20.7.1951; 6.9.1954.	22.50	100.00	—
	c. 19.9.1955-30.11.1959.	7.50	25.00	75.00
	d. 24.10.1960-27.9.1966.	3.00	10.00	35.00
	e. 3.11.1966. 2 sign.	2.00	5.00	22.50
10	**10 SHILLINGS**			
	1941-66. Green on m/c unpt. *TEN SHILLINGS* at l. and r.			
	a. 19.5.1939; 17.10.1941-28.11.1944. 3 sign.	35.00	200.00	—
	b. 9.7.1949-1955.	30.00	125.00	—
	c. 2.5.1956; 22.7.1957; 10.12.1958.	7.50	30.00	—
	d. 24.10.1960; 28.11.1962; 29.7.1964; 22.6.1965.	3.00	10.00	65.00
	e. 3.11.1966. 2 sign.	2.00	7.50	30.00

11 1 POUND
1940-66. Red on m/c unpt. *ONE POUND* at l. and r.

	VG	VF	UNC
a. 3.5.1940-7.11.1944. 3 sign.	35.00	150.00	—
b. 15.6.1951; 11.9.1951; 19.9.1955.	30.00	120.00	—
c. 2.5.1956; 10.12.1958; 30.11.1959; 12.12.1961.	10.00	25.00	85.00
d. 28.11.1962; 30.10.1964; 2.11.1965; 3.11.1966.	5.00	12.00	55.00
e. 2.12.1966. 2 sign.	3.00	10.00	37.50

12 5 POUNDS
1942-66. Dk. blue on m/c unpt. *FIVE POUNDS* at l. and r.

	VG	VF	UNC
a. 11.3.1942-1945. 3 sign.	550.00	1000.	—
b. 15.6.1951; 5.7.1955; 11.9.1956; 26.6.1958.	300.00	650.00	—
c. 30.11.1959; 2.11.1965.	150.00	400.00	—
d. 2.12.1966. 2 sign.	10.00	25.00	70.00

PULE' ANGA 'O TONGA

GOVERNMENT OF TONGA

1967 ISSUE
#13-17 arms at lower l., Qn. Salote at r. Various date and sign. varieties.

13 1/2 PA'ANGA
1967-73. Dk. brown on pink unpt. Back brown and blue; coconut workers.

	VG	VF	UNC
a. 3.4.1967; 10.3.1970; 16.6.1970; 4.2.1971; 24.7.1972. 3 sign.	1.50	7.50	30.00
b. 13.6.1973. 2 sign.	2.00	6.50	37.50

14 1 PA'ANGA
1967; 70-71. Olive on m/c unpt. Back olive and blue; river scene, palm trees.

	VG	VF	UNC
a. 12.4.1967; 2.10.1967; 8.12.1967; 3.4.1967.	2.00	7.50	50.00
b. 10.3.1970; 19.10.1971.	2.50	8.50	60.00

15 2 PA'ANGA
1967-73. Red on m/c unpt. Back red and brown; women making Tapa cloth.

	VG	VF	UNC
a. 3.4.1967; 2.10.1967; 8.12.1967.	3.00	12.00	70.00
b. 19.5.1969; 10.3.1970; 19.10.1971; 2.8.1973.	3.50	15.00	85.00

16 5 PA'ANGA
1967; 1973. Purple on m/c unpt. Back purple and olive-green; Ha'amonga stone gateway.

	VG	VF	UNC
a. 3.4.1967.	7.00	25.00	130.00
b. 13.6.1973.	8.50	30.00	175.00

17 10 PA'ANGA
3.4.1967; 2.10.1967; 8.12.1967. Dk. blue on m/c unpt. Back blue and purple; Royal Palace.

VG	VF	UNC
12.00	50.00	225.00

1974; 1985 ISSUE
#18-22 arms at lower l., Portr. Kg. Taufa'ahau at r. Various date and sign. varieties.

#23 Kg. in new design at ctr. r. and as wmk., arms at r.

Replacement notes: Serial # prefix *Z/1.*

NOTE: #23a was made in limited quantities in celebration of the king's birthday.

18 1/2 PA'ANGA
1974-83. Dk. brown on pale orange unpt. Back like #13.

	VG	VF	UNC
a. 2 sign. 2.10.1974; 19.6.1975.	1.00	2.50	10.00
b. 3 sign. 12.1.1977-29.7.1983.	.50	1.00	10.00

19 1 PA'ANGA
1974-89. Olive-green on m/c unpt. Back like #14.

	VG	VF	UNC
a. 2 sign. 31.7.1974; 19.6.1975; 21.1.1981; 18.5.1983.	FV	1.50	6.00
b. 3 sign. 17.5.1977-11.6.1980; 31.7.1981-28.10.1982; 27.7.1983-30.6.1989.	FV	FV	4.50

20 2 PA'ANGA
1974-89. Red on m/c unpt. Back like #15.

	VG	VF	UNC
a. 2 sign. 2.10.1974; 19.6.1975; 21.1.1981.	FV	2.00	10.00
b. 3 sign. 12.1.1977-27.8.1980; 31.7.1981-30.6.1989.	FV	FV	5.00

21 5 PA'ANGA
1974-89. Purple on m/c unpt. Back like #16.

	VG	VF	UNC
a. 2 sign. 2.10.1974; 19.6.1975; 21.1.1981.	FV	4.00	20.00
b. 3 sign. 21.12.1976-28.11.1980; 27.5.1981-30.6.1989.	FV	FV	10.00

22 10 PA'ANGA
1974-89. Dk. blue on m/c unpt. Back like #17.

	VG	VF	UNC
a. 2 sign. 31.7.1974; 3.9.1974; 19.6.1975; 21.1.1981.	FV	7.50	35.00
b. 3 sign. 12.12.1976-28.11.1980; 19.1.1982-30.6.1989.	FV	FV	18.50

23 20 PA'ANGA
1985-89. Orange on green and m/c unpt. Kg. in new design at ctr. r. and as wmk., arms at r. Tonga Development Bank on back.

	VG	VF	UNC
a. 4.7.1985.	FV	25.00	70.00
b. 18.7.1985; 8.1.1986; 27.2.1987; 28.9.1987.	FV	FV	45.00
c. 20.5.1988; 14.12.1988; 23.1.1989; 30.6.1989.	FV	FV	40.00

KINGDOM OF TONGA

1988-89 ISSUE

#24 Kg. in new design at ctr. r. and as wmk., arms at r.

NOTE: #24a was made in limited quantities in celebration of the king's birthday.

24 50 PA'ANGA
1988-89. Brown and green on m/c unpt. Kg. in new design at ctr. r. and as wmk., arms at r. Vava'u Harbour on back.

	VG	VF	UNC
a. 4.7.1988.	FV	50.00	110.00
b. 14.12.1988; 30.6.1989.	FV	FV	85.00

NATIONAL RESERVE BANK OF TONGA

1992 ISSUE

#25-29 designs like #19-23. 2 sign. w/Tongan titles beneath.

25 1 PA'ANGA
ND (1992-95). Olive-green on m/c unpt.

	VG	VF	UNC
	FV	FV	3.50

26 2 PA'ANGA
ND (1992-95). Red on m/c unpt.

	VG	VF	UNC
	FV	FV	5.50

27 5 PA'ANGA
ND (1992-95). Purple on m/c unpt.

	VG	VF	UNC
	FV	FV	15.00

28 10 PA'ANGA
ND (1992-95). Dk. blue on m/c unpt.

	FV	FV	22.50

29 20 PA'ANGA
ND(1992-95). Orange and green on m/c unpt.

	FV	FV	47.50

1989 COMMEMORATIVE ISSUE

#30, Inauguration of National Reserve Bank of Tonga.

30	**20 PA'ANGA**	**VG**	**VF**	**UNC**
	1.7.1989. Orange on green and m/c unpt. w/commemorative text wmk. area on face and back.	FV	25.00	50.00

1995 ISSUE
#31-34 Kg. Taufa'ahau at upper ctr. r., arms at r.

31	**1 PA'ANGA**	**VG**	**VF**	**UNC**
	ND (1995). Olive-green on m/c unpt. River scene, palm trees on back.	FV	FV	3.00
32	**2 PA'ANGA**			
	ND (1995). Red on m/c unpt. Woman making Tapa cloth on back.	FV	FV	5.00
33	**5 PA'ANGA**			
	ND (1995). Purple on m/c unpt. Ha'amonga stone gateway on back.	FV	FV	12.50
34	**10 PA'ANGA**			
	ND (1995). Dk. blue on m/c unpt. Royal Palace on back.	FV	FV	22.50

COLLECTOR SERIES

NATIONAL RESERVE BANK OF TONGA

1978 ISSUE

CS1	**1978 1-10 PA'ANGA**	**ISSUE PRICE**	**MKT. VALUE**
	#19-22 ovpt: *SPECIMEN* and Maltese cross prefix serial #.	14.00	25.00

The Transdniester Moldavian Republic was formed in 1990, even before the separation of Moldavia from Russia. It has an area of 11,544 sq. mi. (29,900 sq. km). and a population of 742,000. Capital: Tiraspol. Once the Moldavian SSR declared independence in August 1991, the natural independence route for Transdniestria was pushed to a head when Russian occupation forces quelled demonstrations by force in Bendery and Doubossary.

Transdniestria has a president, parliament, army and police forces, but as yet it is lacking international recognition.

The area was conquered from the Turks in the last 18th Century, and in 1792 the capital city of Tiraspol was founded. After 1812, the area called Bessarabia (present Moldova and part of the Ukraine) became part of the Russian Empire. During the Russian Revolution, in 1918, the area was taken by Romanian troops, and in 1924 the Moldavian Autonomous SSR was formed. On 22 June 1941, Romania declared war on the U.S.S.R. and Romanian troops fought alongside the Germans up to Stalingrad. A Romanian occupation area between the Dniester and Bug Rivers called *Transdniestria* was established in October 1941, and was used mainly as a dumping ground for Jews deported by Romania. Its center was the port of Odessa. A special issue of notes for use in Transdniestria was made by the Romanian government. In 1944 the Russians recaptured Transdniestria, advancing into Romania itself and occupying Bucharest in August of that year.

Moldovan Lei were declared legal tender in July 1995.

REPUBLIC

GOVERNMENT

1994 ND PROVISIONAL ISSUES
#1-15 issued 24.1.1994, invalidated on 1.12.1994.

1	**10 RUBLES**	**VG**	**VF**	**UNC**
	ND (1994- old date 1961). Green on pink tint adhesive stamp on Russia #233.	.10	.40	2.00

2	**10 RUBLES**	**VG**	**VF**	**UNC**
	ND (1994- old date 1991). Green on pink tint adhesive stamp on Russia #240.	.30	1.25	2.00

3	**25 RUBLES**	**VG**	**VF**	**UNC**
	ND (1994- old date 1961). Red-violet on buff tint adhesive stamp on Russia #234.	.15	.60	2.00
4	**50 RUBLES**			
	ND (1994- old date 1991). Red on pale green tint adhesive stamp on Russia #241.	.20	.80	5.00

		VG	VF	UNC
5	**50 RUBLES** ND (1994- old date 1992). Red on pale green tint adhesive stamp on Russia #237.	.20	.80	4.00
6	**100 RUBLES** ND (1994- old date 1991). Black on pale blue tint adhesive stamp on Russia #242.	.25	1.00	10.00

		VG	VF	UNC
7	**100 RUBLES** ND (1994- old date 1991). Black on pale blue tint adhesive stamp on Russia #243.	.25	1.00	4.00
8	**200 RUBLES** ND (1994- old date 1991). Green on yellow tint adhesive stamp on Russia #244.	.25	1.00	12.00
9	**200 RUBLES** ND (1994- old date 1992). Green on yellow tint adhesive stamp on Russia #248.	.25	1.00	3.00
10	**500 RUBLES** ND (1994- old date 1991). Blue adhesive stamp on Russia #245.	1.25	3.00	12.00

		VG	VF	UNC
11	**500 RUBLES** ND (1994- old date 1992). Blue adhesive stamp on Russia #249.	.20	.50	1.00
12	**1000 RUBLES** ND (1994- old date 1991). Violet on yellow tint adhesive stamp on Russia #246.	1.00	2.50	12.00

		VG	VF	UNC
13	**1000 RUBLES** ND (1994- old date 1992). Violet on yellow tint adhesive stamp on Russia #250.	.20	.50	1.00

		VG	VF	UNC
14	**5000 RUBLES** ND (1994- old date 1992). Dk. brown on pale blue-gray tint adhesive stamp on Russia #251.	.30	.75	2.00
14A	**5000 RUBLES** ND (1994 -old date 1961). Adhesive stamp on Russia 5 Rubles #224.	.15	.60	2.00
14B	**5000 RUBLES** ND (1994 -old date 1991). Adhesive stamp on Russia 5 Rubles #239.	.20	.75	2.50

		VG	VF	UNC
15	**10,000 RUBLES** ND (1994- old date 1992). Purple on yellow tint adhesive stamp on Russia #252.	.50	1.00	4.00

БАНКЭ НИСТРЯНЭ

BANKA NISTRIANA

1993-94 КУоOH KUPON ISSUE

#16-18 A. V. Suvorov at r. Parliament bldg. at ctr. on back. Wmk: Block design.

#19-24 equestrian statue of A. V. Suvorov at r. Parliament bldg. on back. Wmk: Block design.

NOTE: Postal adhesive stamps have been seen affixed to #16-18 to imitate revalidated notes.

		VG	VF	UNC
16	**1 RUBLE** 1994. Dk. green on m/c unpt.	FV	FV	.30

		VG	VF	UNC
17	**5 RUBLEI** 1994. Blue on m/c unpt.	FV	.10	.35

		VG	VF	UNC
18	**10 RUBLEI** 1994. Red-violet on m/c unpt.	FV	.15	.50

		VG	VF	UNC
19	**50 RUBLEI** 1993 (1994). Olive-green on m/c unpt.	FV	.10	.35

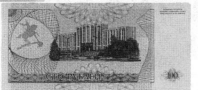

20 **100 RUBLEI**   **VG**   **VF**   **UNC**
      1993 (1994). Dk. brown on m/c unpt.   FV   .15   .50

21 **200 RUBLEI**   **VG**   **VF**   **UNC**
      1993 (1994). Brown and violet on m/c unpt.   FV   .15   .50

22 **500 RUBLEI**   **VG**   **VF**   **UNC**
      1993 (1994). Blue-black on m/c unpt.   FV   .30   1.00

23 **1000 RUBLEI**   **VG**   **VF**   **UNC**
      1993 (1994). Purple and red-violet on m/c unpt.   FV   .50   1.75
24 **5000 RUBLEI**
      1993 (1994). Black on deep olive-green and m/c unpt.   FV   FV   2.50
25 **10,000 RUBLEI**
      (1995).   Expected New Issue

1994 (1995) ISSUE
Currency Reform
1 "New" Ruble = 1000 "Old" Rublei

26 **1000 RUBLEI = 100,000 RUBLES**   **VG**   **VF**   **UNC**
(31)   1994 (1995). Violet and purple. V. Suvorov at r. Parliament bldg. on   FV   FV   3.00
        back.

1995; ND (1996) PROVISIONAL ISSUE

27 **50,000 RUBLEI ON 5 RUBLEI**   **VG**   **VF**   **UNC**
      ND (1996 - old date 1994). Blue on m/c unpt. Hologram w/*50,000* at   FV   FV   1.75
      upper l. on #17.
28 **50,000 RUBLEI = 500,000 RUBLEI**
      1995 (1996). Brown on m/c unpt. B. Chmeinitsky at r. Drama and   FV   FV   7.00
      comedy theatre on back.

1996 ND PROVISIONAL ISSUE

29 **10,000 RUBLEI ON 1 RUBLE**   **VG**   **VF**   **UNC**
      ND (1996 - old date 1994). Dk. green on m/c unpt. Ovpt. on #16.   FV   FV   .75

30 **50,000 RUBLEI ON 5 RUBLEI**   **VG**   **VF**   **UNC**
      ND (1996 - old date 1994). Blue on m/c unpt. Ovpt. on #17.   FV   FV   1.75

31 **100,000 RUBLEI ON 10 RUBLEI**   **VG**   **VF**   **UNC**
      ND (1996 - old date 1994). Red-violet on m/c unpt. Ovpt. on #18.   FV   FV   3.00

TRINIDAD & TOBAGO

Caribbean Sea

North Atlantic Ocean

VENEZUELA

GUYANA

The Republic of Trinidad and Tobago, a member of the British Commonwealth, situated 7 miles (11 km.) off the coast of Venezuela, has an area of 1,981 sq. mi. (5,130 sq. km.) and a population of 1.25 million. Capital: Port-of-Spain. The Island of Trinidad contains the world's largest natural asphalt bog. Birds of Paradise live on little Tobago, the only place outside of their native New Guinea where they can be found in a wild state. Petroleum and petroleum products are the mainstay of the economy. Petroleum products, crude oil and sugar are exported.

Trinidad and Tobago were discovered by Columbus in 1498. Trinidad remained under Spanish rule from the time of its settlement in 1592 until its capture by the British in 1797. It was ceded to the British in 1802. Tobago was occupied at various times by the French, Dutch and English before being ceded to Britain in 1814. Trinidad and Tobago were merged into a single colony in 1888. The colony was part of the Federation of the West Indies until Aug. 31, 1962, when it became an independent member of the Commonwealth of Nations. A new constitution establishing a republican form of government was adopted on Aug. 1, 1976. Trinidad and Tobago is a member of the Commonwealth of Nations. The president is Chief of State. The prime minister is Head of Government.

Notes of the British Caribbean Territories circulated between 1950-1964.

RULERS:
British to 1976

MONETARY SYSTEM:
1 Dollar = 100 Cents

REPUBLIC

CENTRAL BANK OF TRINIDAD AND TOBAGO

SIGNATURE VARITIES

1	J. F. Pierce	5	W. Demas
2	A. N McLeod	6	N. Hareward
3	J. E. Bruce		
4	Linn OHB		

1964 CENTRAL BANK ACT OF TRINIDAD AND TOBAGO

Central Bank Act of Trinidad and Tobago, 1964

#26-29 arms at l., Portr. Qn. Elizabeth II at ctr. Central Bank bldg. at ctr. on back. Wmk: Bird of paradise.

26	**1 DOLLAR**	VG	VF	UNC
	L.1964. Red. Oil rig in water at upper r. on back.			
	a. Sign. 1.	1.50	3.50	20.00
	b. Sign. 2.	2.00	4.50	30.00
	c. Sign. 3.	1.00	2.50	15.00
	s. As a. Specimen.	—	—	175.00

27	**5 DOLLARS**	VG	VF	UNC
	L.1964. Green. Crane loading sugarcane at upper r. on back.			
	a. Sign. 1.	7.50	30.00	250.00
	b. Sign. 2.	5.00	12.50	135.00
	c. Sign. 3.	2.00	7.50	65.00
	s. As a. Specimen.	—	—	250.00

28	**10 DOLLARS**	VG	VF	UNC
	L.1964. Dk. brown. Factory at upper r. on back.			
	a. Sign. 1.	10.00	35.00	450.00
	b. Sign. 2.	9.00	30.00	400.00
	c. Sign. 3.	5.00	15.00	175.00
	s. As a. Specimen.	—	—	325.00

29	**20 DOLLARS**	VG	VF	UNC
	L.1964. Purple. Cocoa pods at upper r. on back.			
	a. Sign. 1.	15.00	50.00	550.00
	b. Sign. 2.	12.50	35.00	450.00
	c. Sign. 3.	7.50	20.00	250.00
	s. As a. Specimen.	—	—	375.00

1977 ISSUE

#30-35 authorization date 1964. Arms at ctr. Back designs like previous issue. Wmk: Bird of paradise.

30	**1 DOLLAR**	VG	VF	UNC
	L.1964 (1977). Red on m/c unpt. 2 flying birds at l.			
	a. Sign. 3.	FV	.50	3.00
	b. Sign. 4.	FV	1.00	4.00

31	**5 DOLLARS**	VG	VF	UNC
	L.1964 (1977). Dk. green on m/c unpt. Branches and leaves at l.			
	a. Sign. 3.	FV	1.00	6.00
	b. Sign. 4.	FV	2.00	12.00

32	**10 DOLLARS**	VG	VF	UNC
	L.1964 (1977). Dk. brown on m/c unpt. Bird on branch at l. Sign. 3.	FV	3.00	13.50
33	**20 DOLLARS**			
	L.1964 (1977). Purple on m/c unpt. Flowers at l. Sign. 3	FV	6.00	27.50
34	**50 DOLLARS**			
	L.1964 (1977). Dk. brown on m/c unpt. Hummingbird at l. Net fishing at upper r. on back. Sign. 3.			
	a. 1963 (error date in authorization).	25.00	40.00	165.00
	b. 1964 (corrected authorization on date).	30.00	75.00	300.00
35	**100 DOLLARS**			
	L.1964 (1977). Deep blue on m/c unpt. Branch w/leaves and berries at l. Huts and palm trees at upper r. on back.			
	a. Sign. 3.	FV	30.00	125.00
	b. Sign. 4.	FV	35.00	150.00

1985 ISSUE
Central Bank Act Chap. 79.02

#36-40 arms at ctr. Twin towered modern bank bldg. at ctr. on back. Wmk: Bird of paradise.

36	**1 DOLLAR**	VG	VF	UNC
	ND (1985). Red-orange and purple on m/c unpt. 2 birds at l. Oil refinery at r. on back.			
	a. Sign. 4.	FV	FV	1.00
	b. Sign. 5.	FV	FV	.85
	c. Sign. 6.	FV	FV	.75

37	**5 DOLLARS**	VG	VF	UNC
	ND (1985). Dk. green on m/c unpt. Bird at l. Women working at r. on back.			
	a. Sign. 4.	FV	FV	3.50
	b. Sign. 5.	FV	FV	3.00
	c. Sign. 6.	FV	FV	2.25

38	**10 DOLLARS**	VG	VF	UNC
	ND (1985). Dk. brown on m/c unpt. Face similar to #32. Cargo ship dockside at r. on back.			
	a. Sign. 4.	FV	FV	7.00
	b. Sign. 5.	FV	FV	6.00
	c. Sign. 6.	FV	FV	4.00

39	**20 DOLLARS**	VG	VF	UNC
	ND (1985). Purple on m/c unpt. Hummingbird in flowers at l. Steel drums at r. on back.			
	a. Sign. 4.	FV	FV	11.50
	b. Sign. 5.	FV	FV	7.00
	c. Sign. 6.	FV	FV	6.00

40	**100 DOLLARS**	VG	VF	UNC
	ND (1985). Deep blue on m/c unpt. Bird at l. Oil rig at r. on back.			
	a. Sign. 4.	FV	FV	50.00
	b. Sign. 5.	FV	FV	33.50
	c. Sign. 6.	FV	FV	28.50

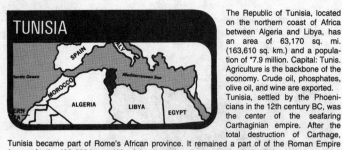

The Republic of Tunisia, located on the northern coast of Africa between Algeria and Libya, has an area of 63,170 sq. mi. (163,610 sq. km.) and a population of *7.9 million. Capital: Tunis. Agriculture is the backbone of the economy. Crude oil, phosphates, olive oil, and wine are exported.

Tunisia, settled by the Phoenicians in the 12th century BC, was the center of the seafaring Carthaginian empire. After the total destruction of Carthage,

Tunisia became part of Rome's African province. It remained a part of of the Roman Empire (except for the 439-533 interval Vandal conquest) until taken by the Arabs, 648, who administered it until the Turkish invasion of 1570. Under Turkish control, the public revenue was heavily dependent upon the piracy of Mediterranean shipping, an endeavor that wasn't abandoned until 1819 when a coalition of powers threatened appropriate reprisal. Deprived of its major source of income, Tunisia underwent a financial regression that ended in bankruptcy, enabling France to establish a protectorate over the country in 1881. National agitation and guerrilla fighting forced France to grant Tunisia internal autonomy in 1955 and to recognize Tunisian independence on March 20, 1956. Tunisia abolished the monarchy and established a republic on July 25, 1957.

RULERS:
French, 1881-1956

MONETARY SYSTEM:
1 Franc = 100 Centimes to 1960
1 Dinar = 1000 Millim, 1960-

REPUBLIC

BANQUE CENTRALE DE TUNISIE

1962 ND ISSUE

#57 and 58 H. Bourguiba at l.
#59-61 H. Bourguiba at r.

57	1/2 DINAR	VG	VF	UNC
	ND. (1962). Purple on m/c unpt. Mosque at r. Ruins at l., arms at r. on back.	4.00	20.00	100.00
58	1 DINAR			
	ND. (1962). Green on m/c unpt. Peasant and farm machine at r. Dam on back.	3.50	17.50	85.00

59	5 DINARS	VG	VF	UNC
	ND. (1962). Brown on m/c unpt. Bridge at l., Arabic numerals 5 and serial #. Archways on back.	2.50	20.00	100.00

60	5 DINARS	VG	VF	UNC
	1.11.1960. Brown on m/c unpt. H. Bourguiba at r., bridge at l. Western numerals 5 and serial #.	7.50	25.00	120.00

1962 ISSUE

61	5 DINARS	VG	VF	UNC
	20.3.1962. Blue on m/c unpt. Like #60.	10.00	25.00	125.00

1965-69 ISSUE

#63-65 H. Bourguiba at r. and as wmk.

62	1/2 DINAR	VG	VF	UNC
	1.6.1965. Blue on m/c unpt. H. Bourguiba at l., Mosque at r. Mosaic from Monastir on back.	5.00	20.00	80.00

63	1 DINAR	VG	VF	UNC
	1.6.1965. Blue on m/c unpt. Factory at l. Mosaic on back.	6.00	20.00	70.00

64   5 DINARS
1.6.1965. Lilac-brown and green on m/c unpt. Sadiki College at l. Mosaic w/woman in sprays at l., arch at ctr., Sunface at lower r. on back.

VG	VF	UNC
10.00	35.00	125.00

65   10 DINARS
1.6.1969. M/c. Refinery at l. Palm trees in field on back.

VG	VF	UNC
15.00	30.00	100.00

1972 ISSUE
#66-68 H. Bourguiba at r. and as wmk. Printer: TDLR.

66   1/2 DINAR
3.8.1972. Brown on m/c unpt. City w/river at l. View of Tunis on back.

VG	VF	UNC
1.00	7.50	15.00

67   1 DINAR
3.8.1972. Purple on m/c unpt. Old fort at l. Minaret at l., girl at ctr. on back.

VG	VF	UNC
2.00	10.00	45.00

68   5 DINARS
3.8.1972. Green on m/c unpt. Modern bldg. at l. Amphitheater at El-Djem on back.

VG	VF	UNC
6.00	21.50	85.00

1973 ISSUE
#69-72 H. Bourguiba at l. ctr. and as wmk.

69   1/2 DINAR
15.10.1973. Green on m/c unpt. Man w/camel and trees at l. Landscape w/sheep and assorted produce on back.

VG	VF	UNC
1.50	8.50	20.00

70   1 DINAR
15.10.1973. Blue and green on m/c unpt. Bldg. at r. Industrial scenes on back.

VG	VF	UNC
1.50	4.50	18.50

			VG	VF	UNC
71	**5 DINARS**				
	15.10.1973. Dk. brown and lilac on m/c unpt. City view at l. Montage of old and new on back.		FV	12.00	25.00

			VG	VF	UNC
72	**10 DINARS**				
	15.10.1973. Lilac on m/c unpt. Refinery in background at ctr. Montage w/students, column, train and drummers on back.		FV	20.00	100.00

1980 ISSUE
#74, 75 and 77 H. Bourgaiba at r. and as wmk.

			VG	VF	UNC
74	**1 DINAR**				
	15.10.1980. Red-brown on dk. red and m/c unpt. Amphitheater at ctr. Town w/sea and mountain on back.		FV	2.50	16.50
75	**5 DINARS**				
	15.10.1980. Brown and green on m/c unpt. Bldgs. at ctr. Bridge and hills at l. on back.		FV	6.50	22.50
76	**10 DINARS**				
	15.10.1980. Blue-green on bistre and m/c unpt. H. Bourguiba at l., bldg. at ctr. Reservoir at ctr. on back.		FV	15.00	43.50

			VG	VF	UNC
77	**20 DINARS**				
	15.10.1980. Dk. blue and brown on m/c unpt. Amphitheater at ctr. Rowboats dockside on back.		FV	30.00	85.00

1983 ISSUE
#79-81 H. Bourguiba on face and as wmk.

			VG	VF	UNC
79	**5 DINARS**				
	3.11.1983. Red-brown on lilac unpt. H. Bourguiba at l., desert scene at bottom ctr. Hydroelectric dam at ctr. r. on back.		FV	6.00	15.00

			VG	VF	UNC
80	**10 DINARS**				
	3.11.1983. Blue and lilac on m/c unpt. Workers at lower l. ctr., H. Bourguiba at ctr., offshore oil rig at r. Modern bldg. at ctr., old city gateways at r. on back.		FV	15.00	35.00

81 **20 DINARS**
3.11.1983. Lt. blue and dk. blue on green unpt. H. Bourguiba at l.,
bldg. at bottom ctr. Harbor on back.

	VG	VF	UNC
	FV	22.00	67.50

1986 ISSUE
#85 Held in reserve.

84 **10 DINARS**
20.3.1986. Yellow-brown on green unpt. H. Bourguiba at l. ctr. and as
wmk., agricultural scene at bottom ctr. Offshore oil rig at l. ctr. on
back.

	VG	VF	UNC
	FV	FV	22.50

1992-94 ISSUE

86 **5 DINARS**
7.11.1993. Black, olive-brown and green. Head of Hannibal at l. ctr.
and as wmk., harbor fortress at r. "Dec. 7, 1987" collage at l. ctr. on
back.

	VG	VF	UNC
	FV	FV	10.00

87 **10 DINARS**
7.11.1994. Purple and red on m/c unpt. Ibn Khaldoun at ctr. and as
wmk. Open book of "7 Novembre" at l. ctr. on back.

		VG	VF	UNC
		FV	FV	18.50

88 **20 DINARS**
7.11.1992. Deep purple, blue-black and red-brown on m/c unpt. K.
Ettounsi on horseback at l. ctr., his head as wmk., bldgs. in
background. Montage of city view; a '7' over flag on stylized dove at
ctr. on back.

		VG	VF	UNC
		FV	FV	35.00

89 **50 DINARS**
199x.

Expected New Issue

TURKEY

The Republic of Turkey, a parliamentary democracy of the Near East located partially in Europe and partially in Asia between the Black and the Mediterranean seas, has an area of 301,382 sq. mi. (780,580 sq. km.) and a population of 59.9 million. Capital: Ankara. Turkey exports cotton, hazelnuts, and tobacco, and enjoys a virtual monopoly in meerschaum.

The Ottoman Turks, a tribe from Central Asia, first appeared in the early 13th century, and by the 17th century had established the Ottoman Empire which stretched from the Persian Gulf to the southern frontier of Poland, and from the Caspian Sea to the Algerian plateau. The defeat of the Turkish navy by the Holy League in 1571, and of the Turkish forces besieging Vienna in 1683, began the steady decline of the Ottoman Empire which, accelerated by the rise of nationalism, contracted its European border, and by the end of World War I deprived it of its Arab lands. The present Turkish boundaries were largely fixed by the Treaty of Lausanne in 1923. The sultanate and caliphate, the political and spiritual ruling institutions of the old empire, were separated and the sultanate abolished in 1922 by Mustafa Kemal Atatürk. On Oct. 29, 1923, Turkey formally became a republic and Atatürk was selected as the first president.

* * * NOTE: This section has been renumbered * * *

MONETARY SYSTEM:
1 Lira (Livre, Pound) = 100 Piastres

REPUBLIC

TÜRKIYE CÜMHURIYET MERKAZ BANKASI

CENTRAL BANK OF TURKEY

1961-65 ND ISSUES

CENTRAL BANK LAW 11 HAZIRAN 1930
#173-175 Pres. K. Atatürk at r. and as wmk. Sign. varieties. Printer: DBM-A (w/o imprint).
#176-178 Pres. K. Atatürk at r. and as wmk. Printer: DBM-A (w/o imprint).

173 (95)	**5 LIRA** L.1930 (25.10.1961). Blue w/orange, blue and m/c guilloche. Back blue; 3 peasant women w/baskets of hazlenuts at ctr.	VG 1.75	VF 4.00	UNC 25.00
174 (96)	**5 LIRA** L.1930 (4.1.1965). Blue-green. Back blue-gray.	1.75	4.00	25.00

175 (106)	**50 LIRA** L.1930 (1.6.1964). Brown on m/c unpt. Different sign. Soldier holding rifle at ctr. on back.	VG 2.50	VF 7.50	UNC 30.00
176 (112)	**100 LIRA** L.1930 (15.3.1962). Olive on orange and m/c guilloche. Park w/bridge in Ankara on back.	5.00	17.50	50.00

			VG	VF	UNC
177 (113)	**100 LIRA** *L.1930* (1.10.1964). Like #176, but guilloche blue, lilac and m/c. Different sign.		5.00	17.50	50.00
178 (114)	**500 LIRA** *L.1930* (1.12.1962). Brown. Square w/mosque on back.		25.00	60.00	200.00

1966-69 ND ISSUE

CENTRAL BANK LAW 11 HAZIRAN 1930

#179-183 Pres. Atatürk at r. and as wmk. 3 sign. Printer: DBM-A (w/o imprint).

			VG	VF	UNC
179 (115)	**5 LIRA** *L.1930* (8.1.1968). Grayish purple on m/c unpt. Waterfalls on back.		.15	.75	1.75
180 (116)	**10 LIRA** *L.1930* (4.7.1966). Green on m/c unpt. Lighthouse at l., town view at ctr. on back.		.30	1.00	3.50

			VG	VF	UNC
181 (117)	**20 LIRA** *L.1930* (15.6.1966). Red-brown on m/c unpt. Back dull brown on pale green unpt., monument at l., tomb of Atatürk at ctr. on back.		1.00	2.25	6.50
182 (118)	**100 LIRA** *L.1930* (17.3.1969). Like #176 but modified guilloche in pinkish red, blue and m/c. Different sign.		7.50	20.00	60.00
183 (119)	**500 LIRA** *L.1930* (3.6.1968). Purple, brown and m/c. Like #114.		10.00	40.00	150.00

1971-82 ND ISSUE

CENTRAL BANK LAW OCAK 14 (JANUARY 26), 1970 AND 11 HAZIRAN 1930

#185-191 Pres. Atatürk at r. and as wmk.
#184 *Deleted*. See #175.

			VG	VF	UNC
185 (121)	**5 LIRA** *L.1970*. Like #181. 2 sign.		.15	.30	1.50

			VG	VF	UNC
186 (122)	**10 LIRA** *L.1970*. Like #182.		.30	1.00	3.00

			VG	VF	UNC
187 (123)	**20 LIRA** *L.1970*. Like #183.				
	a. Black sign. 2 varieties.		.20	.60	1.50
	b. Brown sign.		.20	.40	1.00

			VG	VF	UNC
188 (124)	**50 LIRA** *L.1970*. Dk. brown on m/c unpt. New portr. at r. Fountain on back. 2 sign. varieties.		.50	.75	1.50

189 **100 LIRA**
(125)   *L.1970* 15.5.1972). Blue-green on m/c unpt. Face similar to #188.
      Back brown; Mt. Ararat. 2 sign. varieties.

		VG	**VF**	**UNC**
		.60	1.00	2.00

190 **500 LIRA**
(126)   *L.1970* 1.9.1971). Blue-black and dk. green on m/c unpt. Gate of the
      University of Istanbul on back. 2 sign. varieties.

		VG	**VF**	**UNC**
		1.25	3.50	10.00

191 **1000 LIRA**
(127)   *L.1970.* Deep purple and brown-violet on m/c unpt. River w/boat and
      suspension bridge on back. Sign. varieties.

		VG	**VF**	**UNC**
		1.25	2.50	7.50

1984-97 ND ISSUES

CENTRAL BANK LAW OCAK 14 (JANUARY 26), 1970 AND 11 HAZI-RAN 1930

#192-208 Pres. Atatürk at r. and as wmk.

192 **10 LIRA**
(130)   *L.1970.* Dull gray-green on m/c unpt. Young boy and girl in medallion
      in unpt. at ctr. Children presenting flowers to Atatürk on back.

		VG	**VF**	**UNC**
		.10	.20	.50

193 **10 LIRA**
(130A) *L.1970.* Like #192 but black on m/c unpt.

		VG	**VF**	**UNC**
		.10	.20	.50

194 **100 LIRA**
(132)   *L.1970* (1984). Violet and brown on m/c unpt. Bldg., castle on hill,
      document and M. A. Ersoy on back.

		VG	**VF**	**UNC**
a.	Wmk.: Head sm. bust facing r., dotted security thread.	.15	.30	1.00
b.	Wmk.: Head lg. bust facing 3/4 r.	.10	.25	.75

195 **500 LIRA**
(133)   *L.1970* (1984). Blue on m/c unpt. Tower monument at l. ctr. on back.
      Wmk. varieties.

		VG	**VF**	**UNC**
		.25	.75	2.00

196 **1000 LIRA**
(134)   *L.1970* (1986). Blue-violet on m/c unpt. One dot for blind at lower l.
      Coastline at l., Fatin Sultan Mehmed at ctr. r. on back.

		VG	**VF**	**UNC**
		.35	.85	2.50

197
(135) **5000 LIRA**
L.1970 (1985). Dk. brown and olive-green on m/c unpt. 2 dots for blind at bottom l. Seated Mevlana at l. ctr., Mevlana Museum at ctr. on back.

	VG	VF	UNC
	.50	2.00	6.00

198
(136) **5000 LIRA**
L.1970 (ca.1992). Deep brown and deep green on m/c unpt. Face like #197. Afsin-Elbistan thermal power plant on back.

	VG	VF	UNC
	.40	1.50	4.00

199
(137) **10,000 LIRA**
L.1970. Purple and deep green on m/c unpt. 3 dots for blind at lower l. Back darker green and m/c; mosque at l., Mimar Sinan at ctr. on back.

	VG	VF	UNC
	FV	1.50	5.00

200 10,000 LIRA
L.1970. Like #199 but back pale green.

	VG	VF	UNC
	FV	.75	1.50

201
(138) **20,000 LIRA**
L.1970 (1988). Red-brown and violet on m/c unpt. Central Bank bldg. in Ankara at l. ctr. on back.

	VG	VF	UNC
	FV	FV	7.50

202
(138A) **20,000 LIRA**
L.1970 (1995). Like #201 but w/yellow unpt. on back. Red sign. Series G-.

	VG	VF	UNC
	FV	FV	2.25

203
(139) **50,000 LIRA**
L.1970 (1989). Black and blue-green on m/c unpt. Atatürk at r. National Parliament House in Ankara on back.

	VG	VF	UNC
	FV	FV	15.00

204
(139A) **50,000 LIRA**
L.1970 (1995). Like #203 but w/value in gray on back. Sereis K-.

	VG	VF	UNC
	FV	FV	3.50

205
(140) **100,000 LIRA**
L.1970 (1991). Reddish brown, dk. brown and black on m/c unpt. Equestrian statue of Atatürk at ctr. Children presenting flowers to Atatürk on back.

	VG	VF	UNC
	FV	FV	5.00

206 100,000 LIRA
L.1970 (1997). M/c. Like #205 but w/o security device at upper r.

Expected New Issue

207
(141) **250,000 LIRA**
L.1970 (1992). Blue-gray, dk. green and violet on m/c unpt. Triangular security device at upper r. Kizilkale Fortress at Alunya on back.

	VG	VF	UNC
	FV	FV	12.00

208
(142) **500,000 LIRA**
L.1970 (1993). Purple, blue-black and violet on m/c unpt. Square security device at upper r. Canakkale Martyrs Monument on back.

	VG	VF	UNC
	FV	FV	20.00

209
(143) **1,000,000 LIRA**
L.1970 (1995). Claret red and blue-gray on m/c unpt. Atatürk dam in Sani lurfa on back.

	VG	VF	UNC
	FV	FV	35.00

210 2,500,000 LIRA
L.1970 (1997). M/c.

Expected New Issue

TURKMENISTAN

The Turkmenistan Republic (formerly the Turkmen Soviet Socialist Republic) covers the territory of the Trans-Caspian Region of Turkestan, the Charjiui Vilayet of Bukhara and the part of Khiva located on the right bank of the Oxus. Bordered on the north by the Autonomous Kara-Kalpak Republic (a constituent of Uzbekistan), by Iran and Afghanistan on the south, by the Usbek Republic on the east and the Caspian Sea on the west. It has an area of 186,400 sq. mi. (488,100 sq. km.) and a population of 3.5 million. Capital: Ashkhabad (formerly Poltoratsk). Main occupation is agricultural products including cotton and maize. It is rich in minerals, oil, coal, sulphur and salt and is also famous for its carpets, Turkoman horses and Karakul sheep.

The Turkomans arrived in Transcaspia as nomadic Seluk Turks in the 11th century. It often became subjected to one of the neighboring states. Late in the 19th century the Czarist Russians invaded with their first victory at Kyzyl Arvat in 1877, arriving in Ashkhabad in 1882 resulting in submission of the Turkmen tribes. By Mar. 18, 1884 the Transcaspian province of Russian Turkestan was formed. During WW I the Czarist government tried to conscript the Turkmen; this led to a revolt in Oct. 1916 under the leadership of Aziz Chapykov. In 1918 the Turks captured Baku from the Red army and the British sent a contingent to Merv to prevent a German-Turkish offensive toward Afghanistan and India. In mid-1919 a Bureau of Turkistan Moslem Communist Organization was formed in Moscow hoping to develop one large republic including all surrounding Turkic areas within a Soviet federation. A Turkistan Autonomous Soviet Socialist Republic was formed and plans to partition Turkistan into five republics according to the principle of nationalities was quickly implemented by Joseph Stalin. On Oct. 27, 1924, Turkmenistan became a Soviet Socialist Republic and was accepted as a member of the U.S.S.R. on Jan. 29, 1925. The Bureau of T.M.C.O. was disbanded in 1934. In Aug. 1990 the Turkmen Supreme Soviet adopted a declaration of sovereignty followed by a declaration of independence in Oct. 1991 joining the Commonwealth of Independent States in Dec. A new constitution was adopted in 1992 providing for an executive presidency.

REPUBLIC

TÜRKMENISTANYÑ MERKEZI DÖWLET BANKY

CENTRAL BANK OF TURKMENISTAN

1993 ND; 1996 ISSUE
#1-9 wmk: Rearing Arabian horse.
#3-9 Pres. S. Niazov at r.

		VG	VF	UNC
1	**1 MANAT**			
	ND (1993). Brown and tan on m/c unpt. Ylymar Academy at ctr., native craft at r. Shield at l., temple *ILARSLANYÑ YADY-GARLIGI* at ctr. Wmk: Rearing horse.	FV	FV	.20

		VG	VF	UNC
2	**5 MANAT**			
	ND (1993). M/c. Bldg. Horse and bldg. on back.	FV	FV	.65

		VG	VF	UNC
3	**10 MANAT**			
	ND (1993). M/c. Bldg. at ctr. Bldg. on back.	FV	FV	1.00

		VG	VF	UNC
4	**20 MANAT**			
	ND (1993); 1995. M/c. National library at ctr.			
	a. ND (1993).	FV	FV	3.00
	b. 1995.	FV	FV	1.25

		VG	VF	UNC
5	**50 MANAT**			
	ND (1993); 1995. M/c. Monument at ctr. Anew mosque ruins on back.			
	a. ND (1993).	FV	FV	5.00
	b. 1995.	FV	FV	1.50

		VG	VF	UNC
6	**100 MANAT** ND (1993); 1995. Dk. blue and dk. gray on m/c unpt. Presidential Palace at ctr. Sultan Sanjaryn mausoleum on back.			
	a. ND (1993).	FV	FV	8.50
	b. 1995.	FV	FV	1.75

		VG	VF	UNC
7	**500 MANAT** ND (1993); 1995. Violet, dk. brown, orange and deep olive-brown on m/c unpt. National theatre at ctr. Hanymym mausoleum on back.			
	a. ND (1993).	FV	FV	12.50
	b. 1995.	FV	FV	6.50
8	**1000 MANAT** 1995. M/c. Bldg. at ctr. Coat of arms on back.	FV	FV	11.50
9	**5000 MANAT** 1996. Violet, purple and red on m/c unpt. Bldg. at ctr. Coat of arms on back.	FV	FV	38.50

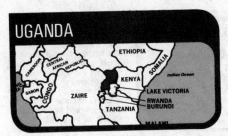

The Republic of Uganda, a former British protectorate located astride the equator in east-central Africa, has an area of 91,134 sq. mi. (236,036 sq. km.) and a population of 16.6 million. Capital: Kampala. Agriculture, including livestock, is the basis of the economy; there is some mining of copper, tin, gold and lead. Coffee, cotton, copper and tea are exported.

Uganda was first visited by Arab slavers in the 1830s. They were followed in the 1860s by British explorers searching for the headwaters of the Nile. The explorers, and the missionaries who followed them into the Lake Victoria region of south-central Africa in 1877-1879, found well developed African kingdoms dating back several centuries. In 1894 the local native Kingdom of Buganda was established as a British protectorate that was extended in 1896 to encompass an area substantially the same as the present Republic of Uganda. The protectorate was given a ministerial form of government in 1955, full internal self-government on March 1, 1962, and complete independence on Oct. 9, 1962. Uganda is a member of the Commonwealth of Nations. The president is Chief of State and Head of Government.

Notes of East African Currency Board circulated before Bank of Uganda notes were available.

Also see East Africa.

MONETARY SYSTEM:
1 Shilling = 100 Cents

CAUTION: The Bank of Uganda recently had sold demonetized notes, most of which were being made available for only $1.00 per note. Condition of notes thus sold is not reported. A listing of some pieces NOT available from the bank include #4, 6a, 7a, 8a and b, 9a and b, 13a, 14a, 16b, 23, and 24a and b.

REPUBLIC

BANK OF UGANDA

1966 ISSUE
#1-5 sign. titles: *GOVERNOR* and *SECRETARY*. Wmk: Hand.

		VG	VF	UNC
1	**5 SHILLINGS** ND (1966). Dk. blue on m/c unpt. Arms at r. River and waterfall on back.	.65	2.00	4.50

2 **10 SHILLINGS**
ND (1966). Brown on m/c unpt. Arms at ctr. Workers picking cotton on back.

VG	VF	UNC
1.35	4.00	10.00

3 **20 SHILLINGS**
ND (1966). Violet on m/c unpt. Arms at l. African animals on back.

VG	VF	UNC
1.00	3.00	7.50

4 **100 SHILLINGS**
ND (1966). Green on m/c unpt. Crested crane at l., w/o *FOR BANK OF UGANDA* just below value at ctr. Bldg. on back.

VG	VF	UNC
20.00	85.00	600.00

5 **100 SHILLINGS**
ND (1966). Green. Like #4 but w/text: *FOR BANK OF UGANDA* under value.

VG	VF	UNC
1.00	2.00	5.00

1973-77 ISSUE

SIGNATURE VARIETIES

1	*[signature]* GOVERNOR	*[signature]* SECRETARY	2	*[signature]* GOVERNOR	*[signature]* SECRETARY

#5A-9 Pres. Idi Amin at l. Wmk: Crested crane.

5A **5 SHILLINGS**
ND (1977). Blue and m/c. Woman picking coffee beans on back.

VG	VF	UNC
.50	1.00	2.75

6 **10 SHILLINGS**
ND (1973). Brown on m/c unpt. Elephants, antelope and hippopotamus on back.

	VG	VF	UNC
a. Sign. titles: *GOVERNOR* and *DIRECTOR*.	5.00	15.00	85.00
b. Sign. titles: *GOVERNOR* and *SECRETARY*. Sign. 1.	1.00	2.50	8.00
c. Sign. titles as b. Sign. 2.	.35	1.00	3.00

7 **20 SHILLINGS**
ND (1973). Purple on m/c unpt. Lg. bldg. on back.

	VG	VF	UNC
a. Sign. titles: *GOVERNOR* and *DIRECTOR*.	7.50	25.00	95.00
b. Sign. titles: *GOVERNOR* and *SECRETARY*. Sign. 1.	1.00	3.00	10.00
c. Sign. titles as b. Sign. 2.	.75	2.25	7.00

8   50 SHILLINGS
ND (1973). Blue on m/c unpt. Hydroelectric dam on back.

	VG	VF	UNC
a. Sign. titles: *GOVERNOR* and *DIRECTOR*.	8.50	40.00	175.00
b. Sign. titles: *GOVERNOR* and *SECRETARY*. Sign. 1.	2.00	5.00	20.00
c. Sign. titles as b. Sign. 2.	.75	2.00	5.00

9   100 SHILLINGS
ND (1973). Green on m/c unpt. Scene of lake and hills on back.

	VG	VF	UNC
a. Sign. titles: *GOVERNOR* and *DIRECTOR*.	8.00	30.00	135.00
b. Sign. titles: *GOVERNOR* and *SECRETARY*. Sign. 1.	3.00	10.00	45.00
c. Sign. titles as b. Sign. 2.	.75	2.00	7.00

1979 ISSUE

#10-14 Bank of Uganda at l. Sign. titles: *GOVERNOR* and *DIRECTOR*. Wmk: Crested crane's head.

10   5 SHILLINGS
ND (1979). Blue on m/c unpt. Back like #5A.

	VG	VF	UNC
	.10	.25	1.25

11   10 SHILLINGS
ND (1979). Brown and m/c. Back like #6.

	VG	VF	UNC
a. Lt. printing on bank.	.25	1.50	5.00
b. Dk. printing on bank.	.30	.90	2.75

12   20 SHILLINGS
ND (1979). Purple on m/c unpt. Back like #7.

	VG	VF	UNC
a. Lt. printing on bank.	.40	2.50	6.50
b. Dk. printing on bank.	.50	1.50	3.75

13   50 SHILLINGS
ND (1979). Dk. blue, purple and dk. blue-green on m/c unpt. Back like #8.

	VG	VF	UNC
a. Lt. printing on bank.	5.00	17.50	100.00
b. Dk. printing on bank.	.75	1.75	4.00

14   100 SHILLINGS
ND (1979). Green on m/c unpt. Back like #9.

	VG	VF	UNC
a. Lt. printing on bank.	1.50	4.00	10.00
b. Dk. printing on bank.	1.00	3.00	7.50

1982 ISSUE

#15-19 arms at l. Sign. titles: *GOVERNOR* and *SECRETARY*. Wmk: Crested crane's head.

15   5 SHILLINGS
ND (1982). Olive-green and m/c. Back like #5A.

	VG	VF	UNC
	.10	.40	1.00

16   10 SHILLINGS
ND (1982). Purple and m/c. Back like #6.

	VG	VF	UNC
	.15	.40	1.75

17   20 SHILLINGS
ND (1982). Green, red and m/c. Back like #7.

	VG	VF	UNC
	.30	1.50	4.50

18   50 SHILLINGS
ND (1982). Brown and m/c. Back like #8.

	VG	VF	UNC
a. Sign. titles: *GOVERNOR* and *SECRETARY*.	.30	1.25	3.50
b. Sign. titles: *GOVERNOR* and *DEPUTY GOVERNOR*.	.25	1.00	3.00

19   100 SHILLINGS
ND (1982). Red-violet, orange and m/c. Back like #9.

	VG	VF	UNC
a. Sign. titles: *GOVERNOR* and *SECRETARY*.	.75	2.50	7.50
b. Sign. titles: *GOVERNOR* and *DEPUTY GOVERNOR*. Sm. or lg. prefix letter and # before serial #.	.25	1.00	3.00

1983-85 ISSUE
#20-23 have Pres. Milton Obote at l. on face. Sign. titles: *GOVERNOR* and *DEPUTY GOVERNOR*. Wmk: Hand.

20   50 SHILLINGS
ND (1985). Brown on m/c unpt. Back like #18.

	VG	VF	UNC
	.50	1.00	2.75

21   100 SHILLINGS
ND (1985). Red-violet on m/c unpt. Back like #19.

	VG	VF	UNC
	1.00	2.50	7.50

22   500 SHILLINGS
ND (1983). Blue and m/c. Cattle and harvesting on back. Serial # prefix varieties as #19b.

	VG	VF	UNC
	.30	1.25	5.00

23   1000 SHILLINGS
ND (1983). Red and m/c. Bldg. on back. Serial # prefix varieties as #19b.

	VG	VF	UNC
	1.50	4.00	15.00

1985-86 ISSUE
#25 and 26 face similar to #24. Wmk: Crested crane's head.

24   5000 SHILLINGS
1985-86. Purple and m/c. Arms at l. Bldg. w/clock tower at ctr. r. on back.

	VG	VF	UNC
a. Wmk: Hand. 1985.	2.50	8.00	24.00
b. Wmk: Crested crane. 1986.	.75	2.25	7.00

25	500 SHILLINGS	VG	VF	UNC
	1986. Blue and m/c. Back like #22.	.25	.75	2.50

29	20 SHILLINGS	VG	VF	UNC
	1987-88. Purple, blue-black and violet on m/c unpt. Modern bldgs. at ctr. r. on back.			
	a. Imprint on back. 1987.	.20	.60	2.50
	b. W/o imprint. 1988.	.05	.25	1.00

26	1000 SHILLINGS	VG	VF	UNC
	1986. Red and m/c. Back like #23.	.35	1.00	3.00

1987-95 ISSUE

#27-32 arms at upper l., map at ctr. Printer: TDLR.

#29-34 wmk: Crested crane's head.

#33-35 arms at upper ctr.

30	50 SHILLINGS	VG	VF	UNC
	1987-89. Red, orange and dk. brown on m/c unpt. Parliament bldg. at ctr. r. on back.			
	a. Imprint on back. 1987.	.20	.50	3.00
	b. W/o imprint. 1988; 1989.	.15	.40	1.50

27	5 SHILLINGS	VG	VF	UNC
	1987. Brown on m/c unpt. Arms at r. also. African wildlife on back.	.10	.35	1.00

31	100 SHILLINGS	VG	VF	UNC
	1987-89. Deep blue-violet, black and aqua on m/c unpt. High Court bldg. w/clock tower at ctr. r. on back.			
	a. Sign. titles: *GOVERNOR* and *SECRETARY, TREASURER.* Imprint on back. 1987.	.25	.60	4.50
	b. As a. but w/o imprint on back. 1988.	.15	.25	1.50
	c. As b. but w/sign. titles: *GOVERNOR* and *SECRETARY.* 1994. W/o imprint. 1988.	FV	.20	1.00

28	10 SHILLINGS	VG	VF	UNC
	1987. Green on m/c unpt. Arms at r. also. 2 antelope grazing, 2 men fishing in canoe at ctr. on back.	.10	.35	1.25

32	200 SHILLINGS	VG	VF	UNC
	1987; 1991. Brown, orange and olive-brown on m/c unpt. Worker in textile factory at ctr. r. on back.			
	a. 1987.	.20	.50	2.25
	b. 1991.	.20	.50	2.25

33	500 SHILLINGS	VG	VF	UNC
	1991. Dk. brown and deep purple on m/c unpt. Elephant at l., arms at upper ctr. and lower r. Uganda Independence Monument at l., municipal bldg. w/clock tower at ctr. on back.			
	a. Sign. titles: *GOVERNOR* and *SECRETARY, TREASURY*.	.65	1.00	2.50
	b. Sign. titles: *GOVERNOR* and *SECRETARY*.	FV	.65	1.75

34	1000 SHILLINGS	VG	VF	UNC
	1991. Black, deep brown-violet and dk. green on m/c unpt. Farmers at l., arms at upper ctr. and lower r. Grain storage facility at ctr. on back.			
	a. Sign. titles: *GOVERNOR* and *SECRETARY, TREASURY*.	1.25	2.00	5.00
	b. Sign. titles: *GOVERNOR* and *SECRETARY*.	FV	1.25	3.00

1993-94 ISSUE
#35-38 wmk: Crested crane's head.

35	500 SHILLINGS	VG	VF	UNC
	1994. Like #36. Segmented foil over security thread. Ascending serial # at l.	FV	FV	2.00
36	1000 SHILLINGS			
	1994. Like #34. Segmented foil over security thread. Ascending serial # at l.	FV	1.25	3.00
37	5000 SHILLINGS			
	1993. Red-violet, deep purple and dk. green on m/c unpt. Lake Bunyoni, terraces at l. Railroad cars being loaded onto Kaawa Ferry at ctr., plant at lower r. on back.	FV	6.00	11.00
38	10,000 SHILLINGS			
	1995. Green and red on m/c unpt. Musical instruments at l. Owen Falls dam, kudu on back.	FV	11.00	20.00

UKRAINE

The Ukraine (formerly the Ukrainian Soviet Socialist Republic) is bordered by Russia to the east, Russia and Belarus to the north, Poland, Slovakia and Hungary to the west, Romania and Moldova to the southwest and in the south by the Black Sea and the Sea of Azov. It has an area of 233,088 sq. mi. (603,700 sq. km.) and a population of 51.9 million. Capital: Kyiv (Kiev). Ukraine was the site of the Chernobyl nuclear power station disaster in 1986. Coal, grain, vegetables and heavy industrial machinery are major exports.

The territory of Ukraine has been inhabited for over 30,000 years. As the result of its location, Ukraine has served as the gateway to Europe for millennia and its early history has been recorded by Arabic, Greek, Roman, as well as Ukrainian historians.

Ukraine, which was known as Rus' until the sixteenth century (and from which the name Russia was derived in the 17th century), became the major political and cultural center of Eastern Europe in the 9th century. The Rus' Kingdom, under a dynasty of Varangian origin, due to its position on the intersection of the north-south Scandinavia to Byzantium and the east-west Orient to Europe trade routes, became a focal point of world trade. At its apex Rus' stretched from the Baltic to the Black Sea and from the upper Volga River in the east, almost to the Vistula River in the west. It has family ties to many European dynasties. In 988 knyaz (king) Volodymyr adopted Christianity from Byzantium. With it came church books written in the Cyrillic alphabet, which originated in Bulgaria. The Mongol invasion in 1240 brought an end to the might of the Rus' Kingdom.

In the seventeenth century, after almost four hundred years of Mongol, Lithuanian, Polish, and Turkish domination, the Cossack State under Hetman Bohdan Khmelnytsky regained Ukrainian independence. The Hetman State lasted until the mid-eighteenth century and was followed by a period of foreign rule: Eastern Ukraine was controlled by Russia, which enforced russification through introduction of the Russian language and prohibiting the use of the Ukrainian language in schools, books and public life. Western Ukraine came under relatively benign Austro-Hungarian rule.

With the disintegration of the Russian and Austro-Hungarian Empires in 1917 and 1918, Eastern Ukraine declared its full independence on January 22, 1918 and Western Ukraine followed suit on November 1 of that year. On January 22, 1919 both parts united into one state that had to defend itself on three fronts: from the "Red" Bolsheviks and their puppet Ukrainian Soviet Republic formed in Kharkiv, from the "White" czarist Russian forces, and from Poland. Ukraine lost the war. In 1920 Eastern Ukraine was occupied by the Bolsheviks and in 1922 was incorporated into the Soviet Union. There followed a brief resurgence of Ukrainian language and culture until Stalin suppressed it in 1928. The artificial famine-genocide of 1932-33 killed 7-10 million Ukrainians, and Stalinist purges in the mid-1930s took a heavy toll. Western Ukraine was partitioned between Poland, Romania, Hungary and Czechoslovakia.

During the period of independence 1917-1920, Ukraine issued its own currency in Karbovanets denominations under the Central Rada of social-democrats (#1-11) and in Hryvnia denominations during the monarchy of Hetman Pavlo Skoropadsky (#12-19 and #29-34). During WW II German occupation forces issued Karbowanez currency.

On August 24, 1991 Ukraine once again declared its independence. On December 1, 1991 over 90% of Ukraine's electorate approved full independence from the Soviet Union. On December 5, 1991 the Ukrainian Parliament abrogated the 1922 treaty which incorporated Ukraine into the Soviet Union. Later, Leonid Kravchuk was elected president by a 65% majority.

During the changeover from the Ruble currency of the Soviet Union to the Karbovanets of Ukraine, as a transition measure and to restrict unlicensed export of scarce goods, coupon cards (202 x 82mm), similar to ration cards, were issued in various denominations They were valid for one month and were given to employees in amounts equal to their pay. Each card contained multiples of 1, 3, 5, 10, 25 and sometimes 50 Karbovanets valued coupons, to be cut apart. They were supposed to be used for purchases together with ruble notes. In January 1992 Ukraine began issuing individual coupons in Karbovanets denominations (printed in France and dated 1991), which are presently functioning as sole currency (#81-).

Ukraine is a charter member of the United Nations and has inherited the third largest nuclear arsenal in the world, which by recent agreement with the USA will be dismantled within the next decade. Ukrainians in the homeland and the diaspora make up 1% of the world's population.

MONETARY SYSTEM:
1 Karvovanets (Karbovantsiv) КАРБОВАНЕЦЬ, КАРБОВАНЦІВ = 1 Russian Ruble, 1991-96
1 Hrynia (Hryvni, Hryven) ГРИВНЯ (ГРИВНІ, ГРИВЕНЬ) = 100,000 Karbovantsiv, 1996-

УКРАЇНСЬКА Р.С.Р.

TREASURY

1990 ND КУПОН RUBLE CONTROL COUPON ISSUE
#68-70 and 72 various authorization handstamps in registry. Uniface.

#71 Held in reserve.

#73 and 74 Held in reserve.

68	50 KARBOVANTSIV	VG	VF	UNC
	ND (1990). Black text on pink unpt. Sheet of 28 coupons and registry. Жовтень.			
	a. Full sheet.	—	—	4.00
	b. Coupon.			.20
69	50 KARBOVANTSIV			
	ND (1990). Black text on pale blue-violet unpt. Sheet of 28 coupons and registry. Листопад.			
	a. Full sheet.	—	—	4.00
	b. Coupon.			.20
70	75 KARBOVANTSIV			
	ND (1990). Black text on pale green unpt. Sheet of 28 coupons and registry. Грудень.			
	a. Full sheet.	—	—	4.00
	b. Coupon.			.20
72	200 KARBOVANTSIV			
	ND (1990). Black text on blue unpt. Sheet of 28 coupons and registry. Червень.			
	a. Full sheet.	—	—	4.00
	b. Coupon.			.20

1991 KYoOH RUBLE CONTROL COUPON ISSUE

#75-79 various authorization handstamps in registry. Uniface.
#80 *Deleted. See #79.*

	82	**3 KARBOVANTSI**	VG	VF	UNC
		1991. Greenish gray and pale orange on yellow unpt. Back greenish gray.			
		a. Issued note.	.05	.10	.20
		b. Error. Uniface.	3.00	10.00	30.00

	83	**5 KARBOVANTSIV**	VG	VF	UNC
		1991. Dull blue-violet and pale orange on yellow unpt. Back lt. blue.			
		a. Issued note.	.05	.20	.40
		b. Error. Uniface.	3.00	10.00	30.00

	84	**10 KARBOVANTSIV**	VG	VF	UNC
		1991. Pink and pale orange on yellow unpt. Back red.	.05	.20	.50

	85	**25 KARBOVANTSIV**	VG	VF	UNC
		1991. Red-violet and pale orange on yellow unpt. Back red-violet.	.15	.50	1.50

	75	**50 KARBOVANTSIV**	VG	VF	UNC
		1991. Black text on green unpt. Sheet of 28 coupons and registry. Лютий.			
		a. Full sheet.	—	—	4.00
		b. Coupon.	—	—	.20
	76	**50 KARBOVANTSIV**			
		1991. Black text on pink unpt. Sheet of 28 coupons and registry. Квітень.			
		a. Full sheet.	—	—	4.00
		b. Coupon.	—	—	.20
	77	**50 KARBOVANTSIV**			
		1991. Black text on pale unpt. Sheet of 28 coupons registry. Травень.			
		a. Full sheet.	—	—	4.00
		b. Coupon.	—	—	.20
	78	**75 KARBOVANTSIV**			
		1991. Black text on pale green unpt. Sheet of 28 coupons and registry. Грудень.			
		a. Full sheet.	—	—	4.00
		b. Coupon.	—	—	.20
	79 (80)	**100 KARBOVANTSIV**			
		1991. Black text on aqua unpt. Sheet of 28 coupons and registry. березень.			
		a. Full sheet.	—	—	4.00
		b. Coupon.	—	—	.20

	86	**50 KARBOVANTSIV**	VG	VF	UNC
		1991. Blue-green and pale orange on yellow unpt. Back blue-green.			
		a. Issued note.	.10	.35	1.00
		b. Error. Uniface.	3.00	10.00	30.00

НАЦІОНАЛЬНИЙ БАНК УКРАЇНИ

UKRANIAN NATIONAL BANK

1991 COUPON ISSUE

Karbovanets System

Originally issued at par and temporarily to be used jointly with Russian rubles in commodity purchases as a means of currency control (similar to Ruble Control Coupons above). They soon became more popular while the ruble slowly depreciated in exchange value. This did not last very long and the karbovanets has now suffered a higher inflation rate than the Russian ruble.

#81-87 Lybed, Viking sister of the founding brothers, at l. Cathedral of St. Sophia in Kiev at l. ctr. on back. All notes w/o serial #. Wmk: Paper. All denominations had the value, i.e. *3 KRB*, printed sideways with indelible ink at l.

	81	**1 KARBOVANETS**	VG	VF	UNC
		1991. Dull brown and pale orange on yellow unpt. Back dull brown.	.05	.10	.20

	87	**100 KARBOVANTSIV**	VG	VF	UNC
		1991. Brown-violet and pale orange on yellow unpt. Back brown-violet.			
		a. Issued note.	.50	1.50	4.50
		b. Error. Uniface.	3.00	10.00	30.00

1992 ISSUE

#88-91 founding Viking brothers Kyi, Shchek and Khoryv w/sister Lebbid in bow of boat at l. Backs like #81-87. All notes w/serial #. Wmk. paper.

Replacement notes: Serial # prefix .../99 in denominator.

88	100 Karbovantsiv	VG	VF	Unc
	1992. Orange on lilac and ochre unpt. Back orange and gray.			
	a. Issued note.	.10	.40	1.75
	s. Specimen.	—	—	40.00

89	200 Karbovantsiv	VG	VF	Unc
	1992. Dull brown and silver on lilac and ochre unpt. Back dull brown and gray.			
	a. Issued note.	.25	.85	2.50
	s. Specimen.	—	—	40.00

90	500 Karbovantsiv	VG	VF	Unc
	1992. Blue-green and silver on lilac and ochre unpt. Back blue-green and gray.			
	a. Issued note.	.25	.85	2.50
	s. Specimen.	—	—	40.00

91	1000 Karbovantsiv	VG	VF	Unc
	1992. Red-violet and lt. green on lilac and ochre unpt. Back red-violet and gray.			
	a. Issued note.	.25	1.00	3.00
	s. Specimen.	—	—	40.00

GOVERNMENT

TREASURY

1992 СЕРТИФІКАТ - PRIVATIZATION CERTIFICATE ISSUE

91A	1,000,000 Karbovantsiv	VG	VF	Unc
	1992. Gray on pale blue-green and pale orange unpt. Church at l.	6.50	8.50	15.00

УКРАЇНСЬКА Р.С.Р.

Ukraine R.S.R.

НАЦІОНАЛЬНИЙ БАНК УКРАЇНИ

UKRANIAN NATIONAL BANK

1993 ISSUE

#92-93 similar to #88-91, but trident symbol added at l. on face; at r. on back.

#94-97 statue of St. Volodymyr standing w/long cross at l. Bldg. facade at l. on back. Trident at l. on face. at r. on back. Wmk: Ornamental shield repeated vertically.

#98-99 statue of St. Volodymyr standing w/long cross at r. Opera house at l. ctr. on back.

92	2000 Karbovantsiv	VG	VF	Unc
	1993. Blue and olive-green on aqua and gold unpt.	.35	1.00	3.00

93	5000 Karbovantsiv	VG	VF	Unc
	1993; 1995. Red-orange and olive-brown on pale blue and ochre unpt.			
	a. 1993.	.10	.35	1.00
	b. 1995.	.05	.15	.40

94	10,000 Karbovantsiv	VG	VF	Unc
	1993-96. Apple green and tan on pale blue and ochre unpt.			
	a. Local printing. 1993.	FV	FV	1.00
	b. Printer: TDLR (w/o imprint). 1995; 1996.	.05	.15	.40

95	20,000 Karbovantsiv	VG	VF	Unc
	1993-96. Lilac and tan on blue and yellow unpt.			
	a. 1993.	.20	.65	2.00
	b. 1994; 1995.	.10	.35	1.00
	c. Wmk: Zig-zag of 4 bars. 1996.	.20	.65	2.00

96	50,000 Karbovantsiv	VG	VF	Unc
	1993; 1994. Dull orange and blue on m/c unpt.	.15	.50	1.50

97	**100,000 Karbovantsiv**	VG	VF	Unc
	1993; 1994. Gray-green and ochre on m/c unpt.			
	a. Prefix letters above serial #. Wmk: *HYB*. 1993.	.25	1.00	4.00
	b. Prefix letters w/serial #. Wmk: Trident shield repeated. 1994.	.25	1.00	3.00

98	**200,000 Karbovantsiv**	VG	VF	Unc
	1993; 1994. Dull red-brown and lt. blue on aqua and gray unpt.			
	a. Prefix letters above serial #. Wmk: *HYB*. 1993.	1.25	2.50	8.00
	b. Prefix letters w/serial #. Wmk: Trident shield repeated. 1994.	1.00	2.00	6.00

99	**500,000 Karbovantsiv**	VG	VF	Unc
	1994. Lt. blue and lilac on yellow and gray unpt. Wmk: Trident shield repeated.	3.50	5.00	10.00

1995 Issue

100	**1,000,000 Karbovantsiv**	VG	VF	Unc
	1995. Dk. brown on pale orange, lt. blue and m/c unpt. Statue of T. G. Shevchenko, arms at lower l. Kyiv State University at l. ctr., arms at lower r. on back.	6.50	8.50	15.00

1992; ND (1996) Issue

#103-109 wmk: Trident repeated. Printer: CBNC (w/o imprint).

103	**1 Hryvnia**	VG	VF	Unc
	1992 (1996). Olive-brown on m/c unpt. Ruins of Kherson at ctr. Prince Vladimir at ctr. on back.	FV	FV	1.50

104	**2 Hryvni**	VG	VF	Unc
	1992 (1996). Brown on m/c unpt. Cathedral of St. Sophia in Kyiv at ctr. Yaroslav "The Wise" at ctr. on back.	FV	FV	2.50

105	**5 Hryven**	VG	VF	Unc
	1992 (1996). Blue-gray on m/c unpt. Village church in Subotiv at ctr. B. Chmielnytski at ctr. on back.	FV	FV	4.50
106	**10 Hryven**			
	1992 (1996). Violet on m/c unpt. Pechersky Monastery at ctr. l. Mazepa at ctr. on back.	FV	FV	8.50
107	**20 Hryven**			
	1992 (1996). Brown on m/c unpt. Opera theater in Lviv at ctr. l. Franko at ctr. on back.	FV	FV	16.50
108	**50 Hryven**			
	ca. 1992.	FV	FV	50.00
109	**100 Hryven**			
	ca. 1992.	FV	FV	95.00

1996 ND ISSUE
#110 and 111 printer: TDLR (w/o imprint).

110	50 HRYVEN		VG	VF	UNC
(108)	ND (1996). Purple and dk. blue-gray on m/c unpt. M. Hrushevski at r. and as wmk. Parliament bldg. at ctr. on back.		FV	FV	40.00

111	100 HRYVEN		VG	VF	UNC
(109)	ND (1996). Brown and dk. green on m/c unpt. T. Shevchenko at r. and as wmk. Cathedral of St. Sophia in Kyiv at ctr., statue of St. Volodymyr standing at l.		FV	FV	75.00

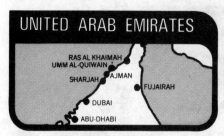

The seven United Arab Emirates (formerly known as the Trucial Sheikhdoms or States), located along the southern shore of the Persian Gulf, are comprised of the Sheikhdoms of Abu Dhabi, Dubai, Sharjah, Ajman, Umm al Qaiwain, Ras al Khaimah and Fujairah. They have a combined area of about 32,000 sq. mi. (83,600 sq. km.) and a population of 1.9 million. Capital: Abu Zaby (Abu Dhabi). Since the oil strikes of 1958-60, the economy has centered on petroleum.

The Trucial States came under direct British influence in 1892 when the maritime truce treaty, enacted after the suppression of pirate activity along the Trucial Coast, was enlarged to enjoin the states from disposing of any territory, or entering into any foreign agreements, without British consent in return for British protection from external aggression. In March of 1971 Britain reaffirmed its decision to terminate its treaty relationships with the Trucial Sheikhdoms, whereupon the seven states joined with Bahrain and Qatar in an effort to form a union of Arab emirates under British protection. When the prospective members failed to agree on terms of union, Bahrain and Qatar declared their respective independence in Aug. and Sept., 1971. Six of the Sheikhdoms united to form the United Arab Emirates on Dec. 2, 1971. Ras al Khaimah joined a few weeks later.

MONETARY SYSTEM:
1 Dirham = 1000 Fils

SHEIKHDOMS

UNITED ARAB EMIRATES CURRENCY BOARD

1973 ND ISSUE
#1-6 dhow, camel caravan, palm tree and oil derrick at l. Wmk: Arabian horse's head. Non-redeemable after 2.2.1989.

1	1 DIRHAM	VG	VF	UNC
	ND (1973). Green on m/c unpt. Police station on back.	1.00	4.00	15.00

2	5 DIRHAMS	VG	VF	UNC
	ND (1973). Purple on m/c unpt. Fort Fujairah on back.	1.25	5.00	25.00

3	10 DIRHAMS	VG	VF	UNC
	ND (1973). Gray-blue on m/c unpt. Umm Al Qaiwain (aerial photograph) on back.	2.00	8.00	35.00

4	50 DIRHAMS	VG	VF	UNC
	ND (1973). Red on m/c unpt. Ruler's Palace of Ajman on back.	8.00	32.50	125.00

5	100 DIRHAMS	VG	VF	UNC
	ND (1973). Olive-green on m/c unpt. Ras al Khaima (village on the Gulf) on back.	14.00	55.00	285.00

1976 ND ISSUE

6	1000 DIRHAMS	VG	VF	UNC
	ND (1976). Blue on m/c unpt. Fortress on back.	150.00	300.00	700.00

UNITED ARAB EMIRATES CENTRAL BANK

1982; 1983 ND ISSUE
#7-11 arms at upper ctr., sparrowhawk at l. on back. Wmk: Sparrowhawk's head.

7	5 DIRHAMS	VG	VF	UNC
	ND (1982). Brown on m/c unpt. Arms at ctr., Sharjah Market at r. Seacoast cove w/tower on back.	FV	FV	5.50

8	10 DIRHAMS	VG	VF	UNC
	ND (1982). Green on m/c unpt. Arms at ctr., Arab dagger at r. Terraces w/trees at l. ctr. on back.	FV	FV	10.00

9	50 DIRHAMS	VG	VF	UNC
	ND (1982). Purple, dk. brown and olive on m/c unpt. Oryx at r. Al Jahilie Fort at l. ctr. on back.	FV	FV	32.50

10	100 DIRHAMS	VG	VF	UNC
	ND (1982). Red, violet and black on m/c unpt. Al Fahidie Fort at r. Dubai Trade Ctr. at l. ctr. on back.	FV	FV	60.00

11	500 DIRHAMS	VG	VF	UNC
	ND (1983). Dk. blue, purple and brown on m/c unpt. Sparrowhawk at r. Mosque in Dubai at l. ctr. on back.	FV	FV	250.00

1989-95 ISSUE
#12-15 and 17 similar to #7-11 w/condensed Arabic text in titles and modified designs. Wmk: Sparrowhawk's head.

12	5 DIRHAMS	VG	VF	UNC
	1993-/AH1414-. Dk. brown, red-orange and violet on m/c unpt.			
	a. 1993/AH1414.	FV	FV	4.00
	b. 1995/AH1416.	FV	FV	3.50

13	**10 DIRHAMS**		VG	VF	UNC
	1993-/AH1414-. Green and pale olive-green on m/c unpt.				
	a.	1993/AH1414.	FV	FV	7.00
	b.	1995/AH1416.	FV	FV	6.00

14	**50 DIRHAMS**	VG	VF	UNC
	1995/AH1415. Purple, black and violet on m/c unpt.	FV	FV	30.00

15	**100 DIRHAMS**		VG	VF	UNC
	1993-/AH1414-. Red, red-violet and black on m/c unpt.				
	a.	1993/AH1414.		FV	50.00
	b.	1995/AH1416.		FV	47.50
16	**200 DIRHAMS**				
	1989/AH 1410. Brown, green and m/c. Sharla Court bldg. and Zayed Sports City on face. Central bank bldg. at l. ctr. on back.		FV	FV	90.00

17	**500 DIRHAMS**	VG	VF	UNC
	1993/AH1414. Dk. blue, black, purple and silver on m/c unpt. Similar to #11.	FV	FV	200.00

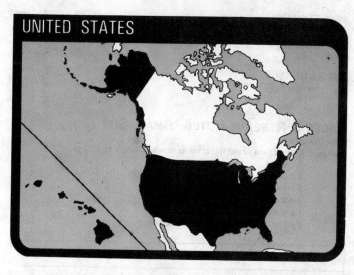

UNITED STATES

The United States of America as politically organized under the Articles of Confederation consisted of the 13 former British-American colonies - New Hampshire, Massachusetts, Rhode Island, Connecticut, New York, New Jersey, Pennsylvania, Delaware, Maryland, Virginia, North Carolina, South Carolina and Georgia - clustered along the eastern seaboard of North America between the forests of Maine (then part of Massachusetts) and the marshes of Georgia. The United States had no national capital; Philadelphia, where the Continental Congress met, was the "seat of the government." The population during this formative phase of America's history (1777-1789) was about 3 million, most of whom lived on self-sufficient family farms. Fishing, lumbering and the production of grains for export were major economic endeavors. Rapid strides were also being made in industry and manufacturing, as well as mining one-seventh of the world's production of raw iron.

On the basis of the voyage of John Cabot to the North American mainland in 1497, England claimed the entire continent. France and Spain also claimed extensive territory in North America. At the end of the French and Indian War (1763), England acquired all of the territory east of the Mississippi River, including East and West Florida. During the colonial and Confederation period individual states each retained the right to issue money and did so. Independence from Great Britain was declared on July 4, 1776 and ratified in 1783 at the end of the American Revolution. The Constitution which organized and governs the present United States was ratified on Nov. 21, 1788 and became effective in 1789, removing from the states the right to issue money.

1775 Declaration of Independence; 1789 George Washington first president; 1861-1865 Civil War and defeat of the Confederate States by the Union. Originally 13 states, in 1959 Alaska joined the Union as 49th and Hawaii as 50th state.

MONETARY SYSTEM:
1 Dollar = 100 Cents

REPUBLIC

UNITED STATES NOTES - SMALL SIZE

Red Treasury seal.

PORTRAIT VARIETIES

1 Dollar: George Washington	100 Dollars: Benjamin Franklin
2 Dollars: Thomas Jefferson	500 Dollars: William McKinley
5 Dollars: Abraham Lincoln	1000 Dollars: Grover Cleveland
10 Dollars: Alexander Hamilton	5000 Dollars: James Madison
20 Dollars: Andrew Jackson	10,000 Dollars: Salmon P. Chase
50 Dollars: U.S. Grant	100,000 Dollars: Woodrow Wilson

SERIES OF 1963

382	2 DOLLARS		VG	VF	UNC
	1963.		2.50	3.00	4.50
	a. 1963A.		2.50	3.00	4.50
383	5 DOLLARS				
	1963.		FV	8.00	10.00

SERIES OF 1966

384	100 DOLLARS		VG	VF	UNC
	1966.		FV	130.00	200.00
	a. 1966A.		FV	150.00	450.00

FEDERAL RESERVE NOTES - SMALL SIZE

Green Treasury seal.

Imprinted #, letter and name (in seal at l.) of 1 of the 12 Federal Reserve Banks:

A-1: Boston	G-7: Chicago
B-2: New York	H-8: St. Louis
C-3: Philadelphia	I-9: Minneapolis
D-4: Cleveland	J-10: Kansas City
E-5: Richmond	K-11: Dallas
F-6: Atlanta	L-12: San Fransisco

SIGNATURE VARIETIES

Series	Treasurer	Secretary
1963	Kathryn O'Hay Granahan	C. Douglas Dillon
1963A	Kathryn O'Hay Granahan	Henry H. Fowler
1963B	Kathryn O'Hay Granahan	Joseph W. Barr
1969	Dorothy Andrews Elston	David M. Kennedy
1969A	Dorothy Andrews Kabis	David M. Kennedy
1969B	Dorothy Andrews Kabis	John B. Connally
1969C	Romana Acosta Banuelos	John B. Connally
1969D	Romana Acosta Banuelos	George P. Schultz
1974	Francine I. Neff	William E. Simon
1977	Azie Taylor Morton	W. Michael Blumenthal
1977A	Azie Taylor Morton	J. William Miller
1981	Angela M. Buchanan	Donald T. Regan
1981A	Katherine Davalos Ortega	Donald T. Regan
1985	Katherine Davalos Ortega	John A. Baker III
1988	Katherine Davalos Ortega	Nicholas F. Brady
1988A	Catalina Vasquez Villapando	Nicholas F. Brady
1993	Mary Ellen Withrow	Lloyd Bentson
1995	Mary Ellen Withrow	Robert E. Rubin

BANKNOTE DESIGNS

1 DOLLAR	Portr. G. Washington. Great Seal flanking ONE on back.
2 DOLLAR	Portr. T. Jefferson. Monticello on back to 1963, signing of the Declaration of Independence, 1976 series.
5 DOLLAR	Portr. A. Lincoln. Lincoln Memorial on back.
10 DOLLAR	Portr. A. Hamilton. U.S. Treasury bldg. on back.
20 DOLLAR	Portr. A. Jackson. White House on back.
50 DOLLAR	Portr. U. S. Grant. U.S. Capital bldg. on back.
100 DOLLAR	Portr. B. Franklin. Independence Hall on back.

SERIES OF 1963

443	1 DOLLAR		VG	VF	UNC
	1963. (A-L).		FV	FV	3.00
	a. 1963A. (A-L).		FV	FV	3.00
	b. 1963B. (B; E; G; J; L).		FV	FV	3.50

444	5 DOLLARS		VG	VF	UNC
	1963. (A-D; F-H; J-L).		FV	FV	14.00
	a. 1963A. (A-L).		FV	FV	12.00

445	10 DOLLARS		VG	VF	UNC
	1963. (A-H; J-L).		FV	FV	20.00
	a. 1963A. (A-L).		FV	FV	20.00

446	20 DOLLARS		VG	VF	UNC
	1963. (A-B; D-H; J-L).		FV	FV	35.00
	a. 1963A. (A-L).		FV	FV	30.00

447	**50 DOLLARS**	VG	VF	UNC
	1963A. (A-L).	FV	FV	70.00

461	**2 DOLLARS**	VG	VF	UNC
	1976. (A-L).	FV	FV	4.00

SERIES OF 1977

NOTE: Since Oct. 1981 the Bureau of Engraving and Printing has made available to collectors uncut sheets of 4, 16 and 32 notes of the $1.00 and $2.00 denominations. A high serial # range is used.

462	**1 DOLLAR**	VG	VF	UNC
	1977. (A-L).	FV	FV	2.00
	a. 1977A. (A-L).	FV	FV	2.00
463	**5 DOLLARS**			
	1977. (A-L).	FV	FV	10.00
	a. 1977A. (A-L).	FV	FV	10.00
464	**10 DOLLARS**			
	1977. (A-L).	FV	FV	17.00
	a. 1977A. (A-L).	FV	FV	16.00
465	**20 DOLLARS**			
	1977. (A-L).	FV	FV	30.00
466	**50 DOLLARS**			
	1977. (A-L).	FV	FV	65.00

448	**100 DOLLARS**	VG	VF	UNC
	1963A. (A-L).	FV	FV	135.00

SERIES OF 1969

449	**1 DOLLAR**	VG	VF	UNC
	1969. (A-L).	FV	FV	2.50
	a. 1969A. (A-L).	FV	FV	2.50
	b. 1969B. (A-L).	FV	FV	2.50
	c. 1969C. (B; D-L).	FV	FV	2.50
	d. 1969D. (A-L).	FV	FV	2.50
450	**5 DOLLARS**			
	1969. (A-L).	FV	FV	10.00
	a. 1969A. (A-L).	FV	FV	12.00
	b. 1969B. (A-L).	FV	FV	14.00
	c. 1969C. (A-L).	FV	FV	10.00
451	**10 DOLLARS**			
	1969. (A-L).	FV	FV	20.00
	a. 1969A. (A-L).	FV	FV	20.00
	b. 1969B. (A-L).	FV	FV	25.00
	c. 1969C. (A-L).	FV	FV	18.00
452	**20 DOLLARS**			
	1969. (A-L).	FV	FV	30.00
	a. 1969A. (A-L).	FV	FV	30.00
	b. 1969B. (B; D-L).	FV	FV	40.00
	c. 1969C. (A-L).	FV	FV	30.00
453	**50 DOLLARS**			
	1969. (A-L).	FV	FV	75.00
	a. 1969A. (A-L).	FV	FV	70.00
	b. 1969B. (A-B; E-G; K).	FV	FV	90.00
	c. 1969C. (A-L).	FV	FV	70.00
454	**100 DOLLARS**			
	1969. (A-L).	FV	FV	130.00
	a. 1969A. (A-L).	FV	FV	130.00
	b. 1969C. (A-L).	FV	FV	125.00

SERIES OF 1974

455	**1 DOLLAR**	VG	VF	UNC
	1974. (A-L).	FV	FV	2.00
456	**5 DOLLARS**			
	1974. (A-L).	FV	FV	10.00
457	**10 DOLLARS**			
	1974. (A-L).	FV	FV	17.00
458	**20 DOLLARS**			
	1974. (A-L).	FV	FV	30.00
459	**50 DOLLARS**			
	1974. (A-L).	FV	FV	65.00
460	**100 DOLLARS**			
	1974. (A-L).	FV	FV	120.00

SERIES OF 1976

#461, Bicentennial of signing of the Declaration of Independence
NOTE: #461 is also available in uncut sheets of 4, 16 and 32 notes. A high series # range is used.

467	**100 DOLLARS**	VG	VF	UNC
	1977. (A-L).	FV	FV	120.00

SERIES OF 1981

468	**1 DOLLAR**	VG	VF	UNC
	1981. (A-L).	FV	FV	2.00
	a. 1981A.	FV	FV	2.00
469	**5 DOLLARS**			
	1981. (A-L).	FV	FV	10.00
	a. 1981A.	FV	FV	10.00
470	**10 DOLLARS**			
	1981. (A-L).	FV	FV	15.00
	a. 1981A.	FV	FV	15.00
471	**20 DOLLARS**			
	1981. (A-L).	FV	FV	30.00
	a. 1981A.	FV	FV	30.00
472	**50 DOLLARS**			
	1981. (A-L).	FV	FV	55.00
	a. 1981A.	FV	FV	65.00
473	**100 DOLLARS**			
	1981. (A-L).	FV	FV	120.00
	a. 1981A.	FV	FV	120.00

SERIES OF 1985

474	**1 DOLLAR**	VG	VF	UNC
	1985. (A-L).	FV	FV	2.00
475	**5 DOLLARS**			
	1985. (A-L).	FV	FV	10.00
476	**10 DOLLARS**			
	1985. (A-L).	FV	FV	15.00
477	**20 DOLLARS**			
	1985. (A-L).	FV	FV	30.00
478	**50 DOLLARS**			
	1985. (A-L).	FV	FV	65.00
479	**100 DOLLARS**			
	1985. (A-L).	FV	FV	120.00

SERIES OF 1988

480	**1 DOLLAR**	VG	VF	UNC
	1988. (A-L).	FV	FV	2.00
	a. 1988A.	FV	FV	2.00
481	**5 DOLLARS**			
	1988. (A-L).	FV	FV	10.00
	a. 1988A.	FV	FV	10.00
482	**10 DOLLARS**			
	1988. (A-L). (Not issued).	—	—	—
	a. 1988A.	FV	FV	15.00
483	**20 DOLLARS**			
	1988. (A-L). (Not issued).	—	—	—
	a. 1988A.	FV	FV	30.00
484	**50 DOLLARS**			
	1988. (A-L).	FV	FV	65.00
	a. 1988A.	FV	FV	65.00
485	**100 DOLLARS**			
	1988. (A-L).	FV	FV	120.00
	a. 1988A.	FV	FV	120.00

SERIES OF 1990

#486-489 w/additional row of micro-printing: *THE UNITED STATES OF AMERICA* repeated around portr. Filament w/value and *U.S.A.* repeated inversely at l.

			VG	VF	UNC
486	**10 DOLLARS**		FV	FV	15.00
	1990. (A-L).				
487	**20 DOLLARS**		FV	FV	30.00
	1990. (A-L).				
488	**50 DOLLARS**		FV	FV	65.00
	1990. (A-L).				
	x. Error w/filament at r.			Reported Not Confirmed	
489	**100 DOLLARS**		FV	FV	115.00
	1990. (A-L).				
	x. Error w/filament at r.		FV	140.00	350.00

SERIES OF 1993

			VG	VF	UNC
490	**1 DOLLAR**		FV	FV	2.00
	1993. (A-L).				
491	**5 DOLLARS**		FV	FV	8.00
	1993. (A-L).				
492	**10 DOLLARS**		FV	FV	15.00
	1993. (A-L).				
493	**20 DOLLARS**		FV	FV	30.00
	1993. (A-L).				
494	**50 DOLLARS**		FV	FV	65.00
	1993. (A-L).				
495	**100 DOLLARS**		FV	FV	115.00
	1993. (A-L).				

SERIES OF 1995

			VG	VF	UNC
496	**1 DOLLAR**		FV	FV	2.00
(495)	1995.				
497	**2 DOLLARS**		FV	FV	4.00
	1995.				
498	**5 DOLLARS**		FV	FV	7.50
(496)	1995.				
499	**10 DOLLARS**		FV	FV	15.00
	1995.				
500	**20 DOLLARS**		FV	FV	30.00
	1995.				

SERIES OF 1996

#503 redesigned face portrait and back building.
#501 and 502 held in reserve.

			VG	VF	UNC
503	**100 DOLLARS**		FV	FV	115.00
	1996.				

MILITARY PAYMENT CERTIFICATES

Replacement Notes: Can be identified by serial # which will have a prefix letter but no suffix letter. All replacement notes are much scarcer than regular issues which have prefix and suffix letters. Issued after World War II for use by American military and certain civilian personnel in 21 various occupied areas or military bases.

SERIES 591

26.5.1961 to 6.1.1964.
#M43-M46 Liberty at r.

			VF	XF	UNC
M43	**5 CENTS**		6.00	13.00	55.00
	ND (1961). Lilac on green and yellow unpt.				
M44	**10 CENTS**		7.00	15.00	65.00
	ND (1961). Blue on lilac unpt.				
M45	**25 CENTS**		28.00	50.00	135.00
	ND (1961). Green on purple unpt.				

			VF	XF	UNC
M46	**50 CENTS**		40.00	85.00	235.00
	ND (1961). Brown on aqua unpt.				

			VF	XF	UNC
M47	**1 DOLLAR**		40.00	85.00	275.00
	ND (1961). Red. Woman at r.				
M48	**5 DOLLARS**		550.00	1500.	4000.
	ND (1961). Blue. Woman at l.				

			VF	XF	UNC
M49	**10 DOLLARS**		175.00	325.00	2000.
	ND (1961). Green. Woman at r.				

SERIES 611

6.1.1964 to 28.4.1969.
#M50-M53 Liberty at l.

			VF	XF	UNC
M50	**5 CENTS**		2.00	3.00	10.00
	ND (1964). Blue.				
M51	**10 CENTS**		3.00	6.00	17.00
	ND (1964). Green.				
M52	**25 CENTS**		5.00	8.00	25.00
	ND (1964). Brown.				
M53	**50 CENTS**		6.00	15.00	55.00
	ND (1964). Lilac				

			VF	XF	UNC
M54	**1 DOLLAR**		6.00	15.00	55.00
	ND (1964). Green. Woman w/tiara at l.				
M55	**5 DOLLARS**		100.00	175.00	600.00
	ND (1964). Red. Woman at ctr.				

M56 **10 DOLLARS**
ND (1964). Blue. Woman at ctr.

	VF	XF	UNC
	130.00	200.00	550.00

SERIES 641
31.8.1965 to 21.10.1968.
#M57-M60 woman at l.

		VF	XF	UNC
M57	**5 CENTS** ND (1965). Violet on blue.	1.00	2.00	5.00
M58	**10 CENTS** ND (1965). Green.	1.00	3.00	6.00
M59	**25 CENTS** ND (1965). Red.	2.00	4.00	12.00
M60	**50 CENTS** ND (1965). Orange.	3.00	6.00	18.00
M61	**1 DOLLAR** ND (1965). Lilac. Woman at r.	3.50	8.00	20.00
M62	**5 DOLLARS** ND (1965). Green. Woman w/wreath of flowers at ctr.	35.00	75.00	275.00

		VF	XF	UNC
M63	**10 DOLLARS** ND (1965). Brown. Woman at ctr .	30.00	60.00	300.00

SERIES 661
21.10.1968 to 11.8.1969.
#M64-68 woman wearing scarf at l.

		VF	XF	UNC
M64	**5 CENTS** ND (1968). Green and lilac.	.50	2.00	6.00
M65	**10 CENTS** ND (1968). Blue and violet.	FINE .25	VF .75	XF 2.00
M66	**25 CENTS** ND (1968). Brown and orange.	VF 2.00	XF 3.00	UNC 10.00
M67	**50 CENTS** ND (1968). Red and green.	FINE 2.00	VF 3.00	XF 6.00

		VF	XF	UNC
M68	**1 DOLLAR** ND (1968). Blue. Woman at r.	3.00	6.00	15.00
M69	**5 DOLLARS** ND (1968). Dk. brown. Woman holding flowers at ctr.	3.00	6.00	14.00

		FINE	VF	XF
M70	**10 DOLLARS** ND (1968). Red. Woman holding fasces at l.	150.00	250.00	450.00
M71	**20 DOLLARS** ND (1968). Black, brown and blue. Woman at ctr.	VF 200.00	XF 300.00	UNC 650.00

SERIES 651
28.4.1969 to 19.11.1973.
#M72A-M74 similar to Series 641 except for colors and the addition of a "Minuteman" at l.

		VF	XF	UNC
M72A	**5 CENTS** ND (1969).	—	—	2800.
M72B	**10 CENTS** ND (1969).	—	—	2800.
M72C	**25 CENTS** ND (1969).	—	—	2800.
M72D	**50 CENTS** ND (1969).	1250.	1500.	2500.

		VF	XF	UNC
M72E	**1 DOLLAR** ND (1969). Green. Woman at r.	3.00	8.00	25.00

		VF	XF	UNC
M73	**5 DOLLARS** ND (1969). Brown. Woman w/wreath of flowers at ctr.	35.00	75.00	150.00
M74	**10 DOLLARS** ND (1969). Violet. Woman at ctr.	35.00	80.00	200.00

SERIES 681
11.8.1969 to 7.10.1970.
#M75-M78 submarine at r.

		VF	XF	UNC
M75	**5 CENTS** ND (1969). Green and blue.	1.00	2.00	6.00

		VF	XF	UNC
M76	**10 CENTS** ND (1969). Violet.	1.00	2.00	6.00
M77	**25 CENTS** ND (1969). Claret and blue.	2.00	5.00	15.00
M78	**50 CENTS** ND (1969). Brown and blue.	3.00	6.00	18.00
M79	**1 DOLLAR** ND (1969). Violet. Air Force pilot at r.	2.00	4.00	12.00

		VF	XF	UNC
M80	**5 DOLLARS** ND (1969). Purple and green. Sailor at ctr.	5.00	12.00	35.00

M81 10 DOLLARS
ND (1969). Blue-green. Infantryman at ctr.

	VF	XF	UNC
	20.00	35.00	160.00

M82 20 DOLLARS
ND (1969). Brown, pink and blue. Soldier wearing helmet at ctr.

	VF	XF	UNC
	20.00	45.00	150.00

SERIES 692
7.10.1970 to 15.3.1973.
#M83-M86 seated Roman warrior at l.

		VF	XF	UNC
M83	**5 CENTS** ND (1970). Brown.	1.00	2.00	7.00
M84	**10 CENTS** ND (1970). Green.	1.50	2.00	7.00
M85	**25 CENTS** ND (1970). Blue.	3.00	4.50	15.00
M86	**50 CENTS** ND (1970). Violet.	4.00	6.00	22.50

		VF	XF	UNC
M87	**1 DOLLAR** ND (1970). Blue green. Woman at l., flowers at bottom ctr.	5.00	10.00	30.00
M88	**5 DOLLARS** ND (1970). Brown. Girl and flowers at ctr.	75.00	150.00	250.00

M89 10 DOLLARS
ND (1970). Blue. Indian Chief Hollow Horn Bear at ctr.

	VF	XF	UNC
	130.00	250.00	475.00

M90 20 DOLLARS
ND (1970). Violet. Indian Chief Ouray at ctr.

	VF	XF	UNC
	100.00	220.00	450.00

URUGUAY

The Oriental Republic of Uruguay (so called because of its location on the east bank of the Uruguay River) is situated on the Atlantic coast of South America between Argentina and Brazil. This most advanced of South American countries has an area of 68,536 sq. mi. (176,220 sq. km.) and a population of 3.12 million. Capital: Montevideo. Uruguay's chief economic asset is its rich, rolling grassy plains. Meat, wool, hides and skins are exported.

Uruguay was discovered in 1516 by Juan Diaz de Solis, a Spaniard, but settled by the Portuguese who founded Colonia in 1680. Spain contested Portuguese possession and, after a long struggle, gained control of the country in 1778. During the general South American struggle for independence, Uruguay's first attempt was led by gaucho soldier José Gervasio Artigas leading the Banda Oriental which was quelled by Spanish and Portuguese forces in 1811. The armistice was soon broken and Argentine forces from Buenos Aires cast off the Spanish bond in the Plata region in 1814, only to be reconquered by the Portuguese from Brazil in the struggle of 1816-20. Revolt flared anew in 1825 and independence was reasserted in 1828 with the help of Argentina. The Uruguayan Republic was established in 1830.

MONETARY SYSTEM:
1 Peso = 100 Centésimos, 1860-1975
1 Nuevo Peso = 1000 Old Pesos, 1975-1993
1 Peso Uruguayo = 1000 Nuevos Pesos, 1993-

REPUBLIC

BANCO CENTRAL DEL URUGUAY

1967 ND PROVISIONAL ISSUE
#42-45 Banco Central was organized in 1967 and used notes of previous issuing authority w/Banco Central sign. title ovpt. All ovpt. notes are Series D.

		VG	VF	UNC
42	**10 PESOS** *L.1939* (1967). Purple on m/c unpt. Like #37b but all sign. titles in name of Banco Central.			
	a. Bank name below title: *Banco Central de la Republica.*	1.00	3.25	10.00
	b. Bank name below title: *Banco Central del Uruguay.*	.75	2.50	7.50
42A	**50 PESOS** *L.1939* (1967). Blue and brown. Like #38b but bank name below sign. at r. Banco Central del Uruguay.			
	a. Bank name below 2 sign. at r.	.75	2.50	7.50
	b. Bank name below all 3 sign.	.75	2.00	6.00
43	**100 PESOS** *L.1939* (1967). Red and brown. Like #39b.			
	a. R. sign. title: *Presidente, Banco Central de la Republica.*	—	—	—
	b. Bank name below 2 sign. at r.: *Banco Central del Uruguay.*	1.00	3.00	10.00
	c. Bank name below 3 titles: *Banco Central del Uruguay.*	1.00	3.00	10.00

		VG	VF	UNC
44	**500 PESOS** *L.1939.* Green and blue. Like #40b but all sign. titles in name of Banco Central.			
	a. Sign. like #42a.	1.50	5.00	15.00
	b. Sign. like #42b.	1.50	5.00	15.00
45	**1000 PESOS** *L.1939.* Purple and black. Like #41b. Bank name under all 3 sign: *Banco Central de la Republica.*	3.00	7.00	20.00

1967 ND ISSUE
#46-51 J. G. Artigas at ctr. Sign. and sign. title varieties.
#48-51 wmk: Arms. Printer: TDLR.

		VG	VF	UNC
46	**50 PESOS** ND (1967). Deep blue on lt. green and lilac unpt. Arms at l. Group of 33 men w/flag on back. Series A.	.10	.25	1.00

		VG	VF	UNC
47	**100 PESOS** ND (1967). Red on lilac and lt. gold unpt. Arms at l. Man presiding at independence meeting on back.	.10	.25	1.00

		VG	VF	UNC
48	**500 PESOS** ND (1967). Green and blue on orange and lt. green unpt. Dam on back.	.50	1.25	5.00

		VG	VF	UNC
49	**1000 PESOS** ND (1967). Purple and black on blue and yellow unpt. Lg. bldg. on back.	.50	1.25	5.00

		VG	VF	UNC
50	**5000 PESOS** ND (1967). Brown and blue-green on lilac and lt. blue unpt. Bank on back.			
	a. Series A; B.	2.00	5.00	20.00
	b. Series C.	1.00	2.00	5.00
51	**10,000 PESOS** ND (1967). Dk. green and black on yellow and lt. orange unpt. Bldg. on back. Series A; B.			
	a. R. sign. title: *PRESIDENTE*.	5.00	12.50	30.00
	b. R. sign. title: *VICE-PRESIDENTE*.	6.00	15.00	35.00

1974 ISSUE
#51A-53 sign. varieties. Wmk: Artigas.
#52 *Deleted*. See #57.

		VG	VF	UNC
51A	**1000 PESOS** ND (1974). Violet and dk. green on m/c unpt. Arms at upper ctr., Artigas at r. Bldg. on back. Printer: CdeM - A.	.30	.90	2.75

		VG	VF	UNC
53	**10,000 PESOS** ND (1979). Orange on m/c unpt. arms at upper ctr., J. G. Artigas at r. Palace Esteze on back. Printer: TDLR. Series A; B; C.	2.00	4.00	8.00
	a. Series A.	.90	2.75	8.00
	b. Series B.	.75	2.25	7.00
	c. Series C.	.65	2.00	6.00

1975 PROVISIONAL ISSUE
#54-58 new value ovpt. on wmk. area.
#53, 56 and 57 replacement notes: Serial # prefix *R*.

		VG	VF	UNC
54	**0.50 NUEVO PESO ON 50 PESOS** ND (1975). Ovpt. on #48.	.10	.35	1.00

55	1 NUEVO PESO ON 1000 PESOS	VG	VF	UNC
	ND (1975). Ovpt. on #49.	.25	.75	2.50
56	1 NUEVO PESO ON 1000 PESOS			
	ND (1975). Ovpt. on #51A.	.25	.75	2.50
57	5 NUEVOS PESOS ON 5000 PESOS			
	ND (1975). Brown on m/c unpt. J. G. Artigas at r., arms at ctr. w/ovpt. new value. Old Banco de Republica on back. Printer: CdM-A.	.75	2.25	7.00

58	10 NUEVOS PESOS ON 10,000 PESO	VG	VF	UNC
	ND (1975). Ovpt. on #53.	1.00	3.25	10.00

1975 ISSUE

#59-60 arms near ctr., J. G. Artigas at r. and as wmk. Old govt. palace on back. Printer: TDLR.

59	50 NUEVOS PESOS	VG	VF	UNC
	ND (1975). Deep blue on m/c unpt. Series A. 3 sign.	2.00	4.50	7.00

60	100 NUEVOS PESOS	VG	VF	UNC
	ND (1975). Olive-green on m/c unpt. Series A. 3 sign.	4.00	8.00	12.00

1978-88 ND; 1986 ISSUES

#61-64A similar to previous issue but w/o text: *PAGARA .... A LA VISTA* at ctr. Printer: TDLR.

#65-67 wmk: J. G. Artigas.

Replacement notes: 8 digit serial # starts w/*9*.

NOTE: on #67, description *Plaza de la Nacionalidad Oriental/Monumento a la bandera and LEY 14.316* was ovpt. out because of a change of government from military to elected civil administration before the notes were released. The new government took the prepared notes, ovpt. the legend relating to the old government and issued them (Series A). Only Specimen notes are known w/o the ovpt.

61	50 NUEVOS PESOS	VG	VF	UNC
	ND (1978-89). Similar to #59.			
	a. 2 sign. Series B (1978).	.40	1.65	5.00
	b. 3 sign. Series C (1980).	.25	1.00	3.00
	c. 2 sign. Series D (1981).	.15	.65	2.00
	d. 3 sign. Series E (1987).	.10	.35	1.00

61A	50 NUEVOS PESOS	VG	VF	UNC
	ND (1988-89). Like #61 but J. G. Artigas portr. printed in wmk. Series F (1988); Series G (1989).	.05	.20	.60
62	100 NUEVOS PESOS			
	ND (1978-87). Similar to #60.			
	a. 2 sign. Series B (1978).	.50	2.00	5.00
	b. 3 sign. Series C (1980); Series D (1981).	.15	.65	2.00
	c. Series E (1985); Series F (1986).	.05	.15	.50

62A	100 NUEVOS PESOS	VG	VF	UNC
	ND. Like #62 but J. G. Artigas portr. printed in wmk. Series G (1987).	.05	.25	.75
63	500 NUEVOS PESOS			
	ND(1978-85). Red on m/c unpt.			
	a. 2 sign. Series A (1978).	.90	3.50	10.00
	b. 3 sign. Series B (1978); Series C (1985).	.20	.80	2.50
63A	500 NUEVOS PESOS			
	ND. Like #63 but J. G. Artigas portr. printed in wmk. Series D (1991).	.15	.45	1.25
64	1000 NUEVOS PESOS			
	ND(1978-). Purple on m/c unpt.			
	a. 2 sign. Series A (1978).	2.00	4.50	10.00
	b. 3 sign. Series B (1981).	.40	1.50	4.50
64A	1000 NUEVOS PESOS			
	ND. Like #64 but J. G. Artigas portr. printed in wmk.			
	a. Series C (1991).	.35	1.00	3.00
	b. Series D (1992).	.10	.35	1.00

65	5000 NUEVOS PESOS	VG	VF	UNC
	ND (1983). Deep brown and blue on m/c unpt. Arms at top ctr., Brig. Gen. J. A. Lavalleja at r. Back m/c; 1830 scene of pledging allegiance at ctr. Series A; B; C. Printer: TDLR.	.35	1.10	3.50

1986; ND ISSUE

66	200 NUEVOS PESOS	VG	VF	UNC
	1986. Dk. and lt. green on brown and m/c unpt. Quill and scroll at l., arms at ctr., J. E. Rodo at r. Back green and brown; Rodo Monument at ctr., statuary at l. and ctr. Series A. Printer: Ciccone S.A.	.10	.35	1.00

67   10,000 Nuevos Pesos
ND (1987). Blue and m/c. Plaza w/flag at ctr. 19 departmental arms on back. Printer: ABNC.

		VG	VF	UNC
a.	Ovpt. gold gilt bars on description and law designation. Series A.	7.50	25.00	75.00
b.	No ovpt. bars and *DECRETO-LEY NO. 14.316* at upper. Series B; C.	FV	2.75	8.00
s.	Entire note as printed and w/o ovpt. Series A. Specimen.	—	—	—

1989-92 Issue

#68-73 arms at upper l. Wmk: Artigas. Printer: TDLR.

#68-73 arms at upper l., silver oval latent image at upper r. w/letters B/CU. Wmk: Portr. J. G. Artigas. Printer: TDLR.

		VG	VF	UNC
68	**2000 Nuevos Pesos**			
	1989. Black and red-orange on m/c unpt. J. M. Blanes, banker at ctr. r. Altar of the Fatherland (allegory of the Republic) on back. Series A.	FV	.50	1.50

		VG	VF	UNC
69	**20,000 Nuevos Pesos**			
	1989; 1991. Dk. green and violet on m/c unpt. Dr. J. Zorilla de San Martin at ctr. r. Manuscript and allegorical victory w/wings on back. Series A.	FV	4.00	7.50

		VG	VF	UNC
70	**50,000 Nuevos Pesos**			
	1989; 1991. Black and violet on m/c unpt. J. P. Varela at ctr. r. Varela Monument at l. on back. Series A.	FV	10.00	17.50

		VG	VF	UNC
71	**100,000 Nuevos Pesos**			
	1991. Purple and dk. brown on m/c unpt. E. Fabini at r. ctr. Musical allegory on back. Series A.	FV	20.00	32.50

		VG	VF	UNC
72	**200,000 Nuevos Pesos**			
	1992. Dk. brown and violet and orange on m/c unpt. P. Figari at ctr. r. Old dance at l. on back. Series A.	FV	37.50	65.00

		VG	VF	UNC
73	**500,000 Nuevos Pesos**			
	1992. Blue-gray, violet and pale red on m/c unpt. A. Vaquez Acevedo at ctr. r. University of Montevideo at l. on back. Series A.	FV	85.00	125.00

1994-97 Issue

Currency Reform

1 Peso Uruguayo = 1000 Nuevos Pesos, 1993-

#73A-77 like #67 and 69-73 but w/new denominations. Arms at upper l. Series A. Wmk: J. G. Artigas. Printer: TDLR.

		VG	VF	UNC
73A	**10 Pesos Uruguayos**			
	ND (1994). Blue on m/c unpt. Similar to 10,000 Nuevos Pesos #67. Printer: G&D.	FV	FV	3.50
74	**20 Pesos Uruguayos**			
	1994. Dk. green and violet on m/c unpt. Similar to #69.	FV	FV	6.00
75	**50 Pesos Uruguayos**			
	1994. Black, red and violet on m/c unpt. Similar to #70.	FV	FV	13.50
76	**100 Pesos Uruguayos**			
	1994. Purple and dk. brown on m/c unpt. Similar to #71.	FV	FV	25.00
77	**200 Pesos Uruguayos**			
	1995. Dk. brown-violet on m/c unpt. Similar to #72.	FV	FV	47.50
78	**500 Pesos Uruguayos**			
	1994. Blue-gray, violet and pale red on m/c unpt. Similar to #73.	FV	FV	87.50
79	**1000 Pesos Uruguayos**			
	1995. Brown and olive-green on m/c unpt. J. de Ibarbourou at r. Palm tree, books on back.	FV	FV	165.00
80	**2000 Pesos Uruguayos**			
	1997.		Expected New Issue	

The Republic of Uzbekistan (formerly the Uzbek S.S.R.), is bordered on the north by Kazakhstan, to the east by Kirghizia and Tajikistan, on the south by Afghanistan and on the west by Turkmenistan. The republic is comprised of the regions of Andizhan, Bukhara, Dzhizak, Ferghana, Kashkadar, Khorezm (Khiva), Namangan, Navoi, Samarkand, Surkhan-Darya, Syr-Darya, Tashkent and the Karakalpak Autonomous Republic. It has an area of 172,741 sq. mi. (447,400 sq. km.) and a population of 20.3 million. Capital: Tashkent.

Crude oil, natural gas, coal, copper and gold deposits make up the chief resources, while intensive farming, based on artificial irrigation, provides an abundance of cotton.

The original population was believed to be Iranian towards the north while the southern part hosted the satrapies of Sogdiana and Bactria, members of the Persian empire and once part of the empire of Alexander of Macedon. In the 2nd century B.C. they suffered an invasion by easterners referred to by the Chinese as Yue-chi and Hiung-nu. At the end of the 7th century and into the 8th century an Arab army under Emir Kotaiba ibu Muslim conquered Khiva (Khorezm) and Bukhara (Sogdiana). Persian influence developed from the Abbasid caliphs of Baghdad. About 874 the area was conquered by the Persian Saminids of Balkh.

In 999 a Turkic Karakhanid dynasty, the first to embrace Islam, supplanted the Samanids in Samarkand and Bukhara. At the beginning of the 11th century the Seljuk Turks passed through Transoxiana and appointed a hereditary governor at Khorezm. In 1141 another dynasty appeared in Transoxiana, the Kara Kitai from north China. Under the Seljuk shahs Khorezm remained a Moslem outpost.

The Mongol invasion of Jenghiz Khan in 1219-20 brought destruction and great ethnic changes among the population. The conquerors became assimilated and adopted the Turkic language "Chagatai." At the beginning of the 16th century Turkestan was conquered by another wave of Turkic nomads, the Uzbeks (Usbegs). The term Uzbek was used in the 15th century to indicate Moslem. In the 18th century Khokand made itself independent from the emirate of Bukhara, but was soon subject to China, which had conquered eastern Turkestan (now called Sinkiang). The khanate of Khiva, in 1688, became a vassal of Persia, but recovered its independence in 1747. While the Uzbek emirs and khans ruled central Turkestan, in the north were the Kazakhs, in the west lived the nomadic Turkmens, in the east dwelled the Kirghiz, and in the southeast was the homeland of the Persian-speaking Tajiks. In 1714-17 Peter the Great sent a military expedition against Khiva which ended in a disaster. In 1853 Ak-Mechet ("White Mosque," renamed Perovsk, later Kzyl Orda), was conquered by the Russians, and the following year the fortress of Vernoye (later Alma-Ata) was established. On July 29, 1867, Gen. C. P. Kaufmann was appointed governor general of Turkestan with headquarters in Tashkent. On July 5 Mozaffar ed-Din, emir of Bukhara, signed a treaty making his country a Russian vassal state with much-reduced territory. Khiva was conquered by Gen. N. N. Golovachev, and on Aug. 24, 1873, Khan Mohammed Rakhim Kuli had to become a vassal of Russia. Furthermore, all his possessions east of the Amu Darya were annexed to the Turkestan governor-generalship. The khanate of Khokand was suppressed and on March 3, 1876, became the Fergana province. On the eve of WW I Khiva and Bukhara were enclaves within a Russian Turkestan divided into five provinces or *oblasti*. The czarist government did not attempt to Russify the indigenous Turkic or Tajik populations, preferring to keep them backward and illiterate. The revolution of March 1917 created a confused situation in the area. In Tashkent there was a Turkestan committee of the provisional government; a Communist-controlled council of workers', soldiers' and peasants' deputies; also a Moslem Turkic movement, Shuro-i-Islamiya, and a Young-Turkestan or Jaddidi (Renovation) party. The last-named party claimed full political autonomy for Turkestan and the abolition of the emirate of Bukhara and the khanate of Khiva. After the Communist *coup d'éin* Petrograd, the council of people's commissars on Nov. 24 (Dec. 7), 1917, published an appeal to "all toiling Moslems in Russia and in the east" proclaiming their right to build their national life "freely and unhindered." In response, the Moslem and Jaddidi organizations in Dec. 1917 convoked a national congress in Khokand which appointed a provisional government headed by Mustafa Chokayev (or Chokaigolu; 1890-1941) and resolved to elect a constituent assembly to decide whether Turkestan should remain within a Russian federal state or proclaim its independence. In the spring of 1919 a Red army group defeated Kolchak and in September its commander, M.V. Frunze, arrived in Tashkent with V.V. Kuibyshev as political commissar. The Communists were still much too weak in Turkestan to proclaim the country part of Soviet Russia. Faizullah Khojayev organized a Young Bukhara movement, which on Sept. 14, 1920, proclaimed the dethronement of Emir Mir Alim. Bukhara was then made a S.S.R. In 1920 the Tashkent Communist government declared war on Junaid, who took to flight, and Khiva became another S.S.R. In Oct. 1921 Enver Pasha, the former leader of the Young Turks, appeared in Bukhara and assumed command of the Basmachi movement. In Aug. 1922 he was forced to retreat into Tajikistan and died on Aug. 4, in a battle near Baljuvan. Khiva concluded a treaty of alliance with the Russian S.F.S.R. in Sept. 1920, and Bukhara followed suit in March 1921. Theoretically, a Turkestan Autonomous Soviet Socialist Republic had existed since May 1, 1918; in 1920 this "Turkrepublic," as it was called, was proclaimed part of the R.S.F.S.R. On Sept. 18, 1924, the Uzbek and Turkmen peoples were authorized to form S.S.R.'s of their own, and the Kazakhs, Kirghiz and Tajiks to form autonomous S.S.R.'s. On Oct. 27, 1924, the Uzbek and Turkmen S.S.R. were officially constituted and the former was formally accepted on Jan. 15, 1925, as a member of the U.S.S.R. Tajikistan was an autonomous soviet republic within Uzbekistan until Dec. 5, 1929, when it became a S.S.R. On Dec. 5, 1936, Uzbekistan was territorially increased by incorporating into it the Kara-Kalpak A.S.S.R., which had belonged to Kazakhstan until 1930 and afterward had come under direct control of the R.S.F.S.R.

On June 20, 1990 the Uzbek Supreme Soviet adopted a declaration of sovereignty, and in Aug. 1991, following the unsuccessful coup, it declared itself independent as the 'Republic of Uzbekistan', which was confirmed by referendum in December. That same month Uzbekistan became a member of the CIS.

* * * NOTE: This section has been renumbered. * * *

Monetary System:
1 СЎМ (Sum) = 100 ТИЙИН (Tiyin)

REPUBLIC

GOVERNMENT

КУПОНГА КАРТОЧКА - 1993 RUBLE CONTROL COUPONS
#43-52 and 58 uniface.
#53-57 Held in reserve.
#59 and 60 Held in reserve.

		VG	VF	UNC
43 **10 AND 25 COUPONS**				
(42A) ND (1993). Black on pale blue unpt.				
a. Full sheet of 35 coupons w/2 registries.		—	—	3.50
b. Top half sheet of 10 coupons w/registry.		—	—	2.00
c. Bottom half sheet of 25 coupons w/registry.		FV	FV	2.00
d. Coupon.		FV	FV	.25
44 **10 AND 25 COUPONS**				
ND (1993). Black on orange unpt.				
a. Full sheet of 35 coupons w/2 registries.		FV	FV	3.50
b. Top half sheet of 10 coupons w/registry.		FV	FV	2.00
c. Bottom half sheet of 25 coupons w/registry.		FV	FV	2.00
d. Coupon.		FV	FV	.25
45 **10 AND 25 COUPONS**				
ND (1993). Black on pink unpt.				
a. Full sheet of 35 coupons w/2 registries.		FV	FV	3.50
b. Top half sheet of 10 coupons w/registry.		FV	FV	2.00
c. Bottom half sheet of 25 coupons w/registry.		FV	FV	2.00
d. Coupon.		FV	FV	.25
46 **50 COUPONS**				
ND (1993). Black on pale ochre unpt.				
a. Full sheet of 50 coupons w/registry.		FV	FV	3.50
b. Coupon.		FV	FV	.15
47 **100 COUPONS**		VG	VF	UNC
ND (1993). Black on violet unpt.				
a. Full sheet of 100 coupons w/registry.		FV	FV	3.50
b. Coupon.		FV	FV	.15
48 **100 COUPONS**				
ND (1993). Black on tan unpt.				
a. Full sheet of 100 coupons w/registry.		FV	FV	3.50
b. Coupon.		FV	FV	.15
49 **100 COUPONS**				
ND (1993). Black on lt. blue unpt.				
a. Full sheet of 100 coupons w/registry.		FV	FV	3.50
b. Coupon.		FV	FV	.15

				VG	VF	UNC
50	**150 COUPONS**					
(43)	ND (1993). Red on pale gray unpt.					
	a.	Full sheet of 150 coupons w/registry.		FV	FV	3.50
	b.	Coupon.		FV	FV	.15
51	**200 COUPONS**					
	ND (1993). Black on pink unpt.					
	a.	Full sheet of 200 coupons w/registry.		FV	FV	3.50
	b.	Coupon.		FV	FV	.15
52	**200 COUPONS**					
	ND (1993). Black on tan unpt.					
	a.	Full sheet of 200 coupons w/registry.		FV	FV	3.50
	b.	Coupon.		FV	FV	.15

			VG	VF	UNC
61	**1 SUM**				
(44)	1992 (1993). Blue-gray on lt. blue and gold unpt. Back gray.		.05	.10	.25

			VG	VF	UNC
62	**3 SUM**				
(45)	1992 (1993). Green and blue. Back green.		.05	.10	.35

			VG	VF	UNC
63	**5 SUM**				
(46)	1992 (1993). Purple on lt. blue and gold unpt. Back pale purple.		.05	.10	.40

			VG	VF	UNC
64	**10 SUM**				
(47)	1992 (1993). Red on lt. blue and gold unpt. Back red.		.05	.15	.60

			VG	VF	UNC
58	**2000 COUPONS**				
	ND (1993). Blue on pink unpt.				
	a. Full sheet of 2000 coupons w/registry.		FV	FV	5.00
	b. Coupon.		FV	FV	.20

УЗБЕКИЧТОН ДАВПАТ БАНКИ

BANK OF UZBEKISTAN

1992 (1993) ISSUE

Sum System

1 Sum (1 Ruble) = 100 Kopeks, 1991-

#61-72 arms at l. Mosque at ctr. on back. Printer: H&S (w/o imprint).

65 (48)	**25 Sum** 1992 (1993). Green on lt. blue and pale orange unpt. Back green.	**VG** .05	**VF** .25	**UNC** 1.00

66 (49)	**50 Sum** 1992 (1993). Rose and blue. Back rose.	**VG** .10	**VF** .45	**UNC** 1.75

67 (50)	**100 Sum** 1992 (1993). Dk. brown and blue. Back blue.	**VG** .10	**VF** .35	**UNC** 1.50

68 (51)	**200 Sum** 1992 (1993). Violet and blue. Back violet.	**VG** .10	**VF** .45	**UNC** 3.00

69 (52)	**500 Sum** 1992 (1993). Orange and lt. blue. Back red-brown.	**VG** .10	**VF** .35	**UNC** 2.50

70 (53)	**1000 Sum** 1992 (1993). Brown and green. Back brown.	**VG** .20	**VF** .75	**UNC** 5.00

71 (54)	**5000 Sum** 1992 (1993). M/c.	**VG** .90	**VF** 3.75	**UNC** 15.00

72 (55)	**10,000 Sum** 1992 (1993). Red-orange on lilac and pale green unpt. Back pale red-orange.	**VG** 1.50	**VF** 6.00	**UNC** 25.00

ЎЗБЕКИЧТОН РЕСПУБЛИКАСИ МАРКАЗИЙ БАНКИ

CENTRAL BANK OF UZBEKISTAN REPUBLIC

1994 ISSUE
Currency Reform, 1.7.1994
1 Sum = 1,000 Sum (Coupons)
#73-80 arms at upper ctr. and as wmk.

73 (56)	**1 Sum** 1994. Dk. green on m/c unpt. Arms at l. Bldg., fountain at ctr. r. on back.	**VG** FV	**VF** FV	**UNC** .50
74 (57)	**3 Sum** 1994. Red-brown on m/c unpt. Mosque of Ça çma Ayub Mazar in Bukhara on back.	FV	FV	1.25

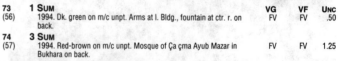

75
(58) **5 SUM**
1994. Dk. blue and red-violet on m/c unpt. Statue under kiosk at ctr. on back.

	VG	VF	UNC
	FV	FV	2.25

76
(59) **10 SUM**
1994. Violet and blue-gray on m/c unpt. Mosque of Mohammed Amin Khan in Khiva on back.

	VG	VF	UNC
	FV	FV	3.50

77
(60) **25 SUM**
1994. Dk. blue and brown on m/c unpt. Mausoleum Kazi Zadé Rumi in the necropolis Shakhi-Zinda in Samarkand on back.

	VG	VF	UNC
	FV	FV	6.00

78
(61) **50 SUM**
1994. Brown and orange on m/c u npt. Esplanade in Reghistan and the 2 Medersas in Samarkand on back.

	VG	VF	UNC
	FV	FV	9.00

79
(62) **100 SUM**
1994. Purple on m/c unpt. Stylized facing peacocks at ctr. "Drugja Narodov" palace in Tarshkent on back.

	VG	VF	UNC
	FV	FV	13.50

80
(63) **200 SUM**
(1994).

Expected New Issue

VANUATU

Vanuatu (formerly the New Hebrides Condominium), a group of islands located in the South Pacific 500 miles (800 km.) west of Fiji, were under the joint sovereignty of Great Britain and France. The islands have an area of 5,700 sq. mi. (14,763 sq. km.) and a population of *154,000, mainly Melanesians of mixed blood. Capital: Port-Vila. The volcanic and coral islands, while malarial and subject to frequent earthquakes, are extremely fertile, and produce copra, coffee, tropical fruits and timber for export.

The New Hebrides were discovered by Portuguese navigator Pedro de Quiros in 1606, visited by French explorer Bougainville in 1768, and named by British navigator Capt. James Cook in 1774. Ships of all nations converged on the islands to trade for sandalwood, prompting France and Britain to relinquish their individual claims and declare the islands a neutral zone in 1878. The New Hebrides were placed under the control of a mixed Anglo-French commission of naval officers during the native uprisings of 1887, and established as a condomiuium under the joint sovereignty of France and Great Britain in 1906. Independence for the area was attained in 1982 under the new name of Vanuatu.

RULERS:
British and French to 1982

MONETARY SYSTEM:
100 Vatu = 100 Francs

SIGNATURE/TITLE VARIETIES

1			3		
	PRESIDENT	GENERAL MANAGER		GOVERNOR	MINISTER OF FINANCE
2			4		
	PRESIDENT	MINISTER OF FINANCE			

INDEPENDENT

BANQUE CENTRALE DE VANUATU

CENTRAL BANK OF VANUATU

1982 ISSUE
#1-4 arms w/Melanesian chief standing w/spear at ctr. r. Wmk: Male Melanesian head. Printer: BWC.

1
100 VATU
ND (1982). Dk. green on m/c unpt. Cattle amongst palm trees at l. ctr. on back. Sign. 1.

	VG	VF	UNC
	1.25	2.50	12.50

2   500 Vatu
ND (1982). Red on m/c unpt. 3 carved statues at l., 2 men beating
upright hollow log drums at l. ctr. on back. Sign. 1.

	VG	VF	UNC
	FV	6.50	20.00

3   1000 Vatu
ND (1982). Black on m/c unpt. 3 carvings at lower l., 3 men in
outrigger sailboat at ctr. on back. Sign. 1.

	VG	VF	UNC
	FV	12.50	35.00

1989 Issue

4   5000 Vatu
ND(1989). Brown and lilac on m/c unpt. Man watching another *Gol*
diving from log tower at ctr. on back. Sign. 2.

	VG	VF	UNC
	FV	50.00	95.00

Banque de Reserve de Vanuatu

Reserve Bank of Vanuatu

1993 Issue
#5-7 like #2-4 but w/new bank name. Sign. 3.

5   500 Vatu
ND (1993). Dk. green on m/c unpt.

	VG	VF	UNC
	FV	FV	13.50

6   1000 Vatu
ND (1993). Red on m/c unpt.

	VG	VF	UNC
	FV	FV	25.00

7   5000 Vatu
ND.

Expected New Issue

1995 ND Issue

8   200 Vatu
ND (1995). Purple on m/c unpt. Arms w/Melanesian chief standing
w/spear at ctr. Statue of family life, 'Traditional parliament in session'
and flag on back.

	VG	VF	UNC
	FV	FV	5.50

1995 ND Commemorative Issue
#9, 15th Anniversary of Independence.

9   200 Vatu
ND (1995). Ovpt. on #8.

	VG	VF	UNC
	FV	FV	10.00

VENEZUELA

The Republic of Venezuela ("Little Venice"), located on the northern coast of South America between Columbia and Guyana, has an area of 352,145 sq. mi. (912,050 sq. km.) and a population of *20.2 million. Capital: Caracas. Petroleum and mining provide 90 percent of Venezuela's exports although they employ less than 2 percent of the work force. Coffee, grown on 60,000 plantations, is the chief crop.

Columbus discovered Venezuela on his third voyage in 1498. Initial exploration did not reveal Venezuela to be a land of great wealth. An active pearl trade operated on the off-shore islands and slavers raided the interior in search of Indians to be sold into slavery, but no significant mainland settlements were made before 1567 when Caracas was founded. Venezuela, the home of Bolivar, was among the first South American colonies to revolt against Spain in 1810. Independence was attained in 1821 but not recognized by Spain until 1845. Together with Ecuador, Panama and Colombia, Venezuela was part of "Gran Colombia" until 1830 when it became a sovereign and independence state.

MONETARY SYSTEM:
1 Bolívar = 100 Centimos, 1879-
1 Venezolano = 100 Centavos to 1879.

REPUBLIC

Banco Central de Venezuela
Issuing notes since 1940. Sign. and date varieties. Notes from 1940-53 bear the legend "E.E.U.U. de Venezuela" in the coat of arms and after 1953 "República de Venezuela." Many specimen notes were "liberated" about 1982. Up to 200 of each are known for many of the more common types which are now incorporated in these listings.

1940-45 Issues
#31-37 arms on back. Printer: ABNC.

34   100 Bolívares
11.12.1940-3.7.1962. Brown on m/c unpt. Portr. S. Bolívar at ctr.
Arms at ctr. on back.

		VG	VF	UNC
a.	1940-52.	20.00	60.00	200.00
b.	1953-58.	15.00	45.00	150.00
c.	1959-62.	10.00	30.00	100.00

1947 Issue

37   500 Bolívares
1947-71. Orange on m/c unpt.

		VG	VF	UNC
a.	14.8.1947-17.1.1952.	60.00	150.00	—
b.	23.7.1953-29.5.1958.	25.00	55.00	165.00
c.	11.3.1960-9.11.1971.	20.00	50.00	135.00

1960 Issue
#42-44 printer: TDLR.

42   10 Bolívares
6.6.1961. Purple on m/c unpt. Portr. S. Bolívar at l., A. J. de Sucre at r.
Monument and arms on back.

		VG	VF	UNC
a.	Issued note.	2.50	9.00	25.00
s.	Specimen.	—	—	11.00

43   20 Bolívares
11.3.1960-10.5.1966. Dk. green on m/c unpt. Portr. S. Bolívar at r.,
bank name in 1 line. Monument at ctr. on back.

		VG	VF	UNC
a.	Issued note.	4.00	12.00	30.00
s.	Specimen (varieties).	—	—	15.00

44   50 Bolívares
6.6.1961; 7.5.1963. Black. Modified effigy of S. Bolívar at l. Back
orange; monument at ctr. on back.

		VG	VF	UNC
a.	Issued note.	8.00	25.00	75.00
s.	Specimen.	—	—	15.00

1963-67 Issue
#45-48 monument on back similar to #42-44. Printer: TDLR.

45 **10 BOLÍVARES**
7.5.1963-27.1.1970. Purple on m/c unpt. Similar to #42 but much
different portr. of A. J. de Sucre at r.

	VG	VF	UNC
	1.00	2.50	7.50

46 **20 BOLÍVARES**
8.8.1967-29.1.1974. Green on orange and blue unpt. Portr. S. Bolívar
at r., and as wmk., bank name in 3 lines. Arms w/o circle at l. on back.

	VG	VF	UNC
a. Issued note.	1.60	4.00	15.00
s. Specimen (varieties).	—	—	11.00

47 **50 BOLÍVARES**
2.6.1964-22.2.1972. Black. Portr. S. Bolívar at l. *CINCUENTA
BOLÍVARES* above *50* at ctr. Back orange.

	VG	VF	UNC
	5.00	12.50	35.00

48 **100 BOLÍVARES**
7.5.1963-6.2.1973. Brown. Portr. S. Bolívar at r.

	VG	VF	UNC
a. Issued note.	5.00	12.50	47.50
s. Specimen (varieties).	—	—	15.00

1966 COMMEMORATIVE ISSUE
#49, 400th Anniversary of Founding of Caracas 1567-1967.

49 **5 BOLÍVARES**
10.5.1966. Blue on green and yellow unpt. Scene of the founding and
commemorative text at ctr. and l., portr. S. Bolívar at r. Back blue; city
arms at l., early map (1578) of the city at ctr., national arms at r.
Printer: ABNC.

	VG	VF	UNC
	2.00	5.00	20.00

1968-71 ISSUE
#51-52 printer: ABNC.

50 **5 BOLÍVARES**
24.9.1968-29.1.1974. Red on m/c unpt. S. Bolívar at l., F. de Miranda
at r. Arms at l., National Pantheon at ctr. on back. Printer: TDLR.

	VG	VF	UNC
a. Issued note.	.75	2.00	6.50
b. Remainder w/o date, sign. or serial #.	—	—	7.50
s. Specimen.	—	—	8.50

51 **10 BOLÍVARES**
1971-79. Purple on green and lilac unpt. Similar to #45.

	VG	VF	UNC
a. Dark blue serial #. 22.6.1971-7.6.1977.	.90	2.25	7.00
b. Black serial #. 18.9.1979.	.75	2.00	6.00
s. Specimen (varieties).	—	—	10.00

52 **20 BOLÍVARES**
22.6.1971; 11.4.1972. Dk. green on m/c unpt. Similar to #46.

	VG	VF	UNC
a. Issued note.	1.35	3.50	10.00
s. Specimen.	—	—	10.00

1971-74 ISSUE

53 20 BOLÍVARES
23.4.1974; 7.6.1977; 18.9.1979. Dk. green on m/c unpt. J. Antonio
Paez at r. and as wmk. Arms at l., monument of Battle of Carabobo at
ctr. on back. Printer: ABNC.

	VG	VF	UNC
a. Issued note.	1.00	2.50	7.50
s. Specimen (varieties).	—	—	7.50

54 50 BOLÍVARES
21.11.1972; 29.1.1974; 27.1.1976; 7.6.1977. Purple, orange and m/c.
Academic bldg. at ctr., A. Bello at r. and as wmk. Back orange; arms at
l., bank at ctr. Printer: TDLR.

	VG	VF	UNC
a. Issued note.	1.65	4.00	12.50
s. Specimen.	—	—	12.50

55 100 BOLÍVARES
1972-81. Dk. brown and brown-violet on m/c unpt. S. Bolívar at r. and
as wmk. National Capitol at l., arms at r. on back. Printer: BDDK.

	VG	VF	UNC
a. Red serial #. 21.11.1972.	6.00	15.00	55.00
b. Wmk: Bolívar. 6.2.1973-5.3.1974.	5.00	12.50	30.00
c. Blue serial #. B-C added to wmk. 27.1.1976-1.9.1981.	2.75	7.00	25.00
s. Specimen (varieties).	—	—	12.50

56 500 BOLÍVARES
9.11.1971; 11.1.1972. Brown, blue and m/c. S. Bolívar at l. and as
wmk., horsemen w/rifles riding at ctr. Back brown; dam at ctr. Printer:
TDLR.

	VG	VF	UNC
a. Issued note.	2.50	10.00	35.00
s. Specimen.	—	—	22.50

1980 ISSUE

57 10 BOLÍVARES
29.1.1980. Purple and m/c. A. J. de Sucre at r. Arms at l., officers on
horseback at ctr. r. on back. Printer: ABNC.

	VG	VF	UNC
a. Issued note.	.50	1.00	4.50
s. Specimen.	—	—	8.50

1980-81 COMMEMORATIVE ISSUES
#58, Bicentennial Birth of Andres Bello 1781-1981
#59, 150th Anniversary Death of Simon Bolívar 1830-1980.

58 50 BOLÍVARES
27.1.1981. Dk. brown and green on m/c unpt. A. Bello at r. and as
wmk. Arms at l., scene showing Bello teaching young Bolívar on back.
Printer: TDLR.

VG	VF	UNC
1.65	4.00	12.50

59 100 BOLÍVARES
29.1.1980. Red and purple on m/c unpt. S. Bolívar at r. and as wmk.,
his tomb at ctr. r. Arms at l., scene of hand to hand combat on back.
Printer: TDLR.

	VG	VF	UNC
a. Issued note.	2.25	6.00	22.50
s. Specimen.	—	—	12.50

1981-87 ISSUES
#60-67 w/o imprint.
Central design in l.h. guilloche: or

60 10 BOLÍVARES
6.10.1981. Purple on lt. blue unpt. Similar to #57 but unpt. is
different, and there are many significant plate changes.

	VG	VF	UNC
a. Issued note.	FV	.75	2.50
s. Specimen.	—	—	9.50

61 10 BOLÍVARES
1986-. Purple on lt. green and lilac unpt. Like #51, but *CARACAS* removed from upper ctr. beneath bank title.

	VG	VF	UNC
a. 18.3.1986.	FV	FV	1.50
b. 31.5.1990.	FV	FV	.75
c. 8.12.1992.	FV	FV	.50
d. 5.6.1995.	FV	FV	.25

62 10 BOLÍVARES
3.11.1988. Purple on ochre unpt. Like #45, but *CARACAS* removed from upper ctr. beneath bank title.

VG	VF	UNC
FV	FV	1.00

63 20 BOLÍVARES
1981-. Dk. green on m/c unpt. Similar to #53 but *CARACAS* deleted under bank title. Title 82mm, horizontal central design in l. ctr. guilloche.

	VG	VF	UNC
a. 6.10.1981.	FV	FV	2.00
b. 7.7.1987.	FV	FV	1.75
c. 7.9.1989; 31.5.1990.	FV	FV	1.50
d. 31.5.1990.	—	—	1.25
e. 8.12.1992.	FV	FV	1.00
s. Specimen.	FV	FV	9.00

64 20 BOLÍVARES
25.9.1984. Like #63, but title 84mm and w/o central deisign in l. ctr. guilloche, also other minor plate differences. Latent image *BCV* in guilloches easily seen.

VG	VF	UNC
FV	FV	2.00

65 50 BOLÍVARES
10.12.1985-16.3.1989. Similar to #54, but *CARACAS* removed under bank name.

VG	VF	UNC
FV	FV	3.00

66 100 BOLÍVARES
1987-. Like #55 but w/o imprint.

	VG	VF	UNC
a. 3.2.1987.	FV	FV	4.00
b. 16.3.1989.	FV	FV	3.00
c. 31.5.1990; 8.12.1992.	FV	FV	2.50
d. 8.12.1992.	FV	FV	2.00

67 500 BOLÍVARES
1981-. Purple and black on m/c unpt. S. Bolívar at r. and as wmk. Back green and m/c; arms at l. of flowers.

	VG	VF	UNC
a. 25.9.1981.	FV	10.00	35.00
b. 3.2.1987.	FV	FV	25.00
c. 16.3.1989.	FV	FV	12.50
d. 31.5.1990.	FV	FV	12.50

1989 ISSUE
#68-70 w/o imprint.

68 1 BOLÍVAR
5.10.1989. Purple on blue and green unpt. Lg. *1* at l., S. Bolívar on coin at r. Arms at l., rosette at r. on back. Wmk. paper.

VG	VF	UNC
FV	FV	.35

69 2 BOLÍVARES
5.10.1989. Blue and black on lt. blue unpt. Coin head of S. Bolívar at r. Lg. *2* at l., arms at r. on back.

VG	VF	UNC
FV	FV	.50

70 5 BOLÍVARES
21.9.1989. Red on m/c unpt. Like #50, but *CARACAS* removed from upper ctr. beneath bank title on face and back. Lithographed.

VG	VF	UNC
FV	FV	.65

1989 COMMEMORATIVE ISSUE
#68, Bicentennial Birth of Rafael Urdaneta (1789)

		VG	VF	UNC
71	**20 BOLÍVARES**	FV	FV	2.00
	20.10.1987 (1989). Deep green and black on m/c unpt. Gen. R. Urdaneta at r. and as wmk. Battle of Lake Maracaibo on back.			

1990-94 ISSUE
#72-73 w/o imprint.
#73-75 arms at upper r. on back.

		VG	VF	UNC
72	**50 BOLÍVARES**	FV	FV	.50
	31.5.1990; 8.12.1992. Similar to #65 but modified plate design, ornaments in "50's". Back, deeper orange.			

		VG	VF	UNC
73	**1000 BOLÍVARES**			
	1991; 1992. Red-violet on m/c unpt. Part of independence text at far l., S. Bolívar at l. and as wmk. Signing of the Declaration of Independence at ctr. r., arms at upper r. on back.			
	a. Dot instead of accent above *i* (error) in *Bolívares* on face and back. 8.8.1991.	FV	27.50	60.00
	b. Accent above *í* in *Bolívares* on face and back. 30.7.1992.	FV	FV	11.00
	c. As b. 8.12.1992.	FV	FV	7.00
	d. As b. 17.3.1994.	FV	FV	5.50
74	**2000 BOLÍVARES**	FV	FV	10.00
	12.5.1994. Dk. green and black on m/c unpt. A. J. de Sucre at r. and as wmk. Gathering of cavalry officers at l. ctr. on back.			
75	**5000 BOLÍVARES**	FV	FV	23.50
	12.5.1994. Dk. brown and brown-violet on m/c unpt. S. Bolívar at r. and as wmk. Gathering at palace at ctr. on back.			

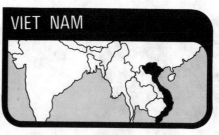

VIET NAM

The Socialist Republic of Viet Nam, located in Southeast Asia west of the South China Sea, has an area of 127,300 sq. mi. (329,560 sq. km.) and a population of *69.3 million million. Captial: Hanoi. Agricultural products, coal and mineral ores are exported.

The Viet Namese originated in North China, from where they were driven southward by the Han Chinese. They settled in the Red River Delta in northern Viet Nam; by 208 BC, much of present-day southern China and northern Viet Nam were incorporated into the independent kingdom of Nam Viet. China annexed Nam Viet in 111 BC and ruled it until 939, when independence was reestablished. The new state then expanded until it included much of Cambodia and southern Viet Nam. Viet Nam was reconquered by the Chinese in 1407; they were finally driven out, but the country was divided into two, not to be reunited until 1802.

During the latter half of the 19th century, the French gradually overran Viet Nam. Cochin-China, an alluvial plain of the Mekong Delta, fell to the French in 1862-67. In 1884, France established protectorates over Annam, an historic kingdom on the east coast of Indochina, and Tonkin in the north. Cambodia, Cochin-China, Annam and Tonkin were incorporated into the Indo-Chinese Union in 1887.

Viet Namese nationalists never really acquiesced to French domination, but continued to resist through a number of clandestine extra-legal organizations. At the start of World War II, many nationalists, communist and non-communist alike, fled to China where Ho Chi Minh organized the League for the Independence of Viet Nam ("Viet Minh") to free Viet Nam from French rule. The Japanese occupied Viet Nam during World War II. As the end of the war drew near, they ousted the Vichy French administration and granted Viet Nam independence under a puppet government headed by Bao Dai, emperor of Annam. The Bao Dai government collapsed at the end of the war, and on Sept. 2, 1945, Ho Chi Minh proclaimed the existence of an independent Viet Nam consisting of Cochin-China, Annam and Tonkin, and set up a provisional Communist government of the Democratic Republic of Viet Nam. France recognized the new government as a free state, but later reneged and in 1949 reinstalled Bao Dai as ruler of Viet Nam and extended the regime independence within the French Union. Ho Chi Minh led a guerrilla war, in the first Indochina war, against the French puppet state that raged on to the disastrous defeat of the French by the Viet Minh at Dien Bien Phu on May 7, 1954.

An agreement signed at Geneva on July 21, 1954, provided for a temporary division of Viet Nam at the 17th parallel of latitude, with the Communist dominated Democratic Republic of Viet Nam (North Viet Nam) to the north, and the US/French-supported Republic of Viet Nam (South Viet Nam) to the south. In October 1955 South Viet Nam deposed Bao Dai by referendum and authorized the establishment of a new republic with Ngo Dinh Diem as president. This Republic of Viet Nam was proclaimed on October 26, 1955, and was recognized immediately by the Western powers.

The Democratic Republic of Viet Nam, working through Viet Cong guerrillas, instigated subversion in South Viet Nam which led to US armed intervention and the second Indochina War. This war, from the viewpoint of the North merely a continuation of the first (anti-French) war, was a bitter, protracted military conflict which came to a brief halt in 1973 (when a cease-fire was arranged and US and its other allied forces withdrew), but did not end until April 30, 1975 when South Viet Nam surrendered unconditionally. The National Liberation Front for South Viet Nam, the political arm of the Viet Cong, assumed governmental power when on July 2, 1976, North and South Vietnam were united as the Socialist Republic of Viet Nam with Hanoi as the capital.

* * * This section has been renumbered. * * *

MONETARY SYSTEM:
1 Hao = 10 Xu
1 Dông = 100 Xu
1 "New" Dông = 10 "Old" Dông

NOTE: HCM - Ho Chi Minh

DEMOCRATIC REPUBLIC OF VIET NAM

NGÂN-HÀNG NHA-NUÔC VIÊT-NAM

STATE BANK OF VIET NAM

1964-75 ISSUE

		VG	VF	UNC
75 (66)	**2 XU**	3.50	10.00	38.50
	ND (1964). Purple on green unpt. Arms at ctr.			

		VG	VF	UNC
76 (67)	**5 XU**			
	1975 (date in lt. brown above *VIET* at lower l. ctr.). Violet on brown unpt. Arms at upper r.			
	a. Wmk: 15mm stars	.30	1.25	6.50
	b. Wmk: 30mm radiant star.	.30	1.25	6.50
	s. Specimen w/o wmk.	—	—	100.00

77	**1 HAO**	VG	VF	UNC
(68)	1972. Violet on m/c unpt. Arms at ctr. Woman feeding pigs on back.			
	a. Wmk: 15mm stars. Series KG-?	.30	1.25	6.50
	b. Wmk: 32mm encircled stars. Series MK-?	.30	1.25	6.50
	c. W/o wmk. Series ML.	.30	1.25	5.00
	s. Specimen w/o wmk.	—		75.00

78	**2 HAO**	VG	VF	UNC
(69)	1975. Brownish purple on green and peach unpt. Arms at ctr. 2 men spraying rice field on back.	.30	1.25	6.50

SOCIALIST REPUBLIC

Working through Viet Cong guerrillas with material help from China and Russia, and finally with years of armed conflict, the Democratic Republic of Viet Nam (North Viet Nam) toppled the U.S.A. supported Democratic government of the South. Reunion of North and South Viet Nam took place on July 2, 1976, and the Socialist Republic of Viet Nam was established.

NGÂN-HÀNG NHA-NUÔC VIÊT-NAM

STATE BANK OF VIET NAM

1976 DATED ISSUE

Issued in 1978, these notes unified the monetary systems of the South with that of the DRVN. Exchanged at par with the old DRVN notes, these replaced South Viet Nam (Ngan Hang Viet Nam) transitional series (see South Viet Nam #37-44) at 1 "new" = 0.8 "old South".

79	**5 HAO**	VG	VF	UNC
(70)	1976. Purple on m/c unpt. Arms at ctr. Coconut palms and river scene on back.	.30	.75	2.50

80	**1 DÔNG**	VG	VF	UNC
(71)	1976. Brown on m/c unpt. Arms at ctr. Factory on back.			
	a. Issued note.	.25	.65	2.00
	s. Specimen.	—	—	50.00

81	**5 DÔNG**	VG	VF	UNC
(72)	1976. Blue-gray and green on pink unpt. Arms at ctr. Back green and yellow; 2 women w/fish, boats in harbor.			
	a. Issued note. Wmk: Flower. Block letter at l., serial # at r.	.30	.75	2.50
	b. Block letter and serial # together. W/o wmk.	.30	.75	2.50
	s. Specimen.	—	—	55.00

82	**10 DÔNG**	VG	VF	UNC
(73)	1976. Purple and brown on m/c unpt. Arms at ctr. Elephants logging on back.			
	a. Issued note.	.15	.50	6.50
	s. Specimen.	—	—	60.00

83	**20 DÔNG**	VG	VF	UNC
(74)	1976. Blue on pink and green unpt. Arms at l., HCM at r. Tractors and dam on back.			
	a. Issued note.	.60	1.25	5.00
	s. Specimen.	—	—	60.00

84	**50 DÔNG**	VG	VF	UNC
(75)	1976. Reddish purple on pink and green unpt. Arms at l., HCM at r. Open pit mining scene on back (in Hongay). 2 serial # varieties.			
	a. Issued note.	.85	1.65	6.00
	s. Specimen.	—	—	75.00

SOCIALIST REPUBLIC OF VIET NAM

NGÂN-HÀNG NHA-NUÔC VIÊT NAM

STATE BANK OF VIET NAM

1980; 1981 ISSUE

85	**2 DÔNG**	VG	VF	UNC
(76)	1980 (1981). Brown on m/c unpt. Arms at ctr. River scene on back.			
	a. Issued note.	.20	.50	1.50
	s. Specimen.	—	—	50.00

86	10 Đồng	VG	VF	Unc
(77)	1980 (1981). Brown on m/c unpt. Arms at r. House at l. on back.	.25	.60	1.75

87	30 Đồng	VG	VF	Unc
(78)	1981 (1982). Purple, brown and m/c. Arms at l. ctr., HCM at r. Harbor scene on back.			
	a. Issued note.	.40	1.00	5.00
	s. Specimen.	—	—	60.00

88	100 Đồng	VG	VF	Unc
(79)	1980 (1981). Brown, dk. blue and m/c. Arms at ctr., HCM at r. Back blue, violet and brown; boats and mountains. Lg. or sm. serial #.			
	a. Issued note.	.45	1.10	4.00
	s. Specimen.	—	—	80.00

1985 ISSUE

Currency Reform, 1985
1 "New" Đồng = 10 "Old" Đồng
#89-93 tower at l. ctr. on face.
#94-99 HCM at r.

89	5 Hao	VG	VF	Unc
(A80)	1985. Red-violet on lt. blue unpt.	.50	1.35	5.00

90	1 Đồng	VG	VF	Unc
(80)	1985. Deep blue on m/c unpt. Boats along rocky coastline on back.			
	a. Issued note.	.10	.25	.85
	s. Specimen.	—	—	40.00

91	2 Đồng	VG	VF	Unc
(81)	1985. Purple on m/c unpt. Boats anchored along coastline on back.			
	a. Issued note.	.15	.40	1.75
	s. Specimen.	—	—	40.00

92	5 Đồng	VG	VF	Unc
(82)	1985. Green on m/c unpt. Sampas anchored in river on back.			
	a. Issued note.	.10	.30	1.00
	s. Specimen.	—	—	45.00

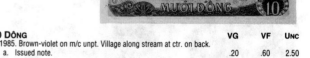

93	10 Đồng	VG	VF	Unc
(83)	1985. Brown-violet on m/c unpt. Village along stream at ctr. on back.			
	a. Issued note.	.20	.60	2.50
	s. Specimen.	—	—	45.00

94	20 Dông		VG	VF	UNC
(84)	1985 (1986). Brown, dk. purple and m/c. One pillar pagoda in Hanoi on back.				
	a. Issued note.		.25	.60	1.75
	s. Specimen.		—	—	45.00

95	30 Dông		VG	VF	UNC
(84A)	1985 (1986). Blue and m/c. Lg. bldg. w/clock tower at ctr. on back.				
	a. Issued note.		.35	.85	3.50
	s. Specimen.		—	—	50.00

96	50 Dông		VG	VF	UNC
(85)	1985. Green, brown and m/c. Reservoir and electric power station on back.				
	a. Issued note.		.50	1.25	5.00
	s. Specimen.		—	—	50.00

97	50 Dông		VG	VF	UNC
(85A)	1985 (1987). Blue-gray on orange and m/c unpt. Bridge at ctr. on back.				
	a. Issued note.		.30	.75	2.50
	s. Specimen.		—	—	45.00

98	100 Dông		VG	VF	UNC
(86)	1985. Brown, yellow and m/c. Planting rice on back. Wmk: HCM.				
	a. Issued note.		1.00	2.50	11.50
	s. Specimen.		—	—	65.00

99	500 Dông		VG	VF	UNC
(87)	1985. Red on blue and m/c unpt. Factory at l. ctr. on back. Wmk: HCM.				
	a. Issued note.		1.25	3.25	10.00
	s. Specimen.		—	—	70.00

1987; 1988 ISSUE
#100-104 HCM at r.
#102-104 wmk: HCM.

100	200 Dông		VG	VF	UNC
(88)	1987. Red-brown and tan on m/c unpt. Peasants and tractor on back.				
	a. Issued note.		.20	.50	1.75
	s. Specimen.		—	—	45.00

101	500 Dông		VG	VF	UNC
(89)	1988 (1989). Red-brown and red on m/c unpt. Dockside view on back.				
	a. Issued note.		.25	.65	3.00
	s. Specimen.		—	—	50.00

		VG	VF	Unc
102 (90)	**1000 Dông** 1987 (1988). Purple, dk. brown and deep olive-green on m/c unpt. Open pit mining equipment on back.			
	a. Issued note.	.40	1.00	4.00
	s. Specimen.	—	—	50.00

		VG	VF	Unc
103 (91)	**2000 Dông** 1987 (1988). Brown, purple and olive-green on m/c unpt. Industrial plant on back.			
	a. Issued note.	.75	2.00	5.00
	s. Specimen.	—	—	50.00

		VG	VF	Unc
104 (92)	**5000 Dông** 1987 (1989). Deep blue, purple and brown on m/c unpt. Offshore oil rigs on back.			
	a. Issued note.	.30	.75	3.00
	s. Specimen.	—	—	60.00

1988-91 Issue
#106-111 HCM at r.
#109-111 wmk: HCM.

		VG	VF	Unc
105 (94)	**100 Dông** 1991 (1992). Brown on m/c unpt. Arms at l. Temple and pagoda at l. ctr. on back.			
	a. Issued note.	FV	FV	.25
	s1. Specimen w/ovpt: *TIEN MAO.*	—	—	100.00
	s2. Specimen w/ovpt: *SPECIMEN.*	—	—	100.00

		VG	VF	Unc
106 (95)	**1000 Dông** 1988 (1989). Purple on m/c unpt. Arms at l. ctr. Elephant logging on back.			
	a. Issued note.	FV	FV	.50
	s. Specimen.	—	—	50.00

		VG	VF	Unc
107 (96)	**2000 Dông** 1988 (1989). Brownish purple on lilac and m/c unpt. Arms at l. Women textile factory on back.			
	a. Issued note.	FV	FV	.75
	s. Specimen.	—	—	50.00
108 (97)	**5000 Dông** 1991 (1993). Dk. blue on m/c unpt. Arms at l. Electric lines on back.			
	a. Issued note.	FV	FV	2.50
	s. Specimen.	—	—	75.00
109 (98)	**10,000 Dông** 1990 (1992). Red and red-violet on m/c unpt. Arms at ctr. Back brown-violet and red; junks along coastline.	FV	FV	4.50
110 (99)	**20,000 Dông** 1991 (1993). Blue-green on m/c unpt. Arms at ctr. Packing factory on back.	FV	FV	8.50

		VG	VF	Unc
111 (100)	**50,000 Dông** 1990 (1993). Dk. olive-green and black on m/c unpt. Armas at upper l. ctr. Date at lower r. Port view on back.	FV	FV	20.00

1992 Monetary Emergency Issue
Negotiable Bank Cheques

		VG	VF	Unc
112 (101)	**100,000 Dông** (ca. Nov. 1992).	FV	12.50	—
113 (102)	**500,000 Dông** (ca. Nov. 1992).	FV	60.00	—
114 (103)	**1 Million Dông** (ca. Nov. 1992).	FV	110.00	—

1993; 1994 Regular Issue

		VG	VF	Unc
115 (104)	**10,000 Dông** 1993. Like #109 but w/optical registry device at lower l., modified unpt. color around arms. Back brown-violet on m/c unpt.	FV	FV	3.75
116 (105)	**50,000 Dông** 1994. Like #111 but w/date under HCM.	FV	FV	12.50

FOREIGN EXCHANGE CERTIFICATES

NGAN HANG NGOAI THUONG

BANK FOR FOREIGN TRADE

1987 ND DONG B ISSUE

			VG	VF	UNC
FX1	**10 DÔNG B**				
	ND (1987). Green on pale blue and yellow unpt. Back pale blue.				
	a. Issued note. Series AA; AB.		.25	1.00	8.00
	s. Specimen. Series EE.		—	—	50.00
FX2	**50 DÔNG B**				
	ND (1987). Green on pale blue and yellow unpt. Back pale blue.				
	a. Issued note. Series AD.		.25	1.00	8.00
	s. Specimen. Series EE.		—	—	50.00
FX3	**100 DÔNG B**				
	ND (1987). Green on pale blue and yellow unpt. Back pale blue.				
	a. Issued note. Series AC.		.25	1.00	20.00
	s. Specimen. Series EE.		—	—	50.00
FX4	**200 DÔNG B**				
	ND (1987). Green on pale blue and yellow unpt. Back pale blue.				
	a. Issued note. Series AD.		.25	1.00	8.00
	s. Specimen. Series EE.		—	—	50.00
FX5	**500 DÔNG B**				
	ND (1987). Green on pale blue and yellow unpt. Back pale blue.				
	a. Issued note. Series AC.		.25	1.00	8.00
	s. Specimen. Series EE.		—	—	50.00

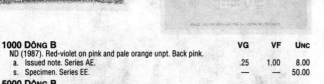

			VG	VF	UNC
FX6	**1000 DÔNG B**				
	ND (1987). Red-violet on pink and pale orange unpt. Back pink.				
	a. Issued note. Series AE.		.25	1.00	8.00
	s. Specimen. Series EE.		—	—	50.00
FX7	**5000 DÔNG B**				
	ND (1987). Brown on ochre unpt. Back ochre.				
	a. Issued note. Series AA; AB.		.25	1.00	8.00
	s. Specimen. Series EE.		—	—	50.00

1981 US DOLLAR A ISSUE

			VG	VF	UNC
FX8	**1 DOLLAR**				
	1981-84.				
FX9	**5 DOLLARS**				
	1981-84.				

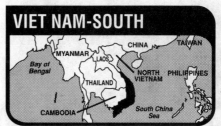

VIET NAM-SOUTH

South Viet Nam (the former Republic of Viet Nam), located in Southeast Asia, bounded by North Viet Nam on the north, Laos and Cambodia on the west, and the South China Sea on the east and south, had an area of 66,280 sq. mi. (171,665 sq. km.) and a population of 20 million. Capital: Saigon (now Ho Chi Minh City). The economy of the area is predominantly agricultural.

South Viet Nam, the direct successor to the French-dominated Emperor Bao Dai regime (also known as the State of Viet Nam), was created after the first Indochina War (between the French and the Viet-Minh) by the Geneva agreement of 1954 which divided Viet Nam at the 17th parallel of latitude. The National Bank of Viet Nam, with headquarters in the old Bank of Indochina building in Saigon, came into being on December 31, 1954. Elections which would have reunified North and South Viet Nam in 1956 never took place, and the North continued the war for unification of Viet Nam under the communist government of the Democratic Republic of Viet Nam begun at the close of World War II. South Viet Nam surrendered unconditionally on April 30, 1975. There followed a short period of coexistence of the two Viet Namese states, but the South was governed by the North through the Peoples Revolutionary Government (PRG). On July 2, 1976, South and North Viet Nam joined to form the Socialist Republic of Viet Nam.

Also see Viet Nam.

* * * **NOTE: This section has been renumbered.** * * *

MONETARY SYSTEM
1 Dông = 100 Xu

VIET NAM - SOUTH

NGÂN-HÀNG QUÔC-GIA VIÊT-NAM

NATIONAL BANK OF VIET NAM

1962 ND ISSUE

			VG	VF	UNC
5	**10 DÔNG**				
	ND (1962). Red. Young farm couple at l. Ornate arch on back.		.20	.60	2.50
6	**20 DÔNG**				
	ND (1962). Brown. Ox cart at l. Woman digging on back.		.30	1.50	5.00

1964; 1966 ND ISSUES

			VG	VF	UNC
15	**1 DÔNG**				
	ND (1964). Lt. and dk. brown on orange and lt. blue unpt. Tractor on back. Wmk: Plant.				
	a. Issued note.		.10	.50	2.00
	s. Specimen.		—	—	150.00

			VG	VF	UNC
16	**20 DÔNG**				
	ND (1964). Green on m/c unpt. Stylized fish at ctr. on back. Wmk: Dragon's head.				
	a. Issued note.		.20	.75	5.00
	s. Specimen.		—	—	150.00

17   50 Đồng

		VG	VF	Unc
ND (1966). Purple on m/c unpt. Leaf tendrils at r.				
a.	Issued note.	1.00	5.00	25.00
s.	Specimen.	—	—	150.00

18   100 Đồng

		VG	VF	Unc
ND (1966). Lt. and dk. brown on lt. blue unpt. Bldg. w/domed roof at r. Quarry and hills on back. Wmk: Plant.				
a.	Issued note.	1.00	5.00	25.00
s1.	Specimen. Red ovpt.	—	—	150.00
s2.	Specimen. Black ovpt.	—	—	150.00

19   100 Đồng
(21)

		VG	VF	Unc
ND (1966). Red on m/c unpt. Le Van Duyet in national costume at l. Bldg. and ornate arch at ctr. r. on back.				
a.	Wmk: Dragon's head.	.50	2.50	10.00
b.	Wmk: Le Van Duyet.	1.00	7.50	20.00
s1.	As a. Specimen.	—	—	250.00
s2.	As b. Specimen.	—	—	250.00

20   200 Đồng
(22)

		VG	VF	Unc
ND (1966). Dk. brown on m/c unpt. Nguyen-Hue, warrior at l. Warrior on horseback leading soldiers on back.				
a.	Wmk: Dragon's head.	2.50	10.00	25.00
b.	Wmk: Warrior's head.	.25	4.00	10.00
s1.	As a. Specimen.	—	—	250.00
s2.	As b. Specimen.	—	—	250.00

21   500 Đồng
(19)

		VG	VF	Unc
ND (1962). Green-blue on gold and pinkish unpt. Palace-like bldg. at ctr. Farmer w/2 water buffalos at r. on back. Wmk: Ngo Dinh Diem.				
a.	Issued note.	50.00	150.00	500.00
s.	Specimen.	—	—	1000.

22   500 Đồng
(20)

		VG	VF	Unc
ND (1964). Brown on m/c unpt. Museum in Saigon at ctr. Stylized creatures at ctr. on back. Wmk: Dragon's head.				
a.	Issued note.	5.00	15.00	50.00
s.	Specimen.	—	—	300.00

23   500 Đồng

		VG	VF	Unc
ND (1966). Blue on m/c unpt. Tran-Hu'ng-Dao, warrior at l. and as wmk. Sailboat and rocks in water on back.				
a.	Issued note.	1.50	5.00	15.00
s.	Specimen.	—	—	200.00
x.	Counterfeit.	—	—	15.00

1969-71 ND ISSUE
#24-29 bank bldg. at r. Lathework on all backs. Wmk. as #23.

24	20 DÔNG	VG	VF	UNC
	ND (1969). Red on m/c unpt.			
	a. Issued note.	.25	.50	2.50
	s. Specimen.	—	—	250.00

25	50 DÔNG	VG	VF	UNC
	ND (1969). Blue-green on m/c unpt.			
	a. Issued note.	.25	.50	2.50
	s. Specimen.	—	—	250.00

26	100 DÔNG	VG	VF	UNC
	ND (1970). Dk. green on m/c unpt.			
	a. Issued note.	.25	.75	5.00
	s. Specimen.	—	—	250.00

27	200 DÔNG	VG	VF	UNC
	ND (1970). Violet on m/c unpt.			
	a. Issued note.	.50	1.25	7.50
	s. Specimen.	—	—	250.00

28	500 DÔNG	VG	VF	UNC
	ND (1970). Orange and black on m/c unpt. Back orange and pale olive-green on m/c unpt.			
	a. Issued note.	.25	.75	5.00
	s. Specimen.	—	—	250.00
28A	500 DÔNG			
	ND (1970). Like #28 but brown and black on m/c unpt. Back brown and pale olive-green on m/c unpt.	5.00	25.00	100.00

29	1000 DÔNG	VG	VF	UNC
	ND (1971). Turquoise on m/c unpt.			
	a. Issued note.	1.00	7.50	20.00
	s. Specimen.	—	—	250.00

1972; 1975 ND ISSUE
#30-36 Palace of Independence at r. Wmk: Young woman's head in profile.
#35 and 36 printer: TDLR.

30	50 DÔNG	VG	VF	UNC
	ND (1972). Blue-gray on m/c unpt. 3 horses on back.			
	a. Issued note.	.50	1.25	7.50
	s. Specimen.	—	—	250.00

34	**1000 Đồng**	VG	VF	UNC
	ND (1972). Blue on m/c unpt. 3 elephants carrying loads on back.			
	a. Issued note.	.25	1.00	5.00
	b. Training note w/non-negotiable ovpt.	5.00	12.50	25.00
	s. Specimen.	—	—	200.00

31	**100 Đồng**	VG	VF	UNC
	ND (1972). Green on m/c unpt. Farmer w/2 water buffalos on back.			
	a. Issued note.	.25	.75	5.00
	s. Specimen.	—	—	250.00

34A	**1000 Đồng**	VG	VF	UNC
	ND(1975). Green and m/c. Stylized fish at l., Truong Cong Dinh at r. Dinh's tomb at upper l., stylized fish at r. on back. Specimen. (Not issued).	—	—	600.00

32	**200 Đồng**	VG	VF	UNC
	ND (1972). Wine red on m/c unpt. 3 deer on back.			
	a. Issued note.	.50	1.25	8.00
	s. Specimen.	—	—	250.00

35	**5000 Đồng**	VG	VF	UNC
	ND (1975). Brown, blue and m/c. Leopard on back. (Not issued).			
	a. Normal serial #.	20.00	40.00	100.00
	s. Specimen.	—	—	300.00

33	**500 Đồng**	VG	VF	UNC
	ND (1972). Orange and olive-green on m/c unpt. Back orange on m/c unpt., tiger at l. ctr.	.25	.75	5.00
33A	**500 Đồng**			
	ND (1972). Like #33 but brown and olive-green on m/c unpt. Back brown on m/c unpt.	3.00	7.50	22.50

36	**10,000 Đồng**	VG	VF	UNC
	ND (1975). Violet and m/c. Water buffalo on back. (Not issued).			
	a. Normal serial #.	27.50	65.00	135.00
	s. Specimen.	—	—	300.00

NGÂN-HÀNG VIỆT-NAM

1966 DATED (1975) TRANSITIONAL ISSUE

#37-44 constitute a transitional issue of the communist National Liberation Front (Viet Cong) government which took over on April 30, 1975. Dated 1966 but not issued until 1975, they were used until the South's economic system was merged with that of the DRVN (North Viet Nam) into a unified Socialist Republic of Viet Nam.

			VG	VF	UNC
37	**10 XU**	1966 (1975). Brown on m/c unpt. Drying salt at ctr. Unloading boats on back.			
	a.	Issued note.	.35	.85	3.00
	s.	Specimen.	—	—	100.00
38	**20 XU**	1966 (1975). Blue on m/c unpt. Workers on rubber plantation at ctr. Soldiers greeting farmers w/oxen on back.			
	a.	Issued note.	.50	2.50	7.50
	s.	Specimen.	—	—	100.00
39	**50 XU**	1966 (1975). Brownish purple on m/c unpt. Harvesting cane at ctr. Women weaving rugs on back.			
	a.	Issued note.	.75	5.00	15.00
	s.	Specimen.	—	—	100.00

			VG	VF	UNC
R2	**20 XU**	ND (1963). Red-brown on aqua and m/c unpt. Star at ctr.	.20	.50	2.00
R3	**50 XU**	ND (1963). Green and m/c. Star at ctr.	.30	1.50	5.00

			VG	VF	UNC
40	**1 ĐỒNG**	1966 (1975). Red-orange on m/c unpt. Boats on canal at ctr. Workers in field on back.			
	a.	Issued note.	1.00	4.00	10.00
	s.	Specimen.	—	—	100.00
41	**2 ĐỒNG**	1966 (1975). Blue and green on m/c. Houseboats under a bridge at ctr. Soldiers and workers on back.			
	a.	Issued note.	3.00	12.50	30.00
	s.	Specimen.	—	—	100.00
42	**5 ĐỒNG**	1966 (1975). Purple on m/c unpt. 4 women in textile factory at ctr. Armed soldiers w/downed helicopters on back.			
	a.	Issued note.	3.00	12.50	30.00
	s.	Specimen.	—	—	100.00
43	**10 ĐỒNG**	1966 (1975). Red on m/c unpt. 3 women and train at ctr. Soldiers and people w/flag on back.			
	a.	Issued note.	8.00	25.00	75.00
	s.	Specimen.	—	—	100.00
44	**50 ĐỒNG**	1966 (1975). Green and blue on m/c unpt. Workers in factory at ctr. Combine harvester on back.			
	a.	Issued note.	20.00	55.00	175.00
	s.	Specimen.	—	—	100.00

			VG	VF	UNC
R4	**1 ĐỒNG**	ND (1963). Lt. brown on m/c unpt. Harvesting at ctr. Schoolroom on back.	1.00	4.00	15.00

REGIONAL

UY BAN TRUNG U'O'NG

CENTRAL COMMITTEE OF THE

NATIONAL FRONT FOR THE LIBERATION OF SOUTH VIET-NAM

1963 ND ISSUE

#R1-R8 were printed in China for use in territories under control of the National Liberation Front. They were never issued, but many were captured during a joint US/South Viet Nam military operation into Cambodia. Except for #R2, relatively few survived in uncirculated condition.

			VG	VF	UNC
R5	**2 ĐỒNG**	ND (1963). Blue on m/c unpt. Women in convoy at ctr. Fishermen w/boats on back.	3.00	10.00	40.00

			VG	VF	UNC
R1	**10 XU**	ND (1963). Purple and m/c. Star at ctr.	.20	.60	3.00

			VG	VF	UNC
R6	**5 ĐỒNG**	ND (1963). Lilac on m/c unpt. Women harvesting at ctr. Line of women fighters on back.	1.50	10.00	25.00

		VG	VF	UNC
R7	**10 ĐÔNG**	3.00	20.00	75.00

ND (1963). Green on m/c unpt. Harvesting scene at ctr. War scene on back.

		VG	VF	UNC
R8	**50 ĐÔNG**	5.00	25.00	100.00

ND (1963). Orange on m/c unpt. Truck convoy at ctr. Soldiers shooting down helicopters on back.

WEST AFRICAN STATES

The West African States, a former federation of eight French colonial territories on the northwest coast of Africa, had an area of 1,813,079 sq. mi. (4,742,495 sq. km.) and a population of about 17 million. Capital: Dakar. The constituent territories were Mauritania, Senegal, Dahomey, French Sudan, Ivory Coast, Upper Volta, Niger and French Guinea.

The members of the federation were overseas territories within the French Union until Sept. of 1958 when all but French Guinea approved the constitution of the Fifth French Republic, thereby electing to become autonomous members of the new French Community. French Guinea voted to become the fully independent Republic of Guinea. The other seven attained independence in 1960. The French West Africa territories were provided with a common currency, a practice which was continued as the monetary union of the West African States which provides a common currency to the autonomous republics of Dahomey (now Benin), Mali, Senegal, Upper Volta, Ivory Coast, Togo and Niger.

* * * NOTE: This section has been partially renumbered. * * *

MONETARY SYSTEM:

1 Franc = 100 Centimes

DATING

The year of issue on the current 500, 1000 and 2500 Francs appears in the first 2 digits of the serial number, i.e. (19)91, (19)92, etc.

SIGNATURE VARIETIES			
	LE PRÉSIDENT	**LE DIRECTEUR GÉNÉRAL**	**Date**
1		R. *Julienne*	Various dates – 1959 20.3.1961
2		R. *Julienne*	20.3.1961
3		R. *Julienne*	2.12.1964
4		R. *Julienne*	2.3.1965; ND
5		R. *Julienne*	ND
6		R. *Julienne*	ND
7		R. *Julienne*	ND
8		R. *Julienne*	ND
9		R. *Julienne*	ND
	LE PRÉSIDENT DU CONSEIL DES MINISTRES	**LE GOUVERNEUR**	**Date**
10		*Harding*	ND
11		*Harding*	ND (1977); 1977
12		*Harding*	ND (1978); 1978; 1979
13		*Harding*	ND (1980); 1980

14		*Mading*	ND (1977); 1977; 1988; 1989
	LE PRÉSIDENT DU CONSEIL DES MINISTRES	**LE GOUVERNEUR**	**Date**
15		*Mading*	ND (1981); 1981; 1982
16		*Mading*	ND (1983); 1983
17		*Mading*	1981; 1983; 1984
18		*Mading*	ND (1984); 1984
19		*Mading*	1984; 1985
20		*Mading*	1986; 1987
21		*Alassane Ouattara*	1989
22		*Alassane Ouattara*	1991
23		*Alassane Ouattara*	1992
24		*Alassane Ouattara*	1992
25		*Alassane Ouattara*	1993
26			
27			
28			

WEST AFRICAN STATES

NOTE: Begining with signatures #21 the position has been reversed on the 500 Francs.

BANQUE CENTRALE DES ETATS DE L'AFRIQUE DE L'OUEST

Notes of this bank were issued both w/and w/o code letters in the upper r. and lower l. corners. The code letter follows the control number and indicates which member country the note was issued for. Those w/o code letters are general issues. The code letters are as follows:

A for Ivory Coast   H for Niger
D for Mali   K for Sengal
E for Mauritania   T for Togo

GENERAL ISSUES W/O CODE LETTER

1958; 1959 ND ISSUE
#1-5 w/o code letters to signify member countries.

2	**100 FRANCS**	VG	VF	UNC
	1959; ND. Dk. brown, orange and m/c. Mask at l., woman at r. Woman at l., carving at lower ctr. on back.			
	a. Sign. 1. 23.4.1959.	10.00	40.00	90.00
	b. Sign. 5. ND.	3.00	10.00	20.00

A FOR IVORY COAST

1959-65; ND ISSUE

101A	**100 FRANCS**	VG	VF	UNC
	1961-65; ND. Dk. brown, orange and m/c. Design like #2.			
	a. Engraved. Sign. 1. 20.3.1961.	12.00	30.00	65.00
	b. Sign. 2. 20.3.1961.	10.00	25.00	60.00
	c. Litho. Sign. 2. 20.3.1961.	10.00	25.00	60.00
	d. Sign. 3. 2.12.1964.	8.00	20.00	50.00
	e. Sign. 4. 2.3.1965.	8.00	20.00	50.00
	f. Sign. 4. ND.	7.00	18.00	40.00
	g. Sign. 5. ND.	7.00	18.00	40.00

102A	**500 FRANCS**	VG	VF	UNC
	1959-64; ND. Brown, green and m/c. Field workers at l., mask carving at r. Woman at l., farmer on tractor at r. on back.			
	a. Engraved. Sign. 1. 15.4.1959.	25.00	55.00	100.00
	b. Sign. 1. 20.3.1961.	15.00	40.00	80.00
	c. Sign. 2. 20.3.1961.	15.00	40.00	80.00
	d. Sign. 3. 2.12.1964.	25.00	55.00	100.00
	e. Sign. 5. ND.	12.00	35.00	75.00
	f. Sign. 6. ND.	10.00	30.00	65.00
	g. Litho. Sign. 6. ND.	10.00	30.00	65.00
	h. Sign. 7. ND.	12.00	35.00	75.00
	i. Sign. 8. ND.	25.00	55.00	100.00
	j. Sign. 9. ND.	8.00	25.00	55.00
	k. Sign. 10. ND.	5.00	15.00	40.00
	l. Sign. 11. ND.	5.00	15.00	40.00
	m. Sign. 12. ND.	20.00	50.00	90.00

103A	**1000 FRANCS**	VG	VF	UNC
	1959-65; ND. Brown, blue and m/c. Man and woman at ctr. Man w/rope suspension bridge in background and pineapples on back.			
	a. Engraved. Sign. 1. 17.9.1959.	—	—	—
	b. Sign. 1. 20.3.1961.	15.00	45.00	100.00
	c. Sign. 2. 20.3.1961.	10.00	35.00	80.00
	d. Sign. 4. 2.3.1965.	30.00	70.00	—
	e. Sign. 5. ND.	8.00	25.00	60.00
	f. Sign. 6. ND.	8.00	25.00	60.00
	g. Litho. Sign. 6. ND.	8.00	25.00	60.00
	h. Sign. 7. ND.	10.00	30.00	70.00
	i. Sign. 8. ND.	12.00	40.00	90.00
	j. Sign. 9. ND.	6.00	20.00	50.00
	k. Sign. 10. ND.	5.00	15.00	40.00
	l. Sign. 11. ND.	5.00	15.00	40.00
	m. Sign. 12. ND.	5.00	15.00	40.00
	n. Sign. 13. ND.	5.00	15.00	40.00

104A 5000 FRANCS

		VG	VF	UNC
1961-65; ND. Blue, brown and m/c. Bearded man at l., bldg. at ctr. Woman, corn grinders and huts on back.				
a. Sign. 1. 20.3.1961.		35.00	75.00	175.00
b. Sign. 2. 20.3.1961.		35.00	65.00	160.00
c. Sign. 3. 2.12.1964.		35.00	65.00	160.00
d. Sign. 4. 2.3.1965.		35.00	75.00	—
e. Sign. 6. ND.		20.00	45.00	130.00
f. Sign. 7. ND.		25.00	55.00	145.00
g. Sign. 8. ND.		35.00	75.00	—
h. Sign. 9. ND.		20.00	45.00	130.00
i. Sign. 10. ND.		20.00	40.00	120.00
j. Sign. 11. ND.		20.00	40.00	120.00

1977-81; ND ISSUE

#105A-109A smaller size notes.

NOTE: #106A w/10-digit sm. serial # were printed by Banque de France (BF) while those w/9-digit lg. serial # were printed by F-CO.

105A 500 FRANCS

		VG	VF	UNC
1979-80. Lilac, lt. olive-green and m/c. Artwork at l., long horn animals at ctr., man wearing hat at r. Pineapple at l., aerial view at ctr., mask at r. on back.				
a. Sign. 12. 1979.		3.00	8.00	17.00
b. Sign. 13. 1980.		2.75	7.00	15.00

106A 500 FRANCS

		VG	VF	UNC
1981-90. Pale olive-green and m/c. Design like #105A.				
a. Sign. 14. 1988.		FV	FV	6.00
b. Sign. 15. 1981. (BF).		6.00	15.00	35.00
c. Sign. 15. 1981. (F-CO).		FV	3.00	7.00
d. Sign. 15. 1982. (BF).		6.00	15.00	35.00
e. Sign. 17. 1981. (F-CO).		6.00	15.00	35.00
f. Sign. 17. 1983.		FV	3.00	7.00
g. Sign. 18. 1984.		FV	3.00	7.00
h. Sign. 19. 1984.		FV	3.00	7.00
i. Sign. 19. 1985.		FV	3.00	7.00
j. Sign. 20. 1986.		FV	FV	6.00
k. Sign. 20. 1987.		FV	3.00	7.00
l. Sign. 21 (reversed order). 1989.		FV	FV	5.00
m. Sign. 22. 1990.		FV	FV	5.00

107A 1000 FRANCS

		VG	VF	UNC
1981-90. Brown on m/c unpt. Artwork at l., open pit mine at ctr., woman at r. Wood carver w/finished works on back.				
a. Sign. 14. 1988.		FV	FV	10.00
b. Sign. 15. 1981.		FV	4.00	11.00
c. Sign. 17. 1981.		FV	4.00	11.00
d. Sign. 18. 1984.		FV	4.00	11.00
e. Sign. 19. 1984.		5.00	11.00	30.00
f. Sign. 19. 1985.		FV	4.00	11.00
g. Sign. 20. 1986.		FV	FV	10.00
h. Sign. 20. 1987.		FV	FV	10.00
i. Sign. 21. 1989.		FV	FV	9.00
j. Sign. 22. 1990.		FV	FV	9.00

108A 5000 FRANCS

		VG	VF	UNC
1977-92. Black and red on m/c unpt. Woman at l., fish and boats on shore at ctr., carving at r. Carvings, fishing boats and mask on back.				
a. Sign. 11. 1977.		18.00	30.00	60.00
b. Sign. 12. 1978.		18.00	30.00	60.00
c. Sign. 12. 1979.		25.00	45.00	80.00
d. Sign. 13. 1980.		30.00	50.00	110.00
e. Sign. 14. 1977.		20.00	35.00	70.00
f. Sign. 14. 1988.		FV	FV	35.00
g. Sign. 14. 1989.		FV	FV	35.00
h. Sign. 15. 1981.		FV	20.00	50.00
i. Sign. 15. 1982.		FV	20.00	50.00
j. Sign. 16. 1983.		35.00	60.00	—
k. Sign. 17. 1983.		25.00	45.00	80.00
l. Sign. 18. 1984.		30.00	45.00	80.00
m. Sign. 19. 1984.		FV	20.00	50.00
n. Sign. 19. 1985.		FV	20.00	50.00
o. Sign. 20. 1986.		FV	20.00	50.00
p. Sign. 20. 1987.		FV	FV	35.00
q. Sign. 21. 1990.		FV	FV	35.00
r. Sign. 22. 1991.		FV	FV	35.00

109A 10,000 FRANCS

		VG	VF	UNC
ND (1977-92). Red-brown on m/c unpt. 2 men seated operating primitive spinning apparatus, woman w/headwear at r. Figurine and girl at l., modern textile spinning machine at ctr. on back.				
a. Sign. 11. ND.		25.00	45.00	85.00
b. Sign. 12. ND.		30.00	50.00	90.00
c. Sign. 13. ND.		30.00	50.00	90.00
d. Sign. 14. ND.		FV	FV	60.00
e. Sign. 15. ND.		FV	25.00	65.00
f. Sign. 18. ND.		FV	25.00	65.00
g. Sign. 19. ND.		30.00	50.00	90.00
h. Sign. 20. ND.		FV	FV	60.00
i. Sign. 21. ND.		FV	FV	55.00
j. Sign. 22. ND.		FV	FV	55.00
k. Sign. 23. ND.		FV	FV	55.00

1991-92 ISSUE

#113A and 114A were first issued on 19.9.1994.

110A 500 FRANCS

		VG	VF	UNC
(19)91-. Dk. brown and green on m/c unpt. Male at r. and as wmk., flood control dam at ctr. Farmer riding spray rig behind garden tractor at ctr., native art at l. on back.				
a. Sign. 22. (19)91.		FV	FV	3.00
b. Sign. 23. (19)92.		FV	3.00	6.00
c. Sign. 25. (19)93.		FV	FV	3.00
d. Sign. 26. (19)94.		FV	FV	3.00
e. Sign. 27. (19)95.		FV	FV	3.00

111A 1000 FRANCS

		VG	VF	UNC
(19)91-. Dk. brown on tan, yellow and m/c unpt. Workman hauling peanuts to storage at ctr., woman's head at r. and as wmk. Twin statues and mask at l., 2 woman w/baskets, elevated riverside storage bins in background at ctr. on back.				
a. Sign. 22. (19)91.		FV	FV	6.00
b. Sign. 23. (19)92.		FV	FV	6.00
c. Sign. 25. (19)93.		FV	FV	6.00
d. Sign. 26. (19)94.		FV	FV	6.00
e. Sign. 27. (19)95.		FV	FV	6.00

112A 2500 FRANCS

	VG	VF	UNC
(19)92-. Deep purple and dk. brown on lilac and m/c unpt. Dam at ctr., young woman's head at r. and as wmk. Statue at l., harvesting and spraying of fruit at l. ctr. on back. Sign. 23.			
a. Sign. 23. (19)92.	FV	FV	14.00
b. Sign. 25. (19)93.	FV	FV	14.00
c. Sign. 27. (19)94.	FV	FV	14.00

113A 5000 FRANCS

	VG	VF	UNC
(19)92-. Dk. brown and deep blue on m/c unpt. Woman wearing headdress adorned w/cowrie shells at r. and as wmk., smelting plant at ctr. Woman w/children and various pottery at l. ctr. on back. Sign. 23.			
a. Sign. 23. (19)92.	FV	FV	26.00
b. Sign. 25. (19)93.	FV	FV	26.00
c. Sign. 27. (19)94.	FV	FV	26.00
d. Sign. 27. (19)95.	FV	FV	26.00

114A 10,000 FRANCS

	VG	VF	UNC
(19)92-. Dk. brown on m/c unpt. Headman w/scepter at r. and as wmk., skyscraper at ctr. Native art at l., woman crossing vine bridge over river at ctr. on back.			
a. Sign. 23. (19)92.	FV	FV	45.00
b. Sign. 27. (19)94.	FV	FV	45.00
c. Sign. 27. (19)95.	FV	FV	45.00

B FOR BENIN (DAHOMEY)

1959-65; ND ISSUE
#201B-209B have letter B for Benin.

201B 100 FRANCS

	VG	VF	UNC
1961-65; ND. Like #101A.			
a. Engraved. Sign. 1. 20.3.1961.	12.00	35.00	85.00
b. Sign. 2. 20.3.1961.	10.00	25.00	65.00
c. Litho. Sign. 2. 20.3.1961.	10.00	25.00	65.00
d. Sign. 3. 2.12.1964.	8.00	20.00	50.00
e. Sign. 4. 2.3.1965.	8.00	20.00	50.00
f. Sign. 4. ND.	7.00	18.00	40.00

202B 500 FRANCS

	VG	VF	UNC
1961-64; ND. Like #102A.			
b. Engraved Sign. 2. 20.3.1961.	25.00	65.00	130.00
d. Sign. 3. 2.12.1964.	—		
f. Sign. 5. ND.	25.00	55.00	120.00
g. Sign. 6. ND.	10.00	30.00	65.00
h. Litho. Sign. 7. ND.	12.00	35.00	75.00
i. Sign. 9. ND.	8.00	25.00	65.00
k. Sign. 10. ND.	5.00	20.00	50.00
l. Sign. 11. ND.	5.00	20.00	50.00

203B 1000 FRANCS

	VG	VF	UNC
1961-65; ND. Like #103A.			
a. Engraved. Sign. 1. 17.9.1959.	35.00	75.00	—
b. Sign. 2. 20.3.1961.	25.00	60.00	125.00
e. Sign. 4. 2.3.1965.	25.00	60.00	125.00
g. Sign. 6. ND.	8.00	30.00	65.00
h. Litho. Sign. 6. ND.	7.00	25.00	60.00
i. Sign. 7. ND.	20.00	55.00	110.00
j. Sign. 8. ND.	10.00	35.00	70.00
k. Sign. 9. ND.	10.00	35.00	70.00
l. Sign. 10. ND.	5.00	15.00	45.00
m. Sign. 11. ND.	5.00	15.00	45.00
n. Sign. 12. ND.	5.00	15.00	45.00

204B 5000 FRANCS

	VG	VF	UNC
1961; ND. Like #104A.			
a. Sign. 1. 20.3.1961.	35.00	80.00	—
b. Sign. 2. 20.3.1961.	35.00	80.00	—
h. Sign. 6. ND.	25.00	65.00	150.00
j. Sign. 7. ND.	25.00	65.00	150.00
k. Sign. 9. ND.	20.00	55.00	135.00
l. Sign. 10. ND.	20.00	55.00	135.00

1977-81; ND ISSUE
#205B-209B smaller size notes.

NOTE: #206B w/10-digit sm. serial # were printed by Banque de France (BF) while those w/9-digit lg. serial # were printed by F-CO.

205B 500 FRANCS

	VG	VF	UNC
1979-80. Like #105A.			
a. Sign. 12. 1979.	6.00	18.00	40.00
b. Sign. 13. 1980.	3.00	8.00	18.00

206B 500 FRANCS

	VG	VF	UNC
1981-90. Like #106A.			
a. Sign. 14. 1988.	4.00	8.00	—
b. Sign. 15. 1981. (BF).	FV	3.00	8.00
c. Sign. 15. 1981. (F-CO).	FV	3.00	8.00
d. Sign. 15. 1982. (BF).	6.00	15.00	35.00
e. Sign. 17. 1981. (F-CO).	6.00	15.00	35.00
f. Sign. 17. 1983. (BF).	6.00	15.00	—
g. Sign. 18. 1984.	FV	3.00	8.00
h. Sign. 19. 1984.	FV	3.00	7.00
i. Sign. 19. 1985.	FV	3.00	8.00
j. Sign. 20. 1986.	FV	FV	6.00
k. Sign. 20. 1987.	FV	FV	6.00
l. Sign. 21. 1989.	FV	FV	6.00
m. Sign. 22. 1990.	FV	FV	6.00

207B	1000 FRANCS	VG	VF	UNC
	1981-90. Like #107A.			
a.	Sign. 14. 1988.	FV	FV	11.00
b.	Sign. 15. 1981.	FV	4.00	12.00
c.	Sign. 18. 1984.	FV	4.00	12.00
d.	Sign. 19. 1985.	FV	4.00	12.00
e.	Sign. 20. 1986.	FV	FV	11.00
f.	Sign. 20. 1987.	FV	FV	11.00
g.	Sign. 21. 1989.	3.00	6.00	—
h.	Sign. 22. 1990.	FV	FV	10.00

208B	5000 FRANCS	VG	VF	UNC
	1977-92. Like #108A.			
a.	Sign. 12. 1979.	22.00	30.00	65.00
b.	Sign. 14. 1977.	22.00	35.00	70.00
c.	Sign. 14. 1988.	FV	FV	35.00
d.	Sign. 14. 1989.	FV	FV	35.00
e.	Sign. 15. 1981.	FV	20.00	55.00
f.	Sign. 15. 1982.	FV	20.00	55.00
g.	Sign. 17. 1983.	35.00	45.00	90.00
h.	Sign. 18. 1984.	25.00	45.00	90.00
i.	Sign. 19. 1985.	25.00	45.00	90.00
j.	Sign. 20. 1986.	FV	40.00	75.00
k.	Sign. 20. 1987.	FV	FV	35.00
l.	Sign. 21. 1990.	FV	FV	35.00
m.	Sign. 22. 1991.	FV	FV	35.00
n.	Sign. 22. 1992.	FV	FV	30.00
o.	Sign. 23. 1992.	FV	FV	30.00

209B	10,000 FRANCS	VG	VF	UNC
	ND (1977-92). Like #109A.	40.00	75.00	150.00
a.	Sign. 11. ND.	40.00	75.00	—
b.	Sign. 12. ND.	FV	FV	65.00
c.	Sign. 14. ND.	FV	75.00	80.00
d.	Sign. 15. ND.	FV	75.00	—
e.	Sign. 16. ND.	40.00	75.00	—
f.	Sign. 18. ND.	40.00	75.00	—
g.	Sign. 19. ND.	FV	35.00	80.00
h.	Sign. 20. ND.	30.00	55.00	110.00
i.	Sign. 21. ND.	FV	FV	60.00
j.	Sign. 22. ND.	FV	FV	60.00
k.	Sign. 23. ND.	FV	FV	60.00

1991-92 ISSUE

210B	500 FRANCS	VG	VF	UNC
	(19)91-. Like #110A.	FV	FV	4.00
a.	Sign. 22. (19)91.	FV	3.00	7.00
b.	Sign. 22. (19)92.	FV	3.00	7.00
c.	Sign. 23. (19)92.	FV	FV	4.00
d.	Sign. 25. (19)93.			
e.	Sign. 26. (19)94.	FV	FV	4.00

211B	1000 FRANCS	VG	VF	UNC
	(19)91-. Like #111A.	FV	FV	7.00
a.	Sign. 22. (19)91.	FV	4.00	10.00
b.	Sign. 22. (19)92.	FV	4.00	10.00
c.	Sign. 23. (19)92.	FV	FV	7.00
d.	Sign. 25. (19)93.	FV	FV	7.00
e.	Sign. 26. (19)94.	FV	FV	7.00
f.	Sign. 27. (19)95.			

212B	2500 FRANCS	VG	VF	UNC
	(19)92-. Like #112A.			
a.	Sign. 23. (19)92.	FV	FV	15.00
b.	Sign. 25. (19)93.	FV	FV	15.00
c.	Sign. 27. (19)94.	FV	FV	15.00

213B	5000 FRANCS			
	(19)92-. Like #113A.			
a.	Sign. 23. (19)92.	FV	FV	28.00
b.	Sign. 25. (19)93.	FV	FV	28.00
c.	Sign. 27. (19)94.	FV	FV	28.00

214B	10,000 FRANCS			
	(19)92-. Like #114A.			
a.	Sign. 23. (19)92.	FV	FV	50.00
b.	Sign. 27. (19)94.	FV	FV	50.00
c.	Sign. 27. (19)95.	FV	FV	50.00

C FOR BUKINA FASO (UPPER VOLTA)

1961; ND ISSUE

#301C-309C have letter C for Burkina Faso.

301C	100 FRANCS	VG	VF	UNC
	1961-65; ND. Like #101A.			
a.	Engraved. Sign. 1. 20.3.1961.	12.00	35.00	85.00
b.	Sign. 2. 20.3.1961.	10.00	30.00	75.00
c.	Litho. Sign. 2. 20.3.1961.	12.00	35.00	85.00
d.	Sign. 3. 2.12.1964.	—	—	—
e.	Sign. 4. 2.3.1965.	8.00	20.00	55.00
f.	Sign. 4. ND.	7.00	18.00	45.00

302C	500 FRANCS	VG	VF	UNC
	1961-65; ND. Like #102A.			
c.	Engraved. Sign. 2. 20.3.1961.	25.00	65.00	130.00
e.	Sign. 4. 20.3.1961.	25.00	65.00	—
g.	Sign. 6. ND.	15.00	40.00	75.00
h.	Litho. Sign. 6. ND.	10.00	30.00	65.00
i.	Sign. 7. ND.	20.00	55.00	120.00
j.	Sign. 8. ND.	15.00	40.00	75.00
k.	Sign. 9. ND.	8.00	25.00	55.00
m.	Sign. 11. ND.	5.00	15.00	45.00
n.	Sign. 12. ND.	5.00	15.00	45.00

303C	1000 FRANCS			
	1961 ND. Like #103A.			
b.	Sign. 1. 20.3.1961.	30.00	70.00	—
d.	Sign. 2. 20.3.1961.	30.00	70.00	—
e.	Sign. 5. ND.	—	—	—
f.	Sign. 6. ND.	20.00	55.00	110.00
i.	Sign. 7. ND.	15.00	35.00	80.00
j.	Sign. 8. ND.	20.00	55.00	110.00
k.	Sign. 9. ND.	10.00	25.00	65.00
l.	Sign. 10. ND.	5.00	15.00	45.00
m.	Sign. 11. ND	5.00	15.00	45.00
n.	Sign. 12. ND.	5.00	15.00	45.00
o.	Sign. 13. ND.	8.00	20.00	55.00

304C	5000 FRANCS			
	ND. Like #104A.			
a.	Sign. 1. 20.3.1961.	35.00	75.00	175.00
h.	Sign. 6. ND.	20.00	65.00	—
i.	Sign. 7. ND.	25.00	65.00	—
k.	Sign. 9. ND.	20.00	55.00	140.00
l.	Sign. 11. ND.	20.00	50.00	130.00

1977-81; ND ISSUES

#305C-309C smaller size notes.

NOTE: #306C w/10-digit sm. serial # were printed by Banque de France (BF) while those w/9-digit lg. serial # were printed by F-CO.

305C	500 FRANCS	VG	VF	UNC
	1979-80. Like #105A.			
a.	Sign. 12. 1979.	3.00	8.00	18.00
b.	Sign. 13. 1980.	2.75	7.00	15.00

306C	**500 FRANCS**	VG	VF	UNC
	1981-90. Like #106A.			
	a. Sign. 14. 1988.	FV	FV	6.00
	b. Sign. 15. 1981. (BF).	FV	3.00	8.00
	c. Sign. 15. 1981. (F-CO).	FV	2.75	7.00
	d. Sign. 15. 1982. (BF).	6.00	15.00	35.00
	e. Sign. 17. 1981. (F-CO).	6.00	15.00	—
	f. Sign. 17. 1983. (BF).	6.00	15.00	—
	g. Sign. 18. 1984.	FV	2.75	7.00
	h. Sign. 19. 1984.	FV	2.75	7.00
	i. Sign. 19. 1985.	4.00	2.75	7.00
	j. Sign. 20. 1986.	6.00	15.00	—
	k. Sign. 20. 1987.	FV	FV	6.00
	l. Sign. 21. 1989.	FV	FV	6.00
	m. Sign. 22. 1990.	FV	FV	6.00

307C	**1000 FRANCS**	VG	VF	UNC
	1981-90. Like #107A.			
	a. Sign. 14. 1988.	FV	FV	10.00
	b. Sign. 15. 1981.	FV	4.00	11.00
	c. Sign. 17. 1981.	5.00	11.00	30.00
	d. Sign. 18. 1984.	5.00	11.00	30.00
	e. Sign. 19. 1984.	5.00	11.00	30.00
	f. Sign. 19. 1985.	5.00	11.00	30.00
	g. Sign. 20. 1986.	FV	FV	11.00
	h. Sign. 20. 1987.	FV	FV	10.00
	i. Sign. 21. 1989.	FV	FV	9.00
	j. Sign. 22. 1990.	FV	FV	9.00
308C	**5000 FRANCS**			
	1977-92 Like #108A.			
	a. Sign. 12. 1978.	18.00	30.00	60.00
	b. Sign. 12. 1979.	18.00	30.00	60.00
	c. Sign. 14. 1977.	20.00	35.00	70.00
	d. Sign. 14. 1988.	FV	FV	35.00
	e. Sign. 14. 1989.	FV	FV	35.00
	f. Sign. 15. 1981.	FV	20.00	50.00
	g. Sign. 15. 1982.	FV	20.00	50.00
	h. Sign. 17. 1983.	FV	20.00	50.00
	i. Sign. 18. 1984.	FV	20.00	50.00
	j. Sign. 19. 1984.	FV	20.00	50.00
	k. Sign. 19. 1985.	FV	20.00	50.00
	l. Sign. 20. 1986.	FV	20.00	50.00
	m. Sign. 20. 1987.	20.00	35.00	70.00
	n. Sign. 21. 1990.	FV	FV	35.00
	o. Sign. 22. 1991.	FV	FV	35.00
	p. Sign. 22. 1992.	FV	FV	35.00
	q. Sign. 23. 1992.	FV	FV	35.00
	r. Sign. 24. 1992.	FV	20.00	50.00
309C	**10,000 FRANCS**			
	ND (1977-92). Like #109A.			
	a. Sign. 11. ND.	45.00	75.00	140.00
	b. Sign. 12. ND.	30.00	50.00	95.00
	c. Sign. 13. ND.	30.00	50.00	95.00
	d. Sign. 14. ND.	30.00	50.00	95.00
	e. Sign. 15. ND.	FV	25.00	65.00
	f. Sign. 20. ND.	FV	FV	60.00
	g. Sign. 21. ND.	FV	FV	55.00
	h. Sign. 22. ND.	FV	FV	55.00
	i. Sign. 23. ND.	FV	FV	55.00

1991 ISSUE

310C	**500 FRANCS**	VG	VF	UNC
	(19)91-. Like #110A.			
	a. Sign. 22. (19)91.	FV	FV	3.00
	b. Sign. 23. (19)92.	FV	3.00	7.00
	c. Sign. 25. (19)93.	FV	FV	3.00
	d. Sign. 26. (19)94.	FV	FV	3.00
	e. Sign. 27. (19)95.	FV	FV	3.00
311C	**1000 FRANCS**			
	(19)91-. Like #111A.			
	a. Sign. 22. (19)91.	FV	FV	6.00
	b. Sign. 22. (19)92.	3.00	6.00	10.00
	c. Sign. 23. (19)92.	3.00	6.00	10.00
	d. Sign. 25. (19)93.	FV	FV	6.00
	e. Sign. 26. (19)94.	FV	FV	6.00
	f. Sign. 27. (19)95.	FV	FV	6.00
312C	**2500 FRANCS**			
	(19)91-. Like #112A.			
	a. Sign. 23. (19)92.	FV	FV	14.00
	b. Sign. 25. (19)93.	FV	FV	14.00
	c. Sign. 27. (19)94.	FV	FV	14.00
313C	**5000 FRANCS**			
	(19)92-. Like #113A.			
	a. Sign. 23. (19)02.	FV	FV	26.00
	b. Sign. 25. (19)93.	FV	FV	26.00
	c. Sign. 27. (19)94.	FV	FV	26.00
	d. Sign. 27. (19)95.	FV	FV	26.00
314C	**10,000 FRANCS**			
	(19)92-. Like #114A.			
	a. Sign. 23. (19)92.	FV	FV	45.00
	b. Sign. 27. (19)94.	FV	FV	45.00
	c. Sign. 27. (19)95.	FV	FV	45.00

D FOR MALI

1959-61; ND ISSUE

401D	**100 FRANCS**	VG	VF	UNC
	20.3.1961. Like #101A. Sign. l.	65.00	125.00	—
402D	**500 FRANCS**			
	1959; 1961. Like #102A.			
	a. Sign. l. 15.4.1959.	90.00	175.00	—
	b. Sign. l. 20.3.1961.	—	—	—
403D	**1000 FRANCS**			
	1959; 1961. Like #103A.			
	a. Sign. l. 17.9.1959.	75.00	150.00	—
	b. Sign. l. 20.3.1961.	75.00	150.00	—
404D	**5000 FRANCS**			
	20.3.1961. Like #104A. Sign. l.	125.00	250.00	—

1981; ND ISSUE

#405D-408D smaller size notes.

NOTE: #405D w/10-digit sm. serial # were printed by Banque de France (BF) while those w/9-digit lg. serial # were printed by F-CO.

405D	**500 FRANCS**	VG	VF	UNC
	1981-90. Like #106A.			
	a. Sign. 14. 1988.	FV	FV	6.00
	b. Sign. 15. 1981. (BF).	FV	2.75	7.00
	c. Sign. 17. 1981. (F-CO).	FV	2.75	7.00
	e. Sign. 19. 1985.	FV	2.75	7.00
	f. Sign. 20. 1986.	FV	FV	6.00
	g. Sign. 20. 1987.	FV	FV	6.00
	h. Sign. 21. 1989.	FV	FV	5.00
	i. Sign. 22. 1990.	FV	FV	5.00
406D	**1000 FRANCS**			
	1981-90. Like #107A.			
	a. Sign. 14. 1988.	FV	FV	10.00
	b. Sign. 15. 1981.	FV	4.00	11.00
	c. Sign. 17. 1981.	FV	4.00	11.00
	f. Sign. 19. 1985.	4.00	11.00	30.00
	g. Sign. 20. 1986.	4.00	11.00	30.00
	h. Sign. 20. 1987.	4.00	11.00	30.00
	i. Sign. 21. 1989.	FV	FV	9.00
	j. Sign. 22. 1990.	FV	FV	9.00
407D	**5000 FRANCS**			
	1981-92. Like #108A.			
	a. Sign. 14. 1988.	FV	FV	35.00
	b. Sign. 14. 1989.	FV	FV	35.00
	c. Sign. 15. 1981.	FV	20.00	50.00
	d. Sign. 17. 1984.	FV	20.00	50.00
	e. Sign. 18. 1984.	25.00	45.00	80.00
	f. Sign. 19. 1985.	FV	20.00	50.00
	g. Sign. 20. 1986.	FV	20.00	50.00
	h. Sign. 20. 1987.	FV	FV	35.00
	i. Sign. 21. 1990.	FV	FV	35.00
	j. Sign. 22. 1991.	FV	FV	35.00
	k. Sign. 23. 1992.	FV	FV	35.00
	l. Sign. 24. 1992.	FV	20.00	50.00
408D	**10,000 FRANCS**			
	ND (1981-92). Like #109A.			
	a. Sign. 14. ND.	FV	25.00	65.00
	b. Sign. 15. ND.	FV	30.00	65.00
	c. Sign. 18. ND.	30.00	50.00	90.00
	d. Sign. 19. ND.	30.00	50.00	90.00
	e. Sign. 20. ND.	FV	FV	60.00
	f. Sign. 21. ND.	FV	FV	55.00
	g. Sign. 22. ND.	FV	FV	55.00

1991-92 ISSUE

			VG	VF	UNC
410D	**500 FRANCS**				
	(19)91-. Like #110A.		FV	FV	3.00
	a. Sign. 22. (19)91.		3.00	6.00	10.00
	b. Sign. 23. (19)92.		FV	FV	3.00
	c. Sign. 25. (19)93.		FV	FV	3.00
	d. Sign. 26. (19)94.		FV	FV	3.00
	e. Sign. 27. (19)95.				

			VG	VF	UNC
411D	**1000 FRANCS**				
	(19)91-. Like #111A.		FV	FV	6.00
	a. Sign. 22.		FV	FV	6.00
	b. Sign. 23. (19)92.		FV	FV	6.00
	c. Sign. 25. (19)93.		FV	FV	6.00
	d. Sign. 26. (19)94.		FV	FV	6.00
	e. Sign. 27. (19)95.		FV	FV	6.00
412D	**2500 FRANCS**				
	(19)92-. Like #112A.		FV	FV	14.00
	a. Sign. 23. (19)92.		FV	FV	14.00
	b. Sign. 25. (19)93.		FV	FV	14.00
	c. Sign. 27. (19)94.		FV	FV	14.00
413D	**5000 FRANCS**				
	(19)92-. Like #113A.		FV	FV	26.00
	a. Sign. 23. (19)92.		FV	FV	26.00
	b. Sign. 27. (19)94.		FV	FV	26.00
	c. Sign. 27. (19)95.				
414D	**10,000 FRANCS**				
	(19)92-. Like #114A.		FV	FV	45.00
	a. Sign. 23. (19)92.		FV	FV	45.00
	b. Sign. 27. (19)94.		FV	FV	45.00
	c. Sign. 27. (19)95.				

E FOR MAURITANIA

1959-64; ND ISSUE

			VG	VF	UNC
501E	**100 FRANCS**				
	1961-65; ND. Like #101A.				
	b. Sign. 1. 20.3.1961.		30.00	90.00	—
	c. Sign. 3. 2.12.1964.		30.00	90.00	—
	e. Sign. 4. 2.3.1965.		25.00	85.00	—
	f. Sign. 4. ND.		25.00	85.00	—
502E	**500 FRANCS**				
	1959-64; ND. Like #102A.				
	a. Engraved. Sign. 1. 15.4.1959.		55.00	120.00	—
	b. Sign. 1. 20.3.1961.		45.00	100.00	—
	c. Sign. 2. 20.3.1961.		45.00	100.00	—
	e. Sign. 4. 2.3.1965.		45.00	100.00	—
	f. Sign. 5. ND.		45.00	100.00	—
	g. Sign. 6. ND.		45.00	100.00	—
	h. Litho. Sign. 6. ND.		45.00	100.00	—
	i. Sign. 7. ND.		45.00	100.00	—
503E	**1000 FRANCS**				
	1961-65 ND. Like #103A.				
	b. Engraved. Sign. 1. 20.3.1961.		60.00	130.00	—
	e. Sign. 4. 2.3.1965.		60.00	130.00	—
	g. Sign. 6. ND.		55.00	120.00	—
	h. Litho. Sign. 6. ND.		55.00	120.00	—
504E	**5000 FRANCS**				
	1961-65 ND. Like #104A.				
	a. Sign. 1. 20.3.1961.		65.00	150.00	—
	b. Sign. 2. 20.3.1961.		65.00	150.00	—
	c. Sign. 4. 2.3.1965.		65.00	150.00	—
	d. Sign. 6. ND.		60.00	130.00	—
	e. Sign. 7. ND.		60.00	130.00	—

H FOR NIGER

1959-65; ND ISSUE

			VG	VF	UNC
601H	**100 FRANCS**				
	1961-65 ND. Like #101A.				
	a. Engraved. Sign. 1. 20.3.1961.		12.00	35.00	85.00
	b. Sign. 2. 20.3.1961.		12.00	35.00	85.00
	c. Litho. Sign. 2. 20.3.1961.		12.00	35.00	85.00
	d. Sign. 3. 2.12.1964.		12.00	35.00	85.00
	e. Sign. 4. 2.3.1965.		10.00	30.00	75.00
	f. Sign. 4. ND.		8.00	25.00	55.00
602H	**500 FRANCS**				
	1959-65; ND. Like #102A.				
	a. Engraved. Sign. 1. 15.4.1959.		25.00	65.00	130.00
	d. Sign. 3. 2.12.1964.		25.00	65.00	130.00
	e. Sign. 4. 2.3.1965.		25.00	65.00	130.00
	g. Sign. 6. ND.		15.00	40.00	85.00
	h. Litho. Sign. 6. ND.		15.00	40.00	85.00
	i. Sign. 7. ND.		25.00	65.00	—
	j. Sign. 8. ND.		15.00	40.00	85.00
	k. Sign. 9. ND.		10.00	30.00	65.00
	m. Sign. 11. ND.		10.00	30.00	65.00

			VG	VF	UNC
603H	**1000 FRANCS**				
	1959-65; ND. Like #103A.				
	a. Sign. 1. 17.9.1959.		30.00	65.00	150.00
	b. Sign. 1. 20.3.1961.		30.00	65.00	150.00
	e. Sign. 4. 2.3.1965.		30.00	65.00	150.00
	f. Sign. 5. ND.		10.00	35.00	80.00
	g. Sign. 6. ND.		15.00	40.00	—
	h. Litho. Sign. 6. ND.		10.00	35.00	80.00
	i. Sign. 7. ND.		30.00	55.00	—
	j. Sign. 8. ND.				
	k. Sign. 9. ND.		8.00	30.00	65.00
	l. Sign. 10. ND.		5.00	18.00	50.00
	m. Sign. 11. ND.		5.00	18.00	50.00
	n. Sign. 12. ND.		5.00	18.00	50.00
	o. Sign. 13. ND.		5.00	18.00	50.00
604H	**5000 FRANCS**				
	ND (1966). Like #104A.				
	b. Sign. 2. 20.3.1961.		40.00	—	—
	e. Sign. 6. ND.		40.00	—	—
	i. Sign. 7. ND.		35.00	75.00	—
	k. Sign. 9. ND.		35.00	75.00	175.00
	l. Sign. 10. ND.		30.00	65.00	155.00
	m. Sign. 11. ND.		25.00	55.00	140.00

1977-81; ND ISSUE

#605H-608H smaller size notes.

			VG	VF	UNC
605H	**500 FRANCS**				
	1979-80. Like #105A.				
	a. Sign. 12. 1979.		6.00	18.00	40.00
	b. Sign. 13. 1980.		3.00	8.00	18.00
606H	**500 FRANCS**				
	1981-90. Like #106A.				
	a. Sign. 14. 1988.		FV	FV	7.00
	b. Sign. 15. 1981. (BF).		6.00	15.00	35.00
	c. Sign. 15. 1981. (F-CO).		FV	3.00	8.00
	d. Sign. 17. 1981. (F-CO).		FV	3.00	8.00
	e. Sign. 18. 1984.		6.00	15.00	35.00
	f. Sign. 19. 1985.		FV	3.00	8.00
	g. Sign. 20. 1986.		FV	FV	7.00
	h. Sign. 20. 1987.		FV	2.75	7.00
	i. Sign. 21. 1989.		FV	FV	6.00
	j. Sign. 22. 1990.		FV	FV	6.00

607H	**1000 FRANCS**	VG	VF	UNC
	1981-90. Like #107A.			
a.	Sign. 14. 1988.	FV	FV	11.00
b.	Sign. 15. 1981.	FV	4.00	12.00
c.	Sign. 17. 1981.	5.00	11.00	30.00
d.	Sign. 18. 1984.	5.00	11.00	30.00
e.	Sign. 19. 1984.	5.00	11.00	30.00
f.	Sign. 19. 1985.	FV	4.00	12.00
g.	Sign. 20. 1986.	FV	FV	11.00
h.	Sign. 20. 1987.	FV	FV	11.00
i.	Sign. 21. 1989.	FV	FV	10.00
j.	Sign. 22. 1990.	FV	FV	10.00

608H	**5000 FRANCS**	VG	VF	UNC
	1977-. Like #108A.			
a.	Sign. 12. 1978.	18.00	30.00	65.00
b.	Sign. 12. 1979.	18.00	30.00	65.00
c.	Sign. 13. 1980.	30.00	50.00	110.00
d.	Sign. 14. 1977.	18.00	30.00	65.00
e.	Sign. 14. 1989.	FV	FV	35.00
f.	Sign. 15. 1981.	FV	20.00	55.00
g.	Sign. 15. 1982.	FV	20.00	55.00
h.	Sign. 17. 1983.	FV	20.00	55.00
i.	Sign. 18. 1984.	20.00	45.00	80.00
j.	Sign. 19. 1985.	FV	20.00	55.00
k.	Sign. 20. 1986.	FV	FV	35.00
l.	Sign. 20. 1987.	FV	FV	35.00
m.	Sign. 21. 1990.	FV	FV	35.00

609H	**10,000 FRANCS**			
	ND (1977). Like #109A.			
a.	Sign. 11.	35.00	55.00	100.00
b.	Sign. 12.	45.00	75.00	—
c.	Sign. 13.	45.00	75.00	—
d.	Sign. 14.	FV	FV	65.00
e.	Sign. 15.	FV	35.00	80.00
f.	Sign. 18.	35.00	55.00	100.00
g.	Sign. 19.	35.00	55.00	100.00
h.	Sign. 20.	FV	FV	65.00
i.	Sign. 21.	FV	FV	60.00
j.	Sign. 22.	FV	FV	50.00

1991-92 ISSUE

610H	**500 FRANCS**	VG	VF	UNC
	(19)91-. Like #110A.			
a.	Sign. 22. (19)91.	FV	FV	4.00
b.	Sign. 23. (19)92.	FV	2.75	7.00
c.	Sign. 25. (19)93.	FV	FV	4.00
d.	Sign. 26. (19)94.	FV	FV	4.00

611H	**1000 FRANCS**			
	(19)91-. Like #111A.			
a.	Sign. 23. (19)91.	FV	FV	7.00
b.	Sign. 23. (19)92.	FV	FV	7.00
c.	Sign. 25. (19)93.	FV	FV	7.00
d.	Sign. 26. (19)94.	FV	FV	7.00
e.	Sign. 27. (19)94.	FV	FV	7.00

612H	**2500 FRANCS**			
	(19)92-. Like #112A.			
a.	Sign. 23. (19)92.	FV	FV	15.00
b.	Sign. 25. (19)93.	FV	FV	15.00
c.	Sign. 27. (19)94.	FV	FV	15.00

613H	**5000 FRANCS**			
	(19)92-. Like #113A.			
a.	Sign. 23. (19)92.	FV	FV	28.00
b.	Sign. 27. (19)94.	FV	FV	28.00

614H	**10,000 FRANCS**			
	(19)92-. Like #114A.			
a.	Sign. 23. (19)92.	FV	FV	50.00
b.	Sign. 27. (19)94.	FV	FV	50.00

K FOR SENEGAL

1959-65; ND ISSUE

701K	**100 FRANCS**	VG	VF	UNC
	1961-65 ND. Like #101A.			
a.	Engraved. Sign. 1. 20.3.1961.	12.00	30.00	70.00
b.	Sign. 2. 20.3.1961	10.00	25.00	60.00
c.	Litho. Sign. 2. 20.3.1961.	10.00	25.00	60.00
d.	Sign. 3. 2.12.1964.	10.00	25.00	60.00
e.	Sign. 4. 2.3.1965.	10.00	25.00	60.00
f.	Sign. 4. ND.	7.00	18.00	50.00
g.	Sign. 5. ND.	7.00	18.00	50.00

702K	**500 FRANCS**			
	1959-65; ND. Like #102A.			
a.	Engraved. Sign. 1. 15.4.1959.	25.00	55.00	100.00
b.	Sign. 1. 20.3.1961.	15.00	40.00	80.00
c.	Sign. 2. 20.3.1961.	15.00	40.00	80.00
d.	Sign. 3. 2.12.1964.	15.00	40.00	80.00
e.	Sign. 4. 2.3.1965.	15.00	40.00	80.00
f.	Sign. 5. ND.	18.00	45.00	90.00
g.	Sign. 6. ND.	10.00	30.00	65.00
h.	Litho. Sign. 6. ND.	10.00	30.00	65.00
i.	Sign. 7. ND.	10.00	30.00	60.00
j.	Sign. 8. ND.	15.00	40.00	80.00
k.	Sign. 9. ND.	8.00	25.00	55.00
l.	Sign. 10. ND.	5.00	15.00	40.00
m.	Sign. 11. ND.	5.00	15.00	40.00
n.	Sign. 12. ND.	5.00	15.00	40.00

703K	**1000 FRANCS**	VG	VF	UNC
	1959-65; ND. Like #103A.			
a.	Engraved. Sign. 1. 17.9.1959.	20.00	65.00	125.00
b.	Sign. 1. 20.3.1961.	20.00	65.00	—
c.	Sign. 2. 20.3.1961.	10.00	50.00	100.00
e.	Sign. 4. 2.3.1965.	10.00	50.00	100.00
f.	Sign. 5. ND.	20.00	65.00	—
g.	Sign. 6. ND.	20.00	65.00	—
h.	Litho. Sign. 6. ND.	5.00	20.00	50.00
i.	Sign. 7. ND.	8.00	30.00	60.00
j.	Sign. 8. ND.	8.00	30.00	60.00
k.	Sign. 9. ND.	5.00	20.00	50.00
l.	Sign. 10. ND.	5.00	15.00	40.00
m.	Sign. 11. ND.	5.00	15.00	40.00
n.	Sign. 12. ND.	5.00	15.00	40.00
o.	Sign. 13. ND.	5.00	15.00	40.00

704K	**5000 FRANCS**			
	1961-65 ND. Like #104A.			
b.	Sign. 1. 20.3.1961.	35.00	75.00	175.00
c.	Sign. 2. 20.3.1961.	35.00	75.00	175.00
d.	Sign. 3. 2.12.1964.	30.00	70.00	160.00
e.	Sign. 4. 2.3.1965.	30.00	70.00	160.00
h.	Sign. 6. ND.	25.00	55.00	145.00
i.	Sign. 7. ND.	30.00	65.00	160.00
j.	Sign. 9. ND.	25.00	55.00	145.00
k.	Sign. 10. ND.	20.00	40.00	125.00
m.	Sign. 11. ND.	20.00	40.00	125.00

1977-81; ND ISSUE

#705K-709K smaller size notes.

NOTE: #706K w/10-digit sm. serial # were printed by Banque de France (BF) while those w/9-digit lg. serial # were printed by F-CO.

705K	**500 FRANCS**	VG	VF	UNC
	1979-80. Like #105A.			
a.	Sign. 12. 1979.	3.00	8.00	17.00
b.	Sign. 13. 1980.	2.75	7.00	15.00

710K	500 FRANCS	VG	VF	UNC
	(19)91-. Like #110A.			
	a. Sign. 22. (19)91.	FV	FV	3.00
	b. Sign. 23. (19)92.	FV	FV	3.00
	c. Sign. 25. (19)93.	FV	FV	3.00
	d. Sign. 26. (19)94.	FV	FV	3.00
	e. Sign. 27. (19)95.	FV	FV	3.00
711K	1000 FRANCS			
	(19)91-. Like #111A.			
	a. Sign. 22. (19)91.	FV	FV	6.00
	b. Sign. 23. (19)92.	FV	FV	6.00
	c. Sign. 25. (19)93.	FV	FV	6.00
712K	2500 FRANCS			
	(19)92-. Like #112A.			
	a. Sign. 23. (19)92.	FV	FV	14.00
	b. Sign. 25. (19)93.	FV	FV	14.00
	c. Sign. 27. (19)94.	FV	FV	14.00
713K	5000 FRANCS			
	(19)92-. Like #113A.			
	a. Sign. 23. (19)92.	FV	FV	26.00
	b. Sign. 25. (19)93.	FV	FV	26.00
	c. Sign. 27. (19)94.	FV	FV	26.00
714K	10,000 FRANCS			
	(19)92-. Like #114A.			
	a. Sign. 23. (19)92.	FV	FV	45.00
	b. Sign. 27. (19)94.	FV	FV	45.00
	c. Sign. 27. (19)95.	FV	FV	45.00

T FOR TOGO
1959-65; ND ISSUE

801T	100 FRANCS	VG	VF	UNC
	1961-65. Like #101A.			
	a. Engraved. Sign. 1. 20.3.1961.	12.00	30.00	70.00
	b. Sign. 2. 20.3.1961.	10.00	25.00	60.00
	c. Litho. Sign. 2. 20.3.1961.	10.00	25.00	60.00
	d. Sign. 3. 2.12.1964.	10.00	25.00	60.00
	e. Sign. 4. 2.3.1965.	10.00	25.00	60.00
	f. Sign. 4. ND.	7.00	18.00	50.00
	g. Sign. 5. ND.	7.00	18.00	50.00

706K	500 FRANCS	VG	VF	UNC
	1981-. Like #106A.			
	a. Sign. 14. 1988.	FV	FV	5.00
	b. Sign. 15. 1981 (BF).	6.00	15.00	35.00
	c. Sign. 15. 1981. (F-CO).	FV	3.00	7.00
	d. Sign. 15. 1982. (BF).	FV	4.00	9.00
	e. Sign. 17. 1981. (F-CO).	FV	3.00	7.00
	f. Sign. 17. 1983. (BF).	FV	4.00	9.00
	g. Sign. 18. 1984.	FV	3.00	7.00
	h. Sign. 19. 1985.	FV	3.00	7.00
	i. Sign. 20. 1986.	FV	FV	6.00
	j. Sign. 20. 1987.	FV	FV	6.00
	k. Sign. 21. (reversed order). 1989.	FV	FV	5.00
	l. Sign. 22. 1990.	FV	FV	5.00
707K	1000 FRANCS			
	1981-90. Like #107A.			
	a. Sign. 14. 1988.	FV	FV	10.00
	b. Sign. 15. 1981.	FV	4.00	11.00
	c. Sign. 17. 1981.	FV	4.00	11.00
	d. Sign. 18. 1984.	FV	4.00	11.00
	e. Sign. 19. 1984.	5.00	11.00	30.00
	f. Sign. 19. 1985.	FV	4.00	11.00
	g. Sign. 20. 1986.	FV	FV	10.00
	h. Sign. 20. 1987.	FV	FV	10.00
	i. Sign. 21. 1989.	FV	FV	9.00
	j. Sign. 22. 1990.	FV	FV	9.00
708K	5000 FRANCS			
	1977-. Like #107A.			
	a. Sign. 12. 1978.	18.00	30.00	60.00
	b. Sign. 12. 1979.	18.00	30.00	60.00
	c. Sign. 13. 1980.	30.00	50.00	110.00
	d. Sign. 14. 1977.	18.00	30.00	60.00
	e. Sign. 14. 1989.	FV	FV	35.00
	f. Sign. 15. 1982.	18.00	30.00	60.00
	g. Sign. 16. 1983.	35.00	60.00	125.00
	h. Sign. 17. 1983.	18.00	30.00	60.00
	i. Sign. 18. 1984.	18.00	30.00	60.00
	j. Sign. 19. 1985.	20.00	35.00	—
	k. Sign. 20. 1986.	20.00	35.00	—
	l. Sign. 20. 1987.	FV	FV	35.00
	m. Sign. 21. 1990.	FV	FV	35.00
	n. Sign. 22. 1991.	FV	FV	35.00
	o. Sign. 22. 1992.	FV	FV	35.00
	p. Sign. 23. 1992.	FV	FV	35.00
	q. Sign. 24. 1992.	FV	FV	35.00
709K	10,000 FRANCS			
	ND. (1977-). Like #109A.			
	a. Sign. 11. ND.	30.00	50.00	95.00
	b. Sign. 12. ND.	30.00	50.00	95.00
	c. Sign. 13. ND.	30.00	50.00	95.00
	d. Sign. 14. ND.	FV	FV	60.00
	e. Sign. 15. ND.	FV	25.00	65.00
	f. Sign. 16. ND.	30.00	55.00	100.00
	h. Sign. 18. ND.	FV	25.00	65.00
	i. Sign. 19. ND.	30.00	50.00	95.00
	j. Sign. 20. ND.	FV	FV	60.00
	k. Sign. 21. ND.	FV	FV	55.00
	l. Sign. 22. ND.	FV	FV	55.00
	m. Sign. 23. ND.	FV	FV	55.00

1991-92 ISSUE

802T	500 FRANCS	VG	VF	UNC
	1959-61; ND. Like #102A.			
	a. Engraved. Sign. 1. 15.4.1959.	25.00	65.00	130.00
	b. Sign. 1. 20.3.1961.	25.00	65.00	—
	c. Sign. 2. 20.3.1961.	25.00	65.00	—
	f. Sign. 5. ND.	25.00	65.00	—
	g. Sign. 6. ND.	10.00	30.00	65.00
	i. Litho. Sign. 7. ND.	20.00	55.00	110.00
	j. Sign. 8. ND.	20.00	55.00	110.00
	k. Sign. 9. ND.	8.00	20.00	55.00
	l. Sign. 10. ND.	15.00	30.00	75.00
	m. Sign. 11. ND.	3.00	10.00	30.00
803T	1000 FRANCS			
	1959-65; ND. Like #103A.			
	a. Engraved. Sign. 1. 17.9.1959.	30.00	70.00	—
	b. Sign. 1. 20.3.1961.	25.00	65.00	130.00
	c. Sign. 2. 20.3.1961.	25.00	65.00	—
	e. Sign. 4. 2.3.1965.	25.00	65.00	130.00
	f. Sign. 5. ND.	15.00	45.00	100.00
	g. Sign. 6. ND.	10.00	30.00	70.00
	h. Litho. Sign. 6. ND.	10.00	30.00	70.00
	i. Sign. 7. ND.	10.00	30.00	70.00
	j. Sign. 8. ND.	15.00	45.00	100.00
	k. Sign. 9. ND.	5.00	20.00	50.00
	l. Sign. 10. ND.	5.00	15.00	40.00
	m. Sign. 11. ND.	5.00	15.00	40.00
	n. Sign. 12. ND..	5.00	15.00	40.00
	o. Sign. 13. ND.	5.00	15.00	40.00

804T 5000 FRANCS
1961 ND. Like #104A.

			VG	VF	UNC
b.	Sign. 1. 20.3.1961.		35.00	70.00	175.00
h.	Sign. 6. ND.		25.00	55.00	145.00
i.	Sign. 7. ND.		30.00	65.00	160.00
j.	Sign. 8. ND.		30.00	65.00	—
k.	Sign. 9. ND.		25.00	55.00	145.00
m.	Sign. 11. ND.		20.00	40.00	125.00

1977-81; ND ISSUE

#805T-809T smaller size notes.

NOTE: #806T w/10-digit sm. serial # were printed by Banque de France (BF) while those w/9-digit lg. serial # were printed by F-CO.

805T 500 FRANCS	VG	VF	UNC
1979. Like #105A. Sign. 12.	3.00	8.00	17.00

806T 500 FRANCS
1981-90. Like #106A.

			VG	VF	UNC
a.	Sign. 14. 1988.		6.00	15.00	—
b.	Sign. 15. 1981. (BF).		FV	3.00	7.00
c.	Sign. 15. 1981. (F-CO).		FV	3.00	7.00
d.	Sign. 15. 1982. (BF).		FV	5.00	11.00
e.	Sign. 17. 1981. (F-CO).		FV	5.00	11.00
f.	Sign. 18. 1984.		6.00	15.00	—
g.	Sign. 19. 1994.		FV	5.00	11.00
h.	Sign. 19. 1985.		FV	3.00	7.00
i.	Sign. 20. 1986.		FV	FV	6.00
j.	Sign. 20. 1987.		FV	FV	6.00
k.	Sign. 21. 1989.		FV	FV	5.00
l.	Sign. 22. 1990.		FV	FV	5.00

807T 1000 FRANCS
1981-90. Like #107A.

			VG	VF	UNC
a.	Sign. 14. 1988.		FV	FV	10.00
b.	Sign. 15. 1981.		FV	4.00	11.00
c.	Sign. 17. 1981.		FV	4.00	11.00
d.	Sign. 18. 1984.		FV	4.00	11.00
e.	Sign. 19. 1984.		5.00	11.00	—
f.	Sign. 19. 1985.		FV	4.00	11.00
g.	Sign. 20. 1986.		5.00	11.00	—
h.	Sign. 20. 1987.		FV	FV	10.00
i.	Sign. 21. 1989.		FV	FV	9.00
j.	Sign. 22. 1990.		FV	FV	9.00

808T 5000 FRANCS
1977-92. Like #108A.

			VG	VF	UNC
a.	Sign. 12. 1978.		18.00	30.00	60.00
b.	Sign. 12. 1979.		18.00	30.00	60.00
c.	Sign. 14. 1977.		18.00	30.00	60.00
d.	Sign. 14. 1989.		FV	FV	35.00
e.	Sign. 15. 1981.		FV	22.50	45.00
f.	Sign. 15. 1982.		18.00	30.00	60.00
g.	Sign. 17. 1983.		25.00	45.00	85.00
h.	Sign. 18. 1984.		FV	25.00	50.00
i.	Sign. 20. 1987.		FV	FV	35.00
j.	Sign. 21. 1990.		FV	FV	35.00
k.	Sign. 22. 1991.		FV	FV	35.00
l.	Sign. 22. 1992.		FV	FV	35.00
m.	Sign. 23. 1992.		FV	FV	35.00
n.	Sign. 24. 1992.		FV	FV	35.00

809T 10,000 FRANCS
ND. (1977-). Like #109A.

			VG	VF	UNC
a.	Sign. 11. ND.		30.00	50.00	95.00
b.	Sign. 12. ND.		30.00	50.00	95.00
c.	Sign. 13. ND.		30.00	50.00	95.00
d.	Sign. 14. ND.		FV	FV	60.00
e.	Sign. 15. ND.		FV	25.00	65.00
f.	Sign. 16. ND.		30.00	55.00	100.00
h.	Sign. 18. ND.		FV	25.00	65.00
k.	Sign. 22. ND.		FV	FV	55.00
l.	Sign. 23. ND.		FV	FV	55.00

1991-92 ISSUE

810T 500 FRANCS
(19)91-. Like #110A.

			VG	VF	UNC
a.	Sign. 22. (19)91.		FV	FV	3.00
b.	Sign. 23. (19)92.		FV	3.00	6.00
c.	Sign. 25. (19)93.		FV	FV	3.00
d.	Sign. 26. (19)94.		FV	FV	3.00
e.	Sign. 27. (19)95.		FV	FV	3.00

811T 1000 FRANCS

		VG	VF	UNC
(19)91-. Like #111A.				
a.	Sign. 22. (19)91.	FV	FV	6.00
b.	Sign. 23. (19)92.	FV	FV	6.00
c.	Sign. 25. (19)93.	FV	FV	6.00
d.	Sign. 26. (19)94.	FV	FV	6.00
e.	Sign. 27. (19)95.	FV	FV	6.00

812T 2500 FRANCS

		VG	VF	UNC
(19)92-. Like #112A.				
a.	Sign. 23. (19)92.	FV	FV	14.00
b.	Sign. 25. (19)93.	FV	FV	14.00
c.	Sign. 27. (19)94.	FV	FV	14.00

813T 5000 FRANCS

(19)92. Like #113A.				
a.	Sign. 23. (19)92.	FV	FV	26.00
b.	Sign. 25. (19)93.	FV	FV	26.00
c.	Sign. 27. (19)94.	FV	FV	26.00

814T 10,000 FRANCS

(19)92. Like #114A.				
a.	Sign. 25. (19)92.	FV	FV	45.00
b.	Sign. 27. (19)94.	FV	FV	45.00

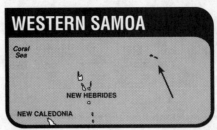

WESTERN SAMOA

The Independent State of Western Samoa (formerly German Samoa), located in the Pacific Ocean 1,600 miles (2,574 km.) northeast of New Zealand, has an area of 1,097 sq. mi. (2,860 sq. km.) and a population of 157,000. Capital: Apia. The economy is based on agriculture, fishing and tourism. Copra, cocoa and bananas are exported.

The Samoan group of islands was discovered by Dutch navigator Jacob Roggeveen in 1772. Great Britain, the United States and Germany established consular representation at Apia in 1847, 1853 and 1861 respectively. The conflicting interests of the three powers produced the Berlin agreement of 1889 which declared Samoa neutral and had the effect of establishing a tripartite protectorate over the islands. A further agreement, 1899, recognized the rights of the United States in those islands east of 171 deg. west longitude (American Samoa) and of Germany in the other islands (Western Samoa). New Zealand occupied Western Samoa at the start of World War I and administered it as a League of Nations mandate and U.N. trusteeship until Jan. 1, 1962, when it became an independent state.

Western Samoa is a member of the Commonwealth of Nations. The Chief Executive is Chief of State. The prime minister is the Head of Government. The present Head of State, Malietoa Tanumafili II, holds his position for life. Future Heads of State will be elected by the Legislature Assembly for five-year terms.

RULERS:
  British, 1914-1962
  Malietoa Tanumafili II, 1962-

MONETARY SYSTEM:
  1 Shilling = 12 Pence
  1 Pound = 20 Shillings to 1967
  1 Tala = 100 Sene, 1967-

NEW ZEALAND ADMINISTRATION

TERRITORY OF WESTERN SAMOA

1920-22 TREASURY NOTE ISSUE
By Authority of New Zealand Government
#7-9 various date and sign. varieties. Printer: BWC.
#8 and 9 *STERLING* appears close beneath spelled out denominations at ctr. until about 1953.
NOTE: Some of these notes may appear to be ND, probably through error or washed out, faded or worn off hand-stamped dates.

7	**10 SHILLINGS**				
	1922-61. Black on brown and green unpt. Palm trees along beach at ctr.				
	a. 3.3.1922.		—	Rare	—
	b. Sign. title: *MINISTER OF EXTERNAL AFFAIRS FOR NEW ZEALAND* at l. 24.4.1939-21.11.1949.		50.00	165.00	350.00
	c. Sign. title: *MINISTER OF ISLAND TERRITORIES FOR NEW ZEALAND* at l. 25.9.1953-27.5.1958.		75.00	250.00	600.00
	d. Sign. title: *HIGH COMMISSIONER* at 1.20.3.1957-22.12.1959.		35.00	140.00	250.00
8	**1 POUND**				
	1922-61. Purple on m/c unpt. Hut, palm trees at ctr.				
	a. 3.3.1922.		—	Rare	—
	b. Sign. title: *MINISTER OF EXTERNAL AFFAIRS FOR NEW ZEALAND* at l. 16.1.1939-12.1.1947.		65.00	175.00	450.00
	c. Sign. title: *MINISTER OF ISLAND TERRITORIES FOR NEW ZEALAND* at l. 21.6.1951-1.4.1958.		85.00	250.00	650.00
	d. Sign. title: *HIGH COMMISSIONER* at l. 20.4.1959; 10.12.1959; 1.5.1961.		50.00	135.00	350.00

BANK OF WESTERN SAMOA

1960-61 PROVISIONAL ISSUE

#10-12 red ovpt: *Bank of Western Samoa, Legal Tender in Western Samoa by virtue of the Bank of Western Samoa Ordinance 1959* on older notes. Various date and sign. varieties.

		Good	Fine	XF
10	**10 SHILLINGS** ND; 1960-61. Ovpt. on #7.			
	a. Sign. title: *HIGH COMMISSIONER* blocked out at lower l., w/*MINISTER OF FINANCE* below. 8.12.1960; 1.5.1961.	25.00	75.00	225.00

		Good	Fine	XF
	b. ND. Sign. title: *MINISTER OF FINANCE* in plate w/o ovpt., at lower l. 1.5.1961.	25.00	75.00	225.00

		Good	Fine	XF
11	**1 POUND** 1960-61. Ovpt. on #8.			
	a. Sign. title: *HIGH COMMISSIONER* blocked out at lower l., w/*MINISTER OF FINANCE* below. 8.11.1960; 1.5.1961.	35.00	100.00	350.00
	b. Sign. title: *MINISTER OF FINANCE* in plate w/o ovpt., at lower l. 1.5.1961.	35.00	100.00	350.00
12	**5 POUNDS** 1.5.1961. Ovpt. on #9.	250.00	950.00	2250.

FALE TUPE O SAMOA I SISIFO

BANK OF WESTERN SAMOA

1963 ND ISSUE

		Good	Fine	XF
13	**10 SHILLINGS** ND (1963). Dk. green on m/c unpt. Arms at l., boat at r. Hut and 2 palms on back.	2.50	8.00	35.00

		Good	Fine	XF
14	**1 POUND** ND (1963). Blue on m/c unpt. Palms and rising sun at l. and r., arms at ctr. Sm. bldg. and lagoon on back. 159 x 83mm.	4.00	15.00	50.00

		Good	Fine	XF
15	**5 POUNDS** ND (1963). Brown on m/c unpt. Flag over arms at r. Shoreline, sea and islands on back. 166 x 89mm.	20.00	45.00	115.00

1967 ND ISSUE

Tala System

#16-18 sign. varieties. Wmk: BWS repeated.

SIGNATURE VARIETIES			
1	*[signature]* MANAGER	**3**	*[signature]* MANAGER
2	*[signature]* MANAGER	**4**	 SENIOR MANAGER

19   1 T<small>ALA</small>

	VG	VF	U<small>NC</small>
ND (1980). Dk. green on m/c unpt. 2 weavers at r. 2 fishermen in canoe on back.	.75	2.00	9.00

16   1 T<small>ALA</small>

	VG	VF	U<small>NC</small>
ND (1967). Dk. green on m/c unpt. Like #13.			
a. Sign. 1.	1.50	3.50	22.50
b. Sign. 2.	1.00	3.00	20.00
c. Sign. 3.	1.00	3.00	17.50
d. Sign. 4.	1.00	3.00	18.50
s. Sign. as b. Specimen.	—	—	30.00

20   2 T<small>ALA</small>

	VG	VF	U<small>NC</small>
ND (1980). Deep blue-violet on m/c unpt. Woodcarver at r. Hut w/palms on sm. island on back.	1.50	3.00	15.00

17   2 T<small>ALA</small>

	VG	VF	U<small>NC</small>
ND (1967). Blue on m/c unpt. Like #14, but 144 x 77mm.			
a. Sign. 1.	2.50	5.00	25.00
b. Sign. 3.	2.25	4.50	22.50
c. Sign. 4.	2.00	3.50	18.50
s. Sign. as b. Specimen.	—	—	40.00

21   5 T<small>ALA</small>

	VG	VF	U<small>NC</small>
ND (1980). Red on m/c unpt. Child writing at r. Sm. port city on back.	3.50	7.00	30.00

18   10 T<small>ALA</small>

	VG	VF	U<small>NC</small>
ND (1967). Brown on m/c unpt. Like #15, but 150 x 76mm.			
a. Sign. 3.	12.00	20.00	75.00
b. Sign. 4.	10.00	17.50	65.00
s. Sign. as b. Specimen.	—	—	50.00

I<small>NDEPENDENT</small> S<small>TATE</small>

K<small>OMITI</small> F<small>AATINO</small> O T<small>UPE</small> A S<small>AMOAI</small> S<small>ISIFO</small>

M<small>ONETARY</small> B<small>OARD OF</small> W<small>ESTERN</small> S<small>AMOA</small>

1980-84 ND I<small>SSUE</small>

#19-23 national flag on face and back. Arms on back. Wmk: M. Tanumafili II.
#24 *Deleted.*

22   10 T<small>ALA</small>

	VG	VF	U<small>NC</small>
ND (1980). Dk. brown and purple on m/c unpt. Man picking bananas at r. Shoreline landscape on back.	7.00	12.50	50.00

23   20 T<small>ALA</small>

	VG	VF	U<small>NC</small>
ND (1984). Brown and orange-brown on m/c unpt. Fisherman w/net at r. Round bldg. at l. on back.	30.00	65.00	185.00

FALETUPE TUTOTONU O SAMOA

CENTRAL BANK OF SAMOA

1985 ND ISSUE
#25-30 similar to #20-23 but w/new issuer's name. Wmk: M. Tanumafili II.
#29-30 M. Tanumafili II at r.

25	2 TALA	VG	VF	UNC
	ND (1985). Deep blue-violet on m/c unpt. Similar to #20.	FV	FV	3.00

26	5 TALA	VG	VF	UNC
	ND (1985). Red on m/c unpt. Similar to #21.	FV	FV	8.50

27	10 TALA	VG	VF	UNC
	ND (1985). Dk. brown and purple on m/c unpt. Similar to #22.	FV	FV	15.00

28	20 TALA	VG	VF	UNC
	ND (1985). Brown and orange-brown on m/c unpt. Similar to #23.	FV	FV	25.00
29	50 TALA			
	ND (ca.1990). Green on m/c unpt. Former home of R. L. Stevenson, current residence of Head of State at ctr. Man performing traditional knife dance on back.	FV	FV	47.50
30	100 TALA			
	ND (ca.1990). Olive-brown and lt. brown on m/c unpt. Flag and Parliament bldg. at ctr. Harvest scene on back.	FV	FV	92.50

1990 COMMEMORATIVE ISSUE
#31, Golden Jubilee of Service of the Head of State, Susuga Malietoa Tanumafili II, 1990

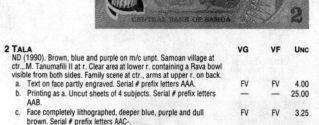

31	2 TALA	VG	VF	UNC
	ND (1990). Brown, blue and purple on m/c unpt. Samoan village at ctr.,.M. Tanumafili II at r. Clear area at lower r. containing a Rava bowl visible from both sides. Family scene at ctr., arms at upper r. on back.			
	a. Text on face partly engraved. Serial # prefix letters AAA.	FV	FV	4.00
	b. Printing as a. Uncut sheets of 4 subjects. Serial # prefix letters AAB.	—	—	25.00
	c. Face completely lithographed, deeper blue, purple and dull brown. Serial # prefix letters AAC-.	FV	FV	3.25
	d. As a. w/special folder.	—	—	7.50

YEMEN ARAB REP

The Yemen Arab Republic, located in the southwestern corner of the Arabian Peninsula, has an area of 75,290 sq. mi. (195,000 sq. km.) and a population of 13 million. Capital: San'a. The industries of Yemen, one of the world's poorest countries, are agriculture and local handicrafts. Qat (a mildly narcotic leaf), coffee, cotton and rock salt are exported.

One of the oldest centers of civilization in the Near East, Yemen was once part of the Minaean Kingdom and of the ancient Kingdom of Sheba, after which it was captured successively by Egyptians, Ethiopians and Romans. It was converted to the Moslem religion in 628 AD and administered as a caliphate until 1538, when it came under Turkish occupation which was maintained until 1918 when autonomy was achieved through revolution.

On Feb. 1, 1958, Egypt and Syria formed the United Arab Republic. Yemen joined on March 8 in an association known as the United Arab States. Syria withdrew from the United Arab Republic on Sept. 29, 1961, and on Dec. 26 Egypt dissolved its ties with Yemen in the United Arab States.

Provoked by the harsh rule of Imam Mohammed al-Badr, last ruler of the Kingdom of Mutawwakkilite, the National Liberation Front seized control of the government on Sept. 27, 1962. Badr fled to Saudi Arabia.

An agreement for a constitution was reached on Dec. 1989 uniting the Yemen Arab Republic with the People's Democratic Republic of Yemen into the Republic of Yemen on May 22, 1990. Both currencies are still valid but the P.D.R.Y. dinars are being phased out.

RULERS:
    Imam Ahmad, AH1367-1382/1948-1982AD
    Imam al-Badr, AH1382-1388/1962-1968AD

MONETARY SYSTEM:
    1 Rial = 40 Buqshas

ARAB REPUBLIC

ARAB REPUBLIC OF YEMEN

1960s ND ISSUES
#1-10 sign. varieties. Wmk: Arms.

		VG	VF	UNC
1	**10 BUQSHAS** ND. Brown on m/c unpt. Child riding on a lion (sculpture) at l. Ancient inscription on back.	2.00	6.00	25.00

		VG	VF	UNC
2	**20 BUQSHAS** ND. Green on m/c unpt. Stylized human head (sculpture) at l. Back olive; tall ruins.	3.50	13.50	40.00

		VG	VF	UNC
3	**1 RIAL** ND. Green on m/c unpt. Arms at l. Bldg. on back.	5.00	25.00	115.00

		VG	VF	UNC
4	**1 RIAL** ND. Green on m/c unpt. Human head (sculpture) at l. Back like #3.	3.50	17.50	85.00
5	**5 RIALS** ND. Red on m/c unpt. Arms at l. Sculpture like #1 face at r. on back.	15.00	65.00	250.00

		VG	VF	UNC
6	**5 RIALS** ND. Red on m/c unpt. Animal sculpture (leopard head) at l. Back like #5.	8.50	37.50	165.00

		VG	VF	UNC
7	**10 RIALS** ND. Blue-green on m/c unpt. Arms at l. Dam on back. 145 x 75mm.	25.00	100.00	375.00

8	**10 RIALS**	VG	VF	UNC
	ND. Blue-green on m/c unpt. Tower at l. Back like #7. 135 x 70mm.	10.00	40.00	150.00

12	**5 RIALS**	VG	VF	UNC
	ND (1973). Red on m/c unpt. Modern bldgs. at l. Back red and lt. olive; bldgs. on high rock hill.	1.00	2.50	9.50

9	**20 RIALS**	VG	VF	UNC
	ND. Violet and blue-green on m/c unpt. House on rocks at l. Back violet and gold; city scene.	25.00	80.00	250.00

13	**10 RIALS**	VG	VF	UNC
	ND (1973). Blue-green on m/c unpt. Human head (sculpture) at l. Lg. bldg. on back. 2 sign. varieties.	1.50	3.00	10.00

10	**50 RIALS**	VG	VF	UNC
	ND. Dk. olive on m/c unpt. Crossed daggers at l. Plants on back.	30.00	85.00	350.00

CENTRAL BANK OF YEMEN

1973-77 ND ISSUES
#11-16A wmk: Arms.

14	**20 RIALS**	VG	VF	UNC
	ND (1973). Purple on m/c unpt. Sculpture (God of Grapes) at l. Back purple and brown; terraces and rock hill.	2.00	4.00	15.00

11	**1 RIAL**	VG	VF	UNC
	ND (1973). Green on m/c unpt. Mosque and minaret (Bekilia dome) at l. Plants in field w/mountains behind on back. 2 sign. varieties.	.15	.40	2.50

15   50 RIALS

	VG	VF	UNC
ND (1973). Dk. olive and m/c. Ancient statue at l. Fortified archway on back. 2 sign. varieties.	FV	5.50	12.00

16   100 RIALS

	VG	VF	UNC
ND (1975). Lilac on m/c unpt. Stone carving of child and mythical beast at l. City and mountain view on back.	7.50	20.00	65.00

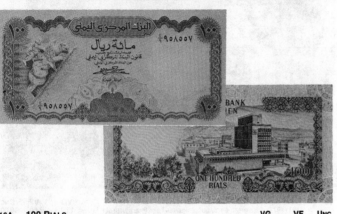

16A   100 RIALS

	VG	VF	UNC
ND (1977). Face like #16 but different sign. Modern bldg. on back.	FV	.10.00	25.00

1979-85 ND ISSUES
#16B-21 wmk: Arms.

16B   1 RIAL

	VG	VF	UNC
ND (1980). Like #11, but darker green and smaller serial #. Clearer unpt. design over wmk. area at r.	FV	.25	1.00

17   5 RIALS

	VG	VF	UNC
ND (1981). Red on orange and m/c unpt. Bldg. at l. City view at foot of mountain fortress on back. 2 sign. varieties.	FV	.60	3.00

18   10 RIALS

	VG	VF	UNC
ND (1981). Blue-green on m/c unpt. City view on rock hill at l. Mosque w/minaret on back. 2 sign. varieties.	FV	1.25	6.00

19   20 RIALS

	VG	VF	UNC
ND (1985). Face similar to #14. View of city w/minarets at l., ctr. and at r. on back.			
a. Bank title on tan unpt. on back.	FV	4.50	11.00
b. Bank title on lt. brown vertical lines unpt. on back.	FV	4.00	10.00

20   20 RIALS
(26)

	VG	VF	UNC
ND (ca. 1994). Face like #19. View of city w/o minarets on back.	FV	FV	4.50

21   100 RIALS

	VG	VF	UNC
ND (1979). Lilac on m/c unpt. City view at l., mosque in foreground. City panorama w/mountains on back.	FV	5.00	27.50

1991-96 ND Issues

#22-29 wmk: Arms.

#26 *Deleted*. See #20.

22	**5 RIALS**	VG	VF	UNC
	ND (ca.1991). Red and orange on m/c unpt. Bldg. at l. City w/mountain behind on back.	FV	FV	2.00

23	**10 RIALS**	VG	VF	UNC
	ND (ca.1991). Blue and black on m/c unpt. Minaret, mosque at l. Dam at ctr. r., *10* at upper corners on back.	FV	FV	3.50

24	**10 RIALS**	VG	VF	UNC
	ND (ca.1992). Face as #23. Back design as #23, but w/*10* at upper l. and lower r. *10* w/Arabic text: *Said Marib* near lower r.	FV	FV	2.50
25	**20 RIALS**			
	ND (ca. 1992). Dk. brown on m/c unpt. Arch ended straight border across upper ctr. Sculpture of God of Grapes at l. Coastal view of Aden, dhow on back.	FV	FV	6.50

27	**50 RIALS**	VG	VF	UNC
	ND (1992). Black on m/c unpt. Face like #15. City in the Hadramawt at ctr. r. on back.			
	a. City w/o Arabic title at lower wer l.	FV	FV	6.50
	b. W/Arabic title *Shibam Hadra dramawt* at lower l.	FV	FV	6.50

28	**100 RIALS**	VG	VF	UNC
	ND (1992). Violet, purple and black on m/c unpt. Ancient water supply installation on island of Aden at l. City view of old San'a w/mountains behind on back.	FV	FV	8.50
29	**200 RIALS**			
	ND (1996). Deep blue-green on m/c unpt. Stone carving of kg. at l. View of San'a at ctr. r. on back.	FV	FV	12.50

The People's Democratic Republic of Yemen, located on the southern coast of the Arabian Peninsula, had an area of 128,560 sq. mi. (332,968 sq. km.). Capital: Aden. It consists of the port city of Aden, 17 states of the former South Arabian Federation, 3 small sheikhdoms, 3 large sultanates, Quaiti, Kathiri and Mahri, which made up the Eastern Aden Protectorate, and Socotra, the largest island in the Arabian Sea. The port of Aden is the area's most valuable natural resource. Cotton, fish, coffee and hides are exported. Between 1200 BC and the 6th century AD, what is now the People's Democratic Republic of Yemen was part of the Minaean kingdom. In subsequent years it was controlled by Persians, Egyptians and Turks. Aden, one of the cities mentioned in the Bible, had been a port for trade between the East and West for 2,000 years. British rule began in 1839 when the British East India Co. seized control to put an end to the piracy threatening trade with India. To protect their foothold in Aden, the British found it necessary to extend their control into the area known historically as the Hadramaut, and to sign protection treaties with the sheikhs of the hinterland. Eventually, 15 of the 16 Western Protectorate states, the Wahidi state of the Eastern Protectorate, and Aden Colony joined to form the Federation of South Arabia. In 1959, Britain agreed to prepare South Arabia for full independence, which was achieved on Nov. 30, 1967, at which time South Arabia, including Aden, changed its name to the People's Republic of Southern Yemen. On Dec. 1, 1970, following the overthrowing of the new government by the National Liberation Front, Southern Yemen changed its name to the People's Democratic Republic of Yemen. On May 22, 1990 the People's Democratic Republic merged with the Yemen Arab Republic into a unified Republic of Yemen. The YDR currency is being phased out.

PEOPLES DEMOCRATIC REPUBLIC

SOUTH ARABIAN CURRENCY AUTHORITY

SIGNATURE VARIETIES			
1	*(signature)*	3	*(signature)*
2	*(signature)*	4	*(signature)*

1965 ND ISSUE

#1-5 show w/coastal town in background. Each back has palm tree at ctr. but different additional plants. Wmk: Camel's head. Printer: TDLR.

			VG	VF	UNC
1	**250 FILS**				
	ND (1965). Brown on m/c unpt.				
	a. Sign. 1.		2.50	6.00	25.00
	b. Sign. 2.		.50	2.00	12.50

			VG	VF	UNC
2	**500 FILS**				
	ND (1965). Green on m/c unpt.				
	a. Sign. 1.		3.00	7.50	40.00
	b. Sign. 2.		2.50	6.00	25.00
3	**1 DINAR**				
	ND (1965). Blue-black on m/c unpt.				
	a. Sign. 1.		5.00	17.50	75.00
	b. Sign. 2.		4.00	15.00	45.00

			VG	VF	UNC
4	**5 DINARS**				
	ND (1965). Red on m/c unpt.				
	a. Sign. 1.		17.50	40.00	160.00
	b. Sign. 2.		15.00	32.50	120.00
5	**10 DINARS**				
	ND (1965). Deep olive-green on m/c unpt.				
	a. Sign. 1.		40.00	100.00	350.00
	b. Sign. 2.		35.00	85.00	275.00

BANK OF YEMEN

1984 ND ISSUE

#6-9 similar to #1-5 but w/o English on face and w/new bank name on back. Capital: *ADEN* added to bottom r. on back. Wmk: Camel's head.

			VG	VF	UNC
6	**500 FILS**				
	ND (1984). Green on m/c unpt. Similar to #2.		.65	2.00	13.50
7	**1 DINAR**				
	ND (1984). Blue-black on m/c unpt. Similar to #3.		1.00	3.00	17.50

8   5 DINARS
ND (1984). Red on m/c unpt. Similar to #4.

		VG	VF	UNC
a.	Sign. 3.	5.00	15.00	50.00
b.	Sign. 4.	3.25	10.00	45.00

9   10 DINARS
ND (1984). Deep olive-green on m/c unpt. Similar to #5.

		VG	VF	UNC
a.	Sign. 3.	10.00	30.00	100.00
b.	Sign. 4.	6.50	20.00	85.00

YUGOSLAVIA

The Federal Republic of Yugoslavia, a Balkan country located on the east shore of the Adriatic Sea bordering Bosnia-Herzegovina and Croatia to the west, Hungary and Romania to the north, Bulgaria to the east, and Albania and Macedonia to the south. It has an area of 39,449 sq. mi. (102,173 sq. km.) and a population of *10.4 million. Capital: Belgrade. The chief industries are agriculture, mining, manufacturing and tourism. Machinery, non-ferrous metals, meat and fabrics are exported.

Yugoslavia was proclaimed on Dec. 1, 1918, after the union of the Kingdom of Serbia, Montenegro and the South Slav territories of Austria-Hungary; and changed its official name from the Kingdom of the Serbs, Croats, and Slovenes to the Kingdom of Yugoslavia on Oct. 3, 1929. It was composed of six autonomous republics: Serbia, Croatia, Slovenia, Bosnia-Herzegovina, Macedonia and Montenegro with two autonomous provinces within Serbia: Kosovo-Melohija and Vojvodina. The Royal government of Yugoslavia attemped to remain neutral in World War II but, yielding to German pressure, aligned itself with the Axis powers in March of 1941; a few days later it was overthrown by revolutionary forces and its neutrality reasserted. The Nazis occupied the country on April 6, and throughout the remaining years were resisted by a number of guerrilla armies, notably that of Marshal Josip Broz Tito. After the defeat of the Axis powers, a leftist coalition headed by Tito abolished the monarchy and, on Jan. 31, 1946, established a "People's Republic".

The collapse of the Federal Republic during 1991-92 has resulted in the autonomous republics of Croatia, Slovenia, Bosnia-Herzegovina and Macedonia declaring their respective independence. Bosnia- Herzegovina is under military contest with the Serbian faction opposed to the Moslem populace. Besides the remainder of the older Serbian sectors, a Serbian enclave in Knin located in southern Croatia has emerged called *REPUBLIKE SRPSKE KRAJINE* or Serbian Republic-Krajina surrounding the city of Knin; it has also declared its independence in 1992. Croatian forces overwhelmed this enclave in August 1995. In 1992 the Federal Republic of Yugoslavia, consisting of the former Republics of Serbia and Montenegro, was proclaimed.

MONETARY SYSTEM:
1 Dinar = 100 Para
1 New Dinar = 100 Old Dinara, 1965-89
1 New Dinar = 10,000 Old Dinara, 1990-92
1 New Dinar = 10 Old Dinara, 1992-93
1 New Dinar = 1 Million "Old" Dinara, 1993
1 New Dinara = 1 Milliard "Old" Dinara, 1.1.1994

FEDERAL REPUBLIC

НАРОДНА БАНКА ЈУГОЛАВИЈЕ

NARODNA BANKA JUGOSLAVIJE

1963 ISSUE

73   100 DINARA
1.5.1963. Red on m/c unpt. Woman wearing national costume at l. View of Dubrovnik at ctr. on back.

VG	VF	UNC
.10	.30	1.50

74   500 DINARA
1.5.1963. Dk. green on m/c unpt. Farm woman w/sickle at l. 2
combine harvesters at ctr. on back.

VG	VF	UNC
.25	.50	3.00

75   1000 DINARA
1.5.1963. Dk. brown on m/c unpt. Male steelworker at l. Factory
complex at ctr. on back.

VG	VF	UNC
.35	1.00	4.00

76   5000 DINARA
1.5.1963. Blue-black on m/c unpt. Relief of Mestrovi at l. Parliament
bldg. (National Assembly) in Belgrade at ctr. on back.

VG	VF	UNC
1.00	3.00	22.50

1965 ISSUE

77   5 DINARA
1.8.1965. Dk. green on m/c unpt. Like #74. 134 x 64mm.

	VG	VF	UNC
a. Sm. numerals in serial #.	.20	.50	7.50
b. Lg. numerals in serial #.	.20	.50	7.50

78   10 DINARA
1.8.1965. Dk. brown on m/c unpt. Like #75. 143 x 66mm.

	VG	VF	UNC
a. Like #77a.	.20	.50	8.00
b. Like #77b.	.20	.50	8.00

79   50 DINARA
1.8.1965. Dk. blue on m/c unpt. Like #76. 151 x 72mm.

	VG	VF	UNC
a. Like #77a.	.50	1.50	10.00
b. Like #77b.	.30	1.75	12.00

80   100 DINARA
1.8.1965. Red on m/c unpt. Equestrian statue "Peace of Augustinci"
statue in United Nations, New York at l.

	VG	VF	UNC
a. Like #77a.	1.00	3.00	9.00
b. Like #77b, but w/o security thread.	.75	3.25	10.00
c. Like #77b, but w/security thread.	.25	1.00	5.00

1968-70 ISSUE

81   5 DINARA
1.5.1968. Dk. green on m/c unpt. Like #77. 123 x 59mm.

	VG	VF	UNC
a. Like #77a.	.05	.20	.50
b. Like #77b.	.05	.20	.50

82   10 DINARA
1.5.1968. Dk. brown on m/c unpt. Like #78. 131 x 63mm.

	VG	VF	UNC
a. Like #77a.	.50	2.00	8.00
b. Like #80b.	.20	.50	1.00
c. Like #80c.	.05	.15	.25

83   50 DINARA
1.5.1968. Blue-black on m/c unpt. Similar to #79 but lg. 50 in circle at
l. ctr. on back. 139 x 66mm.

	VG	VF	UNC
a. Like #77a.	.75	3.00	10.00
b. Like #80b.	.20	.65	4.00
c. Like #80c.	.10	.35	1.00

84	**500 DINARA**	VG	VF	UNC
	1.8.1970. Dk. olive-green on m/c unpt. N. Tesla seated w/open book at l.			
	a. W/o security thread.	.15	.50	2.00
	b. W/security thread.	1.50	6.00	15.00

1974 ISSUE

85	**20 DINARA**	VG	VF	UNC
	19.12.1974. Purple on m/c unpt. Ship dockside at l. 6 or 7-digit serial #.	.15	.40	1.50
86	**1000 DINARA**			
	19.12.1974. Blue-black on m/c unpt. Woman w/fruit at l.	.50	1.65	5.00

1978-85 ISSUE

#87-92 long, 2-line sign. title at l. and different sign.

87	**10 DINARA**	VG	VF	UNC
	12.8.1978; 4.11.1981. Like #82.	.10	.20	.75
88	**20 DINARA**			
	1978; 1981. Like #85.			
	a. 12.8.1978.	.05	.15	.75
	b. 4.11.1981.	.15	.50	5.00
89	**50 DINARA**			
	12.8.1978; 4.11.1981. Like #83.	.05	.15	.75
90	**100 DINARA**			
	12.8.1978; 4.11.1981; 16.5.1986. Like #80.	.05	.15	1.00

91	**500 DINARA**	VG	VF	UNC
	1978; 1981; 1986. Like #84.			
	a. 12.8.1978.	.20	.65	2.00
	b. 4.11.1981.	.10	.40	1.25
	c. 16.5.1986.	.10	.35	1.00

92	**1000 DINARA**	VG	VF	UNC
	1978; 1981. Like #86.			
	a. Sign. title: *Governor* in Cyrillic w/o letter *R* (engraving error). Series AF. 1978.	.25	.75	7.00
	b. As a. Series AR.	3.00	12.50	50.00
	c. Corrected sign. title.	.15	.50	5.00
	d. 1981.	.05	.25	1.00

93	**5000 DINARA**	VG	VF	UNC
	1.5.1985. Deep blue on m/c unpt. Tito at l. and as wmk., arms at ctr. Bldg. on hill at ctr. on back.			
	a. Error date *1930* instead of *1980* (Tito's death year).	4.00	15.00	60.00
	b. Corrected date *1980*.	.10	.25	1.50

1987-89 ISSUE

95	**20,000 DINARA**	VG	VF	UNC
	1.5.1987. Brown on m/c unpt. Miner at l. and as wmk., arms at ctr. Mining equipment on back.	.10	.25	1.50

96	50,000 DINARA	VG	VF	UNC
	1.5.1988. Green and blue on m/c unpt. Girl at l., and as wmk. City of Dubrovnik on back.	.15	.35	3.50

101	50 DINARA	VG	VF	UNC
	1.1.1990. Purple on lilac unpt. Similar to #98.	.40	1.25	7.50
102	200 DINARA			
	1.1.1990. Pale olive-green and brown on lt. orange unpt. Similar to #100.	.60	1.75	10.00

1990 SECOND ISSUE
#107A-111 have lg. portr. at l. and as wmk.. arms at ctr.

97	100,000 DINARA	VG	VF	UNC
	1.5.1989. Violet and red on m/c unpt. Young girl at l. and as wmk. Abstract design w/letters and numbers on back.	.25	.75	4.50

103	10 DINARA	VG	VF	UNC
	1.9.1990. Violet and red on m/c unpt. Similar to #97.	.05	.20	1.50

98	500,000 DINARA	VG	VF	UNC
	Aug. 1989. Deep purple and blue on m/c unpt. Arms at l., partisan monument "Kozara" at r. Partisan monument "Sutjeska" on back.	.35	1.50	8.50

104	50 DINARA	VG	VF	UNC
	1.6.1990. Purple. Young boy at l. Roses on back.	.05	.25	1.50
105	100 DINARA			
	1.3.1990. Lt. olive-green on orange and gold unpt. Similar to #99.	.15	.45	3.00
106	500 DINARA			
	1.3.1990. Blue and purple. Young man at l. Mountain scene on back.	.35	1.00	7.50
106A	500 DINARA			
	Brown and orange. Like #106. (Not issued).	—	—	275.00

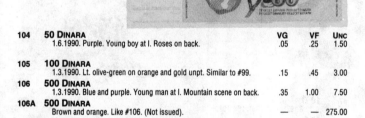

99	1 MILLION DINARA	VG	VF	UNC
	1.11.1989. Lt. olive-green on orange and gold unpt. Young woman at l. and as wmk. Stylized ear of corn on back.	.40	1.25	7.50
100	2 MILLION DINARA			
	Aug. 1989. Pale olive-green and brown on lt. orange unpt. Partisan monument "Kozara" at r. Partisan "V3" monument at Kragujevac at ctr. on back.	3.50	13.50	55.00

1990 FIRST ISSUE

107	1000 DINARA	VG	VF	UNC
	26.11.1990. Brown and orange. N. Tesla at l. High frequency transformer on back.	1.00	3.00	15.00

1991 ISSUE
#108-111 portr. as wmk. Year date only.

107A 10 DINARA
    1991. Purple, black and lilac. Like #97. (Not issued).   —   —   200.00

107B 50 DINARA
    1991. Orange and red. Like #104. (Not issued).   —   —   200.00

		VG	VF	UNC
108	**100 DINARA**	.10	.30	1.50
	1991. Black and olive-brown on yellow unpt. Similar to #105.			

		VG	VF	UNC
109	**500 DINARA**	.25	.75	4.00
	1991. Brown, dk. brown and orange on tan unpt. Similar to #106.			

		VG	VF	UNC
110	**1000 DINARA**	.50	1.50	7.50
	1991. Blue and purple. Similar to #107.			

		VG	VF	UNC
111	**5000 DINARA**	.85	2.50	15.00
	1991. Purple, red-orange and violet on gray unpt. I. Andric at l. Multiple arch stone bridge on the Drina River at Visegrad on back.			

1992 ISSUE
#114-120 new Republic monogram, arms at ctr. Similar to previous issues.

		VG	VF	UNC
112	**100 DINARA**	.10	.25	1.00
	1992. Pale blue and purple. Similar to #105.			

		VG	VF	UNC
113	**500 DINARA**	.30	.50	4.50
	1992. Pale purple and lilac. Similar to #106.			

		VG	VF	UNC
114	**1000 DINARA**	.75	2.00	7.50
	1992. Red, orange and purple on lilac unpt. Similar to #107.			

		VG	VF	UNC
115	**5000 DINARA**	.30	1.50	5.00
	1992. Deep blue-green, purple and deep olive-brown on gray unpt. Similar to #111.			

116	**10,000 DINARA**	VG	VF	UNC
	1992. Varied shades of brown and salmon on tan unpt. Like #103.			2.75
	a. W/dot after date.	.15	.15	2.75
	b. W/o dot after date.	.10	.30	2.00

117	**50,000 DINARA**	VG	VF	UNC
	1992. Purple, olive-green and deep blue-green. Like #104.	.50	1.50	4.50

1993 ISSUE
#118-127 portr. as wmk.

118	**100,000 DINARA**	VG	VF	UNC
	1993. Olive-green on orange and gold unpt. Sunflowers on back.	.50	1.50	5.00

119	**500,000 DINARA**	VG	VF	UNC
	1993. Blue-violet and orange on m/c unpt. Young man at I. Kopornik Sky Center on back.	1.00	3.25	10.00

120	**1 MILLION DINARA**	VG	VF	UNC
	1993. Purple on blue, orange and m/c unpt. Face like #117. Iris flowers on back.	1.25	4.00	12.50

121	**5 MILLION DINARA**	VG	VF	UNC
	1993. Violet, lilac, turquoise and m/c. Face like #116. Vertical rendition of high frequency transformer at ctr., hydroelectric dam at r. on back.	.15	.50	2.50

122	**10 MILLION DINARA**	VG	VF	UNC
	1993. Slate blue, lt. and dk. brown. Face like #115. National library on back.	.20	.60	3.00
123	**50 MILLION DINARA**			
	1993. Black and orange. Face like #116. Belgrade University on back.	.25	.75	4.00

124	**100 MILLION DINARA**	VG	VF	UNC
	1993. Grayish purple and blue. Face like #113. Academy of Science on back.	.20	.60	3.00

125	**500 MILLION DINARA**	VG	VF	UNC
	1993. Black and lilac. Face like #118. Faculty of Agriculture on back.	.45	1.35	6.00

126	**1 MILLIARD DINARA**	VG	VF	UNC
	1993. Red and purple on orange and blue-gray unpt. Face like #123. Parliament bldg. (National Assembly) on back.	.50	1.50	6.00

127	**10 MILLIARD DINARA**	VG	VF	UNC
	1993. Black, purple and red. Face like #121. Back like #114.	.50	1.50	7.50

1993 REFORM ISSUE

128 5000 DINARA
1993. Pale reddish brown, pale olive-green and orange. Face like #110. Museum on back.

	VF	VF	UNC
	FV	FV	5.00

129 10,000 DINARA
1993. Orange, gray and olive-green. S. Kara-dzic at I. Orthodox Church on back.

	VG	VF	UNC
	.50	1.50	3.00

130 50,000 DINARA
1993. Blue and pink. Petar II, Prince-Bishop of Montenegro at I. Monastery in Cetinje on back.

	VG	VF	UNC
	.45	1.25	3.50

131 500,000 DINARA
1993. Dk. green on blue-green and yellow-orange unpt. D. Obradovic at I. Monastery Kholovo on back.

	VG	VF	UNC
	.50	1.25	5.00

132 5 MILLION DINARA
1993. Dk. brown on brown-orange and blue-green and pale olive-brown unpt. K. Petrovich, Prince of Serbia at I. Orthodox Church on back.

	VG	VF	UNC
	.55	1.75	5.00

133 50 MILLION DINARA
1993. Red and purple on orange and lilac unpt. M. Pupin at I. Telephone Exchange bldg. on back.

	VG	VF	UNC
	.85	2.50	7.50

134 500 MILLION DINARA
1993. Purple on aqua, brown-orange and dull pink unpt. J. Cvijich at I. University on back.

	VG	VF	UNC
	.85	2.50	7.50

135 5 MILLIARD DINARA
1993. Olive-brown on red-orange, lt. green, ochre and orange unpt. D. Jaksich at I. Monastery in Vrazcevsnica on back.

	VG	VF	UNC
	.15	.50	4.50

136 50 MILLIARD DINARA
1993. Dk. brown on blue-violet, orange, red-violet and gray unpt. Serbian Prince M. Obrenovich at I. Villa of Obrenovich on back.

	VG	VF	UNC
	.30	.90	4.50

137 **500 MILLIARD DINARA**

	VG	VF	UNC
1993. Red-violet on orange, pale blue-gray and olive-brown unpt. Poet J. J. Zmaj at l. National Library on back.	.35	1.00	7.50

1994 ISSUE

138 **10 DINARA**

	VG	VF	UNC
1994. Chocolate brown on brown and gray-green unpt. J. Panchih at l. Kopaonik Mountain on back. W/o serial #.	.10	.25	1.00

139 **100 DINARA**

	VG	VF	UNC
1994. Grayish purple on purple pink and aqua unpt. N. Tesla at l. Tesla Museum on back.	.10	.30	1.50

140 **1000 DINARA**

	VG	VF	UNC
1994. Dk. olive-gray on red-orange, olive-brown and lilac unpt. Like #130.	.15	.45	2.00

141 **5000 DINARA**

	VG	VF	UNC
1994. Dk. blue on lilac, orange and aqua unpt. D. Obradovic at l. Monastary in Kholovo on back. Similar to #131.	.40	1.25	6.00

142 **50,000 DINARA**

	VG	VF	UNC
1994. Dull red and lilac on orange unpt. Serbian Prince K. Petrovich at l. Orthodox Church on back. Similar to #132.	.45	1.40	6.00

142A **100,000 DINARA**

	VG	VF	UNC
1994. Red-brown on ochre and pale olive-green unpt. Like #133. M. Pupin at l. Telephone Exchange bldg. on back. W/o serial #. (Not issued).	—	—	275.00

143 **500,000 DINARA**

	VG	VF	UNC
1994. Dull olive-green and orange on yellow unpt. J. Cvijich at l. Belgrade Univeristy on back. Similar to #134.	.55	1.75	6.50

1994 PROVISIONAL ISSUE

144 **10 MILLION DINARA**

	VG	VF	UNC
1994 (-old date 1993). Red ovpt: *1994* on face and back w/new silver ovpt. sign. and sign. title on back on #122.	.20	.60	3.00

1994 REFORM ISSUES
#145-147 wmk: Diamond grid.

NOTE: #145-147 withdrawn from circulation on 1.1.1995.

145 **1 NOVI DINAR**

	VG	VF	UNC
1.1.1994. Blue-gray and brown on pale olive green and tan unpt. J. Panchih at l. Kopaonik Mountain on back. Similar to #138.	.25	1.00	3.00

146 **5 NOVIH DINARA**

	VG	VF	UNC
1.1.1994. Red-brown and pink on ochre and pale orange unpt. N. Tesla at l. Tesla Museum on back. Similar to #139.	FV	1.75	5.00

147 **10 Novih Dinara**
1.1.1994. Purple and pink on aqua and olive-green unpt. Petar II, Prince-Bishop of Montenegro at l. Monastery in Cetinje on back. Similar to #130 and 140.

	VG	VF	UNC
	.60	3.00	10.00

1994; 1996 ISSUE

#148-150 arms w/double-headed eagle at upper ctr. Wmk: Symmetrical design repeated.

Replacement notes: Serial # prefix *3A*.

148 **5 Novih Dinara**
3.3.1994. Deep purple and violet. N. Tesla at l. Back like #146.

	VG	VF	UNC
	FV	FV	6.50

149 **10 Novih Dinara**
3.3.1994. Purple, violet and brown. Like #147.

	VG	VF	UNC
	FV	FV	12.50

150 **20 Novih Dinara**
3.3.1994. Greenish black, brown-orange and brown. Similar to #135.

	VG	VF	UNC
	FV	FV	23.50

151 **50 Novih Dinara**
June 1996. Black and blue. Prince M. Obrenovich at l. Villa of Obrenovich on back.

	VG	VF	UNC
	FV	FV	42.50

ZAIRE

The Republic of Zaïre (formerly the Belgian Congo), located in the south-central part of Africa, has an area of 905,568 sq. mi. (2,345,409 sq. km.) and a population of 38.6 million. Capital: Kinshasa. The mineral-rich country produces copper, tin, diamonds, gold, zinc, cobalt and uranium.

In ancient times the territory comprising Zaïre was occupied by Negrito peoples (Pygmies) pushed into the mountains by Bantu and Nilotic invaders. The interior was first explored by the American correspondent Henry Stanley, who was subsequently commissioned by King Leopold II of Belgium to conclude development treaties with the local chiefs. The Berlin conference of 1885 awarded the area to Leopold, who administered and exploited it as his private property until it was annexed to Belgium in 1908. Following the eruption of bloody independence riots in 1959, Belgium granted the Belgian Congo independence as the Republic of the Congo on June 30, 1960. The Belgian Congo attained independence with the distinction of being the most ill-prepared country to ever undertake self-government. Without a single doctor, lawyer or engineer, with no organized unit capable of maintaining law and order, independence disintegrated into an orgy of anarchy. Provinces seceded. Intertribal warfare erupted. Belgian troops intervened to protect Belgian citizens from retributive massacre. By 1961, four groups were fighting for political dominance. The most serious threat to the viability of the country was posed by the secession of mineral-rich Katanga province on July 11, 1960.

After two and one-half years of sporadic warfare with a U.N. military force, Katanga's leaders capitulated, Jan. 14, 1963 and the rebellious province was partioned into three provinces. The nation officially changed its name to Zaïre on Oct. 27, 1971. See also Rwanda and Rwanda-Burundi.

MONETARY SYSTEM:
1 Franc = 100 Centimes to 1967
1 Zaïre = 100 Makuta, 1967-1993
1 Nouveaux Zaïre = 100 N Makuta = 3 million 'old' Zaïres, 1993-

CONGO (KINSHASA)

CONSEIL MONÉTAIRE DE LA RÉPUBLIQUE DU CONGO

1962-63 ISSUE

Various date and sign. varieties.

1 **100 FRANCS**
1.6.1963-8.7.1963. Green and m/c. Dam at l. Dredging at r. on back.

	VG	VF	UNC
	5.00	17.50	40.00

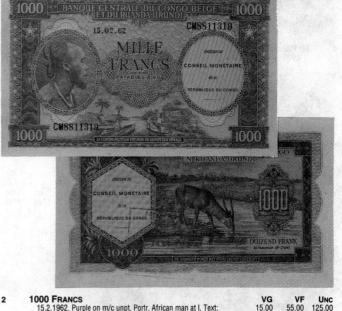

2 **1000 FRANCS**
15.2.1962. Purple on m/c unpt. Portr. African man at l. Text: *EMISSION DU CONSEIL MONÉTAIRE DE LA REPUBLIQUE DU CONGO* in place of wmk. Back deep violet on pink unpt; longhorn animal drinking in stream.

	VG	VF	UNC
	15.00	55.00	125.00

3 5000 FRANCS
  1.12.1963. Gray-green. Portr. African woman at l. Oarsmen on back.

	VG	VF	UNC
	400.00	950.00	2000.

BANQUE NATIONALE DU CONGO

1961 ISSUE
#5-8 have long bldg. at bottom on back.

4 20 FRANCS
  15.11.1961-15.9.1962. Green, blue and brown. Girl seated at r. and as wmk. Stylized tree on back. Printer: JEZ.

	VG	VF	UNC
	2.00	8.00	25.00

5 50 FRANCS
  1.9.1961-1.7.1962. Green. Lion at l., bridge and lake in background.

	VG	VF	UNC
	3.00	20.00	50.00

6 100 FRANCS
  1.9.1961-1.8.1964. Dk. brown on m/c unpt. J. Kasavubu at l., 2 birds at r. Printer: TDLR.

	VG	VF	UNC
	3.00	17.50	40.00

7 500 FRANCS
  15.10.1961; 1.12.1961; 1.8.1964. Lilac. Mask at l. Wmk: Bird.

	VG	VF	UNC
	10.00	35.00	120.00

8 1000 FRANCS
  15.10.1961; 15.12.1961; 1.8.1964. Dk. blue on m/c unpt. J. Kasavubu at l., carving at r. Wmk: Antelope's head. Printer: TDLR.

	VG	VF	UNC
	8.00	25.00	75.00

1967 ISSUE
#9-13 various date and sign. varieties. Printer: TDLR.

9 10 MAKUTA
  2.1.1967-21.1.1970. Blue and olive on m/c unpt. Stadium at l., Mobutu at r. Long bldg. on back.

	VG	VF	UNC
	2.00	6.00	25.00

10 20 MAKUTA
  24.11.1967-1.10.1970. Black on green, blue and m/c unpt. Man w/flag at ctr., P. Lumunba at r. People in long boat on back. Wmk: Antelope's head.

	VG	VF	UNC
	4.00	25.00	60.00

11 50 MAKUTA
  2.1.1967-1.10.1970. Red and olive on m/c unpt. Stadium at l., Mobutu at r. Gathering coconuts on back.

	VG	VF	UNC
	4.50	20.00	60.00

12 1 ZAÏRE- 100 MAKUTA
  2.1.1967-1.10.1970. Brown and green on m/c unpt. Stadium at l., Mobutu at r. Mobutu leading inoculation drive on back. Wmk: Antelope's head.

	VG	VF	UNC
	4.00	15.00	75.00

13	**5 ZAÏRES - 500 MAKUTA**	VG	VF	UNC

1967-70. Green and m/c. Mobutu at r. Long bldg. at l. ctr. on back.
Wmk: Antelope's head.

		VG	VF	UNC
a.	Sign. above title: *LE GOUVERNEUR*. Green date. 2.1.1967; 24.6.1967.	12.50	55.00	200.00
b.	Sign. below title: *LE GOUVERNEUR*. Black date. 2.1.1967; 21.1.1970.	12.50		55.00

1971 ISSUE

#14-15 portr. Mobutu at l. and as wmk., leopard at r. Printer: G&D.

14	**5 ZAÏRES**	VG	VF	UNC

24.11.1971. Green, black and m/c. Carving at l. ctr., hydroelectric dam
at r. on back.

	VG	VF	UNC
	17.50	70.00	175.00

15	**10 ZAÏRES**	VG	VF	UNC

30.6.1971. Blue, brown and m/c. Arms on back w/yellow star.

	VG	VF	UNC
	20.00	75.00	150.00

ZAÏRE

BANQUE DU ZAÏRE

1972-80 ISSUES

#16-25 Mobutu at l. and as wmk. Various date and sign. varieties. Printer: G&D.

16	**50 MAKUTA**	VG	VF	UNC

1973-78. Red, brown and m/c. Man and structure in water on back.
Intaglio printed.

		VG	VF	UNC
a.	Red guilloche at l. on back. 30.6.1973-4.10.1975.	.50	1.50	6.50
b.	Red and purple guilloche at ctr. on back. 24.6.1976-20..5.1978.	.25	.75	4.00

17	**50 MAKUTA**	VG	VF	UNC

24.11.1979; 14.10.1980. Like #16 but slight color differences and
lithographed.

	VG	VF	UNC
	.35	1.00	3.00

18	**1 ZAÏRE**	VG	VF	UNC

1972-77. Brown and m/c. Factory, pyramid, flora and elephant tusks
on back. Intaglio printed. plates.

		VG	VF	UNC
a.	Sign. title: *LE GOUVERNEUR* placed below line. 15.3.1972-27.10.1976.	.50	1.50	5.00
b.	Sign. title: *LE GOUVERNEUR* placed above line. 27.10.1977.	.30	1.00	2.50

19	**1 ZAÏRE**	VG	VF	UNC

22.10.1979; 27.10.1980; 20.2.1981. Like #18 but slight color
differences and lithographed.

	VG	VF	UNC
	.15	.35	1.00

20	**5 ZAÏRES**		**VG**	**VF**	**UNC**
	24.11.1972. Green, black and m/c. Carved figure w/hydroelectric dam on back. Like #14.		15.00	35.00	100.00

21	**5 ZAÏRES**		**VG**	**VF**	**UNC**
	1974-77. Green and m/c. Similar to #20 but Mobutu w/cap.				
	a.	30.11.1974; 30.6.1975; 24.11.1975; 24.11.1976.	2.50	7.50	20.00
	b.	24.11.1977.	.50	1.50	7.00

22	**5 ZAÏRES**	**VG**	**VF**	**UNC**
	20.5.1979; 27.10.1980. Blue, brown and m/c. Like #21.	.50	1.50	4.50

23	**10 ZAÏRES**		**VG**	**VF**	**UNC**
	1972-77. Blue and m/c. Similar to #15 but arms w/hand holding torch on back.				
	a.	30.6.1972; 22.6.1974; 30.6.1975; 30.6.1976.	2.50	7.50	22.50
	b.	27.10.1977.	1.00	3.00	10.00

24	**10 ZAÏRES**	**VG**	**VF**	**UNC**
	24.6.1979; 4.1.1981. Green and m/c. Like #23.	1.00	3.00	10.00

25	**50 ZAÏRES**	**VG**	**VF**	**UNC**
	4.2.1980; 24.11.1980. Red, violet, brown and m/c. Similar to #21. Arms on back.	5.00	17.50	30.00

1982-85 ISSUES

#26-29 leopard at lower l., Mobutu in civilian dress at ctr. r. and as wmk. Sign. varieties.

#28-29 printer: G&D.

#30-31 leopard at lower l., Mobutu in military dress at ctr. r. and as wmk. Printer: G&D.

26	**5 ZAÏRES**	**VG**	**VF**	**UNC**
	17.11.1982. Blue, black and m/c. Hydroelectric dam on back. Printer: G&D.	.25	.60	2.00
26A	**5 ZAÏRES**			
	24.11.1985. Like #26, but printer: HdMZ.	.20	.40	1.25

27	**10 ZAÏRES**	**VG**	**VF**	**UNC**
	27.10.1982. Green, black and m/c. Hand holding torch on back. Printer: G&D.	.40	1.00	2.50
27A	**10 ZAÏRES**			
	27.10.1985. Like #27, but printer: HdMZ.	.20	.40	1.25

28 **50 ZAÏRES**
24.11.1982; 24.6.1985. Purple and m/c. Back blue and m/c; natives
fishing w/stick nets at ctr.

	VG	VF	UNC
	.60	2.00	3.00

29 **100 ZAÏRES**
1983; 1985. Brown, orange and m/c. Bank of Zaïre on back.

	VG	VF	UNC
a. 30.6.1983.	.60	1.75	5.00
b. 30.6.1985.	.25	.75	3.00

30 **500 ZAÏRES**
14.10.1984; 14.10.1985. Brown, purple and m/c. Suspension bridge
over river on back.

	VG	VF	UNC
	1.25	3.50	12.50

31 **1000 ZAÏRES**
24.11.1985. Blue-black and green on m/c unpt. Civic bldg., water
fountain at ctr. on back.

	VG	VF	UNC
	1.00	4.00	12.50

1988-92 ISSUES

#32-46 Mobutu in military dress at r. and as wmk., leopard at lower l. ctr., arms at lower r. Reduced size
notes.

#32-36 printer: HdMZ.

#37 and 38, printer: G&D.

#40 and 41 printer: G&D.

#43 and 44 printer: G&D.

32 **50 ZAÏRES**
30.6.1988. Green and m/c. Natives fishing w/stick nets on back.
Similar to #28.

	VG	VF	UNC
	.10	.25	.85

33 **100 ZAÏRES**
14.10.1988. Blue and m/c. Bank of Zaïre at l. on back.

	VG	VF	UNC
	.15	.25	.85

34 **500 ZAÏRES**
24.6.1989. Brown, orange and m/c. Suspension bridge over river on
back. Similar to #30.

	VG	VF	UNC
	.25	1.00	2.50

35 **1000 ZAÏRES**
24.11.1989. Purple, brown and m/c. Back similar to #31.

	VG	VF	UNC
	.50	1.65	5.00

36 **2000 ZAÏRES**
1.10.1991. Violet on m/c unpt. Structure in water at l., carved figure at
ctr. r. on back. (Smaller size than #35.)

	VG	VF	UNC
	.25	.75	2.00

37 **5000 ZAÏRES**
20.5.1988. Blue, green and m/c. Factory at l., elephant tusks and
plants at ctr. on back.

	VG	VF	UNC
a. Brown triangle at lower r.	2.00	6.00	15.00
b. Green triangle at lower r.	.25	.75	2.00

38 **10,000 ZAÏRES**
24.11.1989. Violet, brown-orange and red on m/c unpt. Complex of
official bldgs. on back.

	VG	VF	UNC
	.35	1.00	2.50

39 20,000 ZAÏRES
1.7.1991. Black on m/c unpt. Bank of Zaïre at l., other bldgs. across
ctr. on back. Printer: HdMZ.

	VG	VF	UNC
39	.25	.50	2.00

40 50,000 ZAÏRES
24.4.1991. Wine and blue-black on m/c unpt. Family of gorillas on
back.

	VG	VF	UNC
40	.75	2.00	4.50

41 100,000 ZAÏRES
4.1.1992. Black and deep olive-green on m/c unpt. Domed bldg. at l.
ctr. on back.

	VG	VF	UNC
41	.50	1.50	4.50

42 200,000 ZAÏRES
1.3.1992. Deep purple and deep blue on m/c unpt. Civic bldg., water
fountain at l. ctr. Printer HdMZ.

	VG	VF	UNC
42	.50	1.50	5.00

43 500,000 ZAÏRES
15.3.1992. Brown and orange on m/c unpt. Hydroelectric dam at l. ctr.
on back.

	VG	VF	UNC
43	.50	1.50	5.00

44 1,000,000 ZAÏRES
31.7.1992. Red-violet and deep red on m/c unpt. Suspension bridge at
l. ctr. on back.

	VG	VF	UNC
44	.50	1.25	3.50

45 1,000,000 ZAÏRES
17.5.1993; 30.6.1993. Like #44 but printer: HdMZ.

	VG	VF	UNC
45	.50	1.25	3.50

46 5,000,000 ZAÏRES
1.10.1992. Deep brown and brown on m/c unpt. Factory, pyramids,
flora and elephant tusks on back. Printer: H&S.

	VG	VF	UNC
46	.40	1.00	4.50

1993 ISSUE

#47-56 leopard at lower l., Mobutu at r., arms at lower r.

#47-48 Independence Monument at l. on back. W/o wmk. Printer: G&D.

#49 and 51 wmk: Mobutu. Printer: HdMZ (CdM-A).

#52-54 wmk: Mobutu. Printer: G&D.

#55-58 wmk: Mobutu.

#55-57 printer: HdMZ (CdM-A)

#50 *Deleted.*

47 1 NOUVEAUX LIKUTA
24.6.1993. Tan on pink and m/c unpt.

	VG	VF	UNC
47	.05	.20	.50

48 5 NOUVEAUX MAKUTA
24.6.1993. Black on pale violet and blue-green unpt.

	VG	VF	UNC
48	.05	.20	.65

49   10 NOUVEAUX MAKUTA
24.6.1993. Green on m/c unpt. Factory, pyramids, flora and elephant
tusks on back.

	VG	VF	UNC
	.10	.30	1.00

51   50 NOUVEAUX MAKUTA
24.6.1993. Brown-orange on lt. green and m/c unpt. Chieftan at l.,
natives fishing w/stick nets at ctr. on back.

	VG	VF	UNC
	.10	.30	.75

52   1 NOUVEAUX ZAÏRE
24.6.1993. Violet and purple on m/c unpt. Banque du Zaère at l. on
back.

	VG	VF	UNC
	.10	.30	1.00

53   5 NOUVEAUX ZAÏRES
24.6.1993. Brown on m/c unpt. Back like #41.

	VG	VF	UNC
	.20	.50	1.50

54   10 NOUVEAUX ZAÏRES
24.6.1993. Dk. gray and dk. blue-green on m/c unpt. Back like #42.

	VG	VF	UNC
	.50	1.00	3.00

55   10 NOUVEAUX ZAÏRES
24.6.1993. Dk. gray and dk. blue-green on m/c unpt. Back like #42.

	VG	VF	UNC
	.15	.40	1.50

56   20 NOUVEAUX ZAÏRES
24.6.1993. Brown and blue on pale green and lilac unpt. Back similar
to #42.

	VG	VF	UNC
	.20	.60	1.75

57   50 NOUVEAUX ZAÏRES
24.6.1993. Brown and deep red on m/c unpt. Back like #43.

	VG	VF	UNC
	.20	.60	1.75

58   100 NOUVEAUX ZAÏRES
1993-94. Grayish purple and blue-violet on aqua and ochre unpt. Back
like #44. Printer: G&D.

		VG	VF	UNC
a.	24.6.1993.	1.00	3.00	5.00
b.	15.2.1994.	FV	2.00	4.50

1994-96 ISSUES

#59-66 leopard at lower l., Mobutu at r. and as wmk., arms at lower r.

#59-61 printer: HdMZ.

#70-75 w/optical device vertical band at l.

59   50 NOUVEAUX ZAÏRES
15.2.1994. Dull red-violet and red on m/c unpt. Like #55.

	VG	VF	UNC
	FV	2.00	6.00

60   100 NOUVEAUX ZAÏRES
15.2.1994. Like #56.

	VG	VF	UNC
	FV	2.00	6.00

61   200 NOUVEAUX ZAÏRES
15.2.1994. Deep olive-brown on m/c unpt. Natives fishing w/stick nets
at l. ctr. on back.

	VG	VF	UNC
	FV	FV	1.25

62   200 NOUVEAUX ZAÏRES
15.2.1994. Like #59. Printer: G&D.

	VG	VF	UNC
	FV	FV	2.25

			VG	VF	UNC
63	**500 NOUVEAUX ZAÏRES** 15.2.1994. Gray and deep olive-green on m/c unpt. Banque du Zaïre at l. ctr. on back. Printer: HdMZ.		FV	FV	1.25
64	**500 NOUVEAUX ZAÏRES** 15.2.1994. Like #61. Printer: G&D.		FV	FV	2.50

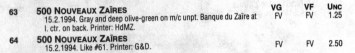

			VG	VF	UNC
65	**500 NOUVEAUX ZAÏRES** 30.1.1995. Blue on m/c unpt.		FV	FV	1.50

			VG	VF	UNC
74 (73)	**50,000 NOUVEAUX ZAÏRES** 30.1.1996. Violet and pale blue on m/c unpt. Printer: G&D.		FV	FV	10.00
75 (74)	**50,000 NOUVEAUX ZAÏRES** 30.1.1996. Violet and pale blue on m/c unpt. Printer: HdMZ.		FV	FV	9.00
76	**100,000 NOUVEAUX ZAÏRES** (1996). M/c.				Expected New Issue
77	**500,000 NOUVEAUX ZAÏRES** (1996). M/c.				Expected New Issue
78	**1,000,000 NOUVEAUX ZAÏRES** (1996). M/c.				Expected New Issue

REGIONAL

Validation Ovpt:

Type I: Circular handstamp: *REPUBLIQUE DU ZAÏRE-REGION DU BAS-ZAÏRE; GARAGE - STA/BANANA* around arms.

BANQUE DU ZAÏRE BRANCHES

NOTE: This is one example of an ovpt. applied to a note being turned in for exchange for a new issue. It appears that in some locations (i.e. Bas Fleuve, Bas Zaïre and Shaba Sons) there were not enough of the new notes to trade for the older ones. In such cases, an ovpt. was applied to the older piece indicating its validity and acceptability for future redemption into new currency. A number of different ovpt. are known, and more information is needed. Market values have ranged from $10-25.

1980s ND ISSUES

			VG	VF	UNC
66	**1000 NOUVEAUX ZAÏRES** 30.1.1995. Olive-gray and olive-green on m/c unpt. Printer: G&D.		FV	FV	4.00
67	**1000 NOUVEAUX ZAÏRES** 30.1.1995. Like #66. Printer: HdMZ.		FV	FV	3.00
68	**5000 NOUVEAUX ZAÏRES** 30.1.1995. Brown-violet and red-violet on m/c unpt. Printer: G&D.		FV	FV	7.00
69	**5000 NOUVEAUX ZAÏRES** 30.1.1995. Like #68. Printer: HdMZ.		FV	FV	5.00
70	**10,000 NOUVEAUX ZAÏRES** 30.1.1995. Blue-violet on m/c unpt. Printer: G&D.		FV	FV	5.00
71	**10,000 NOUVEAUX ZAÏRES** 30.1.1995. Blue-violet on m/c unpt. Printer: HdMZ.		FV	FV	5.00

		VG	VF	UNC
R3	**5 ZAÏRES**			

			VG	VF	UNC
72 (71)	**20,000 NOUVEAUX ZAÏRES** 30.1.1996. Brown on m/c unpt. Printer: G&D.		FV	FV	7.00
73 (72)	**20,000 NOUVEAUX ZAÏRES** 30.1.1996. Brown on m/c unpt. Printer: HdMZ.		FV	FV	6.50

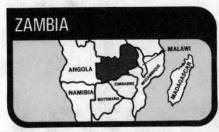

ZAMBIA

The Republic of Zambia (formerly Northern Rhodesia), a land-locked country in south-central Africa, has an area of 290,586 sq. mi. (752,614 sq. km.) and a population of nearly 8.8 million. Capital: Lusaka. The economy of Zambia is based principally on copper, of which Zambia is the world's third largest producer. Copper, zinc, lead, cobalt and tobacco are exported.

The area that is now Zambia was brought within the British sphere of influence in 1888 by empire builder Cecil Rhodes, who obtained mining concessions in south-central Africa from indigenous chiefs. The territory was ruled by the British South Africa Company, which Rhodes established, until 1924 when its administration was transferred to the British government as a protectorate. In 1953, Northern Rhodesia was joined with Nyasaland and the colony of Southern Rhodesia to form the Federation of Rhodesia and Nyasaland. Northern Rhodesia seceded from the Federation on Oct. 24, 1964, and became the independent Republic of Zambia. Zambia is a member of the Commonwealth of Nations. The president is Chief of State.

Zambia adopted a decimal currency system on Jan. 16, 1969.

Also see Rhodesia.

RULERS:
British to 1964

MONETARY SYSTEM:
1 Shilling = 12 Pence
1 Pound = 20 Shillings to 1969
1 Kwacha = 100 Ngwee, 1969-

SIGNATURE VARIETIES

1	C. Hallet, 1964–67	7	Dr. L.S. Chivuno, 1986–88
2	Dr. J.B. Zulu, 1967–70	8	F. Nkhoma, 1988–91
3	V.S. Musakanya, 1970–72	9	J.A. Bussiere, 1991– ca.1993
4	B.R. Kuwani, 1972–76, 1982–84	10	D. Mutaisho, 1993–
5	L.J. Mwananshiku, 1976–81		
6	D.A.R Phiri, 1984–86		

REPUBLIC
BANK OF ZAMBIA
1963 ND ISSUE

A1	1 POUND	VG	VF	UNC
	1963. Blue on lilac unpt. Fisherman w/net and boat at ctr., portr. Qn. Elizabeth II at r. Back purple; bird at l. ctr. Imprint: H&S. (Not issued).	—	—	—

1964 ND ISSUE
#1-3 sign. R. C. Hallet. Arms at upper ctr. Printer: TDLR. Wmk: Wildebeest head.

1	10 SHILLINGS	VG	VF	UNC
	ND (1964). Brown on m/c unpt. Chaplins Barbet bird at r. Farmers plowing w/tractor and oxen on back.	15.00	50.00	225.00

2	1 POUND	VG	VF	UNC
	ND (1964). Green on m/c unpt. Lovebird at r. Mining tower and conveyors on back.	20.00	100.00	550.00

3	5 POUNDS	VG	VF	UNC
	ND (1964). Blue on m/c unpt. Wildebeest at r. Waterfalls on back.	25.00	125.00	1000.

1968 ND ISSUE
#4-8 Pres. Kaunda at r. Period between letter and value. Sign. 2. Printer: TDLR.
#5-8 Arms at upper ctr. Wmk: Pres. Kaunda.

4   50 NGWEE

		VG	VF	UNC
ND (1968). Red-violet on m/c unpt. Arms at l. 2 antelope on back. W/o wmk.		3.00	8.00	57.50

5   1 KWACHA

		VG	VF	UNC
ND (1968). Dk. brown on m/c unpt. Farmers plowing w/tractor and oxen on back.		3.50	12.50	65.00

6   2 KWACHA

	VG	VF	UNC
ND (1968). Green on m/c unpt. Mining tower and conveyors on back.	4.00	15.00	85.00

7   10 KWACHA

ND (1968). Blue on m/c unpt. Waterfalls on back.	15.00	50.00	325.00

8   20 KWACHA

ND (1968). Purple on m/c unpt. National Assembly on back.	25.00	75.00	450.00

1969 ND ISSUE
#9-13 Pres. Kaunda at r., w/o period between letter and value. Backs and wmks. similar to #4-8.

9   50 NGWEE

	VG	VF	UNC
ND (1969). Red-violet. Like #4.		Reported Not Confirmed	
a. Sign. 2.	2.00	6.50	42.50
b. Sign. 3.			
c. Sign. 4.	1.00	4.00	20.00

10   1 KWACHA

	VG	VF	UNC
ND (1969). Dk. brown.			
a. Sign. 2.	2.50	6.00	65.00
b. Sign. 3.	2.00	5.00	45.00

11   2 KWACHA

ND (1969). Green.			
a. Sign. 2.	3.00	10.00	135.00
b. Sign. 3.	2.50	8.50	65.00
c. Sign. 4.	FV	FV	—

12   10 KWACHA

	VG	VF	UNC
ND (1969). Blue.			
a. Sign. 2.	6.00	17.50	175.00
b. Sign. 3.	10.00	35.00	300.00
c. Sign. 4.	8.00	25.00	200.00

13   20 KWACHA

	VG	VF	UNC
ND (1969). Purple.			
a. Sign. 2.	15.00	50.00	300.00
b. Sign. 3.	20.00	70.00	425.00
c. Sign. 4.	10.00	35.00	300.00

1973 ND ISSUE
#14-16, Arms at upper ctr., Pres. Kaunda at r. Printer: TDLR.

14   50 NGWEE

	VG	VF	UNC
ND (1973). Black on purple and m/c unpt. Miners on back. W/o wmk. Sign. 4.	.50	1.50	6.50

16   5 KWACHA

ND (1973). Red-violet. Children by school on back. Sign. 4. Wmk: Kaunda.	15.00	75.00	325.00

1973 ND COMMEMORATIVE ISSUE
#15, Birth of the Second Republic December 13, 1972

15 **1 Kwacha**
ND (1973). Red-orange and brown on m/c unpt. Document signing, commemorative text and crowd on back. Sign. 4. Wmk: Kaunda.

	VG	VF	UNC
	4.00	10.00	35.00

1974 ND Issue
#17-18 Arms at upper ctr; Pres. Kaunda at r. and as wmk. Sign. 4. Printer: BWC.

17 **10 Kwacha**
ND (1974). Blue and m/c. Waterfalls on back.

VG	VF	UNC
17.50	75.00	235.00

18 **20 Kwacha**
ND (1974). Purple, red and m/c. National Assembly on back.

VG	VF	UNC
15.00	60.00	195.00

1974-76 ND Issue
#19-22 earlier frame design, arms at upper ctr. Older Pres. Kaunda at r. but same wmk. as previous issues. Printer: TDLR.

19 **1 Kwacha**
ND (1976). Brown. Back like #5. Sign. 5.

VG	VF	UNC
.50	2.00	10.00

20 **2 Kwacha**
ND (1974). Green. Back like #6. Sign. 4.

1.00	3.25	18.50

21 **5 Kwacha**
ND (1976). Brown and violet. Back like #16. Sign. 5.

VG	VF	UNC
3.00	12.00	40.00

22 **10 Kwacha**
ND (1976). Blue and m/c. Back similar to #17. Sign. 5.

VG	VF	UNC
5.00	20.00	110.00

1980; 1986 ND Issue
#23-28 Pres. Kaunda at r. and as wmk., Fish Eagle at ctr. Printer: TDLR.
Replacement notes: Serial # prefix Z/1.

23 **1 Kwacha**
ND (1980-88). Brown and m/c. Cotton picking on back.

	VG	VF	UNC
a. Sign. 5.	.20	.50	2.50
b. Sign. 7.	.15	.40	2.00

24 **2 Kwacha**
ND (1980-88). Olive and m/c. School bldg. w/teacher and student on back.

	VG	VF	UNC
a. Sign. 5.	.50	1.00	5.00
b. Sign. 6.	.25	.75	4.00
c. Sign. 7.	.10	.25	2.50

25 **5 Kwacha**
ND (1980-88). Brown and m/c. Hydroelectric dam on back.

	VG	VF	UNC
a. Sign. 5.	.40	1.50	5.50
b. Sign. 4.	.50	2.00	8.00
c. Sign. 6.	.25	.75	4.00
d. Sign. 7.	.15	.50	3.50

26 **10 Kwacha**
ND (1980-88). Blue, green and m/c. Bank on back.

	VG	VF	UNC
a. Sign. 5.	1.50	5.00	27.50
b. Sign. 4 in black.	1.25	4.00	17.50
c. Sign. 4 in blue.	1.25	4.00	25.00
d. Sign. 6.	1.00	2.00	7.00
e. Sign. 7.	.40	1.50	5.00

27 20 KWACHA
ND (1980-88). Green and m/c. Woman w/basket at r. on back.

	VG	VF	UNC
a. Sign. 5.	3.00	8.00	32.50
b. Sign. 4 in black.	2.00	6.00	25.00
c. Sign. 4 in dk. green.	2.00	6.00	32.50
d. Sign. 6.	1.00	3.00	11.50
e. Sign. 7.	.50	1.50	7.50

28 50 KWACHA
ND (1986-88). Brown, purple, and m/c. "Chainbreaker" statue at l., modern bldg. at ctr. on back. Sign. 7.

VG	VF	UNC
.90	2.75	9.00

1989 ND ISSUE

#29-33 Fish Eagle at lower l., butterfly over arms at ctr., Pres. Kaunda at r. and as wmk. "Chainbreaker" statue at l. on back.

29 2 KWACHA
ND (1989). Olive-brown on m/c unpt. Rhinoceros head at lower l., cornfield at ctr., tool at r. on back. Sign. 8.

VG	VF	UNC
.30	.75	3.00

30 5 KWACHA
ND (1989). Brown and red-orange on m/c unpt. Back brown; lion cub head at lower l., bldg. at ctr., jar at r. Sign. 8.

VG	VF	UNC
.15	.50	3.00

31 10 KWACHA
ND (1989). Dk. blue and black on m/c unpt. Back dk. blue; giraffe head at lower l., bldg. at ctr., carving of man's head at r.

	VG	VF	UNC
a. Sign. 8.	.15	.40	7.00
b. Sign. 9.	.10	.30	2.00

32 20 KWACHA
ND (1989). Dk. olive-green and brown on m/c unpt. Back dk. green; Dama gazelle head at lower l., bldg. at ctr., carving of man's head at r.

	VG	VF	UNC
a. Sign. 8.	.15	.50	8.50
b. Sign. 9.	.10	.30	2.00

33 50 KWACHA
ND (1989). Red-violet and purple on m/c unpt. Zebra head at lower l., manufacturing at ctr., carving of woman's bust at r. on back.

	VG	VF	UNC
a. Sign. 8.	.50	4.00	22.50
b. Sign. 9.	.45	2.25	12.50

1991 ND ISSUE

#34-35 Fish Eagle at l., tree over arms at ctr., older Pres. Kaunda at r. and as wmk. "Chainbreaker" statue at l. on back. Sign. 9.

34 100 KWACHA
ND (1991). Purple on m/c unpt. Water buffalo head at l., Victoria Falls of Zambezi w/rainbow through ctr. on back.

VG	VF	UNC
FV	.60	7.00

35 500 KWACHA
ND (1991). Brown on m/c unpt. Elephant at l., workers picking cotton at ctr. on back.

VG	VF	UNC
FV	1.50	4.50

1992; 1996 ND ISSUE

#36-42 seal of arms w/date at lower l., Fish Eagle at r. Wmk: Head of Fish Eagle. "Chainbreaker" statue at lower ctr. r. on back. Printer: TDLR.

Replacement notes: Serial # prefix *1/X*.

36 20 KWACHA
1992. Green on m/c unpt. Kudu at l., govt. bldg. at ctr. on back. Sign. 10.

VG	VF	UNC
FV	.20	1.00

37 50 KWACHA
  1992. Red on m/c unpt. Zebra at l., foundry worker at ctr. on back. Sign. 10.

	VG	VF	UNC
	FV	.30	1.75

38 100 KWACHA
  1992. Deep purple on m/c unpt. Water buffalo head at l., waterfalls at ctr. on back. Sign. 10.

	VG	VF	UNC
	FV	.40	3.00

39 500 KWACHA
  1992. Brown on m/c unpt. Elephant head at l., workers picking cotton at ctr. on back.

	VG	VF	UNC
a. Sign. 10.	FV	1.50	5.00
b. Sign. 11.	FV	FV	3.50

40 1000 KWACHA
  1992 (1996). Red-violet, deep orange and dk. olive-green on m/c unpt. Aardvark at l., farmer on tractor at ctr. on back. Sign. 11.

	VG	VF	UNC
	FV	FV	3.00

41 5000 KWACHA
  1992. Purple, dk. brown and deep red on m/c unpt. Lion at l., plant at ctr. Sign. 11.

	VG	VF	UNC
	FV	FV	7.50

42 10,000 KWACHA
  1992 (1996). Aqua, brown-violet and yellow-brown on m/c unpt. Porcupine at l., harvesting at ctr. on back. Sign. 11.

	VG	VF	UNC
	FV	FV	18.50

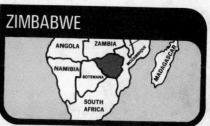

The Republic of Zimbabwe (formerly the "Republic of" Rhodesia or Southern Rhodesia), located in the east-central part of southern Africa, has an area of 150,820 sq. mi. (390,580 sq. km.) and a population of 9.9 million. Capital: Harare (formerly Salisbury). The economy is based on agriculture and mining. Tobacco, sugar, asbestos, copper and chrome ore and coal are exported.

The Rhodesian area, the habitat of paleolithic man, contains extensive evidence of earlier civilizations, notably the world-famous ruins of Zimbabwe, a gold-trading center that flourished about the 14th or 15th century AD. The Portuguese of the 16th century were the first Europeans to attempt to develop south-central Africa, but it remained for Cecil Rhodes and the British South Africa Co. to open the hinterlands. Rhodes obtained a concession for mineral rights from local chiefs in 1888 and administered his African empire (named Southern Rhodesia in 1895) through the British South Africa Co. until 1923, when the British government annexed the area after the white settlers voted for existence as a separate entity, rather than for incorporation into the Union of South Africa. From Sept. of 1953 through 1963 Southern Rhodesia was joined with the British protectorates of Northern Rhodesia and Nyasaland into a multiracial federation. When the federation was dissolved at the end of 1963, Northern Rhodesia and Nyasaland became the independent states of Zambia and Malawi.

Britain was prepared to grant independence to Southern Rhodesia but declined to do so when the politically dominant white Rhodesianas refused to give assurances of representative government. In November 1965, the white minority government of Southern Rhodesia unilaterally declared Southern Rhodesia an independent dominon. The United Nations and the British Parliament both proclaimed this unilateral declaration of independence null and void. In 1970, the government proclaimed a republic, but this too recieved no recognition. In 1979, the government purported to change the name of the Colony to Zimbabwe Rhodesia, but again this was never recognized. Following a conference in London in December 1979, the opposition government conceded and it was agreed that the British Government should resume control. A British governor soon returned to southern Rhodesia. One of his first acts was to affirm the nullification of the purported delcaration of independence. On April 18, 1980, pursuant to an act of the British Parliament, the Colony of Southern Rhodesia became independent within the commonwealth as the Republic of Zimbabwe.

MONETARY SYSTEM:
  1 Dollar = 100 Cents

NOTE: For earlier issues see Rhodesia.

SIGNATURE/ VARIETIES			
1	*signature*	3	*signature*
2	*signature*		

REPUBLIC

RESERVE BANK OF ZIMBABWE

1980 ISSUE
#1-4 Re Matapos Rocks at ctr. r. Sign. varieties. Wmk: Zimbabwe bird.
Replacement notes: Serial # prefix: *AW; BW; CW* or *DW*.

1 2 DOLLARS
  1980 (1981); 1983; 1994. Blue and m/c. Water buffalo at l. Tigerfish at ctr., Kariba Dam and reservoir at r. on back.

	VG	VF	UNC
a. Sign. 1. Salisbury. 1980.	FV	1.50	6.00
b. Sign. 2. Harare. 1983.	FV	FV	2.50
c. Sign. 3. Wmk: Type A. 1994.	FV	FV	1.5
d. Sign. 3. Wmk: Type B.	FV	FV	4

1994-95 ISSUE

#5-6 Wmk: Zimbabwe bird, Type B.

Replacement notes: Serial # prefix *AE*.

			VG	VF	UNC
5	**50 DOLLARS** 1994. Dk. brown, olive-brown and red on m/c unpt. Matapos Rocks at l. Great Zimbabwe ruins on back. Sign. 3.		FV	FV	18.50

			VG	VF	UNC
2	**5 DOLLARS** 1980 (1981); 1983; 1994. Green and m/c. Zebra at l. Village scene w/2 workers on back.				
	a. Sign. 1. Salisbury. 1980.		FV	3.00	15.00
	b. Sign. 1. Harare. 1982.		FV	FV	15.00
	c. Sign. 2. 1983.		FV	FV	3.50
	d. Sign. 3. 1994. Wmk: Type A.		FV	FV	3.00
	e. Sign. 3. 1994. Wmk: Type B.		FV	FV	3.00

			VG	VF	UNC
6	**100 DOLLARS** 1995. Brownish black and purple on m/c unpt. Matapos Rocks at l. ctr. Kariba Dam and reservoir at l. ctr. on back. Sign. 3.		FV	FV	30.00

			VG	VF	UNC
3	**10 DOLLARS** 1980 (1981); 1982-83; 1994. Red and m/c. Sable antelope at l. View of Harare and Freedom Flame monument on back.				
	a. Sign. 1. Salisbury. 1980.		FV	7.50	26.50
	b. Sign. 1. Salisbury. 1982 (error).		FV	12.50	30.00
	c. Sign. 1. Harare. 1982.		FV	FV	30.00
	d. Sign. 2. 1983.		FV	FV	7.00
	e. Sign. 3. 1994.		FV	FV	5.00

			VG	VF	UNC
4	**20 DOLLARS** 1980 (1982); 1982-83; 1994. Blue, black and dk. green on m/c unpt. Giraffe at l. Elephant and Victoria Falls on back.				
	a. Sign. 1. Salisbury. 1980.		FV	10.00	40.00
	b. Sign. 1. Harare. 1982.		FV	30.00	165.00
	c. Sign. 2. 1983.		FV	FV	15.00
	d. Sign. 3. 1994.		FV	FV	9.00

COUNTRY INDEX

ISSUER & BANK INDEX

ISSUER & BANK INDEX

ISSUER & BANK INDEX

HOW TO USE THIS CATALOG

Catalog listings consist of all regular and provisional notes attaining wide circulation in their respective countries for the period covered. Notes have been listed under the historical country name. Thus British Honduras is not under Belize, Dahomey is not under Benin, and so on, as had been the case in past catalogs. Where catalog numbers have changed, and you will find some renumbering in this edition, the old catalog numbers appear in parentheses directly below the new number. The listings continue to be grouped by issue range rather than by denomination, and a slight change in the listing format should make the Bank name, Issue dates as well as catalog numbers and denominations easier to locate. These changes have been made to make the catalog as easy to use as possible for you.

The editors and publisher make no claim to absolute completeness, just as they acknowledge that some errors and pricing inequities will appear. Correspondence is invited with interested persons who have notes previously unlisted or who have information to enhance the presentation of existing listings in succeeding editions of this catalog.

Catalog Format

Listings proceed generally according to the following sequence: Country, Geographic or Political chronology, Bank Name, sometimes alphabetically or by date of first note issue. Release within the bank, most often in date order, but sometimes by printer first.

Catalog number — The basic reference number at the beginning of each listing for each note. For this Modern Issues volume the regular listing require no prefix letters except when an 'A' or 'B' appear within the catalog number. (Military and Regional prefixes are explained later in this section.)

Denomination — the value as shown on the note, as western numerals. When denominations are only spelled out, consult the numerics chart.

Date — the actual issue date as printed on the note; in day-month-year order. Where more than one date appears on a note, only the latest is used. Where the note has no date, the designation ND is used, followed by a year date in parentheses when it is known. If a note is dated by the law or decree of authorization, then these dates appear with a L or D and are italicized.

Descriptions of the note are broken up into one or more items as follows:

Color — the main color(s) of the face, and the underprint are given first. If the color of the back is different, then they follow the face design description.

Design — The identification and location of the main design elements if known. Back color follows only if different than the face color. Back design elements identified if known.

If design elements and or signatures are the same for an issue group then they are printed only once at the heading of the issue, and apply for the group that follows.

Printer — often a local printer has the name shown in full. Abbreviations are used for the most prolific printers. Refer to the list of printer abbreviations elsewhere in this introduction. In these listings the use of the term imprint refers to the logo or the printer's name as usually appearing in the bottom frame or below in the margin of the note.

Valuations — are generally given under the grade headings of Good, Fine and Extremely Fine for early notes; and Very Good, Very Fine and Uncirculated for the later issues. Listings which do not follow these two patterns are clearly indicated. Unc followed by a price is used usually for specimens and proofs when lower grade headings are used for a particular series of issued notes.

A word about renumbering

For this edition, there has been extensive reordering and renumbering of many major countries and sporadic renumbering of smaller sections of many other countries. This will give all an opportunity to look at their collections again, as well as the descriptions and prices and enjoy the changes made in this edition all the more. Sure, you could complain about changing the numbers on your labels, but I don't think you'll complain about the improvement in most prices.

As the cataloging of paper money has matured with more information being shared the editors have endeavored to be as accurate as possible. To ease the task of renumbering, in most cases the previous edition's catalog number appears in parentheses immediately underneath the current number where changes have been made. In addition, an information line noting a catalog renumbering appears at the start of the country's listing.

Catalog prefix or suffix letters

A catalog number preceded by a capital 'A' indicated the incorporation of an earlier listing as required by type or date; a capital letter following the catalog number usually shows the addition of a later issue. Both may indicate newly discovered lower or higher denominations to a series. Listings of notes for regional circulation are distinguished from regular national issues with the prefix letter 'R'; military issues use a 'M' prefix; foreign exchange certificates are assigned a 'FX' prefix. Varieties, specific date or signature listings are shown with small letters 'a' following a number within their respective entries. Some standard variety letters include: 'p' for proof notes, 'r' for remainder notes, 's' for specimen notes and 'x' for errors.

Denominations

The denomination as indicated on many notes issued by a string on countries stretching from the eastern Orient, through western Asia and on across northern Africa often appear only in unfamiliar non-Western numeral styles. Within the listings which follow, however, denominations are always indicated in Western numerals.

A comprehensive chart keying Western numerals to their non-Western counterparts is included elsewhere in this introduction as an aid to the identification of note types. This compilation features not only the basic numeral systems such as Arabic, Japanese and Indian; but also the more restricted systems such as Burmese, Ethiopian, Siamese, Tibetan, Hebrew, Mongolian and Korean, plus other localized variations which have been applied to some paper money issues.

In consulting the numeral systems chart to determine the denomination of a note, one should remember that the actual numerals styles employed in any given area, or at a particular time, may vary significantly from these basic representations. Such variations can be deceptive to the untrained eye, just as variations from Western numeral styles can prove deceptive to individuals not acquainted with the particular style employed.